BRITISH WRITERS

Selected Authors

BRITISH WRITERS

Selected Authors

IAN SCOTT-KILVERT

General Editor

EDITED UNDER THE AUSPICES OF THE BRITISH COUNCIL

VOLUME III

CHARLES SCRIBNER'S SONS
Macmillan Library Reference USA
Simon & Schuster Macmillan
New York

Simon & Schuster and Prentice Hall International
London   Mexico City   New Delhi   Singapore   Sydney   Toronto

5 7 9 11 13 17 19 20 18 16 14 12 10 8 6 4

LIBRARY OF CONGRESS CATALOGING-IN-PUBLICATION DATA

British Writers, selected authors / Ian Scott-Kilvert, general editor.
p. cm.
Edited under the auspices of the British Council.
Includes bibliographical references and index.
ISBN 0-684-80518-9 (set: alk. paper).—ISBN 0-684-80515-4 (v. 1: alk. paper).
—ISBN 0-684-80516-2 (v. 2 : alk. paper).—ISBN 0-684-80517-0 (v. 3 : alk. paper)
1. English literature—Dictionaries. 2. English literature—Biobibliography—Dictionaries.
3. Authors, English—Biography—Dictionaries. I. Scott-Kilvert, Ian. II. British Council.
PR19.B68 1997
820.9'0003—dc21
[B]   97-14303
                                                                                  CIP

0-684-80518-9 (Set)
0-684-80515-4 (Vol. I)
0-684-80516-2 (Vol. II)
0-684-80517-0 (Vol. III)

Printed in the United States of America

The paper in this publication meets the requirements of ANSI / NISO Z39.48-1992
(Permanence of Paper).

Contents

Contents of Other Volumes

GEORGE BERNARD SHAW

(1856-1950)

Margery M. Morgan

BERNARD SHAW created a new art of drama in the 1890's and remained the vigorous center of the British theater for half a century. For much of that period he was regarded throughout the world as the preeminent modern dramatist. After his death there came the usual critical reaction in England; and the eclipse of his reputation was a fortunate and healthy liberation for a new succession of playwrights (starting with John Osborne and Arnold Wesker) that emerged through the Royal Court Theatre in London, where Shaw himself had triumphed between 1904 and 1907. The new writers needed to bury Shaw to gain a hearing for themselves, as he had needed to bury Victorian idolization of Shakespeare. His plays continued to be performed as surefire entertainments for conventional middle-class audiences, a fate that would have exasperated but not surprised the author; and his successors carried on the work of social criticism and political debate to which he, in the wake of Ibsen, had reopened the English stage. Meanwhile, serious scholarly and critical study of his writings was left almost entirely to Americans, and the British have had to fight through years of neglect and ignorance to reach a new perspective on his work and a fresh judgment of its nature and value.

Born in Dublin of Protestant stock in 1856, Shaw became—with Oscar Wilde—the eldest of a galaxy of Irish writers, including William Butler Yeats, John Millington Synge, Sean O'Casey, James Joyce, and Samuel Beckett—who have contributed richly to modern English literature and drama. Political and economic stagnation, following the famines, poverty, and depopulation of mid-nineteenth-century Ireland, were forcing-house conditions for the imagination prior to the romantic revival of nationalism, but drove many of those with artistic talents to seek a more cosmopolitan and hopeful culture overseas.

In Shaw's case there were precipitating family reasons for his departure to England at the age of twenty. He was the son of a loveless marriage between an incompetent father, whose drinking habits won his wife's contempt and ostracism in a narrowly respectable society, and a snobbish, indifferent mother who found her emotional fulfillment in music, as an amateur singer of marked talent. She brought the teacher who trained her voice, and conducted the concerts and operas in which she sang, to live with the family. This man, George John Vandeleur Lee, had a high reputation as a musician in Dublin at the time. When he went to London to advance himself professionally, Mrs. Shaw followed him with her two daughters, the younger of whom died of tuberculosis at the age of twenty-one, while Lucy, the eldest child, made a career as a singer in light opera. For two years her son stayed with his father and worked as a clerk in a land agency. Then he left his job and joined his mother, who was now herself teaching music and becoming disillusioned over Lee's gradual abandonment of his high standards and remarkable principles of voice training.

No one had bothered to teach the rudiments of music to Bernard Shaw, but the home environment had nourished his love and need of it, and he taught himself to play operas on the piano, as he was to teach himself much else. From his father and uncles he had learned a vivid sense of the ridiculous and a quick-witted skepticism that flung reverence and conventional thinking to the winds. This was a survival kit for accommodating plagues and disasters great and small, which more Irishmen than Shaw have turned into a genius for comic fantasy. His formal education was scanty and unsystematic, and he arrived in London untrained for anything, provincial in manners, and very shy.

For the next ten years Shaw lived in his mother's house, surviving on her tolerance and with some initial help from Lee, who set him on the path of journalism by arranging for him to write and be paid for a series of articles on music commissioned from Lee himself by a satirical weekly review, *The Hornet*. Apart from this, Shaw in his twenties read widely, wrote occasional rather hopeless and usually unsuccessful letters of application for jobs, and piled up manuscripts of novels that publishers consistently refused. These "desperate days," as he later described them to Frank Harris, were a severe test of morale and determination, and undoubtedly led to his deliberate cultivation of the bold front, the self-advertising persona, "public Shaw," that was to become a familiar and sometimes exasperating feature of his art as well as a means of self-protection in social life.

Shaw was taken on for regular work by the Edison Telephone Company in the autumn of 1879, an experience reflected in his second novel, *The Irrational Knot*. But what saved him was the plunge he took, at about the same time, into the active life of London's then flourishing societies for philosophical discussion. James Lecky, a civil servant with a strong interest in phonetics, introduced him to the Zetetical Society, where he met his lifelong friend Sidney Webb. Then he joined the Dialectical Society, on which the Zetetical had been modeled. The membership of both was broadly humanist and progressive in opinion, like the congregation of the Ethical Church in South Place, which he sometimes attended. He joined literary societies, too (and through F. J. Furnivall of the New Shakespeare Society he was engaged to make an index and glossary of *The Works of Thomas Lodge*[1] for the scholarly Hunterian Club). Anxious to make his mark, he forced himself to speak at every meeting, as he forced himself to accept social invitations, until his gaucheness gave way to ease.

Shaw became a vegetarian in 1881 in the hope of curing his chronic migraine headaches; the vegetarianism, but not the continuing migraine, became another feature added to the public image, soon well known in London's intellectual circles. He worked at self-improvement: he had learned shorthand; he took drawing lessons (and showed no talent); he studied languages; with his friend Pakenham Beatty he took lessons in boxing at the London Athletic Club. His knowledge of pugilism formed the basis of

his third novel, *Cashel Byron's Profession*, and he continued to make play with the metaphysical value of personal fitness in attack and defense, notably in *Major Barbara* and, late in life, in *The Millionairess*.

Probably the most momentous event of these years was Shaw's conversion to socialism after hearing a lecture by the American Henry George in 1882. George's economic theory, concentrating on the possession and value of land, made immediate sense to one familiar with discussions of the Irish Land Question. Shaw went on to read other economists, but he had been writing and addressing meetings for the Social Democratic Federation for some time before he read the first volume of Marx's *Kapital* in a French translation in 1884. He had already met Marx's daughter Eleanor and her common-law husband, Edward Aveling, translator of *Das Kapital* into English, in the Browning Society, for they had literary and dramatic interests in common and were to share in amateur playreadings. Through the next twelve years, while he spoke as a "socialist agitator" once or twice every week all over London, Shaw became intimate with anarchists and socialists of every persuasion. Yet he and Sidney Webb had committed themselves to the Fabian Society, newly founded in 1884, and in which they soon became controlling voices: it was a deliberate move away from the proletarian element in the S.D.F. into an organization of middle-class intellectuals, "my own class," that shared Marx's "hatred . . . for the middle-class institutions that had starved, thwarted, misled and corrupted them spiritually from their cradles" (*Sixteen Self Sketches*, 1949).

How great a political influence the Fabians exerted and how socialist they were has been debated ever since H. G. Wells's attack from within in 1906, after which he left the society. (It is still functioning today.) They were planners, researchers, teachers, men and women of social conscience who, instead of forming a political party themselves, sought to promote their policies through whatever parliamentary party they could interest and involve, usually the Liberal Party, but also the Tories, before the Labour Party was formed. (Their claim to have promoted most of the progressive social legislation of this century and to have been the architects of the "Welfare State," established by the Labour government after World War II, at least deserves examination.) Although there was great variety of opinion among the early membership, Shaw's and Webb's view that socialism in Britain was more likely to come through

---

[1]Shaw declined acknowledgment for his work because he failed to finish it on time. It was completed by the Shakespearean scholar Thomas Tyler.

gradual reform than through revolution was generally accepted. But the form of Shaw's socialism, his belief in equality and his attitude to revolution, was not immutably fixed and free from ambiguousness. It gave him the purpose outside mere personal ambition that he needed—and he adopted as his telegraph address "Socialist, London"—but he never wrote or spoke simple propaganda from a doctrinaire political viewpoint. The groundwork of his politics, and what his writing expressed throughout his long life, was a faith in reason and humanity, motivating what was to seem an increasingly difficult struggle to turn men from cruel and genocidal courses. He involved himself in the practical work of local government as a councillor "vestryman" for the London borough of St. Pancras from 1897 to 1903.

Shaw's early life of political activity made him many friends, some of them already distinguished people. These included Annie Besant, already a celebrated public speaker for social reform, and William Morris, the great artist-craftsman-poet, who won Shaw's enduring love and admiration. J. L. Joynes and H. H. Champion, editors of the socialist paper *To-Day*, serialized his fifth novel, *An Unsocial Socialist*, in 1884, and *Cashel Byron's Profession* between 1885 and 1886. Annie Besant published *The Irrational Knot* in serial form in her paper, *Our Corner*, between 1885 and 1887, and the fourth novel, *Love Among the Artists*, in 1887 and 1888. However, it was his meeting with William Archer, a man of deep social and ethical convictions, well established as a critic and becoming known as translator and champion of Ibsen, that enabled him to win fame and earn a regular living as a journalist, and then led him on into his career as a playwright. Shaw had published the occasional essay and written some music criticism for the *Dramatic Review, Our Corner*, and the *Magazine of Music*, when in 1886 Archer passed over to him his own commission as staff writer of art criticism for a flourishing weekly review, the *World*. ("He didn't know much more about painting than I, but he thought he did," said Archer, "and that was the main point.") These articles were unsigned but continued from February 1886 to December 1889. Although Shaw was not offered a place on the political staff of the newly founded mass-circulation newspaper the *Star*, he was taken on as its music critic in 1888 and chose the pseudonym "Corno di Bassetto." Two years later he became music critic of the *World* under his own name and continued until the *Saturday Review* enticed him to become its drama critic from 1895 to 1898.

As a critic of painting, Shaw wrote for the average man and woman uninitiated into the technicalities and more purely aesthetic qualities of the art, giving them grounds on which to approach and enjoy pictures with a degree of intelligent discrimination. Pictures that tell stories were still fashionable in this period, and his underlying concern is with the moral qualities implied in how the stories are told. The socialist origins of the Pre-Raphaelites, and John Ruskin's and William Morris' links with the movement, certainly had much to do with the generally favorable attention he gave to works of this native English school. The boxer's comments, in *Cashel Byron's Profession*, on the figure of St. George in Adrian Herbert's picture, pointing out that the artist understands nothing about the physical science of fighting, are typical of Shaw's own art reviews: observant, realistic, sensible, and limited. It was the kind of nonspecialist criticism that James McNeill Whistler, the impressionist painter, virtually killed off, in his notorious "Ten o'Clock" lecture of 1888, though it was Oscar Wilde, not Shaw, who was the object of Whistler's attack.

Shaw's music criticism, much more considerable in volume, also has greater intrinsic value, and most of it is as interesting and entertaining today as when he wrote it. He settled on a style as different as possible from the pontifical formality of the *Times*: it is personal, spontaneous, easy, and vivid, befitting a more democratic paper reaching out, as the *Star* did, toward a newly literate public. Shaw avoids isolating the musical experience from its particular context and may tell his readers about his journey to the concert hall, the chair he sat in, the coughs and fidgetings of the audience; he establishes an everyday frame of mind as natural and appropriate to the occasion.

Yet there is no mistaking Shaw's intense interest in the performance itself. He may be enraged, but he is never bored or indifferent. There is always some passage of quite precise and analytic comment, forthrightly and unhesitatingly expressed, that increases the general reader's confidence in his authority and arrests the attention of musicians. The impression of a considerable background of musical knowledge is secondary to his communication of a great appetite and enthusiasm for the art. He often criticizes with unsparing ridicule—especially famous performers giving less than their very best—yet he is equally ready to express delight in spite of imperfections. His dedication to the raising of standards and improvement in audience discrimination often resulted, even when he was writing for the *World*, in nagging or bullying passages, or comments such as a severe schoolmaster might write in a boy's report:

Richter has no right to stuff a programme with the most hackneyed items in his repertory in order to save the trouble of rehearsing. . . . The orchestra is by no means what it ought to be; and it has been getting worse instead of better for some years past.

There is a certain amount of deliberate clowning in this that can seem boorish in cold and now antiquated print; but usually the amusing exaggerations and farfetched yet curiously evocative comparisons take away some of the sting, as the attentions of a clever caricaturist may be appreciated as almost flattering by his victims.

George Carr Shaw, left alone in Ireland, died in 1885 at the age of seventy-one. None of the family went to the funeral, not even Lucy, who was in Dublin at the time. Her brother responded to the news of their father's death with the mixture of practicality and flippancy that was to serve him as a barrier against emotion on numerous other occasions. Falling in love with Alice Lockett in 1881, and for three years pursuing a volatile relationship and lively correspondence with her that are echoed in *An Unsocial Socialist*, was the beginning of a series of "philanders," as he liked to call them. He enjoyed the flattery of women's interest in him and the fun of flirtation, even the conflict to gain the upper hand, and he was not above playing off one woman against another and getting further pleasure from such intrigues.

If Shaw saw the spirit of farce hovering near all his love affairs, the women did not always share his view. In particular, Mrs. Jenny Patterson, a widow fifteen years his senior, to whom he lost his virginity on his twenty-ninth birthday, pursued him with a frustrated passion he found intolerable. Most of his erotic entanglements remained at the level of flirtation, and possibly the most delightful to both parties was his courtship of the actress Ellen Terry, conducted entirely by letter. He escaped from the threat of sexual capture into a happy celibate marriage with Charlotte Payne Townshend, a wealthy Irishwoman and fellow Fabian, in 1898, when both were over forty: "It ended the old gallantries . . . for both of us."

For Shaw there was to be one more notable exception to this.

Shaw had started the habit of theatergoing in Dublin. He enjoyed whatever was good of its kind: popular entertainment or Shakespearean tragedy. In 1890 he agreed to give a lecture to the Fabian Society on Henrik Ibsen, who had stirred Europe by his dramatic onslaughts on patriarchal society and its idealization of the home. The lecture was the germ of the first book in English on the Norwegian playwright, *The Quintessence of Ibsenism* (1891), and helped to build up interest in the formation of an Independent Theatre Society to present Ibsen's *Ghosts*, which had no chance of public production in England, in current conditions of theatrical censorship. The society mounted *Ghosts* in 1891, and its founder, J. T. Grein, then asked Shaw for a play. Shaw went back to an abortive attempt he had made in collaboration with William Archer and revised and completed it; and, under the title of *Widowers' Houses*, it was presented by the Independent Theatre in 1892. He went on writing plays. Except for one or two private performances by avant-garde groups and the presentation of *Arms and the Man* in 1894 in a short season privately financed by Miss Annie Horniman and starring one of his lady friends, Florence Farr, his plays seemed fated for the same neglect as his novels. Being no longer a poor boy, Shaw was able to publish them at his own expense in two collections under the single title of *Plays: Pleasant and Unpleasant* (1898). So they were read, often enjoyed, but dismissed as unsuitable for the stage. Until the century was over Shaw could retaliate only by citing the single example of Richard Mansfield's New York success in *The Devil's Disciple* (in the next collection, *Three Plays for Puritans*) in 1897.

It was through the campaign to establish a national theater, which had started in the 1860's, that Shaw found conditions for testing and proving the theatrical effectiveness of his drama. Archer, Professor Gilbert Murray, Shaw himself, and their young friend the actor Granville Barker (who in 1917 began to use the name Harley Granville Barker) were all involved in this campaign. Archer and Barker presented their case for a state-subsidized theater of excellence in *A Scheme and Estimates for a National Theatre*, and Barker followed this up by leasing the Royal Court theater in Sloane Square to demonstrate the higher quality of acting, production, and new drama that a theater freed from normal commercial pressures could offer. Charlotte and

Bernard Shaw put up the greater part of the money for this limited experiment; Barker trained and directed the actors, with Shaw coming in for the production of his own plays. By 1907, when the money ran out, the case was proved and the reputations were made.

Shaw lived until 1950 and continued writing almost to the end. Though he was out of public favor at times, on account of his known or supposed political views, his literary eminence was generally accepted, and his fame continued to grow. He had, he said, "no adventures"—except those of the mind, recorded in the continually changing character of his writing.

NOVELS, JOURNALISM, ESSAYS

BEFORE they started on their brief playwriting collaboration, Shaw remarked to Archer that he had difficulty in devising plots. His novels bear this out. They all contain lively scenes, but, with the exception of *Cashel Byron's Profession*, the shortest, they seem largely unplanned, even improvised. Writing to the publisher Swan Sonnenschein in defense of the first, *Immaturity* (not published until 1930), Shaw declared that he had thought of calling it *Quadrille*, as the interwoven narratives of four principal characters made the only artificial construction he cared to impose on the lifelike realism he sought. *Love Among the Artists* has a similar very general design, which does not rescue it from being the dullest of the books. There is a similar dispersal of interest in *The Irrational Knot*, though combined with a more conventional plot that gets somewhat out of hand. *An Unsocial Socialist* falls into two halves, with a number of the characters, including the extraordinary central figure, struggling through from the first half into the second.

Immaturity underwent two thorough revisions and emerged a more readable book than some of the later ones. ("People who read *An Unsocial Socialist* will read anything," said its author.) It contains plenty of good talk and amusing comment and a considerable range of figures, from Lady Geraldine Porter to the comic Irishman Cornelius Hamlet, whose histories and moral character are rapidly and vividly sketched; and it is united by the manner in which it is written, its air of good sense and sweet temper (not least in writing about bad-tempered people), its con-

sistent valuing of good fellowship and laughter at "romance." There is no evident theme beyond a very young man's discovery of society, though an egalitarian tendency is clear. *The Irrational Knot* improves on this by treating the theme of love and marriage through a contrast between two couples. There are signs that the second pair were meant to be figures of comedy, but the woman, Susannah, who is a burlesque actress under the name of Lalage Virtue, is eventually conducted through a rake's progress from strong-minded independence to alcoholic breakdown and death.

It may be that Shaw, having set himself to write a more grimly realistic type of novel, as he was to imitate conventional melodrama at the start of his play *The Devil's Disciple*, aped the conventionally narrow, moralistic attitude of the Victorian public. He shows unexpected disapproval of Susannah's profession and her freedom—not so remote from his own sister's. That he had imbibed some of his mother's puritanical and snobbish attitudes is certain (the Fabian "hatred . . . for the middle-class institutions that had . . . misled and corrupted them spiritually" may reflect his mother's influence), and this novel may well record a usually suppressed emotional shock that accompanied his youthful skepticism and intellectual boldness. There is a prevailing sourness of tone, not confined to the "bitter and flippant humour" of the spinsterish Elinor McQuinch; and characters are satirically exposed without the veil of liking that softens the ridicule through most of Shaw's comedy. Conolly, the engineer hero, and Marian, the lady born and bred, are presented in realistic detail and with a measure of sympathy, but they represent opposite temperaments, the one governed by reason, the other by emotion. Conolly comes close to being an idealized portrait of the wise and just man, but is saved from priggishness by the awareness the author lets his character share: that there is something monstrous, almost tragic, about such perfect consistency.

Cashel Byron's Profession is very different, written throughout with a much lighter and surer touch. As he was often to do later, Shaw started with an unpretentious, popular form: here a boy's adventure tale involving plenty of fistfighting. Improbably, he combined it with a novel of manners, coolly analytical of social morality and distinctly reminiscent of the work of Jane Austen. In all his novels, most of the characters speak with a rather formal precision, "as if all their speeches had been corrected by their governesses and schoolmasters," and it gives them a rather old-fashioned charm, set off in this book by the robuster boyishness of expression and occasional unselfconscious fluency of his hero, a type of the natural man. Only the inadequate development of the secondary plot, the germ of which was lifted directly from Jane Austen's *Emma*, mars *Cashel Byron's Profession*, and it was with good reason that Shaw later commented on his narrow escape from becoming a successful novelist at this point.

While publishers neglected their opportunity, Shaw went on to write the most wildly fantastic of these early works, keeping his hand in practice, but caring less than before to write an acceptable book. *An Unsocial Socialist* is an absurd farrago of incidents, mostly brought about by the "hero," who makes love to a bunch of young women and exercises his sway over them by lecturing them lengthily, but not tediously, on socialism. This character is a curious, comic variant on the psychological double made familiar in R. L. Stevenson's famous "shocker," *Dr. Jekyll and Mr. Hyde* (1886). Shaw's more particular inspiration for the wealthy Sidney Trefusis, who runs away from his young wife and puts on the burlesque disguise of the uncommon workman Jefferson Smilash, was undoubtedly Prince Hamlet in his "antic disposition": "The son of a millionaire, like the son of a king, is seldom free from mental disease," Trefusis explains. "I am just mad enough to be a mountebank." One early reader, at least, remarked on the originality of the book and recorded: "This is the most comical novel I have ever read."

Shaw's ability to create lively women characters, many of them strong-minded and sharp-tongued, is evident through all the novels. Indeed he seems more interested in the women than in his male characters. Other well-marked features that emerge again in his drama are: the governing concern with what is mockingly called "moral science," in *An Unsocial Socialist*; the interest in the philanderer-figure that starts with his first hero's imagining of himself as "Don Juan Lothario Smith"; and respect for the type of conscience that is directed toward mankind in general and runs counter to normal, domestic morality. In the form of the peculiar selfishness of the artist, this last concern provides the main interest of *Love Among the Artists*.

Shaw did not hide his personal tastes in his journalism. The music critic disliked Brahms and championed Wagner; Mozart was the musician he loved above all others. The theater critic reviewed every

kind of dramatic entertainment, including comic opera and pantomime, but identified himself firmly with the intellectual avant-garde that looked to Ibsen as the revolutionary dramatist who would sweep away the nineteenth century. Shaw coined the term *sardoodledom* to describe the "well-made plays" imported in great quantity from France, where they were slickly constructed to an established formula by Victorien Sardou, Eugène Scribe, Alexandre Dumas *fils,* and others. (These dramatists are best known today through the late-nineteenth-century operas *Tosca* and *La Traviata*, among others, based on their stories.) The most distinguished of the contemporary British dramatists that Shaw found himself reviewing, Arthur Wing Pinero, Henry Arthur Jones, and Oscar Wilde, also adopted the well-made play form and, like some of their French colleagues, had started to mix in a little of Ibsen's concern with the condition of society and its pressures on individuals. This gave their plots a superficial seriousness, but all were far from issuing any radical challenge, as Ibsen did, and as Shaw began to do.

The *Saturday Review* gave Shaw plenty of space for his critiques. Though he had not been appointed as an editorial writer, he exercised a license to comment on virtually any topical subject, and his remarks on the plays he had seen were frequently introduced by lengthy discussions of more general interest. This was the period when he acquired his reputation as a highly articulate clown, perhaps an indication that an overforceful presentation of his convictions made him less influential than a quieter, less brash advocacy would have done. But this is hard to determine: he was attacking strongly entrenched opposition, and it seems likely that his wit and liveliness started many of his readers asking new questions and looking more skeptically at old arguments. Certainly he won recognition as the most brilliant of journalists, and he sufficiently identified himself with this profession to continue as a member of the Institute of Journalists until his death. The prefaces he wrote to accompany his plays in their published form were further exercises in the genre in which he had made his name. He included them, at first, in order to sell the plays to a public unaccustomed to reading dramatic texts.

None of the three long essays Shaw published between 1891 and the end of the decade was criticism in the same sense as his regular reviews. *The Quintessence of Ibsenism* is a discussion of social morality that uses Ibsen's plays as its Bible; *The Sanity of Art*

(1895) was Shaw's answer to a sweeping attack on fin-de-siècle symbolism made by Max Nordau under the title *Degeneration* (1893), and presents the case for what we now call modernism; *The Perfect Wagnerite* (1898) translates the music-drama *The Ring of the Nibelungs* as a socialist allegory. The first of these essays isolates the theme of destructive idealism in play after play of Ibsen's. The acceptance of stereotypes and attachment to ideologies are included in "idealism," as this essay uses the term, and so is the idolization of self-righteousness that passes for "public opinion." Writing the preface to the third edition of *Quintessence*, after World War I, Shaw argued:

The war was a war of ideals. Liberal ideals . . . , bourgeois and proletarian, all heaped up into a gigantic pile of spiritual high explosive, and then shovelled daily into every house with the morning milk by the newspapers. . . .

Truthfulness to human nature was the test he saw Ibsen's realism applying to social institutions and conventional behavior, and when he came to introduce to the public his own first collection of plays (in the preface to volume II of *Plays: Pleasant and Unpleasant*), he defined his own attitude:

To me the tragedy and comedy of life lie in the consequences . . . of our persistent attempts to found our institutions on the ideals suggested to our imaginations by our half-satisfied passions, instead of on a genuinely scientific natural history.

Shaw's exposition of Wagner's *Ring* was more peculiar. He argued, with every justification, that Wagner did not write his music-drama merely for the sensual and emotional enjoyment of his audience. Indeed the Nazis were later to demonstrate horrifyingly that the work has a political message. Shaw did not read it their way, as he brought to it a concern for humanity, indeed for all life, nothing as restricted as nationalism or ideas of racial superiority; yet he was guilty, as they were, of imposing a narrow and doctrinaire meaning on an imaginative creation. Admittedly, he points out that no great allegory is ever mechanically consistent, but his whole manner of exposition raises doubts as to whether he understood why this is so. Curiously enough, the explanation is to be found in *The Sanity of Art*. Here he had employed Schopenhauer's notion of the Will as the great motive force in human psychology, inaccessible to reason. It was probably his familiarity with

evolutionary theory that allowed him to regard optimistically the power of feeling and conviction that sweeps aside personal, prudential considerations, and to view it as serving the ultimate interests of the species—or even, beyond the species, of life itself, whatever form it might take. The core of his argument in this essay is summed up in one of the Maxims for Revolutionists that he was to print with *Man and Superman*: "The unconscious self is the true genius."

Throughout his plays, this faith counterbalances the rational temperament that he had examined in his novels in the characters of Edward Conolly and of Lydia Carew, who marries Cashel Byron to make up for her own shortcomings. The result is a drama in which the discussion of public themes is combined with forms of intimate self-examination, and in which the irrational is expressed with comic passion —in laughter.

PLAYS: PLEASANT AND UNPLEASANT *AND* THREE PLAYS FOR PURITANS

BERNARD SHAW had tried his hand at writing dramatic pieces before *Widowers' Houses*, the first of his plays to be performed and published. He had dramatized a novel, *The Gadfly*, by Ethel Voynich, in 1875 (published in 1973); more significantly, he had attempted a *Passion Play* in verse in 1878 (published in 1971). There is no subtlety in Shaw's verse rhythms: only for burlesque purposes could he write effective verse at any period of his life. What is more interesting in *A Passion Play* is a determined attack on the supernatural elements in Christianity through a rather sourly naturalistic presentation of the Holy Family.

At this stage in his life, Shaw was still brashly positivist and antireligious in his outlook. The destructive aspect of his satiric and parodic impulses is still evident in the three plays he published under the general description "Unpleasant." *Widowers' Houses* offers a cynical view of young love readily collaborating with the greed and callousness of capitalist society. *The Philanderer* (written in 1893) turns its attention to the fashionable intellectuals of the day, just such enthusiasts for Ibsen as had supported the Independent Theatre production of Shaw's own previous play, and it moves to an equally disenchanted end in the announcement of a marriage that has no prospect of happiness for either party, but that society approves. Like *Widowers' Houses*, which exposes exploitation of the poor by the wealthy and respected (including the church) who draw rents from slum properties, *Mrs. Warren's Profession* demonstrates how responsibility for social evils extends through society, involving even those who think themselves innocent.

The third play was the most shocking in the means it used to bring home to his audience, or readers, their own guilty complicity. The manners of the day and the fact of theatrical censorship played into Shaw's hands by giving him grounds for suppressing the name of the profession Mrs. Warren had adopted (sexual prostitution) and advanced in (to the directorship of an international chain of brothels). There is evidence that many of the women and some of the men who saw the first performance of this play came away uncertain what the profession was, thus confirming Shaw's point that the unconscious hypocrisy of an innocence protected from knowledge of unpleasant facts can be a strong barrier against social change. Indeed the play was banned in England from public performance, as morally offensive, until World War I.

A purely aesthetic criticism tends to dismiss such works as propagandist, of a topical and so less enduring interest, and too utilitarian in their intention to be good art. Early critics' objections to these socialist "bluebook" plays, as they called them, have left a persisting echo ever since. Yet they have not lost their grip in the theater; indeed audiences of the 1960's and 1970's liked them better than some of Shaw's later, more extravagantly praised work. *Widowers' Houses* and *Mrs. Warren's Profession* further the belief on which he had based *Cashel Byron's Profession*, and that was to contribute to *Major Barbara* (written in 1905): that there is a unity, a self-consistency, in any social system that allows the nature of the whole to be discovered by study of any part. Ibsen may have helped him to this view; Mrs. Alving, in *Ghosts*, speaks of the fabric of received ideas on which society rests, in a homely simile, as like a piece of knitting that is soon totally unraveled if it comes undone anywhere. Shaw's reading of Marx is also reflected in this, though he never regarded Marx as the infallible pope of socialism.

The consequence of this way of seeing the human world is that conventional dichotomies—between private and public, individual and society—evaporate; and they seem to have been absent from the creative processes that brought the plays into being.

The title of *Widowers' Houses* is indicative: Sartorius is a widower whose emotional nature seeks fulfillment in the relationship with his daughter, and the unnatural intensity of his concern for her is the motive force behind his ruthless pursuit of wealth. In *Mrs. Warren's Profession*, Vivie is a young woman whose brittle independence corresponds to ignorance of her father's identity (an ignorance she has to live with, as no one else knows it either) and the fact that her mother, too, is a stranger, little more than a name to her. The psychological need for love and commitment to other individuals has as important a part in these plays as the revelation of how the economic structure of society determines compromises and betrayals, and gives a questionable ambiguousness to every social undertaking, every institution and profession: to marriage and family, to art, and even to the business of earning an honest living.

Shaw is able to make so comprehensive a statement with economy of method in these plays because they rest on a basically simple structure of ideas contained in a form he imitated from Ibsen's modification of the well-made play in *A Doll's House, Ghosts*, and *Rosmersholm*, particularly. The dramatic development involves a progress from apparently contented ignorance to an enlightenment that may have tragic implications for the individual in the short run. Crucial revelations are made about the past, usually in two stages, and these affect understanding of the present. The stages are marked by the appearance and reappearance of a relatively minor character: Lickcheese, in *Widowers' Houses*, has no exact counterpart in *Mrs. Warren's Profession*, though there are corresponding figures in later Shaw plays (for example, Burgess in *Candida*, Doolittle in *Pygmalion*). These features give a rather schematic effect to the plot: the choice of episodes to be presented is governed by the central idea; coincidences and sharply juxtaposed contrasts do little to suggest the unformulated experience of ordinary living, but much to direct and enforce a general argument.

Shaw blends in other styles. The supper episode in *Mrs. Warren's Profession* has a touch of the rambling naturalism to be found in *Immaturity*. Such characters as Cockane and Lickcheese in *Widowers' Houses*, Craven, Cuthbertson, and Paramore in *The Philanderer* are drawn with broad strokes, close to caricature, and they demonstrate themselves in all they say and do, in a frankly theatrical way. Shaw, discussing acting with William Archer, argued for objectivity as preferred by Denis Diderot in *Paradoxe sur le comédien* (written in 1773–1778) against psychological subjectivity, though he did not go to the theoretical extremes that his successor Bertolt Brecht was to put forward in reaction against the subjective approach of the great Russian director Konstantin Stanislavski. Yet it is not only in the major characters, notably Julia Craven and Vivie Warren, that Shaw suggests an individual temperament and some psychological complexity: Paramore is a mean creature of low vitality, and the Reverend Samuel Gardner is a figure of farce—treated as such by his son—whose alcoholic misery and degradation may have been modeled on George Carr Shaw's and set up an uncomfortable undertow to the laughter they provoke.

The inclusion of the son, Frank Gardner, in *Mrs. Warren's Profession* maintains the comic balance of the play, and indeed allows modern productions to play up the artificial coincidences in the plot and to burlesque passages that had a strained seriousness in 1892. Frank is a cool, mischievous observer who takes the world as his entertainment and ridicules the morality of a system he despises. What he objects to in the vicious characters is "their form . . . ever so slovenly," as he might say of horses, when placing his bets. Shaw's comic impulse is evident in each of the plays in this first group, but chiefly in *The Philanderer*, which echoes with the laughter of the central character, Charteris, the first of Shaw's satirical self-portraits to appear in his drama. Charteris belongs to the Don Juan type. The intrigues with women that complicate his life and give the play its bursts of farcical action are linked with a clear-sighted rationality, a combination that recalls Trefusis in *An Unsocial Socialist*. The play exposes more than the ambiguousness of his attitude to women: this is a character who playacts emotional responses and laughs at everything. Shaw has sketched the very type of a comic dramatist, but the character also represents an irresponsible man in private relationships, out of touch with his buried emotions and afraid of emotion in others. *The Philanderer* is not directly concerned with economics, as are the other two plays, but it offers a serious and subtle comment on another topic with political as well as social implications: the struggle of women toward independence and equality with men. Shaw was to return to this in *You Never Can Tell* (written in 1895–1896), one of his "pleasant" plays.

The new group represents his deliberate effort to write for the commercial theater, not just for avant-garde play-producing societies that could evade censorship and were not seeking simple entertainment first and foremost. Though he still failed to break through to the wider audience, the manner he deliberately assumed to this end was to stay with him, a mask becoming indistinguishable from his face: invariably sweet-tempered, however severe he sometimes pretends to be, essentially genial and optimistic. No doubt the ample experience of public success in another field and the welcome into a wide circle of interesting and distinguished friends modified Shaw's character, dispelling bitterness and establishing the positive aspects of his volatile temperament. This laid the foundations of an art that good-humoredly recognizes the humanity of knaves and fools and reserves its scorn for their crimes and stupidities, an art that has been accused of lacking a sense of evil. Certainly two qualities came into prominence now that must put criticism warily on its guard. These are blandness and childishness.

Each of the full-length *Plays: Pleasant* and two of the following *Plays for Puritans* contain at least one very youthful figure with which the childish view or approach can be associated: Raina (*Arms and the Man*)—who gets her own way by playing the spoiled child—and Cleopatra, the boy Ptolemy (*Caesar and Cleopatra*), the puppyish Eugene (*Candida*), Effie in *The Devil's Disciple*, and the twins in *You Never Can Tell*. Shaw was reverting to a technique he had used in the first piece he completed after arriving in London in 1876, the letter of advice to an imaginary five-year-old child, which was ultimately published in 1956 as *My Dear Dorothea*. This was informal moral reflection expressed in practical precepts and conceptually simple explanations. Treating the child as an intelligent and thoughtful being, though of limited and largely domestic experience, resulted in both a demonstration of proper respect for childhood and its rights, and a wise document that may be thoughtfully and profitably read by the adults for whom it was, in fact, intended. Shaw the theater critic had good reason to know that much of the popular, and least debased, theatrical entertainment of the day allowed audiences to relax in a simplified world of fantasy and to regress to an immature level of desire and belief. He had had a marked success in *Cashel Byron's Profession* by writing in a popular mode, while permeating it with his own critical judgment and thoughtfulness. Now he tried the same thing again, though his strong individuality made the difference from the commonplace type greater than he may have planned.

An astute publicist for his latest work, Shaw was always inclined to undervalue what he had written in earlier days. So he frequently dismissed earlier plays as potboilers and in private expressed his doubts about the worth of others that had taken considerable effort. When Alma Murray, who first acted Raina in *Arms and the Man*, was thinking of reviving the play in 1904, Shaw wrote: "I took to reading it the other day . . . and was startled to find what flimsy, fantastic, unsafe stuff it is." The words are recognition of the knife-edge that he sometimes walked and that productions of his plays need to walk, if the critical sense of reality is not to be lost in the entertainment. He claimed later that World War I need never have occurred if the lessons of *Arms and the Man* had been heeded; but how seriously he is concerned with the theme of war in this play may be overlooked by present-day audiences, who cannot even identify the war in Eastern Europe that occasioned it. Shaw does not start with actuality, but takes the then fashionable convention of Ruritanian romance (Ruritania being the imaginary European country in which Anthony Hope set his novel of 1894, *The Prisoner of Zenda*, the best-known example of the type) and attacks it with a farcical treatment in which the absurdities of the plot and puppetlike aspect of the characters are deliberately exaggerated.

Sergius Saranoff is the embodiment of honor, quixotic in his attachment to myths of militarism undoubtedly easier to sustain before World War I than after, though Shaw shows Sergius to be as ludicrously out-of-date as Cervantes' Don Quixote. Alongside this patriot of insane ideals is set Bluntschli, the Swiss mercenary, the man who knows himself to be only a tool, sees fighting as an evil to be avoided, but accommodates himself to the world as it is by soldiering simply for pay, his share of the spoils, for he has the soul of a shopkeeper. A technique of anticlimax is used to ridicule Sergius and more playfully to expose the false attitudes of the heroine, already bored with her own make-believe of romance; but it is the rather cynical subplot, involving the brutally calculating servants, that focuses the questionable nature of the alternative Bluntschli represents, and leaves Raina, the child whose toys these wooden (or candy) figures are, to hold the balance.

A similar demolition of accepted heroic values is attempted in *The Devil's Disciple* through the apparently more realistic and serious convention of melodrama. It was this play, produced in New York in 1897, that give Shaw his first taste of success as a playwright.

Shaw's competence in providing what an earlier public liked is just what may limit his appeal today; such is the risk of his chosen strategy. He did not expect a metropolitan audience of the last decade of the century to take readily to the straightforward, pious hero of old-fashioned melodrama, so he gave Dick Dudgeon a reputation for dissoluteness, evidently unearned; excluded him from decent society; filled him with hatred of his mother; and finished off the portrait with a jeering manner and a bitter tongue, to counterbalance his good looks. A soubrette type like Raina would be out of place in a melodrama; instead, Shaw includes a pathetic, oppressed, and abandoned bastard girl, and the projection of Dick Dudgeon as the scornful hero whose authentic morality is so much higher than that of orthodox society corresponds to Effie's idealizing view of him, taken over by Judith Anderson, the second sentimentalist, old enough to know better. But Dick is a sham diabolonian, a disguised example of true Christian virtue in the midst of corruption. The changing of coats that is crucial to the plot is also emblematic of Shaw's dramatic subterfuge: the parson's coat is fitly transferred to Dick, and the true rebel proves to be Anderson, the natural man of good sense, delivered from his Christian assumptions. Only near the end, with the introduction of General Burgoyne, the sophisticated wit, does the play establish itself as a comedy after all. The strategy has been to indulge childish tastes and lead through this to a more adult consciousness.

That Shaw's conception of wickedness is purely naturalistic can be gleaned through his characterization of Mrs. Dudgeon. She is unloving because unloved; the root of her malignancy is identical with that sacrifice of true love to profitable marriage to which Ibsen traces the bitterness and viciousness of a line of women characters culminating in Gunhild Borkman (*John Gabriel Borkman*, written in 1896). In the preface to *Plays: Pleasant*, Shaw declared his adherence to philosophic naturalism. Yet he rarely keeps to a naturalistic dramatic style. Of all his plays the nearest to consistent naturalism is *Candida*, where the style is part of the blandness it shares with the superficially very different *Captain Brassbound's*

Conversion. Naturalistic drama must seem to be free of domination by abstract ideas and to mean only what it shows. Like Ibsen before him, Shaw in *Candida* had to contrive to comment on dramatic situations and characters by covert means. The result was his most elaborately written and enigmatic play so far, despite its air of being as simple and straightforward as its heroine. Indeed he indirectly confessed as much, on publishing the text in 1898, when he substituted the descriptive subtitle "A Mystery" for the simple "Domestic Play" that classified it in his original manuscript. As Shaw, the working member of the New Shakespeare Society, would have known, contemporary scholarship was interested in the mystery plays of the medieval religious stage, and to Ellen Terry, the actress he wanted to play the role, he confided that Candida Morell was "the virgin mother and nobody else." Ironically, this recalls his early *Passion Play,* with its depiction of the virgin mother of Christian legend as a nagging wife; but Ellen Terry did not know that.

Though Shaw was to refer to the play as his version of *A Doll's House,* in which the man and not the woman was the doll (this being the usual state of affairs in English society as he saw it), and to declare that "Candida seduces Eugene just exactly as far as it is worth her while to seduce him," he encouraged actresses to take the character at her own estimation: as the Reverend James Morell's model wife and the motherly protector of the young poet, Eugene Marchbanks. If the other actors and the director follow the same line, *Candida* lulls audiences into accepting it as Shaw's celebration of the Good Woman and a work of distinctly conservative tendency; for the irony on which he now relies is almost silent, a matter of nuances calculated to make the conventional public just faintly uneasy in its accustomed beliefs. Both her Christian Socialist husband and the poet who loses his bid for her look on Candida with the eyes of worshippers. As neither Morell nor Candida herself shows any awareness that the great monologue in which she tells the truth about their marriage systematically humiliates him and justifies her, it is very likely that theater audiences may be mesmerized into acceptance of this version as Shaw's, forgetting the commonsense remark of the spinster secretary, Prossy, "She's very nice, very good-hearted: I'm very fond of her, and can appreciate her real qualities far better than any man can."

Shaw has been criticized for carelessness in giving Candida the stock comedy figure of Burgess, the wily cockney businessman, as a father. If he had been a thoroughgoing naturalist dramatist, social verisimilitude and realism would have excluded, or taken great pains to explain, the unlikely relationship. But the staginess of Burgess disturbs the bland surface to insinuate a political comment on Candida and the effect of the domestic ideal in delaying social reform. The character of Marchbanks offers a similar choice of interpretation that may lead to artistic failure, mawkish and embarrassing if entirely naturalistically played; or to ironic success, if authorial awareness and fey, almost puckish humor (a generic relation to Frank Gardner and to Philip in *You Never Can Tell*) break through the simple portrait of a shy boy, unused to society. Why unused, if he is indeed an earl's son and not a foundling from outside nature altogether?

Prossy's words, "very nice, very good-hearted," are even more applicable to Lady Cicely Wayneflete of *Captain Brassbound's Conversion* (a character Ellen Terry did eventually play). Not even subdued irony calls into question her selflessness, practical benevolence, and common sense. Yet much of the comedy of this play turns on her blatantly manipulative ways and the capitulation of the male characters to her moral and emotional blackmail. Certainly this makes no pretense of being a naturalistic play: it is essentially a fable, decked out as an adventure story in an exotic setting, with a cast of minor characters that looks and acts like the chorus of a comic opera. It can be argued that Lady Cicely is simply a female mask, a dramatic device for challenging the monstrous ideas of justice and punishment upheld in patriarchal society: Shaw regarded imprisonment, like poverty, as a crime committed by society against the individual, and considered all penal systems barbarous. Whereas Candida triggers speculation about her motives, no level of deep motivation, or unconscious self, is suggested in the drawing of Lady Cicely. Even so, an unpleasant aftertaste is left by Shaw's presentation of female power asserting "feminine" values through the reduction of society to a hospital or a nursery.

It is not that he does not recognize the possibility of a more open and straightforward kind of strength in women. He shows it in the able and independent Mrs. Clandon of *You Never Can Tell,* a character having qualities and experience corresponding to his own mother's, and showing a likeness also to Annie Besant and other "new" women of the day whom he numbered among his friends. She is humane and dignified, but the dramatist chastens her, instead of praising her, and his instrument to this end is the young man, Valentine, who plays a concealed game to net the young woman he desires. This is the most delicately balanced play in Shaw's early collections. The sadness of a human situation—the long-estranged family who meet again by chance only to discover that they are strangers; the unloved man confronting the unloving woman; the poignant contrast between untouched youth and soiled, defeated age—is contained within the gayest of formal comedies. The conflict of the sexes is enacted in the ritual of courtship, and, though troubles remain and problems are unresolved, all ends in a dance.

The whole is a daring, entirely successful blend of commedia dell'arte (the tradition of Italian comedy based on the stock characters of Harlequin and Columbine, young lovers; crabbed father Pantaloon; and the rest), a critique of contemporary manners, and a dialectical play that pits intellect against emotion, with the first of these elements serving to distance and simplify the more realistic content of the play. Valentine, the lover, dismisses with easy arrogance his beloved's education and good brain: "I've a better one myself: it's a masculine speciality." No other character in the play contradicts him, and the statement could pass for Shaw's own view— evidence from outside the play would raise doubts: he chose to make Vivie Warren a brilliant mathematician; he had tremendous respect for the specialist mind of Beatrice Webb. But Valentine's charm is shadowed by the brutal and bullying force of Bohun, "the very incarnation of intellect." It is a silent irony again that indicates the needful poise of thought and feeling.

The Devil's Disciple and the most trifling of the *Plays: Pleasant, The Man of Destiny*, seem to be historical plays and include what purport to be genuine historical figures: General Burgoyne in the one, Napoleon in the other. More ambitious than either of these is the remaining work in *Three Plays for Puritans: Caesar and Cleopatra*. An alternative grouping would place these "historical" plays alongside *Arms and the Man* and *Captain Brassbound's Conversion* as examples of drama that announces itself as make-believe by its use of theatrical costume and, perhaps, by exotic and decorative stage sets. The new prologue Shaw wrote for *Caesar and Cleopatra* in 1912 brushes aside the convention of the transparent fourth wall, dividing the actors from the audience whose presence they ignore; and the statue of the god Ra gibes straight out of "ancient

Egypt" at the twentieth-century theatergoers. Although Shaw takes a different stretch of time, and thus different plot material, from Shakespeare in *Antony and Cleopatra*, he includes frequent allusions to, or reminiscences of, incidents and passages in the Shakespearean original.

Indeed, from the moment when Caesar, apostrophizing the Sphinx, is answered by the girlish voice calling "Old gentleman!" (the echo of a comic moment in Ibsen's moral fantasy of 1867, *Peer Gynt*), Shaw's play unfolds as a double structure of parody on heroic drama spattered with anachronisms, running parallel with a serious commentary on the action. He wrote the play with Forbes Robertson, "the classic actor of our day," in mind, but the date-eating Caesar is truly the chocolate-eating Bluntschli in a toga, while Britannus is the clown and Apollodorus is the harlequin from nineteenth-century pantomime; though it is equally true that Shaw has incorporated tragic themes. The way in which Shakespeare's play straddles two empires gave Shaw the lead toward further theatrical outrageousness: destroying the mold of conventional dramatic form in a deliberately straggling and halting action, and breaking out of the sober room, which is the typical set of modern naturalistic drama, into a frankly spectacular theater like grand opera gone mad and seeming at times like the circus, where characters dive or are pushed into a stage sea and the heroine is rolled around in a carpet. Besides the temple of Ra (in the 1912 version) and the Sphinx, the palace of Alexandria and its roof garden, the greatest library of the ancient world in flames, the Pharos and its lighthouse, and an ancient Egyptian steam-powered crane are borrowed from the pseudoclassical paintings of nineteenth-century Royal Academicians and brought to the stage. The energy of Shavian drama has burst its bounds and flowered into irregularity and extravagance, in the middle of which Caesar stands firm: not a heroic man-of-action, but a patient teacher.

MAN AND SUPERMAN

AFTER this, Shaw felt able to treat a drama of modern life with equal freedom, and the masterpieces *Man and Superman* (written in 1901–1902) and *John Bull's Other Island* (1904) were the result. The larger scale on which he worked in these plays probably reflected his hopes for the establishment of a national theater in which his drama would at last find its proper place. The campaigners certainly did not expect to have to wait until a second world war was over and a Labour government with a massive majority in office to see their plans adopted by the state; indeed Winston Churchill, a leading Liberal at the time, spoke with strong approval of the national theater cause in 1906. Shaw got on with the writing of *Man and Superman*, while Barker, with the *Scheme and Estimates for a National Theatre* already published over his name and William Archer's, proceeded in 1903 with a hilarious production for the Stage Society of *The Admirable Bashville*, a comic play in blank verse on material drawn from *Cashel Byron's Profession*; "Children in arms will find this play peculiarly suited to their taste and capacity" was one of the program notes supplied by the dramatist. Four months later, J. H. Leigh, lessee of the Royal Court theater, and his manager, J. E. Vedrenne, started a series of Shakespeare productions in which Barker was to take part, directing and acting in *Two Gentlemen of Verona*, on condition that he could also present six matinees of *Candida*. This led straight into the Vedrenne-Barker national theater experiment, in 1904. Barker had been involved as an understudy at the Avenue Theatre in 1894, when *Arms and the Man* had been presented in a double bill with W. B. Yeats's *Land of Heart's Desire*. The wealthy theater enthusiast Miss Annie Horniman had set up an Irish National Theatre at the Abbey Theatre, Dublin, by 1904. In this new theatrical climate Shaw had less need to compromise with what the public was used to, and could originate a new kind of play. Yet even in the Vedrenne-Barker seasons, the long dream sequence in the third act of *Man and Superman*, which turns a comedy of manners into a cosmic drama, was played separately.

As Shaw says in the dedicatory letter to the *Times* theater critic, A. B. Walkley, published with this play, he was answering a challenge to write about the legendary figure of Don Juan; and in his dream the millionaire socialist, John Tanner, is stripped of accidentals to reveal the type he belongs to. As we have seen, Tanner, his new satirized antihero, was not Shaw's first version of Don Juan. The outer acts of *Man and Superman* return to the matter of *Candida*: the convinced and eloquent socialist is caught in bondage, called marriage, by a woman who does not respect his principles and regards his zeal with indulgence rather than enthusiasm; *Man and Superman* deals with the process of capture, whereas *Candida* showed possession confirmed. Tanner is not

Don Juan the wayward lover of many women, but Don Juan brought low at last, in punishment for his rebellion against social and divine law. Among Shaw's remains is a two-page reading list of European literature on the Don. Unlike Morell, Tanner is treated as a figure of fun, Shaw's satiric strategy being to implicate the audience, through its laughter, with Ann against Jack, in the assimilation of the rebel by the forces of convention.

The main departure from the comedy of manners pattern is the startling change of scene involved by the motor tour—a form of chase—from England to Spain, which ends in capture by brigands. This plot element had been used in *Captain Brassbound's Conversion*; and the brigands—like the pirates of the earlier play—are a comic-opera chorus, except that these talk left-wing politics and thus offer a key to Shaw's satiric intention. Against this background Jack dreams that he is in hell, under his other identity of Don Juan in seventeenth-century garb, surrounded by other figures from the main play transformed, as in the stock transformation scene of pantomime, into other characters familiar from Mozart's opera *Don Giovanni*. They argue with brilliant, unflagging eloquence, in lengthy, rhetorically patterned speeches that call for virtuoso speaking as well as excellent memory on the actors' part.

The matter of their debate is philosophic, and for it Shaw plundered Schopenhauer (on the struggle of the sexes as a conflict between Intellect and Will) and the vitalist doctrine of Bergson. The manner is unmistakably operatic, the occasional burst of actual music backing up the effortlessly soaring dream-speech and the effervescence of ideas. Hell is defined within the episode as "the home of the unreal" (the setting is a void), and the scene serves a double purpose: as a mentally stimulating entertainment very loosely attached to the main play, a token of Shaw's expressed desire to turn his theater audience into a "pit of philosophers"; and as a satire on the inadequacy of talk and ideas (a more developed version of the attack on Morell in *Candida*), which fits closely into the general drama of Tanner and Ann Whitefield.

MAJOR BARBARA *AND* JOHN BULL'S OTHER ISLAND

IN identifying a particular social and psychological type with a recurrent figure of European legend, Shaw was moving on a general cultural tide that accompanied the decline of Christianity. The growing study of comparative religion and anthropology, as exemplified in James Frazer's *The Golden Bough* (1890), treated the Christian gospel story as one myth among others, and the ground was prepared for the deliberate use of mythic material as a kind of cultural shorthand in literature and art, as in psychoanalytic classification of human motives (most famously in the Oedipus complex).

Shaw went on to devise the plot of *Major Barbara* (1905) on lines that reflect several legends from within the Christian tradition: that of Barbara, the patron saint of gunners and miners, interlinked with a version of the mission, betrayal, passion, and ascension associated with Christ himself, and complicated with elements from the best known of postmedieval myths, that of Faust, who sells his soul to the Devil in exchange for some superhuman power in this world. He dedicated *Major Barbara* to his other close associate (along with Archer and Barker) in the campaign for a national theater and the Royal Court enterprise: Gilbert Murray, professor of Greek, whose translations of Euripides' plays were offered alongside Shaw's as new work appropriate to a national repertoire. It is well known that Professor Cusins in *Major Barbara*, nicknamed Euripides by his antagonist, the formidable Andrew Undershaft, was modeled on Gilbert Murray, to whom "my play stands indebted . . . in more ways than the way from Athens" (prefatory note to the screen version, published in 1945). Murray is known in another context as one of the small group of British classical scholars who gave wide currency to the theory of the ritual origins of Greek drama and were particularly influential on the modernist writers who incorporate myth in literature. The "way from Athens" is most directly seen in the allusions to Dionysus, god of irrational forces, linked with the birth of drama, made by Cusins in Shaw's text: Nietzsche's philosophic campaign against Christian ethics had made the name of Dionysus familiar to contemporaries by using it symbolically. But the reference was broader than that and included Shaw's indebtedness to the dialogues of Plato in his procedures for guiding others to the truth through informal debates lightened by humor and controlled with Socratic irony.

Technically, *Major Barbara* is the culmination and compendium of Shaw's work up to this point. Its three acts belong to different modes. The first is drawing-room comedy, dominated by a splendidly

alive caricature of the grande dame, Lady Britomart, who is played off against three disguised clown-types: the solemn idiocy of her son, Stephen; the silly-ass antics of Charles Lomax; and the clever, ironic clowning of Adolphus Cusins. The second act switches to a Salvation Army shelter in a poor district of London and a Dickensian melodramatic action, accompanied by an intense ironic commentary embedded in the dialogue. Act III is a variation of the abstract debate, against a symbolic background, that Shaw had tried out in the dream episode of *Man and Superman*; but this time he has kept it as an organic part of the main action of the play. If the author has a persona in *Man and Superman* it is John Tanner/Don Juan himself, and the play—like *The Philanderer* before it—is in part a self-directed analysis. He has two personas in *Major Barbara*: Cusins, who grasps the meaning and understands the irony of what is going on, but is himself involved as an actor; and Undershaft, the tempter/devil in the guise of an immensely wealthy manufacturer of armaments, who directs the plot from within the play, remaining essentially detached and a totally ironic consciousness, ultimately unfathomable.

Undershaft is the most formidable character Shaw had yet created—intellectually formidable, despite the mildest of civilized manners; the play as a whole is the most intellectually taut and challenging he ever wrote and has continued to provoke rival interpretations, not because it is confused in thought, but because Shaw has succeeded in leaving it dialectically open. The vision of Perivale St. Andrews (heaven against the hell of *Man and Superman*) is an ambiguous one that points toward a social millennium but remains a cheating simulacrum: Barbara sees that "It only needs a cathedral to be a heavenly city instead of a hellish one." Metaphor and symbol are used throughout the play with a similar dangerous ambiguity, summed up in the paradox of Cusins' intention to "make war on war" and even more sharply illustrated in such explosive aphorisms as "The ballot paper that really governs is the paper that has a bullet wrapped up in it," which are scattered through the text and testify to the influence of William Blake's aphoristic and dialectical *Marriage of Heaven and Hell*, from which Shaw has taken the concept of Energy, here conflated with the Schopenhauerian concept of Will. In doing this he has been able to replace the bland, hypocritical, and self-deceived type of heroine by a new, actively committed, androgynous figure in whom energy is directed by a positive belief. It is the price of this soul that the Faustian bargaining of *Major Barbara* seeks to define.

At the Court Theatre in 1905 *Major Barbara* confirmed the reputation Shaw had achieved with the previous play, *John Bull's Other Island*, a more centrally satirical, less overwhelmingly ironic work. For this he had taken a more specifically political theme: the policy of England, and the Liberal party in particular, toward Ireland, which was then governed entirely from London through Dublin Castle. This topic in itself was calculated to bring into the theater the men of affairs whom the management wanted to win over to the national theater campaign. Shaw, the leading Fabian, together with the Webbs, followed up astute publicity with direct invitations. As a result, all the leading statesmen of the day, the king, and other members of the royal family came, were delighted (Edward VII broke his chair with his paroxysms of laughter), and in many instances repeated the visit several times. The play makes a very serious indictment, but does so in a freer, less structured form, more like a variety show with a large cast of character turns than Shaw had ventured on before. At every point comedy gets under the guard of prejudice and drives criticism home, while the central dramatic idea holds everything in unity. Shaw uses the romantic movement's interpretation of Mephistopheles as the alter ego of a Faust who is blind to reality, including the truth about himself. Both figures appear in modern form as business partners: the English Liberal, Broadbent, genial and foolish, who believes, like Voltaire's Pangloss in *Candide*, that "All is for the best in the best of all possible worlds"; and the embittered, ruthless, self-exiled Irishman, whose consciousness reflects the evil that the other does in the illusion of his benevolence. It is interesting to reflect that the play which established his stature gives the plainest indication that the genial comedian's mask Shaw showed to the world overlaid a different self, formed by the Irish experience of his early years.

THE DOCTOR'S DILEMMA, MISALLIANCE, PYGMALION, ANDROCLES AND THE LION

IN 1906, at the age of fifty, Bernard Shaw could look back on some fifteen years of increasing fame, success, and influence. The production of his plays at the Court Theatre since 1904 had established him as a superb entertainer for intelligent audiences seeking a commentary on modern life and public affairs. The long waiting period, his novels, his journalism, his public speaking and committee work had all been preparation for what now seemed his true métier—as a dramatist. He had written a dozen plays that already showed his virtuosity; a greater number lay ahead, including some of his best work. His ambition was now matched by a sense of his powers and of opportunity at last within his grasp. He saw the next step as official recognition in the form of a national theater, where his work would take its place alongside Shakespeare's, and he wrote *The Dark Lady of the Sonnets* in 1910 as propaganda, and to win campaign funds, for this cause. When the Court Theatre seasons were not immediately followed by a new, major development, he wrote to his ally Barker and encouraged him to accept the directorate of a theater in New York as a step toward the conquest of two nations: "Why not do four years there, and then come back and found the national theatre and opera house of this country? . . . Eventually, simultaneous operations on both sides of the Atlantic might be possible" (21 April 1907).[2]

Instead, Shaw had to endure a number of disappointments: not only did Barker's apparent chance prove illusory, but critical reception of the major new Shaw plays produced in 1908 and 1910 (*Getting Married* and *Misalliance*) was not so favorable, and the public was cool; while in 1909 he ran into trouble with the censorship over *Press Cuttings* and *The Shewing-Up of Blanco Posnet*. Audiences were once more delighted by *Fanny's First Play*, which had a long run at a tiny theater in 1911, but Shaw had already devised tactics to help his subsequent plays along with the right kind of publicity. Starting with *Pygmalion*, he arranged for each to be performed abroad, in translation, before the British premiere. (The translations were initially for the purpose of copyright.) Thus English critics could be refuted by reports of success abroad, and his reputation as an international dramatist was made without interference by grudging English verdicts. Siegfried Trebitsch turned each play into German as it was written; Shaw continued to be performed in Germany during the war, though his royalties were frozen, and he remained easily the most-performed modern

[2]In C. B. Purdom, ed., *Bernard Shaw's Letters to Granville Barker* (London, 1957), p. 83.

playwright in Germany—at least until the rise of Nazism, and again after World War II until the mid-1950's, when he was superseded by Brecht, his most direct successor in more intrinsic ways also.

After the sustained effort and concentration that had gone into *Major Barbara*, Shaw wrote a group of more modestly designed plays that show an easy, near-perfect mastery. These are *The Doctor's Dilemma* (1906), *Fanny's First Play* (1910–1911), *Pygmalion* (1912), and the play he wrote for children young and old, *Androcles and the Lion* (1912). *The Doctor's Dilemma* and *Pygmalion* are problem plays in a special sense: they are logically designed to examine abstract propositions of some social consequence, and much of the pleasure they offer lies in the wit and elegance of an almost mathematically exact demonstration. That Shaw had been schooled in the Platonic dialogues is suggested by his use of a fictional mode to lead others to an understanding of the questions he has isolated; the liveliness and variety of his characters are a constant challenge to the rational scheme, as the opposed parties in *The Doctor's Dilemma* try to bend logic to their own ends and those in *Pygmalion* threaten to kick it to bits. Both plays confront the question of the relative merits of human individuals. (In 1928, Shaw was to propose to readers of his *Intelligent Woman's Guide to Socialism and Capitalism* that they should think out for themselves the most equitable way to distribute the wealth of society. There he advocates economic equality because there can be no absolute judgment of what men are worth.)

The reported incident of a distinguished physician's asking "Is he worth it?" when required to take on an additional patient struck Shaw forcibly, and he devised a play that would reflect on the godlike power that some men may be tempted to exert over others. His satirical portrayal of the doctors who set themselves up as judges exposes the false pretensions of the medical profession at the same time as it delights us with their separate human foibles, rivalries, and eccentricities; and the general point is silently reinforced by the expansive amiability of the greatest fool, Sir Ralph Bloomfield-Bonington (known to his friends as B.B.), which makes him "a born healer." To set up an ironic conflict that would add savor to the play, Shaw drew on his knowledge of the art world and the half-defined debate of the late nineteenth century between ethics and aesthetics carried on through John Ruskin and William Morris, Leo Tolstoy, Henry James, and Oscar Wilde, Shaw's colleague on the *Saturday Review*. So the doctors are

provided with their match in Louis Dubedat, the artist who combines the talent and frail constitution of Aubrey Beardsley with the wit and audacity of Ruskin's antagonist, James McNeill Whistler, and the incorrigible moral carelessness of Edward Aveling. In labeling *The Doctor's Dilemma* a tragedy, Shaw was up to his games again: including a death scene as formal qualification for the description, only to treat that scene with comic poise, and at the same time indicating with full justification that the themes of comedy can be at least as serious as those of tragedy.

Pygmalion examines the assumptions of social superiority and inferiority that underlie the class system, and demonstrates how unconsciously regulated patterns of social behavior (etiquette, opposed to more spontaneous manners) help preserve class distinctions. There is good reason to believe that Shaw had read Thorstein Veblen's *Theory of the Leisure Class* (1899). In particular, this play is concerned with speech differences as hallmarks of class: a professor of phonetics sets up an experiment to prove that he can turn a slum girl into a lady by changing her speech habits, and the comic climax of this scheme—negative proof of the theory—is reached when the elegantly dressed Eliza, in the most ladylike of tones, uses the taboo expression "Not bloody likely!" in the drawing room. The play gains symmetry, and its argument is made more complex, through the introduction of a second scheme, whereby her father is elevated socially and transformed in character by a bequest of money. The schematic element is cut across by a conflict more genuinely desperate than in *The Doctor's Dilemma*: the struggle of the girl to liberate herself from the insensitive tyranny of the professor, who is himself determined to remain comfortably dominant. As in so many of his plays, Shaw guides the audience's response to *Pygmalion* by combining in it echoes of older legends that arouse particular, sometimes discordant, expectations and emotions. Here he links the Cinderella story—the classic of wish-fulfilling transformation from rags to riches in a conventionally hierarchical society—with variations on the Faust legend of the man who assumes forbidden superhuman powers: Frankenstein, who creates a monstrous form of life (a more sinister analogue of the classical Pygmalion, the misogynist sculptor whose statue is brought to life in answer to his prayers), or Svengali (a role played shortly before with much success by Beerbohm Tree, the first English actor to play Professor Higgins), who turns a young girl into a world-renowned singer by the art of hypnotic possession. In every production of the play, the lure of the Cinderella plot is so strong, and Shaw's increasing self-projection as Higgins becomes so enticing, that the theme of the degradation of women and wastage of life in patriarchal society is all but submerged, even though it is spelled out in the dialogue.

The ambivalence of Shaw's attitude to the prewar feminist movement is revealed in a group of plays worth considering alongside *Pygmalion. Fanny's First Play,* as it was produced at the Little Theatre in 1911, masquerades as the work of a suffragette—though the introduction and epilogue written to sustain this pretense soften any challenge with an avuncular playfulness, and divert attention to new, peripheral material through recognizable parodies of leading contemporary theater critics. Inset is a play as "pleasant" as *You Never Can Tell,* in which Shavian idiosyncrasy is subdued to produce a light comedy that could almost have been written by the popular Arthur Wing Pinero and that includes a footman, really the younger brother of a duke, who claims relationship with J. M. Barrie's Admirable Crichton and anticipates the Jeeves of P. G. Wodehouse. Feminist values are assumed in the characterization of Margaret Knox, as in many of the energetic young women, impatient of convention, in Shaw's later drama; perhaps feminism is there, too, in the unabashed merriment of "Darling Dora," euphemistically described as a *fille de joie,* who turns that phrase into an imaginative reality. The explicit interlinked themes are a plea for youth's freedom to live experimentally and a commentary on the folly of class distinctions; but it is the old woman, Mrs. Knox, who is promoted to oracular authority, toward the end of the play—a minor echo of Mrs. George, who, dignified by mayoral robes and fallen into a trance, carries *Getting Married* beyond the range of laws and statute books into more abstract pronouncements on human life.

Among the Fabians, Shaw put up some resistance to the campaign for votes for women, in fearful anticipation that most women would support the Tories. The neglected sketch *Press Cuttings* (1909) is a vivid example of how his own fear of women rendered the idea that they might be given greater power farcical to him. The nearest he comes in this piece to presenting a suffragette is in the entrance of the prime minister, Balsquith (a lampoon on Balfour and Asquith), to the War Office, disguised in women's clothing and having first chained himself to the railings outside. The device has the explosive economy of political caricature, but its commentary on the nervousness of the politicians over the feminist issue preludes the arrival of two women who are contrasted, yet are equally tyrannical and man-despising antisuffrage campaigners. Mrs. Banger fully appreciates the War Office's argument of force in the face of suffragism and concludes: "Give me a regiment of women with sabres, opposed to a regiment of men with votes." The younger Shaw's attitude to the power exerted by Candida Morell and Ann Whitefield (in *Man and Superman*) finds much broader expression at this period, and Androcles and Megaera, in his Roman fable play of 1911–1912, are the henpecked husband and domineering wife of popular mythology, the music hall, pantomime, and comic seaside postcards. In *Misalliance,* the motherly Mrs. Tarleton, who calms down the would-be-revolutionary, is counterbalanced by an improbable apotheosis of free womanhood in the figure of Lina Szczepanowska, who literally takes off into the skies at the end of the play—so remote was the ideal from what actually went on and was likely to go on in the world, to the playwright's way of thinking.

Though he might choose to write the occasional piece, like the self-proclaimed melodrama *The Shewing-Up of Blanco Posnet,* in a conventional guise, Shaw was now demonstrating his mastery of style and form in an increasing eclecticism and freedom of experimentation. The variousness of his output challenged audiences' powers of swift adjustment to the mode of each new work. In particular, his blatant disregard of conventional snobbish distinctions between classical and "low" art carried the principle of equality into a new area, as well as increasing the cultural range embodied in individual plays. He advertised *Getting Married,* on the eve of its first production in 1908, as a return to "the Greek form." What he meant by this—except that he had not divided the play into acts and scenes—was left obscure. It is safe to assume that the dramatist who had used a phrase from Homer in the original to make a curiously erudite joke in *Major Barbara* had again been conferring with the Greek scholar Gilbert Murray. It is generally easier to identify parallels with Aristophanic comedy and the New Comedy of Menander, in *Getting Married,* than with Greek tragedy or Plato. The play has, in effect, two choruses, one male, one female, into which the cast is divided; there is no story plot, as there is no central protagonist, only a situation, much argument, considerable stage movement, and a scatter of incidents that culminate in the "judgment" delivered by the divinely possessed coal merchant's wife; and symbols of fertility are prominent in the stage picture. Many of the actors appear in forms of institutional fancy dress, as Bishop, General, or Beadle, and present a wide range of attitudes to sexual love and marriage, against a semiallegorical stage set representing the great pillars and arches of a Norman undercroft. Some of the elements of this play recur in *The Apple Cart* (1929), where the affinities with types of comic opera may be more easily recognized.

Rehearsing the actress Lillah McCarthy in Murray's version of Euripides' *The Bacchae*[3] led Shaw to incorporate motifs from that play, and fragments of its tragic plot, in *Misalliance*, mixing them up with elements of the companion play, *The Madras House* (both written in 1909), which Barker was writing for inclusion in the same new repertory program to be given by an idealistic commercial manager at the Duke of York's Theatre in 1910. The principle of burlesque, one of the most flourishing genres of English theater in the eighteenth and nineteenth centuries, was always congenial to Shaw, who liked to recall that Henry Fielding had practiced it, before political censorship drove him to novel-writing instead. Shaw preferred improvising playful variations on the work of others, parodying conventional forms and caricaturing familiar public figures, to inventing stories and characters with the primary power of illusion to blot out the actual world. But *Misalliance* takes off from farce into fantasy as no previous Shaw play had done; his comic genius comes into its own in a scintillating blend of nonsense, radical social comment, and gnomic wisdom. No doubt he was anxious, as he had been much earlier with *You Never Can Tell*, to conceal the teacher beneath the mask of an entertainer in order to win a West End audience; he succeeded only in baffling them. The quality of *Misalliance* has been discovered by productions in the second half of the century; the androgynous character of Polish origin who descends in an airplane upon the greenhouse of a wealthy linen-draper's Hindhead mansion and asks for a Bible and six oranges, and the clerk who conceals himself in the portable Turkish bath standing conveniently on stage and emerges brandishing a pistol and declaiming lines of apocalyptic rhetoric, have obvious affiliations with the 1960's farces of Joe Orton, or the highly intelligent craziness of the Monty Python entertainments.

---

[3]Shaw was often involved in rehearsing actors for other productions when he was not at work on one of his own.

Shaw's practice seems less idiosyncratic if it is seen in a wider context that goes beyond drama and beyond the boundaries of Britain. By comparison, in opera, Hugo von Hofmannsthal and Richard Strauss combined classical legend with the comedy of Molière's *Le Bourgeois Gentilhomme* and a harlequinade, in *Ariadne auf Naxos* (1912). The hostile reception given to the postimpressionist exhibition brought to London by Roger Fry in 1910 is evidence of the contemporary English public's ignorance of the artistic ferment that led to the emergence of a variety of now celebrated avant-garde movements in Europe before World War I. (Shaw was well acquainted with Roger Fry and made a considerable financial contribution to the setting-up of the Omega Workshop, which employed Duncan Grant and Vanessa Bell, among other artists, including briefly but prominently Wyndham Lewis, whose vorticist group was England's equivalent of futurism and cubism.) The barbaric vigor of Sergei Diaghilev's Ballet Russe, seen in Paris in 1909, and influential on Granville-Barker's prewar productions of Shakespeare, may be reflected in the figure of Lina Szczepanowska. It is now possible to see that Shaw's rejection of the logic of a cause-and-effect plot and a coherently developed thesis in *Misalliance* was allied to the assaults on bourgeois order and rationality that the futurists had recently started and that were to be continued by the Dada group at the Café Voltaire, in Zurich, when Shaw was at work on his next play in the same mode, *Heartbreak House*. The anarchic zest that found expression in *Misalliance*, the clown aspect of his temperament, was averse to any carefully constructed "organic" unity in art, preferring the effects of spontaneity and improvisation; it is not fundamentally at odds with the humane reservations expressed in *You Never Can Tell* and, later, in *The Doctor's Dilemma* about the doctrinaire application of reason to human life, which he saw as a most insidious form of the supreme enemy, idealism.

WORLD WAR I

THE coming of war largely diverted Shaw from playwriting. He had attacked militarism as early as 1909 in *Press Cuttings*, which takes sideswipes at Lord Kitchener's army and ridicules the fetish of military discipline through the mouth of a conscripted orderly: "It's being made a bloomin sheep of." Incidentally, the sketch anticipates the bringing of the moon into the orbit of power politics; more centrally, it turns around the argument offered with diabolical persuasiveness by Undershaft in *Major Barbara*, four years earlier, and gives it to General Mitchener, reduced to the basic, appalling logic of war and persecution, which he offers as "the secret of government": "Public opinion is mind. Mind is inseparable from matter. Shoot down the matter and you kill the mind." (Curiously enough, Shaw was never in the technical sense a pacifist, but he was later to fall into disrepute as favoring fascism.) Aware of the dangers of intensifying trade rivalries and the arms buildup to which Britain as well as Germany was committed, he used the press early in 1912 and again in the spring of 1913 to advocate a four-power peace-keeping pact between Britain, France, Germany, and the United States. He joined with Sidney and Beatrice Webb and H. D. Harben in founding the weekly review the *New Statesman*; and from its first number, in May 1913, he seems to have regarded it as his personal organ for influencing government and public opinion, overriding the protests of Clifford Sharp, the actual editor, to insist on the publication of his articles unsigned, as though they were editorials.

Immediately upon the outbreak of war, Shaw settled down to write an extended statement of his views on the situation, internal and international, which eventually appeared as "Commonsense About the War," an eighty-page supplement to the *New Statesman*, on 14 November 1914. It was widely read, and much more widely condemned, its reception having been prepared by fragmentary reports in the American press and what was, in effect, an open letter to the American president, Woodrow Wilson, that Shaw had published on both sides of the Atlantic. Although he considered that Britain, having gotten herself into the war, must now complete the business successfully, he would have no part of the hysteria of blind patriotism then sweeping the country. Perhaps his Irish origins helped, as he claimed, to keep him emotionally detached. The fact that he was writing precisely as he would have done before the outbreak of war, with the same critical clarity, the same intention to outrage and provoke, the same humorous exaggeration and sometimes flippancy of style, was now quite intolerable to the great majority, who had embraced the absolute moral imperative of the conflict with Germany, now transformed in their minds into a diabolical power. He was quite widely branded a traitor, even forced to resign from

the Dramatists' Club, and some who had been his friends broke with him temporarily or permanently.

By 1916, opinion was swinging around, and, privately at least, more people were prepared to agree with Shaw's views; early in 1917 he paid an official visit to the front, but it was certainly unrealistic of him to expect to be appointed by the British government as a member of the convention called to discuss the question of Home Rule for Ireland, in the aftermath of the Easter Rebellion in Dublin. A letter from Shaw defending the rebels and warning of the folly of reprisals had been published in the *Daily News*, and his help was sought and offered for the defense of Sir Roger Casement, eventually executed as a traitor for his part in seeking German aid for the Irish patriots. When the Irish Convention sat, in 1917, Shaw, anxious to be on hand in an advisory capacity, stayed in Dublin with its chairman, his friend Sir Horace Plunkett, and wrote the articles immediately collected under the title *How to Settle the Irish Question*, at the request of the *Daily Express*, generally the most antagonistic of newspapers to him and his views. In 1918 the Irish Recruiting Council asked him to write in support of its cause; though the armistice made it useless in any practical way, Shaw printed his characteristically devious arguments for Ireland's fighting alongside England in the European war in the pamphlet entitled *War Issues for Irishmen*, which he dated for historical interest 10 November 1918 but which was never issued to the public. Inevitably, he continued in his self-appointed task of political commentator and national adviser by issuing *Peace Conference Hints* (published in a limited edition in 1919) before Versailles.

Shaw's imaginative writing had been limited to short pieces during these war years. Light entertainment for troops home on leave seemed to be all that the theater wanted. Barker had temporized by taking a company to America in 1915, and the breakup of his marriage to Lillah McCarthy heralded the end of his work as a stage director and manager. This helps to explain the long delay before Shaw got down to writing the major play that he had been planning in 1913 and that did not appear in print or on the stage until after the war. For the Abbey Theatre, Dublin, which had put on *Blanco Posnet* when it was foolishly banned in England, he wrote the one-act *O'Flaherty, V.C.*, which may be classified among his antidomestic comedies—along with the 1913 farce *Great Catherine*—as it reveals that the Irishman's strongest motive for joining the British army is to get away from home and mother, though "home" certainly represents the troubled land of his birth, also; it is equally in line with the early *Arms and the Man* as one of Shaw's attacks on the idealization of war, and it was this aspect of the play that led to a threat from Dublin Castle that the theater's license would be revoked if it were produced. (In the absence of Yeats and Lady Augusta Gregory, who might have risen to the challenge, the theater gave in.) In addition, Shaw added to the farcical sketches he had written before the war *The Inca of Perusalem*, including a caricature of the kaiser, and *Augustus Does His Bit*, lampooning the stupidities of Whitehall bureaucrats, whom officers and men in the trenches were currently seeing as the enemy at their backs. He had also written a story for a Belgian charity, "The Emperor and the Little Girl," using a childlike consciousness for his critical purpose, as he had done in the early essay *My Dear Dorothea*.

Major events had occurred in Shaw's private life, such as it was, shortly before the war. His mother had died in 1913, and he had launched into an affair with Mrs. Patrick Campbell that may not have been wholly platonic and that caused his wife painful jealousy. As earlier in his life, the elation and flirtatious wrangling of being in love found ready expression both in letters to the lady and in his dramatic work: most immediately in *Pygmalion*, in which the part of Eliza was written for and played by Mrs. Campbell (a fact that raises the question of how far Shaw had fallen Pygmalion-like in love with his own creation); and later in his characterization of Hesione, in *Heartbreak House*, and in the "Interlude" of *The Apple Cart*. Possibly related to these events as much as to the general shattering of Edwardian complacency by the nightmare-come-true of the war itself, glimpses of emotional sensitivity appear: in private letters, as when he wrote to Stella Campbell and to Lady Gregory (when each had received the news of a son killed in action); in the general quality of *Heartbreak House*, and especially in Shotover's tenderness toward Ellie and, at last, toward Ariadne when she is troubled by her own unfeeling nature; there is emotion in Shotover's reflections on old age; and these signs anticipate the trial scene in *Saint Joan*, which the public was to find so moving.

HEARTBREAK HOUSE

SHAW had difficulty in getting on with the text of *Heartbreak House*, altering and rewriting more extensively than he was used to doing, perhaps partly because he was following no preconceived plan (as he later told Archibald Henderson). He was working on it through the greater part of 1916, the year before Guillaume Apollinaire coined the term *surréaliste* in his preface to *Les Mamelles de Tirésias (The Breasts of Tiresias)*. The names of some of the characters in the new play—Hector, Hesione (originally Hecuba), and Ariadne—indicate that Shaw was continuing whimsically to derive his work from Greek sources and, in particular, that it was in his mind to suggest an analogy between the fall of Troy and the last days of the British Empire. (The Gunner, in *Misalliance*, had already announced: "Rome fell. Babylon fell. Hindhead's turn will come.") When the text was published in 1919, it carried the descriptive subtitle "A Fantasia in the Russian Manner on English Themes," thus drawing attention to other elements in the design: the symbolist practice of replacing narrative and logical plotting with a patterning of themes in imitation of musical form (a fantastic and improvisatory patterning in this case); the assimilation of Shaw's view of the English leisure class to Anton Chekhov's treatment of the decaying provincial aristocracy of Russia in its country houses (at Shaw's prompting, begun in 1905, the Stage Society had presented *The Cherry Orchard* to London in 1911); and the volume of Shakespeare that Ellie Dunn is reading and that drops from her hand as she nods off, at the beginning of the play (a clue to the principal source from which the English themes are drawn). This is certainly not the end of the medley of materials that Shaw was now bringing together, ranging from an element of science fantasy (old Captain Shotover seeks a mind ray that will destroy his enemies) to Wagnerian cosmic allegory.

Whereas *Misalliance*, the closest anticipation of *Heartbreak House* in Shaw's drama, is generally explicable as a development out of native burlesque tradition in a climate of revolt against sober artistic conventions, the later play seems to draw imaginative and symbolic force from areas of the mind that are obscure to the playwright himself, perhaps half acknowledged in the nickname "the Ancient Mariner," which links Shotover with the weird romantic poetry of Coleridge. The humor—there is still plenty of it—is sometimes shadowed, suffused with dark moods, or clashing against them to grotesque effect. Capitalism is embodied and exposed in the character of Mangan; the more attractive, realistically drawn Mazzini Dunn, who accommodates himself happily to the strange house and its unpredictable inhabitants, represents the spirit of liberalism in its weakness and, ultimately, its strength. The rest of the vivid, strongly defined figures in the play seem for most of the time to be acting out their fantasy selves, larger than life, though occasionally coming down to earth with some commonplace admission. So the outer world of society, politics, and economics is interlocked, throughout, with the dreamlike quality of subjective life. Shaw later referred to *Heartbreak House* as his *Lear*, and indeed the character-constellation of Shotover-Hesione-Ariadne-Ellie is strikingly reminiscent of the old, mad king and his three daughters; but *The Tempest* is more substantially present in the dominant imagery of the ship driving on the rocks, the drunken sailors, the world-ordering sage who has dealt with occult powers and practices magic arts, yet watches tenderly over the young girl. Mangan, cast into a trance and cruelly persecuted, is part Caliban, part dwarfish Alberic mocked by the Rhine maidens and thwarted in his desire for Freya (Ellie) by the combination of Wotan and Loki in the guise of Shotover and Hector. For the tendency of the work is toward a kaleidoscopic quality. So, at the end in the theater, when stage and auditorium blaze in response to the call for more and more light, the mysterious sound in the air, ominously heard twice in Chekhov's *The Cherry Orchard*, is also the noise of raiding zeppelins overhead and a thrilling music: Beethoven is named in the dialogue, but it could as well be Wagner's *Ring of the Nibelungs*, the music of the flashing thunderstroke or the Ride of the Valkyries—until mind ray or "act of God" triggers the explosion.

The oracular Captain Shotover is often interpreted with some justice as Shaw's fantastic self-projection into *Heartbreak House*. Unless this is felt to some extent, the sharp dramatic jolt will be missed when he turns on Ellie: "What did you expect? A Savior, eh? Are you old-fashioned enough to believe in that?"

BACK TO METHUSELAH

THE idea that Shaw's later plays preach doctrinaire solutions to humanity's problems has done much to hamper Shaw criticism, especially in relation to his next and most ambitious play, *Back to Methuselah* (written in 1918–1920). This work's central point of reference is the recently ended European war, close to the characters of part II, which is set in the present;

the aftermath of the war is seen in remote but far from passionless perspective in the epilogue:

Mars blushed as he looked down on the shame of his sister planet: cruelty and hypocrisy became so hideous that the face of the earth was pitted with the graves of little children among which living skeletons crawled in search of horrible food.

Caricatures of Lloyd George and Asquith are introduced into the drawing-room comedy of part II to give topical focus to an exposition of the moral and intellectual bankruptcy of party politics. The design of the whole dramatic cycle is based on two principal conceptual models: Swift's satirical masterpiece, *Gulliver's Travels*, and the Judeo-Christian cosmic myth. The fact that the author called his work "A Metabiological Pentateuch" or, alternatively, a "Bible of Creative Evolution," suggests a more scientifically based replacement for the account of the creation and early history of mankind, which nineteenth-century Christians were having increasing difficulty believing as their Bible related it.

Shaw had earlier, in *Major Barbara*, written a play that took the forms of Christian legend and liturgy and changed their content. In *Back to Methuselah*, his admiration for the Bible as imaginative art is reflected in a new success in writing prose poems under its influence. The familiar story of Adam and Eve in the Garden of Eden and its continuation into the account of Cain and Abel after the Fall are retold in part I, "In the Beginning," with an economy unexpected in Shaw, and with a careful harnessing of the dramatic element to lyrical and reflective ends. The first scene introduces the themes to be developed throughout the play cycle, sounding them in succession, briefly defining them, repeating and linking them in a prose equivalent of sonata form; for the epilogue into which part V passes, the phantasms of Adam and Eve, Cain, and the Serpent return, only to be superseded by the further legendary figure of Lilith from rabbinical tradition, embodiment of the creative spirit outside time, who utters a final, sustained monologue that recapitulates all the themes in developed form. So the end circles back to the beginning and balances it in an aesthetically pleasing way.

Within this frame Shaw uses the notion of relative length (or expectation) of life as the fictive basis for his satirical perspectives, as Swift used relative physical size. The last three sections thus offer variant utopias, or speculative fantasies of human life at distances of 250, 1,080, and 30,000 years beyond the present. Far from showing any increase in wisdom, the government of the British Isles is headed in part III by a burlesque conflation of the Lloyd George and Asquith figures of the previous section viewed with a broader, more contemptuous mockery; technological advance is opportunity for greater silliness among the English, while the serious running of the state is carried on by a civil service of Chinese and blacks. The folly of the generation that had brought about the war persists in the deputation of short-livers that has traveled from the capital of the British Commonwealth at Baghdad to consult the oracle among the long-livers in southern Ireland, in part IV; indeed the Napoleonic figure of the Emperor of Turania appears to be a reincarnation of Cain much degenerated since part I.

In the last section, the vanities and illusions of humanity as we know it persist only in (physically mature) children under the age of five and, in cruder and more vicious form, reappear briefly in the automata made by the scientist-sculptor among them, who is destroyed by his own horrible creation. For the antitheses that he uses critically Shaw went to Plato: the long-livers of part IV are the totally rational Guardians of the *Republic*, who do not understand metaphor and regard imagination as a lying faculty; in part V, the state has withered away and the errors and excesses of self-government are committed by the Ancients only within the boundaries of the self, as part of an endless process of self-development and discovery. As the evolutionary direction is away from beauty toward truth, away from art toward contemplative thought and its more direct material transformations, the playwright's own activity is called into question; it is put into perspective by the miniature inset tragedy acted out by the automata when they have been partially transformed by the breath of life, and at which even the Ancients smile. The function of art is one of the main themes of the cycle, and Shaw is careful from part I to the epilogue to indicate that he belongs among those who "tell beautiful lies in beautiful words" and that what he is now presenting is not a prediction or blueprint for the future, but a fable.

Apart from a common tendency to raise overliteral objections to the substance of *Back to Methuselah*, for which Shaw's exposition of the theory of creative evolution in the preface is partly to blame, there has been much division of critical opinion over this play. In its general conception it is the most impressive, as well as the longest, of Shaw's dramatic achievements, yet critics have often shied away from it. Not surprisingly, the execution of the scheme is uneven, and there are passages, especially in the lengthy duologues of Zoo and Zozim with the Elderly Gentleman, in part IV, when Shaw seems to have forgotten that he was writing for stage production and even falters in his differentiation of characters. It is difficult to be particularly enthusiastic about part III, "The Thing Happens" (corresponding to the Laputa section of *Gulliver's Travels*): the satire is little more penetrating than it is precise, the short-lived characters are two-dimensional, and the clownish comedy lacks engaging geniality; the carrying on of the narrative from part II holds the attention sufficiently to make a bridge to the more important fourth and fifth sections, where philosophic thought gains dominance over the satiric element, though never ousting it completely.

"Tragedy of an Elderly Gentleman" is, despite the length of its expositions, the most moving section of the whole, for the main character, who is, like Gulliver, driven to detest his own Yahoo nature, has genuine moral passion, and Shaw's rhetoric is at its most powerful and various in rhythm and tone in the sweep of his interrupted monologues:

My society has printed an editio princeps of the works of the father of history, Thucyderodotus Macollybuckle. Have you read his account of what was blasphemously called the Perfect City of God, and the attempt made to reproduce it in the northern part of these islands by Jonhobsnoxious, called the Leviathan? Those misguided people sacrificed the fragment of life that was granted to them to an imaginary immortality. They crucified the prophet who told them to take no thought for the morrow and that here and now was their Australia. . . . I accept my three score and ten years. If they are filled with usefulness, with justice, with mercy, with good-will; if they are the lifetime of a soul that never loses its honor and a brain that never loses its eagerness, they are enough for me, because these things are infinite and eternal. . . .

There is concentrated substance in this, not windy inflation, and the immediate detail also serves as commentary on the entire work.

Shaw's images of the remote future are derived from the classical past. "Their dress," he says of the children, "like the architecture of the theatre and the design of the altar and curved seats, resembles Grecian of the fourth century B.C., freely handled." All is contained in "a sunlit glade," and the use of music and formal dance contributes to the pastoral effect, the aesthetic charm and tranquility of this most distanced view of human nature. Shaw did not forget here that the characters were to be played by living actors, but offered them a distillation of familiar qualities to portray in the petulance of Strephon; the boring self-complacency of Pygmalion; the brash, soubrettish eagerness of the Newly Born (in whom both Savvy Barnabas of the twentieth century and Zoo return)—as in part I he offered the touchiness of Adam, the jealousy of Eve, the sly flattery and ironic consciousness of the Serpent. Even in his presentation of the Ancients, those grotesque embodiments of the philosophic mind, laughter and gravity are interwoven; and in part V, as in part IV, a virtually self-contained dramatic action counterbalances the discussion. The kinds of drama Shaw has written in the later parts of *Back to Methuselah* are rare in the theater, and their sophisticated artifice may be an acquired taste; but stage productions have reinforced their claim to a critical appraisal that acknowledges the care and skill with which they have been composed.

It seemed to Shaw, when he had finished *Back to Methuselah,* that he had probably written his last play. He was sixty-five years old, and he had given extended expression to the faith in Creative Evolution that he had derived from Samuel Butler and from Henri Bergson, and that he had come increasingly to speak of as his religion. It is worth noting that he did not call his socialism a religion. Having rejected Marxism, as he rejected the Darwinian version of the evolution of species, as too deterministic, he preferred to stress the pragmatic and provisional nature of his Fabian views and principles. (Incidentally, he associated himself with Ebenezer Howard's Fourierist scheme for changing society through the establishment of cooperative "Garden Cities," which resulted in the founding of Letchworth in the early years of the century and Welwyn between the wars, both within easy distance of the Shaws' country home at Ayot St. Lawrence.) The certainty of continual change, failure, decay, the necessity for renewed efforts and fresh visions were essential articles of the general faith in which he confronted the postwar world, the coming of the second major war, and the arrival of the nuclear age with its sharper threat of universal destruction.

SAINT JOAN—*SHAW'S BELIEFS*

SHAW's wife was largely responsible for interesting him in a further dramatic project: a play on the subject of Joan of Arc. Her legend had been revived in France during the war; and an ambitious Hollywood silent film, *Joan the Woman,* had been made in 1917 with the leading soprano of the Metropolitan Opera, Geraldine Farrar, in the lead. In 1920 Joan was canonized, an event that gave publicity to the original documents to which Shaw chose to go for his materials. There he found a heroine after his own heart: clearheaded and quick-witted, energetic and practical, with a personality that ruled out any crude element of sex appeal. What he produced was not a history, however, so much as another fable play that was to be the principal model for such Brechtian "historical" fables as *Mother Courage* (1936–1939)[4] and *Galileo* (1938–1939)—Brecht's *St. Joan of the Stockyards* (1929–1930) is more closely related to *Major Barbara*—and for Luigi Pirandello's theatrical demonstrations of the relativity of truth and illusion in *Six Characters in Search of an Author* (1921) and, more specifically, his *Henry IV* (1922).

To ensure the perspective of fable, Shaw combined a chronicle-play form with elements from the native tradition of pantomime. He started with a scene based on the same kind of folk legend as the familiar pantomimes of *Dick Whittington, Puss in Boots,* and *Mother Goose:* confronted by the insouciant audacity of the androgynous Principal Boy, whose garb Joan is eager to put on, Baudricourt stamps and fumes like a pantomime ogre; Joan's first triumph is marked by a suitably rustic "miracle," when the hens suddenly start laying in crazy abundance. The Dauphin is the clown of the play, though a particularly shrewd one; and the scattering of verbal anachronisms (from the allusion to "cowboys" in the first passage), and contemporary and often schoolboyish slang expressions, together with Joan's lapses into pantomime dialect (for example, "Coom, Bluebeard. . . . Where be dauphin?" or "Dressing up dont fill empty noddle"), are calculated controls on what might too easily have turned into a tragic pageant play. Shaw admits the possibility of a tragic vision of the materials he is using (the dialogue includes a reference to Joan's hubris), and the succession of scenes leading up to the trial, and into the immediate aftermath of Joan's death at the stake, establishes a gradual increase in gravity; but the epilogue—decried by a majority of contemporary critics, who wanted a more romantic work than the dramatist chose to give—breaks the illusion of a history play, by taking the historical events into a dream realm outside time, and reasserts the perspective of comedy in a culmination of all the earlier comic inciden-

[4]The years cited are those for the first versions of Brecht's plays.

GEORGE BERNARD SHAW

tals. In fact, this last scene, which introduces a modern man in a top hat among the medieval characters, thus revealing them all as actors dressed up, is in part a return to nineteenth-century extravaganza convention, but changes into a new hybrid as it passes into the final, liturgical movement: a *Te Deum* that closes the saint's play, a passion play imitative of Christ's passion (as are all such plays within the Christian tradition), which is also assimilated into Shaw's total scheme.

The heroine is as ambiguous as the form of the play. As a human individual she is "quite innocent," as the Inquisitor privately recognizes; but a similar innocence is caricatured in the person of de Stogumber, the simpleton priest on the English side whose crude nationalism has all the excesses Shaw had deplored in the insensate patriotism he observed around him in the early years of the war with Germany. Joan is a contrast with the priest in that he lacks imagination, while hers is so vivid that it imposes itself upon her as supernatural revelation; but her vision still has its limitations, and her innocence is partly unreflecting ignorance of where her inspiration might ultimately lead. The subtle churchmen see further. Indeed, the tense conflicts of the play are essentially conflicts of perspective: Dunois, the Dauphin, and Warwick all have elements of foxy, Machiavellian political awareness beyond the range of Joan's consciousness; with a modern historian's understanding, Cauchon looks beyond the end of feudalism and the rise of Protestantism to the more distant effects of uncurbed individual self-assertion and nationalism—toward the twentieth century: "a world of blood, of fury, of devastation, of each man striving for his own hand: in the end a world wrecked back into barbarism." The Joan whose suggestion of a second coming appalls the other characters of the epilogue is both the champion of absolutes and herself an idealization, too dangerous a phenomenon to be trusted in any age. The voices she hears and stubbornly insists on obeying are tokens of her authenticity, but, though Shaw may have accepted that "The unconscious self is the true genius" (one of the Maxims for Revolutionists attached to *Man and Superman*), he was very far from equating irrationality with good. Joan's "innocent" arrogance is consequent on her lack of a self-critical faculty. According to the Serpent in *Back to Methuselah*, "The Voice in the garden is your own voice," though Adam's qualification of this claims attention: "It is; and it is not. It is something greater than me: I am

only a part of it." However altruistic its intent, the value of inspiration still needs to be tested critically, as the Inquisition, despite all its confusions and irrelevancies, tests Joan's.

A number of Shaw's plays have been classified as "religious," among them *Major Barbara*, *The Shewing-Up of Blanco Posnet*, *Androcles and the Lion*, *Back to Methuselah*, and *Saint Joan*; and certainly the adolescent Bernard Shaw who mocked all religion as crass superstition stayed, in later life, to discover the truth any religious belief might hold. He numbered among his later friends both the Anglican dean Inge and the Catholic abbess of Stanbrook, Dame Laurentia McLachlan, to whom he presented a copy of his prose fable *The Adventures of the Black Girl in Her Search for God* (1932), in expectation of an understanding it did not receive. Undershaft, in *Major Barbara*, names the subject of religion as "the only one that capable people really care for"; and Tarleton, in *Misalliance*, repudiates Ecclesiastes' association of age with the desire that fails: "Does it? By George! No, sir: it spiritualizes."

Yet an examination of Shaw's later writings makes it clear that he was not among the rebels from traditional belief who revert to some form of it as age draws on. Lavinia, in *Androcles* (the central part of which borrows the form of the sensational melodrama *The Sign of the Cross*, which was written and performed by the actor-manager Wilson Barrett and first published in 1896), discovers her readiness to die for something greater than herself but also realizes that no particular doctrine is great enough to merit total self-sacrifice. As the Archbishop explains away Joan's apparently supernatural powers in the formula "A miracle is an event that creates faith," so the dramatist rationalizes her voices and visions on a psychological basis as forms taken by natural forces, objectifications of her impulses and perceptions. *The Adventures of the Black Girl* is a critical examination of the gods that men have made for themselves that is as close to Voltaire in attitude as in its literary procedures; indeed allusions to Voltaire multiply in Shaw's late writings. Shaw was certainly in pursuit of a longer view than politics affords, but he never abandoned the rational understanding of philosophy for mysticism.

Shaw became a life member of the Royal Astronomical Society, and it fell to him to propose a toast to Albert Einstein at a celebratory dinner in 1931; at the age of ninety-three he applied to join the British Interplanetary Society, with Arthur C. Clarke, a

1076

well-known exponent of popular science, sponsoring him. He submitted the scientific material in the text of *In Good King Charles's Golden Days* (1938–1939) to Sir James Jeans and Sir Arthur Eddington for correction. In fact, he was as concerned as when he wrote *The Irrational Knot* that his view of the world and human life should be scientific. Most of his late plays offer a more distant and abstract view of their subjects (as anticipated by the last section of *Back to Methuselah*), as they take account of the major calamities of the twentieth century and, by the time he reached *Farfetched Fables* (1948), incorporate the atomic bomb and chemical warfare in their range of vision. Using a scale of astronomical change enables the playwright to maintain his philosophic and comedic poise, but as early as *Caesar and Cleopatra*, with its references to Pythagoras, and later, in *Saint Joan*, which identifies Pythagoras as "a sage who held that the earth is round, and that it moves round the sun," Shaw had used scientific theories as tokens of the relativity and provisional nature of any truth that the human mind could—indeed must—grasp.

Saint Joan proved to be the great popular favorite among Shaw's plays, though he himself never rated it so high. The first English production was beautifully staged, with decorative hangings and costumes by the great art nouveau designer Charles Ricketts, and the memory of it unluckily encouraged subsequent overromantic interpretations of the work that, in turn, helped trigger the reaction against Shaw's whole reputation as a dramatist. Meanwhile, in 1925, he won the Nobel Prize for Literature, the only public honor he agreed to accept—on the understanding that he be permitted to use the prize money for the making and publication of translations from Swedish literature, especially August Strindberg's plays, into English. After *Saint Joan* there was a gap of six years before he wrote another play. His major work within this period was the writing, at his sister-in-law's request, of *The Intelligent Woman's Guide to Socialism and Capitalism* (published in 1928; he later added chapters on "Sovietism" and Fascism for the Penguin edition in 1937), which shows the born teacher in Shaw to best advantage: master of an unforced simplicity of exposition and continual vivid yet careful illustration, staying within the bounds of the reader's likely experience. As he presents them, politics and economics are not specialist studies but the daily business of ordinary men and women. The manner he used in this book, as in many of the prefaces written to accompany his plays in printed form, was to make him a very effective broadcaster during the next decade and remained at his command for his last major work, *Everybody's Political What's What?*, published in 1944.

LAST PLAYS AND OTHER WRITINGS

SIR BARRY JACKSON, the wealthy theater enthusiast who gave to Birmingham between the wars a repertory theater of the first order and who was a direct inheritor of Barker's work, was responsible for the extension of Shaw's playwriting career through another eight full-length plays and a number of shorter pieces. It was he who had eventually produced *Back to Methuselah* and brought it to London, and his establishment of an annual Shaw Festival at Malvern gave the dramatist fresh impetus for the creation of new works. (Though he was once more assured of a stage and a company at his disposal in England, he continued to arrange premieres abroad, increasingly by the New York Theatre Guild; and *Geneva*—1936; revised sometime before 1939—was playing in Warsaw when Nazi troops entered the city.) The plays of the final phase still await adequate critical attention: as a group, they remain little known and tend to be briefly dismissed without differentiation as virtually senile relics of a failing talent. But the long practice of his craft stood Shaw in good stead, and although there are echoes of earlier work in most of these plays, there is no repetition of formulas, but continuing inventiveness and incisive criticism. The late work may not have the tight thematic complexity of *Major Barbara* or match the fresh exuberance of *Misalliance* or *Pygmalion*, but most of it compares well in quality with some of the plays Shaw wrote before 1900. Recent productions of *Too True to Be Good* (1931) and *On the Rocks* (1933) have held their audiences as surely as *The Philanderer* or *The Devil's Disciple*; and *The Simpleton of the Unexpected Isles* (1934) is not obviously inferior in interest or skill to *Captain Brassbound's Conversion*.

New concerns come into prominence in the late plays: above all, the theme of individual responsibility recurs in one after another. *The Apple Cart* (1928) and *On the Rocks* are Shaw's main indictments of the ineffectualness of parliamentary democracy. The first of these emulates Aristophanic

1077

comedy and offers a loosely constructed satirical entertainment (with some meticulous patterning of detail) in which a chorus of cabinet members is a major element. By locating the action at an indefinite but not too distant future time, and giving classical names to the characters, Shaw is able to abstract the essentials of the situation he wants to examine. A tendency to such abstraction, which gives the plays the quality of philosophic fables, is another general characteristic of this last phase of his work. In *On the Rocks* he presents the cabinet room at 10 Downing Street on the stage, but his prime minister is not identifiable with any actual politician, and again the effect is to make the play tangential to the actual world and to emphasize the hypothetical nature of the plot. An ultimatum from America, threatening to annex Britain, breaks in upon the petty internal squabbling in *The Apple Cart*; the action of *On the Rocks* turns on the supposition that the prime minister, faced by the economic slump and mass unemployment of contemporary England, is converted to socialism by reading Marx and attempts to deal with his country's problems accordingly. Both plays demonstrate the power of vested interests at work within the party political system. *The Apple Cart* also specifically attacks the passivity of the trade union rank-and-file, which gives excessive power, without adequate accountability, to its leaders. The political maneuverings shown in *On the Rocks* are more intense and subtle, as well as more substantial, than the stylized, token equivalents in *The Apple Cart*; and it is in keeping that the old, disillusioned trade unionist, Hipney, should bring a deadlier irony into the play, as he offers the decade's most dangerous temptations:

. . . if Srarthur means business, then let him come out of Parliament and keep out. . . . The only man that ever had a proper understanding of Parliament was old Guy Fawkes. . . . Adult suffrage: that was what was to save us all. My God! It delivered us into the hands of our spoilers and oppressors, bound hand and foot by our own folly and ignorance . . . now I'm for any Napoleon or Mussolini or Lenin or Chavender that has the stuff in him to take both the people and the spoilers and oppressors by the scruffs of their silly necks and just sling them into the way they should go. . . . You cant frighten me with a word like dictator. Me and my like has been dictated to all our lives by swine that have nothing but a snout for money. . . .

But Chavender has liberal scruples that leave him anticipating some man of iron who will put through the measures he knows are needed: "I'm not the man for the job. . . . And I shall hate the man who will carry it through for his cruelty and the desolation he will bring on us and our like."

The common verdict that Shaw was pro-Fascist in the 1930's was certainly based on careless attention to his writings, a confusion between satirical technique and substance, perhaps compounded by knowledge of the close friendship he developed with the first woman (Conservative) member of Parliament, Lady Astor, whose home became a frequent meeting place for those who favored the policy of appeasing Hitler. In his public utterances Shaw tended to use the dictators as sticks with which to correct the errors of the British, while being little concerned and not very knowledgeable about the evils of their regimes. (He was certainly flattered by Stalin during the visit he paid to Russia, in a small party that also included Lady Astor, in 1931.) The term "extermination" figures quite prominently in his work of this decade; later, in *Farfetched Fables*, it is replaced by "liquidation." Defiantly, his preface to *On the Rocks* argued the case for political purges: he was certainly persisting in his efforts to shock the public into thinking, and his attitude cannot be properly appraised unless the preface is not only weighed against the testimony of the plays but seen in the context of his general opposition to judicial punishment, most fully stated in his preface to the volume on prisons in the Webbs' *English Prisons Under Local Government* (1922), several times separately reprinted. In the course of this radical document he declares that the idea of individual freedom "is as yet unformed":

we conceive Man as being either in authority or subject to authority. . . . The concept of the evolving free man in an evolving society . . . is still unusual, and consequently terrifying, in spite of all the individualist pamphlets of the eighteenth and nineteenth centuries.

His opinion that capital punishment is more humane than imprisonment received a good deal of publicity, and supplied the motivation for Joan of Arc's emotional choice of the stake in his dramatization of her story. The process of extermination, or "weeding the garden," gets its dramatic presentation in *The Simpleton of the Unexpected Isles*: useless people and mere talkers vanish, like Euphorion in the Faust legend, into air; for Shaw's abstract idea lacks the ferocity of Swift's "Modest Proposal" that the ills of Ireland might be cured by encouraging the natives to eat their children, though both display the satirist's necessary ability to be inhumanly rational about what may matter greatly to the man. The garden that is being weeded is an island utopia where the unit of group marriage embraces a blend of the cultures of East and West, subsequent to the death of colonialism. But as all fixed ideas and established systems threaten to tyrannize over "the evolving free man," the whole dream is judged and dismissed before the play ends.

Recognition that King Magnus, in *The Apple Cart*, is not a benign autocrat, but a representative figure of responsible individuality, might have come more easily if Barker's last play, *His Majesty* (1923–1928), on which Shaw drew heavily in his accustomed way in *The Apple Cart* and *On the Rocks*, had been more generally known. Yet Shaw often referred to John Bunyan as his favorite author, a fair enough clue to his own practice of allegory and a warning against overliteral interpretation that is most applicable to his later work. Concentration of the serious thought of *The Apple Cart* in the lengthy arias of the soloists, Magnus and Lysistrata, too sharply distinguishes them from the ridiculous chorus; *Too True to Be Good* may be finally less confusing because the improbabilities and absurdities of plot and matching, disjointed shifts from one stylized theatrical mode to another involve all the characters equally: from the Measles Microbe (the clown) in the prologue to the orating Elder in his cave; the Patient and the Burglar in their changing guises; and old Mrs. Mopply, who is brought to sanity by a blow from an umbrella. The whole of this latter play is acceptable as a wild fantasy version of Britain and the Empire midway between the wars; it is technically a development from *Heartbreak House*, offering Shaw's final version of Jack Tanner (of *Man and Superman*) in the compulsive preacher with nothing to say, on whom the curtain descends, but reserving respect for the energetic female, whose portrait is not now undercut with irony, as happened with Vivie Warren or Ann Whitefield in the earlier plays.

Substantially the same character appears as the Young Woman in *The Simpleton* and the similarly labeled female voice that drives through the comic duologue *Village Wooing* (1933). Amanda, the soubrette of *The Apple Cart*, Aloysia Brollikins, who emerges out of the Aristophanic chorus of *On the Rocks*, and Nell Gwynn, in *In Good King Charles's Golden Days*, are versions of the same type assimilated to vaudeville conventions. Opportunities for actors to give virtuoso displays of highly stylized acting technique are as readily to be found in most of the late work as at any earlier period of Shaw's career. The most considerable star role for an actress, in the last plays, is the part of Epifania in *The Millionairess* (1934), which requires emotional power, not simply controlled energy: a melancholy, operatic grandeur. Yet a general comparison of Epifania with Lulu, Frank Wedekind's personification in the Lulu plays of the life force, points up one aspect of Shaw's work that has particularly dissatisfied the later twentieth century: his failure to deal with sexuality, as distinct from the socially conventionalized forms of eroticism. The marriages to which several of the late plays lead are allegorical happy endings, in which efficiency and productive capacity are united with spiritual values or vision.

The voyages to distant parts of the world that the Shaws took between 1931 and 1934 undoubtedly suggested the exotic settings and elements of adventure among which the philosophic questions are posed in *Too True, The Simpleton of the Unexpected Isles, Buoyant Billions* (1936–1937 and 1945–1947), and the nondramatic fable of *The Adventures of the Black Girl*, which Shaw wrote in South Africa. (*Village Wooing* is evidently a product of shipboard experience.) In subtitling *The Apple Cart* and *Too True to Be Good* "extravaganzas," the dramatist was pointing to connections with nineteenth-century entertainments that relied as much on stage spectacle as on music and comedy. But the movement out of English domestic settings into desert, jungle, or oriental temple scenes is also a superficial token of how the world has become the true and relevant context of the plays. Internationalism is the theme of *Geneva*, the last of Shaw's plays to achieve a long run in the theater during his lifetime. Topicality may have been its chief attraction initially, though its caricatures of Mussolini, Franco, and Hitler are used as lay figures in a burlesque with a moral lesson to deliver that is even more urgent today. The political education of the audience has its surrogate in the stage action, which leads the averagely amiable, ignorant, and prejudiced Begonia Brown to summon the dictators before the World Court, the audience they cannot resist posturing before. In the literal sense the trial is "a farce," but Begonia's discovery of her own power and exposure of her inadequacy to use it wisely is more fundamental to Shaw's purpose. The Judge's verdict, "Man is a failure as a political animal," is promptly followed by news from the astronomical observatories that spells out a judicial

1079

sentence: "Humanity is doomed." Impatient of pessimism even now, and preferring to be a teacher rather than a prophet, Shaw defuses the threat of its terror in order to use it as a warning.

Shaw undoubtedly accepted the view of himself as the greatest playwright of his generation. He had taken upon himself, as if it were a public office, the characteristically Victorian role of keeper of the public conscience, criticizing the state from within and teaching its citizens how to govern; like Ibsen, he kept up a running quarrel with the majority. Being, in his generation, in revolt against Victorian earnestness and the hypocrisy it encouraged, he played the clown to carry out his task. Having inherited a theater that lent itself to the display and the mockery of rhetoric, he created for it a large repertoire of technically innovative, prolifically various, exuberant, and exhilarating works in which his passion for music found expression through torrents of cunningly orchestrated dialogue distributed among a great range of vivid, assertive characters whose home is truly the stage. His was a lopsided genius, certainly, with the virtues of its own defects: he translated his temperamental detachment into breadth of vision and public concern—for the community and, ultimately, for the species; his rejection of suffering released tremendous energy; and the buried stream of powerful feeling was signaled by his effervescent and even anarchic humor. If the intellectual thrust fails, his clowning alone can seem embarrassingly childish. Yet he remains one of the few writers who have had a complete and profound comic vision of the world: it might be "God's joke," he commented to Tolstoy, who did not understand; and being innocent of the worst confusions of the soul, he refused to romanticize as evil the ignorance and folly of men.

SELECTED BIBLIOGRAPHY

Many of Shaw's plays were published in German translations or in some cases in other languages before publication of the English texts. These foreign-language editions are not listed below.

I. BIBLIOGRAPHY.
Writings: G. H. Wells, "A Bibliography of the Books and Pamphlets of Bernard Shaw" (London, 1926; rev., enl. ed., 1929), pamphlet, from *The Bookman's Journal* Supplements (1928–1929); C. L. and V. M. Broad, *Dictionary to the Plays and Novels of Bernard Shaw, with Bibliography of His Works* . . (London, 1929); S. Weintraub, "Shaw,"

in R. J. Finneran, ed., *Anglo-Irish Literature. A Review of Research* (New York, 1976); J. C. Amalric, *Bernard Shaw, du réformateur victorien au prophète édouardien* (Paris, 1977), 423–566; F. E. Loewenstein, *The Rehearsal Copies of Bernard Shaw's Plays* (London, 1950), of more specialist bibliographical interest; D. H. Laurence, comp., *Shaw: An Exhibit* (Austin, 1978), a catalog comp. for the Humanities Research Center of the University of Texas, contains much information.

Works About Shaw: "A Continuing Checklist of Shaviana," issued in the *Shaw Bulletin*, later the *Shaw Review*, published three times a year since 1950; E. Farley and M. Carlson, "George Bernard Shaw: A Selected Bibliography (1945–1955)," in *Modern Drama*, parts I and II (September and December 1959); L. C. Keough, "George Bernard Shaw, 1946–1955: A Bibliography," in *Bulletin of Bibliography* (September–December 1959, January–April 1960, May–August 1960); M. M. Morgan, "Shaw," in S. J. Wells, ed., *English Drama (Excluding Shakespeare)* (London, 1975), discusses a selection of publications on Shaw, see also J. C. Amalric and S. Weintraub, above.

II. COLLECTED WORKS. All of the following eds. were originally seen through the press by Shaw himself: *Collected Edition*, 30 vols. (lim. ed., London, 1930–1932), 3 more vols. added by 1937, lim. to 1,000 sets, known in the U.S. as the Ayot St. Lawrence ed.; *Standard Edition*, 37 vols. (London, 1931–1950), contains items not in the *Collected Edition*; *Complete Plays* (London, 1931; enl., 1934, 1938, 1950; reiss. 1965); *Our Theatres in the Nineties*, 3 vols. (London, 1932), weekly reviews contributed to the *Saturday Review* (5 January 1895–21 May 1898), in the *Standard Edition*; *Music in London*, 3 vols. (London, 1932), weekly articles contributed to the *World*, 28 May 1890–8 August 1894, in the *Standard Edition*; *Prefaces* (London, 1934), the updated and enl. ed. is entitled *Complete Prefaces* (London, 1938; reiss. 1965); *London Music in 1888–1889 as Heard by Corno di Bassetto* (London, 1937), articles originally contributed to the *Star*, in the *Standard Edition*; *The Penguin Edition*, 10 vols. (Harmondsworth, 1946), additional vol. (1956), current reprs. under editorial supervision of D. H. Laurence.

D. H. Laurence, ed., *The Bodley Head Bernard Shaw, Collected Plays and Their Prefaces*, 7 vols. (London, 1970–1974), containing previously unpublished texts in the last vol., also miscellaneous material by Shaw relating to each play, with history of composition, publication, and early performances, is new definitive ed.; D. H. Laurence, gen. ed., *Early Texts: Play Manuscripts in Facsimile*, 9 vols. (New York, 1981); D. H. Laurence, ed., *The Bodley Head Shaw; Complete Musical Criticism*, 3 vols. (London, 1981), definitive.

III. OTHER POSTHUMOUS COLLECTIONS. E. J. West, ed., *Shaw on Theatre* (New York, 1958); D. H. Laurence, ed., *How to Become a Musical Critic* (London, 1960), previously uncollected writings on music, 1876–1950; D. H. Laurence, ed., *Platform and Pulpit* (New York, 1961), previously uncollected lectures, speeches, debates, 1885–1946; D. H. Green and D. H. Laurence, eds., *The Matter with Ireland* (London, 1962), essays, 1886–1950; A. Tauber, ed., *George Bernard Shaw on Language* (London, 1963); W. S. Smith, ed., *The Religious Speeches of Bernard Shaw* (University Park, Pa., 1963); H. M. Geduld, ed., *Bernard Shaw: The Rationalization of Russia* (Bloomington, Ind., 1964); *Selected One-Act Plays,* 2 vols. (Harmondsworth, 1965), Penguin ed.; W. S. Smith, ed., *Shaw on Religion* (London, 1967); L. Crompton, ed., *The Road to Equality* (Boston, 1971), unpublished lectures and essays, 1884–1918; S. Weintraub, ed., *Bernard Shaw's Non-Dramatic Literary Criticism* (Lincoln, Nebr., 1972); L. J. Hubenka, ed., *Practical Politics: Twentieth-Century Views on Politics and Economics* (Lincoln, Nebr., 1976), speeches, 1905–1933; L. Crompton, ed., *The Great Composers: Reviews and Bombardments* (Berkeley, Calif., 1978); B. F. Dukore, ed., *The Collected Screenplays* (London, 1980); *Plays Extravagant* (Harmondsworth, 1981), Penguin ed.

IV. SELECTED SEPARATE WORKS. *An Unsocial Socialist,* serialized in *To-Day* (March–December 1884), first published in book form (London, 1887), new ed. with intro. by Michael Holroyd (London, 1980); *The Irrational Knot,* serialized in *Our Corner* (April 1885–February 1887); *Cashel Byron's Profession,* serialized in *To-Day* (April 1885–March 1886) (Harmondsworth, 1979), Penguin ed.; *Love Among the Artists,* serialized in *Our Corner* (November 1887–December 1888); G. B. Shaw, ed., *Fabian Essays in Socialism* (London, 1889), with two chs. by Shaw, new ed. with intro. by Asa Briggs (London, 1967); *The Quintessence of Ibsenism* (London, 1891), completed to the death of Ibsen (London, 1913), republished (New York, 1959); *Widowers' Houses* (London, 1893), no. 1 of J. T. Grein, ed., Independent Theatre Series of Plays; *The Sanity of Art,* in *Liberty* (New York, July 1895); *The Perfect Wagnerite* (London, 1898); *Plays: Pleasant and Unpleasant,* 2 vols. (London, 1898), vol. I: "Preface: Mainly About Myself," *Widowers' Houses* [rev. ed.], *The Philanderer, Mrs. Warren's Profession;* vol. II: "Preface," *Arms and the Man, Candida, The Man of Destiny, You Never Can Tell.*

The Admirable Bashville, in *Cashel Byron's Profession* (rev. ed., Chicago, 1901), later included in *Translations and Tomfooleries* (London, 1926); *Three Plays for Puritans* (London, 1901), contains "Preface," *The Devil's Disciple, Caesar and Cleopatra, Captain Brassbound's Conversion; Man and Superman: A Comedy and a Philosophy* (London, 1903); *Passion, Poison, and Petrification; or, The Fatal Gazogene,* in H. Furniss, *Christmas Annual* (London, 1905); *John Bull's Other Island and Major Barbara* (London, 1907), includes *How He Lied to Her Husband; Press Cuttings: A Topical Sketch* (London, 1909); *The Shewing-Up of Blanco Posnet: A Sermon in Crude Melodrama* (London, 1909).

The Doctor's Dilemma: A Tragedy (London, 1911); *The Doctor's Dilemma, Getting Married, and The Shewing-Up of Blanco Posnet* (London, 1911); *The Dark Lady of the Sonnets,* in the *English Review* (1911); *Overruled,* in the *English Review* (1913); *Misalliance, The Dark Lady of the Sonnets, and Fanny's First Play* (London, 1914); *Common-sense About the War,* supplement to *New Statesman* (14 November 1914); *Androcles and the Lion,* in *Everybody's* magazine (September 1914); *Pygmalion,* in *Everybody's* magazine (November 1914) and *Noah's* magazine (November and December 1914); *Androcles and the Lion, Overruled, Pygmalion* (London, 1916); *O'Flaherty V.C.,* in *Hearst's* magazine (August 1917); *How to Settle the Irish Question,* in the *Daily Express* (27–29 November 1917); *Peace Conference Hints* (London, 1919); *Heartbreak House, Great Catherine, and Playlets of the War* (New York, 1919).

Ruskin's Politics (London, 1921); *Back to Methuselah, A Metabiological Pentateuch* (London, 1921); *Imprisonment,* published as preface to S. Webb and B. Webb, *English Prisons Under Local Government* (London, 1922); *Saint Joan* (London, 1924); *Translations and Tomfooleries* (London, 1926), contains *Jitta's Atonement, The Admirable Bashville, Press Cuttings, The Glimpse of Reality, Passion, Poison, and Petrification; or, The Fatal Gazogene, The Fascinating Foundling, The Music Cure; The Intelligent Woman's Guide to Socialism and Capitalism* (London, 1928); "Socialism: Principles and Outlook," in *Encyclopaedia Britannica,* 14th ed. (London, 1929).

What I Really Wrote About the War (London, 1930); *Immaturity* (London, 1930); *The Apple Cart: A Political Extravaganza* (London, 1930); *Major Critical Essays* (London, 1930); *Doctors' Delusions, Crude Criminology, and Sham Education* (London, 1931); *Pen Portraits and Reviews* (London, 1931); *The Adventures of the Black Girl in Her Search for God* (London, 1932); *Essays in Fabian Socialism* (London, 1932); *Short Stories, Scraps, and Shavings* (London, 1932); *Too True to Be Good, Village Wooing, and On the Rocks* (London, 1934), *Too True to Be Good,* in *Plays Extravagant* (Harmondsworth, 1981), Penguin ed.; *The Simpleton of the Unexpected Isles, The Six of Calais, and The Millionairess* (London, 1936), *The Simpleton* and *The Millionairess* in *Plays Extravagant* (Harmondsworth, 1981), Penguin ed.; "William Morris as I Knew Him," in M. Morris, *William Morris, Artist, Writer, Socialist,* 2 vols. (Oxford, 1936); *Cymbeline Refinished* (lim. ed., London, 1937); *Shaw Gives Himself Away: An Autobiographical Miscellany* (lim. ed., Newtown, 1939); *Geneva* (London, 1939), illus. by Feliks Topolski, rev. and included in *Geneva, Cymbeline Refinished, In Good King Charles's Golden Days,* see below; *In Good King Charles's Golden Days: A History Lesson* (London, 1939).

Everybody's Political What's What? (London, 1944); *Geneva, Cymbeline Refinished, In Good King Charles's Golden Days* (London, 1946); *Sixteen Self Sketches* (London, 1949); *Buoyant Billions: A Comedy of No Manners in*

Prose (lim. ed., London, 1949), illustrated by Clare Winsten; *Buoyant Billions, Farfetched Fables, Shakes Versus Shav* (London, 1950); *Bernard Shaw's Rhyming Picture Guide to Ayot Saint Lawrence* (Luton, 1950); *My Dear Dorothea: A Practical System of Moral Education for Females* (London, 1956), written in 1878, illus. by Clare Winsten and with a note by Stephen Winsten; "Why She Would Not," in *London* magazine, III (August 1956); S. Weintraub, ed., *An Unfinished Novel by Bernard Shaw* (London, 1958); J. E. Pringle, ed., *A Passion Play, A Dramatic Fragment, 1878* (London, 1971), written in 1878.

V. COLLECTIONS OF LETTERS. *Letters from George Bernard Shaw to Miss Alma Murray*, privately printed (Edinburgh, 1927); C. St. John, ed., *Ellen Terry and Bernard Shaw, a Correspondence*, with a preface by Shaw (London, 1931); *More Letters from George Bernard Shaw to Miss Alma Murray*, privately printed (Edinburgh, 1932); C. Bax, ed., *Florence Farr, Bernard Shaw, W. B. Yeats: Letters* (lim. ed., New York–Dublin, 1941); A. Dent, ed., *Bernard Shaw and Mrs. Patrick Campbell: Their Correspondence* (London, 1952); E. J. West, ed., *Advice to a Young Critic: Letters to Golding Bright, 1894–1928* (New York, 1955); Letters to Dame Laurentia McLachlan, abbess of Stanbrook, in *The Nun and the Dramatist*, by a nun of Stanbrook, in *Cornhill* magazine (Summer 1956); C. B. Purdom, ed., *Bernard Shaw's Letters to Granville Barker* (London, 1957); P. Tompkins, ed., *To a Young Actress: The Letters of Bernard Shaw to Molly Tompkins, 1921–49* (London, 1960); "Beerbohm, Wilde, Shaw and the 'Good-Natured Critic,'" in *Bulletin of the New York Public Library* (New York, 1964), twelve letters to the critic Edward Rose; D. H. Laurence, ed., *Collected Letters*, vol. I: *1874–1897*; vol. II: *1898–1910* (London, 1972–   ), in progress; B. Forbes, *Dame Edith Evans: Ned's Girl* (London, 1978), includes letters to Edith Evans; M. Hyde, ed., *Bernard Shaw and Alfred Douglas: A Correspondence* (New Haven, Conn.–New York, 1982).

VI. SELECTIONS. J. Huneker, ed., *Dramatic Opinions and Essays*, 2 vols. (London, 1907), unauthorized ed. (New York, 1906); [Mrs.] C. F. Shaw, comp., *Selected Passages from the Works of Bernard Shaw* (London, 1912); W. R. Ellis, ed., *Bernard Shaw and Karl Marx: A Symposium, 1884–1889* (New York, 1930); *The Quintessence of G.B.S.* (London, 1949), with commentary by Stephen Winsten; H. G. Bowker, ed., *Shaw on Vivisection* (London, 1949); A. C. Ward, ed., *Plays and Players: Essays on the Theatre* (London, 1952); D. Russell, ed., *Selected Prose of Bernard Shaw* (London, 1952); C. E. M. Joad, ed., *Shaw and Society: An Anthology and a Symposium* (London, 1953); *Selected Plays and Other Writings* (New York, 1956), with intro. by William Irvine; J. F. Matthews, comp., *Dramatic Criticism, 1895–98* (New York, 1959); E. J. West, ed., *Shaw on Shakespeare* (New York, 1961); *G.B.S. on Music* (London, 1962), with a foreword by Alec Robertson; S. Weintraub, comp., *Shaw: An Autobiography*, vol. I: *1856–1898* (London, 1969), vol. II: *1898–1950: The Playwright Years* (London, 1970); W. S. Smith, ed., *Bernard Shaw's Plays: Major Barbara, Heartbreak House, Saint Joan, Too True to Be Good* (New York, 1971), with backgrounds and criticism; H. G. Earnshaw, ed., *A Selection from Shaw's Prefaces* (London, 1977); L. Crompton, ed., *The Great Composers: Reviews and Bombardments* (Berkeley, Calif., 1978); S. Weintraub, ed., *The Portable Bernard Shaw* (London, 1978).

VII. ADAPTATIONS. *My Fair Lady* (New York, 1958), a musical play in two acts based on *Pygmalion* by Bernard Shaw, adap. and lyrics by Alan J. Lerner, illus. by Cecil Beaton; *Dear Liar: A Comedy of Letters* (New York, 1960), adap. by Jerome Kilty from the correspondence of Bernard Shaw and Mrs. Patrick Campbell.

VIII. CONCORDANCE. E. D. Bevan, *A Concordance to the Plays and Prefaces of Bernard Shaw*, 10 vols. (Detroit, 1971), with references to the *Standard Edition*.

IX. RECORD OF PRODUCTIONS. R. Mander and J. Mitchenson, comps., *A Theatrical Companion to Shaw* (London, 1954); R. Huggett, *The First Night of Pygmalion* (London, 1970); E. Stürzl and J. Hogg, *The Stage History of G. B. Shaw's Saint Joan* (Salzburg, 1975).

X. BIOGRAPHICAL AND CRITICAL STUDIES. (Note: The critical literature on Shaw is now so extensive that any selection inevitably has an arbitrary element.) H. L. Mencken, *Bernard Shaw: His Plays* (Boston, 1905), the first book on Shaw; J. G. Huneker, *Iconoclasts* (London, 1906); G. K. Chesterton, *G. B. Shaw* (London, 1909); H. Jackson, *Bernard Shaw* (London, 1909); D. MacCarthy, *The Court Theatre, 1904–1907: A Commentary and a Criticism* (London, 1907), reiss. with a commentary by Stanley Weintraub (Coral Gables, Fla., 1966); J. Bab, *Shaw* (Berlin, 1910; rev. ed., 1926); A. Henderson, *G. B. Shaw: His Life and Works* (London, 1911); A. Harmon, *Le Molière du XXᵉ siècle: Bernard Shaw* (Paris, 1913); G. Norwood, *Euripides and Mr. Shaw* (London, 1913); P. B. Howe, *Bernard Shaw: A Critical Survey* (London, 1915); E. R. Pease, *History of the Fabian Society* (London, 1916).

A. Henderson, *Table Talk of G.B.S.: Conversations on Things in General Between Shaw and His Biographer* (London, 1925); M. Ellehauge, *The Position of Bernard Shaw in European Drama and Philosophy* (Copenhagen, 1931); F. Harris, *Bernard Shaw: An Unauthorized Biography* (London, 1931), with a postscript by Shaw; E. G. Craig, *Ellen Terry and Her Secret Self* (London, 1931); A. Henderson, *Shaw: Playboy and Prophet* (New York, 1932); A. Maurois, *Magiciens et logiciens* (Paris, 1936); S. C. Sen Gupta, *The Art of Bernard Shaw* (London, 1936); C. Caudwell, *Studies in a Dying Culture* (London, 1938); C. M. Shaw, *Bernard's Brethren* (London, 1939).

J. Gassner, *Masters of the Drama* (New York, 1940; 3rd enl. ed., 1954); H. Pearson, *G.B.S.: A Full-Length Portrait* (London, 1942; new ed. with postscript, 1961); E. Strauss, *Bernard Shaw: Art and Socialism* (London, 1942; new ed., 1978); E. Bentley, *The Playwright as Thinker* (New York, 1946); S. Winsten, *G.B.S. 90: Aspects of Bernard Shaw's*

Life and Works (London, 1946), contributors include Gilbert Murray, John Masefield, Lord Passfield (Sidney Webb), H. G. Wells, Sir Max Beerbohm, James Bridie, Lord Dunsany, Lord Keynes (Maynard Keynes), W. R. Inge, Kenneth Barnes, Aldous Huxley, and others; E. Bentley, *A Century of Hero-Worship* (Boston, 1947); E. J. Hobsbawm, "Bernard Shaw's Socialism," in *Science and Society,* 11 (1947); E. Bentley, *Bernard Shaw* (Norfolk, Conn., 1947; reiss., 1967); F. E. Loewenstein, ed., *Bernard Shaw Through the Camera* (London, 1948); E. Wilson, *The Triple Thinkers* (London, 1948); W. Irvine, *The Universe of G.B.S.* (New York, 1949); A. Nicoll, *World Drama from Aeschylus to Anouilh* (New York, 1949); A. C. Ward, *Bernard Shaw* (London, 1950).

A. West, *G. B. Shaw: A Good Man Fallen Among Fabians* (London, 1950; new ed., 1974); I. Fiske, *Bernard Shaw's Debt to William Blake* (London, 1951), Shavian Tract no. 2, with a foreword by G.B.S.; D. MacCarthy, *Shaw's Plays in Review* (New York, 1951); B. Patch, *Thirty Years with G.B.S.* (London, 1951); G. Whitworth, *The Making of a National Theatre* (London, 1951); S. Winsten, *Salt and His Circle* (London, 1951), intro. by G. B. Shaw; L. Kronenberger, *The Thread of Laughter* (New York, 1952); A. Ussher, *Three Great Irishmen* (London, 1952); M. Beerbohm, *Around Theatres* (London, 1953); S. Holberg, *The Economic Rogue in the Plays of Bernard Shaw* (Buffalo, 1953); C. E. M. Joad, ed., *Shaw and Society: An Anthology and a Symposium* (London, 1953), contributors include Kingsley Martin, Leonard Woolf, S. K. Ratcliff, Benn W. Levy, Hugh Dalton; L. Kronenberger, ed., *George Bernard Shaw: A Critical Survey* (New York–Cleveland, 1953), includes commentaries by W. H. Auden, Jacques Barzun, Eric Bentley, Max Beerbohm, G. K. Chesterton, Thomas Mann, V. S. Pritchett, Dixon Scott, Stephen Spender, and others; A. Nethercot, *Men and Supermen: The Shavian Portrait Gallery* (London, 1954; rev. ed., 1966); St. J. Ervine, *Bernard Shaw: His Life, Work and Friends* (London, 1956); A. Henderson, *George Bernard Shaw: Man of the Century* (New York, 1956); G. Roppen, *Evolution and Poetic Belief: A Study in Some Victorian and Modern Writers* (Oslo, 1956); J. B. Kaye, *Bernard Shaw and the Nineteenth-Century Tradition* (Norman, Okla., 1958); L. Simon, *Shaw on Education* (1958); H. G. Farmer, *Bernard Shaw's Sister and Her Friends* (Leiden, 1959); A. Freemantle, *This Little Band of Prophets: The British Fabians* (London, 1959); E. N. Rao, *Shaw the Novelist* (Madras, 1959).

A. H. Nethercot, *The First Five Lives of Annie Besant* (London, 1960); J. Smith and A. Toynbee, eds., *Gilbert Murray, an Unfinished Autobiography* (London, 1960); M. Cole, *The Story of Fabian Socialism* (London, 1961); A. Chappelow, ed., *Shaw the Villager and Human Being* (London, 1961); G. W. Knight, *The Golden Labyrinth* (London, 1962); A. M. MacBriar, *Fabian Socialism and English Poetics* (Cambridge, 1962); R. Ohmann, *Shaw: The Style and the Man* (Middletown, Conn., 1962); M.

Shenfield, comp., *A Pictorial Biography of Bernard Shaw* (London, 1962); J. Dunbar, *Mrs. G.B.S.: A Biographical Portrait of Charlotte Shaw* (London, 1963); M. Meisel, *Shaw and the Nineteenth-Century Theater* (Princeton, 1963); C. B. Purdom, *A Guide to the Plays of Bernard Shaw* (London, 1963); J. I. M. Stewart, *Eight Modern Writers* (London, 1963); S. Weintraub, *Private Shaw and Public Shaw: A Dual Portrait of Lawrence of Arabia and G. B. Shaw* (London, 1963); F. P. W. McDowell, "Heaven, Hell, and Turn-of-the-Century London: Reflections upon Shaw's *Man and Superman,*" in *Drama Survey,* 2 (1963); B. C. Rosset, *Shaw of Dublin: The Formative Years* (University Park, Pa., 1964); B. B. Watson, *A Shavian Guide to the Intelligent Woman* (New York–London, 1964; repr. New York, 1972); D. P. Costello, *The Serpent's Eye: Shaw and the Cinema* (Notre Dame, Ind., 1965); R. J. Kaufmann, ed., *Twentieth-Century Views of George Bernard Shaw* (Englewood Cliffs, N.J., 1965), contributors include Brecht, Ohmann, Bentley, O'Donnell, Crompton, Morgan, Fiske; J. O'Donovan, *Shaw and the Charlatan Genius: A Memoir* (London, 1965); J. P. Smith, *The Unrepentant Pilgrim: A Study of the Development of Bernard Shaw* (London, 1965); K. Muggeridge and R. Adam, *Beatrice Webb: A Life, 1858–1943* (London, 1967); H. Fromm, *Bernard Shaw and the Theater in the Nineties: A Study of Shaw's Dramatic Criticism* (Lawrence, Kans., 1967); F. P. W. McDowell, "Politics, Comedy, Character and Dialectic: The Shavian World of *John Bull's Other Island,*" in *PMLA,* 82 (1967); W. S. Smith, *The London Heretics, 1870–1914* (London, 1968); M. Beerbohm, *More Theatres* (London, 1969); C. A. Carpenter, *Bernard Shaw and the Art of Destroying Ideals: The Early Plays* (Madison, Wis., 1969); L. Crompton, *Shaw the Dramatist* (Lincoln, Nebr., 1969); A. M. Gibbs, *Shaw* (Edinburgh, 1969); A. Mills, *Language and Laughter: Comic Diction in the Plays of Bernard Shaw* (Tucson, 1969); C. Wilson, *Bernard Shaw: A Reassessment* (London, 1969).

E. Bentley, "Ibsen, Shaw, Brecht: Three Stages," in A. Cheuse and R. Koffler, eds., *The Rarer Action: Essays in Honor of Francis Fergusson* (New Brunswick, N. J., 1970); M. Beerbohm, *Last Theatres* (London, 1970); R. F. Dietrich, *Portrait of the Artist as a Young Superman: A Study of Shaw's Novels* (London, 1970); W. B. Furlong, *G.B.S./G.K.C.: Shaw and Chesterton, the Metaphysical Jesters* (University Park, Pa., 1970); V. Pascal, *The Disciple and His Devil* (London, 1970); J. W. Hulse, *Revolutionists in London* (London, 1970); E. B. Adams, *Bernard Shaw and the Aesthetes* (Columbus, Ohio, 1971); B. F. Dukore, *Bernard Shaw, Director* (London, 1971); N. Rosenblood, ed., *Shaw: Seven Critical Essays* (Toronto, 1971), includes important essay by M. Meisel; S. Weintraub, *Journey to Heartbreak: The Crucible Years of Bernard Shaw* (New York, 1971); M. M. Morgan, *The Shavian Playground: An Exploration of the Art of George Bernard Shaw* (London, 1972); D. J. Leary, "Shaw's Blakean Vision: A Dialectic Approach to *Heartbreak House,*" in

Modern Drama, 15 (1972); C. A. Berst, *Bernard Shaw and the Art of Drama* (Urbana, Ill., 1973); B. F. Dukore, *Bernard Shaw, Playwright* (Columbia, Mo., 1973); M. Hardwick and M. Hardwick, *The Bernard Shaw Companion* (London, 1973); P. A. Hummert, *Bernard Shaw's Marxian Romance* (Lincoln, Nebr., 1973); M. J. Valency, *The Cart and the Trumpet: The Plays of George Bernard Shaw* (London, 1973); M. Cole, *The Webbs and Their Work* (London, 1974); M. Goldstein, *The Political Stage* (London, 1974); J. L. Wisenthal, *The Marriage of Contraries: Bernard Shaw's Middle Plays* (Cambridge, Mass., 1974); D. Dervin, *Bernard Shaw: A Psychological Study* (London, 1975); A. Kennedy, *Six Dramatists in Search of a Language* (London, 1975); T. F. Evans, ed., *Shaw: The Critical Heritage* (London, 1976); R. Weintraub, ed., *Fabian Feminist: Bernard Shaw and Women* (University Park, Pa., 1976); A. Turco, Jr., *Shaw's Moral Vision* (London, 1976); R. N. Palmer, *Bernard Shaw's Historical Plays* (New York, 1976); R. P. Arnott, *Bernard Shaw and William Morris* (London, 1977); G. Berquist, *The Pen and the Sword: War and Peace in the Prose and Plays of Bernard Shaw* (Salzburg, 1977); R. F. Whitman, *Shaw and the Play of Ideas* (Ithaca, N.Y.–New York, 1977); B. Green, *Shaw's Champions: G.B.S. and Prize Fighting from Cashel Byron to Gene Tunney* (London, 1978); N. MacKenzie and J. MacKenzie, *The Fabians* (London, 1978); M. Holroyd, ed., *The Genius of Bernard Shaw* (London, 1979); C. D. Sidhu, *The Pattern of Tragicomedy in Bernard Shaw* (Delhi, 1979); M. Peters, *Shaw and the Actresses* (London, 1981).

XI. STUDIES OF INDIVIDUAL PLAYS. S. S. Stanton, ed., *A Casebook on "Candida"* (New York, 1962); G. A. Pilecki, *Shaw's "Geneva": A Critical Study of the Evolution of the Text in Relation to Shaw's Political Thought and Dramatic Practice* (The Hague, 1965); R. Zimbardo, ed., *Twentieth-Century Views of "Major Barbara"* (Englewood Cliffs, N. J., 1970).

XII. PERIODICALS. The leading periodical publication concerned with the study of Shaw began as the *Bulletin* of the Shaw Society of America (New York, 1951–1958) and has continued as the *Shaw Review* (University Park, Pennsylvania State University, 1959–   ). The British Shaw Society published the *Shaw Bulletin* (Dagenham, Essex, September 1946–September 1953) and the *Shavian* (1953–1959, 1960–1963). It was revived in 1976 as the *Shaw Newsletter*.

MARY SHELLEY

(1797–1851)

Anne K. Mellor

WHEN MARY WOLLSTONECRAFT died of puerperal fever on 10 September 1797, she left her newborn daughter with a double burden: a powerful need to be mothered, which was never to be fulfilled, together with a name, Mary Wollstonecraft Godwin, that proclaimed this small child the fruit of the most famous radical literary marriage of eighteenth-century England. As we trace the growth of this baby girl into the author of *Frankenstein; or, The Modern Prometheus* (1818), we can never forget how much her desire for a loving and supportive family defined her character, shaped her fantasies, and structured her fictional idealizations of the nuclear family—idealizations so exaggerated that their impossibility is always apparent.

LIFE

LEFT with two infant daughters to raise, the austere philosopher William Godwin immediately hired a nanny, Louisa Jones, to care for Mary and her half sister Fanny Imlay (Wollstonecraft's daughter by Gilbert Imlay). For three years, Mary enjoyed a happy childhood, beloved both by Louisa and by Fanny. But when Louisa fell in love with George Dyson, one of Godwin's more tempestuous and irresponsible disciples, Godwin strongly objected; when she decided to live with Dyson, Godwin in July 1800 forbade her ever seeing the girls again. Thus, at the age of three, Mary lost the only mother she had ever known. Godwin, desperate to find a wife to care for his family, soon married Mary Jane Clairmont, the unmarried mother of two children, who deeply resented the special attention paid by visitors to Wollstonecraft's and Godwin's only daughter. She favored her own children, refused to provide any special lessons for Mary, and quarreled frequently

with her. The tension between Mary Godwin and her stepmother was so severe that Mary suffered from psychosomatic skin boils at the age of thirteen, boils that disappeared when she and her stepmother were separated. Godwin then decided to send Mary away indefinitely, shipping her to Dundee, Scotland, to stay with the family of a near stranger, William Thomas Baxter, in June 1812.

An outsider in the happy home of the Baxters, Mary nonetheless learned to enjoy the bleak but beautiful landscape of the Tay estuary and gradually became close friends with the Baxter daughters. Nevertheless, she continued to yearn for her father, for whom she had developed by the age of twelve, as she later confessed to Maria Reveley Gisborne, an "excessive & romantic attachment" (letter to Gisborne, 30 October 1834). At the age of sixteen, she returned to London to discover that Godwin had acquired a new disciple, one whom she saw as a youthful incarnation of all she most admired in her father. Within two months, she and the married Percy Shelley had become lovers; on 28 July 1814, they eloped to Paris, taking Mrs. Godwin's daughter Jane Clairmont with them.

The Godwins were furious at this elopement; William Godwin refused to speak to Mary (although he continued to borrow money from Percy Shelley), especially after Jane insisted on living with Mary and Percy. The trio traveled across Europe to Lake Lucerne; Mary and Percy later published their letters describing the sublime landscapes they encountered on this trip in *History of a Six Weeks' Tour Through a Part of France, Switzerland, Germany, and Holland: With Letters Descriptive of a Sail Round the Lake of Geneva, and of the Glaciers of Chamouni* (1817). During this trip Mary became pregnant, Jane and Percy probably became lovers, and all three converted to Percy's fervent belief in free or nonpossessive love and universal benevolence as the solution to every social and political evil.

When they returned to England, Mary gave birth to a baby girl, christened Clara, who lived for only two weeks. After Clara's death on 6 March 1815, Mary had a recurrent dream that she recorded in her journal: "Dream that my little baby came to life again—that it had only been cold, and that we rubbed it before the fire, and it lived—I awake and find no baby—I think about the little thing all day—not in good spirits" (*Journal*, 19 March 1815). Increasingly resentful of Jane's presence in her household, Mary insisted that she leave; Jane then decided to find her own poet and set her cap for the most famous young poet of the day, Lord Byron. By April 1816, Jane (having changed her name to the more romantic Claire) had become Byron's lover, despite his obvious lack of affection for her. She then persuaded Percy (who wanted to meet Byron) and Mary to accompany her to Switzerland in pursuit of Byron. The four spent the summer of 1816, the coldest summer for a century, on the shores of Lake Geneva, engaging in intense conversation and reading ghost stories out loud. On the memorable night of 15 June, they decided to compete in writing the most frightening story each could imagine. The next day, Mary Godwin, as she later reported in her introduction to the 1831 edition of *Frankenstein*, having experienced a "reverie" or waking nightmare in which she saw "the pale student of unhallowed arts" create a living being from dead parts, began to write one of the most powerful horror stories of modern times.

FRANKENSTEIN; OR, THE MODERN PROMETHEUS

MARY Shelley's story of a scientist who creates a monster he cannot control can claim the status of a myth, so profoundly resonant are its implications for our understanding of the modern world. Of course, the media and the average person often mistakenly assign the name of Frankenstein not to the maker of the monster but to his creature. But as we shall see, this "mistake" derives from an intuitively correct reading of the final identity of the creator with his creation.

From the feminist perspective, which has dominated critical discussions of the novel since 1975, *Frankenstein* is in part a book about what happens when a man tries to have a baby without a woman. As such, the novel is concerned with natural as opposed to unnatural modes of reproduction. In 1976, in her *Literary Women*, Ellen Moers drew our attention to the novel's emphasis on birth and "the trauma of the after-birth." Since this is a novel about giving birth, let us first ask why the eighteen-year-old Mary Godwin gave birth to this novel on that night in 1816, the question so frequently put to her, "How I, then a young girl, came to think of, and to dilate upon, so very hideous an idea?" In her author's introduction to the revised edition of *Frankenstein* (1831), she tells us that the night before her dream, she had heard Byron and Shelley discussing certain scientific experiments by Erasmus Darwin, in which he was said to have animated a piece of vermicelli by sending an electrical current though it.

Mary's reverie of creation, which followed this discussion, also drew upon far more personal knowledge. More than fifteen years later, she claimed she could still see vividly the room to which she woke and feel "the thrill of fear" that ran through her. Why was she so frightened? Remember that she had eighteen months earlier given birth to a baby girl whom she had dreamed she had "rubbed . . . before the fire" and brought back to life. Here once again she dreamed of reanimating a corpse by warming it with "a spark of life." Only six months ago this night, Mary had given birth a second time, to a boy named William. And while she wrote out her novel, she was pregnant a third time, with a daughter, again named Clara, who was born in September 1817. Mary's waking dream unleashed her deepest subconscious anxieties, the anxieties of a very young, frequently pregnant mother.

The dream that gave birth to her novel also gave shape to what we might imagine to be her deepest fears: "What if my child is born deformed, a freak, a 'hideous' thing? Could I still love it, or would I be horrified and wish it were dead again (as the 'pale student' does)? What will happen if I cannot love my child? Am I capable of raising a normal, healthy child? Will my child die (as my first baby did)? Could I wish my own child to die, to destroy itself? Could I kill it? Could it kill me (as I killed my mother, Mary Wollstonecraft)?" One reason Mary Shelley's story reverberates so strongly is that it articulates, for perhaps the first time in Western literature, the most powerfully felt anxieties of pregnancy, a topic avoided by male writers and considered improper for women to discuss in public. Mary Shelley's focus on the birth process both educates a male readership about the ways in which pregnant women or new mothers may not desire their own babies, even as it reassures female readers that their fears and hostilities are shared by other women.

Her dream thus generates that dimension of the novel's plot that has been much discussed by feminist critics, Victor Frankenstein's total failure as a parent. Even though he has labored nine months to give birth to his Creature, Frankenstein flees from his child the moment it opens its eyes with the "convulsive motion" of birth. And when like a child, his Creature follows him, grinning, arms open to embrace him, Frankenstein can see his creation only as a devil, a wretch, whom he violently abandons. Throughout the novel, Frankenstein's inability to accept responsibility for his son, his Adam, is contrasted with the examples of two loving fathers, Alphonse Frankenstein and the father in the De Lacey family. Mary Shelley's ideal family, a community of equals joined by love and mutual respect, is represented in the novel especially by the De Laceys: Felix (whose name connotes happiness), Agatha (goodness), and Safie (Sophia or wisdom, a portrait of the liberated woman modeled on Mary Wollstonecraft).

As the novel develops, the author's attention focuses less on the feelings and experiences of Victor Frankenstein and more on those of his Creature, the abandoned child. Mary Shelley powerfully identified with this rejected child. The Creature spends two years peering in on the De Lacey family, just as Mary peered in on the Baxters; the Creature reads the same books as did Mary in 1814 and 1815 (*Paradise Lost, The Sorrows of Young Werther*, Plutarch's *Parallel Lives*, Volney's *Ruins of Empires*, the poetry of Coleridge and Byron); both lack a mother and suffer from distant fathers. The novel powerfully evokes the Creature's pain at the recognition that he will be alone, forever alone; equally powerfully, the novel evokes the anger and desire for revenge that such abandonment and isolation can produce. When the Creature finally loses his last hope of joining the De Lacey family, he commits his first act of violence and burns down their cottage.

Mary Shelley recognized that the experience of parental rejection can produce a desire to retaliate: it is no accident that the Creature's first victim is a young boy named William whom he wished to adopt. By naming this child William Frankenstein, Mary Shelley invoked her father William Godwin, her stepbrother William Godwin, Jr., who displaced her in her father's affections, and her own son William Shelley (of whom William Frankenstein is a portrait, possessing the same blue eyes and blond curls). At the psychological level, the Creature's murder of William Frankenstein manifests Mary Shelley's repressed patricidal, fratricidal, and even infanticidal urges, revealing her horrified recognition of her own capacity for aggression.

Mary Shelley's anxiety about her capacity to give birth to a normal, healthy child that she could mother lovingly surfaces in the novel in another way. In her introduction to the revised edition of *Frankenstein* (1831), she identifies the novel itself as her child, her "hideous progeny." For Mary Shelley, this metaphor of the book-as-baby articulates a double anxiety. In giving birth to a book, she has given birth to herself as an author, and specifically to herself as the author of horror. She is reinforcing the literary tradition of the female Gothic, the association of women with the expression of desire that might better remain hidden, repressed. She is thus defying the decorum of the "proper lady," the domestic ideology that insists that women should remain silent in public.

Mary Shelley's guilt at writing an "improper" book led to extensive self-censorship in her novel. Not only did she repress the female authorial voice, assigning her tale to three male narrators (Walton, Frankenstein, and the Creature), but she also gave her tale to a man, Percy Shelley, to "edit" and "correct." Percy Shelley made numerous changes to the manuscript of *Frankenstein*, changes that both improved and damaged the novel. He corrected occasional factual errors and misspellings, he substituted technical terms for Mary Shelley's less precise ones, and he sometimes improved the continuity of and clarified her text. Everywhere he "heightened" her diction and style, substituting polysyllabic, Latinate words and Miltonic inversions for her vernacular, Anglo-Saxon words and sentence constructions. He is thus responsible for that ornate, Ciceronian prose style employed by Frankenstein and his Creature, a style that many readers have found distancing and stilted, not to say improbable for a Creature who is only two years old!

Percy also distorted Mary Shelley's intentions in two important ways. He tended to see Victor

Frankenstein more sympathetically than did Mary. He called Victor an "author" and regarded him as a tragic hero, whereas Mary saw the scientist as an agent of evil and identified him with the hubristic overreachers Faust, Satan, and Prometheus. Similarly, Percy Shelley regarded the Creature more negatively and introduced the Creature as an "abortion." Finally, he changed the last line of the novel, from Mary Shelley's "I soon lost sight of him in the darkness and distance" to "[he was] lost in darkness and distance." Mary Shelley's ending leaves open the possibility that the Creature is still alive, the more so because his promise to build a funeral pyre at the North Pole is inherently incredible, given the lack of wood for such a pyre. Percy Shelley's ending gives a false sense of closure to the novel. Feminist critics have suggested that Mary Shelley's willingness to accept all of Percy's emendations reflected her sense of psychological and literary inferiority to her older, already published, mentor, father figure, and now husband (Percy and Mary were married on 30 December 1816, after his first wife, Harriet, committed suicide).

As its subtitle suggests and many critics have noted, *Frankenstein; or, The Modern Prometheus* functions as a political critique both of Romantic Prometheanism and of the ideology of the French Revolution. By naming her scientist a modern Prometheus, Mary Shelley called into question the fundamental project of the Romantic poets and philosophers she knew best (Godwin, Coleridge, Byron, Percy Shelley): their attempt to perfect mankind, to transform mortals into godlike creatures, to locate the divine in the human. Victor Frankenstein's quest, to "bestow animation upon lifeless matter" and thereby "renew life where death had apparently devoted the body to corruption," is in fact a quest to become God, the creator of life and the gratefully worshiped father of a new species of immortal beings. This quest parallels Godwin's theory of perfectibility through unfettered rationality, Coleridge's claim that the primary human imagination is an "echo of the Infinite I AM," Blake's vision of the human form divine, Wordsworth's insistence that the "higher minds" of poets "are truly from the Deity," and Percy Shelley's image of the poet as the savior and "unacknowledged legislator of the world."

Invoking the myths both of Prometheus plasticator (the maker of man) and of Prometheus pyr-

phoros (the fire stealer), Mary Shelley identified her modern Prometheus explicitly with Byron and Percy Shelley. In 1816 she had copied out for his publisher Byron's poem "Prometheus" and verse-drama *Manfred*, in which the Faustian Manfred, who cannot escape his incestuous guilt, nonetheless defies the gods and insists that

> The mind, the spirit, the Promethean spark,
> The lightning of my being, is as bright,
> Pervading, and far-darting as your own,
> And shall not yield to yours, though coop'd in clay!
> (*Manfred*, I.i.154–157)

More immediately, she identified Victor Frankenstein with her husband. Percy Shelley had published his first volume of poems under the pen name Victor; like Frankenstein, he had a "sister" named Elizabeth; he had received the same education as Victor, reading Paracelsus, Albertus Magnus, Pliny, and Buffon, and specializing in alchemy, chemistry, and foreign languages; he shared Frankenstein's revolutionary ideals, which are signaled in the novel by Frankenstein's attending the University of Ingolstadt, home of the leading German Jacobin thinker, Adam Weishaupt. Most important, Frankenstein shared Percy Shelley's relative indifference to his children: Shelley had abandoned his first wife and their children and had not grieved for the death of Mary's first child, Clara.

Mary Shelley also included a positive portrait of her husband through the character of Clerval, Victor's other "self." Clerval is a poet who loves nature, is capable of empathy, of parenting others (he nurses Victor when Victor is sick), and does not disobey his father. But this positive image of an altruistic Percy Shelley is torn from the novel when Clerval is murdered, leaving behind only the egotistical, self-absorbed Victor.

As a modern Prometheus, Victor Frankenstein is a fire stealer, someone who usurps nature's "spark of life" to animate a dead corpse, but then refuses to accept responsibility for the Creature he has created. Mary Shelley rejected the Romantic dream of progressing ever upward to human perfection and immortality because she recognized that a commitment to a utopian, future ideal too often entailed an indifference to the responsibilities of the present. She concluded that a Romantic poetics that valued the creative process above the created product too often failed to acknowledge the predictable consequences of that product, once created—for example, the suffering caused by the political and social revolutions that the passionate words of the poet might inspire.

Imbedded in *Frankenstein* is an allegory of the French Revolution and the Terror. Mary Shelley encourages us to see the Creature as the embodiment of the entire progress of the French Revolution. The Creature first invokes Rousseau's noble savage, born free but everywhere in chains: "I was benevolent and good; misery made me a fiend," he claims (p. 95). Were he incorporated into the family of man, he would be entirely virtuous, he insists. But the Creature does not get the female companion he craves and is driven to violence. Just so the French Revolution was driven out of the hands of the well-intentioned Girondists (Mirabeau, Lafayette, Talleyrand) by the September massacres and the execution of Louis XVI and Marie Antoinette, and into the bloodthirsty arms of Marat, Saint-Just, and Robespierre. The identification of the French Revolution as a "monster" had been made by Edmund Burke and Abbé Barruel, both of whom Mary Shelley had read and admired; in his *Reflections on the Revolution in France* (1789), Burke had defined the Revolution as a "vast, tremendous, unformed spectre."

With this allegory, Mary Shelley offers a subtle political argument, crudely stated as "the end does not justify the means." An abstract cause can never be separated from its historical embodiment in events, nor can an ideology be separated from the class interests it serves. If Victor Frankenstein had loved and cared for his child, the Creature might never have become a monster; similarly, if the early leaders of the French Revolution had found a place for the aristocrats, clergy, and king and queen in their new republic, the Terror and the devastations of the Napoleonic campaigns might not have occurred. Mary Shelley sums up her political credo in a central passage in *Frankenstein*:

A human being in perfection ought always to preserve a calm and peaceful mind and never to allow passion or a transitory desire to disturb his tranquillity. I do not think that the pursuit of knowledge is an exception to this rule. If the study to which you apply yourself has a tendency to weaken your affections, and to destroy your taste for those simple pleasures in which no alloy can possibly mix, then that study is certainly unlawful, that is to say, not befitting the human mind. If this rule were always observed; if no man allowed any pursuit whatsoever to interfere with the tranquillity of his do-

mestic affections, Greece had not been enslaved; Caesar would have spared his country; America would have been discovered more gradually; and the empires of Mexico and Peru had not been destroyed.

(p. 51)

Mary Shelley was a political reformist, rather than a revolutionary. She believed that the nation-state ought to be modeled upon the "domestic affections," upon a loving family in which each member is valued and cared for equally. She shared this concept of "family politics" with other women writers of her day, with Mary Wollstonecraft, Maria Edgeworth, and Jane Austen, a concept of the ideal state as a socialist community grounded in an ethic of care that serves the needs of all the community's members.

Frankenstein offers a powerful critique both of scientific thought and of the psychology of the modern scientist. Mary Shelley may have been the first to question the commitment of science to the search for objective truth irrespective of the consequences. What science did Mary Shelley know? Clearly, she had no personal experience with scientific research; she envisioned Frankenstein's laboratory as a small attic room lit by a single candle! Nonetheless, she had a sound grasp of the concepts and implications of some of the most important scientific research of her day, namely the work of Sir Humphry Davy, Erasmus Darwin, and Luigi Galvani.

At the University of Ingolstadt, Victor Frankenstein chooses to specialize in the field of "natural philosophy," or chemical physiology, the field defined by Humphry Davy in his *A Discourse, Introductory to a Course of Lectures on Chemistry* (1802), the source for Professor Waldman's lecture in the novel. In this pamphlet, Davy insisted that modern chemistry had bestowed upon the chemist "powers which may be almost called creative; which have enabled him to modify and change the beings surrounding him, and by his experiments to interrogate nature with power, not simply as a scholar, passive and seeking only to understand her operations, but rather as a master, active with his own instruments" (p. 16). Gendering nature as female, Davy defined two scientific ways of dealing with her. A "descriptive" science would try to understand the workings of Mother Nature. An "interventionist" science, on the other hand, would be an effort to change the operations of nature. Davy clearly preferred the latter and hailed the scientist who modified nature as a "master." Similarly, Professor Waldman urges Victor Frankenstein to "penetrate into the recesses of nature, and show how she works in her hiding places" (p. 42), an effort Victor undertakes so that he might discover the "principle of life" (p. 46) and use it to his own ends. In Mary Shelley's view, such interventionist science is bad science, dangerous and self-serving.

In contrast, good science is that practiced by Erasmus Darwin, the first theorist of evolution and the grandfather of Charles Darwin. In *The Botanic Garden* (1789, 1791) and *Zoonomia; or, The Laws of Organic Life* (1794, 1801), Darwin had described the evolution of more complex life-forms from simpler ones and argued that dual-sex propagation is higher on the evolutionary ladder than single-sex propagation. From Darwin's perspective, Victor Frankenstein's experiment would reverse evolutionary progress, both because Frankenstein engages in single-sex propagation and because he constructs his new species from both human parts (collected from cemeteries and charnel houses) and animal parts (collected from slaughterhouses). Moreover, he defies the entire concept of evolution by attempting to create a "new" species all at once, rather than through the random mutation of existing species.

The scientist who had the most direct impact on Shelley's representation of Frankenstein's experiment was Luigi Galvani, who argued that electricity was the life force and who had performed numerous experiments conducting electrical currents through dead animals in order to revive them. His most notorious experiment was performed in public in London on 17 January 1803, by his nephew Giovanni Aldini. On that day Aldini applied galvanic electricity to the corpse of a human being. The body of the recently hanged criminal Thomas Forster was brought from Newgate Prison, where it had lain in the prison yard for one hour at thirty degrees Fahrenheit, to Mr. Wilson's Anatomical Theatre, where live wires attached to a pile composed of 120 plates of zinc and 120 plates of copper were connected to the ear and mouth of the dead man. At this moment, Aldini reported, "the jaw began to quiver, the adjoining muscles were horribly contorted, and the left eye actually opened." When the wires were applied to the dissected thumb muscles they "induced a forcible effort to clench the hand"; when applied to the ear and rectum, they "excited in the

muscles contractions much stronger. . . . The action even of those muscles furthest distant from the points of contact with the arc was so much increased as almost to give an appearance of reanimation." When volatile alkali was smeared on the nostrils and mouth before the galvanic stimulus was applied, "the convulsions appeared to be much increased . . . and extended from the muscles of the head, face, and neck, as far as the deltoid. The effect in this case surpassed our most sanguine expectations," Aldini exulted, and he concluded remarkably that "vitality might, perhaps, have been restored, if many circumstances had not rendered it impossible" (Giovanni Aldini, *An Account of the Late Improvements in Galvanism*, 1803, pp. 54, 193-194). Here is the scientific prototype for Victor Frankenstein, restoring life to dead human corpses.

By grounding her literary vision of a scientist animating a corpse upon the cutting-edge scientific research of her day, Mary Shelley initiated a new literary genre, what we now call "science fiction." As Brian Aldiss in *Billion Year Spree: The History of Science Fiction* (1973) and Robert Scholes and Eric Rabkin in *Science Fiction: History, Science, Vision* (1977) have argued, *Frankenstein* possesses the three characteristics essential to the genre of science fiction: (1) it is based on valid scientific research; (2) it gives a persuasive prediction of what science might achieve in the future; and (3) it offers a humanistic critique of the benefits and dangers of either a specific scientific discovery/invention or of the nature of scientific thought.

Frankenstein is notable both for its grasp of the nature of the scientific enterprise and for its searching analysis of the dangers inherent in that enterprise. Victor Frankenstein is our first literary portrait of what we might now call the "mad scientist," but it is a far more subtle portrait than that provided by such films as *Dr. Strangelove*. Mary Shelley recognized that Victor Frankenstein's passion for scientific research is a displacement of normal emotions and healthy affections. Significantly, when Victor is working on his experiment, he cannot love—he ignores his family, even his fiancée Elizabeth, and he takes no pleasure in the beauties of nature. Moreover, he becomes physically and mentally ill, subject to nervous fevers.

Mary Shelley also offers a critique of the nature of scientific thought. Inherent in the concept of science is a potent gender identification, as Sir Humphry Davy assumed: nature is female, the scientist is male. Therefore the scientist who analyzes, manipulates, and attempts to control nature is engaging in sexual politics. In his essay "Temporis Partus Masculus," Francis Bacon heralded the seventeenth-century scientific revolution with the words, "I am come in very truth leading to you Nature with all her children to bind her to your service and make her your slave." By constructing nature as female, the scientist feels entitled to exploit her to gratify his own desire for power, money, and status. Frankenstein's scientific quest is nothing less than an attempt to "penetrate into the recesses of nature, and show how she works in her hiding places," to penetrate the womb of nature and to appropriate that womb, to usurp the process of female biological reproduction. In effect, Frankenstein wishes to rape nature in order to gratify his own lust for power. Frankenstein fantasizes, "A new species would bless me as its creator and source; many happy and excellent natures would owe their being to me. No father could claim the gratitude of his child so completely as I should deserve theirs" (p. 49). If Frankenstein were to succeed in stealing the power of female biological reproduction, he would eliminate the biological necessity for females; the human race of males could survive by cloning. For women readers, this is perhaps the greatest horror of Mary Shelley's story: the implicit threat to the social and biological survival of the human female.

By constituting nature as female, Frankenstein participates in a gendered construction of both physical and social reality. Feminist critics have argued that his scientific endeavor to clone human males and eliminate human females reinforces the general devaluation of women in the nineteenth-century European society to which he belongs. The society of Geneva depicted in Shelley's novel is based on the doctrine of the separate spheres, the assumption that men should work outside the home in the public sphere, while women are confined in the private sphere within the home. Notably, the male characters in Shelley's novel all leave home, to go to university (Victor), to explore the planet (Walton), to work as businessmen (Clerval and his father), and to work as public servants (Alphonse Frankenstein). In contrast, the women are kept at home; as much as she would like to, Elizabeth is not permitted to attend university or travel. Inside the home, the women function as housewives (Caroline Beaufort, Margaret Saville),

as nurses, caregivers for children, servants (Justine), or as "pets" (Elizabeth).

Shelley's novel makes it clear that this division of labor on the basis of gender is destructive for both sexes. All of the women associated with Victor Frankenstein die: his mother sacrifices herself to nurse Elizabeth's scarlet fever, Justine is executed for a crime she did not commit, and Elizabeth is killed by Victor's Creature on her wedding night. Similarly, Victor, his father, and his best friend all die, killed by the results of Victor's reckless experiment. In contrast to this mutually destructive construction of gender is the egalitarian family of the De Laceys, in which both son and daughter contribute equally to the welfare of the family and hold all property in common. But this socialist, egalitarian community is wrenched from the novel, as it was from Mary Shelley's own life: in her view, such a social ideal could not survive in the nineteenth-century England she knew.

Why have women been oppressed, in Mary Shelley's view? She offers a particularly subtle answer to this question in the scene where Victor Frankenstein decides to destroy the female creature. His male Creature has begged him for a female companion. Acknowledging the justice of the Creature's claim that, as Adam, he deserves an Eve, Victor Frankenstein collects his instruments together on a desolate island off the coast of Scotland and proceeds to construct a female body. But halfway through his endeavor, he destroys this body and throws it away. He rationalizes his action thus:

I was now about to form another being, of whose dispositions I was alike ignorant; she might become ten thousand times more malignant than her mate, and delight, for its own sake, in murder and wretchedness. He had sworn to quit the neighbourhood of man, and hide himself in deserts; but she had not; and she, who in all probability was to become a thinking and reasoning animal, might refuse to comply with a compact made before her creation. They might even hate each other; the creature who already lived loathed his own deformity, and might he not conceive a greater abhorrence for it when it came before his eyes in the female form? She also might turn with disgust from him to the superior beauty of man; she might quit him, and he be again alone, exasperated by the fresh provocation of being deserted by one of his own species.
Even if they were to leave Europe, and inhabit the deserts of the new world, yet one of the first results of those sympathies for which the daemon thirsted would be children, and a race of devils would be propagated

upon the earth, who might make the very existence of the species of man a condition precarious and full of terror. Had I a right, for my own benefit, to inflict this curse upon everlasting generations?

(p. 163)

What Frankenstein truly fears is that the female he will construct might be independent, that she might refuse to obey laws she did not make. She might be aggressive, ugly, and lustful. Worse, given that she too would be eight feet tall, she would have the physical strength to realize her sexual desires, perhaps even upon Victor Frankenstein himself. Most frightening, she would have the capacity to procreate. Frankenstein's deepest fear is of female sexuality. He evinces traditional patriarchal womb envy, which stems in part from the fact that a child's paternity can be called into question, whereas a female always knows that the child she carries is hers. In reaction to this masculine fear of an independent, uncontrollable female sexuality, Frankenstein rips up the female creature in an act that echoes a violent rape: "trembling with passion, [I] tore to pieces the thing on which I was engaged" (p. 164). Later, he remarks, "I almost felt as if I had mangled the living flesh of a human being" (p. 167).

In Mary Shelley's feminist novel, however, Victor Frankenstein does not succeed in creating a new race of supermen because nature fights back. She begins by plaguing Frankenstein with bad health. As he engages in his two experiments, he is tormented by fevers, heart palpitations, nervous fits, depression, and paranoia. His physical exhaustion is finally so great that he dies at the age of twenty-five. Nature further punishes Victor by preventing him from creating a normal child: his lack of empathy first causes him to create a giant (simply because the "minuteness of the [normal-sized] parts formed a great hindrance to my speed") and then leads to a series of disasters that prevent him from normal procreation with his bride Elizabeth. Finally, nature pursues Victor Frankenstein with the very electricity and fire he has stolen from her. The lightning, thunder, and rain that surround Victor as he carries on his experiments are not just the conventional atmospheric effects of the Gothic novel but also a manifestation of nature's elemental powers. Like the Furies, nature pursues Victor to his hiding places, destroying not only Victor but his family, friend, and servant. Finally, the penalty of violating nature is death.

Encoded in *Frankenstein* is an alternative to Victor's and Walton's view of nature as female and to be penetrated or as dead matter to be reassembled at will. Significantly, the only member of the Frankenstein family still alive at the end of the novel is Ernest, who, rather than becoming a lawyer like his father, wished to become a farmer. His survival, together with Clerval's enthusiastic love of the changing beauty of the seasons, reveals Mary Shelley's view of the appropriate relationship between human beings and nature: an ecological vision of nature as a person with rights and responsibilities who must be treated with respect, even reverence.

Frankenstein persistently raises the two philosophical questions that haunted all the Romantic writers of the period: What is being? And how do we know what we know? These are the ontological and epistemological questions David Hume and Immanuel Kant had tried to answer, and these are the questions with which both Victor Frankenstein and his Creature are wrestling. Victor sets out to answer the question "whence did the principle of life proceed?" And the Creature insistently demands, "Who was I? What was I? Whence did I come? What was my destination?" (p. 124).

As Shelley's characters struggle with these questions, the novel presents two diametrically opposed answers. The Creature, echoing Jean-Jacques Rousseau, insists that human nature is innately good: "I was benevolent and good; misery made me a fiend" (p. 95). On the other hand, Victor Frankenstein insists that the Creature is innately evil: "Abhorred monster! fiend that thou art!" (p. 94). Insofar as the Creature is frequently referred to in the text as "Being," his very existence poses this problem: is human nature innately good or evil?

This question is emphasized in the emblematic scene when the Creature first sees himself, in a forest pool: "At first I started back, unable to believe that it was indeed I who was reflected in the mirror; and when I became fully convinced that I was in reality the monster that I am, I was filled with the bitterest sensations of despondency and mortification" (p. 109). This scene suggests that in this novel, knowing (re-cognition) is a matter of seeing (perception)—the Creature is at first unable to believe that he is what he perceives himself to be. He then decides that he is "in reality" what he appears to be, what his mirror shows him to be, namely, a "monster." The Creature is as he is seen; he functions in the novel as the sign of the unknown, as that which does not exist until it is read or linguistically named. All the characters impose such names upon him; all immediately read this giant with yellow skin and black lips as the monstrous. The creature insists that such a reading is arbitrary; "'Thus I relieve thee, my creator,' he said, and placed his hated hands before my eyes" (p. 96), as if to suggest that when Victor ceases to see the Creature, he may be able to read him more correctly. Similarly, the father in the De Lacey family can interpret the Creature as "sincere" because he is blind. Walton also covers his eyes when he finally encounters the Creature, refusing to impose a single interpretation upon him, but even Walton then "lost sight" of him in "darkness and distance."

By refusing to tell us whether the Creature is innately good and driven to violence by social rejection, or innately evil, Mary Shelley constructs the Creature as the Kantian noumenon, the forever unknowable "thing-in-itself." She thus equates her Creature with the terror of the Romantic or Burkean sublime, that ultimate power in nature which overwhelms human cognition and consciousness. But, unlike Kant or Burke, or such Romantic poets as Wordsworth, Coleridge, and Percy Shelley, Mary Shelley does not represent the sublime as a moment when the mind of the (male) poet or philosopher comes to know its own creative, shaping powers.

Rather, she represents the sublime as posing an ethical problem. The way we read or interpret the Creature determines the way we treat him. Human beings typically construe the unique, the unfamiliar, and the abnormal as frightening, threatening, and evil. As Michel Foucault argues in *Madness and Civilization,* we use language to fix the boundaries between the acceptable and the unacceptable. Linguistic definitions of evil thus create evil. Because Victor Frankenstein reads his newborn child as a "miserable monster," he interprets the Creature as evil and thus becomes the author of evil.

In effect, Victor Frankenstein becomes the monster he constructs. By the end of the novel, Victor and his creature have been fused into one consciousness, each the hunter and the hunted, each driven equally by revenge and remorse. In their chase across the North Pole, both are identified with the fallen Adam and with Satan, until Victor

in his nightmares experiences the Creature as "my own vampire" (p. 72)—"I felt the fiend's grasp *in* my neck" (p. 181), not "around" his neck, as we might expect. The Creature and Victor now inhabit the same body. This is the sense in which popular culture is correct in confounding the Creature with his creator.

Mary Shelley wants us to see that in a world created by linguistic constructions that code the unfamiliar as evil, we create the evil and injustice that we imagine. She is here criticizing the male Romantic poets' celebration of the imagination as divine. A promiscuous imagination is more likely to generate readings based on fear than on love, as Theseus says in Shakespeare's *A Midsummer Night's Dream.* Her answer to the philosophical questions posed in *Frankenstein* is a radical skepticism. Since we can never *know* the thing-in-itself, we must consciously control our interpretations of almighty nature with a nurturing love that can embrace even freaks and monsters. For as the Creature reminds Victor, "You are my creator but I am your master—obey!"

MATHILDA

SHORTLY after Mary Shelley completed *Frankenstein,* her second daughter, Clara Everina, died, on 24 September 1818, as a result of Percy Shelley's refusal to obtain adequate medical care for her; less than a year later, on 7 June 1819, her only surviving child, William, died in Rome of malaria. Mary Shelley entered a prolonged period of profound depression, blaming Percy (in part correctly) for both these deaths and refusing to be reconciled to him. She was roused from this depression only by the writing of her long novella *Mathilda,* which she began in August 1819, and by the birth of her second son, Percy Florence, on 12 November 1819. *Mathilda* is a powerful tale of incestuous father-daughter love and death in which Mary Shelley articulates her deepest and most ambivalent feelings toward both her father and her husband.

Her hostility to her father was immediately aroused by his failure to understand her despair at William's death. In a letter that may rank among the cruelest ever sent by a father to a bereaved daughter, Godwin had written on 9 September 1819:

I cannot but consider it as lowering your character in a memorable degree, and putting you among the commonality and mob of your sex, when I had thought you to be ranked among those noble spirits that do honour to our nature. Oh! What a falling off is here! . . . you have lost a child; and all the rest of the world, all that is beautiful, and all that has a claim upon your kindness, is nothing, because a child of three years old is dead!

(quoted in *Shelley and Mary*,
ed. by Jane Shelley, 1882, I:104A)

In her novella, Shelley writes the story of a young man whose adored wife Diana dies in childbirth; he then abandons his baby daughter Mathilda for sixteen years, returning only to fall passionately in love with the girl who exactly resembles his dead wife. When he confesses his incestuous passion, Mathilda is horrified and immediately dreams of his suicide, only to awaken to find him gone. This novella thus uncovers Mary Shelley's deepest desire: to be passionately loved by the father who had rejected her, and at the same time to reject and even kill him.

Unlike representations of father-daughter incest by men, like Percy Shelley's *The Cenci*, in which incest is a trope for the domination of the tyrant-father over the rights of both his daughters and his sons (whose appropriate "brides" he usurps), Mary Shelley recognizes that in a relationship of incest the daughter may deeply love her father. Mathilda cannot survive her father's suicide; she stages her own suicide and then retires to live like a hermit, dressed as a nun, in a forsaken wood in Scotland. She regards herself as "the bride of death."

There she is found by an idealistic but lovelorn poet, Woodville (modeled on Percy Shelley), who urges her to rejoin the living but fails to understand the depths of her suffering. When she offers Woodville a drink of total communion, a poison, he refuses it, claiming that he must remain alive to give his poetry to the world. He abandons her, as Percy had emotionally abandoned Mary in her suffering. Mathilda then wanders in a storm at night until she becomes ill—she soon expires from self-induced consumption, penning the story of her life as she dies.

THE LAST MAN

MARY Shelley's sufferings were to continue. Her husband's sudden death by drowning on 8 July 1822, off the coast of Livorno, Italy, was a devastating blow to Mary Shelley and left her widowed at the age of twenty-five with a two-year-old son to raise. Worse, Percy Shelley's death followed a long period of emotional estrangement between the couple caused by Mary Shelley's conviction that Percy had been in part responsible for the prior deaths of both her daughter, Clara Everina, and her son, William. As Mary Shelley wrote bitterly to her good friend Marianne Hunt on 29 June 1819: "We came to Italy thinking to do Shelley's health good—but the Climate is not any means warm enough to be of benefit to him & yet it is that that has destroyed my two children" (*Letters*, vol. 1, p. 101). Confronted with his wife's depression and resentment, Percy Shelley had in the months prior to his death found consolation in the company of other women, of Maria Gisborne, Claire Clairmont, and Jane Williams. His death thus occurred at the worst possible time for Mary Shelley, when there was a great deal of emotional turmoil between them.

Overwhelmed by love, guilt, and remorse, blaming herself for having made his final months unhappy, Mary attempted to make reparation to her dead husband by giving him a posthumous life. She immediately collected his manuscripts and published texts for a complete edition of his works and began to write a hagiographic biography. When her father-in-law forebade its publication, she instead appended long biographical notes to her 1824 and 1839 editions of Percy Shelley's poems, notes in which she deified the poet and revised their past history together, asserting that his last two months on earth were "the happiest he had ever known" (1824). She used her fiction to present idealized portraits of Percy Shelley, first and most tellingly as Adrian in *The Last Man* (1826). In financially straitened circumstances, she managed to give her only surviving child the education and upbringing of a future baronet (he inherited his grandfather's title and estate in 1844) by writing novels, essays, and encyclopedia articles, by translating, and by living as economically as possible on her meager inheritance and allowance from Percy's father, Sir Timothy Shelley.

Published in 1826, *The Last Man* is a brilliantly prophetic novel. It draws on Mary Shelley's personal experiences of abandonment and isolation after the deaths of her husband and of Lord Byron, who died on 19 April 1824. At the same time, it articulates a profound critique of the dominant gender, cultural, and political ideologies of the Romantic era. Equally important, *The Last Man* explores the social significance of a worldwide plague that relentlessly annihilates the entire human race, leaving only one last man to tell the story.

At the biographical level, *The Last Man* is a roman à clef in which Mary Shelley projected and tried to come to terms with both Percy Shelley and Lord Byron, in the figures of Adrian, Earl of Windsor, and of Lord Raymond. Adrian, the "hero" of the novel, shares Percy Shelley's democratic principles as well as his face, form, and voice; he arouses universal affection, even among his enemies. But like the poet of Percy Shelley's "Alastor," he is driven mad by despair when his beloved Evadne rejects him, a madness from which he recovers only after a severe fever has permanently impaired his health.

Despite his physical weakness, Adrian ardently supports the cause of freedom, fights for a year with the Greeks against their Turkish oppressors, and urges his countrymen "to introduce a perfect system of republican government into England" (p. 30). But he refuses to use his position as Earl of Windsor to gain personal political power. Not until England is ravaged by the deadly plague does he determine to "sacrifice himself for the public good" (p. 182) and to accept the position of Lord Protector. With courage and unflagging energy, he then comforts the sick, takes what preventive measures he can against the unstoppable epidemic, and when factions develop among his followers, heroically hurls himself between their armed forces, eloquently reminding them that the plague is their common enemy and that each human life is sacred. Like "an angel of peace" (p. 277), he reunites and governs his countrymen.

Even as Mary Shelley lovingly portrays Adrian as a paragon of benevolence, idealism, courage, and self-sacrifice, her underlying resentment toward her husband cracks this perfect facade. Adrian never marries, never accepts responsibility for a family: "the sensitive and excellent Adrian, loving all, and beloved by all, yet seemed destined not to find the half of himself, which was to complete his happiness" (p. 65). Thus Mary Shelley alludes to the narcissistic egoism of her husband, his insatiable demand for that perfect soul mate who could only be his own self.

Moreover, Adrian is incapable of working pragmatically to achieve his political ideals. Only after the plague has brutally eliminated all distinctions

of wealth and class can he assume leadership over a leveled, egalitarian society. As Hugh Luke has observed, he is subtly associated with Merrival, the old astronomer who is "too long sighted in his view of humanity to heed the casualties of the day" (p. 209) and who remains oblivious to the sufferings of his wife and children until poverty, hunger, and the plague have killed them all.

This oblique criticism of Percy Shelley's insensitivity to the needs of his wife and children is also expressed in the final fate of Adrian. After war, disease, and the plague have destroyed all but three of the human race, Adrian urges the reluctant Verney to accede to his niece Clara's request that the three of them sail to Greece to visit the tomb of her parents. Verney warns against the dangers of a storm at sea, but Adrian insists that they can easily make the journey. In the ensuing tempest, Adrian and Clara are both drowned, leaving only Verney alive on earth. Here Mary Shelley vividly focuses her persistent anger at her husband's irresponsibility concerning his family's welfare. Despite her overt celebration of her husband's genius and "angelic" character, Mary Shelley had not forgiven him for contributing to Clara Everina Shelley's death, or to his own.

This critique of male egoism also informs Shelley's characterization of Lord Raymond, in which she comes to terms with her fascination with Lord Byron. After the death of Percy Shelley, Mary had expected Byron to become her protector and eagerly welcomed his offers of help. But Byron disappointed her. Caught up in his plans to fight for Greek independence, Byron could not long be bothered with the distraught widow and abruptly withdrew his financial and emotional support. Nonetheless, Mary Shelley's emotions toward Byron remained charged. When she learned of his death at Missolonghi, she cried out to her journal (15 May 1824):

Byron has become one of the people of the grave— . . . Can I forget his attentions & consolations to me during my deepest misery?—Never.
Beauty sat on his countenance and power beamed from his eye—his faults being for the most part weaknesses induced one readily to pardon them. Albe [the Shelley circle's pun on L. B.]—the dear capricious fascinating Albe has left this desart [*sic*] world.
(*Journals*, vol. 2, p. 478)

Lord Raymond is presented as the antithesis of Adrian: a proud man of personal ambition, practical worldly knowledge, and intense sexual passions. After fighting heroically in the Greek wars of independence and successfully scheming to restore the British monarchy, Raymond throws over his worldly ambitions to marry the woman he loves, the impoverished Perdita Verney. Mary Shelley, who has given many of her own personality traits to Perdita, reveals through this character her own half-conscious fantasies: that Byron would give up his mistress Teresa Guiccioli and his dreams of military glory in order to marry her. Nevertheless, Raymond cannot long be content with a retired life of intellectually stimulating companionship and the domestic affections; drawn back into politics as Lord Protector (with Perdita as a successful hostess at his side), for three years he rules wisely and well.

But when Raymond falls half in love with the impoverished Evadne, he cannot acknowledge his feelings to his wife. Their perfect communion is destroyed, the foundation of their marriage wrecked. Still in love with Perdita but too proud to apologize, Raymond turns to dreams of military glory instead, heroically conquering Constantinople, only to die in a fatal explosion when he courageously enters its streets silenced by plague. In her portrait of Raymond, Mary Shelley reiterated the judgment of masculine political ambition she had earlier attributed to her protagonist, Castruccio, in her novel *Valperga* (1823): military and civic glory is too often won at the expense of family relationships and the suffering of the innocent. At the same time she exorcised her fascination with Byron: his pride and lack of control over his personal passions tainted even his most noble achievements.

The failures of both Adrian and Raymond to protect either their own or their children's lives again expresses Mary Shelley's political criticism of her contemporary society's division of labor on the basis of sex. Mary Shelley again suggests that the domination of such masculine values as ambition, competition, and heroism in the public realm can extinguish human life in both the public and the private sphere and even extinguish the human race itself. Implicit is the political argument that she had made earlier in *Frankenstein:* only if men as well as women define their primary personal and political responsibility as the nurturance and preservation of all human life, even abnormal monsters, will humanity survive.

In *The Last Man*, Mary Shelley further explores the specific consequences for women of the gender ideology of her day. The female characters in *The Last Man* register her perception that the social roles assigned by her culture to women both cripple and destroy them. Perdita and Idris, both in part self-portraits of Mary Shelley, confine their lives to the domestic sphere; they thereby reveal the results of a society that defines women primarily as members of family units, as daughters, wives, or mothers.

Perdita, whose name is drawn from the outcast and "orphaned" child of Shakespeare's *Winter's Tale,* can conceive of herself only as a part of her husband's self: "Her whole existence was one sacrifice to him" (p. 84). When she discovers Raymond's secret visits to Evadne, she knows that they are no longer one. Mary Shelley explicitly denies her husband's self-serving declaration in "Epipsychidion" that "True Love in this differs from gold and clay / That to divide is not to take away" (pp. 160–161). As Perdita insists, the unique love between a devoted husband and wife cannot be shared without destroying the very intimacy and trust on which it is grounded.

Perdita cannot tolerate the sham of living a lost love and leaves Raymond, but her unwavering passion for him forces her back to his side, first to nurse him when he is wounded and then to die and be buried in his tomb in Greece. Perdita's suicide by drowning imaginatively realizes Mary Shelley's own guilt-ridden desire to rejoin her dead husband in a final act of atonement. But it also embodies her recognition that the role of devoted wife within the bourgeois family is inherently suicidal: the wife submerges her identity into that of her husband, sacrificing herself for his welfare.

Idris, Mary Shelley's second self-portrait in this novel, is portrayed almost exclusively as a mother. She is so idealized in her highborn beauty, sensitivity, and loyalty as to be almost an abstraction of female perfection. Idris becomes a rounded character only in her relationships with her children. Here she embodies the overriding maternal anxiety experienced by the very young Mary Shelley, who had been pregnant five times. As the plague advances, Idris is slowly destroyed by this maternal anxiety: "she compared this gnawing of sleepless expectation of evil, to the vulture that fed on the heart of Prometheus" (p. 219). Shelley identifies the modern Prometheus, not with the scientist/creator Victor Frankenstein, but with the biological creator, the mother. By implying that

Idris' maternal suffering is as intense and unending as that of Prometheus, Shelley underlines the heroic but self-destructive dimensions of motherhood. Because Idris identifies so closely with her children, she has no life of her own—her sons' deaths annihilate her as well.

In *The Last Man*, women can find fulfillment neither within the family nor outside it. In contrast to Perdita and Idris, who define themselves entirely as wives and mothers, the Countess of Windsor has strong political ambitions—she wishes to restore the monarchy and to rule over England. But she is defeated by her gender. The English would never accept her, a foreign woman, as monarch. Hence she must channel her ambitions through her son or her daughter's husband. Blocked by her husband's decision to abdicate, her son's republicanism, her daughter's rejection of Raymond, and Raymond's own desire for Perdita, she can never achieve her desires. After Idris' death, she acknowledges that her political ambition has been both futile and counterproductive and has cut her off from the love and nurturance of her children. While Mary Shelley makes it clear that the Countess of Windsor would have been a tyrannical ruler, she also emphasizes that a woman cannot even gain access to the corridors of political power: the countess is notably absent from the parliamentary debates concerning the protectorship.

Mary Shelley thus suggests that in both the future (the novel is set in the years 2073–2100) and the present, a rigid division of sex roles denies women full satisfaction in life. In the public realm, her female characters must depend on and serve men. In the private domestic realm, they again must depend on others, whether their children or their husbands, to gratify their emotional needs. Both in the public and the private spheres depicted in *The Last Man*, women have only a relational identity, as wife or mother. They are never self-centered or self-sufficient. And while this relational identity contributes positively to the welfare and survival of the family, it is also extremely precarious. It is easily destroyed by infidelity (the betrayal of Raymond) or by the greater power that rules over all human experience, that of chance, accident, and death. Mary Shelley here undermines the very ideology of the egalitarian family that she celebrated in her earlier novels (*Frankenstein, Valperga*) by acknowledging that it can oppress and even finally destroy the women who practice it.

This pessimistic assessment of the future of the family and domestic affection is summed up in the fate of Clara, a portrait of the ideal daughter that Mary Shelley desired. Sensitive, loving, exuberant, intelligent, devoted to her uncle, a second mother to her younger cousins, Clara suddenly becomes sad and withdrawn at the age of puberty. Clara's transformation is never explained but we can speculate as to its cause. With her dawning sexuality, Clara may have realized that her future—and the future of the human race—demanded her involvement in a sexual liaison and motherhood. With her choices limited to an incestuous union with her uncle or her cousin, or a legitimate union with Adrian, her inability to contemplate the latter with pleasure is final testimony to Mary Shelley's ambivalence toward Percy. She cannot imagine a satisfying relationship between Adrian and a woman, not even with her ideal future self. When she insists on visiting her parents' tomb, Clara shows that she feels more bonded to death than to Adrian. Significantly, our last glimpse of Clara is as a half-drowned virgin clasped to Adrian's breast (p. 323). But Adrian cannot support her; Lionel last sees Adrian alone, clinging not to Clara but to an oar. Clara's death is Mary Shelley's final comment in this novel on the possibility of female fulfillment and even survival in a family unit to which men do not make an equal commitment.

To the ideology of the domestic affections that sustained her earlier fiction, which she so effectively explodes in *The Last Man*, Mary Shelley offers but one alternative: a stoical solipsism rendered endurable by an optimistic imagination. We must look closely at the way Mary Shelley depicts the creative imagination in this novel, for she gives a far more devastating critique of Romantic poetics than she did in *Frankenstein*. When he loses his family, Lionel Verney becomes a writer, the narrator of the tale we read.

The last man, Lionel Verney, is also the last woman, Mary Shelley—she so identified herself in her journal on 14 May 1824: "The last man! Yes I may well describe that solitary being's feelings, feeling myself as the last relic of a beloved race, my companions, extinct before me" (*Journals*, vol. 2, pp. 476–477). There are numerous parallels between Verney's situation and Mary Shelley's. Both were "outcasts" in childhood, both possessed a scholarly temperament, a literary imagination, and a preference for domestic pleasures and affections. Both were in love with Adrian/Shelley and credited him with their salvation from intellectual ignorance and emotional misery. Both find themselves at last enduring an almost unimaginable experience of isolation and loneliness. As Mary Shelley recorded in the journal she addressed to her dead husband: "At the age of seven & twenty in the busy metropolis of native England I find myself alone—deserted by the few I knew—disdained—insulted" (3 December 1824; *Journals,* vol. 2, p. 487). Deprived of human companionship, Lionel Verney and Mary Shelley both turn to creative composition for comfort. Lionel Verney, inspired by the monuments of Rome and a desire to celebrate the "matchless specimens of humanity" that created such grandeur, receives momentary satisfaction from his decision to write an account of the end of mankind.

Significantly, Verney consciously works within a female literary tradition; he invokes both Ann Radcliffe's *The Italian* and Madame de Staël's *Corinne* as models. In the author's introduction to *The Last Man,* we are told that the author functioned merely as the collector and arranger of the fragmentary leaves of a prophecy found in the cave of the Cumaean Sibyl. Mary Shelley thus invokes the ultimate female literary authority, the oracle of the Sibyl, to authenticate her prophetic vision. Of course, the novel also identifies Verney with a male-authored literary tradition that focuses on the isolated hero: Charles Brockden Brown's egocentric Arthur Mervyn, Shakespeare's dying Macbeth, Defoe's stranded Robinson Crusoe, Coleridge's guilt-ridden and blasted Ancient Mariner. In contrast to these prototypes, Lionel Verney cannot even hope for human communication; he can dedicate his tale only to "the illustrious dead."

Explicit in Mary Shelley's account of the last man is the assertion that her tale has no living readership, no audience. Even as she constructs a female literary tradition, from the Sibyl through her own editorship, she terminates that tradition. Shelley's novel posits the end of writing. It is a manuscript left on the tombs of Rome for no one to read by a writer who has abandoned authorship in order to voyage aimlessly, an ancient mariner encountering no wedding guest but only life-in-death. Shelley thus implies that the female writer—like Lionel Verney—will not be read, her voice will not be heard, her discourse will be silenced forever.

Shelley further suggests that the products of the creative imagination so glorified by the male Romantic poets may be worthless. At best their consolation is temporary, if delusive, as Verney finds when he enters Constantinople, seeking the deceased Raymond: "For a moment I could yield to the creative power of the imagination, and for a moment was soothed by the sublime fictions it presented to me. The beatings of my human heart drew me back to blank reality" (p. 145).

Insubstantial dreams, such fictions become "tales of sound and fury, signifying nothing" when they can reach no living ear or mind. Here Shelley's philosophical skepticism becomes visible. She first posits the idealist epistemology endorsed by Berkeley, Kant, and Percy Shelley. If to be is to be perceived, if the human mind can never know the thing itself but only its own linguistic constructions of it, then reality exists only in the collective minds of all perceivers. As Percy Shelley had put it in "Mont Blanc," "The everlasting universe of things / Flows though the mind." Unlike Bishop Berkeley, Kant, or her husband, Mary Shelley posits no overarching mind of God, no transcendental subject, no eternal power, to guarantee the truth or endurance of mental things. Once all human perceivers are dead, history ends. The death of the last man is the death of consciousness. It is moreover the death of the universe, since the Cumaean Sibyl prophesies a point in the future, "2100 Last Year of the World," when time and space—as experienced duration and extension—terminate. Since reality is a set of language systems, the death of Lionel Verney is the death of narration, the final period.

Underlining her critique of Romantic idealism, Mary Shelley sets the final scene of the plague's devastation on the very banks of the Arve River in the valley of Chamonix where Percy Shelley wrote "Mont Blanc" and raised the epistemological question of whether the universe could have an existence not constituted by human thought:

And what were thou, and earth, and stars, and sea,
If to the human mind's imaginings
Silence and solitude were vacancy?
                    ("Mont Blanc," ll. 142–145)

When Adrian and his few remaining followers cross into Switzerland, they are confronted with one of nature's most sublime Alpine landscapes. Overcome by the sheer grandeur of nature's beauty, many in the group are moved to tears and one cries out, "God reveals his heaven to us; we may die blessed" (p. 305). But Mary Shelley's allusions here to both Christian heavens and pagan naiads serve paradoxically to highlight the fact that no deity presides over this plague, only an indifferent nature. Human efforts to fit their experiences into a preexisting providential design or ontological moral absolutes are here rendered nugatory.

Mary Shelley's conception of the last man thus stands in deliberate contrast to her contemporaries' treatments of the same theme, all of which used the trope of the end of civilization to point to either an ethical or religious moral. Byron's "Darkness" (1816; itself derived from Alexander Pope's vision of chaotic night in "The Dunciad," 1728) and Thomas Hood's "The Last Man" (1826) had satirized mankind's greed, aggression, and cowardice as forceful enough to compel even the last two men on earth to turn against each other. In a more optimistic vein, the paintings of *The Deluge* and *The Last Man* by John Martin and Philippe de Loutherbourg, Cousin de Grainville's novel *The Last Man; or, Omegarious and Syderia, a Romance in Futurity* (1806), and Thomas Campbell's poem "The Last Man" (first published in 1823 and probably the immediate inspiration for Mary Shelley's 14 May 1824, journal entry and title) all invoke a Judeo-Christian framework and the possibility of a finer life elsewhere, either on earth or in heaven. Mary Shelley explicitly denies such theological or millennial interpretations of her plague. In her novel, the illiterate man who insists that the plague is God's punishment for human sin and that he and his followers constitute an "Elect" that will be saved is explicitly condemned as an "Imposter" who is finally driven to suicide and whose deceived followers perish along with everyone else.

Moreover, Shelley's intentions go far beyond satire. Implicit in *Frankenstein* is a belief in the primacy of the domestic affections and in the restorative power of a maternal, "beautiful" nature. But in *The Last Man*, all pastoral idylls—whether set among the woods of Windsor or on the shores of Lake Como—are abruptly shattered by the advent of the plague. Even though nature continues to provide scenes of sublime grandeur and beautiful delight that give pleasure to the human senses, it remains indifferent to the preservation of human life.

Therefore all human values must be engendered out of the human imagination. But such values, including the value of the domestic affections that Lionel Verney celebrates throughout *The Last Man*, finally depend entirely on individual commitment. And since individuals are mutable, often unable to control their passions (as in the case of Lord Raymond) and always unable to control their final destiny, such values are necessarily temporal and mutable. As Verney says at the very beginning of his tale, "My fortunes have been . . . an exemplification of the power that mutability may possess over the varied tenor of man's life" (p. 5). Mary Shelley's novel recognizes only one controlling power, death.

Moreover, when Mary Shelley defines nature (the plague) as the final arbiter of human destiny in *The Last Man*, she undercuts another fundamental Romantic assumption that she had endorsed in *Frankenstein*: the belief that nature can be the source of moral authority, a belief asserted by Wordsworth in *The Prelude* (1805, 1850). Mary Shelley explicitly denies Wordsworth's assertion by portraying her "child of nature," her orphaned narrator Lionel Verney, as an aggressive, embittered outcast, much like the rejected Creature in *Frankenstein*. Deliberately alluding to Wordsworth's celebrations of the life of the shepherd, Shelley portrays her Cumberland sheep boy as a savage whose only law "was that of the strongest" and whose only concept of virtue "was never to submit" (pp. 8–9). Verney eagerly abandons his lonely shepherd life to participate in the social pleasures offered by Adrian—friendship, learning, gamesmanship, military struggle, and politics. But all such social interactions terminate in the destructions of the plague. Verney ends in the solitude in which he began, but he bears it less well, since he has learned to appreciate the value of those social relationships that he can never know again.

Mary Shelley also undercuts the Romantic concept of nature as a source of cultural meaning. The nature imaged in *The Last Man* is closer to Alfred, Lord Tennyson's trope of "Nature, red in tooth and claw" in *In Memoriam* (1850) than to Mary Shelley's earlier image in *Frankenstein* of nature as a sacred female life force that man penetrates and violates at his peril. Here female nature is indifferent to mankind; her agent, the female plague, now "Queen of the World" (p. 252), is a juggernaut: "she proceeds crushing out the being of all who strew the high road of life" (p. 289). In a passage that explicitly refutes Percy Shelley's invocation of nature (in the shape of the west wind) as both destroyer and preserver in his "Ode to the West Wind" (1820), Lionel Verney addresses the omnipotent power of nature: "when any whole nation becomes the victim of the destructive powers of exterior agents, then indeed man shrinks into insignificance, he feels his tenure of life insecure, his inheritance on earth cut off" (pp. 166–167). In this central passage, Mary Shelley undercuts the Romantic assumption that language constructs and communicates meaning. If the human race can be eliminated, as it is in *The Last Man*, then the very concept of meaning is, finally, meaningless. Where human discourse cannot occur, linguistically constituted meaning cannot exist and human consciousness is annihilated. This is Mary Shelley's sweeping critique of the masculine Romantic poetic ideology promoted by Percy Shelley, Blake, Coleridge, and Wordsworth: the constructions of the imagination cannot transcend the human mind, which is inherently finite, mutable, and mortal.

From this position of radical skepticism, *The Last Man* generates a powerful political criticism. The first half of the novel pits Mary Shelley's earlier belief in the domestic affections as the model of good government and the source of human fulfillment against the forces that destroy it: the forces of male egotism, female masochism, and plague-induced death. In undermining the family as the preserver of cultural value and social stability, Shelley does more than undercut her own beliefs. She also reveals the failure of all the dominant political ideologies of her day—both radical (republican and democratic) and conservative (monarchical and theocratic). Ultimately, she denies the authority of all ideologies and systems of belief.

Both her father, the radical philosopher William Godwin, and his disciple Percy Shelley believed that mankind might be perfected through the improvement of reason and love under a democratic government or benevolent anarchy. This belief is tested by Mary Shelley in *The Last Man* through the actions of both Ryland, leader of the people's party, and Adrian, the ardent espouser of republican principles. Ryland, whose appearance and character are based on the radical British journalist and politician William Cobbett, eloquently defends the rights of the common man against Lord Raymond's attempts to restore the monarchy. But equal freedoms mean equal responsibilities, sacrifices, and limitations. In the period of economic expansion celebrated by Ryland, an egalitarian society can provide adequately for all its members. But in a time of scarcity, of restricted resources, all its members must be equally deprived. Mary Shelley subtly unmasks the inability of Ryland's democratic ideology to confront the necessity of distributing the burden of disaster equally. When the limited resource is life itself, freedom from plague, who is to be saved? Initially the wealthier members of English society willingly share their lands and goods with the refugees fleeing from the plague in Europe, even taking up the hoe and plow to till their own fields (p. 172). The plague thus brings about the social leveling advocated by democratic theory, but it also demands that all must die equally. When confronted with the brute reality that, in a classless society, all must suffer as well as benefit equally, Ryland abdicates the Lord Protectorship and barricades himself within his own estate in a futile attempt to save his own life. Ryland's frantic abdication of political responsibility expresses Mary Shelley's skeptical view of the excessive optimism inherent in a democratic ideology: a socialist government succeeds only if there is enough for every individual. In a scarcity economy, she implies, the equal distribution of resources may not be the best way to protect and preserve the human race.

Inherent in Godwin's and Percy Shelley's political ideology were more extreme utopian concepts that Mary Shelley's novel specifically challenges. Adrian repeats the visionary ideas that Godwin had propounded in his *Enquiry Concerning Political Justice* (1793) and that Percy Shelley had endorsed in his epic verse-drama *Prometheus Unbound* (1820): the conviction that the improved powers of the rational mind could conquer disease and even death. As Godwin argued, "we are sick and we die . . . because we consent to suffer these accidents." When the rational mind has achieved its full powers, Godwin claimed, "there will be no disease, no anguish, no melancholy and no resentment." At that point, he speculated, man "will perhaps be immortal" (II: 869, 872, 871).

Adrian endorses these utopian beliefs when he cries out to Verney: "the will of man is omnipotent, blunting the arrows of death, soothing the bed of disease, and wiping away the tears of agony" (pp. 53–54). But Mary Shelley shows that the powers of the human mind are feeble in comparison to those of all-controlling nature. In this novel, no one can determine the cause, the mode of transmission, or the cure of the fatal plague that sweeps across the earth.

Mary Shelley similarly undercuts the conservative political ideology most powerfully articulated during her lifetime by Edmund Burke. Initially, she invokes Burke's arguments for a constitutional monarchy and a traditional class system with approval, assigning them both to the successful politician Lord Raymond (p. 43) and to her narrator Lionel Verney (p. 165). Gazing on the playing fields of Eton, the source of "the future governors of England" (p. 165), Verney explicitly endorses Burke's view in *Reflections on the Revolution in France* that the human race is an organism in "a condition of unchangeable constancy" and "moves on through the varied tenors of perpetual decay, fall, renovation, and progression" (pp. 107–108). Mary Shelley clearly has more sympathy for Burke's vision of an organic society developing naturally toward an ever-higher form of being, guided by enlightened and benevolent rulers who institute gradual reforms in pragmatically effective ways, than she has for the impractical utopianism of Godwin and Percy Shelley.

Nonetheless, she recognizes that Burke's conservative ideology also rests on a heuristic fiction, a trope: the image of the body politic as a natural organism. If society is an organism, then it is subject to disease. Burke had defined this disease as the "plague" of revolution currently festering in France, a plague which "the precautions of the most severe quarantine ought to be established against" lest it infect that "course of succession [which] is the healthy habit of the British constitution" (Burke, pp. 107–108). In *The Last Man*, Mary Shelley takes Burke's metaphor literally. Even the healthy British constitution cannot long resist the ravages of a deadly plague that can be neither confined nor cured. The body politic, like all living organisms, can die as well as grow.

By taking Burke's figure of the plague and the body politic literally, Mary Shelley implies that human consciousness functions within a linguistic universe in which the figural and the literal are but differing signs or linguistic markers. Since in Shelley's radically skeptical view, there is no ontological distinction between the literal and the figurative, between the thing and the word, conscious experience can occur only within the prison house of language. Therefore the destruction of language—or of all speakers of language and recorded texts—is the destruction of human life. In place of the metaphor put forth by both Godwin and Burke, of history as progress toward perfection, Mary Shelley offers the alternative metaphor of human history as a motion that can suddenly stop. By the end of her novel, only one human being remains alive on earth. She thus introduces a powerful image that has increasingly dominated our cultural consciousness: the image of history as a narrative that reaches an abrupt and final conclusion, whether by biological epidemic, chemical warfare, invasion from outer space, or nuclear holocaust. Since this metaphor denies any ultimate significance to all human events, Shelley's novel is on the deepest level antipolitical and anti-ideological. Echoing the radical skepticism of David Hume, she suggests that all conceptions of human history, all ideologies, are grounded on metaphors or tropes that have no referent or authority outside of language.

The Last Man thus foreshadowed twentieth-century existentialism and nihilism. It anticipates the assertion in Albert Camus's *The Plague* (1947) that all meaning resides, not in an indifferent universe, but in human relationships that are inherently temporal and doomed to end. But *The Last Man* went further than Camus in extending this claim to language itself: it is the first literary text to base itself on the philosophical concept we now call deconstruction. It is the first text to demonstrate that all cultural ideologies and human interactions rest on nonreferential signs, signs written as literal but nonetheless inherently figural, signs no more stable or enduring than the mortal mind.

FINAL FICTIONS

IN the novels she wrote to support herself and her son—*Perkin Warbeck* (1830), *Lodore* (1835), and *Falkner* (1837)—Mary Shelley continued to explore the themes that had long obsessed her: the relation of the individual to history and the relationship of daughters to fathers. She details the ways in which daughters fail to escape their dependence on their fathers, marrying father figures and submitting to the demands of powerful men. Again and again, she uncovers the hierarchy implicit in the bourgeois family even as she idealizes the family as the only location in which a woman could find the love and companionship she craved.

Mary Shelley believed the egalitarian family to be the only social context in which both men and women could achieve emotional satisfaction, through powerful husband-wife and parent-child bonding. Such a loving family embodies an ethic of disinterested care that is in her view the necessary foundation of a healthy body politic. It is critical to recognize that, most explicitly in *Frankenstein* and *Lodore*, Shelley insisted that the role of the mother must also be filled by men if the family is to survive. Nevertheless, even as her novels celebrate the egalitarian bourgeois family and an ethic of care, they reveal the limits of her ideology. They consistently show that a woman who defines herself totally in terms of her family relationships is unhappy: either she is cruelly abandoned, or lacks any sense of autonomy or self-esteem, or loses those she loves to disease and death. Even as she overtly celebrates the egalitarian bourgeois family, Mary Shelley acknowledges that it has never existed. There are no detailed examinations of such a family in her novels.

Her lifelong search for a fulfilling family life was never successful. Her surviving son was devoted to her, but she found him dull. In 1848 she found him a satisfactory wife, Jane St. John, a young widow. She moved with them into Field Place, the Shelley estate in Bournemouth, Sussex, in 1849, ensured that a shrine to Percy Shelley would always be kept there, and soon after died of nervous attacks that had produced a partial paralysis, on 1 February 1851.

SELECTED BIBLIOGRAPHY

I. BIBLIOGRAPHY. "Current Bibliography," *Keats-Shelley Journal* (1952–present), an exceptionally complete annual and indexed bibliography to all publications on the Shelley circle; W. H. Lyles, *Mary Shelley: An Annotated Bibliography* (New York, 1975).

II. SEPARATE WORKS. *History of a Six Weeks' Tour Through a Part of France, Switzerland, Germany, and Holland: With Letters Descriptive of a Sail Round the Lake of Geneva, and of the Glaciers of Chamouni* (London, 1817), travel writing; *Frankenstein; or, The Modern Prometheus* (London, 1818; rev. ed. 1831), novel; *Mathilda* (1819), repr. ed. by Elizabeth Nitchie (Chapel Hill, N.C., 1959), novella; *Valperga; or, The Life and Adventures of Castruccio, Prince of Lucca* (London, 1823), historical novel; *The Last Man* (1826), repr. ed. by Hugh J. Luke, Jr. (Lincoln, Nebr., 1965, repr. 1993), novel; *The Fortunes of Perkin

Warbeck* (London, 1830), historical novel; *Lodore* (London, 1835), novel; *Falkner*, 3 vols. (London, 1837); *Lives of the Most Eminent Literary and Scientific Men of France*, for *Lardner's Cabinet Cyclopedia*, ed. by Rev. Dionysius Lardner (London, 1838–1839), encyclopedia entries; notes to *The Poetical Works of Percy Bysshe Shelley* (London, 1839), repr. in *The Complete Poetical Works of Percy Bysshe Shelley*, ed. by Thomas Hutchinson (London, 1905, 1960), biography; *Rambles in Germany and Italy in 1840, 1842, and 1843* (London, 1844), travel writing; *The Choice: A Poem on Shelley's Death*, ed. by H. Buxton Forman (London, 1876); *Proserpine and Midas: Two Unpublished Mythological Dramas by Mary Shelley*, ed. by André Koszul (London, 1922); *Mary Shelley, Collected Tales and Stories*, ed. by Charles E. Robinson (Baltimore and London, 1976).

III. LETTERS AND JOURNALS. Betty T. Bennett, ed., *The Letters of Mary Wollstonecraft Shelley*, 3 vols. (Baltimore, 1980, 1983, 1988); Paula R. Feldman and Diana Scott-Kilvert, eds., *The Journals of Mary Shelley, 1814–1844*, 2 vols. (Oxford, Eng., 1987).

IV. BIOGRAPHICAL STUDIES. Elizabeth Nitchie, *Mary Shelley: Author of* Frankenstein (New Brunswick, N.J., 1953); Emily W. Sunstein, *Mary Shelley: Romance and Reality* (Boston, 1989).

V. CRITICAL STUDIES. General: Jean de Palacio, *Mary Shelley dans son oeuvre* (Paris, 1969), phenomenological approach to Shelley's work; Mary Poovey, *The Proper Lady and the Woman Writer: Ideology as Style in the Works of Mary Wollstonecraft, Mary Shelley, and Jane Austen* (Chicago and London, 1984), thoughtful and perceptive analysis of Shelley's thought and style; Anne K. Mellor, *Mary Shelley: Her Life, Her Fiction, Her Monsters* (New York and London, 1988), feminist approach to life and works; Meena Alexander, *Mary Shelley* (New York, 1993), intelligent, brief overview; Audrey Fisch, Anne Mellor, and Esther Schor, *The Other Mary Shelley: Beyond Frankenstein* (New York, 1993), important collection of essays on Shelley's less familiar works.

On *Frankenstein*: Robert Kiely, *The Romantic Novel in England* (Cambridge, Mass., 1972), on Frankenstein as a tragic hero; Ellen Moers, *Literary Women* (Garden City, N.J., 1976), brilliant discussion of birth myth in *Frankenstein*; Marc A. Rubenstein, "'My Accursed Origin': The Search for the Mother in *Frankenstein*," in *Studies in Romanticism* 15 (1976), the best of the psychoanalytic readings of the novel; Martin Tropp, *Mary Shelley's Monster* (Boston, 1976), useful collection of historical documents; Sandra Gilbert and Susan Gubar, *The Madwoman in the Attic* (New Haven, Conn., 1979), excellent feminist discussion; David Ketterer, *Frankenstein's Creation: The Book, the Monster, and the Human Reality* (Victoria, B.C., 1979), on Frankenstein as a tragic hero; George Levine and U. C. Knoepflmacher, eds., *The Endurance of Frankenstein* (Berkeley, Calif., and London, 1979), extremely influential collection of essays; Jerrold E. Hogle,

"Otherness in *Frankenstein:* The Confinement/Autonomy of Fabrication," in *Structuralist Review* 2 (1980), interesting deconstructionist analysis; Barbara Johnson, "My Monster/Myself," in *Diacritics* 12 (1982), seminal feminist analysis; Franco Moretti, *Signs Taken for Wonders: Essays in the Sociology of Literary Forms* (London, 1983), interesting Marxist analysis; Paul A. Cantor, *Creature and Creator: Myth-making and English Romanticism* (New York, 1984), excellent analysis of Rousseau's influence; William Veeder, *Mary Shelley and* Frankenstein: *The Fate of Androgyny* (Chicago, 1986), Freudian and Lacanian approach; Chris Baldick, *In Frankenstein's Shadow: Myth, Monstrosity, and Nineteenth-Century Writing* (Oxford, 1987), fine study of the text and its impact on later works.

On *The Last Man:* A. J. Sambrook, "A Romantic Theme: The Last Man," in *Forum for Modern Language Studies* 2 (1966), useful treatment of other texts; Lee Sterrenburg, "*The Last Man:* Anatomy of Failed Revolutions," in *Nineteenth-Century Fiction* 33 (1978), superb analysis of politics in the novel; Morton D. Paley, "Mary Shelley's *The Last Man:* Apocalypse Without Millennium," in *Keats-Shelley Review* 4 (1989), excellent discussion of Romantic millenarian thought; Jane Aaron, "The Return of the Repressed: Reading Mary Shelley's *The Last Man*," in Susan Sellers, ed., *Feminist Criticism: Theory and Practice* (New York and London, 1991), on the role of nature; Anne Mellor, introduction to *The Last Man* (Lincoln, Nebr., 1993), overview of the novel.

PERCY BYSSHE SHELLEY
(1792-1822)

G. M. Matthews

I

It is no good making up one's mind too hastily about Shelley. Contemporary reviewers called various of his works a "dish of carrion," "drivelling prose run mad," "the production of a fiend, and calculated for the entertainment of devils in hell." The Victorians thought his lyrics "absolutely perfect"; he was "the Divine" poet. Early twentieth-century critics could see at a glance that there was "no brain work" in Shelley's poetry; it was "antipathetic to the play of the critical mind." Generalizations about him have always differed wildly. To Charles Kingsley, Shelley was "utterly womanish"; to D. H. Lawrence, he was "transcendently male"; and the man whose friends thought him "full of life and fun" while they knew him, T. S. Eliot in 1933 found humorless and pedantic.

Shelley was no perfectibilist. He saw human society in terms of unending struggle, and controversy delighted him, so his work is understandably controversial. But most judgments of it have been impressionistic: rationalizations of instant liking or distaste. The hostile criticism of the 1930's plainly took no trouble to understand the material it was dismissing: that "Alastor," for instance, was not a form of the name "Alastair" but Greek for an avenging fury; that "The Indian Serenade" was Indian, and a serenade; that when a snake renewed its "winter weeds outworn" (in Shelley or in William Shakespeare), it was changing its skin, not raising a fresh crop of nettles. Only in the last fifty years, and chiefly by Americans, has it been shown how complex this deceptively fluent verse often is, and how patiently its symbolic language needs learning.

Poor texts are still a handicap, and there is still room for disagreement. In this language, for example, electricity or "lightning" pervades the physical, as love pervades the moral, world; the fire of sun and stars is the counterpart of the One, the Unity or Spirit that shapes the beauty of the world; and the changing forms of cloud and vapor represent the mutations of matter that "veil" or refract this brightness and resist its influences. Some of the vocabulary is Platonic, perhaps Neoplatonic; but the language is Shelley's. His "Intellectual Beauty" (a phrase from William Godwin and James Burnett, Lord Monboddo, not from Plato) may express itself in revolutionary action (as in the "Ode to Naples," 149–176) and in sexual intercourse (as in *Laon and Cythna*, 2650–2665).

What fascinated Shelley was not *being* but *process*; not John Keats's timeless urn or William Wordsworth's "permanent forms of nature," but the sun-awakened avalanche, the destroying and preserving wind, the "unpastured sea hungering for calm." So it is true that as a poet he never looked steadily at an object for long, and this elusiveness can be irritating to his readers. By a principle of indeterminacy he passed on to what the object was becoming, or to what caused it. But accurate knowledge was generally taken for granted as the starting point of his invention. He was a country boy; most of his life was spent out-of-doors; and he read a good deal about the workings of nature. In many ways he was a very exact poet—more exact and knowledgeable than some of his critics.

Shelley was also a versatile craftsman. Unlike Geoffrey Chaucer, or George Gordon, Lord Byron, he was not interested in the full scope of human activity, but only in the great problem of humanity's place in the universe and of the achievement of happiness. Can man, through self-conquest, master his own future? Shelley's poetry was the changing comment of his own life experience on this unvarying question. But the angle of the comment, the stylistic range, was very wide. He wrote well in many different "kinds": epic, epigram, pastoral elegy, political ballad, familiar epistle, tragedy, lyric, burlesque. He is best known as the poet of fiery imaginings:

And the green lizard, and the golden snake,
Like unimprisoned flames, out of their trance awake[1]
(*Adonais*, 161–162)

The colors are heraldic, and oppressed creatures break like volcanic fire out of the "trance" of winter; yet as a physical picture every detail is vivid and apt. He could also write with a sensuous verbal relish not unlike Keats's:

Blue thistles bloomed in cities; foodless toads
Within voluptuous chambers panting crawled
(*Prometheus Unbound*, I. 170–171)

Again a symbolic description, with a strong undertone of social criticism; yet again it recalls eyewitness accounts of Hiroshima a few months after atomic bombardment. Or his imagery could be plain and familiar: "like a flock of rooks at a farmer's gun"; "as bats at the wired window of a dairy"; "like field smells known in infancy."

One important quality in Shelley's later verse, expressing itself in both rhythm and tone, might be defined as witty play:

Where light is, chameleons change:
Where love is not, Poets do:
("An Exhortation," 14–15)

This "power of entering thoroughly into the spirit of his own humour," as Shelley's cousin Thomas Medwin remembered it, not only informs long poems like "The Witch of Atlas" and the "Hymn to Mercury," but also can be recognized in the absorbed dramatic roles of lyrics such as "The Cloud" and "The Two Spirits." Until recently readers have been unwilling to notice this quality. When Francis Palgrave and Alfred, Lord Tennyson, put "The Invitation" into *The Golden Treasury* in 1861, they left out the playfully mocking middle passage, presumably because they thought it spoiled the serious idealism of the poem.

Shelley was not a particularly self-centered poet. Less than six percent of the poems in his *Collected Works* begin with the first-person pronoun, compared with more than fifteen percent of those in William Butler Yeats's; and only nineteen percent of his first lines contain "I," "me," "my," "mine," compared with nearly twenty-three percent of John Dryden's. The test is a rough one, of course, since the pronoun "I" does not necessarily mean the writer; but that is as true in Shelley as in Yeats or Dryden.

[1] All quotations are from G. M. Matthews, ed., *Shelley: Selected Poems and Prose* (Oxford, 1964).

II

PERCY BYSSHE SHELLEY was born on 4 August 1792 at Field Place, near Horsham, Sussex. His father was the heir of an American-born adventurer who had twice married money, and who became a baronet in 1806. His family called him Bysshe, after his grandfather; his first wife called him Percy; and everyone else has simply called him Shelley.

As the indulged eldest son of a country gentleman and member of Parliament, Shelley became a fair horseman, an excellent shot, and a memorable practical joker; and by his early teens he was already romantically devoted to a pretty cousin, Harriet Grove. But in adolescence he could not take his conventional, rather dim-witted father seriously as an advocate of Whig ideals such as parliamentary reform, and sometimes mocked his shortcomings not only to friends but even—less openly—in letters to his father himself.

Shelley's uncompetitive home life had not fitted him for survival at Eton, where he was savagely ragged for his non-conformism. (He entered in 1804.) But though vulnerable, he was fearless; and it was probably at Eton that the self-commitment recorded in his dedication to *Laon and Cythna* was made:

I will be wise,
And just, and free, and mild, if in me lies
Such power, for I grow weary to behold
The selfish and the strong still tyrannize
Without reproach or check.
(31–35)

He would not learn what his "tyrants" taught, he decided, but would "Heap knowledge from forbidden mines of lore"—from science, for example (then outlawed at Eton), and the writings of Godwin and the French skeptics. His tyrants did succeed in teaching him Latin and Greek.

Just before Shelley entered University College, Oxford, in October 1810, the parents concerned broke off his friendship with Harriet Grove, alarmed at its effects on her beliefs, and she dutifully married the nephew of a clergyman. In the spring of 1811, Shelley was sent down from Oxford for circulating an unsigned leaflet, *The Necessity of Atheism*, written with his friend Thomas Jefferson Hogg, who shared the same fate.

The shock of these arbitrary acts confirmed Shelley's intellectual revulsion from Christianity.

His reaction, in August 1811, was to elope with a sixteen-year-old friend of his sister's, Harriet Westbrook. This marriage failed, but not before it had inspired his first important poem. Even at twenty-one Shelley was a well-published author, with two prose thrillers to his discredit and two volumes of mainly sensational, "gothic" verse.

Queen Mab, never regularly published, was, ironically, the one popular success of Shelley's career. From 1821 on, it was frequently reprinted— more to the author's amusement than dismay—and became one of the most respected texts in the Radical working-class movement, "the Chartists' Bible."

There is much in it to deserve respect. The fairy title was camouflage to cover "long notes against Jesus Christ, & God the Father and the King & the Bishops & marriage & the Devil knows what," as Shelley later remembered them, so that *Queen Mab*, like all his political verse, was solidly buttressed by prose argument. But the poem has a plain, simple structure—a perspective of the past, present, and future conditions of mankind—and the writing, though modeled on the irregular verse of Robert Southey's *Thalaba the Destroyer* (1801), is hard and clear. Many features of *Queen Mab* have a continuous development throughout Shelley's subsequent work. Human society is always seen in a cosmic setting, and human history as inseparable from the history of stars and insects. From the vantage point to which Mab has carried her, the soul of Ianthe (Harriet) is shown

> The flood of ages combating below,
> The depth of the unbounded universe
> Above, and all around
> Nature's unchanging harmony.
>
> (II. 254–257)

The order of nature is unchanging, a "wilderness of harmony," but its constituent parts are "combating below" in a continual storm of change. Thus the ruined civilizations that Mab exhibits are not—as in many eighteenth-century poems—mere illustrations of human pride humbled by time; they are part of a process in which man is endlessly implicated with nature. Necessity, "mother of the world" and moving in it everywhere like the West Wind, rules this "Imperishable change/That renovates the world." Only man does not yet cooperate. "Matter, with all its transitory shapes,/Lies subjected and plastic at his feet"; but he cannot master it, not by reason of his supposed

> evil nature, that apology
> Which kings who rule, and cowards who crouch, set up
> For their unnumbered crimes
>
> (IV. 76–78)

but because his false institutions and superstitions offend the natural law. "Nature rejects the monarch, not the man."

Yet life goes on aspiring, "like hungry and unresting flame," and must triumph in the end. Then the playthings of man's social childhood—thrones, cathedrals, prisons—will be abandoned, and man will take his place among his fellow creatures in the natural order:

> ... Man has lost
> His terrible prerogative, and stands
> An equal amidst equals ...
>
> (VIII. 225–227)

Men and women, too, will be equal, and thus truly free to love; the old quarrel between passion and reason will end once sexual relations are no longer distorted by commercial exploitation or venereal disease. And eventually the nightshade berries will outgrow their old habit of being poisonous, and the lions their customary fierceness.

Much of the egalitarianism of *Queen Mab*, its sun that shines as sweetly on cottage thatch as on the domes of palaces, was traditional. The style, too, was still eighteenth-century rather than romantic. Shelley did not find his way back to this sort of harsh clarity until the very different "Triumph of Life" a decade later.

For some three years after the writing of *Queen Mab*, Shelley's hectic life gave him little time for poetry; and the forms of direct action that he tried first—agitation in Ireland, land reclamation in Wales—resulted in prose tracts and manifestos rather than poems. Harriet's role as wife of a "committed" poet was hard to keep up, and the gap between their interests widened. In 1814, Shelley met Mary Godwin, daughter of Mary Wollstonecraft and the radical thinker William Godwin; and after a brief agony of indecision, they fled to Switzerland together, accompanied by Mary's stepsister Claire Clairmont.

The practical result of this second elopement was a year desperately spent in trying to raise credit on which to live and in dodging creditors. The strain made Shelley ill; he was told he was dying of consumption. Not until the summer of 1815, when his grandfather died, was there a reasonable subsistence for all concerned.

PERCY BYSSHE SHELLEY

But in August, Shelley, now permanently addicted to boats, made a ten-day voyage up the Thames that mended his health and resulted in the first poem of his early maturity. *Alastor* is exploratory, a languidly beautiful product of convalescence. It is broadly in the eighteenth-century tradition of James Beattie's *The Minstrel*, that of moralizing on the way various experiences affect the sensibility of a young genius, but its landscapes are no longer diagrams thrown on a cosmic screen: they are symbolic, inseparable from the psychic and emotional states of the Poet passing through them.

The Greek title "Alastor," an avenging power, applies to the "self-centred seclusion" that tempts the Poet to waste his life in pursuing a dream lover of impossible perfection instead of making do with the love of his fellow beings. Was Shelley thinking mainly of himself? (He had given up direct political action, and a quiet country life certainly tempted him: a little later he was styling himself the "Hermit of Marlow.") Or Wordsworth? Or Coleridge? Short poems critical of both were included in the *Alastor* volume, but Shelley always took care that the minor poems in his collections matched the principal one. In any case, as the preface admits, his sympathies were on both sides; and the poem tends to romanticize what it was supposed to condemn.

Six weeks of the summer of 1816 were spent on the Lake of Geneva, near Lord Byron. The meeting was occasioned by Byron's liaison with Claire Clairmont; but the two poets liked each other, and their mutual literary admiration, at least, remained to the end. At this time Wordsworth's intuition in "Tintern Abbey" of

A motion and a spirit, that impels
All thinking things, all objects of all thought,
And rolls through all things

was beginning to haunt Shelley's imagination. In "Mont Blanc," a poem the obscurity of which is partly due to technical clumsiness, the mountain embodies a secret Power, perhaps identical with Necessity, that, once acknowledged, could regenerate the world. In a companion "Hymn to Intellectual Beauty," reworked after his return home, Shelley celebrates "Intellectual Beauty" almost as the spiritual aspect of this immanent power, a radiance that invests Necessity with sympathy and loveliness, somewhat as Asia in *Prometheus Unbound* spiritualizes the inscrutable Demogorgon.

Back in England, the suicide of Fanny Imlay (Mary Shelley's half sister) on 9 October 1816 was swiftly followed by Harriet's suicide, in obscure circumstances; and early the following year the lord chancellor, John Scott, 1st earl of Eldon, ruled that Shelley was not fit to take care of Harriet's two children, although he had regularized his claim on them by marrying Mary. His friendships with Hogg, Thomas Love Peacock, and especially Leigh Hunt helped Shelley through these disastrous months. Hunt introduced him to John Keats, and the two young poets agreed each to complete a 4,000-line poem during the summer of 1817. Shelley's poem was *Laon and Cythna; or, The Revolution of the Golden City: A Vision of the Nineteenth Century*, a romance epic in Spenserian stanzas. Despite its Turkish setting, it was intended as a lesson to those supporters of the French Revolution who had been disillusioned by events since 1789. There is no easy optimism here (nor, indeed, anywhere else in Shelley's poems). Although the road to egalitarian objectives is always open, it leads through disappointment, bloody defeat, sacrifice, and death. To "break through the crust of those outworn opinions on which established institutions depend," Shelley made his revolutionary lovers brother and sister (the biological hazards not then being understood), and also stressed the bloodthirstiness of Christianity; but his publisher prevailed on him to modify these features, and to adopt a tactfully distancing title, *The Revolt of Islam*.

This poem has had very few to praise, and none to love it. Whereas the realism of its great prototype, *The Faerie Queene*, vitalizes the allegory, Shelley's symbolic treatment undermines the intended human interest. What stay in the mind are single images, as of the sunlit sea depths from which a diver "Passed like a spark sent up out of a burning oven," and single episodes, such as the opening duel between the eagle of darkness and the snake of light, the description of plague and famine in canto X, and Laone's hymn of hope during the "winter of the world" in canto IX, which anticipates the seasonal imagery of the "Ode to the West Wind."

Shelley was very depressed by the failure of *The Revolt of Islam*, still feeling, three years later, that its "date should have been longer than a day." This and the move to Italy in the spring of 1818—partly for the sunshine, partly to take Claire Clairmont's illegitimate daughter Allegra to her father, Byron—temporarily unsettled him. When he could "absolutely do nothing else," he translated Plato's *Sym-*

posium and the *Cyclops* of Euripides. But August brought the stimulus of a reunion with Byron in Venice. Claire wanted to see her little girl again, and Shelley had gone alone to negotiate a meeting. He succeeded—but when his family joined him at the villa near Este that Byron had lent them, the long, hot journey from Leghorn proved too much for his own year-old daughter Clara. She died of dysentery soon after arrival.

Out of this loss came the "Lines Written Among the Euganean Hills," a minor masterpiece. From the highest point of the Colli Euganei, on the lower slopes of which the Shelleys were living, could be seen Padua and Venice to the east, the Alps to the north, and the Apennines to the south. Islanded in space, making one October day an island in the flux of time, Shelley moves out of the storms of his own life to prophesy over the cities of the plain, enslaved and corrupted by foreign occupation, yet transfigured momentarily under the eternal sunlight. As usual he writes best when his private feelings dissolve into feeling for others; but even the "mariner" of the opening lines is not himself only, for the date is only a week from the anniversary of Fanny Imlay's suicide.

Just as individual lives are wrecked because love is willfully withheld until it is too late, so Venice and Padua face destruction because they lack the will to assert their ancient greatness. The line "Men must reap the things they sow" is bitterly ironical, for the harvests are being gathered—to supply the invader. The meter is that of John Milton's "L'Allegro," a favorite measure in the eighteenth century used, for instance, in John Dyer's Grongar Hill poems, and one with a flexibility that appealed to Shelley:

> And of living things each one,
> And my spirit which so long
> Darkened this swift stream of song,
> Interpenetrated lie
> By the glory of the sky:
> Be it love, light, harmony,
> Odour, or the soul of all
> Which from heaven like dew doth fall,
> Or the mind which feeds this verse
> Peopling the lone universe.
>
> (310–319)

There was reason for the new note of artistic assurance in this poem. Act I of *Prometheus Unbound* had just been finished.

Prometheus Unbound, Shelley's central poetic achievement, was composed over three widely spaced sessions that it will be necessary to treat as one. All but this first act was written during 1819: Acts II and III in the spring, at Rome, and Act IV in the autumn, at Leghorn and Florence. The "myth" of the poem is the great European humanist myth of the Titan who steals fire from the sun and teaches man all the arts and sciences, in defiance of an outraged deity. Shelley's version derives from that of Aeschylus' *Prometheus Bound* (and it is Aeschylus' Prometheus, not Shelley's, that is discussed in the preface); but he reminds readers of his great predecessor partly in order to underline the differences. *Prometheus Bound* was one play of a trilogy in which the hero eventually compromised with Jupiter; Shelley reorders the myth so that it will incorporate the knowledge gained in the struggle for human emancipation since the fifth century b.c.

Prometheus Unbound, as Shelley explained in the preface, was not a program of action, which could better be provided in prose tracts such as the "Essay on Christianity" and the "Philosophical View of Reform"; it was an "idealism"—an imaginative picture of "what ought to be, or may be"—meant to condition people's minds for the stupendous changes that society must undergo in becoming truly human. "Man must first dream the possible before he can do it." So even where the poem is closest to allegory, its characters cannot be translated exactly into moral or political terms, and different aspects of their significance are emphasized at different moments. Nor can the poem be summed up as a "drama in the mind"—or even in a universal Mind—although some of its actions are mental, such as Prometheus' renunciation of the curse, and his torture by the Furies, who represent his own temptations to despair.

At one level the poem mirrors the contemporary social order. Jupiter represents the ruling classes of Europe with their apparatus of repression and propaganda:

> Thrones, altars, judgement-seats, and prisons; wherein,
> And beside which, by wretched men were borne
> Sceptres, tiaras, swords, and chains, and tomes
> Of reasoned wrong, glozed on by ignorance . . . .
>
> (III. iv. 164–167)

Freedom can come only when this entrenched order is overthrown from below. But from another viewpoint all these repressive institutions, and the prestige that makes them effective, exist because mankind installed them and tolerated them: they "were, for his will made or suffered them," and man is able to undo his own mistakes. Jupiter is in this sense the creation of Prometheus. This is why he is described at his fall as "sunk, withdrawn, covered, drunk up/By thirsty nothing"—a mere hole in social and moral space that Love fills up.

At the beginning of the drama, the position is deadlocked. To defy power keeps hope alive, yet defiance alone cannot either dislodge the old regime or create a new one. Necessity, the natural law, cannot operate as one day it must, until the right conditions are met; and one essential condition is that Prometheus should give up his adversary's vindictive attitude of mind. Milton's God in *Paradise Lost* had allowed Satan freedom to act, "That with reiterated crimes he might/Heap on himself damnation." But Prometheus learns through centuries of suffering to forgo revenge; then Asia (Love, his wife and natural counterpart) can be inducted willingly into the realm of Demogorgon. Thus Love, the law that governs the moral world, interacts with Necessity, the law that governs all other worlds, and the Hour of liberation is released.

The imaginative implications of this unusual "plot" are many-sided. Appropriately in a drama about Prometheus, Shelley made part of the action into a geophysical metaphor. The scientist James Hutton had recently explained how the earth recreated itself by periodic cycles of volcanic activity, and it was believed that eruptions were triggered by the entry of water from the sea. So when Asia and her sea sisters penetrate the mountain of Demogorgon, who is described as if he were made of molten lava, they activate an eruption out of which the old earth is reborn. As Sir Humphry Davy had observed of volcanoes in 1811, "The evil produced is transient; the good is permanent. The ashes which buried Pompeii have rendered a great country continually productive. The destruction is small and partial—the benefit great and general." Shelley constantly used volcanic imagery in his poetry. Christianity placed God in Heaven and the Devil in the Pit; but for Shelley evil was rained from above, while the ultimate source of power and energy was located below, at the center. So the earth produced "fountains," or springs, and breathed up exhalations; these might be mischievous, corrupted as earth was under Jupiter, but in origin they were the "wine of life," sources of inspiration, prophecy, and action.

The dramatic center of Act I is the confrontation between Prometheus and the Furies, who are brought by Mercury to force him into despair. The contrast between the mealy-mouthed, self-indulgence of Mercury and the tight-lipped, dismissive irony of Prometheus is very effective:

> *Mercury.* Thou canst not count thy years to come
>   of pain?
> *Prometheus.* They last while Jove must reign; nor
>   more, nor less
> Do I desire or fear.
>   *Mercury.* Yet pause, and plunge
> Into Eternity, where recorded time,
> Even all that we imagine, age on age,
> Seems but a point, and the reluctant mind
> Flags wearily in its unending flight,
> Till it sink, dizzy, blind, lost, shelterless;
> Perchance it has not numbered the slow years
> Which thou must spend in torture, unreprieved?
>   *Prometheus.* Perchance no thought can count them,
>   yet they pass.
>   *Mercury.* If thou might'st dwell among the Gods the
>   while
> Lapped in voluptuous joy?
>   *Prometheus.* I would not quit
> This bleak ravine, these unrepentant pains.
>   *Mercury.* Alas! I wonder at, yet pity thee.
>   *Prometheus.* Pity the self-despising slaves of
>   Heaven,
> Not me, within whose mind sits peace serene,
> As light in the sun, throned: how vain is talk!
> Call up the fiends.
>   (I. 414–432)

To the Furies, Prometheus is curt and laconic:

> Pain is my element, as hate is thine;
> Ye rend me now: I care not.
>   (I. 477–478)

And there is equal economy of language in a Fury's demoralizing summary of human impotence: even the greatest human figures

> . . . dare not devise good for man's estate,
> And yet they know not that they do not dare.
> The good want power, but to weep barren tears.
> The powerful goodness want: worse need for them.
> The wise want love, and those who love want wisdom;
> And all best things are thus confused to ill.
>   (I. 623–628)

The wintry poetic language of the alpine first act matches the dramatic situation; the language of the second act, borrowing its scenery from the luxuriant area around Naples, opens with a burst of colors to match the revitalizing forces set in motion by Prometheus' change of heart. In one dialogue—virtually a monologue—Asia is inspired to speculate, to the limit of her own insight (and Shelley's), on the authorship of evil; but some of the most original writing in this act is lyrical. In the "Semichorus of Spirits," a key passage with its remarkable reconcilement of free will and determinism in the final stanza, the clogged movement, the intricate syntax, the images of vegetation, gloom, and moisture aptly suggest the dense forest surrounding the causal source of material life:

> Nor sun, nor moon, nor wind, nor rain
> Can pierce its interwoven bowers,
> Nor aught, save where some cloud of dew,
> Drifted along the earth-creeping breeze
> Between the trunks of the hoar trees,
> Hangs each a pearl in the pale flowers
> Of the green laurel, blown anew;
>
>   . . .
>
> And the gloom divine is all around;
> And underneath is the mossy ground.
>   (II. ii. 5–11; 22–23)

The "Voice in the Air, Singing" in celebration of Asia is at another extreme, for here Asia is to Demogorgon as spiritual light is to physical heat:

> Child of Light! thy limbs are burning
> Through the vest which seems to hide them,
> As the radiant lines of morning
> Through the clouds ere they divide them;
> And this atmosphere divinest
> Shrouds thee wheresoe'er thou shinest.
>   (II. v. 54–59)

In Act III, after Jupiter has fallen, the gradual change to a new civilization is abridged for formal reasons; there seems to be little difference in things at first, but by the end the old idols are moldering ruins. And as in *Queen Mab*, not only is man reaching out into the deeps of space, but his morality is affecting the ecology of nature. The precision and quality of the lines in which the Spirit of the Earth rejoices over this development prove how seriously Shelley took it:

> All things had put their evil nature off:
> I cannot tell my joy, when o'er a lake

> Upon a drooping bough with nightshade twined,
> I saw two azure halcyons clinging downward
> And thinning one bright bunch of amber berries
> With quick long beaks, and in the deep there lay
> Those lovely forms imaged as in a sky . . . .
>   (III. iv. 77–83)

Act IV, the lyrical "cosmic dance" added to the poem when it was already half-copied for the printer, is patchy, but fascinating, as Mary Shelley said, for its "abstruse and imaginative theories with regard to the Creation." The extraordinary song of the Moon to the Earth, which turns gravitation into a metaphor of sexual love, is an example of the unique kind of analogical vitality that Shelley could derive from physical science:

> I, thy crystal paramour
> Borne beside thee by a power
> Like the polar Paradise,
> Magnet-like, of lovers' eyes;
>
>   . . .
>
> Sheltered by the warm embrace
> Of thy soul, from hungry space . . . .
>   (IV. 463–466; 479–480)

The end of the act is, in effect, a proclamation by Demogorgon to his reclaimed empire, summarizing the central experience of the poem:

> To defy Power, which seems omnipotent;
> To love, and bear; to hope, till Hope creates
> From its own wreck the thing it contemplates;
>   Neither to change, nor falter, nor repent;
> This, like thy glory, Titan! is to be
> Good, great and joyous, beautiful and free;
> This is alone Life, Joy, Empire and Victory.
>   (IV. 572–578)

From Este, with *Prometheus* one-quarter finished, the Shelleys traveled south to winter in Naples, an obscure and unhappy period in which only the "Stanzas Written in Dejection" were completed. But it is probable that "Julian and Maddalo," though planned at Este, was mostly written between Acts I and II of *Prometheus*; if so, Shelley was already experimenting consciously in a very different, familiar style, and a *"sermo pedestris* way of treating human nature," in the middle of his lyrical drama. The successful parts are in fact its vivid descriptions of Venice and its imitations of "the actual way in which people talk with each other"—in this case Julian

(Shelley) and Maddalo (Byron), on the shores and canals of Venice:

> Of all that earth has been or yet may be,
> All that vain men imagine or believe,
> Or hope can paint or suffering may achieve,
> We descanted, and I (for ever still
> Is it not wise to make the best of ill?)
> Argued against despondency, but pride
> Made my companion take the darker side.
>
> (43–49)

So Julian maintains, once more, that men are enslaved to evil because they make no effort to be otherwise; "it is our will/That thus enchains us to permitted ill." "You talk Utopia," Maddalo retorts; men are too weak ever to control their own destinies. And he supports his case by showing Julian someone whose reason has been destroyed by personal suffering. Perhaps the concept of this maniac derives from the madness of Torquato Tasso, and parts of his story from the private affairs of Shelley or Byron, but the episode as a whole is a "comment for the text of every heart." The poem ends with the argument still unsettled.

"Julian and Maddalo," subtitled "A Conversation," was a stylistic bridge between *Prometheus Unbound* and the "sad reality" of *The Cenci*, which Shelley wrote for the stage. All that he ironically called "mere poetry" was banished from the script, which was to be objective and lucid, "a delineation of passions which I had never participated in, in chaste language," and the principal part was angled toward a particular actress, Eliza O'Neill. But the true-life plot proved too unchaste for the theater management; Miss O'Neill could not be asked even to read it.

The heroine, Beatrice, is a mortal Prometheus who, because her oppressor is hateful, cannot help hating him, and answers rape with murder. Her conviction that a just God endorses her deed is so sustained and passionate that a puzzling dramatic tension is set up by "the restless and anatomizing casuistry with which men seek the justification of Beatrice, yet feel that she has done what needs justification." She is given other motives for her pose of innocence, including the fear of death. In the Old Vic production of 1959, Barbara Jefford spoke Beatrice's final words of the play, "Well, 'tis very well," with a stinging derision that epitomized the vitality and complexity of this remarkable heroine. *The Cenci*

cannot properly be judged away from the theater, and in the theater it is powerful but defective. It is also memorably original. Except in the most trivial ways it is quite un-Shakespearean, in versification as in content.

Most of *The Cenci* was written near Leghorn. Mary Shelley had been grief-stricken by the death of their son William in June 1819; and the Shelleys had fled from Rome, now childless, to seek consolation from an old friend, Maria Gisborne, who had nursed Mary as a baby. Shelley did, of course, write private verses to express his feelings, but the two public poems composed during this unhappy summer were entirely objective. The second of these was "The Masque of Anarchy," a vigorous fusion of biblical prophecy, poetic vision, and street balladry:

> As I lay asleep in Italy
> There came a voice from over the Sea,
> And with great power it forth led me
> To walk in the Visions of Poesy.
>
> (1–4)

Asleep at his post of duty to others, Shelley meant. The news of the Peterloo massacre of 16 August, when a peaceful reform demonstration in Manchester was ridden down by drunken yeomanry, had reached him on 5 September; next day he told his publisher, "The torrent of my indignation has not yet done boiling in my veins"; and within three weeks a ballad of ninety-one stanzas was on its way to Leigh Hunt for publication. Again a poem was addressed to a popular audience, and again it was held back for fear of the consequences. Perhaps with reason, for although its appeal is to the advantages of passive resistance and (shrewdly) to "the old laws of England," the refrain "Ye are many—they are few" would hardly have tranquilized the frightened leaders of Lord Liverpool's government, nor would the opening stanzas, in which each leader is made to seem a mere "front" for the evil that inhabits him:

> I met Murder on the way—
> He had a mask like Castlereagh . . . .
>
> (5–6)

Murder wears the face of Lord Castlereagh (foreign secretary); Hypocrisy, that of Lord Sidmouth (home secretary and builder of churches for the starving poor); Fraud is a mock-up of Lord Eldon (a judge). Thus the title is a pun: "masque," pageant play, and "mask," disguise. Once more the constructive side of the poem takes the form of a prophetic vision, but the writing is forceful and concrete. "Freedom" is no abstract slogan: it means bread on a table, a home, and clothes.

Shelley's other political songs are less interesting than the long, incomplete prose essay "A Philosophical View of Reform," written soon after "The Masque of Anarchy." Its modest proposals to abolish the national debt, to disband the army, to make religious intolerance illegal, to extend the jury system and the franchise were not, of course, all that Shelley wanted, but only what he thought it possible to get. The long-range aspirations of his poetry always have somewhere behind them this sort of short-term prose practicality.

From this time on, with minor exceptions, Shelley gave up trying to reach a wide audience on subjects of topical concern, as he had earlier given up direct action. But one major poem, the "Ode to the West Wind," ends this period of passionate commitment. Shelley had just read an attack on *The Revolt of Islam* in the *Quarterly Review*, full of innuendo against the poet's private life and concluding, "Instead of relying on his own powers, he must feel and acknowledge his weakness, and pray for strength from above." Shelley takes this advice with ironic literalness: he acknowledges his weakness, and prays to the wind. The West Wind he invokes is the "breath of Autumn's being," the essence of seasonal change, one aspect of that universal Power operating at every level in all the elements, from the star-fretted sky to the weed on the seabed: the Power that destroys leaves and people of all colors but also resurrects them as children of another spring.

The reviewer (who had known Shelley at Eton) called him "unteachable in boyhood." If only he could be an unteachable boy again, or if the Wind would simply order him about, as it orders all inanimate things: wave, leaf, and cloud! So it does, for he too is subject to the universal Law; his own leaves are falling. But he is a man, not a leaf, and must use the Wind as well as serve it, just as Asia on her journey used as well as obeyed the "plume-uplifting wind" steaming from Demogorgon's mountain. He is a poet, and must give back music to the Wind; he is a prophet, and the Wind must trumpet his words abroad. Cause and effect interpenetrate to proclaim the same message of hope.

The ode is one of the great lyrics of the language, unique for its athletic swiftness within a tightly con-

troling form. Its imagery and diction, which a few critics have thought suspiciously beautiful, have turned out on closer inspection to be equally exact and subtle.

The day "West Wind" was begun in Florence was probably the day after *Peter Bell the Third* was finished, this last a shrewd joke at Wordsworth's expense, with much hard-hitting contemporary satire:

> Hell is a city much like London—
>   A populous and a smoky city;
> There are all sorts of people undone
> And there is little or no fun done;
>   Small justice shown, and still less pity.
>   (147–151)

There was also a literal "new birth" in November 1819. Percy Florence Shelley, who survived his father, owed his second name to the suggestion of a visiting friend, Sophia Stacey. Sophia flirted amicably with Shelley, sang to him, and was courted in a resourceful variety of poetic attitudes: with playful practicality in "Love's Philosophy," with oriental sensuality in "The Indian Serenade," and ethereally in "Thou art fair and few are fairer" (a lyric evidently once intended for Asia, but re-addressed from a "nymph of air" to a "nymph of earth"). Perhaps the unclaimed flowers of "The Question" would have been Sophia's too, if she had stayed to accept them.

In January 1820, Shelley took his family to Pisa, where a small group of friends later began to gather: Edward Williams and Jane Johnson early the following year, he a young officer on half-pay, she a refugee from her real husband; and in 1822, Edward Trelawny, a supposed former privateer who was as devoted as his credentials were unreliable.

The severe winter in Florence, and perhaps Miss Stacey's departure, influenced Shelley's first poem of 1820, "The Sensitive Plant" (*Mimosa pudica*), a parable of man's precarious situation within nature. This was followed by the grandiloquent "Ode to Liberty," inspired by news of the revolution in Spain against Ferdinand VII. Perhaps some of the shorter poems of this spring were more successful within their limits. Shelley obviously enjoyed the challenge to his craftsmanship of commissioned work, and it was probably after writing what is known as the "Hymn of Apollo," which the sun god sings in the first person, for a verse play of his wife's that Shelley went on to write, in the same manner but just for fun, his dazzling meteorological nursery rhyme "The Cloud."

The other long poems written in 1820 are all light in tone, especially the accomplished (and funny) translation of Homer's "Hymn to Mercury." "The Witch of Atlas" is more serious than it seems, but is still a holiday poem. And early in July, Shelley wrote the verse letter that Maria Gisborne called "that delightful and laughable and exquisite description in verse of our house and Henry's workroom"—the poem generally entitled "Letter to Maria Gisborne," although it was sent to the family. It was not that he was especially lighthearted. What the playful tone represents is a new artistic maturity in Shelley, a sort of Mozartian wryness, compounded of sadness and self-mockery, that is characteristic of some of his best work from 1820 on.

The Gisbornes had gone to London, and Shelley was writing from the workroom of Maria's son Henry, who was a nautical engineer. It is a true letter to close friends, not a public poem, and its deceptively careless form gives the illusion of spontaneous informality. The spider and silkworm of the opening introduce several themes—"threads of friendship," "machinery," and "habitation"—that permeate the poem. These verses are not to catch readers, Shelley says; they are just an expendable way of making my friends remember me. What really counts is not the apparatus of constraint, but the ties of affection, natural beauty, and domesticity. Later the spider's meretricious web becomes equivalent to London, and the silkworm's mulberry tree to the peaceful environment of Italy (silk was the chief industrial product of Italy). All this with playful courtesy— for instance, in the recollection of how Maria Gisborne, who had cared for Shelley's wife as a baby, had nursed him also through his infancy in the Spanish language. Topics of every degree of seriousness grow effortlessly out of one another: torture, toy boats, tea, life after death, prostitution, mince pies; and the appropriate modulations of tone are managed with a happy confidence:

> You will see Coleridge, he who sits obscure
> In the exceeding lustre and the pure
> Intense irradiation of a mind
> Which, with its own internal lightning blind,
> Flags wearily through darkness and despair—
>   . . .
> But we will have books, Spanish, Italian, Greek,
> And ask one week to make another week

> As like his father as I'm unlike mine,
> Which is not his fault, as you may divine.
>   (202–206; 298–301)

There is throughout a concrete particularity—a sense of locality and of things—which is not often credited to Shelley:

> . . . a shabby stand
> Of hackney coaches, a brick house or wall
> Fencing some lordly court, white with the scrawl
> Of our unhappy politics . . .
>   (265–268)

The poem is a triumph of graceful craftsmanship and civilized feeling.

A more intense but much narrower poem resulted from Shelley's celebration of a young Italian girl, Emilia Viviani, as the final embodiment of the Ideal Beauty he had been seeking all his life. In a way *Epipsychidion* ("a little soul beside a soul") is the most "typical" of all Shelley's works, an extreme concentration of a single element in his genius. But Keats would have called it "too smokeable"—too easy to smile at. When, eventually, Shelley found Emilia "a cloud instead of a Juno," he reacted against the poem too, and sent word to stop its further publication.

He was still under the spell of this platonic friendship when he wrote his best-known prose work, "A Defence of Poetry," unpublished until 1840. It was part of an answer to Thomas Love Peacock's half-serious argument that poetry in a utilitarian age was obsolescent, and his treatment is therefore very general. But his metaphors are generally used, as in Francis Bacon, not for mere eloquence but in order to make complex meanings intelligible ("the mind in creation is as a fading coal, which some invisible influence, like an inconstant wind, awakens to transitory brightness"); and some of the incidental discussions are of much interest: for example, the question why a great poem such as *Paradise Lost* will go on revealing new significances long after its social context, and even the religion that inspired it, have disintegrated. "Veil after veil may be undrawn, and the inmost naked beauty of the meaning never exposed." This is an important commentary on Shelley's own adaptations of myth.

News came in April 1821 of Keats's death in Rome. Shelley had not known him well; but he had seen from *Hyperion* that Keats was a major poet, and the supposed primary cause of his death—the *Quarterly*

Review attack on *Endymion* in 1818—roused him to fury. Yet *Adonais* is "a highly wrought *piece of art*," for in this most complimentary of English elegies, Shelley purposely followed Keats's advice to "curb his magnanimity" (that is, his humanitarian zeal) and "be more of an artist." So it is statelier, more conscious of its own verbal substance, than many of Shelley's poems.

To counter the reviewers' dismissal of Keats as an illiterate Cockney, Shelley chose to honor him by adopting the graceful classical artifice of the pastoral elegy, as Edmund Spenser had mourned Sir Philip Sidney in *Astrophel*, and Milton his friend Edward King in "Lycidas." The classical pastoral transfers personal emotions and relationships to a more or less idealized country community; the shepherd with his pipe, living in close contact with nature, becomes a type of the poet, and the death of a shepherd-poet is lamented by his fellow shepherds and by nature itself. The convention derives from Theocritus and his Latin imitator Vergil; but Shelley's more immediate influences were Moschus' elegy on the Greek poet Bion, and Bion's own *Lament of Venus for Adonis*, lines from both of which he had translated. Thus *Adonais* belongs to a tradition extending from the Greek idyll to Matthew Arnold's "Thyrsis"—and even, in some respects, to T. S. Eliot's *The Waste Land*.

Keats had used the myth of Adonis, whose name suggested "Adonais," in his *Endymion*. He was a boy loved by the goddess Venus, but one day a boar killed him while he was hunting. He was permitted to return to life for half the year, spending the other half asleep in the underworld. This was a close fit: Keats was loved by immortal Poetry (Urania) and killed by a reviewer, yet in death he had rejoined the Spirit whose "plastic stress" shapes the beauty of the material world. Like Asia, Urania is composite. She is not Adonais' love but his mother, and she is imagined as being Milton's spiritual widow, with Adonais as their youngest offspring. This is because Shelley regarded the author of *Hyperion* as the poetic heir of Milton, who had adopted Urania as his single "heavenly born" Muse in *Paradise Lost*; so, after Milton's death, Keats was the "nursling of her widowhood." But at times she is also Venus Genetrix, goddess of love and organic life.

The almost unrelieved grief of the opening stanzas, expressed in imagery of cloud and vapor, is not to be dispelled by the return of spring, although

> The leprous corpse touched by this spirit tender
> Exhales itself in flowers of gentle breath;
> Like incarnations of the stars . . .
>
> (st. 20)

The flowers are earthly versions of the stars, radiating perfume instead of light. But for the dead man there is no renewal of life, as Moschus had said in his lament for Bion. Death is the price paid on earth for the colors of sky and field. Even Urania, undying mother of generation, cannot revive Adonais.

Adonais' own poetic imaginings lament him, and there are many references to Keats's poems: the "pale flower by some sad maiden cherished" is "Isabella"; Adonais is washed from a "lucid urn"; his spirit's sister is the nightingale; like his own Hyperion he could scale Heaven. His fellow poets lament him, too, mountain shepherds in honor of Endymion, who kept sheep on Mount Patmos; these include Byron, Thomas Moore, and Leigh Hunt. Shelley's own presence among them is often thought an embarrassment to the poem, and there is some evidence that he meant to omit these stanzas in a second edition. But the episode is not irrelevant; an obscure mourner, who identifies his fate with that of Adonais, asks: If the enemies of the imagination could not even discriminate between the extremes represented by Cain and Christ, what justice can be expected for any of us? Yet, in some sense at least, Adonais is with the "enduring" dead, like pure metal melted down and returned to the furnace, whereas the reviewer and his kind are ashes only:

> Thou canst not soar where he is sitting now—
> Dust to the dust! but the pure spirit shall flow
> Back to the burning fountain whence it came,
> A portion of the Eternal . . . .
>
> (st. 38)

So the poem reaches its final affirmation, expressed in imagery of light and fire. Adonais has "awakened from the dream of life"—this life the flowers, arts, and cultures of which can only partially embody the Power working through them—and has become identified with that Power:

> He is a portion of the loveliness
> Which once he made more lovely: he doth bear
> His part, while the one Spirit's plastic stress
> Sweeps through the dull dense world, compelling there
> All new successions to the forms they wear;

Torturing the unwilling dross that checks its flight
To its own likeness, as each mass may bear;
And bursting in its beauty and its might
From trees and beasts and men into the Heavens' light.

(st. 43)

In death the white sunlight of Unity is no longer refracted into colors by the "dome" of the mundane atmosphere. And that Unity, to attain which Shelley would almost accept a death like Keats's ("why shrink, my Heart?"), touches him in the act of writing his poem and authorizes its final daring paradoxes of grammar and metaphor:

That Light . . .

. . .

Which through the web of being blindly wove
By man and beast and earth and air and sea,
Burns bright or dim, as each are mirrors of
The fire for which all thirst, now beams on me,
Consuming the last clouds of cold mortality.

(st. 54)

In the autumn Shelley completed *Hellas* ("Greece") in honor of the Greeks' insurrection against their Turkish overlords. It was written, like W. H. Auden's *Spain*, for the cause; and though it has some fine lyrical choruses, the blank verse tends to be strained. Shelley called it "a mere improvise."

Byron had moved to Pisa late in 1821, to write for *The Liberal*, which Leigh Hunt was coming from England to edit; and in March and April 1822, Shelley translated some scenes from Pedro Calderón de la Barca and from *Faust* for publication in the new journal. But he was again in a very unsettled state. He had already abandoned work on a new play, *Charles I.* Some of his uncertainty related to Edward and Jane Williams—especially Jane, whom he found increasingly attractive. As the months of 1822 passed, the eight lyrics he gave her came to form the best—indeed, the only—group of unequivocally personal love poems he ever wrote. For all their tact and delicacy, these poems have a new undertone of skepticism, almost earthiness:

. . . the sweet warmth of day
Was scattered o'er the twinkling bay;
And the fisher with his lamp
And spear, about the low rocks damp
Crept, and struck the fish who came
To worship the delusive flame.

(43–48)

These "Lines Written in the Bay of Lerici" were composed when the Williams and Shelley families were in joint occupation of Casa Magni, the only house available to them on that beautiful coast. Claire's little Allegra had died of fever, and it had been imperative to get her mother well away from Byron, whom she was bound to blame for this tragedy. In May, Shelley's new boat, the *Don Juan*, arrived; and the outward things of life seemed very favorable to him, for once:

Williams is captain [he wrote], and we drive along this delightful bay in the evening wind, under the summer moon, until earth appears another world. Jane brings her guitar, and if the past and the future could be obliterated, the present would content me so well that I could say with Faust to the passing moment, "Remain, thou, thou art so beautiful".[2]

(letter to John Gisborne, 18 June 1822)

Inwardly it was otherwise. His poetry had failed, and the popular cause had been defeated over almost all of Europe. Four children he had loved were dead; his wife was ill and unhappy; and he was in love with someone unobtainable. In this complex of troubles he began "The Triumph of Life."

Shelley's last, unfinished, poem is difficult and enigmatic. Stylistically it is like a combination of "The Masque of Anarchy" and *Adonais*—that is, of directness and economy with a "highly wrought" verbal texture—but the literary influences behind it are no longer English or Greek, but Italian: Petrarch and Dante. Although most of the poem exists only in rough draft, the movement of the verse is so fluent that Shelley's technical mastery of the terza rima goes almost unnoticed. The homage of all creation to the sun, at the opening, is followed by a vision of the car of light, in front of which the young execute a frenzied erotic dance, until

One falls and then another in the path
Senseless, nor is the desolation single,

Yet ere I can say *where*, the chariot hath
Passed over them; nor other trace I find
But as of foam after the ocean's wrath

Is spent upon the desert shore.—Behind,
Old men and women foully disarrayed
Shake their grey hair in the insulting wind,

[2]From F. L. Jones, ed., *The Letters of Percy Bysshe Shelley* (Oxford, 1964), vol. II, pp. 435–436.

Limp in the dance and strain with limbs decayed
    To reach the car of light which leaves them still
Far behind, and deeper in the shade.

    But not the less with impotence of will
They wheel, though ghastly shadows interpose,
    Round them and round each other, and fulfil

Their work, and to the dust whence they arose
    Sink, and corruption veils them as they lie,
And frost in these performs what fire in those.
                       (159–175)

One fallen worshipper, Jean Jacques Rousseau, describes how the car seduced him from what seemed an early ideal, a "fair Shape" brighter than the sun, and then destroyed him as it had destroyed these others.

What is being repudiated in this poem? The "suicidal selfishness" of *Queen Mab*, the "loathsome mask" of *Prometheus Unbound*, all the moral and social targets of Shelley's earlier attacks? These, certainly; but some feel that earthly life is now being rejected altogether, that Rousseau's "fair Shape" was a double agent, a delusive embodiment of the true Ideal. The poem breaks off, and no one knows whether there would have been another side to this somber vision, or whether it was already almost complete.

Leigh Hunt's arrival must have interrupted the answer to that final question, "What is Life?" After a busy but happy reunion with him in Leghorn, Shelley and Williams sailed for home on 8 July; but on the way the boat was wrecked in a squall. Because of the quarantine laws, the bodies of Shelley and his friend were burned on the foreshore under Trelawny's supervision; and Shelley's ashes were interred in the Protestant cemetery in Rome on 21 January 1823, that "flame transformed to marble" that had been celebrated in *Adonais*. At about the same age of twenty-nine, Wordsworth, who considered Shelley "one of the best *artists* of us all," was just thinking of writing a preface to his *Lyrical Ballads*.

SELECTED BIBLIOGRAPHY

I. Bibliography. H. B. Forman, *The Shelley Library* (London, 1886), pt. I: "Shelley's Own Books, Pamphlets and Broadsides; Posthumous Separate Issues; and Posthumous Books Wholly or Mainly by Him"; no pt. II was published; W. Sharp, *Life of Percy Bysshe Shelley* (London, 1887), includes bibliography by J. P. Anderson, still useful for critical articles 1822–1887; F. S. Ellis, comp., *A Lexical Concordance to the Poetical Works of Shelley* (London, 1892), repr. with app. by T. Saito (Tokyo, 1963), based on H. B. Forman's 1882 ed. of the poems; R. Granniss, *A Descriptive Catalogue of the First Editions in Book Form of the Writings of Shelley* (New York, 1923), with 30 plates; T. J. Wise, *A Shelley Library. A Catalogue of Printed Books, Manuscripts and Autograph Letters* (London, 1924), privately printed, essentially vol. V of *The Ashley Library* (London, 1924); S. de Ricci, *A Bibliography of Shelley's Letters, Published and Unpublished* (Paris, 1927), privately printed; *Keats-Shelley Journal* (1952–), contains an annual bibliography; L. Patton, *The Shelley-Godwin Collection of Lord Abinger, Duke University Library Notes*, 27 (1953), 11–17; C. H. Taylor, *The Early Collected Editions of Shelley's Poems: A Study in the History and Transmission of the Printed Text* (New Haven, Conn., 1958); K. N. Cameron, ed., *Shelley and His Circle 1773–1822* (Cambridge, Mass.–London, 1961–), vols. I–II (1961); D. H. Reiman, ed., vols. III–IV (1970); vols. V–VI (1973); to be completed in about 8 vols.; D. B. Green and D. E. G. Wilson, comps., *Keats, Shelley, Byron, Hunt and Their Circles: A Bibliography 1 July 1950–30 June 1962* (Lincoln, Nebr., 1964); I. Massey, *Posthumous Poems of Shelley: Mary Shelley's Fair Copy Book, Bodleian MS. Shelley Adds. d.9* (Montreal, 1969); C. Dunbar, *A Bibliography of Shelley Studies: 1823–1950* (Folkestone, 1976).

II. Principal Collected Editions. *The Poetical Works of Coleridge, Shelley, and Keats* (Paris, 1829), the Galignani ed., with a memoir by C. Redding; M. W. Shelley, ed., *The Poetical Works*, 4 vols. (London, 1839), *Queen Mab* printed with omissions; new rev. ed. in 1 vol., adding *Swellfoot, Peter Bell the Third*, and *Queen Mab* complete (London, 1839 [title page dated 1840]); W. M. Rossetti, ed., *The Poetical Works, Including Various Additional Pieces from MS and Other Sources, the Text Carefully Revised, with Notes and a Memoir*, 2 vols. (London, 1870; rev. ed., 3 vols., 1878); H. B. Forman, ed., *The Poetical Works*, 4 vols. (London, 1876–1877), new eds. in 2 vols. (London, 1882), with Mary Shelley's notes, and in 5 vols. (London, 1892), the Aldine ed.; H. B. Forman, ed., *The Works in Prose and Verse*, 8 vols. (London, 1880); G. E. Woodberry, ed., *Complete Poetical Works*, 4 vols. (Boston, 1892; London, 1893), also in 1 vol. (Boston, 1901), the Cambridge Poets ed.; T. Hutchinson, ed., *Complete Poetical Works* (London, 1904), with textual notes by Hutchinson, also published in Oxford Standard Authors ed. (London, 1905), with intro. by B. P. Kurtz (New York, 1933), and without intro. (London, 1934; 2nd ed., 1970), the latter rev. by G. M. Matthews; A. H. Koszul, ed., *The Poetical Works*, 2 vols. (London, 1907), with intro. by Koszul, also rev. ed. with new intro., 2 vols. (London,

1953), in Everyman's Library, poems published in chronological order; C. D. Locock, ed., *The Poems*, 2 vols. (London, 1911), with intro. by A. Clutton-Brock, the only complete ed. with explanatory notes; R. Ingpen and W. E. Peck, eds., *The Complete Works*, 10 vols. (London, 1926–1930; repr. New York, 1965), the Julian ed.; D. L. Clark, ed., *Shelley's Prose* (Albuquerque, N. M., 1954; repr. with corrs., 1967), a usefully full collection, but very unreliable textually and in dating; N. Rogers, ed., *The Complete Poetical Works*, vol. I: *1802–1813* (Oxford, 1972); vol. II: *1814–1817* (Oxford, 1975); to be completed in 4 vols.

III. SELECTIONS. R. Garnett, ed., *Select Letters* (London, 1882); E. Rhys, ed., *Essays and Letters* (London, 1886); J. Shawcross, ed., *Shelley's Literary and Philosophical Criticism* (London, 1909), with intro. by Shawcross; H. F. B. Brett-Smith, ed., *Peacock's Four Ages of Poetry; Shelley's Defence of Poetry; Browning's Essay on Shelley* (London, 1921; expurgated ed., 1923); A. M. D. Hughes, ed., *Poetry and Prose, with Essays by Browning, Bagehot, Swinburne, and Reminiscences by Others* (London, 1931); C. Baker, ed., *Selected Poetry and Prose* (New York, 1951), the Modern Library ed.; A. S. B. Glover, ed., *Selected Poetry, Prose and Letters* (London, 1951), the Nonesuch ed.; M. Spark and D. Stanford, eds., *My Best Mary: The Selected Letters of Mary W. Shelley* (London, 1953), with intro. by the eds.; E. Blunden, ed., *Selected Poems* (London, 1954), with a long intro. and notes; K. N. Cameron, ed., *Selected Poetry and Prose* (New York, 1956); J. Holloway, ed., *Selected Poems* (London, 1960), with intro. by Holloway; D. S. R. Welland, ed., *Selections from Shelley's Poetry and Prose* (London, 1961); G. M. Matthews, ed., *Shelley: Selected Poems and Prose* (Oxford, 1964), contains a new poem; H. Bloom, ed., *Selected Poetry and Prose* (New York, 1966); B. R. McElderry, ed., *Shelley's Critical Prose* (Lincoln, Nebr., 1966); P. Butter, ed., *Alastor and Other Poems: Prometheus Unbound with Other Poems: Adonais* (London, 1970); R. A. Duerksen, ed., *Political Writings Including "A Defence of Poetry"* (New York, 1970); N. Rogers, ed., *Selected Poetry* (London, 1970), an Oxford Paperback; D. H. Reiman and S. B. Powers, eds., *Shelley's Poetry and Prose* (New York, 1977), includes new texts and fifteen critical articles; T. Webb, ed., *Selected Poems* (London, 1977), with new texts.

IV. SEPARATE WORKS IN VERSE AND PROSE. *Original Poetry by Victor and Cazire* [Shelley and his sister Elizabeth] (Worthing, 1810), photofacs. in S. J. Hooker, *Shelley, Trelawny and Henley* (Worthing, 1950); John Fitzvictor [P. B. Shelley], ed., *Posthumous Fragments of Margaret Nicholson, Being Poems Found Amongst the Papers of That Noted Female Who Attempted the Life of the King in 1786* (Oxford, 1810), also privately printed by H. B. Forman (London, 1877); *Zastrozzi: A Romance* (London, 1810), repr. in E. Chesser, *Shelley and Zastrozzi: Self-Revelation of a Neurotic* (London, 1965); *The Necessity of Atheism* (Worthing, 1811), published anonymously

by Shelley and T. J. Hogg, photofacs. in S. J. Hooker, *Shelley, Trelawny and Henley* (Worthing, 1950); *St Irvyne or the Rosicrucian: A Romance, by a Gentleman of the University of Oxford* (London, 1811; reiss., 1822); *An Address to the Irish People* (Dublin, 1812); *Declaration of Rights* (Dublin, 1812), an unsigned broadside, two copies are in the Public Record Office; *The Devils' Walk: A Ballad* (Barnstaple [?], 1812), unsigned broadside, one copy in the Public Record Office and one at the University of Texas, Austin; *A Letter to Lord Ellenborough* (London, 1812), privately printed, one copy in the Bodleian Library; *Proposals for an Association of . . . Philanthropists . . .* (Dublin, 1812); *Queen Mab: A Philosophical Poem, with Notes* (London, 1813), privately printed, many unauthorized eds. 1821–1857; *A Vindication of a Natural Diet, Being One in a Series of Notes to Queen Mab, a Philosophical Poem* (London, 1813); *A Refutation of Deism, in a Dialogue* (London, 1814), published anonymously; *Alastor: or The Spirit of Solitude, and Other Poems* (London, 1816).

History of a Six Weeks' Tour Through a Part of France, Switzerland, Germany and Holland (London, 1817), published anonymously by Percy and Mary Shelley; *A Proposal for Putting Reform to the Vote Throughout the Kingdom, by the Hermit of Marlow* [Shelley] (London, 1817), facs. of the MS published by H. B. Forman (London, 1887); *Laon and Cythna; or, The Revolution of the Golden City: A Vision of the Nineteenth Century in the Stanza of Spenser* (London, 1818), suppressed, rev. and reiss. as *The Revolt of Islam: A Poem in Twelve Cantos* (London, 1818), some copies dated 1817; *The Cenci: A Tragedy in Five Acts* (Leghorn, 1819; 2nd ed., London, 1821), repr. by G. E. Woodberry (Boston, 1909), with bibliography; *Rosalind and Helen: A Modern Eclogue; with Other Poems* (London, 1819); *Oedipus Tyrannus: or, Swellfoot the Tyrant: A Tragedy in Two Acts, Translated from the Original Doric* (London, 1820), this unsigned ed. was suppressed; *Prometheus Unbound: A Lyrical Drama in Four Acts, with Other Poems* (London, 1820), the principal separate modern eds. are V. Scudder, ed. (Boston, 1892), R. Ackermann, ed. (Heidelberg, 1908), A. M. D. Hughes, ed. (Oxford, 1910; repr. 1957), L. J. Zillman, ed. (Seattle, 1959; New Haven, Conn.-London, 1968); *Adonais: An Elegy on the Death of John Keats, Author of Endymion, Hyperion, etc.* (Pisa, 1821; 2nd ed., Cambridge, 1829), annotated ed. by W. M. Rossetti (Oxford, 1890) was rev. by Rossetti and A. O. Prickard (London, 1903), photofacs. in N. Douglas, ed. (London, 1927); *Epipsychidion: Verses Addressed to the Noble and Unfortunate Lady Emilia V—Now Imprisoned in the Convent of——* (London, 1821; facs. ed., Menston, 1970), this unsigned ed. was withdrawn; *Hellas: A Lyrical Drama* (London, 1822).

V. POSTHUMOUS WORKS. M. W. Shelley, ed., *Posthumous Poems* (London, 1824), this ed. was suppressed; *The Masque of Anarchy: A Poem Now First Published* (London, 1832), with preface by L. Hunt, photofacs. of the

"Wise" MS published by H. B. Forman (London, 1887); *The Shelley Papers: Memoir by T. Medwin and Original Poems and Papers by Shelley* (London, 1833), includes a spurious poem, "To the Queen of My Heart"; M. W. Shelley, ed., *Essays, Letters from Abroad, etc.*, 2 vols. (London, 1840), includes "A Defence of Poetry"; *An Address to the People on the Death of Princess Charlotte, by the Hermit of Marlow* (London, *ca.* 1843), probably from a MS written *ca.* 1817 and now lost; Lady J. Shelley and R. Garnett, eds. *Shelley Memorials* (London, 1859), includes "An Essay on Christianity"; R. Garnett, ed., *Relics of Shelley* (London, 1862); H. B. Forman, ed., *The Daemon of the World* (London, 1876), privately printed; H. B. Forman, ed., *Notes on Sculptures in Rome and Florence, Together with a Lucianic Fragment and a Criticism on Peacock's Poem "Rhododaphne"* (London, 1879), privately printed; B. Dobell, ed., *The Wandering Jew* (London, 1887); C. D. Locock, *An Examination of the Shelley Manuscripts in the Bodleian Library* (Oxford, 1903); A. H. Koszul, ed., *Shelley's Poetry in the Bodleian Manuscripts* (Oxford, 1910), "A Defence of Poetry," "Essay on Christianity," and fragments; *Note Books of Shelley, from the Originals in the Library of W. K. Bixby*, deciphered, transcribed, and edited by H. B. Forman, 3 vols. (Boston, 1911), privately printed; T. W. Rolleston, ed., *A Philosophical View of Reform* (Oxford, 1920); W. E. Peck, ed., "An Unpublished Ballad by Shelley" ("Young Parson Richards"), in *Philological Quarterly*, 5 (1926), 114–118; G. E. Woodberry, ed., *The Shelley Notebook in the Harvard Library* (Cambridge, Mass., 1929), a photofacs., autograph ascriptions were corrected by H. Darbishire in *Review of English Studies*, 31 (July 1932), 352–354.

J. C. E. Shelley-Rolls and R. Ingpen, eds., *Verse and Prose from the Manuscripts of Shelley* (London, 1934), privately printed; D. Cook, ed., "'Sadak the Wanderer': An Unknown Shelley Poem," in *Times Literary Supplement* (16 May 1936), 424; E. H. Blakeney, ed., *A Shelley Letter* (Winchester, 1936), Shelley's verse epistle to Feargus Graham (1811); J. A. Notopoulos, *The Platonism of Shelley* (Durham, N. C., 1949), includes "Shelley's Translations from Plato: A Critical Edition," edited by the author, and unpublished material; G. M. Matthews, ed., "The Triumph of Life: A New Text," in *Studia Neophilologica*, 32 (1960), 271–309; K. N. Cameron, ed., *The Esdaile Notebook: A Volume of Early Poems* (New York, 1964; slightly rev., London, 1964); D. H. Reiman, *Shelley's "The Triumph of Life": A Critical Study Based on a Text Newly Edited from the Bodleian MS* (Urbana, Ill., 1965); N. Rogers, ed., *The Esdaile Poems* (Oxford, 1966); J. Chernaik, "Shelley's 'To Constantia,'" in *Times Literary Supplement* (6 February 1969), 140, a new text of "To Constantia Singing"; T. Webb, ed., "Shelley's 'Hymn to Venus': A New Text," in *Review of English Studies*, n.s. 21 (August 1970), 315–324; J. Chernaik and T. Burnett, eds., "The Byron and Shelley Notebooks in the Scrope Davies Find," in *Review of English Studies*, 29 (February 1978), 36–49.

VI. LETTERS AND JOURNALS. Lady J. Shelley and Sir P. F. Shelley, eds., *Shelley and Mary*, 3 (or 4) vols. (London, 1882), privately printed; R. Ingpen, comp. and ed., *The Letters*, 2 vols. (London, 1909), new ed., adding five letters (London, 1912; rev. ed., 1914); R. H. Hill, ed., *The Shelley Correspondence in the Bodleian Library* (Oxford, 1926), contains lists of MSS, letters, and relics; L. Hotson, ed., *Shelley's Lost Letters to Harriet* (London, 1930), with intro. by Hotson; S. Norman, ed., *After Shelley. The Letters of T. J. Hogg to Jane Williams* (Oxford, 1934); F. L. Jones, comp. and ed., *Letters of Mary W. Shelley*, 2 vols. (Norman, Okla., 1944); F. L. Jones, ed., *Mary Shelley's Journal* (Norman, Okla., 1947); W. S. Scott, ed., *New Shelley Letters* (London, 1948), letters by Shelley and members of his circle from the papers of T. J. Hogg; F. L. Jones, ed., *Maria Gisborne and Edward E. Williams, Shelley's Friends: Their Journals and Letters* (Norman, Okla., 1951); F. L. Jones, ed., *The Letters of Percy Bysshe Shelley*, 2 vols. (Oxford, 1964); M. K. Stocking, ed., *The Journals of Claire Clairmont* (Cambridge, Mass., 1968).

VII. BIOGRAPHICAL AND CRITICAL STUDIES. T. Medwin, *Journal of the Conversations of Lord Byron* (London, 1824), in E. J. Lovell, ed. (Princeton, N. J., 1966); L. Hunt, *Lord Byron and Some of His Contemporaries* (London, 1828), also in J. E. Morpurgo, ed. (London, 1949), see also Hunt's *Autobiography*, 3 vols. (London, 1850); W. Bagehot, *Estimates of Some Englishmen and Scotchmen* (London, 1858), repr. in his *Literary Studies*, vol. I, R. B. Hutton, ed. (London, 1879); T. J. Hogg, *Life of Shelley*, 2 vols. (London, 1858), the MS of two further vols. has been lost; T. L. Peacock, "Memoirs of Shelley," in *Fraser's* magazine (June 1858–March 1862), in H. F. B. Brett-Smith, ed. (Oxford, 1909); E. J. Trelawny, *Recollections of the Last Days of Shelley and Byron* (London, 1858; repr. 1906, 1952), rev. as *Records of Shelley, Byron and the Author*, 2 vols. (London, 1878; repr. London, 1905; New York, 1968); Lady J. Shelley and R. Garnett, eds., *Shelley Memorials* (London, 1859); T. Hunt, "Shelley, by One Who Knew Him," in *Atlantic Monthly*, 11 (February 1863), 184–204; D. F. MacCarthy, *Shelley's Early Life, from Original Sources* (London, 1872), Shelley's activities and publications in Ireland; E. Dowden, *Life of Shelley*, 2 vols. (London, 1886), the 1-vol. rev. and abr. version (1896) in H. Read, ed. (London, 1951); M. Arnold, *Essays in Criticism*, 2nd ser. (London, 1888), includes an essay on Shelley; H. S. Salt, *Shelley: Poet and Pioneer* (London, 1896).

W. B. Yeats, *Ideas of Good and Evil* (London, 1903), includes "The Philosophy of Shelley's Poetry," repr. in his *Essays and Introductions* (London, 1961); A. Droop, *Die Belesenheit Shelleys* (Weimar, 1906); E. S. Bates, *A Study of Shelley's Drama "The Cenci"* (New York, 1908; repr. 1969); A. C. Bradley, *Oxford Lectures on Poetry* (London, 1909), includes "Shelley's View of Poetry"; *Bulletin of the Keats-Shelley Memorial, Rome*, vol. I (1910), vol. II (1913), both repr. (1961), journal subsequently published yearly from vol. III (1950); A. Clutton-Brock, *Shelley: The Man and the Poet* (London, 1910; rev. ed., 1923); A. H. Koszul, *La jeunesse de Shelley* (Paris, 1910); H. R. Angeli, *Shelley and His Friends in Italy* (London, 1911); H. N. Brailsford, *Shelley, Godwin and Their Circle* (London, 1913; rev. ed., Oxford, 1951); R. Ingpen, *Shelley in England: New Facts and Letters from the Shelley-Whitton Papers* (London, 1917); S. de Madariaga, *Shelley and Calderón and Other Essays* (London, 1920); A. T. Strong, *Three Studies in Shelley* (Oxford, 1921); O. W. Campbell, *Shelley and the Unromantics* (London, 1924); E. Blunden, *Shelley and Keats as They Struck Their Contemporaries* (London, 1925); M. T. Solve, *Shelley: His Theory of Poetry* (Chicago, 1927; repr. New York, 1964).

C. H. Grabo, *A Newton Among Poets: Shelley's Use of Science in Prometheus Unbound* (Chapel Hill, N. C., 1930); *The Life of Percy Bysshe Shelley as Comprised in the "Life of Shelley" by T. J. Hogg, "The Recollections of Shelley and Byron" by E. J. Trelawny, "Memoirs of Shelley" by T. L. Peacock*, 2 vols. (London, 1933), with intro. by H. Wolfe; B. P. Kurtz, *The Pursuit of Death: A Study of Shelley's Poetry* (New York, 1933); C. H. Grabo, *Prometheus Unbound: An Interpretation* (Chapel Hill, N. C., 1935); C. H. Grabo, *The Magic Plant: The Growth of Shelley's Thought* (Chapel Hill, N. C., 1936); H. Read, *In Defence of Shelley and Other Essays* (London, 1936), rev. and repr. as *The True Voice of Feeling* (London, 1953); E. Barnard, *Shelley's Religion* (Minneapolis, 1937; repr. New York, 1964); R. G. Grylls, *Mary Shelley: A Biography* (Oxford, 1938); N. I. White, *The Unextinguished Hearth: Shelley and His Contemporary Critics* (Durham, N. C., 1938; repr. 1968), a full collection of the early reviews of Shelley.

N. I. White, *Shelley*, 2 vols. (New York, 1940; rev. ed., London, 1947), abr. to the 1-vol. *Portrait of Shelley* (New York, 1945), the standard biography; E. Blunden, *Shelley: A Life Story* (London, 1946); J. Barrell, *Shelley and the Thought of His Time* (New Haven, Conn., 1947); A. M. D. Hughes, *The Nascent Mind of Shelley* (Oxford, 1947); C. Baker, *Shelley's Major Poetry: The Fabric of a Vision* (Princeton, N. J., 1948); D. G. James, *The Romantic Comedy* (Oxford, 1948), has a section on *Prometheus Unbound*; R. H. Fogle, *The Imagery of Keats and Shelley* (Chapel Hill, N. C., 1949); J. A. Notopoulos, *The Platonism of Shelley* (Durham, N. C., 1949).

K. N. Cameron, *The Young Shelley: Genesis of a Radical* (New York, 1950; London, 1951), Shelley's life and work up to 1814; P. H. Butter, *Shelley's Idols of the Cave* (Edinburgh, 1954); S. Norman, *Flight of the Skylark: The Development of Shelley's Reputation* (Norman, Okla., 1954); C. E. Pulos, *The Deep Truth: A Study of Shelley's Scepticism* (Lincoln, Nebr., 1954); N. Rogers, *Shelley at Work: A Critical Inquiry* (Oxford, 1956; rev. ed., Oxford, 1968); H. Bloom, *Shelley's Mythmaking* (New Haven, Conn., 1959); D. Perkins, *The Quest for Permanence: The Symbolism of Wordsworth, Shelley and Keats* (Cambridge, Mass., 1959); E. R. Wasserman, *The Subtler Language* (Baltimore, 1959), essays on "Mont Blanc," "The Sensitive Plant," and *Adonais*; M. Wilson, *Shelley's Later Poetry: A Study of His Prophetic Imagination* (New York, 1959).

D. King-Hele, *Shelley: His Thought and Work* (London, 1960); L. S. Boas, *Harriet Shelley: Five Long Years* (Oxford, 1962); H. Lemaitre, *Shelley, poète des éléments* (Paris, 1962); G. M. Ridenour, ed., *Shelley: A Collection of Critical Essays* (Englewood Cliffs, N. J., 1965); E. R. Wasserman, *Shelley's Prometheus Unbound: A Critical Reading* (Baltimore, 1965); B. Wilkie, *Romantic Poets and Epic Tradition* (Madison, Wis., 1965), on *The Revolt of Islam* as epic; E. J. Schulze, *Shelley's Theory of Poetry: A Reappraisal* (The Hague, 1966); R. B. Woodings, ed., *Shelley* (London, 1968), 17 critical essays (1943–1968), in the Modern Judgments series; D. H. Reiman, *Percy Bysshe Shelley* (New York, 1969); J. P. Guinn, *Shelley's Political Thought* (The Hague, 1969); G. McNiece, *Shelley and the Revolutionary Idea* (Cambridge, Mass., 1969); S. Curran, *Shelley's "Cenci": Scorpions Ringed with Fire* (Princeton, N. J., 1970); E. R. Wasserman, *Shelley: A Critical Reading* (Baltimore, 1971); J. Chernaik, *The Lyrics of Shelley* (Cleveland, Ohio, 1972), new texts of 25 lyrics, with full commentary; K. N. Cameron, *Shelley: The Golden Years* (Cambridge, Mass., 1974); R. Holmes, *Shelley: The Pursuit* (London, 1974), a full biography; J. E. Barcus, ed., *Shelley: The Critical Heritage* (London, 1975); G. Carey, *Shelley* (London, 1975); S. Curran, *Shelley's Annus Mirabilis: The Maturing of an Epic Vision* (San Marino, Calif., 1975); C. E. Robinson, *Shelley and Byron: The Snake and Eagle Wreathed in Fight* (Baltimore, 1976); T. Webb, *The Violet in the Crucible: Shelley and Translation* (Oxford, 1976); T. Webb, *Shelley: A Voice Not Understood* (Manchester, 1977); N. Brown, *Sexuality and Feminism in Shelley* (Cambridge, Mass., 1979); E. Duffy, *Rousseau in England: The Context for Shelley's Critique of the Enlightenment* (Berkeley, 1979), a study of "The Triumph of Life"; J. V. Murphy, *The Dark Angel: Gothic Elements in Shelley's Works* (Lewisburg, Pa., 1979).

EDMUND SPENSER

(ca. 1552-1599)

Alastair Fowler

I

"SAGE Homer, Virgil, Spenser laureate." Spenser is one of our few classics. For that very reason, although his status has never been very seriously threatened, ideas of him have changed. Different ages and critics have given very different accounts of his work. Up to the eighteenth century, his reputation depended far more than it would now on *The Shepherd's Calendar*. Spenser was consequently a pastoral and love poet: even in *The Faerie Queen* he was "Heroic Paramour of Faerie Land," to be compared with Ariosto or Petrarch. On the other hand he was also a learned poet, an English Virgil, edited, cited as a classical author, and widely imitated. This posed problems for neoclassically minded readers, who had a blindingly clear idea of exactly what a classic work ought to be. *The Faerie Queen* could easily seem a bit too "uncultivate" and Gothic. Their solution was to turn attention away from Spenser's design, which broke too many rules, to the serious moral content—or else to his descriptive pictorial art. *The Faerie Queen* became "an excellent piece of morality, policy, history"—or Mrs. Spence's "collection of pictures." The influential John Hughes completed this development by combining both approaches. He showed how Spenser could be valued both as an "imager of virtues and vices" and a "rough painter" ("The embellishments of description are rich and lavish . . . beyond comparison.") without looking to him for epic or romance coherence. Unfortunately Spenser's morality was largely embodied in allegory. If the neoclassical critics were prepared to accord this element a lowly but secure place, "allegories fulsome grow," and the romantic critics were inclined to jettison it altogether. For William Hazlitt the allegory was

something that would not bite so long as one left it alone. Even the perceptive critic James Russell Lowell followed this approach, recommending *The Faerie Queen* to those who wished "to be rid of thought." Spenser's sensuous vividness has always remained, together perhaps with the dazzling ease of transitions, and a deeper, more elusive imaginativeness, closer to dream. However variously described and subject to misunderstanding, he has occupied a special place in our literature as a nourisher of other poets' work. He was Cowley's first introduction to poetry; Pope's "mistress"; Wordsworth's "inspiration"; and a model to Milton, Dryden, Thomson, Yeats, and countless others. By almost common consent he is one of our most "poetic" poets, so that he serves as a sounding board even for those of a very different temper: his words run softly even through the lines of T. S. Eliot.

Twentieth-century criticism has been better equipped historically to interpret the poetry that Spenser wrote. Sharing a common view of him as a great and serious poet, it has mostly been taken up with explaining. The explanation tends to be detailed: the picture-gallery view has given way to iconographical studies. The best modern criticism is technically remarkable; but it usually lacks the proportion achieved in the eighteenth century by John Upton, still Spenser's best reader. Perhaps in consequence some judicious critics, who would not quite deny the greatness of Spenser, have nevertheless thought his poetry too much in need of difficult explanation to be worth the effort for modern readers. They have renewed and reinforced Ben Jonson's objections to his poetic diction and the Augustan charges of structural faults; or fallen back on the position that "the wittiest poets have been all short" (Owen Felltham).

Neocritical, in fact, is neoclassical writ small. Recently, however, critics have shown more interest in longer poems. At the same time, a better appreciation of Gothic interlace—interweaving of linear narratives—is allowing revaluation of Spenser's complex neo-Gothic form. Very early on, John Hughes and Richard Hurd guessed that Spenser's Gothic cathedral might have its own kind of unity. But the implications of that valuable analogy can only now be fully developed. Poetry such as Spenser's is too central to our literature to be really threatened by critical opinion; some of it is too profound even to need much conscious understanding. Still, it is as well, from time to time, to revise our notion of the achievement. Where are Spenser's excellences, for us? We are beginning to have more interest than our predecessors in his vision of the totality of human experience—a vision as wide, in its way, as Milton's, or Blake's, or Hugh MacDiarmid's. We should be more inclined to see him as pursuing the highest and most philosophical ends of poetry.

II

NOT much is known about Spenser's life. He was born in London, his "most kindly nurse," probably in 1552. Although related to the noble Spencers of Warwickshire and Northamptonshire, his immediate family circumstances seem to have been poor. He was educated at Merchant Taylors' School, an outstanding new grammar school, which he attended for eight years from its foundation in 1561. There the curriculum included a great deal of Latin, some Greek (certainly Homer), and the Hebrew psalter. As in other grammar schools, the Latin would be not only classical but Renaissance: Erasmus, Vives, perhaps Mantuanus' pastorals or Palingenius' *Zodiacus vitae*. Exceptionally, the curriculum extended to music and possibly even to English. For the headmaster was an advanced educationalist, the great Richard Mulcaster. No doctrinaire humanist, Mulcaster had a strong and original mind, which he expressed in a fine though sometimes obscure style. The ideas developed in *Positions* and *The Elementary* are sometimes ahead of any that have even yet been

realized; nevertheless, they are compatible with a deep sense of history. The latter gave Mulcaster a reverence for such fragile institutions as customs and languages. Thus, his classicism allowed for the possibility of different classical periods in modern literatures. He read Ariosto: he advocated regular teaching of the vernacular ("I honour Latin, but worship English"); he defended the education of women. Many of Mulcaster's ideas seem to find a later echo in Spenser's writing: not least the belief that literature and learning may form the character of the individual for the public good.

Together with Lancelot Andrewes, Spenser left school in 1569 for Pembroke Hall, Cambridge, where he was a sizar (an undergraduate receiving an allowance from the college to enable him to study), paying no fees but performing certain chores. The next four years were spent in completing the trivium begun at school—by reading rhetoric, logic, and philosophy; the three years after on the quadrivium—arithmetic, geometry, astronomy, and music. These studies centered on a small number of set authors, all classical. In 1573 Spenser proceeded B.A.; in 1576 M.A. At Cambridge an oral tradition then vigorously prevailed of lectures and public disputation. The level of learned eloquence was high, fitting an excessive number for the administrative offices available. (The size of the university was small by modern standards: about 1,800, of whom 250 were sizars.) Spenser's contemporaries included the much older Thomas Preston, author of *Cambyses*; the younger Abraham Fraunce, poet, rhetorician, literary theorist; and Gabriel Harvey.

Harvey, who was Spenser's senior by about three years, became a fellow of Pembroke Hall in 1570, praelector (or professor) of rhetoric in 1574. His *Ciceronianus* and *Rhetor* show him to have been a brilliant scholar and writer, surely possessing one of the sharpest minds of his time. And he was probably, as Virginia Woolf surmised, a brilliant talker. Yet his Cambridge career was erratic, and in the end unsuccessful. This may have been not altogether to his discredit: he had ideas progressive enough to provoke opposition—including Ramist reform in logic, and unsound "paradoxes" such as Copernicus' heliocentric hypothesis. But he was also arrogant, quarrelsome, tactless, vain, silly, and a misfit. The man who could write "Sometime my book is unto me a god / Sometime I throw it from me a rod" was too restless for mere scholarship. In another age he might have been a literary critic, or even a columnist. As it was, he went after preferment with the desperation of frustrated greatness, perpetually encouraging himself the while, in countless Machiavellian marginalia, to futile circumspections.

In spite (or perhaps because) of our knowing so many of his private thoughts, he remains a baffling figure. Most—like Nashe in their public quarrel, and perhaps Shakespeare, in Holofernes—have regarded him as a foolish pedant. He took himself seriously; so that others have tended not to. But it is not Harvey who seems pedantic when Spenser and he differ about quantity in English verse. His greater experience and wide reading enabled him to enlarge Spenser's tastes and perhaps to make him more contemporary, more European. Harvey came to recognize the quality of an early version of *The Faerie Queen*, although he preferred (rightly or wrongly) Spenser's lost "Comedies." But this advice was resisted. Spenser was well able to exert his own taste decisively, using a bet, for example, to press Harvey to read *Lazarillo de Tormes*. Their friendship, which mattered to both men, was reciprocal and not dependent.

How did Spenser regard Harvey? The sonnet he addressed to him from Dublin in 1586 seems comically inappropriate now: "happy above happiest men . . . sitting like a looker-on / Of this world's stage," wielding his "critic pen," careless of suspicion. But Harvey, who was not yet the failure of later years, nor demeaned by controversy with the unfair and clever Nashe, perhaps had still an outsider's early idealism. However that may be, this strange man also cherished ambitious hopes of following in the footsteps of Cheke and Smith, and of becoming great in the councils of the mighty. From 1576 he pursued the favor of Leicester and, from 1578, of Sidney. He was thus in a position to introduce Spenser to two of the greatest patrons of the age. And when Spenser's *Shepherd's Calendar* appeared anonymously in 1579, it bore a dedication to Sidney.

Although the Cambridge of Spenser's day was dominated by radical Puritans of Thomas Cartwright's stamp, Spenser emerged a moderate but fervent Protestant, with views comparable to those of Richard Hooker or gentle Archbishop Grindal (the Algrin of *The Shepherd's Calendar*). In 1578, after some time in the north, Spenser became secretary to Edward Young, the former master of Pembroke Hall. By October 5, 1579, however, he had entered the household of the earl of Leicester and was familiar with Leicester's nephew Sir Philip Sidney. Together with Sidney and Sir Edward Dyer he made the experiments in "artificial" or quantitative verse that are discussed and developed in the correspondence with Harvey, published in 1580 as *Three proper, and witty, familiar Letters*. (This spirited but unsuccessful attempt to capture in the vernacular the sophisticated obliquity of smart neo-Latin epistles got Gabriel Harvey into a great deal of trouble with the authorities.) Probably about the same time, Spenser was writing his "lost" works ("Epithalamion Thamesis," "The Court of Cupid," "Dreams," "Pageants," etc.), some of which may be early versions of parts of *The Faerie Queen*. Also in 1579 he married, almost certainly, Machabyas Childe, by whom he was to have two children, Sylvanus and Katherine.

Then, in 1580, Spenser went to Ireland as secretary to the new governor, Arthur Lord Grey. (The English were making another of their incoherent attempts to anglicize barbarous Ireland, partly by colonial settlement, partly by the sword.) Inexplicably this move has been represented as exile consequent on some disgrace (perhaps Spenser offended Leicester, as his *Virgil's Gnat* hints?). But humanistically trained men of letters expected and hoped to exercise their pens in administrative tasks. A career's success was gauged by the minor offices collected, and the estates. Spenser was clerk of faculties in the Court of Chancery (1581: a sinecure); commissioner for musters (1583); deputy to Lodowick Bryskett as clerk of the Council of Munster (1584); prebendary of Limerick Cathedral (1585: a sinecure); and justice of the County of Cork (1594). From 1582 he leased New Abbey near Dublin; in 1586 he was assigned, and in 1590 formally granted, the very large estate of Kilcolman (3,000 acres, or about 1,214 hectares). Kilcolman was Spenser's real and emotional home: its landscape finds reflection in many passages of his poetry. In fact, he should be regarded as one of our great Irish writers.

Even in Ireland, however, he still belonged to the literary milieu of the court. Lodowick Bryskett, whose dialogue *Discourse of Civil Life* (1583) has Spenser as one of its interlocutors, was a poet and former tutor of Sidney's. Ralegh visited his nearby estate in 1589. And manuscript circulation of Spenser's work is argued by Abraham Fraunce's ability to quote from *The Faerie Queen*, book 2, before its publication.

In 1589 and again in 1595 or 1596 Spenser made visits to London that occasioned flurries of publication, partly of old work revised: 1590, *The Faerie Queen*, part 1, and *Muiopotmos*; 1591, *Daphnaida* and *Complaints*; 1595, *Amoretti and Epithalamion* and *Colin Clout's Come Home Again*; 1596, *The Faerie Queen*, part 2 (books 4–6), *Prothalamion*, and *Four Hymns*. *The Faerie Queen* may never have been finished. Of the six missing books, only the Cantos of Mutability (published posthumously) remain.

The *Complaints* volume was suppressed, probably because Spenser had criticized William Cecil, lord Burghley, in *The Ruins of Time* and *Mother Hubberd's Tale*. Burghley was nevertheless included, although cautiously, among the sixteen nobles to whom *The Faerie Queen* was presented (it was dedicated to the queen herself). He seems not to have liked it. The queen, however, did. She paid Spenser the unique honor in 1591 of a life pension of £50 a year (a considerable sum—more than twice the rent for Kilcolman). In 1594 Spenser was remarried, to Elizabeth Boyle. He solemnized the wedding day, June 11, in *Amoretti and Epithalamion*. 1596 finds him celebrating with *Prothalamion* the spousals of the earl of Worcester's daughters at Essex House in London. The poem expresses "old woes," the loss of his patron Leicester, who had died in 1588, and his consequent friendlessness; but it also looks forward to the favor of a new patron, the earl of Essex. Spenser's successful career culminated with his nomination (as one "with good knowledge in learning and not unskilful or without experience in the service of the wars") to the post of high sheriff of Cork, on September 30, 1598. But within a month the rebels had overrun Munster and burned Kilcolman. Spenser returned to London with dispatches on Christmas Eve; and

on January 13, 1599, he died. He was buried in Westminster Abbey, near Chaucer, at the expense of Essex, "his hearse being carried by poets, and mournful verses and poems thrown into his tomb." There was an early tradition that Spenser died in want; but it seems to have been without basis.

III

The Shepherd's Calendar (1579) was Spenser's first considerable published work. This fact is a little misleading, in that he already had behind him the lost works, not to speak of the schoolboy translation of Van der Noodt's Protestant emblem book. Spenser was early drawn to poetry, yet had a slow development as a poet. Traditionally, pastoral offered an unassuming mode that might be attempted in prelude to more ambitious flights. *The Shepherd's Calendar*, however, is far from being apprentice work. It shows a high sense of control, and yet an astonishing freedom in the treatment of genre. It is far from mere imitation or combination of Theocritus, Virgil, Mantuan, and Marot. Indeed, considered historically, its achievement is so considerable as to make it a watershed on any map of English verse.

Spenser enlarged the pastoral tradition in several ways. The Renaissance eclogues by Mantuan and Barclay had already treated moral or religious matters: pastoral could be microcosmic and satiric rather than idyllic. Spenser took up this option and invested in it heavily. The landscape that he makes a mirror of his shepherd's plight is "barren ground, whom winter's wrath hath wasted": a land suffering from adverse weather, wolves, and disease. In fact, it is real country. And he introduces many fresh images from nature, such as the oak's top "bald and wasted with worms" and the bee "working her formal rooms in waxen frame," besides many country phrases not previously heard in serious poetry.

Most creative of all is his approach to the structure. Instead of the usual collection of independent "eclogues" (the term anciently implied separateness) Spenser has made a single work, unified by the structural principle of the natural year, and of seasons that symbolize stages in human life. As Pope noted, "the addition he has made of a calendar to his eclogues is very beautiful." The calendrical form not only holds the eclogues together, but contributes to their special character of endless variety combined with complex, elusive order. It works multifariously: in the changing weather; in seasonal customs (April's flower gathering was the occupation for that month by the conventions of visual art); explicitly astronomical imagery (Sol appears in July, the month of his own sign Leo, "making his way between the Cup,/ and golden Diadem"); and even in physical proportions (May is by far the longest eclogue, since the sun was known to stay longer in Gemini than in any other sign). Spenser also achieved controlled variety by varying the meter, all the way from rough alliterative lines to the gentle, grave stateliness of November's elegy for Dido:

But now sike [such] happy cheer is turned to heavy
    chance,
  Such pleasance now displaced by dolour's dint:
All music sleeps, where death doth lead the dance,
  And shepherds' wonted solace is extinct.
    The blue in black, the green in grey is tinct
      [tinged],
    The gaudy garlands deck her grave,
    The faded flowers her corse embrace.
      O heavy hearse,
Mourn now my muse, now mourn with tears
    besprint [sprinkled].
      O careful verse.

                  (November 103–112)

Inset songs and fables introduce further variation. Then there is the alternation of three modes or categories—"plaintive," "moral," and "recreative"—and the interweaving of three large subjects: love, poetry, and religious politics. The command with which genres are deployed makes for admiration, even where this is not accompanied with understanding or enjoyment. Everything seems in scale, and orchestrated, giving a sense of various modes of life in harmony. January's love complaint gives way to February's *débat* between youth and age, which encloses (and perhaps underlies too) the fable of an episcopal oak and a Puritan briar. March offers an exploit of Cupid; April, an inset ode in praise of Elizabeth, with some delicately Skel-

tonic flower poetry; and May, a beast fable and more controversy.

The poetic statement made on this complex instrument is itself complex. For one thing, the shepherds enact a roman à clef, to which the key has been lost. Algrin is Archbishop Grindal and Hobbinol Gabriel Harvey; but others remain unidentified, even with the help of fashionably elaborate annotation by "E.K." (himself unknown). Moreover, some of the roles are multivalent. Thus, besides being a persona for Spenser, Colin Clout is a highly idealized laureate (combining poetic names from Skelton and Marot). Tityrus is both Virgil and Chaucer. And Pan figures severally as Henry VIII, as the pope, and as Christ. Nevertheless, the topical allegory is probably not intricate; Spenser seems to have tended to political simplicity as much as to intellectual subtlety.

Nowhere is there more subtlety than in the poem's structural pattern. To begin with, it sets out two calendars: the astronomical, running from March to February, and the Christian, from January to December. Circularity is suggested by the linking of the January and December eclogues, each of which has the single speaker Colin. They are "proportionable" in the octave ratio of perfect harmony, one being exactly twice as long as the other. Then, the plaintive (*p*), the moral (*m*), and the recreative (*r*) eclogues are arranged, with their speakers, in interlocking symmetries. For example, January to June (corresponding astrologically to the six "lunar" signs) form the sequence *p/m/r/r/m/p*. Moreover, Colin's concluding motto in June, as E.K. notes, answers that in January. Thus, the first half of the *Calendar* also forms a circle, a subsidiary "world," which may be interpreted as the mundane world of natural life. It begins with Colin's "wilfully" breaking his pipe and ends with his giving up false love and the unworthy Rosalind. Within this world are conflicts between the old and the new (February: oak versus briar), or between worldly pleasure and censorious morality (May: Palinode versus Piers). June, however, makes the challenges to an earthly paradise explicit, leading to July's myth of the Fall, and fatal disorders in nature. Here, at the poem's center, stands a mountain, the high place of God: there is mention of Sinai, Olivet, and "mighty Pan" or Christ.

The *Calendar*'s second half becomes increasingly dark, the secular idyll more and more plainly illusion. Art's solace now replaces that of nature. But the mirror of art, which itself mirrors nature, brings deeper disenchantments still. October questions the use of poetry and even the possibility of literary life. Its talk of war contradicts the olive coronal of April, the matching month (with sign in opposition) of the *Calendar*'s first half. To lighten this gloom there emerges the theme of grace. In September, Diggon Davie repents; in December, Colin himself. Indeed, one might see the whole *Calendar* as a confession of Colin's developing religious consciousness: as his palinode or retraction from earlier secularity. But the poem is more inclusive, more Chaucerian perhaps, than this would suggest. It finds room, after all, for natural beauty, for the worldly Palinode, for the retired Hobbinol. And it is the reformer Piers who overstates his case. The *Calendar* leaves us, in the end, with a sense of manifold fictive worlds, all comprehended in Spenser's detached vision of mutability.

This marvelous intellectual structure unfortunately no longer quite succeeds as poetry. This is not merely because of its coterie aspects—these are no insuperable obstacle with Shakespeare's poems. The reasons have to do with certain critical theories, fashionable in Spenser's day, about the language of literature. Following ideas of Joachim Du Bellay and others, he believed that a classical English style could be based on Chaucer's language. Hence his interweaving of rustic expressions appropriate to pastoral, Chaucerian archaisms, and ancient poetic words ("grieslie," "moe," "astert"), together with contrastingly easy conventional epithets ("riper age," "doleful verse"), to form a lexical tapestry of great, perhaps even excessive, richness. Especially desirable were dialectal or pseudodialectal words, parts, or mere spelling variants that preserved Chaucer's, Gavin Douglas', and earlier forms ("swincke," "sayne"). This diction was not quite so experimental then as it has since come to look; but intensified as it was by archaic syntax and combined with a style of plain pithy statement, its effect must always have been singular enough. Jonson says that Spenser "writ no language." Spenser might appeal to Theocritus' precedent—and to

the many poets who have followed his, rather than Jonson's, example. The smooth element of Spenser's diction has influenced poetic taste ever since. But some of his rougher innovations now seem as decisively wrongheaded as any in Wordsworth's *Lyrical Ballads:*

My ragged ronts [bullocks] all shiver and shake,
As doen high towers in an earthquake. . . .
(February 5–6)

Another unfortunate theory concerned Chaucer's versification. At a time when the Chaucerian canon was uncertain, and accessible only in bad texts, his verse was universally held to be rough. It was imitated by such devices as the addition of final -*e*. Spenser's fashionably rough verse now seems almost as dated as that of his contemporaries. At best it is workmanlike. Above its shaggy lowliness, as above a rusticated ground story, rises the piano nobile of inset songs (April, August, November). Here, and in only a few other passages, the *Calendar* displays a liquid ease and subtlety of movement adequate to the brilliant rhetoric:

Why do we longer live, (ah why live we so long)
(November 73; cf. 81, 111)

Note how the *correctio,* or restatement, puts a different accent on "we" and "live," reinforcing the meaning yet also making a tenderly elegiac music. In such passages Spenser achieves a remarkably mellifluous flow. His special gift was for counterpointing a great many structures and textures: rhetorical, phonetic, metrical. So in

The mantled meadows mourn,
Their sundry colours turn.
(November 128–129)

the lines are matched by their similar clause length, their words of equivalent syllables symmetrically distributed, their rhetorical parallelism, and their literal meaning; so that the switch from alliteration (monochromatic consonants) to assonance (monochromatic vowels) mimes the drab change of color. Spenser's later verse is full of such correspondences, in which form continuously accompanies sense in a ceremony of meaning. His smooth style, indeed, has so dominated taste that we take it for granted and hardly notice the first beginnings. These should not be exaggerated either. The *Calendar* is high art, certainly; but only locally higher than that of Sidney. Overall, it is the *Calendar's* ambitious encyclopedic content that bodes well, not its poetic language. It already shows a very special combination of complicated medieval structure with Renaissance hyperconsciousness about consistency. But it has attracted too much attention for the good of Spenser's modern reputation.

Spenser continued to write pastoral throughout his life. In 1591 *Astrophel. A Pastoral Elegy* appeared as the framing introduction to a volume of elegies on Sidney. Certainly later than 1586, and probably later than 1590, it is a finer work than most of *The Shepherd's Calendar*, although it has not usually been valued so highly. The first part (lines 1–216) relates, under the allegory of a boar hunt, Sidney's death from a wound received at the battle of Zutphen (1586). Astrophel is gored by one of "the brutish nation" (the Spanish oppressors); mourned by his widow; and metamorphosed into a flower. This part, while always felicitous, preserves so impersonal a tone as to seem now a shade pallid, a little too consciously Bionesque. It is another matter with the Lay of Clorinda. This part, exactly half as long as the first—the proportions of harmony—purports to give the mourning song of Sidney's sister Mary, countess of Pembroke. It is a deeply serious expression of grief, from which Milton learned for *Lycidas*. Who is the mourner to address? She can hope for comfort neither from men nor from gods ("From them comes good, from them comes also ill"), so that she addresses her complaint to herself:

> The woods, the hills, the rivers shall resound
> The mournful accent of my sorrow's ground.
> (lines 23–24)

The resonance of "ground" ("ground bass," "basis") is characteristic of the Lay's self-referring style, which can be poignant—as in "The fairest flower . . . Was Astrophel; that *was*, we all may rue." The resolution in this second part is deeper and darker: Clorinda reflects that when we grieve we may be self-regarding, "Mourning in others, our own miseries". Sid-

ney is better where he is. If this part was by Mary herself, as some have suggested, she wrote a better poem than Spenser on this occasion.

In December 1591, from Kilcolman, Spenser dedicated to Sir Walter Ralegh *Colin Clout's Come Home Again*, a pastoral eclogue about a recent visit to court. This popular yet incompletely appreciated work is directly autobiographical, if not so literally as some have thought (it transports Gabriel Harvey, surely in wish-fulfillment, to Ireland). Its engaging method is that of general conversation, with no fewer than ten shepherds and shepherdesses interrupting and questioning Colin. These familiar exchanges establish a sense of Spenser's social and literary circle. They also, by their distancing or alienating effect, allow transitions through a wide range of tones, from the strangely exalted to the quietly humorous. The humor of Colin's account of his voyage is quite broad: the sea ("A world of waters heaped up on high"), ships ("Glued together with some subtle matter"), and mythologized admirals (Triton and Proteus) are consistently described as they might appear to an innocent, quite unironic shepherd's eye. Less obvious is the joke whereby the most extensive piece of alliteration—lines 25–26—comes in a speech of Hobbinol's. Harvey disliked this device.

Most good eclogues are deeper than they look; and this one, probably the longest and most complex in the language, is no exception. It has an elaborate symmetrical structure to reflect its various but carefully balanced moods. There is even an inset eclogue, an account of a previous conversation with Ralegh, "the Shepherd of the Ocean," in which the narrative's doubly reported status expresses the remoteness of a primitive river myth of sexual rivalry in the far past. The first half is divided between nature (the watery wilderness; wild Ireland) and art (epitomized by a catalogue of England's twelve chief poets). This passage, where Spenser authoritatively reviews his literary milieu and freely reveals his tastes, has an interest similar to that of, say, W. H. Auden's *Letter From Iceland*. Most praise goes to Daniel and Alabaster (both named), to Astrophel, Alcyon (Sir Arthur Gorges), and to the mysterious Aetion. The second half answers with a catalogue of twelve ladies, courteously praised, and a lofty encomium of the queen. Why then did Colin ever leave the court? His reply offsets the gallantry with a sharp attack on the court's incivility: "it is no sort of life," and all its glory is "but smoke, that fumeth soon away." Hobbinol speaks up for Leicester, giving a well-informed review of his patronage program; but Colin responds with renewed attacks, this time on the court's immorality.

All this has been seen as Spenser's ambivalence; and so in a way it may have been, in personal terms. But the poem's effect seems not so much ambiguous as poised. Peaceful England is excellent, by comparison with disordered Ireland: the court is frivolous, by comparison with true civility. More delicately poised still is Colin's balance of Rosalind's cruelty to him with the queen's to Ralegh (whose suffering carries conviction—"Ah my love's queen, and goddess of my life"). He even reconciles a near-blasphemous panegyric of Elizabeth with the elevation of another vassalage to a higher place within the poem's little world. Its sovereign center honors not the queen, but the courteous grace of an unnamed "maid" (probably Elizabeth Throckmorton, later Lady Ralegh), to whom Spenser pays ardent homage:

> And I hers ever only, ever one:
> One ever I all vowed hers to be,
> One ever I, and other's never none.
> (lines 477–479, of 955)

"Ever one . . . one ever . . . one ever" is no mere decorative rhetoric of chiasmus[1] or anaphora[2] but mimes the iconographic attitude of the three Graces, one facing forward, two turned in outgoing. For the rest, the poem glances at several of the main interests of Spenser's mature work: cosmogonic myth; a metaphysic of "Beauty the burning lamp of heaven's light"; and a passionate theology of love, with a myth of the androgynous Venus. He condemns the court's lewdness not from a puritanical standpoint, but because it profanes the "mighty mysteries" of love, "that dread lord." The

poem's range of feeling is immense; no work gives a better sense of the possibilities of eclogue.

IV

IN *Amoretti and Epithalamion* (1595) Spenser lays aside the pastoral weeds of Colin Clout to sing in his own person, as the lover of Elizabeth Boyle. Considering his early reputation as a love poet, it is strange how few now think him one of the great sonneteers. The *Amoretti* can easily seem low-pressure work, lacking the dramatic intensity of Sidney's *Astrophel and Stella*. However, interest grows when one appreciates how far Spenser's quieter virtues and more deeply poetic qualities have been missed. Take *Amoretti* 18, for example, in which the lover complains that whereas "The rolling wheel. . . . The hardest steel in tract of time doth tear" and raindrops wear the "firmest flint," yet he cannot move his lady. Stock images of obduracy; but how originally and deceptively they are put to work. Is the lady really discouraging? If tears are "but water," then the proverb holds and she will yield: only if tears are contrasted with rain would she be unmoved. Similarly when she "turns herself to laughter," who now is "the rolling wheel" and who "doth still remain"? Again, what association have flint and steel together, but kindled fire? The poetic indirection here is quite unlike anything in the other sonneteers of Spenser's time.

And in deeper ways too he is unlike them. Indeed, he came late enough in the vogue—after a dozen other English "sonnet sequences"—to have something different to offer. Shakespeare responded to a similar challenge by writing sonnets that seem to be about friendship and jealousy. But Spenser's are not about passion at all, in the ordinary sense, but about a love that ends happily, in marriage: the British romantic love, mingling friendship with sexual desire, in praise of which he wrote at greater length in *The Faerie Queen*. The lover of the *Amoretti* (partly followed by the reader) gets to know Elizabeth Boyle well, forming a full personal relation with her. And a keenly intelligent, witty person she is—an Elizabeth Bennett rather than a Penelope

---

[1] A figure of speech in which the word order in one clause is inverted in another phrase soon after.
[2] The repetition of a word or phrase at the beginning of successive clauses or verses.

Rich—with a firm, unmistakable character. Unlike the usual Petrarchist lady, who is a trigger of passion and little else, Elizabeth does not wound with Cupid's darts, but calms passion's storm (8), and, characterized herself by "goodly temperature" (13), frames and tempers her lover's feelings too. Even after they are mutually committed (84), we hear of her "too constant stiffness." This intense but tender courtship of a young girl by a middle-aged lover has the air of reality. (The general situation is probably autobiographical. In *Amoretti* 60, Spenser implies that he is forty; and Elizabeth in fact outlived him, to have children by a second marriage at dates that make it likely that she was at least fifteen years younger.) Their love is deep, but too serious, too responsible, for passion.

Nevertheless, Elizabeth must receive every tribute usually paid to a slavishly worshipped sonneteer's goddess. In performing this contract Spenser shows an astonishing capacity to fulfill the forms of love complaint, and yet all the time to be free from them, above them—not so much through irony or travesty (although these are sometimes not far away) as through the direct, open refusal of conventional literary attitudes. To the latter, he prefers the more complex human comedy. Sometimes, it is true, he carries the Petrarchist commonplaces far enough towards absurdity to expose their false logic, as in 32: "What then remains but I to ashes burn . . . ?" But more often the commonplaces—the fire and ice, the tyrant and captive, the storm and cruel tigress—are taken up with just a hint of distancing humor, a bantering tone or self-deprecating smile, to remind us that they belong to only one of the ways of wooing. The lover knows Elizabeth too well to think that she is really a tigress (in that way, at least). Not that the pains of love are merely acted, in a sense that would make them unreal. Indeed, where the idea of acting becomes most explicit, in the theatrical conceit of 54, the lady—who as unmoved spectator does not act—sits admonished; she is less than alive: "a senseless stone." Alternatively, the commonplaces may be taken up seriously but transformed. So it is with the erotic "blazon," or item-by-item portrait, which had generated much loose poetry, particularly in French and Italian. Spenser has extremely sensuous sonnets of this type, such as the complete blazon in 64. There are several on Elizabeth's eyes, hair, and breasts. In each case, however, the idea is elevated. In 76, her breasts are a "bower of bliss," *pome acerbe* ("unripe apples"), "like early fruit in May," between which the lover's frail thoughts dive "through amorous insight." But the very next sonnet shows the same apples in a dream, now ripe and "golden," laid out for a sacred feast. For they surpass even those that Hercules came by in the Hesperidean garden of chastity: "sweet fruit of pleasure brought from paradise / By love himself." It is the exalted desire of the *Song of Solomon*. Meanwhile, as he waits and woos, the lover is concerned to allay Elizabeth's anxiety about the loss of freedom that marriage would involve:

The doubt which ye misdeem, fair love, is vain,
That fondly fear to lose your liberty,
When losing one, two liberties ye gain,
And make him bond that bondage erst did fly.
Sweet be the bands, the which true love doth tie,
Without constraint or dread of any ill:
The gentle bird feels no captivity
Within her cage, but sings and feeds her fill.
There pride dare not approach, nor discord spill
  [destroy]
The league 'twixt them, that loyal love hath bound:
But simple truth and mutual good will,
Seeks with sweet peace to salve each other's wound:
There faith doth fearless dwell in brazen tower,
And spotless pleasure builds her sacred bower.

(*Amoretti* 65)

There is a tenderness and reciprocity of feeling here that would be impossible to match anywhere else in the Renaissance sonnet.

Spenser could hardly have given such a love simple dramatic expression. Instead of Sidney's individually intense sonnets forming moments in a narrative, he has written what seems much more obviously a long stanzaic poem (as is expressed formally by linked rhyme schemes). This continuity between sonnets, allowing complex large-scale imagery and amplitude of thematic development, goes back beyond the Petrarchists to the prolonged meditations of Petrarch's *Rime* themselves. Like Petrarch (and like Shakespeare), Spenser uses a calendrical structure to suggest the variety and natural growth of emotion. Thus there are New Year and Easter sonnets, set in their appropriate numerological places. The contradictory feelings that some have seen as problematic or indicative of revision all belong to this "whole year's work," leading to the marriage day celebrated in *Epithalamion*. Like other Elizabethan "sonnet sequences," *Amoretti* is really part of a composite work, combining sonnets with other stanza forms. Linking it to *Epithalamion* are four "anacreontic odes," or sweet epigrams, which languish for the bliss of the wedding night. These serve as generic transition to the major ode that follows.

Amoretti may fascinate as an interesting departure from the usual sequence or as a shorter treatment of themes developed in *The Faerie Queen*. But *Epithalamion* is unique. Nothing shows Spenser's creativity better than this poem, which most agree to be the finest major ode in English, and to be surpassed in ancient literature—if at all—only by Pindar. Classical comparisons are inevitable, because Spenser here invented for English literature the humanist ceremonial mode that was to be so important for Michael Drayton, Robert Herrick, and others—and carried it at once to its greatest height. Like Catullus' *Carmina* 61, Spenser's poem moves in festal exaltation through the events of a wedding day. But its structure is very different, rising as it does through a crescendo of gathering voices and sounds and excitement to the roaring organs and public affirmation of the marriage service at the altar, in the central two stanzas or strophes; before the feasting, the public "bedding" of the bride, consummation, and soft recession into the silence and darkness of the night. Each stage is due and accepted:

Now welcome night, thou night so long expected,
That long day's labour dost at last defray,
And all my cares, which cruel love collected,
Hast summed in one, and cancelled for aye:
Spread thy broad wing over my love and me,
That no man may us see,
And in thy sable mantle us enwrap,
From fear of peril and foul horror free.
Let no false treason seek us to entrap,
Nor any dread disquiet once annoy
The safety of our joy:
But let the night be calm and quietsome,
Without tempestuous storms or sad affray:

Like as when Jove with fair Alcmena lay,
When he begot the great Tirynthian groom:
Or like as when he with thy self did lie,
And begot Majesty.
And let the maids and young men cease to sing:
Ne let the woods them answer nor their echo ring.
(stanza 18)

What audacity for a poet to dare to speak to the goddess Night about her lovemaking!—and yet how apt, at the juncture when he is about to become intimate with his own wife. Throughout, mythological imagery mingles with real, external with psychological. Indeed, the comprehensiveness takes in even negative feelings, such as dread of an "affray," and sexual fears of "Medusa's mazeful head." Spenser's robust yet sensitive personal address is unflinchingly inclusive, as he faces both day and unconscious night in the ritual of love. His ceremony remains reverent; yet it affirms nature and finds authenticity in the role of Jupiter, spouse of Night. These and other deep archetypes and powers are recognized and profoundly composed: the *Horae*, the *Gratiae*, the *amorini* of passion, Cynthia the chaste destroyer yet patroness of childbirth, and, in the one stanza, Juno foundress of marriage and female genius, together with Genius himself, god of pleasure and generation. As Spenser invokes them in turn, or turns from one wedding scene to another, he dwells on each in such a way that the stanzas acquire their own characters and modalities. They are like the dances of a suite. Now all is private communing with the "learned sisters"; now expectant bachelors wait for Hymen's torchlit masque to move off; now pristine garlanded "nymphs" make final arrangements. One stanza will be a blazon of Elizabeth's beauties admired by all ("lips like cherries charming men to bite"), the next a mysterious praise of her chaste inner character. The poem's movement through this variety is fluid but calm and firm and sure. It is as if everything had its inevitable place.

And so, in numerological terms, it had. The spatial disposition of *Epithalamion* mimes with extraordinary precision the astronomical events of the day that it celebrates. Thus the 24 stanzas represent its 24 hours, with night falling at the right point for Saint Barnabas' Day, the summer solstice, "the longest day in all the year." Then, after stanza 16, the refrain changes from positive to negative: "The woods no more shall answer, nor your echo ring." And the *canzone*-like stanzas consist of pentameters and occasional trimeters, with the long lines numbering just 365 to represent the days of the year, during which the sun completes its journey round the 24 sidereal hours. The ceremony of time has never been realized so fully as in this most musical of Spenser's poems. It is indeed an "endless monument" to the poignantly short time of his day. Yet before the end it has carried the torches of its masque up to join the "thousand torches flaming bright" in the temple of the gods. It aspires to commemorate an anticipated cosmic event, addition to the communion of saints, eventual "stellification."

Prothalamion (1596), written for an aristocratic betrothal, has similar ceremonial qualities and a form almost as highly wrought. It too is a masterpiece of occasional art in the grand mannerist style. But, in spite of autobiographical references to "old woes," it is more public, more philosophical, and harder at first to warm to. Only after prolonged consideration and the effort of attending to its closely overdetermined images does its profundity emerge. It not only sums up the whole river-epithalamium genre, but sings the mutability of the height of life.

Spenser wrote other short works, notably the medievalizing satire *Mother Hubberd's Tale* and the lofty Christian-Platonic *Hymns*. The former is not dull; but neither does it show Spenser to have been a great satirist. As for the *Hymns*, they challenge more attention, as a vastly ambitious undertaking, a poetic theology of love and generation. Their extreme difficulty (and the correspondingly glorious opportunity they offer to the commentator) is not their only interest for Spenserians. They cast much cloudy light on Spenser's unexpected, syncretistic thinking. But this is not enough to make them great poems. Whether their metaphysical puzzles yield to solution or remain attributed to blunders, the *Hymns* must be counted noble failures. When all is said and done (and much has still to be said, for the love poems particularly), the work in which Spenser chiefly lives is *The Faerie Queen.*

V

The Faerie Queen occupies a very special place in English literature. Yet far more would acknowledge its classic status than would count themselves among its readers. There are doubtless several reasons for this, some of which I mention below. One may be a misconception about the kind of work *The Faerie Queen* is. Another, closely related, may be the disablement inflicted by much reading of "probable report" novels, which seems to produce insensitivity to less novelistic sorts of fictive realism. A third may be its length. For my own part, I was fortunate enough to come upon the poem during a convalescence: I could read without interruption. But there are other ways of reading such a work, which were not unknown to the Elizabethans themselves. In his translation of *Orlando Furioso*, Sir John Harington gives directions "for the several tales, where to begin and end, those that may conveniently be read single." Of course such a method will not give a very adequate idea of the work, unless it is complemented by reading *in extenso*. Much of the characteristic quality of *The Faerie Queen* depends on juxtaposition of stories and episodes of different kinds, on interrupted, interwoven narrative, on multiplication.

And this is perhaps the first point to take hold of: that it is a work of interlaced art. Suppose you are following the story of Belphoebe. You pick it up in book 2, canto 3, stanzas 21–42, a luscious ten-stanza description of the heroine, broken up by a comic encounter with Trompart and the upstart Braggadocchio. Belphoebe explains that true honor comes by hard work and is more likely to be found in the forest (or studying at home) than at court. But when she has fiercely rebuffed an improper advance, and fled, she makes no further appearance in book 2—nor in the next, until 3.5.57, where she cares for the wounded Timias. Her parentage and relation to Amoret are explained in the canto following, through the myth of Chrysogone. But then she disappears again until book 4, by which time several other stories have been woven into the fabric. If the reader loses track of these windings he should on no account despair: all is going according to plan; the sense of labyrinthine unsearchability is a desired effect.

Some degree of incomprehension is as deliberate a feature in Spenser's art as it is in certain types of medieval romance, or in the visual interlace of the *Book of Kells*. The reader may follow the pattern again and again, and have the experience, as in life, of gradual understanding.

To enjoy Spenser's *entrelacement*, feel free, first, to reread. Second, attend closely to the distant connections (whether of resemblance, variation, or contrast) between widely separate parts of the poem. As in most interlaced narratives, such internal allusions carry a great deal of the content. Third, notice the transitions between stories and between episodes. It is often at these points of juncture that Spenser indicates the fictive status of the various milieus that are brought into relation, and implies a deeper import. So the beautiful description of achieved true honor, Belphoebe alone, confronts the farcical pretensions of Braggadocchio (a thin character) and his sycophant. And this scene is in turn followed by Guyon's adventures on quite a different scale—far more minutely psychological—as he overcomes a series of difficulties in the pursuit of honor. The formal relation of interlaced narrative strands can offer a pleasure of its own, like that of abstract art. But with Spenser the interruptions of the story generally also give reminders of further reality. The breaks in his tapestry disclose glimpses of windows that look out on larger, more complex worlds. When Artegall returning victorious encounters the Blatant Beast (5.12.37), the juncture of stories shows how military success and administrative success are not enough: there is also a social world, with reputation to be won or lost. In this sense, polyphonic narrative serves the deeper purpose of comprehensiveness, of inclusiveness, of Renaissance epic's aspiration to complete unity. It is not quite the same as *entrelacement* in the older romances.

At one time, *The Faerie Queen* used to be thought of as the last great medieval work in English—although it was also supposed to have been written without much access to medieval literature. Now the manner of its medievalism is more problematic. Many would agree that Spenser knew Malory, together with other late romances. And there can be no doubt at all of his respect for old traditions: of his deep passion for "old records from ancient times derived," and of his avidity, as greedy as Guyon's, for romantic antiquities—chronicles and armor and heraldry and ruins and hermitages. *Ancient*—or, even older, *auncient*—is indeed one of his favorite words, which he is capable of using twice in the same line: "Ancient Ogyges, even the ancientest." There is some justice in C. S. Lewis' view that Spenser was "the first of the romantic medievalists." Certainly the retrospective Gothic taste in literature was identified from the start, in Pope and Thomas Warton for example, with a taste for *The Faerie Queen*. It should not be forgotten, however, that Spenser's own medieval enthusiasm was also coupled with a rather sharp stylishness. We miss a great deal of what he was about unless we appreciate his sophisticated modernity too. Not that Spenser was ever a merely fashionable writer. But he wrote in part to overgo Ariosto, who had established a vogue for Gothic costume narrative. It might be more accurate to characterize *The Faerie Queen* as mannerist neo-Gothic, rather than medieval. This stylistic character is reflected in the form, which is not romance but romantic epic.

Epic was supposed to give a sense of life's totality. And each Renaissance epicist in turn aimed at further, fuller inclusiveness, both by reaching out to a progressively more diverse or encyclopedic content, and by subsuming, whether through allusion or other means, contents already enclosed in the poetic domain of previous epics. Thus the commentators taught that Virgil's *Aeneid* combined an *Odyssey* (books 1–6) with an *Iliad* (7–12). Moreover, Julius Caesar Scaliger and other literary theorists had developed the doctrine that epic contains a wide variety of inset smaller forms. Spenser gave a creative turn to this idea: anticipating Milton's *Paradise Lost*, he included several different epic and romance forms in *The Faerie Queen*. Ariostan epic—all scramble and bravura and surprise—is probably his principal Italian ingredient. But he also uses Tasso's larger scale, especially for elaborate set pieces with luxuriant detail, such as the Bower of Bliss. Then there are passages of obscure Boiardan epic, burlesque, and puns like Pulci's, and even a few static hieroglyphs reminiscent of Trissino's *L'Italia Liberata dai Goti*. Ancient epic is represented not only in its Virgilian form—complete with descents into hell, games, extended similes, and stylistic formulas of the sort that Ford Madox Ford called "marmoreal Latinisms," but also in its Ovidian form (metamorphoses and loves of the gods). And it would risk Polonius's folly to enumerate the other types, such as pastoral epic, meandering through the world of the *Aethiopica* and the *Arcadia;* allegorical quests distantly resembling Deguilleville's or Hawes's; and (in the Cantos of Mutability) a procession like the ones in Du Bartas's Christian epic of creation.

All this should not be taken to mean that Spenser merely pillaged biblical, classical, medieval, and Renaissance epics for source material. (His sources are a separate topic, which hardly lends itself to brief treatment, being so poorly understood. Some of the poetical sources are beyond doubt. But the informational sources may have been fewer and more compendious, murkier and less literary, than scholars have assumed.) Allusion would be a better term than borrowing. Spenser is the first great allusive poet in English. And his mastery of generic variation goes further than I have suggested. With never a hint of pastiche, he deploys different kinds, almost as a composer scores for different instruments, to render life's various modes. Spenser is not always superior in handling a particular form. Ariosto's adventures, for example, run more easily; although Spenser's come very close in such an episode as Timias' skirmish with the foresters (3.5), and in any case are carrying more weight. But in shading such adventures into writing of other kinds, in using his far wider generic palette, in mixture, Spenser shows fictive genius of a different order altogether.

VI

THE detachment of *The Faerie Queen* from previous epics is reflected in its decisive formal individuation. Its meter, the "Spenserian stanza," that great legacy to Thomson and Shelley and Keats, contrives to be at once novel and traditional. By comparison with the brisk heroic stanza of Ariosto and Tasso, *ottava rima*—*a b a b a b c c*—the larger English stanza is spacious

and unhurried; while its more intricately interlaced rhymes—*a b a b b c b c c*—further slow its pace (usually: exceptions include the sprightly cadence at 7.7.46) and knit it more closely together. The final alexandrine, which determines much of the effect of stateliness and weight, allows us to think not only of a nine-line stanza, but of an eight-line stanza rounded off: *a b a b b c b c C*—the ballade or *Monk's Tale* stanza, in fact, extended and transcended. Chaucer's stanza consists of two separate, symmetrical, couplet-linked halves: *a b a b / b c b c.* But the notional halves of the indivisible Spenserian stanza are united by its shared central line:

a b a b b
  b c b c C.

An Elizabethan critic describing it—as Drayton described his own *Barons' Wars* stanza—might also have observed how it rests like a column on its hexameter base (six feet, a number of perfection), or how its rhymes occur two, three, and four times: the numbers grouped by Macrobius and others as forming the ratios of the fundamental musical concords.

Right in the midst the goddess' self did stand
Upon an altar of some costly mass,
Whose substance was uneath [difficult] to understand:
For neither precious stone, nor dureful brass,
Nor shining gold, nor mouldering clay it was;
But much more rare and precious to esteem,
Pure in aspéct, and like to crystal glass,
Yet glass was not, if one did rightly deem,
But being fair and brickle [brittle], likest glass did seem.

(4.10.39)

The Spenserian stanza has been well compared to a wave falling on a beach: breaking, it runs to implement the full alexandrine mark and to give, where needed, a meditative lull. It "closeth not but with a full satisfaction to the ear for so long detention." It is the greatest of all stanzas.

The Italianate division into cantos tends to be taken for granted, but it was an innovation in English. Spenser offset it against a different division, of antique association, into books. Within each book, the cantos may vary greatly in representational mode. This is indeed the poem's most copious source of variety. It relies on formal variegation more than on multiplication of narrative incident.

This point calls for enlargement. The stanza just quoted, describing a mysterious altar of Venus, comes from a canto about Scudamour's entry into the Temple of Venus, a fully realized allegorical place in the manner of medieval dream vision. Book 4 in general treats friendship; but this canto initiates us into the very sanctum of the virtue, its inner nature, foundation, ideals, meaning. In the same way, each book has some such medullary or "core" canto, in which, usually, the champion of a virtue visits a place that symbolizes its essential character. Saint George, the patron of Holiness, visits the House of Holiness in 1.10; Guyon, the patron of Temperance, the castle of Alma in 2.9; and Artegall Mercilla's Court in 5.9. In such cantos the virtue is developed visually through an orderly procession, a pageant tableau, or its descriptive equivalent. It is a special symbolic mode that goes back to medieval vision allegories. Valuations of it now differ sharply, usually according to the critic's familiarity with its subtle conventions. But few would question that in the fiction of a Chaucer or a Colonna or a Spenser it can be a profoundly eloquent, although very oblique, form. The expressionist mysteriousness of the Garden of Adonis or the Temple of Venus is quite unlike almost anything in Ariosto; it is more like Colonna's enigmatic *Hypnerotomachia*, that strange work of sexual mysticism, whose psychological intuitions fascinated many writers and artists of the Renaissance. To explain some features of Spenser's symbolic places it may help to compare the material of Venus' altar with the rich shining substance of the Fountain of Will in the Bower of Bliss (2.12.60), or to know that in erotic poetry, glass might figure the female pudendum (as, for example, in *Greek Anthology* 5.36). But schematic interpretation of the Temple of Venus would be unthinkable. Too much is deeply implicit or indirectly conveyed for that. How is the brittle glass related to Ptolomae's glass tower of marital fidelity at 3.2.20? And Phidias, whose Paphian idol is introduced to amplify the greater beauty of this living god: does his wretched love for a mere image belong with the

many unhappy loves about the altar? Again, why do the lovers outside the Temple sport their pleasures, while those within, and closest to the strange hermaphroditic goddess, suffer and complain? If Spenser invites such questions, he does not encourage quick answers.

The strange symbolic places stand out prominently, each like a *temenos* or sanctuary or *arcanum* set in the deep forest of romance. But they form one kind of episode only, one component of the Spenserian book. Another sort, coming in an early position, serves to join the adventures and to show the relations between the virtues that the knights strive for. Thus Saint George, patron of holiness, and Guyon, patron of temperance, meet and almost fight at 2.1.26; and Britomart (chaste love) shows herself superior to Guyon in a trial of strength at 3.1.6. Then there are early passages that announce the book's subjects by developing emblems of the virtues in their abstract or common acceptation: Saint George's encounter with Error in 1.2, Guyon's visit to Medina's castle of moderation in 2.1, Cambina's reconciliation of combatants in 4.3. These passages pose the books' topics in broad terms. The subjects thus stated undergo modification as well as expansion, however, so that the virtues of the early emblems are by no means identical with those realized in the "core cantos." The latter present insights reached only after the experience (that is, adventures) of attempting the virtue. As for the intervening adventures themselves, they superficially appear like Ariosto's. But in reality they also contribute a medieval (or medievalizing) element. They have a far more continuous moral sense than the adventures of most romances—even of many medieval romances. The Spenserian hero encounters obstacles to his virtue, or aspects of the opposing vice, which are thus analyzed into branches or subdivisions like those familiar from older moral works such as Frère Lorens' *Somme le Roi*. (Sometimes the categories are surprising and thought-provoking, as when Sansloy, a brother of Sansfoy and Sansjoy—developed characters in book 1—makes a perfunctory appearance in book 2 on the quite different scale of an aberration from Medina's golden mean.) Certain of the vices are explored fully enough to call for "places" of their own, such as the Cave of Mammon (2.7) or the House of Busirane (3.11–12). Finally, there are "digressive" episodes, such as the inset chronicle histories at the Castle of Alma and the river-god spousals of Thames and Medway, or the subplot adventures of Florimell, Marinell, and Belphoebe.

If some such repertoire of forms gives variety within a book, each book has, nevertheless, its own individual character. And each seems so distinct in emotional key as to compose with the others a sequence of complementary movements. The apocalyptic book 1 runs a vast gamut of spiritual extremities, from dark to light. But in book 2 we move to a world at once more schematically controlled and more sensuously vivid, with a tendency to frequent confrontations between its single (almost single-minded) hero and his many, minutely problematic emotions. Book 3's ardors are in the ordinary proportion of romance. Its characters disperse in ramifying adventures; but they are regathered by the centripetal tendency of book 4, through which accumulating groups of four friends (true or false) join by aggregation in a movement towards the great nuptial feast of Thames and Medway. Book 5 is Draconian in its severity. But book 6 is unbraced and vulnerable, its knights disarmed or dressed in shepherds' clothes. Throughout, the atmosphere alters in the interests of variety, and alters again for a balanced view of the wholeness of human experience.

Perhaps for the same reason, the emotional colorations change without any hard-edged divisions. They shade into one another with a subtlety and delicacy that is one of the chief marks of Spenser's art. He seems to achieve the effect partly by running stories and themes over to blur the divisions, by arranging trailers or anticipations of any change of mood, and by suturing in the overlaps with an astonishing fineness and obliquity. (Metrically this finds reflection in a system of liaison of rhyme between stanzas.) Thus, although *The Faerie Queen* is manneristically composite and complicated outwardly, as a reading experience it is not like that at all. Inwardly it moves with an almost baroque fluidity. Its wonderful transitions, for example, have none of the alienating abruptness of Ariosto's, which, as scholars have noted, go back to medieval formulas such as "Mes a tant

laisse li contes a parler de . . . et retorne a . . ." ("Now I stop telling the story of . . . and return to . . ."). Instead we move by a smooth, imperceptible progression from episode to episode, mode to mode, with even the explicit junctures, where these occur, accomplishing more than a mere narrative cut-and-join.

Thus, 3.6 begins with the geniture of Belphoebe and her twinship with Amoret—an inset Ovidian tale of Chrysogone provides the canto's first mythological treatment of generation, inside an *occupatio* (a pretended refusal to discuss):

> It were a goodly story, to declare,
> By what strange accident fair Chrysogone
> Conceived these infants, and how them she bare,
>
> (3.6.5)

The work then slides into a lost Cupid myth. This naturally leads to a burlesque quarrel between the distraught Venus and the at first censorious then relenting Diana, until their accord brings discovery of the twin births of Belphoebe and Amoret and arrangements for their separate fostering: a separation that implies an emotional polarity corresponding to that which exists between the traditionally opposed goddesses (3.6.11–28). Cupid has been found, divided or "unfolded" into two forms. Then an apparently casual transition takes us into the famous Garden of Adonis: "She brought her to her joyous Paradise, / Where most she wonces [stays], when she on earth does dwell." Besides introducing a second mythological treatment of generation, however, this stanza adds a psychological, individually sexual strand, by its personal confession:

> Whether in Paphos, or Cytheron hill,
> Or it in Gnidus be, I wot not well;
> But well I wot by trial, that this same
> All other pleasant places doth excel, . . .

In the Garden itself (30–50), the metaphysical, physical, and mythic elements interweave with formidable ease yet without ever seeming clever—suggesting, rather, Virgil's profundity of feeling and suggestion.

> There wont fair Venus often to enjoy
> Her dear Adonis' joyous company,
> And reap sweet pleasure of the wanton boy;

There yet, some say, in secret he does lie,
Lappèd in flowers and precious spicery,
By her hid from the world, and from the skill
Of Stygian gods, which do her love envy;
But she her self, when ever that she will,
Possesseth him, and of his sweetness takes her fill.

And sooth it seems they say: for he may not
For ever die, and ever buried be
In baleful night, where all things are forgot;
All be he subject to mortality,
Yet is etern in mutability,
And by succession made perpetual,
Transformèd oft, and changèd diversely:
For him the father of all forms they call;
Therefore needs mote [must] he live, that living
    gives to all.

(3.6.46–47)

The Garden is where an individual participates, through the act of sex, in making new life;
and where the relation of form and matter, of
permanence and change, declares itself. It is a
Christian-Platonic-Pythagorean vision of the
soul's vocation in a world of accident. At the
same time, the canto is full of Spenser's own
characteristic bittersweet cheerful melancholy.
Wicked Time destroys the Garden's goodly
things; but the pity of that cannot make it other
than a gloriously creative place. Time's scythe
mows, but Venus can still "reap sweet pleasure." The canto began with explanation of
Belphoebe's inherited qualities, which led,
through the confrontation of Venus and Diana,
to the Garden of Adonis. But Spenser leaves the
Garden for the story of Belphoebe's vulnerable
twin, Amoret (52–53), and then (by a more distant modulation) for that of the still more fearful
Florimell. We have moved from Belphoebe almost to her opposite, with hardly a break.

VII

THE movement of *The Faerie Queen* seems
fluid and unpredictable, almost like human experience. To get this realistic effect it must
avoid obvious regularities of the composite
parts. Consequently order, although everywhere discoverable, is everywhere hidden.
Thus, placement of the so-called core cantos

varies from book to book: 1.10, 4.10, and 6.10,
but 2.9 and 5.9. Yet the variation is not random
either, since it follows a number symbolism (the
core cantos in ninth place enshrine cardinal virtues, Temperance and Justice). Similarly, the
contents of books broadly follow the sequence
of the planetary week, with book 1 as the book
of Sol, book 2 as Luna, and so forth. Truth
(troth, faith), the subject of book·1, was a usual
association or meaning of the sun; just as Una's
lion attendant—the terrible aspect of truth—
would have been recognized as Sol's astrological
house. The planetary series is interrupted, however, when book 3 proves to be not a book of
Mars but of his feminine and wiser counterpart
Minerva (a cult image of Queen Elizabeth). The
overall narrative pattern of yearly quests shows
a similarly regular irregularity. Saint George's
mission against the dragon and Guyon's against
Acrasia lead us to expect one adventure per
book. But books 3 and 4 have between them
only one, Scudamour's. Again, most of the
books feature the titular patron of a virtue, sent
out from Gloriana's court. In book 3, however,
it is Britomart, not Scudamour, who defeats Busirane and frees Amoret; while book 4 has two
other heroes, Cambel and Triamond, who do
not belong to Gloriana's order of knighthood.
These variations can easily seem random and
confused. But they turn out to be governed by a
structural logic, related to Christian-Platonic or
Neoplatonic concepts such as the Triad. The latter not only informs many groupings of characters—Sansfoy, Sansjoy, Sansloy, for example—
but also a division, confirmed by the order of
publication, into three-book parts.

Another structural pattern that runs throughout is the arrangement of thematic images in as-
cending sequence, from evil, through less evil
(or mixed), to good. In book 6 the series is of
human "garlands" ranging from the cannibals
gathered round Serena, through the lusty shepherds and lovely lasses round Pastorella, to the
"hundred naked maidens lily white, / All ranged
in a ring" round the three Graces—who themselves encircle "another damsel," Spenser's own
love. The theme makes connection through the
common figure of a garland, whose oblatory
meaning becomes explicit in the primitive ritual
(6.8.39, 6.9.8, 6.10.12, and 6.10.14). In the same
way bad Venuses taking pleasure at the Bower

of Bliss and the House of Malecasta precede the good Venus enjoying the Garden of Adonis. And the pains of a cruel Cupid triumphing at the House of Busirane (3.11–12) goes before the painful sentence pronounced by the "wise" Cupid at 6.8.22–25. It is a law of Fairyland. The quests are always making gradual labyrinthine approaches, or ascents in Platonic fashion, from perverse and dark images towards the reality of virtues themselves. The virtues have to be composed, step by step, in a process of integration. It is a remarkably inclusive vision. At the Temple of Venus are held in concord not only love and hate, "brethren both of half the blood" (4.10.32), but Venus and Cupid, potentially, and the pleasure and pain of love.

It is Spenser's Christian Platonism, his conception of things as images of reality, that makes sense of dwelling on symbolic objects rather than on probable action. Certainly *The Faerie Queen* is pictorial in the extreme. When Joseph Spence read it to his aged mother she said that he "had been showing her a collection of pictures;" and Pope appreciatively concurred. Not all post-Victorian critics have cared for this picturesque quality. Some have felt quite superior to the naïveté of speaking pictures. But we should remember that in the Renaissance—even partly in Ruskin's time—pictures spoke conceptually and articulately. Whether or not our ancestors were also in closer touch with the images of the unconscious, they demonstrably used a conscious and conventional iconographical language. The adventure of the champion of temperance is full of emblems of that virtue, such as the bridle or collar, which appears in the "gorgeous barbs" of Guyon's horse Brigador (*briglia d'oro*), in the bridle put on Occasion's tongue, and perhaps in the elaborately described "silken camus lily white" worn by Belphoebe (Latin *camus*, "bridle, collar"; English *camis*, "tunic"). Belphoebe also wore

> a golden baldric, which forelay
> Athwart her snowy breast, and did divide
> Her dainty paps; which like young fruit in May
> Now little gan to swell, and being tied
> Through her thin weed their places only signified.
> (2.3.29)

The half-exposed bosom regularly emblemized true honor, so that an Elizabethan reader was prepared in advance to recognize the values latent in Belphoebe's confrontation with Braggadocchio and Trompart.

Spenser does not always give explanatory labels to such relatively simple iconography. And even when he seems explicit, as with the cruel hag Occasion, the labeling abstraction by no means exhausts the image's meaning. Literature dominated iconography, rather than the reverse: Spenser was forming images not yet in any handbook. His figure was not Occasion in general (who would have been a young girl), but a very specific Occasion, incorporating such additional features as the lameness of Poena (slow retribution). Possibly Spenser himself could not have identified the composite figure much more fully, in other terms than he has actually used. He was exploring psychological depths: the springs of impatience, the penalties of guilt. His emblematic pictures and hieroglyphs were not, after all, merely quaint, but a means to self-discovery. Having only a smattering of the language of emblem, our best approach is to meditate on the scene as a whole and to take in details of mood and appearance. We need to feel Occasion's intemperate readiness to blame—perhaps to guess at the suggestion of self-punishing remorse in the cruelty of her son Furor—before we know how to bring iconography to bear.

In a fiction that uses images as its words in this way, language is apt to be of secondary importance, at least compared with an epic such as *Paradise Lost*. I do not mean that *The Faerie Queen* is carelessly or flatly written. Its style can reach intensity when a grand theme calls for it—as in the description of

> Death with most grim and grisly visage seen,
> Yet is he nought but parting of the breath;
> Ne ought to see, but like a shade to ween [suppose],
> Unbodièd, unsouled, unheard, unseen.
> (7.7.46)

And it varies with every change of mode— lyrical, narrative, descriptive. But much of the time it makes little conscious impression on the casual reader. Like the clean window glass that you do not notice so long as you focus on a distant object, the language of *The Faerie Queen* is usually transparent. Every now and them comes a more noticeable stanza, such as the intricately eloquent, densely patterned, much quoted description of the Cave of Sleep (1.1.41). But such "opaqueness" is unrepresentative of a narrative style that mostly effaces itself. This shaven manner of the narrative allegory contrasts with the richer sonority of description sustained in the "core" cantos. There, epiphanies stand out with the dense force of language of a major ode. The disparity is of course deliberate. For the discriminating reader, indeed, this balance of plane surfaces and enriched areas offers one of the main pleasures of the poem.

Not that the diction is neutral or colorless, even in the narrative allegory. It has too marked a medieval tinge for that. Still, the notorious archaisms are fewer and less frequent than critics suggest: many stanzas have none, and others have only the token ne or eke of the poem's soon-familiar idiolect. On the other hand, there is a good deal more sly wordplay than used to be recognized. Sometimes Spenser draws on proverbial lore, which may provide the basis of a whole episode, in the manner of Langland or Nashe or Brueghel. But more often the wit takes the form of what Hazlitt called "an allegorical play upon words": a punning ambiguity, that is, with one meaning in the story and the other in the allegory; as at 6.9.5, where Calidore, who brought the faults of the court with him in his courtly nature, inquires after the Blatant Beast, "If such a beast they saw, which he had thither brought." Altogether the language, which owes much in this to Gavin Douglas, brilliantly compounds the high-flown and the vernacular.

VIII

I have left until now the problems of the allegory, since these have been exaggerated into unnecessary stumbling blocks. Victorian and Georgian critics were predisposed against what they saw as didactic and mechanical "naïve allegory." But Spenser's poem would now be generally exonerated from these charges. If its moral seems in any sense too bare, it is not in the sense of being crude or obvious. Besides, there is now more feeling for what was a dominant form of literature in the Middle Ages, and at least one of the most prominent in the Renais-

sance. Spenser, however, wrote a special sort of allegory, whose characteristics should be distinguished. He himself called The Faerie Queen "a continued allegory, or dark conceit" and noticed "how doubtfully all allegories may be construed" (Letter to Ralegh).

Like much Elizabethan criticism, this calls for sympathetic interpretation. When he calls the allegory "continued," Spenser probably means that it is not merely local, but kept up by the author all through. In this his poem differs from, say, Orlando Furioso. Ariosto has occasional allegories, such as that of Logistilla; and he was freely allegorized, by such anti-intentionalists de ses jours as Fornari and Bononome. But Spenser wrote throughout what was meant allegorically or symbolically. Unlike the strange places and marvels of medieval romance (and, to a large extent, those in Ariosto), Spenser's are interpreted. In consequence they are brought into unity with the rest of the work. Thus, the improbably numerous foundlings in book 6 are not left as a matter of surprise and delightful wonder. Spenser makes it plain that the marvel, anything but arbitrary, is designed to explore various relations between natural inheritance and "nurture" (environmental influences). To the various structures of the Orlando, therefore, The Faerie Queen adds another, quite distinct.

Moreover, this extra strand is itself manifold. Unlike Bunyan's allegory (which has only one sphere of reference, the religious), Spenser's may be religious or moral or psychological or philosophical or political. Most often, perhaps, it is moral, setting out virtues and vices, or distinctions within virtues and vices, in the narrative mode by which ethics used to be understood. Lucifera and the Giant Orgoglio present different kinds of pride; the six knights of Malecasta six steps into lechery. Other figures, however, such as Pyrochles and Cymochles, or Elissa and Perissa, treat polarities of a more psychological order. In Shamefastness and Praisedesire, indeed, Spenser explores the springs of moral behavior in two contrasting temperamental dispositions. It is often observed, and rightly, that his psychological insights seldom issue in character studies. But we should recall that each book really studies a single "super-character," its hero, whose traits are the individual allegorical characters. (And the Letter to

Ralegh hints that Arthur himself composes a superhero from the hero parts of individual books.) Regarded in this light, Spenser's poem is seen to analyze psychological experience in unusual depth. Even so, some of his greatest passages tend in another direction altogether, belonging to a philosophical allegory enacted either by abstract personifications (Mutability) or by mythological figures (Adonis).

There is also, particularly in book 5, a political allegory, which many have found repellent in its severity. The iron man Talus with his flail seems uncomfortably proleptic of the harshest modern riot police. What is one to think, in particular, of Spenser's attitude to Ireland? As a patriot, he worked for the English oppressors. Yet he hated violence and loved peace and justice. Such an attitude wins few friends now. It has even been asserted, by Yeats and others, that Spenser hated the Irish. The fact remains that in his prose *View of the Present State of Ireland* Spenser attempted what few British and American writers have emulated: to understand the Irish. It does not do to forget the magnitude of the disorders or the weakness of government in Spenser's time.

The allegory, of course, often has multiple implications. Indeed, the same character may have a political or topical, as well as a moral, meaning. Artegall, for example, combines Sovereign Power, Justice, and Maleness-in-generation (not portrayed as a superior role) with Leicester, Essex, Grey, and perhaps other historical figures. Similarly, Belphoebe represents Queen Elizabeth, but also Virginality. But in approaching these "antique praises unto present persons fit" we must not be tempted into looking for a key. Such figures represent insights into life; they should not be reduced to system, but responded to with a correspondingly personal intuition.

This is true of all Spenser's allegories. You cannot be too subtle in interpreting them; but you can easily be subtle in the wrong way. Alertness is everything. In the Cave of Mammon episode, Guyon's refraining from combat with golden Disdain (who resembles "an huge Giant") has attracted ingenious explanations: Guyon is learning that martial heroism is not enough, et cetera. But the alert reader will sense that the supercilious hero has blundered. Per-

haps what prompts him is a remembered law of Fairyland, that Giants are for fighting (as witness Orgoglio, Argante, Ollyphant, Corflambo, the Giant with the Scales, Geryoneo, and others). Or perhaps he reflects that Mammon's advice to "abstain from perilous fight" is unlikely to be dependable. (Another law: evil figures give bad advice.) In any event, by not fighting, Guyon has gone disastrously wrong. His moral heroism has degenerated into mere aristocratic *sdegno:* he is literally reconciled to disdain; and he rejects the world because he feels superior to it. He may be doing the right thing, but for the wrong reason. A really wakeful reader will also see Spenser's joke, that all the time golden Disdain is really not aristocratic but a "villain." Such a point is a matter for the attention of the third ear. The laws of Fairyland are not those of deductive logic.

IX

No sooner has one drawn attention to the complicated manifold character of *The Faerie Queen* than the balance must be righted by affirming its simplicity. Mere formal complication seems almost irrelevant to Spenser's serious purpose: his sophisticated detachment from forms serves other than formal values. He uses any means that will illustrate the deepest truth of the matter. Hence his easy freedom with sources. Since he is more concerned with truth than with elegance or poetic success, great predecessors never intimidate him. He has had his own glimpse of life; and in the end it is for his unified vision that we read *The Faerie Queen*.

Spenser's reliance on chivalric values may appear to contradict what I have just written, and to make any very high seriousness impossible. How can we take seriously a knighthood that was already outgrown in the poet's own time— that he himself presents, indeed, in anachronistic terms? Well, a reinterpreted knighthood, offering ideals for courtiers and administrators, may have formed a part of Spenser's purpose. But it would be a mistake to think of this as merely an aspiration to some Indian summer of English chivalry. At the very least, the adventures are moral psychomachies. And their content is quite as much private as public. They continually press behind virtues to the growth of "the fresh bud of virtue," to the "sacred nursery / Of virtue" "deep within the mind," and even to "the root" of all virtue, in love (4 Proem 2). In Spenser, virtues, and especially symbols of virtue, are "secret" or "hidden" (1.11.36, 3.1.10, 2.8.20). We may conclude that the heroes' approaches to the "sacred virtue(s)" pursue quests of self-discovery. Moreover, the virtues themselves, when discovered, are numinous mysteries that may even be described as "resembling God" (5 Proem 10). In fine, the adventures go to form a greater self: to fashion a person.

At the deepest level, therefore, the poem's narrative paradigm must be discovery: the discovery that characterizes romance, rather than the conflict of epic. Of course there are many battles, and the frequency of revenge is conspicuous. But *The Faerie Queen* usually avoids any simple *enantiodromia* or war of contraries. Indeed, its most striking moral feature is reconciliation or transcendence of opposites. It pursues wholeness. Is it more antipapist or more Catholic? More devoted to pleasure or to virtue? Traditional or innovative? Such questions have only to be formulated for us to see their inappropriateness. Spenser combines the great antipodes—reason and emotion, sovereignty and equity, male and female—into a single larger world of integrated identity. Not a bad emblem of *The Faerie Queen* would be Dame Concord's tempering of the fearful siblings Love and Hate (4.10.32). Unquestionably such *coincidentia oppositorum*, or union of opposites, runs the danger of limitless abysses. Perhaps in consequence, it arouses disagreeable apprehensions in some. Indeed, dislike of *The Faerie Queen*, when it arises, may have much to do with this feature. To lovers of the poem, distaste for it seems incomprehensibly perverse—like a distaste for life. But (again like life) *The Faerie Queen* can be difficult, dark with shades of half-thought meanings. The Victorian critics may not have been far wrong in calling it dreamlike. Only, its dream analysis is more worthwhile than they cared to admit—and already expressed by Spenser in what is more alert meditation than languid fantasy.

One of the pervasive antinomies that *The Faerie Queen* attempts to combine is the one between order and change. That Spenser shared Mulcaster's and Camden's reverence for ancient tradition needs no argument. His feeling for the sanctity of civilized order finds continued and varied expression, in metaphysical celebrations, in happy ceremonies, and in praises of Queen Elizabeth, not to mention execrations of savagery and disordered license. Nevertheless, Spenser may also be the first English poet to have written favorably of change, in any sense even remotely like what we should now call historical. In the Cantos of Mutability, Nature dismisses, it is true, Dame Mutability's claim to cosmic supremacy. But she does so for a strange and subtle reason: namely, that all things indeed change, "But by their change their being do dilate [implement]." Mutability, which generations of poets had taken as a subject of complaint, was for Spenser something quite different: a creative process, almost a subject of encomium. Her witnesses form the grand procession of the parts of time that has offered inspiration to many subsequent poets, and that all would now concede to be a high point of Spenser's oeuvre. Moreover, it sums up a vision informing the entire poem, of nature in multifarious transformation.

I well consider all that ye have said,
And find that all things steadfastness do hate
And changèd be: yet being rightly weighed
They are not changèd from their first estate;
But by their change their being do dilate:
And turning to themselves at length again,
Do work their own perfection so by fate:
Then over them change doth not rule and reign;
But they reign over change, and do their states maintain.

Cease therefore daughter further to aspire,
And thee content thus to be ruled by me:
For thy decay thou seek'st by thy desire;
But time shall come that all shall changèd be,
And from thenceforth, none no more change shall see.
So was the Titaness put down and whist [silenced],
And Jove confirmed in his imperial see.
Then was that whole assembly quite dismissed,
And Nature's self did vanish, whither no man wist [knew].   (Cantos of Mutability, 7.58–59)

The Faerie Queen as a whole could be said to hymn creation in process, rather than created nature. It aspires to unifying change; and, by exploring far back into historical origins, ancient myths, causes of wrath, and the deepest relations of "cousin passions," it searches, beneath outward and partial metamorphoses, for the changes of heart that could release life's fullness.

The world of *The Faerie Queen* is never vague. It may seem unsearchably vast and uncertain in measurement; but it is emotionally sure and distinctive in atmosphere. This has something to do with the long epic similes, which, like Homer's, introduce ordinary domesticities, but which have also a crisp, concentrated particularity that is Spenser's own ("The watery southwind from the seaboard coast"). From time to time, too, precise sensible details come into the story itself. These would be striking but for their immediate rightness: Arthur's savage squire shook his oaken plant so sternly "That like an hazel wand, it quiverèd and quook"; Glauce "the drunken lamp down in the oil did steep."

In general, of course, Spenser's poem needs the unfeatured continuum of romance. This is usually, with him, a fortuitous Brocéliande-like forest, "a forest wide, / Whose hideous horror and sad trembling sound / Full grisly seemed." This dark verdure serves as an unassertive background, from which marvels stand out in highlight: a Rich Strand, perhaps, heaped with "the wealth of the east," or a castle with magical flames guarding its porch. But the symbolic environments themselves are as distinct as places of the mind can well be. They are varied decisively, with a sharp discrimination that will be inherited (at whatever removes) by Dickens and Stevenson, Borges and de la Mare. One of Spenser's forests or caves is not like another. Here the "surges hoar, / . . . 'gainst the craggy clifts did loudly roar"; there dolphins drew the chariot of sad Cymoent so smoothly "that their broad flaggy fins no foam did rear, / Ne bubbling roundel they behind them sent." (Spenser is almost always specific about weather, being the first English, although not the first British, poet to notice it much.) The House of Busirane, with, its grandeurs and longueurs; Malecasta's

fun house; and the difficult but desirable Temple of Venus: these are all places we should recognize instantly. As in dream, the presence of place is intense:

That house's form within was rude and strong,
Like an huge cave, hewn out of rocky clift,
From whose rough vault the rugged breaches [fractures] hung,
Embossed with massy gold of glorious gift,
And with rich metal loaded every rift,
That heavy ruin they did seem to threat;
And over them Arachne high did lift
Her cunning web, and spread her subtle net,
Enwrappèd in foul smoke and clouds more black than
　jet.
(2.7.28)

Unlike the world of common dreams, however, Spenser's Fairyland combines emotional precision with intense lucidity. We breathe in it a purer air that imparts not only excitement to the intellect but vigor to all the faculties. Its impression is fresh; yet it has been formed by thought, long brooded, deeply meditated. Its places and landscapes are symbolic rather than allegorical in a schematic way. And if it is pondered sufficiently, it is discovered to have a profundity that justifies the stress in early criticism on Spenser's "deep conceit."

Such poetry has never been easy to locate on the map of Parnassus. *The Faerie Queen* contrasts, in this respect, with the work of the more fashionable Sidney, who can quite readily be related to the mannerist literary movement of his time. Spenser fits in nowhere. Neither classical nor romantic, neither medieval nor merely neo-Gothic, neither historical nor wholly imaginary, neither fanciful nor rationally intelligible, his visionary work awaits the understanding and the judgment of ages. It has already shown an astonishing capacity to speak to our own century. How inadequate, we are bound to think, and yet how splendid too, was the inscription put on Spenser's monument in Westminster Abbey, naming him "the prince of poets in his time."

SELECTED BIBLIOGRAPHY

I. BIBLIOGRAPHIES, ETC. C. G. Osgood, *A Concordance to the Poems* (Washington, D.C., 1915; repr. Gloucester, Mass., 1963); C. H. Whitman, *A Subject Index to the Poems* (New Haven, 1918; repr. New York, 1966); Frederic I. Carpenter, *A Reference Guide to Edmund Spenser* (Chicago, 1923), with supplement by D. F. Atkinson (Baltimore, 1937; repr. New York, 1967); F. R. Johnson, *A Critical Bibliography of the Works Printed Before 1700* (Baltimore, 1933; repr. London, 1966; Folcroft, Pa., 1969); *Spenser Newsletter*, vols. 1–5, University of Western Ontario (1970–1974), vols. 5– , University of Massachusetts, Amherst and Holyoke Community College (1974–). R. M. Cummings, *Spenser: The Critical Heritage* (London, 1971); W. F. McNeir and F. Provost, *Edmund Spenser: An Annotated Bibliography 1937–1972* (Pittsburgh, 1975).

II. COLLECTED WORKS. *The Faerie Queen: The Shepherd's Calendar: Together With the Other Works of England's Arch-Poet, Edm. Spenser: Collected Into One Volume, and Carefully Corrected* (1611 or 1617), folio eds. of the collected poetry, consisting of seven separate sections independently printed at various dates, each with two main states, issued as single vol. bearing the date 1611 or 1617; *The Works of That Famous English Poet, Mr Edmond Spenser* (1679), the third folio but the first collected ed. of the poetry and prose, with glossary; J. Hughes, ed., *The Works of Mr. Edmund Spenser*, 6 vols. (1715), with glossary and essays; H. J. Todd, ed., *The Works*, 8 vols. (1805), a variorum ed., reviewed by Walter Scott, in *The Edinburgh Review*, 7 (1805); R. E. N. Dodge, ed., *The Poetical Works* (Boston, 1908), sparsely annotated; J. C. Smith and E. de Sélincourt, eds., *The Poetical Works*, 3 vols. (Oxford, 1909–1910), Oxford English Texts series, with textual and bibliographic notes; J. C. Smith and E. de Sélincourt, eds., *The Poetical Works* (London, 1912), Oxford Standard Authors ed., with textual notes, glossary, and critical intro. by E. de Sélincourt, contains the Spenser-Harvey letters, first printed as *Three proper, and witty, familiar Letters* (1580); W. L. Renwick, ed., *The Complete Works of Edmund Spenser*, 4 vols. (London, 1928–1934), omits *The Faerie Queen*, but includes all the other poems; E. Greenlaw *et al.*, eds., *The Works: A Variorum Edition*, 9 vols. (Baltimore, 1932–1949; repr. with index vol. by C. G. Osgood, 1957; and with A. C. Judson, *Life of Spenser*, in 11 vols., 1966).

III. SEPARATE WORKS IN VERSE. S. J. van der Noodt, *A Theatre for Worldlings* (1569), containing "Epigrams" and "Sonnets" trans. by Spenser, rev. in *Complaints* (1591); *The Shepherd's Calendar. Containing Twelve Eclogues Proportionable to the Twelve Months* (1579; repr. 1581, 1586, 1591, 1597; subsequently in the folio eds., and in 1653, with Latin trans.), includes preface and glosses by "E. K."; *The Faerie Queen* (1590), containing books 1–3 and Letter to Ralegh; 2nd ed., rev. (1596); *Daphnaida. An Elegy Upon the Death of . . . Douglas Howard . . . Wife of Arthur Gorges* (1591), repr. with the *Hymns* (1596); *Complaints. Containing Sundry Small Poems of the World's Vanity* (1591), including *The Ruins of Time, The Tears of the Muses, Virgil's Gnat, Prosopopoia: or Mother Hubberd's Tale, Ruins of Rome: by Bellay, Muiopotmos: Or the Fate of the Butterfly, Visions of the World's Vanity, The Visions of Bellay,* and *The Visions of Petrarch; Colin Clout's Come Home Again* (1595), containing the title poem, *Astrophel. A Pastoral Elegy Upon the Death of . . . Sidney* (including *The Doleful Lay of Clorinda* without a separate title), and other elegies, one by L[odovick] B[ryskett]; *Amoretti and Epithalamion* (1595); *Prothalamion: Or: A Spousal Verse* (1596); *Four Hymns* (1596), containing *An Hymn in Honour of Love, An Hymn in Honour of Beauty, An Hymn of Heavenly Love,* and *An Hymn of Heavenly Beauty; The Second Part of the Faerie Queen* (1596), containing books 4–6 (more copies printed than of the 1596 ed. of the first part), facs. of both parts of 1596 ed., G. Hough, ed., 2 vols. (London, 1976), folio ed. of *The Faerie Queen* (1609), first to include the Cantos of Mutability; J. Upton, ed., *The Faerie Queen. A New Edition With a Glossary, and Notes Explanatory and Critical*, 2 vols. (1758), a great and classic ed.; E. Welsford, ed., *Spenser: Four Hymns: Epithalamion* (Oxford, 1967); R. Beum, ed., *Epithalamion* (Columbus, Ohio, 1968); A. C. Hamilton, ed., *The Faerie Queen* (London, 1977), Longman Annotated Poets series; T. P. Roche, ed., *The Faerie Queen* (in press).

IV. SELECTED VERSE. C. S. Lewis, with essay "Edmund Spenser, 1552–1599," in G. B. Harrison, ed., *Major British Writers*, 2 vols. (New York, 1954), repr. in C. S. Lewis, *Studies in Medieval and Renaissance Literature* (Cambridge, 1966); P. C. Bayley, ed., *Spenser: "The Faerie Queen,"* book 2 (London, 1965); R. Kellogg and O. Steele, eds., *Books 1 and 2 of "The Faerie Queen": The Mutability Cantos and Selections From the Minor Poetry* (New York, 1965); P. C. Bayley, *Spenser: "The Faerie Queen,"* book 1 (London, 1966); A. C. Hamilton, ed., *Edmund Spenser: Selected Poetry* (New York, 1966); S. P. Zitner, *The Mutability Cantos* (London, 1968); A. K. Hieatt and C. Hieatt, eds., *Edmund Spenser: Selected Poetry* (New York, 1970); D. Brooks-Davies, ed., *Edmund Spenser: "The Faerie Queen": A Selection* (London, 1976).

V. CRITICAL AND BIOGRAPHICAL STUDIES. T. Warton, *Observations on "The Faerie Queen"* (London, 1754; enl., 1762; 2nd ed., repr. New York, 1968, 1969; Farnborough, 1969); R. Hurd, *Letters on Chivalry and Romance* (London, 1762), edited by E. J. Morley (1911); W. Hazlitt, *Lectures on the English Poets* (London, 1818); J. Ruskin, *The Stones of Venice*, vol. II (London, 1853), chs. 7, 8; J. Ruskin, *Modern Painters,* vol. III (London, 1856), ch. 8; James Russell Lowell, "Spenser," in *The Writings of James Russell Lowell*, IV (1892); E. Legouis, *Edmond Spenser* (Paris, 1923; rev. ed., Paris, 1956), English trans. (London, 1926); W. L. Renwick, *Edmund Spenser: An Essay on Renaissance Poetry* (London, 1925; repr. London, 1965); P. Henley, *Spenser in Ireland* (Cork, 1928; repr. New York, 1969); M. Y. Hughes, *Virgil and Spenser* (Berkeley, Calif., 1929; repr. Port Washington, N.Y., 1969); H. S. V. Jones, *A Spenser Handbook* (New York, 1930; repr. London, 1947); E. Greenlaw, *Studies in Spenser's Historical Allegory* (Baltimore, 1932; repr. New York, 1967); H. G. Lotspeich, *Classical Mythology in the Poetry of Edmund Spenser* (Princeton, 1932; repr. 1965); J. Spens, *Spenser's Faerie Queen: An Interpretation* (London, 1934; repr. New York, 1967); T. M. Raysor, ed., *Coleridge's Miscellaneous Criticism* (London, 1936); C. S. Lewis, *The Allegory of Love* (London, 1936); I. E. Rathborne, *The Meaning of Spenser's Fairyland* (New York, 1937; repr. New York, 1965); J. W. Bennett, *The Evolution of "The Faerie Queen"* (Chicago, 1942; repr. New York, 1960); V. K. Whitaker, *The Religious Basis of Spenser's Thought* (Stanford, Calif., 1950; repr. New York, 1966); H. Smith, *Elizabethan Poetry: A Study in Convention, Meaning and Expression* (Cambridge, Mass., 1952; repr. Ann Arbor, 1968); C. S. Lewis, *English Literature in the Sixteenth Century Excluding Drama* (Oxford, 1954); J. Arthos, *On the Poetry of Spenser and the Form of Romances* (London, 1956; repr. New York, 1970); H. Berger, *The Allegorical Temper. Vision and Reality in Book 2 of Spenser's "Faerie Queen"* (New Haven, 1957; repr. Hamden, Conn., 1967); W. R. Mueller, *Spenser's Critics: Changing Currents in Literary Taste* (Syracuse, N.Y., 1959), criticism of *The Faerie Queen* from 1715 to 1949, with intro.; S. T. Coleridge, *Shakespearian Criticism*, T. M. Raysor, ed., 2 vols. (London, 1960); A. K. Hieatt, *Short Time's Endless Monument. The Symbolism of the Numbers in Edmund Spenser's "Epithalamion"* (New York, 1960; repr. Port Washington, N.Y., 1972); R. Ellrodt, *Neoplatonism in the Poetry of Spenser* (Geneva, 1960), reviewed by C. S. Lewis, in *Études anglaises*, 14 (1961); A. W. Satterthwaite, *Spenser, Ronsard and Du Bellay* (Princeton, 1960); A. C. Hamilton, *The Structure of Allegory in "The Faerie Queen"* (Oxford, 1961); P. E. McLane, *Spenser's "Shepherd's Calendar": A Study in Elizabethan Allegory* (Notre Dame, Ind., 1961); G. Hough, *A Preface to "The Faerie Queen"* (London, 1962); T. Greene, *The Descent From Heaven: A Study in Epic Continuity* (New Haven, 1963); N. Frye, *Fables of Identity: Studies in Poetic Mythology* (New York, 1963); W. Nelson, *The Poetry of Edmund Spenser: A Study* (New York, 1963); T. P. Roche, *The Kindly Flame: A Study of the Third and Fourth Books of Spenser's "Faerie Queen"* (Princeton, 1964); A. Fowler, *Spenser and the Numbers of Time* (London–New York, 1964); A. B. Giamatti, *The Earthly Paradise and the Renaissance Epic* (Princeton, 1966); C. S. Lewis, *Spenser's Images of Life*, A. Fowler, ed. (Cambridge, 1967); E. A. F. Watson, *Spenser* (London, 1967); P. J. Alpers, *The Poetry of "The Faerie Queen"* (Princeton, 1967); T. K. Dunseath, *Spenser's Allegory of Justice in Book Five of "The Faerie Queen"* (Princeton, 1968); R. Sale, *Reading Spenser: An Introduction to "The Faerie Queen"* (New York, 1968); H. Maclean, ed., *Edmund Spenser's Poetry: Authoritative Texts; Criticism* (New York, 1968), texts and selections from 1590 to 1963; K. W. Grandsen, *A Critical Commentary on Spenser's "Faerie Queen"* (London, 1969); J. Aptekar, *Icons of Justice: Iconography and Thematic Imagery in Book 5 of "The Faerie Queen"* (New York, 1969); S. Meyer, *An Interpretation of Edmund Spenser's "Colin Clout"* (Notre Dame, Ind., 1969); M. Evans, *Spenser's Anatomy of Heroism: A Commentary on "The Faerie Queen"* (Cambridge, 1970); R. Freeman, *"The Faerie Queen": A Companion for Readers* (Berkeley, Calif., 1970); P. Bayley, *Edmund Spenser: Prince of Poets* (London, 1971); A. Fletcher, *The Prophetic Moment: An Essay on Spenser* (Chicago–London, 1971); J. E. Hankins, *Source and Meaning in Spenser's Allegory: A Study of "The Faerie Queen"* (Oxford, 1971); H. Tonkin, *Spenser's Courteous Pastoral: Book Six of "The Faerie Queen"* (Oxford, 1972); J. B. Bender, *Spenser and Literary Pictorialism* (Princeton, 1972); P. Cullen, *Infernal Triad: The Flesh, the World, and the Devil in Spenser and Milton* (Princeton, 1974); A. Fowler, *Conceitful Thought: The Interpretation of English Renaissance Poems* (Edinburgh, 1975); A. B. Giamatti, *Play of Double Senses: Spenser's "Faerie Queen"* (Englewood Cliffs, N.J., 1975); A. K. Hieatt, *Chaucer: Spenser: Milton: Mythopoeic Continuities and Transformations* (Montreal–London, 1975); M. Rose, *Spenser's Art. A Companion to Book 1 of "The Faerie Queen"* (Cambridge, Mass., 1975); I. G. MacCaffrey, *Spenser's Allegory: The Anatomy of Imagination* (Princeton, 1976); J. Nohrnberg, *The Analogy of "The Faerie Queen"* (Princeton, 1976).

VI. ARTICLES. W. R. Mueller and D. C. Allen, eds., *That Sovereign Light. Essays in Honor of Edmund Spenser, 1552–1952* (Baltimore, 1952; repr. New York, 1967); D. C. Allen, "The March Eclogue of *The Shepherd's Calendar*" and "*Muiopotmos*," in *Image and Meaning, Metaphoric Traditions in Renaissance Poetry* (Baltimore, 1960; rev. 1968); W. Nelson, ed., *Form and Convention in the Poetry of Edmund Spenser* (New York, 1961), Selected Papers From the English Institute; H. Berger, ed., *Spenser: A Collection of Critical Essays* (Englewood Cliffs, N.J., 1968); R. R. Elliott, ed., *The Prince of Poets: Essays on Edmund Spenser* (New York, 1968); A. Fowler, ed., *Silent Poetry: Essays in Numerological Analysis* (London–New

York, 1970), contains M. Baybak *et al.*, "Placement 'in the middest', in *The Faerie Queen*" and A. Dunlop, "The Unity of Spenser's *Amoretti*"; Editors of the *Journal of English Literary History, Critical Essays on Spenser From ELH* (Baltimore, 1970); J. F. Kermode, *Shakespeare, Spenser, Donne: Renaissance Essays* (London–New York, 1971); A. C. Hamilton, ed., *Es-sential Articles for the Study of Edmund Spenser* (Hamden, Conn., 1972); J. M. Kennedy and J. A. Reither, eds., *A Theatre for Spenserians: Papers of the International Spenser Colloquium, Fredericton, 1969* (Toronto, 1973); P. Bayley, ed., *Spenser: "The Faerie Queen"* (London, 1977).

SIR RICHARD STEELE
(1672-1729)

JOSEPH ADDISON
(1672-1719)

A. R. Humphreys

THE PERIODICAL ESSAYIST

It is a salutary principle, in judging a work of art, not to confuse its historical with its aesthetic importance. Anyone writing on the eighteenth-century periodical essay, even at its best in the *Tatler* and the *Spectator*, needs to remind himself of this principle; here is a case where the historical importance is very great but where the modern reader, if led to expect more than a charming humor and vivacity, is likely to feel cheated. Induced to expect too much, he will dismiss what he finds as too little.

Yet in doing so he will miss much in a delightful minor mode that is worth having, as well as a historical phenomenon that can give much food for reflection. Let us take this latter point first. In Britain's cultural life, few alliances have been more fruitful than that between the writers and the readers of these essays, few relationships more thoughtfully and responsibly adjusted. To study the best Augustan[1] periodicals leaves one, if not responding to a profound literary achievement, at least admiring the skill with which enlightenment was spread on a broad front of morals and letters. This was achieved by authors who gave their public what it wanted (they had to), but gave it something consistently better than it could have imagined. Entertainment went hand in hand with improvement; if human nature demanded amusement, it had its better self to be considered too. There is here a code of behavior, as well as a skill of achieve-ment, which in our own times, and with our own standards of practice, should cause us an earnest and critical self-searching.

For what was happening was the direct and highly effective application to social life, and to a popular audience, of the best efforts literary men could bring to bear. By the late seventeenth century many forces were striving for a peaceful society, for a widely disseminated intelligent culture, and for a prose that would communicate clearly and pleasantly. Yet these forces strove against great odds, and one of the impressive things about the period is the ardor with which writers fought for better things. When violent politicians were "throwing Whig and Tory at one another" (the phrase is from the antifanatic statesman George Savile, marquess of Halifax), uni-ty and sanity were needed; when the focus of culture was wavering between court and city, and a large but ill-defined reading public was coming into view, a common basis of intelligence was needed; and when prose was seeking to free itself from uncertain tone, technique, and aim, an assured acceptable style was needed. To see how the periodical essay-ists attended to these needs it is necessary to glance briefly at some historical circumstances.

First are the political and religious circumstances. From 1685 to 1715 there were thirty years of dan-ger. In 1688, James II, swiftly deposed and exiled by a revolution, was replaced by his daughter Mary II and her foreign husband William III. James's son was further excluded from the throne by the impor-tation of a second foreign ruler, George I of Hanover, in 1714; and in 1715 an abortive invasion was attempted in his favor. Party rancor was fierce. Of the political temper about 1690 Halifax writes:

---

[1]This term refers to the most accomplished period of a literature, like that in Rome under the Emperor Augustus; it normally in-dicates the period 1680–1750 in English literature.

There is a flying Squadron on both sides, that are afraid the World should agree, that raise angry Apparitions to keep Men from being reconciled, like Wasps that fly up and down, buzz and sting to keep Men unquiet.

Party journalism, seen at its strongest in Jonathan Swift's *Examiner* papers (1710–1711), was bitter in the early eighteenth century, and Daniel Defoe in his *Review* of 2 August 1712 draws a picture of extreme dissension:

What Distractions in what we expect! What Disorder in what we feel! What Confusion of Counsels! What Division of Parties! What Animosities in these Disputes! And in General what Clashings of Interest are to be found just now, among all the People of this Age! How are the Blessings of Charity, good Neighbourhood, Natural Affections, Civility, good Manners, and in short every Temper necessary to maintain Peace and Prosperity among a Society of People sunk and gone among us!

An equal danger showed itself in religious as in political affairs (the two were often connected), a danger that had exploded in the Civil War (1642–1649) and that still showed itself in violent sermons by High Church extremists and recriminations by the Dissenters against whom they were directed. Here again, men of goodwill felt the need for reconciliation. "No other thing is the better for being *Sower*; and it would be hard that religion should be so, which is the best of things," Halifax observed. His belief was shared by enlightened churchmen—the Latitudinarians (men of the Broad Church movement, who were inspired by the spiritual ideals of the Cambridge Platonists)—who propounded charity and toleration under their renowned leader John Tillotson, archbishop of Canterbury, and whose mildness Gilbert Burnet's *History of My Own Times* (first volume, 1723; second volume, 1734) contrasted with the "narrower thoughts and fiercer temper" of their opponents. In these circumstances Sir Richard Steele and Joseph Addison worked for latitude; the *Tatler* and the *Spectator*, as Samuel Johnson put it, "were published at a time when two parties, loud, restless and violent . . . were agitating the nation: to minds heated with political contest they supplied cooler and more inoffensive reflections."

Men of sense were not content with hauling the nation back from the brink of disaster; they had a large campaign of improvement to promote. There were triumphs of the new science to proclaim; there

was a civilized literary style to practice; there was a busy and advancing civic life to record; there was a whole morality of social conduct to explore in relation to the growing demand for harmony. It was this complex of tasks that the periodical essayists undertook.

EVOLUTION OF THE ESSAY

THE evolution of the essay form first needs a comment. Montaigne's *Essais* (1580) had established the word "essay," and a taste for the form; his method, though resulting sometimes in a long composition, is characteristically easygoing, almost haphazard. In the essay "Of Democritus and Heraclitus" he remarks:

The judgement is a tool adapted for all subjects, and meddles with everything. Therefore, for these trials I make of it, I grasp at any kind of opportunity. . . . I take the first subject that chance offers; they are all equally good to me. And I never purpose to treat them exhaustively.

This is, in fact, the typical method of the essay writer. The first English practitioner was Francis Bacon, whose first ten *Essays* appeared in 1597—"grains of salt which will rather give an appetite than offend with satiety," he called them. Pithy, aphoristic, and stiff at first, Bacon developed in later essays such as "Atheism," "Superstition," and "Truth" a majestic and continuous eloquence. Yet one is not quite at ease with him; eloquent he may be, but with a magisterial eloquence. Nearer to Montaigne's familiar reflectiveness, and the easy manner of the Augustans, are the *Essayes* (in two series, 1600 and 1601) of Sir William Cornwallis. They reach no great heights; they are a personal and honest self-examination, a friendly and unassuming communication. But it is interesting to note this early naturalization in English of the friendly, private manner we credit rather to Abraham Cowley sixty years later, and the readable social advice we credit rather to the Augustans. The essay "Of Discourse" contains, though in a more picturesque idiom, advice an Augustan might well have given:

A Gentleman should talk like a Gentleman, which is, like a wise man. His knowledge ought to be general: it becomes him not to talk of one thing too much or to be weighed down with any particular profession. . . . One knowledge is but one part of a house, a bay-window or a gable-end. Who builds his house so maimed, much less himself? No, be complete.

Cornwallis seems to foreshadow some aspects of Sir Thomas Browne, like the whimsical revelations of *Religio Medici*, the improving precepts of *Christian Morals*; this familiar, Montaigne-like commentary became a favorite mode in the seventeenth century and has ever since remained so. One of its most pleasant exponents was Cowley in his *Discourses by Way of Essays* (1668). Like Horace (whom he often echoes, and translates) he praises the middle way of life, and the following Horatian passage exemplifies the lightness of his tone and touch:

> I know very many men will despise, and some pity me, for this humour as a poor-spirited fellow; but I'm content and, like Horace, thank God for being so. . . . I confess, I love littleness almost in all things. A little convenient Estate, a little cheerful House, a little Company, and a very little Feast, and if ever I were to fall in love again (which is a great Passion, and therefore I hope I have done with it) it would be, I think, with Prettiness, rather than with Majestical Beauty!
>
> ("Of Greatness")

Friendly anecdotes, agreeable displays of his reading, rallying comment on social life, and unfailing charm—these ingredients make his essays a landmark in appealing discourse. They are too light to carry ideas far; instead, they while away the time in good sense and cultured companionship.

Cowley's distinction includes a clear and natural style. The periodical essay could not have arisen without such a style, and its evolution is one of the most notable achievements in English literature after 1660 (though not entirely unknown before). Its first monument is John Dryden's *Essay of Dramatick Poesy* (1668), which is good conversation and fair-minded argument. In the preface to the *Fables* (1700), his last prose work, Dryden refers to "the practice of honest Montaigne," and his own personal commentary, frank manner, well-stored mind, and roaming spirited intelligence recall his predecessor. By the time he wrote the preface, with its famous praise of Chaucer, prose was prepared for all the purposes of social comment, discussion, and entertainment. By that time other writers had

practiced it well, like Tillotson in his sermons, and Halifax in his cogent *Advice to a Daughter* and *Character of a Trimmer*, and Swift's employer, the once-esteemed diplomat Sir William Temple, whom Johnson (overgenerously) called "the first writer who gave cadence to English prose." "Temple," remarks Oliver Goldsmith in the *Bee* (24 November 1759), "wrote always like a man of sense and a gentleman; and his style is the model by which the best prose writers in the reign of Queen Anne formed theirs." "Very harmonious and sweet, full of Spirit and *Raciness of Wit*" was the view of John Hughes in his *Of Style* (1698). Temple's most admired work consists of four essays in the second part of *Miscellanea* (1690)—"Upon Ancient and Modern Learning," "Upon the Gardens of Epicurus," "Upon Heroick Virtue," and "Upon Poetry"—and for the scholar these are still interesting specimens of what the enlightened man of the period thought. Temple uses the essay as a methodical demonstration of serious subjects; he goes through his book learning and treats his topics academically, "like popular lectures," Sir Edmund Gosse devastatingly comments, "by a very ignorant man who presumes upon his genteel appearance and elegant delivery." His matter is now unimportant, but his manner at best has wit and charm, with a good-tempered easy thoughtfulness that was to mean much to Steele and Addison. He can be favorably represented by his best-known passage, the end of the essay "Of Poetry":

> I know very well that many who pretend to be Wise, by the Form of being Grave, are apt to despise both Poetry and Music, as Toys and Trifles too light for the Use or Entertainment of serious Men. But whoever find themselves wholly insensible to their Charms, would I think do well to keep their own Counsel, for fear of Reproaching their own Temper, and bringing the Goodness of their Natures, if not their Understandings, into Question. . . . When all is done, Human Life is at the greatest and best but like a froward Child, that must be play'd with, and Humor'd a little, to keep it quiet, till it falls asleep, and then the Care is over.

Gosse, rightly severe on Temple's contents, is rightly impressed by his style. "If we must not say that Addison was taught by Temple," he observes, "at least it was Temple who taught the public to be ready for Addison." That was no small contribution to public taste.

The credit for establishing the social essay in the periodical, the particular vehicle Steele and Addison were to use, is largely Defoe's. Other men had worked toward it. Sir Roger L'Estrange's *Observator* papers (1681–1687) had question-and-answer dialogues that somewhat dramatized problems of the day, though in a violent party spirit. Edward (Ned) Ward's monthly *London Spy* (November 1698–April 1700), supposedly written by a country scholar who has "found an itching inclination in myself to visit London," describes what he finds there in a lively grotesque way, like the Elizabethan satirists on the one hand (Robert Greene, Thomas Nashe, or Ben Jonson), and the picaresque novelist such as Tobias Smollett on the other. It is vivid, and highly entertaining, but not "polite" letters; one thinks rather of William Hogarth's brilliant caricatures. The same may be said of Tom Brown's agreeable *Amusements Serious and Comical* (1700). The most promising performer before Defoe was his brother-in-law, the bookseller John Dunton, who has been rather too decisively called the father of English journalism. Dunton started the *Athenian Mercury* on 17 March 1690, originally called the *Athenian Gazette*; its title echoed St. Paul's remark that the Athenians "spent their time in nothing else, but either to tell or to hear some new thing." Besides news, the paper contained answers to correspondents, and in them Dunton provided numerous brief essays on social, ethical, and intellectual topics. On these (especially on such as are apt to arouse prejudice, like religion, superstition, and the status of women) he is thoroughly enlightened, a vigorous propagandist for the increasingly vocal conscience of the middle classes.

Defoe drew up his remarkable *Review* (February 1704–June 1713) on similar lines. In the first number he explained that the news ("real History, and just observation") would be followed by "a little Diversion," and this diversion, originally called "*Mercure Scandale*: or advice from the Scandalous Club" (later merely "Advice from the Scandal Club") was to be "*A Weekly History* of Nonsense, Impertinence, Vice and Debauchery." Starting as satire on rival newswriters it soon turned into commentary on social folly, seeking its main targets in drunkenness, inhuman magistrates, the folly of dueling, civil violence (with the outrages of the hooligan "Mohocks"), and the evils of seduction, adultery, and prostitution. As a Whig Dissenter, Defoe was against High Church extremists, but his paper's political tone was quite moderate (much more so than Swift's *Examiner*), and he did his best to spread common sense in political as in social conduct. In a practical, citizenly way, and with the religious earnestness of the Nonconformist, for nine years he urged moderation, humanity, and good behavior on his readers, and sometimes encouraged them to good literature, as when he paid tribute to Addison's *Spectator* papers on "the famous Mr. Milton" (29 March 1712). The title of the club is more titillating than its activities; the "Scandalous Club" is not in itself scandalous, nor does Defoe spread "scandalous" stories. The club is a court of reference, a company of sensible men, who adjudicate on incidents reported to them. These incidents Defoe describes with unfailing realism even when, as sometimes happens, they are allegorical, like the splendidly told story of the "young Lady brought before the Society this Week, in a very strange Condition," wasting away, unfashionably dressed, friendless, expelled from home, excluded from society, shunned in her walks, left "the last of her House, and afraid she should be the last in the Nation." "Her Name," we learn, "was *Modesty*" (8 August 1704). Defoe writes unaffectedly, directly, convincingly; the "Club" device allowed his subjects to be dramatized and was an important lead for future clubs like that of the *Spectator*; and his vivacious but responsible treatment of social morals proved, as his modern editor observes, "an important civilising force among simple readers."[2] He showed what the periodical could do.

THE TATLER

It is with the *Tatler* that the periodical and its essays really emerge into distinction. Steele was one of the remarkable writers of genius with whom Ireland provided England (others, in the eighteenth century, were George Farquhar, Swift, George Berkeley, Goldsmith, Edmund Burke, Laurence Sterne, and Richard Brinsley Sheridan; William Congreve, though born in Yorkshire, had his education at Kilkenny and Dublin). Educated at Oxford, a cap-

[2]Arthur Wellesley Secord, ed., the Facsimile Text Society edition, 22 vols. (New York, 1938). The most convenient form in which to study the *Review* is in W. L. Payne, ed., *The Best of Defoe's Review* (New York, 1951)—a most useful selection.

tain in the Life Guards, writer of comedies, and a political journalist, Steele was a man of warm, impulsive, generous temper, given to heavy drinking and plagued by debts, but, with all his improvidence, an endearing person. His paper ran from April 1709 to January 1711 (271 issues) and, like Defoe's *Review*, was published, the first number explains, on Tuesday, Thursday, and Saturday "for the convenience of the post"—that is, the mail coaches leaving London on those days for the country. The title, the supposed author Isaac Bickerstaff announces, has been taken to honor "the Fair Sex," for the *Tatler* was to appeal not only to the predominantly masculine tastes for politics and economics served by previous papers, but to women as well, and was to comment in a familiar, friendly way on matters of general social interest. Each contribution was to come from the most appropriate source, from the coffeehouse or chocolate house identified with that particular interest: accounts of "Gallantry, Pleasure, and Entertainment" from the fashionable White's Chocolate-House; literary matters from Will's, which Dryden had established as the center of letters; learning from the Grecian, haunt of the clergy; foreign and home news from St. James's, the center of political Whiggery. Above the text appeared the famous motto from Juvenal— *Quicquid agunt Homines nostri Farrago Libelli*— translated in the collected edition as

> Whate'er men do, or say, or think, or dream,
> Our motley paper seizes for its theme.

The *Tatler*'s range is not quite as wide as its motto suggests. It keeps to the normal range of social comedy, pathos, and moral improvement; as Samuel Johnson observes in the *Life of Addison*, its authors are the first "masters of common life," determined to "survey the track of daily conversation and free it from thorns and prickles, which tease the passer though they do not wound him." But within that familiar range it gradually creates a wonderfully complete picture, and the charm with which it does so differentiates it from its predecessors. 'The exceptional feature of *The Tatler*," Peter Smithers comments in his biography of Addison, "was its air of gentlemanly unconcern, its appeal to the world of fashion, and hence, subtly, to that of unfashion." By the multiplicity of its social portraits (continued in later journals) it created a lively comic population of great vivacity and interest.

Addison detected the person of Steele behind the

pseudonym of Bickerstaff, and began to contribute with No. 18. He had been a friend of Steele's since school and Oxford days, and had become well known for political and literary work. Both men tried their hands at comedies for the stage, but they show themselves far better comic dramatists in the essay form, in the animated social scenes and the entertaining persons who populate their pages. Neither tried the novel (which, indeed, was not truly created until Defoe produced *Robinson Crusoe* in 1719), but the spirit and manner of domestic-social fiction—as Henry Fielding was to provide it in *Joseph Andrews*, Goldsmith in *The Vicar of Wakefield*, and Jane Austen in all of her novels— begins to rise from the crisscross of relationships and events in the affairs of the Bickerstaffs (Isaac and his half-sister Jenny), whose comic genealogy by Heneage Twisden appears in the *Tatler* No. 11, and who, among their Staff ancestors, from their native county of Staffordshire, count Falstaff as a forebear.

The aims of the *Tatler*—entertainment and improvement—were strikingly furthered by its authors' ability to place their ideas in concrete situations, to discuss ethical, political, or commercial subjects in realistic or allegorical stories, and in living characterization. Sir Leslie Stephen, in *English Literature and Society in the Eighteenth Century*, points out that the philosophical trend of the time was making intellectual discourse abstract. The periodical essayists reversed this trend; they embedded it in real life. And they did so with a natural ease. Earlier "character" writers such as Sir Thomas Overbury and John Earl had presented vivid social types as set pieces, extracted from the context of normal life. Steele and Addison worked differently. Their portrait gallery is in action, and their moral commentary arises from a living scene. Open the *Tatler* or the *Spectator* where one will, one meets not stiff set descriptions but vivacious dramatic scenes, amusing on the whole, but sometimes (for both Steele and Addison were men of feeling) pathetic and touching. The following, brief as it is, may serve to show the social comedy in action; it is the sketch of the "Pretty Fellow" in the *Tatler* No. 21, and it follows the portrait of Sophronius, "a gentleman of sweet diosition," whose natural, unaffected bearing "that animal we call a pretty fellow" tries unsuccessfully to imitate:

Jack Dimple is his [Sophronius'] perfect mimic, whereby he is, of course, the most unlike him of all men living. Sophronius just now passed into the inner room directly forward: Jack comes as fast after as he can for the right and left looking-glass, in which he had but just approved himself by a nod at each, and marched on. He will meditate within for half an hour, until he thinks he is not careless enough in his air, and come back to the mirror to recollect his forgetfulness.

This has the right economy, the right bantering note, the right familiar style. The manner is skillful; no one could take offense at the humor, but everyone must ask himself whether he looks thus to an amused observer who nevertheless does not plume himself on his superiority, but who represents the pleasant good sense that everyone should approve.

The "Pretty Fellow" is Addison's creation, and the fuller sketch of him in No. 24 helped to make the paper very popular; the same number, in addition to the lively comedies of the "Pretty Fellow," "Very Pretty Fellow," and "Happy Fellow," contains the famous account of the Toasts of the Town, with an anecdote of their origin in Bath, and the rival claims of the vivacious Mistress Gatty and the grave Mistress Frontlet. Addison is not always to modern tastes, least of all in his sermonizing (nor was he, in this respect, to all his contemporaries; "a parson in a tye-wig," the sardonic Bernard Mandeville called him). But for his social comedy, and for Steele's, there must be high praise; there is a spiritedness of fun, a lightness of touch, and an affectionateness of humor that compare well with the same qualities in Goldsmith, William Cowper, or Charles Lamb.

The *Tatler* began with short-winded essays and very miscellaneous contents, including current news. But the last "Continental Intelligence" occurs in No. 83, and as the paper won its hold it concentrated on the social and moral essay, reduced the contents to two themes, or even one, with correspondingly greater fullness, and introduced a generous sprinkling of literary discussion, usually by Addison. Much of this concerns classical reading, but there are comments on plays of Shakespeare and passages of Milton, and treatments of subjects like "the sublime" (No. 43), the expression of grief in tragedy (No. 47), true and false wit (No. 62), the treatment of love (No. 90), the moral power of poetry (No. 98), and poetical commonplaces (Nos. 106, 143, and 163, the particularly amusing paper on Ned Softly).

Though this criticism came mostly from Addison, there is no need here to distinguish methodically between his work and that of Steele, who wrote the majority of the *Tatler* essays. What is more important is the achievement of the paper as a whole. And its liveliest modern impact is made not by its literary criticism but by its social comedy. The material is dramatized excellently, like the entertaining account of Tom Wildair and his father (No. 60), or the philandering Tom Varnish (No. 136), or the visit made to Bickerstaff by some country grandees (No. 86), or the satire on dappers, mettled fellows, coffeehouse statesmen, and others (No. 96), or the political upholsterer (No. 155), or Ned Softly (No. 163). A portrait like the following, in No. 96, is as lively as anything a dramatist could stage:

About two days ago I was walking in the Park and accidentally met a rural Squire . . . with a carriage and behaviour made entirely out of his own head. He was of a bulk and stature larger than ordinary, had a red coat, flung open to show a gay calamanco waistcoat. His periwig fell in a very considerable bush upon each shoulder. His arms naturally swang at an unreasonable distance from his sides; which, with the advantage of a cane that he brandished in a great variety of irregular motions, made it unsafe for any one to walk within several yards of him. In this manner he took up the whole Mall, his spectators moving on each side of it, whilst he cocked up his hat, and marched directly for Westminster.

When Mr. Bickerstaff wishes to reprehend swearing he will do so not in a formal exhortation but in a discussion at his club with a friend, providing a lively anthology of illustrative curses and a richly comic tableau of irate coach passengers in a traffic jam (No. 137). When he discourages sour tempers between husbands and wives he presents the tart comedy of trivial dissension in a dramatic conversation piece (No. 150). And to provide a social context he draws the members of his Trumpet Club (No. 132), Bickerstaff with four garrulous veterans—"the talkative humour of old men"—though the full development of the club idea had to await the *Spectator*.

Characteristically, the Trumpet Club paper ends with a moral reflection on age and wisdom—characteristically, because the *Tatler* does more than hold a mirror up to nature. Steele's first publication, *The Christian Hero* (1701), sought to discover "why the Pagan struts, and the Christian sneaks." Dedicated to his commanding officer, Lord Cutts, as one not sullied by "the fashionable Vice of Exploding [pooh-poohing] Religion," it pleaded not for unthinking credulity but for real religious responsibility. Christianity, not pagan stoicism, is the creed for the man of courage; the life of Christian conscience is better than any amount of classical virtue; and "a certain neglected book which is call'd . . . THE SCRIPTURE" is the best guide to conduct. Steele is one of the earliest and most attractive propagandists for social sympathy, and his generous sense of human nature makes him argue for it warmly, persuasively, though still clear-headedly. He wants a harmonious social life, on religious principles:

God presses us by a Natural Society to a close Union with each other, which is methinks a sort of enlargement of our very selves, when we run into the Ideas, Sensations, and Concerns of our Brethren.

Dedicating to Arthur Maynwaring the first volume of the collected *Tatler*, he explains that he has made it his aim "to pull off the disguises of cunning, vanity, and affectation." When in No. 271 he winds up his task as Bickerstaff he asserts that "the general purpose of the whole has been to recommend truth, innocence, honour, and virtue, as the chief ornaments of life." In No. 3 Bickerstaff says he is "of the 'Society for the Reformation of Manners'"; he is an enemy of viciousness and boorishness—"for, merely as a well-bred man, I cannot bear these enormities." What impressed the reading public was the stress that "as a well-bred man" he laid on decency. Dunton and Defoe had done so, as plebeian journalists; Jeremy Collier, who forcefully arraigned the indecencies of Restoration comedy in his *Immorality and Profaneness of the English Stage* (1698), did so as a High Church parson and was widely supported by the godly. But little had been heard from well-bred men, though, contemporaneously with Steele, one of the best bred, the third earl of Shaftesbury (1671–1713), was writing some extremely elegant persuasives to virtue, collected as his *Characteristicks* in 1711. Moral improvement coming from a popular periodical, urged with politeness, humor, and intelligence, was a new thing—how new, and how influential, John Gay reveals in *The Present State of Wit* (1711):

It would have been a jest, some time since, for a man to have asserted that anything witty could be said in praise of a married state, or that Devotion and Virtue were any way necessary to the character of a Fine Gentleman. . . . His [Bickerstaff's] writings have set all our Wits and Men of Letters on a new way of Thinking. . . . Every one of them writes and thinks much more justly than they did some time since.

The reformed wits, it will be noticed, now think "more justly" than before, more in accordance with true humanity. The *Tatler* and the *Spectator* hold vice, cynicism, ungenerosity, and infidelity to be distortions of man's real self; in *Tatler* No. 111 Addison objects to La Rochefoucauld as one concerned "to depreciate human nature." Fashion and sophistication have gone wrong, as they habitually do. Dr. Johnson's tribute to Addison applies equally to the joint "Bickerstaff" personality Addison shared with Steele:

He not only made the proper use of wit himself, but taught it to others; and from this time it has been generally subservient to the cause of reason and of truth. He has dissipated the prejudice that had long connected gaiety with vice, and easiness of manner with laxity of principles. He has restored virtue to its dignity, and taught innocence not to be ashamed.

What did the *Tatler* do in this regard? It never for long overlooked its moral duty of enlightening as well as its commercial necessity of interesting. In No. 96 Addison mentions "a false opinion, that what I write is designed rather to amuse and entertain, than convince or instruct." Amusingly, but instructively also, he then distinguishes "living" from "dead" men (those with from those without useful lives). "In short," he concludes, "whoever resides in the world without having useful business in it, and passes away an age without ever thinking on the errand for which he was sent hither, is to me a dead man." Common failings and vulgarities are laughed at—practical joking, swearing and vulgar colloquialism, coquetry and pose, the frivolity of society ladies, affected dress, fashionable extravagances of deportment, boorishness, selfishness, swashbuckling, pedantry or dandyism, commercial meanness or narrow-mindedness, and a hundred other impediments to the good society. At the same time evils, as well as follies, are discredited—the recklessness of gambling, the inhumanity of seduction and of dueling, the brutality of hooliganism, the hideousness of cruelty to animals as well as to men. On such subjects the *Tatler*, though not invariably grave in manner (after all, it had to allure its readers), speaks quite forthrightly. Steele had shown courage in courting his fellow officers' mockery by writing *The Christian Hero*; Addison was more discreet, even demure; but neither of them was prepared to let decency and humanity go by default. So in No. 134, having gained the readers' attention with an amusing petition from an incarcerated cock, Steele goes on to show up cockfighting, bear-baiting, and similar popular sports for the ugly things they are. "The virtues of tenderness, compassion, and humanity," he concludes,

> are those by which men are distinguished from brutes, as much as by reason itself; and it would be the greatest reproach to any nation, to distinguish itself from all others by any defect in these particular virtues. . . . When any of these ends [safety, convenience, or nourishment] are not served in the destruction of a living creature, I cannot but pronounce it a great piece of cruelty, if not a kind of murder.

While on the one hand vices are condemned, on the other hand goodness is exalted. In No. 74 Steele prints a letter from a correspondent protesting against destructive or venomous forms of satire and praising "your designed attempt of 'raising merit from obscurity, celebrating virtue in distress and attacking vice in another method, by setting innocence in a proper light.'" Satire abounds in these papers but (as will have been seen) it is satire to tease rather than to infuriate its victims. It may not have turned the vicious from their courses, but it doubtless prevented waverers from following them. And the satire is coupled with encouragements to goodness. Studies of "the noble character of Verus the magistrate" (No. 14), Sophronius the true gentleman (No. 21), Paulo the generous merchant (No. 25), Aspasia the ideal woman (Nos. 42, 49), the value of good breeding (No. 30)—these and many other studies of virtue, often drawn from real life and only thinly disguised, are dispersed through the essays. The institutions of the good society are to be defended against fashionable denigration. "The Wits of this Island, for some fifty years past, instead of correcting the vices of the age, have done all they could to inflame them," Steele protests (No. 159). Marriage, marital harmony, obedience to conscience rather than worldliness, charity, and religious earnestness have been the butts of ridicule. To Steele in particular, devotedly warmhearted toward his wife (his endearments in his letters are delightful), married love was one of the saving values of life. Again and again the *Tatler* speaks out in its favor, as it does also in favor of honor toward women in general. Probably the best-known phrase anywhere in Steele's work is that which concludes

the following praise of Lady Elizabeth Hastings, under the guise of Aspasia (*Tatler* No. 49):

> In this accomplished lady, love is the constant effect, because it is never the design; yet, though her mien carries much more invitation than command, to behold her is an immediate check to loose behaviour; and to love her is a liberal education.

The "Scene of Domestic Felicity" (No. 95), the "Happiness . . . secured in the Married State" (No. 104), the "Characters of an Affectionate Couple" (No. 150)—these and similar papers have a charm of sentiment one hardly expects before Goldsmith. Steele is particularly good at these family companionships. If his best-known single phrase comes in the Aspasia extract above, his best-known single passage is in No. 181, on his childhood memories of his father's death. This has a truth and tenderness of feeling that anticipate Lamb.

THE REGULATION OF VIRTUE

BENEATH the social humor, beneath the generous feeling, there is something deeper. The *Tatler*, like its immediate successors the *Spectator* and the *Guardian*, and Dr. Johnson's *Rambler* and *Idler* later, does not hesitate to recommend religious faith. Among Aspasia's virtues it is related that "without the least affectation she consults retirement, the contemplation of her own being, and that supreme Power which bestowed it. . . . She goes on in a steady course of uninterrupted piety and virtue" (No. 42—the passage is Congreve's). Good conscience alone "can make us pass our days in our own favour and approbation" (No. 48). No. 111, "On the Prevalence of Irreligious Principles," is a midnight meditation on current "looseness of principles" fostered supposedly by would-be scientists and modish "freethinkers." In No. 108 Addison seeks in the arts of life ("the very design of dress, good-breeding, outward ornaments and ceremony . . . as indeed every art and science") the means "to lift up human nature, and set it off to advantage." He concludes:

> But there is nothing which favours and falls in with this natural greatness and dignity of human nature so much as religion, which does not only promise the entire refinement of the mind, but the glorifying of the body, and the immortality of both.

Few tasks are more taxing than to retain a large public for moral exhortations. The *Guardian* (No. 87, 20 June 1713) confessed that "the grave Discourses which I sometimes give the Town do not win so much Attention as lighter Matters." Here the *Tatler*'s strategy was very skillful, and the judgment in linking gravity and frivolity was admirable. As Gay's tribute shows, it was immediately effective. This was largely, one surmises, because of the utter blandness of its assumption, or purported assumption, that of course men of sense were men of virtue; that virtue, though it needed cultivation, was natural to the gentleman. The tone of this assumption may sometimes seem too nonchalant; for instance, No. 5 recommends Swift's *Project for the Advancement of Religion* as "written with the spirit of one who has seen the world enough to undervalue it with good-breeding." "Good-breeding," one may feel, has not much to do with religion's undervaluing of the world. Yet Steele and Addison might well reply in the words "Bickerstaff" uses to explain his light tone in attacking dueling, that "you have chiefly to do with that part of mankind which must be led into reflection by degrees, and you must treat this custom with humour and raillery to get an audience" (No. 26). On these same grounds Johnson defends Addison against the charge of superficiality—"his instructions were such as the character of his readers made proper." Many otherwise unremarkable essays have an amiable presentation of such qualities as modesty, kindliness, and reverence, to encourage the conclusion that "life without the rules of morality is a wayward, uneasy being . . . but under the regulation of virtue, a reasonable and uniform habit of enjoyment" (No. 49). The recommendation of virtue as "enjoyment" is part of the temper of the times. Religion inspired "the soul's calm sunshine and the heartfelt joy" (Pope); a benevolent God attached happiness to the practice of goodness. "Religion is a cheerful thing," Halifax had remarked, "so far from being always at *Cuffs* with *Good Humour*, that it is inseparably united to it." Conventionally, the code of pleasure was that of the rake; Steele and Addison wished to equate it with virtue, and virtue with religion. Man was to be, as Shaftesbury recommended, in "the sweetest disposition" when he thought of spiritual things; religion was to be treated not with the fiery or the gloomy ardors of the seventeenth century but with an air of sweetness and light. Social and religious virtues were to coincide; good sense, good nature, good conscience, even "that inferior art of life and behaviour called good-breeding," were things of Christian even more than of pagan morals. In the next century Cardinal John Henry Newman was to insist on a difference of category—"Liberal Education makes not the Christian . . . but the gentleman." But the *Tatler* insists rather on the equivalence among the three terms. The true gentleman, liberally educated, is to be the true Christian; equally, the true Christian, liberally educated, is to be the true gentleman. And as Steele concluded his enterprise he expressed happily the outlook and manner of the periodical he had created (No. 271):

I must confess it has been a most exquisite pleasure to me to frame characters of domestic life, and put those parts of it which are at least observed into an agreeable view; to inquire into the seeds of vanity and affection, to lay before the readers the emptiness of ambition: in a word, to trace human life through all its mazes and recesses, and show much shorter methods than men ordinarily practise, to be happy, agreeable, and great.

THE SPECTATOR

HARDLY had the *Tatler* expired (January 1711) than the *Spectator* came to birth (March 1711), published six times weekly until December 1712 (555 numbers) and revived in 1714 thrice weekly for a further eighty. It is more famous than its forerunner, and its principal author, Addison, makes a greater, though not more attractive, literary figure than Steele. Son of a clerical father who became dean of Lichfield, educated with Steele at Charterhouse and at Oxford, he became a good classical scholar, a good Latin poet, and a fellow of Magdalen College. While Steele was serving in the Guards, Addison was preparing himself for a diplomatic career by traveling in Europe (1699–1704), and thereafter he held some prominent political offices, being undersecretary of state (1705), member of Parliament (1708–1719), chief secretary to the lord lieutenant of Ireland (1708–1710), and a secretary of state (1718). His verse gained him fame when he celebrated Marlborough's victory at Blenheim in *The Campaign* (1705); his high-minded classical tragedy, *Cato*, had a dazzling reception (1713). But were it not for his essays, Addison's literary reputation would be insignificant; into them, diluted and sweetened for popular consumption, went his classical and modern reading, his study of philosophy and natural science, reflections culled from French critics, and indeed anything that might make learning "polite."

Despite his career, Addison preferred to be a man of letters rather than a man of affairs. The *Tatler* and the *Spectator* show few signs of journalism's normal interest in news, and indeed on the whole they avoided it. The *Spectator*, being a sequel, lacks a touch of the *Tatler's* exhilarating freshness, but from the beginning it had an advantage in being sure of its aim. Instead of the sheaf of short essays with which the *Tatler* had begun, it consists generally of a single one, which allows some length of presentation. The social portraits, good-humored raillery, and moral improvement that the *Tatler* had evolved were the *Spectator's* aims too; it took its stand on a firm idea of what human nature needed. As Addison observed in No. 10:

I shall leave it to my Reader's consideration, whether it is not much better to be let into the knowledge of one's self than to hear what passes in Muscovy or Poland; and to amuse ourselves with such writings as tend to the wearing out of ignorance, passion and prejudice, than such as naturally conduce to inflame hatreds, and make enmities irreconcileable.

Whereas the *Tatler* had included some foreign news, the *Spectator* concerns itself throughout with the social scene and with moral and intellectual themes. "The knowledge of one's self" is that of the best self; it does not include partisanship, and "Mr. Spectator," though leaning occasionally to the Whigs (for example, in No. 3 "The Vision of Public Credit") dissociates himself from political strife. "A man makes an odious and despicable figure, that is violent in a party," he remarks (No. 58); "there cannot be a greater judgment befall a country than such a dreadful spirit of division as rends a government into two distinct people [nations]" (No. 125). Nor does "the knowledge of one's self" include self-centeredness of interest or specialization—among which is included rakishness, the specialization of pleasure. "Bar him [the rake] the play-house, a catalogue of the reigning beauties, and an account of a few fashionable distempers that have befallen him, and you strike him dumb" (No. 105). Mr. Spectator would echo Cornwallis—"Be complete." The standards Dryden had laid down in prefacing the *Miscellaneous Essays* (1692) of Charles de St. Évremond are now not only achieved in essay style but are to be the measures of man in society— "Fineness of Expression and a Delicateness of Thought, the Easiness of a Gentleman, the Exact-

ness of a Scholar, and the Good Sense of a Man of Business."

But lest this all sound too general and abstract, the same point is to be made here as was made about the *Tatler*, that the material is vividly realized in the social scene. The very first account of Mr. Spectator reads like the opening of an autobiographical novel (No. 1):

I was born to a small Hereditary Estate,[3] which I find, by the Writings of the Family, was bounded by the same Hedges and Ditches in *William* the Conqueror's Time that it is at present, and has been delivered down from Father to Son whole and entire, without the Loss or Acquisition of a single Field or Meadow, during the Space of six hundred Years. There goes a Story in the Family, that when my Mother was gone with Child of me about three Months, she dreamt that she was brought to Bed of a Judge: Whether this might proceed from a Law-Suit which was then depending in the Family, or my Father's being a Justice of the Peace, I cannot determine; for I am not so vain as to think it presaged any Dignity that I should arrive at in my future Life, though that was the Interpretation which the Neighbourhood put upon it. The Gravity of my Behaviour at my very first Appearance in the World, and all the Time that I sucked, seemed to favour my Mother's Dream: For, as she has often told me, I threw away my Rattle before I was two Months old, and would not make use of my Coral 'till they had taken away the Bells from it.

Thereafter, Mr. Spectator tells his readers, he has been a studious and silent schoolboy and college scholar, an observant traveler, and a quiet onlooker at social resorts, "rather as a Spectator on mankind than as one of the Species"; from points of discreet advantage he comments on the lives of others. Yet, onlooker though he may be, he immediately surrounds himself with company, the famous Spectator Club drawn first by Steele in No. 2 and by its varied interests improving greatly on the *Review's* Scandal Club and the *Tatler's* Trumpet Club. At its head is Sir Roger de Coverley, the jovial, eccentric, kindly, elderly, Tory country squire. Then there is Sir Andrew Freeport, "a merchant of great eminence," embodying city interests, Whig commerce, and progressiveness; then an Inner Temple lawyer; then Captain Sentry, "a gentleman of great courage, good understanding, but invincible modesty";

---

[3]This account is fictional. It is true that Addison was born in the remote West Country village of Milston, in Wiltshire, where his father, Lancelot Addison, was rector; but the "estate," a church living, was not and could not be hereditary. In fact his father came from Westmorland in the north of England.

then Will Honeycomb, a sociable man-about-town; and finally "a clergyman, a very philosophic man, of general learning, great sanctity of life, and the most exact good-breeding." The club is not, in fact, much used as a device, though Sir Roger is developed through a series of papers that is the *Spectator*'s most enduring attraction;[4] but it symbolizes the range and sympathy of outlook that the paper displayed, appreciative equally of professional worth, social manners, and religious seriousness, and of the old-fashioned country Tory and the enterprising city merchant (both types apt to be butts of satire). Addison speaks of the club as "very luckily composed of such persons as are engaged in different ways of life," so that different members of the public may be assured "that there is always somebody present who will take care of their respective interests" (No. 34). The club reminded readers, in an age of sectarian passion, that they should live together as a family, reproving real vice but looking on harmless differences of outlook and interest as a rich variegation of the nation's essential unity.

The *Spectator*, even more than the *Tatler*, is famous for the variety and vividness of its social panorama. The scope of London's life, and something of the country's, is mirrored—coffeehouse life with its debates, news sheets, clubs of common interests (even the common interests of oddities), and indeed its whole routine (Sir Roger sits down to "a clean pipe, a paper of tobacco, a dish of coffee, and the supplement" [of Defoe's *Review*]). We observe street scenes; commercial houses (No. 69 creates a splendid pattern of Royal Exchange activity and the romance behind the process of trade); moneyed and trading interests (Nos. 21 and 108 recommend business); theaters with accounts of performers and performances (and fun at the extravagances of the reigning Italian opera); current gossip; street cries; churches great and small; the ships and traffic of the Thames; fashions and fashionable affectations; and, beyond the town, the country with its sports, superstitions, and the comedy of its old-fashioned social life. The figure of Sir Roger flits through these scenes with his amiable eccentricities, tiffing good-humoredly with Sir Andrew at the club, distrusting any but elderly coachmen, engaging none but war-

wounded ferrymen when he goes on the Thames, discoursing in old-fashioned commonplaces upon the great men buried in Westminster Abbey, choosing to stay at uncomfortable Tory inns rather than comfortable Whig ones, and so on.

The series in which Mr. Spectator visits Sir Roger in the country (Nos. 106–132) provides an attractive picture of country manners. The Coverley household is served by veteran retainers who have grown old in Sir Roger's service, and indeed by veteran dogs and horses too; his old valet de chambre is like a brother, his butler is gray-haired, his coachman has "the looks of a privy counsellor." They love him, as he does them and indeed all his tenants, after whose welfare he solicitously inquires when he meets them at church. His chaplain is a venerable and kindly man, a good shepherd to his flock, an equally good backgammon opponent for Sir Roger, a seeker of charity for his parishioners but never for himself. Sir Roger is seen in his occupations and amusements, guiding his estate, conversing with fellow country gentlemen like Will Wimble, the expert in matters of game, or the acquaintances whose touchiness over precedence he must not offend. He is presented in his portrait gallery with his ancestors, in his hall with the trophies of the chase, on the judgment bench as a justice of the peace, having his palm read and pocket picked by gypsies, furnishing the church with texts and hassocks and prayer books as well as keeping the congregation in order, and being "a little puzzled" as to whether an old crone is a witch or not. We walk through his fields, attend his church services, are romantically impressed by a ruined abbey on his grounds, with aged elms and a rookery, and feel "a certain transport which raises us above ordinary life" in his country scenes. One of the brightest papers, No. 116, is by neither Addison nor Steele but Addison's cousin Eustace Budgell; it is a truly delightful account of Sir Roger's pack of hounds and a hunting scene, a vivid, lively, colorful, and traditionally English episode.

In No. 16 Addison had set his target high—"It is not my intention to sink the dignity of this my paper with reflections upon red heels or topknots, but rather to enter into the passions of mankind and to correct those depraved sentiments that give birth to all those little extravagancies which appear in their dress and behaviour." But this, though true, is too restrictive. In the first place, a large part of the paper's charm lies in its red heels, topknots, and so on—in the vivid externals of life; and in the second,

---

[4]The main series runs from No. 106 to No. 132, but Sir Roger makes scattered appearances up to No. 517 when Addison, foreseeing the end of the paper, caused his death to be reported to save him from maltreatment by other pens.

it goes higher than "little extravagancies." A famous statement of aims in No. 10 speaks of bringing philosophy out "to dwell in clubs and assemblies, at tea-tables and in coffee-houses." "Philosophy" is a comprehensive term for many kinds of knowledge and wisdom, and on many matters the *Spectator* conveys to its readers the best thought of its time. If its treatment is somewhat glib, Johnson's defense is still a just one, that "that general knowledge which now [1779] circulates in common talk was in his time rarely to be found . . . and in the female world any acquaintance with books was distinguished only to be censured." Delicate tactics of presentation were called for; as the *Tatler* had assumed it to be self-evident that self-respect and virtue go together, so the *Spectator* purports to assume that self-respect naturally goes with intelligence and a taste for "polite writing" (No. 58). By this simple flattery Addison and his collaborators were able to introduce a large circle of readers to such subjects as the criticism of tragedy (Nos. 39, 40, 42, 44), true and false wit (Nos. 23, 38, 59–63), recommendations of ballad simplicity (Nos. 70, 74), the morality or immorality of comedy (Nos. 65, 270, 446), "the Pleasures of the Imagination" (Nos. 411–421, a very significant and long-influential set on the subjects that inspire the mind), and a repeated treatment of Milton (over twenty papers between Nos. 267 and 463).

Not least impressive of the *Spectator*'s campaigns was that by which it popularized science, "the new philosophy," as a reinforcement of religious faith. No. 120 sees in the natural adaptation of animals a demonstration of God's beneficence; No. 387 rejoices in the beauties the microscope reveals in the minutest creatures; No. 393 asserts that natural philosophy "raises such rational admiration in the soul as is little inferior to devotion." In No. 465 Addison quotes Psalm 19—"The heavens declare the glory of God; and the firmament sheweth his handiwork"—and ends with his fine hymn on the stars in their courses, "The spacious firmament on high." No. 565 again quotes the Psalms (Psalm 8—"When I consider thy heavens, the work of thy fingers: the moon and the stars, which thou hast ordained"), and then dwells on the vastness of stellar space as astronomy was revealing it, concluding with confidence in God's omnipresence and omniscience.[5] The presiding geniuses of the new thought are saluted: Copernicus, René Descartes, Francis

Bacon, John Locke, Christiaan Huygens, Robert Boyle, and particularly Isaac Newton, still alive and boundlessly revered. In the *Guardian* No. 175, Steele adds William Derham, author of *Physico-Theology* (1713), who "does, as with a wand, show us the wonders and spectacles of all nature, and the particular capacities with which all living creatures are endowed for their several ways of life." Most important of all, science fed faith and imagination too. The finest of many statements of its power, in these papers, is Addison's praise in the *Spectator* No. 420 of "the authors of the new philosophy" for demonstrating, through the whole range from infinitesimally small to infinitely vast, the wonders of God in creation, by which we are "confounded with the immensity and magnificence of nature." On such themes the *Spectator* achieves a high eloquence.

A few years earlier it would have seemed inconceivable that such extended intellectual themes should appear in a popular journal, and if the language is somewhat bland the conviction of purpose behind it is impressive. It is equally so in the many papers that encourage social harmony and good sense, that "endeavour to enliven morality with wit, and to temper wit with morality" (No. 10), or satirize national prejudices (No. 50), or attack political violence (No. 125), or recommend good nature (Nos. 169, 177), or meditate on the transience of life (No. 26, on the tombs in Westminster Abbey; No. 159, the "Vision of Mirza," on life and death). The tone may be light, but it induces a serious idea, as when amusing anecdotes of credulous superstitions lead to recommendations of confidence in a merciful God (Nos. 7, 12), or light comedy on political passions in women turns into a plea for true womanly distinction at home (Nos. 57, 81). In particular, Addison, the "parson in a tyewig," campaigned for charitable religion against narrow fanatics or mocking skeptics.[6] In No. 445 he spoke with sturdy confidence of his aims and methods:

If I have any other merit in me, it is that I have new-pointed all the batteries of ridicule. They have been generally planted against persons who have appeared serious rather than absurd; or at best, have aimed rather at what is unfashionable than what is vicious. For my

---

[5]To similar effect are Nos. 571, 580, 590, and 628.

[6]For example, in Nos. 93, 106, 111, 112, 147, 185, 186, 201, 257, 356, 378, 381, 441, 459, 461, 465, 519, 531, 538, 543, 571, and 600; the list is far from exhaustive.

own part, I have endeavoured to make nothing ridiculous that is not in some measure criminal. I have set up the immoral man as the object of derision. In short, if I have not formed a new weapon against vice and irreligion, I have at least shown how that weapon may be put to a right use.

LATER PERIODICALS

STEELE's and Addison's subsequent periodicals can only be touched on. Between the suspension of the *Spectator* in December 1712 and its resumption in June 1714, Steele launched the *Guardian*, which ran daily from March to October 1713 (175 issues). Addison came in with No. 67 (having been preoccupied with his tragedy *Cato*) and thereafter wrote more than fifty papers. The most distinguished of the other contributors were Pope and Berkeley. The *Guardian* is not particularly distinguishable from the *Tatler* or the *Spectator*: the formula had been found satisfactory and the recipe continued as before. "The Guardian" himself is an elderly gentleman, "Nestor Ironside," friend of the country family of the Lizards and guardian to an excellent young landowner, Sir Harry Lizard, whose kindly but efficient estate owning is the model for other country gentlemen (No. 6). This family circle, under the excellent Lady Aspasia (No. 2), with her lively daughters (No. 5) and variously gifted sons (No. 13), gives Steele the chance he likes for domestic sentiment, coming appropriately from the kindly, elderly Nestor. One other portrait is notable, that of the wealthy merchant Mr. Charwell (No. 9), retiring to a country estate and increasing the countryside's prosperity with a practical wisdom that would have pleased Defoe. The range of the *Guardian* is the normal one: there are outright attacks on seduction (Nos. 17, 45, 123), dueling (Nos. 20, 129), and cruelty (No. 61, by Pope), and particularly an earnest but witty campaign by Berkeley (seconded by Steele) for a benign religious faith and against freethinkers. The tone of this latter campaign is light, for tactical reasons—"I must not be rough to gentlemen and ladies, but speak of sin as a gentleman," says Steele demurely (No. 17); even so, it considerably reduced the paper's popularity. Good miscellaneous essays are those on the miseries of the poor, and charity (Nos. 79, 166), charity schools (No. 105), rival periodical essayists (No. 98), natural phenomena as evidence of God's goodness (Nos. 103, 169, 175), and natural taste in gardens (No. 173, by Pope). Some papers discuss literature and poetic style (Nos. 4, 12, 15, 16, 25), and Thomas Tickell contributed five on the pastoral (Nos. 22, 23, 28, 30, 32). His praise of Ambrose Philips roused Pope to send anonymously to Steele the very humorous No. 40, an ironic puff for Philips' pastorals at the expense of Pope's own. Not penetrating the irony, Steele sought Pope's permission before publishing and was gravely encouraged to proceed. This paper, with Pope's famous "Receipt to make an Epic Poem" (No. 78), is the *Guardian*'s most entertaining exercise in comedy.

Steele launched several papers of less significance—the *Reader* (1714), *Town Talk* (1715), *Chitchat* (1716), the *Tea-Table* (1716), and, as his last venture, the *Theatre* (1720). Addison was to assist in one other, the *Lover* (February–May 1714), though of forty numbers he furnished only two. The main theme of this is one dear to Steele, "the softer affections of the mind" (No. 1), and the main contents relate to affairs of the heart, a novel and attractively managed bias of interest. Addison contributed No. 10, on women and their craze for the newly fashionable chinaware ("playthings for women of all ages"), and No. 39, on the love-crossed Will Wormgood, and on Theophrastus' *Characters* as translated by Budgell.

Steele's further relationship with Addison was less happy. Suddenly terminating the *Guardian*, he started the *Englishman* without Addison's aid (two series with a total of ninety-five numbers; October 1713–February 1714; July–November 1715). This calls itself "a sequel of the GUARDIAN" and claims to have taken over Nestor Ironside's assets. The first series keeps up some *Guardian* traits with appearances of the Lizard family and the usual comic, pathetic, or moralizing papers on social and religious topics, though the most interesting single number relates the adventures of Alexander Selkirk, the shipwrecked sailor (No. 26), and perhaps prompted Defoe to write *Robinson Crusoe*. But intermittently through the first series, and unremittingly through the second, runs "a particular regard to the Protestant interest in the world" (No. 53), a strong Whig campaign against the Tory *Examiner*, the pope, Louis XIV, and the exiled Stuart line. "This Paper," Steele admits in winding up the first series, "has exposed me to much Hatred and Invective," but politics had gripped him, and it was a political quarrel that estranged the former friends.

Addison himself was meanwhile proving to be a party publicist of skill; his *Whig Examiner* (September–October 1712; five numbers) counterblasts the Tory *Examiner*, which, it says, should rather be called the *Executioner*. In it Addison shows, as Johnson remarks, "all the force of gay malevolence and humorous satire." Much more important was his *Free-Holder* (December 1715–June 1716; fifty-five numbers). This stoutly supports the new Hanoverian king, George I, praising him as guardian of civil liberties and constitutional government, and it attacks the "Popish Pretender" and despotic power. "Every Englishman," it asserts, "will be a good subject to King George, in proportion as he is a good Englishman, and a lover of the constitution of his country" (No. 18). The paper's great merit is that it is written with much dignity and spirit, and a rollicking good humor. In circumstances of pressing political crisis, when other men were angry and bitter, Addison shows his best qualities; he is extremely amusing, but reasonable and constructive too. In No. 8 he addresses not only irritated politicians but society women at their tea tables, and does so with little of the irritating patronage that is elsewhere disagreeable in him:

It happens very luckily for the interest of the Whigs, that their enemies acknowledge the finest women of Great Britain to be of their party. The Tories are forced to borrow their toasts from their very antagonists, and can scarce find beauties enough of their own side, to supply a single round. . . . One may, indeed, sometimes discover among the malignants of the sex a face that seems to have been naturally designed for a Whig lady: but then it is so often flushed with rage, or soured with disappointments, that one cannot but be troubled to see it thrown away upon the owner. Would the pretty malecontent be persuaded to love her king and country, it would diffuse a cheerfulness through all her features and give her quite another air.

Among the best-known *Free-Holders*, and rich examples of partisan comedy, are the three papers on the Tory foxhunter (Nos. 22, 44, 47), the ludicrous, blundering reactionary countryman with all the comic ignorance of rustic bigotry, whom the Whigs liked to equate with the Tory squirearchy.

Addison, then, as well as Steele, could show his powers in politics. Unfortunately, in the last year of his life (1719), Steele and he quarreled over a point of constitutional procedure, in the *Plebeian* and the *Old Whig* respectively. No journals could have been much shorter-lived: the *Plebeian* ran for four

issues, the *Old Whig* for two. But the damage was done; the old friends were estranged, and before a reconciliation could take place, Addison died. Steele, harassed by debts, left London for Wales, and there, isolated, died in 1729.

CONCLUSION

I f any literary form is the particular creation and the particular mirror of the Augustan age in England it is the periodical essay. It was immensely popular; the *Cambridge Bibliography of English Literature* lists ninety periodicals founded between the *Tatler* in 1709 and 1720. Nathan Drake's *Essays Illustrative of The Tatler* (1805) enumerates 221 papers in the *Tatler* tradition current during the eighteenth century, though of course many were almost stillborn. "It may well be called the age of Counsellors, when every Blockhead who could write his own name attempted to inform and amuse the public," said Lewis Theobald. Circulations are hard to calculate; modern scholars put Defoe's *Review* somewhere between 3,000 (which Addison claims in No. 10) and 9,000 at its height. Each of the many copies displayed in coffeehouses would be read by many readers, so the effect of the papers would far outstrip their relatively small circulation.

The modern response to them is naturally cooler than the contemporary, for reasons that must almost always apply to ephemeral writing. And while Steele's personality still appeals warmly, Addison's has lost much favor since the idolizing Victorian days when Thomas Macaulay confessed for him "a sentiment as much like affection as any sentiment can be which is inspired by one who has been sleeping a hundred and twenty years in Westminster Abbey." "Always a somewhat superior person," say A. E. Dyson and John Butt;[7] "undoubtedly something of a prig," comments Bonamy Dobrée. T. S. Eliot feels "something very like antipathy" for him; C. S. Lewis thinks he would be "the most hated of our writers" if he were not so little read. There is something in this; the historical estimate is bound to put him higher than the literary one. "Neither Steele nor Addison is really a great writer," is Oliver Elton's verdict.[8] Yet even the literary estimate, though discovering in the

---

[7] In *Augustans and Romantics* (London, 1940), p. 57.
[8] In *The Augustan Ages* (London, 1899), p. 295.

essays little that is for all time, must admit the responsibility of aim, the comprehensiveness of grasp, and often the richness of comedy, that these papers show. The didacticism, with the genteel tone and the patronizing "fair-sexing it," may indeed irritate, but any modern journal that in three years produced a cultural revolution comparable with that the *Tatler* or the *Spectator* achieved would be a remarkably welcome phenomenon. The modern writer is not likely to follow Johnson's famous advice and "give his days and nights to the volumes of Addison"; it is nevertheless true that Addison developed prose with great skill, a skill excellently analyzed in Jan Lannering's *Studies in the Prose Style of Joseph Addison* (1951). His easy continuity and coherence were what prose was looking for, after the more spasmodic, even if more spirited, manner of even his greatest contemporaries like Dryden and Swift. From a study of his work and Steele's we may gain, first, an intimate, varied, and vivid picture of Augustan society, and, second, a renewed faith that men and women of intelligence, by striving for the good society, can bring it nearer, and indeed must do so.

SELECTED BIBLIOGRAPHY

I. BIBLIOGRAPHY. Detailed bibliographical information can also be found in the appropriate volume of the *Cambridge Bibliography of English Literature* and the *Oxford History of English Literature*. R. S. Crane and F. B. Kaye, *A Census of British Newspapers and Periodicals, 1620–1800* (Chapel Hill, N. C., 1927); K. K. Weed and R. P. Bond, *Studies in British Newspapers and Periodicals from Their Beginning to 1800: A Bibliography* (Chapel Hill, N. C., 1946).

II. COLLECTIONS AND ANTHOLOGIES. A. Chalmers, *The British Essayists; with Prefaces, Historical and Biographical*, 45 vols. (London, 1802–1803); R. Lynam, ed., *The British Essayists*, 30 vols. (London, 1827); G. Carver, ed., *Periodical Essays of the Eighteenth Century* (New York, 1930); M. G. Segar, ed., *Essays from Eighteenth Century Periodicals* (London, 1947).

III. GENERAL STUDIES. N. Drake, *Essays Biographical, Critical, and Historical, Illustrative of the Tatler, etc.*, 3 vols. (London, 1805); W. C. Hazlitt, *The English Comic Writers* (London, 1819); J. Spence, *Literary Anecdotes*, S. W. Singer, ed. (London, 1820); W. M. Thackeray, *The English Humourists of the Eighteenth Century* (London, 1853); L. Stephen, *English Literature and Society in the Eighteenth Century* (London, 1904); H. Walker, *The English Essay and Essayists* (London, 1915); G. S. Marr, *The Periodical Essayists of the Eighteenth Century* (London, 1923); W. Graham, *English Literary Periodicals* (New York, 1930), contains a useful bibliography; A. Beljame, *Men of Letters and the English Public, 1660–1744*, E. O. Lorimer, trans., B. Dobrée, ed. (London, 1948), originally published in French (Paris, 1881); R. P. Bond, *Contemporaries of the Tatler and Spectator* (Los Angeles, 1954), the Augustan Reprint Society; W. B. Ewald, *The Newsmen of Queen Anne* (London, 1956); D. H. Bond and W. R. McLeod, eds., *Newsletters to Newspapers: Eighteenth-Century Journalism* (Morgantown, W. Va., 1977), includes important essays on Addison and Steele.

IV. ESSAYISTS. *Before Defoe*: F. Bacon, *Essayes* (London, 1597; enl. eds., 1612, 1625); W. Cornwallis, *Essays* (London, 1600, 1601), in D. C. Allen, ed. (Baltimore, 1946); J. Florio, trans., *The Essayes, or Morall, Politike, and Militairie Discourses of Lo: Michaell de Montaigne* (London, 1603); T. Sprat, ed., *The Works of Mr. Abraham Cowley* (London, 1668), in A. R. Waller, ed., 2 vols. (Cambridge, 1905–1906); W. Temple, *Miscellanea*, 3 parts (London, 1680, 1690, 1701), the second is the most relevant to the periodical essay; R. L'Estrange, *The Observator, in Question and Answer* (London, 1681–1687); J. Dunton, *The Athenian Gazette; or, Casuistical Mercury, Resolving All the Most Nice and Curious Questions Proposed by the Ingenious* (London, 1690–1697), retitled *The Athenian Mercury* with the second number though each vol. bore the whole original title, anthologized as *The Athenian Oracle*, 3 vols. (London, 1704); E. (Ned) Ward, *The London Spy* (London, 1698–1700), in A. L. Hayward, ed. (London, 1927), with some expurgation; T. Brown, *Amusements Serious and Comical* (London, 1700), in A. L. Hayward, ed. (London, 1927), with other works; W. P. Ker, ed., *The Essays of John Dryden*, 2 vols. (Oxford, 1900); J. E. Spingarn, ed., *Essays on Ancient and Modern Learning and on Poetry by Sir William Temple* (Oxford, 1909); W. A. Raleigh, ed., *The Complete Works of George Savile, First Marquess of Halifax* (Oxford, 1912); G. Kitchen, *Sir Roger L'Estrange: A Contribution to the History of the Press in the Seventeenth Century* (London, 1913); F. J. C. Hearnshaw, ed., *Social and Political Ideas of Some English Thinkers of the Augustan Age* (London, 1928); C. Marburg, *Sir William Temple: Seventeenth-Century "Libertin"* (Chicago, 1929); H. E. Woodbridge, *Temple: The Man and His Work* (New York, 1940); H. W. Troyer, *Ned Ward of Grub Street* (Cambridge, Mass., 1946).

Defoe: D. Defoe, *A Weekly Review of the Affairs of France* (London, 1704–1713), continued successively as *A Review of the Affairs of France* and *A Review of the State of the English Nation*, in A. W. Secord, ed., 22 vols. (New York, 1938), complete facs. repr. for Facsimile Text Society, *Index* by W. L. Payne (New York, 1948); W. L. Payne, ed., *The Best of Defoe's "Review": An Anthology* (New York, 1951), contains a useful intro.; J. Sutherland,

Defoe (London, 1937), see also Sutherland's essay in this vol.; F. Watson, *Defoe* (London, 1952); J. T. Boulton, ed., *Selected Writings of Daniel Defoe* (London, 1965; repr. Cambridge, 1975); J. Sutherland, *Daniel Defoe: A Critical Study* (Cambridge, Mass., 1971).

Steele: R. Steele, *The Christian Hero: An Argument Proving that No Principles but Those of Religion Are Sufficient to Make a Great Man* (London, 1701), in R. Blanchard, ed. (Oxford, 1932), with a good intro.; "Isaac Bickerstaff" [R. Steele, J. Addison, et al.], *Tatler* (12 Apr. 1709–2 Jan. 1711), 271 nos. of which Steele wrote about 188 alone and shared about 36 with Addison, often repr. either with other periodicals (see "Collections and Anthologies" above) or separately as in G. A. Aitkin, ed., 4 vols. (London, 1898–1899), selections in Everyman's Library; "Mr. Spectator" [J. Addison, R. Steele, et al.], *Spectator* (1 Mar. 1711–6 Dec. 1712; 18 June–29 Sept. 1741), 635 nos. of which Steele wrote about 236 nos., often repr. either with other periodicals (see "Collections and Anthologies" above) or separately as in Bohn's Standard Library (London, 1854–1856), G. G. Smith, ed., 8 vols. (London, 1897–1899), and in Everyman's Library— D. F. Bond, ed., 5 vols. (Oxford, 1965), with intro. and notes, the definitive ed.; *Guardian* (12 Mar.–1 Oct. 1713), 175 nos. of which Steele wrote 82, repr. with other periodicals (see "Collections and Anthologies" above); *The Englishman: Being the Sequel to the Guardian* (6 Oct. 1713–15 Feb. 1714), 57 nos. of which Steele wrote 41, in R. Blanchard, ed. (Oxford, 1955), contains a good intro.; *The Englishman: Volume II* (11 July–21 Nov. 1715), all 38 nos. by Steele, included in R. Blanchard's ed. above; "Marmaduke Myrtle, Gent." [R. Steele], *Lover* (25 Mar.–27 May 1714), 40 nos. including 2 by Addison; *Reader* (22 Apr.–10 May 1714), 9 nos. including 2 by Addison; *Town-Talk* (17 Dec. 1715–13 Feb. 1716), 9 nos.; R. Blanchard, ed., *Periodical Journalism, 1714–1716* (Oxford, 1959), reprints *Lover, Reader*, and *Town-Talk*; *Plebeian* (14 Mar.–6 Apr. 1719), 4 nos.; *Theatre* (2 Jan.–5 Apr. 1720), 28 nos., in J. Loftis, ed. (Oxford, 1962); J. Gay, *The Present State of Wit* (London, 1711), in D. F. Bond, ed. (Ann Arbor, Mich., 1947), the Augustan Reprint Society, repr. in E. Arber, ed., *An English Garner*, vol. VI (Birmingham, 1883); N. Drake, *Essays . . . Illustrative of the Tatler*, 3 vols. (London, 1805); A. Dobson, *Selections* (London, 1885), contains an intro.; A. Dobson, *Richard Steele* (London, 1886); G. A. Aitkin, *Richard Steele*, 2 vols. (London, 1889), the standard biography.

L. E. Steele, *Selected Essays* (London, 1902); W. Connely, *Sir Richard Steele* (London, 1934); C. Winton, *Captain Steele* (London, 1964); D. F. Bond, ed., *Critical Essays from "The Spectator"* (London, 1970); C. Winton, *Sir Richard Steele, M. P.: The Later Career* (Baltimore, 1970); R. P. Bond, *"The Tatler": The Making of a Literary Journal* (Cambridge, Mass., 1971); D. McDonald, ed., *Joseph Addison and Richard Steele: Selected Essays from*

"The Tatler," "The Spectator," and "The Guardian" (Indianapolis, 1971); D. Kay, *Short Fiction in "The Spectator"* (University, Ala., 1975).

Addison: *Tatler*, see under "Steele" above, Addison wrote about 46 nos. alone and about 36 with Steele; *Whig Examiner* (14 Sept.–12 Oct. 1710), 5 nos.; *Spectator*, see under "Steele" above, Addison wrote about 298 nos.; *Guardian*, see under "Steele" above, Addison wrote about 51 nos.; *Lover*, see under "Steele" above, Addison wrote 2 nos.; *Reader*, see under "Steele" above, Addison wrote 2 nos.; *Free-Holder* (23 Dec. 1715–29 June 1716), 55 nos., in J. Lenehy, ed. (Oxford, 1979), with intro. and notes, the definitive ed.; *Old Whig* (19 Mar.–2 Apr. 1719), 2 nos.; T. Tickell, ed., *Works*, 4 vols. (London, 1721), in R. Hurd, ed., 6 vols. (London, 1811), repr. in the Bohn Standard Library, 6 vols. (1854–1856); S. Johnson, *Lives of the English Poets* (London, 1779–1781); T. B. Macaulay, *Critical and Historical Essays* (London, 1843); J. R. Green, ed., *Essays* (London, 1880); W. J. Courthope, *Addison* (London, 1884), in the English Men of Letters series; W. Lewin, ed., *The Lover, with Other Papers of Steele and Addison* (London, 1887); A. Symons, ed., *Sir Roger de Coverley, and Other Essays from "The Spectator"* (London, 1905); A. Dobson, *Selected Essays* (London, 1906); J. G. Fraser, ed., *Essays*, 2 vols. (London, 1915); B. Dobrée, *Essays in Biography, 1680–1726* (Oxford, 1925); W. Graham, ed., *Letters* (Oxford, 1941); *Essays on the Eighteenth Century Presented to David Nichol Smith* (Oxford, 1945), contains an essay by C. S. Lewis on Addison; J. Lannering, *Studies in the Prose Style of Joseph Addison* (Uppsala, 1951); P. Smithers, *The Life of Joseph Addison* (Oxford, 1954; repr. 1968), the standard life; E. A. Bloom and L. D. Bloom, *Joseph Addison's Sociable Animal: In the Marketplace, on the Hustings, in the Pulpit* (Providence, 1971); J. Loftis, ed., *Essays in Criticism and Literary Theory* (Northbrook, Ill., 1975).

Swift: T. Scott, ed., *The Prose Works of Jonathan Swift*, vol. IX (London, 1902), contains Swift's contributions to the *Tatler*, the *Examiner*, the *Spectator*, and the *Intelligencer*; H. Davis, ed., *Political Tracts, 1711–1713* (Oxford, 1951), contains some *Examiner* papers, this and three following collections are separate vols. in the Shakespeare Head ed. of *The Prose Works of Jonathan Swift*; H. Davis and I. Ehrenpreis, *Political Tracts, 1713–1719* (Oxford, 1953), contains Swift's onslaught on Steele, "The Importance of the *Guardian* Considered"; J. M. Murry, *Jonathan Swift* (London, 1955; rev. ed., 1965; repr. 1979); H. Davis, *The Examiner and Other Pieces Written in 1710–1711* (Oxford, 1957), contains an excellent intro.; H. Davis, *Bickerstaff Papers* (Oxford, 1957), contains some *Tatler* papers; I. Ehrenpreis, *Swift: The Man, His Works, the Age*: vol. I, *Mr. Swift and His Contemporaries* (London, 1962); vol. II, *Dr. Swift* (London, 1967), the standard biography, third vol. in progress.

ROBERT LOUIS STEVENSON

(1850-1894)

G. B. Stern

ROBERT LOUIS STEVENSON was born on 13 November 1850; he died in 1894. His stepdaughter remembers a note he wrote his wife bidding her not delay too long with his biography after his death, for "my fame will not last more than four years." By this modest and perfectly sincere estimate, we can imagine how astonished he would have been in 1935 at a set of Samoan stamps showing his grave on the crest of Mount Vaea and his house, Vailima; and another, rarer issue in 1939 commemorating the twenty-fifth anniversary of the Australian landing on the island at the outbreak of the 1914–1918 war, somewhat irrelevantly pictured with a head of Robert Louis Stevenson. Even more amazed would he have been by the centenary in 1950 that in print and on the air honored his name and proclaimed a longer life than even a hundred years for *Treasure Island* (1883), *The Strange Case of Dr. Jekyll and Mr. Hyde* (1886), and the two brief verses of "Requiem" (1887), if for no other of his writings.

It is hardly possible now to open a newspaper or a magazine without seeing "Jekyll and Hyde" quoted either as a caption or in illustration of some debatable point of modern schizophrenia. "Home is the sailor, home from the sea" is quoted nearly as often; in fact, at moments it becomes quite a struggle not to quote it. And the films have given *Treasure Island* as vivid a resurrection as any nineteenth-century writer could have desired who unconsciously employed such an excellent film technique as Stevenson; he said himself that he visualized his novels in a series of small, bright, restless pictures; "Thus with imagined wing our swift scene flies / In motion . . ." says the Chorus in Shakespeare's *Henry V*. And *The Wrecker* (1892), for instance, employing the speed, energy, and facility of the camera "on location," might certainly have been originally planned in terms of celluloid.

The Wrecker, however, is not to be listed among his books that have survived in equal popularity with *Treasure Island* and *Jekyll and Hyde*. Survival and popularity, as we are all aware, are capricious matters and play tricks that no one can ever foresee. Without doubt, his finest work was poured into the first few chapters of *Weir of Hermiston* (1896), *Kidnapped* (1886), two-thirds of *The Master of Ballantrae* (1888), a half-dozen of his short stories, about three poems, a generous handful of the letters he wrote spontaneously from all over the world to his friends and family, and one immortal letter that he sent to be published with the title *An Open Letter to the Revd. Dr. Hyde in Defence of Father Damien* (1890).

The London in which Stevenson pretended to have set the drama of *Jekyll and Hyde*, had it been called Timbuktu or Athens, would even then have been clearly recognizable as his native Edinburgh. G. K. Chesterton was probably the first to stress the significance of this, noticing how strangely Stevenson always produced his most vital work under the stimulus of banishment—strangely, because creative artists are said to draw constant nourishment from the soil where their roots are deeply planted and to wilt in exile—yet if we except *Treasure Island*, Stevenson was not dominated by an urgent need to write stories of Scotland till he left it behind him for good. And in comic proof that his nostalgia was reversible, *Treasure Island*, an aching for adventure in the fierce tropical heat of the Caribbean, was mostly written in the mists and gray cold of Braemar. Certainly when he conceived *Kidnapped* and *Jekyll and Hyde* in Bournemouth, his exile from Scotland was not yet such a histrionic affair as it would be in future years, when a sudden view from his high, snowy hut at Saranac was so poignantly to remind him of the Solway shore that straightway he began to write *The Master of Ballantrae*. It was a masterpiece even though he kept the scene at Durrisdeer—the enemy brothers fighting their duel by candlelight "in a windless stricture of frost" provides one of those unforgettable scenes of literature which have been far too often overlooked, to be classed with that other tremendous fight in *Kidnapped*, when Alan Breck and David Balfour defend themselves against a crew of fifteen in the roundhouse of the brig *Covenant:*

The sword in his hand flashed like quicksilver into the huddle of our fleeing enemies. . . . "And O, man," he cried in a kind of ecstasy, "am I no a bonny fighter?"[1]

The Master of Ballantrae can be read as a story of a dual personality less obviously confined in one body than Jekyll and Hyde. Two brothers stand for good and bad, love and hate. And in the course of time, hate wins. Henry, the gentle and the kind, is justified in hating James, incarnation of fascinating evil, if hate were ever justified. But James grows no less wicked while we have to watch Henry, a slave to his obsession, gradually drained of all good . . . till in the end, Henry and James are the same—and again Hyde has conquered Jekyll. Sir Arthur Quiller-Couch was later to develop that sinister idea in a novel called *Foe-Farrell*, which may well have been inspired by *The Master of Ballantrae;* for Quiller-Couch was one of Stevenson's ardent disciples; he it was who exclaimed for all the band of younger writers, on hearing of the death of Stevenson: "Now there's no one left to write for!" And to him was entrusted the task of finishing Stevenson's *St. Ives* (1897), the book which started with a breathtaking narrative of a French prisoner's escape from Edinburgh Castle.

"Inspiration": the act of drawing air into the lungs. So says the dictionary. Thus a vivid memory of Edinburgh, its force and impact, its authentic speech, character, and flavor, was enough of inspiration for those magnificent scenes in *Weir of Hermiston* between the stern old Justice-Clerk and his rebellious only son. It may truthfully be said of Stevenson that all his days were brave, but that in his early youth they were also days of bravado; and it had taken him more than twenty years to realize how his own father had suffered in the clash of opinions with a headstrong only son. In that one scene of *Weir*, Thomas Stevenson, engineer to the Commissioners of Northern Lights, stern Puritan and deeply loving father, was at last triumphantly understood.

And in the same book, the pure moorland air up by the Praying Weaver's Stone at Cauldstaneslap, where Archie Weir and Christina Elliot discover and confess their love, put an end to a notion that Stevenson could not write a great love scene. Indeed, his special genius may be described as this useful power of identification with each of his characters; "A Lodging for the Night,"[2] where François Villon, after assisting in a brutal tavern murder, stumbles in terrified flight through the snow-covered streets of medieval Paris, does not merit our praise for its virtuosity alone, nor for its strict economy of phrase and adjective, but because the same man who at the end of his life could plunder the soul of Adam Weir, here, fairly near the beginning of his career, could also by inspiration—identification—what you will!—enter fully into the motives, philosophy, and rationalizations of a fifteenth-century poet and scamp. And Villon's sardonic reactions to normal good treatment, displayed in argument with his courteous host, the Seigneur de Brisetout, are as exciting as the pace and action of the earlier half of the story.

One can find many similar examples of Stevenson's uncanny coalition with villainy. All the people in *The Ebb-Tide* (1894) are horrible—one does not so much read the last few chapters as feel them crawling up one's spine; and Long John Silver, James Durie of Ballantrae, or Jekyll's schizophrenic double, Hyde, might really cause readers to wonder whether he could present Brother Good without Sister Dull as an inevitable companion . . . till David Balfour, Jim Hawkins, Kirstie and her enchanting niece Christina join the procession of his living characters. In *Notes on Novelists* (1914) Henry James said of Stevenson, "he belongs to the class who have both matter and manner, whom life carries swiftly before it, and who communicate and signal as they go." He very rarely "communicated" in poetry, and when he did he wrote his verses literally like an amateur; that is to say, like an impetuous fellow in love; not, as when he wrote prose, with the severe self-discipline of a professional unremittingly engaged in a life-and-death struggle with style. Which is probably why critics are rather apt to underrate the stature, or rather the depth, of an occasional poem embodying his creed.

[1]*The Works of Robert Louis Stevenson*, Tusitala ed., 35 vols. (London, 1923–1924), vol. VI, p. 67. All references are to this edition unless otherwise noted.

[2]Appeared originally in *Temple Bar*, October 1877; included in *New Arabian Nights*, 2 vols. (London, 1882), vol. I.

To thrill with the joy of girded men
To go on for ever and fail and go on again,
And be mauled to the earth and arise,
And contend for the shade of a word and a thing not
　　seen with the eyes:
With the half of a broken hope for a pillow at night
That somehow the right is the right
And the smooth shall bloom from the rough:
Lord, if that were enough?[3]

To browse through any of the several uniform editions of Stevenson's works must bring the conclusion that there is nothing uniform about them except their bindings. As we race through the titles, it emerges clearly, however, that to dismiss him as the author of "no more than a handful of stories for boys" is not only a fallacy, but a fallacy so preposterous that only Stevenson himself could be forgiven for such a statement, spoken once to his stepson, Lloyd Osbourne, in a mood of weariness shortly before his death. True that when he had grown to be a celebrity in a big way, a midshipman from H.M.S. *Curaçao,* hospitably made free of the library at Vailima, suddenly exclaimed, "Good Lord, I never realized! *He's* the josser who wrote *Treasure Island."* True, also, that elderly men gulped down *Treasure Island,* unashamed to have become boys for a spell; though when it was reported to the author how William Gladstone read it through in a night, he merely remarked coldly that Gladstone would have done better to have attended to the business of the Empire. For Stevenson was by nature a hero-worshiper, a passionate champion of lost causes, and he could not forgive the prime minister responsible for General Charles Gordon's death on the steps of the Residency at Khartoum.

But setting aside *Treasure Island* and *Kidnapped,* nobody in his senses would benevolently produce *The Ebb-Tide* as suitable literature for juveniles; nor, with all its promising title, *The Wrecker;* nor the tale of what happened on the Beach of Falesà; nor *The Master of Ballantrae;* nor *Weir of Hermiston;* nor *Jekyll and Hyde;* nor *Father Damien.* In short, and after a brief biographical sequence of events and dates, one could draw up a fairly adequate survey of the life and works of Robert Louis Stevenson by investigating and if necessary clearing away every fallacy that has grown up to surround and obscure the truth.

[3]From "If This Were Faith," poem no. 24 of *Songs of Travel* in *Works,* vol. XXII, p. 147.

But first the sequence.

His father, Thomas, was a son of Robert Stevenson, founder of the family of lighthouse engineers who built Skerryvore, Bell Rock, and other famous towers round the rocky coast of Scotland. His mother was Margaret, youngest daughter of the Reverend Lewis Balfour, minister at Colinton. A French strain in the Balfours became evident in the appearance of Robert Louis Stevenson and in his gaiety and resilience that conflicted with the Scottish strain of melancholy, integrity, and forthrightness inherited from the Stevenson side. He was a delicate only child, adored by his parents and "Cummy," his devoted nurse, a strongly religious woman with a dramatic vein, from whose fund of stories about the Covenanters he drew his passionate interest in that dour portion of his country's history. To her he dedicated *A Child's Garden of Verses* (1885): ". . . From the sick child now well and old"—but the sick child was rarely to be well and never old. It is strange that the Stevensons remained so long in 8 Howard Place, the gloomy, sunless house where Louis was born; much mischief had been done by the time he was three and they moved to Inverleith Terrace, and four years later to 17 Heriot Row. Thomas Stevenson had no rigid ideas about education; he was a delightful playmate, content that Louis' attendance at school should be irregular and undistinguished. Sometimes his mother took him abroad for his health and hers, and often he stayed with a throng of cousins at Colinton Manse, holidays happily commemorated in *A Child's Garden of Verses.* Several of his essays, notably "A Penny Plain and Twopence Coloured" and "The Lantern Bearers," would never have been written had he not played enthusiastically with a toy theater or joined other boy adventurers with evil-smelling lanterns strapped under their coats.

When Louis was seventeen, his father bought Swanston Cottage in the Pentland Hills near Edinburgh. Louis loved Swanston, loved his long rambles with his father or alone over the slopes of Allermuir, Caerketton, and Halkerside—his "hills of home." Thomas Stevenson took it for granted that presently he would enter the family profession, but Louis soon showed that he was temperamentally and physically unsuited for superintending the construction of harbors and lighthouses on the bleak windswept coast of Fife; so he was allowed to go to Edinburgh University on condition that he study law and leave writing to be a sideline. The young man idled, loafed, took up with the wrong companions, and caused serious anxiety at home and grimly disapproving looks from the "unco' guid" citizens of Edinburgh by his wayward, extravagant behavior; he did eventually obtain his law degree and, surprisingly, even a Silver Medal from the Royal Scottish Society of Arts for reading a paper on a new form of intermittent light.

Violent quarrels with his father on conduct and religion led to their tragic estrangement; and seriously affected by the unhappiness and misunderstandings that surrounded him, Louis fell ill. He was sent for convalescence to some cousins in Suffolk. Here, in 1873, he met Mrs. Sitwell, who, until he married, was to be the strongest influence in his life. Mrs. Sitwell made him consult a lung specialist. "Ordered South" was the verdict, and he stayed for several months in the south of France, writing and slowly recuperating. But before he went, she introduced him to Sidney Colvin, and they encouraged young Stevenson to become a professional writer. Through Colvin's good offices, he succeeded in getting his first essay, "Roads," published in *The Portfolio* (vol. 4, November 1873), using the initials that were to become his signature tune: R.L.S.

Back again from the Riviera, some of his essays were accepted by the *Cornhill* magazine; and he was taken by the editor, Leslie Stephen, to see another contributor, William Ernest Henley, who was having treatment under Dr. Joseph Lister at the Edinburgh Infirmary. A memorable friendship sprang up; and when Henley was appointed to the editorship of the *London* magazine, R.L.S. contributed the *New Arabian Nights*. This, however, did not immediately follow their first encounter; for in 1876, R.L.S. joined his cousin R. A. M. "Bob" Stevenson in a long, careless sojourn with the artists' colony at Barbizon. From a canoe trip through the canals, waterways, and rivers of northern France, he gained material for his first book, *An Inland Voyage* (1878). On his return to the Forest of Fontainebleau, he saw and fell in love with Fanny Osbourne, a beautiful married woman from Indiana, staying at the inn at Grez with her two children, Isobel and Lloyd. The next two years he spent his summers with her in France, his winters in Edinburgh, and established a growing reputation as a writer, mainly with essays on a variety of literary subjects. In 1878, Fanny Osbourne felt she had to return to her husband in California, and R.L.S. went on his lonely travels with a donkey in the Cevennes (Modestine was chosen by several children in a centenary competi-

tion for an essay on Stevenson's most bewitching character!).

A year later, hearing that Fanny, ill and unhappy, was starting divorce proceedings, Stevenson wrenched himself from his home, his parents, and his potential career, and against the strong advice of all his friends (Henley's went beyond all reason), followed her to California. He chose to travel steerage to New York and again fell dangerously ill from the further drastic experience of crossing the plains of America in the emigrant train. Twice he nearly died, first at Monterey and then in San Francisco, where he struggled through conditions of stark poverty to maintain himself by his writing without appealing for help from home. Finally, gaunt as a wolf and hardly able to stand, he married Fanny. The doctor told her he could not live more than a few months; she kept him alive and creative for fourteen years. After their honeymoon in the California mountains, where he wrote *The Silverado Squatters* (1883), a longed-for reconciliation with his parents drew him back again to Scotland, bringing his wife and his stepson, Lloyd Osbourne. Mr. and Mrs. Thomas Stevenson soon became tenderly attached to Fanny; and she and Louis alternated between summers spent with them at Pitlochry and Braemar, and winters in Davos, Switzerland. On a rainy day in the Highlands, Stevenson began writing *Treasure Island* to amuse Lloyd—and himself. He finished it at Davos in 1882, and it ran as a serial in *Young Folks*, where it was oddly unsuccessful with its juvenile readers. His lungs could not stand the climate of Scotland, and three times they had to go on those weary pilgrimages to the Swiss mountains; but in whatever state of bad health, except when he was nearly dying, he could not afford to let up on his writing. Besides finishing *Treasure Island* at Davos, he produced a first-class biography: the "Memoir" of Fleeming Jenkin (1887), tribute of gratitude to a dead friend, the university professor who had had the perception to stand by him in "the coiled perplexities of youth," during his wild odyssey through the taverns and brothels of Edinburgh.

In 1882, he and Fanny moved to the South of France. Châlet la Solitude at Hyères was their first home together and he said of it, years afterward, in a letter, "I've only been happy once, at Hyères." There he wrote *Prince Otto* (1885) and exultantly put on record that he received a hundred guineas from Cassells for the publishing rights of *Treasure Island*, which seemed to him then a very large sum.

A dangerous hemorrhage brought him to the state

of lying in a dark room, forbidden to speak, his arm strapped to his side; rendered incapable of sterner efforts as a wage earner, he scribbled a great many letters, a lot of gay nonsense, and most of *A Child's Garden of Verses*. On receiving news that Thomas Stevenson was failing, they returned and settled down at Bournemouth in a house his father bought for Fanny, which Louis chose to call Skerryvore.

During most of their three years in Bournemouth, Stevenson was confined to his detested bed, an apparently incurable invalid. *Kidnapped* brought him an unsensational meed of fame; but there was the desperate nightmare of perpetually needing money that probably evoked the actual nightmare, which was to find it. *The Strange Case of Dr Jekyll and Mr Hyde* leapt at once into amazingly big sales; it was pirated in America, where its popularity brought Stevenson his first experience, half astonished, half amused, as an idol of the public. For in 1887, after his father's death, he crossed the Atlantic on board the *Ludgate Hill*, with his mother, Fanny, Lloyd, and a merry cargo of apes and stallions.

In New York he soon had enough of adulation; his health collapsed once more, and he was banished to Saranac, the American equivalent of Davos, a small health resort high in the Adirondacks. Here was born *The Master of Ballantrae*, and, in collaboration with young Lloyd Osbourne, a gorgeous piece of buffoonery, *The Wrong Box* (1889).

After a biting winter in the snows, his American publisher, Scribners, commissioned a volume on the South Seas. Stevenson used his patrimony to charter a luxury yacht in San Francisco, and, still accompanied by his family, sailed on the *Casco* for the Marquesas, Tahiti, and the Sandwich (Hawaiian) Islands, a voyage that was a significant success from every point of view except the book itself; commissioned work never suited him, for the results were always labored, overly scrupulous, and disappointing, and he then had to cope with misgivings as to whether in honesty he should return the advances and cancel the contracts.

Once at sea, his health and activities were always miraculous to those who had hitherto only known him as an invalid on land. He struck up enduring friendships with native kings, dark warriors and princesses, traders and sailors and missionaries of all nations, and with a touching group of lepers, old men and children, whom he encountered on his visit to the island of Molokai. In 1889, he paid off the *Casco*, Mrs. Thomas Stevenson returned to Scotland, and he stayed on with Fanny and Lloyd for

nearly six months at Honolulu, where he finished *The Master of Ballantrae* and *The Wrong Box*. Then he went on a further exploration of the more uncharted archipelagos of the South Pacific, finally making harbor at Apia, on Opolu, one of the Samoan Islands (the sequence of Robert Louis Stevenson's addresses is a horror to any conscientious biographer). They were so delighted with the climate and the beauty of the place that they bought an estate halfway up Mount Vaea, where he and Fanny proposed to build a house in which to spend their winters. It fell out, however, that another serious hemorrhage at Sydney, on their way home in 1890, caused him to be forbidden on pain of death ever to revisit Europe or any temperate zone; the tropics were his only chance. So with what grace he could muster—and to accept misfortune with good grace was among his happier talents—he built Vailima; sent Lloyd back to Edinburgh and Bournemouth to collect their furniture; and joined by his mother and Fanny's daughter, Isobel Strong, with her little son Austin, settled in Samoa till his death. During this last fruitful period he wrote *Catriona* (1893), *The Wrecker, The Ebb-Tide, Records of a Family of Engineers* (1912), *St. Ives*, several poems and ballads, four striking South Sea tales to be published as *Island Nights' Entertainments* (1893), and those immortal chapters of *Weir of Hermiston* published posthumously in 1896. His stepdaughter, Belle, to whom he dictated them, relates how instinctively he found the right word, the right sentence, and the right incident, as though he had written it all before and only had to reel it off from memory.

At Vailima he lived as a sort of chieftain, visited by pilgrims and friends from all over the world. His native staff were devoted to him, and he had all the generous instincts of a Scottish clansman in his abundant hospitality toward his own kin, friends, and strangers—"distance no object." In the troubled politics and wars of Samoa, the weaker side as usual claimed his quixotic support; and he could not bear to remain a mere spectator at the defeat and banishment of the rebel King Mataafa whom he knew to be "the one man of governing capacity among the native chiefs, and whom, in the interest alike of whites and natives, he had desired to see the Powers not crush, but conciliate."

It would be literally true to say that since 1888, Stevenson's friends and readers had lost sight of him; which must mean that a man is either forgotten or becomes a legend while he is still alive. The spate and vitality of his intimate letters made it impossible that he should be forgotten, and his situation contributed to a tuppence-colored legend that he would have repudiated with real exasperation, for it was alien to his nature to assume importance. John Steinbeck relates an incident heard from an old woman who in her childhood had had an encounter with R.L.S. at Monterey. "It's not bad fun," he remarked, after the little girl had cheated him over a sale of blueberries, "it's not bad fun, to be made a fool of for ten cents!"

But the man was overstrained and overworked, and his friends' project for an Edinburgh collected edition failed to reassure him that he might now safely take a rest for a while. On 3 December 1894, he was struck down by a cerebral hemorrhage and died within two hours.

Certain men have provocative personalities: H. G. Wells once remarked a little sadly, "I don't know how it is, but whenever [a famous contemporary's] name is mentioned, there's a respectful hush, but when it's mine, there's a dog-fight!" The remark would be as true of Stevenson as of Wells; mention his name, and still, where anything is known about him at all, the result will not be indifference or calm, high hymns of praise, but a dogfight; for his centenary revealed that far from being moribund, a casual reference to Robert Louis Stevenson will cause as much red blood to spurt as made the decks slippery on board the brig *Covenant*.

Jekyll and Hyde was his first huge selling success in England and America; he wrote it as a shilling shocker, and it became popular at once and ever after as a symbolic portrayal of the dual nature of man, with the moral inverted: not to impress us by the victory of good over evil, but to warn us of the strength and ultimate triumph of evil over good once sin is suffered to enter human habitation. Yet neither was Jekyll intended as a simple personification of good, but as good trying to keep up appearances, good wishing to maintain its prestige while it stealthily enjoys "going to the bad"; the author obviously regarded him as a contemptible Quisling who failed to put up any resistance movement against the invader. He once remarked to Andrew Lang, with admirable brevity: "I want to write about a fellow who was two fellows"; and in a letter discussing the interdependence of Jekyll and Hyde, he admitted to an old dingdong battle which perpetually preoccupies the disreputable human soul: "the only thing I feel dreadful about is that damned old business of the war in the members." It cannot be denied that he was inordinately fond of sermoniz-

ing—"I shall preach on my death-bed"—but he always found a more vivid medium in fiction, through narrative and character, than when he indulged himself with composing half-hour sermons for an imaginary pulpit.

It is well known how he originally dreamed "this fine bogey tale" and finished it in three days of furious writing, and then burned the draft and rewrote it in another three days, deferring to his wife's objection that he had left out the allegory. Long afterward, Stevenson alluded to the book, casually, as the worst thing he had ever done; he never harbored pretty illusions about his own work. Although rueful and ashamed that his own angel always seemed to put up such a poor show, he was no hypocritical weakling like Jekyll; and whatever enemy he carried within him, it utterly lacked the callous cruelty of Hyde.

"The legend goes" is a scornful phrase used with conviction by both sides in a battle; for nearly every biography will reveal a small but willful partiality, an almost invisible pendulum swing toward this pile of evidence or that: "Codlin's the friend, not Short." . . . And where the matter rests upon surmise, the subconscious has to choose between a discreet and somewhat irritating type of biographical softpedaling—"we need touch but lightly on"—or an inevitable swing over to the brutal realism of the Debunking School, which has found a peculiar satisfaction in stressing the early swashbuckling period of an author whom they considered had received more than his share of sentimental idolatry. Stevenson's fellow Scot, James M. Barrie, referred to "R.L.S., these familiar initials . . . the best beloved in recent literature"; and this has helped toward an odd notion that to think of Stevenson by his surname, not by his initials, made all the difference between a realistic approach or an attitude of whimsical tenderness— which seems to indicate that every biography of George Bernard Shaw referring to him as G.B.S. must necessarily mean that we are dandling him in our arms!

Probably Robert Louis Stevenson signed his earlier essays with his initials for the sake of convenience and brevity; he could hardly have known that after his death they would be condemned as a culpable form of petting party. On the other hand, the pro-Stevenson brigade often damage their own cause by reproducing portraits of a picturesque invalid with untidy hair lapping his shoulders and a smile of ineffable sweetness. (It must have been one of those that the little Samoan boy Pola threw on the floor when, directly after Tusitala's[4] death, he begged for his "sun-shadow." "'I will not have that!' he cried. 'It is pig-faced. It is not the shadow of our chief.' He leaned against the door and wept.") That long hair of Stevenson's has become the favorite object of ridicule for the scornful. He may have started it in a period of youthful folly, from the desire to be unconventional; and later, while he lived in a northern climate, in perpetual danger of tuberculosis, his doctors would not allow him out for fear of cold. But every portrait extant from the South Seas during the four years before his death shows the fallacy of still considering this fantastically thin man as an invalid: his hair was short, his clothes as normal as comfort and the tropical climate permitted; he spent hours every day in the saddle without fatigue, galloping over rough country; and he spent days and weeks at sea on a tramp steamer, never noticing the lack of amenities in the questionable jollity of thrashing through typhoon and hurricane.

Gardening in its herbaceous-border sense had never appealed to him at Bournemouth, but at Vailima this feeble dilettante hacked down trees and tore up masses of jungle growth before he even settled down to his morning's professional work. He laughed when threatened with expatriation by the furious German officials at Apia, but there was no laughter in his reaction to the news that Mataafa's warriors were being foully treated in prison. Everyone was afraid to interfere till Stevenson went storming down to the rescue in one of his crusading rages, bringing his men loaded with food, setting them to light the great ovens and clean out the stinking cells, attending to the victims who had been flogged through the streets, bringing the doctor to attend to them (and paying for it), and finally shaming the officials till they could no longer look the other way while these monstrous abuses were not only denounced but remedied by that troublesome writer who so maddeningly refused to mind his own business and remain writing nice books in his nice home halfway up a mountain.

For at all instances of cruelty or injustice to the oppressed, he flared up in a moment. From his childhood he had wanted to be a soldier; he loved fighting, but, he said, hated people to be angry with him—"the uncomfortable effect of fighting"—shrewdly laying his finger on the weak spot. And

[4]Tusitala was the Samoan name for Stevenson.

should one appear to dwell overlong on Stevenson's personality at the expense of concentrating on his work—or works—it would only be a false detachment to allot him a final place in literature without an attempt to understand that what he was, and why, must include so much of what he did and how. Writers like Byron or Robert Burns, Percy Bysshe Shelley or Stevenson are handicapped through the possession of a certain exciting quality in their makeup and the involuntary drama of their death. Neither was he at all the type conveyed in that nauseating phrase, "a man with the heart of a boy"; his faults were essentially those of an adult male: a strong, hot temper with frequent use of strong, hot language; inconsiderate on a really grand scale (despite all his natural kindness) as regards the physical comfort of those around him, having himself no use for physical comfort; improvident in his generosity; wildly extravagant, and then given to moods of deep melancholy at the resulting state of his affairs.

When we encounter Henley's "assassin" review in the *Pall Mall* magazine, eight years after Stevenson's death, his lament for a lost friend whose genius had (apparently) been thwarted, hampered, enslaved, intimidated, deluded, badgered, and forced into mere wage earning by the gloomy, respectable, material-minded woman with whom he had been press-ganged into marriage, we are up against another fallacy of such controversial proportions that it would take several volumes to go into the matter thoroughly and sift delusion from fact. Fanny Stevenson's place has often been in the doghouse; but Colvin left behind, for the guidance of "all future biographers of R.L.S.," a round authoritative statement beginning:

With reference to the causes of estrangement and in the actual quarrel, between Stevenson's widow and sometime old friend William Ernest Henley, it ought to be publicly known that the wife had ample and just cause for regarding the friendship as one that entailed risks to Louis's health and should be discouraged accordingly.

As we are most concerned with the indictment that his wife ruined his writing for the sake of material gain, let us point out that Stevenson certainly did write many promising essays before he married, and also *Travels with a Donkey* (1879), *An Inland Voyage*, *New Arabian Nights* (1882), *The Amateur Emigrant* (1895), and *Across the Plains* (1892). But *after* he married Fanny Osbourne, besides the best of his short stories, he wrote *Treasure Island, Kidnapped, Catriona, Jekyll and Hyde, The Master of Ballantrae, Father Damien, The Ebb-Tide,* and *Weir of Hermiston*—titles that speak for themselves. As for deploring her continual wary eye on the main chance, letters extant show that it was Colvin, not Fanny, who tried to hold him back from publishing *The Ebb-Tide,* a grim, squalid, powerful tale which might easily have spoiled his sales as a purveyor of juvenile fiction. And when Stevenson flamed out into his *Open Letter in Defence of Father Damien* and read it to his family, gravely warning them that its publication might result in a libel action and the loss of all they had, she was the first to cry in a white heat of enthusiasm, "Print it! Publish it!" In the dedication to *Weir of Hermiston,* he set down what may surely be taken for fair corroboration of his wife's influence.

> Take thou the writing; thine it is. For who
> Burnished the sword, blew on the drowsy coal,
> Held still the target higher . . . who but thou?
> (*Works*, vol. XVI, p. xxi)

Another absurd fallacy has been that he hated his father, whom, nevertheless, he speaks of in a letter as "ever my dearest"; and in an essay of wonderful tenderness and perception, from *Memories and Portraits* (1887), he pays him a tribute of which any father might be proud. For undoubtedly R.L.S. honors the sound achievement of the "Lighthouse Stevensons" far beyond his own as an author.

> Say not of me that weakly I declined
> The labours of my sires and fled the sea,
> The towers we founded and the lamps we lit,
> To play at home with paper like a child.[5]

His summing-up of Lord Justice Weir—"steadfastly mounting the great bare staircase of his duty, uncheered and undepressed"—betrays again that no man could hope to win Stevenson by flamboyant exploits; he may have created Alan Breck for our delight, but we cannot suppose he thought him a character to emulate. Furthermore, in a letter to Henry James, he underlines his steady preference: "The world must return some day to the word 'duty,' and be done with the word 'reward.' There are no rewards, and plenty duties."

And that he was never, in the responsible sense of the phrase, the breadwinner and head of his own household is a fallacy so damaging to his good repute that it should still be examined, contradicted, and once and for all thrown away. A hundred quotations from published letters, as well as from those not intended for publication, endorse his despair when illness tore gaps in his financial independence and corroborate his passionate desire, at whatever expense of sweat and toil, to stand on his own feet and support a family without having to appeal for money to a wealthy father. Curious that the swashbuckling author of *Treasure Island* should have been in essence "a family man"; he liked having his family always around him—his mother, his wife, his two stepchildren, Lloyd and Belle, and Belle's little son Austin; liked to gather them under his roof-tree, declaring that they alone made exile bearable. His native staff looked up to Tusitala with more reverence as a father and a wise man than as a teller of tales; and as a father, he took trouble to make them see the ethics of why certain things may not be done: when any of them was caught out in wrongdoing, he held a formal court of justice to make sure of the full truth before inventing a mild punishment to fit the crime. The collection of prayers he wrote, so often derided as merely fit for the nursery, were indeed deliberately written for the nursery; that is, for the clear understanding of those native converts to Christianity. This aspect of the white man's burden, combined with running a large estate, local politics, entertaining recklessly, and writing for a living, make it the more remarkable that he should have remained all his life so passionately preoccupied with the campaign for upholding literary style.

There are those who often contemptuously dismiss Stevenson as "a mere stylist"; as though a talent that was in the highest degree competent and fastidious counted for no more than a prinking among words, stepping daintily along an imitation pergola, a sort of picot edging to the silk. When he was young he scribbled that fatal phrase, "I have played the sedulous ape"; Sir Max Beerbohm, with his nonchalant gift for hitting the nail on the head, supposed that this must be "permanently kept in type in the journalistic offices . . . so frequently is it quoted against him." Yet a neophyte who was later to develop into a magnificent stylist could ill afford *not* to play the sedulous ape; it meant no more than that

---

[5]Poem no. 38 from *Underwoods,* book I, in *Works,* vol. XXII, p. 95.

he did not tumble into style as a child tumbles into water, but studied it more consciously and conscientiously than young writers usually do, by examining the technique of his great masters in craftsmanship. Speaking of himself as "a working man," he assumed a title which he thoroughly deserved; he treated words courteously, not mangling them, though he confessed that his chief temptation was always "to cut the flesh off the bones." An old lady, Miss Adelaide Boodle, to whom he gave lessons in style when she was a girl and who was persona grata at their house in Bournemouth, wrote a delightful book about the Stevensons, where the very voice of R.L.S. can be heard teaching her how to write and breaking her heart twenty times on every page: "Never let a long sentence get out of hand," he said to her. Did he ever think to say it to his friend Henry James?

The friendship between Stevenson and Henry James, those unlikely bedfellows in literature, is brilliantly discussed in *A Record of Friendship and Criticism*, published in 1948 by Janet Adam Smith. Both these writers cared intensely about style, and believed in the future of literature as warriors go on believing in a cause that might sometimes look as though it were already lost. Stevenson's amusing piece of doggerel, "The Pirate and the Apothecary," might well stand for their prototypes; for it would be difficult to find a greater contrast than the pirate in his characteristic mood of courage and laughing despair, and the apothecary, meticulously weighing out his scruples and his sentences, tasting, measuring, conscientiously concerned as to their exact effect. This volume should rate high among the first half-dozen of a vast Stevenson bibliography, revealing how in their too rare conversation pieces as well as in their voluminous correspondence both men recognized that a work of imagination must live by its own laws and only take so much from life as serves its purpose. Apothecaries do not, however, always dose themselves, and James's own style is a fairly potent reason why one would be more likely to choose G. K. Chesterton's estimate of Stevenson as a stylist.

The real defect of Stevenson as a writer, so far from being a sort of silken trifling and superficial or superfluous embroidery, was that he simplified so much that he lost some of the complexity of real life. He treated everything with an economy of detail and a suppression of irrelevance which had at last something about it stark and unnatural. He is to be commended among authors for sticking to the point; but real people do not stick quite so stubbornly to

the point as that. . . . Though he may seem to describe his subject in detail, he describes it to be done with it; and he does not return to the subject. He never says anything needlessly; above all, he never says anything twice.[6]

Nevertheless, and after all this, it must be admitted that, for some perplexing reason, Stevenson is not always *readable*; he demands an effort—no, fairer to say an initial effort; humor is not lacking, nor irony, nor the element of surprise, nor a plenitude of swift, exciting action; and the characters are sometimes disconcertingly alive—look at Alan Breck. The fault may be in our laziness to take trouble over an author already removed from contemporary interest, but not yet dead so long that we can surrender our reluctance to be rushed back from the present into the past.

But these strictures do not apply to his letters, which are undated in both senses of the word and wholly delightful, excepting only a batch published separately as *Vailima Letters* (1895), containing densely packed descriptions of his existence in Samoa, the scenery, climate, manners, customs, politics, flora, and fauna of the place. Not having time to waste in writing of these twice over, he suggested to Sidney Colvin that they should be kept and docketed for publication after his death and thus help provide for his family. But the hundreds of his other letters were intimate and spontaneous, not deliberately produced; they have been miscalled the letters of an egoist—again a fallacy; certainly they show a healthy—we underline the word—a *healthy* interest in himself and his mental processes, in his changes of heart as well as his actual doings, but nothing to compare with their vital interest in his friends, displayed in a fury of questions as to their affairs and their work; delight in their successes, compassion for their personal news, indignation over wrongs done to them, eagerness to help at any cost to himself. Surely here is no record of egoism? And surely no egoist had friends as he had friends?

Friendship is a keepsake word, but it must form an essential feature of a writer's biography if we are to understand the different influences at different times of his life. Thus without his friend Henley, Stevenson might never have wasted his small reserve of nervous energy on writing plays, very bad, very rumbustious plays. Or he might have written better

[6]G. K. Chesterton, *Robert Louis Stevenson* (London, 1927; repr. New York, 1955), pp. 127–128, 131.

plays, for he was fundamentally a dramatist; all the most famous scenes of his novels and tales could be acted with hardly any change. Henley has contributed generously and far more than a small share toward Stevenson's growth as a writer, but little to the Stevenson biography except that one mysterious ill-judged attack in the *Pall Mall* and one heartbroken poem: "When we that were dear are all too near / With the thick of the world between us. . . ." His nostalgic longing that one day they may "lie in the peace of the Great Release as once in the grass together" quickens our glimpses of two young men idly sprawling on a slope of the Pentlands, talking and talking of the wonderful things they were to achieve. Yet still one cannot write a biography of either without feeling that their war is not over. Final and visible causes for quarrel are always a little obscure; they begin many years before their protagonists are aware of them, and if we say heaven only knows when and where they end, it is in the hope that heaven at least does know. Kinder, meanwhile, to remember how Henley, after reading the posthumous fragment of *Weir of Hermiston*, wrote to Colvin a triumphant "I have found my Lewis [*sic*] again and in all his glory."

On the whole, even in his profligate youth, Stevenson chose friends to match his strength, not his weakness; they make quite an impressive roll call headed by Colvin, Fleeming Jenkin, Henley, Will Low (the American artist), and Charles Baxter (writer to the signet).[7] Henry James and Edmund Gosse came later. The last published letter of Stevenson's—it may be the last he ever penned—was written to Gosse in deep affection and sadness.

It is all very well to talk of renunciation, and of course it has to be done. But, for my part, give me a roaring toothache. . . . I have very little use for either watching or meditation. I was not born for age.

(*Works*, vol. XXXV, pp. 183, 184)

Henry James included in *Notes on Novelists* a highly perceptive review of Stevenson's letters:

He had incurred great charges, he sailed a ship loaded to the brim, so that the strain under which he sailed and wrought was immense; but the very grimness of it all is sunny, slangy, funny, familiar; there is as little of the florid in

his flashes of melancholy as of the really grey under the stress of his wisdom. . . . He has . . . a soundness all liberal and easy and born of the manly experience, that it is a luxury to touch.

(p. 17)

A solemn young Scots writer called J. M. Barrie once hauled him over the coals for his want of proper seriousness, in a somewhat impertinent essay published in *An Edinburgh Eleven:*

Mr. Stevenson has reached the critical point in his career, and one would like to see him back at Bournemouth, writing within high walls. We want that big book; we think he is capable of it, and so we cannot afford to let him drift into the seaweed.

(p. 103)

Three years afterward, Stevenson wrote to him from Samoa in a spirit to serve as example to all famous writers of how to take with humorous good nature the attacks of their lofty-minded juniors:

. . . I have been off my work for some time, and re-read the *Edinburgh Eleven*, and had a great mind to write a parody and give you all your sauce back again, and see how you would like it yourself.

(*Works*, vol. XXXIV, p. 273)

Another letter warmly praises Barrie's *A Window in Thrums* ("There are two of us now who the Shirra might have patted on the head!"—the Shirra was, of course, Sir Walter Scott, their hero) and ensured that Barrie, being human, became Stevenson's adoring, uncritical "pen friend"; and we hear no more in his former lofty vein.

Andrew Lang, who frankly preferred the books to the man, wrote an introduction to the Swanston edition, which should be read by the discriminate for its unbiased discrimination:

Many circumstances caused Stevenson, when at his best, to be a historical novelist, and he is, since Scott and Thackeray, the best historical novelist whom we have.

Add to all this his notable eminence in tales of shorter scope; in essays, whether on life or literature, so various and original, so graceful and strong; add the fantasies of his fables, and remember that almost all he did is good. . . . With his faith, whatever its tenets may have been, was implicated his uneasily active conscience; his sense of duty. This appears to have directed his life; and was practically

[7]A lawyer who conducts cases before the court of sessions.

the same thing as his sense of honour. Honour, I conceive, is, in a phrase of Aristotle's, duty "with a bloom on it."[8]

Sidney Colvin handed over his literary executor's privilege of writing the official *Life of Stevenson* (1901) to Graham Balfour, a cousin on the distaff side, who had stayed a year with Stevenson at Vailima. He did, however, himself edit the *Letters* with notes and introduction. J. A. Steuart's *Life of Stevenson* (1924), without overstressing those "revelations" so dear to the Debunking School, has certainly freed itself from the affectionate partisan spirit of kinsman or personal friend. Rosaline Masson, too, has written a *Life* (1923) which is almost free from it; the Masson family knew him personally, for her father was a distinguished professor at Edinburgh University at the same time as young Stevenson was cutting lectures and painting the town red. She wrote with authority and knowledge of her subject, rather than with intimacy; possibly she had not been allowed much intercourse with such a ne'er-do-well. She also edited a volume to which she gave the somewhat too sentimental title *I Can Remember Robert Louis Stevenson* (1922), containing nevertheless a variety of interesting matter that otherwise would have slipped through the grating and been swirled away; such as his comment, too wise not to be sad, to a servant eager to escape blame: "Hush. . . . You know when one tries to justify oneself, one puts someone else in the wrong—and life is not possible under those conditions."

For any student lost and bewildered by the multitude of Stevensoniana, a collection actually called *Stevensoniana* (1903), by Sir John Hammerton, a notable beachcomber in the quest of contemporary material, ought not to be missed. But the "sideline" biographies, with something of innocence—or shall we say naiveté—in their treatment, unprofessional and uncritical, with no literary "approach," not out to "refute" anything, nor swayed by post-mortem "research," are often the most revealing provided they are written with integrity, free from the sweetness of marshmallow. In our selection, therefore, of the Hundred Best Books on Stevenson, we should include *A Chronicle of Friendships* (1908), by Will Low, delightfully covering the Barbizon and Grez

period; and Lloyd Osbourne's prefaces to the Tusitala edition; *This Life I've Loved* (1937), by Isobel Field; *The Life of Mrs. Robert Louis Stevenson* (1920), by Nellie Sanchez (Fanny's sister); *R.L.S. and His Sine Qua Non*, by Adelaide Boodle (especially recommended); and *Memories of Vailima* (1902), by both his stepchildren.

The most distinguished contributions to Stevensoniana produced by the centenary year were a localized study by Moray MacLaren on *Stevenson and Edinburgh* (1950); a preface by John Hampden to *The Stevenson Companion*, felicitous title to a summing-up that is often shrewd and always courteous to the best companion in the world; and preeminently the *Collected Poems* (1950), edited by Janet Adam Smith, with an introduction and notes.

But the best assessment of Stevenson remains G. K. Chesterton's biography, written in 1927. Chesterton's appreciation of Stevenson every now and then might be comically inverted and read as Stevenson's appreciation of Chesterton, for they are extraordinarily similar in their outlook and aims: ". . . why should he be treated as a liar," Chesterton asks, "because he was not ashamed to be a story-teller?"

He had often said he wanted to be buried on top of Mount Vaea, but no way existed through the impenetrable tangle of scrub and undergrowth; so on the night of his death, Lloyd Osbourne summoned the chieftains and told them Tusitala was dead, and what he had wished. With the first light of dawn, the stronger men set themselves to hew a track up the steep slope. By noon it was ready, and a long procession of mourners set out to climb the mountain road in the blazing heat, following the coffin carried shoulder-high on the spears of Samoan warriors.

The other road was opened only a couple of months before his death: until then, there had been no more than a path up to Vailima, branching off the main road which crossed the island. But when Mataafa's men were released from prison, they chose to remain behind, instead of returning straight to their homes and families, and replace the path by a connecting road sixty feet wide, themselves paying for all the necessary materials and maintenance while they built it. Then they set up a board with an inscription:

Considering the great love of Tusitala in his loving care of us in our distress in the prison, we have therefore prepared a splendid gift. It shall never be muddy, it shall endure for ever, this road that we have dug.

[8]*The Works of Robert Louis Stevenson*, Swanston ed., 25 vols. (London, 1911-1912), with an introduction by Andrew Lang, vol. I., pp. lii, liii–liv.

Two roads. Two letters. Ori, sub-chief of the island of Tautira, had grown to love "Rui" like a brother, and after Stevenson's departure in the *Casco*, he wrote:

I make you to know my great affection . . . you looked from that ship, and I looked at you on the ship with great grief until you had raised the anchor and hoisted the sails. When the ship started, I ran along the beach to see you still. . . . I did not sleep that night, thinking continually of you, my very dear friend, until the morning. . . . Afterwards I looked into your rooms; they did not please me as they used to do. . . . I will not forget you in my memory. Here is the thought: I desire to meet you again. . . . It must be that your body and my body shall eat together at our table; there is what would make my heart content.

The second letter, a torn-off scrap written to Fanny in December 1894, needs no explanation:

Dear Madam: Many thousands mourn the death of Robert Louis Stevenson, but none more than the blind leper of Molokai.

The final item for this random collection appeared in the *Reader's Digest*. The author was telling of his unregenerate boyhood in Chillicothe, Missouri. The little town had no public library, so the boy and his gang read nothing but forbidden dime novels, shockers from the book-and-stationery shop.

One day when I went into the shop to select a new Nick Carter, Mr. McIllwrath spoke to me in a lowered voice. "You like to read exciting stories, don't you?" he said, and his eyes narrowed behind their smeared spectacles.

"Why, yes, sir," I said.

"All right, I'm going to tell you something I wouldn't tell just anybody. Back in the store here, I've got the most exciting dime novel you ever read." He led me to the rear of the store. "This book will cost you five times as much as a Buffalo Bill, but there's five times as much reading in it and it's about five times as exciting. Pirates, murder, hidden treasure—everything."

He took from a shelf a cheap red, clothbound book and slapped it affectionately. I read the title—*Treasure Island*.[9]

The rest is quickly told; the whole of the gang came under the spell of Long John Silver and Jim Hawkins; they were converted; they learned to read. But they kept *Treasure Island* hidden from the

[9]Clyde Brion Davis, *The Age of Indiscretion*, condensed in the *Reader's Digest*, vol. 57, August 1950, pp. 162–164.

adults, quaintly assuming that any exciting story would be considered bad.

". . . don't let your mother or sisters catch you with it. They might look inside and then there'd be a big stink and Mr. McIllwrath would get in trouble."

. . . It was with astonishment that I learned some years later that *Treasure Island* actually was a respectable book which could be read openly, and that some even regarded it as a classic.

Mr. McIllwrath later sold us *Kidnapped*. . . . I suspect the sour-faced old man was deliberately trying to develop a taste for literature in us.

(pp. 163–164)

There must be hundreds of Old Chillicothians and their like who could contribute similar experiences. Perhaps, after all, Stevenson sometimes wrote books for boys.

If any of these gestures were merely bogus, acts of nothingness that viewed from here and now would seem as impotent as a radio playing in an empty room, then one would have no reply to those of Stevenson's critics who maintain that he was little more than a pseudoromantic. But on the contrary, they are in a true romantic tradition we have met before, of unselfconscious service to the human race (memory may set up the names of Chinese Gordon and Lawrence of Arabia), a tradition that appears to be founded on solid sense. Providing the right nourishment for a boy's mind makes sense; and to inspire a road to materialize where no road was before. And Stevenson's address to the chiefs on the opening of the Road of Gratitude in 1894, can surely be read and reread for its contemporary message that begins with an echo from Ecclesiastes.

For there is a time to fight and a time to dig. You Samoans may fight, you may conquer twenty times, and thirty times, and all will be in vain. There is but one way to defend Samoa. Hear it before it is too late. It is to make roads, and gardens, and care for your trees, and sell their produce wisely, and, in one word, to occupy and use your country. If you do not, others will.

. . . because all things in a country hang together like the links of the anchor cable, one by another: but the anchor itself is industry.

(*Works*, vol. XXXV, pp. 191, 193)

Probably in another hundred years, if the conduct of the world has not changed beyond recognition, it may still be as relevant.

ROBERT LOUIS STEVENSON

SELECTED BIBLIOGRAPHY

I. BIBLIOGRAPHY. W. F. Prideaux, *A Bibliography of the Works of Robert Louis Stevenson* (London, 1903), a new ed., rev., ed., and supplemented by Mrs. L. S. Livingstone (London, 1917), is a standard work—only the specialist in Stevensonian bibliography will need to consult, in addition, the important catalogs of the Widener and Beinecke collections (see below); *A Catalogue of the Books and Manuscripts of Robert Louis Stevenson in the Library of the Late H. E. Widener* (Philadelphia, 1913), with a memoir by A. S. W. Rosenbach; G. L. McKay, ed., *A Stevenson Library* (New Haven, Conn., 1951–1964), catalog of a collection of writings by and about Stevenson, formed by E. J. Beinecke, 6 vols., vols. I and II: printed books, pamphlets, broadsides, etc.; vol III: autograph letters by Stevenson and his wife; vol. IV: letters to and about R.L.S.; vol. V: MSS by R.L.S. and others; vol. VI: addenda and corrigenda, the catalog describes in detail the comprehensive collection of Stevenson's writings and Stevensoniana presented to Yale University on and since its 250th anniversary, indispensable for the specialist.

II. COLLECTED EDITIONS. S. Colvin, ed., *Works*, 28 vols. (London, 1894–1898), the first collected ed., known as the Edinburgh ed.; S. Colvin, ed., *A Stevenson Medley* (London, 1899); *Novels and Tales*, 26 vols. (New York, 1902), the Thistle ed., issued to subscribers only; *Essays and Criticisms* (Boston, 1903); *Tales and Fantasies* (London, 1905); *Essays of Travel* (London, 1905); *Essays in the Art of Writing* (London, 1905); *Works*, 20 vols. (London, 1906–1907), with bibliographical notes by E. Gosse, the Pentland ed., Gosse's biographical and bibliographical notes were issued separately in a 1908 privately printed ed.; *Works*, 25 vols. (London, 1911–1912), the Swanston ed., with an intro. by A. Lang; *Poems and Ballads* (New York, 1913), complete ed.; *Complete Poems* (New York, 1923), includes reprs. of the three collections of poems privately printed for members of the Bibliophile Society, Boston (2 vols., 1916; 1 vol., 1923), for an account of the fate of Stevenson's poetical MSS after his death see introduction to *Collected Poems* (London, 1950); F. van de Grift Stevenson and Lloyd Osbourne, eds., *Works*, 26 vols. (New York, 1921–1923; London, 1922–1923), the Vailima ed., with prefatory notes by F. van de Grift Stevenson, and portraits, limited ed. of 2,000 copies; *Works*, 35 vols. (London, 1923–1924), the Tusitala ed., the best and most complete ed., fully annotated; *Works*, 30 vols. (London, 1924–1926), the Skerryvore ed.; *Works*, 21 vols. (London, 1926–1927), the Lothian ed.; J. Adam Smith, ed., *Complete Poems* (London, 1950), with intro. and notes, the definitive ed., valuable notes; J. Hampden, ed., *The Stevenson Companion* (London, 1950), with an intro., contains *Weir of Hermiston* and a large selection of Stevenson's work; G. B. Stern, ed., *R.L.S., An Omnibus* (London, 1950); G. B. Stern, ed., *Selected Poems* (London, 1950); G. B. Stern, ed., *Tales and Essays* (London, 1950).

III. SEPARATE WORKS. *The Pentland Rising: A Page of History, 1666* (Edinburgh, 1866), essay; *A New Form of Intermittent Light for Lighthouses* (Edinburgh, 1871), essay, first printed in the Transactions of the Royal Scottish Society of Arts, vol. VIII (1871); *On the Thermal Influence of Forests* (Edinburgh, 1873), essay, first printed in Proceedings of the Royal Society of Edinburgh, vol. VIII (1873); *An Appeal to the Clergy of the Church of Scotland* (London, 1875), essay; *An Inland Voyage* (London, 1878), travel; *Edinburgh: Picturesque Notes* (London, 1879), essays; *Travels with a Donkey in the Cevennes* (London, 1879), travel.

Virginibus Puerisque and Other Papers (London, 1881), twelve essays repr., with one exception, from magazines; *Familiar Studies of Men and Books* (London, 1882), nine essays repr. from magazines; *New Arabian Nights*, 2 vols. (London, 1882), fiction, vol. I: "The Suicide Club," "The Rajah's Diamond"; vol. II: "The Pavilion on the Links," "A Lodging for the Night," "The Sire de Maletroit's Door," "Providence and the Guitar"; all these stories had previously appeared in magazines; *The Silverado Squatters: Sketches from a Californian Mountain* (London, 1883), travel, originally published in *Century* magazine (November–December 1883); *Treasure Island* (London, 1883), fiction, originally published as by "Captain George North" in *Young Folks* (1882), also in Scribner Illustrated Classics series (New York, 1911; reiss. 1981); *Prince Otto: A Romance* (London, 1885), fiction, originally published in *Longman's* magazine (April–October 1885); *A Child's Garden of Verses* (London, 1885), more than half of the text had previously appeared in a trial ed. with the title *Penny Whistles; More New Arabian Nights: The Dynamiter* [in collaboration with F. van de Grift Stevenson] (London, 1885), fiction, Stevenson's wife was the sole author of "The Destroying Angel" and "The Fair Cuban."

The Strange Case of Dr. Jekyll and Mr. Hyde (London, 1886), fiction; *Kidnapped: Being Memoirs of the Adventures of David Balfour in the year 1751 &c.* (London, 1886), fiction, originally published in *Young Folks*, May–July 1886; *The Merry Men, and Other Tales and Fables* (London, 1887), fiction, includes "The Merry Men," "Will O' the Mill," "Markheim," "Thrawn Janet," "Olalla," "The Treasure of Franchard," all these stories had previously appeared in magazines; *Thomas Stevenson, Civil Engineer* (London, 1887), essay, privately printed, also in the *Contemporary Review* (June 1887); S. Colvin, ed., *Papers Literary and Scientific by the Late Fleeming Jenkin*, 2 vols. (London, 1887), contains Stevenson's "Memoir," published separately in New York (1887); *Memories and Portraits* (London, 1887), sixteen essays, mostly repr. from magazines, and including "Thomas Stevenson, Civil Engineer" and the "Memoir" from *The Papers of H. Fleeming Jenkin*; *Underwoods* (London, 1887), contains poems in English and Scots; *Ticonderoga: A Poem* (Edinburgh, 1887), privately printed, originally published in *Scribner's* magazine (December 1887), repr. in *Ballads* (London,

1890); *The Misadventures of John Nicholson: A Christmas Story* (New York, 1887), fiction, piratically repr. from *Cassell's Christmas Annual* (1887); *The Black Arrow: A Tale of the Two Roses* (London, 1888), fiction, originally published as by "Captain George North" in *Young Folks* (1883); *The Master of Ballantrae: A Winter's Tale* (London, 1889), fiction, originally published in *Scribner's* magazine (November 1888–October 1889); *The Wrong Box* [in collaboration with Lloyd Osbourne] (London, 1889), fiction.

Father Damien: An Open Letter to the Revd. Dr. Hyde of Honolulu (London, 1890), essay, originally published in the *Scots Observer* (May 1890) and privately printed in the same year in Sydney and Edinburgh; *Ballads* (London, 1890), verse, includes "The Song of Rahero," "The Feast of Famine," "Ticonderoga," "Heather Ale," "Christmas at Sea"; *Across the Plains, with Other Memories and Essays* (London, 1892), twelve essays repr. from magazines; *The Wrecker* [in collaboration with Lloyd Osbourne] (London, 1892), fiction, originally published in *Scribner's* magazine (August 1891–July 1892); *A Footnote to History: Eight Years of Trouble in Samoa* (London, 1892), essay; *War in Samoa* (London, 1893), privately printed essay, originally published in the *Pall Mall Gazette* (September 1893); *Island Nights' Entertainments* (London, 1893), fiction, includes "The Beach of Falesá," "The Bottle Imp," "The Isle of Voices," preceded by publication in periodicals from 1891 to 1892, and by a privately printed ed.; *Catriona: A sequel to Kidnapped, being the Memoirs of the Further Adventures of David Balfour at Home and Abroad, &c.* (London, 1893), fiction, originally published as "David Balfour" in *Atlanta* (1892); *The Ebb-Tide: A Trio and Quartette* [in collaboration with Lloyd Osbourne] (London, 1894), fiction, originally published in *To-Day* (November 1893–January 1894); *The Body Snatcher* (New York, 1895), fiction, originally published in *Pall Mall* (Christmas 1894); *The Amateur Emigrant: From the Clyde to Sandy Hook* (Chicago, 1895), travel, originally published in vol. III of the Edinburgh ed. of Stevenson's works.

Four Plays [in collaboration with W. E. Henley] (London, 1896), drama, contains *Deacon Brodie, Beau Austin, Admiral Guinea, Robert Macaire,* each play was originally issued separately in a small privately printed ed. in 1880, 1884, 1884, 1885, respectively, the first three were published together as *Three Plays* (London, 1892); *The Strange Case of Dr. Jekyll and Mr. Hyde, with Other Fables* (London, 1896), the *Fables* were originally published in *Longman's* magazine (August–September 1895) and first published separately (New York, 1895); *Weir of Hermiston: An Unfinished Romance* (London, 1896), fiction, originally published in *Cosmopolis* (January–April 1896); *A Mountain Town in France: A Fragment* (London–New York, 1896), essay; S. Colvin, ed., *Songs of Travel and Other Verses* (London, 1896), originally published in vol. XIV of the Edinburgh ed. of Stevenson's works; *St. Ives: Being the Adventures of a French Prisoner in England*

[completed by A. T. Quiller-Couch] (New York, 1897; London, 1898), fiction, the first thirty chapters, by Stevenson, were originally published in the *Pall Mall* magazine.

Prayers Written at Vailima (New York, 1904; London, 1905), with an intro. by Mrs. Stevenson, originally published in vol. XXI of the Edinburgh ed. of Stevenson's works; *Lay Morals and Other Papers* (London, 1911), ten essays originally published in magazines; *Memoirs of Himself* (Philadelphia, 1912), biography, privately printed from the original MS in the possession of H. E. Widener; *Records of a Family of Engineers* (London, 1912), essays; *The Hanging Judge: A Drama in Three Acts and Six Tableaux* [in collaboration with F. van de Grift Stevenson] (London, 1914), drama, privately printed, with an intro. by E. Gosse; *The Waif Woman* (London, 1916), fiction, originally published in *Scribner's* magazine (December 1914); *On the Choice of a Profession* (London, 1916), essay, originally published in *Scribner's* magazine (January 1915); *New Poems and Variant Readings* (London, 1918), unedited repr. of the two carelessly compiled vols. issued in 1916 to members of the Bibliophile Society, Boston; for a severe but justified stricture on this compilation and its sequel, see introduction to *Collected Poems* (London, 1950); J. C. Bay, ed., *The Manuscripts of Robert Louis Stevenson's Records of a Family of Engineers: The Unfinished Chapters* (Chicago, 1930), with an intro. *Note:* The above list does not include many of the authorized privately printed eds. in which some of Stevenson's stories, essays, and poems first appeared, among them the pamphlets printed on a hand press at Davos, 1881–1882, by Lloyd Osbourne, then a schoolboy; or a number of "manufactured rarities" for the collectors' market, consisting of small, privately printed eds. of occasional pieces of verse and prose from private collections in the United States.

IV. LETTERS. *Vailima Letters: Being Correspondence Addressed by Robert Louis Stevenson to Sidney Colvin, November 1890–October 1894* (London, 1895); *In the South Seas* (New York, 1896; London, 1900), an account of experiences and observations in the Marquesas, Paumotus, and Gilbert Islands in the course of two cruises, on the yacht *Casco,* 1888, and the schooner *Equator,* 1889, originally published in the *New York Sun* (1891) and privately printed in part in *The South Seas* (London, 1890); S. Colvin, ed., *Letters to His Family and Friends,* 2 vols. (London, 1899), with an intro. and notes, a new ed. (London, 1911), rearranged in 4 vols., has 150 new letters; L. Osbourne, ed., *Some Letters* (London, 1914); *Autograph Letters, Original Mss., Books, Portraits and Curios from the Library of the Late R. L. Stevenson,* 3 vols. (New York, 1914–1916), catalog of the sale of the Anderson Galleries, by Isobel Strong, of her stepfather's literary property; one of the consequences of this sale was the unauthorized and ill-considered production of the "manufactured rarities" referred to in the *Note* above; J. A. Smith, ed., *Henry James and Robert Louis Stevenson: A Record of Friendship and Criticism* (London, 1948), with an intro.; D. Ferguson and M. Waingrow, eds., *RLS: Stevenson's Letters to Charles Baxter* (New Haven, Conn., 1956).

V. BIOGRAPHICAL AND CRITICAL STUDIES. W. Raleigh, *Robert Louis Stevenson* (London, 1895), lecture given at the Royal Institution, 1895, with additions; M. Fraser, *In Stevenson's Samoa* (London, 1895); M. Armour, *The Home and Early Haunts of Robert Louis Stevenson* (Edinburgh, 1895); J. Geddie, *The Home Country of R. L. Stevenson* (Edinburgh, 1898); E. B. Simpson, *Robert Louis Stevenson's Edinburgh Days* (London, 1898); M. M. Black, *Robert Louis Stevenson* (Edinburgh, 1898), *Famous Scots* series; L. C. Cornford, *Robert Louis Stevenson* (Edinburgh, 1899), Modern English Writers series.

H. B. Baildon, *Robert Louis Stevenson: A Life Study in Criticism* (London, 1901); Sir G. Balfour, *The Life of Robert Louis Stevenson*, 2 vols. (London, 1901); I. Strong and L. Osbourne, *Memories of Vailima* (New York, 1902; London, 1903), by Stevenson's stepchildren; W. R. Nicoll and G. K. Chesterton, *Robert Louis Stevenson* (London, 1902), *The Bookman* booklet no. 2; J. A. Hammerton, ed., *Stevensoniana* (London, 1903), new and revised ed. (Edinburgh, 1907), uniform with the Pentland ed. of Stevenson's works; Sir L. Stephen, *Robert Louis Stevenson: An Essay* (New York–London, 1903); A. W. Pinero, *Robert Louis Stevenson: The Dramatist* (London, 1903); L. Stubbs, *Stevenson's Shrine: A Record of a Pilgrimage* (London, 1903); A. H. Japp, *Robert Louis Stevenson: A Record, an Estimate, and a Memorial—with Hitherto Unpublished Letters from R. L. Stevenson in facsimile* (London, 1905); A. Johnstone, *Recollections of Robert Louis Stevenson in the Pacific* (London, 1905); E. B. Simpson, *Robert Louis Stevenson* (London, 1906); H. J. Moors, *With Stevenson in Samoa* (Boston, 1910; London, 1911).

K. D. Osbourne, *Robert Louis Stevenson in California* (Chicago, 1911); I. Strong, *Robert Louis Stevenson* (London, 1911), Little Books on Great Writers series; E. B. Simpson, *The Robert Louis Stevenson Originals* (London–Edinburgh, 1912); W. H. Low, *A Chronicle of Friendships, 1873–1900* (London, 1908), with illus. by the author; A. Webster, *R. L. Stevenson and Henry Drummond* (London, 1912); *Robert Louis Stevenson: The Man and His Work* (London, 1913), extra number of *The Bookman*, includes repros. of many portraits; F. Watt, *R.L.S.* (London, 1913); R. O. Masson, *Robert Louis Stevenson* (London, 1914), rev. ed. in People's Books series (London, 1920); F. Swinnerton, *R. L. Stevenson: A Critical Study* (London, 1914); A. W. Pinero, *Robert Louis Stevenson as a Dramatist* (New York, 1914), lecture ed. by C. Hamilton; C. Hamilton, *In the Trail of Stevenson* (London, 1916); C. Eaton, *A Last Memory of Robert Louis Stevenson* (New York, 1916); S. Chalmers, *The Penny Piper of Saranac: An Episode in Stevenson's Life* (Boston–New York, 1916); E. Brown, *A Book of R.L.S.: Works, Travels, Friends and Commentators* (London, 1919).

C. J. Guthrie [Lord Guthrie], *Robert Louis Stevenson: Some Personal Reflections and Recollections* (Edinburgh,

1920); H. H. Harper, *Robert Louis Stevenson: An Appreciation* (Boston, 1920); N. van de G. Sanchez, *The Life of Mrs. Robert Louis Stevenson* (London, 1920); C. Eaton, *Stevenson at Manasquan* (Chicago, 1921), with a note on the fate of the yacht *Casco*, by F. Dickie, and six portraits from Stevenson (in verse) by G. S. Seymour; M. Balfour [later Stevenson], *Stevenson's Baby Book: Being the Record of the Sayings and Doings of Robert Louis Balfour Stevenson*, K. D. Osbourne, ed. (San Francisco, 1922); R. O. Masson, ed., *I Can Remember Robert Louis Stevenson* (Edinburgh–London, 1922), enlarged ed. containing approximately 100 short articles by as many contributors (1925); R. O. Masson, *The Life of Robert Louis Stevenson* (Edinburgh–London, 1923); C. Sarolea, *Robert Louis Stevenson and France* (Edinburgh, 1923); L. Osbourne, *An Intimate Portrait of R.L.S.* (New York, 1924); A. St. John Adcock, ed., *Robert Louis Stevenson: His Work and His Personality* (London, 1924), essays by Adcock, H. C. Beeching, S. Colvin, S. R. Crockett, A. Gordon, E. Gosse, J. A. Hammerton, C. Lowe, I. MacLaren, N. Munro, W. Robertson Nicoll, A. Noyes, L. Osbourne, E. B. Simpson, Y. Y. (R. Lynd); J. A. Steuart, *Robert Louis Stevenson: Man and Writer, A Critical Biography* (London, 2 vols., 1924; 1 vol., 1926); G. Hellman, *The True Stevenson: A Study in Clarification* (Boston, 1925), with portraits and facs.; A. A. Boodle, *R.L.S. and His Sine Qua Non* [i.e., Stevenson and his wife]: *Flashlights from Skerryvore* (London, 1926); A. Cunningham, *Cummy's Diary*, R. T. Skinner, ed. (London, 1926), diary kept by Stevenson's nurse while traveling with him on the Continent during 1863, with preface and notes; J. A. MacCulloch, *R. L. Stevenson and the Bridge of Allan, with Other Stevenson Essays* (Glasgow, 1927); G. K. Chesterton, *Robert Louis Stevenson* (London, 1927; repr. New York, 1955); D. B. Morris, *Robert Louis Stevenson and the Scottish Highlanders* (Stirling, 1929).

H. D. MacPherson, *R. L. Stevenson: A Study in French Influence* (New York, 1930); L. E. Chrétien, *La Vocation de Robert-Louis Stevenson: Étude de psychologie littéraire* (Paris, 1930); S. Dark, *Robert Louis Stevenson* (London, 1931); F. Fabre, *Un Ami de la France: R. L. Stevenson dans le Velay* (Clermont-Ferrand, 1932), étude, suivie des Lettres écrites du Monastier en 1878; W. G. Lockett, *Robert Louis Stevenson at Davos* (London, 1934); T. M. MacCallum, *Adrift in the South Seas: Including Adventures with Robert Louis Stevenson* (Los Angeles, 1934); C. MacLean, *La France dans l'Oeuvre de R. L. Stevenson* (Paris, 1936); J. A. Smith, *R. L. Stevenson* (London, 1937); I. Field, *This Life I've Loved* (London, 1937); D. N. Dalglish, *Presbyterian Pirate: A Portrait of Stevenson* (London, 1937); S. Gwynn, *Robert Louis Stevenson* (London, 1939), English Men of Letters series; A. R. Issler, *Stevenson at Silverado* (Caldwell, Ida., 1939).

H. J. Cowell, *Robert Louis Stevenson: An Englishman's Re-Study, After Fifty Years, of R.L.S. the Man* (London, 1945); L. U. Cooper, *Robert Louis Stevenson* (London,

1947); D. Daiches, *Robert Louis Stevenson* (Glasgow, 1947); J. A. Smith, *A Record of Friendship* (London, 1948), discusses Stevenson's friendship with Henry James; *Essays Mainly on the Nineteenth Century* (London, 1948), presented to Sir Humphrey Milford, contains the essay "The Poetry of R. L. Stevenson" by H. W. Garrod; J. Bowman, *Robert Louis Stevenson* (London, 1949).

M. Elwin, *The Strange Case of Robert Louis Stevenson* (London, 1950); M. S. Lawson, *On the Bat's Back: The Story of Robert Louis Stevenson* (London, 1950); M. MacLaren, *Stevenson and Edinburgh: A Centenary Study* (London, 1950); A. R. Issler, *Our Mountain Heritage: Silverado and Robert Louis Stevenson* (Stanford, Calif., 1950); D. Daiches, *Stevenson and the Art of Fiction* (New York, 1951), privately printed, Frances Bergen memorial lecture, Yale University, May 1951; J. C. Furnas, *Voyage to Windward: The Life of Robert Louis Stevenson* (London, 1952), contains interesting, authoritative matter only recently discovered, and sets forth in a clear, dispassionate style that carries conviction a point of view defending Mrs. R. L. Stevenson in considered opposition to her detractors; R. Aldington, *Portrait of a Rebel: The Life and Work of R. L. Stevenson* (London, 1957); G. L. MacKay, *Some Notes on Robert Louis Stevenson, His Finances and His Agents and Publishers* (New Haven, Conn., 1958).

E. N. Caldwell, *Last Witness for Robert Louis Stevenson* (Norman, Okla., 1960); R. Kiely, *Robert Louis Stevenson and the Fiction of Adventure* (Cambridge, Mass., 1964); A. Nakajima, *Light, Wind and Dreams: An interpretation of the life and mind of Robert Louis Stevenson* (Tokyo, 1965); D. Butts, *R. L. Stevenson* (London, 1966); J. D. Hart *R.L.S.* (San Francisco, 1966); E. M. Eigner, *Robert Louis Stevenson and the Romantic Tradition* (Princeton, N.J., 1966); E. M. Compton Mackenzie, *Robert Louis Stevenson* (London, 1968); M. M. MacKay, *Island Boy: Robert Louis Stevenson and His Step-Grandson* [i.e., Austin Strong] *in Samoa* (London, 1969); L. U. Cooper, *Robert Louis Stevenson* (London, 1969); D. Daiches, *Robert Louis Stevenson and His World* (London, 1973); P. Binding, *Robert Louis Stevenson* (London, 1974); J. Pope-Hennessy, *Robert Louis Stevenson* (London, 1974); M. McGaw, *Stevenson in Hawaii* (Westport, Conn., 1978); J. Calder, ed., *A Robert Louis Stevenson Companion* (London, 1980).

TOM STOPPARD

(1937–   )

C. W. E. Bigsby

I

Don't you see that nowadays tragedy isn't possible any more? . . . Today farce is the only thing possible.
            (*Tango*, by Slawomir Mrozek, adapted by
                                        Tom Stoppard)

In the early 1960's the English theater seemed suddenly to have found itself. It celebrated with naive enthusiasm its belated discovery of naturalism and its new-found social concern. For a brief period playwrights tended to regard themselves as the cutting edge of a social revolution in which they would articulate the frustration of a new generation growing up in a society that seemed not merely complacent to the point of inertia but dangerously blind to the vital forces that lay encysted within a decaying art. Despite the fact that this fervor gave birth to disturbing sentimentality rather than hard-edged social or political analysis, the energy that had been released so suddenly created a compelling paradigm for the new writer. As Tom Stoppard has said, "after 1956 everybody my age who wanted to write, wanted to write plays —after Osborne and the rest at the Court."

But if increased financial support for the arts, the creation of major subsidized companies, the expansion of television services, and the growth of regional drama encouraged many young writers to work for the stage, it did not create an avant-garde studiously dedicated to fracturing the mold of twentieth-century drama. The newly liberated imagination largely turned to familiar forms; the revolution, it seemed, had more to do with renewal than iconoclasm. Certainly, despite the much-publicized working-class and Jewish origins of some new writers, the public school and Oxford and Cambridge continued to provide the majority of British dramatists. What these new writers did offer, however, was a control of language that placed them in a recognizable English tradition that

in the previous half-century had produced Oscar Wilde, George Bernard Shaw, and Noël Coward. Preeminent among these is Tom Stoppard, who combines considerable talents as a parodist and wit with a genuinely personal vision. Recognizably derivative in his early work, he has since emerged as a writer of genuine originality.

Stoppard was born on 3 July 1937 in Zlin, Czechoslovakia. His father worked for the internationally famous Bata shoe company, and when the Germans threatened invasion, the family was transferred to the Singapore branch. Three years later they were forced to move again when Japanese troops captured the city. Stoppard's father was killed; with his mother and brother he was evacuated to India. Here his mother remarried and the family name, Straussler, became Stoppard.

On their return to England in 1946, he attended a preparatory school in Nottinghamshire and a boarding grammar school in Yorkshire, and in 1954 he began his career as a journalist, working first for the *Western Daily Press* and subsequently for the *Bristol Evening World*. As a theater reviewer he became interested in writing for the stage: in 1960 he resigned from his job and in three months wrote *A Walk on the Water*. This was eventually bought by a commercial television company, and Stoppard's public career as a playwright began, in November 1963. After several rewrites and a brief production in Hamburg, the play was finally produced on the London stage in 1968, two years after the success of *Rosencrantz and Guildenstern Are Dead*, under a new title, *Enter a Free Man*.

II

STOPPARD is a self-confessed aesthetic reactionary. That is, at a time when the avant-garde in theatre is deemphasizing language, stressing performance over text, preferring group composition to the insights of the individual author, he believes in the primacy of words. At a time when committed artists are asserting that art necessarily derives from social commitment, he regards it at times as a formalist exercise and at others as a moral gesture. As he has explained, "I don't set out . . . to write a play that will demand a new kind of theatre or a new kind of audience. But my feeling still is that the theatre ought to start from writing, come what may, even though in my view it is a delusion that a play is the end product of an idea; in my experience the idea is the end product of the play." In an article in the *Sunday Times* (25 February 1968) entitled "Something to Declare," Stoppard confessed that he had "very few social pre-occupations," writing, instead, out of a love of language and an avowedly intellectual fascination with "things I find difficult to express." "Some writers," he continued, "write because they burn with a cause which they further by writing about it. I burn with no causes. I cannot say that I write with any social objective. One writes because one loves writing." When he adds that he is "hooked on style," however, he is not only describing his own concern as a writer but also identifying the desperate strategy of so many of his protagonists, who feel, in the words of a character from his only novel, *Lord Malquist and Mr Moon* (1966), that "since we cannot hope for order let us withdraw with style from chaos."

Lord Malquist and Mr Moon is an exuberant farce, an absurdist romp that displays Stoppard's considerable talent for parody. The opening chapter offers a collage of literary styles used to ironic effect. His methodology is reminiscent of Salvador Dali's insofar as he treats improbable situations in a realistic manner, bringing together radically dissimilar elements. He peoples his novel with a black Irish Jew, two cowboys who stage a shoot-out in Trafalgar Square, a man who regards himself as the Risen Christ, and a peer of the realm who insists on behaving as though he were living in the eighteenth century, while assiduously seducing the wife of his biographer, Mr. Moon, a historian turned anarchist. This latter has set himself the somewhat daunting task of writing a history of the world, in the conviction that with perseverance it will manifest a coherent order that he not unnaturally finds hard to distinguish in the chaotic events that buffet him daily. The first and only sentence

he has thus far composed for his great work has unfortunately so unnerved him, however, that he is unable to get any further. Having written the confident words, "History is the progress of Man in the World, and the beginning of history is the beginning of Man," he can write only the word "Therefore" before the demonstrable absurdity of his premise overwhelms him.

Half-recognizing the fallacy implicit in his own capital letters, he wanders through London equipped with a homemade bomb, none too sure whether he wishes to precipitate the chaos he feels to be implicit in human affairs, or to rectify some mistake that has inadvertently caused an otherwise reliable system to malfunction. He finds himself "without possibility of reprieve or hope of explanation," bemused by the bewildering anarchy of existence, and uncertain whether life would be more absurd if it were random or simply the mechanical enactment of a determined scenario. It is thus entirely consistent that the novel should be full of characters more distinguished for their bizarre life styles than for their authentic humanity, for they, like Moon, appear to have grasped a truth that Stoppard himself adheres to with apparent conviction, until *Jumpers* and *Travesties* reveal the tentative humanism that had in fact always lurked beneath his absurdist stance: Stoppard's characters have understood, that is, that "substance is ephemeral but style is eternal"—an assumption that, although it "may not be a solution to the realities of life . . . is a workable alternative."

Stoppard seems to suggest with Wilde that life may best be regarded as an imitation of art, that in a situation where nothing can be taken seriously farce is both the true realism and, by a kind of homeopathic logic, the only valid strategy for artist and individual alike. Yet this conviction seems to battle with a more deep-seated humanism that leads him not only to reveal a compassionate concern for his characters but also to advocacy of such a concern within otherwise absurdist dramas. For, after all, as one of his characters observes in *Jumpers*, "the whole point of denying the Absolute was to reduce the scale, instantly, to the inconsequential behaviour of inconsequential animals." Yet this logic is too implacable for Stoppard. He creates a series of characters who, although ultimately defeated by social and metaphysical forces, provoke or themselves embrace a human compassion that transcends the relativistic ethics of an absurd universe.

III

In his early plays Stoppard presents a series of images of the individual trapped inside a mechanistic world, warped and destroyed by a logical system that fails to accommodate itself to human aspirations. *If You're Glad I'll Be Frank* (1969) details the ineffectual rebellion of the telephonist who works as the automatic time-giver. In the battle between her fragile individualism and the social and mechanical forces, there can be only one victor. Like her lover, whose protests have to be accommodated to the schedules of his regular bus route, the most she can do is stutter out her protest before retreating once more into her social role. In *Albert's Bridge* (1969) the same battle is repeated, except that Albert actually embraces his mechanical job as a release from the alarming disorder of his mundane existence. Albert takes great pleasure in his career as painter on the Clufton Bay Bridge, discovering poetry in the bridge's symmetry and meaning in its geometrical precision. His own life lacks this coherence; human relations stubbornly refuse to display the patterned grace and predictable order of the machine. He abandons his wife and withdraws into the reassuring world of the bridge, attracted by the fact that it is "separate—complete—removed, defined by principles of engineering which make it stop at a certain point, which compel a certain shape, certain joints—the whole thing utterly fixed by the rules that make it stay up . . . complete." But the same logical rules that enable the bridge to be built also lead to its collapse when an army of painters march across it without breaking step. In other words, the existence of order and system do not of themselves imply purpose and meaning. Albert discovers order in narcissism only to perish like Narcissus.

The note in these early plays is one of compassionate irony. Faced with a situation that seems to offer "nothing, absolutely nothing," in which "I give nothing, I gain nothing, it is nothing," George Riley's conviction in *Enter a Free Man* that "a man must resist. A man must stand apart, make a clear break on his own two feet," that "faith is the key —faith in oneself" becomes merely ironic. It is a faith that can be sustained only so long as he refuses to recognize his absolute dependence on those around him, on the absurd fictions that he chooses to embrace. Like Willy Loman, the leading character in Arthur Miller's *Death of a Salesman*, Riley

seems to feel that the stars projected on the clouds from the rooftops are real stars. As with Willy Loman the consequence is a combination of pathos and a curious dignity. In such a world the only value is indeed compassion.

Stoppard has confessed that *A Walk on the Water* was in fact *Flowering Death of a Salesman* (a combination of Robert Bolt's *Flowering Cherry* with *Death of a Salesman*), admitting that "I don't think it's a very true play, in the sense that I feel no intimacy with the people I was writing about. It works pretty well as a play, but it's actually phony because it's a play written about other people's characters."[1] Certainly *Enter a Free Man*, the rewritten stage version eventually produced in 1968 following the success of *Rosencrantz and Guildenstern Are Dead*, is a curiously eclectic work. Indeed, a number of speeches could have come straight out of Miller, as, for example, when the play's protagonist, George Riley, laments that

my life is piled up between me and the sun, as real and hopeless as a pile of broken furniture. Thirty years ago I was a young man ready to leave the ground and fly. Thirty years. . . . More, perhaps much more than the time I have left, and when a man's past outweighs his future, then he's a man standing in his own shadow.

(Act I)

There is the same tension between father and child as in *Death of a Salesman*, the same desperate attachment to illusion sustained by a wife every bit as compassionate and understanding as Linda in Miller's play. Stoppard even retains the name Linda, transferring it to the daughter.

Yet, despite this, Stoppard's own voice is clear enough, and in the figure of George Riley he creates the first of many portraits of a modern hero. Riley is a man who has dedicated his life to perfecting such devices as a reusable envelope (with gum on both sides of the flap) and an elaborate system of pipes designed to utilize rainfall to water indoor plants. Unaware of the logical flaws that make his inventions useless, he nonetheless pits his "tattered dignity" against a world that seems designed merely to taunt him. Described in the stage directions as "a smallish untidy figure in a crumpled suit . . . certainly not mad but . . . definitely odd," he is, we are assured, "unsinkable, despite the slow

---

[1]"Ambushes for the Audience," *Theatre Quarterly*, May–July 1974.

leak." And this "tattered dignity" is what characterizes the Stoppard hero, for while it is clear that none of his characters control their own destiny, that neither logic nor faith can confer meaning on their lives, it is equally obvious that their unsinkable quality, their irrepressible vitality and eccentric persistence, constitute what Stoppard feels to be an authentic response to existence. They are marginal men, uncertain of their own role and unsure of the true nature of the mechanism in which they feel caught. Like Samuel Beckett's clowns, John Osborne's music-hall entertainer, Harold Pinter's caretaker, David Mercer's morally confused minister, and Joe Orton's faithful retainer, they are the pathetic but touching remnants of a broken system. Dislodged from history even in the act of recognizing their own insignificance, their own inability to control events, they nonetheless assert a vestigial identity that they hold up against the flux of events. Even if their identities are disintegrating or scarcely exist (as is clearly the case with Rosencrantz and Guildenstern), they still pit their wounded psyches against a world they despair of understanding. And because the world that exists indistinctly and threateningly just beyond the focus of their vision is a brutal and uncompassionate one, the remnants of individuality that they can scrape together from the detritus of their hopes and fears make them heroes—ironical and inadequate, but heroes nonetheless, in a world that is presented as systematic and logical but devoid of moral purpose.

Yet there is a problem here, since in his first play Stoppard is drawn to both comedy and farce, the one implying a world in which values exist, the other an antinomian world of ethical relativity. In the former world, heroes, even those who can deploy only a tattered dignity, may not only survive but in doing so imply the survival of certain moral principles; in the latter, the most they can do is inhabit an autonomous world of their own creation. In *Enter a Free Man* Stoppard tries to have it both ways. The title is of course ambiguous. By all external standards George Riley is not free. He survives on handouts from his daughter, and his self-confidence is a fragile product of his family's compassion. But in another sense he is free. His imagination and self-respect survive repeated blows. He resists social pressure. And yet, although Stoppard seems to be celebrating Riley's self-sufficiency and his oddball courage, he is shown as

inhabiting a genuine social environment replete with real psychological problems. Where Willy Loman sustained his illusions precisely because of the social pressures to which he was submitted, George Riley recognizes no social obligations at all. He inhabits his own "definitely odd" world, and thus the psychological and social realism of other sections of the play seem not merely irrelevant but fragments of a different work. Willy Loman could arguably have been a different man in other circumstances. He, too, wanted to make things, but in his case this was to establish a real identity in a world that dealt only in images. If George Riley had been a different man, if he had moved back into the moral world, he would have disappeared. His illogic is his prime virtue; it is his defense against the world.

IV

STOPPARD began work on *Rosencrantz and Guildenstern Are Dead* in 1964. During a five-month stay in Berlin on a Ford Foundation grant he wrote a one-act Shakespearean pastiche in blank verse. On his return he rewrote it, abandoning verse for prose, and it was duly performed by the Oxford Theatre Group as a "fringe" production at the Edinburgh Festival in 1966. Following favorable reviews it was subsequently staged by the National Theatre Company in London.

Few writers can have been accorded such instant recognition. Harold Hobson, in the *Sunday Times*, described this play as "the most important event in the British professional theatre of the last nine years"—in other words, the most important event since Osborne's *Look Back in Anger* had supposedly changed the direction of British drama. *The Observer* endorsed this view, calling it "the most brilliant début of the sixties."

A play that seemed to combine the brittle wit of Wilde with the mordant humor of Beckett, *Rosencrantz and Guildenstern Are Dead* takes as its main characters two of literature's most marginal figures, attendant lords who, as several critics pointed out, are actually excluded from some productions of *Hamlet*. Stoppard himself has said that "the chief object and objective was to exploit a situation which seemed to me to have enormous dramatic and comic potential—of these two guys who in

Shakespeare's context don't really know what they are doing. The little they are told is mainly lies, and there's no reason to suppose that they ever find out why they are killed." As he points out, "probably more in the early 1960s than at any other time, that would strike a young playwright as being a perfectly good thing to explore."

These two "bewildered innocents" act out a scenario that they cannot understand, uncertain of their own roles and increasingly disturbed by the apparent meaninglessness of their lives. Although aware that "the only beginning is birth and the only end is death," they are forced to believe that there is some purpose in their existence or to capitulate to a growing sense of terror. Like the Players who are to perform before Hamlet, they act out their assigned roles with diminishing confidence as they begin to suspect that life lacks both a transcendent dimension and an enabling logic. As the Player says:

We're actors. . . . We pledged our identities, secure in the conventions of our trade; that someone would be watching. And then, gradually, no one was. We were caught, high and dry. . . . Even then, habit and a stubborn trust that our audience spied upon us from behind the nearest bush, forced our bodies to blunder on long after they had emptied of meaning, until like runaway carts they dragged to a halt. No one came forward. No one shouted at us. The silence was unbreakable, it imposed itself upon us; it was obscene.

(Act II)

The theatrical metaphor is the dominant one in the play. The pointless prospect of actors without an audience expands to incorporate mankind in general. This is not a disordered world to be restored to consonance by self-sacrifice and heroic action; it is an arbitrary existence in which resolute action decays into mere performance. As Guildenstern observes, "We don't question . . . we don't doubt . . . we perform." The chief problem becomes the need to survive from moment to moment without succumbing to panic.

The strategies that they adopt in the face of this situation are familiar enough, particularly to audiences familiar with Beckett's *Waiting for Godot.* They blot out their incipient terror by playing Wittgensteinian language games, flipping coins, conversing, reaching out to one another for momentary contact. They attempt to discover pattern and pur-

pose in their existence by use of scientific logic. But all these defenses crumble. The language games lead them to real and disturbing questions about their own identity, the coins persistently and alarmingly come down heads every time in defiance of the laws of chance, and conversation drains away until Guildenstern shouts out in despair, "Do you think conversation is going to help us now?" Logic is similarly ineffectual, for although Guildenstern asserts that "the scientific approach to the examination of phenomena is a defense against the pure emotion of fear," the logical explanations he laboriously constructs collapse under their own weight.

They are caught, then, trapped inside a play they did not write and doomed to enact roles they can never understand, lacking as they do vital clues as to the meaning of the total drama. Yet even the autonomous identity of the supposed author of that play is cast in doubt when Rosencrantz anachronistically recalls the famous analogy for the law of probability whereby, given time, six monkeys typing at random could produce the entire works of Shakespeare. In other words, the entire scenario may be simply the consequence of chance and not the ordered product of an omniscient creator. The metaphysical implications are obvious.

Rosencrantz and Guildenstern are forced to conclude that the only freedom they possess is that of sailors on a ship, free to move around on the vessel but unable to influence the wind and current that draw them inexorably onward. Or, more bleakly, theirs is the freedom to exist in a coffin, aware that one day the lid will be screwed down but able in the meantime to breathe, converse, exist. As Rosencrantz suggests, "Life in a box is better than no life at all. I expect. You'd have a chance at least. You could lie there thinking—well, at least I'm not dead! In a minute someone's going to bang on the lid and tell me to come out." This is the last resort: illusion, willed self-deceit of the kind Edward Albee had indicted in *Tiny Alice.* But even this cannot be sustained. When Guildenstern tries to convince himself that "we are not restricted. No boundaries have been defined, no inhibitions imposed. . . . We can breathe. We can relax. We can do what we like or say what we like to whomever we like, without restriction," Rosencrantz adds the necessary and deflating proviso: "Within limits, of course."

And as confidence drains away, as the ship, literal and metaphoric, nears its destination, so the defensive illusions begin to disintegrate, flake by flake. Language itself begins to collapse. Sigmund Freud saw speech not as a path to truth, as a means of destroying barriers between individuals, but as a means of holding truth at bay, of evading the vulnerability that is a necessary corollary of communication. This, indeed, is how Rosencrantz and Guildenstern deploy it. But as the terror of their situation becomes more and more compelling, this membrane between themselves and truth becomes permeable. The tissue begins to dissolve, and their loss of control is mirrored in a fragmentation of their language:

ROS: I want to go home.
GUIL: Don't let them confuse you.
ROS: I'm out of my step here—
GUIL: We'll soon be home and high—dry and home—
      I'll—
ROS: It's all over my *depth*—
GUIL: —I'll hie you home and—
ROS: —out of my head—
GUIL: —dry you high and—
ROS: *(cracking, high)*   —over my step over my head body!—I tell you it's all stopping to a death, it's boding to a depth, stepping to a head, it's all heading to a dead stop—
GUIL: *(the nursemaid)* There! . . . and we'll soon be home and dry . . . and *high* and dry . . .

                         (Act I)

It is essentially the same technique as that used by Pinter in *The Birthday Party*, although here the menace is not objectified; it remains vague, generalized.

The play is full of theatrical references. There are plays within plays within plays, a device that implicitly raises questions about the nature of truth. Apart from the obvious references to *Hamlet*, there are others to Albee ("good old east," derived from "good old north" in *The Zoo Story*) and Osborne ("Don't clap too hard. It's a very old world," derived from Archie Rice's rather less metaphysical comment in *The Entertainer*: "Don't clap. It's a very old building"). We are, indeed, constantly reminded of the unreality of what we are watching. Rosencrantz on several occasions shows awareness of the presence of the audience, and the conventions of the stage are repeatedly mocked. The consequence is that the audience is reminded that it too is playing a role, collaborating in the establishment of contingent truths. As the Player reminds

us, "truth is only that which is taken to be true. It's the currency of living. There may be nothing behind it, but it doesn't make any difference so long as it is honoured. One acts on assumptions." It is, in fact, precisely the existence of a world in which the only fixed points are birth and death that creates the need for fictions, for self-sustaining pretense; precisely the need for an ordering of experience that sends people to art, whose hermetic structures imply both a sequential code and a sustainable set of values. The willing suspension of disbelief thus applies not only to the content of a work but also to the assumptions about form, causality, and moral progress that have been corollaries of liberal art. Absurdist drama is thus not merely a rejection of liberal convictions about society and the nature of man; it is an implicit critique of the role ascribed to the artist. For he is no less a clown than Vladimir and Estragon, the two central characters in Beckett's *Waiting for Godot;* his audience is, for the duration of the play, in a temporal void as real as that occupied by Rosencrantz and Guildenstern and as pathetically dedicated to "passing the time" while awaiting with absolute faith, like the absurdist characters they observe, for structure to cohere into meaning.

Nor can one feel that Rosencrantz and Guildenstern's fate derives from their unique position as marginal individuals. For, as we discover, marginality is a matter of focus. In this play Hamlet is marginal, and if the two attendant lords face imminent death, this is no less than Hamlet, Polonius, Gertrude, Ophelia, and Laertes face. Hamlet's observations while holding Yorick's skull contain the essence of Stoppard's play, for it is precisely the existence of the grave that retrospectively deprives life of meaning. As Hamlet observes, what is the meaning of a beauty that simply conceals the skull; what the purpose of humor if it merely cloaks the black comedy of death? Yet such questions pursued too far lead to genuine madness, and having mocked passion and justified inaction, Hamlet acts with vigor and by doing so not only restores a secular order but reanimates the concept of order itself. This is not true of the world that Rosencrantz and Guilderstern inhabit. Here there is no definable truth, no established pattern, no tradition of morality to be pursued. Their individual qualities are irrelevant to their plight. One is intellectual, incisive, disturbed; the other obtuse, contented, placid. One is a leader; the other is led. It makes no difference. Such characteristics cannot alter their plight. Consequently they display an alarming uncertainty as to their identities, and as the pressure on them increases, they exchange roles, thus emphasizing that these are indeed roles, assumed modes of action generated by the exigencies of situation rather than by the compulsions of authentic character.

Is Stoppard, then, an absurdist? Like most arbitrary categories this is frequently more misleading than helpful, as has proved to be the case with writers such as Pinter and Albee. Yet the iconography of *Rosencrantz and Guildenstern Are Dead* is familiar to audiences who cut their critical teeth on Beckett and Eugene Ionesco. The absurdists captured a deracinated world—a world in which the potential for action and communication has been irrevocably eroded. The setting is timeless, the landscape an expressionistic desert reminiscent of Dali's lapidary wilderness[2] or the claustrophobic living room of modern, uncommunal living. The capacity for action is minimal and ironic. Language itself is simply an elaborate papering over of cracks, which constantly threaten to open up beneath those who remain either blithely unaware of their plight or numbed with despair. That anguish obviously exists in Stoppard's play —a work in which two men are seen "passing the time in a place without any visible character," clinging fiercely to the conviction that they "have not been picked out . . . simply to be abandoned," that they are "entitled to some direction," only to confess at the end of their "play" that "it is not enough. To be told so little—to such an end—and still, finally, to be denied an explanation." The only resources available to these abandoned characters are the compassion with which they respond to one another and the humor they deploy as a means of neutralizing their fear. Reinhold Niebuhr's comment that laughter is a kind of no-man's-land between faith and despair is clearly applicable to *Rosencrantz and Guildenstern Are Dead.* For Rosencrantz and Guildenstern themselves, humor is a means of preserving sanity; for Stoppard it is a natural product of disjunction—of the gulf between cause and effect, aspiration and fulfillment, word and meaning, which is the root alike of pain, absurdity, and laughter, and a clue

[2]The adjective refers to Dali's paintings, which often picture desolate landscapes dominated by rocks and stones.

to the relativity of truth—itself a subject to which Stoppard has repeatedly returned.

Stoppard has said that

what I try to do is to end up by contriving the perfect marriage between the play of ideas and farce or, perhaps, even high comedy . . . to that end I have been writing plays which are farcical and without an idea in their funny heads, and I have also written plays which are all mouth . . . and don't bring off the comedy. And occasionally, I think *Jumpers* would be an example, I've got fairly close to a play which works as a funny play and which makes coherent, in terms of theatre, a fairly complicated intellectual argument.

("Ambushes for the Audience," *Theatre Quarterly,* May–July 1974)

While it is true that the argument behind *Rosencrantz and Guildenstern Are Dead* is not complex, its strength lies precisely in the skill with which Stoppard blends humor with metaphysical inquiry, the success with which he makes the play's theatricality an essential element of its thematic concern. It is, indeed, a kind of *Waiting for Godot* in which Vladimir and Estragon become university wits.

V

YET, as Stoppard has indicated, not all his plays have such serious aspirations. He followed *Rosencrantz and Guildenstern Are Dead* and *Enter a Free Man* with two adroit and well-constructed works (*The Real Inspector Hound* and *After Magritte*), whose chief fascination resides in the skill with which he unravels his own aesthetic conundrums. As he has said, "*After Magritte* and *The Real Inspector Hound* are short plays and they really are an attempt to bring off a sort of comic coup in pure mechanistic terms. They were *conceived* as short plays."

The ostensible subject of *The Real Inspector Hound* (1968) is the rivalry of two drama critics who, somewhat bewilderingly, are drawn into the action of the play they are reviewing. But we have Stoppard's warning that "the one thing *The Real Inspector Hound* isn't about, as far as I am concerned, is theatre critics. . . . I just got into it, and I knew that I wanted it somehow to resolve itself in a breathtakingly neat, complex and utterly comprehensible way." He does, admittedly, give free rein to his considerable talents as a parodist, mocking both the conventions of antiquated drawing-room whodunits and the critical styles of drama reviewers (Birdboot works for a popular paper: "let us give thanks and double thanks for a good clean show without a trace of smut"; Moon writes for a rather more pretentious readership: *"Je suis,* it seems to be saying, *ergo sum* . . . and here one is irresistibly reminded of Voltaire's cry, *Voilá!"*). But once again he is concerned with raising more fundamental questions about the nature of truth and theatricality, although no longer with the same degree of seriousness that he had brought to his first successful play. Once again he creates a play within a play; the audience, by a trick of the eye, is projected into the play that it is watching, as the two critics themselves will be later in the work. The opening stage direction indicates that "the audience appear to be confronted by their own reflection in a huge mirror." In many ways the play is cast from the same die as *Rosencrantz and Guildenstern Are Dead.* Birdboot, like Rosencrantz, is a literal-minded man whose reach does not extend beyond his grasp. Metaphysics disturb him, and he retains his grip on reality by reducing all experience to banalities. Moon, on the other hand, is reminiscent of Guildenstern. He sees significance in everything and is dominated by a growing sense of his own insecurity. Yet, however they may differ, both find themselves occupying the same stage, desperately trying to understand what they are doing, cast suddenly and without appeal in a second-rate drama.

Critics have inevitably invoked the name of Luigi Pirandello in relation to Stoppard's work, and there is, indeed, considerable similarity in their concern with the nature of reality, the relativity of truth, and the fluid nature of identity. Both writers have repeatedly resorted to the theatrical metaphor in expressing the conviction that individual existence consists of a number of overlapping roles, that appearance and reality are inevitably and instructively divorced from one another, and that life is more usefully regarded as a series of improvisations than as the acting out of a prepared scenario. Nor is it without significance that the play Birdboot and Moon are reviewing is a whodunit, the supreme example of rational art that, particularly in the parody version Stoppard offers us, derives its whole effect from the conviction that individuals are justifiably identified with their roles (victim, murderer, detective)—indeed gain their meaning purely in terms of the part they play in a highly structured scenario. It is also a form that rests on the conviction that reality is susceptible to rational analysis, since it turns so clearly on causality. But, as a character in *Jumpers* remarks, "unlike mystery novels, life does not guarantee a denouement." Thus, when the prepared text is suddenly disturbed, when the hapless reviewers find themselves on stage, these conventions are threatened. Stoppard then offers his audience a difficult choice, in that in order to restore a sense of order, to maintain the conventions, to avoid the conviction that the action has become irrational, arbitrary, and improvised, the audience is forced to accept a number of wholly absurd assumptions. It is placed, in other words, in the position of Rosencrantz and Guildenstern, who are forced for their own peace of mind to presume the paradigmatic nature of theater, to accept the conviction that performance at all levels implies the existence of an audience.

The Real Inspector Hound is not a wholly satisfactory play. It is more adroit than convincing. The parody, although at times brilliant, is too often facile; the metaphysical dimension, deliberately underplayed, is nonetheless too often sacrificed to the witty remark. A confessedly lightweight comedy, the play finally stops annoyingly short of examining the implications of its central premise.

VI

IT is not surprising to learn that René Magritte is Stoppard's favorite artist, for both men secure their particular effects by essentially the same method. The wrenching of object from setting, of event from context, results not merely in a revealing absurdity but also in a perception of the contingent nature of truth. Yet Stoppard is no surrealist. The tableau at the beginning of his one-act play *After Magritte* (1971) is not a surrealist image designed to liberate the imagination, to energize the subconscious, but a teasing problem in logic, a conundrum to be unraveled. Its metaphorical significance remains largely unexamined, but, as Stoppard himself commented, it is "not an intellectual play, it's a nuts-and-bolts comedy."

The play opens with an old woman lying prone on an ironing board with her foot resting against an iron and with a bowler hat on her stomach. Of the two other people in the room, one is dressed for ballroom dancing and the other, a man equipped with thigh-length waders, is apparently trying to blow out an electric light bulb. The remaining furniture is piled against the front door, and a policeman is staring through the window. The play itself consists of an elaborate explanation for this apparently absurd situation. It is an adroit demonstration of the fact that truth is a matter of perspective. As one of the characters observes, "there is obviously a perfectly logical explanation for everything." Yet although logic does indeed hold, as it does in the radio plays *Albert's Bridge* and *If You're Glad I'll Be Frank,* it has no connection with the inner life of the characters. As George remarks in *Jumpers,* "if rationality were the criterion for things being allowed to exist, the world would be one gigantic field of soya beans! . . . In a wholly rational society the moralist will be a variety of crank." As a consequence these shorter plays are little more than five-finger exercises, displays of virtuoso talent that hint at a metaphysical dimension that they forebear to examine. The same could not be said of Stoppard's more recent work.

Stoppard has said that *Jumpers* (1972) was the first play in which he specifically set out to "ask a question and try to answer it, or at any rate put the counter question." And although once again he chooses a comic framework, the question is a serious one, and one moreover that leads on to the more avowedly political questions of *Travesties.* It is a play about the growingly materialist base of modern society and the desperate attempt by its protagonist to establish the existence and reality of transcendent values.

His protagonist, another bewildered individual assailed by authority and threatened by the positivist assumptions of his society, struggles manfully to establish by logical means the existence of moral absolutes and the credibility of God. As a professor of moral philosophy, George Moore tries to oppose the rationalist assumptions of his age by deploying a blend of intuitionist philosophy, deductive reasoning, and empirical evidence. He does so, however, in the most unpromising circumstances. The radical liberal party has just won an election and has begun the process of rationalizing society by appointing a veterinary surgeon as archbishop of Canterbury. A British moon landing, itself a victory for technology, has ended in near disaster, the captain pragmatically abandoning his

companion in order to return to the equally pragmatic earth. And George's wife, Dotty, a well-known singer, who may or may not have murdered the professor of logic, has retired from show business, her lyrical invocations to the moon effectively destroyed not merely by an antinomian science that daily appropriates further aspects of human experience, but by a perspective that suddenly reduces human significance. As she explains:

. . . it's all over now. Not only are we no longer the still centre of God's universe, we're not even uniquely graced by his footprint in man's image. . . . Man is on the Moon, his feet on solid ground, and he has seen us whole . . . and all our absolutes . . . that seemed to be the very condition of our existence, how did *they* look to two moonmen? . . . Like the local customs of another place.
(Act II)

All George's convictions seem to be invalidated by events. As he tries to construct his logical defense of illogic and substantiate his faith in a nonrelativistic ethic, a group of acrobatic philosophers are busily engaged in disposing of the corpse of one of their colleagues—a logician who has come to doubt the morality of his own denial of moral values. Even the language he uses subverts his intention, since it too is relativistic, a pragmatic approximation. He is, in other words, in an absurd situation building logical structures as flawed as those of the bewildered George Riley in *Enter a Free Man.* Yet he and Dotty remain dedicated to humane values as well as to preserving an element of mystery in a society that regards human experience as wholly classifiable in rational terms. As he confesses:

When I push *my* convictions to absurdity, *I* arrive at God. . . . All I know is that I think that I know that I know that nothing can be created out of nothing, that my moral conscience is different from the rules of my tribe, and that there is more in me than meets the microscope —and because of *that* I'm lumbered with this incredible, indescribable and definitely shifty *God,* the trump card of atheism.
(Act II)

The irony of George's situation, however, resides in the fact that while he elaborates his defense of values in the admittedly somewhat limited privacy of his own study, the world outside is renouncing all interest in the matter. Engaged only on a theoretical level, he implicitly compounds the forces that he deplores. Just as life inevitably evades his attempt to pin it down with words, his elaborate arguments sliding off into anecdote and parenthetical byways, so his grasp on the real world is seen to be tenuous at best. Obsessed with validating an abstraction, he fails to grasp the totalitarian nature of the forces that have just come to power, blinded, ironically, by their use of the word "liberal." The fact that George succeeds ironically in destroying his own overelaborate proofs (when he kills the rabbit and crushes the tortoise with which he had planned to clinch his rational justification of irrationality) is evidence of his own ironic contradictions. As Dotty suggests, he is "living in dreamland."

Indeed, the final scene of the play is presented in what Stoppard calls "bizarre dream form." It consists of the symposium for which George has been preparing himself throughout the rest of the play. Following a parodied and semi-coherent statement of a materialist view of man by the decidedly materialist and incidentally lecherous vice-chancellor, the new secular archbishop of Canterbury is summoned. Himself an atheist, he proceeds to imitate Thomas Becket and voices the opinion, heretical in a rational state, that "surely belief in man could find room for man's beliefs." When the archbishop is consequently murdered for this affront to rationality and political expediency, George fails to intervene, unwilling to make the necessary connection between theory and practice. He simply excuses his detachment by asserting that "that seems to be a political quarrel. . . . Surely only a proper respect for absolute values . . . universal truths . . . *philosophy*—." His desperate desire to get the conversation back onto an abstract plane is interrupted by a gun shot, as the archbishop is deftly removed from the human pyramid into which the gymnastic philosophers had carefully incorporated him. Unmoved, George launches into his prepared text on the existence of moral values only to be interrupted again—this time, finally, by the vice-chancellor. He in turn glibly outlines a pragmatic defense of a positivist stance that, in its justification for baseless optimism over the plight of modern man, ironically applies not only to the radical liberals intent on eradicating an inefficient individualism but also to George.

George is so caught up in his own confident assertions of moral values that he fails to see the collapse of everything that gives those values meaning. This society is nothing if not pragmatic.

The police force seems likely to be "thinned out to a ceremonial front for the peace-keeping activities of the Army," and the Chair of Divinity at the university no longer invites applicants and can be offered as a bribe to an overinquisitive policeman or as a reward for a particularly diligent porter. Against such a situation George's confused liberalism seems no defense. His convictions paradoxically lead him to contradiction and equivocation. His respect for reason leads him to attempt a rational justification for faith, and his commitment to tolerance makes him endorse the very forces that threaten his philosophy most directly. "It would be presumptuous," he says, "to condemn radical ideas simply because they appear to me to be self-evidently stupid and criminal, if they do happen to be at the same time radical." His passion is deflected into his work, into finding the right word, the right image, into creating a convincing structure. In many ways his problem is that of the playwright himself, in love with words and ideas but detached from the real world by virtue of his craft, as is the philosopher by virtue of his need to deal in abstractions rather than concrete realities. (At any rate, this question becomes central to Stoppard's later work, *Travesties*, which attempts to examine the whole question of the role of the artist.)

George inevitably fails in his attempt to prove the existence of God, as he does in his effort to establish the absolute nature of moral values. His convictions remain nothing more than an expression of faith disguised as logical inferences. But, after all, as the wholly irrational relationship of George and Dotty would seem to suggest, "the irrational, the emotional, the whimsical . . . are the stamp of humanity which makes reason a civilizing force." The anarchic energy of this embattled couple, alarmed as they are by the threatened collapse of their world but resisting with sporadic displays of affection, humor, and faith, contrasts sharply with the crudely rational world that intrudes on the television screen and in the pointless precision with which the philosophical jumpers turn their literal and metaphorical somersaults. As George remarks, "now and again, not necessarily in the contemplation of polygons or new-born babes, nor in the extremities of pain or joy, but more probably in some quite trivial moment, it seems to me that life itself is the mundane figure which argues perfection at its limiting curve." And if perfection is in fact unreachable, the existence of such moments is enough to justify the faith and lyrical yearnings of George and his vulnerable wife.

The real advance in *Jumpers* is not merely that Stoppard succeeds in fusing a comic approach with metaphysics, but that he begins to control the resources of theater with greater confidence and skill than before. The philosophical acrobats, performing their various contortions and constructing human pyramids, constitute a perfect image of the intellectual processes they enact. The huge television screen that projects the external world into the frenetic private life of the Moores is both an assertion of that connection between public and private morality which Stoppard is anxious to establish, and itself evidence of an alienating technology. Even the word games, the ambiguities, the puns, which are all recognizable marks of Stoppard's work, are entirely functional in a play that is in large part concerned with the inadequacy of attempts to capture reality with words, the palpable absurdity of measuring with a rule whose length obstinately varies from moment to moment. The apparent absurdity of the opening scene—during which a stripper flies across the stage on a trapeze, Dotty flounders through a bewildering medley of "moon" songs, and the yellow-uniformed gymnasts perform their feats until the death of one of their number precipitates an abrupt end—resembles the bizarre opening of *After Magritte.* Indeed, as in that play, these impossibly incongruous elements are shown to be capable of a perfectly rational explanation; but whereas in the earlier work Stoppard was largely content with his display of ingenuity, here the unraveling of confusions is endemic to the style and purpose of the play's protagonist. And although once again it becomes apparent that events can be shown to sustain a logical explanation, the simple unraveling of that logic leaves a residual problem, since it can offer no explanation for the irrational yearnings that torture both Dotty and George but which, it is increasingly apparent, are seen by Stoppard as constituting the essence of human nature, the core of individual resistance to reification.

VII

THE moral dimension of Stoppard's work appears at times to suffer from his own commitment to farce. He seems afraid to take himself seriously, to allow

his humor to become a consistent critique—hence his penchant for parody rather than satire, his technique of building scenes through contradiction. As he once remarked, "I write plays because dialogue is the most respectable way of contradicting myself."

It follows that he feels "committed art" to be "a kind of bogus exercise." As he has explained, "I get deeply embarrassed by the statements and postures of "committed" theatre. There is no such thing as "pure" art—art is a commentary on something else in life—it might be adultery in the suburbs, or the Vietnamese war. I think that art ought to involve itself in contemporary social and political history as much as anything else, but I find it deeply embarrassing when large claims are made for such an involvement: when, because art takes notice of something important, it's claimed that the art is important. It's not."

Travesties (1975) attempts to debate essentially this problem. As Stoppard has said, "it puts the question in a more extreme form. It asks whether an artist has to justify himself in political terms *at all,*" "whether the words 'revolutionary' and 'artist' are capable of being synonymous or whether they are mutually exclusive, or something in between." It is a play that brings together the opposite extremes of the debate in the persons of James Joyce (whom Stoppard elsewhere quotes as saying that the history of Ireland, troubles and all, is justified because it led to a book such as *Ulysses*) and Lenin, who felt that the only justification for art lies in its political utility. Mediating between the two is Tristan Tzara, drawn simultaneously in both directions—on the one hand spinning neologisms and cascades of words like Joyce, convinced that the artist constitutes the difference between brute existence and any sense of transcendence, and on the other hand seeing the writer as the conscience of the revolution and justifying the brutality of its servants. However, the question is effectively begged by the form in which Stoppard chooses to conduct the debate. For the most part we see the characters only as they are refracted through the febrile imagination of a minor British consular official, Henry Carr. Just as *Hamlet,* viewed through the eyes of Rosencrantz and Guildenstern, is drained of tragic meaning, so too this clash of ideas loses much of its urgency seen from the perspective of a deluded, prejudiced, and erratic minor functionary. In this context, perforce, they become mere performers in a Wildean comedy, which jolts along with all the manic energy and manifest dishonesty of a bogus memoir.

In "The Critic as Artist," Wilde remarks of memoirs that they are "generally written by people who have either entirely lost their memories, or have never done anything worth remembering." This proves all too accurate a description of Carr's memoirs, which tend to confuse his own fictions with those of *The Importance of Being Earnest,* in which he had once scored a minor success. Indeed, apart from appropriating dialogue and even two of his characters directly from Wilde's play, he even restructures history so that it conforms to the requirements of high comedy. The title is thus an appropriate one as Stoppard, through Carr, presents a travesty of both literary styles and historical events.

Carr erroneously remembers himself as having been British consul in Zurich during World War I, at a time when Lenin, Joyce, and Tzara were living out an expatriate existence, plotting their various revolutions in art and society. In juxtaposing these forces, Stoppard seems to be suggesting that history is no less a fiction than Joyce's parodic constructions; that it has no more logic than Tzara's poems, which are themselves the product of pure chance. But something about this equation of literary performance and bravura politics fails to convince. In picking Lenin as the embodiment of political fabulism, Stoppard engages not merely a historically bound figure who can be parodied as a none-too-competent role player, but also a palpable reality whose particular fictions have assumed an implacable form. There is a degree, therefore, to which Stoppard seems to have been unnerved by the ineluctable consequences of revolutionary conviction. We know, or think we know, that the opinions expressed by the various characters in the play are those which Carr constructs. The single exception is Lenin, who stands, perhaps, as a corrective to those fictions—massive, real. The grand claims of Tzara, the self-confident assertiveness of Joyce, real or illusory, can only inhabit a world defined by the prosaic realities identified by Lenin. The massive scale of his impact on history, an impact that transcends the banality of both his life style and his literary style, is a fact tucked away in the mind of the audience. Just as his presence seems to neutralize the play's anarchic humor, to inhibit the irresponsible contempt for social reali-

ties, so his presence in the real world does much the same. He is a materialist, and the material has no time for fantasy, as Dotty had realized in *Jumpers.* The details of Lenin's career, solemnly narrated by Nadya, his Russian secretary (a narration that Stoppard incautiously invites his directors to edit to taste), contrast markedly with the anarchic frivolity of those other revolutionaries who surround him in Zurich, and whose revolutions are contained by the boundaries of artistic concern.

From his initial description of the characters through to Lenin's departure for Russia, it is the political activist alone who for the most part escapes parody. Carr's imagination makes both Joyce and Tzara perform a series of bizarre antics. Indeed, they become the chief actors in a baroque farce, likely at any moment to lapse into song and dance. Lenin remains stolidly detached. His speeches are authentic, a point that Stoppard is at pains to stress. He is the only character, in other words, who is not controlled by Carr's distorting imagination, although according to the conventions of the play he too should be molded to fit the elderly diplomat's psychic needs. And although this is perhaps a conscious comment on the nature of the difference between the artist and the social revolutionary, a difference that makes the fusion of the two roles unlikely, it also has the effect of dislocating the play. The second act is not merely less funny than the first, containing a detailed documentary account of Lenin's career (accompanied by objectifying photographs) as well as a debate about the role of the artist between Carr on the one hand and Tzara and Cecily (a librarian) on the other; it is also less effective. The sources for the first act are Wilde's play *The Importance of Being Earnest,* James Joyce's *Ulysses,* and the documented excesses of Dada; the source for the second is Lenin's biography. The change in mood is inevitable. The result is a curiously reverential treatment of the political leader, an approach quite at odds with the tone of a play that seems to suggest his poverty of imagination, his disregard for moral values, and his misconceptions about the function of art and history. Farce drains away as Stoppard comes to the heart of his concern, and although he is careful to conceal his own commitments by refusing to resolve the contradictory views expressed by his characters, the stylistic dislocation exposes the seriousness of his concern, as the play becomes at moments a genuine debate about the importance of being earnest—of adopting a humorless dedication to social realities.

Stoppard has called his distinguishing mark an "absolute lack of certainty about almost anything." This detachment, unnerving in some respects, gives him the freedom most of the time to criticize the materialist inhumanity of Lenin, the spurious artistic arrogance of Joyce, the cavalier socialism of Tzara, and the aristocratic hauteur of Carr. All seem squarely rooted in self-concern. But Stoppard's detachment slips once or twice. Despite his failure to locate a satisfactory mode of parody with regard to Lenin, his distrust of ideologists surfaces at moments, cutting through the comic banter that otherwise for the most part defuses any attempt at moral seriousness. Carr's rebuttal of Marxist analysis and Cecily's disingenuous justification for Lenin's inhumanity are too studied to sustain a credible commitment to ethical distance. The assumptions of farce come up against the moral presumptions of comedy, and the resulting clash disturbs not merely stylistic unity but also the momentum of the humor.

In a conflict between a materialistic view of history and an approach that translates the substantial realities of human life into fictions, fantasies, and plots, there can be little doubt where Stoppard's sympathies will lie—nor, by the end, can we be in any doubt that these two views are so clearly antithetical that the notion of a revolutionary artist is a demonstrable contradiction in terms. Yet, in his own way, Carr is as dedicated to a simplistic view of reality as is Lenin. He wants to believe in a world in which he can play a central role. Language must provide a precise symbolism, the artist must be a beautifier of reality, a licensed hedonist. He resists reality with as much dedication as either Joyce or Tzara. He is, of course, in a real sense a playwright. He "creates" the drama in which he casts himself as the central character (as, essentially, does each individual). He claims the same right to refuse social liability as he believes the true artist must do. As he remarks, "to be an artist *at all* is like living in Switzerland during a world war."

In this respect, also, he is close kin to Rosencrantz and Guildenstern, to George Riley and Professor Moore. Like Stoppard himself, these characters choose to respond to the bewildering vagaries of existence by creating games, plays, by remaking the world until its absurdities dissolve in simple performance. Lenin, Joyce, Tzara, Carr, all are equally pathetic and heroic as they inhabit with such apparent conviction the fictions they choose to regard as reality. Role players all, they seek to construct plots that will make sense of their urge for personal, social, or metaphysical order. Art, politics, philosophy, logic are deployed with varying degrees of conviction. But behind it all there lurks the savage joke that is implicit in the figure of the aging Carr, who reconstructs his past out of the same compulsions that led Beckett's Krapp to turn the switch of his tape recorder to replay the hopes and aspirations of his youth. It is Carr's distinction that he glimpses this truth for a moment and is still able to justify his challenge to reality.

VIII

THE pressure of history and the coercive power of the public world are such that at times humor seems to find less and less room to operate. Ironies are too apparent, language too obviously corrupt and corrupting, public fictions too evidently paraded as verities to require the writer to underscore them. So it seemed, at any rate, in 1982, when Stoppard responded to a request to write a television film about the situation in Poland. Martial law had been in force for a month; Solidarity had shown its first real signs of vulnerability. The problem was to write a play that addressed this situation without seeming to create the impression of a documentary realism for which the film could claim no authority. The solution lay in the creation of a "fallible narrator," whose expressed opinions and confident possession of fact could be undermined by the flow of events. But at the same time there was no doubt as to Stoppard's own position. *Squaring the Circle* was based on the conviction that freedom as defined by Solidarity could no more be reconciled with state socialism than a circle can be turned into a square with the same area. There was also no doubt as to where his sympathy lay.

Defined thus, the play might seem to be little more than an exercise in propaganda, and there were indeed those on the left in British cultural life who had begun to expect little more from Stoppard, seeing a certain irony in the sight of a playwright who, like the British prime minister, seemed to defend the rights of trade unions abroad while attacking their privileges at home. It certainly came as little surprise when he urged voters to support Margaret Thatcher in the 1983 elections. But the play was never to be simply this. It was, at least in intent, a play as much about colliding languages as about a conflict of values; a play that concerned itself with the differing models of reality that are a product of point of view.

Stoppard has written amusingly of the difficulties attending the film's production—an Anglo-American enterprise that suffered most of the problems implicit in such ventures. And it is tempting to see in the circumstances of the film's production—which required Stoppard to make flying visits to conferences at the Beverly Hills Hotel and to tolerate alterations to his work—an irony as sharp as any within the play. For, plainly, while he chose to focus on the shortcomings of an East European system that finds the concept of personal freedom and individual vision difficult to understand, let alone tolerate, his own battles with production companies and commercial interests (not to mention ideological presumptions) showed that the West is hardly immune to a similar myopia. Certainly, in the introduction to a collection of his plays, a disproportionate amount of space is devoted to an account of negotiations over the status and content of a film that purports to dramatize negotiations between the creator of a union and those with the power to deny that union access to the media.

That aside, however, the play seeks to show the incompatibility of systems of thought that no more share a common language than they do a common conception of freedom, democracy, or meaning. Lech Walesa is presented as sincere if naive; as honest, confused, courageous, and occasionally arrogant. The various party functionaries and political figures are seen as baffled, wily, Machiavellian. They control the vocabulary of the state, hence its power. But where in *Every Good Boy Deserves Favour* that fact becomes the basis of both the play's humor and politics, little is made of it in *Squaring the Circle.* The play is not without its humor, but this seems somewhat desperately worked for in a series of artful but ultimately, I think, unconvincing scenes, which attempt to find images commensurate with the political processes that the play dramatizes. The material was there to create either a powerful drama of colliding moralities or a work that exposes the contingent nature of all value systems, the fictionality of ideological convictions and

political faiths. It ends up by choosing neither option, or failing to examine either with real wit or conviction. In fact, the drama remains inert, the metaphysical implications of Stoppard's own dramatic strategy unexplored, the humor uninspired and in some senses the political analysis disabled, as the creators of Gulag become comic puppet masters, more amusing than threatening.

There is no doubting the strength of Stoppard's conviction or his grasp of the subtleties, no less than the crudities, of power. He has increasingly involved himself in the battle and has written powerfully of a society in which "control over information aspires to the absolute and where reality can be rewritten." Indeed, in calling for a boycott of the 1980 Moscow Olympics, he insisted that "we have the chance to let it be known throughout the Soviet Empire that, contrary to appearances, there is some bread we will not break with the saviours of Eastern Europe and Afghanistan, not to mention Greater Russia; that morality has not yet been stood on its head on planet earth . . . there is still a decent way to govern people and an indecent way, that the difference is not relative but absolute."[3] The sentiments are unexceptionable, but curiously the anger that generated them dissipates in the artifices of *Squaring the Circle.* To be sure, it was not written as protest drama. For all the distance Stoppard has come since *Rosencrantz and Guildenstern Are Dead,* when notions of absolute values, clear political allegiances, and an assumed system of morality would have seemed irrelevant if not wholly without meaning, he has not become a purely political writer. The Marxist playwright Edward Bond chooses to characterize him as a "Fascist" and a "clown in a charnel house," but this description is painfully wide of the mark and does little to elucidate the paradoxes of Stoppard's work. He is, indeed, right-wing—in the sense that an eighteenth-century liberal might be said to be. That is to say, he apotheosizes the individual, seemingly accepts the inequities generated by a society that relates political freedom to what passes, in twentieth-century terms, for laissez-faire economics, and implicitly asserts a moral function for art. He deplores the erosion of the concept of the self that he sees as a corollary of state socialism, and he distrusts definitions of the real offered by

[3]"Tom Stoppard on the KGB's Olympic Trials," the *Sunday Times,* 6 April 1980, p. 16.

those who equate truth with ideology. But for the most part his plays have set themselves the task of exploring the processes whereby we create the worlds we inhabit through the language with which we choose to describe them; the extent to which we invent the determinism to which we willfully submit ourselves; the degree to which we deceive ourselves into believing ourselves agents rather than principals; and above all—and not in contradistinction to his own political and moral values—that the real and the true are ultimately only fictions, albeit fictions whose superiority is instinctively felt. In other words, in some final sense, he deals in faith. It is that which lies at the heart of *Squaring the Circle,* as it does of *Professional Foul, Every Good Boy Deserves Favour,* and, in some senses, *Jumpers.* It is a faith that in another sense underlies his commitment to humor, which, after all, crucially depends upon the ambiguity rather than the total authority of language, and which frequently, in intent and effect, resists precisely that humorless commitment to a singular interpretation of the real, which he increasingly sees as a primary enemy.

IX

STOPPARD began his career with witty, absurdist dramas. His work was distinguished by its humor, by brilliance and originality of construction, and by intellectual fleetness of foot. Then, having in effect argued for the primacy of aesthetics over ethics, he began to wish to find a way in which his moral convictions could find space to operate. And this meant reinventing the values he had so carefully evacuated from *Rosencrantz and Guildenstern Are Dead, After Magritte,* and so on. It was a process that he began in *Jumpers,* which continued in the debate, explicit and implicit, between Lenin and Joyce in *Travesties,* and which then found a clear focus in *Professional Foul, Every Good Boy Deserves Favour,* and *Night and Day*—in every one of which, beyond the political questions posed, he considers the possibility that a mere facility with language may in some sense be at the heart of corruption. The linguistic philosophers of *Professional Foul* (1978), the KGB colonel who is also a professor of philology in *Every Good Boy Deserves Favour,* the journalists of *Night and Day* (1978) are all people who, like Stoppard him-

self, create their own worlds of meaning with words. These are, in effect, all plays that, beyond their immediate political frisson, at least simulate a debate about the nature of the real and the extent to which language can capture it. And that remains true in *The Real Thing* (1982), in which two playwrights—one supposedly a mere wordsmith, content to amuse with his wit and entertain with his intellectual sophistication, the other a committed writer, crude in his construction of character but supposedly sincere in his beliefs—are contrasted with one another.

The former, Henry, is married to Charlotte, an actress currently appearing with an actor called Max in one of her husband's plays. Indeed, *The Real Thing* actually begins with a scene from that play, a fact that is, of course, lost on the audience, which takes as real the scene played out in front of them. In that scene Charlotte plays a woman whose marriage is collapsing, a fact whose hidden ironies become apparent only later, when we learn that Henry is in love with Max's wife, an actress called Annie. She, in turn, is involved with another actor, Billy, who plays the role of a young soldier called Brodie in yet another play in which he appears with Annie. Brodie, however, is not merely a character in this play; he is also its author, having been moved to write it by his somewhat confused involvement in an antiwar protest.

The complexities of plot, which make this such a difficult play to describe, are deliberate in a play that seeks to problematize the notion of the real while apparently staging a debate about the nature and role of the writer. The claim now discussed is whether the urgency of the subject justifies the work it provokes—in this case Brodie's less than competent play about his own antiwar protest—or whether clever construction, humor, and the elaboration of private and inconsequential dilemmas have their own justification. The dice are loaded with respect to both options. Brodie writes in clichés; Henry creates brittle plays about adultery in which character is subordinated to wit; in other words, he writes plays not entirely remote from those which had characterized Stoppard's own early career. Thus, Annie accuses her husband of being "bigoted about what writing is supposed to be like. You judge everything as though everyone starts off from the same place, aiming at the same prize. . . . Brodie isn't writing to compete like you. He's writing to be heard.

TOM STOPPARD

. . . He's a prisoner shouting over the wall." Elsewhere she insists that he is

jealous of the idea of the writer. You want to keep it sacred, special, not something anybody can do. . . . *You're a writer*. You write *because* you're a writer. Even when you write *about* something, you have to think up something to write about just so you can keep writing. More well chosen words nicely put together. . . . You teach a lot of people what to expect from good writing, and you end up with a lot of people saying you write well. Then somebody who isn't in on the game comes along . . . who really has something to write about, something real, and you can't get through it. Well, *he* couldn't get through *yours*, so where are you? To you, he can't write. To him, write is all you *can* do.

(II.v)

Since this is essentially the accusation once leveled at Stoppard, it seems precisely set up to enable him to justify himself, the more especially since Annie incautiously compares him to a writer who has something "real" to write about in a play in which the substantiality of reality is in question, and Brodie's commitment is itself seen as unreal because unfelt and unmotivated. Henry's reply, however, at least initially, has little substance, as he insists that writing is indeed a craft and that sincerity of feeling does not justify misuse of language. His more significant response is that slogans have no human content and that the committed writer is liable to fail to inspect his own motives, position, and deceits. He insists, centrally, that a willful abuse of language is itself actually an assault on the very implied contract that links people together. Words exist, he insists, so that "you can build bridges across incomprehension and chaos." Such a respect for language becomes crucial because, as he says, "if you get the right ones in the right order, you can nudge the world a little or make a poem which children will speak for you when you're dead. . . . If you know this and proceed with humility, you may perhaps alter people's perceptions." In other words, he has adroitly usurped the position of the committed writer, simply asserting that values reside in the imagination and in a commitment to language and not the mere authenticity of emotions—that aesthetic values may be the root of ethical values.

The only problem with this is that, at the very moment of making this speech, Henry is actually engaged in writing a totally banal movie script for purely monetary motives. He is also fully aware

that words are themselves plastic, dependent for their meaning on context, inflection, nuance, and that as his own adultery and his play about adultery make plain, language is frequently deployed to conceal as well as to reveal truth: it is often enrolled in the service of private and public betrayals. And if the state can be indicted for its abuse of language, for its propensity to create fictions within which the rest of us must live our lives, then so, too, can the writer. Indeed, in *The Real Thing* there seems to be no irreducible reality. If we seek it in personal relationships, in the moment when, apparently, masks are removed and there is a nakedness of souls no less than bodies, then this, too, can become simple deceit, mere role playing. It certainly proves to be so in a play in which personal betrayal is a norm. And that raises another question: in a world of unreality, of competing fictions in which from moment to moment we are unable to distinguish the real, how can morality exist or express itself? Stoppard's only answer elsewhere in his work had been to insist on the superior nature of certain fictions; but even this required some irreducible value by means of which such judgment could be made, and increasingly this seemed to amount to little more than a simple declaration of faith.

In *The Real Thing* there is no irreducible reality, and it follows that the debate it contains is itself factitious, and that not merely because he chooses to parody both his writers, who are, anyway, themselves simple fictions. But insofar as it becomes anything more than a witty, inconsequential play, of the kind it contains, this is because the destabilizing of the real may itself be a moral act. Realistic theater presumes the knowability of the self and the transparency of social process; it presumes, in particular, that the real offers itself readily to our understanding. As Jean-Paul Sartre once observed, "The error of realism has been to believe that the real reveals itself to our contemplation, and that consequently one could draw an impartial picture of it. How could that be possible, since the very perception is partial since by itself the meaning is already a modification of the object." That perception does not deny the substance of experience, nor, in Sartre's case, the necessity to reinject meaning into language ("If words are sick," he once remarked, "it is up to us to cure them"). Indeed, he distrusted the incommunicable, seeing it as the root of social despair, hence of violence. But Sartre's remarks do indicate his belief that the real is not immediately apparent and that art works by indirection. What Stoppard is doing is to insist that our map of the world is an invented one, that states are no less factitious than our own lives, no less theatrical constructions. That is not to say that they do not have observable results. Writers are arrested, as they are in *Professional Foul;* dissidents are imprisoned in mental hospitals, as they are in *Every Good Boy Deserves Favour.* Myths can kill. But if we recognize them for what they are, it becomes possible for us to acknowledge their sheer contingency: the debate between the Soviet state and the prisoner assigned to a mental hospital, because his vision of the real differs from that of the state, is in essence a debate about which fiction we should be permitted to live by. It begins with the assumption that the fictions of the state have no ultimate authority.

Stoppard is attacked by the left not for being a bad playwright but for choosing to disregard the seriousness of moral issues, for being either a mere entertainer or, worse, an entertainer whose moral seriousness is reserved for threats to freedom deriving from the left. But if he is undoubtedly conservative in his politics, there is a radicalism to his work that tends to be disregarded. For his assault on the real is in effect an implied critique of those for whom the real presents itself in simple terms, those for whom complexity is a mere mask and the role of the writer to expose that reality. It was Sartre who said that "the work of art does not have an end . . . it is an end"; and while he, like Theodore Adorno, was aware that "there is no material content, no formal category of artistic creation, however mysteriously transmitted and itself unaware of the process, which does not originate in the empirical reality from which it breaks free," it is clear that the question of language and the manner in which it constitutes the real remained a crucial concern for him as it does for Stoppard. Indeed, it was Adorno who insisted that the real revolutionaries were Beckett and Franz Kafka because they assaulted from within, destabilizing our sense of the real, what others attack only from without.

Less surprisingly, in 1957 Alain Robbe-Grillet insisted that "to believe that the novelist has 'something to say,' and that he then tries to discover how to say it, is the gravest misconception. For it is precisely this 'how,' this way of saying things, that constitutes the whole, obscure project of the writer, and that later becomes the dubious content of his book. And in the final analysis it may

well be this dubious content of an obscure project that best serves the cause of freedom."[4] True commitment, he insists, is to be aware of the problems of language, to be resistant to "fixed and ready-made meanings"; true hope lies in man and "the forms he creates that give meaning to the world." It sounds like a defense of formalism, but that same essay, in which he argues for the contingency of meaning and insists that it is the ability of art to declare its freedom from other structures of meaning which constitutes its power as a paradigm, ends with a disturbing question: "But how long," he asks, "will we have to wait?"

The cogency of Robbe-Grillet's argument for the centrality of language and form, as well as for the significance of the fictionalizing process in the construction of what we take for reality, is balanced by an awareness of the urgency of certain social demands, of the justice of those who advance the need for a frontal, if crude, assault on a system of power no less dangerous for its contingency. And it is the pressure of that question that has increasingly made itself felt in Stoppard's work. To some degree Brodie and Henry now coexist in Stoppard's sensibility, as once they did not (if we mean by that not the crude aesthetic values and political bad faith with which he chooses to parody the left-wing writer, but an acknowledgment of the justice of both ethical and aesthetic claims on the writer). Stoppard also seems to accept, as once he did not, that the writer is complicit in that manipulation of freedom which has become a central theme in his recent work. But he tends to locate his moral concerns in fictions whose very inventiveness constitutes the basis of their moral claim. In that way he has sought to accommodate his patent and unrivaled skills as a writer of witty, articulate, and brilliantly constructed comedies to a moral and even a political commitment, with which such skills might seem to be incompatible.

SELECTED BIBLIOGRAPHY

I. SEPARATE WORKS. *Introduction 2: Stories by New Writers* (London, 1964), includes "Reunion," "Life, Times, Fragments," and "The Story"; *Lord Malquist and Mr Moon*

4Alain Robbe-Grillet, *Snapshots and Towards a New Novel,* trans. by B. Wright (London, 1965), p. 70.

(London, 1966), fiction; *Rosencrantz and Guildenstern Are Dead* (London, 1966), play; *Enter a Free Man* (London, 1968), play; *The Real Inspector Hound* (London, 1968), play; *Tango* (London, 1968), play by S. Mrozek, adapted by Stoppard from the trans. from Polish by N. Bethell; *Albert's Bridge* (London, 1969), radio play; *If You're Glad I'll Be Frank* (London, 1969), radio play; *A Separate Peace* (London, 1969), play; *After Magritte* (London, 1971), play; *Jumpers* (London, 1972), play; *Artist Descending a Staircase* (London, 1973), radio play; *Where Are They Now?* (London, 1973), radio play; *Travesties* (London, 1975), play; *Every Good Boy Deserves Favour* (London, 1978), play; *Professional Foul* (London, 1978), play; *Night and Day* (London, 1978), play; *Dogg's Our Pet* and *The (15-Minute) Dogg's Troupe Hamlet* (London, 1979), in *Ten of the Best British Short Plays*; *Dogg's Hamlet, Cahoot's Macbeth* (London, 1980), plays; *Undiscovered Country* (London, 1980), adaptation of play by A. Schnitzler; *On the Razzle* (London, 1981), adaptation of play by J. Nestroy; *The Real Thing* (London, 1982), play; *Squaring the Circle* (London, 1982), play; *The Dog It Was That Died and Other Plays* (London, 1983).

II. ARTICLES. "The Writer and the Theatre: The Definite Maybe," in *Author*, 78 (Spring 1967); "Something to Declare," in the *Sunday Times* (25 February 1968); "Doers and Thinkers; Playwrights and Professors," in the *Times Literary Supplement* (13 October 1972); "Dirty Linen in Prague," in the *New York Times* (11 February 1977); "Looking-Glass World," in the *New Statesman* (28 October 1977); "Tom Stoppard on the KGB's Olympic Trials," in the *Sunday Times* (6 April 1980).

III. CRITICAL STUDIES. J. R. Taylor, *Anger and After: A Guide to the New English Drama* (London, 1962), includes a chapter on Stoppard; J. Simon, "Theatre Chronicle," in the *Hudson Review*, 20 (Winter 1967–1968); K. Harper, "The Devious Route to Waterloo Road," in the *Guardian* (12 April 1967); J. Weightman, "Mini-Hamlets in Limbo," in *Encounter* (29 July 1967); I. Wardle, "A Grin Without a Cat," in the *Times* (22 June 1968), on *The Real Inspector Hound*; V. L. Cahn, *Beyond Absurdity: The Plays of Tom Stoppard* (London, 1969); J. F. Dean, *Tom Stoppard: Comedy as a Moral Matrix* (London, 1981); F. H. Londré, *Tom Stoppard* (London, 1981); T. R. Whitaker, *Tom Stoppard* (London, 1983); "Tom Stoppard Moves into Political Writing," in *Newsday* (7 October 1978); "Faith in Mr. Stoppard," in *Queens Quarterly*, 86 (1979); "The Real Stoppard," in *Encounter* (February 1983).

JONATHAN SWIFT

(1667-1745)

A. Norman Jeffares

LIFE

JONATHAN SWIFT was born in Dublin on 30 November 1667. His father was the fifth son of Thomas Swift, vicar of Goodrich and rector of Bridstow, in Herefordshire, and an ardent royalist who had been ejected from his two livings and imprisoned by the Cromwellians. After Thomas' death, the Swifts, attracted by the possibilities of making themselves lucrative careers, removed to Ireland. But Swift's father died in the March or April before his son's birth, and the widow had merely twenty pounds a year on which to live. Swift described his parents' marriage as "on both sides very indiscreet, for his wife brought her husband little or no fortune, and his death happening so suddenly before he could make a sufficient establishment for his family." He remarked that he felt the consequences of that marriage, not only through the whole course of his education but during the greatest part of his life. He did not have a home in the ordinary sense of the word; and when he was about a year old his wet nurse took him from Dublin to Whitehaven (of which she was a native), where he stayed for nearly three years. Swift thought he had been in effect kidnapped by the nurse because she "was extremely fond of the infant," and his mother sent orders he was not to hazard another sea voyage back to Dublin until he "could be better able to bear it."

When Swift returned to Ireland he did not stay long with his mother. She returned to her home in Leicestershire with his sister, and Swift was then brought up by his uncles in Ireland. He was sent, probably at the age of six, to Kilkenny College, an excellent school established by the Ormonde family. He entered Trinity College, Dublin, on 24 April 1682. His tutor was St. George Ashe, who later became provost and subsequently held several

bishoprics. Swift's own account of his undergraduate days gives a gloomy picture:

. . . by the ill treatment of his nearest relations, he was so discouraged and sunk in his spirits, that he too much neglected some parts of his academic studyes, for which he had no great relish by nature, and turned himself to reading history and poetry. So that when the time came for taking his degree of batchelor, although he had lived with great regularity and due observance of the statutes, he was stopped of his degree for dullness and insufficiency, and at last admitted in a manner little to his credit, which is called in that college *speciali gratia*.

Swift had found being a poor relation humiliating. When he was young he had wanted to be famous. His unhappiness is recorded in a memory of one youthful moment of frustration, itself an example of other events and emotions:

I remember when I was a little boy, I felt a great fish at the end of my line which I drew up almost on the ground, but it dropt in, and the disappointment vexeth me to this very day, and I believe it was the type of all my future disappointments.

In fact he had the best possible education in Ireland; and he had not done so badly at Trinity College as he made out in his old age. He found the curriculum dull; the most likely career to which it led—the Anglican Church of Ireland—did not necessarily offer the prospect of rapid advancement: and he was short of money. He spent nearly seven years at Trinity and was about to take his master's degree when public events intervened.

The tensions of impending revolution no doubt explain some of Swift's unsettled state as a student. Admonished for neglect of duties and for "frequenting the town" in March 1687, he started tumults at Trinity and, with five others, insulted the junior dean in November of that year, for which their degrees were suspended, and they had to beg the junior dean's pardon publicly on bended knees. James II's appointment of Richard Talbot, earl of

[All quotations are from H. Davis, ed., *The Prose Works* (Oxford, 1939-1964) and H. Williams, ed., *The Poems* (Oxford, 1937).]

Tyrconnel, as lord lieutenant led to a withdrawal of the college's annual grant when the authorities refused to appoint a Roman Catholic to a fellowship on the king's orders. Most of the fellows and students, Swift among them, joined the general exodus of Protestants for England and Scotland.

After staying some time with his mother in Leicester, Swift became private secretary to Sir William Temple in 1689. Temple had family connections with Ireland. His grandfather had been provost of Trinity College, Dublin; his father, Sir John Temple, was educated there, became master of the rolls in Ireland, but eventually lived in London; Temple himself was elected to the Irish convention of 1660 and became a member of the Dublin Parliament in 1661. He pursued a diplomatic career, and was the architect of the Triple Alliance between England, Sweden, and the United Provinces; he next served as ambassador to Holland, where he became a close friend of William of Orange. Finally, in dislike of public life, he retreated to the country in 1681. Temple's effect on Swift was profound, for his experience of court life and diplomacy and the elegant mode of life he created at Moor Park, his country home in Surrey, enlarged the young man's horizons and, no doubt, his ambitions. After Swift had experienced his first attack of what we now know as Ménière's disease (its etiology was not fully recognized until 1861; its symptoms are giddiness, vomiting, deafness, and noises in the head), he returned briefly to Ireland. He thought his giddiness had been caused by eating too many apples (his later deafness he put down to the effects of a severe cold), and the doctors thought the effects of the English climate might have caused his illness. But he was soon back. Life at Moor Park, in a dependent position, was not enough for him. Not unnaturally, he wanted to make his own way in the world and Temple was "less forward" than Swift hoped in aiding him to obtain a position in the church. But he had "a scruple of entering the church meerly for support" so, once he had managed to get Temple to offer him a minor clerkship in the office of the master of the rolls in Ireland, he felt he could enter the church from choice rather than necessity. He refused the clerkship and left Moor Park in May 1694. Sir William Temple was "extremely angry" and still would not promise the young man anything firmly.

Swift returned to Ireland, not realizing that he would have difficulty in becoming ordained. There was a need to explain why he had not entered the church at once after taking his degree. What had he been doing in England? He had to humble himself, to write to Temple for a testimonial testifying to his good life and behavior, and giving the reasons for his leaving Temple's household. (Temple's sister, Lady Giffard, endorsed the ensuing dignified appeal to Temple as Swift's "penitential" letter.) Temple wrote in support of his former secretary; and Swift was ordained as deacon in October 1694, and as priest in January 1695. Two weeks later he became prebend of Kilroot. He found the experience of living in a rural parish in Northern Ireland with but a few parishioners, and surrounded by Presbyterians, disheartening, and he gave up the living at Temple's persuasion and returned to Moor Park in 1696.

In 1699, Temple died without having obtained a living for Swift in England, as he had promised he would, and so Swift again traveled to Ireland, this time as chaplain to the earl of Berkeley (who had become one of the three Lords Justice). The following year he was appointed vicar of Laracor, in County Meath, and became a prebend of Dunlavin in St. Patrick's Cathedral in Dublin. Again he was in a parish very thinly peopled with Church of Ireland Protestants, but this time he was surrounded by Catholics. He liked the place, and set about gardening, planting and improving his grounds.

When he was at Kilroot he had courted Jane Waring of Belfast, whom he knew as Varina. It was a curious courtship. He wrote her eloquent letters; but she did not fancy living in Kilroot on Swift's income. He managed to extricate himself by asking her to commit herself immediately when he was going back to Moor Park in 1696, though he was obviously fairly confident she would not do so. He had realistic views about marriage. He had earlier been involved in heavy flirtations in Leicester, but regarded himself as naturally temperate; and there were always "a thousand household thoughts" to drive matrimony out of his mind whenever it chanced to enter it. In 1699 he wrote a series of seventeen resolutions entitled "When I come to be old," the first, fifth, and fifteenth of which are part of what John Forster calls in his biography "the mystery" of Swift's life; they are: "Not to marry a young woman"; "Not to be fond of children, or let them come near me hardly"; "Not to hearken to flatteries, nor conceive I can be beloved by a young woman; *et eos qui haereditatem captant, odisse ac vitare.*[1] When Swift was once more in Laracor, in 1700, Varina wrote to inquire why he had not visited her in Belfast, and, in effect, he dismissed her in a devastating letter full of challenging questions: as to whether she had good enough health, the ability to manage a household on perhaps less than £300 a year, and an adequate inclination to his person and humors for marriage with him. There was another reason for ending their relationship. He had first met Esther Johnson, whom he later called Stella, at Moor Park, when she was a child of thirteen (some critics have agreed that Sir William Temple may have been her father); he now persuaded her to move to Ireland in 1701 with her friend and companion, Rebecca Dingley. He had taught Stella at Moor Park; she was intelligent, truthful, and courageous: she fitted into his idea of friendship. He never saw her alone, though the two ladies lived at Laracor and in his Dublin residences when he was not there. It was an unusual relationship. Swift wrote on 20 April 1704 to William Tisdall, a clergyman and friend of his who wished to marry Stella, that if his own fortunes and humor "served me to think of that state, I should certainly among all persons on earth, make your choice; because I never saw that person whose conversation I entirely valued but hers; this was the utmost I ever gave way to." When he wrote to her, he addressed his letters to both ladies, and his close and tender friendship with Stella lasted, with perhaps one break, until her death in 1728.

Swift was in London with Berkeley in 1701, and he then wrote his first political pamphlet, *A Discourse of the Contests and Dissensions between the Nobles and the Commons in Athens and Rome*. He praised the Whig leaders, Baron Somers and the earl of Halifax (disguised under Roman names), and the following year Swift let himself be known in London as the author. He made several visits to England between 1701 and 1704. In 1704 came the anonymous publication of *A Tale of a Tub* and *The Battle of the Books* (even in the fifth edition the anonymity was kept up), though the identity of the author was known to Swift's peers. Swift intended *A Tale of a Tub* as a satire on what he thought the gross contemporary corruptions in religion and learning: in it he satirized the worldliness of Rome and the immoderacy of the Presbyterians and Nonconformists. He was himself a churchman of the center, though he called himself a "high churchman." Although he thought the Church of England far from perfect, it was the best church he knew; its doctrine and discipline were moderate and cautious. It offered the middle way between Rome and Puritanism. He valued the Anglican church as the voice of reason, and reason seemed very necessary in an age when the Stuarts and the Puritans had recently tried to seize power: both royalist and Puritan causes were regarded as leading to absolutism and tyranny. But Swift knew that man's management of Christianity was all too human; and he was not above exercising his wit on religious absurdity, while remaining a good churchman.

During the period from 1707 to 1709, Swift was in London endeavoring to persuade the Whig government to grant a concession—remission of the firstfruits[2] and tithes—to the Church of Ireland. His efforts were unsuccessful, and he was also disappointed in his attempts to gain preferment. It was hinted to him that the remission of the firstfruits might be granted if the Test Act were to be repealed in Ireland. The Whigs' policy was to repeal the sacramental Test; and by removing it in Ireland they might have a useful example to support removal of the measure in England also. It was an act that excluded non-Anglicans from political power. Through its operation the Dissenters and Catholics could not, for instance, accept commissions in the army and the militia. Swift, however, was deeply concerned about the position of the Anglican church. He believed there was a danger of upsetting what had been achieved; he disliked the potential for corruption that might be generated by change; equilibrium was a condition for the continuance of the Anglican church and balanced government. But in Ireland the number of Protestant churchmen in the Pale[3] was small, the Establishment was insecure, and Swift felt the Dissenters of Scottish descent in the north had an innate industry and bravery as well as "a most formidable notion of episcop[ac]y," which they thought, "as most surely they did," three degrees worse than popery. It is clear from *A*

---

[1]Translation: "and to hate and avoid those who practice legacy-hunting."

[2]The first year's income or profits, formerly paid by each new holder of a benefice, or any office of profit, to some superior.

[3]That part of Ireland over which English jurisdiction was established.

Letter from a Member of the House of Commons in Ireland to a Member of the House of Commons in England Concerning the Sacramental Test (which Swift dated as being written from Dublin in December 1708) that his distrust of the Presbyterians was far greater than any worry about the Catholics, who had, after all, been defeated:

'Tis agreed among naturalists that a lion is a larger, a stronger, and more dangerous enemy than a cat; yet if a man were to have his choice, either a lion at his foot, bound fast with three or four chains, his teeth drawn out, and his claws pared to the quick, or an angry cat in full liberty at his throat; he would take no long time to determine.

It was probably in the summer of 1708 that Swift's friendship with Joseph Addison ripened into close intimacy: it was then that he complained of increased governmental work preventing Addison from meeting him as often as he would wish: their respect and liking for each other was mutual. Addison had inscribed a copy of his *Travels in Italy* (1705) to "the most Agreeable Companion, the Truest friend and the Greatest Genius of his Age"; and Swift regarded Addison as the man who had "worth enough to give reputation to our age." A remark is attributed to Swift that when he and Addison spent an evening together they "neither of them ever wished for a third person": they were, however, often in the company of wits (largely Whigs), and Swift also formed a friendship with Addison's friend and schoolfellow Richard Steele. He aided Steele in the creation of the *Tatler* and wrote pieces for it. Ambrose Philips and Matthew Prior were other friends of this period, and he had met many other literary figures in the coffeehouse society of the time, in which his schoolfellow William Congreve, a member of the Whigs' Kit Kat Club, also moved freely. Yet another friend was Charles Ford, a smart young intellectual and Irish landowner.

In the summer of 1709 Swift returned to Ireland in a depressed state. The symptoms of Ménière's disease, the giddiness, nausea, deafness, and noises in his head, continued throughout his life, and there are many entries in his memoranda book that show his occasional utter despair, two poignant examples being the entries for April 1709—"Small giddy fitt and swimming in the head MD [his name for Stella] and God help me"—and July 1710—'Terrible fitt.

God knows what may be the event. Better towards the end." Despite these attacks, he enjoyed his time at Laracor, planting trees, improving his garden, mending his canal. He had much social life. Addison was secretary to the lord lieutenant, and Swift saw a good deal of him in Dublin, introducing him to Stella—they liked each other—and there were many other friends with whom to dine and play cards.

When, somewhat reluctantly ("I never went to England with so little desire in my life"), he returned to London in 1710, things began to change. Though the letters to Stella and Miss Dingley continued with all their openness, their constant account of his doings and ideas, they did not convey the complication of a new friendship he began or, perhaps, drifted into with Esther Vanhomrigh. His relationship (he was forty-two, she twenty) with Esther—he called her Hessy or Vanessa—was based on a teasing, didactic, almost fatherly concern for her intellectual and moral development: and she (whose father was dead) found it irresistible. He dined frequently at the Vanhomrighs' in the autumn and winter of 1710; in the spring, Mrs. Vanhomrigh set aside a room for him. Stella was surprised at his frequenting them; he replied in a letter, jocosely but perhaps also defensively, "You say they are of no consequence: why, they keep as good female company as I do male; I see all the drabs of quality at this end of town with them. . . ." On the one hand, he taught Vanessa to despise orthodox views of conventional behavior; on the other, he valued discretion; he was probably quite sure of his own propriety, he had no intention of marrying, but he did enjoy his intimate friendship with this attractive girl. It is possible that she declared her love for him in 1712; it was probably in the autumn of 1713 that he wrote the poem *Cadenus and Vanessa*, which gives us an idea of his evasive tactics when Vanessa indicated her preference for passion rather than a Platonic friendship:

> But friendship in its greatest height
> A constant, rational delight
> On virtue's basis fix'd to last,
> When love's allurements long are past;
> Which gently warms but cannot burn;
> He gladly offers in return:
> His want of passion will redeem,
> With gratitude, respect, esteem:
> With that devotion we bestow
> When goddesses appear below.   (780–789)

Conversations with Vanessa, those meetings "over a pott of coffee or an orange and sugar in the sluttery,[4] which I have so often found to be the most agreeable chamber in the world," provided a relief from the world of politics, where Swift was rapidly becoming so successful. The new Tory ministry realized the value of his combination of cold reason and explosive logic and agreed to remission of the firstfruits (though Swift did not get the credit for this). He became a close friend of Robert Harley and Henry St. John and was put in charge of the Tory journal *Examiner*. This was the beginning of his period of political power.

After the Tory administration came into office, Swift had used his influence on behalf of Whig writers, as he told Stella in a letter:

And do you know I have taken more pains to recommend the Whig wits to the favour and mercy of the ministers than any other people. Steele I have kept in his place; Congreve I have got to be used kindly, and secured. Rowe I have recommended and got a promise of a place. Philips I could certainly have provided for, if he had not run party mad and made me withdraw my recommendation; and I got Addison so right at first, that he might have been employed, and have partly secured him the place he has; yet I am worse used by that faction than any man.   (18 December 1812)

He tried to reconcile Steele and Harley, but Steele did not keep the appointment. Later in 1713 he quarreled fiercely with Swift. Relations with Addison were not easy because of party differences, and John Arbuthnot, the queen's physician, became Swift's closest companion and friend. He shared Swift's love of hoaxes, of paradox, of irony. Swift had met him at Windsor. His friendship with the ministers had led him to court, where he had a wide range of acquaintances. He dined with the great, indeed he was included in the Society, a dining club set up by St. John for men of "wit and interest," whose members called each other "brother." Another grouping, the Scriblerus Club, was made up of leading writers, Swift, John Arbuthnot, Alexander Pope, John Gay, and Thomas Parnell, who allowed Harley and St. John to attend their meetings. A love of satiric literature and erudite jesting was shared by these authors, and their meetings obviously gave Swift very great pleasure. It was an ex-

[4]A workroom.

citing period in his life, and portions of "The Author upon Himself" convey this:

Swift had the sin of wit, no venial crime;
Nay 'twas affirm'd he sometimes dealt in rhyme.
Humour and mirth had place in all he writ;
He reconcil'd divinity and wit:
He moved and bow'd, and talk'd with too much grace;
Nor show'd the parson in his gait or face;
Despis'd luxurious wines and costly meat;
Yet still was at the tables of the great;
Frequented lords; saw those that saw the queen,
At Child's or Truby's never once had been.   (9–18)

Though he did not bother to frequent the favorite taverns of the clergy, Child's and Truby's, he worked hard for his view of how the interests of church and state should be preserved. His skill as a political propagandist greatly aided the acceptance of Tory policies and, notably, his attacks on the duke of Marlborough, which helped to bring about the conclusion of the war against France. *The Conduct of the Allies*, which went through many editions, supplied the arguments for the debate in the House of Commons: as he told Stella, "The Resolutions printed t'other day in the Votes are almost quotations from it; and would never have passed, if that book had not been written." But his pen had harmed his own career as well as Marlborough's, for *A Tale of a Tub* had been described to Queen Anne as profane. The "royal prude," as Swift called her, was reluctant that he should occupy high office in the church. He had used this phrase in a lampoon upon the duchess of Somerset, the mistress of the robes, who henceforth became his implacable enemy. This was partly because Swift had published the third part of Sir William Temple's *Memoirs* against the wishes of the family; these reflected upon the character of Lord Essex, husband of the duchess' favorite aunt. So he was not given the fat English deanery or slim bishopric he desired, but instead was made dean of St. Patrick's Cathedral, Dublin, in April 1713. Swift regarded this post as a kind of exile, deeply regretting the distance from his friends in London. He was back in London in September, vainly trying to patch up affairs between the two estranged Tory leaders, then withdrew to the country in May 1714 to stay with a friend in Berkshire, hoping to be made historiographer royal. He offered to accompany Harley, now earl of Oxford, to Herefordshire, for Viscount Bolingbroke (St. John) had won and Oxford had been dismissed by the queen.

Then the queen died, and the Whigs were back in power with the Hanoverian king enthroned.

Returning to Ireland in August, Swift occupied himself with administration. "You are to understand," he wrote to Pope,

that I live in the corner of a vast unfurnished house. My family consists of a steward, a groom, a helper in the stable, a footman, and an old maid, who are all at board wages, and when I do not dine abroad, or make an entertainment, which last is very rare, I eat a mutton-pie, and drink half a pint of wine. My amusements are defending my small dominions against the Archbishop, and endeavouring to reduce my rebellious choir.

He worked on *Gulliver's Travels* and, after about three years, had found congenial company in two young clergymen who were wits and scholars, Thomas Sheridan and Patrick Delany. It was not as brilliant a society as he had left in London, he wrote to Pope in 1722:

The best and greatest part of my life, until these eight years, I spent in England, there I made my friendships, and there I left my desires. I am condemned for ever to another country; what is in prudence to be done?

A crisis arose in his relationship with Vanessa, who had crossed to Ireland in 1714, despite the stern warning he had given her in England, "If you are in Ireland while I am there, I shall see you very seldom. It is not a place for any freedom, but where everything is known in a week, and magnified a hundred degrees." She seemed to have accepted earlier his conditions for friendship; but despite his warnings she was importunate; and he reminded her again that he would see her seldom. There was some final break, perhaps because she realized that the friendship with Stella came first with him. In June he vanished to the south of Ireland for several months. Vanessa had died, on 31 May 1723, making no mention of him in her will. He was in the depths of depression when he wrote to Pope in September:

I read the most trifling books I can find, and whenever I write, it is upon the most trifling subjects; but riding, waking, and sleeping take up eighteen of the twenty-four hours. I procrastinate more than I did twenty years ago, and have several things to finish which I put off to twenty years hence.

Irish politics roused him from his inertia, the Drapier[5] was born, and *Gulliver's Travels* finished. He wrote a famous letter to Pope about them on 29 September 1725, which contained his rationale as man and writer:

I have ever hated all nations, professions and communities, and all my love is towards individuals: for instance, I hate the tribe of lawyers, but I love Counsellor Such-a-one, and Judge Such-a-one. . . . But principally I hate and detest that animal called man, although I heartily love John, Peter, Thomas, and so forth.

He arrived in London in 1726, took up his old friendships after twelve years, and argued Ireland's case unsuccessfully with Sir Robert Walpole.

He was deeply disturbed at the news of Stella's illness and wrote some letters, to his vicar, John Worrall, to James Stopford, and to Richard Brinsley Sheridan, that show how affected he was. "We have been perfect friends these thirty-five years," he wrote, explaining how he had realized how ill she was and how much her death would mean to him. "I am of the opinion that there is not a greater folly than to contract too great and intimate a friendship, which must always leave the survivor miserable." He tried to rationalize the situation, but Stella "excelled in every good quality," and he confessed that "violent friendship is much more lasting, and as much engaging, as violent love." She recovered, but the ordeal of her death was deferred only for a year. In that year he offered her a last birthday poem:

> From not the greatest of divines
> Accept for once some serious lines.

In this he allowed his affection to have its head. He was again in London—his last visit to England—in 1727 and was himself ill when the news of Stella's being again in a precarious state reached him in September. Ill as he was, he rushed off to Holyhead as soon as he could, only to find himself, with wind and tide unfavorable for a week, raging at the delay. Stella died in January, and he immediately wrote an account of her life, finding it impossible to attend the burial service, the lights of which he saw through the deanery window as he recorded Stella's

---

[5]Swift adopted the persona of an imagined Dublin shopkeeper, M. B. Drapier, for his famous Drapier *Letters*.

JONATHAN SWIFT

qualities. This brief biography is haunting in its simplicity and sorrow.

Swift's last years were filled with more activity on behalf of Ireland. To this period belongs *A Modest Proposal* (1729) and *Verses on the Death of Dr. Swift* (1731), virtually a posthumous survey of his own life. He was also involved in *A Complete Collection of Genteel and Ingenious Conversations* and the *Directions to Servants* (posthumously published, 1745). He was often ill now, irascible at times, and yet his fierce anger flared out as effectively as ever in "The Legion Club," his scathing attack on the Dublin Parliament. His popularity, he wrote to Pope, was "wholly confined to the common people who are more constant than those we miscall our betters." When he walked the streets, he was received with acclaim, his seventieth birthday celebrated with illuminations, bonfires, and salutes of guns. And yet his attitude to the "ordinary" people of Ireland was ambivalent, indeed paradoxical; while condemning their governors, he despised them for their inability to help themselves. As his friend Arbuthnot recorded, he was a sincere, honest man who spoke truth when others were afraid to speak it. He himself wrote of his hate

> Whose lash just Heaven had long decreed
> Shall on a day make sin and folly bleed.

At the age of fifty, Swift had said to Edward Young, when gazing at an elm tree withered and decayed in its upper branches, "I shall be like that tree: I shall die at the top." His memory went; a letter, written in 1740 to his cousin Mrs. Whiteway, described his miserable state: extremely deaf and full of pain. He was "so stupid and confounded" he could not express the mortification he was under in body and mind. He was sure his days would be few. He lived another five years, legally declared of unsound mind in May 1742, not capable of taking care of his person or fortune. He died on 19 October 1745, and was buried in St. Patrick's Cathedral, with the Latin epitaph he wrote for himself placed over his grave. Yeats's version of it gives us the essence of the man:

> Swift has sailed into his rest;
> Savage indignation there
> Cannot lacerate his breast.
> Imitate him if you dare,
> World-besotted traveller; he
> Served human liberty.

THE PROSE SATIRES

SWIFT finished "the greatest part" of *A Tale of a Tub* in 1696 and published it anonymously in 1704. It was wrapped around in the mystery with which Swift loved to tease his readers; he seems to have assumed a false identity—a persona. In the fourth document, fitted in between "The Dedication to Lord Somers" and "The Epistle Dedicatory . . . to Prince Posterity," and entitled "The Bookseller to the Reader," it is stated that no satisfaction can be given as to the author, the bookseller being credibly informed that the publication is "without his knowledge" and whether the author had finished it or intended to fill up the defective places "is like to remain a secret." This challenging the curiosity of readers about the identity of the supposed author was matched by the mass of learned allusions in which the book abounds. The supposed annotator says, "I believe one of the Author's Designs was to set curious Men a-hunting thro Indexes and enquiring for Books out of the Common Road." He issued a warning to those "whom the *Learned* among Posterity will appoint for Commentators upon this elaborate Treatise" and, as Professor Nichol Smith, himself one of Swift's most notable modern editors, remarked, "the modern editor must always be conscious of the shade of Swift finding amused pleasure in the false surmises that send him searching on the wrong track, and when the hunt is successful, as often by luck as by skill, in the explanations that sometimes come perilously near to pedantry."

Swift's reading was extremely wide and in his own words "indefatigable"; he kept commonplace books, he abstracted from authors, he epitomized, but ultimately he was his own man, skeptical yet creative, insisting proudly that he had not borrowed hints from any other writers in the world. His originality is borne out by his own style, highly individual even in the midst of its mocking parodies. In *A Tale of a Tub* Swift involved himself in satirizing abuses in religion with digressions that mocked abuses in learning, literature, and language. He wrote in the manner of earlier seventeenth-century prose writers, echoing their complexity and the magnificent manner of their rhetoric. The following passage on man's fancy is characteristic: it is metaphysical in its imaginative energy, its paradoxical exaggeration, and contradictory in that it condemns the very fancy or free imagination that gives it exuberant life:

1201

AND, whereas the mind of Man, when he gives the Spur and Bridle to his Thoughts, doth never stop, but naturally sallies out into both extremes of High and Low, of Good and Evil; his first flight of fancy, commonly transports Him to Idea's of what is most Perfect, finished, and exalted; till having soared out of his own Reach and Sight, not well perceiving how near the Frontiers of Height and Depth, border upon each other; With the same Course and Wing, he falls down plum into the lowest Bottom of Things; like one who travels the *East* into the *West*; or like a strait line drawn by its own length into a Circle. Whether a Tincture of Malice in our Natures, makes us fond of furnishing every bright Idea with its Reverse; Or, whether Reason reflecting upon the Sum of Things, can, like the Sun, serve only to enlighten one half of the Globe, leaving the other half, by Necessity, under the Shade and Darkness; Or, whether Fancy, flying up to the imagination of what is Highest and Best, becomes over-shot, and spent, and weary, and suddenly falls like a dead Bird of Paradise, to the Ground.   (sec. VIII, p. 99)

He could draw upon earlier writers. For instance, this passage from *Antony and Cleopatra* (IV. xiv):

> Sometimes we see a cloud that's dragonish;
> A vapour sometime like a bear or a lion,
> A tower'd citadel, a pendant rock,
> A forked mountain, or blue promontory
> With trees upon't, that nod unto the world
> And mock our eyes with air . . .

was pressed into his service:

If I should venture in a windy Day, to affirm to *Your Highness*, that there is a large Cloud near the *Horizon* in the Form of a *Bear*, another in the *Zenith* with the Head of an *Ass*, a third to the Westward with Claws like a *Dragon*; and *Your Highness* should in a few Minutes think fit to examine the Truth, 'tis certain, they would all be changed in Figure and Position, new ones would arise, and all we could agree upon would be, that Clouds there were, but that I was grossly mistaken in the *Zoography* and *Topography* of them.

Swift was a firm believer in common sense; he wrote as a wit and a literary man. He naturally deflated what he thought dangerous and stupid. Thus he moved to a simpler style when he recounted the actual tale. This is the allegorical story—it begins "Once upon a time"—of the man "who had Three Sons by one Wife, and all at a Birth, neither could the Mid-Wife tell certainly which was the Eldest." The father leaves his triplet sons each a coat, instructing them not to alter them in any way. These coats represent the Christian faith; the sons Peter, Martin, and Jack, the three churches: Peter, the Roman Catholic; Martin, the Lutheran, which becomes the Anglican after the Reformation; and Jack, the Calvinist. Peter departs from the terms of the will after ingenious interpretations of it, so that silver fringes, embroidery, and shoulder knots are added. He hides the will and goes mad. The others, ejected from his house, get copies of the will and realize how they have departed from its conditions. Martin takes away as much as he can of the added decoration without damaging the original cloth; but Jack damages his coat by tearing off the extra material, being more bent on removing Peter's influence than keeping to the will. Peter's belief in the infallibility of the pope and Jack's in his own interpretation of the Bible lead to corruption in religion; but Martin, who represents the Anglicanism in which Swift believed, is rational in his attitude to religion—the compromise achieved was between Christianity and the world, and based upon the actual historical situation. The dangers to the Anglican position from Catholicism and Dissent were added to by the effects of the Deists, notably John Locke, the author of the *Essay Concerning Human Understanding*, and the Skeptics, notably Thomas Hobbes, author of *Leviathan*. Swift attacked both viewpoints in *A Tale of a Tub*, particularly in the Digression on Madness. Ironically he praises man's capacity for self-delusion:

. . . when a Man's Fancy gets *Astride* on his Reason, when Imagination is at Cuffs with the Senses and Common Understanding, as well as Common Sense, is Kickt out of Doors; the first Proselyte he makes, is Himself, and when that is once compass'd, the Difficulty is not so great in bringing over others; A Strong Delusion always operating from *without*, as vigorously as from *within*. For, Cant and Vision are to the Ear and Eye, the same as Tickling is to the Touch. Those Entertainments and Pleasures we most value in life, are such a *Dupe* and play the Wag with the Senses.   (sec. IX, p. 108)

Swift had developed his own style: he depended in part upon lulling his reader into false security and then exposing the falsity of his reasoning, his happiness that "*is a perpetual Possession of being well Deceived.*" There is a passage that praises the pursuit of truth despite the pain this may cause:

And therefore, in order to save the Charges of all such expensive Anatomy for the time to come; I do here think fit low# JONATHAN SWIFT

to inform the Reader that in such Conclusions as these, Reason is certainly in the Right; and that in most Corporeal Beings which have fallen under my cognizance, the *Outside* hath been infinitely preferable to the *In*: Whereof I have been farther convinced from some late Experiments. Last week I saw a Woman *flay'd* and you will hardly believe how much it altered her Person for the worse. (sec. IX, p. 109)

Despite the anonymity of its authorship, *A Tale of a Tub*, reprinted twice in 1704 and again in 1705, made Swift's reputation, but it marred his career in the church, for, although we can now see its essential morality, it offended many by what Francis Atterbury called its "profane strokes." Swift defended it in the Apology that prefaced the fifth edition of 1710; but he had not perhaps fully realized how few people could—and still can—accept a relationship between satire and genuine religion such as that which he put forward with what Nigel Dennis has described as "so much coarseness and vehemence." He had to create an audience for his particular invention, the persona, the "author"; his apparent irreverence, his variety of viewpoint, and his shatteringly satiric comments on stupidity have meant that the audience has sometimes shared Queen Anne's unamused disapproval. And Swift knew it. He wrote in "The Life and Character of Dean Swift" in 1731:

> 'Tis own'd he was a *Man of Wit*-,
> Yet many a *foolish thing* he writ-;
> And, sure he must be deeply learn'd-!
> That's more than ever I discern'd-;
> I know his nearest friends complain
> He was too *airy* for a *Dean*. (74–79)

Along with *A Tale of a Tub* was published *The Battle of the Books*, which reflects some of Swift's unease at the corruptions he thought had invaded English life and letters after the Civil War: he was particularly concerned about the corruption of the language. He had also a certain skepticism about the value of the new sciences. His defense of Sir William Temple's essay *Of Ancient and Modern Learning* (1690) involved him in an argument in which Temple had cited *Aesop's Fables* and the *Epistles of Phalaris* to prove the superiority of the ancients in prose. William Wotton defended the modern age in his *Reflections upon Ancient and Modern Learning* (1694), and Richard Bentley argued in the second edition of that book that neither the *Fables* nor the

Epistles were as old as Temple thought. Robert Boyle supported Temple, and Swift joined in the fray—but was strongly aware of what *was* important: he used the mock heroic form to allow sufficient distance from the actual controversy. Into his account of the battle in St. James's Library (Bentley had been keeper there) he introduced a digression—the fable of the spider and the bee, which was based upon a proverb frequently used in the seventeenth century: "where the bee sucks honey, the spider sucks poison." Temple had used the image of the bee in his essay "Of Poetry" (1690), and Swift, after dismissing the spider as a symbol of modernity, produced an echo of Temple's poem in praise of the bee, ending with an elegant phrase that was itself echoed a century and a half later by Matthew Arnold in *Culture and Anarchy*:

> . . . As for *Us*, the *Ancients*, We are content with the *Bee*, to pretend to Nothing of our own beyond our *Wings* and our *Voice*: this is to say, our *Flights* and our *Language*; For the rest, whatever we have got, has been infinite Labor, and search, and ranging thro' every corner of Nature: The Difference is, that instead of *Dirt* and *Poison*, we have rather chose to fill our Hives with *Honey* and *Wax*, thus furnishing Mankind with the two Noblest of Things, which are *Sweetness* and *Light*. (p. 151)

The spider represents the overweening, self-sufficient pride of an age concerned with artifice, rejecting the wisdom of the past, relying on intellect to create new ways of thought. Swift looked back to "the peaceable part" of the reign of Charles I as the highest period of politeness in England, and when he measured by that standard the world of his own time, he found it sadly lacking:

> Whether is the nobler Being of the two, That which by a lazy Contemplation of Four Inches round; by an overweening Pride which feeding and engendering on itself, turns all into Excrement and Venom; producing nothing at last, but Fly-bone and a Cobweb: Or That, which, by an universal Range, with long Search, much Study, true Judgement, and Distinction of Things, brings home Honey and Wax. (p. 151)

Swift wrote most of *Gulliver's Travels* between 1721 and 1725, not, as used to be thought, between 1714 and 1720 (a theory that led to the idea that Swift wrote the book on his return to Ireland in disappointment, and that the fourth book was the culmination of his misanthropy. The fourth book, in fact, was written before the third). Some parts may possibly derive from earlier drafts associated with a project of the Scriblerus Club to produce the *Memoirs of Martin Scriblerus* (1741), the satiric remembrances of an invented traveler.

The first edition, printed in London by Benjamin Motte, appeared in 1726; two editions followed in 1727, though Swift was dissatisfied with the text and himself later corrected the version published in 1735 by the Dublin printer George Faulkner (the third in a four-volume edition of Swift's *Works*). Swift's friend Gay wrote to him describing it as "the conversation of the whole town" since its publication, with all agreed "in liking it extremely." And he alluded to the fiction that Swift had nothing to do with it:

'Tis generally said that you are the author, but I am told, the Bookseller declares he knows not from what hand it came. From the highest to the lowest it is universally read, from the Cabinet-council to the Nursery.

Swift himself enjoyed the situation. In a letter to Mrs. Howard he remarked that he could not understand a letter of hers "till a bookseller sent me the Travells of one Captain Gulliver, who proved a very good Explainer, although at the same time, I thought it hard to be forced to read a Book of seven hundred Pages in order to understand a Letter of fifty lines."

Gulliver's Travels begins with two prefatory items, "A Letter from Captain Gulliver to His Cousin Sympson" and 'The Publisher to the Reader." These are designed to give authenticity to the accounts of Gulliver's four voyages that follow. Swift was writing in well-established genres, the traveler's tale, and parodies of it. He drew upon a very entertaining parody of fabulous voyages (such as those we find in the *Odyssey* and elsewhere in classical literature)—probably the first of its kind—written by Lucian in the second century A.D. The hero of Lucian's *True History* had many adventures, including being blown up to the moon and living for two years inside a whale. Sir Thomas More's introduction to *Utopia* (1516), the fourth and fifth books of François Rabelais (*ca.* 1552; *ca.* 1564), and Cyrano de Bergerac's *L'Autre monde on les états et empires de la lune* (1657) were other works of this nature, while Daniel Defoe's *Robinson Crusoe* (1719), written two years before *Gulliver's Travels* was begun, put the traveler's tale into the form of a realistic novel. Travelers' tales of

his own time were also parodied by Swift—notably William Dampier's *A New Voyage Round the World* (1697) and *A Voyage to New Holland* (1703-1709).

The *Travels* appeal to the reader on many levels. There is the simple attraction of the story. It is funny; it is filled with ingenious inventions; and it is exciting. Swift used a literary genre in order to criticize his contemporaries, and he also produced profound comments on human life in general. The story shows us humanity from four different points of view. In the first book Gulliver, among the Lilliputians, sees mankind as ridiculously small. In the second book, he is himself minute in comparison with the Brobdingnagians. For instance, when Gulliver is brought home by the farmer and shown to his wife, she screams and runs back "as women in England do at the sight of a Toad or a Spider." He is terrified of falling off their thirty-foot-high table, and is disgusted by the sight of a nurse with a monstrous breast feeding a Brobdingnagian baby. In the third book, the absurdity of human activities is seen from a commonsensical attitude, the whole book being a species of science fiction in its attitude to time, its mockery of philosophical belief in progress, its dislike of government by experts, its ridicule of experimental science. The fourth book describes rational animals, the Houyhnhnms; they regard mankind as irrational, as bestial as the Yahoos. Swift, as he wrote to Pope in 1725, had "got Materials Towards a Treatis proving the falsity of that Definition *animal rationale*; and to show it should be only *rationis capax*. Upon this great foundation of Misanthropy (though not in Timon's manner) the whole building of my Travells is erected" (*Correspondence*, book III). Since he considered man capable of reason but not a rational creature (like the Houyhnhnms), Swift did not hate mankind, as has sometimes been alleged, indeed as he wrote to Pope "it is *vous autres* who hate them because you would have them reasonable Animals, and are angry for being disappointed" (*Correspondence*, book III).

We need to remember, as we read the *Travels*, that Gulliver is not Swift; he is an invented character, and not always an admirable one. He himself is an object as much as an instrument of satire. This is true also of the characters in the first voyage, though there are different views on how the allegory is to be worked out in terms of English politics in the early eighteenth century. For example, Sir Charles Firth and A. E. Case have offered different identifications of the ministers at the Lilliputian court; and scholars have theorized at length on the likely identities of Bolgolam and Reldresal, and on whether Flimnap, the court treasurer, who is the most expert at a rope dance, is Sir Robert Walpole or perhaps Lord Godolphin. It is easier for the general reader to realize that the High heels, the majority party, are the Tories, and the Low heels, favored by the emperor, the Whigs. The religious parties, the Big Endians and the Little Endians (who break their eggs at the large or the small end respectively), represent the Catholics and the Protestants, and while Lilliput is obviously England, Blefuscu resembles France.

The Lilliputians are cruel, and gradually their treacherous nature is revealed, as we can see them (and, of course, human vice and stupidity) from a detached distance. But the tables are turned in Brobdingnag, where our human weaknesses become obvious in relation to the giants and the crude insensitivity of some of them. There are exceptions to this: for Glumdalclitch is consistently kind to Gulliver, and the king expresses his horror at European modes of life and the corruptions of Gulliver's society. Though the king is also kind, taking Gulliver into his hands and stroking him gently, his comment on the historical account Gulliver has given him of the politics of Europe in the last century is one of revulsion, "protesting it was only an Heap of Conspiracies, Rebellions, Murders, Massacres, Revolutions, Banishments; the very worst Effects that Avarice, Rage, Madness, Hatred, Envy, Lust, Malice, and Ambition could produce." The king continues:

"As for yourself . . . who have spent the greatest part of your Life in travelling; I am well disposed to hope you may hitherto have escaped many vices of your country. But, by what I have gathered from your own Relation, and the Answers I have with much Pains wringed and extorted from you; I cannot but conclude the Bulk of your Natives, to be the most pernicious Race of little odious Vermin that Nature ever suffered to crawl upon the Surface of the Earth."   (ch. VI)

Gulliver finds the physical presence of the Brobdingnagians repulsive, but his attempt to ingratiate himself with the king, by giving him an account of gunpowder and offering to build cannon for him, is received with intellectual horror:

He was amazed how so impotent and groveling an Insect as I (these were his Expressions) could entertain such inhuman Ideas, and in so familiar a Manner as to appear wholly unmoved at all the Scenes of Blood and Desolation, which I had painted as the Common Effect of those destructive Machines, whereof he said, some evil Genius, Enemy to Mankind, must have been the first Contriver.
                                                                    (ch. VII)

And he commanded Gulliver, as he valued for his life, never to mention this secret anymore.

Swift enjoyed himself in parodying the scientists and projectors of the Royal Society in his account of the grand Academy of Lagado in the third book; he mocked the experiments on animals (blood transfusion had been unsuccessfully performed on a dog, and Swift recounts an experiment of deflating and inflating a dog's intestines by the insertion of a bellows in its anus—"the Dog died on the Spot, and we left the Doctor endeavouring to recover him by the same operation") as well as current theories of language. The flying island anticipated science fiction. And for sheer horror little can match the depressing account of the Struldbrugs, immortal, yet regarded as dead in law after eighty, forgetful. "They were not only opinionative, peevish, covetous, morose, vain, talkative, but uncapable of Friendship and dead to all natural affection. . . . Beside the usual Deformities in extreme old Age, they acquired an additional Ghastliness in Proportion to their Number of Years, which is not to be described. . . ."

It is the fourth book of the *Travels* that has caused most critical ink to be spilled. Here Swift splits human qualities between the Houyhnhnms and the Yahoos, the former rational, benevolent, and the latter brutish, selfish. The argument is not complete, for we see an occasional comic view of the horses, though Gulliver treats them with respect and reverence, accepting their view of him as a Yahoo, yet trying to meet their approval and his own self-approval by imitating "their gait and gesture which is now grown into a *Habit*, and my Friends often tell me in a blunt Way, that I *trot like a Horse*; which, however, I take for a great compliment: Neither shall I disown, that in speaking I am apt to fall into the Voice and manner of the *Houyhnhnms*, and hear my self ridiculed on that Account without the least Mortification."

Gulliver is banished from the Houyhnhnms' island by the horses and when he returns—saved by a benevolent and truly Christian Portuguese cap-

JONATHAN SWIFT

tain, Don Pedro, who persuaded him that his duty is to return to his family—we are given Swift's complex, ironic attitude to his relatively simple creation.

> As soon as I entered the House, my Wife took me in her Arms, and kissed me; at which, having not been used to the Touch of that odious Animal for so many Years, I fell in a Swoon for almost an Hour. At the Time I am writing, it is five Years since my last Return to *England*: During the first Year I could not endure my Wife or Children in my Presence, the very Smell of them was intolerable; much less could I suffer them to eat in the same Room. To this Hour they dare not presume to touch my Bread, or drink out of the same Cup; neither was I ever able to let one of them take me by the Hand. The first money I laid out was to buy two young Stone-Horses, which I keep in a good Stable, and next to them the Groom is my greatest Favourite; for I feel my Spirits revived by the Smell he contracts in the Stable. My horses understand me tolerably well; I converse with them at least four Hours every day.
>
> (ch. IX)

In the last chapter we realize that Gulliver is himself suffering from what he attacks in others—pride. He is oversimplistic; and his misanthropy and misogyny are absurd. Swift's own view of humanity is larger, ultimately, than the rational, satiric view of man Gulliver put forward in his *Travels*.

TORY PROPAGANDA IN ENGLAND AND HISTORICAL WRITINGS

SWIFT was well received in London by the new, largely Tory, cabinet led by Harley and St. John in 1710. His apprehensions about the future position of the Anglican church after the Whigs' Toleration Act of 1689 had been expressed in *The Sentiments of a Church-of-England Man* (1704), *An Argument to Prove that the Abolishing of Christianity in England, May, as Things Stand, be Attended with some Inconveniences* (1708), and *A Project for the Advancement of Religion and the Reformation of Manners* (1709). His ability to write matched what Harley told Swift was the great difficulty of the new ministry, "the want of some good pen, to keep up the spirit raised in the people, to assert the principles, and justify the proceedings of the new ministers." And so from November 1710 onward Swift wrote for the *Examiner* those pungent and

persuasive articles that had such an effect on a small, though highly influential, readership. The gentry, the clergy, and business and professional men were generally tired of the war against France and the taxes raised for it; they were suspicious of the Whigs' attitude to the Anglican church; they feared for the position of the crown. There was a rift between landed and financial interests. It was obvious to Swift, and he made it equally clear to his readers:

> Let any man observe the equipages in this town; he shall find the greater number who make a figure, to be a species of man quite different from any that were ever known before the Revolution, consisting either of Generals or Colonels, or of such whose whole fortunes lie in funds and stocks: so that power, which according to the old maxim, was used to follow land, is now gone over to money.

The only answer to a situation where, as Swift put it, "through the contrivance and cunning of stock-jobbers, there has been brought in such a complication of knavery and cozenage, such a mystery of iniquity, and such an unintelligible jargon of terms to involve it in, as were never known in any other age or country of the world; was the conclusion of a peace." And Swift's *Examiner* of 23 November 1710 attacked the duke of Marlborough, "the great Commander," and also his wealth. In December he turned to Marlborough's request for lifetime employment in the post of captain-general. This, he argued, was criminal.

The *Examiner* was most influential, but it had served its purpose by July 1711. The delicate secret negotiations for peace went on; jealousies had developed between Harley and St. John; Marlborough had to be deceived into thinking the war could be prosecuted. Swift returned to England during the height of Grub Street pamphleteering, when the secret negotiations had reached their climax, and then his pamphlet *The Conduct of the Allies and of the Late Ministry in Beginning and Carrying on the Present War* was published on 27 November 1711. This devastating attack on Marlborough put forward a conspiratorial view, that the war had been a deception practiced by Marlborough and the Whigs:

> We have been fighting to raise the wealth and grandeur of a particular family; to enrich usurers and stockjobbers; and to cultivate the pernicious design of a faction by

1206

destroying the Landed Interest. The nation begins to think these blessings are not worth fighting for any longer, and therefore desires a peace.

The pamphlet had an immediate effect, and further editions carried its message to more and more readers; it culminated in Marlborough's dismissal on the last day of the year, and this led the way to the Peace of Utrecht. Swift recorded the captain-general's fall in "The Widow and Her Cat"; he respected the achievements of Marlborough, despite his own detestation of war. The whole story is one of the power of the printed word, and, as Winston Churchill pointed out in his life of Marlborough, those "were not days when public men could afford to disdain the Press."

The Tory ministry, despite Swift's efforts to patch up some peace between Oxford and Bolingbroke, appeared to be doomed. Swift thought "A Ship's Crew quarelling in a Storm, or while their Enemies are within gun shott" was but a "faint Idea of this fatal Infatuation." So he wrote *Some Free Thoughts upon the Present State of Affairs* (1714), which supported St. John's policies. Swift's last statements of the Tory point of view were *The History of the Four Last Years of Queen Anne* and his *Memoirs Relating to that Change which happened in Queen Anne's Ministry in the year 1710*; but the death of the queen, who had thwarted his ambition of preferment in England, brought in George I and the Whigs. To his historical writings Swift brought a firm belief, reinforced by Temple's experience and views, that history depended upon individuals, and a firm conviction that divine intervention could, no matter how hopeless the position of church and state, alter the history of England. He possessed a superb historical perspective, his knowledge of the past illuminated, he believed, his attitude to the present, and his desire to get the record straight by preserving facts was part of his historiographical method.

IRISH ANTICOLONIAL WRITINGS

Swift returned to Ireland to become dean of St. Patrick's Cathedral in 1713; twenty years later he referred to the greatest unhappiness of his life: "I mean, my banishment to this miserable country." Not only did he miss his literary friends in Lon-

don—Pope, Prior, Arbuthnot, and Gay; not only did he regret not being virtually at the center of political power; but he disliked being, in effect, a colonial, in "wretched Dublin, in miserable Ireland." He had earlier recorded his feelings in *The Story of the Injured Lady*, written in 1707 but not published till after his death. In this he had deplored the effect of English legislation on Ireland, particularly on the Irish wool trade. The "injured lady" (Ireland) alleges she has been undone by the gentleman (England), "half by Force and half by Consent after Solemn Vows and Protestations of Marriage": she has been jilted in favor of an inferior rival (Scotland). The Act of Union of 1707 between England and Scotland was something many of the governing Anglo-Irish would then have wished repeated in a union between England and Ireland. Swift's answer to Ireland's plight was that since the gentleman had got possession of her person, obliged her to place her estate under the management of his servants, and reduced her and her tenants to poverty, she should act legally, have the same steward (i.e., the king), and regulate her household "by such methods as you shall both agree to." This stemmed from the ideas of William Molyneux, a philosopher and member of the Irish Parliament, whose *The Case of Ireland Being Bound by Acts of Parliament in England, Stated* (1698) had put the view that Ireland had its own Parliament and owed allegiance to the king, but not to the Parliament at Westminster. Swift also argued that Ireland should assert her rights to export her goods where she wished, and he attacked the appointment of Englishmen to office in Ireland.

During Swift's first years in the deanery, he had no wish to play any part in Irish politics, but in 1720 his *Proposals for the Universal Use of Irish Manufacture . . .* put the case for using Irish goods and avoiding importation from England, which had restricted Irish trade. He had much sympathy with the plight of the Dublin weavers, though he thought that Ireland had the right remedies at hand, if she would use them. His polemical style had lost none of its force:

the fable, in *Ovid*, of *Arachne* and *Pallas*, is to this Purpose. The Goddess had heard of one *Arachne*, a young Virgin, very famous for *Spinning* and *Weaving*: They both met upon a Tryal of Skill; and *Pallas* finding herself almost equalled in her own Art, stung with Rage and Envy, knockt her *Rival* down, turned her into a *Spyder*, enjoining her to *spin* and *weave* for ever, *out of her own Bowels*, and *in a very narrow Compass*. I confess, that from a Boy, I always pitied poor *Arachne*, and could never heartily love the Goddess, on account of so *cruel and unjust a Sentence*; which, however, is *fully executed* upon *Us* by *England*, with further Additions of *Rigor* and *Severity*. For the greatest part of our *Bowels* and *Vitals* is extracted, without allowing us the Liberty of *spinning* and *weaving* them.

The government prosecuted the printer, but though this prosecution was dropped, the pamphlet did not have much direct success. Swift entered the fray again, when there seemed some chance of rallying and encouraging opposition to a patent granted to an English ironmaster, William Wood, in July 1722, to allow him to coin copper money for Ireland. The Irish Privy Council, the Lords Justice, the commissioners of revenue, and the two Irish houses of Parliament had declared against the patent; and Swift made devastating attacks on the project, in the adopted persona of a Dublin shop-keeper, M. B. Drapier, in a series of letters, the first of which was entitled *A Letter to the Shop-Keepers, Tradesmen, Farmers, and Common-People of Ireland* (1724), while the fourth was addressed to "the Whole People of Ireland." By this phrase Swift probably meant the Irish Protestant "garrison"; in his own words, the "true English people of Ireland"; those whom he was to describe in his letter of June 1737 to Pope as "the English gentry of this kingdom," as opposed to the "savage old Irish." While arguing that the people of Ireland are and ought to be as free as their brethren in England ("Am I a *Free-Man* in *England*, and do I become a *Slave* in Six Hours by crossing Channel?"), attacking the theory that Ireland was *"a depending kingdom,"* and destroying any credibility that might have attached to Wood's coinage, he was creating an active public opinion, and in September 1725 it was announced that Wood's patent had been withdrawn. Swift had become a popular Irish hero, an Irish patriot.

Irish affairs, however, despite the defeat of Wood's coinage, did not greatly change, as the pessimistic attitude that permeates *A Short View of the State of Ireland* (1727–1728) indicated. There followed a series of bad harvests—"three years dearth of corn, and every place strowed with beggars . . . the kingdom is absolutely undone," as Swift described the situation to Pope in a letter of 11 August 1729—and his sense of horror is recorded in what is perhaps the most stirring satire, *A Modest Proposal for Preventing the Children of Ireland from Being Burdensome, and for Making Them Beneficial* (1729). In this he argues his case as if he were an economist, putting forward his politico-economic project coolly and reasonably, with statements of the situation and some persuasive statistics. His appeal to the reader on moral grounds makes his suggestion for a solution of the Irish problem the more devastating when he reveals in a matter-of-fact manner:

I have been assured by a very knowing *American* of my Acquaintance in *London*; that a young healthy Child, well nursed, is, at a Year old, a most delicious, nourishing and wholesome Food: whether *Stewed, Roasted, Baked,* or *Boiled*; and, I make no doubt, that it will equally serve in a *fricasie*, or *Ragoust*.

The scheme is carefully calculated:

I do therefore humbly offer it to *publick Consideration* that of the Hundred and Twenty Thousand Children already computed, Twenty thousand may be reserved for Breed. . . . That the remaining Hundred thousand may, at a Year old, be offered in Sale to the *Persons of Quality* and *Fortune*, through the Kingdom; always advising the Mothers to let them suck plentifully in the last Month, so as to render them plump and fat for a good Table.

The *Modest Proposal* records Swift's disgust with the poverty of Ireland, but he thought that Irish apathy and selfishness and greed created it as much as English policy. His *saeva indignatio*, his fierce indignation, emerges through his scathingly ironic use of metaphor:

I grant this food will be somewhat dear, and therefore very *proper for Landlords*; who, as they have already devoured most of the parents, seem to have the best title to the children.

THE PROSE STYLE AND SWIFT'S SATIRE

In *Gulliver's Travels* Swift wrote of the style of the Brobdingnagians, which he described as "clear, masculine and smooth but not florid; for they avoid nothing more than multiplying unnecessary words, or using various expressions." This description could be applied to his own writing after *A Tale of a*

Tub, when he allowed his sense of comedy, irreverence, and particularly parody its head. He became deeply disturbed about the degeneration of the English language in his own day; he thought the peaceable part of King Charles I's reign was the time when English was at its best. This was very different from the attitude of those who had altered the language for the purposes of scientific communication, those who had produced the close, naked speech praised by Thomas Sprat in his *History of the Royal Society*. Swift thought that

During the Usurpation, Such an Infusion of Enthusiastick Jargon prevailed in every Writing, as was not shaken off in many Years after. To this succeeded that Licentiousness which entered with the *Restoration*; and from infecting our Religion and Morals, fell to corrupt our Language: Which last was not like to be much improved by those who, at that Time, made up the Court of King Charles the Second; either such who had followed him in his Banishment, or who had been altogether conversant in the Dialect of those *Fanatick Times*.

Swift tended to associate language with history, with politics, with religion. He wrote on English in *Tatler* No. 280 (1710) and his *Proposal for Correcting, Improving and Ascertaining the English Tongue* (1712), his *Letter to a Young Gentleman . . .* (1720), and his *Complete Collection of Genteel and Ingenious Conversation . . .* (1738) show his concern with language. For his political purposes and for his pamphlets, he needed a middle style, which would, in effect, avoid the extremes of decadent courtier or disloyal dissenter, of licentiousness and fanaticism. He thought that an academy, founded on the example of the Académie Française, might act prescriptively, to define correct English and fix it—a thing we now think virtually impossible to achieve. But for him language was not only associated with history, politics, and religion: it was part and parcel of morality as he saw it. So clarity was to be sought above all: "propriety and correctness of speech." What this meant in his case was the right word in the right place. He distrusted rhetoric that appealed to passion: his own plain style was nonetheless rhetorical, designed to provoke, to vex, to rouse. He translated arguments into literal terms; he pursued them to their limits. He was aware of his audience; he offered it concrete examples that could be understood. He is said to have summoned his servants, had his proofs read aloud to them, and then

to have altered his writing until the servants fully understood it. He aimed, then, not only at the educated classes but at ordinary intelligent people; he therefore had to use an English that was, above all, normal—that is to say uneccentric, commonplace, simple, and generally acceptable; a prose that could evoke decent, tolerant responses and could, paradoxically, provide a vehicle for what is perhaps Swift's main contribution to English literature, his departure from the normal, the peculiarly powerful irony that carried his satire so effectively.

Satire in Swift's hands was a great cleansing force: it shifted the rubbish, it cut clear channels through the corruption of his own day—the hypocrisy and cant, the sheer stupidity and dullness of many of his contemporaries—and it remains with us, for the things he attacked are with us still. He was profoundly aware of the absurdities of human life; he found injustice and irrationality revolting; and he dwelt with disgust upon the ugly, unhygienic aspects of eighteenth-century life. And yet he had two main approaches: he described one as lashing vice, the other as ridiculing. The latter was natural for "a man of mirth," as many of his friends saw him, exuberant in his invention and sense of comic absurdity.

He could rail directly at the men whom he distrusted or disliked: this kind of satire runs the risk of seeming abusive or crude, and his other methods better stand the test of time. His indirect methods of irony led him into impersonating his enemies, or to achieving his effects indirectly with a deadpan style, or else to either diminishing or inflating an enemy's argument. And there was his habit of shifting his style from the reasonable and urbane to the disturbingly violent. He could also surprise his readers by omitting normal or expected human qualities, notably, for instance, in *A Modest Proposal*, which avoids any humanitarian sense of pity. This is part of one of his techniques—of being allusive, or forcing the reader to face for himself the problems presented by the printed word. In short, his methods possess immense variety, informed by that intensity of feeling he brought to bear on the temporary and the lasting issues of his age. The imperishable qualities of his satire are in part achieved by the quality of his imagination that imbues his inventions with the qualities of fact and of reality, and, therefore, even now, with that of convincing contemporaneity.

THE POETRY

SWIFT's poetry has an engaging directness: he wrote occasional poems to amuse himself and others, to pay tribute and to denigrate, to capture details of the life about him, and to justify himself. He regarded his verses as written "upon trifles," though they were never composed "without a moral view." Trifles they may have seemed to him, but the total impact of his poetry gives us insight into the way his mind worked, shows us his skill with words (the fun he got out of punning and out of rhyming, not always very precisely) as well as his sense of realism. In the "Ode to Mr. Congreve" he offered advice:

> Beat not the dirty paths where vulgar feet have trod
> But give the vigorous fancy room.

And he took his own advice to heart. His fancy played with a wide range of subjects, and he could parody well-trodden, heroic, or pastoral paths with acute irony, as well as adapting classical models—notably, poems of Horace—to his own uses.

What beats through all his verse, even the early odes, is the accent of direct speech. The formal structure of the Pindaric ode that he used in his early poems was not suitable in his kind of poetry; yet in the "Ode to Sir William Temple" he contrived to convey his genuine respect and, at the close of that poem, to express his own feelings. Nature, he says, has tied him to the Muse's galleys:

> In vain I strive to cross this spacious main,
> In vain I try and pull the oar
> And when I almost reach the shore
> Strait the Muse turns the helm, and I launch out again;
>   And yet to feed my pride,
> Whene'er I mourn, stops my complaining breath
> With promise of a mad reversion after death.

He offers Temple the tribute of a humbler Muse:

> Nature the hidden spark did at my birth infuse
> And kindled first with Indolence and Ease,
> And since too oft debauch'd by praise,
> 'Tis now grown an incurable Disease:
> In vain to quench this foolish fire I try
> In Wisdom and Philosophy;
> In vain all wholesome Herbs I sow,
> Where nought but weeds will grow.
> Whate'er I plant (like Corn on barren Earth)

> By an equivocal Birth
> Seeds and runs up to Poetry.   (192–198; 202–212)

This should be contrasted with a poem of 1733, "On Poetry: A Rhapsody," which exhibits an old man's frenzy:

> Not Beggar's Brat, on Bulk begot;
> Not Bastard of a Pedlar Scot;
> Not Boy brought up to cleaning shoes,
> The Spawn of Bridewell, or the Stews;
> Not Infants dropt, the spurious Pledges
> Of Gipsies littering under Hedges,
> Are so disqualified by Fate
> To rise in Church or Law, or State,
> As he, whom Phebus in his Ire
> Hath blasted with poetick Fire.   (33–42)

These early odes show his desire to get below surface appearances: they contain his fierce awareness of human mortality. For him poetry was a means of clarifying, even of condensing, experience, of arriving at truth. But it had to seem casual—paradoxically, both concise and conversational, direct and clear. Thus in two poems, "A Description of the Morning" and "A Description of a City Shower" (both published in the Tatler in 1710, Nos. 9 and 238 respectively), he gives an impression of movement and noise, assembling details into a general and convincing pattern of city life, ironically mocking, in the process, aspects of heroic and pastoral poetry. The rhythm and the rhymes give an urgency to the lines on the shower:

> Now from all Parts the swelling Kennels flow,
> And bear their Trophies with them go:
> Filth of all Hues and Odours seem to tell
> What Streets they sailed from, by the Sight and Smell.
> They, as each Torrent drives, with rapid Force
> From Smithfield, or St. Pulchre's shape their Course,
> And in huge Confluent join at Snow-Hill Ridge,
> Fall from the Conduit prone to Holborn-Bridge.
> Sweepings from Butchers Stalls, Dung, Guts, and Blood,
> Drown'd Puppies, stinking Sprats, all drench'd in Mud,
> Dead Cats and Turnip-Tops come tumbling down the
>   Flood.   (53–63)

Here Swift is insisting upon the crude reality of ordinary objects. Human attitudes to life are captured equally well in the speech he created in colloquial monologues—as, for example, the famous "Humble Petition of Frances Harris" (1710) with all its breathless account of the loss of her money:

Now you must know because my Trunk has a very
    bad lock
Therefore all the Money, I have, which, *God*
    knows, is a very small stock,
I keep in a Pocket ty'd about my Middle, next
    my smock.
So when I went to put up my Purse, as *God* would
    have it, my smock was unript,
And, instead of putting it into my Pocket, down it
    slipt . . .   (5–9)

And the poem moves to her real problem, the
possible loss of the chaplain as a husband. No less
effective is a later poem in this genre, "Mary the
Cook-Maid's Letter to Mr. Sheridan" (1718), which
captures the rattling speech of a forthright Irish
servant.

Swift adopted octosyllabic couplets, and in so
doing found the right form for expressing himself.
The directness and control of his lines are noteworthy. He wrote some political poems during his
stay in London: these lampoons were clever,
notably the attack on Marlborough in "A Fable of
the Widow and Her Cat" (1712) or "The Virtues of
Sid Hamett the Magician's Rod" (1710) on Lord
Godolphin. He continued his attack on Marlborough, even after his death, in "A Satyrical Elegy
on the Death of a Late Famous General":

    Let pride be taught by this rebuke
    How very mean a thing's a Duke
    From all his ill-got Honours flung
    Turn'd to that dirt from whence he sprung. (29–34)

These poems chimed with his political prose, and
later, when he was involved in combating Wood's
halfpence with *The Drapier's Letters*, his poems (of
1724–1725) again displayed a satiric liveliness of invention, a vitality of interpretation, which emerged
in the bursting vigor of "Mad Mullinix and Timothy" (1728) and "A Character, Panegyric, and
Description of the Legion Club" (written in 1736), a
comment on the Irish Parliament, matched only by
the bitter view expressed in "Ireland" (1727).

Before Swift settled in Dublin, as dean of St.
Patrick's, he wrote *Cadenus and Vanessa*, his
longest poem, in 889 lines, an account of his relationship (Cadenus is an anagram of *decanus*, Latin
for dean) with Esther Vanhomrigh. This poem contrasts Vanessa's perfections and the imperfections of
contemporary women that correspond to the failings of society, by means of setting this moral fable
in a mythological setting where the two sexes

dispute before Venus. The poem tells of Cadenus'
surprise at Vanessa's falling in love with him:

    Vanessa, not in Years a Score
    Dreams of a Gown of forty-four;
    Imaginary Charms can find,
    In Eyes with Reading almost blind;
    Cadenus now no more appears
    Declin'd in Health, advanc'd in Years.
    She fancies Musick in his Tongue
    Nor further looks but thinks him Young. (525–532)

He is flattered, but his dignity and age forbid him
to engage in love:

    But friendship in its greatest Height,
    A constant, rational Delight,
    On Virtue's Basis fix'd to last,
    When Love's allurements long are past;
    Which gently warms but cannot burn;
    He gladly offers in return.   (780–785)

Vanessa sees the situation of pupil and tutor is
reversed:

    But what success Vanessa met,
    Is to the world a Secret yet:
    Whether the Nymph to please her Swain,
    Talks in a high Romantick Strain;
    Or whether he at last descends
    To like with less Seraphick Ends;
    Or, to compound the Business, whether
    They temper Love and Books together;
    Must never to Mankind be told,
    Nor shall the conscious Muse unfold.   (818–827)

The poem pays its compliments to Vanessa, but
the interest for us is its autobiographical account of
the problems of one of Swift's close relationships.
Swift's friendship with Stella gave rise to revealing
poems, some written for her birthdays, in which he
pays tribute to her character, her intelligence, and
her care for him. In these he pays her compliments
("On Stella's Birth-day, Written A.D. 1718–[19]"),
praises her kindness ("To Stella, Visiting Me in My
Sickness"), stresses their friendship:

    Thou *Stella* wert no longer young
    When first for thee my Harp I strung;
    Without one Word of Cupid's Darts,
    Of killing Eyes, or bleeding Hearts:
    With Friendship and Esteem possesst,
    I ne'er admitted Love a guest. . . .
        ("To Stella, Who Collected and
              Transcribed His Poems," 9–14)

Other poems stress the lasting quality of her intellect ("Stella's Birthday, Written A.D. 1720–21"), tease her ("Stella's Distress on the 3rd Fatal Day of October 1723," rewritten as "Stella at Wood-Park") when she finds her Dublin lodgings small after staying at Wood Park, praise her for missing him on her birthday—a self-pitying poem ("To Stella . . . Written on the Day of Her Birth, but not on the Subject, When I Was Sick in Bed") on his being fifty-six, she forty-three ("Stella's Birth Day, 1725"), on her being too thin ("A Receipt to Restore Stella's Youth, Written in the Year 1724–5"), and, perhaps the most moving of all, as Stella was dying in 1727 ("Stella's Birthday, March 13, 1727"):

> This Day whate'er the fates decree,
> Shall still be kept with Joy by me:
> This Day then, let us not be told,
> That you are sick and I grown old,
> Nor think on our approaching ills,
> And talk of Spectacles and Pills;
> To morrow will be time enough
> To hear such mortifying stuff.
> Yet since from Reason may be brought
> A better and more pleasing thought,
> Which can in spite of all Decays
> Support a few remaining Days:
> From not the gravest of Divines,
> Accept for once some serious lines
> Although we now can form no more
> Fond schemes of Life, as here to fore;
> Yet you, while Time is running fast,
> Can look with Joy on what is past. . . .

Perhaps the deepest sign of his care for Stella is to be found in "Holyhead, September 25, 1717," the moody, angry poem he wrote when, deeply anxious about her "On whom my fears and hopes depend," he was held up by contrary winds:

> Lo here I sit at holy head
> With muddy ale and mouldy bread
> All Christian vittals stink of fish
> I'm where my enemies would wish. . . .

Swift's last poems return to his basic interest in the difference between truth and illusion. "The Problem," a poem of 1699, deals with the animal side of love, and such poems as "The Lady's Dressing Room" (1732) stress his loathing of untidiness and lack of hygiene. "A Beautiful Young Nymph Going to Bed" (1734) develops the attack on appearance and reality by showing how Erinna dismantles her artificial aids at night while "Strephon and Chloe" (1734), describing Strephon's shock at discovering that his bride is all too human, stresses the need for maintaining decency.

Swift did not accept a persona in poetry as in prose. Thus his attitude toward himself appears unequivocally in several poems. "The Author upon Himself" (1714) was a straightforward, if ironic, account of his life in London, and his retiring from political life, "The Life and Character of Dr. Swift" (1731) exhibited a frank desire to weigh up his achievement, albeit laughingly, but the "Verses on the Death of Dr. Swift" (1739) had its sadness as it considered how quickly he will be forgotten. While playing cards the ladies

> Receive the news in doleful dumps,
> The Dean is dead, (and what is *Trumps*?)
> Then Lord have mercy on his Soul
> (Ladies I'll venture for the *Vole*)
> Six Deans they say must bear the Pall
> (I wish I knew what *King* to call). . . .

He defended his satire and his moral view, remarked how he had exposed the fool and lashed the knave:

> Yet malice never was his Aim
> He lash'd the Vice but spar'd the Name.

And finally, ironically, he linked himself yet again with the land he hated:

> He gave the little Wealth he had,
> To build a House for Fools and Mad:
> And show'd by one satyric Touch,
> No nation wanted it so much.
>   (227–231; 459–460; 479–483)

THE CORRESPONDENCE

SWIFT's letters have an immediacy about them; they too reflect his desire to write unaffectedly and intimately, and they are written in a graphic, lively style. He provided his recipients with what he might have offered them in conversation. Thus he seems to talk out loud to Stella and her friend Rebecca Dingley in the *Journal to Stella*. He returns from his days among the great and relaxes in telling the ladies in Dublin about the events of his day in London, as well as relaying the gossip of the town.

From them we can piece together his care over money, coupled with his generosity, his fiery independence, his desire to be treated like a lord. He could tell Stella how he called on Secretary St. John and told him "never to appear cold to me, for I would not be treated like a school boy." St. John "took all right; said I had reason" and would have had Swift dine with him "to make up matters; but I would not. I don't know, but I would not." Stella knew him well. He had taught her to despise the shows of the world; so to her he could recount his sorrows—the death of Lady Ashburnham, for instance. He could scold her and tease her, and demand from her news of his garden in Ireland, of his fruit trees and willows and the trout stream.

Swift emerges from these letters in all his complexity, coarse and sensitive, proud yet ready to serve; humanly despairing and yet ready to endure. To Stella he could be imperious and instructive, gay and scathing, tender and scathing, tender and tolerant. We hear of his health, his troubles with servants, his forebodings about the government.

In letters to others we learn of his domestic situation, as dean in Dublin, for instance; he is often depressed by the effects of Ménière's disease, yet energetically taking vast exercise. There is one charming vignette:

I often ride out in fair weather, with one of my servants laden with a Joynt of meat and a bottle of wine, and Town bread, who attends me to some rural parson 5 or 6 miles round this Town.

There were many letters to Archbishop King, filled with the latest political views, yet discreet, for he knew well the man to whom he was writing. There were the letters to his younger friend Charles Ford, and the jesting, punning letters to Sheridan. Swift wrote many letters: and through them, as through his poems, there runs a nimbleness and drive, whether he is dispensing a moral view or enjoying some piece of raillery. The taut language of his letters reinforces his desire for simplicity; they are always concise. They range from statesmanship to literary satire; to his friends he showed his jocosity, his natural inventiveness, and, at times, his moods of deep depression.

He fought for health. There is a touching letter to Charles Ford advising him to take exercise and be temperate for his health's sake. In this Swift argues that life is not of much value but health is

everything. For his part, he wrote, he labored for daily health "as often and almost as many hours as a workman does for daily bread, and like a common labourer can but just earn enough to keep life and soul together." It was to Ford he wrote that he had finished *Gulliver's Travels* and was transcribing them. As always there is the query of how far to accept his literal meaning, for he commented on them: "they are admirable Things, and will wonderfully mend the World." And in a letter to Pope he wrote a sentence that does more to explain him than the writings of most commentators:

All my endeavours from a boy, to distinguish myself, were only for want of a great title and fortune, that I might be used like a Lord by those who have an opinion of my parts—whether right or wrong, it is no great matter, and so the reputation of wit or great learning does the office of a blue ribbon, or of a coach and six horses.

THE ULTIMATE ACHIEVEMENT

LORD BATHURST, writing in 1730 of Swift's achievement in his time, summed up his success in words that are still useful:

You have overturned and supported Ministers. You have set Kingdoms in a flame by your pen. Pray, what is there in that but having the knack of hitting the passions of mankind?

A fair comment and query; but it does not solve the problem of the elusive man behind the masks. Swift remains elusive, apt to rouse the passions of his readers into admiration or dislike. The evils of existence, as Bonamy Dobrée well put it, are combated with laughter by men such as Swift, who balance their critical, satiric spirits and their savage indignation with an exuberant, fantastic humor. And when there was no need for indignation at the irrationality and injustice of men, when reasonableness prevailed and life ran in smooth social currents, the humor was urbane, teasing where tacit, protective affection existed; creating mirth out of irony when fierce passions were temporarily lulled. Swift moved between moods, as Vanessa knew to her cost: she recorded how he could shake her with prodigious awe so that she trembled with fear, but at other times her soul was revived by the charming compassion that shone through Swift's soul. His *saeva indignatio* was matched by what Ford called his capacity "for mirth and society"; and Arbuthnot once wrote that it was not Swift's wit and good conversation that he valued him for, but for being a sincere, honest man and speaking truth when others were afraid to do so.

SELECTED BIBLIOGRAPHY

Detailed bibliographical information will also be found in the appropriate volume of the *Cambridge Bibliography of English Literature* and the *Oxford History of English Literature*.

I. BIBLIOGRAPHY. H. Teerink, *A Bibliography of the Writings in Prose and Verse* (The Hague, 1937), revised by A. H. Scouten, ed. (Philadelphia, 1963), a comprehensive work that supersedes W. S. Jackson's bibliography in T. Scott, ed., *Prose Works*, vol. XII (London, 1908) and contains extensive lists of doubtful and supposititious writings as well as of critical and biographical studies; L. L. Hubbard, *Contributions towards a Bibliography of "Gulliver's Travels"* (London, 1922); H. Williams, *The Motte Editions of "Gulliver's Travels"* (London, 1925), see also Sir H. Williams' authoritative bibliography of the early eds. in his ed. of *Gulliver's Travels* (First Edition Club, 1926); D. M. Berwick, *The Reputation of Swift, 1781-1882* (Philadelphia, 1941); L. A. Landa and J. E. Tobin, comps., *Jonathan Swift: A List of Critical Studies, 1895-1945* (New York, 1945), a valuable guide to numerous articles in learned journals, with an account by D. H. Davis of Swift MSS in American libraries; *The Rothschild Library*, 2 vols. (London, 1954), contains full descriptions of the important collection of printed books, pamphlets, and MSS by Swift formed by Lord Rothschild, with references to bibliographical studies of separate works published since Teerink; M. Voigt, *Swift and the Twentieth Century* (Detroit, 1964); J. J. Stathis, comp., *A Bibliography of Swift Studies 1945-1965* (Nashville, 1967); A. Norman Jeffares, ed., *Fair Liberty Was All His Cry* (London, 1967), includes C. Lamont's "A Checklist of Critical and Biographical Writings on Jonathan Swift, 1945-65."

II. COLLECTED WORKS. *Miscellanies in Prose and Verse* (London, 1711), the earliest collection of Swift's writings, apart from a sixteen-page pamphlet (1710), a number of unauthorized and pirated Swiftian "Miscellanies" of varied content were published during the following quarter of a century; *Miscellanies in Prose and Verse*, 3 vols. (London, 1727), these vols. of the "Swift-Pope Miscellanies" were extended by a 4th vol. (1732) and 5th vol. (1735), in 6-vol. ed. (1736), in 13 vols. (1751); *The Drapier's Miscellany* (Dublin, 1733), miscellaneous pieces

in verse and prose relating to the Irish economy; *Works*, 4 vols. (Dublin, 1735), published by Faulkner with Swift's tacit approval, extended to 6 vols. (1738), 8 vols. (1746), 11 vols. (1763), and 20 vols. (1769); *Poetical Works* (Dublin, 1736), a separate reprint of Faulkner's 2nd ed. of *Works*, vol. II (above), a number of separate eds. of Swift's poetical works were published during the eighteenth century and his poems were included in the well-known series edited by Bell et al.; J. Hawkesworth, ed., *Works* (London, 1755-1775), a rival of Faulkner's ed., published simultaneously in 6 quarto vols. and 12 octavo vols., subsequently extended by 8 quarto vols. and 13 octavo vols., also published later in 27 eighteenmo vols.; T. Sheridan, ed., *Works*, 17 vols. (London, 1784), based on Hawkesworth's text.

Works, 19 vols. (London, 1801, 24 duodecimo vols., 1803), Sheridan's ed. corrected and revised by J. Nichols; Sir W. Scott, ed., *Works*, 19 vols. (Edinburgh, 1814; 2nd ed., 1824; repr., 1883), vol. I contains Scott's long biographical essay; T. Scott, ed., *Prose Works*, 12 vols. (London, 1897-1908), vol. XII is W. S. Jackson's bibliography; H. Davis, ed., *The Drapier's Letters to the People of Ireland against Receiving Wood's Halfpence* (Oxford, 1935), the definitive ed.; H. Davis, ed., *Prose Works*, 15 vols. (Oxford, 1939-1964), the definitive Shakespeare Head ed., with valuable intros. and bibliographical and textual notes; H. Williams, ed., *Poems*, 3 vols. (Oxford, 1937; 2nd ed., rev., 1958), the definitive ed.; J. Horrell, ed., *Collected Poems*, 2 vols. (London, 1958), in the Muses' Library.

III. SELECTED WORKS. Among the many selections from Swift's writings, ranging from school texts to deluxe limited eds. and including vols. in such series as Everyman's Library and Collins' Classics, the following are noteworthy: W. A. Eddy, ed., *Satires and Personal Writings* (London, 1932); J. Hayward, ed., *Gulliver's Travels and Selected Prose and Verse* (London, 1934), the Nonesuch Press ed.; J. Hayward, ed., *Selected Prose Works* (London, 1949), the Cresset Library ed.

IV. LETTERS. *Letters to and from Dr. J. Swift, 1714-1738* (Dublin, 1741), also published as Faulkner's ed. of *Works*, vol. VII; J. Hawkesworth, ed., *Letters* (London, 1766); J. Hawkesworth and D. Swift, eds., *Letters*, 6 vols. (London, 1768-1769), published as part of Hawkesworth's ed. of *Works*; G. B. Hill, ed., *Unpublished Letters* (London, 1899); A. M. Freeman, ed., *Vanessa and Her Correspondence with Swift* (London, 1921), the first publication of the "love letters" of Swift and Esther Vanhomrigh; D. Nichol Smith, *Letters to Charles Ford* (Oxford, 1935), edited for the first time from the originals, now for the most part in *The Rothschild Library*; H. Williams, ed., *The Journal to Stella*, 2 vols. (Oxford, 1948), the definitive ed., the letters to Esther Johnson were first printed, more or less inaccurately, in Hawkesworth's *Works*, vol. X, letters 1 and 41-65, and in vol. XII, letters 2–40; later eds. are G. A. Aitken, ed. (London, 1901), F. Ryland, ed. (London, 1905), which is vol. II of T. Scott's ed. of *Works*, and J. K. Moorhead, ed. (London, 1924), in Everyman's Library; H. Williams, ed., *The Correspondence of Jonathan Swift*, 5 vols. (Oxford, 1963–1965).

V. SEPARATE WORKS. This section does not include single pieces printed as broadsides or as folio halfsheets; contributions to periodicals (e.g., *The Tatler* and *The Examiner*) and to books by other writers, for which see H. Davis, ed., *Prose Works* and H. Williams, ed., *Poems*; or any of the numerous doubtful or supposititious works that at various times have been ascribed to Swift. For titles of the latter see Teerink's *Bibliography* (above) and the excellent short-title list by H. Williams in the *Cambridge Bibliography of English Literature*.

A Discourse of the Contests and Dissensions between the Nobles and the Commons in Athens and Rome (London, 1701), politics; *A Tale of a Tub* [and *The Battle of the Books*] (London, 1704), polemical satire, annotated ed. with plates (1710); *The Battle of the Books* was Swift's contribution to the famous quarrel of the ancients and the moderns, the definitive ed. of both works is A. Guthkelch and D. Nichol Smith, eds. (Oxford, 1920); *Predictions for the Year 1708* (London, 1708), parody, the first of several jesting satires against almanac-makers (and one, Partridge, in particular) written under the pseudonym of Isaac Bickerstaff during 1708–1709; *A Project for the Advancement of Religion and the Reformation of Manners* (London, 1709), moral instruction; *A Letter . . . Concerning the Sacramental Test* (London, 1709), church politics; *Baucis and Philemon* (London, 1709), verse, Swift's first separately printed poem, reprinted with other poems and with the prose parody *A Meditation upon a Broom-Stick* (London, 1710).

The Examiner (London, 1710–1711), political journalism, 32 weekly issues, beginning with No. 14, 26 Oct. 1710, written by Swift; *A Short Character of . . . [the Earl of Wharton]* (London, 1711), invective; *Some Remarks upon a Pamphlet* (London, 1711), politics; *A New Journey to Paris* (London, 1711), politics; *A Learned Comment upon Dr. Hare's Excellent Sermon* (London, 1711), church politics; *The Conduct of the Allies* (London, 1712), politics, the definitive ed. was edited, with intro. and notes, by C. B. Wheeler (Oxford, 1916); *Some Advice Humbly Offer'd to the Members of the October Club* (London, 1712), politics; *Some Remarks on the Barrier Treaty* (London, 1712), politics; *A Proposal for Correcting . . . the English Tongue* (London, 1712), criticism; *Some Reasons to Prove that No Person Is Obliged by His Principles as a Whig, etc.* (London, 1712), politics; *A Letter of Thanks . . . to the . . . Bishop of S. Asaph* (London, 1712), church politics; *Mr. C[olli]n's Discourse of Free-Thinking* (London, 1713), polemics; *Part of the Seventh Epistle of the First Book of Horace Imitated* (London,

1713), verse; *The Importance of the Guardian Considered* (London, 1713), politics; *The First Ode of the Second Book of Horace Paraphras'd* (London, 1713), verse; *The Publick Spirit of the Whigs* (London, 1714), politics; *An Argument to Prove that the Abolishing of Christianity in England, etc.* (London, 1717), first published in *Miscellanies* (London, 1711).

A Proposal for the Universal Use of Irish Manufacture (London, 1720), political economy, *A Defence of English Commodities* (London, 1720), an answer to this pamphlet, was probably written by Swift; *A Letter . . . to a Gentleman Designing for Holy Orders* (London, 1720), criticism; *The Swearer's Bank* (London, 1720), satire; *The Bubble* (London, 1721), verse; *A Letter of Advice to a Young Poet* (Dublin, 1721), criticism, long ascribed to Swift but probably not by him; *Some Arguments against Enlarging the Power of the Bishops* (London, 1723), church politics; *A Letter to the Shop-Keepers* (London, 1724), political economy, the first of the celebrated Drapier's letters; *A Letter to Mr. Harding the Printer* (London, 1724), political economy, the second of Drapier's letters; *Some Observations upon a Paper* (London, 1724), political economy, the third of Drapier's letters; *A Letter to the Whole People of Ireland* (London, 1724), political economy, the fourth of Drapier's letters; *A Letter to . . . Viscount Molesworth* (London, 1724), political economy, the fifth and last of Drapier's letters, which were published together in *Fraud Detected: or, The Hibernian Patriot* (Dublin, 1725); the definitive ed. of *Drapier's Letters* was H. Davis, ed. (Oxford, 1935); *The Birth of Manly Virtue* (London, 1725), verse; *Cadenus and Vanessa: A Poem* (London, 1726), verse; *[Gulliver's] Travels into Several Remote Nations of the World*, 2 vols. (London, 1726), satirical fantasy, Faulkner's text (*Works*, vol. III), which was revised with Swift's cooperation, was first reprinted in modern times in the Nonesuch ed. of *Swift*, and later in the Cresset Library *Swift*, in the Shakespeare Head *Swift*, vol. XI, and in Collins' Classics; the definitive ed. of the text of the first ed. (1726) was elaborately edited by H. Williams for the First Edition Club (1926); *A Short View of the State of Ireland* (Dublin, 1727–1728), political economy; *An Answer to a Paper Called "A Memorial of the Poor Inhabitants"* (Dublin, 1728), political economy; *The Intelligencer* (Dublin, 1728), political journalism, 20 weekly numbers by Swift and Sheridan, published as a single vol. (1729), No. 19 printed separately as *A Letter . . . to a Country Gentleman in the North of Ireland* (1736); *A Modest Proposal* (Dublin, 1729), sociological satire; *The Journal of a Dublin Lady* (Dublin, 1729), verse, reprinted in London as *The Journal of a Modern Lady*; *A Panegyric on . . . Dean Swift* (Dublin, 1729–1730), verse.

An Epistle to . . . Lord Carteret (Dublin, 1730), politics; *An Epistle upon an Epistle* (Dublin, 1730), verse; *A Libel on D[octor] D[elany]* (London, 1730), verse; *A Vindica-*

tion of . . . *Lord Carteret* (London, 1730), politics; *Traulus*, 2 parts (Dublin, 1730), verse; *Horace, Book I: Ode XIV* (Dublin, 1730), verse; *A Soldier and a Scholar* (London, 1732; repr., Dublin, 1732), verse, reprinted as *The Grand Question Debated*; *Considerations upon Two Bills* (London, 1732), church politics; *An Examination of Certain Abuses* (Dublin, 1732), sociological satire, the title of the London ed. begins *City Cries, Instrumental and Vocal . . .* ; *The Lady's Dressing Room* (London, 1732), verse; *The Advantages Proposed by Repealing the Sacramental Test* (Dublin, 1732), church politics; *An Elegy on Dicky and Dolly* (Dublin, 1732), verse; *The Life and Genuine Character of Doctor Swift. Written by Himself* (London, 1733), verse; *On Poetry: A Rapsody* (London, 1733), verse; *The Presbyterians' Plea of Merit* (Dublin, 1733), church politics; *Some Reasons against the Bill for Settling the Tyth of Hemp by a Modus* (Dublin, 1734), political economy; *An Epistle to a Lady . . . also a Poem . . . Called the Universal Passion* (London, 1734), verse; *A Beautiful Young Nymph Going to Bed* (London, 1734), verse, also contains "Strephon and Chloe" and "Cassinus and Peter"; *A Proposal for Giving Badges to the Beggars . . . of Dublin* (Dublin, 1737), sociology; *An Imitation of the Sixth Satire of the Second Book of Horace* (London, 1738), verse, written in 1714 and completed by Pope; *The Beasts' Confession to the Priest* (Dublin, 1738), verse; *A Complete Collection of Genteel and Ingenious Conversation* (London, 1738), social satire, published under the pseudonym of Simon Wagstaff; *Verses on the Death of Dr. Swift. Written by Himself* (London, 1739), verse, incorporates part of *The Life and Genuine Character . . .* (above), the text of the 4 folio eds. of 1739, published by Bathurst in London, is inferior to the text of the 6 octavo eds. published in Dublin by Faulkner in the same year.

Some Free Thoughts upon the Present State of Affairs (Dublin, 1741), politics; *Three Sermons* (London, 1744), theology, a fourth sermon was added to the 2nd ed. of the same year; *Directions to Servants* (Dublin, 1745), social satire; *Brotherly Love: A Sermon* (Dublin, 1754), theology; *The History of the Four Last Years of the Queen* (London, 1758), history; *Polite Conversation* (London, 1963), with intro., notes, and extensive commentary by E. Partridge; S. Le Brocquy, ed., *Stella's Birth-Days: Poems* (Dublin, 1967).

VI. BIOGRAPHY AND CRITICISM. *Memoirs [of Laetitia Pilkington]*, 3 vols. (London, 1748–1754), lively but somewhat fanciful firsthand reminiscences; John Earl of Orrery, *Remarks on the Life and Writings of Jonathan Swift* (London, 1752), see also P. Delany's more important *Observations on Lord Orrery's Remarks* (London, 1754); J. Hawkesworth, *Life of Dr. Swift* (Dublin, 1755), first printed in Hawkesworth's ed. of *Works*, vol. I; *An Essay upon the Life, Writings and Character of Dr. Jonathan Swift* (London, 1735), by Swift's cousin Deane Swift; W. H. Dilworth, *Life* (London, 1758); S. Johnson,

Life, in his *Lives of the Poets*, vol. III (London, 1781); T. Sheridan, *Life* (London, 1784); J. Barrett, *Essay on the Earlier Part of the Life of Swift* (London, 1808); Sir W. Scott, *Memoirs of Jonathan Swift*, 2 vols. (Paris, 1826), first printed in Scott's ed. of *Works*, vol. I; Sir W. Wilde, *The Closing Years of Dean Swift's Life* (London, 1849); W. M. Thackeray, *The English Humourists of the 18th Century* (London, 1851), contains a famous essay on Swift; L. Prévost-Paradol, *Jonathan Swift: sa vie et ses oeuvres* (Paris, 1856); J. Forster, *Life* (London, 1875), only vol. I was published, the Forster Collection in the library of the Victoria and Albert Museum contains important manuscript and printed material by and relating to Swift; L. Stephen, *Swift* (London, 1882), in the English Men of Letters series; H. Craik, *Life* (London, 1882; 2 vols., 1894); J. C. Collins, *Jonathan Swift: A Bibliographical and Critical Study* (London, 1893); G. P. Moriarty, *Dean Swift and His Writings* (London, 1893); R. A. King, *Swift in Ireland* (London, 1895).

The Orrery Papers, 2 vols. (London, 1903); C. Whibley, *Swift* (London, 1917), the Leslie Stephen lecture; C. H. Firth, 'The Political Significance of *Gulliver's Travels*" in *Proceedings of the British Academy* (1919–1920); W. A. Eddy, *Gulliver's Travels: A Critical Study* (Princeton, 1923); S. Goulding, *Swift en France* (Paris, 1924); E. Pons, *Swift: Les années de jeunesse et "Le Conte du Tonneau"* (Strasbourg, 1925), the first installment of a massive but incomplete critical biography; F. E. Ball, *Swift's Verse* (London, 1928); A. Huxley, *Do What You Will* (London, 1929), contains an essay on Swift; C. Van Doren, *Swift* (London, 1931); H. Williams, *Dean Swift's Library* (London, 1932), contains a facsimile of the catalog of Swift's library; S. Gywnn, *The Life and Friendships of Dean Swift* (London, 1933), a popular biography; W. D. Taylor, *Jonathan Swift: A Critical Essay* (London, 1933); W. B. Yeats, *The Words upon the Window Pane: A Play in One Act* (Dublin, 1934), a play about a seance in which the spirit of Swift appears, the intro. has many comments on Swift, whom Yeats read with deep interest in the 1920's and 1930's; S. Leslie, *The Script of Jonathan Swift and Other Essays* (Philadelphia, 1935); C. Looten, *La Pensée Religieuse de Swift et ses antinomies* (Lille, 1935); R. Quintana, *The Mind and Art of Jonathan Swift* (London, 1936; rev., 1953), an important critical study; M. B. Gold, *Swift's Marriage to Stella* (Cambridge, Mass., 1937), a careful analysis of all the available evidence relating to this vexed problem; B. Newman, *Jonathan Swift* (London, 1937); B. Dobrée, ed., *From Anne to Victoria* (London, 1937), valuable essay on Swift by J. Hayward; R. W. Jackson, *Jonathan Swift, Dean and Pastor* (London, 1939).

H. Davis, *Stella* (New York, 1942); R. W. Jackson, *Swift and His Circle* (Dublin, 1945); L. A. Landa and J. E. Tobin, *Jonathan Swift: A List of Critical Studies Published from 1895 to 1945* (New York, 1945); A. E. Case,

Four Essays on "Gulliver's Travels" (Princeton, 1945), defends the 1726 text against Faulkner's revised text of 1735; E. Hardy, *The Conjured Spirit: Swift: A Study in the Relationship of Swift, Stella and Vanessa* (London, 1949); H. Davis, *The Satire of Jonathan Swift* (New York, 1947); G. Orwell, *Shooting an Elephant* (London, 1950), includes the essay "Politics vs. Literature" on Gulliver; M. K. Starkman, *Swift's Satire on Learning in "A Tale of a Tub"* (Princeton, 1952); M. Johnson, *The Sin of Wit: Jonathan Swift as a Poet* (Syracuse, 1950); B. Fitzgerald, *The Anglo-Irish: Three Representative Types: Cork, Ormonde, Swift, 1602–1745* (London, 1952), F. R. Leavis, *The Common Pursuit* (London, 1952), contains an important study entitled "Swift's Irony"; H. Williams, *The Text of "Gulliver's Travels"* (London, 1953), the Sanders lectures, a defense of Faulkner's text of 1735; J. M. Bullitt, *Jonathan Swift and the Anatomy of Satire: A Study of Satirical Technique* (Cambridge, Mass., 1953); M. Price, *Swift's Rhetorical Art: A Study in Structure and Meaning* (New Haven, 1953); J. M. Murry, *Jonathan Swift: A Critical Biography* (London, 1954); W. M. Ewald, Jr., *The Masks of Jonathan Swift* (London, 1954), a study of the personae adopted by Swift; L. A. Landa, *Swift and the Church of Ireland* (London, 1954), an important piece of research; R. Quintana, *Swift: An Introduction* (Oxford, 1955; ppb. ed., 1962), a masterly condensation; P. Greenacre, *Swift and Carroll* (New York, 1955), a psychological study according to Freudian principles; M. M. Foot, *The Pen and the Sword* (London, 1957); I. Ehrenpreis, *The Personality of Jonathan Swift* (London, 1958); D. Johnston, *In Search of Swift* (Dublin, 1959); K. Williams, *Jonathan Swift and the Age of Compromise* (London, 1959).

R. Paulson, *Theme and Structure in Swift's "Tale of a Tub"* (New Haven, 1960); D. F. R. Wilson, *Dean Swift* (Dublin, 1960); C. A. Beaumont, *Swift's Classical Rhetoric* (Athens, Ga., 1961); B. A. Goldgar, *The Curse of Party: Swift's Relations with Addison and Steele* (Lincoln, Nebr., 1961); P. Harth, *Swift and Anglican Rationalism: The Religious Background of "A Tale of a Tub"* (Chicago, 1961); O. W. Ferguson, *Jonathan Swift and Ireland* (Urbana, Ill., 1962); J. Fletcher, *Samuel Beckett et Jonathan Swift: vers une étude comparée* (Toulouse, 1962); S. Le Brocquy, *Cadenus: A Reassessment . . . of the Relationship between Swift, Stella and Vanessa* (Dublin, 1962); J. L. Snethlage, *Jonathan Swift: De Englese Voltaire* (The Hague, 1962); N. S. Subramanyam, *Jonathan Swift* (Allahabad, 1962); I. Ehrenpreis, *Swift: The Man, His Works and the Age* (London, 1962–), vol. I: *Mr. Swift and His Contemporaries*, vol. II: *Dr. Swift*; J. A. Mazzeo, ed., *Reason and Imagination* (London, 1962), contains an essay by R. S. Crane on book 4 of *Gulliver's Travels*; J. Traugott, ed., *Discussions of Jonathan Swift* (Boston, 1962); W. A. Eddy, *"Gulliver's Travels": A Critical Study* (New York, 1963); E. W. Rosenheim, *Swift and the Satirist's Art* (London, 1963); H. Davis, *Jonathan Swift* (New York, 1964), contains essays on Swift's satire and other studies; H. Davis, *Jonathan Swift: Essays on His Satire and Other Studies* (London, 1964); N. Dennis, *Jonathan Swift: A Short Character* (New York, 1964; London, 1965); P. Frédérix, *Swift, le véritable Gulliver* (Paris, 1964); E. Tuveson, *Swift: A Collection of Critical Essays* (Englewood Cliffs, N.J., 1964); M. Voight, *Swift and the Twentieth Century* (Detroit, 1964).

C. A. Beaumont, *Swift's Use of the Bible: A Documentation and Study in Allusion* (Athens, Ga., 1965); D. Donoghue, ed., *Swift Revisited* (Cork, 1965); M. E. Novak, *The Uses of Irony: Papers on Defoe and Swift* (Los Angeles, 1966), includes H. Davis' "Swift's Use of Irony"; J. G. Gilbert, *Jonathan Swift: Romantic and Cynic Moralist* (London, 1966); R. J. MacHugh and P. W. Edwards, eds., *Jonathan Swift, 1667–1967: A Dublin Tercentenary Tribute* (Dublin, 1967); P. Wolff-Windegg, *Swift* (Stuttgart, 1967); L. T. Milic, *A Quantitative Approach to the Style of Jonathan Swift* (The Hague, 1967); R. I. Cook, *Jonathan Swift as a Tory Pamphleteer* (London, 1967); G. Y. Goldberg, *Jonathan Swift and Contemporary Cork* (Cork, 1967); A. N. Jeffares, ed., *Fair Liberty Was All His Cry: A Tercentenary Tribute to Jonathan Swift* (London, 1967); A. N. Jeffares, ed., *Swift: Modern Judgements* (London, 1968); B. Vickers, comp. and ed., *The World of Jonathan Swift: Essays for the Tercentenary* (Oxford, 1968); K. Williams, *Jonathan Swift* (London, 1968), the Profiles in Literature series; S. Le Brocquy, *Swift's Most Valuable Friend* (Dublin, 1968); D. Donoghue, *Jonathan Swift: A Critical Introduction* (Cambridge, 1969); W. A. Speck, *Swift* (London, 1969), the Literature in Perspective series; K. Williams, ed., *Swift: The Critical Heritage* (London, 1970); D. Donoghue, ed., *Jonathan Swift: A Critical Anthology* (Harmondsworth, 1971); C. J. Rawson, ed., *Swift* (London, 1971); D. Ward, *Jonathan Swift: An Introductory Essay* (London, 1973); C. J. Rawson, ed., *Gulliver and the Gentle Reader: Studies in Swift and Our Time* (London, 1973); R. Gravil, ed., *Swift: "Gulliver's Travels": A Casebook* (London, 1974); A. L. Rowse, *Jonathan Swift: Major Prophet* (London, 1975), a lively biography, particularly good about Swift's relationships with Stella and Vanessa; C. T. Probyn, ed., *Jonathan Swift: The Contemporary Background* (Manchester, 1978) and *The Art of Jonathan Swift* (London, 1978).

ALFRED TENNYSON

(1809-1892)

Brian Southam

I

FOR many years the prevailing image of Tennyson has been of one of the great corruptors of English poetry, of a writer with a style so meretricious and insidiously molding that he misshaped the taste of generations of readers and the practice of generations of poets. A succession of influential critics, from Matthew Arnold to F. R. Leavis (and their many disciples), have condemned Tennyson as a second-rater, as an artist of Tennysonian verse—polished, melodious, and decorative; and in this artistry marooned, isolated from the central vitality of English poetry, cut off from the resources of the living language as Keats, immediately before him, was not. In this perspective the creative effort of Yeats, Eliot, and Pound, at the beginning of the century, is seen as a disinfection of poetic language and style, a breaking away from the Tennysonian embrace and the foundation of the modern movement as a counterforce to the Victorian poetic: the old style characteristically escapist, weakly romantic, medievalizing, moralizing, sentimental, simple, and unsubtle in its thought and feeling, the new style characteristically intelligent, unromantic, subtle, and complex in its tones and irony, realistic in its approach to human experience, seeking not to escape but to confront.

Broadly, this is an acceptable theory of action and reaction. Tennyson's popular style was indeed swamping; it formed public taste and set a standard by which poetry was to be judged; and a great deal of his writing can be described as Tennysonian, the heavy hand against which the modern poets turned in protest, just as there was a widespread reaction against Victorianism in general. Tennyson suffered particularly as the representative Victorian poet. His rejection was part of a historical process. But the continuing prejudice against Tennyson is as indefensible as the romantics' rejection of Pope and Dryden.

Difference is not inferiority. Although there is a good deal of Tennyson that is pompous, banal, grotesquely sentimental, and in many other ways laughably or unpleasantly Victorian, there is a sufficient body of his finest work to place him among the great poets of English literature. The refreshing challenge for anyone coming to Tennyson in the 1980's is precisely in this question, for there is no commonly accepted view of his achievement. Many critics see him as a minor poet of a minor period, of historical interest only. Others see him as an early symbolist poet, with modern affinities, a writer whose work repays the closest attention and responds to the kind of detailed analysis that we put to poetry of richness and complexity.[1]

Whatever we or posterity may decide on these questions, as a cultural and intellectual figure Tennyson occupies a unique position in English history. No writer has ever dominated his age so completely as Tennyson dominated Victorian England; no poet has ever been so completely a national poet. His writing entered the consciousness of the age. As Henry James said in 1875, his verse had become "part of the civilization of his day." To illustrate the true quality of faith, George Eliot quoted from the opening to *In Memoriam*; to discuss the capacities of women, she quoted from *The Princess*. Tennyson, she wrote in 1885, voiced "the struggles and the far reaching thoughts of this nineteenth century"; *In Memoriam* "enshrines the highest tendency of this age." Matthew Arnold prophesied that in a time of science and spiritual doubt, poetry would come to take the place of religion. How close the poetry of

[1]See particularly M. McLuhan, "Tennyson and Picturesque Poetry" (1951) and "Tennyson and the Romantic Epic" (1959); C. Brooks, *The Well-Wrought Urn* (1947); F. W. Bateson, *English Poetry* (1950); G. Hough, "Tears, Idle Tears" (1951); L. Spitzer, "'Tears, Idle Tears' Again" (1952). All are reprinted in J. Killham, ed., *Critical Essays on the Poetry of Tennyson* (London, 1960).

ALFRED TENNYSON

Tennyson came to fulfilling that prophecy we can judge from the words of the historian J. A. Froude:

Your father in my estimate stands and will stand far away by the side of Shakespeare above all other English Poets, with this relative superiority even to Shakespeare, that he speaks the thoughts and speaks *to* the perplexities and misgivings of his own age.

Froude was writing to Hallam Tennyson in 1894, when the biographer-son was compiling the monumental *Memoir*. But this is something more than obituary homage; the comparison with Shakespeare was not mere lip service; nor was Froude a critical simpleton (as anyone can see from his discussion of Shakespeare in "The Science of History").[2] What he says here is an assertion of Tennyson's hold upon the Victorian mind.

Tennyson's domination of the later nineteenth century is partly to be explained by the prosaic fact of his longevity. His career extended over seventy-five years, from childhood until his death in 1892, and he was a known poet, through his published work, from 1830 onward. He began in the shadow of the great romantics and lived to be the older contemporary of Hardy and Yeats. He came to an open field. The earlier generation was dead: Keats in 1821, Shelley in 1822, Byron in 1824; Scott, turned novelist, in 1832; Coleridge, turned philosopher, in 1834. Only Wordsworth survived, the young Wordsworth dead, until 1850, when he was succeeded as poet laureate by Tennyson, the then supreme poet of *In Memoriam*. In these terms Tennyson opened a fresh, post-romantic period in English poetry, a period further defined by historical events, notably the Reform Bill of 1832, the first real step toward modern parliamentary democracy, and the accession of Queen Victoria in 1837. Victorian England developed an unmistakable character. Its sustaining dynamic was the idea of Progress—full-blooded material progress in the growth of industry and trade; social progress in concern for the poor; nervous political progress in the direction of responsible democracy; fearful scientific progress toward the facts of creation and evolution; moral progress, as it was seen, in the ideals of purity and of family life, of paternalism, motherhood, and domesticity; religious progress, again, as it was seen, in the pietism of the Anglican church. There was also a higher, more speculative ideal of progress arising out of the grandiose vision of man's nature and destiny formulated by Thomas Carlyle, the "thinker" of the century, in "Signs of the Times" (*Edinburgh Review*, June 1829):

We have a faith in the imperishable dignity of man; in the high vocation to which throughout his earthly history, he had been appointed. . . . Doubtless this age also is advancing. Its very unrest, its ceaseless activity, its discontent contains matter of promise. Knowledge, education are opening the eyes of the humblest; are increasing the number of thinking minds without limit. This is as it should be; for not in turning back, not in resisting, but only in resolutely struggling forward, does our life consist.

Whether Tennyson read these words, we have no direct evidence. But only four years later, he was using this same cluster of ideas about man's "imperishable dignity" and the "unrest" and "ceaseless activity" of the age in the dramatic monologue "Ulysses," where the aged hero of Homer and Dante becomes a mouthpiece for the nineteenth century, rallying his shipmates with a Carlylean cry:

One equal temper of heroic hearts,
Made weak by time and fate, but strong in will
To strive, to seek, to find, and not to yield.[3]
(68–70)

In this poem, as in many others, Tennyson shows himself to be emphatically a modern poet, immersed in the circumstances of the age, its currents of thought and feeling, its way of life. Sometimes his involvement was in the line of duty. As poet laureate he was required to provide verses for the comings and goings of the royal family, and celebratory pieces for great events, such as the funeral of the duke of Wellington and the opening of the International Exhibition of 1862 (where he faced the technical problem of composing an ode suitable for a choir of four thousand). He met these demands with style and a sure sense of rhetoric and public verse.

Outside his official capacity Tennyson came to see himself as a kind of national watchdog. Early in 1852, for example, he thought that the government was not sufficiently alert to the threat of invasion from France. So he fired off a series of squibs to the

[2]In *Short Studies of Great Subjects* (London, 1867).

[3]All quotations of poetry are from C. Ricks, ed., *The Poems of Tennyson* (London, 1969).

press, calling on the ministers to wake up and rousing the country to arms. The archenemies were the "vile" Napoleon III and "bastard Christianity," his term for Roman Catholicism, to be opposed by the stout English virtues of traditional liberty and the strength of national character. In 1854–1855, sections of *Maud* were written against the "peace-at-any-price" party in the Crimean War; and other sections of the poem were directed against contemporary scandals—the adulteration of food, the condition of the poor in the industrial cities, the worship of money (then vilified as Mammonism). Later in the century, in "Politics," he encouraged the former prime minister, Gladstone, to take back the reins of government with a firm hand; this was in 1889, at the end of a troublesome decade which had seen the Irish home rule issue and the Reform Bill of 1884. Occasionally these poems rise above doggerel and survive for some quality of verse. "The Charge of the Light Brigade" is one such poem. It sprang from a report in the *Times* for 2 December 1854; was written, said Tennyson, "in a few minutes"; and appeared in the *Examiner* seven days later.

Tennyson was also determinedly up-to-date in his science and scholarship. The twentieth-century nightmare is the horror of the nuclear age. The nineteenth-century nightmare was the discovery of man's place in the universe, the discrediting of the biblical story of creation, the realization of man's animal origin. These were some of the questions that Tennyson faced in *In Memoriam*, bringing to his poetic task the latest state of scientific knowledge. Readers in the 1850's were reassured that their poet laureate was no warbling songster but a poet-philosopher whose trains of thought involved cold fact and hard speculation—the cataclysmic theory of creation and its refutation in Sir Charles Lyell's counter-theory of uniformitarian creation, the nebular hypothesis of the origin of the stars, the biological theory of mutability. What they read in Elegy CXXIII was not a string of poetic images but an account of the earth's past and future which they could substantiate in the textbooks of geology; reading in "Locksley Hall," in 1842, of the weighing of the sun, they would think of the astronomer Baily, who had been attempting that calculation since 1838.

In *In Memoriam* Tennyson set out to provide the nineteenth century with a moral interpretation of the universe, the meaning of life, and the nature of faith in a scientific world. In "Locksley Hall," he shows the impact of science and technology upon the imagination of contemporary man. The prospect of the future brings an uneasy excitement:

For I dipt into the future, far as human eye could see,
Saw the Vision of the world, and all the wonder that would be;

Saw the heavens fill with commerce, argosies of magic sails,
Pilots of the purple twilight, dropping down with costly bales;

Heard the heavens fill with shouting, and there rain'd a ghastly
  dew

From the nations' airy navies grappling in the central blue. . . .

(119–124)

This is the lesson of history, of man morally incapable of controlling his inventions. But the pattern takes a new turn. War is quelled in "the Federation of the world," "the Parliament of man."

In *The Princess* the scientific-technological vision is domesticated, playfully, to a fete day in the Kentish countryside of the 1840's:

                    and somewhat lower down
A man with knobs and wires and vials fired
A cannon: Echo answer'd in her sleep
From hollow fields: and here were telescopes
For azure views; and there a group of girls
In circle waited, whom the electric shock
Dislink'd with shrieks and laughter: round the lake
A little clock-work steamer paddling plied
And shook the lilies: perch'd about the knolls
A dozen angry models jetted steam:
A petty railway ran: a fire-balloon
Rose gem-like up before the dusky groves
And dropt a fairy parachute and past:
And there thro' twenty posts of telegraph
They flash'd a saucy message to and fro
Between the mimic stations; so that sport
Went hand in hand with Science, otherwise
Pure sport: a herd of boys with clamour bowl'd
And stump'd the wicket; babies roll'd about
Like tumbled fruit in grass; and men and maids
Arranged a country dance, and flew thro' light
And shadow, while the twangling violin
Struck up with Soldier-laddie, and overhead
The broad ambrosial aisles of lofty lime
Made noise with bees and breeze from end to end.
(prologue, 64–88)

This is Tennyson's social vision of midcentury life, in the mixing of the classes, the squire among his tenants and their families; in the mingling of the countryfolk with the workingmen of the nearby town. Past, present, and future join hands in the encounter between newfangled science and the world of country sports, songs, and dances. This is the Victorian holiday Arcadia of harmony between man and man, between man and his inventions, and, in the closing lines, of an attendant harmony in nature.

Tennyson's distinctive Victorianism is most clearly shown in a large group of descriptive-narrative poems which he called his "English Idyls."[4] He borrowed the term from the Greek idyll, a type of pastoral poem presenting a scene or event in country life. He knew the form well from his reading of Theocritus and the Latin imitation in Vergil. Nothing quite like it had ever existed in English poetry. Perhaps the closest equivalent was in Crabbe and Wordsworth, telling of "man's inhumanity to man," the harsh realities of country poverty and despotism, and of the human and spiritual values of life in simple communities close to nature. In Tennyson these realities and intuitions are Victorianized. Nature is picturesque, ruralized; man is domesticated, his spiritual and emotional life cozily bounded by the pieties of the cradle, the family hearth, and the parish church. Inhumanity, where it occurs, is often in the shape of the seducer or the oppressive snob. The scenes and stories are carried in poetry of extraordinary descriptive power, such as this passage from "The Gardener's Daughter":

> Not wholly in the busy world, nor quite
> Beyond it, blooms the garden that I love.
> News from the humming city comes to it
> In sound of funeral or of marriage bells;
> And, sitting muffled in dark leaves, you hear
> The windy clanging of the minster clock;
> Although between it and the garden lies
> A league of grass, wash'd by a slow broad stream,
> That, stirr'd with languid pulses of the oar,
> Waves all its lazy lilies, and creeps on,
> Barge-laden, to three arches of a bridge
> Crown'd with the minster-towers.
>   The fields between
> Are dewy-fresh, browsed by deep-udder'd kine,
> And all about the large lime feathers low,
> The lime a summer home of murmurous wings.
>   (33–48)

Here language is pushed to its fullest expressive reach. The weight and density and richness of the water meadows and the "deep-udder'd kine" are car-

ried toward and over us in the embracing onomatopoeia; it is a highly sensuous verbal gesture the effect of which we can compare with another kind of virtuosity in this delicate atmospheric image from "The Miller's Daughter":

> I loved the brimming wave that swam
>   Through quiet meadows round the mill,
> The sleepy pool above the dam,
>   The pool beneath it never still,
> The meal-sacks on the whitened floor,
>   The dark round of the dripping wheel,
> The very air about the door
>   Made misty with the floating meal.
>   (97–104)

This stanza, like so many passages in Tennyson, can be read quite on its own as a beautiful vignette.

This style of pictorialism, applied to English country life and the English scene, was a feature of Tennyson's poetry that shaped nineteenth-century sensibility, although his own practice was shaped in turn—very directly so—in response to advice and criticism of individual poems. We can follow this process closely in the revisions he effected to certain pieces in the volumes of 1830 and 1833. When they were reprinted in *Poems* (1842), many were changed verbally and metrically, sometimes much for the worse, as with "The Miller's Daughter." The narrator is a man country-born and bred. In the 1833 version he is given a touching simplicity of style, a rustic quaintness of diction and phrasing. In the 1842 version this quality is lost. The language is decorated, poeticized; and the story of the fresh and innocent joy of first love is overlaid with what we come to recognize as a typically Victorian celebration of filial ties and domesticity. One such addition is the stanza in which the young man, a squire's son, seeks the consent of his widowed mother:

> And slowly was my mother brought
>   To yield consent to my desire:
> She wished me happy, but she thought
>   I might have looked a little higher;
> And I was young—too young to wed:
>   "Yet must I love her for your sake;
> Go fetch your Alice here," she said:
>   Her eyelid quivered as she spake.
>   (137–144)

It is probably fair to say that an important side to Tennyson's Victorianism was his willingness to con-

---

[4]Including "The Gardener's Daughter," "Audley Court," "Edwin Morris," "The Miller's Daughter," and many other poems.

form to popular taste, to write a style of poetry that was easily understood and enjoyed, both in its poetic technique and in themes and subject matter which fell within the popular notion of what poetry should be about. To a degree he was able to create and extend these limits by the force of his own writing. One excursion was into dialect poetry, rude eccentricity, perhaps, for a poet of such refined art. Whether the motive was experiment or a nostalgic return to the language of his Lincolnshire childhood (the thick twang of which he never lost) the poems themselves[5] are masterpieces of characterization and irony, Chaucerian in their gusto, their wit, their observation, and their penetration of human nature. They are portraits that Browning would have envied and Dickens enjoyed.

Tennyson's major innovation was to bring to English poetry a very remarkable and sophisticated experience of classical literature, something quite apart from his English-Vergilianism, the characteristics of which are neatly itemized in his official tribute, "To Virgil," written in 1883. He refers there to some of the qualities he most admired in the Roman poet and which he tried to imitate in his own choice of subject matter and in the musicality of his diction: Vergil the "Landscape-lover," the "lord of language," of "many a golden phrase," "majestic in thy sadness," "Wielder of the stateliest measure ever moulded by the lips of man." Much of Tennyson's poetry is decoratively and melodiously Vergilian in these ways. But not his best and most interesting work. There the Vergilian element is often assimilated in a larger, more complex classical presence, to be manipulated as a device of style and meaning, as it is in Elegy IX of *In Memoriam*, where the classical-Augustan surface is a deliberate aestheticism, a contrived face of art, which is destroyed by the sudden breakthrough of emotion, the encroachment of grief. Sometimes the classical presence excludes Vergil altogether for the social tones, the ease, and urbanity of Horace; and the voice we hear again and again in many of the finest lyrics is the voice of Catullus—not Catullus imitated or merely alluded to, but received and controlled in Tennyson's experience, as it is in Elegy LIX, Tennyson's formal and nonetheless beautiful version of the famous song of Catullus, "Vivamus, mea Lesbia, atque amemus," a

favorite among English poets (as we see in Marlowe's "The Passionate Shepherd to his Love," Jonson's "To Celia," Donne's "The Baite"):

> O Sorrow, wilt thou live with me
>   No casual mistress, but a wife,
>   My bosom-friend and half of life;
> As I confess it needs must be;
>
> O Sorrow, wilt thou rule my blood,
>   Be sometimes lovely like a bride,
>   And put thy harsher moods aside,
> If thou wilt have me wise and good.
>
> My centred passion cannot move.
>   Nor will it lessen from to-day;
>   But I'll have leave at times to play
> As with the creature of my love;
>
> And set thee forth, for thou art mine,
>   With so much hope for years to come,
>   That, howsoe'er I know thee, some
> Could hardly tell what name were thine.
>
>   (1–16)

Each poet has his distinctive version. Marlowe's shepherd sings a seductive account of the pleasures they will "prove" together. Jonson's lover is a logic-chopping seducer—love stolen is no sin, only stolen love discovered. Donne is seductive in metaphysical style, in paradoxical hyperbole. This witty and sophisticated tradition is the ironic context, part of the meaning of Tennyson's poem, which has its own internal wit, sad and sardonic, turning the not-a-mistress-but-a-wife joke through the tones of resignation, pleading, stoic fatalism, and fearful wonder as the poet woos Sorrow, the classical muse Melpomene.

The allusive subtlety and literary sophistication of this poem are new in nineteenth-century literature. Ezra Pound thought that he was the discoverer of Catullus for the modern world, the Latin poet he most admired and judged untranslatable. But would he have been quite so contemptuous of Tennyson if he had taken account of Elegy LIX, or "Frater Ave atque Vale," or "Prefatory Poem to my Brother's Sonnets," or "Hendecasyllabics," a brilliant pastiche of Catullus' favorite meter in which Tennyson slyly rebuked the reviewers for their inability to attune to his poetic effects?

> O you chorus of indolent reviewers,
> Irresponsible, indolent reviewers,

[5] "Northern Farmer, Old Style" (written 1861), "Northern Farmer, New Style" (1865), "The Spinster Sweet-Arts" (1884), "The Church-warden and the Curate" (1890).

Look, I come to the test, a tiny poem
All composed in a metre of Catullus,
All in quantity, careful of my motion,
Like the skater on ice that hardly bears him,
Lest I fall unawares before the people,
Waking laughter in indolent reviewers.
Should I flounder awhile without a tumble
Thro' this metrification of Catullus,
They should speak to me not without a welcome,
All that chorus of indolent reviewers.
Hard, hard, hard is it, only not to tumble,
So fantastical is the dainty metre.
Wherefore slight me not wholly, nor believe me
Too presumptuous, indolent reviewers.
O blatant Magazines, regard me rather—
Since I blush to belaud myself a moment—
As some rare little rose, a piece of inmost
Horticultural art, or half coquette-like
Maiden, not to be greeted unbenignly.

This is no more than a skit. But, playful as it is, it illustrates as well as any of the lyrics or any of the classical monologues—"Ulysses," "Tithonus," "Tiresias," or "Demeter and Persephone"—that Tennyson's essential classicism is in his view of the poem as a work of art, with form as its distinguishing characteristic. It is this concern that sets him apart from the romantic poets and from the beginnings of the modern movement.

II

TENNYSON's poetry can be divided chronologically into three distinct groups: the poetry written before the death of Arthur Hallam in September 1833; the poetry written from the autumn of 1833 to the publication of *Maud* in 1855, including *The Princess* and *In Memoriam*; and the later writing, including his largest and most ambitious work, the *Idylls of the King*, the first section of which appeared in 1859 and which was virtually complete by 1872. Reading the works in this order, we can watch the poet's emergence from the imitative and derivative stage of his earliest childhood writing; and, in the late 1820's and early 1830's, the development of his own special kind of art poetry, the pictorializing treatment of scenes and situations and the highly expressive technique in the handling of language and verse form. The death of Arthur Hallam, his closest friend, in September 1833 was the immediate inspiration for his finest work in the 1830's and 1840's, leading to the collec-

tion of the elegies and their publication together in *In Memoriam* (1850). *Maud* marks a turning point in his career. It is a poem of great emotional violence and remarkable originality of form—as Tennyson described it, a lyric "Monodrama"—a strange work as original and unprecedented in English literature as *The Waste Land*. At the time the critics rejected *Maud* as a mistake, tainted by morbidity, a work of spasms. Thereafter Tennyson's creative drive was slackened, his fieriness burned out. A harsher, pessimistic note sounds increasingly in his public poetry, a disenchantment with materialism, a fear of overwhelming social and moral chaos following in the train of democracy, fear of contamination from the new freedoms in literature and art. In 1886, in "Locksley Hall Sixty Years After," he delivered his report on the state of Victorian civilization, a ranting diatribe against modern man and his creations: risen "from out the beast," to bestialism he is returning via atheism, radicalism, and the sewer realism of Zola. The idyllic serenity of pastoral England is blotted out by the canker of industrialism and its city-infernos of human degradation. All he could conjure against this was the countervision of the *Idylls*, an attempt to recreate the Arthurian story as a moral and spiritual allegory; and the series of historical plays—*Queen Mary, Harold, Becket,* and *The Foresters*—published between 1875 and 1892, in which he set out to portray periods of crisis in the struggle between right and might in what he called "the making of England." His ambition was to complement the history plays of Shakespeare. But Tennyson's grasp of drama and character was feeble, his sense of history incomplete; and his imagination and lyrical genius were never at home in these surroundings.[6]

The poetry of Tennyson's middle and later years is unmistakably the work of an aging man, finally of an old man—world-weary, reflective, disillusioned, sometimes wise and humane, an ancient sage, sometimes peppery and intolerant, a castigating Timon, sometimes just silly. Yet from the 1830's onward until the end of his life, Tennyson's poetry reveals a curious lack of development. The language, imagery, form, and imaginative vision of the best of the later poetry are not essentially different from the best of the middle years, and this in turn from the best of the early poetry. There is not, for example,

[6]G. W. Knight has argued strongly for the power of these plays in *The Golden Labyrinth* (London, 1962).

the line of radical development that we find in Yeats: the Tennysonianism of his earliest poetry and the Celtic Twilight of the 1880's and 1890's are followed by a purging sharpness and clarity which give way to the rich symbolism of the Byzantium poems, followed in turn by the Crazy Jane poetry and the masks and gnomism of the later 1930's. This development was partly a consequence of the literary situation. Whatever his own impulse toward change, Yeats had change thrust upon him by Eliot and Pound and by the twentieth-century demand for a new poetry, whereas Tennyson's public, by contrast, clung to the style and taste that the poet had himself created and which remained the poetic norm, at a popular level, until the end of the century. This historical, circumstantial explanation is of some value. But the inertia in Tennyson is more than stylistic; its center is in a strange recessive quality of his imagination which we come to recognize in his poetry in the recurrence of certain situations and moods around the experience of doubt, horror, isolation, and loss, of friends absent or dead, of loved ones yearned for, of scenes and events recalled from long ago.

This is naturally the poetry of old age—of "To the Rev. W. H. Brookfield" (1874), of "Vastness" and "To Mary Boyle" (1888), of "The Roses on the Terrace" and "Merlin and the Gleam" (1889), of "The Silent Voices" (1892). Yet this valetudinarian experience is also a feature of Tennyson's early poetry. Declarations of loneliness and deep melancholy are a phase of adolescence and a favorite stance of the Romantic Agony. But there is a note of genuine imaginative morbidity in "The Outcast," in "In Deep and Solemn Dreams," and in the "Ode to Memory," which date from 1826; and among the trivia of the *Poems* (1830 and 1833), the individual poetic voice sounds darkly in the "Mariana" poems, "Song," "The Kraken," "The Dying Swan," and "The Lady of Shalott," where the themes of death, abandonment, and isolation are so closely, sometimes obsessively, explored. So dramatically convincing is the note of depression and desperation in "The Two Voices" that critics have always accepted at face value the statement of Hallam Tennyson that the poem "was begun under the cloud" of his father's "overwhelming sorrow after the death of Arthur Hallam." In fact, the poem, then known as "Thoughts of a Suicide," was largely in existence by June 1833. Similar questions of style make it impossible to decide whether "Youth" and "From Sorrow Sorrow

Yet Is Born," both written in 1833, date from before or after Hallam's death.

Insofar as there can be any clue to the peculiar cast of Tennyson's imaginative temper, it is probably in the renowned "black-bloodedness" of the family, a hereditary melancholia, and in the circumstances of his home life at Somersby. His father was neurotic and took to drink to escape the fits of depression which overwhelmed him increasingly into the 1820's and drove him to homicidal violence. Tennyson recalled how as a child he used to run from the rectory on such occasions, throwing himself down among the gravestones in the churchyard, praying for a release in death. We can only conjecture about the impact of these experiences upon his creative imagination. What Tennyson does discuss about his childhood is "the passion of the past," a phrase which he used to describe the inspiration for "Tears, Idle Tears," and it is this "passion" which provides our best understanding of the recessive quality of his imagination, of which the melancholic and morbid aspects are only a part:

It is what I have always felt even from a boy, and what as a boy I called "the passion of the past". And it is so always with me now; it is the distance that charms me in the landscape, the picture and the past, and not the immediate today in which I move.

The poetic elaboration of this idea comes in "The Ancient Sage," written in 1885:

> Today? but what of yesterday? for oft
> On me, when boy, there came what then I called,
> Who knew no books and no philosophies,
> In my boy-phrase "The Passion of the Past".
> The first gray streak of earliest summer-dawn,
> The last long stripe of waning crimson gloom,
> As if the late and early were but one—
> A height, a broken grange, a grove, a flower
> Had murmurs "Lost and gone and lost and gone!"
> A breath, a whisper—some divine farewell—
> Desolate sweetness—far and far away—
> What had he loved, what had he lost, the boy?
> I know not and I speak of what has been.
>   (216–228)

Tennyson's "for oft" is a playful echo of the "For oft" that opens Wordsworth's remembered vision of the "golden daffodils." But there is no pretension to a mystical or philosophical interpretation, no move to penetrate the nature of the experience. He remains content to contemplate its reminders and images—of half-light, of solitariness, remoteness, and neglect— and to ascribe to them a strange evocative power, as of something loved and lost, which he cannot and will not explain. Three years later, in 1888, Tennyson wrote "Far—Far—Away," a poem which contemplates, with similar delicacy, the "strange charm" that these three words held for him since childhood, a charm inexpressible (he says) in poetry, its meaning only to be guessed at:

> What vague world-whisper, mystic pain or joy,
> Through those three words would haunt him
> when a boy,
> Far—far—away?
>
> (7–9)

In "Tears, Idle Tears," Tennyson defined "the passion of the past" more precisely: its origin and compelling force are located not in childhood but in the adult experience of unassuageable love:

> Dear as remember'd kisses after death,
> And sweet as those by hopeless fancy feign'd
> On lips that are for others; deep as love,
> Deep as first love, and wild with all regret;
> O Death in Life, the days that are no more.
>
> (16–20)

This poem was written in 1845, and "the days that are no more" is almost certainly a reference to his years of friendship with Arthur Hallam, the "Death in Life" a reference to the years after Hallam's death.

The memory of Hallam remained a haunting, obsessive presence for the remainder of Tennyson's life, a focal point for all his sadness and passion, his feelings of yearning, desolation, and loss, the emotional experiences at the heart of his finest work. The Hallam origin can be surprising. For example, it is a recent discovery that the lyric "Oh! That 'Twere Possible," the nucleus around which *Maud* was built in 1854–1855, was first written, in a slightly shorter version, in the winter of 1833–1834. We can see in the opening stanzas that only a matter of weeks or months after his death, Hallam, in Tennyson's imagination, had already been transformed into a symbolic figure, here an androgynous lover:

> Oh! that 'twere possible,
> After long grief and pain,
> To find the arms of my true-love
> Round me once again!

> When I was wont to meet her
> In the silent woody places
> Of the land that gave me birth,
> We stood tranced in long embraces,
> Mixt with kisses sweeter, sweeter,
> Than any thing on earth.
>
> (1–10)

Hallam's death was a precipitating experience rather than an experience in itself. Tennyson's rhetoric of affection, sometimes strongly sexual, can be properly interpreted only if we understand that the Hallam of the poet's imagination was invested with many roles—wife, lover, consoler, savior, muse. In "Vastness," written almost sixty years later, Tennyson reviewed the history of man's existence, the unending succession of revolution and change—"what is all of it worth?"

> What the philosophies, all the sciences, poesy, varying
> voices of prayer?
> All that is noblest, all that is basest, all that is filthy with all
> that is fair?
>
> What is it all, if we all of us end but in being our own
> corpse-coffins at last,
> Swallow'd in Vastness, lost in Silence, drown'd in the deeps
> of a meaningless Past?
>
> What but a murmur of gnats in the gloom, or a moment's
> anger of bees in their hive?—
>
> . . .
>
> Peace, let it be! for I loved him, and love him for ever: the
> dead are not dead but alive.
>
> (31–36)

For Tennyson, so many years later, the simple affirmation of continuing love is offered as a sufficient and final answer; pathetically, we may think. It was the only answer he could give, a flat, assertive statement. His deepest experiences of Hallam are in the "dark house" sections of *In Memoriam* (VII, XCIX), in the "Valley of Cauteretz," most powerfully of all in "Cold and clear-cut face" in *Maud*, a single, sustained lyric sentence projecting the haunted mind, the psychological reality of a nightmare vision, unequaled in English literature from Shakespeare's *Pericles* to Eliot's *Marina*:

> Cold and clear-cut face, why come you so cruelly meek,
> Breaking a slumber in which all spleenful folly was
> drown'd,
> Pale with the golden beam of an eyelash dead on the cheek,

Passionless, pale, cold face, star-sweet on a gloom
    profound;
Womanlike, taking revenge too deep for a transient wrong
Done but in thought to your beauty, and ever as pale as
    before
Growing and fading and growing upon me without a
    sound,
Luminous, gemlike, ghostlike, deathlike, half the night
    long
Growing and fading and growing, till I could bear it no
    more,
But arose, and all by myself in my own dark garden
    ground,
Listening now to the tide in its broad-flung shipwrecking
    roar,
Now to the scream of a madden'd beach dragg'd down by
    the wave,
Walk'd in a wintry wind by a ghastly glimmer, and found
The shining daffodil dead, and Orion low in his grave.

                  (88–101)

III

On the evidence of Tennyson's early poetry, up to 1833, it would have been inconceivable to predict the emergence of a great national poet. The quality of imagination is introspective and withdrawn; the poems themselves, highly aesthetic. They announce a writer devoted to exploring language as the medium of art and the forms of poetry as the forms of art distancing and art stylization, with the single poem as an art object, shaped and constructed, to be admired for its formal qualities of shapeliness and poise. *Poems* (1830) also reveals a writer whose sense of his poetic identity is very uncertain. There is an extraordinary unevenness in the collection, with a number of laughable album verses (today's ladies' magazine doggerel), trivially sentimental. At Cambridge he was surrounded by a group of high-minded idealists, the Apostles, who believed (according to one of their members) that it was their mission "to enlighten the world upon things intellectual and spiritual" and "to interpret the oracles of transcendental wisdom to the world of Philistines." Hallam was the born leader, Tennyson the poetic spokesman; and it is easy to understand the kind of pressure to which he was subjected. A neat illustration of this is in "The Palace of Art," his first important discussion of the artist's outward responsibility, his duty toward society.

According to Tennyson himself, the poem was written in response to the challenging remark of a fellow Apostle—"Tennyson, we cannot live in Art." Tennyson's poetic answer is on this same level of platitude: of course, it tells us, we cannot live alone, away from mankind, within our own world of created beauty. The soul that tries to do this is tormented by its conscience and quits the art palace for the humility and down-to-earthness of a country cottage. The art/life question left Tennyson's imagination untouched. The formal argument of the poem exerts no apparent control over its structure, which is largely a succession of isolated pictorial images, projecting the soul's fantasies as individual scenes. Some of these are symbolic landscapes in miniature:

One seemed all dark and red—a tract of sand,
And some one pacing there alone,
Who paced for ever in a glimmering land,
Lit with a low large moon.

        . . .

A still salt pool, locked in with bars of sand,
Left on the shore; that hears all night
The plunging seas draw backwards from the land
Their moon-led waters white.

        (65–68; 249–252)

This is the neurotic vision of "Mariana," the psychological setting of "Mariana in the South," with the strange, uncanny horror of isolation and abandonment. But the poem's structure is elaborative, not defining; the images might have been continued endlessly; and Tennyson's real answer is implicit in the poem's failure—the artist cannot work by slogans, and imagination will have its say, whatever the artist intends.

His positive response to the art/life question is in "The Lady of Shalott," written, unsolicited, at about the same time, in 1831–1832. The allegory is simple and lucid. It stresses the "magic" of art, and its necessity. The "fairy" lady weaves the "magic" sights from her mirror into a "magic" tapestry. But at last she grows weary of mirror images. Her attention is seized by the brilliant figure of Sir Lancelot. She leaves the tapestry and the mirror to look at him directly. These objects break and she suffers the "curse." She surrenders herself to the swollen river and the stormy night and is carried down to Camelot singing into death. The meaning of this fable is clear. The artist has no choice. He follows his calling, and fate decides the rest. His moral stance is not dedication but submission. His artistic stance is reverence for the magic and mystery of his art. The artist is both the magician and the enchanted, the wielder of the magic power and its subject. The poem asserts this in the fable and in its own poetic magic—the power of its images, its insistent and subtly varied rhythms, its intricately shaped stanzas and patterned lines, its sharp pictorialism, its brilliance of detail. It effects the verbal illusion of a new art experience, of a Pre-Raphaelite tapestry-enamel finely and glowingly colored. It is Tennyson's "Kubla Khan," the creation of the possessed, visionary poet, working his spell of words with such insinuating memorability.

As a quality of poetry and of the poetic imagination, the "magic" of art was a familiar idea to the romantic poets and their critics. Matthew Arnold found "natural magic" to the highest degree in Shakespeare and Keats. The "something magic" Tennyson himself found in Keats belonged, he said, to "the innermost soul of poetry." In turn, Whitman was to find a magic in Tennyson, in his "finest verbalism," in his evocation of the "latent charm of mere words, cunning collocutions, and in the voice ringing them." To appeal to magic and the spell of words in the 1980's may seem like critical antiquarianism. But no amount of technical analysis of sound effects and rhythms can explain the mysterious process whereby certain kinds of poetry are able to engage us, as "The Lady of Shalott" has engaged generations of readers. Its effects are the effects of art. Its figures, scenes, and events are pictorialized. It is a story from the legendary past and, stylized picturesquely, is kept there. There is nothing familiar, no human motivation, nothing for the reader to identify with or to understand in terms of his own experience or any imaginable experience other than the experience of the artist and his art. Perhaps this very exclusiveness and concentration are the secrets of its power, its symbolism so compelling that the allegory and fable assume the universality of myth. Certainly the poem carries Tennyson's personal myth of the artist's isolation, his loneliness and vulnerability, his "magic" of creation, his surrender to its working, his fatalism, his submission to necessity, to Camelot's river of life, which is for him the dark river of dissolution.

The imaginative reality of these experiences became fact with the death of Arthur Hallam. This was the tragedy, according to Hallam Tennyson, which "for a while blotted out all joy from his life, and made him long for death." Tennyson's immediate grief was poured into "Speak to Me,"

"Hark! the Dog's Howl," "Whispers," "On a Mourner," "Oh! That 'Twere Possible," and the earliest of the elegies. These are subjective, emotional utterances, the private poetry of desolation and mourning. At the same time he was searching for ways in which to answer his private needs, to carry his personal vision, in poetry addressed outward to the public at large, thereby attempting to fulfill his Apostolic sense of duty within the resources and compulsions of his own poetic character.

His first invention was a special form of dramatic monologue or dramatic narrative, adapting some classical or legendary situation, reinterpreted obliquely in terms of his own predicament. This group includes "Ulysses," "Morte d'Arthur," "Tiresias," "Tithon" (and possibly "St. Simeon Stylites," which was completed by November 1833, but may have been commenced before Hallam's death). The first two poems carry a message for the age. The Carlylean aspect of "Ulysses" has been referred to earlier. For Tennyson personally, the poem was an act of survival. Written at a time of depression and annihilating grief it gave his feeling, he said, "about the need of going forward and braving the struggle of life." This resolve is echoed in Ulysses' rallying cry to his fellow adventurers:

> One equal temper of heroic hearts,
> Made weak by time and fate, but strong in will
> To strive, to seek, to find, and not to yield.
> (68–70)

But there is a discrepancy between this declared moral stance and the character of the poem itself, which is curiously unresolved and undetermined. Its rhythms are long and swelling, lyrical in their larger movement, its imagery expansive and dissolving:

> The long day wanes: the slow moon climbs: the deep
> Moans round with many voices. Come, my friends,
> 'Tis not too late to seek a newer world.
> Push off, and sitting well in order smite
> The sounding furrows; for my purpose holds
> To sail beyond the sunset, and the baths
> Of all the western stars, until I die.
> It may be that the gulfs will wash us down:
> It may be we shall touch the Happy Isles,
> And see the great Achilles, whom we knew.
> Tho' much is taken, much abides; and tho'
> We are not now that strength which in old days
> Moved earth and heaven; that which we are, we are;
> (55–67)

The one distinct objective is Achilles-Hallam, the comrade in arms who died at Troy. But this aim is far distant. The pervasive experience is the voyager's extinction into eternity, his glorious dissolution "beyond the sunset":

Yet all experience is an arch wherethro'
Gleams that untravell'd world, whose margin fades
For ever and for ever when I move.

. . .

And this gray spirit yearning in desire
To follow knowledge like a sinking star,
Beyond the utmost bound of human thought.
(19–21; 30–32)

The discrepancy is between defiance and surrender, between the rousing moral and the poetic counter-pull, between the blunt, prosaic, robust good sense of Ulysses' final words and the large, vague, romantic mirage toward which he will endlessly sail, endlessly hopeful. The Homer-Dante Ulysses is Tennysonianized. The poem becomes a metaphor for the poet's own voyage of self-discovery. He knows what, responsibly, he should be doing, what moral sinews should be flexed. Yet his deepest need is not for exhortation or exercise but for consolation.

The allegorical circumstances of "Morte d'Arthur" are very exact. King Arthur-Arthur Hallam is dying; the Round Table-Apostolic brotherhood is breaking up; Sir Bedivere's questions are Tennyson's own. What is left in the world when the leader is gone? What hope remains when fellowship is destroyed? Arthur's answer is Tennyson's poetic rationalization:

The old order changeth, yielding place to new,
And God fulfils Himself in many ways,
Lest one good custom should corrupt the world.

. . .

Pray for my soul. More things are wrought by prayer
Than this world dreams of. Wherefore, let thy voice
Rise like a fountain for me night and day.
For what are men better than sheep or goats
That nourish a blind life within the brain,
If, knowing God, they lift not hands of prayer
Both for themselves and those who call them friend?
(240–242; 247–253)

In delivering these words Tennyson was addressing his contemporaries as well as seeking a shred of comfort for himself. In an age of intellectual doubt and oppressive materialism, what were to be the guiding values? To these questions "Morte d'Arthur" returns no precise answer, only a general sense of good advice in the air and a readiness to believe. Tennyson's own uncertainty, and his limited means of assuaging it, are sounded in Arthur's final, puzzled, consolatory farewell. The visionary promise of Avilion, in all its poetic beauty, is offered as the one substantial comfort:

But now farewell. I am going a long way
With these thou seest—if indeed I go—
(For all my mind is clouded with a doubt)
To the island-valley of Avilion;
Where falls not hail, or rain, or any snow,
Nor ever wind blows loudly; but it lies
Deep-meadow'd, happy, fair with orchard-lawns
And bowery hollows crown'd with summer sea,
Where I will heal me of my grievous wound.
(256–264)

The interest of these poems is their statement of dilemma and, equally, their acceptance of dilemma as a condition of experience. Tennyson acknowledges his need for inspiration, whether in the heroics of the Carlylean message or in the Christian-Stoic resignation of Arthurian pulpit oratory. Yet he was too good a poet, too faithful to his weaker, more pathetic self, to deny his need for consolation, for an un-Christian, unmoral, unrespectable escape into fantasy and myth, into the wan, wistful illusion of Hallam's immortality.

Whereas both "Ulysses" and "Morte d'Arthur" carried a prominent and acceptable public message, and duly appeared in the next collection, *Poems* (1842), the other two poems of this group were held back: "Tithon" until 1860, when it was published, in a revised and lengthened form, as "Tithonus," and "Tiresias," also revised, until 1885. They are not notably inferior poems, and Tennyson's reluctance to make them public in 1842 was almost certainly on account of their lack of a theme more positive than the burden of existence, the appeal of death, and, for Tiresias, the longing for ennoblement in the heroic realms of the afterlife. Possibly Tennyson judged these dramatizations to be too indulgent, too confessional; and his great imaginative effort in the later 1830's, in "Locksley Hall" (written 1837–1838) and *The Princess* (begun by 1839), until *In Memoriam* and *Maud*, was the attempt to write poetry more securely distanced, to create verse structures in which he could develop a more optimistic countervision to the dilemma of "Ulysses" and "Morte d'Arthur" and to the inert withdrawal of "Tithon" and "Tiresias." Tennyson's task was to reconcile his Apostolic sense of duty with his interior nature as the poet of Shalott; and the creative cost of this ambition is clearly marked in the poetry of these years.

During the 1840's, especially after the success of *Poems* (1842), Tennyson's friends and reviewers (sometimes, significantly, the same people) urged him to change course, to engage with one of the great subjects of modern life, something with a human touch. His answer was *The Princess*, published in 1847. Since 1839, possibly earlier, he had been interested in the idea of a poem on women's education, a topic then much in the air. This was to provide the core of the work. Tennyson enlarged on this social theme, taking in the high Victorian notion of womanhood, its proper rights and duties. At a more profound level he considered the false ambitions and delusive ideals that can lure woman along the unnatural path of sexual and intellectual solitude, and within this moral theme, he explored the emotional implications of such separation. Described in this way, *The Princess* is neat and schematic. But for all the poem's ideas, and its seriousness of theme, and, on occasion, its seriousness of treatment, it reveals Tennyson's uneasiness, his inability to dramatize a public theme which touched him so deeply. His recourse is to a mock archaic style, quaint and fanciful, an evasive playfulness, a deprecatory whimsicality.

The modern social picture in the prologue and the conclusion is playful and naively idyllic, unpretentiously so. The message is universal harmony—between the classes, the sexes, mankind and science and nature, and a harmony of all creation with "the Heaven of Heavens." But the assertion is rhetorical; the poem itself is grossly unharmonious—stylistically and imaginatively it remains, as it is subtitled, *A Medley*. In effect it merely serves as a showcase for some of the great lyrics—"Tears, Idle Tears," "Ask Me No More," "Now Sleeps the Crimson Petal."

Tennyson's most ambitious structure and most embracing countervision was achieved in the formation of *In Memoriam*. When he wrote the first elegies in the winter of 1833–1834, it was with no thought of publication or any larger design. But the poems in this common stanza form accumulated until, eventually, in the 1840's, Tennyson introduced narrative-chronological sections and arranged the poems sequentially, so that they recounted a spiritual biography: the first prostration of grief, the onset of

religious doubt and hopelessness, checked by the intimation of a new and tempered faith, leading to a happy sense of God's purpose. The poem's crown is the epilogue, an epithalamium in which there is the fullest exposition of Tennyson's grand myth of consolation and comfort, involving Hallam, nature, and mankind in a triumphant single vision. He looks forward to the child of the marriage, destined to bring the human race one step closer to its highest state. The mood is serene and joyful, with the *Princess*-like harmonies of man, nature, and the universe beyond. Tennyson's prophetic myth is constructed from contemporary evolutionary thought adjusted to the romantic idealism of the age; and both these elements joined to his private fantasy of Hallam as forerunner of the "noble type," the link between later nineteenth-century man and his evolved form as "the crowning race."

The epilogue is a tour de force, a beautiful and suave conclusion to the poem's line of argument. But it has no more than a formal connection with the center of experience of the finest elegies, the poems that arise from Hallam. *In Memoriam* is a construct, an exploitation of the early elegies for the sake of Tennyson's ambition to deliver the great philosophical poem of the age and his need to ameliorate the Hallam experience, just as in *The Princess* the central core of emotion is separated off in the lyrics, contained in a Chinese-box extravaganza.

Tennyson's other recourse, in "Locksley Hall" and *Maud*, was not the escape from personality but its indulgence; not the measured, composed voice of the lyrical seer, nor the indirection of the virtuoso, with his "medley" of artful tones and styles, but the dense psychological and temperamental expression of confused or disordered minds, a thin ventriloquial disguise for the poet's own violence of feeling. Tennyson insisted that "Locksley Hall" was a "dramatic impersonation," not autobiography, a denial repeated more vehemently with *Maud*. But there are striking similarities in the circumstances of both heroes, with a common background story of tyrannical relations, frustrated love, and the power of money; and recent studies of these poems put it beyond doubt that Tennyson was writing out of his own bitterness and frustration in love, his poverty, and the feud with another, snobbishly superior, branch of the family.

Tennyson himself gave a very tepid account of "Locksley Hall": that it "represents young life, its good side, its deficiencies, and its yearnings"; and it was probably in this spirit that he included it in *Poems* (1842) as a young Victorian's view of the years ahead, of accelerating change and the promise of a new age of science and invention. What comes across, however, is not a representative point of view, not a neutrally Victorian response to the future, but the portrait of a disturbed mind, of someone dizzied and terrified by the vistas of change, yet cursing and rejecting the past embodied in the hall, whose name carries this symbolic, "locked" meaning:

Howsoever these things be, a long farewell to Locksley
　　Hall!
Now for me the woods may wither, now for me the roof-
　　tree fall.
Comes a vapour from the margin, blackening over heath
　　and holt,
Cramming all the blast before it, in its breast a thunderbolt.
Let it fall on Locksley Hall, with rain or hail, or fire or
　　snow;
For the mighty wind arises, roaring seaward, and I go.

(189–194)

As in the opening section of *Maud*, we are faced here with an unaccountable violence, a fantasy of rejection and denial for which there is no explanation either in the circumstances of the poem or in the character of the speaker. We have the impression of something left unsaid or imperfectly rendered, of effect without cause. In *Maud*, Tennyson allowed himself greater license in the persona of a madman; artistically, a dangerous license, for verisimilitude could justify the fragmentation of experience, the disassociation of thought and feeling, the lurchings and incoherences and wildness of a mind out of control—ironically so, since the poem itself is an outstanding exhibition of lyrical virtuosity and technical command over a great range of feeling and tone, from the fine ironies of "She came to the village church" (I.viii) to the sensuous lyricism of "I have led her home" (I.xviii) and the intense psychological realism of "Cold and clear-cut face" (I.iii) and "I heard no sound" (I.xiv. 516–526). One would guess that these sections of the poem, together with "Come into the garden" and several others, belong to the Hallam experience (remembering that the poem's starting point was "Oh! that 'twere possible") and to Tennyson's positive emotional life of the 1830's. The sections of madness come from another part of his experience altogether, from his hurt and pain, from the bitterness and injury of those years, feelings

which rankled and which he was unable to exploit creatively, other than in the madman's ravings:

And the vitriol madness flushes up in the ruffian's head,
Till the filthy by-lane rings to the yell of the trampled wife,
And chalk and alum and plaster are sold to the poor for
　　bread,
And the spirit of murder works in the very means of life,

And Sleep must lie down arm'd, for the villainous
　　centre-bits
Grind on the wakeful ear in the hush of the moonless
　　nights,
While another is cheating the sick of a few last gasps, as
　　he sits
To pestle a poison'd poison behind his crimson lights.

When a Mammonite mother kills her babe for a burial fee,
And Timour-Mammon grins on a pile of children's bones,
Is it peace or war? better, war! loud war by land and by
　　sea,
War with a thousand battles, and shaking a hundred
　　thrones.

(I.i. 36–47)

Of course, this is not Tennyson in person. But in a strange sense it is. The images of horror are figments of a demented mind; yet they have a rational, external, historical existence. The adulteration of bread was a current scandal much written about in the period 1851–1855. The "Mammonite" mother was a horrible reality. Children had indeed been murdered for the sake of the "burial fee" of £3 or £4. It is impossible to judge where Tennyson's revulsion ends and the dramatic character of the madman begins. In those closing lines war is a symptomatic image of the hero's own divided, disruptive personality. Yet in the concluding sections of the poem, when the hero has emerged into sanity, war is presented as the ennobling cause, the great destiny which will raise and unify the nation:

For the peace, that I deem'd no peace, is over and done,
And now by the side of the Black and the Baltic deep,
And deathful-grinning mouths of the fortress, flames
The blood-red blossom of war with a heart of fire.

Let it flame or fade, and the war roll down like a wind,
We have proved we have hearts in a cause, we are noble
　　still,
And myself have awaked, as it seems, to the better mind;
It is better to fight for the good than to rail at the ill;
I have felt with my native land, I am one with my kind,
I embrace the purpose of God, and the doom assign'd.

(III.iv–v. 50–59)

There is nothing remarkable in the fact of Tennyson's warmongering; it is exactly in character with his newspaper squibs of 1852; and he was an opponent of those who wanted peace in the Crimea. What is remarkable is the apparent ease and confidence with which this rousing finale is delivered, so alike in style and manner to the endings of *The Princess* and *In Memoriam*, but to what different harmonies! There the vision was idyllic and spiritual; here it is the glorification of war as a moral force, as the destiny to uplift society and assert the nation's strength, and to join the individual to this great common purpose. This is Tennyson's secular, propagandizing, energizing countervision, to ward off the Hallam experience, to deny the poet of Shalott, to fulfill the Apostolic mission. We must admire the synthesizing power of the verse in answering these complex demands; but we can only regret the imaginative necessity that drove Tennyson to seek a solution so unworthily and triumphantly expedient.

Maud was an act of catharsis. Whatever the personal and imaginative pressures that drove him to this strange, inventive creation, there was no return after this to the anguish and yearning for Hallam or to the powerful eroticism of the lyrics. The lyrical vein continues, much subdued, in poems of friendship—"To Mary Boyle," "To E. Fitzgerald," "To the Master of Balliol," "June Bracken and Heather," "The Roses on the Terrace." These Horatian lyrics are graceful, charming, and witty. But the impulse is low-powered. We see this too in the elegiac poems and the reminiscences of Hallam—"In the Garden at Swainston," *In Memoriam* XXXIX (written in 1868), "Prefatory Poem to my Brother's Sonnets," "Frater Ave atque Vale"—beautiful and moving tributes from which the anguish and poignance have gone.

For the public of the 1850's, *Maud* was an aberration. Tennyson redeemed himself, became once again the poet of *In Memoriam*—and, more than that, a modern Vergil, a great national poet—in the *Idylls of the King*. Tennyson regarded the story of Arthur as "the greatest of all poetical subjects" and Malory's version the best of the existing accounts, full of "very fine things but all strung together without Art." The Arthurian stories had fascinated him since childhood and he planned and hesitated for over twenty years, from about 1833 to the mid-1850's, before seriously embarking upon the poem entire, of which "Morte d'Arthur" had appeared as a separate piece in 1842. Eventually, the *Idylls* came out in four volumes between 1859 and 1885, when they were first collected and placed in their final order.

The "Art" which he applied to his sources, principally to Malory, was characteristically Tennysonian. The cycle of stories is drawn upon to provide the raw material for a group of pictorialized scenes and events, each one isolated and presented rather like a stage tableau, showing a step in the rise and fall of Arthurian society, from Arthur's "Coming" to his "Passing." The moral allegory is pronounced: this is what happens to the ideals of chivalry and Christian heroism—brotherhood degenerates into enmity, love into lust, honor into pride, courage into brutality, vision into delusion. This is the cost of man's all-too-human humanity.

Tennyson is successful in the *Idylls* where we would expect him to be—in the descriptive writing, in establishing atmosphere and mood and the reality of particular disturbed states of mind and feeling. His failure is in the treatment of the figures. On the one hand, he was unable to distance and stylize them allegorically, in the accomplished manner of Chaucer or Spenser; on the other hand, he was unable to bring them to life naturally and realistically (as he did successfully in the Lincolnshire poems); nor could he even manage the halfway dramatization that Wordsworth discovered as the perfect medium for his beggars, leech gatherers, shepherds, and other countryfolk who have both a symbolic and a natural role. It was not simply a technical deficiency but a failing in dramatic sense, which is really an absence of human sympathy. This comes across very sharply, for example, in the confrontation between Arthur and Guinevere. After listening to his wife's plea for forgiveness for her unfaithfulness with Lancelot, Arthur delivers a reprimand two hundred lines long, veering between his allegorical function as the conscience of society:

> Yet must I leave thee, woman, to thy shame.
> I hold that man the worst of public foes
> Who either for his own or children's sake,
> To save his blood from scandal, lets the wife
> Whom he knows false, abide and rule the house:
> ("Guinevere," 508–512)

and his part in the human drama:

> I cannot touch thy lips, they are not mine,
> But Lancelot's: nay, they never were the King's.
> I cannot take thy hand; that too is flesh,
> And in the flesh thou hast sinn'd; and mine own flesh,

Here looking down on thine polluted, cries
"I loathe thee":

(548–553)

Arthur sounds no better than an outraged husband in a Victorian melodrama—shades of Mr. Collins! If we try to localize the problem, it is in Tennyson's decision to purify the legendary Arthur, to transform him into a being sent by God and returning to Him unsullied by his earthly passage. Tennyson was proud to point out this purification in a dedicatory poem "To the Queen," published in the 1872 edition, in which he underlined the fact that his Arthur was not Malory's "Touched by the adulterous finger of a time/That hovered between war and wantonness, / And crownings and dethronements," and later he inserted a line exactly describing Arthur's allegorical character: "Ideal manhood closed in real man."

To be precise, Tennyson's crucial act of censorship was to ignore the stories of Arthur's adulterous conception and of his unwitting incestuous relationship with his half sister, of which the offspring is Modred. These elements in the Arthurian story constitute the doom of the house, the cruel and tragic destiny, which any Greek dramatist would have lighted upon as a fable as strong and significant as that of Oedipus. Whether or not we judge this to be a fair analogy,[7] the *Idylls* face us squarely with the question of Tennyson's later achievement, its scope and limitations, its timelessness in placing the poet as a teller of old tales, its peculiar Victorianism in the adaptation of the tale and the style of its telling.

SELECTED BIBLIOGRAPHY

I. BIBLIOGRAPHY. Detailed bibliographical information can also be found in the *New Cambridge Bibliography of English Literature*, vol. III (Cambridge, 1969). T. J. Wise, *A Bibliography of the Writings of Alfred, Lord Tennyson* (London, 1908), privately printed, the most detailed, analytical bibliography, includes Wise's forged eds.; F. E. Faverty, ed., *The Victorian Poets: A Guide to Research* (Cambridge, Mass., 1956; rev. ed., 1968), contains a sound account of modern research and criticism by P. F. Baum, the latter contains an updated account by E. D. H. Johnson; C. Tennyson and C. Fall, *Alfred Tennyson: An Annotated Bibliography* (Athens, Ga., 1967), the only

classified bibliography, useful but with many inexplicable omissions; A. E. Dyson, ed., *English Poetry: Select Bibliographies* (Oxford, 1971), contains the best descriptive and critical bibliography of the works of Tennyson, comp. by J. D. Hunt.

II. REFERENCE WORKS. A. E. Baker, *A Concordance to the Poetical and Dramatic Works of Alfred, Lord Tennyson* (London, 1914; supp. 1931; reiss. 1966); A. E. Baker, *A Tennyson Dictionary* (London, 1916); G. O. Marshall, *A Tennyson Handbook* (New York, 1963).

III. COLLECTED WORKS. *Poetical Works*, 4 vols. (Leipzig, 1860); *Works*, 10 vols. (London, 1870), the Pocket Volume (Miniature) ed., augmented by one vol. in 1873 and two more in 1877; A. C. Loffelt, ed., *Complete Works* (Rotterdam, 1871); *Works*, 6 vols. (London, 1872–1873; reiss. 1877), the Imperial Library ed.; *Works*, 12 vols. (London, 1874–1877), the Cabinet ed., augmented by an additional vol. (1881); *Works*, 7 vols. (London, 1874–1881), the Author's ed.; *Works* (London, 1878), the Crown ed.; *Works* (London, 1884), the Macmillan ed., often repr.; *Works* (London, 1894), the standard complete one-vol. ed. of the poems and plays, also issued in the Oxford Standard Authors series as *Tennyson: Poems and Plays* (London, 1965); *Life and Works of Alfred, Lord Tennyson,* 12 vols. (London, 1898–1899), the Edition de Luxe, the "Life" by Hallam, second Baron Tennyson; Hallam, Lord Tennyson, ed., *Poems, Annotated by Alfred, Lord Tennyson,* 9 vols. (London, 1907–1908), the Eversley ed.; C. Ricks, ed., *The Poems of Tennyson* (London, 1969), supersedes all previous "complete" eds. of the poetry, presenting all the known poems, published and unpublished, omitting only MS material still under restriction, has full textual, historical, and bibliographical notes and can properly be regarded as the basic document in any study of Tennyson.

IV. SELECTED WORKS. F. T. Palgrave, ed., *Lyrical Poems* (London, 1885), in the Golden Treasury series, important because Tennyson advised Palgrave on the selection; J. C. Collins, ed., *The Early Poems* (London, 1900); H. J. C. Grierson, ed., *Poems* (London, 1907); B. C. Mulliner, ed., *Shorter Poems and Lyrics, 1833–42,* 2 vols. (Oxford, 1909); J. C. Thompson, ed., *Suppressed Poems, 1830–68* (London, 1910); T. S. Eliot, ed., *Poems* (Edinburgh, 1936); W. H. Auden, ed., *A Selection from the Poems* (New York, 1944); D. Bush, ed., *Tennyson: Selected Poetry* (New York, 1951); C. Tennyson, ed., *Poems* (London, 1954); M. McLuhan, ed., *Selected Poetry* (London, 1956); J. H. Buckley, ed., *Poems* (Cambridge, Mass., 1958); B. C. Southam, ed., *Selected Poems* (London, 1964), the only ed. apart from the complete one by Ricks to place the poems in order of composition and to attempt comprehensive historical and explanatory notes; D. Cecil, ed., *A Choice of Verse* (London, 1971); J. D. Jump, ed., *In Memoriam, Maud and Other Poems* (London, 1975), the Everyman ed.

V. SEPARATE WORKS. *Poems by Two Brothers* (Lon-

---

[7]Swinburne's discussion of this point in *Under the Microscope* (London, 1872) is the most sustained criticism of Tennyson as a poet reduced by his own notion of morality.

1233

don–Louth, 1827), by Alfred and Charles, with three or four pieces by Frederick; 2nd ed., H. Tennyson, ed. (London, 1893); *Timbuctoo* (Cambridge, 1829), in *Prolusiones Academicae*; *Poems, Chiefly Lyrical* (London, 1830); *The Lover's Tale* (London, 1833; 1st authorized ed., London, 1879), the former was privately printed; *Poems* (London, 1833); *Poems*, 2 vols. (London, 1842), contains many poems repr., and some rev., from *Poems* of 1830 and 1833; *The Princess: A Medley* (London, 1847; rev. eds., 1850, 1851, 1853); *In Memoriam* (London, 1850), an additional poem in the 4th ed. (London, 1851), and another inserted in 1870; *Ode on the Death of the Duke of Wellington* (London, 1852; rev. ed., 1853); *Maud, and Other Poems* (London, 1855; rev. eds., 1856, 1859); *Idylls of the King* (London, 1859; enl. eds., 1862, 1869, 1872, 1885), early eds. consisted of "Enid," "Vivien," "Elaine," "Guinevere"; *Enoch Arden, and Other Poems* (London, 1864); *The Holy Grail, and Other Poems* (London, 1870); *Gareth and Lynette* (London, 1872); *Queen Mary: A Drama* (London, 1875); *Harold: A Drama* (London, 1877); *Ballads and Other Poems* (London, 1880); *Becket* (London, 1884), drama; *The Cup, and, The Falcon* (London, 1884), dramas; *Tiresias, and Other Poems* (London, 1885); *Locksley Hall Sixty Years After* (London, 1886); *Demeter, and Other Poems* (London, 1889); *The Death of Oenone, Akbar's Dream, and Other Poems* (London, 1892); *The Foresters: Robin Hood and Maid Marian* (London, 1892), drama; C. Tennyson, ed., *The Devil and the Lady* (London, 1930); C. Tennyson, ed., *Unpublished Early Poems* (London, 1931).

VI. Letters. H. Tennyson, *Alfred Lord Tennyson: A Memoir*, 2 vols. (London, 1897), vol. I, ch. 10, contains letters 1842–1845, and vol. II, chs. 16 and 23, letters 1862–1864; F. A. Mumby, ed., *Letters of Literary Men* (London, 1906), vol. II, pp. 561–567; L. Pierce, ed., *Alfred Lord Tennyson and William Kirby: Unpublished Correspondence* (Toronto, 1929); M. J. Ellmann, "Unpublished Letters of Tennyson," in *Modern Language Notes*, 65 (1950).

VII. Biographical and Critical Studies. Some of the following articles are repr. in J. D. Jump, ed., *Tennyson: The Critical Heritage* (London, 1967) or in J. Killham, ed., *Critical Essays on the Poetry of Tennyson* (London, 1960). They are referred to under the titles given in those publications. A. H. Hallam, "Poems, Chiefly Lyrical, 1830," in *Englishman's Magazine*, 1 (August 1831), an unsigned review, repr. in Jump, further discussed in M. McLuhan, "Tennyson and Picturesque Poetry" (see below); G. Eliot, "Maud and Other Poems," in *Westminster Review* (October 1855); W. Bagehot, "Idylls of the King, 1859," in *National Review*, 9 (October 1859), an unsigned review, repr. in Jump; M. Arnold, *On Translating Homer: Last Words* (London, 1862), includes a section on Tennyson's simplicity that is repr. in Jump; H. Taine, *Histoire de la littérature anglaise*, 4 vols. (Paris, 1863–1864), trans. by H. Van Laun

into English, 2 vols. (London, 1871), contains the ch. "Poetry—Tennyson," repr. in Jump; W. Bagehot, "Wordsworth, Tennyson and Browning: Or, Pure, Ornate and Grotesque Art in English Poetry," in *National Review*, n.s. 1 (November 1864), an unsigned article, repr. in Jump, contains a review of Tennyson's *Enoch Arden*, further discussed in M. Dodsworth, "Patterns of Morbidity: Repetition in Tennyson's Poetry," in I. Armstrong, ed. *The Major Victorian Poets* (see below); R. Simpson, "Mr. Tennyson's Poetry," in *North British Review* (January 1871); A. C. Swinburne, *Under the Microscope* (London, 1872), includes comments on *Idylls of the King* that are repr. in Jump; H. James, "Tennyson's Drama," in *Galaxy* (September 1875); A. C. Swinburne, *Miscellanies* (London, 1886), includes the essay "Tennyson and Musset," a reply to Taine (above), extracts repr. in Jump; R. H. Hutton, *Literary Essays* (London, 1888), contains the ch. "Tennyson," replying to Swinburne (above) and repr. in Jump; H. Tennyson, *Materials for a Life of A. T.*, 4 vols. (London, 1896), privately printed, basic source material for the author's later official biography; H. Tennyson, *Alfred Lord Tennyson: A Memoir*, 2 vols. (London, 1897).

A. C. Bradley, *A Commentary on Tennyson's "In Memoriam"* (London, 1901; rev. eds., 1902, 1930); A. Lang, *Alfred Tennyson* (London, 1901); G. K. Chesterton and R. Garnett, *Tennyson* (London, 1903); W. P. Ker, *Tennyson* (Cambridge, 1909), the Leslie Stephen Lecture, Cambridge, 11 November 1909; G. K. Chesterton, *The Victorian Age in Literature* (London–New York, 1913); A. C. Bradley, *The Reaction Against Tennyson* (London, 1917), English Association pamphlet no. 39; H. Nicholson, *Tennyson: Aspects of His Life, Character and Poetry* (London, 1923; 2nd ed., 1925), the most popular and influential account, very readable and convincing as a psychological-literary portrait, but must be read with caution; F. R. Leavis, *New Bearings in English Poetry* (London, 1932; rev. ed., 1950), together with his *Revaluation* and *The Common Pursuit* (below), contains this author's influential views; T. S. Eliot, *Essays Ancient and Modern* (London, 1936), contains the essay "In Memoriam," which is repr. in Killham; F. R. Leavis, *Revaluation: Tradition and Development in English Poetry* (London, 1936); G. M. Young, *Victorian England: Portrait of an Age* (London, 1936); J. N. D. Bush, *Mythology and the Romantic Tradition in English Poetry* (Cambridge, Mass., 1937), Harvard Studies in English no. 18; C. C. Abbott, ed., *Further Letters of Gerard Manley Hopkins* (London, 1938), includes a letter dated 10 September 1864 that discusses Tennyson's language and is repr. in Jump; G. M. Young, *The Age of Tennyson* (London, 1939), the Warton Lecture on English Poetry, 1939, also printed in *Proceedings of the British Academy*, 35 (1939).

W. D. Paden, "Tennyson and the Reviewers, 1827–35," in *University of Kansas Publications, Humanistic Studies*, 6, no. 4 (1940), 15–39; W. D. Paden, *Tennyson in Egypt: A*

Study of the Imagery in His Earlier Work (Lawrence, Kans., 1942); C. Brooks, The Well-Wrought Urn (London, 1947), includes the ch. "The Motivation of Tennyson's Weeper," on "Tears, Idle Tears," which is repr. in Killham; P. F. Baum, Tennyson Sixty Years After (Chapel Hill, N. C., 1948); C. Tennyson, Alfred Tennyson (London, 1949), the standard biography, excellent both historically and interpretatively; F. W. Bateson, English Poetry: A Critical Introduction (London, 1950), contains the ch. "Romantic Schizophrenia: Tennyson's 'Tears, Idle Tears'"; A. J. Carr, "Tennyson as a Modern Poet," in University of Toronto Quarterly, 19 (1950), repr. in Killham; J. H. Buckley, The Victorian Temper: A Study in Literary Culture (Cambridge, Mass., 1951); G. Hough, "Tears, Idle Tears," in Hopkins Review (1951), repr. in Killham; M. McLuhan, "Tennyson and Picturesque Poetry," in Essays in Criticism, 1 (January 1951), repr. in Killham, relates to Hallam's review (above); E. D. H. Johnson, The Alien Vision of Victorian Poetry: Sources of the Poetic Imagination in Tennyson, Browning and Arnold (Princeton, N. J., 1952); F. R. Leavis, The Common Pursuit (London, 1952); E. F. Shannon, Tennyson and the Reviewers: A Study of His Literary Reputation and of the Influence of the Critics upon His Poetry, 1827–1851 (Cambridge, Mass., 1952); L. Spitzer, "'Tears, Idle Tears' Again," in Hopkins Review (1952), repr. in Killham, a reply to Hough (above); C. Tennyson, Six Tennyson Essays (London, 1954); R. Langbaum, The Poetry of Experience: The Dramatic Monologue in Modern Literary Tradition (London, 1957); W. W. Robson, "The Dilemma of Tennyson," in The Listener, 13 (June 1957), repr. in Killham; B. Ford, ed., The Pelican Guide to English Literature, vol. VI (London, 1958), contains R. Mayhead's "The Poetry of Tennyson"; J. Killham, Tennyson and the Princess: Reflections of an Age (London, 1958); M. McLuhan, "Tennyson and the Romantic Epic," in Killham (London, 1960).

J. H. Buckley, Tennyson: The Growth of a Poet (Cambridge, Mass. -London, 1960), an important biographical-historical study giving a detailed scholarly and critical account of Tennyson's development; J. Killham, ed., Critical Essays on the Poetry of Tennyson (London, 1960), a representative collection of the best modern criticism, repr. studies by T. S. Eliot, G. M. Young, C. Brooks, M. McLuhan, G. Hough, L. Spitzer, A. J. Carr, and W. W. Robson; H. S. Davies, comp., The Poets and Their Critics: Blake to Browning (London, 1962), gives extracts of adverse criticism of Tennyson; G. W. Knight, The Golden Labyrinth: A Study of British Drama (London, 1962); V. Pitt, Tennyson Laureate (London, 1962); J. Richardson, The Pre-eminent Victorian: A Study of Tennyson (London, 1962); R. W. Rader, Tennyson's Maud: The Biographical Genesis (Berkeley–Los Angeles, 1963), explores the significant relationship of the poet's private life and art; J. B. Steane, Tennyson (London, 1966); J. D. Jump, ed., Tennyson: The Critical Heritage (London, 1967), reprs. a selection of reviews, essays, and other comments for the period 1831–1891 and discusses the contemporary response and critical reception in an extensive intro., selections include criticism by A. Hallam (reviewing Poems, 1830), W. Bagehot, M. Arnold, G. M. Hopkins, A. C. Swinburne, H. Taine, R. H. Hutton, and many others; C. Ricks, "Tennyson's Methods of Composition," in Proceedings of the British Academy, 52 (1967); I. Armstrong, ed., The Major Victorian Poets: Reconsiderations (London, 1969), includes essays by M. Dodsworth, B. Bergonzi, A. Sinfield, and A. S. Byatt; J. D. Hunt, ed., Tennyson's "In Memoriam": A Casebook (London, 1970), a collection of documents and critical essays on the poem; C. Ricks, Tennyson (London, 1972); D. J. Palmer, ed., Tennyson (London, 1973); F. E. L. Priestley, ed., Language and Structure in Tennyson's Poetry (London, 1973); C. Tennyson and H. Dyson, The Tennysons: Background to Genius (London, 1974); P. Kincaid, Tennyson's Major Poems: The Comic and Ironic Patterns (New Haven, Conn., 1975); A. D. Culler, The Poetry of Tennyson (New Haven, Conn., 1977); P. Henderson, Tennyson: Poet and Prophet (London, 1978); J. S. Hagen, Tennyson and His Publishers (London, 1979); R. Pattison, Tennyson and Tradition (Cambridge, Mass., 1980); R. B. Martin, Tennyson: The Unquiet Heart (London, 1980).

WILLIAM MAKEPEACE THACKERAY
(1811-1863)

John Carey

INTRODUCTION

Vanity Fair is arguably the greatest English novel of the nineteenth century, and the only one that, in epic sweep, can challenge comparison with the masterpieces of Stendhal and Leo Tolstoy. That alone would make William Makepeace Thackeray worth studying. But he had, also, an extremely likable personality—wry, warm, disillusioned, self-deprecating—that colors almost everything he wrote. As with a handful of other great writers—Samuel Johnson, Robert Louis Stevenson, G. K. Chesterton, George Orwell among them—it is eventually not just the writer but the man that you value.

Like Honoré de Balzac, from whom he learned, and whose *Cousine Bette* influenced *Vanity Fair*, Thackeray was imaginatively excited by the externals of life—what people wore, ate, earned, spent; their jobs, marriages, postal addresses, and social connections. These data teem in his fiction: he can evoke whole careers and genealogies in a few sentences. Behind his main characters we glimpse swarms of remoter figures, not nightmarish or fantastic, as in Charles Dickens, but busily pursuing realistic vocations. For the first time in English literature, Thackeray gives us a sense of living in a crowded and diverse world.

His ideas, too, are more modern than those of any previous novelist. Thomas Carlyle said that he had no convictions, and that is true—but only because Thackeray realized that convictions come easiest to those who are dull, self-satisfied, and unseeing. He questioned, at some time or other, the value of almost everything his Victorian contemporaries held dear—including literature and art. The notion that painters or writers were more loftily engaged than ordinary people and consequently should not have to earn their living, provide for their children, or treat their fellow men with decent consideration, attracted his untiring scorn. A literary man, he

declared, was no better or worse than a man writing in a ledger. He loved poking fun at the cult of romantic genius (of which Byron was for him the most deplorable example). He disparaged classical culture and the educational system based on it. He found William Shakespeare's tragedies boring and exaggerated, and he insisted that nothing was so overrated as the fine arts.

Like our age, he found doubt in religion easier than certainty. The God his countrymen worshiped caused him grave misgivings, and he pointed out that the Old Testament was largely a chronicle of crimes and slaughters sanctioned by the Almighty. In ethics, too, he tended to skepticism. Moral choice, he suggested, was illusory, and moral judgment consequently misguided. When one considered the unequal fortunes of men and how completely genetic factors and environment mastered their actions, the concepts of vice and virtue, as generally understood, became irrelevant, as did punishment. The loyalty of Englishmen to their country and their readiness to fight for it were other nineteenth-century ideals he eyed quizzically. Patriotism, he said, was the faith of dullards. His poem "The Chronicle of the Drum" calls war "The noble art of murdering" and ridicules poets and historians who glorify it. He distrusted all political dogma, decrying the "humbug" of both right and left. Since selfishness was the universal human motive, any change in the distribution of wealth was likely, he argued, to end in a system as unjust as the one it had replaced.

His unflattering opinions of life displeased the Victorians. John Ruskin complained that he "settled like a meat fly on whatever one had got for dinner and made one sick of it." We are likelier to regret that he did not remain faithful to his disturbing insights. As time went on, he suppressed his satirical side for the sake of popularity. Even before that happened, his basic lack of conviction made him irresolute. The skeptical views, summarized above, alternate in his writing with postures that are rigid, pompous, and conservative. Instead of confronting this dilemma, he tended increasingly to shuffle off into jocular cynicism and conformity. His flippant side shows up in his light verse, which is often both comic and winningly irresponsible. Significantly, his poem "A Failure" defines life as "a laugh disguising a defeat." These shortcomings and inconsistencies, however, only make him a more authentic and recognizable human being. He had no pretensions to systematic thought; indeed, he mistrusted it, for he believed that every human viewpoint was isolated, limited, and personal. "A distinct universe," he said, "walks about under your hat and under mine." Ultimately all his writing is a study of the factors—pride, greed, selfishness, class—that divide people from one another. But he does not hold out any hope that things could be very different. He was too realistic to be an optimist.

LIFE

THACKERAY's life encompassed unusually violent ups and downs of fortune, and these developed his awareness of the sharp divisions between different social groups. He began opulently. His father, Richmond Makepeace Thackeray, was highly placed in the East India Company, with a palatial residence near the Esplanade in Calcutta, where William Makepeace Thackeray, his only legitimate child, was born on 18 July 1811. William retained only vague memories of India—ballrooms, fireworks, elephant rides—for his father soon died, and at the age of five he was sent back to school in England. Meanwhile, his mother stayed in India, taking as her second husband an officer in the Bengal Engineers, Henry Carmichael-Smyth. She had known and loved him as a girl, but her family had prevented the match on financial grounds and married her off to Thackeray's wealthy father. Nearly four years passed before she and her new husband rejoined young William in England.

This period of separation marked Thackeray deeply. School was horrible. He never forgot the misery, the canings, the fat yellow soap floating in ice and water each morning. Every night he prayed that he might dream of his mother. His later fictional portraits of her—Helen Pendennis, Rachel Esmond—show the sacred place she occupied in his imagination. The story of her family's mercenary treatment of her gave him a phobia about money-marriages that is apparent in the novels.

In 1822, he went to Charterhouse, his stepfather's old school. He found it brutal, snobbish, and depraved, and he made little progress as a student. Being nearsighted, he was no good at games, and his nose was broken in a fight, which disfigured him for life. His hostility to public schools and classical education was bred at Charterhouse. However, his memories of it grew rosier with the years, and it features much in his books—most celebratedly as Grey Friars in *The Newcomes*. It was at school that he began making comic sketches to amuse his classmates. Drawing and, to a lesser degree, painting remained lifelong passions: he often felt he should have been an artist, not a writer.

Leaving Charterhouse, Thackeray entered Trinity College, Cambridge, in 1829, where he was again a failure academically. As the heir to his father's fortune, he could afford to cut an aristocratic figure. He mixed with gilded youths and cultivated his taste in wines, fine foods, jewelry, and cigars. At the time, rich Anglo-Indians were envied and somewhat shunned in good English circles, and this quickened Thackeray's desire to hobnob with young men of rank. He scorned the humbler, hard-working undergraduates, telling his mother that they "smelt of the shop."

He spent his first long vacation in Paris—a turning point in his life, for he fell in love with the city and the glittering realms of opera and ballet that he found there. Marie Taglioni, the great ballerina, enchanted him: she always remained one of his ideals. At Frascati's he discovered the excitement of *rouge et noir*, and he returned from Paris a compulsive gambler. Over the next four years his gaming debts mounted dizzily. He fell victim to a group of professional cardsharpers who descended on Cambridge and tricked him out of a large part of his patrimony. Sharks, gulls, and foolish young wastrels were to become, when he turned to writing, constant inhabitants of his fictional world.

After five terms he abandoned Cambridge and began a life of leisured idleness. He sailed up the Rhine and spent six months in Weimar, captivated by the cultured, old-world society with its sedan chairs and court entertainments. It seemed a fragment of the eighteenth century, miraculously preserved, and his memories of it helped to kindle his affection for that historical period. Back in London, he started legal studies at the Middle Temple, but soon gave them up, preferring the comforts of luxurious gaming houses and brothels. He studied art, rather negligently, in Paris, and he bought up an ailing London paper, the *National Standard*, which he ran for a few months until it collapsed, learning the rudiments of journalism from William Maginn, one of the "low literary men" whom Thackeray always felt distaste for, even when his livelihood depended on them.

At the end of 1833, disaster struck. The Indian banks in which his stepfather had invested Thackeray's fortune failed, and he was suddenly poor. To make matters worse, he fell in love with a penniless girl, Isabella Shawe, daughter of an Irish military widow living in Paris. Her mother's mercenary opposition to their union (fictionalized, much later, in *Philip*) was bound, given Thackeray's views on money and marriage, to drive him into wedlock. But much as he loved Isabella, he soon realized how unwise their marriage had been. She was a sweet, limp little thing (Amelia in *Vanity Fair* is partly modeled on her) and could offer Thackeray no intellectual companionship. For her mother, he developed a profound loathing: she permanently poisoned his view of mothers-in-law and the Irish. Despite these drawbacks, his early wedded life with Isabella was blissful, and he celebrated it in the "Ballad of Bouillabaisse," where his memory of his young bride is characteristically mingled with wining and dining and the Parisian elegancies he so loved.

To earn his living in these anxious years Thackeray turned to journalism. His stepfather secured him the job of Paris correspondent on a radical London paper, the *Constitutional*, in which capacity he was expected to express abhorrence of Louis Philippe and to champion liberty against French despotism. In 1837, the paper ceased publication, and Thackeray became a free-lance writer. He wrote under tremendous pressure, but enjoyed the challenge. "I love to have the press thumping, clattering, and banging in my rear," he declared; "it creates the necessity which always makes me work best." Certainly the sketches, reviews, and articles that he dashed off during the next ten years contain much of his most brilliant and vivacious writing, though they are virtually unknown today. He wrote for various periodicals, most notably the conservative *Fraser's* and, from 1844 onward, the left-wing *Punch*. He adopted the facetious nom de plume Michael Angelo Titmarsh, partly as a protest against undue solemnity and partly to keep an amused, gentlemanly distance from the business of authorship.

As a relief from the strain of hack work he turned increasingly to clubland, bachelor society, and the joys of haute cuisine, leaving his wife to cope with the trials of motherhood alone. Their eldest child, Anne, had been born in 1837; a second daughter, Jane, was born in 1838, but died within a year. Shortly after Isabella had given birth to their third child, Harriet, in 1840, Thackeray left for a continental pleasure trip. In retrospect he blamed himself severely for this neglect. Isabella suffered acute depression following Harriet's birth, and attempted suicide by throwing herself into the sea when Thackeray was taking her to visit her mother in Ireland. He accompanied her to the continent, seeking a cure for her mental breakdown, but none was found. She remained hopelessly insane for the rest of her long life, and in 1845 was placed in a home at Camberwell. Thackeray's self-reproach is reflected in his account of George's desertion of Amelia in *Vanity Fair*, but the tragedy had more far-reaching effects on him than this. He felt prematurely aged and became a prey to nostalgia. Also, he depended more and more on wine and gastronomic excesses to keep himself going. His girth increased accordingly—he was, as he put it, a "Big Blubber man"—and this, together with his exceptional height and piping treble voice, gave him, in his maturity, rather a distinctive social presence.

Meanwhile, he went on struggling to earn a living by his pen. He begged advances from his publishers, and was reduced to humiliating expedients—depositing, on one occasion, his household silverware with them as security. The knowledge of genteel poverty displayed in the closing chapters of *The Newcomes* was firsthand. But his reputation grew steadily. By 1845 he was earning £1,200 a year, and was able to rent a house in Kensington, so that his daughters, who had been boarded with his mother in Paris, could come and live with him. In February 1845 he began the first draft of *Vanity Fair*.

Published in monthly parts from January 1847 to July 1848, this novel made him a celebrity. Its success, however, did not have a wholly beneficial effect on his writing. He found himself courted by the great and a frequent guest in their grand houses. Society hostesses competed for him. "I reel from dinner party to dinner party. I wallow in turtle and swim in Shampang," he wrote jocularly to a friend. He felt that he had won his way back to the patrician status he had enjoyed before he lost his fortune, and he came to feel ashamed of the "misanthropical" and satirical strains in his work. He parted company with *Punch*, describing its leading light, Douglas Jerrold, as a "savage little Robespierre," and he decided to strike a "kinder" and more solemn note in his books. To be "comic and grinning" was now, he decided, "below my rank in the world."

The loss of sparkle in his writing after *Vanity Fair* can be traced to this deliberate change of policy and also to a sudden decline in his health. He had suffered for some time from digestive disorders and from the painful aftermath of a venereal infection—a relic of his prodigal youth. Then, in September 1849, he was stricken with a near-fatal illness, diagnosed as "bilious fever" but probably typhoid, from which he made a slow recovery. Another source of upset was his frustratingly unphysical love affair, extending over several years, with Jane Brookfield, the wife of his clergyman friend Henry Brookfield. Eventually Thackeray realized that Jane had merely played with his affections and never intended to be unfaithful to her husband. The knowledge hurt him: "the thought I have been made a fool of is the bitterest of all," he wrote. He felt resentful toward Henry Brookfield too, believing he had treated Jane tyrannically. The coarsely inconsiderate husband Lord Castlewood, in *Henry Esmond*, is a stab at Brookfield.

The softening of Thackeray's mind after *Vanity Fair* and his obsequious relations with high society are sadly apparent in his sentimental lectures *The English Humourists*, written during 1851. He gave them before a genteel audience in Willis's Rooms, St. James's, a fashionable venue, and the third lecture (as Charlotte Brontë sardonically records) was postponed for a week because it clashed with Ascot. As his social views became more complacent and his prosperity increased, he found writing less and less attractive. It became a joyless grind, and he groaned over the dullness of it, complaining that he had no new ideas. Money seemed the only worthwhile goal. Seized with the urge to amass a fortune that he could leave to his daughters, he toured the English cities with his lectures and, in 1852, took them to America, netting handsome profits.

The disasters of the Crimean War in 1854–1855 put a stop, temporarily, to Thackeray's flirtation with England's governing class. Indignant at the appalling mismanagement, he joined the Administrative Reform Association, demanding that the educated middle classes should take over the running of the country, and with this in mind he stood for Parliament at the Oxford election in 1857, but he was defeated. To express his new impatience with monarchy and aristocracy he wrote his series of lectures *The Four Georges*, with which he made his second American tour in 1855. The lectures antagonized

some highly placed friends, but Thackeray's brief return to the radical attitudes of his *Punch* period did not signal any real inclination toward democracy. It always alarmed him to think of the masses having power. Significantly, he was much less taken with America on his second trip than on his first: "the rabble supremacy turns my gorge," he remarked.

The great success of his final years was his editorship of the *Cornhill* magazine, launched in 1859, which allowed him to present his ideal of the middle-class gentleman to a large audience. He carefully censored the paper's political views, cutting short the serialization of Ruskin's *Unto This Last*, which had offended readers by its attacks on orthodox political economy. Sales of the *Cornhill* soared, as did the editor's salary, and Thackeray was able to build himself a splendid house, in his beloved Queen Anne style, at Palace Green, Kensington.

These last years also saw a rift between Thackeray and his great rival Dickens. At bottom he had always disliked Dickens and envied his unmatchable popularity. He objected to Dickens' sentimentalization of low and criminal types (Nancy, in *Oliver Twist*, for instance), his dandified dress, and his rabble-rousing politics. Dickens was not, in his eyes, a gentleman—though he acknowledged his genius. When a young friend of Dickens, Edmund Yates, wrote a sarcastic article referring to Thackeray's leftward swing in *The Four Georges*, a furious row ensued, which ended with Thackeray severing relations with Dickens and getting Yates expelled from the Garrick Club.

The two novelists did not speak again until late in 1863 when, seeing Dickens in the Athenaeum, Thackeray ran to him and shook his hand. A few days later, coming home late from dinner on Christmas Eve, Thackeray suffered an apoplectic stroke and died instantly. By his own request he was buried in Kensal Green next to his infant daughter Jane, who had always held a special place in his heart. His mother, whose influence on him had been so great, lived for one more year, and was laid to rest on Christmas Eve 1864, beside her son.

EARLY WORKS, 1837–1843

WHAT spoils Thackeray's earliest works is that he is so keen to sound superior to what he is writing about that you wonder why he is writing about it at all. He chooses lower-class subjects and treats them in a way that amounts to a protracted sneer. This is understandable, given his recent fall from fortune, but it is still regrettable. "The Professor" (1837), his first published story, is a facetious, disparaging account of a romance between two h-dropping cockneys; *The Yellowplush Correspondence* (1837–1838) is the memoir of a mercenary, snobbish footman, couched in uneducated spelling; "Barber Cox" (1840) is the tale of a barber and his wife who come into a fortune and make fools of themselves by trying to live like gentlefolk; "The Fatal Boots" (1839) is the autobiography of an unbelievably base, cowardly, and bullying youth, intent on marrying for money. Fortunately, even these works have stretches where, despite himself, Thackeray has allowed his imagination to become engaged. The details of the oyster shop in "The Professor," with the gas lamps gleaming on the ruby lobsters; the portrait in "Yellowplush" of the smooth, revered old hypocrite, the Earl of Crabs; and in "Barber Cox" the chaos of dirt and glitter backstage at the ballet: all open up subjects that Thackeray was to pursue later. The most remarkable early piece in this respect is "Captain Rook and Mr. Pigeon" (1840), a tale of a dandy card-sharper and his victim, which is based on Thackeray's own dearly bought experience and bristles with incidents and items of food, clothing, and jewelry that were to become fixtures in his fictional workshop.

Two early works that shift the focus to the middle classes and adopt a more sympathetic attitude are *The Bedford-Row Conspiracy* (1840) and *Samuel Titmarsh and the Great Hoggarty Diamond* (1841). The first, an adaptation of a *nouvelle* by Charles de Bernard, follows the fortunes of John Perkins, a good-natured but simple young barrister, and his sweetheart, Lucy. Thackeray directs his satire against the establishment figures who confront these two—notably William Scully, a double-dealing Whig MP, and General Gorgon, a haughty Tory militia officer whose wife, Lady Gorgon, resembles a "healthy, broad-flanked, Roman-nosed white drayhorse." Giving yourself airs and living above your station are anathema in all these works, and the Gorgons exhibit them on a grand scale.

Sam Titmarsh in *The Great Hoggarty Diamond* belongs to the clerkly, commercial-traveler class and is presented as a likable chap who improbably falls in with some aristocrats while shopping. They take to him because he is cocky, yet respectful, and disdains affectation. Eventually Sam goes bankrupt through speculation, and his infant son dies, whereupon Lord and Lady Tiptoff generously employ him as their steward while his wife, Mary (an angelic girl who,

though poor, is voted a true lady by everyone), is taken on by the Tiptoffs as a wet nurse. This rather absurd tale, with its stress on humility and charity, is in some respects (such as the child's death) autobiographical, and for Thackeray to cast himself as Titmarsh suggests his worries about class. While scorning those who aped their betters, he was unsure where, in the social scale, he himself fitted. He realized that he had made a fool of himself by acting the grandee at Cambridge, so he adopted, defensively, a jauntily unpretentious persona.

The most successful of these social fictions is *A Shabby Genteel Story* (1840), which brings two parts of Thackeray's past life into fruitful conflict. The heroine, Caroline Gann, is an idealized portrait of Isabella. Set against her is her villainous seducer, Brand Firmin (alias George Brandon), based on Harry Matthew, a young roué who had been Thackeray's idol at Cambridge. Caroline, though pure-souled, comes, like Isabella, from a grubby background and has coarse relatives. Her stepmother (modeled on Mrs. Shawe) is a military widow of the deepest vulgarity, perpetually boasting of her noble lineage, and her father, James Gann, is a bankrupt oil merchant, eking out a flyblown existence in his wife's Margate boardinghouse. Thackeray's portrayal of the dirt and meanness in the Gann family shows his recoil from the kind of people his marriage had dragged him down among, and his depiction of Firmin shows his disenchantment with his Cambridge values. A snobbish idler and glutton, contemptuous of the *canaille*, Firmin is presented by Thackeray as a typical product of the "accursed system" of public school and university education that teaches, we are told, selfishness, irreligion, and scorn for natural affections. Yet Firmin is also, Thackeray assures us, "innately a gentleman," and his polished mockery of the Ganns is close to Thackeray's own style. This tension, suggesting Thackeray's divided feelings about his affluent past, lends complexity to the tale. The minor figures are profusely imagined—Andrew Fitch, for instance, the rhapsodic cockney painter, or the decayed James Gann, with his telescope for examining the bathing machines from the esplanade. For the first time in Thackeray's work, this story makes us aware of the varied, receding depths of other lives, beyond the doings of the main characters.

Though Thackeray was still, at this stage, unsure of his own stance as a writer, he was quite clear where others had gone wrong, and he developed a talent for burlesque. Exaggeration and unreality are what he derides in the authors he picks on, and his burlesques build up their own fantastic momentum accordingly. *The Tremendous Adventures of Major Gahagan* (1838–1839) ridicules military adventure novels, particularly those with an Indian setting, through the person of Major Goliah O'Grady Gahagan, commander of the Ahmednuggar Irregular Horse, who kills four tigers with his bare hands, enters the enemy camp disguised with bootblacking, and performs other valorous feats—for all of which we have only the major's decidedly questionable word. Throughout, Thackeray makes great play with the routine articles of local color and the scattering of Hindustani words by which novelists strive to convey the mysterious East.

Much less funny is *Catherine* (1839–1840), the story of the "idlest, dirtiest and most passionate little minx" of a servant girl, who is ruined, betrayed, and finally burned at the stake for murdering her husband. Thackeray based it on an actual case, and meant it as an attack on the "Newgate School" of novelists (a category in which he included Dickens), which glamorized the lives of criminals. He admitted, though, a "sneaking kindness" for his heroine, and the book outgrows its satirical purpose. Set in the early eighteenth century, it is the earliest of Thackeray's stories to show his fascination with the luxuriously artificial life of Europe in that period, epitomized in Catherine's seducer, the shady nobleman von Galgenstein, with his ruffles and rings, and the "chestnut-coloured, orange-scented pyramid of horsehair" that forms his wig.

Thackeray's series of *Punch's Prize Novelists* (1847) added to the tally of his burlesques. It includes brilliant take-offs of Bulwer-Lytton's *Eugene Aram* and Benjamin Disraeli's *Coningsby*, and a piece called "Crinoline" by Jeames Plush Esq. (the footman from *Yellowplush*), which exposes, through Jeames's enthusiasm, the vulgarity and ignorance upon which novels of high society depend for their appeal:

Add I the penn of the hawther of a Codlingsby himself, I coodnt dixcribe the gawjusness of their aboad. They add twenty-four footmen in livery, besides a boy in codroys for the knives & shoes. They had nine meals aday—Shampayne and pineapples were served to each of the young ladies in bed before they got up.[1]

(vol. VIII, pp. 91–92)

[1]All quotations of prose and verse are from *The Works,* 26 vols. (London, 1910–1911).

As this suggests, Thackeray was always just as interested in the motives and social conditions that produce and popularize literature and art as he was in literature and art themselves. The topic satisfied his instinct to dissect society. It is treated in sketches like "The Fashionable Authoress" and "The Artists" (both 1841), where he harps on the insincerity of newspaper editors and reviewers (a favorite grumble) and describes in his zestful, knowing, impressionistic way the lives of the painting fraternity and the London districts they frequent. Also in this line, though more factual, is "Half-a-Crown's Worth of Cheap Knowledge" (1839)—a survey based on a reading of several penny and twopenny newspapers produced for the working class. The liveliness of the original idea is, unfortunately, counteracted by Thackeray's scornful response both to the radical political papers in his sample and to the "inconceivably dirty" journals like the *Town,* which circulated information about gin shops, barmaids, pawnbrokers, and tripe vendors. Still, as Thackeray was writing for *Fraser's,* a more liberal stance could scarcely be expected.

This brings us to Thackeray's role as social observer, which accounts for his most enjoyable writing in these years. In *The Paris Sketch Book* (1840) he presents France as a ridiculous but lovely playground and the French as absurd political animals whose nature it is to knock down omnibuses and build barricades. On the other hand, they are far more cultured and artistic, Thackeray emphasizes, than the English. A theme uniting the book is the healthiness of the commonplace, by comparison with high or romantic art. Thackeray scoffs at Racine, Victor Hugo, George Sand, and the German mystics and transcendentalists, and ridicules the ostentation of Versailles with its "thousands of yards of the worst pictures the eye has ever looked on." The circus or the spectacles at Franconi's, where the battles of the Empire were replayed for a popular audience, seem to him by contrast "good and right-hearted."

Apart from the *Sketch Book* there are three other outstanding pieces of similar date that exploit Thackeray's quick eye for foreign culture. *The Second Funeral of Napoleon* (1841), which he thought, with some reason, his best thing so far, gives a marvelously deflating account of the ceremonial surrounding the collection of Napoleon's body from St. Helena and its conveyance to Les Invalides; "Shrove Tuesday in Paris" (1841) describes a masked ball where Thackeray met a young woman called Madame Pauline, ex-governess to an English family, who, some have conjectured, became his mistress and contributed to his portrait of Becky Sharp; and "Memorials of Gormandising" (1841) takes us on a lyrical tour of the Café Foy, the Trois Frères, the Rocher de Cancale, and other temples of Parisian haute cuisine. Any of these pieces would be a good place for someone ignorant of Thackeray to start reading him, and so would "Going to See a Man Hanged" (1840), where the subject is, for a change, English—the public execution of the murderer Courvoisier in July 1840. In its vividness and mastery of atmosphere this challenges comparison with George Orwell's "A Hanging."

Finally, art criticism was a branch of his trade that Thackeray relished, for it went some way to answering his wish to be a painter himself. He wrote about pictures and exhibitions for several magazines, employing a chatty, discursive, irreverent manner that still retains, when we read it, some of the fun and sparkle of the day it was written. He adopted this tone quite deliberately, to express his distrust of sublimity and aggrandizement and his opinion that art should be rooted in everyday life. To the same end his picture reviews give glimpses of the author strolling out of the National Gallery for a cigar, or bolting gin and ham sandwiches while he writes up his copy, and they use commonplace language (alluding to Hill's "spinach pastures" or to Stone's painting of a dog "with no more bones than an apple dumpling") to keep the knockabout, forthright figure of Michael Angelo Titmarsh in the front of the reader's mind.

MATURING YEARS, 1843–1848

As he grew more confident, Thackeray's involvement in what he was writing about became richer and deeper. In these years, too, his association with *Punch* sharpened his sense of society's shams and injustices, while the breakdown of his marriage made him more reflective about the effects of time on people and about the loves and choices that shape our lives.

In the series of short stories called *Men's Wives* (1843), which show his increased misgivings about marriage and women, we can feel a new sympathy in the characterization that clearly foreshadows a full-scale novel. "Mr. and Mrs. Frank Berry" is set in Versailles, where the narrator comes across a former school friend, now married and living in a house in the Avenue de Paris, a crumbling old pleasure dome with a grotto, a fountain, plaster-of-Paris nymphs, damp Cupids, and cracked gilt cornices. The presiding genius of this ruin, reflecting its genteel decay, is the friend's wife, Mrs. Berry, a skinny killjoy with no lips—her mouth a mere "feeble pucker" in her face. Berry is dominated by this specter, and the point of the story is the contrast between his feeble manhood and the bonny lad the narrator remembers at Slaughter House School (Charterhouse), who once vanquished Biggs, the school champion, in an epic scrap, when raspberry tarts and ginger beer changed hands prodigiously in wagers. (This fight represents an early version of that between Dobbin and Cuff in *Vanity Fair*.)

"The Ravenswing," a novelette, also anticipates Thackeray's masterpiece in numerous details, and its heroine, Morgiana, combines characteristics of both Becky and Amelia. But the imaginative heart of the piece lies in the aura of theatrical reminiscence that Thackeray weaves around the characters. Morgiana goes on the stage, and is rapturously received in *The Brigand's Bride*, an opera by Sir George Thrum (a figure based partly on Sir George Smart, one of the leading musical impresarios of the day), and Morgiana's mother, behind the bar of the Bootjack Hotel, is surrounded by mementos of early nineteenth-century dancers, evoking the wonderland of tutus and bouquets that Thackeray so loved. At the end we enter another of Thackeray's dream realms—the German Rhineland. The narrator spots Morgiana, her little boy, and her faithful old suitor, to whom she is now married, at a café in Koblenz, where the stepfather is cramming the boy with cherries and cakes—a scene replayed by Amelia, little George, and Dobbin in the "Am Rhein" chapter of *Vanity Fair*.

In violent contrast is "Dennis Haggarty's Wife," a savage piece, expressing Thackeray's hatred of his mother-in-law and exasperation at his wife's decline. Haggarty marries the daughter of a pretentious, lodging-house-haunting Irish widow, glistening with cheap baubles, and the narrator later finds him and his wife occupying a wretched cottage near Dublin. The place stinks of onions and peat smoke, and Mrs. Haggarty, now blind and ravaged by smallpox, puts on for the visitor a ghastly show of simpering affectation, waving a lace handkerchief before her scarred features, and screeching the girlish ballads with which she used to captivate Haggarty. Eventually mother and daughter take all Haggarty's money and decamp, leaving him broken with grief. Thackeray's failed marriage and lost fortune take on here, it seems, the fictional guise of cause and effect.

The hazards of wedlock occupy Thackeray in several other pieces. "Bob Robinson's First Love" (1845) is about a lad who plans to elope with his tutor's daughter until his uncle, an apoplectic, dandified little military man, dashes to the rescue in his yellow post chaise and cuts short the romance. (Major Pendennis' mission to save his nephew is clearly anticipated.) "Bluebeard's Ghost" (1843), which is about a young widow's unmerited devotion to her dead partner, looks forward to Amelia's mourning for George, and her slighted wooer, Captain Whiskerfield, with his virtues and his squint, foreshadows Dobbin. Thackeray's love for Jane Brookfield and his jealousy of her loyalty to her spouse find an outlet in this tale too, as they do in the twin stories "The Partie Fine" (1844) and "Arabella," which concern an undeserving husband and his sweet, faithful wife, who is left at home to do the sewing while he is out on a spree. "The Partie Fine," with its gas lamps, actresses, and elegant nightlife, is in effect a more sardonic and observant version of "Memorials of Gormandising."

Thackeray's interest in rogues' lives and in the eighteenth century (as exhibited in *Catherine*), his personal worries about the harmful effects of doting mothers and gentlemanly education, his fascination with gambling, and his phobia about lying Irishmen all come together in *Barry Lyndon* (1844), his most successful piece of fiction of these years. Lyndon starts out as a spoiled, naive youth, but his experiences turn him into an unscrupulous adventurer. He flees from home, thinking he has killed a man in a duel, is rooked by cardsharpers (that unavoidable Thackerayan fate), enlists, fights at Minden, finds himself press-ganged into Frederick the Great's army, becomes a professional gambler, travels round Europe running a faro bank with his uncle, returns to Ireland where he terrorizes Honoria, countess of Lyndon, into marrying him, squanders her estate, and dies in the Fleet prison of delirium tremens.

Lyndon tells his own story, and the reader has to guess at the truth through a fog of lies and boasts. But Thackeray's attitude to his antihero is enrichingly divided. He allows Lyndon real courage and spirit, and Lyndon's social criticisms (his scorn, for instance, for young diplomats: "little pink-faced boys from school with no other claim than mamma's title") reflect Thackeray's. His accounts of eighteenth-century life show Thackeray's imagina-

tion deeply stirred—the young bloods shaking their Mechlin ruffles over the green tables at faro; the brutalized soldiery, flogged into battle, their hair plastered with flour and candle grease; the dandies with rouged cheeks and apricot velvet coats and white fishskin sword-scabbards; the ladies with hoopskirts eighteen feet in circumference. Through these glamorous externals Thackeray felt that he had reentered a world that was more dashing and depraved, more cruel and courtly, than the Victorian era.

Social pretension, that bugbear of the young Thackeray, is a root evil in *Barry Lyndon*. Barry's mother dresses him like a little lord, keeps a footman, and otherwise encourages the boy's fatal ambitions. Two near-contemporary stories, *Mrs. Perkins's Ball* (1847) and *A Little Dinner at Timmins's* (1848) (which Orwell called "one of the best comic short stories ever written"), similarly attack the middle classes for getting above their station. Perkins and Timmins, both distantly related to noble persons, both allow this to seduce them into throwing grand entertainments in their ridiculously cramped suburban villas, with catastrophic results. But Thackeray's main assault on swanks and toadies comes in the *Book of Snobs* (1848 and 1852) (first published in *Punch* in 1846–1847 as *The Snobs of England*)—a scintillating indictment of English society, shot through with the *Vanity Fair* spirit. University snobs and military snobs, clerical snobs and city snobs, sporting snobs and holidaying snobs—the categories proliferate, showing us a nation of emulous dupes and fools, rotten with pride and peerage-worship. Thackeray, for all his flippancy, has his finger on the great acquisitive pulse of mid-nineteenth-century England. It is a documentary that keeps sliding sympathetically into fiction, as Thackeray fleshes out his victims with lives, loves, and personal identities. But there is no mistaking the work's radical animus. Thackeray's remedy for the ills he portrays is social equality: "the table of ranks and degrees is a lie, and should be flung into the fire." A tradesman is as good as you, and you are as good as a lord: let us be done with cringing and crawling and court circulars. That is Thackeray's message in the mid-1840's, and we can well understand why, ten years later, he had come to hate the *Book of Snobs* and said he could not bear to read a word of it.

Thackeray's social reporting for *Punch* in this period exposes some of the destitution and starvation upon which the affluent society of the *Book of*

Snobs was built. His articles show his awareness of a side of life that readers of his novels would suppose he was completely blind to. "The Curate's Walk" (November–December 1847) recounts a visit, in the company of clergyman Brookfield, to some artisan dwellings—a bookbinder's, a shoemaker's—in Great Guelph Street. In one, only the children are at home, with some pieces of dry bread and a jug of water to sustain them during the day; in another, the visitors find an emaciated woman and her shriveled baby. Thackeray's tone is uneasy, striving to retain balance, and making one or two unhappy attempts at jocularity. Dickens, less guarded in his response to such scenes, wrote to say that he had "cried most bitterly" over the article. In "Waiting at the Station" (March 1850), a companion piece, Thackeray interviews a group of poor women emigrants, off to seek a better life in Australia, and expresses his shame at the "bitter cold and hunger, constant want and unavailing labour" that have driven them out of their own country. By contrast, "A Dinner in the City" (December 1847) describes the gargantuan consumption of foodstuffs at one of the great livery companies' entertainments—the guests working their jaws in a dizzy mist of gluttony, while rich fluids stream down their chins. News of the popular revolutions of 1848 on the continent alarmed this prosperous section of the community, and Thackeray gives us a glimpse of their fright in "A Club in an Uproar" (March 1848), set in one of those bow-windowed conservative havens so favored in his later writing. He watches the members snatching the newly arrived newspapers in panic, and he notices, while listening to their talk, how bloodthirsty and oppressive fear makes them.

Thackeray was honest enough to acknowledge, though, that his own tastes and instincts, as well as his background, united him with such people, rather than with society's victims. To express his impatience with his own snobbishness while simultaneously indulging it, he invented the persona of the Fat Contributor, whose travels in England and abroad amused *Punch* readers in 1844 and 1845. The Fat Contributor's prejudices are often identical with Thackeray's, but his pomposity and egotism are also unsparingly delineated.

The same uncomfortable sense that he is alienated from the lower orders, and that they arouse his sympathy and his distaste in almost equal quantities, can be felt throughout *The Irish Sketch Book* (1843). In his tour of Ireland, Thackeray found an unprecedented display of beggary, dirt, inefficiency, idleness, superstition, idolatry, and blackguardism—which, as he well realizes, is only another way of saying that he found starvation, unemployment and their natural consequences. His confused reactions—now furious, now compassionate—are recorded with scrupulous frankness. He is "perpetually made ashamed of being happy," yet the beggars howling for his money exasperate him, and he suggests, only half humorously, that policemen should be stationed near the beauty spots to drive such "vermin" away or fling them into the sea. Meanwhile, the Irish landscape—the huge red moon over "white purple flats" at the mouth of the Shannon; the lean, solitary crags at the Giant's Causeway—keep exciting his painter's eye, though he is far from bowled over by the tourist attractions, retaining a chaffing, cockney matter-of-factness in the face of sublimity.

This also pervades his finest travel book, *Notes of a Journey from Cornhill to Grand Cairo* (1846)—the record of a Mediterranean voyage sponsored by the Peninsular and Oriental Steam Navigation Company. Offhand, haphazard, full of sun and surprises, it radiates life the more strongly because it gives its attention to undignified things—greasy food, bedbugs, primitive modes of transport—at the expense of the great buildings and works of art en route, which Thackeray tends to find tedious. Yet even when bored, he makes you feel what it was like to be there, through the brilliant scatter of impressions he records—the tawdry chapels, with their striped calico, gilt paper, and snuffling priests, in the Holy Land; the women in Smyrna, shuffling about in "black nosebags" and yellow slippers; the melon boats heaped with golden fruit on the Bosphorus. Enlivening, too, are Thackeray's robust social views—his reflections on the offensiveness of the English abroad; or his resistance to the "magic" of the Orient, which he sees as a compound of despotism, sensuality, and female enslavement. For the newcomer to Thackeray, this book is an ideal starting point: it sparkles with his vivacity, irreverence, and swift coloring.

VANITY FAIR

WHEN Thackeray talks about *Vanity Fair* (1848) in his letters, we notice an intriguing inconsistency. On the one hand, he maintains that it is a darkly moral tale, that all its characters (except William Dobbin) are meant to be "odious"—greedy, mean, and godless—and that their story should leave us "dissatisfied and unhappy," as "we ought to be with our own and all other stories." Yet writing to Jane Brookfield from Brussels, he expresses delight at revisiting the scenes these characters have frequented: "How curious it is! I believe perfectly in all those people, and feel quite an interest in the Inn in which they lived." This vacillation between imaginative involvement and satirical detachment can be readily detected in the story itself. It is one of the things that keeps a reader's interest in it fresh, and it gives Thackeray scope for the irony and the tenderness that were both natural to him.

He does not make us feel simple approval or disapproval of any of his main figures—least of all Becky Sharp, who is the most interesting character he ever created (and the most objectionable to the Victorian reading public, whose prejudice deterred him from trying anything so intelligent again). Clever, brave, underprivileged, selfish, heartless, and amoral, Becky has the unpredictable quality of a living mind. She could surprise even her creator. When Rawdon Crawley, Becky's husband, rushes in and knocks Lord Steyne down in the great discovery scene (chapter 53), Becky, though aghast, feels a thrill of admiration at seeing her husband "strong, brave, and victorious"—and this reaction, so revealing of Becky's inner needs, came to Thackeray out of the blue, causing him to slap the table and cry out, "*That is a touch of genius!*" Becky, too, expresses Thackeray's resentment against English society, especially the ruling class, as she hoodwinks the purse-proud Crawleys or triumphs over the insolent, aristocratic Bareacres (chapter 32). Her one unforgivable defect is her lack of motherly love (much worse in Thackeray's eyes—and ours—than her adultery with Lord Steyne or her murder of Jos Sedley, supposing she is guilty of these).

On the contrary, motherly love is practically Amelia Sedley's only virtue. Apart from that, she is an empty little thing, and her self-indulgent devotion to George Osborne's memory is positively annoying. But as she clings to her little son, or, having relinquished him to the Osbornes, toils half across London to see the light in his bedroom window, she shows a capacity for love that makes Becky, by comparison, seem scarcely alive at all. That Thackeray, the deserted child, who used to pray that he would dream of his mother, should make motherliness the pivot of his story suggests the depths from which its planning came.

Amelia's failings of character and intelligence, for which maternal love has to compensate, make her unworthy of Dobbin's devotion, and, when roused, he tells her this (chapter 66). Yet she has only to cry for help, and Dobbin comes running once more. Thackeray declared that such an attachment should lessen our regard for Dobbin. We should see, he told the critic Robert Bell, that Dobbin's love is "vanity," and Dobbin "a fool for his pains." No doubt Thackeray sometimes felt like that about himself, looking back on his love for Isabella; but, of course, we do not agree. We do not expect men to fall in love with "worthy" women, and, besides, we recognize that it is Dobbin's nobility that makes him value other people (George Osborne, as well as Amelia) more highly than he values himself. His character illustrates the close connection between modesty and magnanimity.

George, though not the paragon Dobbin takes him for, is not just contemptible either—or, rather, Thackeray makes us feel his youth and callowness so acutely that we blush for him at his worst moments rather than indulging in anything as simple as blame. When he boasts of the dinner he gave the Bareacres ("rather a nice thing"), or demands of Amelia at the opera ("Emmy, why didn't you have a bouquet?") in chapter 29, his vanity and his wish that his wife should do him credit expose themselves so naively that we feel almost protective in the face of such innocence. He is redeemingly capable of shame (see the end of chapter 29, describing his feelings on the eve of Waterloo), and he dies heroically.

About Rawdon Crawley our feelings are again divided. A stupid young heavy dragoon, with savage little eyes, he is also affectionate, fearless, and vulnerable. When we watch him, before Waterloo, toting up his assets, for Becky's benefit, in his big schoolboy handwriting, and going off to battle in a shabby uniform to preserve the better one for his widow; or when later he is shown playing with little Rawdon (chapter 37), cramming his nursery with toys and giving him rides on his chest while the child uses his great mustache as driving reins, we appreciate the essential healthiness of Rawdon's nature. But these winning scenes cannot disguise the fact that he is a fraud and a parasite, whose idleness and dishonesty ruin others. Raggles goes to prison, and his children are flung on the street, because Rawdon wishes to "live well on nothing a year" (chapter 37).

The impact of *Vanity Fair* comes partly from the lifelike complications of these main characters, but even more so from the swarm of minor ones. It is an affirmation of the fertility and fascination of human life, and in this respect its puritanical title (taken from John Bunyan's *Pilgrim's Progress*) is wildly inappropriate. Of course, some members of its huge cast do display the vanity of mankind's aspirations, but love and goodness are much in evidence too— witness Major and Mrs. O'Dowd (through whose shining qualities Thackeray atones for his former treatment of Irish military types); or poor Briggs, weeping over her momentos of the young writing master she loved at eighteen; or tough old Macmurdo, sticking by Rawdon in his distress and touched by his love for his boy; or the young stockbrokers who, when Sedley's effects go under the hammer, buy up his spoons and forks and send them to Mrs. Sedley—a gesture that reduces the old man to tears. Even the wholly worthless characters are not viewed morosely but with keen enjoyment. They are either spectacularly dissolute, like Lord Steyne, or comic, like Jos Sedley, or both, like old Sir Pitt Crawley.

Thackeray surveys this variegated crowd with an exuberant but penetrating gaze. He shows us how little his human beings understand their true motives and how much selfishness is involved even in their kindest acts. His most searing portrait is of old Osborne, a baffled, tigerish man whose one generous feeling, his love for his son, is inextricably enmeshed with self-regard—so that he is horribly torn, when George dies, between grief that he will see his son no more and rage that his desire to avenge himself on the disobedient boy should have been balked.

By combining a broad canvas with intricate personal studies like this, *Vanity Fair* is able to perform one of the main functions of the novel form—it helps its readers to cope with life. As temporary inhabitants of an unknowably complex world, we are all (if we think at all) threatened by feelings of insignificance and self-obliteration. The novelist's task is to save us from this abyss by enthroning us at the perceptual center of an alternative but recognizable world that, through his guidance, we can dominate and understand, and in which we may gain the knowledge and confidence to survive when we return to the world of actuality. The multiplication of minor figures in *Vanity Fair* serves the purpose of making the fictional world seem as profuse and disorganized as the world in which we live, and so it increases the illusion of control we get when we are able to fit it inside our heads.

The other purpose of Thackeray's crowd of extras is that they seem to authenticate by their presence the main action. Thackeray invents a history for the Gaunt family (chapter 47); for instance, he shows us Gaunt Square with its statue in Roman costume of the eighteenth-century Lord Gaunt, who fought at Minden; tells us of Lord George Gaunt, "the brilliant dandy diplomatist of the Congress of Vienna," now locked in a madhouse and playing with children's toys; and pretends that there is a present-day Lord Steyne who lives in Naples. And he concocts this whole fascinating rigmarole (taking up page after page and quite unconnected with the story) simply to supply the Lord Steyne who crosses Becky's path with credentials of actual existence. Equally typical of the method is the family called Scape—prosperous Anglo-Indians who encounter financial troubles and have to go and live in Boulogne—who occupied, we are told, Jos's Gillespie Street house before he moved in (chapter 60). Jos's move is a minor incident, but Thackeray invents a whole family of displaced persons to give it verisimilitude. The principle behind this prolific realism is not just that the more lies you tell the more you will be believed but also that the most circumstantial lies succeed best.

This brings us to Thackeray's treatment of the Battle of Waterloo. By selecting a major historical event as his topic, a novelist—provided he can carry it off—adds greatly to the stature of his book, since he creates for his readers the illusion that they are viewing, from a commanding eminence, a decisive moment in the world's destiny. In real life, wars and revolutions sweep over individuals, leaving them with only a vague sense of the impersonal forces that have engulfed them. This unregarding impetus of history is one of Thackeray's themes in *Vanity Fair*. When the eagles of Napoleon Bonaparte disembark at Cannes, they bring ruin to the little corner of Bloomsbury where Amelia and her family live (chapter 18). But the novelist, if he is sufficiently gifted and intrepid, can turn the tables on history, treating it as masterfully as it treats us and restoring to his readers a sense of superiority to historical events. The greatness of *Vanity Fair* accrues to a considerable degree from the magnitude of its subject; and not until *Denis Duval* (his last and unfinished novel) did Thackeray again choose a subject (the French Revolution) that might have sustained a comparable achievement.

But a big subject brings perils too, increasing the risk of falsity and bombast; and for Thackeray there was an additional problem of artistic integrity, for having no personal experience of battle he thought it would be bogus to write about it. To launch into scenes of shot and shell would be to usurp the glamor of militarism without its dangers, like the clownish Jos Sedley. Accordingly, he decided on a behind-the-scenes view of hostilities—a wartime version of the backstage life he always found so appealing (chapter 30). We see Peggy O'Dowd getting her husband's kit together; the distraught Emmy holding the blood-red sash to her bosom as George packs. We watch the troops march away; hear the thunder of the cannon; see the fugitives and the cartloads of wounded arriving back in Brussels. But of the battle itself we hear only later, in hints and anecdotes.

By this means Thackeray remains true to his central idea, which was to show the effects of war upon the noncombatants. He also gains greatly in suspense, achieving that muted, devastating end to chapter 32—the news of George's death—that is one of the supreme moments in English fiction. In this part of the book, too, we find Thackeray's most telling use of minor characters. Through them he creates the impression of the panic-stricken activity on the battle's edge. In fact, the subsidiary figures he introduces for this purpose are remarkably few: Isador, Jos's servant, fancying what a dash he will cut in his master's lace coat after the French victory; the fugitive Belgian hussar, sweetheart of the Osbornes' cook, who arrives in the kitchen spreading alarm; the Bareacres, fuming and trembling in their immobilized carriage. But through these few, vividly caught figures, and the clutter of circumstantial detail around them, Thackeray conveys, in chapter 32, the bustle of a whole threatened city.

The idea that *Vanity Fair* was not prefigured at all by Thackeray's earlier writings will not, as we have seen, stand much scrutiny. Its satire, and the broad range of its characterization, which make it virtually the portrait of a nation, connect it clearly with the *Book of Snobs;* its continental scenarios reflect enthusiasms Thackeray had long been voicing; and the choice of Becky as a central figure reminds us of the rogues' lives (*Catherine, Barry Lyndon*) that had intrigued him for some years. After *Vanity Fair,* he never again placed a character so dubious, tainted, and controversial in a leading role, and that is an indication of the great change that came over his fiction.

But though hindsight allows us to identify the growth points of *Vanity Fair* in the miscellaneous

productions that preceded it, its advent is still astonishing. We should never have guessed that Thackeray was on the point of writing a masterpiece so ripe, sustained, and serious, or so rich in characters who overcome their creator's criticisms and achieve a life of their own. Had Thackeray followed *Vanity Fair* with four or five books of equal quality, he would be England's greatest novelist. In the event, enjoyable though much of his later work is, he never reached such heights again.

PENDENNIS *AND* THE NEWCOMES

The History of Pendennis (1848–1850) and *The Newcomes* (1853–1855) are appropriately treated together. Characters from one recur in the other, so that they may be said to depict the same extended social circle. Thackeray grew fonder, as time went on, of linking his stories together in this way. Already in *Barry Lyndon* (chapter 5) he had reintroduced Galgenstein, the German recruiting officer, from *Catherine,* and in his later works his reversion to old names and faces becomes almost obsessive. This has struck some critics as a sentimental indulgence. But it is more intelligently seen as a bid to extend the authenticity of his fictional world by giving us a fuller understanding of the lives and ancestries of the figures who pass through his pages, so that our grasp of social complications and the interactions of class and personality may be deepened.

After *Vanity Fair,* the chief disappointment for readers of these two novels is Thackeray's apparent loss of satirical edge. As we have seen, his retreat from satire was quite deliberate, and his attempt to appeal instead to the hearts and tear ducts of his Victorian public, in such scenes as the deaths of Helen Pendennis and Colonel Newcome, is, for a modern audience, distinctly trying. But though he made his fictions softer, Thackeray had not, essentially, changed very much. He hid his satirical awareness rather than lost it, and the harsh comments he offers about his fictional characters in private correspondence can surprise readers who have taken the cordial tone of the novels at face value. We find him confessing, in letters, that he does not like "dearest Laura," and that Arthur Pendennis' admiration for her shows "he is a weak character and led by women." Such opinions should encourage us to look more suspiciously at the post-*Vanity Fair* novels, and consider ways of reading them that are less flattering to the participants than Thackeray's generally bland treatment might suggest.

Pendennis and *The Newcomes* (along with *The Virginians* and *Philip*) are all stories about a youth of generous instincts (Pen, Clive, Harry, Philip) who is corrupted by relatives and by snobbery, and develops into a cynic or a wastrel or both. Thackeray, looking back, felt that this was how he had developed in his younger days, and all the stories have a greater or lesser autobiographical ingredient.

Pen's corrupters are his mother and his uncle, Major Pendennis. Chapter 2 is important to our understanding of the story, for there we learn that Pen's father was an apothecary in Bath, who made money, bought a small estate and bogus family portraits, married Helen Thistlewood, "a very distant relative of the noble house of Bareacres" (the abominable Bareacres of *Vanity Fair*), and set up as a gentleman. Social pretension is, accordingly, instilled in Pen as a child (as it was in the young Barry Lyndon). The "vice" of his mother (the Bareacres' relative) is, we are told, pride in her family, and this "unfortunate superstition and idol-worship" caused "a great deal of the misfortune which befell" her son. "Vice" is hardly a word we should associate with the angelic mother-figure Helen Pendennis, as she is later developed; but this clear early statement alerts us to the satirical element in Thackeray's initial conception of the character, which his subsequent sanctification rather glossed over.

Major Pendennis is an even greater snob than Helen, and together they break off, in the first part of the story, Pen's "unsuitable" attachment to an actress, Miss Fotheringay. Thackeray does not simplify the social issues here by putting Helen and the major in the wrong. The match with Miss Fotheringay really would have been a mistake, because she is coarse and stupid, and her father is a drunk. Yet Pen's passion for her is genuine and has all the agony of first love. He never, in the rest of the novel, feels anything so deeply again. The barrier between the middle and the lower classes, Thackeray wants to show us, is sustained by pride and snobbery, yet it also reflects—and perpetuates—real social differences, so that if the middle class step across it they find themselves among people whose speech and habits repel them. It is this kind of uncomfortable truth, distasteful to our liberal instincts, that the later Thackeray is keen to bring out.

There is a barrier between the middle and the upper classes, too, and Pen tries to cross this next. Encouraged to think well of himself by his mother and uncle, he mixes with aristocrats at university, neglects his studies, runs up debts, and leaves in disgrace, unqualified for any employment (just as Thackeray had done). Thackeray condemns his "wicked extravagance and idleness," but he also presents Pen's profligacy as the overflow of a free and generous spirit, which scorns anything mean. As in the Fotheringay episode, Pen's natural impulses are shown to run counter to cautious, worldly class considerations, and they land him in a mess.

This pattern is repeated in the affair with Fanny Bolton, daughter of a lodgekeeper and Pen's second lower-class love. This time, however, conscious of the difference in their stations and hardened by his experience of the world, he feels ashamed of his passion, suppresses it, contracts a fever, and almost dies—being pulled through only by the devoted nursing of Fanny, who is dismissed ignominiously, like a presumptuous servant, when Helen Pendennis arrives on the scene.

This is the novel's emotional climax, and Thackeray discusses at some length (chapter 51) whether Pen was justified in stifling his fondness for a "penniless girl out of the kitchen." He is sarcastic about the "respectable" persons who will applaud Pen's circumspection, and he suggests that a blind, self-sacrificing love on Pen's part might have been nobler. But in the end Thackeray comes to no decision: "in fine, let this be a reserved point, to be settled by the individual moralist who chooses to debate it." This cannot help but strike us as shuffling and equivocal. For if Thackeray is not prepared to say that Pen ought to have flouted respectability, then by what right is he sarcastic at respectability's expense? He wishes, it seems, to remain comfortably ensconced in his middle-class values, but to have the pleasure of poking fun at them at the same time.

Our suspicion that Thackeray's protests against class barriers are insincere is deepened by the support for them that Pen's friend George Warrington expresses. A ludicrous concoction of bluff heartiness, Warrington is evidently intended by Thackeray as an absolutely dependable spokesman on social and moral issues, and he gives it firmly as his opinion (chapter 61) that a "high-souled man" doesn't associate with housemaids, laundresses, or the like—or, if he does, "bitterly rues it afterwards." What's more, Warrington has reason to know, for he reveals (chapter 57) that he married, at eighteen, a woman of "low degree," discovered too late that she was a "boor," and eventually had to settle all his money on her and her children, provided that they would "hide themselves away." This melodramatic flashback is the only attempt the novel makes to examine the actual results of marrying out of one's class, and its handling of the question necessarily appears evasive by consequence.

Evasive, too, is the story's winding-up. By a crude plot mechanism Pen is rescued at the last moment from the natural consequences of his worldliness. We see him growing more and more cynical, sucking up to aristocrats whom he secretly despises, and aspiring to a seat in Parliament. But Blanche Amory, the rich girl whom he plans to marry—though he does not love her—is opportunely revealed as the daughter of a returned convict, and Pen, in a final flurry of pseudoreligious uplift, weds instead his stepsister Laura, who appears as a sort of reincarnation of his mother ("arms as tender as Helen's once more enfolded him," in chapter 74).

The impression *Pendennis* leaves, then, is of halfhearted social criticism, coupled with a genial but condescending attitude to its characters (particularly those representing the world of journalism—Bacon, Bungay, Shandon) that contrasts with the sharper vision of *Vanity Fair*.

From a technical viewpoint, *The Newcomes* illustrates even better than *Pendennis* the extraordinarily roundabout manner of narration that Thackeray developed in his fiction—the wanderings to and fro in time, the side-turnings and interpolations, the letters from people we know nothing about, the passersby who somehow catch Thackeray's attention and are fascinatedly pursued far away from the main story. These tactics can exasperate readers unprepared to trust themselves to Thackeray's "discursive muse," but their purpose is to enhance realism by creating the impression of an actual world of bustle and gossip, flooding over and around the foreground characters, into which Thackeray is free to dip at any point.

In subject matter, *The Newcomes*, like *Pendennis*, is largely about the styles and conventions that separate people from one another. Its most touching scene (chapter 21) shows Colonel Newcome, bewildered by Clive's avant-garde artistic tastes and feeling estranged from his son, standing before the pictures in the National Gallery "desperately praying to comprehend them." Mostly, though, the separating factor the novel examines is not taste or age, as here,

but class. It resembles *Pendennis*, again, in warning its readers at the start that the class aspirations of its characters are bogus: they are "jackdaws" in "peacocks' feathers" (chapter 1). The name "Newcome" itself suggests their parvenu status. The father of Colonel Newcome and his two half brothers was, we learn, in trade as a cloth merchant.

When this humble origin is kept in mind, the half brothers Sir Brian and Hobson can readily be seen as social climbers, especially the former, who (like Pendennis' father) marries an aristocratic girl (the granddaughter, we are told, of old Lady Kew, who is sister to Lord Steyne of *Vanity Fair*). It is the pride of Sir Brian's family that generates catastrophe in the book. His son Barnes is an odious dandy, whose lofty ways infuriate the simple, honest colonel; and Barnes's sister, the lovely Ethel, is destined by her family to marry the young Lord Kew—another bitter pill for the colonel, for he wants her to marry his son Clive, seeing quite well that the two young people are mutually attracted. As the colonel has to stomach more and more indignities from his wealthy relations, hatred and thirst for revenge gradually take possession of him, and he engages recklessly in the Indian moneymaking schemes that bring him to ruin.

Thackeray does not succeed, though, in showing the poisoning of the colonel's heart convincingly. We are informed that "hate and suspicion had mastered him" (chapter 64), but in fact he remains, to our eyes, the rather poignant old duffer he has always been. The Thackeray of *Vanity Fair*, who showed poverty embittering old Sedley and his wife, would have been equal to the task, but the softer, new-style Thackeray cannot bring himself to do it.

More successfully handled is the corruption of Clive by his loving and munificent father. Clive's wealthy indolence and his toying with an artistic career are described so indulgently by Thackeray (who was remembering his own youth) that we are deceived into thinking he approves. And of course, in a way, he does. He warms nostalgically to Clive's hedonism, while recognizing that it is morally indefensible. Gradually we are brought to see that Clive is a spoiled, bored, aimless lad, a parasitic "capitalist" (as Thackeray calls him in chapter 50), with no function, no talent, and no inclination to earn his living. He has not even the energy to choose a wife for himself: his father does it for him, marrying him off (partly to spite Ethel) to the colorless

Rosey Mackenzie. So this novel, unlike *Pendennis*, does not shirk the disastrous marriage toward which the logic of the plot leads the hero, and the subsequent domestic scenes (chapters 73–75, 78–80) are the most powerful Thackeray had written since *Vanity Fair*, with Clive and his father being hounded by Rosey's coarse, tyrannical mother (based, needless to say, on Thackeray's own mother-in-law).

These scenes alone would make *The Newcomes* superior to *Pendennis*. True, it is sometimes evasive, like that novel. We are never quite sure, for example, how culpable the colonel's pride in social rank is meant to appear. His lofty patronage of J. J., the artistic genius whose father is a butler, seems intended as amiable stuffiness, less blameworthy, somehow, than the pride of his half brothers. With certain, favored individuals Thackeray is prepared, it seems, to take an indulgent view of such snobbery. But this, though inconsistent, has the advantage of allowing him a richer sense of the mixture of good and bad within people. In this respect, Lord Kew is one of the triumphs of Thackeray's later art, for in Kew he shows us how a man can be noble-minded and generous, yet also dangerously wrong on every social issue. Kew defends money-marriage (chapter 30). He puts a stop to the affair between penniless Jack Belsize and Clara Pulleyn—though they love each other—and he supports Clara's family in marrying her to Barnes Newcome, whom she hates (chapter 29). When the marriage comes to grief (chapter 58), Kew's ineptitude appears plainly. He is also shown up by Ethel. For when he reprimands her for flirting at the ball (chapter 34), she confronts him with a letter giving details of his own dissolute youth, and having exposed his double standard of morality, she breaks off her engagement to him. In these transactions Kew is stupid, unjust, and hypocritical, but Thackeray's skill lies in presenting him at the same time as gallant and honorable. He is a true product of his class, reflecting its virtues and its faults, which are inextricably intertwined.

The complications surrounding Kew also bring into the novel its most exciting minor characters—the shady, scandalous, arty set headed by the Duchesse d'Ivry (chapters 31, 33–34, 36). Some of them, we are told, knew Becky in her Gaunt House days. They breathe the atmosphere of *Vanity Fair*, and contrast sparklingly with the unfortunately more preponderant characters (Pen, Laura, Warrington) who insert themselves into *The Newcomes* from *Pendennis*.

HENRY ESMOND *AND* THE VIRGINIANS

THACKERAY's fascination with the eighteenth century, which these two novels indulge, was a mixture of attraction and repulsion. Years back, in some of his early *Times* (London) reviews, he had remarked that there was no "meaner page in history" than that period. He envisaged it as a garish cavalcade, rife with corruption and intrigue. To the Victorians, eighteenth-century gentlefolk—duelists, murderers, rakes—must seem, he confessed in his *English Humourists* lectures (1853), as savage as ancient Britons. Yet this wildness added spice to his notion of the "grand Old World," where gentlemen were still gentlemen and the leveling effect of railways and parliamentary democracy had not yet been felt. In those days, he records half-wistfully in *Henry Esmond* (book I, chapter 12), men of breeding would spend a quarter of their time at cards, and another at drink, and could often write no more than their names. They rode roughshod over justice. Lord Mohun, Lord Castlewood's slayer, is released unpunished; and the same day, we are reminded, a woman is hanged at Tyburn for shoplifting (book II, chapter 2). Such enormities gave Thackeray a pleasurable frisson, allowing him to escape, in fancy, from the moral restrictions imposed by civilization.

One interest in *Henry Esmond* (1852), then, is that it introduces us to yet another Victorian fantasy world, as liberating for its inventor as Tennyson's Arthurian Britain or Browning's Italy. A further thing *Henry Esmond* can teach us, alas, is how transient literary judgments are. Though the book seems, as George Orwell put it, "barely readable" nowadays, it was for long considered a masterpiece. George Saintsbury pronounced Beatrix "the one complete woman in English prose fiction." Most moderns would presumably award that title to Molly Bloom. But even if we could not expect that of Saintsbury, it still seems astonishing that he should have imagined Beatrix a worthier claimant than Charlotte Brontë's or George Eliot's heroines—or, indeed, more deserving than Becky Sharp. Beatrix is, in fact, a purely masculine confection, got up to appease the male taste for willful, pettish young women. The book as a whole has all the falsity of costume drama, without the thrills—for Thackeray affects the reserve of a polished Augustan gentleman, and the various campaigns Esmond fights in are relayed to us in self-deprecating summaries that studiously exclude anything that might excite.

It is worth remembering, though, that Thackeray said, apropos of *Henry Esmond*, "it is the unwritten part of books that would be the most interesting." If, taking the hint, we look beneath the surface of this austere and courtly narrative, we come upon orgies of wish-fulfillment, as extravagant as anything we could find in pantomime or fairy tale. Esmond, the waif who is really a lord's son, belongs to the world of goosegirl princesses, and he is also Oedipus—a dashing Oedipus in wig and regimentals, who weds his mother and prospers.

To take these themes separately—first, the sexual one. When little orphaned Henry Esmond, twelve years old, first sets eyes on Rachel, she is a dazzling vision of motherhood, with two children of her own and a grand, haughty husband, Viscount Castlewood. Henry loves her as a son, and she is repeatedly identified as his surrogate "mother." But as time goes on the relative ages of son and mother are reversed, so that he becomes senior. Already by book I, chapter 9 he is acting as Rachel's "tutor"; he seems "older" than her by book II, chapter 6; and by book III, chapter 4 he feels like the "grandfather" of the whole family. So when he marries Rachel at the end (when, if we stop to work it out, we find that he is thirty-five and she forty-three), he seems a rather mature husband for her, and she looks younger than her own daughter. Clearly something perverse and subliminal is afoot here, such as is normally countenanced only in the confused, private world of dreams. Thackeray's ardent love for his mother, with its crisis of early separation and blissful reunion, has procured satisfaction for itself within the innocuous confines of a historical novel, leaving evident traces of the miraculous and the unnatural. Victorian reviewers were quick to scent something indecent about Henry's marriage. It "affects us somewhat like a marriage with his own mother," objected the *Athenaeum*.

Mrs. Carmichael-Smyth's suspicious vigilance in the matter of the governesses Thackeray hired for his daughters perpetuated an element of sexual jealousy in the mother-son relationship, which is reflected in Rachel's anger about Nancy (book I, chapter 8), as it had been in Helen Pendennis' treatment of Fanny Bolton. Meanwhile, young Thackeray's guilt over his resentment of Carmichael-Smyth (he thought his mother's second marriage "immodest" and was "disgusted" to hear his stepfather snoring in her room) finds fictional atonement in Henry's noble behavior toward Rachel's husband, Castlewood. Here, too, the resolution of difficulties has the perfection and self-glorification of a child's dream. Though the stepfather is unworthy, the child fights and is wounded on his behalf (book I, chapter 14); the "mother" unfairly blames the child for her husband's death (book II, chapter 1), but kneels and "worships" him when she discovers the truth (book III, chapter 2).

In the region of social, as of sexual, relations the story offers gratifications normally available only in dream or daydream. For Henry discovers (book I, chapter 14) that he is the real Lord Castlewood—the legitimate son of the third viscount. Out of consideration for Rachel and her children, though, who would be disinherited if he claimed the title, he conceals his identity, experiencing a "glow of righteous happiness" as he does so. When his secret comes out, the aristocrats who have slighted him do him homage. Rachel's daughter, the haughty Beatrix, previously scornful of humble Colonel Esmond's advances, repents her mistake; her betrothed, the great Duke of Hamilton, unbends, deeming it an "honour" to know Esmond; and the foppish, dissolute son of James II, arriving on the scene, to make his unsuccessful bid for the English throne, appears, as Rachel's son Frank exclaims, far less like a king than Esmond (book III, chapter 9). *Henry Esmond* represents, then, the acme of middle-class wish-fulfillment, for it offers a hero who is nobler than the nobles, yet voluntarily remains a commoner. Esmond, at the end, emigrates to the New World, rejecting the institutions of monarchy and peerage altogether.

The Virginians (1857–1859) continues the story. Its twin heroes, Harry and George Warrington, are Henry Esmond's grandsons, born in America, and when they return to England they find themselves treated with mercenary calculation by the present inheritors of the Castlewood estates. Of all Thackeray's longer fictions, this is the least successful. The characters do not gain our sympathy, and their activities seem mostly trivial. Thackeray's eighteenth-century idyll has gone sour: the round of drinking, betting, and courtliness now strikes even its chronicler as tedious. The English historical figures, in their period dress, are pale ghosts of the troop who once reveled and fought in *Barry Lyndon*, and the American scenes are featureless voids. Thackeray is sick of writing novels, and admits it (book I, chapter 18). He dawdled over the plot, so that the American War of Independence (with George fighting for the English, and Harry for the Americans) has to be polished off in a couple of chapters at the end, instead of supplying a central feature.

The plan of the book rests on a number of contrasts. The raw young world of the Virginians comes up against the dissipated routines of the English aristocracy. Savage forests, Indians, and scalpings give way to powder, brocade, and wax candles. The twins themselves are markedly dissimilar. Harry, dashing and soldierly, is corrupted by English life, drinking and gambling his way to a debtors' prison before the end of the first half. George, more thoughtful, marries into the kindly Lambert family, who stand for middle-class virtue in opposition to the arrogant Castlewoods. Meanwhile, in the American scenes, George, Harry, and their mother, Rachel (widowed daughter of Henry Esmond), bring the pride and exclusiveness of the English class system into contention with a sturdy, rebellious land. Rachel, a Negro-whipping despot, retains an English upper-class contempt for books and brains, as against blood, and spurns Harry for eventually marrying Hetty Mountain, her housekeeper's daughter. Set against Rachel is her neighbor George Washington, whom young George absurdly challenges to a duel when he suspects that he is presumptuously aspiring to Rachel's hand.

These contrasts might have endued the novel with genuine conflict and variety—yet they are the qualities it conspicuously lacks. Thackeray cannot manage the switches of viewpoint such a plan would demand. His tone remains equable, lofty, and complacent. He applauds the lordly ways of his young gentlemen—as when Harry treats the lawyer Draper with open contempt (book I, chapters 46–48), or when George is deliberately offensive to Garrick, on the grounds that he is merely an actor (book II, chapter 31). Such displays of class distinction warm Thackeray's heart now. He no longer even pretends to deplore them, as he did in *Pendennis*. On the contrary, he disparages, by comparison, modern egalitarianism, declaring that he finds it objectionable to be hailed as a fellow author by "Tom Garbage" (book I, chapter 43). The defiant impudence of this social comment (which could be matched in the flaunted snobbishness of a twentieth-century reactionary like Evelyn Waugh) is ultimately an expression of wounded feeling, traceable in Thackeray's case to upset over the Garrick Club affair and to resentment at his own obligation to turn out novels—by now a hated chore. What he could seldom bring himself to investigate was the contradiction between his dislike of aristocratic pride (as exhibited in this novel by the Castlewoods) and his approval of middle-class pride (as exhibited by Harry, George, and himself).

But some things worthy of Thackeray can be salvaged from *The Virginians*. The book improves, the further we get from the main story. The incidental characters have more life than the central ones—hook-nosed Mrs. Quiggett, for example, laughing her strident laugh "like a venerable old cockatoo," till her ribs seem to jingle; or Museau, the French officer who helps George to escape, and who plays an asthmatic flute, while dreaming of his native Normandy and tripes à la mode de Caen.

Among the Castlewoods, Maria, the woman who inveigles Harry into a liaison, bears the closest relation to Thackeray's deeper fears and obsessions. Being considerably older than Harry, she is the menacing counterpart of the mother-bride celebrated in *Henry Esmond*. Thackeray transforms her into a siren—eyes cold as fishponds—dragging men to the depths and crunching their bones (book I, chapter 18). This horror (a recurrent one with Thackeray) is compounded by the offensive detailing of Maria's physique. Her teeth are allegedly false (whether they are or not becomes an important factor in the intrigue), and when she is taken sick in the coach (book I, chapter 20), she visibly decays, her eyelids growing wrinkled and her yellow cheeks betraying their metallic streaks of rouge. The contemplation of female decomposition leads Thackeray to one of his greatest pieces of associative writing (the penultimate paragraph of book I, chapter 26), where women and love merge with ashes, corpses, and ghouls, dead limbs stick out from sofa cushions, and death's-head moths flutter over winding sheets.

The mood of generalized reverie in this passage, turning from a single story to muse upon the countless other stories that might be told, became increasingly congenial to Thackeray. Its inherent expansiveness was one factor that gradually unfitted him for the novelist's task, because it made him impatient of any single novel's confines.

LAST YEARS

Roundabout Papers (1860–1863), which Thackeray started to write when he undertook the editorship of the *Cornhill* magazine, provided the ideal medium for his wandering, later mood. They are full of nostalgia. He remembers his boyhood and the incidentals that are, for children as for writers, all-important: the jam tarts and brandyballs, the treasured marbles and pencil cases, the stagecoach rides. He muses upon his passion for pantomimes (which he never outgrew) and upon the vanished ballet dancers and opera singers—Marie Taglioni, Maria Caradori, Pauline Duvernay, and lovely Ronzi de Begnis—who shimmered through his youthful dreams. He remembers being behind the scenes at the opera in 1828 and seeing the great Henriette Sontag let her hair fall over her shoulders, ready for her murder scene with Domenico Donzelli in *Otello;* and further back, he remembers the day George IV was crowned, and how he sat reading in the summerhouse at his great-grandmama's, in a town that might have come out of a Jane Austen novel; and further back still, lies that aching memory of a small boy parting from his mother on the river steps at Calcutta, before he had seen England at all.

There are loving evocations of his travels in Europe and America: Paris; Weimar, where as a youth he met Goethe; the little city of Chur in the Grisons, with its vines and great moldering gates; New Orleans in springtime, when the orchards flush with peachblossom, and sweet herbs sprout to flavor the juleps. The Low Countries, the setting for much of his greatest novel, have a special hold over him. His painter's eye delights in their wide landscapes—the pea-green canals appear so full that a pailful of water would overset them. And in their galleries are the masterpieces of Peter Paul Rubens and Rembrandt, which he has stood before for hours.

These subjects jostle together with a host of other chance interests, so that we seem to watch Thackeray riffling aimlessly but wistfully through a lifetime's joys and sorrows. On social questions he takes, as we might expect, an amused, tolerant line. The essay "On Ribbons" starts out as if it were going to advocate the abolition of titles and decorations, but by the end Thackeray is content that the "Ornamental Classes" (as he calls the aristocracy) should retain their splendors. In "On a Chalk Mark on the Door" he again upholds social divisions, and does it

again with the wry humor of a man who recognizes that in an ideal world things would be different. It is natural, he says, that servants should hang together, tell lies on behalf of their fellows, and adopt a hypocritical air before their masters. Indeed, that is what is required of them, for if servants were to speak their minds, few employers would find it palatable. We must realize, he observes, that servants have their own dependents and loyalties in "the vast, silent, poverty-stricken world outside your comfortable kitchen fire, the world of darkness, and hunger, and miserable cold, and dank, flagged cellars, and huddled straw, and rags, in which pale children are swarming." Thackeray sees how guilty and fragile are the privileges of his own class: it is part of his realism.

The Four Georges (1860), another product of this Indian summer of Thackeray's genius, shares the musing tone of the *Roundabout Papers.* Though a historical work, describing the origins of the Hanoverian line and the manners of English society from the reign of George I to that of George IV, it has the imaginative breadth of fiction and the informality of personal monologue. Thackeray looks back over the revolutions that, almost within living memory, have changed his world—the American Revolution, the French Revolution, and the "silent revolution" of early nineteenth-century England, which has brought industrialization, created the urban mass with its political discontents, and inaugurated the conflict between capital and labor. Thackeray is not concerned to analyze the social implications of all this: his brain was not analytic. Instead, he spreads before us a patchwork of a departed age—the glamor and bustle, the cards and coaches, the flaring lights and gilding of the "vast, busy, brilliant" society. This is Thackeray's last visit to the eighteenth century (except for the unfinished *Denis Duval*), and his divided feelings about it are more acute than ever. He deplores its depravity, its flaunting vice, its brutality to the common people. He declares himself appalled by its excesses. Yet he also fancies that it was a "merrier" England, and we cannot miss the enchantment in his accounts of that "brilliant, jigging, smirking Vanity Fair." It seems, curiously, closer to him than the Victorian age. As he grew older, he lived increasingly in the past, and his own youth—affluent and carefree—seemed to merge with the eighteenth-century world. He had, after all, grown up under the last of the Georges. He had known a lady, he tells us, who had been patted on the head by George I and had knocked on Dr. Johnson's door. His celebration of that bygone era is, in the last resort, personal and possessive. That is why his denunciations of it are so tinged with love.

This quality of involvement, which makes him see and feel the pros and cons deeply, reminds us of *Vanity Fair*, and *The Four Georges* is in some ways his richest achievement since that novel. But the most fascinating (and the most undervalued) of his late works is *Lovel the Widower* (1860), which recasts in the form of a novel (or, rather, of a complex narrative monologue) an unsuccessful play Thackeray had written, *The Wolves and the Lamb*. Like the *Roundabout Papers* and *The Four Georges*, *Lovel the Widower* escapes from the restrictions of the novel form, which Thackeray had come to find oppressive. It does so partly by keeping its characters somewhat flat, so that they belong to fable or burlesque rather than novel, but chiefly by enfolding them within the bewilderingly prolific stream-of-consciousness of the narrator, Mr. Batchelor, who wanders backward and forward in time, and who surrounds Fred Lovel's story in a radiant mist of his own memories and regrets.

Batchelor has, of course, much in common with Thackeray—or, rather, with the composite, fantasized Thackeray who lives in and through his stories. He has had an unhappy love affair with Glorvina O'Dowd (the girl who angles for Dobbin in *Vanity Fair*); a friend of his youth was Warrington (from *Pendennis*); another was Honeyman (from *The Newcomes*). His career (misspent college days, extravagance, debts, early struggles for a living) is a representative one, combining elements from Thackeray's own with those of his various heroes. We seem to have penetrated to the substrata of Thackeray's imagination and to be stumbling on fragments and figures we have met before in other guises. For example, Batchelor's landlord, Captain Prior, a drunken ex-paymaster in the queen of Portugal's service who is now a clerk to a coal merchant, is a battered mutation of Howard Walker from "The Ravenswing" in *Men's Wives*.

The story combines two themes that have always attracted Thackeray—the scheming female with a bohemian past (Becky) and the love of a gentleman for a lower-class girl (Miss Fotheringay and Fanny Bolton). But these themes are given a new, socially emancipating turn. For this time the scheming female wins, and the gentleman marries her, defying snobbish objections. Elizabeth Prior, the heroine, has

been a dancer, twirling in spangles in the corps de ballet at the Prince's Theatre, and then traipsing home to cook mutton broth for her worthless old pa. She has lived by her wits, picking up French and Italian and becoming a governess in the family of the wealthy widower Lovel. Batchelor and Lovel's butler, Dick Bedford, both fall for her, but she keeps them on a string and succeeds in marrying her employer, to the horror of his mother-in-law, Lady Baker. Batchelor ends up feeling cowardly and classbound, for he hesitated when he might have won Elizabeth; and he is conscious of his inferiority to Dick Bedford, who knocks down a relative of Lovel's for pestering her. Bedford was modeled on Thackeray's own butler, Samuel James, a widely read, self-educated man, whom Thackeray much admired and, according to his daughter, treated rather as a friend than as a servant.

The Adventures of Philip on His Way Through the World (1861–1862), the most closely autobiographical of his novels, handles the class question more warily. It is a continuation of *A Shabby Genteel Story*, narrated by Arthur Pendennis. Philip, the son of Dr. Firmin, is a typical Thackerayan young gent —a high-handed but noble-minded fellow who loses his fortune, has to drudge at journalism for a living, and yet feels he is a cut above the people he works for. His life in Paris, wooing of Charlotte, and hostilities with his mother-in-law are all richly atmospheric parts of the novel drawn from Thackeray's personal memories. A key figure in the fiction is Caroline Gann, the girl Dr. Firmin seduced in *A Shabby Genteel Story*, who is now a sick-nurse. We are told she had a baby by Dr. Firmin, and it died. She nurses Philip through a childhood illness and is seized with the delusion that he is really her child. Accordingly, she sacrifices her welfare for him and conceals the fact that Dr. Firmin went through a form of marriage with her, so as not to deprive Philip of his inheritance. Further, when the blackmailing Tufton Hunt, who wants Caroline to expose Dr. Firmin, gets hold of a document Firmin has forged, Caroline steals it from him and destroys it, thus preserving the good name of the Firmins.

Philip does not know of Caroline's sacrifice and treats her with kindly condescension, as a natural inferior. Moreover she acquiesces in this. When the Pendennises, who are Philip's friends, offer her a home, she refuses, insisting she is not fit company for them. "My parents did not give me the education you have had ma'am," she tells Mrs. Pendennis, and she addresses the Pen children as "Miss" and "Master" (book II, chapter 2). We are clearly meant to regard this as commendable and realistic on her part. Pen and his wife agree in private that Caroline, "good as she is," is not a "fitting companion" for Philip (book II, chapter 12), and it is her peculiar virtue, in Philip's eyes, that she "makes no pretence at equality" (book II, chapter 14). Caroline is thus an ideal lower-class person, from the middle-class viewpoint, for she is loyal yet subservient. She dies an appropriately selfless death, catching an infection from a patient she is nursing (book II, chapter 23).

The importance of all this is that it reveals as sham Thackeray's intermittent regrets about Philip's "hauteur and arrogance." For his hauteur and arrogance consist only in maintaining that lower-class people, such as his employer, the self-educated Mugford (book II, chapter 14), are not fit to be his friends—and this, as the Caroline episode demonstrates, is the novel's official view. Thackeray also depicts Philip as a sturdy egalitarian, on the grounds that he refuses to kowtow to Lord Ringwood. To Philip, we are assured, "all folk were alike, great and small" (book I, chapter 19). But, as Caroline and Mugford could testify, that is simply untrue. What it boils down to is that all folk are alike if the folk concerned are the middle and upper classes, but not if they are the middle and lower classes.

This snobbery, it might be retorted, is to be laid not to Thackeray's charge but to Pendennis' since he relates the story and is responsible for all the comments on Philip's behavior. And there are, indeed, indications that Thackeray sees, and means us to see, the social issues more fully than the smug Pendennis or the arrogant Philip do. Thus the woman Philip insults at Mugford's party (book II, chapter 15)—an ex-actress now married to a wealthy tailor named Woolsey—is, the keen reader of Thackeray realizes, none other than Morgiana from "The Ravenswing." This is perhaps the finest instance of Thackeray purposefully reusing a character from another story, for we know the worth of Morgiana and her husband, and can see Philip's rudeness from their angle. Thackeray does not mean us to miss, either, the superior magnanimity of the socially inferior characters, Caroline and Mugford (who forgives Philip and gives him his job back in book II, chapter 22). For all this, Thackeray compromises on the class issue. He is not prepared openly to disown Pendennis' "realistic" view of the gulf between the middle and lower classes. Further, the story's disparaging treatment of the dark-skinned Grenville Woolcomb (a deliberately offensive surname), which is repellent to modern readers, clearly recalls Thackeray's observations about the inferiority of blacks to whites on his American trip.

Of *Denis Duval* (1864), Thackeray's last novel, there is less to say, for he died after completing only eight chapters. A tale of smugglers and spies, highwaymen and sea fights, it represents a bid on Thackeray's part to break away from the repeated remodelings of his own youth, which stretch from *Pendennis* to *Philip*. Beginning in mid-eighteenth-century Rye, where Duval grows up, it was to culminate on the streets of revolutionary France, and Duval, a poor boy who becomes an admiral, was to claim as his bride his childhood love, the aristocratic Agnes de Saverne. Despite this highly charged subject matter, the narrative is dilatory and "roundabout" in Thackeray's late manner, being presented as the reminiscences of Duval, written after retirement. "Why do I make zigzag journeys? 'Tis the privilege of old age to be garrulous," Duval explains in mitigation.

That explanation is distinctly complacent, as is the narrative method it excuses—a method designed not to come to grips with experience but to savor it from a serene distance. In other words, Thackeray's late manner had, in addition to its undoubted personal charms, deeply conservative political implications that were, for its original public, part of its appeal.

CONCLUSION

IT is no exaggeration to say that without a knowledge of Thackeray it is impossible to understand Victorian England. True, there are large areas of the historical picture that he virtually ignores—the slums, the factories, the rural community, the great imperialist adventure. But the fact that he can ignore them is itself historically significant, and he presents more fully than any other writer the social mores of the middle and upper-middle classes, which were to dominate the age. Moreover, born as he was on a watershed between two historical periods, he allows us a unique awareness of what was involved in the transition from the Regency to the Victorian era, from the aftermath of romanticism and revolution to mid-century stability. His works illustrate this transition as well as describe it, which is why we notice a loss of vivacity and irony when we pass from the early miscellaneous writings to the large-scale novels that followed *Vanity Fair*.

But his writings are not, of course, just an illustration of social history. They are the record of a vast imaginative enterprise—an expanding universe of people and places, evoked in his swift, brilliant, seemingly careless manner. Within this expanse we can identify particular regions of space and time—Paris, the old German provinces, the eighteenth century, the demimonde of ballet dancers and opera singers—that had an appeal for him at once worldly and poetic, escapist and eagerly documentary.

He was continually aware of the inadequacy of language, and that is why we have the hundreds of sketches and drawings, which are an integral part of his vision and, especially in a work like *A Journey from Cornhill to Grand Cairo*, provide an essential complement to the written word. He was aware, too, of the artificiality of the whole fictional endeavor, and this, together with his pursuit of realism, led to his experiments in oblique and circuitous methods of narration and to the evolution of a highly personal voice that (as in *Lovel the Widower*) eventually threatened to swamp the novel altogether. It is, finally, in the four volumes of his *Letters and Private Papers*, which no lover of Thackeray should miss, that we find this voice at its most uninhibited. Unflaggingly enjoyable, they offer on page after page that mingling of enchantment and disenchantment, flippancy and seriousness, quick observation and caricature, for which the only adjective is—Thackerayan.

SELECTED BIBLIOGRAPHY

I. BIBLIOGRAPHY. "Lewis Melville" [Lewis Saul Benjamin], *William Makepeace Thackeray*, 2 vols. (London, 1910); H. S. Van Duzer, *A Thackeray Library* (New York, 1919); D. Flamm, ed., *Thackeray's Critics. An Annotated Bibliography of British and American Criticism, 1836–1901* (Chapel Hill, N. C., 1966), with intro. by D. Flamm; J. E. Olmsted, ed., *Thackeray and His Twentieth-Century Critics. An Annotated Bibliography, 1900–1975* (New York–London, 1977), with intro by Olmsted. *Note:* There is no full, definitive bibliography. Important Thackeray collections, which have been cataloged, are housed at Princeton University (Parrish Collection) and in the New York Public Library (Berg Collection).

II. COLLECTED WORKS. *Miscellanies: Prose and Verse*, 4 vols. (London, 1855–1857; repr. 1861, 1865), this selection was made by Thackeray himself; for other collections of miscellaneous essays and stories see the *Cambridge Bibliography of English Literature*, vol. III (1969), cols. 856–859; *Works*, 22 vols. (London, 1867–1869; 2 supp. vols., 1885–1886), the Library ed.; *Works*, 26 vols. (London, 1878–1886), with a memoir by Sir L. Stephen; *Works*, 13 vols. (London, 1898), the Biographical ed., with biographical intros. by Thackeray's daughter Anne Ritchie; *The Works*, 17 vols. (London, 1908), the Oxford ed., intros. by G. Saintsbury, with original and rev. readings, and additional material; *The Works*, 26 vols. (London, 1910–1911), the Centenary ed., with biographical intros. by Lady Ritchie, and a memoir by Sir L. Stephen; G. N. Ray, coll. and ed., *The Letters and Private Papers*, 4 vols. (Cambridge, Mass., 1945–1946); G. N. Ray, ed., *W. M. Thackeray* (Urbana, Ill., 1955), contributions to the *Morning Chronicle*.

III. SEPARATE WORKS. [Goliah Gahagan], "The Professor. A Tale," short story, first published in *Bentley's Miscellany* (July 1837); *The Yellowplush Correspondence* (Philadelphia, 1838), comic pieces, first published in *Fraser's* magazine (November 1837–August 1838), repr. in *Comic Tales and Sketches* (London, 1841) as *Papers by Mr. Yellowplush*; "Strictures on Pictures," art criticism, first published in *Fraser's* magazine (June 1838); *Some Passages in the Life of Major Gahagan*, burlesque short novel, first published in the *New Monthly* magazine (February 1838–February 1839), repr. as *The Tremendous Adventures of Major Gahagan* in *Miscellanies*, vol. I (London, 1855); "Half-a-Crown's Worth of Cheap Knowledge," survey, first published in *Fraser's* magazine (March 1839); "Stubb's Calendar: or, The Fatal Boots" (New York, 1850), comic story, first published in Cruikshank's *Comic Almanack* (London, 1839), repr. as "The Fatal Boots" in *Miscellanies*, vol. I (London, 1855); *Catherine, A Story, by Ikey Solomons, Esq., Junior*, short novel, first published in *Fraser's* magazine (May 1839–February 1840).

The Bedford-Row Conspiracy, short novel, first published in the *New Monthly* magazine (January–April 1840); [Mr. Titmarsh], *The Paris Sketch Book*, 2 vols. (London, 1840), prose sketches; [Michael Angelo Titmarsh], "A Pictorial Rhapsody," art criticism, first published in *Fraser's* magazine (June 1840); *An Essay on the Genius of George Cruikshank* (London, 1840), art criticism, first published in the *Westminster Review* (June 1840); "Going to See a Man Hanged," journalism, first published in *Fraser's* magazine (August 1840); *A Shabby Genteel Story* (New York, 1857), short novel, first published in *Fraser's* magazine (June–October 1840); "Barber Cox and the Cutting of His Comb," comic story, first published in G. Cruikshank's *Comic Almanack* (London, 1840), repr. as "Cox's Diary" in *Miscellanies*, vol. I (London, 1855); "Captain Rook and Mr. Pigeon," "The Fashionable Authoress," "The Artists," prose sketches, first published in K. Meadows, *Heads of the People* (London, 1840–1841).

"On Men and Pictures: A Propos of a Walk in the

Louvre," art criticism, first published in *Fraser's* magazine (July 1841); "Shrove Tuesday in Paris," journalism, first published in *Britannia* (June 1841); [Mr. M. A. Titmarsh], *The Second Funeral of Napoleon . . . and The Chronicle of the Drum* (London, 1841), reportage; [M. A. Titmarsh], "Memorials of Gormandising, In a Letter to Oliver Yorke, Esq.," culinary journalism, first published in *Fraser's* magazine (June 1841); *The Great Hoggarty Diamond* (New York, 1848), short novel, first published in *Fraser's* magazine (September–December 1841) as *The History of Samuel Titmarsh and the Great Hoggarty Diamond. Edited and Illustrated by Sam's Cousin, Michael Angelo*; "Miss Tickletoby's Lectures on English History," comic journalism, first published in *Punch* (July–October 1842); "The Fitz-Boodle Papers," comic journalism, first published in *Fraser's* magazine (June 1842–February 1843) as "Fitz-Boodle's Confessions," repr. in *Miscellanies*, vol. IV (London, 1857), as "The Fitz-Boodle Papers"; [George Fitz-Boodle], *Men's Wives*, short stories and a novelette, first published in *Fraser's* magazine (March–November 1843); [M. A. Titmarsh], *The Irish Sketch Book*, 2 vols. (London, 1843), travel; [M. A. Titmarsh], "Bluebeard's Ghost," short story, first published in *Fraser's* magazine (October 1843).

[Fitz-Boodle], *The Luck of Barry Lyndon, A Romance of the Last Century*, 2 vols. (New York, 1852), novel, first published in *Fraser's* magazine (January–December 1844), rev. as *The Memoirs of Barry Lyndon, Esq.* (New York, 1856), also in M. Anisman, ed. (New York, 1971); "The History of the Next French Revolution," satirical journalism, first published in *Punch* (February–April 1844); [Lancelot Wagstaff, Esq.], "The Partie Fine," short story, first published in the *New Monthly* magazine (May 1844); [Mr. Wagstaff], "Greenwich—Whitebait," journalism, first published in the *New Monthly* magazine (July 1844); [Titmarsh], "Little Travels and Roadside Sketches," travel, first published in *Fraser's* magazine (May 1844–January 1845); "The Fat Contributor Papers," journalism, first published in *Punch* (August 1844–October 1845) as "Wanderings of Our Fat Contributor"; [Lancelot Wagstaff, Esq.], "Bob Robinson's First Love," short story, first published in the *New Monthly* magazine (August 1845); [Michael Angelo Titmarsh], *A Legend of the Rhine*, comic journalism, first published in G. Cruikshank's *Table-Book* (June–December 1845).

[Michael Angelo Titmarsh, Esq.], *Jeames's Diary, or, Sudden Wealth* (New York, 1846), comic journalism, first published in *Punch* (August 1845–January 1846), repr. in *Miscellanies*, vol. II (London, 1855), as *The Diary of C. Jeames De La Pluche, Esq.*; *Notes of a Journey from Cornhill to Grand Cairo . . . by Mr. M. A. Titmarsh* (London, 1846), travel; *The Book of Snobs* (incomplete, London, 1848; complete, New York, 1852), satire, first published in *Punch* (February 1846–February 1847) as *The Snobs of England, By One of Themselves*, also in J. Sutherland, ed. (Santa Lucia, 1978); [M. A. Titmarsh], *Mrs. Perkins's Ball*

(London, 1847), short novel; *Punch's Prize Novelists*, burlesque, first published in *Punch* (April–October 1847); *Sketches and Travels in London* (London, 1856), journalism, first published in *Punch* (November 1847–March 1850) as *Travels in London*; *Vanity Fair. A Novel Without a Hero* (London, 1848), novel, first published in 20 monthly parts (January 1847–July 1848), also in G. Tillotson and K. Tillotson, eds. (London, 1963), and J. I. M. Stewart, ed. (Harmondsworth, 1972); *A Little Dinner at Timmins's*, short novel, first published in *Punch* (May–July 1848); [Mr. M. A. Titmarsh], *Our Street* (London, 1848), prose sketches; *The History of Pendennis. His Fortunes and Misfortunes, His Friends and His Greatest Enemy*, 2 vols. (London, 1849–1850), novel, first published in 24 monthly parts (November 1848–December 1850), also in D. Hawes, ed. (Harmondsworth, 1972); "Mr. Brown's Letters to a Young Man About Town," journalism, first published in *Punch* (March–August 1849); [Mr. M. A. Titmarsh], *Doctor Birch and His Young Friends* (London, 1849), prose sketches.

[Mr. M. A. Titmarsh], *Rebecca and Rowena, A Romance Upon Romance* (London, 1850), parody; [Mr. M. A. Titmarsh], *The Kickleburys on the Rhine* (London, 1850), short novel; *The History of Henry Esmond, Esq. A Colonel in the Service of Her Majesty Q. Anne. Written by Himself*, 3 vols. (London, 1852), novel; *The English Humourists of the Eighteenth Century* (London, 1853), lectures; [Arthur Pendennis, Esq., ed.], *The Newcomes. Memoirs of a Most Respectable Family*, 2 vols. (London, 1854–1855; rev. 1863), novel, first published in 24 monthly parts (October 1853–August 1855); *Ballads* (London, 1855), poems; [Mr. M. A. Titmarsh], *The Rose and the Ring . . . A Fire-side Pantomime for Great and Small Children* (London, 1855), children's story.

The Virginians. A Tale of the Last Century, 2 vols. (London, 1858–1859), novel, first published in 24 monthly parts (November 1857–September 1859); *Lovel the Widower* (London, 1861), novel, first published in the *Cornhill* magazine (January–June 1860); *The Four Georges: Sketches of Manners, Morals, Court and Town Life* (New York, 1860; London, 1861), lectures; *Roundabout Papers* (London, 1863), essays, first published in the *Cornhill* magazine (January 1860–November 1863), also in J. E. Wells, ed. (New York, 1925); *The Adventures of Philip on His Way Through the World*, 3 vols. (London, 1862), novel, first published in the *Cornhill* magazine (January 1861–August 1862); *Denis Duval* (New York, 1864; London, 1867), unfinished novel, first published in the *Cornhill* magazine (March–June 1864).

IV. BIOGRAPHICAL AND CRITICAL STUDIES. A. Trollope, *Thackeray* (London, 1879), in the English Men of Letters series, a portrait of Thackeray by a friend; G. Saintsbury, *A Consideration of Thackeray* (Oxford, 1931), a repr. of the intros. to the Oxford ed. of *The Works*; R. Las Vergnas, *Thackeray. L'Homme, le penseur, le romancier* (Paris, 1932); D. Cecil, *Early Victorian Novelists* (London, 1934);

J. W. Dodds, *Thackeray. A Critical Portrait* (New York, 1941); J. Y. T. Greig, *Thackeray: A Reconsideration* (Oxford, 1950), unsympathetic; G. N. Ray, *The Buried Life* (London, 1952), suggests real-life originals for many of Thackeray's characters; G. Tillotson, *Thackeray the Novelist* (London, 1954), a perceptive study, particularly good on Thackeray's style; K. Tillotson, *Novelists of the Eighteen-Forties* (Oxford, 1954); G. N. Ray, *Thackeray. The Uses of Adversity* (London–New York, 1955); G. N. Ray, *Thackeray. The Age of Wisdom* (London–New York, 1958), the standard biography, authorized by the Thackeray family; the 1955 vol. carries the story up to *Vanity Fair*; the 1958 vol. completes it; J. Loofbourow, *Thackeray and the Form of Fiction* (Princeton, N. J., 1964); G. Tillotson and D. Hawes, eds., *Thackeray: The Critical Heritage* (London, 1968), invaluable for tracing the growth of Thackeray's reputation; J. S. McMaster, *Thackeray. The Major Novels* (Manchester, 1971); B. Hardy, *The Exposure of Luxury. Radical Themes in Thackeray* (London, 1972), a brilliant study, if at times overly moralistic; J. A. Sutherland, *Thackeray at Work* (London, 1974), reconstructs Thackeray's working methods from a study of the MSS; J. Carey, *Thackeray: Prodigal Genius* (London, 1977), argues for the superior imaginative vitality of the younger Thackeray; E. F. Harden, *The Emergence of Thackeray's Serial Fiction* (London, 1979), the closest study of the MSS to date, somewhat indigestible; A. Monsarrat, *An Uneasy Victorian: Thackeray the Man 1811–1863* (London, 1980), sympathetic and lively, but adds little to G. N. Ray.

DYLAN THOMAS

(1914–1953)

Leslie Norris

DYLAN THOMAS was born in Swansea, Wales, on 27 October 1914. No examination of his work can ignore the importance of his birthplace. Even his death in New York in 1953 is less a simple fact than an allegory of how far from home the poet had traveled. From this distance in time it is very easy to see that all his work is based on an assumption that Swansea and its surrounding green county is the center of the world, that all the poet saw and said resulted from the relation of his experience to the small miles of Wales in which he grew up.

No poet of our time lived more in the eye of the world than Thomas. His early recognition—he was famous in the little community of modern poets when he was nineteen—the accounts of his bohemian life-style, the impact of his work on critics and on other poets, all made him a public figure. At the time it seemed that readers waited for the small collections he published every few years as if starved of poetry. As his fame spread, Thomas was regarded as the very type of the romantic poet, wild, dissolute, inspired. This was not the complete truth, but when he died in 1953, tragically and sensationally after a bout of drinking, it was as if Dionysus had died again.

That was a long time ago. We ought to be able to look more objectively at the verse, to see it as it is presented to us in the *Collected Poems* (1952), to realize that it is the whole life's work. It should be possible to decide how much of Thomas' poetry has stood up against insidious time and against changing fashion in verse. We should, moreover, realize that the man's prose has grown in importance since his death, that it is easier to see him as a more interesting figure, more complex and complete, developing marvelous gifts of narrative and humor, than as a poet dead before his time. It has long been acknowledged that Thomas was a conscious artist, well aware of what he was doing,

industrious, serious, and dedicated. His letters to his friend Vernon Watkins, particularly the earlier ones, are clear proof of how seriously he took his craft. To read through the *Collected Poems* is to experience a continuous development and refining of Thomas' technical skills, from the rather heavy iambic early verse through the conscious experiments of his middle period to the extraordinary mastery of his late poems. The truth is that Thomas was always an artist, not only aware of what he was doing but delighting in it. He would have agreed with William Butler Yeats that there is no art without toil.

He realized early that he could write, and he was serious about the possession of such a gift. His father, David John Thomas, was an English master at the local grammar school, a man of taste and intelligence, widely read. Although he came from a Welsh-speaking background, he made his home one in which English was the sole language and its literature valued above all others. A fine reader, he introduced his son to the great poets at an early age. His example, together with the splendid voice he passed on to Dylan, was to result in the extraordinary public readings that made Thomas' work familiar to many people who would normally not have been interested in poetry. D. J. Thomas came of a family famous in South Wales. His uncle, William Thomas, had been a prime mover in the Unitarian movement in western Wales and had been politically active in the unrest between landlords and tenants in the years after 1867. He was, moreover, a good poet in the Welsh language, using the bardic title of Gwilym Marles.

It was a proud inheritance, and D. J. Thomas paid tribute to Gwilym Marles when he gave his son the middle name of Marlais. Yet he tried to ensure that any trace of Welsh language influence was erased when he insisted his two children have elocution lessons. Thomas grew up without the distinctive

Swansea accent. He spoke an English untouched by any regional tinge.

Similarly, he remained unaware of much of what was happening to his country outside his immediate experience. It was a bad time for Wales, and other young poets—a little older than Thomas, it is true—were aware of the despair of the miners, of ruinous unemployment, and wrote about these subjects. He seemed sublimely uninterested in politics. If he knew no Welsh, he had a traditional Welsh attitude toward poetry. It must be rich in sound, it must be beautifully crafted, it must be glorious and as far as possible immortal. He prepared himself to write such poetry. His verse had been influenced, too, by the great English poets, particularly the romantics. The modern poets he read were those whose work his father possessed, Walter de la Mare, John Masefield, the Georgians. From his wide reading he had already mastered a formidable technique, but it was a technique quite unlike that of his contemporaries. David Daiches, in his essay on Thomas in *Dylan Thomas: A Collection of Critical Essays,* writes: "No modern poet in English has had a keener sense of form or has handled stanza and verse-paragraphs—whether traditional or original—with more deliberate cunning." This is an indication of the individuality of Thomas' voice and his technique. Of all the poets of his generation, he alone seemed to have been uninfluenced by the work of T. S. Eliot, then preeminent in English poetry. For Thomas it was as if Eliot had never written. We know from his letters, however, that the younger poet was very well aware of Eliot's work, and it is possible that he wrote differently because he knew his own gifts well, realized that he would travel in other directions.

The unusual thing is that Thomas came to this knowledge while still very young. The *Collected Poems* of 1952, prepared by Thomas himself, contains a total of ninety poems. When the poet's friend Dr. Daniel Jones published his edition of *The Poems* in 1971, he included many more poems; even so, he was at pains to state that this was still a selection. Most of these additional poems were written while Thomas was yet a schoolboy, but so were many of the poems Thomas selected for the collection he chose himself.

Between the years 1930 and 1934, that is, between the ages of fifteen and nineteen, Thomas wrote "at least four times more poetry than in the remaining nineteen years of his life" (*The Poems,* introduction, p. xvi), according to Dr. Jones. Thomas' published *Notebooks* offer convincing evidence of his astonishing early industry, as well as showing how this wealth of early work was revised, sometimes only very slightly revised, to become the poems from which the poet formed his successive books. Although he did write new poems for each new book, a surprising number were rescued from the poems of his adolescence.

It is obvious, then, that the majority of the poems remain the work of a very young man, a provincial young man untouched by London literary society or the discipline of a university. In a sense, despite the influence of his father, Thomas was an autodidact, unaware of the very latest in poetical fashions. He had trained himself in the orthodox metrical forms of English verse and was far away from the current new poets, W. H. Auden, Stephen Spender, and C. Day-Lewis. Working almost alone in Swansea—for he did not meet Watkins, perhaps the most helpful of his friends, until after the publication of *Eighteen Poems* in 1934—his most interesting subject matter was himself. So that when he began to publish, both his matter and his manner, traditional though they were, seemed astonishingly new and very exciting.

Certainly *Eighteen Poems* was received with unusual attention. "I was in London with him," wrote Glyn Jones in *The Dragon Has Two Tongues* (p. 183), "soon after his book appeared . . . and it was a delight to me to witness the excitement with which the book, and its author, were received." Jones had very early recognized the unique quality of the poetry and remains one of the most acute and objective of Thomas' admirers.

It is as well to consider here, since we have stressed that much of Thomas' verse is orthodox and traditional, just what was unique in the work of the new arrival. First there is the important influence of Thomas' environment. Hard though D. J. Thomas fought to give his son the sense of an English language culture, the boy was exposed every day of his formative years to an atmosphere very largely based on Welsh values and mores. He would have heard the language even, since it was more commonly spoken in Swansea during his boyhood than it is today, and in the country districts to the west of the town it was very largely the first language. This means that the English Thomas heard in the streets and classrooms, even that he would use when with his friends, was in a sense a transitional language, its syntax and its rhythms very slightly askew when compared to the language of Englishmen. The poet's usage thus acquires a kind of exotic strangeness and power, adding to his awareness of language—in Thomas' case, an obsession with language that might have been the most obvious facet of his poetry. "I wanted to write poetry in the beginning," wrote Thomas in 1951, in reply to a student's questions, "because I had fallen in love with words" (*Modern Poets on Modern Poetry*, p. 195). He was never to fall out of love with them.

And if his language was exotically rich and musical when we think of the thin, political poetry popular at the time, then its form too was unusual, again for what we might think of as Welsh reasons. Welsh poetry is complex and difficult in form, its poets skilled in the craft to a high degree, the traditional meters demanding long training. I do not suggest that Thomas knew very much about the forms of Welsh language poetry, despite efforts by a few critics to show a deliberate use of some of the constructions, but he grew up in a community in which formal poetry—the belief that poems must be well made—was universal. This is a not an unusual circumstance among poets from Celtic countries. "Irish poets, learn your trade, / Sing whatever is well made" ("Under Ben Bulben," V), admonished Yeats. Certainly Scottish, Irish, and Welsh poets seem for these reasons to use poetic form and language sufficiently unlike that of their English contemporaries to make their work recognizably Celtic. It is not entirely fanciful to suggest that Thomas' mastery of intricate forms had something to do with his nationality and his background.

So his work was significantly novel in both word and form. It is true that there were poets writing at that time who were influenced by the current interest in surrealism; despite superficial similarities— the use of striking imagery is an example— Thomas' extreme control is enough to show that he has no place in such a group. Nor was his adolescent interest in himself, and in particular in his own sexuality, a common subject for verse in 1934. This was a period in which many young writers were greatly concerned with social and political themes. In prose and verse many of them were

trying to analyze the causes of great political upheaval in Europe, and to warn about the war that they saw as inevitable. Thomas seemed untouched by this concern, just as he was not influenced by savage unemployment and poverty in his own country. And if these young people, some of whom were to go on to fight in the Spanish Civil War in a few years time, seemed to represent that call for individual and political freedom which had been so potent a charge in the early nineteenth century to poets like William Blake and William Wordsworth, to Percy Shelley and Lord Byron, then Thomas perhaps represented the viewpoint of even younger poets, who had not outgrown the natural interest in self, shown not only in budding lyrical poets but in all normal adolescents. We have to remember just how young Thomas was at this time, and to recall, moreover, just how much younger he had been when he had written the work in *Eighteen Poems*. Whatever the reasons, young poets found his work exciting and in a sense liberating. His work influenced that of poets in England and America to an extraordinary extent, as a reading of almost any anthology of poetry of the time will show. In retrospect it seems that he changed the direction of contemporary English poetry with his first book, although its real virtues were not always recognized.

In addition to all these factors, Thomas came of families long settled in the Swansea and Carmarthenshire areas. He had a familiar, age-old environment of sea and shore and surrounding hills in which to place his work. His very provincialism, far from being a handicap, gave him safety and strength. His is a recognizable country. His advantages were formidable.

All this is more easily seen from a reading of *The Collected Poems* than from a study of the work in his first book alone. The poems in *Eighteen Poems*, though, are still exciting enough to help us understand some of the furor they caused in the small world of poets, and a few of them remain among the best that Thomas ever wrote.

An old poet has told me how, when he was an undergraduate, he and his friends would walk the streets chanting the poems of Algernon Charles Swinburne, and a similar, almost mesmeric, incantatory quality is felt when one reads these early poems of Thomas. I, as a boy of thirteen, read "The force that through the green fuse drives the flower" in an anthology, and could not believe that it was a poem. It seemed like something alive and physical, too vital for the page to contain. It could well be that such an immediate effect, a feeling that the words contained something beyond meaning and appealing with enormous power to the senses, is not only the first quality of Thomas' early verse, but its most permanent quality, still to be felt. Yet there was, too, a certain confidence in the statement of the poetry, something in addition to the music and the mystery, which persuaded many of us that Thomas was saying something important. How strong some of the opening lines still seem: "I see the boys of summer in their ruin"; "A process in the weather of the heart / Turns damp to dry"; "Where once the waters of your face / Spun to my screws." The poetry was obscure, but with a peculiar kind of obscurity. John Bayley has pointed out ("Chains and the Poet," *New Critical Essays,* p. 57) that we were hearing once again "the Bard's voice" and that even if the words seem obscure, the message is very simple. "Thomas," wrote Bayley, "was the first great and evident talent of the modern movement . . . to concentrate on what it felt like to be himself, to make his poetry the feeling of his being."

But no poet can be entirely absorbed in self. We know from the evidence of his friends in the Swansea of his youth that Thomas was observant, fond of company, funny. His later stories and broadcasts demonstrate very clearly that little went by his keen and tolerant eye, so it is fair to assume that his adolescent concern with himself was abnormal only in that it formed the matter for much of his poetry, that he was very much aware of the external world and his place in it. Like other intelligent young people he was concerned with the great imponderables, time, sex, life, religion. His poetry could be said to attempt to balance such forces within himself and in the world in which he lived.

That effort is serious and arduous. Early critics who felt that Thomas worked thoughtlessly and without effort saw neither the skill, for so young a man, nor the struggle throughout poem after poem to find a conclusion that satisfied his doubts. He certainly knew what he was doing. In many of his poems he uses man as a microcosm and himself as a mirror of the huge and inexplicable world in order to assert some order over chaos. It is not mere rhetoric that he intends (nor, it seems to me, did he

ever intend mere rhetoric) when he ends a superbly serious poem, "If I were tickled by the rub of love," with a simple declaration—"Man be my metaphor." It is a truth he remained loyal to throughout his career. If we remember this, some of the difficulties of the work in *Eighteen Poems* seem less perplexing when we read:

> Light breaks where no sun shines;
> Where no sea runs, the waters of the heart
> Push in their tides;
>   ("Light breaks where no sun shines")

or, even more illuminating, these lines from the same poem:

> Dawn breaks behind the eyes;
> From poles of skull and toe the windy blood
> Slides like a sea.
>
>   (13–15)

It is not, however, simply that Thomas saw himself as the world or the world as himself; he saw himself as being subject to the same forces as the world, and his effort is to understand those forces and to see how they affect him. Much of his poetry, then, is a journey in self-discovery. Those strong, confident lines are also paths of doubt and uncertainty, and the poem was successful only when he had successfully negotiated a way to a conclusion the poem had found for him. Much of the supposed obscurity of the early poetry is the result of the division between the confidence of the technique and the uncertainty—more correctly, the innocence—of the thought. But we can certainly understand more readily now just why these poems use so many images of blood and body. They are not merely images, they form the subject matter of Thomas' first public utterances.

And when the poem works, it is very successful. Such an example would be "The force that through the green fuse drives the flower," in which everything combines to produce a remarkable unity. Here Thomas makes his complete identification with the natural world even more apparent than in other poems. It is not merely an identification with the external world that Thomas understands; it is an interrelationship so firm that its very statement is the poem. The poem opens with something that is almost a definition of the life force, in that the poet shows us how it affects both the flower, representative of external life, and himself:

> The force that through the green fuse drives the
> flower
> Drives my green age; that blasts the roots of trees
> Is my destroyer.

He shows us, then, his place in the natural world. It is precisely that of every other living thing, subject to growth and decay. He links his youth to that of the flower by his use of the common adjective "green"; he anticipates the hardening of age by aligning himself with "the roots of trees." But he does not understand the force he is considering; in fact, he is unable to explain to the rose marred by winter that he is subject to the same fate:

> And I am dumb to tell the crooked rose
> My youth is bent by the same wintry fever.
>   (4–5)

The next two stanzas follow a repetitive pattern, insisting not only on the poet's relationship with the natural world and its laws—

> The force that drives the water through the rocks
> Drives my red blood;

but on his inability to explain the nature of relentless time, of inevitable decay. He is "dumb" for these purposes; not only is he unable to explain to the dying rose the reason for its death, he is identically powerless to explain it to himself:

> And I am dumb to mouth unto my veins
> How at the mountain spring the same mouth sucks.
>   (9–10)

Water and blood, the springing liquids of external and internal worlds, both are ruled by the same inexplicable forces.

Paradoxically, it is the realization of his inability to do more than recognize the intricate relations of natural things ruled by time, to be unable to explain any more than this, which gives power and assurance to the poem, qualities reinforced by the relentless drive of the rhythm, by the repetition of the formal pattern, and by the separated couplet with which he ends the poem. This last piece of virtuosity also brings out clearly the hidden pun the poet intends when he uses "dumb" to describe his helplessness. In it he ironically accuses himself of being stupid when he fails to persuade the dead lover of the universality of death:

> And I am dumb to tell the lover's tomb
> How at my sheet goes the same crooked worm.
>   (21–22)

All in all, this is a most subtle and engaging poem, well worth lengthy study. Even in small matters, as in the manner the poem is rounded off by the final image of the "crooked" worm echoing that of the "crooked" rose—and both, possibly, reminding us of William Blake's "sick rose"—the poem is the work of a young man of great ability, writing at the top of his form.

It is this topic of death and decay that is most frequently examined in the first poems, and the universality of the subject in some measure helps to disguise the extreme introspection of much of the work. Yet it is clear that in all these poems, Thomas is firmly at the center of his world, relying almost entirely on his own sense perceptions. He is hardly ever objective in the ordinary meaning of the word, his thought and his emotion seeming to be an amalgam of these qualities, almost a new and highly individual power. His poems arise, as he tells us, straight out of his senses—"I see the boys of summer"—and we are tempted to think that without that first sight the boys would not have existed at all, nor the poem either. As it is, they can go on living in thoughtless and careless folly, blind to their certain ruin:

> I see the boys of summer in their ruin
> Lay the gold tithings barren,
> Setting no store by harvest, freeze the soils;
> There in their heat the winter floods
> Of frozen loves they fetch their girls,
> And drown the cargoed apples in their tides.

But not all the first poems can be so classified. "Especially when the October wind" is made more recognizably from the visible world in and about Swansea (and is probably the first of several poems written in succeeding October months when the poet celebrated his birthday) and, by some process of relation, from the act of writing poems. "Where once the waters of your face" also seems a more direct and external poem than most. What difficulties exist in the reading of this poem ease when it is realized that we are listening to a boat (or perhaps the owner of a boat) speaking to the ghost of a water that has dried up.

> Where once the waters of your face
> Spun to my screws, your dry ghost blows,
> The dead turns up its eye;

Here, too, we are given such a wealth of sea and tidal images that we are reminded that Thomas lived most of his life by the sea, was increasingly influenced by seascape in his work. It is in this poem that we find the poet perhaps for the first time offering some measure of protection against time and dissolution, even if it is to a dry pool:

> There shall be corals in your beds,
> There shall be serpents in your tides,
> Till all our sea-faiths die.
>
> (22–24)

I have suggested that despite the energy and strength of the rhythms of these poems, they are sometimes less than sensitive, sometimes monotonous and heavy, and I believe this to be true. Yet the best, and the best made (for these are nearly always identical with Thomas), are free of this charge, and an examination of his rhymes would show how cleverly he avoids any suggestion of monotony here. His use of half-rhyme and false rhyme, easily to be seen in the lines already quoted, will show how successful he was. Admirable, too, is his strict search for accuracy; one can only be delighted by the combination of "dry" and "ghost," for instance, in "Where once the waters of your face."

All this meant that Thomas had established at once an easily recognized style and a highly individual voice, strange, exciting, and genuinely poetic. The poems to be found in *Twenty-five Poems* (1936) support and confirm the nature of his gifts, although there are some that seem simpler and more direct and a few that suggest a sadder and less convinced poet. Examples of the first kind are "This bread I break," "Ears in the turrets hear," "The hand that signed the paper," "Should lanterns shine," "I have longed to move away," and "And death shall have no dominion." They form

no small proportion of the work, and while a few of them are new, some are poems that Thomas had rejected for his first collection and revised for this later publication. The poems of melancholy can be represented by the beautiful "Out of the sighs," with its wavering cadences, its slow melody:

> Out of the sighs a little comes,
> But not of grief, for I have knocked down that
> Before the agony; the spirit grows,
> Forgets, and cries;
> A little comes, is tasted and found good;
> All could not disappoint;
> There must, be praised, some certainty,
> If not of loving well, then not,
> And that is true after perpetual defeat.

Perhaps not sufficient attention has been paid to this poem, one of the few pieces that contains none of the famous Thomas images, indeed hardly any images at all, yet no other poet could have written it.

There are more typical poems, some of them going over old ground, looking once again at the apparent division of flesh and soul, exhibiting the presence of death in the newborn:

> I, in my intricate image, stride on two levels,
> Forged in man's minerals, the brassy orator
> Laying my ghost in metal,
> The scales of this twin world tread on the double,
> My half ghost in armour hold hard in death's
>   corridor,
> To my man-iron sidle.
>
> Beginning with doom in the bulb, the spring
>   unravels. . . .
>
> ("I, in my intricate image")

And there are a few poems so frankly obscure ("Now," "How soon the servant sun,") that they are almost jokes. I do not pretend to understand them at all.

But the most important and substantial work of this period are the ten religious stanzas called "Altarwise by owl-light." Written between December 1935 and the summer of 1936, these poems, or rather this poem (since I agree with Dr. Jones that this is a single poem with ten sonnet-like stanzas [*The Poems*, p. 262]), is something of a watershed in Thomas' work. It is his longest piece up to this time, and also the most compressed and the most highly metaphorical. It has been the subject of controversy and explication since it first appeared as a whole in 1936, and opinion has ranged from outright dismissal to prolonged and complex analysis such as that by Elder Olson (*The Poetry of Dylan Thomas,* pp. 63–87). Experts are even divided about how it should be read, some of them (for example, Marshall W. Stearns, "Unsex the Skeleton," *Transformation* 3, 1946) convinced that it is a series of separate sonnets despite Thomas' own statement that "this poem is a particular incident in a particular adventure" (*Sunday Times,* September 1936). Obscure it certainly is, compressed it certainly is. Afterwards, as if he had gone as far as he wished in those directions, Thomas' verse became more free, its music more varied and lyrical.

"We were both religious poets," wrote Watkins (*Letters to Vernon Watkins,* p. 17), and there is enough proof of this statement throughout the work of both poets to sustain this assertion. In Thomas' case we have the example of his early poem, "Before I knocked," in which he speaks for the Christ-child even before His birth:

> Before I knocked and flesh let enter,
> With liquid hands tapped on the womb,
> I who was shapeless as the water
> That shaped the Jordan near my home
> Was brother to Mnetha's daughter
> And sister to the fathering worm.

And there are references to his continued absorption with religion right up to the final statement of his prefatory note to *The Collected Poems.* "These poems, with all their crudities, doubts, and confusions, are written for the love of Man and in praise of God."

Thomas was twenty-one when he wrote "Altarwise by owl-light." It represents a remarkably sustained and unified effort by the young poet. The poem came quickly to him, when one considers its density and complexity, but it is in no way an easy poem and remains one of the most challenging for the reader. Dr. Jones suggests that we should think of it as "absolute" poetry, and that "comprehension is irrelevant" (*The Poems,* p. 263). Its difficulty he considers akin to that of a Bach fugue, and certainly the intricate weaving of images and the stern control of the sonnet form give this opinion some credence. But the poem is also made of words and possesses the properties of meaning.

What seems evident is that Thomas has taken for his subject the biblical themes of divine redemption and the reality of human sacrifice in an attempt to reconcile them. He has not confined his resources, his imagery, his information, to the material of the Old and New Testaments; the poem is made of all his concerns, and part of its difficulty is the wide range of Thomas' curious and personal learning and our difficulty in relating its disparate elements.

Each of the fourteen-line stanzas is organized into an octet and a sestet, the rhymes regular in pattern but not in sound, Thomas using the half-rhymes common with him:

> Altarwise by owl-light in the half-way house
> The gentleman lay graveward with his furies;
> Abaddon in the hangnail cracked from Adam,
> And, from his fork, a dog among the fairies,
> The atlas-eater with a jaw for news,
> Bit out the mandrake with to-morrow's scream.

This is Thomas' version of the Nativity. It is no traditional Christmas scene, full of radiance and the light of promise. Christ's mortality is recognized as early as line 2. He is not surrounded by angels, but by furies. He is descended from Adam, so already aware of sin. Abaddon is an unlikely figure here; he is the Angel of the Bottomless Pit, so the Christ-child, born at dusk, or owl-light, is in dangerous and cast-out company from the time of his birth. His half-way house is already one of dreadful omen.

The second stanza continues the story, so it is possible to see that Thomas, wrestling with words and meaning, was on a journey of understanding as profound as any he had yet made. The child whose birth we attended in the first stanza is growing up:

> Death is all metaphors, shape in one history;
> The child that sucketh long is shooting up

—but we are told again of death toward the end of this stanza:

> Hairs of your head, then said the hollow agent,
> Are but the roots of nettles and of feathers

It is, too, a precise and horrible prophecy that Death ("the hollow agent," a skull) gives, since we are reminded that Christ will wear on his head a crown of thorns, or nettles.

I cannot pretend that it is other than very difficult to trace Thomas' thought through these extraordinarily powerful stanzas, but some of them treat the theme more directly than others. One such is the eighth stanza, which states its message with urgency:

> This was the crucifixion on the mountain,
> Time's nerve in vinegar, the gallow grave
> As tarred with blood as the bright thorns I wept;
> The world's my wound, God's Mary in her grief,
> Bent like three trees and bird-papped through her
>   shift,
> With pins for teardrops is the long wound's woman.

There is little of the extreme difficulty here of some of the other stanzas, since Thomas has followed closely the Gospel accounts of the Crucifixion. The images are those we would expect and at the same time reinforce and interrelate with each other: for example, Christ's tears are as savage as the thorns he wears, Mary's are as sharp and hard as pins. In her grief, Mary is bowed with that invisible weight exactly as the three trees are bent with the weight of three men. The stanza ends with Christ's statement that he is there to heal the world:

> I, by the tree of thieves, all glory's sawbones,
> Unsex the skeleton this mountain minute,
> And by this blowclock witness of the sun
> Suffer the heaven's children through my heartbeat.

He first unsexes "the skeleton" of Death, and then, as the blowclock witness (which I take to be a seeding dandelion, something to be found everywhere, and whose seeds are carried everywhere by the wind, a symbol of delicate and silent power), measures that eclipse of the sun which accompanied the execution; Christ suffers "the heaven's children" through his "heartbeat." This is quite explicit. His suffering allows us into heaven; as his heart stops, we, "the heaven's children," are promised immortality.

This stanza is for me, perhaps because it is the easiest to read, the high point of the poem. Stanza nine is extremely difficult and does not seem to continue, as the first eight do, a retelling and examination of events. But the final stanza, puzzling as it is in its confused syntax and images, ends on a note of hope, a prayer almost, in which Thomas asks that the garden, essentially the garden of Eden, which he has imagined sunken beneath the sea, shall rise again and, holding Adam's tree and Christ's tree, allow the serpent to build "a nest of mercies" in "the rude, red tree," the bloodstained tree upon which Christ died.

This was the last poem in *Twenty-five Poems*. After this, Thomas was never again as fertile a poet. He was at this time living in dire poverty, newly married—he married Caitlin MacNamara in October 1937—and despite the marvelous reception given to *Twenty-five Poems*, the book made little money. He began to work on the autobiographical stories later collected in *The Portrait of the Artist as a Young Dog* (1940), in the hope that these would be more successful financially; but first he put together a volume of seven stories and sixteen new poems, called *The Map of Love*. This was a beautiful book, the stories a selection from Thomas' early prose and the poems including some most exciting work, all proving an even greater technical virtuosity, a number—for example, "After the funeral"—destined to be among his most famous. But ill-luck of the most unhappy kind attended the appearance of this book. Coming out at the end of August 1939, it was overwhelmed by the outbreak of World War II. Neither this nor *The World I Breathe*, a sizable collection of his poetry and prose that appeared in December of the same year and was his first American volume, did very much to relieve his financial straits.

The poems in *The Map of Love* do, however, mark a departure. Much more varied in theme and in style, they form a most interesting group. Still completely personal, they demonstrate a much greater interest in the external world. There are still poems that aroused the conservative critics to anger—particularly the opening poem, "Because the pleasure-bird whistles"—and there are fine poems of the sort we have met before, like the splendid sonnet "When all my five and country senses see," but through them all there runs like a slender narrative thread a suggestion that the poet is no longer alone. "We lying by seasand" begins a poem of recognition that the poet cannot disturb the ravages of time, but it is also a poem of tender resignation, allowing that "wishes breed not" and that the poet and his companion should watch "yellow until the golden weather / Breaks." We are in fact being given a map of love. "If my head hurt a hair's foot" is a poem in which his unborn child speaks to its mother, and the mother responds. "Twenty-four years"—another of the poems for his own birthday—is a celebration of his journey toward death ("sewing a shroud for a journey") and of his responsibilities as husband and father:

Dressed to die, the sensual strut begun,
With my red veins full of money,
In the final direction of the elementary town
I advance for as long as forever is.

(6–9)

It seems that the poet has new directions to explore as well as a new viewpoint for his perennial themes. His love, too, extends outside his immediate concerns. The aunt with whom he had spent much time when a child, on the farm he was to immortalize in "Fern Hill," had died, and he made for her the passionate elegy, "After the funeral."

The original version of this poem was written on 10 February 1933, a few days after his aunt's death. Five years were to pass before Thomas went back to the poem and transformed it into the deeply felt elegy we now have. He is bitter and angry at what he feels to be an insufficient sorrow among the mourners, calling their conventional sadness

. . . mule praises, brays,
Windshake of sailshaped ears, muffle-toed tap
Tap happily of one peg in the thick
Grave's foot, blinds down the lids . . .

(1–4)

But he moves through his memories of the living Ann Jones into a noble eloquence, assuming for her a position as "Ann's bard on a raised hearth," calling all

The seas to service that her wood-tongued virtue
Babble like a bellbuoy over the hymning heads,
Bow down the walls of the ferned and foxy woods
That her love sing and swing through a brown chapel.

(22–25)

And he offers her his continual service of love and eloquence until the dead return to life:

. . . until
The stuffed lung of the fox twitch and cry Love
And the strutting fern lay seeds on the black sill.

(38–40)

It is in these poems that we see for the first time a poet who is part of the outside world, offering as a partial solution to all the puzzles of life his personal love. In "After the funeral," for instance, we are shown a most careful ordering of the imagery, all the properties being those in and about the farm, the "stale fern," "the stuffed fox," the woods behind the house. Dr. Jones has told us that Thomas was not a ready observer of the world of nature, but that "if observation was directly relevant to his central interests, and only in that case, he could observe, and where the relevance was great, his observation could be keen" (*My Friend Dylan Thomas,* p. 56). The force of this remark can be appreciated when we remember that the flower in "The force that through the green fuse" remains an unnamed flower, but that in "After the funeral" a wealth of observed images are identified and ordered into powerful use. This ability was to be used more and more often, reinforcing Thomas' great auditory gifts. Thomas' changed status as a husband gave to him a wider range of subject and a greater involvement with other people.

This was part of a process that led to the comparative clarity and luminosity of the later poems. For a variety of reasons, possibly related to Thomas' work as a film-script writer and to the lack, until he removed to the Boathouse, Laugharne, in 1949, of a settled home, fewer poems were written. These years saw the growth of his reputation as a reader of poetry, not only his own. In February 1946 he published *Deaths and Entrances,* a tiny volume in size but great in achievement and influence. Here were such anthology pieces as "The Hunchback in the Park," which drew on his childhood memories of Cwmdonkin Park; the few war poems included in his work; two long narrative poems, "A Winter's Tale" and "Ballad of the Long-legged Bait"; poems of superb virtuosity like "There was a Saviour," in which a complex rhyme scheme is incredibly maintained; and, amid a whole galaxy of wonderful things, "Poem in October" and "Fern Hill."

It has been fashionable to think that Thomas' early work is superior to these later poems. That must be mistaken opinion. That they are different in many respects, while retaining Thomas' highly individual style, is fairly obvious. The main reason for this difference is one that the poems in *Deaths and Entrances* reflects. Previous to these poems, Thomas had been busily adapting the work contained in his early notebooks, that series of exercise books now in the Lockwood Memorial Library in Buffalo. For seven years these books had held the material for his poetry, but in the spring of 1941 he sold them to a London dealer in rare books and manuscripts. "It would be hard," wrote Constantine FitzGibbon, "to imagine a more significant gesture on Dylan's part, a greater renunciation of his past, than this. Those notebooks were his youth, those notebooks were his poems, those notebooks were Dylan the young poet. . . . The boy-poet, the Rimbaud of Cwmdonkin Drive, had ceased to exist (*The Life of Dylan Thomas*, p. 247)." What we have from this time on are the poems of the mature poet. They demonstrate his presence in wartime London, prey to "many married London's estranging grief," and his growing concern with other sufferers ("The conversation of prayer," "A refusal to mourn," "Ceremony after a fire raid"). Among such resonant elegies, the most personal is probably the best known, the touching poem to his father, "Do not go gentle into that good night." For many of his admirers, the new clarity of these poems, the recognizable scenes of his meditations, were increasing virtues.

By almost any standards the poems in *Deaths and Entrances* are remarkable. They display technical virtuosity of dazzling proportions, ranging from the strict villanelle in which Thomas contained his love for his father in "Do not go gentle," through the ode-like forms of "Into her Lying Down Head" and "Unluckily for a Death"; the revived medieval patterns of "Vision and Prayer"; the invented stanza of "A Winter's Tale"; and the relatively simple shapes of "The Hunchback in the Park" and "In my Craft or Sullen Art." As a demonstration of the poet's craft they are almost unique, and Thomas himself suggests the importance of his skill when he places "craft" before "art":

> In my craft or sullen art
> Exercised in the still night
> When only the moon rages
> And the lovers lie abed
> With all their griefs in their arms,
> I labour by singing light
> Not for ambition or bread
> Or the strut and trade of charms
> On the ivory stages
> But for the common wages
> Of their most secret heart.

And surely there cannot be a more complete statement of the poet's calling than that, nor a more complete refutation of any possibility of Thomas' lack of utter seriousness as an artist. Here he even tells us that he writes now for an audience, even though such people may not be aware of his existence. The young poet who sang himself only is certainly gone.

There are, however, two poems that are personal, not from the absorbed, fascinated examination of self that had characterized the young poet, but poems filled with a piercing melancholy because time has taken away the innocence of childhood. They are "Poem in October" and "Fern Hill."

These famous poems have much in common. Their structure is similar; the verse stanza in each is complex, formal, and invented by Thomas. The difficulty of such forms must have been most challenging, yet Thomas succeeded in making them lyrical, musical, their intricacy and complexity never obtrusive but necessary to the unity of the poetry. To read them aloud is almost to have to sing them. "Poem in October" has seven stanzas, each of ten lines. The lines are syllabic; that is, Thomas, as he had been doing for some time, did not write them in regular rhythmic patterns but adopted the method of counting the syllables, so that the first line in every stanza has nine syllables, the second line twelve syllables, the third nine, the fourth three, and so on. The rhyme scheme is both unusual and far from obvious. Thomas is using a convention that can be seen in other poems of this period, in "There was a Saviour," for example. He rhymes the vowels only—in our example he rhymes "saviour" with "radium." In "Poem in October" the rhymes are not quite as easily recognized, yet they are there and tactfully hold together the verse stanzas despite the variety of line lengths and the strength and dance of the rhythms. We can see that "heaven" in line 1 rhymes with "heron" in line three, "beckon" in line 5, and "second" in line 9. Similarly, "wood," "rook," and "foot" share the same quality of vowel sound, as do "shore" and "forth." One can easily identify this technique in the other stanzas.

The poem is one of that series of October poems in which Thomas celebrates his birthday; others have already been noted. Here he is not so much celebratory as apprehensive, looking back from the anniversary of his "thirtieth year to heaven" to earlier birthdays, those of his innocence, when he

... saw in the turning so clearly a child's
Forgotten mornings when he walked with his mother
    Through the parables
      Of sun light
    And the legends of the green chapels

          (46–50)

What he sees is "the true joy of the long dead child" who was himself. His final lines express the hope that his "heart's truth" may "Still be sung / On this high hill / In a year's turning."

The poem is unashamedly nostalgic, something that has caused some critics to minimize its importance; yet it is also beautiful and perfectly written. It is possible that Thomas idealizes the innocence of childhood, creating a brief moment of visionary happiness in which "a boy . . . whispered the truth of his joy / To the trees and the stones and the fish in the tide." But this is a startling achievement, and he has offered us the vision in highly sophisticated verse, from an adult point of view, and in the hope that he can retain such perfection of truth in the future. Imperfect though his life may have been, his aim is both the perfection of his art and, through it, a vision of perfection.

"Fern Hill" seems to me an even better poem. "Poem in October" includes merely a glimpse of the child's heaven; here he makes heaven as the boy knew it palpable and visible for us. Like the children in Blake's *Songs of Innocence,* the child Dylan on his aunt's farm, in a country world flawless and shining and without enemies, plays in ignorance that he is a prisoner of time:

. . . nothing I cared, at my sky blue trades, that time
    allows
In all his tuneful turning, so few and such morning
    songs,
    Before the children, green and golden
      Follow him out of grace

          (42–45)

The poem is much more than a paean of regret for times past and lost. Sensuous, opulent in language, rich in imagery and music, it paradoxically mourns the passing of an innocent vision that has made a heaven from a poor hill farm in rough country, something possible only for a child who loves the place, and even while mourning its passing re-creates that very heaven, its brilliance of color, the music of its smoke, its magical horses and foxes.

Thomas knows that he has made Eden once again: "So it must have been after the birth of the simple light / In the first spinning place." To lose such a condition, and to know one has lost it, is an appalling plight. It was Thomas' strength and his fate that he never lost such knowledge, that he kept the child's vision and the man's knowledge. His poem possesses both. He has made both his innocence and his sense of loss clear for all of us as long as his language remains.

There are not many poems after this. Whatever the reasons, Thomas wrote few poems in the last years of his life. He includes in his *Collected Poems* only six more poems, if we count the prologue written specially for that volume. Among them are two that few of his admirers would wish to be without, "Poem on His Birthday" and "Over Sir John's Hill." Both reflect the landscape about his house on the shore—"his house on stilts"—at Laugharne; both are calmer, more resigned. It is tempting to see in them some foreknowledge of the poet's death:

    And freely he goes lost
In the unknown, famous light of great
    And fabulous, dear God.
    ("Poem on His Birthday," 46–48)

and to suggest that his frequent references to God mean that he has made his peace and no longer fears time, that he possesses some consolation. But it seems to me that these are probably the more mature manifestations of his old obsessions: death, religion, the inevitability of time. If he had some peace, it was, as he says in his "Author's Prologue," a poor peace.

    In my seashaken house
    On a breakneck of rocks . . .
    At poor peace I sing
    To you strangers. . . .
        (4–5; 23–24)

His "true joy" remains what it always was, that his "ark sings in the sun."

Although poems were few in his later years, he was not idle. Apart from his reading tours and his broadcasts, he continued to write prose, and he was a superb prose writer. His letters are joyous documents, his telegrams even. Having left his shirts in Dr. Jones's house, he sent his friend a wire that read, "For Pete's sake send my shirts, Love Pete" (*My Friend Dylan Thomas,* p. 114). Prose was the medium in which he found an outlet for his narrative skill, for his humor, for all the sides of his life for which poetry—and it will be remembered that for him poetry was used only for the most serious and profound and mysterious work—was not possible. He had a great deal to offer. He was a born teller of tales.

From the very beginning of his career he knew this. He thought of himself as a writer of poems and stories. This is how he describes himself in a letter, written when he was nineteen, to Glyn Jones: "You ask me to tell you about myself, but my life is so uneventful it is not worth recording. I am a writer of poems and stories" (*The Dragon Has Two Tongues,* p. 172). His life did not remain uneventful, but he was to remain a writer of poems and stories. He had contributed stories as well as poems to *The Swansea Grammar School Magazine.* In an appendix to *The Collected Stories* (1984), the editor, Walford Davies, includes three of these schoolboy pieces, the earliest having appeared in the school magazine in April 1931. There is plenty of evidence that Thomas considered poems and stories equal products of his talent, drawing no distinctions between them, knowing they came from the same source. The magazine he hoped to found and edit, on which he spent some time in the effort to promote it, was to be called *Prose and Verse.* It never appeared, but it is noteworthy that he allows prose to appear first in its title. And Glyn Jones and other friends have told us that when they visited him at his parents' house he was as eager to read his stories to them as he was his poems. They were, indeed, very like his poems.

If we read "The Tree," or any of the stories that eventually appeared in *The Map of Love,* it is evident that they possess the same obsessive imagery, are written in the same heightened rhythms, deal very largely with the same interior world as the poems of that period. It is true that, since they are narratives, Thomas had to pay more attention to the observable world; but it remains largely a place of dreams, the details not very clearly the result of observation; nor do the events of the story necessarily proceed from each other with the force of the inevitable. But they have the same sensuous power as the poems, and their very texture is exciting to discover.

Rising from the house that faced the Jarvis hills in the long distance, there was a tower for the day-birds to build in and for the owls to fly around at night. From the village the light in the tower window shone like a glow-worm through the panes; but the room under the sparrows' nests were rarely lit.

("The Tree," *Collected Stories,* p. 5)

When Thomas first went to London in November 1934, he had already published stories in the magazines. Arriving in Soho, he found his poetry and prose equally admired. In "Where Tawe Flows," one of the autobiographical stories yet to be written and which would be included in *Portrait of the Artist as a Young Dog,* Thomas remembers this period: "Young Mr Thomas was at the moment without employment, but it was understood that he would soon be leaving for London to make a career in Chelsea as a free-lance journalist; he was penniless and hoped, in a vague way, to live on women."

But all this was in the future. And if the appearance of his first book of poems in December 1934 meant there was to be a comparative neglect of his prose, Thomas was not aware of it. He continued to write his stories, to send them to editors. From the room off the Fulham Road he shared with his Swansea friend Fred Janes, and where "for yards around" there was "nothing but poems, poems, poems, butter, eggs, mashed potatoes, mashed among my stories and Janes's canvases," he wrote with pride of the stories that had been accepted by various periodicals. He was a teller of stories all his life.

They were not, however, collected into a volume as the poems were, and when *Eighteen Poems* was followed by *Twenty-five Poems,* Thomas was firmly established as a poet, not a prose writer. He tried to persuade Richard Church, his editor at Dent's, to publish a collection of stories, but Church refused, judging the work obscene. This opinion was shared by the printers, who refused to set the stories for another publisher a little later. It was not until 1939 that a representative sample of Thomas' stories appeared in book form, when seven were included with the poems of *The Map of Love.* In December of the same year *The World I Breathe,* a collection of the poems of the first three books and three stories in addition to those in *The Map of Love,* was published in America. At last the early prose, or those stories which were considered suitable, had found a home.

Thomas, too, had found a home. He and Caitlin had moved into a small house in Laugharne, the little seaside town in Carmarthenshire that was to be his home for much of the rest of his life. They were very poor, and Thomas set about earning money by writing a different kind of story altogether. Glyn Jones recalls that in the summer of 1938 he mentioned to Caitlin Thomas that he was engaged on a volume of stories about childhood: "She seemed very surprised and told me that Dylan had already started doing the same thing. His were the autobiographical stories which in 1940 appeared as *Portrait of the Artist as a Young Dog*" (*The Dragon Has Two Tongues*, p. 191). The new stories were direct, uncomplicated evocations of the Swansea in which Thomas had grown up. They were not at all dreamlike; instead they revealed a most observant eye for the oddities of behavior, and an ear for the eccentricities within patterns of ordinary speech, that allowed Thomas to create credible and individual characters for the men, women, and children who people his stories. And while Thomas had written these stories—there were ten of them—at great speed and in the hope that they would be more commercial than his previous narratives, they also proved that this was the medium he could use for all his skills as a commentator on the world in which he lived, for his sense of fun, for his understanding of the small inevitable tragedies that fill ordinary lives.

Just as he had learned his trade as a poet from his reading of the great poets, particularly those of the nineteenth century, so he had served his willing time with the short-story writers. Among other authors, he knew the work of D. H. Lawrence, H. E. Bates, and Liam O'Flaherty; he had read James Joyce's *Dubliners;* he was an admiring student of Charles Dickens. Among Welsh writers he had a particular interest in the work of Caradoc Evans, whose stories had already used a Welsh background with success. With Glyn Jones he had visited the older man in 1936. They had driven north to Aberystwyth, the two young men wearing each other's hats, to speak to "the great Caradoc Evans," as Thomas called him in a story included in *The Portrait of the Artist as a Young Dog.* There is no direct influence of the Cardiganshire writer's work on Thomas, but he is probably important as someone whose example may have inspired the poet to write about Swansea and its people.

Again, Thomas had been living unprotected in the world for a number of years, his eye and his wits sharpened, his naturally alert senses alive to what was about him. He had already abandoned in many ways the interior universe of his early work and, as we have seen in his poems, was ready to create a world more related to that in which he lived. Above all, he had become a great storyteller, famous (as he almost said himself) about the bars. He realized that there were great areas of his ability and his personality that he would never use for lyric poetry, but he could use them in his stories. From this time on, the difference between his poetry and prose was marked.

Thomas believed that poetry is a solemn art, and he was a serious poet, dedicating his life to the service of his muse, restricting his themes to a few great and inevitable subjects. There is a great deal of word-play in his verse, of ecstatic delight in the combination of opulent sounds and highly exact, unusual meaning, in the presence in his lines of serious puns, but there is no room for laughter. Yet he was also a brilliantly funny man, and it is in the ten stories we are considering that a comic Thomas made his appearance. The stories, united in that they have as a central character "young Mr Thomas," move from the innocence of the first three stories ("The Peaches," "A Visit to Grandpa's," "Patricia, Edith, and Arnold"), through two splendid stories of his school days (in one of which, "The Fight," we meet Dr. Daniel Jones as a boy), to a more complex and jaunty person, Thomas as a cub reporter, his cigarette worn in admiring imitation of the old reporter he accompanies through the public houses of the town ("Old Garbo"). We see him as a haunter of deserted winter beaches, as a young man about to leave the town for London. It is with this portrait of himself that Thomas takes as decisive a leave of his younger self as he did with his sale of his notebooks.

The stories are full of wonderful talk, something in which Thomas himself excelled. We hear and recognize the characters as they preach from the back of a cart:

I sat on the hay and stared at Gwilym preaching, and heard his voice rise and crack and sink to a whisper and break into singing and Welsh and ring triumphantly and be wild and meek. The sun through a hole shone on his praying shoulders, and he said: "O God, Thou art everywhere all the time, in the dew of the morning, in the frost of the evening, in the field and the town, in the preacher and the sinner, in the sparrow and the big buzzard."

("The Peaches," *Collected Stories*, p. 128)

They are irreverent to school teachers, joke and wisecrack their way to the shore, stare in sadness and despair at the sea. A great mimic, Thomas realized his exceptional narrative skills in these stories: his sense of place, his fine ear for speech, and his love, appreciative and unjudging, for the people he creates. These are the qualities that make him a fine writer as distinct from a fine poet, and they are the qualities that helped to make him generally popular. Had he not written his stories he would have been a lesser, and a less interesting, figure.

Portrait of the Artist as a Young Dog is a title that pays clear tribute to Joyce, but it is not Joyce's *Portrait of the Artist as a Young Man* that one is reminded of when reading Thomas' book. Rather, the stories are clearly of the same type as those in Joyce's *Dubliners*, and Thomas is surely telling us this. Both books are set in provincial cities, both relate the important small events in unimportant lives and make them important. Stylistically, however, they are very different. Thomas himself denied that there was any Joycean influence on his work:

I cannot say that I have been "influenced" by Joyce, whom I enormously admire, and whose "Ulysses," and earlier stories, I have read a great deal. . . . As you know, the name given to innumerable portrait paintings by their artists is, "Portrait of the Artist as a Young Man." . . . I myself made a bit of doggish fun of the painting title and intended no possible reference to Joyce.

("Notes on the Art of Poetry," *Texas Quarterly*, Winter 1961)

Be that as it may, it is certain that "the bit of doggish fun" is his own. Although Thomas' title is said to have been the suggestion of Richard Hughes, the distinguished author of *A High Wind in Jamaica* and other fine work, Thomas had almost used it years before when he wrote, in 1933, to his friend Trevor Hughes. In that letter Dylan had advised his friend to "dive into the sea of yourself like a young dog." In his own stories, Thomas had taken his own advice and dived into the sea of his childhood and youth.

Portrait was published in 1940, the last of Thomas' books to appear until the war was over. He was—after a short period in which things looked very uncertain—working fairly regularly as a writer of film scripts and a broadcaster, his own writing pushed aside somewhat. He was, however, working intermittently on a novel, and was sending parts of it to London publishers, without success. This was the comic novel, just as autobiographical as his stories, eventually called *Adventures in the Skin Trade*. It was never completed and was published posthumously in 1955.

Despite its late public appearance—an extract had been published in *Folios of New Writing* in 1941 —most of it seems to have been written in the summer of 1941. Its hero, Samuel Bennet, seems to be none other than the young Mr. Thomas of the *Portrait*, and he continues where that young man left off, departing from Swansea by the very train that Thomas himself left home in "to make a career in Chelsea as a free-lance journalist." Vernon Watkins, who wrote an interesting foreword to the novel when it eventually appeared, thought that it remained unfinished because of the impact of the war, particularly of the air raids on London, on what he called Thomas' "essentially tragic vision," but he also thought that Thomas mistrusted his own facility. Certainly Thomas was able to write this sort of prose very quickly, but I feel that there may well have been other reasons for the failure to continue the adventures of Samuel Bennet. The novel is loosely structured as picaresque and moves forward in an arbitrary and rather casual manner. Thomas, that deliberate artist, must have felt very dubious about it; it is impossible to see, for example, any serious reason for it to end anywhere, or indeed to continue. It is funny and inventive, with passages of brilliant slapstick, but Thomas may simply have come to the end of what he had to say. He was, moreover, not a natural novelist; he was a natural short-story writer; the novel was too long for him. The very nature of his talent, selective, concentrated, meant that he was not at home with the novel, a form into which one can pack almost anything. And while Thomas recognized his kinship with Dickens when he called *Adventures in the Skin Trade* "a mixture of Oliver Twist, Little Dorrit, Kafka, Beachcomber, and 3-adjectives-a-penny belly-churning Thomas," it was Dickens' energy and humor that he was acknowledging, the furious poetry. Thomas never actually put his novel away entirely. As late as 1953, the year of his death, he was still suggesting that he might continue it.

For all practical purposes the novel was abandoned when Thomas went to London to work, and the demands on his time from then on resulted in there remaining only seven short narratives from this last period of his life, and six of the seven were written for broadcasting. It is ironic that his great popular reputation may rest on one or two of these and on *Under Milk Wood,* his "play for voices." It is also understandable, for they are entirely memorable pieces, bringing us the whole man, his warmth, the wide range of his humor, his pathos, his brilliant images, his incredible memory for the days and places of his childhood, his moving sadness for what had gone forever, and even enough magic to remind us that he was a great poet.

The first of these late pieces, "Quite Early One Morning," reads like a first draft of *Under Milk Wood,* for it deals with the dreams of a small sleeping town in the early morning, where Captain Tiny Evans, a trial Captain Cat, sleeps and dreams of "a rainbow of flying fishes." But it is "A Child's Christmas in Wales" that everyone knows. All over the world, in the days immediately before Christmas, we can hear from schools and houses the poet's voice rebuilding for us an impossible and utterly satisfying Christmas. Compounded of two similar stories, "Memories of Christmas" and "Conversation about Christmas," this was first published in *Harper's Bazaar* as "A Child's Memories of Christmas in Wales" in December 1950. It is a rich confection, as rich with gifts as any Christmas can hope to be, its snow untouched, its parties warm and musical, packed as a pudding with fruit and brandy. Dickens is not far away, but there are unforgettable Thomas moments too, like that when "with dog-disturbing whistle and sugar fags, I would scour the swatched town for the news of the little world, and find always a dead bird by the white Post Office or the deserted swings; perhaps a robin, all but one of his fires out" (*The Collected Stories,* p. 300).

"The Followers" is a ghost story of the most cunning and surprising sort. On a wet night, so beautifully realized that we must believe it, two bored young men, almost penniless but bravely keeping up appearances, one with a gallant cap, the other with a rolled umbrella and an attempted mustache, follow an ordinary girl home through the soaked, domestic streets. In such a world, so

solid and convincing, ghosts should not happen, and it is all the more credible and terrifying when they do—and also funny. Thomas has learned how to select and create his detail; he has looked hard and lovingly at his world.

"The Followers" is the only one of these late narratives not written for broadcasting, and perhaps the only one that does not have the sound of Thomas' unique voice in it as a result. Certainly the uproarious events of "A Story" were made for him alone to tell, and the very structure of the sentences as they lie on the page seems to carry with them the man's own telling:

> But there he was, always, a steaming hulk of an uncle, his braces straining like hawsers. . . . As he ate, the house grew smaller; he billowed out over the furniture, the loud check meadow of his waistcoat littered, as though after a picnic, with cigarette ends, peelings, cabbage stalks, birds' bones, gravy.
>
> (*The Collected Stories,* p. 337)

Reading again these short narratives, as personal as any he wrote as a young man, it is impossible not to regret the loss of the work he might have written, and to wonder in what direction Thomas might have moved. We have not considered yet *Under Milk Wood,* the play for radio that was successively broadcast, adapted for the stage, and filmed. This might suggest that Thomas would have turned more and more to the stage for his work. His death put an end to the projected opera libretto he was to write for Igor Stravinsky, but we know he was enormously excited by the prospect. *Under Milk Wood* was first performed, in almost its final form, in New York only weeks before Thomas died there. He was working on it even during its performance, sending altered and additional lines to the actors as they read, and Thomas continued to tinker with it almost to his death.

Yet it is astonishly complete and unified, its cast of daft characters amiably dependent one on the other, the laws of its self-contained community thoroughly justifiable in the terms of that community. It cannot be said to have a plot. Its events are those of a single day in a small sea town in South Wales, Laugharne maybe, with echoes of New Quay, in Dyfed, where Thomas also lived. Raymond Williams has distinguished "three kinds of writing" in the play, "narrative, dialogue, song," an observation that helps to define the simplicity of its structure and to point the subtlety of the writing. The unity of the play, its corresponding and related oppositions, of darkness to light, of public chorus to individual musing, of song to prose, of innocence to innocent guilt—these make it remarkable. In it, suggests Williams, "Thomas wrote his adequate epilogue, his uproarious and singing lament" ("Dylan Thomas's Play for Voices," in *Dylan Thomas,* C. B. Cox, ed., p. 98).

There are always difficulties in measuring the stature of a poet. It seems to me that Thomas wrote enough remarkable poetry to justify our calling him great. There are poems that have enriched our literature, and his work has influenced a whole generation of poets. He changed the direction of English language poetry, his example being just as powerful in America as in Britain; nor were they always poets younger than himself who followed his lead. His life may well seem chaotic and without direction, yet it was purposeful and direct when we think of his one aim, to wait for his poems and to write them to the very best of his ability. All his working life he "laboured by singing light" to refine and perfect his skill; he was a great craftsman. For nearly a year he worked on the "Author's Prologue" to his *Collected Poems,* refusing to allow the book to go forward until he had completed to his satisfaction the almost impossibly difficult task of writing a poem of one hundred and two lines, in which line 102 rhymes with line 1, line 101 with line 2, and so on, until they meet in a couplet at the heart of the poem. My belief is that the poetry is as remarkable as the technical ability. And there may be another test of greatness, perhaps one that is more important than the opinion of any critic. On 1 March 1982, when the ceremony for the dedication of the poet's memorial stone took place in Westminster Abbey, the great hall was full. People stood in the aisles, at the pediments of pillars, wherever there was a foot of room. Hundreds stood outside in the rain, unable to hear a word of the proceedings. Ordinary people as well as the great and famous had come to pay their respects, many years after his death, to the poet. "He was loyal to the poem," said Theodore Roethke (*Encounter,* January 1954, p. 11), "he was

one of the great ones." And the people had come to agree with that judgment, to affirm that poetry was necessary for the language and to honor the man who had proved it for them. That may well be greatness.

SELECTED BIBLIOGRAPHY

I. Separate Works. *Eighteen Poems* (London, 1934); *Twenty-five Poems* (London, 1936); *The Map of Love* (London, 1939); *The World I Breathe* (Norfolk, Conn., 1939); *Portrait of the Artist as a Young Dog* (Norfolk, Conn., and London, 1940); *New Poems* (Norfolk, Conn., 1943); *Deaths and Entrances* (London, 1946); *Selected Writings of Dylan Thomas* (New York, 1946); *In Country Sleep and Other Poems* (New York, 1952); *Collected Poems 1934–1952* (London, 1952); *Under Milk Wood* (London, 1954); *Quite Early One Morning* (London, 1954); *A Prospect of the Sea* (London, 1955); *Letters to Vernon Watkins* (London, 1957); "Notes on the Art of Poetry," in *Texas Quarterly* (Winter 1961); *The Notebooks of Dylan Thomas* (New York, 1967), ed. by R. Maud, also pub. as *Poet in the Making* (London, 1968); *The Poems* (London, 1971), ed. by D. Jones; *The Death of the King's Canary* (London, 1976), with J. Davenport; *The Collected Stories* (London, 1984), ed. by W. Davies.

II. Biographical and Critical Works. H. Treece, *Dylan Thomas, "Dog Among the Fairies"* (London, 1949); E. Olsen, *The Poetry of Dylan Thomas* (Chicago, 1954); J. M. Brinnin, *Dylan Thomas in America* (Boston, 1955); C. Thomas, *Leftover Life to Kill* (Boston and London, 1957); E. W. Tedlock, ed., *Dylan Thomas: The Legend and the Poet* (London, 1960); H. H. Kleinmann, *The Religious Sonnets of Dylan Thomas* (Berkley, Calif., 1963; New York, 1979); C. FitzGibbon, *The Life of Dylan Thomas* (Boston and London, 1965); C. B. Cox, ed., *Dylan Thomas: A Collection of Critical Essays* (New York, 1966), includes essay by D. Daiches; J. Scully, ed., *Modern Poets on Modern Poetry* (London, 1966); G. Jones, *The Dragon Has Two Tongues* (London, 1968); R. Maud, *Dylan Thomas in Print* (Pittsburgh, Pa., 1970); W. Davies, *Dylan Thomas* (Cardiff, 1972); W. Davies, ed., *Dylan Thomas: New Critical Essays* (London, 1972); R. M. Kidder, *Dylan Thomas: The Country of the Spirit* (Princeton, N. J., 1973); R. B. Kirshner, Jr., *Dylan Thomas, The Poet and His Critics* (Chicago, 1976); D. Jones, *My Friend Dylan Thomas* (London, 1977); P. Ferris, *The Life of Dylan Thomas* (London, 1977); J. Ackerman, *Welsh Dylan* (Cardiff, 1979); C. Thomas, *Caitlin* (London, 1986), with G. Tremlett.

J. R. R. TOLKIEN
(1892–1973)

Karl Kroeber

In 1954 the British publishers Allen and Unwin, in association with Houghton Mifflin in the United States, issued an edition of 3500 copies of *The Fellowship of the Ring*, the first volume of a lengthy fantasy by J. R. R. Tolkien, a professor at Oxford known only to a handful of philologists and medievalists. But the book was so popular that the publishers quickly brought out the second and third volumes, *The Two Towers* (1954) and *The Return of the King* (1955). The trilogy, known as *The Lord of the Rings,* was so immediately successful that a new, larger printing was required, and soon another, still larger printing became necessary. In 1965 when the first paperback edition of *The Lord of the Rings* was issued, its 50,000 copies were instantly sold out. Since then millions more have been printed and the trilogy has been translated into a dozen languages. So popular had Tolkien become that over a million hardback copies of his posthumously published *The Silmarillion* (1977) were purchased in the first year of its publication. Tolkien's work, in fact, initiated the success of the mass marketing of literary fantasy, now a major part of the publishing industry.

How did so reclusive, even pedantic, a scholar produce such an innovative and commercially successful book? What qualities of *The Lord of the Rings* have made it so esteemed by so many for more than a generation, especially by students and young adults? Do those qualities suggest that Tolkien's book, like analogous literary sensations of earlier times, is likely to fade into obscurity, or will it endure as a classic? Answers to such questions probably are to be found in the nature and social function of literary fantasy in the second half of the twentieth century.

LIFE AND WORK

JOHN RONALD REUEL TOLKIEN (always called Ronald by his family) was born on 3 January 1892, at Bloemfontein, South Africa, where his father Arthur had taken a position with the Bank of Africa. The Tolkien family had been prosperous piano manufacturers, but the business had failed. Mabel Suffield, Arthur's wife, was the daughter of a once successful drapery manufacturer in Birmingham, England, who had gone bankrupt and survived by selling disinfectant to shopkeepers around the city.

In the spring of 1895 Mabel sailed back to England because the African climate was damaging Ronald's health. Arthur hoped to return to England soon, but he contracted rheumatic fever the following autumn and died early in 1896. After a few months of living with her parents, Mabel rented a cottage on the edge of Birmingham, and from then until her death in 1904, she and her two sons lived in rented houses on the edges of the city. In 1900 Mabel Tolkien had converted to Roman Catholicism, and after her death her parish priest, Father Francis Morgan, took responsibility for the upbringing and education of her sons.

Ronald's only means of escape from a lower-middle-class commercial life was by winning an academic scholarship, which, with some difficulty, he did in 1910, gaining entrance to Exeter College, Oxford. In 1908 Tolkien fell in love with Edith Bratt, like him an orphan, three years his senior, but in 1910 Father Francis forbade him to communicate with her until he was of age. Tolkien obeyed. At Oxford he began studying classics but soon concentrated on English language and literature, being awarded first-class honors in his final examination in 1915. He revisited Edith five days after his twenty-first birthday, and they were formally betrothed in 1914 when, at Tolkien's insistence, she converted to Roman Catholicism.

With the rise of patriotism at the outbreak of the First World War, Tolkien's decision to stay at the university to earn his bachelor's degree was an act of moral courage—he was condemned by both family and friends for not at once enlisting. But since he was engaged and had no money he felt he had to obtain his degree before volunteering. As soon as he received it he entered the army, receiving a commission as a second lieutenant and being given training as a signal officer. When his battalion was notified it was being sent to France in March 1916, he used his last leave to marry Edith. In France he was caught up in the bloody horror of the Somme offensive that gained no ground and cost the British 600,000 casualties in four months. Tolkien was not wounded, but in November he was evacuated back to England suffering from a severe case of trench fever. His recovery was slow, and he never returned to the battlefields of France. While convalescing in early 1917 he began to develop "The Book of Lost Tales," imaginative writings he had begun in 1914, work that would become *The Silmarillion,* published more than sixty years later.

The first of Tolkien's four children was born in November 1917. After the Armistice Tolkien joined the staff of the *Oxford English Dictionary,* and in 1920 he was appointed Reader in English Language at Leeds University, where, with E. V. Gordon, he shaped an edition of *Sir Gawain and the Green Knight,* a work that helped lead to his election as Professor of Anglo-Saxon at Oxford University in 1925. For the next thirty-four years Tolkien taught at Oxford, where he became known as an eccentric and often incomprehensible lecturer but one dedicated to helping advanced students. Not a highly published scholar, Tolkien's most significant academic accomplishment was the Gollancz Memorial Lecture at the British Academy in November 1936, "Beowulf: The Monsters and the Critics," which was influential in establishing the Anglo-Saxon poem as a masterpiece of world literature.

At Oxford Tolkien enjoyed informal meetings with small groups of academics who shared his interest in translating medieval literature, such as Norse sagas, or in reading to each other their own unpublished writings—stories, poems, sections of novels—which would then be discussed and criticized. The best known of these groups in which Tolkien participated was the Inklings, a shifting collection of Oxford scholars and writers, of whom the most talented was Tolkien's best friend, C. S. Lewis, who from their earliest meetings until the end of his life admired Tolkien's stories and encouraged him both to write and to publish.

Except for a few poems, however, Tolkien published none of his creative work until, in 1936, he was persuaded by friends to let the firm of Allen and Unwin consider his typescript of *The Hobbit; or, There and Back Again* (1937), a story that had delighted all those to whom he had read it, including his own children. Since it was a children's book, Sir Stanley Unwin, the chairman of the company, employed his ten-year-old son Rayner as reader of the manuscript for the fee of a shilling. Rayner's one-paragraph critique of the book is as good as any brief review that has ever appeared, concluding that the book "should appeal to all children between the ages of 5 and 9" (quoted in Carpenter, p. 181). *The Hobbit* was published to excellent reviews, a couple written anonymously by C. S. Lewis, and it sold so well that Unwin asked Tolkien to write a sequel.

Tolkien wished to oblige, but it took him fifteen years to complete that sequel, which we know as the trilogy *The Lord of the Rings. The Hobbit,* in fact, had been an aberration in Tolkien's creative career. In the summer of 1928, earning a little extra money to support his growing family by reading examinations of secondary school students seeking university admissions, he happened on an examination with a blank page, and in a moment of relief he wrote on the page, "In a hole in the ground there lived a hobbit." Where that sentence came from he never understood, and it was some time before he began developing, slowly, that now famous opening sentence of his first book into a narrative—began, indeed, to imagine what hobbits might be and do.

Tolkien had written his first story, about a dragon, when he was seven. But it was not until he was recuperating from his experiences in the First World War that he began composing in earnest, although only for his private satisfaction or, later, to entertain his children. What he wrote after the war and throughout the entire decade of the 1920's and into the 1930's was published posthumously as *The Silmarillion,* followed by a series of "Lost Tales" volumes—*The Book of Lost Tales Part I* (1983), *The Book of Lost Tales Part II* (1984), *The Lays of Beleriand* (1985), and *The Shaping of Middle-Earth* (1986). These writings shall be referred to in this essay as "Silmarillion materials." None of this writing contained anything to do with hobbits. *The Hobbit,* however, includes some references to the history and mythology of the Silmarillion material that throughout his life was the primary focus of Tolkien's imaginative activity.

To write what became the 600,000-word sequel to *The Hobbit,* between 1937 and 1952, Tolkien had to imagine the relationship of his relatively recently imagined creatures to the vast, complicated world of Silmarillion materials that he had created over the previous two decades. Following the enormous success of *The Lord of the Rings,* when his publishers were clamoring for anything Tolkien cared to write, he spent nearly twenty years procrastinating and not perfecting the intricate Silmarillion material. *The Silmarillion,* which was finally published four years after Tolkien's death on 2 September 1973, was edited by his son Christopher.

The Hobbit, under wartime pressure of paper shortages, went out of print in 1942, and its subsequent popularity largely derives from the success of *The Lord of the Rings.* Tolkien's fame, and whatever critical repute is awarded him, depends principally on the trilogy. "On Fairy-Stories" (1947) is the most intellectually original and provocative modern discussion of fantasy, and seems sure to gain in esteem of historians of criticism. "Beowulf: The Monsters and the Critics" (1936) will hold a distinctive place in Anglo-Saxon studies, having confirmed beyond question *Beowulf*'s artistic merit, and having used the poem to establish fundamental differences between the heroic literatures of northern and southern Europe. The former, Tolkien argued persuasively, centers on martial heroism as its own end in full recognition that the wages of heroism is death. Furthermore, Tolkien's essay proved that Grendel, his mother, and the dragon are brilliant successes of artistic imagination.

Tolkien's few short stories all have charm, though none is a masterpiece. "Leaf by Niggle" (1945; collected in *Tree and Leaf,* 1964) dramatizes the difficulties of being an artist such as Tolkien was, obsessed with details even while worriedly striving to attain a large, dominating form. And he was unsure of his own artistic ability, evidenced in his own self-criticism and self-parody. In *Farmer Giles of Ham* (1949) Tolkien parodies medieval literary forms and conventions, making special fun of *Sir Gawain and the Green Knight* and Chaucer's *Canterbury Tales,* but also entertainingly spoofs academic scholarship and his own fantasies. *Smith of Wootton Major* (1967) is a late story evocative of the bereavements of old age. *The Silmarillion,* and to a much lesser extent the subsequent books retrieved from his father's manuscripts by Christopher Tolkien (who makes use of his father's original, won-

derfully apt title for *The Silmarillion, The Book of Lost Tales*), will always be a joyous resource to enthusiasts. But the material in these volumes remains the matrix for Tolkien's most perfected artistry, of which *The Hobbit* and *The Lord of the Rings* are the dominant expressions.

A way of explaining Tolkien's curious talent of writing enormous numbers of stories but then being slow, even reluctant, to publish is to examine his reaction to the success of *The Lord of the Rings.* Although he was grateful for the wealth it brought him, and sometimes flattered by his fame, he was, unlike most bestselling authors, embarrassed and troubled by the popularity of his books, and did virtually nothing to exploit it. He never, for example, visited the United States, where he would have been lionized and could have earned a fair sum of money through a few lectures. Why not? One reason was that Tolkien was more than anything else a professor.

Many hours of a professor's life are spent in preparing classes, lecturing, and reading and writing on students' work. In addition, university professors find themselves engaged in an array of departmental and university meetings that often leave little time for what initially lured them to the university—research, the analysis and the re-evaluation of a narrow field of knowledge. But Tolkien loved the professorial life, despite its time-consuming responsibilities, as a life motivated by passionate commitment to an intellectual discipline that goes on forever. His specialty was philology, the study of the history of words, and he observed that we do not know with certainty the origin of *any* ancient word. The imaginative reconstructions of verbal origins devised by each philologist are gradually absorbed, and lost, within the ever-developing history of the discipline: one finds oneself by losing oneself within an imaginative tradition.

There is a further source of pleasure for a scholar like Tolkien principally concerned with literary texts: the delight of the great art that is his constant study. There is a difference, however, between studying literary art and making literary art, being an artist. Indeed, the occupations are almost adversarial, as Tolkien demonstrates in his two finest critical essays, "Beowulf: The Monsters and the Critics" and "On Fairy-Stories," since the artist primarily pursues beauty, as does the painter Niggle in Tolkien's story *Leaf by Niggle.* It is rare that a genuine professor, such as Tolkien was, achieves success as a creative artist. But the peculiar accomplishment of Tolkien's imaginative creations can only be understood as having emerged from and having been shaped by the special focus of a professorial life that Tolkien himself recognized as, nevertheless, hostile to artistic activities.

ORIGINS OF THE SILMARILLION MATERIAL

THE Silmarillion material that Tolkien began to compose in 1914, and that he added to and emended for the rest of his life, consists of invented legends about the creation of the world and its early history. These stories are like the myths and wonder-laden tales of the northern European peoples—Finnish, Anglo-Saxon, Norse, Germanic and Celtic—whose literatures were the center of Tolkien's professional studies. Some of his invented legends were written in prose, some in various verse forms, as was true of the myths and stories he studied. Moreover, he regarded his invented legends as having been "originally" composed in invented languages. Tolkien devised several of these languages, the most important being Quenya (which was influenced by Finnish in the complexity of its declensions) and Sindarin (whose closest analogue is Welsh), which possess large vocabularies, complete systems of tense and declension, a complex syntax, as well as coherent phonological structures. Tolkien even composed a few works in these languages.

The conclusion of a poem, "The Last Ark," which Tolkien recited to an Esperanto Congress to illustrate his "secret vice" of the pleasure in linguistic invention (which for him lay in the new relations thus created between sounds and notions), exemplifies his practice:

Man kiluva lómi sangane,   Who shall see the clouds gather,
telume lungane   the heavens bending
tollalinta ruste   upon crumbling hills,
vea qualume   the sea heaving
mandu yáme,   the abyss yawning,
aira móre ala tinwi   the old darkness
lante no lanta-mindon?   beyond the stars falling upon fallen towers?

Man tiruva rusta kirya   Who shall heed a broken ship
laiqa ondolissen   on the green rocks

nu karne vaiya   under red skies,
úri nienaite híse   a bleared sun blinking
pike assari silde   on bones gleaming
óresse oilima?   in the last morning?

Hui oilima man kiluva   Who shall see the last evening?
hui oilimaite?

(*The Monsters and the Critics and Other Essays,* pp. 214–215)

Mostly, however, in composing stories he fantasized that he was translating and reconstructing, as he did in his scholarly work with Norse sagas, the Anglo-Saxon *Beowulf,* or the Finnish *Kalevala.* He thus fused his creative imagining and his professional scholarship.

Tolkien is the only major fantasy writer to have created his fantasy world from a beginning in the systematic invention of languages. And he did this on the basis of a profound scholarly study of medieval northern European philology and literature. Critics without his knowledge tend to misjudge the form of his art. The difficulty in describing the Silmarillion material points to its essential nature of not being entirely coherent. It is deliberately inchoate. That is to say, Tolkien makes the Quenya and Sindarin legends exist as do the medieval legends and myths of northern European peoples in Germany, Scandinavia, Ireland, and Britain for twentieth-century scholars. *The Kalevala,* which fascinated Tolkien and was an important inspiration for him, has often been called the Finnish national epic. But in fact it is a collection of diverse traditional songs, some narrative, some lyric, some magical incantations, which was painstakingly gathered together and edited in the middle of the nineteenth century by a Finnish doctor, Elias Lonnröt, to serve as a poetical museum of vanishing Finnish rural life. Tolkien created the Silmarillion material as an analogous collection of remnants of the various songs and stories of what he called Elvish people. From both Elves and medieval Finnish peasants only fragments of historical and cultural coherence could be reconstructed by even the most diligent present-day philologist-collector.

Quenya and Sindarin are Elvish languages, and the Silmarillion material consists of Elvish myths, legends (on the edge between history and fairy tales), and songs. Elves, as Tolkien presents them, are the "first-born," like men (the "followers") but a little taller and handsomer, more sensitive to the beauty of the world, and doomed to be immortal. Elves who bring the world to high achievements of beauty and courage gradually fade away as the followers grow and absorb the life the Elves have shaped, the special gift (or doom) of men, the followers, being mortality.

Tolkien's conception of an immortal, humanlike race that precedes mankind as we know it, fading as our world comes into being, becoming like carved "figures barely visible in weathered stone in unpeopled lands" (*Lord of the Rings*, vol. 3, bk. 6, ch. 6), imaginatively repeats an idea very widespread in human mythologies—although so far as one can tell, Tolkien was unaware of this universality, since his knowledge of mythology was limited to Europe, where the conception has been somewhat concealed by the superimposition of later philosophical/religious systems. Many Native American cultures, for example, conceive of a world inhabited by firstborn and then followers in a fashion similar to that described by Tolkien. The difference lies in angle of imagination. Whereas Tolkien conceives of a different kind of person, Elves, inhabiting our familiar world, some Native Americans thought of their firstborn as inhabiting a world different from ours, one in which, for example, animals could speak. Native Americans did not, therefore, make modern man's distinction between myth and history, between what we call fictional and factual stories. All the Native American stories are realistic—it is just that the conditions of reality were different when their firstborn were living here. The distinction is worth noticing because it illuminates what Tolkien wished to accomplish, what he means by the "secondary world" produced by the "subcreation" of a writer of fantasy. To write a fantasy, or to tell a story about the firstborn, is to imagine a different kind of reality from that currently prevailing for the imaginer and his audience. Such imagining can be a way of escaping from the actual conditions in which the imagining takes place. But it also can be a way of assessing those conditions, and even of finding ways to improve them. Preliterate cultures, such as those of medieval northern Europeans, recognized the practical advantages of creating such perspectives on their own culture, and modern fantasy, Tolkien believed, could function in an analogous fashion.

The origins of contemporary fantasy may be found in a reaction to Enlightenment rationalism in the eighteenth century. In the middle of the century James Macpherson became famous through his popular European work, *Fragments of Ancient Poetry Collected in the Highlands of Scotland*. These fragments purported to be translations of ancient Gaelic legends unearthed by scholarship. Attractive to eighteenth-century readers because of its pseudo-biblical poetic prose that appealed more to sentiment than to logic, its many romantically exotic names of peoples and places, and its themes of failed grandeur, unhappy love, and heroic enterprise amidst the storms of a bleak northern landscape, Macpherson's work claimed to be "authentic," not an imaginative invention, and it was in fact very loosely based on Gaelic historical materials.

A few years later William Blake in a series of books combining brilliantly colored etchings and startling poetry created a bewildering "death-filled hellish" world through parody of the Bible and traditionally religious literary works such as *Paradise Lost*. Blake, a devout Protestant who lived during a time of enthusiastic utopianism, utilized his personal re-imaginings of myths central to Western civilization to challenge both orthodox religious and scientific thought of his day, hoping to reconstitute Western culture by reestablishing imagination as the primary human capacity.

Like other writers who survived the First World War, Tolkien was more pessimistic, willing to settle for the recovery of a little imaginativeness to lighten the hyperrationalizing of modern, industrial culture. So the tone of his works is closer to the nostalgic melancholy of Macpherson, just as his medium is a somewhat archaic prose, not bewilderingly innovative poetry. Yet the analogy to Blake ought not to be entirely dismissed, for both Tolkien and Blake understood that the imagination does not operate freely unless its possessors have the energy and courage to try reinventing the world around them—and its history.

This view helps to distinguish Tolkien from other writers of fantasy of the later nineteenth and early twentieth century, such as George Macdonald, Lord Dunsany, or William Morris. The latter's *Earthly Paradise* makes use of both Greek and Norse myths in a decorative poem that evades confronting the real difficulties of imaginatively reconstituting earlier mythological or legendary practices. The anthropological comparative analyses of James Frazer in *The Golden Bough* at the turn of the century in fact are closer to Tolkienian imaginings. But Tolkien never developed a deep interest in the Eastern or classical myths that were among Frazer's chief concerns. And Tolkien's way of inventing stories was by inventing languages which the stories embodied. He had no interest in simply retelling old stories, which is one reason he found the tales of King Arthur unadaptable to his purposes.

This point suggests how Tolkien's training as a comparative philologist, one who analyzes texts in terms of the history of the forms of its words and grammatical structures, paradoxically associates him with contemporaneous literary artists and literary trends he consciously ignored or disdained. It is less important that T. S. Eliot drew on Frazerian anthropology for *The Waste Land,* or that William Butler Yeats's poetry was founded on the basis of an original mythopoetic vision, than that while Tolkien was writing *The Silmarillion,* James Joyce was writing *Finnegans Wake.* This is no mere coincidence. The intellectual life of the first years of the twentieth century was dominated by a fascination with language, as is demonstrated by the psychology of Sigmund Freud and the philosophy of Ludwig Wittgenstein. This salient characteristic of modern intellectualism is highlighted by the work of Ferdinand de Saussure, who revolutionized the study of linguistics by turning it from philology to structuralism, a turn Tolkien's work seeks to counteract.

Comparative philology was the first historical science, having its origins in a monograph by Sir William Jones in 1786 which argued that Germanic and Celtic languages, as well as Greek, Latin, and Sanskrit, so closely resembled each other formally that they must have arisen from a common source—what soon came to be called Indo-European. This study of linguistic phenomena, therefore, depends on comparisons between languages and the reconstruction of processes of historical change, extrapolated backward behind any existent language to sources that can only be imagined. Tolkien pointed out that this approach permits an appreciation of a dead language, such as Homeric Greek, unavailable to those who used it when it was alive. Of course the later scholar cannot recover the nuances and meaning and connotations of the original speakers, nor the subtleties of pronunciation, but the scholar does have a perspective from which to see, with a special clarity that was formerly unavailable, the complexities of word

forms, the interrelationship of those forms, and their connection to word meanings.

Tolkien recognized that a keen source of pleasure for a philologist is perceiving relationships of word sounds and word forms to the ideas they express. This pleasure is intensified in the invention of languages, because, as all linguists agree, the meaning of words is arbitrary. "Arbitrary" here means that it is perfectly reasonable for the Romans, for example, to have called what we refer to as a tree by the name of arbor. It is reasonable because "arbor" is part of a complete, intricately organized linguistic system, a language, a human construct. But it is characteristic of languages that their intricate systems contain subtle complexities of meaning that change in time, taking on a history. To imagine a language as Tolkien did is to practice imagining complexities in words' meanings, how these change in time, and how particular words relate to or differ from words with similar meanings in other languages. This practice accounts for Tolkien's peculiar skill, for example, in deploying commonplace words so as to exploit their complicated metaphoric connotations. A simple but striking instance in *The Lord of the Rings* is "shadow," a word (like the phenomenon to which it refers) that we encounter casually every day, but which carries a rich freight of connotations, of fear, of doubt, of moral darkness, dangerous supernatural forces, and so on. It is these connotations of the ordinariness of "shadow" that Tolkien uses to evoke our imagination of Sauron's evil which, we realize when the Ring is destroyed, is also "shadowy" in being insubstantial.

Comparative philology requires imaginative contemplation of words, leading as it does inevitably to reconstruction, the speculative creation of a source word in a vanished language, such as Indo-European. This imagining is the reverse of irrational. It adheres to severely logical systems of morphology and phonology. Tolkien's fiction is an extension of that combination of rigorous logic and fantasy. He understood when he once overheard a man murmur thoughtfully to himself, "Yes, I think I shall express the accusative case by a prefix," that the speaker shared what Tolkien called his "secret vice" of inventing languages. He understood because he and the other man shared a knowledge of the strict discipline of linguistic science.

Most of the best poets and novelists of the early twentieth century experimented—"radically"—with language. Tolkien, too, was intrigued by what language could be made to do, for in good measure increased interest in what language is and how it works had been stimulated by the scholarship of philologists, culminating in works such as Milman Parry's discovery of the formulaic system of Homeric poetry and the production of the *Oxford English Dictionary*. But whereas Gertrude Stein or James Joyce manipulated language of the present day, Tolkien clung to the philological tradition of exploring the developmental, historical nature of words—even when he worked as an artist. Joyce, for example, seems to have been ignorant of scientific linguistics. He plays with words, principally by punning, as verbal counters that may have a symbolic, that is, unhistorical, significance, but he almost never draws upon their morphological history. Joyce's inventiveness with language is purely semantic, as in the sentence from *Finnegans Wake*, "There's many's the ice-polled globetopper is haunted by the hottest spot under his equator like Ramrod, the meaty hunter, always jaeger for a thrust." Tolkien's experimenting with language, contrarily, seeks to develop the *historical* (not symbolic) implications within the forms of ordinary words used in ordinary ways, even when he is describing imaginary places with invented names:

They entered the circle of white trees. As they did so the South Wind blew upon Cerin Amroth and sighed among the branches. Frodo stood still, hearing far off great seas upon beaches that had long ago been washed away, and sea-birds crying whose race had perished from the earth.
(*The Lord of the Rings*, vol. 1, bk. 2, ch. 6)

Here it is worth noting the strange analogy in Tolkien's art with Wittgensteinian language philosophy, of which he appears to have been ignorant. One of Wittgenstein's simplest but most resonant insights was that a private language is an impossibility. Tolkien had his "secret vice" of making up private languages. But in fact Tolkien recognized (in accord with Wittgenstein's perception) that to invent anything truly resembling actual language one must imagine it as used by a specific society and expressive of a distinctive historical culture. Tolkien's stories of unusual peoples are necessary validations of his philological imaginings.

This is why names are so important in his fanta-

sies. A name, of course, is a word that refers to a specific thing, place, or person, but specific persons are part of a society with a particular occupation, a set of relationships to family and others, living in a determinate way in a particular place, all of which characteristics have historical-cultural dimensions that can be suggested by the name and its relation to other names—as is most obvious in names such as John-son, or simply Smith. The implication of social dimensions intrinsic to names is more subtly illustrated by Tolkien's fondness for emphasizing that a particular person or place is named differently by different peoples. Thus "Rohan" is the Gondorian name given to the country inhabited by famous horsemen, who themselves call their homeland "the Riddermark." The place called "Rivendell" in our language, is called "Imladris" in the invented language Sindarin.

Even more revealing is the name Gollum, the hobbit Frodo's principal antagonist in *The Lord of the Rings*. "Gollum" is, in fact, an onomatopoeic nickname derived from a sound he began to make in his throat after acquiring the Ring by murdering his brother, who had found it. His real name was Trahald, meaning "worming in," of which the Anglicized version is Sméagol. These different names for the same character, which are extended by Sam Gamgee's calling him Slinker and Stinker, help to dramatize the changes in Gollum after he obtains the Ring, is driven out by his family after his brother's murder, loses the ring to Bilbo, and so on. For Gollum, like Bilbo and Frodo, is a hobbit, but both his physical form and his moral character are transformed by his history; his name-history represents his character-history.

Significant, too, is the first legendary figure Tolkien invented, one who appears in Shelleyan verses he wrote in 1914, "The Voyage of Eärendil the Evening Star," inspired by his reading of Cynewulf's Old English poem, *Crist*. Tolkien's poem portrays Eärendil's journey across the darkened firmament until he disappears in the light of dawn, and it puzzled Tolkien's friend G. B. Smith, who asked him what it was about. "I don't know," replied Tolkien. "I'll try to find out." *The Silmarillion* can be understood as his attempt to discover the fullest meaning of the name that had aroused his imagination, as the several hundred pages of *The Hobbit* are his attempt to discover what he meant when he wrote on a blank examination page, "In a hole in the ground there lived a hobbit."

J. R. R. TOLKIEN

THE earliest events treated by the Silmarillion material are parts of a cosmogonic myth, of which the most important elements are the Valar, powers deriving from divinity, like angels in Christian theology, existing before the making of the world. That world inhabited primarily by humankind Tolkien came to call Middle-earth. But first it was the scene of Elves' activity, the principal concern of *The Silmarillion* proper. The history of the Elves, who confront the griefs and burdens of deathlessness in a world of time and change, originates in a series of falls, like that initiated by the Christian angels. The first falling away from Eru or Iluvatar, "Father of All," is of Vala Melchar, or Morgoth, who creates his own music in discord with the cosmic music deriving from Eru. This "creative discord" is continued by those deriving from Morgoth. Of these the most significant is Fëanor, finest of Elven craftsmen and leader of the greatest of the Elven peoples, the Noldor. He succeeds in capturing the wondrous light of the Two Trees of the Valar in three jewels, the Silmarils. The story of these events and the subsequent self-exile of the most gifted of the Elves and their followers from Valinor, the home of the gods in the far west, and their reentry into Middle-earth, the place of their origin but now dominated by Melchar/Morgoth's evil creations against which they strive, constitute the history of the beginning of Middle-earth's First Age.

The struggles of this era are focused on the Silmarilli jewels, crafted by Fëanor and imprisoning within them the "radiance of pure light" (the meaning of Silmaril) of Valinor. The downfall of the Elves comes from the possessiveness of the creator of the Silmarilli, Fëanor, and his seven sons. When the jewels are captured by the Morgothian Enemy and set in his Iron Crown and Fëanor is slain, the sons of Fëanor take a disastrous oath of vengeance against any, even gods, who shall claim any part of the Silmarilli. They pervert most of their kindred, who rebel against the gods, leave Valinor, and wage desperate war against the Enemy in the northwest portion of Middle-earth. The evil of the oath of vengeance dogs all the Elves' efforts, and, despite many victories and much heroism, their efforts lead to the catastrophe of Elves slaying Elves.

The next stories concern men resisting the evil ruler of Middle-earth who retreat to the West, where they have heard they may find allies. There they encounter the self-exiled Elves in the midst of their war against the great Enemy. The central story of this part of the First Age (and keystone narrative of *The Silmarillion*) tells of Beren, an orphaned, outlawed mortal, who with the help of his lover Lúthien, an Elf maiden, penetrates the stronghold of the Enemy and wrests one of the Silmarilli from the Iron Crown. The marriage of Beren and Lúthien is the first between mortal and immortal. But—and this is an aspect of the tale that focuses a recurrent motif in Tolkien's cycles—the supreme triumph of the recapturing of the Silmaril leads to disaster, for the oath of the sons of Fëanor comes into play, and lust for the Silmaril brings the kingdoms of the Elves to ruin, as we learn from stories such as the *Children of Húrin* and *The Fall of Gondolin,* which are found in the *Lost Tales* series (a version of the latter story appears in *The Silmarillion*).

The Second Age is a dark one, much of west Middle-earth being desolated. The exiled Elves return to the island of Eressëa, within sight of Valinor, but from which they have excluded themselves. For their valor and good faith men of the Three Houses were permitted to inhabit the great western island of Númenor. Meanwhile, in Middle-earth Sauron, originally a noble being of Valinor perverted to evil, repents but, instead of returning to Valinor, lingers, disregarded by the Valar, and slowly he rebuilds Middle-earth. In the process Sauron becomes the reincarnation of evil lusting for complete power. During the Second Age his shadow grows and extends over Middle-earth. Meanwhile the Elves who remain become obsessed with fading, and as they grow sadder they become friendly with Dwarfs, to whom they had traditionally been hostile, and with them develop smithcraft (the art of forging in smithies) to its apogee. Some (though not all) allow themselves to be persuaded by Sauron that they could make Middle-earth as beautiful as Valinor, and these Elves fall into ways of magic and machinery. Their supreme product are the Rings of Power, whose chief potency is to arrest change, preserving what is loved as beautiful.

But secretly Sauron himself manufactures one Ruling Ring that contains and controls the power of the others and makes its wearer invisible while rendering things of the invisible world visible to him. Aware of what Sauron had done, the Elves hide their chief three Rings of Power and try to destroy the others. Sauron wars on the Elves and seizes many of the Rings of Power thus becoming almost supreme in Middle-earth, the last Elf Kingdom being that ruled by Gil-galad on the extreme west shores near the Havens of ships, while Elrond, son of Eärendil, maintains an enchanted sanctuary of Imladris (Rivendell, in English). But Sauron, through the power of the One Ring rules a growing empire from his great, black tower of Barad-dûr in Mordor, next to fire-riven Orodruin, Mount Doom, within which the greatest Ring was secretly forged.

This One Ring, unbreakable by any smithcraft and indissoluble in any fire, except that in which it was forged, determines the plot of *The Lord of the Rings*, which is the story of how, in fact, the One Ring was brought back to Barad-dûr in Sauron's Mordor (black land) and annihilated when thrown back into the fires in the Crack of Doom out of which it was created. Sauron's own being is thereby made to disintegrate, his power dematerializing as he becomes truly a shadow, an ominous, insubstantial memory of possessive will.

In the latter part of the Second Age the focus is on the glory and fall of Númenor, where dwell the only men who speak in an Elvish tongue. The Númenoreans rise to great wealth and wisdom, but eventually become overbearingly proud and try to gain dominion over the world. Outraged by this perversion of the gifts they have bestowed on the Númenoreans, the Valar consent to the island-continent's destruction by a great flood. From this only Elendil and a few faithful followers escape on their ships to Middle-earth, where he establishes and rules the kingdoms of Arnor and Gondor. The Second Age ends with the Last Alliance of Elves, led by Gil-galad, and Men, led by Elendil, resulting in a siege of Mordor, the seat of evil, and the destruction of Sauron in a great battle. Gil-galad and Elendil, however, are also slain in defeating Sauron, and Isildur, Elendil's son, cuts the One Ring from Sauron's hand. But Isildur, worked on by the temptation embodied in the Ring, refuses to cast it into the fires that will dissolve it. He marches away with it, but is soon drowned, and the Ring is lost to all knowledge.

The Third Age begins with Mordor and its Dark Tower empty, but not obliterated, while the Enemy's monstrous servants, including counterfeit creatures of illusion such as trolls, balrogs, and orcs, persist. Gradually the world becomes literally shadowed as Sauron regains existence and power. In this age the hobbits appear, chiefly in what is called the Shire. Through an odd chance an undistinguished hobbit, Bilbo Baggins, becomes possessed of the One Ring, and eventually his nephew and heir, Frodo Baggins, carries the Ring back to the Dark Tower just as the revived Sauron appears to have attained mastery over all of Middle-earth. As the Ring disintegrates in its founding fires Sauron and all his powers of evil crumble and disappear—at least for a time.

COMPOSITION OF THE LEGENDS

EVEN so schematic a sketch suggests what Tolkien himself recognized, that the hobbits for which he is most celebrated not only had no part in his original imaginings, but remained always secondary and peripheral features of his mythology. *The Hobbit* was written as a children's story, whereas the Silmarillion material was never directed to children. *The Hobbit*, moreover, contains relatively few references to either the details or general structure of *The Silmarillion*. But it is the hobbit books on which Tolkien's fame is based, and it seems unlikely that *The Silmarillion* would even have been published, let alone strengthened Tolkien's celebrity, without the success of the two hobbit books.

Understanding the order in which Tolkien's legends were invented illuminates an interesting feature of Tolkien's art. All that has been said about the One Ring appears nowhere in the Silmarillion material composed roughly between 1914 and 1937. The whole concept of the One Ring and how it was made and the effects of its unmaking was only imagined by Tolkien in the process of writing *The Lord of the Rings* between 1937 and 1952. Bilbo Baggins, the protagonist of *The Hobbit*, which was written between 1930 and 1936, happens upon a ring that makes him invisible and plays some part in his adventures, but which is not tremendously important. It was only when trying to devise a sequel to *The Hobbit* that Tolkien thought to make Bilbo's ring the One Ring with all its powers and significance. This new idea in fact required Tolkien for later editions to rewrite part of *The Hobbit* to make the role of the Ring congruent with its enhanced importance in *The Lord of the Rings.* Even so, careful readers notice that the role of this Ring in the first book is inconsistent with what is made of it in the trilogy.

What makes this peculiarity of composition so interesting is that it is a private, as it were miniaturized, version of what happens all the time in actual legends of preliterate peoples, illuminating the mode of what might be called inchoate composition that distinguishes genuine mythological literatures. These are formed by a variety of storytellers over a considerable span of time. Such living myths are not repeated verbatim; they are constantly being made anew by retellings, retellings that can vary enormously. The living myths of preliterate peoples, the original form of even the Greek and Norse myths, which we know only in their written, systematized, belated forms, were only to a degree systematic. Living myths are hospitable to innovation and radical change because human societies have to contend with changing conditions and new situations, climatological and geographical and social, in relations to other societies and cultures, as well as to interior economic and political self-transformations. The study of any large mythological system reveals, therefore, countless instances of the kind of rethinking and revaluation Tolkien's imagining of the One Ring epitomizes. Suddenly an unimportant object, character, or motif is given prominence in a new version of an old story to meet the exigencies of some change in the circumstances of the teller and his audience. Sometimes an important figure, even a divinity, abruptly vanishes from a traditional narrative. Or a central story of the mythology begins to be told in a new way radically incongruent with its original form.

The existence of the analogy between Tolkien's composition of his fantasies and this inchoateness of living oral mythologies is not merely coincidental. Tolkien was a profound, lifelong student of works such as the *Kalevala* and the Norse sagas that function thus inchoately. These works are fascinating, and indeed aesthetically attractive, precisely because they are so open, able to accommodate radical differences and shifts in perspective, structure, and meaning while remaining expressive of the ways and beliefs of specific peoples. Tolkien was aware that myths are genuinely alive only so long as they retain this power of self-reconstituting creativeness and do not attain the self-sufficient, self-contained perfectedness of form modern criti-

cism tends to identify as the highest achievement of art. The chief reason why Tolkien never "completed" *The Silmarillion* was his commitment to this quality. The book published posthumously under that title, for example, includes material on Sauron and the One Ring supporting the description given above, because after the publication of *The Lord of the Rings* in the mid 1950's Tolkien added to and revised the Silmarillion material to make it congruent with *The Lord of the Rings,* which is supposed to deal with a later period.

Tolkien's fantasy is the only modern fantasy that is composed according to principles equatable with the way in which myths and legends are created by oral cultures. This uniqueness is especially impressive because a large number of modern works of fantasy and science fiction—*Islandia,* Isaac Asimov's *Foundation* series, Frank Herbert's *Dune* novels, for instance—present carefully developed whole cultures and complete geographies. Indeed, many fantastic romances attempt to recreate complete societies, many with far more scrupulosity of concrete detail than Tolkien. He is, in fact, sparse and vague on many practical details of ordinary life and the processes by which things are done or made; one senses that he does not have the faintest idea of how in practice a ring might be forged. But no other fantasy writer has reproduced, as Tolkien has, the *method* of imagining characteristic of oral cultures.

No other writer of modern fantasy has had the knowledge to do what Tolkien thus did. No other writer of modern fantasy has spent a lifetime studying in an intensely scholarly way the "fantasies" of sophisticated preliterate peoples, the northern medieval peoples for whom what we call "fantasy"—the use of imagination to conceive of what one was unlikely to experience in everyday existence—was an important part of their life, perhaps the most important part. Tolkien's profession of philologist is decisively significant for Tolkien's art. For it is through the historical analysis of words in texts representing, with varying degrees of accuracy, accounts and stories originally told orally, that philologists are able imaginatively to reconstruct how particular tales and accounts came into being and their probable relation to other tales and accounts.

Both *The Hobbit* and *The Lord of the Rings,* especially the latter, gain from the Silmarillion-material references a peculiar resonance, or a beauty like that of a glimpse of distant towers in a sunlit mist. Almost all other works of fantasy are in themselves exhaustive—the full extent of the fantasist's imagination is realized in the book we read. One feels that there is no more that is significant for *this* invented world than what is depicted. The hobbit books appear as amidst both a nimbus and penumbra of history, genealogy, and other, untold, stories—facts and imaginings far more extensive and of a different kind from what we read. And the inchoateness is helpful to this resonating effect, because many of the implications and references in the hobbit books are vague, uncertain, inconsistent, seldom exactly fitting any determinate structure.

MODERN INFLUENCES

YET the inspiration (no other word seems appropriate) of hobbits also enabled Tolkien to realize his Silmarillion fantasies with a vividness and cogency that would otherwise have been impossible. The imaginary hobbits, paradoxically, enable Tolkien to link a twentieth-century readership to the ancient Silmarillion world. In Tolkien's stories hobbits are frequently referred to as halflings, that is half-humans—and they are at least that. Except that they are usually only three or three and half feet tall, and that because of their rather large and hirsute feet they prefer not to wear shoes, hobbits are anatomically, in their dress, social life, and habits—notably their fondness for smoking tobacco and drinking beer—identical to humans—very English bourgeois humans. More exactly, perhaps, hobbits are, except for height and feet, like lower middle-class Tolkiens and Suffields holed up in and around Birmingham in the first half of the twentieth century.

Tolkien once remarked that the name "hobbit" owed something to Sinclair Lewis' character George F. Babbitt. If we turn to the opening two pages of *Babbitt* (1922) we will see what Tolkien meant:

The towers of Zenith aspired above the morning mist; austere towers of steel and cement and limestone, sturdy as cliffs and delicate as silver rods. They were neither citadels nor churches, but frankly and beautifully office-buildings. . . . pouring out the honest wares that would be sold up the Euphrates and across the veldt. The whistles rolled out in greeting a chorus cheerful as the April dawn; the song of labor in a city built—it seemed—for giants. . . .

Plainly enough, prosperous, well-fed Bilbo Baggins, the original hobbit, owes something to the creation of Sinclair Lewis. Tolkien set himself the problem of constructing a connected body of legendary tales, ranging from the cosmogonic to the fairy story, "cool and clear" and possessing a "fair elusive beauty" as he confessed to one correspondent, that would form a majestic whole, yet leave scope for imaginative work by "other minds and other hands"—and this in a world in which the dominant literary form was realistic fiction! Tolkien himself observed the absurdity. Yet he tried to make this gift to England, his native land he loved so deeply that he almost never voluntarily left it, by combining his knowledge of its medieval past with his experience of the contemporary bourgeois world in a fashion that would allow the former historically to enoble the latter. This ambition also explains the vein of comedy that runs through the hobbit books, and the remarkably unobtrusive fact that in them two different styles of speech coexist. Bilbo, for instance, speaks in the modern idiom: "Don't wait to knock! Tea is at four." But characters like Gandalf, Thorin Oakenshield, and Aragorn speak archaically. And their speech reflects patterns of thought and behavior such as one encounters in *Beowulf*, *The Niebelungenlied*, and the Norse Sagas. Thus Gandalf tells Aragorn:

It is not our part to master all the tides of world, but to do what is in us for the succour of those years wherein we are set, uprooting the evil in the fields that we know, so that those who live after may have clean earth to till. What weather they shall have is not ours to rule.

Then Gandalf asks the king, "For do I not guess rightly, Aragorn, that you have shown yourself to him in the Stone of Orthanc?" and receives a "kingly" answer: "I did so ere I rode from the Hornburg. . . . I deemed that the time was ripe . . ." (*The Lord of the Rings*, vol. 3, bk. 5, ch. 9,).

Against the heroic codes emphasizing rank, courage, and sheer will expressing itself in joy at violence and personal combat, Bilbo and Frodo are modern middle-class figures concerned about respectability; they are self-distrustful, and capable, like protagonists of that modern form the bildungsroman, of radical personality change, whereas their more archaic peers define themselves by unyielding adherence to traditional patterns of behavior. Aragorn can be himself only by behaving royally, Gandalf by behaving as a wizard.

Absurd as it may have been to try to link these two historically distinct ways of life, the ideal of a continuity of English civilization fired Tolkien's imagination, as can be seen in his 1929 essay "Ancrene Wisse and Hali Meiðhad" (published just after Tolkien had written "In a hole in the ground there lived a hobbit"), which remained his most elegant piece of scholarly writing. In that article, on the basis of a rigorously logical analysis of carefully marshalled linguistic details, Tolkien arrives at a vision of the survival, somewhere in the west of England, of a small group of isolated people adhering to the oldest English language traditions, undisturbed by the Danish and Norman invasions that distorted the pure lines of development from Old English to our present speech. It is that recognizedly visionary ideal on which the hobbit's Shire is founded, but because it is an ideal, Tolkien's "escape" to it is more than a mere evasion of modern life.

There are, of course, as with any work of art, many sources for The Hobbit and The Lord of the Rings, some ancient, some contemporary. "Mirkwood" and the "Misty Mountains" are lifted directly from Norse sagas—Dwarf names and Gandalf's come from the Voluspa. Yet it seems a fair guess, both because rats, moles, and badgers live in holes, and because we know Tolkien's Inkling associates, especially C. S. Lewis and Charles Williams, were deeply influenced by the book, that some inspiration for hobbits came from Kenneth Grahame's The Wind in the Willows. That book combines in a peculiarly English way fantasizing with amusing (because the characters are, after all, rather unattractive animals) representations of the most egregiously ordinary aspects of middle-class life—with the women left out. The accessibility of the hobbit books owes much to this kind of sub-fantasy, one might call it, of gently satiric representation of the most conventional of English conventionalities—to which Sam Gamgee, Frodo's chief supporter in his adventures, also contributes.

That Sam's quietly selfless loyalty, good-humored tenacity under difficulties, and thick-headed unimaginativeness about what does not immediately impinge on him, his master, and their families, are traits of an enduring British type was dramatized by the letter to Tolkien written by a real Sam Gamgee, inquiring how he had become a character in the professor's book. The real Sam, of course, had not read the book—he had picked up his name from a dramatization his daughter heard on the radio. He was not offended, or especially interested, that Tolkien's Sam was heroic, only mildly curious—as Tolkien's Sam would have been.

The difficulty with Tolkien's Sam is the overtness of his literary heritage; he is a later example of English forelock-tugging retainers who defend to the death the class system at its most rigid. Worse, as his girl Rosie and old Gaffer back in the Shire remind us, he is modeled directly on Charles Dickens' Sam Weller. It is unwise to imitate an incomparable performance, and what makes this imitation especially painful is Sam's incapacity for Dickensian humor. The independence implicit in Weller's shrewd humorousness, moreover, is missing from Gamgee—and from Tolkien's world. Gamgee's loyalty to Frodo is blind (as are all Tolkienian loyalties), whereas Weller's to Mr. Pickwick is not. Sam Weller freely chooses to serve Mr. Pickwick, thereby teaching us much about the dignity of service to others and the human rewards that may accrue to good people even if they behave ridiculously. That kind of wisdom is beyond Tolkien, and this failure has encouraged condemnations of his work as both psychologically and ethically simpleminded.

THE SIGNIFICANCE OF ADULT FANTASY

THE charge seems to carry weight because Tolkien's moral system appears crude and superficial. For example, he has no taste for the contradictoriness of trickster figures—in Norse mythology superbly embodied in the figure of Loki. Because Tolkien was incapable of challenging his own system of belief, he imagines "goodness" and "badness" in terms of the simplest popular stereotypes; they are not arranged to compel his readers to reassess their firmest presuppositions about what constitutes goodness and badness.

Yet the student revolutionaries of the 1960's invoked Tolkien the pious Catholic as often as Blake the radical Protestant—who became a popular poet only in that decade, two centuries after his birth. I remember at the University of Wisconsin in Madison in the late 1960s perceiving through a tear-gas haze the conjunction of a sign hoisted by the occupiers of the Education Building quoting Blake's Proverb of Hell, "The Tygers of Wrath are Wiser than the Horses of Instruction" with a giant graffiti scrawled on an unfinished building looking like a ruined tower at the foot of the hill, FRODO LIVES. The vast majority of student protestors were by neither temperament nor background very radical: what they principally desired was the revival of some moral commitments in a world increasingly demoralized because entirely rationalized and pragmatized. Tolkien's moralism, less energetic and demanding than Blake's calls to active self-examination, was in important respects more congenial exactly *because* it was so conventionalized.

The young people of the 1960's were attracted to Blake and Tolkien by these writers' unashamed imaginativeness. The young people were imaginatively starved to emaciation, and the avidity with which they, and their successors, seized on *The Lord of the Rings* is a symptom of the imaginative undernourishment to which modern society subjects its youth.

The bravest and the brightest were drawn to daring innovators such as Blake, but for the majority, to whose suburbanized sensibilities Blake's authentic radicalism and uncompromising passionateness could only be troubling, Tolkien's quieter, far more conventionalized stories, encouraging escape rather than confrontation, were more congenial. Perhaps the least attractive aspect of Tolkienian conventionality is its sexism. Females play very minor parts in both *The Hobbit* and *The Lord of the Rings,* and most of their appearances are somewhat embarrassing, the most painful being that of Shelob. Sam and Frodo's encounter with this spider monster reads like an elementary Freudian text describing male fear-fantasies of female sexual power.

Tolkien's biography is not in these matters attractive. He was one of those good, responsible husbands whose unwitting selfishness damaged a long-suffering wife. One must not forget, however, that in these matters Tolkien adhered to long-established attitudes and patterns of behavior dependent on male-bondings fostered by the English public-school system and universities. The pipe-smoking, beer-drinking, all-male groups, such as the Inklings, served to protect and sustain male imaginativeness. In the modern world, which began earliest in England, the social systems sustaining masculine public fairy-tale telling had been increasingly destroyed. And many men, too. When the Armistice came in 1918 only one of Tolkien's friends from school and university was still alive. Tolkien's conventional attitudes toward women were a price he (and his wife) paid for being free to imagine dragons in the company of other men. And a degree of conventionality in a writer of fantasy is not necessarily a bad thing.

Take dragons for example. No story with a dragon in it can be a total failure. Because dragons are not real, an author who includes one has exercised *some* imagination. But precisely because dragons are human artifacts, not natural creatures, they take shape through conventions of art. And Tolkien's great dragon, Smaug, the best part of *The Hobbit,* is wonderful because carefully crafted to the conventions of dragon depiction. We perceive the care because Smaug is so unlike the terrific dragon in *Beowulf* that Tolkien publicly admired. Beowulf's dragon, after all, came from a time when the imaginariness of dragons was not firmly established. He is truly frightening. When he blasts out of his burrow a fury of claws, scales, and searing flame, one does not approve of Beowulf's companions' pell-mell desertion of their leader, but one understands it. Bravely, Tolkien sacrificed most of what distinguishes the dragon he loved in *Beowulf* (retaining principally his deep malice and stupid exactness as to the contents of his hoard) to produce a more conventional, and therefore for our age, a more convincing and interesting, dragon. For example, Smaug is a clever wordsmith, like many subsequent dragons in twentieth-century literature. Tolkien deserves the credit for having restored dragons to a respectable place in literature: every dragon that has appeared after *The Hobbit* is a direct descendant of Smaug.

That *The Hobbit* is a book for children is no longer ground for denigrating its aesthetic accomplishment, since children's literature has become the object of increased scholarly attention. But *The Hobbit* is not quite in the top rank of children's stories, though as young Rayner Unwin predicted, it satisfies the five-to-nine-year-old crowd. Its weakness lies not in occasional condescensions of style, which Tolkien later deplored more strongly than anyone else. Nor is it the poetry, which is as undistinguished as most—though not all—of Tolkien's verse. (It seems oddly characteristic of comparative philologists to lack the ear needed for the music of genuine poetic form.) *The Hobbit* does not triumph as a children's book because Tolkien was so polemically committed to the recreation of *adult* fantasy. His conservatism and conventionality were enlivened by his conviction that there was inherent value in imaginary stories for everyone living in the modern world. Twentieth-century existence was not so unmitigatedly splendid, Tolkien suggested in his essay on fairy tales, that imaginative escapes from it should be programmatically condemned. And he was consistently explicit that his purpose in *The Lord of the Rings* was to create a long story that would simply amuse, delight, and quicken the emotions of his readers. Tolkien hated the allegorization of imaginative narrative (even resisting W. H. Auden's praise of his work as a splendid realization of the quest archetype). For Tolkien allegory degraded storytelling by imposing some extrinsic meaningfulness upon narrative that could be entirely satisfying intrinsically.

Exactly contrary to Bruno Bettelheim, the psychologist who wrote that fairy tales were composed primarily for the benefit of children, Tolkien wished to reclaim fairyland as an abandoned province of adulthood. This being his heroic quest, he could never hope to address children with that sincere innocence distinguishing the finest of children's writers, such as Beatrix Potter and Jean de Brunhoff.

Tolkien's purposes are revealed by the intriguing fact that the plot structure of *The Hobbit* and *The Lord of the Rings* is identical. The earlier work begins with an "Unexpected Party," which results in Bilbo Baggins learning of the treasure it will become his task to steal from Smaug. The later story begins with a "Long-Expected Party" that leads to Frodo Baggins learning of the Ring it will be his doom to carry back to Sauron's tower. In the first part of the journey from the Shire each hobbit picks up a valuable sword and reaches Rivendell, where there is a conference with the Elf Elrond and the wizard Gandalf. Both hobbits leave Rivendell with a party led by Gandalf that is prevented by storms from passing over the Misty Mountains, so that they must pass through the mountains by means of caverns in which they fend off an attack by Orcs,

encounter Gollum for the first time, and lose Gandalf. The latter portion of both quests involves journeying down a river to a desolated land dominated by powerful evil, climbing a mountain, and penetrating through another tunnel to their goal. The climax of both quests is marked by huge battles engaging a variety of peoples and creatures, in which a king atones for previous errors by a heroic death after leading a decisive charge, and the arrival of a flight of eagles assuring victory for the good. Celebrated for their heroism by Elfs, Dwarfs, and Men, both Bilbo and Frodo return to the Shire to find that in their absence those hostile to them have gained power, so they must struggle to regain their home and restore the tranquility of earlier hobbit life.

Few readers notice this structural identity because the *Lord of the Rings* is so much longer and richer in incidents and diverse characters; it is, in fact, the fulfillment of the hobbit history that Tolkien did not yet know he was trying to write when he undertook his children's story. And the parallelism dramatizes an extraordinary inversion. Bilbo's quest fits the traditional pattern: he seeks out and wins something precious to himself and those with whom he is associated. Frodo's quest is unusual in being an attempt to return and get rid of a dangerous burden. Bound up in that twist is Tolkien's most important contribution to modern fantasy.

It is Gollum, the marvelously slimy-sympathetic, vicious but victimized last possessor of the Ring before Bilbo, who calls the Ring "My Precious," and it is Gollum's relentless quest to recover the Ring that has debased him which finally destroys him and allows Frodo to succeed. In a climactic struggle Gollum bites off the hobbit's finger on which he wears the ring, leaps back, and falls into Sauron's fiery Crack of Doom. The true "power" of the Ring is not that it bestows longevity and invisibility, or even that it controls other powers, but that it becomes overwhelmingly precious to its wearer—and therefore deadly. Modern commentators are reminded of Lord Acton's aphorism on how political power corrupts, but Tolkien is reviving an ancient truth known to many peoples but overlooked in the modern consumerist world— that every gift is a curse, like Helen's beauty that left so many Greeks and Trojans dead. Many cultures have recognized more perceptively than ours the dangers inherent in powers to cure: often the healing doctor through exercise of restorative forces is transformed into a destructive demon. For change and chance, despite the delusions of stability fostered by modern industrialized society, is the rule of life, and it is a function of fantasy to remind us of that rule.

To do this, fantasy writers must resist the lures of psychology and symbolism. Frodo and Bilbo (like most of Tolkien's characters) are little more individualized than Cinderella, or the disregarded youngest son who finally slays the monsters and wins the princess. Bilbo and Frodo are, simply, hobbits, halflings, representatives of small, unnoticed people, upon whom, all unrecognized, the destiny of great events frequently depends. Characters in fantasy are not individuals as are the characters in realistic novels, but the representatives of social subgroups, such as outcasts, or embodiments of social types, such as stuffy stay-at-homes who do not want adventures, or dramatic illustrations of how patterns of force, such as the accidents of life, can suddenly distort normal existence. The portrayal of fantasy characters tells us little or nothing about personal psychology because their function is to enable us to imagine how unimportant individuals, like ourselves, may affect and be affected by the interplay of vast natural or cultural forces—an interplay more difficult to conceive, and to explain, than personal motives or idiosyncrasies of behavior.

In the modern world, where nature is supposedly conquered and life is supposedly entirely rationally ordered, only the realm of personal psychology seems free and untrammeled, and with what imaginativeness it has left, modern literature concentrates on personal psychology. It is this focus from which the fantasist must escape, in part because it leads to an overvaluation of symbolism. One's private hangups, for example, have no significance for anyone else except so far as they embody universal principles. So Freudian psychology isolates individuals in secret rooms to bring to light the specific case of a meta-historical pathology needing to be exorcised. The modern psychologist is in this sense like the modern structural linguist (not philologist), a definer of universal principles that reduce the particular incident, usage or person, to relative unimportance, no more than a case. As Tolkien reactionarily clung to comparative philology, imagining reconstructions from minute particulars of language usage, so his stories reac-

tionarily return to premodern forms and styles in which what a story means, what it may symbolize, is less important than simply what it is.

The weakness of most contemporary fantasy is a determination to be meaningful, to symbolize beyond itself. Here Tolkien's center of scholarly interest, northern European sagas, legends, myths, and folktales, saved him, for this literature has been little contaminated by a quest for symbolic significance. We are still able to read *Beowulf* and many of the Norse sagas simply as gripping stories. And a major function of storytelling is to renew our appreciation of events as events, the potency of living in a world where things happen all the time, where everything always changes. Narrative art, Tolkien thought, degenerates into magic or machinery, when it strives to overcome, not simply confront, that endlessly transformative activity.

Let us return for a moment to the climactic moment in *The Lord of the Rings* to clarify fantasy's resistance to symbolism. Gollum inadvertently saves Frodo from the evil potency of the Ring by inadvertently destroying himself and the Ring. This emphasis upon chance at the story's climax is consistent with the prominence of contingency throughout the book. Neither aesthetic nor ethical patterning is allowed to outweigh happenstance. There is, of course, much order and logic in the trilogy, and even the possibility of a spiritual system, a "logic" of forgiveness and retribution, is raised, but never, as the climax demonstrates, is sheer chance eliminated. It is this characteristic above all else that makes Tolkien's work bothersome to many readers, for whom imagining is justified only if the fantasizing possesses significance. Tolkien's willingness to accept contingency as contingency in his stories derives from his profound knowledge of medieval literature, in which this characteristic often prevails, and from his commitment to philology, which is a severely logical discipline that finally compels the scholar to make an imaginative leap.

For example, in *"Sigelwara land,"* a scholarly essay published before Tolkien had begun *The Lord of the Rings,* he deployed an intricate array of philological evidence to prove that the first part of an Anglo-Saxon word, "Sigelhearwan," *sigel,* had originally meant both "jewel" and "sun." But in combination with *hearwan* it came to refer to creatures "with red-hot eyes that emitted sparks, with faces black as soot." Such monsters, produced by Tolkien's imaginative word-history, suggest the terrible bal-rog who almost destroys the magician Gandalf in *The Lord of the Rings,* while the *silmarils,* the jewels filled with light from which *The Silmarillion* derives its name, find a source in Tolkien's speculation about *sigel.*

Philology encourages this kind of imagined history because a philologist must deal simultaneously with two separate variables, meanings of words and the forms of words. The developments of forms and meanings remain independent even when affecting one another. Tolkien cites the example of "yelp," which for a long time meant "to speak proudly" and was most often linked to major promises, as when a knight vowed to undertake a dangerous deed. Quite suddenly, without any change in form, for no discernible reason, "yelp" began to mean the noise made by foxes or dogs. Because the philologist can find no reason for this change, he must learn to live with the sheer fact, the contingency. In the study of *any* word, moreover, the philologist must keep in mind that there may always be homophones, phonetically indistinguishable elements that possess different meanings and therefore are simultaneously the same word and different words—Tolkien's example is the Indo-European stem (or stems) *men,* meaning "stick out" and "think." And he must remember that semantic change, as in the case of "yelp," is often radical, but may have left no evidence of its violence (if, for instance, the earlier usage of "yelp" as "proud speaking" had not chanced to survive in what texts remain). Seldom can a philologist know whether to weight form or meaning more heavily in tracing linguistic developments, and more often than not the very rigor of his systematic methods compels him to recognize that no fully coherent explanation is possible, that he must use his imagination to deal with inescapable contingencies if he is to be true to his scientific procedure.

This is why Tolkien insists in "On Fairy-Stories" that "fantasy does not destroy or even insult Reason . . . nor obscure the perception of Scientific verity" (*The Tolkien Reader,* p. 54). He argues that "the clearer is the reason the better fantasy it will make," because fantasy is founded on "recognition of fact, but not slavery to it" (p. 55). The strengths and weaknesses of Tolkien's fantasy stories, and the admiration and distaste they have aroused, derive from his carrying into his art his pleasure in imagining provoked by philological uncertainties.

Upon that transfer depends, finally, Tolkien's understanding of the function of fantasy fiction, most forcefully stated in his preface to the first paperback edition of *The Lord of the Rings.* The book, he asserts, has no symbolic meaning or message, no purpose other than to "hold the attention of readers, amuse them, delight them, and at times maybe excite them or deeply move them" (p. ix). Admitting his "book is too short" (p. x)—a splendidly medieval view of a 200,000-word story—Tolkien goes on to observe that he prefers history "true or feigned" (p. xi) to allegory; the latter implies domination by the author, whereas history bestows freedom on the reader, since it represents accidents, real or imagined, as accidents, things that just happen to happen.

Tolkien's preference for history over symbolism explains why in *The Lord of the Rings* magic appears, at best, as a dubious skill, even though Tolkien had argued in "On Fairy-Stories"—composed just as he was beginning *The Lord of the Rings*—that fantasy depends upon enchantment. The art of fantasy for Tolkien is subcreation that aspires to "the elvish craft, Enchantment" which, however much it may resemble magic, is "wholly different from the greed for self-centered power which is the mark of the mere Magician" ("On Fairy-Stories," p. 53). Magic in Tolkien's view is not true art but technique, craft, and its purpose is power, not the delight of joint enchantment. Unlike enchantment, magic produces, or claims to produce, an alteration in the primary world. Tolkien defines enchantment in terms of joining and sharing of creator and audience "in making and delight," whereas magic can only establish separateness and power relations. So he associates magic with technology and manufacturing and their evil consequences.

Among these the worst for Tolkien is possessiveness and materialism, Babbitt's disease, with which Bilbo was dangerously infected, and which, theoretically at least, the youthful protestors of the 1960's rejected. Resistance to possessiveness is the ground for Tolkien's readiness to defend fantasy as "escape," which he identified with recovery, his version of what literary critics call defamiliarization. The "drab blur of triteness or familiarity" ("Of Fairy-Stories," p. 57) of the modern world Tolkien thought originated in our possessiveness: what is familiar is what we have appropriated mentally or legally. What we "know" in some way we "own," whether it be our car or our spouse. In no sense, then, does fantasy deny the facts of the primary world, especially its accidents. To the contrary, fantasy arises from a recognition of the intractability of chance that our familiarity with the rationalized organizations of modern life has obscured, and which we prefer obscured so as to feel secure of our possessions.

For Tolkien, therefore, "escape" in the contemporary world is not, as most literary critics assert, the flight of a deserter. The "realism" these critics applaud, he felt, means behaving like a collaborator, accommodating oneself to a reality recognized to be, if not detestable, needing radical improvement. The escape of the fantasist is a resistance to accepting what the currently dominant (but of course evanescent) fashion of defining reality treats as inexorable. In such arguments Tolkien's cordial dislike for many features of the modern world surfaces, particularly his scorn of improved means to deteriorated ends, and his grumpy professorial opinion that much of today's "serious" literature is only play under a glass roof beside a swimming pool.

CONCLUSION

Tolkien's strengths and weaknesses depend upon his conservatism, even his reactionariness. He is an erratic writer, sometimes awkward, often prolix, occasionally portentously unprogressive in telling his tale, at other moments brilliant, as in the riddling match between Bilbo and Gollum, or in his conception of the Ents, great tree-creatures whose language is composed of enormously long words used to tell very slowly long, long, long stories. But Tolkien's primary virtue is his steady resistance to any temptation to be led away from the satisfaction of the imaginative story. Sauron's evil has no more significance as evil than shadows have significance—other than marking the absence of light we need and love, although we can scarcely conceive of human love in a shadowless land.

How Tolkien's reputation will thrive or dwindle, then, depends largely on whether his conception of the function of storytelling—embodied in his endeavors to recover something of northern medieval narrative art—gains or loses support. Nothing defines more clearly his sense of historical fantasy's opposition to what is dominant in contemporary

literature than his insistence on a happy ending, what he called, coining a new critical term, the "eucatastrophe" essential to fairy stories. The eucatastrophe does not deny the existence, even the probability, of sorrow and failure, but it lifts the heart with a glimpse of possible joy.

Tolkien ends his essay "On Fairy-Stories" with a characteristic reference to an ancient, little-known poem, "The Black Bull of Norroway"; it represents exactly the ultimate effect he thought art could attain and toward which all his fiction aimed.

"Seven long years I served for thee,
The glassy hill I clamb for thee,
The bluidy shirt I wrang for thee,
And wilt thou not wauken and turn to me?"
He heard and turned to her.

Happy endings are not assured; they depend on luck, on chance, and for just that reason they bring a catch in the breath at finding in this harsh world a momentary deliverance or beauty's grace or the heart's desire.

SELECTED BIBLIOGRAPHY

I. BIBLIOGRAPHY. J. A. Johnson, *J. R. R. Tolkien: Six Decades of Criticism.* Bibliographies and Indexes in World Literature, 6 (Westport, Ct, 1986), comprehensive, with succint, accurate annotations for the hundreds of entries, and excellent indexes.

II. SEPARATE WORKS. *The Hobbit; or, There and Back Again* (London, 1937), literary fantasy, illustrated by the author; *Farmer Giles of Ham* (London, 1949), literary fantasy, illustrated by P. Baynes; *The Fellowship of the Ring: Being the First Part of The Lord of the Rings* (London, 1954; Boston, 1955), literary fantasy; *The Two Towers: Being the Second Part of The Lord of the Rings* (London, 1954; Boston, 1965), literary fantasy; *The Return of the King: Being the Third Part of The Lord of the Rings* (London, 1955; Boston, 1956), literary fantasy; *The Adventures of Tom Bombadil and Other Verses from the Red Book* (London, 1962; Boston, 1963), poems, illustrated by P. Baynes; *Tree and Leaf* (London, 1964; Boston, 1965), essays and short fiction, reprints "Leaf by Niggle," an expanded version of "On Fairy-Stories," "The Homecoming of Beorhtnoth Beorhthelm's Son," and "Smith of Wooton Major." *The Tolkien Reader* (New York, 1966), illustrated by P. Baynes, includes "The Homecoming of Beorhtnoth," "On Fairy-Stories," "Leaf by Niggle,"

"Farmer Giles of Ham," and "The Adventures of Tom Bombadil;" *Smith of Wootton Major* (London, Boston, 1967), short fantasy, illustrated by P. Baynes.

Posthumous Works: *The Silmarillion* (London, Boston, 1977), a collection of epic poems and fantasies; *Unfinished Tales of Númenor and Middle-Earth* (London, Boston, 1980), short fiction, ed. by C. Tolkien; *The Book of Lost Tales Part I* (London, 1983; Boston, 1984), ed. by C. Tolkien; *The Book of Lost Tales Part II* (London and Boston, 1984), ed. by C. Tolkien; *The Lays of Beleriand* (London and Boston, 1985), ed. by C. Tolkien; *The Shaping of Middle-Earth: the Quenta, the Ambarkanta, and the Annals, together with the two earliest "Silmarillion" and the First Map* (London and Boston, 1986), ed. by C. Tolkien. The last four entries contain previously unpublished stories, poems, plans, and notes primarily relevant to *The Silmarillion* and *The Lord of the Rings*.

III. Essays. "Ancrene Wisse and Hali Meiðhad," *Essays and Studies by Members of the English Association*, 14 (1929); "Beowulf: The Monsters and the Critics," *Proceedings of the British Academy*, 22 (1936), reprinted in *The Tolkien Reader*; "On Fairy-Stories," in C. S. Lewis, ed., *Essays Presented to Charles Williams* (Oxford, 1947; Grand Rapids, Mich., 1966), revised and reprinted in *Tree and Leaf* and *The Tolkien Reader; The Monsters and the Critics, and Other Essays* (London, Boston, 1984), critical and biographical essays, ed. by C. Tolkien.

IV. Letters. *The Letters of J. R. R. Tolkien* (London, Boston, 1981), ed. by H. Carpenter with C. Tolkien.

V. Biographical and Critical Studies. N. D. Issacs and R. A. Zimbardo, eds., *Tolkien and the Critics* (Notre Dame, Ind., 1968), among the best of critical essays, including essays by W. H. Auden and C. S. Lewis; C. R. Stimson, *J. R. R. Tolkien*, Columbia Essays on Modern Writers series (New York, 1969), a cogent but hostile critique.

P. H. Kocher, *Master of Middle-earth: The Fiction of J. R. R. Tolkien* (Boston, 1972), detailed and thoughtful study; R. Sale, *Modern Heroism: Essays on D. H. Lawrence, William Empson, and J. R. R. Tolkien* (Berkeley, Calif., 1973), interesting comparisons, somewhat critical of Tolkien; R. Foster, *A Guide to Middle-earth* (New York, 1971), annotated glossary with page references; H. Carpenter, *Tolkien: A Biography* (London and Boston, 1977), judicious, perceptive, factually accurate account.

P. H. Kocher, *A Reader's Guide to the Silmarillion* (Boston, 1980); R. Noel, *The Languages of Tolkien's Middle-Earth* (Baltimore, Boston, 1980), includes glossaries, guides to grammars and pronunciation; R. Helms, *Tolkien and the Silmarils: Imagination and Myth in "The Silmarillion"* (Boston, 1981), a thorough guide; N. D. Issacs and R. A. Zimbardo, eds., *Tolkien: New Critical Perspectives* (Lexington, Ky., 1981); T. A. Shippey, *The Road to Middle-Earth* (London, 1982), highly opinionated, but informed analysis of the philological basis of Tolkien's art; R. L. Purtill, *J. R. R. Tolkien: Myth, Morality, and Religion* (San Francisco, 1984), analysis of the religious dimension of Tolkien's art; L. D. Rossi, *The Politics of Fantasy: C. S. Lewis and J. R. R. Tolkien* (Ann Arbor, Mich., 1984), useful comparison of the two friends and very different writers of fantasy.

Note: There are Tolkien societies in both Great Britain and the United States. Each publishes its own journal:

Mallorn, published by the Tolkien Society of Great Britain, 9 Kingston Road, Ilford, Essex, England.

Mythlore, published by the Mythopoeic Society, Box 24560, Los Angeles, Calif. 90024. In 1973 *The Tolkien Journal*, a publication of the Tolkien Society of America, P. O. Box 373, Highland, Mich. 48031, merged with *Mythlore*.

ANTHONY TROLLOPE

(1815-1882)

Hugh Sykes Davies

I

ANTHONY TROLLOPE was born on 24 April 1815. His father was a barrister, learned in law, but of difficult temper and impractical in the management of his affairs. The first twenty years of his son's life were overshadowed by the gradual failure of the legal practice and by a series of ill-planned and worse-executed maneuvers to make money in other ways.

The ruin of the family was delayed, and at the last made less ruinous, by Anthony's mother, Frances Trollope. One of her husband's weirdest schemes was to set up a great bazaar in Cincinnati; and he dispatched his wife to America to supervise its building, in a striking medley of classical and oriental styles. Funds were exhausted before it could be stocked with goods, and Mrs. Trollope found herself in penury. She learned from this crisis not only that she must herself take on a great part of the task of supporting her family, but also a possible means of performing it. On her return to England, she wrote her first book, a racy and rather acid study of the American way of life. It was successful, and she went on at once to write novels and other travelogues. When her husband finally became bankrupt in 1834, she took the family to Belgium and supported them by her pen, never laying it aside for long, even while she saw to the housekeeping and tended the deathbeds of her favorite son, her husband, and her youngest daughter. Her later days were happier and more prosperous, but she went on writing indefatigably when the financial need had passed. When she died, at the age of eighty-three, she had written forty-one books, and her annual rate of production had not been far below that achieved by Anthony himself. They were both late starters in literature: he was forty when his first book was published, and she fifty-two. For both of them the first conscious aim in writing was to make money; but once started, they both found that it satisfied in them needs much deeper than that of money.

Possibly Trollope inherited from his mother some qualities of mind and spirit that favored quick and copious writing, and certainly he had before him her example of what might be made of these qualities. But the deeper needs that writing came to satisfy were the unhappy by-product of his father's misfortunes. When he was seven, he went to Harrow as a day boy. At twelve, he was moved to his father's old school, Winchester, but taken away three years later because the bills had not been, and could not be, paid. Long before his departure, the other boys had known of the unpaid bills and had made use of their knowledge. "It is the nature of boys to be cruel," he mildly observed of their doings when he wrote of them in later life.[1] But worse was to follow, for he went back to Harrow again as a day boy. By this time his mother was in America, and he was living with his father, unkempt and uncouth, in a gloomy tumbledown farmhouse, from which he tramped twice a day through muddy lanes to sit among the well-fed and smartly dressed boarders. "The indignities I endured are not to be described," he wrote later.

> But I was never able to overcome—or even attempt to overcome—the absolute isolation of my school position. Of the cricket-ground or racket-court I was allowed to know nothing. And yet I longed for these things with an exceeding great longing. I coveted popularity with a coveting which was almost mean. It seemed to me that there would be an Elysium in the intimacy of those very boys I was bound to hate because they hated me. Something of the disgrace of my school-days has clung to me all through life.
> (vol. I, pp. 22–23)

He was removed from Harrow at last by the bankruptcy of his father and went with the rest of the family to Belgium, to become a useless and aimless witness of their successive deaths. At the age of nine-

[1]A. Trollope, *An Autobiography*, 2 vols. (London, 1883), vol. I, p. 12. All quotes from the autobiography are from this edition.

teen, however, he was wangled by family friends into the Post Office as a junior clerk, with competitive examinations to the civil service still to come. In later life he wrote and spoke vehemently against that mode of recruitment, on the grounds that it would certainly have excluded him and that the service would have lost a good official by his exclusion. Probably he was right on both points, yet it would not have been easy for any department to function with more than one or two Anthony Trollopes on its strength. He was unpunctual and insubordinate, and he got into "scrapes." Once, in an argument with the secretary, he banged a table so hard that it catapulted an inkwell into his chief's face; since the Post Office was at that time ruled by a retired colonel, he was lucky to have escaped dismissal or something worse. And one day the office was invaded by a lady under a vast bonnet, with a basket on her arm, crying loudly, "Anthony Trollope, when are you going to marry my daughter?" He did not have to marry the young lady, but he admitted that "these little incidents were all against me in the office."

This period of his life lasted for seven years, and it is the one period of which he has told us very little. He lived in poor lodgings, spent much time in bars, got into debt, and made his one and only acquaintance with a moneylender. He began, however, to make friends, and after the disgrace of his schooldays, it meant much to him that men of his own age were willing to like him, to talk with him, and to spend their weekends walking with him. In the office, he kept his place, largely because he turned out to be very good at writing letters, and in the end even his "scrapes" did him a backhanded service, for the ink-stained colonel recommended him for a job in Ireland, as the best way to be rid of him.

It was a very great service, however backhanded. Ireland accomplished a transformation in him hardly less dramatic than that which characterizes the life cycles of insects. Hitherto, his state had been dark and larval, or chrysalid at best, and his days had been spent in obscurity and lonely poverty. "From the day on which I set foot in Ireland," he wrote, "all these evils went away from me. Since that time who has had a happier life than mine?" The essence of the Irish magic was that for the first time he found himself among people who liked him, who did not regard him as a shameful and useless encumbrance. The work was not in an office under superiors, but in the open air on his own, riding up and down, making arrangements or putting disarrangements to rights.

He became good at the work itself, and passionately fond of riding. He took to hunting and found a hobby that was his only major addiction to the end of his life. After three years of this new life, he married, was promoted, and soon began to write his first novel.

He spent most of his time in Ireland until 1859, and remained in the Post Office until 1867. He rose from being an ill-reputed and difficult clerk to being an efficient but still rather difficult public servant, with a flair for negotiating with all kinds of people, of many nations. He had a fine eye for the practical—he was the inventor of the English pillar-box. Above all, he made himself useful to his department in ways that meant that he was kept on his travels, rather than in an office. He came to know many parts of Britain itself, and visited Egypt, America, and the West Indies on postal business. He hunted two days a week, and became a haunter of London clubs, partly for the sake of whist, partly because his acquaintance was now reaching up into higher circles of society and letters. And on top of all this, he wrote at the average rate of 1.7 books per annum and made money by them.

In middle life, he found all that he had missed as a boy—respect, friendship, and worldly success. And he enjoyed it all, hugely and noisily. He banged about the world, rode about Essex and other hunting counties, fell off his horse and lost his spectacles and laughed, dined at the club and laughed, dined at home or with his friends and laughed. In 1882, he was laughing at a comic book read aloud with his family after dinner when he had a stroke, from which he died a month later, on 6 December.

He had been successful and had valued his success all the more because of his early failures. "To be known as somebody,—" he wrote, "to be Anthony Trollope if it be no more,—is to me much." But to understand both the man and his work, it is necessary to set this beside that other verdict: "Something of the disgrace of my school-days has clung to me all through life."

II

THE above quotations are all from Trollope's *Autobiography*, written in 1875–1876, but not published until 1883, a year after his death. Its reputation has kept pace with the recent revival of respect for his novels, and it is now probably one of the most widely read of English autobiographies. This modest popularity it well deserves. As an account of his life, it is so complete and so just that his biographers have added little to its detail and less to its broad outline. It is in no sense a work of intimate self-revelation, and was not intended to be. It is rather a tour de force of self-description by a man who, sitting for his own portrait, drew it with that deceptive first appearance of prosaic fidelity that serves as the clue to the undermining irony of his male portraits (he is rarely ironic about women). To the serious business of self-regard he brought the same standards that inform his portraits of others, with results hardly less fictional.

Yet the self-portrait is a little uneven, clearly delineated where his habitual perceptions were strong, but fainter and more confused where they were weak. His strength lay in describing the manners and morals of the world in which he was so anxious to bear—and even more anxious to deserve—a good name; and in his account of his dealings with this world, he had a natural rightness and honesty that enabled him to behave well, and to describe clearly. His moral standards were not, perhaps, very profound or very subtle, but they were worthy and workable, and they made his conduct better than that of many men who were his superiors in moral perception. His weakness lay rather in his attitude to his own writing and to literature in general. Here he fell into confusions and distortions that have harmed his reputation and—what is worse—damaged his work.

The problem for him lay in a simple contradiction. On the one hand, he was trying to rise in the world by writing novels; on the other hand, the world into which he wished to rise did not have a high regard for novels, or for those who wrote them. "Thinking much," he said, "of my own daily labour and of its nature, I felt myself at first to be much afflicted and then to be deeply grieved by the opinion expressed by wise and thinking men as to the work done by novelists." To this problem, he found two possible answers. Very early in his career as a novelist he proposed to write a history of English prose fiction, which was to have "vindicated my own profession as a novelist" by demonstrating in the work of his predecessors and contemporaries "that high character which they may claim to have earned by their grace, their honesty, and good teaching." But this history was never written, though a few of its leading

ideas are suggested briefly in chapters 12 and 13 of the *Autobiography*. The other possible answer, on the contrary, was given fully, loudly, and insistently throughout the book. It was that novel writing should be regarded as a profession like any other and that the object of the novelist, like that of every other professional man, was to make money for himself and his dependents. This object was not an unworthy nor a base one. He wrote:

But it is a mistake to suppose that a man is a better man because he despises money. Few do so, and those few in doing so suffer a defect. Who does not desire to be hospitable to his friends, generous to the poor, liberal to all, munificent to his children, and to be himself free from the carking fears which poverty creates?

(vol. I, p. 142)

This was the answer to which he committed himself, and it was elaborated in almost every account he gave of his dealings with publishers, up to the last page of the *Autobiography*, with its detailed financial statement of his earnings from each of his books, meticulously totaled to £68,939 17s. 5d.

It was, perhaps, the answer most likely to impress the world that he sought to impress. The men he met in the hunting field, or over the card table at his club, were more likely to accept it than that other argument about the good done by novelists in the moral education of their readers; and they were more likely to welcome among them a professional man just such as they were themselves—barristers, clergymen, engineers—who made no claim to be doing more than earning a good living. But though it was perhaps well fitted for this purpose, it was wrong, even perversely wrong. The novelist is not, of course, exempt from the common necessity of earning a living. But he earns it as a novelist, rather than as a barrister, a clergyman, an engineer, a politician, or a confidence trickster, because his tastes and abilities carry him to the novel rather than to any of these other lucrative activities. Yet although Trollope could not or would not see this, it is typical of him that he gave a faithful report of the manner in which his own tastes and abilities were turned in this direction. Writing of those disgraced schooldays, and of the hardly less-disgraced years as a clerk in the Post Office, he said:

I was always going about with some castles in the air firmly built within my mind. Nor were these efforts at architecture spasmodic or subject to constant change from day to day. For weeks, for months, if I remember rightly, from year to year, I would carry on the same tale, binding myself down to certain laws, to certain proportions. . . . Nothing impossible was ever introduced,—nor anything which, from outward circumstances, would seem to be violently improbable. . . . This had been the occupation of my life for six or seven years before I went to the Post Office, and was by no means abandoned when I commenced my work. There can, I imagine, hardly be a more dangerous mental practice; but I have often doubted whether, had it not been my practice, I should ever have written a novel. I learned in this way to maintain an interest in a fictitious story, to dwell on a work created by my own imagination, and to live in a world altogether outside the world of my own material life.

(vol. I, pp. 57–58)

It is here, and not in the passages on moneymaking, that Trollope describes his real impulse to write novels. He became a writer, not because of his need for money but because of his talent for imaginative daydreams. It was natural that he should have confused the need with the talent, for both drew their strength from the same source. The former was a conscious passion, almost an obsession, because it was the outward symbol of his desire to rise above those early outward troubles, and the latter also was passionate, but more obscurely, because it had been his hidden inner resource against them. The confusion was natural, but nonetheless unfortunate. At first it prevented him from discovering where his true gift lay, and even after this discovery, he underrated its value in himself. In deference to the standards of the hunting field and the club, he abused and exploited it by writing too much and too quickly, without waiting for his imagination to gather weight and depth. Like some of the more enterprising bankers of his time, he possessed genuine gold, but made it serve to support a recklessly diffuse paper circulation.

III

MISCONCEIVING both his own powers and the nature of fiction, Trollope fell an easy prey to the shallower notions of his age about the way novels should be written. It was his job, he supposed, as an honest professional man, to provide his customers with the commodity they expected; and what they expected, he was taught to believe, was "realism," slices of life faithfully observed and entertainingly told, with a few touches of wholesome morality. When he first resolved to write a novel, the life that lay under his eyes was that of Ireland, so he cut a few slices from it, observed them industriously, and wrote them down as best he could. His two Irish novels were failures, as they deserved to be. A historical novel followed, as dismally cluttered up with book learning as the Irish novels had been by unimaginative reporting. Then he tried his hand at a guidebook; but the publishers to whom specimens were sent omitted to read them, and the project was dropped.

He was turned from these false starts, from his conception of the novel as a mere animated guidebook, not by any growth of literary perception on his own part, but by a lucky accident of his official career. In 1851, he was given the task of organizing country posts in South West England, and for two happy years he rode up and down and about in six or seven counties, visiting many places, meeting many people, but always in a hurry. It was his first experience of England outside London, and its combination of variety and hurry was exactly what his imagination needed to work upon; the materials offered to it were extensive, but he moved too quickly to become bogged down anywhere. From these wanderings he got not another careful slice of life, but a hazy, rich impression of towns and villages, of churches and country houses, of clergy and laity, and of the quietly intricate patterns of their manners and social life. It was upon this impression that he based his first truly imaginative novel, *The Warden* (1855), the first of the Barsetshire series, which has come to be regarded as his highest achievement. The book was conceived one summer evening in Salisbury, but the Barchester of the novels was never merely Salisbury, nor was the county round it any one of the counties through which he had traveled. It was pieced together from memories of them all, and though it grew to be so clear in his head that he once drew a very detailed map of it, its air of convincing reality was imaginative, not geographical. In the same way, the clergy who were its main characters were not of his acquaintance. He tells us in the *Autobiography:*

I never lived in any cathedral city,—except London, never knew anything of any Close, and at that time had enjoyed no peculiar intimacy with any clergyman. My archdeacon, who has been said to be life-like, and for whom I confess I have all a parent's fond affection, was, I think, the simple

1298

result of an effort of my moral consciousness. . . . I had not then even spoken to an archdeacon.

(vol. I, p. 124)

Similarly, the great journalist Tom Towers was thought to be very like an eminent man of the staff of the *Times* (London), and the *Times* itself, in its review of *The Warden*, mildly rebuked the author for indulging in personalities. Trollope protests:

But at that time, living away in Ireland, I had not even heard the name of any gentleman connected with *The Times* newspaper, and could not have intended to represent any individual by Tom Towers. As I had created an archdeacon, so I had created a journalist. . . . my moral consciousness must again have been very powerful.

(vol. I, p. 133)

This gift for the imaginative creation of character by the use of his "moral consciousness" was revealed for the first time in *The Warden*, but it had been developed through those long years of daydreaming, and in its own rather unusual direction. His private fantasies had not been adventurous, nor had they conferred upon him glittering social status. "I never became a king," he tells us,

or a duke . . . a learned man, nor even a philosopher. But I was a very clever person, and beautiful young women used to be fond of me. And I strove to be kind of heart, and open of hand, and noble in thought, despising mean things; and altogether I was a very much better fellow than I have ever succeeded in being since.

(vol. I, pp. 57–58)

This passionate and genuinely imaginative concern with moral existence was the essence of his approach to the novel, from *The Warden* onward. Above all, it was his chief means of insight into character and its depiction. The physical characteristics of his personages are rarely made clearly visible, though they are often conscientiously described. It is their moral physiognomies that are sharply drawn, through what they do and say, what they are said to think and feel, and not seldom by direct comments upon them from their maker.

In the type of moral character chosen for portrayal, *The Warden* set the pattern to which he kept in nearly all his later novels. There was no villain, indeed no character much below the middle range of the moral scale, nor was there anyone conspicuously above it, save the Warden himself. Trollope became

exactly what he wished, the moral historian of men and women in the middle range, the usual run of humanity—"with no more of excellence, nor with exaggerated baseness—so that my readers might recognize human beings like to themselves, and not feel themselves to be carried away among gods or demons."

Finally, *The Warden* was typical of all the novels that were to follow in its disregard for plot. It would, indeed, have been incompatible with his choice of the middle range of characters to have involved them in sensational and complicated situations: ordinary people commonly lead ordinary lives. But apart from this, the elaboration of remarkable incident was quite irrelevant to his main purpose—the depiction of moral character. It mattered little to him how his creatures were set in motion, for once they were on the move they had so great a capacity for living their own lives. In *The Warden* itself, he posed them a problem about the proper use of church endowments, a contemporary, if not a burning, issue: just such a case had arisen in Winchester when he was at school there, and was still before the courts many years after he had written this book. But he himself had no clear view of its rights and wrongs, nor did he need one. All that he needed was the opportunity to let his imagination play upon its issues and cross-issues, as they would appear to differing modes and degrees of moral sensibility. And it was in the process of doing this that men and women—not issues—came alive under his hand.

IV

THE intense moral realization of his characters gave them, once created, a very tenacious hold upon his imagination: so tenacious that he was often unwilling, almost unable, to let them go. His two most notable creations in *The Warden* were of this kind, and they were carried on into *Barchester Towers* (1857), *Doctor Thorne* (1858), *Framley Parsonage* (1861), and *The Last Chronicle of Barset* (1867). Other characters were added, of course, and some of them obtained almost as close a grip on their author's affections. Many other novels were written in the same period. But Archdeacon Grantly and his father-in-law went on leading their lives in his imagination, growing older as he grew older, yet always themselves as he remained himself. Of the two, the archdeacon was the more prominent and active, and much more akin to Trollope. His father-in-law, who had been Warden in the first book, stood at the upper limit of Trollope's moral range, and once he had made his great decision in that first episode, there was little for him to do in the world but be gentle to his family and friends, play his cello, and take good care of the music in the cathedral. Yet he did all this in such a way that we are made to feel his virtue, his religion even, beyond any description that Trollope felt able to give. The archdeacon was coarser in grain, quick to anger, but quick to forget his anger, more worldly, but generous and warmhearted. The two existed side by side, as characters must often do in fiction, making a richer pattern by their contrasting qualities than they could ever have made separately. When the older man came to die, it was through the mouth of the archdeacon that Trollope expressed his estimate both of the dying man and of the archdeacon:

"I feel sure that he never had an impure fancy in his mind, or a faulty wish in his heart. His tenderness has surpassed the tenderness of woman; and yet, when occasion came for showing it, he had all the spirit of a hero. I shall never forget his resignation of the hospital. . . . The fact is, he never was wrong. He couldn't go wrong. He lacked guile, and he feared God,—and a man who does both will never go far astray. I don't think he ever coveted aught in his life,—except a new case for his violoncello and somebody to listen to him when he played it." Then the archdeacon got up, and walked about the room in his enthusiasm; and, perhaps, as he walked some thoughts as to the sterner ambition of his own life passed through his mind. What things had he coveted? Had he lacked guile? He told himself that he had feared God,—but he was not sure that he was telling himself the truth even in that.

(*The Last Chronicle of Barset*, ch. 81)

Nothing is more like Trollope himself than this moment of explosive self-perception. The archdeacon, like his creator, had standards by which to measure his fellow men, and he was tolerably sure of their general rightness. But when he came to ask how far he himself measured up to them, he had his awkward moments. He had coveted many things greatly: a bishopric, power, the ruin of his enemies, wealth, and, above all in his later days, the glory of his children. He had indeed done his best for them, and they had not done badly for him. His daughter was a marchioness, and though her husband the marquess was unquestionably a moron, she was still unques-

tionably a marchioness. His eldest son, Henry, had done well in the Indian Army, had won the Victoria Cross and a wife with a little money. The wife had died, leaving the young widower with a baby daughter, but Henry still had his fine record, some money of his own, and a handsome allowance from his father. He had retired from the army, and settled in Barsetshire as a country squire, with land and farms and horses and foxes of his own.

All this had been achieved by stern ambition, and not without guile; and whatever God might think about it, the archdeacon was usually well pleased with his achievements. In *The Last Chronicle of Barset*, he was sorely tried because Henry fell deeply in love with a young woman, the daughter of a cleric who was the very opposite of himself—pious, very poor, unworldly, and, to make the worst of an already bad job, awaiting his trial on a charge of stealing a check. So outrageous was Henry's choice that his father opposed this new marriage, even threatened to stop the allowance. The struggle between father and son was long and obstinate on both sides, and even the mother's intervention was not able to end it. It was brought to its climax, and at the same instant to its solution, in an interview between the archdeacon and the girl herself, which illustrates as comprehensively as any passage in Trollope both the emotional force of which he was capable and the moral standards that he accepted without question. The first part of the interview does her credit—more credit than the archdeacon had expected. She refers to her father's disgrace, and gives her promise that unless his name is cleared, she will marry nobody:

The archdeacon had now left the rug, and advanced till he was almost close to the chair on which Grace was sitting. "My dear," he said, "what you say does you very much honour—very much honour indeed." Now that he was close to her, he could look into her eyes, and he could see the exact form of her features, and could understand—could not help understanding—the character of her countenance. It was a noble face, having in it nothing that was poor, nothing that was mean, nothing that was shapeless. It was a face that promised infinite beauty, with a promise that was on the very verge of fulfilment. There was a play about her mouth as she spoke, and a curl in her nostrils as the eager words came from her, which almost made the selfish father give way. Why had they not told him that she was such a one as this? Why had not Henry himself spoken of the speciality of her beauty? No man in England knew better than the archdeacon the difference between beauty of one kind and beauty of another kind in a woman's face—the one beauty, which comes from health and youth and animal spirits, and which belongs to the miller's daughter, and the other beauty, which shows itself in fine lines and a noble spirit—the beauty which comes from breeding. "What you say does you very much honour indeed," said the archdeacon.

"I should not mind at all about being poor," said Grace.

"No; no; no," said the archdeacon.

"Poor as we are—and no clergyman, I think, ever was so poor—I should have done as your son asked me at once, if it had been only that—because I love him."

"If you love him you will not wish to injure him."

"I will not injure him. Sir, there is my promise." And now as she spoke she rose from her chair, and standing close to the archdeacon, laid her hand very lightly on the sleeve of his coat. 'There is my promise. As long as people say that papa stole the money, I will never marry your son. There."

The archdeacon was still looking down at her, and feeling the slight touch of her fingers, raised his arm a little as though to welcome the pressure. He looked into her eyes, which were turned eagerly towards his, and when doing so he was sure that the promise would be kept. It would have been sacrilege—he felt that it would have been sacrilege—to doubt such a promise. He almost relented. His soft heart, which was never very well under his own control, gave way so far that he was nearly moved to tell her that, on his son's behalf, he acquitted her of the promise. . . . As he looked down upon her face two tears formed themselves in his eyes and gradually trickled down his old nose. "My dear," he said, "if this cloud passes away from you, you shall come to us and be my daughter." And thus he pledged himself. There was a dash of generosity about the man, in spite of his selfishness, which always made him desirous of giving largely to those who gave largely to him. He would fain that his gifts should be bigger, if it were possible. . . . He had contrived that her hand should fall from his arm into his grasp, and now for a moment he held it. "You are a good girl," he said—"a dear, dear, good girl. When this cloud has passed away, you shall come to us and be our daughter."

(*The Last Chronicle of Barset*, ch. 57)

It was thus that Trollope created the most solid of his male characters, by a temporary merging of his own personality in theirs: here, he has all but put himself into the archdeacon's shoes and gaiters. But the merging was never uncritical, because he was critical of himself; he was always capable of qualifying a virtue, of noting an unworthy doubt, and took frequent pleasure in slight backhanded ironies at the expense of their inner weaknesses, as he did at the expense of his own.

As for the girls, he was inclined to be in love with

them in the same vicarious fashion. His contemporaries, we are informed by a review written in 1867, liked to make gentle jokes about his intimacy with the minds of his heroines: How, they asked, had he managed to "find it all out"? And shortly after Trollope's death, Henry James accurately noted the nature of his relation with them:

Trollope settled down steadily to the English girl; he took possession of her, and turned her inside out. He never made her the subject of heartless satire . . . he bestowed upon her the most serious, the most patient, the most tender, the most copious consideration. He is evidently always more or less in love with her. . . . But . . . if he was a lover, he was a paternal lover. . . .[2]

It was, indeed, the English girl who saved Trollope from the labor of devising plots. She was there to be loved, and love for her was enough to set in motion not only one or two young men, but their families too. For only if the love went hand in hand with an income large enough to support marriage—and marriage in the style to which both parties were accustomed—could it run smoothly. All that was needful, then, to produce a story with situations full of doubt and perplexity was to bring the power of love into conflict with the demands of property and social status. The ensuing confusion would involve not only the lovers, but their families and friends, and as wide a circle of acquaintance as might be needed to fill a three-volume novel. Trollope made this discovery early in the Barsetshire series, and thenceforward he never bothered his head with plots. "When I sit down to write a novel," he blandly observed, "I do not at all know, and I do not very much care, how it is to end." For this relief, he was almost entirely indebted to the English girl with her ability to inspire love, and to the Victorian sense of property with its inveterate tendency to make love injudicious. As the great tragic conflicts in French classical plays tend to arise from the opposition of love and honor, so Trollope's arose from love and property.

But it would be unjust to present him as becoming thus involved only with young lovers, or with characters on the whole amiable and admirable. Such was his involvement in any creation of his own that he was almost equally capable of becoming devoted to personages neither young nor amiable. In the Barsetshire novels, for example, the archdeacon's

[2]H. James, *Partial Portraits* (London, 1888), p. 127.

archenemy is Mrs. Proudie, wife of the bishop and mistress of the palace that the archdeacon had coveted so much, and that his father had held before him. Mrs. Proudie is probably the best-known virago in English fiction, above all for her achievements in henpecking her husband, yet even to her, Trollope developed a powerful attachment. The manner of her death was curious. One night at his club, he heard two clergymen criticizing him for carrying the same characters from novel to novel, and they were very hard on Mrs. Proudie. "I got up, and standing between them, I acknowledged myself to be the culprit. 'As to Mrs Proudie,' I said, 'I will go home and kill her before the week is over.' And so I did. . . . but I have never dissevered myself from Mrs Proudie, and still live much in company with her ghost" (vol. II, pp. 109–110).

V

THE Barsetshire novels have come to be regarded as Trollope's chief, if not his only, contribution to literature, both by the common reader and by the general run of critics and literary historians. They hold this position partly through their own merits of character and milieu, but partly because they can so easily be made to satisfy the common reader's most common weakness in his choice of fiction, his liking for some more or less adult fairyland where he can take a well-earned holiday from the tougher and duller realities of his own life. "Barset," J. B. Priestley has observed, "is a haven of rest." It is natural enough that novels whose main setting was rural England, and whose main characters were so often country clergy, should have been appreciated in this way. But it is an injustice to this series of novels to perceive in them no more than pleasant placidity, and it can easily lead to a still greater injustice in estimating Trollope's work. For the more solid qualities in this series are to be found in many of his other novels, where the milieu is less obviously fairylike, but where his central virtue of moral imagination shows itself both with greater depth and with wider range.

These qualities are nowhere more massively developed than in the linked series of novels that ran through his later life, much as the Barsetshire series had run through his earlier years, the "political" novels whose central characters are Plantagenet

Palliser and his wife, Glencora: *Can You Forgive Her?* (1864–1865), *Phineas Finn* (1869), *The Eustace Diamonds* (1873), *Phineas Redux* (1874), *The Prime Minister* (1876), and *The Duke's Children* (1880).

The main setting has moved from Barsetshire to London, and the main characters are men of wealth and high social status, leaders in their professions and in the House of Commons. The general impression is one of greater "realism," at any rate insofar as this world is clearly more remote from any conceivable fairyland than Barsetshire had been. But, in following Trollope's achievement in this less idyllic milieu, it is even more necessary to realize how much it issued from his imagination. It had been the dread of his boyhood, as he walked to Harrow along the muddy lanes, that "mud and solitude and poverty" would be his lot through his whole life. "Those lads about me would go into Parliament, or become rectors and deans, or squires of parishes, or advocates thundering at the Bar," he supposed; and he told himself that he would never live among them. But with the success of his middle years, he had after all risen to live among them. He knew members of Parliament, thundering barristers, and the brother of his closest friend was dean of Ely. And in 1868, he tried to rise still higher, by standing as a candidate for Parliament himself, at Beverley. He was defeated, and both the fact and the manner of his defeat left a very sore place in his spirit. But if he could rise no further himself, his imagination could go where it liked, and its expeditions were the main impulse of the political novels. This was his own view of them, and as usual he saw himself with accuracy:

By no amount of description or asseveration could I succeed in making any reader understand how much these characters [Palliser and Lady Glencora] with their belongings have been to me in my later life; or how frequently I have used them for the expression of my political and social convictions. They have been as real to me as free trade was to Mr Cobden, or the dominion of a party to Mr Disraeli; and as I have not been able to speak from the benches of the House of Commons . . . they have served me as safety-valves by which to deliver my soul.

(vol. I, pp. 240–241)

In this way, his defeat at Beverley gave him a new imaginative impulse, and at the same time ensured that his imagination would not get itself bogged down in too much minute observation. His acquaintance with the political world, like his earlier survey of South West England, was both wide and vague enough to give him precisely the kind of rich but hazy impression that left his imagination neither starved nor shackled.

In the political novels, as in the earlier series, there is a vast array of characters, and most of them are set and kept in motion by Trollope's usual forces, love and property. But in the central character, Plantagenet Palliser, the chief interest is subtler and deeper. It is a long, full study of a conscience, delicate in itself, and even more perplexed because its owner has wealth, a dukedom, political power, and a very thin skin. The close of *The Prime Minister* is a good example of what Trollope's "moral consciousness" could make of this material. Palliser has been prime minister for three years, as head of a coalition government. When it falls, his old friend and ally, the duke of St. Bungay, expresses the hope that he will take some office in the next cabinet. "I don't think I could do that," Palliser told him, "Caesar could hardly lead a legion under Pompey." But when their talk was over, he found himself regretting "that apparently pompous speech by Caesar. . . . Who was he that he should class himself among the great ones of the world." In the days that followed, this moment of unintended arrogance irked him almost more than the end of his power and the formation of a new administration. A few weeks later, he was talking with his former chancellor of the exchequer, one of the few political allies he respected, and by him he was given this assurance:

"If the country is to lose your services for the long course of years during which you will probably sit in Parliament, then I shall think that the country has lost more than it has gained by the Coalition."

The Duke sat for a while silent, looking at the view, and, before answering Mr Monk,—while arranging his answer, —once or twice in a half-absent way called his companion's attention to the scene before him. But, during this time he was going through an act of painful repentance. He was condemning himself for a word or two that had been ill-spoken by himself, and which, since the moment of its utterance, he had never ceased to remember with shame. He told himself now, after his own secret fashion, that he must do penance for these words by the humiliation of a direct contradiction of them. He must declare that Caesar would at some future time be prepared to serve under Pompey. Then he made his answer.

(ch. 80)

This is a more interesting process of the moral life than any studied in the Barset novels, and the obser-

vation is more penetrating: few moralists have noted so clearly the part that a small phrase, almost a chance phrase, can play in bringing the fluid confusions of the inner life to a point where they crystallize into decision.

But the fine conscience of Plantagenet Palliser is more than an individual study. It is also at the center of Trollope's political world, and he finds in it the explanation of a process of change in England that was otherwise mystifying. He was himself a Liberal, though with many touches of the Tory in his temperament. He approved in general of the slow process of amelioration that was going on in his day, the gradual spread of democracy and of education to wider sections of the population. He even approved of the extension of the franchise, but at the same time he wondered at the fact that some of the great Whigs, especially those of wealth and title, should be willing to use their political influence for its destruction, by encouraging it to pass into the hands of millions of men with votes to be cast in secret ballot. Palliser is that type of Whig, and in his exact and exacting conscience Trollope finds the explanation of this remarkable change. No other English novelist, and few historians, saw the problem so clearly and advanced so convincing a solution for it.

It is this extension of his "moral consciousness" to the whole pattern of English life that informs the political novels and justifies to the full the remarkable tribute that Henry James paid Trollope a few years after his death:

Trollope will remain one of the most trustworthy, though not one of the most eloquent, of writers who have helped the heart of man to know itself. . . . His natural rightness and purity are so real that the good things he projects must be real. A race is fortunate when it has a good deal of the sort of imagination—of imaginative feeling—that had fallen to the share of Anthony Trollope; and in this possession our English race is not poor.

(*Partial Portraits*, p. 133)

VI

TROLLOPE wrote forty-seven novels, and since few readers will wish to read them all, some answer is needed to the question, which are most worth reading? It is not easy to find one, for quite apart from the large number involved, there are few that fall markedly below his usual level, and perhaps even fewer that rise much above it.

The verdict of the common reader has always been that the Barset series should be regarded as his best and most typical work, and that there is little point in going much further with him. His more serious and persistent readers, however, generally believe that the "political" series is at least as good and very probably better. Beyond this, there is confusion. Are the other three dozen novels merely an extension of the Trollopian world over a wider area, a repetition of his favorite themes and his familiar types of character under new names and against slightly shifted scenery? Or do some of them present qualities not to be found anywhere in the two central series?

The second argument has been urged with much force in a study by A. O. J. Cockshut, which sets out to alter radically the accepted view of Trollope's whole work.[3] It contends that Trollope's outlook was, especially in the later part of his life, much less superficial than has usually been supposed, less orthodox, less bluffly optimistic, and more prone to question the assumptions of the age about morality and property. In the light of this contention, the emphasis of attention is changed both within the two main series and in the novels outside them. In the Barset novels, it falls above all on the lonely agony of Mr. Crawley, the clergyman wrongly accused of stealing a check, but not sure within himself that he is innocent. In the "political" series, it falls upon the madness of Mr. Kennedy in *Phineas Finn* and *Phineas Redux,* and the appalling loneliness of his wife, Lady Laura, who has married him for his money—or at least refused to marry the man she really loved because he had no money. And in *The Eustace Diamonds,* Cockshut finds Trollope's first decisive movement toward satire, and to a view of goods and chattels not wholeheartedly Victorian. With this alteration of emphasis in the better-known novels, there goes the claim that what is most important in them was often more fully developed elsewhere. The gloom and loneliness of the individual, for example, was explored most deeply in *He Knew He Was Right* (1869), which traces the degeneration of a husband from unreasonable jealousy of his wife into actual madness. The fullest development of satire is in *The Way We Live Now* (1875), and of the attack on property and inheritance in *Mr. Scarborough's Family*

[3]A. O. J. Cockshut, *Anthony Trollope: A Critical Study* (London, 1955).

(1883). These and other of the outlying novels Cockshut would place in the forefront of Trollope's work.

This study has been usefully done; it provokes a more careful reading of some perhaps unduly neglected novels in the later period and corrects some wrong impressions about those which have been widely read. Cockshut, moreover, has drawn together very skillfully the evidence of Trollope's passionate interest in certain situations and characters: the almost inevitably bad relations between fathers and sons, the "snarling intimacy of family life," the desperation of girls whose only future is marriage and whose labor in life is to entrap a suitably endowed husband. And yet the direction of the emphasis is wrong; it runs too directly against the main current of criticism. In his own day, Trollope's reviewers constantly stressed his choice of the middle range of humanity, of the ordinary man or woman, even of the commonplace; they only wondered at his power of making it interesting, without distortion and without much apparent imaginative heightening of color. Henry James's phrase succinctly comprehends the whole contemporary impression: "His great, his inestimable merit was a complete appreciation of the usual." The judgment is the more weighty because a writer's contemporaries very rarely mistake the nature of his merit, though they often misjudge its degree. In concentrating so much attention upon Trollope's handling of the unusual, the heterodox, Cockshut has indulged in an exaggeration, even if a useful one.

My own conviction is that all the essential qualities of Trollope are to be found in the two central series, and that there they are balanced in their right proportions. Outside them, only a few novels appear to me to have a really strong claim on the general reader.

The first is *The Way We Live Now*. It was written in 1873, and it savagely satirized the new power of financiers and speculators in English life. Trollope saw them compassing the ruin, or at least the degradation, of the landed gentry, literature, the press, social life, even the court itself. It is a magnificently sustained piece of anger, imaginatively realized and dramatically presented. The last act of its great villain, Augustus Melmotte, ruined, drunk, and defiant, trying to speak in Parliament, and glowering angrily but speechlessly round the House, has a force, both immediate and symbolic, beyond Trollope's usual range. In 1876 *The Prime Minister* appeared, and in it the new corruption of finance was represented by a small-scale swindler, Lopez. Had Trollope but waited for his imagination to devise and select, he might have put the far greater figure of Melmotte in the same place. A novel in which Plantagenet Palliser was opposed to Melmotte, politically, morally, and imaginatively, would in all probability have been Trollope's unquestioned masterpiece, his most complete comment on the values of his age. That it did not get written is the heaviest single penalty he paid for his precipitation in covering the daily stint of paper. But even so, *The Way We Live Now* deserves to be read more widely and to be allowed a distinguished place beside the main political novels.

The second novel that I would specially commend is *The Claverings*, published in 1867. It is a work of a very different kind. It is short and has a concentration of effect unusual in Trollope. There is no subplot to distract the development of the central situation, and all the characters play real parts in it. The main problem it explores, the hesitations and weaknesses of a young man caught between a beautiful but poor young girl to whom he is engaged and an equally beautiful but rich widow whom he had loved before her marriage, is exactly of the kind to display at its best Trollope's ability to analyze the unheroic but not quite base man of common mold. But it is above all in its style that it is distinctive. For the most part, Trollope's manner of writing is adequate rather than eloquent, and so impersonal that one often feels it might have been practiced by almost anyone else in the same period: though it is remarkable how surely, in fact, a fair specimen of his work can be recognized for what it is. In *The Claverings*, however, more than in any other book, he showed what he could do when he was neither writing against the clock, nor merely "for length" (the dreadful phrase is his own). It is not merely that as a whole the book is better written than most of the others, but that it also shows some of his subtler qualities of style more clearly than the rest.

There is, for example, a turn of phrase almost peculiar to him, and very characteristic of his ironically intimate report of the inner life: it depends upon the addition of some slight qualification to a previous statement. An example has been given already from the archdeacon's reflections:

He told himself that he had feared God,—but he was not sure that he was telling himself the truth even in that.

Here are the others:

"If I were to name the class of men whose lives are spent with the most thorough enjoyment, I think I should name that of barristers who are in large practice and also in Parliament."

"Isn't it a great grind, sir?" asked Silverbridge.

"A very great grind, as you call it. And there may be the grind but not the success. But—" He had now got up from his seat at the table and was standing with his back against the chimney-piece, and as he went on with his lecture,—as the word "But" came from his lips—he struck the fingers of one hand lightly on the palm of the other as he had been known to do at some happy flight of oratory in the House of Commons. "But it is the grind that makes the happiness."

(*The Duke's Children,* ch. 25)

Colonel Osborne knew that his visit had been very innocent; but he did not like the feeling that even his innocence had been made the subject of observation.

(*He Knew He Was Right,* ch. 23)

It cannot be said of him that he did much thinking for himself;—but he thought that he thought.

(*The Prime Minister,* ch. 2)

In *The Claverings*, this characteristic Trollopian turn of phrase is used frequently, and especially in the depiction of the wavering hero. "He told himself that he was an ass, but still he went on being an ass." Thus he got himself into his trouble between the old love and the new, and in the midst of it, when he was being true to neither, Trollope concludes an address to the reader on the failings of his hero: "He should have been chivalric, manly, full of high duty. He should have been all this, and full also of love, and then he would have been a hero. But men as I see them are not often heroic."

Another of Trollope's characteristic devices is the repetition of a short phrase, at brief intervals but with such shifts of context, such exaggeration, that it acquires the ironic power conferred in the same manner on the phrase "honorable men" in Antony's speech in *Julius Caesar*. In *The Claverings* there are two fine examples of its use. One is in the twelfth chapter, describing the visit of the beautiful young widow to the splendid estate she had won by her loveless marriage, and the phrase woven through it is: "She had the price in her hands." It gathers weight continually through the chapter, which ends upon the final bitter variation: "She had the price in her hands, but she felt herself tempted to do as Judas did, to go out and hang herself." Five chapters later, the same device is put to more openly comic and hostile uses, when the best mode of wooing this same rich young widow is discussed by Captain Clavering and Captain Boodle, after dinner at their club:

"Well, now, Clavvy, I'll tell you what my ideas are. When a man's trying a young filly, his hands can't be too light. A touch too much will bring her on her haunches, and throw her out of step. She should hardly feel the iron in her mouth. But when I've got to do with a trained mare, I always choose that she shall know that I'm there! Do you understand me?"
"Yes; I understand you, Doodles."
"I always choose that she should know I'm there." And Captain Boodle, as he repeated these manly words with a firm voice, put out his hands as though he were handling the horse's rein.

(ch. 17)

After the phrase has been relished a further half-dozen times, Boodle leaves his friend alone to meditate upon it:

He sat the whole evening in the smoking-room, very silent, drinking slowly iced gin-and-water; and the more he drank the more assured he felt that he now understood the way in which he was to attempt the work before him. "Let her know I'm there," he said to himself, shaking his head gently, so that no one should observe him; "yes, let her know I'm there." Everything was contained in that precept. And he, with his hands before him on his knees, went through the process of steadying a horse with the snaffle-rein, just touching the curb, as he did so, for security. It was but a motion of his fingers and no one could see it, but it made him confident that he had learned his lesson.

(ch. 17)

And in this way the phrase is made to undermine these two men, to reveal all their coarseness, their monotony of mind, their pompous ineptitude.

An acquaintance with *The Claverings*, then, is worth making not only for its own sake; it is probably the readiest way for a reader to sensitize himself to the subtler aspects of Trollope's style, and above all to his characteristic modes of irony. Without this sensitivity, none of his novels can be read rightly, for even in his dealings with the characters he knew and loved best—indeed especially with them—this irony is never far away. But its quality is so quiet, its onset so unostentatious, that it can easily be missed.

For these reasons, then, these two novels seem to deserve attention. But it must at once be added that many of the others are as good and very possibly better. *Ralph the Heir* (1871), for example, has some fine political scenes and at least one character, Sir Thomas Underwood, profounder in conception than any in *The Way We Live Now*. *The Belton Estate* (1866) is comparable with *The Claverings* in its compression; it has a parallel theme, the hesitations of a young woman between two lovers, developed with all that power of creating a dramatic scene that has been illustrated above in the encounter between the archdeacon and Miss Crawley. Others of the lesser-known novels that certainly deserve to be much better known are *Orley Farm* (1862), *Sir Harry Hotspur of Humblethwaite* (1871), *Is He Popenjoy?* (1878), *Dr. Wortle's School* (1881), and *Ayala's Angel* (1881). But for the attention of American readers there is one novel that has special and powerful claims, *The American Senator* (1877). Its main plot hangs on visits to a typical piece of rural England by an inquiring and inquisitive American senator, with his reflections on what he sees and hears, often expressed in letters. These descriptions and comments offer very convenient and lively cover for some of Trollope's own tilts at some treasured British windmills, and his implied opinions on America are more tolerant and perceptive than those of his mother's first book. As an early example of fictional sociology it is well worth reading, but the main plot is soon nearly submerged in a powerful study of the struggle to entrap a husband waged by an aristocratic pauper. The bitterness of the battle and its ruthlessness are both explored with a horror and sympathy that are hardly matched anywhere else in Trollope's work, and not often equalled anywhere. The list could easily be made much longer, but the reader who wishes to explore these novels further has no lack of guides. If he is interested in the gloomier and less "usual" aspects in them, he cannot do better than follow Cockshut; if, on the other hand, he prefers a more orthodox and central view, he should consult the *Commentary* of Michael Sadleir, to whom this generation owes much for defending and explaining a writer who seemed on the very point of slipping into oblivion.

But whatever he may choose to read, he should guard against two misconceptions that can prevent him from giving both himself and Trollope a fair chance. He should not, under the impression of length and weight of circumstance, mistake what is before him for mere photography, and so miss the real, though unostentatious, imagination that has molded it; nor should he let the apparent uniformity and directness of the style lull him into a hypnotic automatism, insensitive to those subtler turns of phrase that are so characteristic an expression of Trollope's "moral consciousness," of his kindly but ironic perception of the gap between what we are and what we ought to be, wish to be, or believe ourselves to be.

SELECTED BIBLIOGRAPHY

I. BIBLIOGRAPHY. M. L. Irwin, *Anthony Trollope: A Bibliography* (New York, 1926), contains useful references to early reviews, articles in periodicals, etc.; M. Sadleir, *Trollope: A Bibliography* (London, 1928), based on the compiler's renowned collection now in the Parrish Collection in the Princeton University library: *Supplement* (1934), and additional material in Sadleir's *XIX Century Fiction* (1951), final authority on the works of Trollope themselves, with a fascinating section on the extent of their popularity, as measured by the book market; W. G. Gerould and J. T. Gerould, *A Guide to Trollope* (Princeton, N. J., 1948), contains bibliographical tables and a dictionary of characters, places, and events in the novels; D. Smalley, ed., "Trollope," in L. Stevenson, ed., *Victorian Fiction: A Guide to Research* (Cambridge, Mass., 1964); J. C. Olmsted and J. E. Welch, eds., *The Reputation of Trollope: An Annotated Bibliography. 1925–1975* (New York, 1978).

II. COLLECTED WORKS. *Note:* There is no complete ed. of Trollope's works, and it now seems unlikely that there ever will be, for the Oxford University Press has been forced to discontinue *The Oxford Trollope* that was begun in 1948, at a point when it included only nine titles (in fifteen vols.). Many of the novels, along with the *Autobiography*, are published in the World's Classics series by the same publishers, and for most purposes this can be regarded as the standard, if not complete, ed. Several of the novels are also available in Everyman's Library and in Nelson's Classics. Several other reprints of the more popular novels have appeared under several imprints, such as Zodiac, Panther, Dover. Their choices have been influenced largely by the appearance of the novels on radio and television programs. While they have certainly helped to make Trollope more widely known and even read, they have created a severe problem for those who wish to find a particular passage. Page references, if given at all, would have to be given for seven or eight different eds., which might not include the one the reader might possess. If inclusive, they would be very cumbrous. It has seemed better, therefore, to give only references to chapters, which are generally uniform. To find a short passage it may be necessary to read through a whole chapter. But this is nearly always well worth doing.

F. Harrison, ed., *The Barsetshire Novels*, 8 vols. (London, 1906); M. Sadleir, ed., *The Barsetshire Novels*, 14 vols. (Oxford, 1929), Shakespeare Head ed.; M. Sadleir and F. Page, eds., *The Oxford Trollope*, 15 vols. (London, 1948–1954), includes the following: *Can You Forgive Her?* 2 vols. (1948); *Phineas Finn*, 2 vols. (1949); *The Eustace Diamonds*, 2 vols. (1950); *An Autobiography . . .* (1950); *Phineas Redux*, 2 vols. (1951); *The Prime Minister*, 2 vols. (1952); *The Warden* (1952); *Barchester Towers*, 2 vols. (1953); *The Duke's Children* (1954); B. A. Booth, ed., *The Letters of Anthony Trollope* (London, 1951), uniform with vols. of the Oxford ed.

III. SELECTIONS. E. C. Dunne and M. E. Dodd, eds., *The Trollope Reader* (New York, 1947), gives few of his dramatic scenes, but exemplifies very well his range of observation; J. Hampden, ed., *The Parson's Daughter and Other Stories* (London, 1949), includes *Katchen's Caprices*, not repr. since its first appearance in *Harper's Weekly* (1866–1867), and four other stories; L. O. Tingay, ed., *The Bedside Barsetshire* (London, 1940), has its uses, but proves very clearly that Trollope needs space and time to develop his effects; J. Hampden, ed., *Mary Gresley and Other Stories* (London, 1951), includes five stories.

IV. SEPARATE WORKS. *The MacDermots of Ballycloran*, 3 vols. (London, 1847), novel; *The Kellys and the O'Kellys: A Tale of Irish Life*, 3 vols. (London, 1848), novel; *La Vendée: An Historical Romance*, 3 vols. (London, 1850), historical novel; *The Warden* (London, 1855), Barsetshire novel, also with an intro. by A. O. J. Cockshut (London, 1955); *Barchester Towers*, 3 vols. (London, 1857), Barsetshire novel, also with an intro. by P. Hansford Johnson (London, 1952); *The Three Clerks*, 3 vols. (London, 1858), novel; *Doctor Thorne*, 3 vols. (London, 1858), Barsetshire novel; *The Bertrams*, 3 vols. (London, 1859), novel; *The West Indies and the Spanish Main* (London, 1859), travel.

Castle Richmond, 3 vols. (London, 1860), novel; *Tales of All Countries*, 2nd series (London, 1861–1863), short stories; *Framley Parsonage*, 3 vols. (London, 1861), Barsetshire novel; *Orley Farm*, 2 vols. (London, 1862), novel; *North America*, 2 vols. (London, 1862), travel, also in D. Smalley and B. A. Booth, eds. (New York, 1951); *Rachel Ray*, 2 vols. (London, 1863), novel; *The Small House at Allington*, 2 vols. (London, 1864), Barsetshire novel; *Can You Forgive Her?* 2 vols. (London, 1864–1865), political novel; *Miss Mackenzie*, 2 vols. (London, 1865), novel; *Hunting Sketches* (London, 1865), sketches, also in J. Boyd, ed. (London, 1934) and L. Edwards, ed. (London, 1952); *The Belton Estate*, 3 vols. (London, 1866), novel; *Travelling Sketches* (London, 1866), sketches; *Clergymen of the Church of England* (London, 1866), essays; *Nina Balatka: The Story of a Maiden of Prague*, 2 vols. (London, 1867), novel; *The Last Chronicle of Barset*, 2 vols. (London, 1867), Barsetshire novel; *The Claverings*, 2 vols. (London, 1867), novel; *Lotta Schmidt: and Other Stories*

(London, 1867), short stories; *Linda Tressel*, 2 vols. (London, 1868), novel; *Phineas Finn, the Irish Member*, 2 vols. (London, 1869), political novel; *He Knew He Was Right*, 2 vols. (London, 1869), novel; *Did He Steal It?* (London, 1869), drama, privately printed, an adaptation by Trollope from the central episode of *The Last Chronicle of Barset*, also in R. H. Taylor, ed. (Princeton, N. J., 1952).

The Vicar of Bullhampton, 2 vols. (London, 1870), novel; *An Editor's Tales* (London, 1870), short stories; *The Struggles of Brown, Jones and Robinson: By One of the Firm* (London, 1870), novel, a pirated ed., repr. from the *Cornhill* magazine, had appeared in the U. S. in 1862; *The Commentaries of Caesar* (London, 1870), translation; *Sir Harry Hotspur of Humblethwaite* (London, 1871), novel; *Ralph the Heir*, 3 vols. (London, 1871), novel; *The Golden Lion of Granpère* (London, 1872), novel; *The Eustace Diamonds*, 3 vols. (London, 1873), political novel; *Australia and New Zealand*, 2 vols. (London, 1873), travel; *Lady Anna*, 2 vols. (London, 1874), novel; *Phineas Redux*, 2 vols. (London, 1874), political novel, also in the Oxford Illustrated ed., 2 vols. (London, 1951); *Harry Heathcote of Gangoil: A Tale of Australian Bush Life* (London, 1874), novel; *The Way We Live Now*, 2 vols. (London, 1875), novel; *The Prime Minister*, 4 vols. (London, 1876), political novel; *The American Senator*, 3 vols. (London, 1877), novel; *Christmas at Thompson Hall* (New York, 1877), short story; *South Africa*, 2 vols. (London, 1878), travel; *Is He Popenjoy?* 3 vols. (London, 1878), novel; *The Lady of Launay* (New York, 1878), short story; *How the "Mastiffs" Went to Iceland* (London, 1878), travel, privately printed; *An Eye for an Eye*, 2 vols. (London, 1879), novel; *Thackeray* (London, 1879), criticism; *John Caldigate*, 3 vols. (London, 1879), novel; *Cousin Henry*, 2 vols. (London, 1879), novel.

The Duke's Children, 3 vols. (London, 1880), political novel; *The Life of Cicero*, 2 vols. (London, 1880), biography; *Dr. Wortle's School*, 2 vols. (London, 1881), novel; *Ayala's Angel*, 3 vols. (London, 1881), novel; *Why Frau Frohmann Raised Her Prices and Other Stories* (London, 1882), short stories; *Lord Palmerston* (London, 1882), biography; *The Fixed Period*, 2 vols. (London, 1882), novel; *Marion Fay*, 3 vols. (London, 1882), novel; *Kept in the Dark*, 2 vols. (London, 1882), novel; *Mr. Scarborough's Family*, 3 vols. (London, 1883), novel; *The Landleaguers*, 3 vols. (London, 1883), novel; *An Autobiography*, 2 vols. (London, 1883); *An Old Man's Love*, 2 vols. (London, 1883), novel.

M. Sadleir, ed., *The Noble Jilt: A Comedy* (London, 1923), drama, written in 1850 but never acted, used as the main plot of *Can You Forgive Her?* and mentioned in *The Eustace Diamonds*; M. Sadleir, ed., *London Tradesmen* (London, 1928), sketches, from the *Pall Mall Gazette* (1880); M. L. Parrish, ed., *Four Lectures* (London, 1938); B. A. Booth, ed., *The Tireless Traveller* (Cambridge, 1941), letters contributed to the *Liverpool Mercury* (1875);

J. Hampden, ed., *The Two Heroines of Plumplington* (London, 1953), short story.

V. Biographical and Critical Studies. E. Montégut, *Revue des Deux Mondes* (1855 and 1858), studies by a French critic who specialized in the interpretation of English literature. The first of these reviews contains a long study of *The Warden*, the second deals fully with *Barchester Towers* and *Doctor Thorne*. They illustrate very clearly the general superiority of the French critical approach to fiction over that of the English reviewers of the same period. It was this superiority in skill and seriousness that enabled Montégut to perceive Trollope as not simply a naive realist but a writer who imposed upon his report of life a pattern of his own, with a style of his own. Both reviews were repr. in the first vol. of his *Écrivains Modernes de l'Angleterre* (Paris, 1892); H. James, *Partial Portraits* (London, 1888), the most perceptive of the early estimates of Trollope's quality; F. Harrison, *Studies in Early Victorian Literature* (London, 1895), a short essay of special interest because it gives a firsthand impression of Trollope himself and of the surprise felt by the writer that such fine qualities should have happened to lodge in so bluff and noisy a man; G. Saintsbury, *Corrected Impressions* (London, 1895), the short discussion of Trollope in the essay "Three Mid-Century Novelists" is a shallow and contemptuous attempt to record his "comparative oblivion"; may be of some interest as marking the nadir of his reputation; in his "Trollope Revisited," in *Essays and Studies by Members of the English Association*, VI (1920), the same author copiously but indecisively admits that the oblivion had been, after all, only very comparative.

L. Stephen, *Studies of a Biographer*, vol. IV (London, 1902), the essay on Trollope is short and pleasantly nostalgic, and treats him as a pleasing record of a peaceful but bygone age, the earliest expression of this mode of appreciating him; G. S. Street, *A Book of Essays* (London, 1902), a short essay on Trollope claims for him a higher place than was usual at the time and discusses his "realism" with some penetration; T. H. S. Escott, *Anthony Trollope: His Work, Associates and Literary Originals* (London, 1913), the first full-length biography, many details were filled in by a writer who knew Trollope personally; M. E. Speare, *The Political Novel: Its Development in England and America* (New York, 1924), some interesting points are made about Trollope's treatment of politics, but the author is prevented from doing justice to him by his admiration of Disraeli, whom Trollope disliked both as a politician and as a novelist; S. van B. Nicholas, *The Significance of Anthony Trollope* (New York, 1925), only 490 copies of this booklet were printed, some of its literary judgments are too enthusiastic, but it contains one of the first attempts to draw a map of Barsetshire and to classify the novels; M. Sadleir, *Trollope: A Commentary* (London, 1927; rev. eds. 1945, 1961); H. Walpole, *Anthony Trollope* (London, 1929).

D. MacCarthy, *Portraits* (London, 1931); C. C. Koets, *Female Characters in the Works of Trollope* (Amsterdam, 1933); D. Cecil, *Early Victorian Novelists* (London, 1934), a judicious estimate of Trollope is given, containing some valuable comparisons between him and some of his contemporaries, especially Jane Austen, who was his favorite novelist in his youth; B. A. Booth, ed., *The Trollopian* (Los Angeles, 1945–1949), a quarterly, continued after 1949 as *Nineteenth Century Fiction;* L. P. Stebbins and R. P. Stebbins, *The Trollopes: The Chronicle of a Writing Family* (London, 1945), contains much biographical information about Trollope's mother and his eldest brother, Thomas Adolphus, one of the first attempts to emphasize the gloomier and less orthodox strains in Trollope himself; E. Bowen, *Trollope: A New Judgement* (Oxford, 1946); B. C. Brown, *Anthony Trollope* (London, 1950), a sympathetic attempt to define the "theme" common to the novels, some illuminating suggestions about the effect of civil service experience upon Trollope's approach to life and people; A. O. J. Cockshut, *Anthony Trollope: A Critical Study* (London, 1955); R. Helling, *A Century of Trollope Criticism* (Helsinki, 1956), a detailed survey of the ups and downs of Trollope's reputation from his own day to the present, with a good selection of quotations from the original reviews and a good bibliography of Trollope criticism; M. Praz, *The Hero in Eclipse in Victorian Fiction* (London, 1956), a long ch. on Trollope is perhaps the most favorable and discriminating judgment so far made by a writer neither English nor American; B. A. Booth, "Orley Farm: Artistry Manqué," in R. C. Rathburn and M. Steinmann, eds., *From Jane Austen to Joseph Conrad* (Oxford, 1958); A. Mizener, "Anthony Trollope: The Palliser Novels," in R. C. Rathburn and M. Steinmann, eds., *From Jane Austen to Joseph Conrad* (Oxford, 1958); B. A. Booth, *Anthony Trollope: Aspects of His Life and Work* (London, 1959), this very learned study is specially interesting on the social background and vagaries of Trollope's fame.

H. Sykes Davies, "Trollope and His Style," in *A Review of English Literature*, I, no. 4 (October 1960); R. Arnold, *The Whiston Matter* (London, 1961); R. J. Polhemus, *The Changing World of Anthony Trollope* (Berkeley, Calif., 1968); D. Smalley, ed., *Trollope: The Critical Heritage* (London, 1969); R. Roberts, *Trollope: Artist and Moralist* (London, 1971); J. P. Hennessy, *Anthony Trollope* (London, 1971; New York, 1972); D. Skilton, *Trollope and His Contemporaries* (London, 1972); J. W. Clark, *The Language and Style of Anthony Trollope* (London, 1975); J. Halperin, *Trollope and Politics: A Study of the Pallisers and Others* (London, 1977); R. Terry, *Anthony Trollope: The Artist in Hiding* (London, 1977); P. D. Edwards, *Anthony Trollope: His Art and Scope* (London, 1978); A. Pollard, *Anthony Trollope* (London, 1978); T. Bareham, ed., *Anthony Trollope* (London, 1980); N. J. Hall, *Trollope and His Illustrators* (London, 1980); G. Harvey, *The Art of Anthony Trollope* (London, 1980); W. M. Kendrick, *"Novel Machine": The Theory and Fiction of Anthony Trollope* (Baltimore, 1980).

EVELYN WAUGH

(1903-1966)

William Myers

EVELYN WAUGH seems always to have realized that as a writer and probably as a man he needed a lot of attention. "How badly I write when there is no audience to arrange my thoughts for," he noted in his diary (18 April 1926).[1] With his first two novels he secured just such an audience, and for the rest of his life he was a public figure, continually invited to make pronouncements on a vast range of topics, which he willingly, if somewhat cantankerously, did. Nor did he keep his views out of his novels. Fiction, he maintained, is an "exercise in the use of language"; an author can expect his readers to want the same effects as he does, and, prompted by his material, he can "throw out a number of personal opinions and theories" for their consideration (*Spectator*, 6 November 1942). From the beginning, therefore, Waugh was a didactic writer.

His first novel, *Decline and Fall* (1928), tells the story of a young innocent, Paul Pennyfeather, who is unjustly sent down from Oxford and finds himself teaching at Llanabba Castle, a ludicrous Welsh boarding school. There he meets the exquisite Margot Beste-Chetwynde, the mother of a favorite pupil. They are on the point of being married when he is arrested for organizing the international prostitution racket that is the source of her considerable wealth, and sent to prison. However, his death is faked, and he returns to Oxford to start his life anew. Margot marries a retired politician, Lord Metroland—but takes as a lover the very Alastair Digby-Vane-Trumpington whose drunken party first set Paul off on his adventures. Waugh structures this absurd story around a series of comic characters who keep reappearing. The novel opens and closes with

descriptions of a drunken undergraduate party. The central figure at the first is Alastair—handsome, decent, not very bright; the second is dominated by Margot's son, Peter (now Lord Pastmaster), an intelligent, attractive young man who lost his innocence too soon. (When we first meet him, his favorite books are a children's story and a pioneering study in sexual psychopathology.) Without compromising the novel's effortless amorality, these opening and closing scenes provide the framework of a genuine fall from innocent freshness to worldly-wise knowledge.

Vile Bodies (1930) is structurally less satisfactory. It tells the story of Adam Fenwick-Symes's engagement to Nina Blount. In a succession of parties, hangovers, and fatal motorcar races (Adam is temporarily a gossip columnist), they keep getting and losing the thousand pounds that will enable them to marry. Finally, to pay a hotel bill, Adam "sells" Nina to a man called Ginger. Later he and Nina spend an adulterous Christmas together, but war breaks out, and Adam finally gets possession of his (now worthless) money on the field of battle. In spite of its weak ending *Vile Bodies* shares many memorable qualities with *Decline and Fall*, including an economy of statement and incident reminiscent of the furniture and buildings of the interwar years—a style Waugh mocks but which his technique reflects. Much of his reputation for heartlessness comes from this economical style. Lady Circumference's brief remarks in *Decline and Fall* about the trivial injury, cruel decay, and painful death of her son, Tangent, are typical. So are the passing references to Adam's money in *Vile Bodies*.

Another of Waugh's devices is to use flagrantly inappropriate language. The descriptions of the Welsh bandsmen in *Decline and Fall*, for example, are staggeringly offensive: "On seeing the Doctor they halted and edged back, those behind squinting and moulting over their companions' shoulders" (1.8).

[1]All quotations are from Penguin Books editions, as the most generally available, except for quotations from the travel books, which are from first editions. References are to the dates of entries in the *Diaries*, to page numbers of the *Letters* and travel books, and to part and chapter numbers of other works.

Equally characteristic is the slangy exchange between Adam and Ginger over Nina's "sale." Waugh's incidents and characters are quite as outrageous as his vocabulary. In *Decline and Fall*, a pederastic public school man, Captain Grimes, is forced into bigamous marriage with the headmaster's hideous daughter and has to fake suicide to escape. Later a prison chaplain has his head sawn off by a madman.

Not all this extravagance succeeds. The stories of Philbrick the mad butler in *Decline and Fall* and the ludicrous scenario of a film about John Wesley in *Vile Bodies* are overdone, but Waugh's grotesquerie generally pleases. So does his celebration of glamour, laced as it is with high eroticism. The future Margot Metroland's first appearance—"two lizard-skin feet, silk legs, chinchilla body, a tight little black hat, pinned with platinum and diamonds, and the high invariable voice that may be heard in any Ritz Hotel from New York to Budapest" (*Decline and Fall* 1.8)—is justly celebrated.

Astonishingly, much of the material of these early novels has a basis in personal experience. As an undergraduate, Waugh at first lived a relatively respectable life, like Paul Pennyfeather. He then joined a fashionable set, more decadent than Alastair Trumpington's, and came down with a poor degree and a taste for drunken parties. He taught in two schools; in one he formed a faintly amorous attachment to two boys, models for Peter Beste-Chetwynde; in the other he met the original Captain Grimes, and himself attempted the farcical suicide he attributes to the latter. Later he worked briefly on the *Daily Express*. More significantly, his relations with his first wife, whom he married in 1928 and from whom he was divorced a year later, were very like those between Adam and Nina. All of Waugh's later books were to be similarly based on his experiences.

But there is an even more personal element in his writings. They are full of private jokes and portraits of friends and acquaintances. Waugh wrote for two kinds of reader—the public and a group of initiates, not all friends but all in his social circle. Some of these jokes are relatively trivial. He introduces the names of his Oxford tutor, C. R. M. F. Cruttwell, and the critic Cyril Connolly, for example, into deliberately undignified contexts. More seriously, in *Black Mischief* (1932), he gives his own nickname, Boaz, to the leader of fashion among "cosmopolitan blacks . . . and . . . the decayed Arab intelligentsia" (ch. 5); Boaz ends up murdering the young emperor

and being himself murdered. There are similarly ambiguous allusions to friends. The amoral Basil Seal of *Black Mischief*, *Put Out More Flags* (1942), and *Basil Seal Rides Again* (1963) is recognizably the one-time husband of Waugh's close friend Nancy Mitford. Sebastian Flyte in *Brideshead Revisited* (1945) is partly based on the great friend of Waugh's youth, Alastair Graham (his mother is the original Lady Circumference). And both Harold Acton and Brian Howard contribute to the ambivalent figures of Ambrose Silk in *Put Out More Flags* and Anthony Blanche in *Brideshead Revisited*. There is little doubt that Waugh and his friends realized that in time this side of his work would become known to the public, and that the effects he achieved by thus weaving personal allusions into books designed for general consumption would cease to be a merely private pleasure. That, however, was for the future.

What struck the readers of his first two novels was their bright, modern surface. Waugh builds his narrative out of short sequences of externally observed incidents and snatches of dialogue that expose, excite, and conceal with the impersonality of the film or the gossip column. Thus the first four chapters of *Vile Bodies* are constructed around the secret that the mousy Miss Brown, who urges the bright young things to finish their party at her house, is in fact the prime minister's daughter. Waugh reveals this important detail at exactly the right moment. The ensuing scandal brings down the government, an unforeseeable event mysteriously anticipated by the Jesuit Father Rothschild. Meanwhile a customs officer burns Adam's manuscript autobiography as obscene, his friend Agatha Runcible—later to die after a car crash and a hospital drinking party—is strip-searched, and the appalling evangelist Mrs. Melrose Ape arrives in England with the chorus girls she dresses as angels at her revivalist meetings. Margot Metroland later appraises them "one by one, with an expert eye" (ch. 6). The adroitness with which Waugh edits this material makes the first six chapters of *Vile Bodies* one of the funniest tours de force in English fiction.

A no less subtle ingredient of these first two novels, however, is their recognition of human vulnerability. Paul Pennyfeather is a generally colorless character, but he becomes touchingly alive once he is attracted to Margot. Margot herself is allowed her moments of vulnerability too—in a reference to her as a "romantic young heiress who had walked entranced among the cut yews, and had been wooed, how phlegmatically, in the odour of honeysuckle" (2.1) and when she visits Paul in prison. The most serious character in *Decline and Fall*, however, is Margot's son, Peter, capably greeting his mother's degenerate guests while she lies in her room fragrantly sedated, yet unable to stop admiring himself before Paul's wedding, and turning white when Paul is arrested. His final scene with Paul, in which he keeps referring to Margot's marriage to the recently ennobled Lord Metroland, is especially well written. "You know you ought never to have got mixed up with me and the Metroland," he tells Paul (epilogue): it is painful to hear Peter referring to his mother so crudely. In *Vile Bodies* Peter bitterly tells his stepfather to "go to hell" when the latter draws attention to Alastair's hat on the hall table (ch. 5). The lovers in *Vile Bodies* also have their moments of vulnerability: Adam when he dances by himself in Margot's hall, Nina when she nervously admits to being a virgin. Touches such as these are crucial to Waugh's art. Thus the entire history of Margot's first marriage is encapsulated in the two words "how phlegmatically."

Waugh is less adroit, however, in "throwing out" his "personal opinions and theories" in the two early novels. Like T. S. Eliot's *The Waste Land*, a poem Waugh greatly admired, both *Decline and Fall* and *Vile Bodies* present a series of fragmented images of English society in decay. In addition (and unlike Eliot) Waugh tries to give explicit expression to some of the values against which modernity offends. He uses Professor Silenus in *Decline and Fall* and Father Rothschild in *Vile Bodies* for this purpose, but the key speeches of both are inchoate and shallow, and are dressed up in pretentious symbolism: Silenus compares "life" to "the big wheel at Luna Park" (3.7); Father Rothschild speaks of the "almost fatal hunger for permanence" shown by divorce (ch. 8).

The world of *Vile Bodies* is a kind of vorticist nightmare: "I thought we were all driving round and round in a motor race and none of us could stop," says the dying Agatha Runcible (ch. 12). *Vile Bodies* ends literally in nightmare—an invented world war—an indication, perhaps, that fashionable modernity on its own was insufficient to sustain Waugh's art. He himself hated *Vile Bodies*, which he had to complete while his marriage was breaking up. He told Harold Acton that he felt "chained" to it: "It is a welter of sex and snobbery" (*Letters*, p. 37). To Henry Yorke he wrote: "It all seems to shrivel up & rot internally and I am relying on a sort of cumula-

tive futility for any effect it may have" (*Letters*, p. 39).

Waugh's imagination, however, had resources other than the contemporary scene, resources ultimately attributable to his roots in a traditionally minded upper-middle-class home. He was the son of a publisher and writer, Arthur Waugh. Before the drunken orgies and homosexual romances of his undergraduate days, he had had an excellent education at a High Anglican boarding school, which gave him a thorough grounding in the classics and encouraged his talents as a draftsman, and from which he won a history scholarship to Oxford. He was naturally religious; even in his dissolute post-Oxford days he thought about ordination. He was also a natural craftsman. In one of his early travel books, *Ninety-Two Days* (1934), he compares the writer's desire to reduce the amorphous experience of life into communicable form with the carpenter's itch to shape a piece of rough timber. More surprisingly for a young man of his generation, he was a connoisseur of Victorian painting and furniture. In 1926 he published *P.R.B., An Essay on the Pre-Raphaelite Brotherhood 1847-1854*, and in 1928 his first book, *Rossetti*, on the Victorian painter and poet. In all his books his descriptions of buildings are careful and technically accurate.

Granted this interest in traditional craftsmanship and the Victorian period, the influence of Victorian novelists on his work is to be expected, notably that of Charles Dickens, whom Waugh often ridicules but whom he also calls "the most daemonic of the masters" in *The Ordeal of Gilbert Pinfold* (1957). The headmaster's daughter in *Decline and Fall* is reminiscent of Fanny Squeers in Dickens' *Nicholas Nickleby*, and the fantasies of Philbrick are told with a Dickensian relish. Another Victorian influence is William Makepeace Thackeray. Like Waugh, Thackeray was of middle-class origins and made his reputation writing about the lives of the very well-to-do—city merchants and a decaying nobility. Thackeray's view of the social scene was cynically detached; he highlighted the artificiality of his texts and was a gifted parodist. From him Waugh learned the art of casually introducing characters from earlier novels as background figures in later ones. This gives the reader a sense of privileged familiarity with the author's world and provides the writer with an invaluable shorthand for making moral points or achieving comic effects.

Important as these mid-Victorian influences are,

however, Waugh is better understood as a novelist of the age immediately following it. The world of the mid-Victorian novel is insular, commercial, and optimistic. From about 1870 English culture became increasingly imperialist, pessimistic, and inclined to decadence. (Waugh parodies Decadent works like Aubrey Beardsley's *Under the Hill* in *Decline and Fall*, 1928.) The novelists of this "age of imperialism"—the seventy-year period from about 1870 to 1940—were less insular than their Victorian predecessors. Foreigners were no longer "comic" Frenchmen, "heavy" Germans, and "brash" Americans, but Chinese, Indians, Arabs, and black Africans—by turns exotic, savage, possessed of the ancient wisdom or the ancient terrors of "primitive" man, or informed with cultural traditions at least as venerable as those of Europe.

Victorian confidence in the rightness of Western science and Western religion was undercut by these new cultural perspectives. Yet it fell to many of the most intelligent of the British, educated first at boarding schools and then at Oxford, Cambridge, or the military academies, to govern where they were emotionally, intellectually, and sometimes even morally least secure. The fiction of this time returns repeatedly to stories of isolated individuals stumbling against the limitations of their class-based and race-based beliefs, and then staking out for themselves a new area of order, psychological and political, against a background of incipient anarchy and personal disintegration. In Britain itself, of course, this territory of order was secured institutionally, in schools, country houses, London society, the armed services, and possibly the Church of England. But Waugh and his generation were unable to identify themselves wholly with the blander assumptions and professed self-confidence of this English world. Waugh himself was too conservative and pessimistic, too fearful of the consequences of anarchy, to wish to see it overthrown as some of his contemporaries did. On the other hand he was not afraid to observe it with the satirical detachment of a disillusioned initiate.

This certainly is the stance of the travel books and his two historical works, the biography *Edmund Campion: Jesuit and Martyr* (1935) and *Helena* (1950), the postwar novel about the emperor Constantine's mother, reputed discoverer of the cross on which Christ was crucified. Taken together, these works offer a full account of "imperialist" geography, history, and psychology, as interpreted by a writer who openly admitted his fascination with "distant lands and barbarous places, and in particular . . . the borderlands of conflicting cultures and states of development" (*Ninety-Two Days*, p. 13). For Waugh and many of his contemporaries, travel was a way of putting both their own characters and Western culture to the test. It also had overtones of sexual license and personal liberation. Waugh was a habitué of foreign brothels and was excited by perversion, slavery, primitive nudity, and the sexual implications of racial dominance.

Indeed it was precisely because travel liberated such feelings in himself that it also confirmed his commitment to law, order, and "civilization." "Civilization . . . is under constant assault," he writes in *Robbery Under Law* (1939); we are all "potential recruits for anarchy." The "positive work" required of the conservative, therefore, is to keep that anarchy at bay. In *Helena* the future emperor Constantius sees the great wall protecting the imperial frontiers in just these terms, as "a single great girdle round the civilized world; inside, peace, decency, the law, the altars of the Gods, industry, the arts, order; outside, wild beasts and savages, forest and swamp, bloody mumbo-jumbo, men like wolf-packs" (ch. 3).

Precisely because he felt the attractions of "bloody mumbo-jumbo" so strongly in himself, Waugh was able to despise the racialist attitudes of those of his countrymen who pretended they did not. "What," he wonders in his first travel book, *Labels* (1930), "gives the Anglo-Saxons, alone among the colonists of the world [their] ungenerous feeling of superiority over their neighbours?" (p. 187). Of the Arabs in Port Said he writes: "Their intensely human joviality and inquisitiveness, their animal-like capacity for waking-up and sleeping in the dust, their unembarrassed religious observances, their courtesy to strangers, their uncontrolled fecundity, the dignity of their old men, make an interesting contrast with the wrangling and resentment of northern slums" (p. 86).

While writing *Labels* Waugh had come to believe that the superficiality and triviality of contemporary attitudes were such as to vitiate almost entirely Western claims to cultural superiority over most other peoples. What particularly dismayed him was the sense of history characteristic of his generation:

It consists of a vague knowledge of . . . social, religious, and political institutions, of drama, of the biographies of the chief characters of each century, of . . . scraps of diaries and correspondence and family history. . . . This sense of the Past . . . colours our outlook on our own age. We wonder . . . how . . . this absurd little jumble of antagonising forces, of negro rhythm and psycho-analysis, of mechanical invention and decaying industry, of infinitely expanding means of communication and infinitely receding substance of the communicable, of liberty and inertia, how will this ever cool down and crystallise out?

(p. 40)

The world, in other words, is opaque and chaotic; reason and order are necessary illusions. This is a common "imperialist" view, but Waugh was not to hold it for long. Before the publication of *Labels*, he had become a Roman Catholic, an event of the first importance in his life and for his art, the implications of which require separate consideration.

The church that Waugh joined in 1930 was in many respects itself an imperialist institution. In 1870 papal authority had been reinforced by the First Vatican Council's definition of papal infallibility. Throughout the next seventy years, Catholic missionary activity expanded steadily. Everywhere Waugh traveled he encountered Catholic priests imposing their little patches of ecclesiastical law and order alongside the functionaries of secular empires. Catholicism also fitted happily into Waugh's sense of the Mediterranean as the historical center of civilization. (He refers to it in *The Ordeal of Gilbert Pinfold* as that "splendid enclosure which held all the world's history and half the happiest memories of his own life" [ch. 6].)

More parochially, English Catholicism appealed to Waugh's sense of social class. Most of his fellow Catholics in England were Irish and working class or lower middle class. But there were Catholics also among the most ancient and socially superior families in the country, families that had held onto the old faith during the dark days of Tudor persecution. In addition, a number of distinguished Englishmen had become Catholics in the nineteenth century. There was much in English Catholicism, therefore, to appeal to the worldling and the snob in Waugh

The real appeal of the church, however, was that it apparently solved the problem of historical and moral insecurity expressed in *Labels*. Here were an eternal empire and certitudes that commanded profounder assent than the provisional pragmatism of beleaguered conservatism. Nor was the faith anti-intellectual: anyone familiar with traditional Catholic thought can recognize allusions in Waugh's work

(sometimes ironic, sometimes serious) to highly recondite ideas. Besides, it was not in his nature to become a tamely conformist Catholic. Some of his clerical characters, notably in *Helena*, are as unattractive as they are typical, and the *Letters* and *Diaries* contain many tart references to churchmen and church affairs, including a less than overawed account of his private audience with the pope in 1945.

Nevertheless, Catholicism gave Waugh a sense that at bottom things were simple. Helena roundly declares her preference for facts over ideas; in *Remote People* (1931) Waugh contends that theology is "the science of simplification by which nebulous and elusive ideas become formalised and made intelligible and exact" (p. 88); at "the root of all Catholic apologetics," he writes in *Edmund Campion*, lies "the claim . . . that the Faith is absolutely satisfactory to the mind, enlisting all knowledge and all reason in its cause; that it is completely compelling to any who give it an 'indifferent and quiet audience'" (ch. 3).

Waugh realized, however, that that word "any" had dangerous implications for traditional conservatism: in the end Christianity leaves no room for human hierarchies. In the nineteenth century Cardinal Newman, in his *Apologia*, had claimed that the illiterate peasant or naked savage had ways of grasping the truth as rational as the philosopher's, and that in any case "a lazy, ragged, filthy, story-telling beggar woman . . . had a prospect of heaven, such as was absolutely closed to an accomplished statesman, or lawyer, or noble, be he ever so just, upright, generous, honourable, and conscientious, unless he had also some portion of the divine Christian graces."

Christianity thus pulls down the walls of the empire and obliterates distinctions of race and class. In *Helena*, Waugh writes:

A Thracian or a Teuton might stop a fellow countryman in the streets, embrace him and speak of home in his own language. Not so Helena and the Christians. The intimate family circle of which she was a member bore no mark of kinship. The barrow-man . . . in the gutter, . . . the lawyer or the lawyer's clerk, might each and all be one with the Empress Dowager in the Mystical Body. And the abounding heathen might in any hour become one with them.

(ch. 8)

The church is not a substitute for human empires, against which it is in any case powerless. *Helena* is full of ironic indications that all the folly, corruption, and self-importance of Roman imperial politics will reappear in later empires, the victory of Christianity notwithstanding. Similarly in *Edmund Campion* worldly success follows the self-aggrandizing "new men" of Tudor England; the Catholics, of "good" family or of none, are rendered powerless. This comprehensive dismissal of all political effort has, of course, conservative implications. If "no form of government is ordained of God as better than any other" (*Robbery Under Law*, pp. 16–17), there are no grounds in principle for radical political change. Is it possible, then, after all, that Catholicism makes no difference? Critics have been tempted to draw such a conclusion on the strength of Waugh's next two novels, *Black Mischief* (1932) and *A Handful of Dust* (1934). Only a careful reading shows them to be wrong.

Black Mischief is set in Azania, a fictitious African island peopled by Arabs and Africans. It boasts an ancient, heretical Christian church and a new ruling dynasty, founded by Amurath, the son of a slave, who was in turn succeeded by his daughter and her son, Seth. But when the novel opens, Seth's throne is in danger because education in the West has left him insecure and incompetent. He is saved by a white mercenary called Connolly, the rival claimant (who is actually Seth's father) being killed and eaten by mountain tribesmen. But Seth falls under the influence of Basil Seal, whom he knew as an undergraduate. Basil makes love to the British minister's daughter, Prudence, and negotiates cynical commercial deals with various parties. He quarrels with Connolly over the issue of boots to the army, which are eventually eaten by the soldiers; Seth backs Basil and alienates the Nestorian patriarch and the old black nobility by campaigning for the introduction of birth control into Azania. A long-forgotten son of Amurath (kept naked and in chains for decades by Nestorian monks) is wheeled out and crowned. Two English ladies campaigning against cruelty to animals have to be rescued during the ensuing disturbances, as a prelude to the flight by air of the entire British legation. But their plane crashes. Basil meanwhile tries to save Seth but finds that he has been murdered, and that he himself has inadvertently dined on the remains of Prudence. Unabashed, he returns to London. Britain and France take over Azania, Connolly is exiled (largely on account of his African wife, Black Bitch), and the sole beneficiary of all this turmoil seems to be the charming and sublimely selfish Armenian trader Mr. Youkoumian.

In language as in plot, *Black Mischief* seems at first to be a thoroughly offensive book. In a Port Said brothel Basil discusses the monetary systems of the world with a Dutch South African while four native dancing girls huddle together "in the corner like chimpanzees" (ch. 3). Later Connolly's black wife lifts "her dress and wipes her hands on her knickers" before accepting an invitation to dine at the French legation (ch. 5). We are even asked to believe that the Azanians are capable of assuming that the visiting English ladies are in *favor* of cruelty to animals: "Ladies and gentlemen, we must be Modern," declares Viscount Boaz at the banquet in their honor, "we must be refined in our Cruelty to Animals. That is the message of the New Age" (ch. 6). The joke seems to be that the primitive, animal-like Azanians are ludicrously inept in their attempts to assimilate Western culture. Seth's only comment on the Wanda's method of disposing of his father, for example, is that they are "barbarous . . . totally out of touch with modern thought. . . . They need education. . . . We might start them with Montessori methods" (ch. 1).

The novel seemed particularly offensive to Waugh's fellow Catholics. The *Tablet*, a Catholic weekly, objected to Prudence's affair with Basil; his eating her "stewed to pulp among peppers and aromatic roots" (ch. 7); a scene in which Alastair Trumpington and his wife, Sonia, entertain their friends in a bed on which their dog keeps making a mess; the birth control pageant; the ridicule of the two humane ladies; and Waugh's treatment of the Nestorian monastery, with its venerated cross "which had fallen from heaven quite unexpectedly during Good Friday luncheon some years back" (ch. 6). In his own defense Waugh maintained that he was attacking the corruptions of a heretical and schismatic church, not his own. This argument is a little disingenuous since the Nestorian church has a great deal in common with European Catholicism, including "muscular Christians" eager "to have a whack at the modernists and Jews" (ch. 6).

It is not just European Christianity but the whole of Western society that is gruesomely mirrored in the world of Azania. The Earl of Ngumo, who arrives late and drunk at Seth's victory ball demanding "some gin and some women and some raw camel's meat for my men outside" (ch. 4), is obviously a caricature, and not just of a cannibal chief but of a Tory backwoods peer as well. As such, however, he and other characters like him in the novel, notably

Boaz, the Youkoumians, and the British minister, help to resolve some of the difficulties it raises. They belong to the world of farce, not of satire. Accordingly Waugh's second line of defense is that the novel's characters are not "real people" at all (*Letters*, p. 73). He is no more attacking ecclesiastical corruption or African primitivism or the diplomatic service in this novel than he was attacking boarding schools and British prisons in *Decline and Fall*. Finally, to those who accuse him of racism, he can point to the barren absurdity of life in the French and British legations compared to the natural fecundity and vigor of the Azanians. It is Seth's European education, not his African blood, that has left him "strapped down to mean dimensions" (ch. 1).

None of these arguments, however, has more than limited force. Seth might have been more comfortable in the naked intimacy of a mud hut, but Azanian life remains unutterably cruel. (Waugh was disgusted by the brutalities he encountered on his visit to Abyssinia for the imperial coronation in 1930.) Nor are all the novel's characters as unreal as the humane ladies and Prudence's parents. Seth is real enough; so is the wildly romantic Prudence during her seedy little affair with Basil. This makes it quite impossible to compare her death with that of the prison chaplain in *Decline and Fall*, whose unreality is unquestionable. The cannibal scene is thus irreducibly serious.

We can come to terms with it, however, if we read the text as an arrangement of Waugh's thoughts for the audience that had read and relished his two earlier novels, an audience he clearly expects to be seduced by the "corker" Basil Seal, to delight in the stealing of Lady Seal's emeralds, to relish Basil's sadistically terrifying the ladies in the besieged legation, and to feel relieved and justified when he proves unexpectedly loyal to Seth. But that audience has then to face the fact that Basil eats Prudence and emerges unscathed from the experience. This is the point at which Waugh in effect challenges the reader. In *Black Mischief* Waugh hardly alludes to his new faith, but he knows that the novel will be read as the work of a notorious man-about-town, divorcé, and Catholic convert, and he therefore offers the reader in the person of Basil an embodiment of a universality that perversely reflects that of the church. Basil moves freely on both sides of the imperial frontier, and in a horrifying parody of the Eucharist he obliterates distinctions between the primitive and the civilized on which secular imperialism is based. Im-

plicitly Waugh says to his readers: "You liberals, colonialists, and decent agnostic pragmatists—you laugh at my jokes, and are excited like me by wealth, sex, barbarity, and power—but can you face the implications, for society and for yourselves, of identifying with Basil Seal and recognizing him as Everyman? If you cannot, then perhaps I have resources you lack. However, I leave it to you to find out what they are."

Waugh's next novel, *A Handful of Dust*, makes essentially the same points by exactly opposite means. It too mingles an English upper-class world with that of a primitive people, but in proportions that reverse those of *Black Mischief*. Like Basil, its hero, Tony Last, is the only character to unite the two worlds; but unlike Basil he is naive, honorable, and innocent, the creature, not the maker, of circumstance. Yet he is a universal figure, too, in his fashion. What sort of world is it, the reader asks, in which such decency can end up as wretchedly as Tony does? And the answer, of course, is, the same sort of world as that in which a man like Basil Seal can flourish, a world comprehensively in need of redemption.

When the novel opens, Tony Last's life seems perfect. He is married to Brenda; has a son, John Andrew, and an ugly neo-Gothic country house called Hetton; and loves all three. But Brenda takes a lover, a worthless young man called John Beaver. She spends an increasingly large amount of time in a flat she has rented in London, and during one of her absences her son is killed in a riding accident. A family friend, Bruce Scott-Menzies, brings her the news. Momentarily she thinks he is referring to Beaver, and when she realizes that he means John Andrew she says "Thank God" and bursts into tears. After the boy's funeral, she leaves Tony and they agree on a divorce for which Tony is to provide the evidence. After a disastrous trip to Brighton, on which he and his supposed mistress are accompanied by her little girl, Tony learns that Brenda, at Beaver's instigation, is demanding such heavy alimony that he will have to sell Hetton; so he calls off the divorce and sails to Latin America with an absurd explorer, Dr. Messinger, in search of a mythical lost city. He has a futile shipboard romance with a young Catholic girl, and the expedition goes fatally wrong. The final stages of the novel alternate between Tony's fever-dreams in the jungle and Brenda's deprivations in London after Beaver deserts her. Brenda at least ends up married to Bruce Scott-Menzies, now an M.P., whereas Tony is imprisoned by a madman, Mr. Todd, who forces him to read Dickens aloud for the remainder of his days.

The novel takes its title from Eliot's poem *The Waste Land*, certain features of which reappear in it. Thus *The Waste Land* represents the decay of ancient fertility myths into such degenerate forms as telling fortunes with Tarot cards; the fortune-teller in *A Handful of Dust* reads the soles of her clients' feet. *The Waste Land* looks behind the medieval Arthurian story-cycle to the Celtic rituals from which it derives. *A Handful of Dust* gives us a degraded modern version of the same material: Tony is King Arthur, Brenda Guinevere, and Beaver her lover, Lancelot. (The rooms in Hetton are named after the characters in Tennyson's heavily Victorian version of the same story.) And just as Eliot's poem contrasts the "Unreal City" of London with the great cities of legend—Jerusalem, Athens, Alexandria, Vienna: all "fallen," all finally unreal—so Waugh's novel ends with Tony, like a knight searching for the Holy Grail, vainly seeking his mythical city and finding nothing but his own special hell on earth.

This sustained body of literary allusion gives *A Handful of Dust* a greater range of ironic implication than Waugh was ever again to attempt. It is in parts exceptionally funny. The vicar of Tony's church had originally written his sermons while serving in India, and he mindlessly repeats them each Sunday at Hetton to hilarious effect; but his wordy fatuities about the unity of the servants of a far-flung empire have a cruel bearing on the appalling isolation that is Tony's ultimate fate. At least as funny are the absurdities of Tony's supposedly adulterous weekend with Milly and her horrid daughter. The final section is brilliantly edited. The text cuts between Tony's sufferings in the jungle and the loneliness of Brenda in London (or alternatively between Bruce Scott-Menzies asking fatuous questions in the Commons about Japanese pork pies and the explorers' Indian guides gorging themselves on pig meat after a hunt). Finally, in a phantasmagoric fever-dream Tony blends the worlds of London, the jungle, and his dream city (a fantastically elaborated Hetton) only to wake in the hands of Mr. Todd, and to the knowledge he has gained "in the forest where time is different. There is no City" (ch. 6).

Two points remain. Clearly this story of marital betrayal bears closely on Waugh's personal experience. Putting it on public record, however indirectly, was a new instance of his willingness to outface his public. It is remarkable for its generosity

toward Brenda. The moment when she discovers that Beaver is alive and John Andrew is dead is handled with great delicacy. Once she has made her terrible remark, she weeps helplessly, pressing her forehead against the gilt back of a hard little empire chair. Her behavior is clearly compulsive. Later she is for a time impoverished and demoralized, but her real punishment has been to see her situation for what it is from the beginning. Nor is this handled with any vindictiveness. Waugh gives Brenda the dignity of self-knowledge. "I was never one for making myself expensive," she says in chapter 3 when Beaver lets her see herself home. Wit of this kind is a sign of grace in Waugh, though not quite the grace that sanctifies. In all his later writing (with one exception in *Brideshead Revisited*) he remained uncensoriously compassionate in his attitude to faithless women. For a humiliated cuckold, the stance was a fundamentally honorable one.

Far more problematical is the treatment of Tony. The Mr. Todd sequence was originally published in the United States as a short story before work on the novel began. Consequently an American serialization of *A Handful of Dust* has a different ending, in which Tony returns to London, is reunited with Brenda, and cynically takes over her flat in London in order to prosecute his own infidelities. The novelist Henry Yorke felt the English version too "fantastic. . . . The first part is . . . a real picture of people one has met and may at any moment meet again." With his own recent travels in South America in mind (he actually met the original Mr. Todd in 1933), Waugh replied that for him savages were just such people: "the Amazon stuff had to be there" (*Letters*, p. 88). The American version is certainly more urbane, but its effect is cynically to restore, not subvert, civilization. Waugh's scheme, however, was to show "Gothic man in the hands of savages—first Mrs Beaver [John's mother] etc. then the real ones." Even when Tony's happy cousins inherit Hetton, the vixens on their silver-fox farm keep having their brushes bitten off; barbarism can never really be kept at bay. What Tony learns but fails to understand is that, in the words of the Epistle to the Hebrews: "we have not here a permanent city but we seek that which is to come" (13:14, Douai). Waugh's strength as a novelist is that, precisely as a sophisticated inhabitant of the city of man, he was prepared to face all the consequences of its being, in the end, an illusion.

While writing these two novels and for several years thereafter, Waugh lived a restless, self-indulgent life. He made three journeys to Ethiopia and others to Latin America, Morocco, and Europe. His friends included the Roman Catholic Lygon sisters, the fashionable and attractive Diana Guinness (later the wife of the Fascist leader Sir Oswald Mosely), and Lady Diana Cooper, wife of a Conservative Member of Parliament. The *Letters* and *Diaries* record (and jokingly exaggerate) a life of calculated promiscuity and serious repentance. In 1931 he fell in love with "Baby" Jungman, but she was a Catholic and he was divorced; this incident is reflected in Tony Last's shipboard romance. Later Waugh discovered that his first marriage was invalid in church law, and when this was confirmed in 1936 he married another Catholic, Laura Herbert. While house-hunting in the West Country and immediately after their marriage, he was at work on his fifth novel, *Scoop* (1938).

Compared with its predecessors, *Scoop* is a minor work. Combining the formulas of *Decline and Fall* and *Black Mischief*, it tells the story of William Boot, the naive young writer of nature notes for the *Daily Beast*, who is sent to report a war in the African state of Ishmaelia in place of John Courtney Boot, a successful writer. When William Boot returns after pulling off an enormous scoop, it is John Courtney Boot who is knighted and William's uncle, Theodore, who is feasted and rewarded by the press baron Lord Copper. Like Paul Pennyfeather, William is back where he started. Based on Waugh's undistinguished record as a war correspondent in Abyssinia, the novel joyfully seizes on the absurdity of "cablese" (the grotesque abbreviations and neologisms that journalists resorted to when cabling their stories), the ignorance of newspaper proprietors, and the irresponsibility of newspapermen.

The book is largely farcical; no one suffers. William Boot's sexual initiation, for example, is neither touching like Paul's nor sad like Prudence's. The vitality of the book derives from its extravagance of incident, character, and language. The denouement is effected by an absurdly athletic millionaire and parachutist of mixed racial origins who has modestly assumed the name of the former British prime minister, Mr. Baldwin. He is an impishly successful reworking of the Father Rothschild figure in *Vile Bodies*. The most famous incident in the book is the performance of Mrs. Julia Stitch (based on Lady Diana Cooper) in driving her car safely into the gentlemen's lavatory in Sloane Street.

Some excellent comedy concerns Boot Magna Hall, from which William writes his nature notes,

"Lush Places." All his relations are ill-mannered, unmarried, and self-absorbed. Their house is decaying in a riot of fertility. This bears out the view of the *Daily Beast*'s foreign editor, who regards the country as a jungle "where you never [know] from one minute to the next that you might not be tossed by a bull or pitch-forked by a yokel or rolled over and broken up by a pack of hounds" (1.2). Magna thus matches the other wildernesses in the novel, Fleet Street and Ishmaelia. But the blending of tropical and English disorder in *Scoop* carries none of the solemn implications of such fusions in earlier novels.

Nevertheless, even in this most cheerful book a somber note is sounded. As usual there are a number of insolently offensive references to blacks in the novel: "The black-backed, pink-palmed, fin-like hands beneath the violet cuffs flapped and slapped" (1.4). Ishmaelia is governed by an unprincipled black family called Jackson, all inappropriately named after eminent British liberals (Garnett, Huxley, Gollancz, Earl Russell). But the Communists imprison the Jacksons and threaten Mr. Baldwin's and Western interests. They are led by a "short and brisk and self-possessed" man, "soot-black in face, with piercing boot-button eyes" (2.2) called Benito, the only seriously competent man in the whole novel. He controls the journalists like a headmistress subduing schoolgirls ("What's that blackamoor got to be superior about?" mutters one). In Mr. Baldwin's operatic counterrevolution, however, Benito is unceremoniously killed.

Married, settled, and starting a family, Waugh had hardly worked his way into his new role of opinionated country gentleman when war broke out in 1939. He at once abandoned the novel he was writing and talked his way into the Royal Marines. He was later transferred to the Commandos and participated in a futile assault on Dakar by the Free French forces and later in the retreat from Crete. Sailing home from Cairo via the Cape he found time to write one more novel about "Metroland," the world that up to now had been his imaginative base. The dedication of *Put Out More Flags* describes the novel's protagonists as "no longer contemporary" and "disturbed in their habits by the rough intrusion of current history." Many old characters make virtually valedictory appearances: Alastair and Sonia, Peter Pastmaster and his mother, Lady Seal and her booby friend Sir Joseph. New characters appear, notably Poppet Green, Communist and sculptress, much preoccupied with the departure to America of the poets Parsnip and Pimpernell (W. H. Auden and

Christopher Isherwood), and a homosexual dilettante, Ambrose Silk.

The central character, once again, is Basil Seal, the chief preoccupation of his mother, Lady Seal, his sister, Barbara Sothill, and his mistress, Angela Lyne. Barbara, we are told, married Freddie, who is "gifted with that sly, sharp instinct for self-preservation that passes for wisdom among the rich" (1.1), because she loved his exquisite house; in her eyes Hitler is just a mean-minded ascetic whose heart is bent on its destruction. She and Basil are of a kind: when they kiss "Narcissus [greets] Narcissus from the watery depths" of their equally clear blue eyes (2.2). Indeed, a knowing evacuee child thinks Barbara fancies Basil. This child is one of a singularly repellent family, the Connollys, refugees from the city whom Barbara has the duty of billeting on her neighbors. Taking this job over from her, Basil imposes the Connollys on the most respectable local families until bribed to remove them. Faced with the prospect of having them in her home, one pretty young wife stares at Basil "like a rabbit before the headlights of a car" (1.9). This he finds delicious, and he makes love to her instead. His relations with Angela, the "golden daughter of fortune" (1.3), are equally without moral bearings. Angela's passion for Basil is her curse: only death will part them; and with the war, that possibility does arise. But it is Cedric, her husband, who dies. Angela is in many ways a splendid person. Driven literally to drink by her infatuation and teetering on the edge of social humiliation, she stages an impressive social recovery at Peter Pastmaster's wedding. But her neglect of her aesthetically sensitive husband and her lively, lonely son is chilling. So is the joylessness of her union with Basil.

Then there is Ambrose, the great love of whose life, a half-Jewish Brownshirt, is now in a concentration camp. In his honor Ambrose writes a limp novella, which Basil persuades him to edit so that it reads like a hymn of praise to Nazi youth. Basil then reports the matter to Colonel Plum, for whom he works in the Ministry of Information. To escape internment Ambrose flees to Ireland (where he goes melancholy-mad); his publisher is comfortably ensconced in prison for the duration; and Basil, who was denied the promotion he was scheming to obtain, joins Peter and Alastair in the newly formed Commandos. "There's only one serious occupation for a chap now," he says, "that's killing Germans. I have an idea I shall rather enjoy it" (epilogue).

And that of course is the problem. Some critics have found *Put Out More Flags* too optimistic. But the booby Sir Joseph, Lady Seal's confidant, sees "a new spirit on every side" in the closing scene. He is right in one respect: the premiership has passed to Churchill and the "phoney war" is over. But we have just left Alastair and Peter boyishly plotting to go to war, and Basil relishing the thought of killing people. In the book as a whole the two recurring themes are immaturity and savagery: the Ministry of Information is an officially sanctioned Azania in the middle of London; the Connellys are a domestic species of savage. The novel ends with the central characters still absorbed in their money, their prospects, and their fantasies. Cedric is dead, and the one character who knows what the war is really about—Ambrose—because his beloved is among "the prisoners rolled away to slavery" in Europe (2.1), is prevented by his "singularity" from doing anything at all. Barbaric emotions, Waugh wrote in 1939, invade the territory of civilized man by assuming "the livery of the defence"; they "pass through the lines . . . [and] there is always a Fifth Column . . . ready to receive them. . . . That is how the civilized man is undone." In *Put Out More Flags*, the moral defenses of London at war are betrayed in just such a fashion. The novel does not contradict but anticipates the pessimism of Waugh's later work.

The words just quoted are from *Work Suspended* (1942, 1.4), the novel Waugh abandoned when war broke out. Its chief character, John Plant, is a writer of detective fiction who, following his father's death, fails to finish a novel. In the story as we have it, Plant's defenses are threatened in three ways. Having spent his professional life preserving his privacy by writing in the most impersonal genre he knows and avoiding all confidences (he even lies about himself in the Moroccan brothel he patronizes), he is betrayed into emotion when he verbalizes his grief for his father. Later he falls in love with the pregnant wife of a friend, her complete emotional openness further weakening his defenses. At the same time he has to cope with Atwater, whose atrocious driving killed the elder Plant and whose lonely, innocent, egotistic vulgarity—he is a brilliant comic characterization—completely overwhelms Plant's gentlemanly aloofness. Emotional, artistic, and class barriers are thus all under pressure.

A startling departure, not only for Plant but also for Waugh, whose technique hitherto had been flawlessly impersonal, is that *Work Suspended* is a first-person narrative. This in itself is almost a betrayal of the insolent refusal to explain that makes Waugh's such a powerful but suppressed presence in the prewar novels. Now Plant and, insofar as he is Waugh's surrogate, Waugh himself are lured into the treacherous area of explanation, justification, and self-betrayal. In all the novels after *Put Out More Flags* there is a central character whose point of view invites comparisons with that of the author, where the earlier novels prohibited them; and in most of the later fiction, too, that central character is like an imperial city under siege to the forces, divine and human, by which civilized man is undone.

By 1944 Waugh was ready at last to produce another major work. The previous year had been a bad one. He had aroused fiercely negative feelings in his subordinates and superiors and had been forced to resign from the Commandos. The authorities were probably well pleased when he sought special leave from regimental duties to write what was to become his most celebrated novel, *Brideshead Revisited.*

Like *Work Suspended*, *Brideshead Revisited* is a first-person narrative, written purportedly by an architectural painter, Charles Ryder. At the beginning of book 2, Ryder describes artistic inspiration as an unexpected flooding of consciousness by "the memorials and pledges of the vital hours of a lifetime," and he likens such moments to those "epochs of history" in which an unknown race for a brief generation or two stupefies the world by bringing "to birth and nurture a teeming brood of genius" (2.1). The novel itself represents just such an explosion in Waugh's career. It teems with an abundance of new characters, incidents, settings, and even meals. Above all it teems with words, elaborately developed metaphors and descriptions. Most surprisingly of all, it teems with speeches, not just of paragraph length, but flowing on, page after page. Some speeches are comic—as in the case of Charles Ryder's cunning, selfish, mad old father; some sinister—as in the case of the homosexual Anthony Blanche; and some hysterical—as in the case of Julia Flyte, when she is brutally reminded of her position in the eyes of the Catholic church as the faithless wife of a divorced man. The economy of the earlier novels has been abandoned, and Waugh puts on a virtuoso display as a stylist, which he counterpoints with a series of comically unglamorous characters: Hooper, an ungainly wartime officer in Charles Ryder's company; Charles's prosy cousin Jasper; Mr. Samgrass, a syco-

phantic don; Rex Mottram, a political upstart from Canada who marries Julia Flyte; and Celia, Charles's ambitious, well-born, adulterous wife. It is as if Atwater's absurd insensitivity in *Work Suspended* had released an entire tribe of equally repugnant, comic, and vulnerable characters in Waugh's imagination.

But language assumes the livery of the defense and undoes the civilized man. Its abundance in this novel is inextricably involved in a series of interrelated failures and betrayals. The central betrayal, both symbolic and actual, is that of Brideshead itself, ancestral home of the Flytes, which is violated and degraded when requisitioned by the army during the war. Other fine houses are actually pulled down in the course of the narrative, something Charles Ryder sees as "just another jungle closing in" (2.1). But Brideshead is not only the Flytes' home; it would have become Charles's if he had married Julia: barbed wire in the dry, litter-filled fountain therefore symbolizes the betrayal and failure of a grand passion. And it is not just the house and the lovers that have been betrayed, but the family by its own members. The eldest son, Brideshead, a logic-chopping religious fanatic, marries a spiteful, respectable widow who is past childbearing; his younger brother, Sebastian, the beautiful, pagan friend of Charles's youth—"forerunner" of his passion for Julia—ends up a hanger-on in a Moroccan religious house, a lonely, alcoholic homosexual. Of the two Flyte daughters, one gives up her religion to marry Rex Mottram and then returns to it rather than marry the love of her life; the other, the effervescent, affectionate Cordelia, successfully prevents herself from falling in love by devoting herself to good works. And finally art is betrayed—and not just Charles's. Brideshead itself is full of aesthetic resonances—of Troilus and Cressida, of classical comedy, of Pre-Raphaelite painting. All are swept away at the novel's end. In Cordelia's words (she quotes from the Vulgate translation of the Book of Lamentations): "*Quomodo sedet sola civitas*"—"How doth the city sit solitary." Brideshead is Tony Last's dream city, derelict and abandoned to the barbarians.

Words, however, are above all the betrayers of those who utter them. "Thank God I think I am beginning to acquire a style," Waugh wrote in his diary (21 March 1944) as he was working on the novel. When it was published, however, there were elements of malice, curiosity, amusement, and dismay in its reception. The style Waugh had acquired seemed too ornate; the scenes of sexual passion between Charles and Julia were thought ill-judged; the deathbed repentance of Lord Marchmain was parodied; and the novel was believed to reveal aspects of Waugh's own youthful involvements and his moral seduction by the English upper class. Waugh was sensitive to such criticisms and constantly revised the novel in their light, but the charges against it remain to be answered. They are in essence that it is simultaneously too worldly and too religious.

Central to both aspects of the problem is the figure of Lady Marchmain. Nancy Mitford asked Waugh if he was on Lady Marchmain's side. He replied that he was not, but that God was. Nevertheless, the deathbed repentance of her husband looks very much like a posthumous victory for her and all she stands for—the remorseless manipulation of others by means of beauty, charm, and wealth, which presents itself as sincere religious faith and practice but in fact is egocentric, snobbish, and consumed with a hatred of sexuality and life. The portrait of Lady Marchmain can thus be read as an unwitting revelation of what Waugh's Catholicism really was, and it was indeed meant to be read as a kind of literary temptation for the unbelieving reader, an excuse for rejecting God. "I sometimes think," says Cordelia, "when people wanted to hate God, they hated Mummy . . . she was saintly but she wasn't a saint" (1.8). In any case, Lady Marchmain's world is overthrown in the closing stages of the novel. The reopening of the family chapel for the troops is represented as the goal toward which two ambitious aesthetic projects —Brideshead itself, and the working out of the "fierce little human tragedy" that constitutes the novel—have been moving. Yet it is a grossly democratic and aesthetically vulgar goal, from which Lady Marchmain herself would have shrunk.

Replacing the great and terrible chant of Holy Week, "Quomodo sedet sola civitas," are the brazen cries of army bugles, "Pick-em-up, pick-em-up, hot potatoes" (epilogue)—all so that Catholic Hoopers can have their mass while Britain is at war. For as Waugh told Nancy Mitford, Brideshead Revisited is "about God" (Letters, p. 196). In a notorious passage Charles reads Mr. Samgrass' edition of Lady Marchmain's brother's writings—all of her brothers had died in World War I—and reflects bitterly on how such men had to be sacrificed like "garlanded victims . . . to make a world for Hooper . . . so that things might be safe for the travelling salesman, with his

polygonal pince-nez, his fat wet hand-shake, his grinning dentures" (1.5). Mr. Samgrass sees Lady Marchmain's brothers in pagan terms. Charles, however, goes on to wonder if the rest of the family might not also be marked out for destruction "by other ways than war." And of course they are, but only so that the purposes of a Christian God might be fulfilled, purposes that include the saving of their souls, Charles's conversion, and the relighting of "a beaten-copper lamp of deplorable design" (epilogue) before the tabernacle at Brideshead in time of war. Unlike Lady Marchmain, the God of Brideshead Revisited has little use for charm, nor is he put off by grinning dentures as Charles is.

But if God thus overrides human notions of beauty and propriety, a novel "about" him must necessarily declare its own unsatisfactoriness. It is in these terms that the deathbed repentance has to be seen. Critics have traditionally argued that a simple change of mind is an unsatisfactory way of ending a story. Lord Marchmain's repentance, Julia's contrition, and Charles's conversion constitute a kind of ill-designed sanctuary lamp in the very text of the novel. Perhaps the nonbelieving reader can "save" Brideshead Revisited from this in-built fault in design by seeing in it an ultimate irony consistent with the novel's other formal complexities. But if the offense it causes is too serious to be outweighed by mere considerations of form, then a reader holding such views is entirely justified in regarding the novel as morally and aesthetically flawed. This, of course, need not worry the Catholic reader, since, outside the city of man, artistic notions of success have no meaning anyway: that is the point the novel has all along been seeking to make.

After writing Brideshead Revisited, Waugh accompanied Randolph Churchill (the wartime prime minister's son, to whom Put Out More Flags is dedicated) on a mission to the partisan forces in Yugoslavia. Like all his other wartime activities, it was not entirely successful. With that episode his career as a soldier came to an end, and he returned to civilian life. A Labour government was in office, "Metroland" had vanished forever, and Waugh had difficulty in settling down. His family continued to grow. He and Laura had had four children by 1944 (one died) and were to have three more, but Waugh proved a remote and eccentric father, not least because he deliberately adopted the manners and attitudes of an unpredictably irascible old man. This was the time when his offensiveness to strangers, particularly Americans and journalists, both by letter and face to face, became notorious. Some of his least tolerable behavior is triumphantly recorded in his diary.

His disgust with the postwar world was given prompt expression in two short works of fiction. After the stylistic and thematic elaborations of *Brideshead Revisited*, Waugh returned to a purely comic mode in *Scott-King's Modern Europe* (1947), though in a new manner. His innocent central character is no longer the pliable youth of earlier novels but an aging classics schoolmaster, who is invited to Neutralia for celebrations commemorating an obscure sixteenth-century Neutralian poet. (Waugh himself had accepted a similar invitation to Spain.) Scott-King finds himself first the victim of a ludicrous political intrigue, then a refugee who has to disguise himself as a nun, and ends up a bewildered inmate of "No. 64 Jewish Illicit Immigrants Camp Palestine." The story is light farce, the tone one of wry fatalism, but Scott-King's final refusal to change from the teaching of classics to economic history, because "it would be very wicked indeed to do anything to fit a boy for the modern world," makes its point.

The comedy of *Scott-King's Modern Europe* is almost benign; not so that of Waugh's next work of fiction, *The Loved One* (1948). It is the story of Denis Barlow, a young English writer in Hollywood who is reduced to working in an animal cemetery. Denis meets a dedicated morticians' make-up artist called Aimée Thanatogenos (a name that means "the loved one of the people of death") when he goes to arrange the funeral of an expatriate English scriptwriter who has committed suicide. Aimée works at the famous burial park Whispering Glades (based on Forest Lawn in Hollywood) and is half in love with the chief embalmer, Mr. Joyboy. Wooed by Denis with scraps of famous English love-poetry that she takes to be his own, she eventually breaks with him when she discovers his shameful place of work. Amid great publicity in the morticians' social world, she and Mr. Joyboy become engaged, but guilt and a drunken advice-columnist drive her to suicide in Whispering Glades itself. This sacrilege threatens Mr. Joyboy's career. Denis, whose plans to set up as an interdenominational minister have shocked the English community into paying his fare home, then milks Mr. Joyboy of his savings before agreeing to dispose of Aimée's body at his own disreputable workplace. He returns to England in style, leaving behind

"something that had long irked him, his young heart." In its place he carries back "the artist's load, a great, shapeless lump of experience."

This chilling little phrase establishes a significant link between character and writer: the exchange is one that the reader is expected to imagine Waugh himself as having made. In Hollywood, which he visited in 1947, Waugh found an abundance of that modern world he had represented in Neutralia with comparative lightheartedness. It was uncivilized in a way that invited treatment such as he had given distant places in the prewar novels. But California money, California guilelessness, California insensitivity, California paganism—a world in which corpses are painted to look like whores—is too absurd and unnatural, too divorced from traditions of any kind, for the tonal shifts into compassion and seriousness that so enrich *Black Mischief* and *A Handful of Dust*. The only points at which the text touches seriousness, therefore, are when it is uncompromisingly heartless. But for all its scandalous indifference to the taboos surrounding death and mourning, *The Loved One* is an ebullient book. Denis Barlow's hardness of heart is a condition of his art. He and Waugh have a secret they cannot share with the human souls they rub along with in day-to-day living—the rare, classic periods of artistic inspiration.

It is not really surprising, therefore, that Waugh's most uninhibitedly happy fiction, *Helena*, should follow two such apparently disenchanted books as *Scott-King's Modern Europe* and *The Loved One*. This is not a generally well-regarded book, though Waugh was fond of it. It needs to be read sympathetically as a joke about serious subjects. It was followed by another travel book, *Holy Places* (1952).

In some ways, then, the late 1940's and the early 1950's were a satisfying time for Waugh, particularly as a writer. This is the period of his most buoyant and engaging letter writing. In public he entered into a spirited foray against modern art, and thoroughly outwitted the historian Hugh Trevor-Roper (now Lord Dacre) in a correspondence in the *New Statesman* in 1953–1954. In private his letters to Nancy Mitford and other friends maintained a constantly high standard. Waugh was a passionate, uncalculating letter writer, intemperate at times, a vicious gossip, but also, on occasion, vulnerable. By the mid-1950's, however, things started to go badly for him. He had all along intended to turn his wartime experiences to artistic advantage. His plan was to write a series of novels based on the experiences of a central character, but with each volume also focusing on a second major figure. From the start he felt uneasy with the scheme. The first volume did not satisfy him while he was writing it. In 1953 he published a bleak tale of the future, *Love Among the Ruins*, the story of an arsonist who works for the Euthanasia Department of the Welfare State and whose mistress has a lovely flowing beard; Waugh illustrated the story himself. It has some sprightly gibes at favorite targets, but it lacks the energy and verve of *The Loved One*. Waugh then had a breakdown. He was drinking too much and taking uncontrolled doses of a mixture of drugs that had been prescribed for him at various times. While on a cruise to recover his health he began hearing voices and imagined that he was the victim of a monstrous and wicked conspiracy. He recovered, and the second of the war novels, *Officers and Gentlemen*, came out in 1955, but for a time it seemed that he would be unable to continue the series. What he did next, however, was in many ways one of the most significant and courageous acts of his life: he turned his experience of madness into a novel, *The Ordeal of Gilbert Pinfold*.

At one level, *The Ordeal of Gilbert Pinfold* is virtually plotless. Mr. Pinfold is a Catholic novelist living in the country with his wife and large family. His memory starts failing him; he is drinking too much and dosing himself indiscriminately with drugs. After a BBC radio interview set up by a man called Angel, Mr. Pinfold goes on a cruise for his health and on board ship is beset by hallucinations. His behavior embarrasses his fellow passengers. He discovers that there is a family called Angel on board, attributes the voices he has been hearing to a plot by the Angels and the BBC to control his mind, and leaves the ship. The voices pursue him; he sends alarming letters to his wife and receives an urgent summons home, which he obeys. The voices try to persuade him to keep quiet about his experiences, but he decides to tell his wife. His local doctor attributes the experiences to the drugs Mr. Pinfold has been taking—but Mr. Pinfold rejects this simpleminded diagnosis: "he had endured a great ordeal, and unaided, had emerged the victor" (ch. 8). So he sets briskly to work to write the narrative account *The Ordeal of Gilbert Pinfold*.

Uncomplicated as this basic narrative is, however, the novel about his madness is the most intensely plotted of all Waugh's works, a breathtaking account of how inspiration and craftsmanship interact in the mind of a gifted writer. The characters whose voices surround Mr. Pinfold on board ship have the autonomous, self-generating power of the imagination. They are brilliantly inventive, accusing Mr. Pinfold of being a Jew, a homosexual, a social climber, and a snob; they threaten to horsewhip him or to hand him over to a Spanish boarding party (Spain is supposed to be threatening to seize Gibraltar by force). Alternatively they offer him a deliciously nubile young virgin for his pleasure. But these disorganized "inspirations" have to be sorted out and made consistent with one another and integrated with the day-to-day, nonhallucinatory life aboard ship. Otherwise Mr. Pinfold's madness will become apparent to him. Sometimes the solution to these "technical" problems is generated by the voices themselves. Sometimes we see the crafty consciousness of Mr. Pinfold himself working out suitable explanations of what is happening to him. His victory, therefore, is not exclusively located in the crucial decision to tell his wife about the voices. The unfolding of the hallucination, its articulation and development, are themselves achievements of a mind with its twin powers of inspiration and organization working at full stretch.

The excitement of reading the book is thus in part the excitement of suspense. Mr. Pinfold's fantasies get themselves into impossible situations. At one point, for example, he hears a Spanish corvette pull alongside the SS *Caliban*. He bursts from his cabin, fully dressed in tweed and brandishing his blackthorn, only to find the ship in perfect order and no other vessel in sight: "He had been dauntless a minute before in the face of his enemies. Now he was struck with real fear. . . . He was possessed from outside himself with atavistic panic. 'O let me not be mad, not mad, sweet heaven,' he cried" (ch. 5). We are convinced that he will be unable to explain *this* away and the spell will be broken. But no. His cry is a quotation from Shakespeare's *King Lear*; it puts him in mind of one of the voices he had heard earlier, that of a sadistic woman he had named Goneril after Lear's vicious eldest daughter. All he has to do is to "hear" Goneril laughing at him and an explanation of the entire "Spanish" incident is at hand: it was all a trick to break his spirit.

Equally brilliant is the resolution of the defloration episode. Here we see Mr. Pinfold in a state of intense and ludicrous sexual expectation. A delightful

and obedient virgin is being disrobed for his pleasure, but she fails to come to him. Again he leaves his
cabin; the corridor is empty, but he can hear the
voices still, mingled with a sleeping passenger's
snores. It is crucial, of course, that the device of the
hoax should not be repeated. So Mr. Pinfold gets
cross. He refuses to chase the girl around the ship and
returns to his bunk to wait for her in his pyjamas.
Then he hears her weeping; she has heard the other
passenger's snores and mistaken them for Mr. Pinfold's, who, she thinks, has rejected her. "It was
Glover snoring," says Mr. Pinfold, and though
nobody hears him, he is safely restored to his nightmare (ch. 6).

An important element in the novel's comedy is
that of parody. When he "discovers" that Angel is on
board, Mr. Pinfold feels "as though he had come to
the end of an ingenious, old-fashioned detective
novel which he had read rather inattentively" (ch. 7),
but the genre most enthusiastically imitated is that of
the boy's adventure story, in which vigorous, board-
ing-school-educated young Britishers battle heroically against the scheming, caddish, and usually foreign enemies of the empire. Mr. Pinfold's consciousness thus locates itself in two worlds: the deluded,
ridiculous, and morally reductive world of imperialist fantasy, and that other world—Mediterranean, classical, and Catholic—in which his true self
lives and moves and has its being. His superficial
madness and underlying resources are thus a statement about historical as well as psychological situations and possibilities. In addition, of course, there is
the openly autobiographical element in the book.
Waugh faces the unbelieving, liberal reader and
acknowledges the extent to which his representations of a mad world, in Azania or California, are
simultaneously representations of the chaos in his
own mind. His defense of himself, however, as a
man, an artist, and a Catholic, is precisely that his
capacity to admit the presence in his own soul of the
madness and vice he observes also in the world is the
measure of the strength he derives from his art and
his faith.

For this reason the first chapter of the novel is
among the most important of his writings. It is
remarkable for its combination of frankness,
astuteness, and vivid phrasing:

He looked at the world *sub specie aeternitatis* and he found
it flat as a map; except when, rather often, personal an-
noyance intruded. Then he would come tumbling from his

exalted point of observation. Shocked by a bad bottle of
wine, an impertinent stranger, or a fault in syntax, his mind
like a cinema camera trucked furiously forward to confront
the offending object close up with a glaring lens.
(ch. 1)

Even those who only saw Waugh interviewed on
television can vouch for the unnerving accuracy of
this description. What surprised those who did not
know him better was the sensitively understated portrait of Mrs. Pinfold. This tribute to Laura Waugh is
perhaps the most effective demonstration in the
book of Mr. Pinfold's—and of Waugh's—underlying soundness of mind and heart.

However, for the very reason that it treats of both
the author's everyday irascibility and actual
madness with an audacious cold-heartedness as uncompromising as the treatment of California attitudes to death in *The Loved One*, *The Ordeal of
Gilbert Pinfold* is ultimately protective of its author:
the man who originally experienced these disorders
is different from the man who assimilates them and
puts them on display. Thus the novel considerably
enriches the public persona Waugh had created for
himself, but it also limits and controls those elements
of explanation and justification by which an author's
personal privacy is ultimately betrayed.

There was a real possibility that after *The Ordeal
of Gilbert Pinfold* Waugh's career as a novelist had
come to an end. Disliking the first volume of the wartime series, he found in writing the second that
material he had planned to use in two books was
needed to complete one. Then the project went dead,
and he turned to nonfiction instead, producing in
1959 the official biography of his friend Msgr.
Ronald Knox, wit, preacher, detective novelist,
linguist, and translator of the Bible. This was followed by his last travel book, *A Tourist in Africa*
(1960). Eventually, however, the third and last novel
of the wartime series, *Unconditional Surrender*, was
published in 1961. Waugh then set about revising his
earlier novels, particularly *Brideshead Revisited*,
and in 1964 started work on turning the war trilogy
into a single continuous work which was published
in 1965 under the title of *Sword of Honour*. This final
version of the wartime novels is the most authoritative, but the original versions of the three novels
continue to circulate widely. In the following discussion, therefore, references are to the trilogy in its
original and not its final version, unless otherwise
indicated.

The great difference between the *Sword of Hon-*

our novels and *The Ordeal of Gilbert Pinfold* is that the trilogy is drawn into the treacherous territory of explanation and justification. It is true that it is also less overtly autobiographical. The hero, Guy Crouchback, shares Waugh's opinions but has a different personality. However, the distinguishing characteristic of the trilogy is its insistent development of a comprehensive and Catholic view of the moral life and of history. For Waugh such explicitness was undoubtedly riskier than the ironically crafted self-portrayal of *The Ordeal of Gilbert Pinfold.*

This is not to suggest that he abandoned his technique of skillfully pointing his text with small clues about his larger intentions and meanings. Indeed some of the most important changes in the final *Sword of Honour* version of the trilogy relate to such moments. In the first volume, *Men at Arms*, for example, Guy hears some gossip about the sole survivor of an illustrious old Catholic family who was left childless when his wife abandoned him for another man. Years later, however, after her remarriage, she had an affair with her first husband, to whom in church law she was still married. A child was conceived, and, the wife's second marriage being childless also, this son by the first husband succeeded in time to the second husband's title. Moreover by marrying a Catholic he ensured the continuance of an ancient family under a new name but in the old faith. The man Guy is talking to calls this providential. Guy, however, cannot believe that Divine Providence concerns itself with the perpetuation of the English Catholic aristocracy. But of course it does, comes the reply: "And with sparrows too, we are taught" (1.10). The immediate effect of this conversation is to stir Guy to seek out his own former wife—the only woman he may lawfully sleep with because he too is a Catholic—but his scheme is a failure. Virginia is rightly disgusted by the implications of such a seduction, and that apparently is that.

In the second volume, *Officers and Gentlemen*, Virginia has an affair with a vulgar sexual braggart named Trimmer, a former ladies' hairdresser, and in the third, *Unconditional Surrender*, she becomes pregnant by him. She and Guy meet. Guy agrees to marry her and to acknowledge Trimmer's child as his own. Of her own volition Virginia becomes a Catholic and, after the baby's birth, is killed in an air raid. Guy is thus free to marry again, and in the original version he has two sons by his second marriage. Some readers have interpreted these later children as the reward of Guy's generosity, which weakens the

point Waugh wished to make. Consequently, in *Sword of Honour*, Guy has no children by his second wife, and the providential pattern outlined in *Men at Arms* is thus almost exactly reversed. The sole heir of an ancient Catholic name is the bastard son of a ladies' hairdresser—but a Catholic nonetheless.

This indicates clearly enough the lesson Guy learns in the course of the war, namely the worthlessness of all merely human conceptions of honor, and in particular the ultimate insignificance of the traditional English idea of the gentleman. The eclipse of gentlemanliness as a value and a significant fact of English social life is symbolized by the rise of Trimmer. An officer but not a gentleman, he becomes involved in an absurd foray into occupied France, set up in the first place as a publicity stunt by Ian Kilbannock, a Scottish peer and former sporting journalist. By thus cynically establishing Trimmer as a popular hero, Kilbannock connives at the extinction of his own class, and in this his behavior is representative. Paralleling the rise of Trimmer is the self-inflicted disgrace of Ivor Clair, the handsome, decadent embodiment of the ideal of the gifted gentleman-amateur. In all three novels the wealthy and privileged reveal themselves to be completely without a sense of history or a sense of values. Even the glamorous Julia Stitch is prepared to ruin Guy's career to protect Ivor's reputation and is too self-preoccupied to forward the identity disc of a dead soldier to the proper authorities as Guy requests her to.

What dismays Guy above all as the war proceeds is the complete indifference of all around him to its purposes and conduct. No one recognizes how the opportunistic alliances of the Western Powers deprive them of their moral standing as belligerents. This issue comes into focus in *Unconditional Surrender* with the appearance of a ruthlessly ambitious young American officer known as "Loot" and a group of upper-class Communists, including Sir Ralph Brompton and Frank de Souza, a gifted Jewish fellow officer of Guy's. Both are involved in furthering the cause of the Communist partisans in Yugoslavia, where against much opposition Guy works hard to relieve a party of Jewish refugees. Waugh evidently regards Loot and de Souza as embodiments of the powers destined to inherit the earth when the war is over.

Over and against all these self-preoccupied or conspiratorial representatives of a decaying past and a valueless present stand the Catholic characters, and it is with them that Waugh's difficulties begin. There are fewer "bad" and "sad" Catholics in the trilogy than in *Brideshead Revisited*. Nearly all the minor Catholic characters are overtly sympathetic—notably Guy's sister, Angela Box-Bender, and her lively, eager son, Tony, both of them a puzzle to Angela's non-Catholic husband, Arthur, a Conservative M.P. One of the minor motifs in the narrative is the news that trickles through about Tony after he is taken prisoner early in the war. In the end, to his father's dismay, he decides to become a monk. The Catholic background to the trilogy is thus less troubled than that in *Brideshead Revisited*, and, if less glamorous, it is socially rather more select. In a minor way, Waugh may be fairly accused of painting too selective and favorable a picture of English Catholicism in these novels.

More serious are the problems raised by the exceptional goodness of Guy's father, the conversion of Virginia, and Guy himself: Mr. Crouchback because he is didactic as well as holy, Virginia because her conversion seems gratuitous and her death too convenient, and Guy because he seems to be too often, and somewhat priggishly, in the right. All this has suggested to some readers that Waugh glamorizes Catholicism in the trilogy by making it socially superior, sanctifies social superiority by making it Catholic, and sentimentalizes both by having Guy forgive Virginia and Virginia die a Catholic.

Some of these charges are undoubtedly sound. The account of Mr. Crouchback's difficulties with the management of the hotel where he lives after the sale of his home confuses vice with vulgarity and virtue with old-world good manners. On the other hand, to anyone familiar with old men and women who spend a lot of time in prayer, his ruminative gentleness seems almost commonplace. The real difficulty is his willingness to talk uninhibitedly with Guy about "the spiritual life." Father and son are interested in much more than the rightness and coherence of Catholicism in principle; they are concerned most of all with salvation as a practical experience of the consciousness and the will. "The Mystical Body"—the church—"doesn't strike attitudes," Mr. Crouchback writes to Guy. "It accepts suffering and injustice. It is ready to forgive at the first hint of compunction" (*Unconditional Surrender*, prologue). At his father's funeral Guy realizes that his sense of God's presence in the world has been too passive, that God "commanded all men to *ask*" (2.3), and he prays to be shown what to do. Like Lord Marchmain, Guy changes his mind, but he lacks the tact of Marchmain. Instead of making a sign, he works out his salvation discursively, in his head.

To understand his position, however, it is necessary also to attend to the clues in the narrative itself as well as to explicit argument. Sometimes these clues take the form of silences—the absence of explanation. In Virginia's case, for example, there is the matter of her feelings about Trimmer's baby. After the birth, she packs him off to the country to be looked after by others. We are not told why. However, in one laconic sentence we learn that she expects to be killed by a flying bomb, as indeed she is. Later some Catholic acquaintances remark that her death may be regarded as providential, since her future was not to be counted on. Be that as it may, her indifference to the child saves its life. Is that providential too? The reader is left with the task of drawing his own conclusions.

There is a comparable challenge in the remark of Box-Bender's with which *Unconditional Surrender* concludes: "Yes . . . things have turned out very conveniently for Guy." To the extent that Guy was joyless and alone in 1939 and (childless or not) is happily married and among friends in 1951, this is true enough. But Box-Bender's remark also voices the complaint that critics of the text are most likely to make against it: that Waugh has made things too easy for Catholicism and for God. A consideration of this problem requires a careful examination of the first and last stages of Guy's story.

The account of the trilogy that has been given so far has failed to indicate the range and inventiveness of its comedy, from the wild excesses of Ben Ritchie-Hook, Guy's alarmingly ferocious, one-eyed commanding officer in *Men at Arms*, to the comic set piece in *Officers and Gentlemen* in which Guy and Tommy Blackhouse (Virginia's second husband) are entertained at dinner by a mad Scottish laird. *Unconditional Surrender*, however, is more somber than its predecessors. At its close Ben Ritchie-Hook gets himself stupidly killed in a tragic replay of his farcical invasion of enemy territory with Guy in *Men at Arms*. This is an indication of how carefully organized the entire narrative in fact is. Wild and extraneous as much of the farce in the trilogy may seem, it is generally integral to a grand design, and of no character is this more true than that of Apthorpe, the central secondary character in *Men at Arms*.

Apthorpe is a great comic creation. He is also a remarkably well-observed study of a recognizable type—innocent, pathetically self-absorbed, and boastful. In spite of his claims to extensive and arduous experiences in the African bush, it is Apthorpe who is taken ill in West Africa. With the best of intentions Guy smuggles a bottle of whiskey into the hospital, and Apthorpe dies as a result, leaving Guy the solemn duty of delivering a grotesque collection of tropical gear to Apthorpe's equally grotesque friend "Chatty" Corner. Because of the sheer absurdity of much of *Men at Arms* we do not take any of this very seriously. In *Unconditional Surrender*, however, Guy's interventions have no less disastrous results. He nearly gets a priest arrested by the partisans when he has mass said for the repose of Virginia's soul, while his efforts on behalf of the Jews have even more serious consequences when his particular friends, the Kanyis, are tried and apparently executed by a people's court for being in possession of some American illustrated magazines that he had given them as a parting gift.

The Kanyis' tragedy is all the more significant because it is Mrs. Kanyi who enables Guy to take the last and decisive step in his spiritual life—to repent of his sins. At the beginning of *Men at Arms*, he welcomes the German-Soviet pact because it enables him to see the war in moral terms and so find a purpose in life. Hence his horror when the Soviet Union enters the war on the side of the Allies: "I don't think I'm interested in victory now," he tells his father in *Unconditional Surrender* (prologue). "Then you've no business to be a soldier," Mr. Crouchback replies, by which he means that a Christian may fight only if he believes in what he is fighting for. The clear implication is that Guy's whole military career is a sin, but Guy himself lacks the spiritual insight to see this: *Men at Arms* opens with his making a singularly shallow and arid confession. At the end of *Unconditional Surrender*, however, Mrs. Kanyi remarks that even "good men thought their private honour would be satisfied by war," and Guy answers, "God forgive me. I was one of them" (3.4). If things turn out conveniently for Guy, it is here, when he is given the grace to confess his sins and beg forgiveness in the presence of a Jewish woman whom inadvertently he is going to send to her death. This is the moment when he realizes at last that history is the territory not of vindication but of trust, where, in his father's words, "Quantitative judgements don't apply" (*Unconditional Surrender*, prologue). Convenience of this kind is beyond Box-Bender's imagining.

Things did not, however, turn out conveniently for Evelyn Waugh. In the closing years of his life he was enraged by changes in the Roman Catholic Church: the great chant "*Quomodo sedet sola civitas*" was replaced by the "Pick-em-up, pick-em-

up, hot potatoes" of the Divine Office sung in English. His friends died, his children grew up, his health deteriorated. In 1963 he published his last short story, *Basil Seal Rides Again*. He was not a great short-story writer: his work is chilling without the implicit qualifications possible in an expansive text; but *Basil Seal Rides Again* has a special interest in the final glimpses it gives us of the Metroland characters. Peter Pastmaster flourishes; Ambrose Silk has been given the Order of Merit; and Margot Metroland spends her days watching television in a darkened room. It is all rather joyless. The 1960's seemed to vindicate Waugh's past forebodings and present fears. There were some compensations, however. Some of his letters to and about his children at this time are engaging and affectionate, and in 1964 he published *A Little Learning*, the first volume of a projected autobiography. But he made no progress with the second volume, and church affairs cut him to the quick. "The Vatican Council has knocked the guts out of me," he wrote; he clung "to the Faith doggedly without joy" (*Letters*, pp. 638–639). He died on Easter Sunday 1966, after hearing mass in the old rite. Like Virginia Crouchback, he was not tried beyond his limits.

He left behind a body of work of immense importance. It is grounded in endlessly inventive comic powers, in a love of craftsmanship and reason, in an astringent economy of expression, and in an appetite for the pleasures of art, friendship, and love. But his most significant gift was the sense of history that his religion gave him. His versions of the past may be fanciful and prejudiced, but his awareness of the human condition as fundamentally historical made him intimately responsive to the history of his own times. He caught up into his comic gift the myths and ideologies of the post-Victorian world and gave them a dramatic significance for an audience whose attention he had captured with his first two novels. This is why his work will last: whether one agrees with him or not, his writings are among the most vivid instances in this century of the way in which English literature receives and preserves the impressions of time.

SELECTED BIBLIOGRAPHY

I. BIBLIOGRAPHY. R. M. Davis, P. A. Doyle, H. Kosok, C. E. Linck, Jr., *Evelyn Waugh: A Checklist of Primary and Secondary Material* (Troy, N.Y., 1972); R. M. Davis,

A Catalog of the Evelyn Waugh Collection at the Humanities Research Center, University of Texas at Austin (Troy, N.Y., 1981).

II. SELECTED WORKS. M. Davie, ed., *The Diaries of Evelyn Waugh* (Boston–London, 1976); D. Gallagher, *Evelyn Waugh: A Little Order* (London, 1977), essays and reviews; M. Amory, ed., *The Letters of Evelyn Waugh* (London, 1980).

III. SEPARATE WORKS. *P.R.B., An Essay on the Pre-Raphaelite Brotherhood 1847–1854* (London, 1926); *Rossetti, His Life and Works* (London, 1928), biography; *Decline and Fall, An Illustrated Novelette* (London, 1928; rev. ed., 1962), novel.

Vile Bodies (London, 1930; rev. ed., 1965), novel; *Labels: A Mediterranean Journey* (London, 1930), travel, new ed. with intro. by K. Amis (London, 1974), published in U.S. as *A Bachelor Abroad* (New York, 1930); *Remote People* (London, 1931), travel, published in U.S. as *They Were Still Dancing* (New York, 1932); *Black Mischief* (London, 1932; rev. ed., 1962), novel; *Ninety-Two Days: The Account of a Tropical Journey Through British Guiana and Part of Brazil* (London, 1934), travel; *A Handful of Dust* (London, 1934; rev. ed. with variant ending, 1964), novel; *Edmund Campion: Jesuit and Martyr* (London, 1935), biography; *Mr. Loveday's Little Outing, and Other Sad Stories* (London, 1936), short stories; *Waugh in Abyssinia* (London, 1936), travel; *Scoop, A Novel About Journalists* (London, 1938; rev. ed., 1964); *Robbery Under Law, the Mexican Object-Lesson* (London, 1939), travel, published in U.S. as *Mexico: An Object-Lesson* (Boston, 1939).

Put Out More Flags (London, 1942; rev. ed., 1967), novel; *Work Suspended* (London, 1942), novel, rev. and repr. with *Scott-King's Modern Europe* in the collection *Work Suspended, and Other Stories Written Before the Second World War* (London, 1949); *Brideshead Revisited: The Sacred and Profane Memories of Captain Charles Ryder* (London, 1945; uniform ed., 1949; rev. ed., 1960), novel; *When the Going Was Good* (London, 1946), repr. of parts of some prewar travel books; *Scott-King's Modern Europe* (London, 1947), novel; *Wine in Peace and War* (London, 1947), essay; *The Loved One: An Anglo-American Tragedy* (London, 1948; rev. ed., 1965), novel.

Helena (London, 1950), novel; *Men at Arms* (London, 1952), novel, rev. version forms first part of *Sword of Honour*; *The Holy Places* (London, 1952), travel; *Love Among the Ruins: A Romance of the Near Future* (London, 1953), story; *Tactical Exercise* (Boston, 1954), stories, includes *Work Suspended, Love Among the Ruins*, etc.; *Officers and Gentlemen* (London, 1955), novel, rev. version forms second part of *Sword of Honour*; *The Ordeal of Gilbert Pinfold* (London, 1957), novel; *The Life of the Right Reverend Ronald Knox, Fellow of Trinity College, Oxford, and Pronotary Apostolic to His Holiness Pope Pius XII* (London, 1959), biography.

A Tourist in Africa (London, 1960), travel; *Unconditional Surrender* (London, 1961), novel, published in U.S. as *The End of the Battle* (Boston, 1962), rev. version forms third part of *Sword of Honour; Basil Seal Rides Again, or The Rake's Regress* (London, 1963), short story; *A Little Learning* (London, 1964), autobiography; *Sword of Honour* (London, 1965), novel, one-vol. version of *Men at Arms, Officers and Gentlemen,* and *Unconditional Surrender;* "Charles Ryder's Schooldays," in *Times Literary Supplement* (5 March 1982), pp. 255–258, included in *Work Suspended* (Harmondsworth, 1982), Penguin ed., literary fragment.

IV. BIOGRAPHICAL AND CRITICAL STUDIES. Arthur Waugh, *One Man's Road, Being a Picture of Life in a Passing Generation* (London, 1931); D. S. Savage, "The Innocence of Evelyn Waugh," in B. Rajan, ed., *Focus Four: The Novelist as Thinker* (London, 1947); H. Acton, *Memoirs of an Aesthete* (London, 1948); G. Mikes, "Evelyn Waugh," in *Eight Humorists* (London, 1954); S. Marcus, "Evelyn Waugh and the Art of Entertainment," in *Partisan Review*, 23 (Summer 1956); S. O'Faolain, *The Vanishing Hero: Studies in Novelists of the Twenties* (London, 1956); A. A. De Vitis, *Roman Holiday: The Catholic Novels of Evelyn Waugh* (New York, 1956); H. Breit, *The Writer Observed* (Cleveland, 1957); F. J. Stopp, *Evelyn Waugh, Portrait of an Artist* (London, 1958).

A. E. Dyson, "Evelyn Waugh and the Mysteriously Disappearing Hero," in *Critical Quarterly*, 2 (Spring 1960), repr. in *The Crazy Fabric: Essays in Irony* (London, 1965); P. Green, "Du Côte de chez Waugh," in *Review of English Literature*, 2 (1961); G. Martin, "Novelists of Three Decades: Evelyn Waugh, Graham Greene, C. P. Snow," in *The Pelican Guide to English Literature*, vol. VII: B. Fox, ed., *The Modern Age* (London, 1961); R. Wasson, "*A Handful of Dust:* Critique of Victorianism," in *Modern Fiction Studies*, 7 (1961–1962); Alec Waugh, *The Early Years of Alec Waugh* (London, 1962); B. Bergonzi, "Evelyn Waugh's Gentleman," in *Critical Quarterly*, 5 (Spring 1963); J. Jebb, interviewer, "The Art of Fiction 30. Evelyn Waugh," in *Paris Review*, 8 (Summer–Fall 1963); M. Bradbury, *Evelyn Waugh* (London, 1964); K. Allsop, "Pinfold at Home," in *Scan* (1965); S. J. Greenblatt, *The Modern Satirists: Waugh, Orwell, and Huxley* (New Haven, Conn., 1965); A. Kernan, *The Plot of Satire* (New Haven, Conn., 1965); J. M. Cameron, "A Post-Waugh Insight," in *Commonweal*, 83 (October 1966); R. Delasanta and M. L. Avanzo, "Truth and Beauty in *Brideshead Revisited*," in *Modern Fiction Studies*, 11 (1965–1966); P. Hinchcliffe, "Fathers and Children in the Novels of Evelyn Waugh," in *University of Toronto Quarterly*, 35 (1966); F. Donaldson, *Evelyn Waugh: Portrait of a Country Neighbor* (London, 1967); Alec Waugh, *My Brother Evelyn and Other Profiles* (London, 1967); P. A. Doyle, *Evelyn Waugh* (Grand Rapids, Mich., 1969).

T. Eagleton, *Exiles and Emigrés* (London, 1970); H.

Acton, *More Memoirs of an Aesthete* (London, 1970); D. Lodge, *Evelyn Waugh* (New York, 1971); W. J. Cook, *Masks, Modes, and Morals: The Art of Evelyn Waugh* (Rutherford, N.J., 1971); D. Price-Jones, ed., *Evelyn Waugh and His World* (London, 1973); J. St. John, *To the War with Waugh* (London, 1974); B. W. Wilson, "*Sword of Honour:* The Last Crusade," in *English,* 23 (Autumn 1974); G. D. Phillips, *Evelyn Waugh's Officers, Gentlemen, and Rogues: The Fact Behind His Fiction* (Chicago, 1975); D. P. Farr, "The Novelist's Coup: Style as Satiric Norm in *Scoop,*" in *Connecticut Review,* 8 (April 1975); C. Sykes, *Evelyn Waugh: A Biography* (London, 1975); Dom H. van Zeller, "The Agreeable Mr. Waugh," in the *Critic,* 13 (Fall 1976); M. Stannard, "Davie's Lamp," in *New Review,* 3 (December 1976); Y. Tosser, *Le Sens de l'absurde dans l'oeuvre d'Evelyn Waugh* (Lille, 1977); W. Myers, "Potential Recruits: Evelyn Waugh and the Reader of *Black Mischief,*" in *Renaissance and Modern Studies,* 21 (1977), repr. in *The 1930s: A Challenge to Orthodoxy,* ed. J. Lucas (Brighton, 1978); J. Meckier, "Evelyn Waugh," in *Contemporary Literature,* 18 (Winter 1977); A. Powell, *Messengers of Day* (London, 1978); S. G. Auty, "Language and Charm in *Brideshead Revisited,*" in *Dutch Quarterly Review,* 6 (August 1978); M. Stannard, "*Work Suspended,* Waugh's Climacteric," in *Essays in Criticism,* 28 (October 1978); J. Meckier, "Cycle, Symbol, and Parody in Evelyn Waugh's *Decline and Fall,*" in *Contemporary Literature,* 20 (Winter 1979).

P. Fussell, *Abroad* (New York–Oxford, 1980); R. Davis, *Evelyn Waugh, Writer* (Norman, Okla., 1980); J. Heath, *The Picturesque Prison. Evelyn Waugh and His Writing* (London, 1982); R. Johnstone, *The Will to Believe: Novelists of the Nineteen-Thirties* (Oxford, 1982); M. Stannard, "Debunking the Jungle: The Context of Evelyn Waugh's Travel Books 1930–39," in *Prose Studies,* 5 (1982), repr. in *The Art of Travel,* ed. P. Dodd (London, 1982); I. Littlewood, *The Writings of Evelyn Waugh* (Oxford, 1983).

Note: Several important articles on Waugh have been published in *Evelyn Waugh Newsletter* (Garden City, N.Y., Spring 1967–   ). Other articles will appear in M. Stannard, ed., *The Critical Heritage,* in progress.

H. G. WELLS

(1866-1946)

Kenneth Young

INTRODUCTION

WHO now reads H. G. Wells, critics sometimes inquire, expecting the answer: Very few. They are wrong. The scientific romances, so-called even though some of these fantasies dating from the 1890's have no element of even pseudoscience, attract yearly a new crop of young devotees in a period when science fiction has attained extraordinary popularity.

Less fashionable are the best of Wells's realistic novels, mostly written between 1900 and 1916; even so, examination of copies of *Kipps* (1905) or *Mr. Polly* (1910) in any public library shows that they are constantly taken out. Many are in paperback; they are stocked in half a dozen hardback series.

Undeniably, however, none of his politico-economico-sociological tracts, his utopias, his calls for world government are much read. As for his massive tomes *The Science of Life* (1929–1930) and *The Work, Wealth and Happiness of Mankind* (1931), which sold in millions, one might agree for once with the critics—who now reads them? Yet two or three generations ago, Wells was the great liberator, educator, visionary.

I do not suppose, either, that his 238,000-word *Experiment in Autobiography* (1934) is much in demand, which is a pity. Although, in the strictly autobiographical sense, it scarcely carries us beyond 1900, its first half is a revealing account of his early years, self-perceptive, brilliantly descriptive, frank "about my difficulties and blunders, about preposterous hopes and unexpected lessons, about my luck and the fun of the road." It is his life in those early years, repeatedly woven and rewoven, expanded here, muted there, which forms the substance, often little disguised, of his best novels, *Kipps, Tono-Bungay* (1909), *Mr. Polly*—and of some of his weakest. As time went on, his once acute interest in people other than himself and his power (or pa-

tience) to portray them declined sadly. He wrote far too much and too quickly for continuous excellence—no less than 114 volumes as well as endless journalism.

LIFE

HERBERT GEORGE WELLS was born a third son on Saturday, 21 September 1866, at 4:30 in the afternoon, in Atlas House, 47 High Street, Bromley ("a suburb of the damnedest") in north Kent, now part of Greater London. His parents, Sarah, then forty-three, whose ancestors came from Northern Ireland, and Joseph, thirty-eight, were poor shopkeepers. She had been brought up as a strict Protestant (which may account for Wells's apocalyptic turn of mind), had been a lady's maid, and to this sort of employment she returned, as housekeeper to the Fetherstonhaugh family at Up Park, Sussex, when her somewhat feckless husband, originally a gardener and later a professional club cricketer, drifted off.

Wells's mother, not ill-educated for her class and time, taught him the alphabet and brought him books from the public library. He was sent to a small village school, then to the Bromley Academy, one of those "frail vessels that often made more sound than sense," as the MacKenzies, his biographers, felicitously remark, or, as Wells put it, "a beastly little private school." Some parts of his holidays were spent at a riverside inn near Windsor kept by his mother's second cousin, where he learned to punt and row—"summer paradise," Wells called it. Around this time he read—significantly for his early fiction—Nathaniel Hawthorne's *The House of the Seven Gables*, Eugène Sue's *The Mysteries of Paris*, William Beckford's *Vathek*, Samuel Johnson's *Rasselas*, and Jonathan Swift's *Gulliver's Travels*.

At fourteen he left school and was apprenticed to a draper at Windsor, where he lived above the shop and had sixpence a week pocket money. He was soon discharged. The next few years he was tossed from pillar to post—a pupil teacher; back with his mother at Up Park, where he saw, albeit from below-stairs, the spacious life of the gentry, which he admired: "behind their screen of deer park and park wall and sheltered service, men could talk, think and write at their leisure." Briefly he was a chemist's assistant, studying dispensers' Latin: for six weeks a full-time pupil at Midhurst School in 1881. Once more he was apprenticed to a draper, at Southsea, "the most unhappy hopeless period of my life," working thirteen hours a day and despising the irksome, toilsome routines. He read "popular educators" from the YMCA library, and, like Mr. Polly, contemplated suicide.

When he was seventeen he abandoned his apprenticeship and became a pupil teacher at Midhurst. Here at last, in the evenings, he could read to his heart's content—Plato, Henry George's *Progress and Poverty* (1880), geology, physiology, chemistry, math. In 1884, when he was eighteen, he won a scholarship to the Normal School of Science in South Kensington, part of London University, with a maintenance grant of £1 a week. There he listened to lectures by the aging T. H. Huxley, heretical Grand Old Man of Science, at once optimistic about science and pessimistic about man, the Huxley who said in his Romanes lecture of 1900 that "the ethical progress of society depends not on imitating the cosmic process, still less in running away from it, but in combating it." Of him, Wells wrote that "he was the greatest man" he ever met. Huxley was a deep influence on his whole work.

Other lecturers were less inspiring, and Wells slacked, leaving the university with poor qualifications. But he joined the debating society (concluding one debate by saying that there was every reason to suppose that Mars had "living beings"), wrote sketches for his later science fiction, and fell in love with a cousin, Isabel, whom he married in 1891. He was small and thin, and his voice was reedy, but his ideas and enthusiasms and sheer fun attracted people throughout his life.

He became ill with tuberculosis. He worked for a London tutorial college, wrote two scientific textbooks, and began to contribute to the periodicals and newspapers then being produced in some profusion to attract the pence of the large public newly literate as a result of the Forster and subsequent educational reforms (1870).

Within months of his marriage that sexual voraci-ty evident all the rest of his long life began to inflame and torment him. He left Isabel in 1894 and eloped with Amy Catherine Robbins (Jane), whom he later married and who, through all his many sexual adventures, remained his wife until her death in 1928.

He published his first fiction in book form in 1895. As was the custom then, these novels were serialized in advance in magazines. *The Time Machine* appeared in 1895, as did *The Wonderful Visit* and a short-story collection, *The Stolen Bacillus*, earning in all £792 that year. *The Time Machine* caused him to be hailed as "a man of genius," and in 1895 the *Bookman* published his portrait with a note about him.

These early fantasies appealed, as T. S. Eliot commented, to readers in both the first-class and third-class compartments of trains. Inside five years, with half a dozen other fantasy stories—including *The Invisible Man* (1897) and *The War of the Worlds* (1898)—behind him, he was building an expensive house, designed by the fashionable Charles F. A. Voysey, at Sandgate near Folkestone, Kent. He had "got on." At Sandgate he wrote: "I want to write novels and before God I *will* write novels." He did: the best of his work dates from these years.

His social life expanded enormously in the years from 1896. Among his acquaintances were the novelists George Gissing, Dorothy Richardson (with whom he had a brief affair), Arnold Bennett, John Galsworthy, Joseph Conrad, Ford Madox Ford, Henry James, Stephen Crane, Frank Swinnerton; though "you," he wrote to Bennett, "are the best friend I ever had." He knew the Fabian Socialists, G. B. Shaw, Sidney and Beatrice Webb, Graham Wallas; and that society mainly of aristocrats, dubbed "The Souls," among them Arthur Balfour, prime minister from 1902 to 1905, for whom he conceived an ambiguous admiration, picturing him under the smallest of disguises in his novel *The New Machiavelli* (1911) and again in *Men Like Gods* (1923). Wells was a member of the Co-efficients, a dining club to which, as well as the Socialist Webbs, belonged such diverse people as Richard Haldane (from 1906, Liberal war minister), the noted Tories Leo Amery and Lord Milner, and the maverick philosopher Bertrand Russell.

Wells had become a social lion. With the Fabians, however, he did not last long; he sought to dominate them and was opposed, especially by Shaw; and he left. With a young member of the Fabians he had a love affair and an illegitimate child, as he did later with Rebecca West. Yet his family life was usually happy. He had two small sons and enticed his many guests into charades, shadow plays, and war games, of which he gave an account in *Floor Games* (1911) and *Little Wars* (1913). But it was as much for himself as for his children that he indulged his delight in such imaginative play.

He began, too, the long series of books, fiction and nonfiction, setting the world to rights—*Anticipations of the Reaction of Mechanical and Scientific Progress upon Human Life and Thought* (1901), *Mankind in the Making* (1903), *A Modern Utopia* (1905), and so on for forty years. These were stimulating to his contemporaries; today they are valuable mainly to those who would understand the period.

Scandal about his love affairs came to a head with the publication of *Ann Veronica: A Modern Love Story* (1909), which had a heroine who seduced the hero and which implied that polygamy was justifiable. Wells had already in *Anticipations* condemned monogamy and *In the Days of the Comet* (1906) optimistically forecast the end of sexual jealousy—at least so far as wives were concerned. *Ann Veronica* and its author were denounced. "A community of scuffling stoats and ferrets," "literary filth," "this poisonous book," screamed the reviewers. The libraries banned it. Publishers—and he had always hopped from one to another—looked at him askance.

Restless as ever, he took a house at Great Easton, Essex, on the estate of Daisy, countess of Warwick, erstwhile mistress of Edward VII. When war came in 1914, he, unlike his Socialist acquaintances, welcomed it, especially in an article whose title became a national, self-comforting slogan, "The War That Will End War"—though he did not persist in that opinion.

Many of his fantasies contained accurate prophecies—of fighting in the air before the first aircraft was off the ground; of space exploration sixty years before men first visited the moon. The novel *In the Days of the Comet* describes among other things a situation very like that of Europe in August 1914. Perhaps most remarkable of all was that in 1914 in *The World Set Free* he prophesied a war with atomic bombs for 1958—a war between the "Free Nations" and the "Central Powers" that would end with the destruction of most cities, after which the survivors would meet in the Swiss Alps to plan a world state. Though the disintegration of the atom had long been a subject of speculation, it was not until 1934 that the Joliot-Curies produced radioactive phosphorus from aluminum. The book was more than prophetic. "Leo Szilard—one of the scientists whose work lay behind the Hiroshima bomb—said that when the idea of chain reaction first occurred to him in 1934 he was influenced by *The World Set Free* which he had read the year before." Thus wrote Wells's biographers Norman and Jean MacKenzie.

When war broke out, Wells was forty-eight, too old to fight. In *Boon* (1915), he savagely satirized, among others, the old and ill Henry James. He spent a few months in the Enemy Propaganda department run by Northcliffe under Beaverbrook as minister for information. His lasting achievement—and his last thoroughly worthwhile novel—was *Mr. Britling Sees It Through* (1916), although to the end his novels, however given over to his hobbyhorses, seldom failed to have flashes of his genuine gift of literary creativity. In *Mr. Britling* and *God the Invisible King* (1917) he had a brief flirtation with religion; both before and after he was agnostic, if not atheist.

After the war, the League of Nations, world government, and his huge historical compilations preoccupied him. By now he was an international figure, interviewing Lenin (whose ideas he propagated for a time), Maxim Gorki, and, later on, Stalin and Franklin Roosevelt. His accounts of these meetings were lapped up and grotesquely overpaid by the world press. Vanity and strain overcame him. His love affairs grew ever more diverse and less satisfying; yet as Beatrice Webb observed, "he is the same brilliant talker and pleasant companion—except that he orates more than he used to and listens less intelligently. . . . He has become a sort of 'little God' . . . he feels himself to be a chartered libertine." Rebecca West described him in 1922 as "practically off his head; enormously vain, irascible and in a fantasy world." At least Wells recognized his symptoms; and he describes his near-psychosis in *Christina Alberta's Father* (1925) and elsewhere.

When Wells learned in 1927 that his wife, Jane, was dying of cancer he wrote to her: "My dear, I love you much more than I have loved anyone else in the world." If love means anything more than sexual intercourse, it was the lie of a sentimental philanderer, even though he supported her and their two sons generously with money. He was always generous with money, giving away large sums from his earnings.

In the 1930's and early 1940's, though he continued to write voluminously, he felt a decline in his physical powers. He resented criticism that he was "a thinker who cannot think"; he resented the coolness of reviewers of his novels. His journalism was still remunerative; but "compulsive repetition revealed his mental sterility," as the MacKenzies comment.

The film of his novel *The Shape of Things to Come* (1933), produced in 1936, was a financial success and an artistic failure. "A mess of a film," Wells observed. All that is remembered of it now is the music by Sir Arthur Bliss, whom Wells himself proposed to the producers, the Korda brothers. It was, once more, prophetic, with its scenes of an air attack on London in 1940; ironically, it was, as the MacKenzies note, "one of the factors which created public support for the policy of appeasement."

The times had passed Wells by; there were newer idols—D. H. Lawrence, Virginia Woolf, Aldous Huxley, Evelyn Waugh. To the intellectuals Wells had become tedious; to those of them who were Communists, a petit-bourgeois humbug. In the aptly named *The Anatomy of Frustration* (1936) he revealed his dismay at death, mankind's "primary frustration." Sex was but a temporary alleviation. He was in some ways an early existentialist. *The Wonderful Visit* (1895) attacks the absurdities inherent in the human condition, as Bernard Bergonzi points out. Existentialist, too, was his perception, in *Babes in the Darkling Wood* (1940), that there was not one John Smith but many John Smiths within the single organism. The individual's belief that he is an independent personality is an illusion—the only reality lies in the collective existence of the species. More and more he despaired of the future of that species, writing in *The Fate of Homo Sapiens* (1939) that he had always been pessimistic but had tried "to live as though it were not so." The mood continued almost to the end of his life; *Mind at the End of Its Tether* (1945) prophesied that "the end of everything we call life is at hand and cannot be evaded." The dropping of the atom bomb in August 1945 seemed to affirm it.

When the Second World War began, Wells told Sir Ernest Barker that he had already composed his epitaph; it was: "God damn you all: I told you so." But quite another epitaph must be composed for the author of, among others, *The Time Machine*, *Tono-Bungay*, and *Mr. Britling Sees It Through*.

Wells, within a month of eighty, died at his London home in 1946.[1]

---

[1]For biographical information required in the writing of this essay, I am chiefly indebted to Wells's *Experiment in Autobiography* (London, 1934) and N. MacKenzie and J. MacKenzie's *The Time Traveller* (London, 1973).

FANTASY FICTION

WELLS began to write fantasy fiction because he wanted to make money and to "get on"; and, to use one of his favorite words, "woosh," he did. But why this particular genre? It was partly because in those final years of the nineteenth century there was an unusually large appetite among readers for the spine-chiller, the bizarre, the weird, and the apocalyptic. Even the great Henry James wrote "The Turn of the Screw" (1898) and William Morris, *News from Nowhere* (1890); others who helped satisfy the appetite were such half-forgotten storytellers as William Le Queux, M. P. Shiel, Edward Bellamy, Arthur Machen, and Algernon Blackwood.

The reasons why readers were avid for this kind of fiction at that time are exhaustively detailed by Bergonzi, but one he omits is that the public that had heard with astonishment of the invention of Edison's "talking machine," the first practical electric light bulb, Daimler's and Benz's internal combustion engined motorcars, Marconi's wireless transmissions, was ready to believe anything possible. They had been stampeded into credulity; to them, that a man could, for example, make himself invisible seemed no more nor less impossible than wireless communication.

Wells knew some of the early tales of the miraculous—they had been popular from classical times; he had read Mary Shelley's *Frankenstein* and *The Last Man*, and Edgar Allan Poe and Eugène Sue. From all these and others he garnered ideas like a magpie, as Ingwald Raknem has shown in *H. G. Wells and His Critics* (1962).

There was another reason why Wells wrote in this genre: he had an innate gift for it. In his preface to *The Country of the Blind, and Other Stories* (1911), he tells us how these stories originated:

I found that, taking almost anything as a starting point and letting my thoughts play about it, there would presently come out of the darkness, in a manner quite inexplicable, some absurd or vivid little nucleus. Little men in canoes upon sunlit oceans would come floating out of nothingness, incubating the eggs of prehistoric monsters unawares; violent conflicts would break out amidst the flower beds of suburban gardens. I would discover I was peering into remote and mysterious worlds ruled by an order, logical indeed, but other than our common sanity.

(p. iv)

This is like Samuel Taylor Coleridge dreaming "Kubla Khan"; or the scientist Friedrich Kekule waking from a nap in front of the fire with a clear picture of the solution to the problem that had so long teased him, how atoms are linked. In short, inspiration.

How different this was from the method of the writer to whom he was sometimes compared—Jules Verne—both men saw clearly. "There is no literary resemblance whatever," wrote Wells, "between the anticipatory inventions of the great Frenchman and these fantasies. He always dealt with the actual possibilities of invention and discovery." Verne agreed, saying of Wells: "His stories do not repose on very scientific bases. I make use of physics. He invents!" Nevertheless Wells was well aware of the latest thought in science. Also some of his fantasies *are* concerned with science in a broader sense; they express a deep pessimism about science's means and ends.

Wells's own conscious aim, however, was to write a mind-boggling, rattling good yarn. Even so, perhaps partly unknown to himself, these tales may be interpreted psychologically, symbolically, moralistically, even poetically: it was the great poet T. S. Eliot who observed that Wells's imagination was of a very high order and found the description of sunrise on the moon in *The First Men in the Moon* (1901) "quite unforgettable." It is doubtless the multiplicity of meanings to be found in the best of these tales that ensures their continuing readability.

Consider *The Time Machine*, the first and among the best of these fantasies. The book opens with a cozy dinner party in Richmond of men friends where, in the postprandial atmosphere when "thought runs gracefully free of the trammels of precision," the host explains, in a manner even now convincing to the nonmathematician, the principles of fourth-dimensional geometry. Amid their skepticism he shows them a machine which, he says, enables him to travel in time. And travel in time he does, forward to the year 802,701 A.D. and to a location resembling the Thames Valley.

There he finds decaying palaces and a little pixie-like people called the Eloi, living on fruit (cattle have disappeared), doing no work, somewhat epicene, easily fatigued, a sort of flower people, "beautifully futile," happy as the day is long—but at night fearful, huddling together. What they fear is the subterranean-dwelling, apelike race called the Morlocks, whom Wells describes in words that his novelist friend Gissing might almost have used for London slum dwellers—"those pale, chinless faces and great, lidless, pinkish-grey eyes." To his horror, the Time Traveller discovers that the Morlocks are still meat-

eaters—human meat—emerging from deep shafts on moonless nights to seize their provender, the Eloi. Yet out of "an old habit of service" they still provide the Eloi with their garments "and maintained them in their habitual needs."

Wells himself—or the Time Traveller—points out the obvious symbolism: the workers, driven underground and become bestial, are taking their revenge on their former masters, who themselves over millennia had become degenerate, incapable of defending themselves, living only for the day and fearful of the night. Indeed he writes of the haves and the have-nots, observing that instead of the "great triumph of Humanity I had dreamed of," the "splitting of our species along lines of social stratification" had become complete and the "exchange between class and class" that had kept society on a more or less even keel had long ago ended. To this had post-Darwinian optimism about evolution come.

The novel is no mere Marxist parable in reverse. The Time Traveller *regrets* that he has no occasion to use his crowbar on the Morlocks. It cannot be justly said that this is Wells hating the class from which he sprang, though all these elements play a part. It is much more a cry of despair:

. . . how brief the dream of the human intellect had been. It had committed suicide. . . . Once, life and property must have reached almost absolute safety. The rich man had been assured of his wealth and comfort, the toiler assured of his life and work. No doubt in that perfect world there had been no unemployed problem, no social question left unsolved. . . . There is no intelligence where there is no change and no need of change.

(ch. 10)

The Time Traveller, after an exciting search in the best Rider Haggard style for his stolen machine, moves yet further into the future, where man has totally disappeared and the earth is left to huge white butterflies and malign crabs as big as tables: "Abominable desolation . . . the stony beach crawling with these foul, slow-stirring monsters, the uniform poisonous-looking green of the lichenous plants, the thin air that hurts one's lungs." And so, thirty million years on, to a great darkness, cold, snow, silence, the only moving object "a round thing, the size of a football perhaps, or, it may be, bigger, and tentacles trailed down from it; it seemed black against the weltering blood-red water, and it was hopping fitfully about."

When the Time Traveller has returned and told his

story to his skeptical friends, he vanishes again, this time for good, perhaps into the past of "the blood-drinking, hairy savages"; and the author himself comments in an epilogue that the Time Traveller "thought but cheerlessly of the Advancement of Mankind, and saw in the growing pile of civilization only a foolish heaping that must inevitably fall back upon and destroy its makers in the end. If that is so, it remains for us to live as though it were not so." This was Wells's own stoicism.

Yet, he adds, referring to the "two strange white flowers" the female Eloi, Weena, had put into the Time Traveller's pocket, "even when mind and strength had gone, gratitude and a mutual tenderness still lived on in the heart of man." Inconsequential? But much of *The Time Machine* is as inconsequential as a dream and that is in part due to hasty, awkward writing. Yet, eighty years on, it grips the reader no less than the centuries-older *Revelation* of St. John the Divine, with which in some aspects it may be compared.

The Wonderful Visit, published in the same year, 1895, is *The Time Machine* run backward, as it were, though it has no element of even pseudoscience in it. The vicar of a Sussex village, "Siddermorton," shoots down what he takes to be a giant bird but which turns out to be an angel or, in Wells's intention, the "natural man," the Great Simpleton. The novel is really an ironical study of life in the English countryside. "I tried to suggest to people the bitterness, the narrow horizon, of their ordinary lives by bringing into sharp contrast with typical characters a being who is free from ordinary human limitations." Thus we see Lady Hammerglow patronizing the angel, the squire warning him off for trespassing, the villagers militant against a stranger they cannot identify, and the village doctor interested only in the angel's "deformed" shoulder blades and proposing manipulative surgery to make him more human. Only Delia, the vicar's simple maid, loves the angel and with him she ascends to heaven. The satire—on ownership, on the ugliness of people's lives—is gentle, though there is a dark passage on the "readiness of you Human Beings to inflict pain" to which the vicar replies: "The whole living world is a battlefield. We are driven by Pain." From the point of view of Wells's literary development, the novel is a first sketch for some of the purely human characters he was to draw with much greater effect in *Kipps* and *Mr. Polly*.

The Island of Doctor Moreau (1896) is the most horrifying of Wells's fantasies and one of the best written and most tautly constructed. It marks the introduction into his fiction of the mad or immoral scientist. The doctor of the title is seeking to make animals half human by means of vivisectional surgery, the transplantation of organs and grafts; the pain involved is vividly described. He explains his methods by snatches of physiology that sound no less convincing than the Time Traveller's new geometry. Moreau has succeeded in making some of his ghastly man-animals talk and even read; but they tend to revert to the beast, so Moreau continues his quest to "burn out all the animal . . . to make a rational creature of my own."

As well as talking, the travesty men, the "Beast People," build huts for themselves and have certain fixed ideas implanted by Moreau known as the Law, which they chant as litany: "Who breaks the law goes back to the House of Pain":

> *His* is the House of Pain.
> *His* is the hand that makes.
> *His* is the hand that wounds.
> *His* is the hand that heals.
> *His* is . . . the lightning-flash. . . .
> *His* is the deep salt sea. . . .
> *His* are the stars in the sky.
>   (ch. 12)

It was this litany with its blasphemous echoes, as much as the repulsive horrors, that caused many reviewers to castigate the novel: "to parody the work of the Creator of the human race and cast contempt upon the dealings of God with his creatures," wrote one critic. Wells, however, is more concerned with Huxley's point that suffering is "the badge of all the tribe of sentient things, attaining its highest level in man." Through this purgatory man must pass on his evolutionary way; nature itself is both cruel and blind, and the scientist himself is affected. In Moreau's words: "The study of Nature makes a man at last as remorseless as Nature."

Much of Moreau's work must inevitably remind present-day readers of the Nazi doctors' vile experiments, the even viler surgical alteration of personality in the Russian psychiatric wards, and perhaps of the more dubious of contemporary organ transplants.

After the exciting climax of the book when Moreau is killed, the grafts are gradually rejected, the Beast People's speech and carriage revert, they hold things more clumsily, "drinking by suction, feeding by gnawing," and, the females leading, begin to disregard decency, even attempting public outrages on the institution of monogamy. Finally, as Wells states in the introduction, when some years later H.M.S. *Scorpion* visits the island, there is nothing alive there except some "curious white moths, some hogs and rabbits and some rather peculiar rats."

But *The Island of Doctor Moreau* is not merely a savage attack on science and unethical experiments: "His curiosity, his mad aimless investigations . . . and the things were thrown out to live a year or so, to struggle, to blunder, and suffer; at last to die painfully." It is a broader attack—as in the fourth book of Jonathan Swift's *Gulliver's Travels*—on the nature of humanity itself.

While the narrator is still on the island he has observed "the Fox-Bear Woman's vulpine, shifty face, strangely human in its speculative cunning, and even imagined I had met it before in some city by-way." And back in England:

I could not persuade myself that the men and women I met were not also another, still passably human, Beast People. . . . Prowling women would mew after me, furtive craving men glance jealously at me, weary pale workers go coughing by me, with tired eyes and eager paces like wounded deer dripping blood, old people, bent and dull, pass murmuring to themselves and all unheeding a ragged tail of gibing children. . . . [In] some library the intent faces over the books seemed but patient creatures waiting for prey.

(ch. 22)

In the end—somewhat contradictorily and after help from a mental specialist—the narrator finds solace in

wise books, bright windows, in this life of ours lit by the shining souls of men. . . . A sense of infinite peace and protection in the glittering hosts of heaven . . . in the vast and eternal laws of matter . . . [there] whatever is more than animal within us must find its solace and its hope.

(ch. 22)

The "shining souls" were conspicuous by their absence in the novel itself where there were only varying degrees of blackness.

Wells was extraordinarily versatile. In the same year as the black fantasy *The Island of Doctor Moreau*, he published the light, cheerful, literally meandering novel *The Wheels of Chance: A Holiday Adventure* (1896). This concerns a gauche young Cockney draper's assistant—a type we shall see

more of in Wells's fiction of the next decade—who sets out for a cycling[2] holiday in Surrey and Sussex and comes to the rescue of a maiden in distress—he who has always "regarded the feminine sex as something to bow to or smirk at from a safe distance."

That is no more than the gist of what plot there is. The charm lies elsewhere, especially in the character of the young draper himself, whose very name, Arthur Hoopdriver, in his dark moments seems to him as absurd as its owner. Still, he sets off blithely with four gold sovereigns in his pocket for ten whole days of freedom from the drudgery and servility of "step this way please" or "no trouble, madam, I assure you." And "his heart sang within him," within this small man "of a pallid complexion, hair of a kind of dirty fairness, greyish eyes and a skimpy, immature moustache under his peaked, indeterminate nose."

His gawkiness, of which he is all too conscious, shows as soon as he mounts his bicycle, for he—like his creator—was just learning to ride; and comical, embarrassing, small misadventures pursue him throughout the book. He "wabbles" (Wells's expressive word for a neophyte cyclist's erratic path) through a countryside most lovingly depicted: "grasses flowering, white campions and ragged robins . . . little cottages, and picturesque beer-houses with the vivid brewers' boards of blue and scarlet . . . a pebbly rivulet that emerged between clumps of sedge, loosestrife and forget-me-nots under an arch of trees": this was the premotor, prebungalow southern countryside that Wells loved.

In his new, brown cycling outfit Hoopdriver sometimes feels himself to be "a bloomin' Dook." He has always been addicted to daydreaming, and, the narrator observes somewhat sententiously: "Self-deception is the anaesthetic of life while God is carving out our beings." More down-to-earth, he adds: "His real life was absolutely uninteresting and if he had faced it as realistically as such people do in Mr. Gissing's novels, he would probably have come by way of drink to suicide in the course of a year." As indeed Mr. Polly and Wells himself almost did, though not via alcohol.

On his joyous "wabbling" jaunt, Hoopdriver keeps coming across two other cyclists, a young girl

[2]The bicycle, then being manufactured at prices only the poorest could not afford, gave the lower classes the freedom of travel; it also freed the middle-class young of chaperonage, for men and women set forth together. So the bicycle symbolized the "new freedom."

and a man in his thirties, who seem to be at loggerheads. In fact the man, Bechamel, is her would-be seducer, a typically mid-Victorian villain down even to the moustache he twirls—and married withal. The girl, Jessie, described variously as sixteen or seventeen, is a would-be emancipated maiden who has left home partly because she can no longer put up with her widowed stepmother, a literary lady of Surbiton, but also because, in the feminist spirit of the 1890's, "I want to lead a Free Life and Own myself . . . I want to do something in the world, something vaguely noble, self-sacrificing, and dignified"—perhaps, ironical as it may seem to journalists, become a journalist. As elsewhere in Wells, Jessie has curiously existential sensations: "I find myself in life and it terrifies me. I seem to be a little speck whirling on a wheel, suddenly caught up. 'What am I here for' I ask. . . . The wheels of the world go on turning, turning. It is horrible." (There is a curious parallel here with some remarks by Ursula in D. H. Lawrence's *The Rainbow*.)

Don Juan Hoopdriver, in tremulous adoration and presenting himself as a well-to-do colonial, snatches her from her would-be seducer with the usual absurdities that cling to his every action, and they cycle off together. Hoopdriver has a fight in a pub, which bucks him up enormously because his opponent (who has made a "remark" about the couple) runs away. Soon the two cyclists are being pursued inefficiently and yet more ridiculously by her stepmother, always on the edge of the vapors, and her small coterie of literary gentlemen, more concerned with winning her exclusive favors than with finding her errant stepdaughter.

The innocent pair of cyclists after a comic chase are eventually confronted. Hoopdriver is accused of abducting a girl under age but—here Wells derides suburban manners—above all everything must be kept quiet. If Jessie's escapade were to become known, ". . . you would be *ruined*," says her stepmother: "No one in Surbiton would ask you anywhere! . . . You would be an outcast."

"But I've done nothing wrong," said Jessie, "It's just a Convention—"

"But everyone will *think* you have."

"Am I to tell lies because other people *think*? stupids. And besides—who wants to know people like that?"

(ch. 39)

While this goes on, "Hoopdriver made a sad figure in the sunlight outside." Once more Jessie has become "an inaccessible Young Lady."

So they part. He dare not declare his love except to kiss her fingers. She will send him books; he will work. "What can a man make of himself in six years time?" she says. Naturally, as he leaves her, he puts his foot in a rabbit hole and almost falls. He knows it is over and done with: "Suppose a chap *was* to drive himself jest as hard as he could—what then?" As for books—"What's books?" And he returns to his apprentice quarters over the draper's shop, "the gate closes upon him with a slam, and he vanishes from our ken."

The Wheels of Chance is light, good-natured fun-poking at some diverse sections of English society—not excluding its hero—in the 1890's, a trial run for the greater *Kipps* and *Mr. Polly*. One criticism, and it applies to some later novels as well: the narrator is the old-style "buttonholer," permitting himself too many flourishes and a jocosity that can grate.

The next year, 1897, Wells returned to the fantastic genre with *The Invisible Man*. It is a less satisfactory story than *The Time Machine* partly because, for present-day readers, it has been overexposed in films and television serials often only crudely based on it; partly, however, because it lacks the poetry, the multiplication of meanings, of its predecessor. Though it was no less appreciated by its early readers, there is now an air of staleness about it; even the pseudoscientific explanation of how Griffin made himself invisible seems unconvincingly nebulous.

The first part is, like *The Wonderful Visit*, more a village comedy than anything else. Wells lovingly establishes his locals and acutely imitates their vernacular—so acutely that their talk may well baffle even an Englishman from another part of the country than Kent and Sussex. Outstanding among these characters is the tramp, Mr. Thomas Marvell.

To the villagers, Griffin—bandaged all over his head, wearing dark blue glasses and what turns out to be a false nose—is at the start merely a baffling curiosity who has, like the central figure of *In the Days of the Comet*, inexplicable outbursts of petulant rage. He is even rather comic; the tramp inquires whether he had been eating bread and cheese; he can see it in the invisible man's stomach because food does not become invisible until it is assimilated.

Gradually Griffin's frustrations, particularly his need for money, lead him to crime and violence, though much of the violence is part of the senseless rage that devours him. On the run, he enters the house of a Dr. Kemp, quietly working for his FRS

H. G. WELLS

(Fellow of the Royal Society)—one of the several "normal" scientists Wells portrays. Griffin recognizes Kemp as having been at "University College" in his time and decides to trust him with his story. It is here that we learn of his ignominious, even ludicrous, adventures when he first became invisible in London; London's weather is hard on a nude invisible man, he cannot easily buy clothing and has to turn criminal to steal some. Snow will stick to his invisible body and give him away. But worse still, he is a disenchanted Faustus:

> "I went over the heads of the things a man reckons desirable. No doubt invisibility made it possible to get them, but it made it impossible to enjoy them when they are got. Ambition—what is the good of pride of place when you cannot appear there? What is the good of the love of woman when her name must needs be Delilah? . . . I had become a wrapped-up mystery, a swathed and bandaged caricature of a man!"
>
> (ch. 23)

He has sought a formula to reverse his invisibility at will but has not found it.

Now Kemp, archetype of the man of honor, breaks his word that he will not give him away; he betrays him in a note surreptitiously sent to the local chief constable, Colonel Adye; but this is what an honorable man would do since Griffin is a dangerous criminal. As Kemp waits in secret agitation for the police, Griffin confirms that he is a homicidal megalomaniac. An invisible man, he can "strike as I like, dodge as I like, escape as I like!" But why kill? "Because that invisible man, Kemp, must now establish a Reign of Terror. He must take a town, like your Burdock, and terrify and dominate it. He must issue his orders. . . . And all who disobey his orders he must kill and kill all who would defend them."

The police arrive. With a shout of "traitor," Griffin disrobes, so becoming invisible, and then begin a siege and a chase such as John Buchan might have written. The area is roused; and in the end the coup de grace for the invisible man comes from the village folk by means of the spade of a stalwart navvy.

Griffin is a less effective portrait of the amoral scientist than is Dr. Moreau. As a character he exists uneasily between farce and melodrama. He is never quite credible.[3] His return, when dying, to visibility

is imaginatively done. But to compare this tale, as does one critic, to the tragic farce of Christopher Marlowe's *The Jew of Malta* is an exaggeration.

There is at least one link between *The Invisible Man* and the otherwise very different *The War of the Worlds*, which appeared in the next year, 1898. In the former, Griffin terrorizes a county; in the latter, the Martians, arriving from their planet in ten cylinders at twenty-four-hour intervals, not only terrorize but devastate the whole country and particularly its heart, London.

The scientific background is plausible. That Mars was populated was then a scientific hypothesis. Astronomers supported the theory that the planet was drawing farther away from the sun and was therefore getting colder. Wells merely added the corollary that the Martians would naturally cast around for some warmer climate and turn envious eyes on Earth. Scientists also thought that Mars was an older spin-off from the sun than was Earth. It was therefore reasonable to deduce that its inhabitants were more developed, cleverer than men. So Wells's Martians are mainly brain floating in a brown liquid with nerves to a pair of protuberant eyes, an auditory organ, and sixteen long, sensitive tentacles arranged about the mouth. Instead of eating they suck fresh living blood from other creatures; thus, they need no apparatus of digestion, and so, unlike Mr. Polly, can suffer no dyspepsia.

Even "intellectual readers" and scientists, wrote Wells's friend Sir Richard Gregory, FRS, found the book "stimulating to thought" and were never repelled by any obvious disregard of scientific principle.

The Martian invaders fight ensconced in vast spiderlike engines a hundred feet high, mounted on a tripod and moving as fast as an express train. Their weapons include a poisonous black smoke with which they smother cities; their heat rays pulverize artillery and battleships. The ray, wrote a contemporary reviewer, was "a sort of searchlight which burned." Today we have something very like it in a laser beam.

Through such devices, the Martians quickly establish that reign of terror of which the invisible man only dreamed. Naturally it is the Martians who are the focal interest in the novel. Of human characterization there is little; the narrator and his brother are clever nonentities; and the vacuous curate is no more than a conventional anticlerical butt.

Humankind exists in the novel mainly as a mob, at first disbelieving, then panicked:

---

[3]Wells, despite revisions of this novel, twice uses "creditable" when he clearly means "credible." Bennett was constantly chiding him about such solecisms.

H. G. WELLS

So you understand the roaring wave of fear that swept through the world just as Monday was dawning—the stream of flight rising swiftly to a torrent, lashing in a foaming tumult round the railway stations, banked up into a horrible struggle about the shipping in the Thames, and hurrying by every available channel northward and eastward. . . . By three, people were being trampled and crushed even in Bishopsgate Street; a couple of hundred yards or more from Liverpool Street station, revolvers were fired, people stabbed. . . . By mid-day a Martian had been seen at Barnes, and a cloud of slowly sinking black vapour drove along the Thames and across the flats of Lambeth, cutting off all escape over the bridges in its sluggish advance.

(ch. 16)

These scenes of what amounts to the breakup of metropolitan life are powerful; anyone who was in France in 1940 (or who has studied the history) will be irresistibly reminded of the panic-stricken civilians driven, as the Germans advanced, ever southward, jamming the roads—targets for low-flying aircraft.

There are obvious dangers for a novel without characters. An early reviewer, Basil Williams, in the *Athenaeum* (February 1898), commented: "Mr. Wells is content with describing the cheap emotions of a few bank clerks and newspapers, and the jostling in the road might very well do for an account of a Derby crowd going to Epsom." With regard to the novel's method, an American reviewer said: "It is an Associated Press dispatch, describing a universal nightmare." This is partly true; yet the narrative gains from the bulletinlike attention to time and the detailed topographical background. And the ultimate destruction of the Martians has a tellingly scientific ring: since on Mars they had long ago eliminated microbacteria, they were unprotected against the germs to which man had become largely immune. Their death agonies are unforgettably described—the howling sound, "a sobbing alternation of two notes 'Ulla, ulla, ulla, ulla,'" coming eerily across deserted, devastated London.

The War of the Worlds greatly impressed its first readers not merely because it coincided with speculation about Mars but because of regular scares about the invasion of England by France or Germany. Among the educated, too, an end-of-the-world mood was rife. The artilleryman in *The War of the Worlds* puts it thus: "Cities, nations, civilizations, progress—it's all over. That game's up. We're beat." And so—what? Of course, he says, we must fight the Martians. There must be underground resistance. But such resistance is not for weaklings; it is for able-bodied men and women willing to obey orders. And such resistance "makes life real again." But he goes on to say that "the useless and cumbersome and mischievous have to die. . . . It's a sort of disloyalty, after all, to live and taint the race."

The novel almost immediately demonstrates the ineffectualness of the artilleryman, whose contribution was added by Wells when it passed from serial form to hardback. Yet its authoritarian tone finds an echo in Wells's speculation, for example, in *A Modern Utopia*, that the country would be best dictatorially ruled by an elite.

By the end of the century Wells's creative energies began to flag, which is scarcely surprising after the almost frenzied productivity of the preceding four years; and he was also quite seriously ill. *When the Sleeper Wakes* (1899) lacks the inventiveness and the descriptive powers of the earlier fantasies. In short, it is dull; one cannot but agree with Wells himself, who called it "one of the most ambitious and least satisfactory" of his books.

By 1901 his health had been much improved by the bracing air of Folkestone, and he published *The First Men in the Moon*. Here in the descriptions of lunar scenery his imaginative gifts were at full blast—and remarkably prophetic, as we saw in the color television pictures sent back by American astronauts in the 1960's. There is narrative excitement, too—another race against time—yet something is lacking, possibly the multiple meanings I mentioned earlier. Wells has regaled us so fully that we resent any diminution in diet. The Selenites (the native inhabitants of the moon) themselves, subject from birth to systematic biological conditioning, have the sinister ring of the so-called social engineering of today. Wells himself thought it was "probably [his] best 'scientific romance.'" Certainly it is entertaining, but not the equal of *The Time Machine*.

There were several more fantasies to come, the last in this decade being *The War in the Air* (1908). But long before this his mind was elsewhere, in nonfictional visions of the future, such as *A Modern Utopia*, and in straight fiction.

This account of Wells's fantastic genre would not be complete without a note of the many short stories he wrote in it. Some are fanciful rather than imaginative (though "The Country of the Blind" is certainly the latter), and some are merely trivial. As in his full-length stories, he blends in some comedy (for example, in "The Man Who Could Work Miracles"). "Lord of the Dynamos" is curiously Kiplingesque, and the psychological "The Door in the Wall" might have been no better written by Henry James. Many odd fancies fill the short stories: eyes that suddenly see the near-future; a man whose anatomy is reversed, his heart going over to the right, who becomes left-handed; a half-painted picture comes to life; an irregular movement of the planets causes catastrophe on earth. There are ghost stories, tales of the occult and the remote past.

What a feast, as Eliot said, for first-class and third-class railway travelers as they chose at the bookstall from the *Strand*, *Pearson's*, *Cassell's*, the *Windsor*, and many other magazines in that golden age of the short story.

REALISTIC FICTION

WHEN Wells turned to writing realistic fiction he did not lack for competitors. Many excellent novelists flourished—Thomas Hardy, James, Conrad, Rudyard Kipling, Galsworthy, Bennett, George Moore, Ford Madox Ford—though not all had yet done their best work. And the market was there. Not for almost half a century would fiction take second place to biography in readers' favors.

In one way Wells was an innovator. From *The Wheels of Chance* to *Mr. Britling Sees It Through*—indeed to the end of his life—his novels are about what happened to him personally and to people he knew. Before Wells, good novelists had taken a hint here, an observation there, a little introspection, and had invented their characters. Wells had many successors in sticking to more or less concealed autobiography, notably D. H. Lawrence and later C. P. Snow and Anthony Powell.

This style is no derogation. The house of fiction has many mansions. I shall not waste time by indicating upon what person such and such a character was based; in the biographical section above I have identified some real persons so blatantly portrayed as to have affected Wells's career. Who, in any case, now cares that the assistant usher at the Whortley Proprietary School on £40 a year in *Love and Mr. Lewisham* (1900) was Wells at Midhurst?

The novels today stand or fall on their literary merits. The present-day reader rightly asks only: Does *Mr. Lewisham* interest me? Is it a good read? I think it is. It is a story of young love, mainly in adversity, joyful sometimes, quarrelsome sometimes, ending always in doubt; the only certainty in the mind of Lewisham, whose wife is pregnant, is: "The future is the child. . . . Career! In itself it is a career—the most important career in the world. Father! Why should I want more?"

Lewisham, however, *has* wanted more; he has had a schema of progress; he has wanted to be a successful science student at the Normal College in South Kensington. But he has been distracted, though sometimes resisting, by his amorous obsession for Ethel—walking her home, even occasional nights at plush restaurants in the glamorous London, vividly depicted, of the 1890's.

The novel also concerns, as K. B. Newell has shown, the corruption—or declension—of an honest assistant usher into a liar ("I'm not so honest now") or at any rate a compromiser, to the point where Lewisham observes that "the enormous seriousness of adolescence was coming to an end." Corruption is shown in a more sophisticated way in the character of Chaffery, more sophisticated since Chaffery is not merely an exposed cheat but a cheat who *defends* cheating and lying. Chaffery is a medium, with tambourine, little green box, odor of violets, and white "ectoplasmic" glove, and he is caught out. As it happens—largely from the plot point of view—Wells makes Chaffery Lewisham's stepfather-in-law, and they relax together over small beer and grog in the connubial home.

Chaffery maintains that

honesty is essentially an anarchistic and disintegrating force in society, that communities are held together and the progress of civilization made possible only by vigorous and sometimes even violent lying; that the Social Contract is nothing more or less than a vast conspiracy of human beings to lie to and humbug themselves and one another for the general good. Lies are the mortar that bind the savage individual man into the social masonry.

(ch. 23)

As for man, he is no more than a compound of "lust and greed tempered by fear and an irrational vanity." Characteristically, Chaffery abandons Ethel's mother (life at Clapham "has irked me for some time") and goes off "to live my own life."

The novel is an unusual mixture of love's young dream and disillusion. This, along with its depiction of an age so innocently inhibited about sexual relations, at least in the lower-middle and middle-middle classes, and its vivid awareness of London from the point of view of those classes, gives it a unique flavor.

Kipps was, said Wells himself, "the complete study of life in relation to England's social condition." It is not quite that; apart from a fleeting reference to the earl of Beauprès's irritability, neither the aristocracy nor the upper-middle classes come much into its purview. Where it is strongest and most observant is with its lower-middle class and shopkeepers, and the genteel and somewhat pretentious middle class.

But to speak thus is to make *Kipps* sound dull, and it never is. It is a riveting story of a young, ill-educated, but mainly happy young man, who, having become a draper's assistant, like Hoopdriver, is sacked for being late in the shop; discovers that he has been left a £24,000 legacy and a house by his natural father; begins to learn some of the mysterious "social niceties"; becomes engaged to a superior and somewhat domineering young lady whom he ditches when he meets his childhood sweetheart, now a servant girl, and elopes with her; and then finds out that the brother of his former fiancée to whom he has entrusted his financial affairs has speculated with his money, been ruined, and fled the country.

This, however, is not the end. Some of the money is rescued and, his social aspirations now comfortably shed, Kipps and his wife, Ann, settle down contentedly with their baby son to run a bookshop, after which Kipps has always hankered. As an extra bonus, the £2,000 he had invested in his affluent days in the plays of a raffish, unsuccessful playwright suddenly bear fruit; one of the plays becomes an overnight success, and so Kipps at the end of the novel "is almost as rich as he was in the beginning." A pleasurably happy ending! No wonder that a film of the novel, made in 1941, entranced its audiences, and that the musical comedy based on the book and called *Half a Sixpence* had a long run in England and abroad.

Academic critics have referred to *Kipps* as a comedy of pretenses, a study in vanity, an exposition of the operation of chance; critics at the time of its publication saw it as a fictional materialization of the "social impeachment" of Wells's *Mankind in the Making,* an essay on "spiritual squalor," and accused the novel of portraying "an utter imperviousness to ideas of any kind." These diverse attitudes can all be attested; it is a novel with many dimensions. But surely Wells's friend Henry James

comes, without any literary jargon, nearest to its essence in a letter:

A brilliancy of *true* truth. . . . You have for the very first time treated the English "lower middle" class etc. without the picturesque, the grotesque, the fantastic and romantic interference of which, e.g. Dickens is so misleadingly full. . . . Such extraordinary life; everyone in it, without exception, and every piece and part of it is so vivid and sharp and *raw.*

One can only point to particular excellences: Chitterlow, the playwright, for instance, who is pictured at first as a rambunctious alcoholic phony and turns out in the end to be heartwarmingly honest; Chester Coote, the snobbish artistic dilettante who takes Kipps in hand for his education in the ways of "society" and who toward the end is responsible for "murdering friendships." The hopelessness of Kipps's fellow drapery apprentices—"we're in a blessed drainpipe and we've got to crawl along it until we die"—is movingly shown; yet both Kipps and Buggins are lifted out of it. There is the Apemantus-like raillery of the sick socialist, Masterman, forecasting "the beginning of the Sickness of the World." Only one positive villain is depicted: Walsingham, who makes away with the bulk of Kipps's legacy.

How fresh, too, is the writing, at least in the first two-thirds of the novel. "Wanderings in the hedgeless reedy marsh, long excursions reaching even to Hythe, where the machine-guns of the Empire are forever whirling and tapping, and to Rye and Winchelsea perched like dream cities on their little hills."[4] Fine, too, the childhood love of Kipps for Ann; and, toward the end of the book, when Kipps's heart cries out for her, for "the lights that lurked in Ann Pornick's eyes," and when he revolts against the middle-class habit of "calling" when a printed card is left, and against such forgotten oddities as the anagram tea.[5]

The final part of the novel is less well done. This was due to the fact that Wells had planned and partly written the book seven years before (when he called it *The Wealth of Mr. Waddy*) and his viewpoint had changed; he wanted to make more of Masterman, have him indeed turn Kipps into a socialist, for by this time Wells was seeking how to use his characters

[4]The marsh is Romney Marsh; Hythe was until recently the main small-arms training school for the army.
[5]A tea party at which each guest wore an anagrammatized name tag and was given a card on which to solve as many names in the company as possible.

to voice his own beliefs. Most critics have noticed this; only one that I know of, K. B. Newell, has sought, by using themes as key signatures, to suggest that the novel *is* a unified whole. I do not think it is. All the same, *Kipps* comes up, fresh and sparkling, one of the three best novels that Wells wrote.

In the Days of the Comet, which came out a year after *Kipps*, has been variously regarded as the tail-end of his fantasies, a fictionalized version of some of his ideas in *A Modern Utopia*, and a satire on politicians. It is possibly trying to be all of these, which would account for its schematic incoherence and justifies Henry James's comment that he did not find it "an artistic fact, quite, as it is my habit to yearn to find suchlike."

The nub and the strength of it lies elsewhere: in the passion and violent jealousy, leading almost to murder, of the central character, Leadford, who sees his childhood sweetheart, Nettie, carried off by Verrall, a young, handsome sprig of the aristocracy. These passages, though occasionally perilously close to Victorian novelettish (remember the moustache-twirling seducer in *The Wheels of Chance*), have a sustained force that compels us to regard the book as novel rather than fantasy. Leadford is as furious, flailing a being as the invisible man or the devil incarnate of Elizabethan imaginings.

After the emanations of the comet—described with all Wells's gifts for evoking the weird—pacify the passions and stupidities of men, there is a great destruction of the sordid, inconvenient houses such as Leadford (and Wells) had been brought up in, and of unsanitary dress and ill-fitting boots. Men and women become "exalted," beautiful Arcadian figures.

What, then, of love and jealousy? At first Leadford proclaims to Nettie that he has "a new mistress . . . the coming City of the World." But after the death of his mother he needs human comfort and finds it in the arms of Anna, the girl who has looked after her. And Nettie? For her he retains a "hunger of the heart." . . . So? The four of them "from that time were very close, you understand, we were friends, helpers, personal lovers in a world of lovers." And, adds the narrator, it occurred to him that "the thoughts that stirred in my mind were sinister and base, that the queer suspicions, the coarseness and coarse jealousies of my old world were over and done with for these more finely living souls."

Small wonder that one periodical primly commented: "Socialistic men's wives, we gather, are, no less than their goods, to be held in common." It was not quite that. Leaving aside the autobiographical obtrusion, Wells was suggesting only that mutual sexual relations between "friends" were permissible, indeed welcome; he was not proposing a sexual free-for-all. Nevertheless, *In The Days of the Comet*, along with *A Modern Utopia*, is another Wells prophecy that has come true: not in respect of an appeasing comet but of the hippie commune.

Tono-Bungay is a jumble. Its narrator calls it "an agglomeration" and, in what is probably a reference to the methods of Wells's friends James, Ford, and Conrad, "comprehensive rather than austere . . . I must sprawl and flounder, comment and theorize." All the same, it is a jumble of genius, for, as Peter Quennell writes: "Despite his attitudes to art he had uncommon artistic aptitude; the gift of selecting and placing words; and unusual faculty of description and a fancy at once precise and sweeping."[6] Some have seen *Tono-Bungay* as Wells's greatest novel.

In form it is the autobiography of a man in the middle years called George Ponderevo who has seen life from butlers' pantries to the dinner tables of the titled and the great (as had Wells). Wells hoped that *Tono-Bungay* would be "a powerful instrument of moral suggestion." Perhaps, indeed, in its day it was. Now we read it as a remarkable picture of mid-Edwardian life. Here is Bladesover, the great country estate, serene yet already "overtaken by fatty degeneration and stupendous accidents of hypertrophy"; here meretricious gentry and nobility, "sold for riches"; there the poor, ill-educated masses, unkind to each other, wide open to exploitation.

Exploitation indeed, and big business followed by a financial crash is the main story line. Edward Ponderevo, the narrator's uncle, is a failed country chemist who sets up in London and begins to market a patent medicine he has invented. The medicine has little or no value and might even cause harm. The narrator has scruples about it, but eventually joins his uncle, even though he never quite accepts his uncle's argument—that all trade is good for the country, that it gives employment, and that for the consumers "we mint faith." The business booms, and Ponderevo becomes a very rich and powerful financier. Then comes the crash; he escapes to France and there dies.

Uncle Ponderevo is only a "character" in his country chemist days. In book III he changes into a rogue

6In *The Singular Preference* (London, 1952).

financier, based possibly on a contemporary fraudulent operator, Whittaker Wright. His wife, Aunt Susan, is always a character, human, kindly, a "natural." One is pleased with her and, when the crash comes, sorry for her.

There are many other strands to the novel. For instance, the narrator surprisingly invents a new naval destroyer said by him to be a symbol of "Truth." There is much about love, particularly with Beatrice, a young woman of the upper class—a figure almost in the mold of Hemingway's Brett—with whom the narrator has a passionate affair. She is a spoiled woman, "spoiled by this rich idle way of living . . . I'm a little cad—sold and done"; and, it is hinted, she is dependent on drugs. Despite the narrator's urgency, despite her physical passion for him, she will not marry him.

Change and decay are the keynotes that most critics have seen in the novel, certainly visible in the narrator's final remarks: "Light after light goes down. England and the Kingdom, Britain and the Empire, the old prides and the old devotions . . . pass, pass. . . . Crumbling and confusion, of change and seemingly aimless swelling, of a bubbling up of futile loves and sorrows." Yet something "drives" through the confusion: call it science, truth, austerity, beauty: "the heart of life. The one enduring thing."

But the *tone* of the novel supports neither the rhetorical pessimism nor the one ray of light presented by the narrator. It says something different. It bespeaks the brimming vitality of life—however, from the moralist's point of view, misdirected—in these Edwardian years. Of course they were not the golden years they have sometimes been painted, but certainly they seem from *Tono-Bungay* to have had energy and adventurousness.

The narrator says, "There's no humour in my blood," but there is plenty in the author's, and to that extent the narrator is *not* H. G. Wells. What one remembers of the novel is not despair, not the "witless waste" of men and of Earth's resources, but the excitement of the rise to fortune of Edward Ponderevo, of his "getting on," and of his decline. One remembers, too, the swirling, "irresoluble" complexity "of things and relations" conveyed. Nor can one deny Wells's prophetic gift once again: England and the empire *would* in the years to come crumble; "the old devotions" *would* pass.

What a worker he was! In the same year as *Tono-Bungay*, Wells published *Ann Veronica*, a novel much abused in its time for its "immorality," and rather slighted by recent critics. Yet its evocation of middle-class life in a London suburb has a springlike quality even though the eponymous heroine finds that life excessively restrictive, because in the most innocent way, like the girl in *The Wheels of Chance,* she wants to be free.

Her father is the Victorian paterfamilias of legend and occasionally, doubtless, of reality. She escapes him but—how to live? Her experiences in murky London lodgings are unpleasant, and she throws herself upon the mercies of kind Mr. Ramage (a suburban neighbor), who tries to seduce her in the best Edwardian style, first in a Covent Garden box watching *Tristan and Isolde* and later in the private room of a restaurant—with an "obtrusive sofa" and a locked door. Her study of jujitsu comes to her aid.

Meanwhile she has been drawn into Fabian circles, some of whose members are cattily portrayed, and into love with her married biology instructor. She takes part in a suffragette escapade, is arrested, persuades her lover that she is ready for the taking—and is taken, to the Swiss Alps. Four years later the liaison is respectable—and Father comes to dinner.

This evokes a particular section of London life, seen largely from the point of view of a young girl seeking tentatively, fearfully, to become the "new woman," to shake off the excess of modesty that inhibited females at the time, to become, in brief, a person. And succeeding.

When *The History of Mr. Polly* came out in 1910, the American wit H. L. Mencken observed that it was not so much a history of Mr. Polly as of Mr. Polly's stomach; and this is only partly a joke. The novel begins with him, another unsuccessful small shopkeeper, sitting on a fence suffering from indigestion as a result of his wife's crude cooking and the unwise diet common in the lower classes of the time.[7] Wells's friend Ford Madox Hueffer (Ford) had noted of the villagers on Romney Marsh that "as children they were starved, as men they were to a man dyspeptic through eating the fat pork and cheese that form the chief of their diet. Thus, in old age, they are crabbed and crippled with rheumatism, they have no blood in their veins."[8]

So Mr. Polly's indigestion is no mere novelistic

---

[7]As John Burnett's *Plenty and Want: A Social History of Diet in England from 1815* (London, 1966) makes clear, the appalling adulteration of foodstuffs had by this time ceased as a result of stringent laws during the last quarter of the nineteenth century. But lower-middle-class cooking continued to be poor because of lack of skill and inadequate kitchen equipment.

[8]*The Cinque Ports* (Edinburgh, 1900).

device. It is reflected in his equally flatulent mental condition produced by the educational fodder at school, which had bored him yet left him no less voracious for reading, especially tales of high adventure and heroism, than his physical dyspepsia made him voracious for food. And he has, too, "an insatiable hunger for bright and delightful experiences, for the gracious aspects of things, for beauty."

The novel ends as it begins, with Mr. Polly's stomach: it ends with him happy and fit on "honest" roast beef and omelettes and wheaten bread, living in the open air, contentedly helping run a remote, riverside pub. (In this respect *Mr. Polly* belongs to that ever-lengthening literary tradition of "back to the simple life, wind on the heath.")

Mr. Polly, undeniably, *is* an escape story. It has a happy ending. Yet much in between is far from happy. Mr. Polly, like many of Wells's characters, drifts into becoming a draper's apprentice, drifts into marriage (backed by a small legacy), drifts into being a near-insolvent shopkeeper. At last he decides to act rather than drift: he will commit suicide. He gets his razor ready and in so doing knocks over an oil lamp that sets his shop on fire and ignites those of his neighbors. The fit of action once upon him, Mr. Polly turns into a hero and, forgetting his death wish, saves a deaf, comic old lady from an upper room. The fire scene is descriptively the high point of the novel—and a turning point, too, since it results in Mr. Polly's freedom. The shop is heavily insured. He gives his wife the bulk of the payment and tramps off into the countryside he has always loved. The narrator comments: "If the world does not please you, *you can change it*"—perhaps for the worse, perhaps for the better, "and at the worst for something more interesting." After all, Wells himself had proved it.

The bliss of being a handyman at the Potwell Inn is not at first unalloyed. The plump, comfortable landlady has a violent psychopathic nephew who appears from time to time to demand money with menaces; she pays. Mr. Polly, nervously, blunders once more into success; through his courage the villainous nephew ("Uncle Jim") is driven off, never to return.

Mr. Polly is related to Hoopdriver and Kipps and other, more minor, characters in the Wells opus; yet he is different in one interesting way: he is, like James Joyce, fascinated by mixed-up words. Kipps and Hoopdriver, of course, had their difficulties with the English language: Mr. Polly goes much further. Not being equipped by his education to assimilate words or to pronounce them properly, "he avoided every recognized phrase in the language, and mispro-

nounced everything in order that he shouldn't be suspected of ignorance but of whim"—an odd ambition. The results are sometimes amusingly surrealist, throwing out hints and half-suggestions, multi-forked: "Elegant Rhapsodooce," "Raboloose" (Rabelais); sometimes they are baffling even to the native English speaker—"skeptaceous," and "I'm going to absquatulate." No less recondite are Wells's phonetic renderings of the Kentish accent of his time: "Elfrid" for "Alfred," "Pass the mustid," "Swelpme." But it is notable that when important action is afoot, these dialogue condiments vanish.

The New Machiavelli is in part yet another revamping of early autobiographical material with long, discursive passages on politics and socialism. It is also reminiscent of *Ann Veronica*, except that we are given more of the pathos of the narrator Remington's relations with his wife, Margaret, once he has fallen in love with Isabel; and except that it is a political, not a teaching, career that Remington must renounce when he elopes with Isabel. The regrets of the two lovers over what they have done to Remington's wife are somewhat lachrymosely long drawn out; but genuine emotion is not lacking. And there are some very acute observations of such public figures as Balfour and the Webbs, concealed by little more than a change of name. This kind of ruminative novel could scarcely be written today; but its many felicities make it readable still.

Boon is a curious incident rather than a novel. It is a ragbag of pieces written over a decade by Wells and allegedly the work of "the popular novelist George Boon," who secretly craves the respect of littérateurs in addition to his achieved monetary success. *Boon*, wrote Lovat Dickson, is "the confession of faith of a tired, troubled and depressed mind, maintaining dispiritedly, against his own questioning, the certainties to which he has clung for so long"; Wells himself referred to it as the most revealing book he ever wrote. From the literary point of view what remains to interest the general reader today are the parodies, some of them bitter, of such writers as Edmund Gosse, George Moore, Hugh Walpole, Ford Madox Ford, G. B. Shaw, W. B. Yeats, and, most hurtful of all, Henry James, then ill, who died the year after *Boon* appeared.

The parodies *are* funny—as funny as the comedy in *The Wheels of Chance, Kipps,* and *Mr. Polly*. For instance, James and Moore returning from a stroll are both in full verbal spate, but neither heeds what the other says: Moore is describing in loving detail, Sterne-fashion, a little sexual adventure in the south of France; James, booming away in an endlessly qualified sentence. But Wells also sneers at James the writer, who regards "the whole seething brew of life as a vat from which you skim, with slow, dignified gestures, works of art. Works of art whose only claim is their art." And he describes James's style, not without some grain of truth, as being like "a hippopotamus trying to pick up a pea."

There is only one more Wells novel—there were many so-called novels still to come—that can be thoroughly recommended as fiction rather than an allegorical tract-for-the-times: *Mr. Britling Sees It Through.* It caught the mood of the well-to-do middle classes in the first months of the war and went into thirteen editions before Christmas of the year of publication. It also describes very closely Wells's own life at Easton Glebe: how Britling kept open house and how among his semipermanent guests were a young German tutor, Heinrich, and a young American sent to sign up Britling for an American publisher.

Heinrich is killed in the German army; Britling's eldest son is reported killed, and his grief and that of the boy's fiancée are told with every gift that Wells ever had as a novelist. Britling's son in fact returns from the war; and the last pages refer to Britling's sending Heinrich's violin to his parents. No less good and fresh are the evocations of the English countryside and its people during the war; the description of trench warfare (written before Wells went to France); Britling's eighth love affair, and his finding of God: "The master, the Captain of Mankind . . . God was beside him and within him and about him"; Britling says that he has thought too much "of what I would do by myself, I have forgotten *that which was with me.*"

Mr. Britling is Wells's equivalent of Shaw's *Heartbreak House.* There is scarcely a false note; the argument about the future, of world government—England in the vanguard—fits naturally, not obtrusively; and he expresses English patriotism as few others have done, which was a considerable shock to some of his socialist friends, just as was his finding a semimystical religion, though in Wells himself this did not long persist.

This is his last true novel in the writing of which all his great gifts were fully deployed, though none of the later novels are totally lacking a touch here, a spark there, witty dialogue, sharp observation, not least in *Apropos of Dolores* (1938). The rest are largely written to a scheme—*Joan and Peter* (1918), for example, presents Wells's opinions on education.

Men Like Gods is not a return to the manner of the early fantasies; it is a picture of Wellsian utopia. It is perfectly possible to write propaganda that is also good fiction, for example, Charles Kingsley's *Alton Locke* or Mark Rutherford's *The Revolution in Tanner's Lane.* But Wells did not. André Malraux's proposition is generally valid: "It is not passion which destroys a work of art, but the desire to prove something."

WELLS AS THEORIST

WELLS was never in the philosophical sense a thinker, nor was he a discoverer. His mind, despite his scientific training, was too undisciplined. He was more a magpie-like picker-up of ideas that he absorbed, developed, popularized, and scattered to the four winds in the form of journalism, even if the journalism was often book length.

However stale and often ill-expressed some of these ideas—ideas that E. J. Mishan has dubbed those of the "Established Enlightenment"—seem to us today, they had enormous impact on readers of the time,[9] and not only in Britain. Indeed it is said that one French publishing house founded its fortunes on the sale of Wells in translation. It was, wrote George Orwell, not perhaps without irony, wonderful for a young person to read a man "who *knew* that the future was not going to be what respectable people imagined." Indeed it may be claimed that the reason Wells's nonfiction seems stale now is that the ideas expressed were simply assimilated into the modern mind, another example of the adage that nothing fails, in the long run, like success.

Nor, to his worldwide public, did it seem to matter that his ideas were often inconsistent and sometimes self-contradictory; he was for a quarter of a century or so taken seriously, from *Anticipations of the Reaction of Mechanical and Scientific Progress upon Human Life and Thought* until, approximately, *The Open Conspiracy: Blueprints for a World Revolution* in 1928.

We noted above the deep strain of pessimism in the famous fantasies of the 1890's. *Anticipations* is notably optimistic—a fact not perhaps unconnected with his financial success—and might have taken as

---

[9]Margaret Cole was only one of very many when she said that by reading Wells she had "tumbled straight into socialism overnight."

its text the sentence quoted above from *Mr. Polly:* "If the world does not please you, you can change it," or, as one critic interpreted it, "whatever is, is certain to give way to better." Wells went even further when in *A Modern Utopia* he asserted that "will is stronger than fact, it can mould and overcome fact." It was a short distance from "can" to "must." The world *must be* changed and with it human nature.

How, then, was the world to be changed? By a group of men and women, whom he sometimes called "samurai" (Japanese swordsmen) and sometimes the "new republicans," the "open conspirators," and even, later on, "the mind of the race," who would "take the world in hand" and create "a sane order." Plato's "guardians" were no doubt Wells's models. There is no reference to democratic election. Wells was that accursed being of present-day socialist demonology, an elitist.

The elite would ensure the proper education (not merely literacy or mathematical skills) of all; and such an educated community would establish rational relationships with others elsewhere. A world community[10] would develop, a sense of kinship among all men, and instead of pointless, wasteful wars, differences would be settled by negotiation and agreement. Racial, regional, and national frictions would disappear. Men would work happily together to bring each other a fair share of the world's abundant wealth. Utopia indeed.

The benevolent dictators, a sort of upper civil service on the lines of Auguste Comte's sociocrats, would ultimately operate through a world state and—sinister adumbration of the Russian dictatorship and Orwell's *1984*—would maintain a central index keeping track of every person in the world. The dictators would abjure alcohol, trade, the stage, and games, in short be a latter-day version of the Cromwellians. Indeed, in his novel *The Shape of Things to Come*, Wells refers to the dictatorship of the airmen as a "Puritan Tyranny," which by its "Act of Uniformity" would stamp out "every facile system of errors."

The books in which Wells propounded these basic thoughts are swarming with ideas; I can mention only a few. For example, the state must control procreation and eliminate the unfit. Sex should be "a straight and clean desire for a clean and straight fellow creature"—no more "uxorious inseparable-

ness." Wives were to have economic equality; husbands, however, were given sexual freedom so long as there was no "emotional offence to the wife . . . if she does not mind, nobody minds."

On less fundamental matters Wells did focus public attention on some real problems of the near future. He foresaw the age of motors, the congestion of cities, the need for throughways. Wells never believed, as G. K. Chesterton did, that the gasoline engine was the vilest invention; he pointed out that their grandfathers had hated railways, which were now everywhere accepted as a boon. So it should be with the motorcar.

He railed, too, against the conservatism that would not admit that the "ordinary domestic house" could be built with elevators and automatic sanitary appliances that would relieve servants of the worst part of their labors. To aid cleaning, rooms should be constructed without corners—a necessary innovation still far from general. Wells mapped out "human ecology"; only in the 1970's did a British government create a department of the environment. As Beatrice Webb wrote of *Anticipations,* he ranged "from the future direction of religious thought to the exact curve of the skirting round the wall of middle-class abodes."

Where doubtless he lost the sympathy of some of his socialist pacifist friends was in his justifiably hard lambasting of military men for failing to adopt "scientific appliances" with which to wage war. Perhaps he was reflecting the views of his acquaintance Balfour, who as prime minister (1902–1905) sacrificed his party's electoral future for the sake of updating Britain's defenses. As we noted in the biographical section, Wells supported Britain against Germany in 1914; it is interesting that, according to his son Anthony West, again in 1939 "Wells took the line that once the country was at war the citizen's job was to do what he was told to do without argument."[11] Wells, for all his internationalism, was at heart a patriot; he might have said, with that other rebel D. H. Lawrence, "I really think that the most living clue of life in us Englishmen is England."

Even so, though he sometimes wandered from the Fabian Socialist hard line, his basic ideas remained theirs. His methods of implementing those ideas were often *not* theirs. For example, he wanted people to have military training so as to enforce world

[10]Wells had perhaps been converted to internationalism, a comparatively new idea, by Havelock Ellis's *The Nineteenth Century: A Dialogue in Utopia* (London, 1906).

[11]See the perceptive essay in Anthony West's *Principles and Persuasions* (London, 1958).

government and to suppress what he calls in *The Open Conspiracy* "nationalist brigandage." The Fabians were cleverer than the impatient Wells. They saw that their aims could better be achieved by gradually infiltrating the media; by backstairs influence on politicians, industrialists, and students; by a quiet, evasive sapping. Wells, for instance, railed at Roman Catholics in *Crux Ansata* (1943) and elsewhere, and wanted them all removed immediately from any influential position. The Fabians simply penetrated them and their seminaries. It is interesting that on a visit to President Roosevelt in 1934 he noticed with pleasure the large number of open conspirators, that is, Fabians, surrounding the president. And this was true.[12]

As for Wells's Fabian aims, George Orwell was near the mark in writing in the 1930's: "Much of what Wells has imagined and worked for is physically there in Nazi Germany. The order, the planning, the State encouragement of science, the steel, the concrete, the aeroplanes." Orwell had correctly seen that the achievement of Wells's ideas would be far from the frivolity of "Utopiae full of nude women" and visions of "super garden cities." In essence, Wells stood close to both the Nazis and the Communists. There was the same millenarian rhetoric, contempt for the bourgeois, and a streak of destructiveness. In real life, despite his laudatory Stalin interview, Wells regarded the leaders of both dictatorships as "primitives," not men like gods.

His attitude to Marxism and Marx was changeable. In *New Worlds for Old* (1908) he pays tribute to Marx. Later on he refers to him as "a Jew who was kept by the tradesman Engels." A more reasoned critique of Marxism came in *The Open Conspiracy*: "In practice Marxism is found to work out in a ready resort to malignantly destructive activities and to be so uncreative as to be practically impotent in the face of material difficulties." Yet, curiously, he gave money to Communist causes and had many friends in the party. In 1945 he wrote to the *Daily Worker* saying that he was "an active supporter of the reconstituted Communist Party," but by then his mind was increasingly wandering—or revealing the true logic of his Fabianism.

Orwell also observed that Wells "is too sane to understand the modern world," by which he meant too rational. This was not quite true. What he had come to realize—and it made him very unhappy—

was that, discounting violent revolution and drastic brainwashing and surgery such as took place in Russia, human nature itself was the greatest stumbling block to the achievement of his objectives. As Conrad had told him long ago: "You do not take sufficient account of human imbecility which is cunning and perfidious"; and again, "You don't care for humanity but think they are to be improved; I love humanity but know they are not."

But Wells *did* know, even if he did not particularly love, humanity and its imbecility: he had shown it comprehensively in the novels of his Edwardian period. Was he to write as he saw or as he thought? Here was the crux of his painful dilemma; and it was not merely in the despairing and somewhat incoherent pamphlet *Mind at the End of Its Tether* (1945) that he despaired. As early as *The Undying Fire* (1919), while expressing his loathing of things as they were, he wrote: "I talk . . . I talk . . . and then a desolating sense of reality blows like a destroying gust through my mind, and my little lamp of hope blows out." It shows, writes Anthony West, "the pendulum of his mind swinging away from its natural despairing bent over to the side of determination to construct something better out of human opportunities and back, again and again."

Such doubts about the sacred cow of progress damned him in the eyes of all good progressives. But *Mind at the End of Its Tether* goes far beyond doubt. He has no doubt anymore: "The end of everything we call life is close at hand and cannot be evaded. A frightful queerness has come into life. . . . Something is happening so that life will never be *quite* the same again. The attempt to trace a pattern of any sort is absolutely futile."

Wells claimed with some justice in a letter in 1939 that all his books had insisted on "the insecurity of progress and the possibility of human degeneration and extinction. I think the odds are against man but it is still worth fighting against them." The trouble is that he fought under the wrong banner. His ideals were frequently undesirable and happily unattainable. The plain fact was that most Englishmen did not want to be regimented by Fabians or any other authoritarian, unelected group, however wise. They did not want dictatorship, nor central world government. Most particularly they did not want to change their character, except in the slow way that nature itself changes it. Only long after Wells's death were they to wake up to what was being put across them by Wells's disciples and successors.

[12]See Rose L. Martin's *Fabian Freeway* (Santa Monica, 1968).

Yet Wells's ideals sprang from goodwill and humanity; he had known poverty and all that went with it; he had been at the receiving end of bad education; he had seen the wastefulness of wars and the irresponsibility of financiers. He wanted to save others from such things, as he had saved himself (for neither wars nor economic collapse really touched him personally). During the Second World War Wells continued to write on the old themes. The MacKenzies sum it up neatly: "The world was in flames and H. G. was trying to beat them out with a Fabian pamphlet."

CONCLUSION

It was unfortunate for Wells's reputation as a novelist—and for the enjoyment of potential readers—that his fiction was given the cold shoulder by two such writers as D. H. Lawrence and Virginia Woolf, both fashionable with the literary intelligentsia in the 1920's. By that time what may be termed the snobbery of letters had gained a real hold. Writers not on the OK list were banished to critical darkness, however high their sales were. Indeed the higher the sales the more likely they were to be looked down on; it was notable that those on the approved list were usually poor sellers. The result was that when Virginia Woolf discovered Wells's work to be "already a little chilled" the word was quickly passed round: Wells is out.

Happily the tide has turned. Some first-class critics have spent time demonstrating Wells's many excellences. Some of the more academic critics, it is true, propound somewhat eccentric views of Wells. But many of them think him worth serious attention, and so they play a part in persuading contemporary readers that the best of Wells's fiction is still good reading. And it is.

I do not know whether he was a "great" writer because I am not sure, below the topmost level of, say, Dickens, Dostoyevsky, Flaubert, what "great" means; and in any case writers are not to be assessed in a sort of football league table. What I am sure of is that a reader who picks up *The Time Machine*, *Kipps*, *Mr. Polly*, and *Mr. Britling Sees It Through* will not put them aside until he has read to the end. Fiction is for enjoyment. Alas, halfway through his career Wells decided it was for teaching.

SELECTED BIBLIOGRAPHY

The H. G. Wells archive, comprising his private papers, correspondence, many MSS of his writings, etc., was acquired from his family by the University of Illinois in 1956. See LETTERS for correspondence with particular individuals published so far from this archive. The H. G. Wells Society, London, publishes occasional papers and a journal (no. 1, Spring 1972).

I. BIBLIOGRAPHY. F. A. Chappell, *Bibliography of the Works of H. G. Wells* (Chicago, 1924); G. H. Wells [G. West], *A Bibliography of the Works of H. G. Wells* (London, 1925), with notes and comments; G. H. Wells, *The Works of H. G. Wells, 1887–1925* (London, 1926), bibliography, dictionary, and subject index; G. A. Connes, *A Dictionary of Characters and Scenes in the Novels, Romances and Short Stories of H. G. Wells* (Dijon, 1926); K. R. Menon, *A Guide to H. G. Wells's Short Stories* (Singapore, 1957); H. G. Wells Society, *H. G. Wells: A Comprehensive Bibliography* (London, 1966).

II. COLLECTED EDITIONS. *The Works of H. G. Wells*, 28 vols. (London, 1924–1927), the Atlantic ed.; *The Works of H. G. Wells*, 24 vols. (London, 1926–1927), the Essex Thinpaper ed.; *Works*, 24 vols. (Geneva, 1968–1969).

III. SELECTED EDITIONS. *Tales of the Unexpected* (London, 1922); *Tales of Life and Adventure* (London, 1923); *Tales of Wonder* (London, 1923); *The Short Stories* (London, 1927); *A Quartette of Comedies* (London, 1928), contains *Kipps, The History of Mr. Polly, Bealby, Love and Mr. Lewisham; The Scientific Romances* (London, 1933), contains *The Time Machine, The Island of Doctor Moreau, The Invisible Man, The War of the Worlds, The First Men in the Moon, The Food of the Gods, In the Days of the Comet*, and *Men Like Gods; Stories of Men and Women in Love* (London, 1933), contains *Love and Mr. Lewisham, The Passionate Friends, The Wife of Sir Isaac Harman, The Secret Places of the Heart; The Wheels of Chance and The Time Machine* (London, 1935), Everyman Library ed.; *Selected Short Stories* (Harmondsworth, 1958); W. Warren Wagar, ed. and comp., *Journalism and Prophecy, 1893–1946* (Boston, 1964; London, 1965).

IV. SEPARATE WORKS. *Text-book of Biology*, 2 vols. (London, 1893); *Honours Physiography* (London, 1893), in collaboration with R. A. Gregory; *Select Conversations with an Uncle, Now Extinct, and Two Other Reminiscences* (London, 1895), sketches and stories, contains twelve conversations and the two short stories "A Misunderstood Artist" and "The Man with a Nose"; *The Time Machine: An Invention* (London, 1895), fantasy; *The Wonderful Visit* (London, 1895), fantasy; *The Stolen Bacillus, and Other Incidents* (London, 1895), short stories, contains "The Stolen Bacillus," "The Flowering of the Strange Orchid," "In the Avu Observatory," "The Triumphs of a Taxidermist," "A Deal in Ostriches," "Through a Window," "The Temptation of Harringay,"

"The Flying Man," "The Diamond Maker," "Aepyornis Island," "The Remarkable Case of Davidson's Eyes," "The Lord of the Dynamos," "The Hammerpond Park Burglary," "A Moth—Genus Novo," "The Treasure in the Forest"; *The Red Room* (Chicago, 1896), short story, only twelve copies printed; *The Wheels of Chance: A Holiday Adventure* (London, 1896), novel, first published serially in *Today* (London, 1896); *The Island of Doctor Moreau* (London, 1896), science fiction; *The Plattner Story, and Others* (London, 1897), short stories, contains "The Plattner Story," "The Argonauts of the Air," "The Story of the Late Mr. Elvesham," "In the Abyss," "The Apple," "Under the Knife," "The Sea-Raiders," "Pollock and the Porroh Man," "The Red Room," "The Cone," "The Purple Pileus," "The Jilting of Jane," "In the Modern Vein," "A Catastrophe," "The Lost Inheritance," "The Sad Story of a Dramatic Critic," "A Slip under the Microscope"; *The Invisible Man: A Grotesque Romance* (London, 1897), science fiction, first published serially in *Pearson's Weekly* (June–July 1897); *Text-Book of Zoology* (London, 1898), in collaboration with A. M. Davies, rev. by J. T. Cunningham (London, 1913); *Certain Personal Matters* (London, 1898), mainly autobiographical; *Thirty Strange Stories* (New York, 1897), contains three new stories: "The Reconciliation," "The Rajah's Treasure," and "Le Mari terrible"; *The War of the Worlds* (London, 1898), science fiction, first published serially in *Pearson's* (April–December 1897); *When the Sleeper Wakes* (London, 1899), science fiction, first published serially in the *Graphic* (1898–1899), rev. as *The Sleeper Awakes* (London, 1910); *Tales of Space and Time* (London, 1899), short stories, contains "The Crystal Egg," "The Star," "A Story of the Stone Age," "A Story of the Days to Come," "The Man Who Could Work Miracles."

Love and Mr. Lewisham (London, 1900), novel, first published serially in the *Weekly Times* (November 1899–1900); *The First Men in the Moon* (London, 1901), science fiction, first published serially in the *Strand* (December 1900–August 1901); *Anticipations of the Reaction of Mechanical and Scientific Progress upon Human Life and Thought* (London, [1901]), prognostication; *The Discovery of the Future* (London, 1902), lecture, given at the Royal Institution on 24 January 1902; *The Sea Lady: A Tissue of Moonshine* (London, 1902), first published serially in *Pearson's* (July–December 1901); *Twelve Stories and a Dream* (London, 1903), contains "Filmer," "The Magic Shop," "The Valley of Spiders," "The Truth about Pyecraft," "Mr. Skelmersdale in Fairyland," "The Story of the Inexperienced Ghost," "Jimmy Goggles the God," "The New Accelerator," "Mr. Ledbetter's Vacation," "The Stolen Body," "Mr. Brisher's Treasure," "Miss Winchelsea's Heart," "A Dream of Armageddon"; *Mankind in the Making* (London, 1903), education, first printed serially in the *Fortnightly Review* (September 1902–September 1903); *The Food of the Gods, And How It Came to Earth* (London, 1904), science fiction, first published serially in *Pearson's* (December 1903–June 1904).

A Modern Utopia (London, 1905), sociology, first published serially in the *Fortnightly Review* (October 1904–April 1905); *Kipps: The Story of a Simple Soul* (London, 1905), novel, first published serially in *Pall Mall* (1905); *In the Days of the Comet* (London, 1906), science fiction, first published in the *Daily Chronicle* (1905–1906); *Socialism and the Family* (London, 1906), political tract; *The Future in America: A Search after Realities* (London, 1906), sociology, first printed serially in *Harper's Weekly* (14 July–6 October 1906); *This Misery of Boots* (London, 1907), political tract, a Fabian Society pamphlet, repr. from the *Independent Review* (December 1905); *New Worlds for Old* (London, 1908), prognostication; *The War in the Air and Particularly How Mr. Bert Smallways Fared While It Lasted* (London, 1908), science fiction, first printed serially in *Pall Mall*; *First & Last Things: A Confession of Faith and Rule of Life* (London, 1908; rev. ed., 1917), philosophy; *Tono-Bungay* (London, 1909), novel, first published serially in the *English Review* (December 1908–March 1909); *Ann Veronica: A Modern Love Story* (London, 1909), novel.

The History of Mr. Polly (London, 1910), novel; *The Country of the Blind, and Other Stories* (London, 1911), contains five new stories: "A Vision of Judgment," "The Empire of the Ants," "The Door in the Wall," "The Country of the Blind," and "The Beautiful Suit"; *The Door in the Wall, and Other Stories* (New York, 1911), short stories, lim. ed. of 600 copies, eight stories selected from previous collections; *Floor Games* (London, 1911), juvenile; *The New Machiavelli* (London, 1911), novel, first printed serially in the *English Review* (May–October 1910); *Marriage* (London, 1912), novel; *Little Wars: A Game for Boys* (London, 1913), juvenile; *The Passionate Friends: A Novel* (1913); *The Wife of Sir Isaac Harman* (London, 1914), novel; *The World Set Free: A Story of Mankind* (London, 1914), fantasy, first published serially in the *English Review* (December 1913–May 1914); *The War That Will End War* (London, 1914), essays; *An Englishman Looks at the World* (London, 1914), contains twenty-six essays, thirteen repr. from the *Daily Mail* and already collected in two pamphlets, *The Labour Unrest* (1912) and *War and Common Sense* (1913), ten published in weeklies and monthlies, three in book form as occasional contributions.

Boon (London, 1915), sketches, contains "The Mind of the Race," "The Wild Asses of the Devil," "The Last Trump: Being a First Selection from the Literary Remains of George Boon, Prepared for Publication by Reginald Bliss" [H. G. Wells]; *The Peace of the World* (London, 1915), commentary, first published in the *English Review* (March 1915); *The Research Magnificent* (London, 1915), novel; *Bealby: A Holiday* (London, 1915), novel, first published serially in *Grand* (August 1914–March 1915); *What Is Coming? A Forecast of Things after the War* (London, 1916), commentary; *Mr. Britling Sees It Through* (London, 1916), novel, first published serially in the *Nation* (May–October 1916); *The Elements of Reconstruction* (London, 1916), commentary, series of articles repr. from the *Times* (July–August 1916); *The Soul of a Bishop: A Novel* (London, 1917), first published serially in *Collier's Weekly* (1917); *War and the Future: Italy, France, and Britain at War* (London, 1917), commentary; *God the Invisible King* (London, 1917), commentary; *In the Fourth Year: Anticipations of a World Peace* (London, 1918), commentary, eleven chs. mostly repr. from daily newspapers; *Joan and Peter: The Story of an Education* (London, 1918), novel; *The Undying Fire: A Contemporary Novel* (London, 1919), first published serially in the *International Review* (March–June 1919); *The Outline of History: Being a Plain History of Life and Mankind,* 2 vols. (1919–1920), originally iss. fortnightly, rev. ed. (1920), 5th rev. (1930), rev. and ext. by R. Postgate (1951).

Russia in the Shadows (London, 1920), politics, originally serialized in the *Sunday Express* (October–November 1920); *The Salvaging of Civilization* (London, 1921), politics; *A Short History of the World* (London, 1922), history; *The Secret Places of the Heart* (London, 1922), novel, first published serially in *Nash's* and *Pall Mall* (December 1921–July 1922); *Washington and the Hope of Peace* (London, 1922), commentary, articles written at the time of the Washington Arms Conference, first published in the *New York World* (November–December 1921); *Men Like Gods* (London, 1923), science fiction, first printed serially in the *Westminster Gazette* (December 1922–February 1923); *The Story of a Great Schoolmaster: Being a Plain Account of the Life and Ideas of Sanderson of Oundle* (London, 1924), biography; *A Year of Prophesying* (London, 1924), commentary; *The Dream* (London, 1924), novel, first published serially in *Nash's* and *Pall Mall* (October 1923–May 1924).

A Forecast of the World's Affairs (London, 1925), commentary; *Christina Alberta's Father* (London, 1925), novel; *The World of William Clissold: A Novel at a New Angle,* 3 vols. (London, 1926); *Meanwhile: The Picture of a Lady* (London, 1927), novel; *Democracy under Revision* (London, 1927), lecture given at the Sorbonne; *The Way the World Is Going: Guesses and Forecasts of the Years Ahead* (London, 1928); *Mr. Blettsworthy on Rampole Island* (London, 1928), novel; *The Book of Catherine Wells* (London, 1928), Wells's tribute to the memory of his wife; *The Open Conspiracy: Blueprints for a World Revolution* (London, 1928; rev. ed., 1930), politics; *The King Who Was a King: The Book of a Film* (London, 1929); *Imperialism and the Open Conspiracy* (London, 1929), politics; *The Adventures of Tommy* (London, 1929), juvenile; *The Treasure in the Forest* (London, 1929), novel; *The Common Sense of World Peace* (London, 1929), lecture, an address to the Reichstag; *The Science of Life: A Summary of Contemporary Knowledge about Life and Its Possibilities* (London, 1929–1930), biology, in collaboration with J. Huxley and G. P. Wells, originally iss. fortnightly.

The Autocracy of Mr. Parham (London, 1930), novel; *What Are We To Do with Our Lives?* (London, 1931), sociology, the final rev. of *The Open Conspiracy; The*

Work, Wealth and Happiness of Mankind, 2 vols. (New York, 1931; London, 1932; rev. ed., 1934), economics; *After Democracy: Addresses and Papers on the Present World Situation* (London, 1932), politics; *The Bulpington of Blup* (London, 1932), novel; *The Shape of Things to Come: The Ultimate Revolution* (London, 1933), prognostication; *Experiment in Autobiography: Discoveries and Conclusions of a Very Ordinary Brain—Since 1866,* 2 vols. (London, 1934; new ed., 1966).

The New America: The New World (London, 1935), travel; *The Idea of a World Encyclopaedia* (London, 1936), lecture given at the Royal Institution; *The Croquet Player: A Story* (London, 1936); *The Anatomy of Frustration: A Modern Synthesis* (London, 1936), commentary; *Star Begotten: A Biological Fantasia* (London, 1937), science fiction; *Brynhild* (London, 1937), novel; *The Camford Visitation* (London, 1937), satire; *World Brain* (London, 1938), essays and addresses; *The Brothers: A Story* (London, 1937); *Apropos of Dolores* (London, 1938), novel; *Travels of a Republican Radical in Search of Hot Water* (London, 1939), polemics; *The Holy Terror* (London, 1939), novel; *The Fate of Homo Sapiens: An Unemotional Statement of the Things That Are Happening to Him Now, and of the Immediate Possibilities Confronting Him* (London, 1939), commentary.

The Rights of Man: Or, What Are We Fighting For? (London, 1940), commentary; *All Aboard for Ararat* (London, 1940), commentary; *Babes in the Darkling Wood* (London, 1940), novel; *The Common Sense of War and Peace: World Revolution or War Unending* (London, 1940), commentary; *The New World Order: Whether It Is Attainable, How It Can Be Attained and What Sort of World a World at Peace Will Have to Be* (London, 1940), commentary; *You Can't Be Too Careful: A Sample of Life, 1901–1951* (London, 1941), story; *Guide to the New World: A Handbook to Constructive World Revolution* (London, 1941), commentary; *Science and the World-Mind* (London, 1942), science; *The Conquest of Time* (London, 1942), commentary, written to replace *First and Last Things* (London, 1908); *The Outlook for Homo Sapiens* (London, 1942), commentary, an amalgamation of *The Fate of Homo Sapiens* (London, 1939) and *The New World Order* (London, 1940); *Phoenix: A Summary of the Inescapable Conditions of World Reorganisation* (London, 1942), politics; *Crux Ansata: An Indictment of the Roman Catholic Church* (London, 1943), polemics; *'42 to '44: A Contemporary Memoir upon Human Behaviour During the Crisis of the World Revolution* (London, 1944), politics, lim. to 2,000 copies, Wells's doctoral thesis at London University, written in 1942 and entitled "A Thesis on the Quality of Illusion in the Continuity of the Individual Life in the Higher Metazoa, with Particular Reference to the Species *Homo Sapiens,*" was printed as an appendix to this work; *The Happy Turning: A Dream of Life* (London, 1945), commentary; *Mind at the End of Its Tether* (London, 1945), commentary.

V. LETTERS. H. A. Jones, *My Dear Wells: A Manual for*

the Haters of England. Being a Series of Letters upon Bolshevism, Collectivism, Internationalism, and the Distribution of Wealth Addressed to Mr. H. G. Wells (London, 1921); L. Edel and G. N. Ray, eds., Henry James and H. G. Wells: A Record of Their Friendship, Their Debate on the Art of Fiction, and Their Quarrel (London, 1958); H. Wilson, ed., Arnold Bennett and H. G. Wells: A Record of a Personal and a Literary Friendship (London, 1960); R. A. Gettmann, George Gissing and H. G. Wells: Their Friendship and Correspondence (London, 1961). The three latter collections are from H. G. Wells papers at the University of Illinois, excellently edited and invaluable for students of Wells's relations with the literary world of his time.

VI. BIOGRAPHICAL AND CRITICAL STUDIES. A. H. G. Craufurd, The Religion of H. G. Wells, and Other Essays (London, 1909); J. D. Beresford, H. G. Wells (London, 1915); Van Wyck Brooks, The World of H. G. Wells (London, 1915).

E. Guyot, H. G. Wells (Paris, 1920); R. T. Hopkins, H. G. Wells: Personality, Character, Topography (London, 1922); S. Dark, The Outline of H. G. Wells: The Superman in the Street (London, 1922); I. J. C. Brown, H. G. Wells (London, 1923); G. A Connes, Étude sur la pensée de Wells (Paris, 1926), includes bibliography; F. H. Doughty, H. G. Wells, Educationist (London, 1926); H. Belloc, A Companion to Mr. Wells's "Outline of History" (London, 1926); H. Belloc, Mr. Belloc Still Objects to Mr. Wells's "Outline of History" (London, 1926), by the most acute critic of Wells's humanistic approach; P. Braybrooke, Some Aspects of H. G. Wells (London, 1928).

G. West [G. H. Wells], H. G. Wells: A Sketch for a Portrait (London, 1930); J. H. S. Rowland, Talk with H. G. Wells (London, 1944), with special reference to Crux

Ansata; N. C. Nicholson, H. G. Wells (London, 1950); V. Brome, H. G. Wells: A Biography (London, 1951); P. Quennell, The Singular Preference: Portraits and Essays (London, 1952); M. Belgion, H. G. Wells (London, 1953); V. Brome, Six Studies in Quarrelling (London, 1958), on the literary quarrels of Shaw, Wells, and others.

F. K. Chaplin, H. G. Wells: An Outline (London, 1960); W. W. Wagar, H. G. Wells and the World State (New Haven, Conn., 1961); B. Bergonzi, The Early H. G. Wells: A Study of the Scientific Romances (Manchester, 1961), illuminating and erudite; I. Raknem, H. G. Wells and His Critics (Oslo–Bergen, 1962); J. Kagarlitski, The Life and Thought of H. G. Wells (London, 1966), trans. from Russian by M. Budberg; R. Costa, H. G. Wells (New York, 1967); M. R. Hillegas, The Future as Nightmare: H. G. Wells and the Anti-Utopians (New York, 1967); K. B. Newell, Structure in Four Novels by H. G. Wells (The Hague–Paris, 1968); L. Dickson, H. G. Wells: His Turbulent Life and Times (New York, 1969), frank and entertaining account.

P. Parrinder, H. G. Wells (Edinburgh, 1970); W. Bellamy, The Novels of Wells, Bennett and Galsworthy, 1890–1910 (London, 1971); J.-P. Vernier, H. G. Wells et son temps (Paris, 1971); P. Parrinder, ed., H. G. Wells: The Critical Heritage (London, 1972), well-chosen selection of reviews of Wells's works as they came out; A. Borrello, H. G. Wells: Author in Agony (Carbondale–Edwardsville, Ill., 1972); N. MacKenzie and J. MacKenzie, The Time Traveller: The Life of H. G. Wells (London, 1973), the essential full-scale biography; J.-P Vernier, H. G. Wells at the Turn of the Century: From Science Fiction to Anticipation (Dagenham, 1973), H. G. Wells Society Occasional Paper no. 1; G. N. Ray, H. G. Wells and Rebecca West (London, 1974).

OSCAR WILDE

(1845-1900)

John Stokes

To reveal art and conceal the artist is art's aim.

No artist desires to prove anything. Even things that are true can be proved.

No artist is ever morbid. The artist can express everything.
(From the preface to *The Picture of Dorian Gray*)

I

THE liberating potential of art that is extolled in these epigrams was Oscar Wilde's most constant theme, and it is as the high priest of aesthetic freedom that he has found his place in cultural histories. In his own life, however, Wilde was a consciously professional writer whose literary ideas were expressed within a particular situation, whose art was effectively a mediation between hopes and possibilities. Wilde's belief that his art could save him from his times turned out to be a disastrous error of judgment, but he was surely close to the truth when he announced that "to be premature is to be perfect," an ironical boast that was to become an established creed with avant-garde artists in general.

If Wilde's devotion to an ideal future served to justify his pose at the time, it now invites us to consider his ideas in their historical moment. By prolonging the tradition of the nineteenth-century dandy and developing the doctrine of the mask, he was, after all, only acting in accordance with his own evaluation of his period. As he wrote in 1894:

To the world I seem, by intention on my part, a dilettante and dandy merely—it is not wise to show one's heart to the world—and as seriousness of manner is the disguise of the fool, folly in its exquisite modes of triviality and indifference and lack of care is the robe of the wise man. In so vulgar an age as this we all need masks.
(*Letters of Oscar Wilde*, p. 353)

This response to the age was entirely characteristic of the Decadent movement to which Wilde belonged.

Self-disguise coupled with an active nostalgia offered the Decadent a shelter from the facile optimism that he felt surrounded him. His conviction that he was living through a period of transition not only provided an ironical perspective on history but encouraged him to invoke the styles of the past in his writing. Although his field of operation was the modern city, the Decadent's language was often archaic, his images grotesque and macabre, and he favored episodic techniques suitable for rendering discontinuous dreamlike experience.

To these tendencies Wilde brought his own unfailing zest for wit and paradox, his dramatic way of throwing into relief the ideas with which he was most seriously engaged. Consequently, even in its most Decadent phases, Wilde's career continued to be an ingenious solution to the problems of being a professional writer, and his essential concerns—integrity, the creation of an audience, and the function of art—did not change, even when they appeared to him, as to others, to be thoroughly compromised by social circumstance. Wilde's answer to circumstance, self-dramatization, was an implicit attack upon the widespread belief that there was some natural contract between the artist and his audience, and a challenge to the utilitarian notion that likened the relationship to the one between a manufacturer and his market. In his refusal to issue moral edicts, Wilde exposed the myth that art performs a simple social service, disdaining to prove in his narrative conclusions of which his audience was already persuaded.

At the same time Wilde could not rest with the kind of pessimism that actually took comfort from alienation. A writer, he chose to become an entertainer, thereby granting himself the freedom to claim the attention of his audience without sharing its pious expectations. An inevitable condition of this choice was that he should seem to remove himself from commitment to any definite social program.

Oscar Wilde was a one-man band, his art a public show in which he played all the instruments and more often than not was one of the spectators too. His versatility depended in part upon shameless plagiarism; but we should view him now as we do a period anthology, remembering that its form and content have been shaped as much by the preferences of the compiler as by the age that it tries to represent. A careful reading of the texts allows us to see more of Wilde than he wanted us to and more perhaps than he could see of himself. For all his professed delight in his own escapades, he was at heart a most reluctant product of his age.

II

OSCAR FINGAL O'FLAHERTIE WILLS WILDE was born in Dublin on 16 October 1854. His father, Sir William Wilde, was a distinguished surgeon, author of several books on the history and topography of Ireland, and, incidentally, a notorious seducer of women. Oscar's mother was also remarkable: deeply versed in Irish literary traditions, she achieved fame through her own writings, in particular for *Jacta Alea Est*, a patriotic outburst written in 1848 that exhorted the Young Ireland Movement to active rebellion against English oppression. His older brother, known as Willie, later became a London journalist and something of a reprobate. A younger sister, Isola Francesca, died when still a child, causing Oscar much grief. His moving poem "Requiescat" is in her memory.

The Wilde household was an eccentric, sometimes scandalous, but unquestionably learned milieu in which to grow up. At this period Dublin, as so often throughout its history, was a city whose cultural interests were a mixture of the cosmopolitan and the parochial. Wilde benefited from the best that Irish education had to offer: he attended the famous Protestant public school Portora Royal and Trinity College, Dublin, to which he won a scholarship in 1871.

At Trinity he quickly established himself as a brilliant student, attracting the attention of two outstanding classical scholars, Robert Yelverton Tyrrell and John Pentland Mahaffy. When Mahaffy published his pioneering and influential book *Social Life in Greece from Homer to Menander* (1874), he acknowledged the advice given to him by his instructive pupil. Precocity, a quality that the mature Wilde was always to hold in the greatest esteem, was something for which he had himself been acclaimed.

Wilde left Trinity laden with honors, among them the prestigious Berkeley Gold Medal for Greek, and in the autumn of 1874 he took up a classical scholarship at Magdalen College, Oxford. Oxford gave him his formative years. It was there that he was impressed by powerful minds such as John Ruskin, Walter Pater, and Benjamin Jowett, whose classical studies attempted to reconcile Socratic method with Christianity and with modern philosophy.

In the essays and lectures that Wilde wrote after leaving Oxford, Ruskin tends to be offered as a precursor. The austere, at times strident, moralism of the professor of fine art could hardly be accommodated within Wilde's glamorous Aestheticism, and as early as 1882 he was announcing that "the younger school" had departed from Ruskin in its "love of art for art's sake." The connection between art and work, however, the pivot of Ruskin's beliefs, was one that Wilde was never entirely to lose sight of.

A considerably more dominant influence was Walter Pater, whom Wilde revered as a father figure yet is sometimes said to have betrayed. The truth is that Pater, who never allowed himself to become a spokesman for others and was unwilling even to speak directly for himself, played the Ghost to Wilde's Hamlet, and was as much a realization of the son's own needs as a distinct presence. Of all the echoes in Wilde's work, the insistent cadences of the conclusion to Pater's *Studies in the History of the Renaissance* (1873) are by far the most pervasive:

High passions give one this quickened sense of life, ecstasy and sorrow of love, political or religious enthusiasm, or the "enthusiasm of humanity." Only, be sure it is passion, that it does yield you this fruit of a quickened, multiplied consciousness. Of this wisdom, the poetic passion, the desire of beauty, the love of art for art's sake has most; for art comes to you professing frankly to give nothing but the highest quality to your moments as they pass, and simply for those moments' sake.

(pp. 212–213)

Pater deals in injunctions so tentative and yet so intensely felt that he bestows on his readers the pleasant sensation that they are hearing their own inner promptings voiced through another. Reading Pater's prose Wilde discovered himself.

Pater's basic concerns, of course, were as typically Victorian as those of Ruskin, Matthew Arnold, or the other sages: progress, community, belief. His nervous attempt to reestablish the interdependence of aesthetics and conduct was to be seen as a premonition of the need for a "New Hellenism," a progressive slogan that denoted the reunion of the spiritual life with its natural roots and a revival of a classical vision unburdened by the moral hypocrisy, sexual puritanism, and aesthetic philistinism of nineteenth-century England. (A related phrase, sometimes used by Wilde, the "New Hedonism," expressed a more individualistic and scientifically based version of the same idea.)

At Oxford, Wilde made contact with two other trends with which Paterian aestheticism was somewhat uneasily associated. One was a practical application of sensibility to life-style, the burgeoning Aesthetic movement, which embraced Japanese art, blue-and-white china, and William Morris furnishings. The other was the homoerotic cult, sometimes known as "uranianism," which celebrated romantic attachments between men and boys.

As an undergraduate Wilde led an extremely full life. In the spring of 1877 he embarked on a tour of Italy and Greece with Mahaffy, his old Trinity tutor, and in 1878 he was awarded the Newdigate Prize for "Ravenna," a long poem inspired by the trip. In the following year he submitted for the Chancellor's English Essay Prize "The Rise of Historical Criticism," a repetitious piece that nevertheless demonstrates a remarkable breadth of knowledge and a precocious ease with abstract ideas that Wilde was later to distill into epigram. The essay displays his wide reading in the classics and is liberally scattered with references to modern thinkers such as Johann Fichte, Georg Hegel, Alexis de Tocqueville, and Herbert Spencer. Its most impressive qualities are its concern with the relationships between art and history, its implicit admiration of relativistic thought and its commitment to the idea of progress.

Surprisingly Wilde did not win the essay prize nor, in spite of a first-class degree, was he invited to become a fellow of his college. He transferred his attention to London.

Conquest of the capital was by no means immediate, and Wilde seems at first to have been somewhat vague about his future plans. He set up a male household off the Strand with the artist Frank Miles and began to cultivate that fringe of high society then operating between the court, as represented by the rakish Prince of Wales, and the theater, where Wilde's expansive charm endeared him to the actress Lily Langtry and other prominent personalities of the day. And of course he wrote—a play, entitled *Vera; or, The Nihilists* (1880); journalism, which he had taken up even before leaving Oxford, with accounts of exhibitions at the fashionable Grosvenor Gallery; and poetry.

In 1881 he brought out a collection simply entitled *Poems*. Despite, or perhaps because of, energetic promotion by its author, the volume met with an extremely mixed reception. The most common, and not inaccurate, complaint was that the poems were scandalously derivative—though one of the most powerful resonances came not from other poetry but from Pater's prose. No more than others could Wilde resist transforming the "poetic passion" into the poetry of passion, and the facility with which he adapted Pater's most famous phrases is enough to make one wonder afresh what Pater himself really meant by them.

In the opening poem, "Hélas," the attractions of hedonism are opposed to an "ancient wisdom and austere control," which might stand for either the Christian or the pagan ideal, either the poet's Celtic inheritance or his responsibilities as a writer; while a later phrase, "the honey of romance," links hedonism with moral susceptibility. In Wilde's poetry even political options mirror the indecisiveness of the self. In "Sonnet to Liberty," for instance, the appeal of young revolutionaries resides in their passion rather than in their cause, and the call they make upon the unruly emotions of the poet has to be suppressed. The sonnet ends in melodrama: "These Christs that die upon the barricades, / God knows it I am with them, in some things."

"The Garden of Eros" is Wilde's most frankly Aesthetic poem, honoring, in the kind of reconstructive word-painting that the Victorians much admired, the leaders of the romantic tradition as an Aesthete might conceive of them: John Keats (Wilde's favorite poet), Percy Bysshe Shelley, Morris, Dante Gabriel Rossetti, and Algernon Swinburne. But the mood is listlessly elegiac, suggesting that these revered artists have fought a losing battle in the face of the modern world, and the poet concludes that to evoke beauty is necessarily to court transience and failure.

In the other long poems, "Panthea," "Humanitad," and "The Burden of Itys," the endeavor would seem to be to answer the modern nightmare vision of a universe lacking all purpose (borrowed in part from Alfred Tennyson) with a vague mystical pantheism that is largely derived from Shelley and

William Wordsworth, but is sometimes expressed in purely sensual terms. In "Humanitad" the Greek ideal of perfect form ("Which curbs the passion of that level line / Of marble youths, who with untroubled eyes / And chastened limbs ride round Athena's shrine / And mirror her divine economies") is opposed to Christian immanence ("Where we behold, as one who in a glass / Sees his own face, self-slain Humanity"). The hope is that man will transcend the image of suffering that he has created out of his own self-division and that, in a favorite formula taken from Johann Wolfgang von Goethe, he will "make the Body and the Spirit one."

In his early poetry Wilde mines the romantic tradition and looks to nature and to art for images that reciprocate his inner confusion. *Poems* is a deliberately portentous volume, which can be seen as Wilde's way of viewing his own situation in the light of the achievements of others to the point where plagiarism becomes a species of narcissism. One cannot even claim for him that faculty of creative borrowing for which T. S. Eliot or more recently Harold Bloom has professed an admiration, because for the most part Wilde's self-dramatization remains at the level of mimicry. His eclecticism sometimes causes him to lose control of his ideas and even his syntax: he is an inflationary poet who devalues what he takes. An indiscriminate proliferation of the first person pronoun, endless relative clauses, and continual qualification mark this as the poetry of an indecisiveness that goes beyond the professed options of Christianity or paganism, asceticism or sensuality, to a more basic uncertainty about emotion itself. For all the talk of conquest and submission the reader has little sense of passion actually experienced. Interestingly enough, that absence of reliable feeling is a sign of Decadent attitudes to come. Each one of the vital principles that Wilde attempts to espouse—art, religion, politics, and love—turns out to be already infected with its own failure.

The influence of the fine arts is always in evidence in Wilde's poetry, from a Pre-Raphaelite obsession with natural detail in "The Garden of Eros," through the exercises in classical archaeology that imitate painters such as Lord Leighton and Alma-Tadema, to the Whistlerian or Japanesque "impressions" that mark a later stage in Aesthetic taste. Wilde also frequently employs "the comparison of the arts," a familiar topic in the late nineteenth century. In the hands of the Aesthetes, adjudication between the competing claims of the different arts became a way of justifying art as a whole. Each art could be said to manifest superiority in a particular mode of representation: sculpture because its permanence conveys essence; painting because it faithfully reflects the color, detail, and rhythms of natural perception; poetry because language is tied to thought; music because it is least bound to the representation of a flawed reality; drama because it includes all the other arts. The permutations could be juggled continually, and Wilde expressed alternative preferences at various times. But in the lectures that he gave in the 1880's he followed a powerful direction in Aesthetic thought, and saw the decorative arts as offering an example that all the other arts should emulate.

III

"I'VE put my genius into my life; I've put only my talent into my works," runs Wilde's famous remark to André Gide. Even today opinion polls frequently make him the guest that most people would like to encounter at a dinner party. But some of his contemporaries were affronted by his dominating presence. The mature Wilde had no qualms about declaiming his own prose-poems at the table, and some of his best-known epigrams are sharp reversals of polite exchanges that rebuke the dull and presumptuous. Accosted by a persistent journalist, he is said to have excused himself with: "You will pardon me: I remember your name, but I can't recall your face." In the 1890's Laurence Housman noted "a certain decorative solemnity, in excess of what the occasion required," but later marveled at Wilde's "smooth-flowing utterance, sedate and self-possessed, oracular in tone, whimsical in substance, carried on without halt, or hesitation, or change of word." Much of Wilde's apparently impromptu wit has this same extravagant quality which, by playing manner off against meaning, turns common speech into drama. A glassy, self-regarding creation, Wilde's social personality was to develop according to the opportunities of the moment.

In the metropolitan world through which he sailed in the early 1880's, style and appearance certainly did much to create identity. To be seen was as important as to produce, and Wilde was always conscious of the relation between the two. And he was seen in several guises: affable country-house guest, happy, indeed eager to join in the weekend sport; top-hatted man-about-town at a private view or public reception; and, more daring but now socially recognizable, languorous, velveted Aesthete. It was this last role that was to offer him some immediate financial reward.

Although Wilde did not invent the Aesthetic movement, it is true to say that for a time he allowed it to invent him. The manner in which this occurred was essentially satirical. The cartoonist George du Maurier had begun a series in *Punch* featuring a comic Aesthete called Postlethwaite, who, as the series continued, came to bear an increasing resemblance to Wilde. At about the same time the actor Herbert Beerbohm Tree adapted some of his performances to mimic Wilde's well-known gestures and expressions. The climax of this satirical process was reached in 1881 with Gilbert and Sullivan's *Patience,* and its outrageous Aesthete, Bunthorne. It was thanks to the great popular success of *Patience* that Wilde was invited to lecture in the United States in 1882. This tour, which took him from coast to coast, had a considerable impact. For the most part a bemused America matched his condescending posture with rambunctious parodies in popular songs and cartoons, but he was granted an interview with the laureate of the democratic self, Walt Whitman, and a minority evidently took him very solemnly indeed. "I am an *intense lover* of the *beautiful,*" wrote one earnest admirer, "and have spent much time and thought over it." "Let me thank you sincerely for your fructifying lecture," wrote another. "I call it fructifying because it teaches a gospel hitherto not heard here, and one which I believe will have a better effect than the foundation of a cotton factory—a compliment which may sound ambiguous to you but it is the highest I can pay in this place enamoured of cotton factories."[1] Self-conscious, precious, and occasionally homoerotic in tone, Wilde's fan letters show the stirrings of an American Aestheticism that was to feed into the culture as a whole. His American manner, a calculated mix of European sensitivity and brash individualism, had obvious attractions for that perennial American type: the cultural exile.

The lectures that Wilde delivered in America were unsystematic and partly extemporized, hasty oracles that often emerged as oppositions, each set leading to the next by way of historical or intellectual contingency. In the most developed of the lectures, "The

English Renaissance of Art," he maintains the common nineteenth-century distinction between the Hellenic and medieval spirits—aesthetic repose against mysterious vision—and proposes that these two currents have been synthesized in modern romanticism, which is characterized by *individualism*—community and history felt through the isolated consciousness—and *relativism*—the belief that all perceptions, emotions, and ideas are constantly evolving and can be understood only by reference to each other and to temporal change. The most celebrated locus for the concept of relativism—a vitally important one in the middle and late nineteenth century—is the opening passage of Pater's essay on Samuel Taylor Coleridge: "Modern thought is distinguished from ancient by its cultivation of the 'relative' spirit in the place of the 'absolute.' . . . To the modern spirit nothing is, or can be rightly known, except relatively and under conditions." Behind Pater's summing up lay influences with which Wilde too had become familiar—Darwinian science and Hegelian metaphysics. "In the work produced under the modern romantic spirit," declared Wilde in his lecture, "it is no longer the permanent, the essential truths of life that are treated of, it is the momentary situation of the one, the momentary aspect of the other that art seeks to render," and he linked this ambition with democratic aspirations: the desire felt by every man since the French Revolution to express himself according to his mood and the moment. In the survey of English romantic poetry that follows, Wilde tends to dismiss Shelley for being overanxious to escape from the circumstances of life, preferring William Blake for his belief that art must be specific and Keats for pursuing the perfection of beauty. Blake and Keats were revolutionary poets because their work reflected the influence of intellectual change upon art, and their immediate descendants are the Pre-Raphaelites and the members of the Aesthetic movement.

Wilde goes on to say that the artist's individualistic dedication to beauty has led inevitably to his estrangement from a public that no longer perceives the revolutionary origins of his art. The artist, moreover, has been obliged to make use of new techniques and new conditions, to reexamine his own creative activities. The emerging proposition, —which borders upon paradox—is that the spontaneous production of art can only be preserved by self-consciousness on the part of the artist. At this point we might seem to have come some way from

---

[1]From letters housed in the William Andrews Clark Memorial Library, Los Angeles.

the revolutionary spirit that Wilde originally projected as the source of the romantic movement, and we move on to what might initially look like an entirely different matter: the elevation of form over feeling, cornerstone of "art for art's sake." This shift is signaled by the mention of Théophile Gautier and Charles Baudelaire. Yet Wilde's argument is not inconsistent: art is a product of the imagination, not simply of the passions, and the artist is distinguished from the rest of mankind by his imaginative capacity to produce inspiring forms. The dicta that follow, that painting is merely "a beautifully colored surface," for example, stem from the precept that the artist must first of all respect his own imagination and his material if he is to avoid the public demand for consumption, for trivial meanings and conventional morality. Only by so doing will he ultimately be of any real value to that public.

Within Wilde's argument there lie many ironies, of which the most profound is the way in which he has rescued idealism from the implacable forces of relativism with which he began. Not only has he moved from society as a whole to individualism and then back again, but in the course of his purposive meanderings he has lit upon several aesthetic formulas, few of them his own invention, which he will repeat again and again throughout his career. "To most of us the real life is the life we do not lead"—this is because the life we do not lead is the life that we desire. The poet can express this desired life by becoming "the spectator of all time and of all existence." Hence the distinctive responsibilities of the critic, who must teach the public "the spirit in which they are to approach all artistic work." Yet art does have its interactions with life: in the drama, for instance, we discover "the meeting-place of art and life." Although "one should never talk of a moral or an immoral poem—poems are either well written or badly written, that is all" (here Wilde is translating directly from Gautier), there is crucially "la consolation des arts" (also taken from Gautier), which makes life endurable.

IV

In 1883, soon after his return from America, Wilde spent three months in Paris, working on poems and plays and discussing literature with Stéphane Mallarmé, Paul Verlaine, and other members of the symbolist and Decadent schools. On his return he devoted his energies to consolidating his position as a writer. In 1884 he married Constance Lloyd, who came from a family of Dublin lawyers, had a moderate inheritance, and was interested in Aesthetic furnishings and fashions. Wilde described her as "quite young, very grave and mystical, with wonderful eyes, and dark brown coils of hair." The following year they moved into a house in Tite Street, Chelsea, decorated for them with dramatic simplicity by the Aesthetic architect E. W. Godwin. The Wildes had two sons in quick succession: Cyril, born in 1885, and Vyvyan in 1886, and they seem, at least to start with, to have led a happy and not unconventional domestic life. Yet W. B. Yeats's memory of the Wilde household in his *Autobiographies* (1926) suggests something more troubling, as if an effort of will were involved in the creation of an ideal environment: "It was perhaps too perfect in its unity, his past of a few years before had gone too completely, and I remember thinking that the perfect harmony of his life there, with his beautiful wife and his two young children, suggested some deliberate artistic composition."

Wilde's professional life—that of a tolerably industrious and versatile free-lance writer and journalist—was altogether less ordered. In 1887 he became editor of *The Woman's World*, a magazine that supported such progressive movements as Rational Dress; and elsewhere he reviewed books on many subjects. A combination of financial pressure and professional expediency obliged him to reconsider his métier, and it is with his changing ambitions in mind that we should assess the diversity of writings that belong to this period in his career. The tone of his work, too, had begun to change and some critics have suggested that this may have had to do with his initiation—or reinitiation—into the homosexual world.

He started producing short stories about survival in Victorian London, with its glamor, its squalor, its public opportunities, and its secret lives. It is an eerie world, where decay and expansion, plenitude and suffering exist side by side. Although Wilde's theme is success in fashionable orbits, an edgy interplay between style and concealment mirrors the larger duplicities of society as a whole. Many of his characters are possessed by a divided consciousness, but division is also implicit in the way that his narrative tone exploits the gulf between the lives that they lead and the beliefs that they profess to hold. As a general rule the survivors are those who have an ironic awareness of social hypocrisy, but that by no means guarantees their moral blamelessness.

The hero of "Lord Arthur Savile's Crime" (first published in periodical form in 1887) is told by a fortune-teller that he is destined to commit murder. This prophecy puts him in an alien state of mind in which he perceives, for the first time, terrifying discrepancies between the self and its roles. Concluding that the world is beyond his rational understanding, he resolves to act according to superstition, and fulfills and assuages the augury by killing the fortune-teller. Luckily for Lord Arthur, "Life to him meant action, rather than thought. He had that rarest of things, common sense." Had he possessed a superior mind—the mind of Hamlet, say, Wilde's favorite comparison—and confined himself to thought, the potential for self-destruction might have been greater. It was perhaps with his own disquieting sense of the imbalance between thought and action that Wilde proceeded with his secret life.

In the essays that Wilde wrote in the 1880's, the distinction between ideas and morality becomes an adjunct to a more immediate concern: the artist's realization of his own personality in a repressive and philistine society. The concepts of art and personality become almost, but not quite, synonymous; together they take priority over all other considerations and maybe justify all means. An increased stress upon antinomian, even illegal, behavior no doubt derived from his involvement with Verlaine, his continuing study of Baudelaire, and the stresses of his own sexual life.

In 1886 he delivered a lecture on Thomas Chatterton, doomed boy poet and literary forger, which was never published, and in 1889, "Pen, Pencil and Poison," an account of Thomas Wainewright, author and murderer. Both men became ironical models of the artistic personality: the forger Chatterton because he "claimed for the artist freedom of mood. He saw the realm of the imagination differed from the realm of fact,"[2] and the murderer Wainewright because in the pursuit of a fulfilling identity he flouted the most basic of social taboos. Wilde was exploring a theoretical paradox, which, although easy to summarize, was put to many uses. The artist is either congenitally unlike other people or is obliged to become unlike them because of his special

needs: "he is lacking in wholeness and completeness of nature," and he can fulfill himself only in his art. Yet to estimate fulfillment in terms of production alone would be to act like the philistine, the governor of the society from which he is estranged; and so it turns out that the artist, by extending his art into life, finds his true completion in style, in his very refusal to produce. He seeks to "be somebody, rather than to do something"; Wilde's modification of the Paterian emphasis on "being" joins Baudelaire's idea of the dandy to supply a definition of the artist that scorns the three major shibboleths of the philistine: fixed morality, material production, and innovation as the measure of social progress.

In Wilde's interpretation Chatterton and Wainewright subvert the rules of society first by concealing their activities and later by flaunting them. The fact that these were fictionalized portraits with no claim to precise historical accuracy helped him to manipulate an ambiguity between "crime" in the sense of evil deeds and crime as simply that which the law forbids. There was a parallel ambiguity in his use of the word "sin," which might denote either a theological or a social offense. Either way the association of such words with art places the artist outside a society that in Wilde's view flattered itself with the belief that civil and moral laws were largely in coincidence. As we shall see, society's willful myopia on that score had particular significance for homosexuals, and in Wilde's next experiment with fiction, homosexual undertones became much more audible.

"The Portrait of Mr. W.H. " (1889) opens a series of narrative Chinese boxes worthy of the Argentine writer Jorge Luis Borges. A brilliant exposition of a developing aesthetic theory, a credible hypothesis conceived within a fiction that is itself based upon a forgery, the story propounds the idea that it was the actor Willie Hughes who provided Shakespeare with his major inspiration. In their researches Wilde's spokesmen encounter many aesthetic riddles, of which the most important is the notion that just as Shakespeare found in the actor a living projection of his own aspirations as an artist, an incarnation of the multiple possibilities of his art, so it is true for all sensitive men that "consciousness, indeed, is quite inadequate to explain the contents of personality. It is art, and art only, that reveals us to ourselves." The playwright creates the forms that the actor embodies; the actor provides the playwright with inspiration. In the objective or "impersonal" forms of literature, in a theatrical role, for example, the ar-

---

[2]From manuscript notes in the William Andrews Clark Memorial Library.

tistic personality is made visible. Thus the impersonal turns out to be an aspect of the personality: the paradox is explicit, but in Wilde's theory, to which he was to remain faithful, the impersonal and the personal continue to confront each other in a perplexing series of exchanges where art is both the means and the end.

The sexual implications of theatrical metamorphosis are to be seen in an extreme form in the case of Elizabethan boy actors, who were of course required to portray women. Wilde's story suggests that sexual encounters parallel the creative interchange, most pertinently perhaps in homosexual relationships, where, it is sometimes said, since both partners are of the same sex, the subject might more easily rediscover itself in the object of its desire.

One curious feature of "The Portrait of Mr. W.H.," which Wilde may not have fully admitted to himself, is that these potent sexual myths run the risk of being undermined by the very flexibility of the aesthetic theory. The objective ideal may be a necessary fiction, opposed to those dull or misleadingly verifiable facts that confine the personality to restrictive circumstance, yet to locate that ideal in a mirroring object who is also another person is not simply to practice solipsism but to court ultimate fragmentation of the self: other people are themselves prone to treacherous shifts of personality, and none more so than actors, who are called upon to embody a wide range of personalities. Fortunately the art of the theater incorporates the element of illusion that accompanies this psychological truth, when it returns its participants and its spectators to mutable experience.

That early remark, "To most of us the real life is the life we do not lead," offers a clue to the importance of fantasy in Wilde's thought; and in his fairy tales, as in his murder, mystery, and ghost stories, Wilde found that fantasy and parable could combine—though his method was to take the reader to the brink of a moral insight without quite introducing him to it. Wilde used the fantastic modes as a means of projecting his own concerns upon readers whose responses were already engaged by familiar literary conventions.

The first audience for the fairy tales was probably Wilde's own sons. Children are of all people the most bound up with their own behavior, yet the most oblivious to what is expected of them, and in that respect alone, as Wilde liked to point out, they are father to the man. His stories take the consciousness of a child as their subject but in a thoroughly unpatronizing way: these are sophisticated works, attractive to all generations, and they have recently been submitted to rigorous critical analysis. Some of the stories have to do with dreams of a return to a primeval universe and the difficulties in isolating a pure motive, others with the mixed blessings of self-awareness and the illusions that follow any attempt to preserve a mirror relationship with the natural world. These are the problems of what Wilde calls the "soul," and although they are normally resolved with a wry acceptance of the dualities of human life, the specific problem of aesthetic experience remains intransigent within them.

"The Young King" (first published in periodical form in 1881) is an Aesthete who gains his greatest pleasure from contact with beautiful things; he finds in them an "anodyne to pain." In his dreams he discovers the unsettling truth that beautiful objects are made by the poor for the rich. Yet when he acts upon this revelation and dresses as a beggar he is resented by his people; and it is only when he is transfigured after gazing at an image of Christ that they recognize his saintliness. In "The Happy Prince" (1888) a swallow and a statue renounce material beauty to satisfy their charitable impulses. The statue loses his gilded surface, the swallow forgoes the sensuality of Egypt, yet when they die the pair are rewarded with permanent residence in an Aesthetic paradise, a city of gold, where the swallow, like one of Yeats's mechanical birds, will sing forever more.

In these stories Wilde outlines two realms of beauty: the transient and the permanent, the meretricious and the meritorious, but he gives no indication that noble deeds will bring forth any reward other than the embodiment of a higher Aesthetic ideal. The progression is rather from an innate capacity to appreciate beautiful things to an awareness of what the creation of that beauty involves in human terms, to a final point, reached only after suffering and sacrifice, when a transcendent beauty is attained. The fairy tales tell of the refinement of Aesthetic principle; the beauties of the moral life, which in themselves compensate for nothing, are only discovered when Aesthetic indulgence has been transformed. This makes Wilde's parabolic fantasies simultaneously liberating and repressive. His Aesthete-martyrs achieve their transcendence only after partial confrontation with repressed knowledge—the knowledge of "cost." If satisfaction is at first unwittingly at the expense of others—their labor and suffering—in its later moral phase it is at the expense of the Aesthete himself—the renunciation of beauty. Finally, in the dream of art and sympathy reconciled, transcendence becomes collaborative, since the Aesthete's charity is rewarded by admiring love, and the quality of beauty is attributed to his personality. Whether the Aesthete should ever forgo that admiration and beauty, the remaining demands of his voracious individualism, was an issue that was so sensitive as to be entrusted only to the wisdom of children.

The problematic reciprocity between the Aesthete and his fellow men mirrors the relationship between an artist and his audience, the inevitability of which Wilde was obliged to point out in his dealings with the painter James McNeill Whistler. Early in his career Wilde had borrowed from Whistler the principle that beauty lies in appearance as it is rendered by an artist and is not an essential quality of the subject, but when the two men quarreled in the mid-1880's—largely in fact over Wilde's supposed plagiarism—it was Wilde who showed himself to have advanced to the more complex position. Whistler's claim, heard at its most provocative in the famous "Ten O'Clock Lecture" of 1885, was that "the master stands in no relationship to the moment at which he occurs—a moment of isolation—hinting at sadness—having no part in the progress of his fellow men." In reviewing the lecture Wilde pointed out that the artist could not escape his conditions quite so easily:

An artist is not an isolated fact; he is the resultant of a certain *milieu* and a certain *entourage,* and can no more be born of a nation that is devoid of any sense of beauty than a fig can grow from a thorn or a rose blossom from a thistle.[3]

As we consider Wilde's extended critical statements we find that they are all concerned with the problems that result when an emergent formalism (the belief that the artist has complete freedom to transform the appearance of the world in his art) is juxtaposed with an equal conviction that art cannot be disengaged from the circumstances of its production, including of course the circumstances of the artist himself.

[3]From "Mr. Whistler's Ten O'Clock," in the *Pall Mall Gazette* (21 February 1885).

V

FOR his two major investigations into aesthetic theory Wilde fittingly chose a dialogue form. "The Decay of Lying" (1889) features "Cyril" and "Vivian" (the names of Wilde's sons); "The Critic as Artist," "Ernest" and "Gilbert." Both were printed first in periodicals and then in a volume called *Intentions* (1891), along with "Pen, Pencil and Poison" and an uncharacteristic essay on the "archaeological" method of staging, "Shakespeare and Stage Costume," now known as "The Truth of Masks." Dialogue serves a double purpose: it dramatizes a pedagogic method on Socratic lines, and it places the reader in the role of eavesdropper instead of addressing him directly. The title *Intentions* suggests that the dialogues are in some sense unfulfilled, and, as we shall see, they both end in paradox and not in formal resolution. Although Wilde leaves himself free to express an internal dialectic (so that the speakers together compose Wilde himself), there is still a clear division into master and pupil. The "pupil" (Cyril or Ernest) expresses conventional wisdom, the tedious consistency of public opinion (or more specifically of the edicts of its intellectual leaders), which the "master" (Vivian or Gilbert) exposes and replaces. At the same time Wilde protects himself from the dangers of proposing a new orthodoxy because the dialogue as a whole retains its literary autonomy: it is a "mask" that confesses "intentions" as yet unrealized.

"The Decay of Lying" is primarily an attack against the principles of realism on the ground that they assume a collusion between the artist and his audience that is socially and imaginatively inhibiting. Wilde's aim is to free art from the constraints of a previously conditioned audience, but in order to do so he has to give art an independent value; he has to resort yet again to "the ideal," although he remains opposed to the kind of social attitudes that idealize present knowledge. First of all he refutes the critical position that appeals to nature as the basis for art. Nature, says Vivian, presents us with a dull uniformity, whereas the human imagination is capable of an infinite variety. A lie is an expression of this variety because it spurns external evidence, and art is like a lie because it too refuses to be subjected to empirical proof, and need not be explained by reference to an affective or utilitarian function. Life can only benefit when it follows the variety of art rather than the monotony of nature.

Art remains in advance of life: consequently life imitates art more than art imitates life. We have reached the central paradox, the hinge of the dialogue.

The argument grows more obscure when we arrive a little later at its formal justification, and the pronouncement that "scientifically speaking, the basis of life—the energy of life as Aristotle would call it—is simply the desire for expression, and Art is always presenting various forms through which the expression can be attained." A page or so later we read that "art never expresses anything but itself." All this seems very muddling unless we are prepared to accept a perfect circularity: art is the source, the means, and the end of its own energy, and it develops by converting everything into itself, forever inventing new forms. The conclusion to "The Decay of Lying" seems to suggest a slight qualification of that extreme position, however, for there Vivian tells Cyril that "the self-conscious aim of life is to find expression."

The second dialogue, "The Critic as Artist," takes the problems of "self-consciousness," "expression," and "development" as far as they will go, blithely replacing Arnold's maxim that it is the aim of criticism to "see the object as in itself it really is" with an assertion that "the primary aim of the critic is to see the object as in itself it really is not." What Wilde means by this paradox is that it is the function of the critic to see the object as it might be, as other people fail to see it, especially when they conceive of themselves as a homogeneous mass. The critic is the ideal audience because he is independent of his time, free from the coercions of popular taste, and therefore supremely individual. Yet on a biological model he is a perfect specimen, summing up within himself the inherited wisdom of the past and projecting it into the future. Moreover he is an embodiment of the principle by which relativism leads to the ideal, since his subjective freedom multiplies the meanings of art through imaginative associations. The more complex, indeed the more contradictory, his impressions, the more complex and vital art will be seen to be.

Furthermore Gilbert is adamant that the realization of art takes place not in action but in contemplation. The critic does not implement his impressions, he does not forcibly apply them to any aspect of life outside the experience of art. (Although we might recall that according to "The Decay of Lying" the appearance, if nothing else, of life will be changed by exposure to art.) Nor does the critic make the fatal mistake of judging art by moral values, even if his very passivity, "being" rather than "doing," does allow an inner progression—"becoming."

Wilde adds several more twists to an already mazy pattern. The view that by "intensifying" his "impressions" within his "personality" by means of his "curiosity" (the vocabulary is Pater's but exaggerated), the critic increases the mystery of art, allows for the reintroduction of "sin," "an essential element of progress," which carries the argument to the point where it issues forth in the most notorious of all Wilde's pronouncements, "All art is immoral." Just as the meaning of "sin" hovers between the theological and the secular, so "immortal" can equally be taken to mean "amoral," that is, oblivious to socially validated codes, and "imagination" can be substituted for "art." Yet Wilde himself admits the interaction between art, ideas, and value, for Gilbert is soon to announce, as he draws into his closing movement, that the imagination is "simply concentrated race-experience." It is through their ever increasing consciousness of themselves, fed by their contemplation of art, their ability to turn first the objective into the subjective (from "art" to "impression") and then the subjective back into the objective (the "mask"), that the critical spirits are able to express within themselves the gropings toward the ideal that less developed intelligences still search for in a consensus response to art. "The Critical and the World Spirit are one": now in the very final moments comes the Hegelian transfiguration of the Aesthetic critic, the dreamer who has as his punishment and his reward that "he sees the dawn before the rest of the world."

Despite the undoubted circularity of Wilde's system we are still free to enjoy the manner of its exposition. The most interesting questions relate to Wilde's need to perform in this way. Why should a writer of such incisive intelligence get himself in such a tangle? There is a general answer to that question. We have seen that Wilde never attempts to distinguish art from what is not art, nor does he examine the reference of the word "beauty," though he does on occasion lend it to what was not generally thought to be beautiful. Both "art" and "beauty" are, in a word, *absolutes*, whose meaning exists apart from their application. The philosophical problem here—the relationship between word and thing—is as old as aesthetics itself, but it had become acute in the later part of the nineteenth century as the romantic tradition confronted a world in which both the nature of production and the very appearance of human surroundings had radically altered. Wilde's nominalism no less than his satirical tactics was a brilliantly evasive reaction to this changed environment, and his vision of a world that is fit for critics to live in is utopian. But then "England will never be civilised till she has added Utopia to her dominions." In "The Soul of Man Under Socialism" (1891) he was a little more precise about where it might lie.

On this single occasion Wilde entered the public arena wearing no other mask than his subversive wit. "The Soul of Man" is prescriptive in the manner of someone who is making his own polemical contribution to a general debate. This after all was the period of the Fabian Society lectures, to which George Bernard Shaw contributed, and of William Morris' *News from Nowhere*.[4] The essay opens with a few smacks at favorite targets: bogus altruism, charity, and all the false virtues that try "to solve the problem of poverty . . . by keeping the poor alive"; as well as at "a very advanced school" who try to solve the problem "by amusing the poor" (possibly a reference to the People's Palace, a philanthropic organization in the East End of London whose aim was to bring culture to the working classes; Wilde had himself applied for the post of secretary in 1886).

Probably influenced by the anarchist tradition, Wilde strongly attacks private property, conceding only that under present circumstances the prophetic freedom of the individualist-aesthete is likely to depend upon his creating the material conditions that will help him to realize his "beautiful and intellectual life." Wilde's system proposes a progression from the individualism of the few to socialism, which is the individualism of the many. This was a common enough idea at the time, although just how it might come about always remained obscure: individualism would have to be a motive force for change in itself. In "The Critic as Artist" Wilde had referred to "the just rancour of the criminal classes"; in "The Soul of Man" he compares the virtuous poor, so degraded that they accept their state, with the criminal classes, who have reached that point of self-awareness where rebellion sets in. (Elsewhere Wilde equated the "criminal" and the working classes in a rather crude way, largely because he considered the law to be exclusively a repressor of freedom and not, even in a

class-dominated society, as guarantor of certain minimal liberties. Already he may have had one particular piece of legislation in mind: the Criminal Law Amendment Act of 1885, which penalized public and private indecencies between adult males.)

"The Soul of Man" endorses the complete individualist, who, like an artist, stands apart from life, adapting it to his own expression, and who, like a criminal, is opposed to the ordering principles of his society. The most perfect embodiment of this type is Christ, yet even he should be seen as transitional, since suffering and pity will disappear altogether from the future ideal society. As a final flourish proclaims, "The new Individualism is the new Hellenism."

VI

BEGUN in Oxford, almost completed in Paris in 1883 but not published until 1894, when it appeared in a superb edition with illustrations by Charles Ricketts, Wilde's long poem *The Sphinx* straddles this crucial period in his life, and we should not look to it for tight formal coherence. Rather, the poem anthologizes the images of Decadence with which he had familiarized himself by reading French literature, and frames them with a structure taken from Edgar Allan Poe's *The Raven*.

The Sphinx is a riddling *imago*, half-woman and half-beast, who, as Wilde described her elsewhere, is "as old as the world itself, and lives in the desert, and knows everything." Wilde's talent for improvisation enables him to sustain an interminable litany of images that conjure up the ancient wisdom, images that are culled from many sources, of which Baudelaire is the most obvious. The rampant inventiveness of the poet's imagination responds to the monstrous sexual energy of the Sphinx, with sacrificial invocations to fecundity of the kind that are associated with primitive sacrificial rites. A roll call of talismanic proper names and increasingly excited apostrophe mesmerize the will of poet and reader alike in authentic symbolist fashion. When the permutations are finally cut short with a return from pagan to Christian images, we are as disappointed as we are skeptical, for the power of myth to displace so thoroughly the controlling mind of the poet suggests some unspoken ground shared between him and the reader: Yeats's *Anima Mundi* perhaps or, in another vocabulary, the "unconscious."

[4]R. Shewan, *Oscar Wilde. Art and Egoism* (London, 1977), a study of Wilde's unpublished commonplace book, also shows the important influence of the essays and lectures of W. K. Clifford.

But the Sphinx keeps her secrets, and the poet must keep his too—which is that he alone might know what the secret is. A similar use of symbolist techniques to convey mysterious temptations is to be found in "The Harlot's House," also written in Paris (and first published in the *Dramatic Review,* April 1885). Here the occupants of a brothel appear to the poet like puppets in some ghastly tableau, shadowy figures whose mechanical dance of death flaunts the power of lust to destroy the individual will. When confessional fantasy manifests itself in poetry in this way, the motivation remains a secret that lies between the writer and his text, explicable only to the reader who keeps himself at one remove. A comparable approach must operate in a reading of Wilde's only novel, *The Picture of Dorian Gray* (1891).

VII

Dorian Gray comes to us obscured by a scandal that was largely of Wilde's own making. The novel was first serialized in *Lippincott's* magazine in 1890 and then revised (probably to remove overt homosexual emphases) before it reached hard covers. Nevertheless the book was greeted on publication with a storm of protest against the supposed immorality of the story and, even more, of Wilde's preface to it. Indeed the preface has attracted so much attention over the years that the story has sometimes been taken as merely a demonstration of its precepts. However, as a novel, much of the interest of *Dorian Gray* resides in its narrative method. It should be read obliquely, with a ready eye for collusion and disparity between author and character.

Wilde uses the first person very rarely, and by far the greater part is recounted in a third-person narration, which appears to be distanced from the characters yet knowingly at ease with their world. Even so the central consciousness of the novel is Dorian's: he is the most important, the most interesting, and probably the most intelligent of the characters. In contrast to Basil Hallward and Lord Henry Wotton, moral idealist and amoral cynic respectively, both condemned to failure and regret, Dorian alone has the capacity for growth through change. As Wilde himself confessed: "Basil Hallward is what I think I am: Lord Henry what the world thinks me: Dorian what I would like to be—in other ages, perhaps." Dorian, though not an artist, is deeply interested in art. His great mistake, of which he is at least inter-

mittently aware, is to abuse both art and life by forestalling their potential in order to preserve the present. That Dorian should ultimately fail to halt the process of aging in himself is biologically inevitable, but the problematic relationship of art to the processes of change is more difficult to understand; indeed it might not appear as a problem had not Wilde already made it one. In his critical essays Wilde retains a commitment to the absolute value of art, while affirming that it is an organic expression of the mood of its maker. He tries to explain subsequent difficulties with the theory that the meaning of a work is realized only within the changing consciousness of the person who views it. Dorian reverses this idea when he renounces change in himself and transfers that potential to a picture, although he finds that he cannot help but retain some of the feelings that initiate and accompany change. His experiment thus paradoxically reveals the problems within his author's aesthetic theory, and the maxims that Wilde put forward in his preface act as a kind of smoke-screen to the honorable confusions within the novel. Where the preface plays with intellectual divisions, the novel restores their interrelatedness. "There is no such thing as a moral or an immoral book," says the preface, separating art from the terms of life; Dorian encounters the illogicality of an Aesthetic life—life as art—that does not encompass moral choice, which, as Pater conventionally pointed out in his review of the book, is an essential part of man's higher function. Dorian's discoveries about art are very pertinent indeed to his author's speculations.

Let us take a single example. Dorian falls in love with an innocent young actress who commits suicide when later he brutally rejects her. He explains his response to her death to Basil Hallward in this way:

"And besides, my dear old Basil, if you really want to console me, teach me rather to forget what has happened, or to see it from the proper artistic point of view. Was it not Gautier who used to write about *la consolation des arts?* I remember picking up a little vellum-covered book in your studio one day and chancing on that delightful phrase. Well, I am not like that young man you told me of when we were down at Marlow together, the young man who used to say that yellow satin could console one for all the miseries of life. I love beautiful things that one can touch and handle. . . . But the artistic temperament that they create, or at any rate reveal, is still more to me. To become the spectator of one's own life, as Harry says, is to escape the suffering of life."

(ch. IX)

It is possible to read that passage as a symposium of opinions, so organized that the authority for voicing them is continually being shifted. Dorian might have been thinking of Gautier's comment about his own poems that "l'art est ce qui console le mieux de vivre" ("art is the greatest consolation for living"), or perhaps of Gautier's observation in his highly consequential preface to Baudelaire's *Les Fleurs du Mal* (1857) about certain phrases that seem, like music, "chuchoter des consolations pour les douleurs inavouées et les irrémédiables désespoirs" ("to whisper consolations for unacknowledged sorrows and despairs without remedy"). Certainly Dorian would also have found in Gautier's preface, as Pater and Wilde no doubt did, an account of a crucial stage in Baudelaire's development: the discovery of his own estrangement from human life, when he becomes "the spectator of life," when "every sensation becomes subject to analysis," and when he "divides" ("se dédouble") and begins to "spy upon" himself.

The novel identifies Dorian as the modern type represented in Gautier's image of Baudelaire. But at the same time Dorian's entreaties to Hallward suggest that he is reaching toward a more advanced version of the idea of the "spectator," for his language also evokes Pater. The astute reader will spot ironies that lie beyond the consciousness of the character. In conversation with Hallward, Dorian outlines his development as he perceives it: his progression from the consolations of the confident "art for art's sake" that Gautier found in Baudelaire, the self-analyzing modern poet, to the restless position of the modern critic as defined by Pater, deeply engrossed with the creative personality that works of art bring into view, and the age of which that personality is a summing up. Dorian seems to aspire to the condition of the ideal critic as Pater described him in *Studies in the Renaissance,* who possessed "the power of being deeply moved by the presence of beautiful objects. . . . The question he asks is always: In whom did the stir, the genius, the sentiment of the period find itself!" In Pater's later book *Marius the Epicurean* (1885), however, the hero progresses from youthful curiosity ("even in his most enthusiastic participation . . . still essentially but a spectator") to a mature wisdom in which the capacities of the observer encompass the magnitude of the world: "the vision of men and things, actually revealed to him on his way through the world, had developed, with a wonderful largeness, the faculties to which it addressed itself, his general capacity of vision." Wilde's novel represents this Paterian striving only by reducing it to the complacent figure of Lord Henry, who observes the world without self-development. Sadly Dorian can do little more than execute Lord Henry's abused and incomplete version of the Paterian ideal.

There is a complex of ideas at work here: an initial proposition that art will console the sensitive man for the suffering in the world, that he can retreat from life and view himself as an object; and there is the larger idea that because art reveals the artist, the man who appreciates art will become a participant in life—the ultimate consolation. The problem for Wilde lay in finding empirical justification for the shift from one vision to the other, when the life that surrounded him appeared fraught with deception and threats to the self. In order to shock his public and to make it aware of its own illusions, he would sometimes exalt the first, concealing his failure to master the second.

Dorian is very like the young Marius, but he is trapped in a transitional moment, a moment that Wilde could perceive but not resolve. Phrases such as "la consolation des arts" and "the spectator of life" are part of the repertoire that Wilde deployed throughout his career, and noting their interchange here helps us to grasp the ironies of the novel and the ways in which the thoughts of its central consciousness enact the impasse of its author. None of Wilde's literary mentors, neither Gautier nor Pater, could solve the immediate historical problem of participation for him, not even by offering him the consolation of ideas.

VIII

THE drama is "the meeting-place of art and life," as Wilde had defined it early on; in later versions he added the rider "where art returns to life." In the 1890's the theater offered him a daring means of self-projection: an immediate involvement with the audience coupled with limitless opportunity for disguise. In the years from 1892 to 1895 Wilde replaced the pose of the Aesthete with a new and triumphant public role: monarch of the West End theater, dandy supreme, impresario of his times. But in other respects his hold on life was far from sure.

In 1891 he had met Lord Alfred Douglas, a sulkily beautiful youth, petulant and unstable, whose father, the marquess of Queensberry, was renowned for the violence of his temper and for the eccentricity of his attitudes to sex, which he saw as directly connected with heredity and purity of the line. Wilde became infatuated with Douglas, and although he continued, in fact increased, his contacts with the London homosexual underground, the two men became extremely dependent upon each other.

In 1892 *Lady Windermere's Fan* opened at the St. James's Theatre to enthusiastic notices, and in the same year a very different kind of play was put into rehearsal, though it was not to reach the stage: *Salomé.* Both plays show Wilde to be as intent as ever on his search for an appropriate form even though the medium had changed, and *Salomé* is Wilde's most extreme and personal expression of Decadent feeling.

"Death," claimed the poet Wallace Stevens, "is the mother of beauty," catching in a phrase a romantic and symbolist obsession; but for the Decadent there was an equal truth to be found in a converse speculation: might not beauty, he wondered, be the mother of death, might not there be some remorseless progression from the kind of life that art demanded to the ignominious and unresolved oblivion that would follow it? The Decadent's concern with his own demise was precipitated by uncertainties about the nature of the artistic life, and it is these that *Salomé* explores.

Notwithstanding the wealth of contextual material to be found in Mario Praz's *Romantic Agony* (1933) and the many insights in Frank Kermode's *Romantic Image* (1957), it may still be hard for us to respond to Wilde's play seriously, knowing of the several rival treatments of the theme, and perhaps concurring with the opinion that in the hands of Richard Strauss an overwritten drama became a powerful opera. Thanks in part to Aubrey Beardsley, who provided a famous set of illustrations to the published text, and to the busy imaginations of set designers, *Salomé* comes to us as the epitome of kitsch. But there can be no doubt that Wilde himself took his play with the utmost seriousness. Whatever the precise influences upon him (and scholars are still divided on the question) his choice of subject was not simply opportunist; nor was his choice of language—he wrote the play in French—a mere whim. Wilde deliberately sought the kind of hieratic cadence and monotonous simplicity most satisfactorily achieved in French symbolist poetry and drama. His belief in the artistic integrity of the play was ironically confirmed when the English censor forebade its perform-

ance in London on the ground of sacrilege, even though rehearsals were already underway with Sarah Bernhardt in the title role. Wilde's threat to leave the country in protest was not entirely empty.

When *Salomé* was published in French in 1893 (an English translation did not appear until the following year), the reviewers greeted it as an entirely representative product of Decadence. "It belongs indeed to the black art," wrote Richard Le Gallienne, then a gauche but ambitious young literary man. "Its motives are monstrous, its colour is evil, its language is lovely and accursed, the very harlotry of language. . . ." Le Gallienne continued in facetious vein with a summary of plot and character. Herodias

is an unimaginative worldly creature. The moon is like the moon, that's all, she says. . . . And amid all the various interests comes the refrain of Jokanaan's voice from his pit proclaiming the day of the Lord. Herod inquires as to who this Son of Man is, and is told of the miracles at Cana and Capernaum and of his raising the dead. Mr. Wilde is amusing here. Herod exclaims that he has no objection to Christ's changing water into wine, and healing the blind—on the whole they are meritorious actions—but he cannot allow him to raise the dead. It would be terrible if the dead were to return!

To this account Wilde replied with some stern, fatherly rebukes:

Why is it that you describe the chill, sceptical, rationalistic Herodias as an "unimaginative worldly creature"? She is far more than that—she is reason in its tragic raiment—reason with its tragic end—and oh! Richard, why say that I am amusing, when Herod hears that in his royaume there is one who can make the dead come to life and filled with the terror at so hideous a prospect says in his insolence and his fear "that I do not allow." "It would be terrible if the dead came back."[5]

Wilde's placing of Herodias helps us to see why he thought of his play as a religious drama whose overall subject includes a clash between rational and imaginative modes of perception.

That is partly expressed in the dialogue, which plays constantly upon the different meanings of the word "look": "You would fancy she was looking for dead things"; "She has a strange look"; "He is look-

[5]From an unpublished letter in the William Andrews Clark Memorial Library. Le Gallienne's review appeared in the *Star* (22 February 1893).

ing at something." In *Salomé* characters are defined by the way they "look." In the major confrontation between Iokanaan and Salomé, two kinds of creative perception meet: the prophetic—aesthetics as an aspect of morality—and the imaginative—aesthetics as an aspect of sensuality. Iokanaan, the ascetic male, renounces and is destroyed; Salomé, the libidinous female, destroys, consummates, and is herself destroyed. We can interpret them as the spiritual consciousness, which attempts to transcend the call of the moment, replacing it with an apocalyptic trust in the future, and the aesthetic consciousness, whose passionate desire to capture the present negates it in the process. But an additional irony suggests the interaction of the two modes, for Salomé is associated, proleptically, with the sterile white moon, and Iokanaan is burning with a passionate black rage. The inclusive antinomies are expressed theatrically in typically symbolist fashion by continual reference to mysterious external phenomena, the moon and the wings of the angel of death. Thus the whole drama—character, decor, and language—is infused with the same set of meanings.

Although death awaits both main characters, the most benighted of all are Herod and Herodias, who are so morally and aesthetically primitive that they dare not pursue the implications of either mode of consciousness. This couple, the clumsy provokers of the action, rely upon empiricism to conceal themselves from themselves. Allowing nothing beyond their immediate needs, they deny their own possibilities, ignoring the fact that others will see in them qualities they prefer not to see in themselves. They are, in short, a pair of pragmatic philistines: Herod, a superstitious and comic voyeur who tries to control everything but his own lust; Herodias, a rationalist who mixes jealousy with self-serving politics. Far less tragic, although they are also "onlookers," are the young Syrian who sacrifices himself for Salomé, naively apostrophizing her as an image of purity, and the page who, with a possibly homosexual motive, attempts to protect the Syrian from involvement.

Which is not to suggest that this is all the play contains. *Salomé* has always attracted commentary, and convincing arguments have been put forward that it is a compromised expression of homosexual guilt, a manipulation of the incest taboo, and Wilde's attempt to expiate the opposing influences of Ruskin and Pater. As a Decadent text, however, the play is characteristic, in that art and sex become all the more

compelling, and all the closer to each other, when contemplated in a mood of deathly foreboding. As Le Gallienne remarked, more wisely this time, "To those who talk of the immorality of the theme, Mr. Wilde might well ask: Is it not a virtuous act to transform evil things to beauty? Doesn't one thus, so to say, *redeem* them?" Finding beauty in ugliness was certainly a Decadent achievement, and so too was Wilde's discovery in religious and dramatic ritual of a perverse means of dramatizing his own state.

When Aubrey Beardsley provided illustrations for the play he included within them caricatures of Wilde himself—as jester and as Herod; most pertinently he turned the round moon into a cypher for the playwright's artful face. Beardsley's purpose was probably malicious, and Wilde was displeased by the illustrations; but a point had been made, and it was one that incriminated Wilde in his work in a way that he should surely have been prepared to admit. The symbolist approach aspired to an overall impersonality that would rid the drama of intrusive moral bias. If Salomé represents the destructive impulses of the Decadent artist, the mode of the play in which she appears aspires to a symbolic wholeness that will appease the artist's hellish solipsism. No wonder then that Wilde took his play seriously. It was his final attempt to become a dramatic writer on his own terms, that is to say, to dominate his audience by transforming the conditions of the theater. But in "The Soul of Man" he had already acknowledged that the theater is inescapably a matter of conditions, and in his four major prose dramas he was to adapt himself to its requirements.

Like Shaw's *Mrs. Warren's Profession* (1893), *Lady Windermere's Fan* relates to a topical genre exemplified by Arthur Wing Pinero's *The Second Mrs. Tanqueray* (1893), the problem play that concerns itself with the sexual morality of women. The play's originality does not lie in its plot nor, though there is much witty dialogue, in wit alone. What gives it its distinctive character is the way in which wit is seen as a part of the moral problem—an interest that links Wilde with the Restoration playwrights. Although it is customary for plays of this type to contain indolent observers (Cayley Drummle in *Mrs. Tanqueray*, Praed in *Mrs. Warren*), Wilde makes more of them than is usually the case and aligns them more generally with other characters. In *Lady Windermere's Fan* the life-style of the dandy, Lord Darlington, becomes a practical option: "If you pretend to be good," he says, "the world takes you very seriously. If you pretend to be bad, it doesn't." This sense of the witty deceit that escapes the hypocrisy of society is shared by almost everyone in the play except the puritanical heroine Lady Windermere, and indeed in Wilde's plays many of the characters sound like Wilde himself. In the dramatic rendering of social convention, the spoils logically go to the person who manipulates his role with the greatest ingenuity, who dupes all the other role-players. Wit is an aspect of this role-playing because it disengages the speaker from the responsibilities of his own identity, and exploits the naive view that upholds the value of sincerity. Yet the play undeniably contains melodramatic and sentimental passages where wit is most noticeable by its absence, and even Darlington is soon arguing, admittedly while attempting to seduce Lady Windermere, that the opinion of the world is of less importance than love. In its final reversals the play is equivocal. Mrs. Erlynne, a woman who has atoned for her dubious past with an act of noble self-sacrifice, chooses to suppress her true feelings behind a brittle façade—a wise person knows that being good means allowing society to think you bad—and Lady Windermere comes to realize that concealment and compromise, if not actual dissembling, are sometimes morally inevitable. She emerges somewhat more tolerant and correspondingly advanced.

In Wilde's next play, *A Woman of No Importance* (1894), we have another dandy, Lord Illingworth; another puritanical young woman, Hester Worsley; and a genuine fallen woman, Mrs. Arbuthnot, whose son, Gerald, is the focus of the drama. In the space of a single day Gerald is offered a position as Lord Illingworth's companion-secretary and discovers that his would-be employer is not only his father but is also attempting to seduce Hester, with whom Gerald is in love. These main characters are surrounded by a bevy of society ladies whose subversive wit confirms the difficulty of performing an authentic act. If Gerald is to reach maturity his only hope is to renounce the cynicism of Lord Illingworth and the society that admires it, without sacrificing his intelligence and gaiety. Guided by his mother, who refuses Lord Illingworth's belated offer of marriage, Gerald opts for morality, but on the basis of experience rather than of innocence.

Gerald's potential might appear to be realized in *An Ideal Husband* (1899) by Lord Goring, a dandy who comes to the aid of his friend Robert Chiltern, a rising young politician. Chiltern is being blackmailed about his past connections with the late Baron Arnheim, an unscrupulous financier; and Chiltern's wife, yet another idealistic puritan, insists that he make a public confession. In conversation with Goring, Chiltern cannot bring himself to deny the fascination that Arnheim's career still holds for him. Indeed he describes their relationship in terms that are reminiscent of that between Lord Henry Wotton and Dorian Gray. But whereas Lord Henry preached "the New Hedonism," the cultivation of sensual pleasure, Baron Arnheim had seduced the young Chiltern with a doctrine based upon the accumulation of power and money. This has acquired heroic proportions in Chiltern's memory. (One is reminded of the financial overreaching of Bernick in Henrik Ibsen's *The Pillars of Society* [1877]: Wilde probably wanted his audience to recognize the type with all its sinister attractions.) Chiltern is torn between lingering admiration for the courage of the ambitious rule-breaker and pitiful attempts to redeem his past through beneficent political acts. Either way, as Goring points out, he is allowing himself to be defined by the rules of society. Goring calls Arnheim's creed "thoroughly shallow"; nevertheless he realizes that the Chilterns must be rescued, and he carries this mission out successfully despite the risks to his own reputation.

Goring's altruism is enough to make one wonder if he should be counted among the dandies at all. He is supremely sensitive to the fluctuations of his own behavior and unswerving in his conviction that it is deference to the idealistic pretensions of public opinion that destroys personal integrity, but he represents a considerable departure from Lord Illingworth. Wilde's initial stage direction—"He is fond of being misunderstood. It gives him a point of vantage"—although carrying the familiar ring of dandyism, is virtually contradicted at a later stage when Goring himself remarks: "I am always saying what I shouldn't say. In fact, I usually say what I really think. A great mistake nowadays. It makes one so liable to be understood."

At the close of the play the Chiltern marriage has been saved, and Goring's own marriage is imminent. Chiltern will continue in politics, a chastened though not necessarily changed man, for he has recanted only his deeds and not the principles upon which they were based. Private values have been restored without any major disturbance to the public system.

What has changed is Wilde's sense of the dandy's

scope. At the very end Goring's fiancée offers him the freedom to "be what he chooses." But we already know that Goring's chosen role is to be a drastically limited one. In reply to his father's remonstrances at his lack of career he has replied, "I prefer it domestic" (an ironical echo of the claim that Wilde had made about *The Sphinx*, that it would "destroy domesticity"). Goring is the most attractive, alternately the most brilliant and the most candid, of all Wilde's surrogates. But this candor is achieved only by presuming a sentimental connection between the realms of human value (love) and public achievement (the great career). The dandy has been driven into a corner; he has triumphed over the moment but now he must retire; his function is fulfilled, and unfortunately it is left to the morally feeble Chilterns to lead society into the future.

An Ideal Husband is quite as eager to expose the "claims of the ideal" as any of Ibsen's plays—at least as they had been interpreted by Shaw—and quite as critical of the coercion that social ambitions exercise upon those people who are misguided enough to respect them. But exposure is as far as Wilde will allow himself to go. Those critics who have variously suggested that Goring fulfills the individualistic ethic foretold in "The Soul of Man," or that he has no need to develop, underestimate the significance of his disappearing act. Goring, wise and honorable man though he is, can have only a marginal claim on our admiration: secure in his inherited rank, sustained by his private income, cushioned by a tolerant wife and understanding valet, he passes into the land of dreams, a smile of sweet insouciance upon his face.

IX

COMEDY is like ignorance as defined by Lady Bracknell: "a delicate exotic fruit; touch it and the bloom is gone." Critics have always claimed, with something like relief, that Wilde's last and greatest play, *The Importance of Being Earnest* (1899), achieves the summit of comic form without the vestigial blemishes of moralism and sentimentality that had marred the earlier plays—a perfection so complete that comment is almost unnecessary. And it is certainly true that the plot precisely fits the traditional requirements of comedy: there is a lost heir miraculously recovered, there is pairing (cousins and brothers), there is a pastoral interlude, there is con-

tinual misidentity. But the presence of these elements proves little in itself—most can also be found in Dion Boucicault's *London Assurance* (1841), for instance, which Wilde may well have had in mind. At the same time critics have enjoyed pointing out that aspects of the play can be related to its author's own activities: that Jack's habit of "Bunburying," for example— avoiding family duties on the pretext of visiting a sick friend—matches the double life that Wilde himself had been living. This makes the play a fantasy about a fantasy: Jack is discovered, as Wilde was to be, but unlike Wilde he survives. The optimism of *The Importance* embraces the dream that duplicity will go unpunished, that everybody's best interests will finally coincide, that reconciliation is the natural order of things. Here pessimism is an attitude that belongs exclusively to the lower orders, who nevertheless obey their masters.

But the secret meanings have never interfered with the play's popularity: it has an immediate reference that gives it distinction within the genre. The miraculous symmetry holds more than a merely personal relationship to the world as Wilde knew it. For Wilde it was "a fanciful, absurd comedy," "so trivial, so irresponsible," but *The Importance* is trivial only in the sense that it laughs at irreducible problems, and absurd in the classic fashion, in that it turns the world upside down. The play is structured as a gigantic paradox in which Wilde's hierarchy of types finds itself the right way up. The dandies are now the true creators of society, who drag even the puritans and the cliché-mongers (Chasuble and Prism) behind them. They invent a world that matches their own needs, and reality obligingly concedes to their demands. But the needs are real enough: from first to last they are financial. Money is an obsessive concern in this play, and it is only when the need for money coincides with its availability that we achieve the ideal state. (By a natural irony this fantasy of solvency was being contradicted by the reality of Wilde's own life even as he wrote, for he was grossly overspending.) Money actually changes the way things look, so that Lady Bracknell's reaction on being told of Cecily's fortune is entirely to the point: "Miss Cardew seems to me a most attractive young lady, now that I look at her. Few girls of the present day have any really solid qualities that last, and improve with time." Inherited investments can of course be waylaid by marriage, which is an investment in heredity and in how people look. But money also changes the way things are, and sometimes things really are the way they look, as Cecily may be beginning to learn:

Chasuble: I suppose you know all about the relations between Capital and Labour. . . .

Cecily: I am afraid that I am not learned at all. All I know is about the relations between Capital and Idleness—and that is merely from observation. So I don't suppose that it is true.

Miss Prism: Cecily, that sounds like Socialism! And I suppose that you know where Socialism leads to?

Cecily: Oh, yes! That leads to Rational Dress, Miss Prism. And I suppose that when a woman is dressed rationally, she is treated rationally—She certainly deserves to be.

(Act II)[6]

But Cecily's innocent wisdom (based on some of Wilde's past enthusiasms) must be contrasted with Gwendolen's wily aesthetic ambition. Gwendolen, the girl who intends "to develop in many directions," quotes her author too: "In matters of grave importance, style, not sincerity, is the vital thing." When Wilde invokes his own past, it is in order to trick his audience into an appreciation of his own contrariness. *The Importance* delights in its display of a comic world in which appearance and reality are continually in exchange with one another; and it seems to suggest that in dealing with that world the mores of the aristocracy offer us, absurdly, the best example.

So the play gratifies a peculiarly English fantasy: it proffers an aristocratic style that successfully derides the pressing worries of the bourgeois life, demoting them to vulgar irritants. Debts are magically paid, relatives ("a sort of aggravated form of the public") are pacified, solicitors are insulted, and women are appeased. On the sunlit Hertfordshire lawns, male eccentricity is the norm, elegance an ultimate and effective defense. Riposte is all. If the nineteenth-century dandy is the bourgeois imagining himself as an aristocrat, then the aristocratic dandy redoubles the fantasy, making it all but impregnable. When Wilde subtitled his play "a serious comedy for trivial people" he was honoring us with an invitation to join a blessed company. Yet to say all this and to enthuse that *The Importance* disarms criticism is to deny it

[6]From the original four-act text, available in the ed. of S. A. Dickson (New York, 1956). The play is usually performed now in a reduced three-act version.

the highest compliment—a final paradox remains for us to appreciate, a paradox within a paradox, a grave truth about the upside-down world. As Wilde's best interpreters, such as Sir John Gielgud, have realized, these people are not finally likeable. They are childish, greedy, often insulting—they are simple. The fantasy world is inhumane, only a callous snob would wish to live in it, and despite everything Wilde was not really a snob—that label among others must be reserved for the solicitor-general who, at Wilde's trial for homosexual indecency in May 1895, asked him, "What pleasure could you find in the society of boys much beneath you in social position?"

X

WE come now to the events that were to change Wilde's life utterly and that have inevitably determined the ways in which he has been remembered. *The Importance* opened on 14 January 1895 and on this, the night of Wilde's most resounding success, the marquess of Queensberry deposited a bouquet of vegetables at the theater. Soon afterward he delivered a card at Wilde's club with the misspelt message: "For Oscar Wilde posing somdomite." Wilde's answer was to sue the marquess for libel, but he lost his case when, during a remorseless cross-examination, it emerged that he had associated with well-known homosexual prostitutes. Almost immediately after the verdict was pronounced, Wilde was arrested and charged with committing indecent acts. Two trials resulted: at the first the jury failed to agree; at the second he was found guilty of several acts of gross indecency with young men and sentenced to two years' imprisonment with hard labor. The belief, on both sides, that Wilde was being tried as much for his aesthetic attitudes as for his sexual activities was greatly reinforced by the considerable use made by the prosecution of his published writings.

At first Wilde was held in London prisons, but he was soon moved to Reading, where, in spite of his friends' efforts to have his sentence commuted, he served the full term. When he emerged from the gates of Reading Gaol in May 1897 he carried with him a long handwritten letter to Douglas, which, for complicated reasons, Douglas probably never read in full. (The complete text was not in fact made public until 1962.) Later known as *De Profundis* (1905), this extraordinary document—which reads more like a manifesto than a personal communication—is by turns acrimonious and maudlin, nostalgic and portentous, despairing and aggressive. Although its ostensible purpose is to confront Douglas with much of the blame for the catastrophe, its psychological origin lies in Wilde's need to confront himself, and in that respect it is, alas, only partially successful. For reasons that are still not entirely clear, Wilde had taken great offense at Douglas' attempts to rally support in France, which, either by accident or design, had tended to center upon the publication of his own poems and of some of Wilde's more fulsome letters.

But it must be stressed that not once in *De Profundis* does Wilde make homosexuality per se the cause of his suffering, and the attack on Douglas refers less to his sexual conduct than to his inherited temperament: "decadence" in its simpler sense of indolence and triviality. Douglas becomes not only Wilde's evil genius but a frightening example of waste and a nightmare reflection of Wilde's own admittedly ironical "cult of idleness"—a thing, a fatal puppet whose purpose is nil, quite literally mindless. "The supreme vice is shallowness," Wilde bewails over and over; "everything that is realised is right," smothering in a Hegelian pun his old belief that only in self-consciousness does the creative act reach fruition. "To be entirely free, and at the same time entirely dominated by law, is the eternal paradox of human life that we realise at every moment," continues that same idea in an attempt to make universal, vatic, what may seem to us merely an expression of fin de siècle anguish or, more narrowly, an epitaph for Wilde's own situation. "I was a man who stood in symbolic relations to the art and culture of my age"; by turning himself into a symbol, Wilde retains yet another concept in the form that he had always known it: the symbol as multifaceted prism that, by refracting the views cast upon it, displays the ideal. So although Wilde is, as he says, "the child of my age," in his life and work he can still claim to transform the forces that have made him what he is. But *De Profundis* exposes these earlier principles to the harsh light of a prison cell.

In the preface to *Dorian Gray* Wilde had claimed that, as an artist, he could express everything. In *De Profundis* he fails to assimilate the contradictory lesson of the novel itself: expression depends upon experience, and experience is limited and affective, changing the artist even as he expresses it. All that Wilde can offer now is change as a transcendent cycle, apotheosis rather than development. As for the artist, Wilde maintains that a gospel of suffering will have to replace the old gospel of hedonism, so that a universal joy can eventually be attained in some ideal future. The sacrificial model, superseded in fact, is Christ. Wilde's final prose mask is a pathetic absurdity, and one can only regret that the comedy of his self-identification is not more fully "realized." It is this protective ambivalence toward himself—passive egocentricity, epigrammatic piety—that makes Wilde's prison letter not revelation but gossip, at first embarrassing, then disappointing.

In prison Wilde endured the most extreme mental and physical discomfort. On his release he was unwilling to admit the extent of the psychological damage, but it was soon to become only too apparent. He made a brief stop in London, then journeyed to France, and the final phase began. It was to take him from Dieppe to Naples, to Rome, to Switzerland, finally to Paris. These last years present an unappealing spectacle. Wilde was plagued by financial worries, his relationship with Douglas went through a series of death throes interspersed with short periods of ecstatic reunion, he became paranoid about his friends' loyalty, and he was forever haunted by his loss of the one talent that had never previously let him down: his ability to write wittily, swiftly, fluently. For Wilde the final consolations lay not in art but in alcohol, boys, and—on his deathbed in a seedy hotel room in 1900—the Roman Catholic church. Yet it is possible to find some dignity in what he wrote after 1895: however lacrimose and distracted, the need for historical self-knowledge persisted.

The only completed piece of writing from these last years is *The Ballad of Reading Gaol* (1898). Critics have habitually complained that the poem alternates between an elegy of the human condition and a protest against the inhumanity of man-made laws. It is as if Wilde had lost his usually deft control over the transactions between actor and spectator and the multiple personality had become all but unmanageable. As the poem declares, "For he who lives more lives than one / More deaths than one must die." In his efforts to place himself in some appropriate relationship to a condemned man, Wilde suppresses the knowledge that the man's crime—murder—is of a radically different kind from his own alleged offenses. It would not be surprising, given his extreme misery, if Wilde had lost sight of ethical and legal distinctions, may perhaps even have wished to forget them. We have already noticed how, in *De Profundis*, he makes indulgence and betrayal, and not homosexuality, his crimes against himself.

Two especially puzzling stanzas seem to claim that sympathy with the criminal means identifying with the crime and hence repeating it:

> But there were those amongst us all
> Who walked with downcast head,
> And knew that, had each got his due,
> They should have died instead:
> He had but killed the thing that lived,
> Whilst they had killed the dead.
>
> For he who sins a second time
> Wakes a dead soul to pain,
> And draws it from its spotted shroud,
> And makes it bleed again,
> And makes it bleed great gouts of blood,
> And makes it bleed in vain!
> (*The Ballad of Reading Gaol*, pt. 4, 25–36)

The moral point here is obscure, suggesting perhaps a deeper level of sensibility than that of corporate guilt, as if Wilde were desperate to increase his alienation from the commonplace maxims, or perhaps to push beyond the comforts of vicarious emotions to the harsher realities of physical sacrifice exemplified by the crucifixion. In Wilde's work sympathy had always been a deceptive virtue that easily turned itself into a means of possession through emotional patronage, and sacrifice had already been retained for the superior man. In his final writings it is as if Wilde had to identify himself with Christ because with no other example could he do himself justice. Alternatively, in a mockery at such pretension, he would sometimes offer himself as a clumsy anomaly, "like ape or clown." On the seesaw of personality there was no longer any chance of poise, only an endless sickening alternation of roles. One section of *The Ballad* echoes *The Harlot's House*, reconvening the images of the dance of death in order to present the prison as a deterministic hell in which the structure of a microcosmic social life takes on the patterned finality of a doomed universe.

The emotional vertigo of Wilde's last poem is counterbalanced by two letters that he wrote to the *Daily Chronicle* protesting against prison conditions: these are full of a passionate common sense. Although it may have been inevitable that in the process of dramatizing his own isolation he turned sympathy into a deadly thing, in his daily practice Wilde,

paradoxical to the end, was too spontaneous a man ever to carry the principle through, too scrupulously aware of the fortunate discrepancies between the possibilities of art and the more pressing claims of life. Our own sympathetic response, prompted by the lasting power of its refrain—"each man kills the thing he loves"—must be to say that *The Ballad* reproduces the perplexities born of moral desperation.

Yet it is more than sympathy that Oscar Wilde inspires in us today; it is gratitude. In any optimistic reckoning of the way we live now there is a considerable debt to be paid to him. At a time when it seemed to many that a creative life could be lived only by the individual artist cut off from his audience, Wilde's literary strategies, for all their contradictions, their lingering idealism, and their tendency to take refuge in mere antithesis, were a bold response to intolerable options. History may yet confirm the prediction for Wilde that an American poet recently ascribed to Walt Whitman:

> Maybe yours will be an essential life—
> one needing *to have been lived*![7]

SELECTED BIBLIOGRAPHY

I. Bibliography. "Stuart Mason" [C. S. Millard], *A Bibliography of the Poems* (London, 1907); *Two Hundred Books from the Library of Richard Butler Glaenzer* (New York, 1911); "Stuart Mason" [C. S. Millard], *Bibliography* (London, 1914), reprinted (London, 1967) with intro. by T. d'A. Smith, still the standard bibliography; *A Collection of the Original Manuscripts, Letters and Books of Oscar Wilde* (London, 1928), catalog of Dulau and Co., Booksellers, lists material from the collections of Robert Ross, C. S. Millard, and Vyvyan Holland; *Catalogue of an Exhibition of Books and Manuscripts in Commemoration of the Centenary of the Birth of Oscar Wilde* (Dublin, 1954); A. Horodisch, *Oscar Wilde's "Ballad of Reading Gaol": A Bibliographical Study* (New York, 1954); J. C. Finzi, *Oscar Wilde and His Literary Circle. A Catalog of Manuscripts and Letters in the William Andrews Clark Memorial Library* (Berkeley and Los Angeles, 1957), supersedes an earlier catalog, *The Library of William Andrews Clark, Wilde and Wildeana* (1922); *Wilde and the 90s* (Princeton, N. J., 1966), exhibition catalog; R. J. Finneran,

---

[7]From R. Howard, "Wild Flowers," in his *Two-Part Inventions* (New York, 1974).

ed., *Anglo-Irish Literature. A Review of Research* (New York, 1976), contains an extensive bibliographical essay by I. Fletcher and J. Stokes, a suppl. is in progress; E. H. Mikhail, *Oscar Wilde. An Annotated Bibliography of Criticism* (London, 1978), the most complete bibliography of secondary material.

II. COLLECTED EDITIONS. *The Writings of Oscar Wilde*, 15 vols. (New York, 1907); R. B. Ross, ed., *The Works of Oscar Wilde*, 14 vols. (London, 1908), an additional vol. containing the apocryphal *For the Love of the King* published in 1922; *The Works of Oscar Wilde*, 12 vols. (New York, 1923), individual vols. contain intros. by W. B. Yeats, A. Symons, and others; G. F. Maine, ed., *The Works of Oscar Wilde* (London and Glasgow, 1948); *Complete Works of Oscar Wilde*, with intro. by V. Holland, new ed. (London–Glasgow, 1966).

III. SELECTED WORKS. *Oscariana: Epigrams* (London, 1895), aphorisms supposedly chosen by Mrs. Wilde; R. B. Ross, ed., *Selected Poems* (London, 1911); R. B. Ross, ed., *Selected Prose* (London, 1914); H. Pearson, ed., *Plays, Prose Writings and Poems* (London, 1930); G. de Saix, ed., *Les Songes Merveilleux du Dormeur Éveillé. Le Chant du Cygne: Contes parlés d'Oscar Wilde* (Paris, 1942; New York, 1979), stories, prose poems, etc., reputedly told by Wilde; R. Aldington, ed., *Selected Works* (London, 1946); H. Pearson, ed., *Essays* (London, 1950); K. Amis, ed., *Poems and Essays* (London, 1956); R. Ellmann, ed., *Selected Writings* (London, 1961); R. Ellmann, ed., *The Artist as Critic* (London, 1968), the major critical essays together with a selection of little-known reviews; S. Weintraub, ed., *The Literary Criticism of Oscar Wilde* (Lincoln, Neb., 1968), a selection of Wilde's reviews; I. Murray, ed., *Plays, Prose Writings and Poems* (London, 1975); R. Gasson, ed., *The Illustrated Oscar Wilde* (London, 1977); I. Murray, ed., *Complete Shorter Fiction* (London, 1979).

IV. SEPARATE WORKS. *Newdigate Prize Poem: "Ravenna"* (Oxford, 1878); *Vera; or, The Nihilists* (London, 1880), drama; *Poems* (London, 1881); *The Duchess of Padua* (London, 1883), drama, first published in Paris (1905), repr. 1908; *The Happy Prince and Other Tales* (London, 1888); *Intentions* (London, 1891), essays; *The Picture of Dorian Gray* (London, 1891), novel, originally appeared in a different version in *Lippincott's Monthly* magazine (July 1890); *Lord Arthur Savile's Crime, and Other Stories* (London, 1891); *A House of Pomegranates* (London, 1891), story; *Lady Windermere's Fan* (London, 1893), drama, produced 1892, also in I. Small, ed. (London, 1980), annotated with an important intro. and cross-references to various versions; *Salomé* (Paris, 1893), drama, English trans. by Lord A. Douglas (London, 1894); *The Sphinx* (London, 1894), verse; *A Woman of No Importance* (London, 1894), drama, produced 1893; *The Soul of Man* (London, 1895), essay, privately printed, originally published as "The Soul of Man Under Socialism" in *Fortnightly Review* (February 1891); *The Ballad of Reading Gaol*, by "C.3.3" (London, 1898), verse; *The Importance of Being Earnest*, three-act version (London, 1899), drama, produced 1895, also in R. Jackson, ed. (London, 1980), annotated ed. of 1899 text with an important intro. and cross-references to various other versions; *An Ideal Husband* (London, 1899), drama, produced 1895.

Essays, Criticisms, and Reviews (London, 1901), privately printed; *De Profundis* (London, 1905), autobiography, an incomplete text, a supposedly complete and accurate version edited and introduced by V. Holland appeared in 1949, but the only reliable text is printed by R. Hart-Davis in *The Letters* (1962); *The Harlot's House* (London, 1905), poem; *The Rise of Historical Criticism* (Hartford, Conn., 1905), essay; R. B. Glaenzer, ed., *Decorative Art in America: A Lecture* (New York, 1906), criticism; "Stuart Mason" [C. S. Millard], ed., *Impressions of America* (Sunderland, 1906); *Constance*, intro. by G. de Saix, in *Les Oeuvres Libres*, no. 101 (Paris, 1954), a play based on Wilde's scenario; *Mr. and Mrs. Daventry*, by F. Harris, intro. by H. Montgomery Hyde (London, 1956), a play based on Wilde's scenario; S. A. Dickson, ed., *The Importance of Being Earnest*, 2 vols. (New York, 1956), four-act version, with facs. of the original MS; *The Portrait of Mr. W. H.* (London, 1958), story, complete version with intro. by V. Holland, originally published 1889; M. Ewing, ed., *Remorse: A Study in Saffron* (Los Angeles, 1961); W. Edener, ed., *The Picture of Dorian Gray* (Nürnberg, 1964), the *Lippincott's* text with variorum notes; *Irish Poets and the Poetry of the Nineteenth Century* (San Francisco, 1972), an 1882 lecture reconstructed by R. D. Pepper; "The House Beautiful: A Reconstruction of Oscar Wilde's American Lecture," by K. H. F. O'Brien, *Victorian Studies* 17 (June 1974); I. Murray, ed., *The Picture of Dorian Gray* (London, 1974), with informative intro. and textual notes; *Some Early Poems and Fragments* (Edinburgh, 1974).

V. LETTERS. *Wilde v. Whistler* (London, 1906), their published exchanges; R. Hart-Davis, ed., *The Letters of Oscar Wilde* (London, 1962), masterly ed., the most important source for all aspects of Wilde's life and work, supersedes all previous selections of the letters, except when they contain significant intros.; R. Hart-Davis, ed., *Selected Letters of Oscar Wilde* (London, 1979).

VI. BIOGRAPHICAL AND CRITICAL STUDIES. R. H. Sherard, *Oscar Wilde: The Story of an Unhappy Friendship* (London, 1902, 1905); F. Blei, ed., *In Memoriam Oscar Wilde* (Leipzig, 1905), contains essays by E. La-Jeunesse, A. Symons, and F. Blei; R. H. Sherard, *The Life of Oscar Wilde* (London, 1906); *Recollections of Oscar Wilde* (Boston-London, 1906), trans. and intro. by P. Pollard, a variation of *In Memoriam Oscar Wilde*; L. C. Ingleby, *Oscar Wilde* (London, 1907), see also Ingleby's *Oscar Wilde: Some Reminiscences* (London, 1922); St. J. Hankin, "The Collected Plays of Oscar Wilde," in *Fortnightly Review*, n.s. 83 (May 1908).

R. Laurent, *Études Anglaises* (Paris, 1910), contains essay on Wilde; Anna, comtesse de Brémont, *Oscar Wilde and His Mother: A Memoir* (London, 1911); "Stuart

Mason" [C. S. Millard], *Oscar Wilde: Art and Morality* (London, 1912), newspaper correspondence and other material relating to *Dorian Gray*; A. Ransome, *Oscar Wilde: A Critical Study* (London, 1922); "Stuart Mason" [C. S. Millard], *Oscar Wilde: Three Times Tried* (London, 1912); W. W. Kenilworth, *A Study of Oscar Wilde* (New York, 1912); R. T. Hopkins, *Oscar Wilde: A Study of the Man and His Work* (London, 1913); E. Bendz, *The Influence of Pater and Matthew Arnold in the Prose Writings of Oscar Wilde* (Göteburg, 1914); A. Douglas, *Oscar Wilde and Myself* (London, 1914); A. Wood, "Oscar Wilde as Critic," in *North American Review* 202 (December 1915); F. Harris, *Oscar Wilde: His Life and Confessions* (New York, 1916), entertaining but unreliable account of Harris' dealings with Wilde, later eds. include a comment by G. B. Shaw; E. Saltus, *Oscar Wilde: An Idler's Impression* (Chicago, 1917); R. H. Sherard, *The Real Oscar Wilde* (London, 1917).

"Stuart Mason" [C. S. Millard], *Oscar Wilde and the Aesthetic Movement* (Dublin, 1920); E. Bendz, *Oscar Wilde: A Retrospect* (Vienna, 1921); L. Housman, *Echo de Paris. A Study from Life* (London, 1923), contains a convincing evocation of Wilde's manner of speech; L. F. Choisy, *Oscar Wilde* (Paris, 1927); H. Davray, *Oscar Wilde: La Tragédie finale* (Paris, 1928); *The Autobiography of Lord Alfred Douglas* (London, 1929).

P. Braybrooke, *Oscar Wilde: A Study* (London, 1930); A. Symons, *A Study of Oscar Wilde* (London, 1930); L. Lemonnier, *La Vie d'Oscar Wilde* (Paris, 1931); A. J. Farmer, *Le Mouvement Esthétique et "Décadent" en Angleterre 1873–1900* (Paris, 1931); L. Lemonnier, "La Condemnation de Oscar Wilde et l'opinion française," in *Revue Mondiale* 102 (January 1931); "J. P. Raymond" and C. S. Ricketts, *Oscar Wilde: Recollections* (London, 1932); M. Praz, *Romantic Agony* (London, 1933; 2nd ed., 1951), repr. with new forward by F. Kermode (1970); G. J. Renier, *Oscar Wilde* (London, 1933); K. Hartley, *Oscar Wilde: L'Influence française dans son oeuvre* (Paris, 1935); M. L. Cazamian, *Le Roman et les idées en Angleterre* (Paris, 1935), has good discussion of *Dorian Gray*; J. Charbonnier, "L'Intellectualisme d'Oscar Wilde," in *Revue Anglo-Américaine* 12 (August 1935); V. O'Sullivan, *Aspects of Wilde* (London, 1936); L. Lewis and J. Smith, *Oscar Wilde Discovers America* (New York, 1936), still the best account of the U.S. tours; L. Lemonnier, *Oscar Wilde* (Paris, 1938); B. Brasol, *Oscar Wilde: The Man—The Artist* (London, 1938); Lord A. Douglas, *Without Apology* (London, 1938).

F. Winwar, *Oscar Wilde and the Yellow Nineties* (London, 1940); Lord A. Douglas, *Oscar Wilde. A Summing Up* (London, 1940); H. Pearson, *The Life of Oscar Wilde* (London, 1946), one of the better biographies; E. Roditi, *Oscar Wilde* (Norfolk, Conn., 1947); R. Merle, *Oscar Wilde* (Paris, 1948); H. Montgomery Hyde, *The Trials of Oscar Wilde* (London, 1948; new and enl. ed., 1962, repr. 1973), still the classic treatment of the trials; G. Woodcock, *The Paradox of Oscar Wilde* (London, 1948); G. Hough, *The Last Romantics* (London, 1949); A. Gide, *Oscar Wilde* (London, 1949), collects in translation Gide's various discussions of Wilde; the marquess of Queensberry and P. Colson, *Oscar Wilde and the Black Douglas* (London, 1949).

H. Montgomery Hyde, *Cases that Changed the Law* (London, 1951); St. J. Ervine, *Oscar Wilde: A Present Time Appraisal* (London, 1951); G. C. Leroy, *Perplexed Prophets* (Philadelphia, 1953), contains section on Wilde; A. Ojala, "Aestheticism and Oscar Wilde," in *Annales Academiae Scientarum Finnicae*, 2 vols. (Helsinki, 1954–1955); V. Holland, *Son of Oscar Wilde* (London, 1954); *Adam* 22 (1954), special Oscar Wilde issue; A. Harris, "Oscar Wilde as Playwright: A Centenary Review," in *Adelphi* 30 (May 1954); R. Merle, *Oscar Wilde; ou la "Destinée" de l'homosexuel* (Paris, 1955); A. Wilson, "Oscar Wilde," in *London* magazine 2 (February 1955), searching investigation of Wilde's personality and sense of comedy; J. D. Thomas, "Oscar Wilde's Prose and Poetry," *Rice Institute Pamphlet* no. 42 (October 1955); O. Reinert, "Satiric Strategy in *The Importance of Being Earnest*," in *College English* 18 (October 1956); M. Peckham, "What Did Lady Windermere Learn?" in *College English* 18 (October 1956); R. Foster, "Wilde as Parodist: A Second Look at *The Importance of Being Earnest*," in *College English* 18 (October 1956); F. Kermode, *Romantic Image* (New York, 1957; ppbk ed., 1961); A. West, *The Mountain and the Sunlight* (London, 1958), contains a perceptive ch. on Wilde; B. Ford, ed., *The Penguin Guide to English Literature* 6 (London, 1958), contains "The Last Phase" by A. E. Rodway, which has sensible comments on Wilde's poetry; V. O'Sullivan, *Opinions* (London, 1959).

V. Holland, *Oscar Wilde: A Pictorial Biography* (London, 1960); T. R. Spivey, "Damnation and Salvation in *The Picture of Dorian Gray*," in *Boston University Studies in English* 4 (Autumn 1960); A. Ganz, "The Divided Self in the Society Comedies of Oscar Wilde," in *Modern Drama* 3 (May 1960); E. B. Partridge, "The Importance of Not Being Earnest," in *Bucknell Review* 9 (May 1960); R. Croft-Cooke, *Bosie: The Story of Lord Alfred Douglas* (London, 1963); H. Montgomery Hyde, *Oscar Wilde: The Aftermath* (London, 1963); V. Wyndham, *The Sphinx and Her Circle. A Memoir of Ada Leverson* (London, 1963); B. Charlesworth, *Dark Passages: The Decadent Consciousness in Victorian Literature* (Madison–Milwaukee, 1965), contains ch. on Wilde; H. Schiff, "Nature and Art in Oscar Wilde's *Decay of Lying*," in *English Studies* 18 (1965); J. D. Thomas, "The Soul of Man Under Socialism: An Essay in Context," in *Rice University Studies* 51 (Winter 1965); S. Sontag, *Against Interpretation* (New York, 1966), contains her essay "Notes on Camp"; I. Gregor, "Comedy and Oscar Wilde," in *Sewanee Review* 74 (April–June 1966), perhaps the best single essay on the plays; B. Borelius,

"Oscar Wilde, Whistler and Colours," in *Scripta Minora* 3 (1966–1967); E. San Juan, *The Art of Oscar Wilde* (Princeton, N. J., 1967); R. Ellmann, *Eminent Domain* (London, 1967), contains a subtle exploration of Wilde's influence on Yeats; T. de V. White, *The Parents of Oscar Wilde* (London, 1967), largely supersedes earlier books on the Wilde family; J. B. Gordon, "'Parody as Initiation': The Sad Education of Dorian Gray," in *Criticism* 9 (Fall 1967), first of Gordon's several discussions of the novel; J. Korg, "The Rage of Caliban," in *University of Toronto Quarterly* 37 (1967), on *Dorian Gray*; J. Lester, *Journey through Despair* (Princeton, N.J., 1968), contains discussion of Wilde; A. J. A. Symons, *Essays and Biographies* (London, 1969), contains three chs. on Wilde; P. Jullian, *Oscar Wilde* (London, 1969), an unreliable, gossipy biography; R. Ellmann, ed., *Oscar Wilde: A Collection of Critical Essays* (Englewood Cliffs, N. J., 1969); J. D. Thomas, "The Intentional Strategy in Oscar Wilde's Dialogues," in *English Literature in Transition* 12 (1969).

K. Beckson, ed., *Oscar Wilde: The Critical Heritage* (London, 1970), good selection of contemporary reviews; J. A. Ware, "Algernon's Appetite: Oscar Wilde's Hero as a Restoration Dandy," in *English Literature in Transition* 13 (1970); P. Rieff, "The Impossible Culture: Oscar Wilde and the Charisma of the Artist," in *Encounter* 35 (September 1970); L. J. Poteet, "Romantic Aesthetics in Oscar Wilde's *Mr. W. H.*," in *Studies in Short Fiction* 7 (Summer 1970); R. J. Jordan, "Satire and Fantasy in Wilde's *The Importance of Being Earnest*," in *Ariel* 1 (July 1970); J. B. Gordon, "Wilde and Newman: The Confessional Mode," in *Renascence* 22 (Summer 1970), the best analysis of *De Profundis*; W. V. Harris, "Arnold, Pater and Wilde and the Object As in Themselves They See It," in *Studies in English Literature, 1500–1900* 11 (Autumn 1971); K. Richards and P. Thomson, eds., *Nineteenth Century Drama* (London, 1971), contains J. W. Donohue, Jr., "The First Production of *The Importance of Being Earnest*: A Proposal for a Reconstructive Study"; R. Croft-Cooke, *The Unrecorded Life of Oscar Wilde* (London, 1972); J. E. Chamberlin, "Oscar Wilde and the Importance of Doing Nothing," in *Hudson Review* 25 (Summer 1972); N. Joost and F. E. Court, "*Salomé*, the Moon and Oscar Wilde's Aesthetics: A Reading of the Play," in *Papers on Language and Literature* 8, suppl. (Fall 1972); I. Murray, "Some Elements in the Composition of *The Picture of Dorian Gray*," in *Durham University Journal* 64 (June 1972), compares the 1890 and 1891 texts.

R. Ellmann, *Golden Codgers* (London, 1973), important essays on *Salomé*, Wilde as critic, and Wilde and Gide; M. Fido, *Oscar Wilde* (London, 1973); H. Sussman, "Criticism as Art: Form in Oscar Wilde's Critical Writings," in *Studies in Philology* 70 (January 1973); R. J. Green, "Oscar Wilde's *Intentions*: An Early Modernist Manifesto," in *British Journal of Aesthetics* 13 (Autumn 1973); C. Nassaar, *Into the Demon Universe* (New Haven, Conn.–London, 1974), has

useful insights despite an overstrained thesis; D. Parker, "Oscar Wilde's Great Farce: *The Importance of Being Earnest*," in *Modern Language Quarterly* 35 (June 1974); A. Gardner, "Oscar Wilde's Swansong," in *Dalhousie Review* 55 (Spring 1974), reading of *The Ballad of Reading Gaol*; H. Montgomery Hyde, *Oscar Wilde. A Biography* (London, 1975), the most detailed and trustworthy life so far; J. de Langlade, *Oscar Wilde, écrivain français* (Paris, 1975), Wilde's influence on French writers.

S. Morley, *Oscar Wilde* (London, 1976); E. Bentley, "The Homosexual Question," in *Canadian Theatre Review* 12 (Fall 1976), argues that the condemnation of Wilde was ideologically motivated; D. J. Spininger, "Profiles and Principles: The Sense of the Absurd in *The Importance of Being Earnest*," in *Papers on Language and Literature* 12 (Winter 1976); G. Stone, "Serious Bunburyism: The Logic of *The Importance of Being Earnest*," in *Essays in Criticism* 26 (January 1976); J. Meyers, *Homosexuality and Literature 1890–1930* (London, 1977), contains ch. on *Dorian Gray*; R. Shewan, *Oscar Wilde. Art and Egoism* (London, 1977), ingenious criticism and diligent new research; R. Ellmann and J. Espey, *Oscar Wilde. Two Approaches* (Los Angeles, 1977); A. Bird, *The Plays of Oscar Wilde* (London, 1977), surveys the complete dramatic output; J. E. Chamberlin, *Ripe Was the Drowsy Hour: The Age of Oscar Wilde* (New York, 1977), stimulating attempt to discuss the aesthetic and historical implications of Wilde's ideas; D. Lodge, *The Modes of Modern Writing* (London, 1977), contains an unusual reading of *The Ballad of Reading Gaol*; D. H. Eriksen, *Oscar Wilde* (New York, 1977), critical biography; B. Bashford, "Oscar Wilde, His Criticism and His Critics," in *English Literature in Transition* 20 (1977); P. K. Cohen, *The Moral Vision of Oscar Wilde* (Cranbury, N.J., 1978), fairly conventional literary criticism; K. Worth, *The Irish Drama of Europe from Yeats to Beckett* (London, 1978), has an interesting ch. on *Salomé*; M. S. Helfand and P. E. Smith, "Anarchy and Culture. The Evolutionary Turn of Cultural Criticism in the Work of Oscar Wilde," in *Texas Studies in Literature and Language* 20 (Summer 1978), makes use of Wilde's unpublished notebooks; E. Bentley, "Lord Alfred's Lover," in *Canadian Theatre Review* 18 (Spring 1978), a play; K. Powell, "Oscar Wilde 'Acting': The Medium as Message in *The Picture of Dorian Gray*," in *Dalhousie Review* 58 (1978–1979); B. Bashford, "Oscar Wilde and Subjectivist Criticism," in *English Literature in Transition* 21 (1978).

E. H. Mikhail, ed., *Oscar Wilde. Interviews and Recollections*, 2 vols. (London, 1979); T. Wratislaw, *Oscar Wilde, A Memoir* (London, 1979), with an apt intro. and notes by K. Beckson; J. McCormack, "Masks Without Faces: The Personalities of Oscar Wilde," in *English Literature in Transition* 22 (1979); R. K. Martin, "Oscar Wilde and the Fairy Tale: 'The Happy Prince' as Self-Dramatization," in *Studies in Short Fiction* 16 (Winter 1979); B. Fong, "Oscar Wilde: Five Fugitive Pieces," in

English Literature in Transition 22 (1979); H. Kail, "The Other Half of the Garden: Oscar Wilde's *De Profundis* and the Confessional Tradition," in *Prose Studies 1800–1900* 2 (1979); M. C. Kotzin, "'The Selfish Giant' as Literary Fairy Tale," in *Studies in Short Fiction* 16 (Fall 1979); N. Kohl, *Oscar Wilde. Das Literarische Werk zwischen Provokation und Anpassung* (Heidelberg, 1980), immense survey of Wilde's works with copious references to other critics; K. Powell, "Hawthorne, Arlo Bates and *The Picture of Dorian Gray*," in *Papers on Language and Literature* 16 (1980), intriguing source material; L. Dowling, "Imposture and Absence in Wilde's 'Portrait of Mr. W. H.,'" in *Victorian Newsletter* 58 (Fall 1980), an outstanding piece of "deconstructive" criticism; J. C. Oates, "*The Picture of Dorian Gray*: Wilde's Parable of the Fall," *Critical Inquiry* 7 (Winter 1980); M. Nichols, *The Importance of Being Oscar* (London, 1981), biographical narrative based upon Wilde's witticisms.

P. G. WODEHOUSE

(1881–1975)

David Damrosch

PELHAM GRENVILLE WODEHOUSE—"Plum" to his many friends—wrote ninety-eight books over a period of seventy-five years, virtually inventing the modern comic novel. In his fiction he developed an extraordinarily rich and supple prose, with which he detailed the adventures of a world of eccentric characters, most notably the bumbling Bertie Wooster and his masterful valet Jeeves, and the circle of friends and relations gathered around Clarence, the potty Earl of Emsworth, at his ancestral estate of Blandings Castle. Yet during the 1920s and 1930s Wodehouse was equally prominent as a writer for the stage, and he had a major influence on the development of the Broadway musical. He collaborated on the book and lyrics for thirty-one musicals, in addition to writing seventeen staged plays, not to mention occasional verse and essays for many newspapers and magazines.

Wodehouse's phenomenal output has been viewed in widely differing ways. Immensely popular from around 1915 onward—with sales of more than fifty million volumes at last count, in more than thirty languages—Wodehouse has been cherished by many intellectuals but dismissed by others, and his work has received little critical analysis. His readers are divided between those who admire him as the creator of a perfectly unreal comic universe, existing on its own terms and by its own laws, and those who see in his books a loving—or reactionary—recreation of the vanished late-Victorian and Edwardian world of his childhood and youth. Writing on the occasion of Wodehouse's eightieth birthday, Evelyn Waugh insisted that "Mr. Wodehouse's characters are not, as has been fatuously suggested, survivals of the Edwardian age. They are creations of pure fancy. . . . the language of the Drones was never heard on human lips. It is all Mr. Wodehouse's invention, or rather inspiration. . . . His characters have never tasted the forbidden fruit. They are still in Eden.

The Gardens of Blandings Castle are that original garden from which we are all exiled" (*The Sunday Times Magazine,* 16 July 1961). Against this view, others have observed that Wodehouse always based his locations on places he personally knew and drew many characters from life; while he took care not to specify dates, many details even in his late stories recall the turn of the century. George Orwell went so far as to describe him as "fixated" on his schooldays in the 1890s, and others have followed Orwell in seeing Wodehouse as a schoolboy who, like Peter Pan, refused ever to grow up.

The contradictions in Wodehouse's life began early. He always insisted that he had enjoyed a happy childhood, including a good relationship with a father who was "normal as rice pudding," and yet he was essentially abandoned by his parents during his childhood. His father, Henry Ernest Wodehouse, was a magistrate in Hong Kong; born on 15 October 1881 in the town of Guildford in Surrey, England, P. G. Wodehouse was taken to Hong Kong in infancy, but when he was two, his mother brought him and his two older brothers back to England. She rented a house for them in Bath and engaged a nanny to look after them. She then returned to Hong Kong; Wodehouse scarcely saw his parents during the ensuing dozen years. He was shuttled about among nannies, schools, and aunts and uncles— he had no fewer than fifteen uncles and twenty aunts, by birth or marriage—and his relations with his mother, Eleanor Deane Wodehouse, remained minimal for the rest of her life.

Parents are few and far between in Wodehouse's fiction, and mothers are almost unknown; most of his heroes and heroines are dependent upon their aunts and uncles, especially their aunts, most of whom are irritable, domineering figures. As Bertie Wooster remarks in a story called "The Aunt and the Sluggard" (1916):

It's a curious thing how many of my pals seem to have aunts and uncles who are their main source of supply.... These things cannot be mere coincidence. They must be meant. What I'm driving at is that Providence seems to look after the chumps of this world; and, personally, I'm all for it. I suppose the fact is that, having been snootered from infancy upwards by my own aunts, I like to see that it is possible for these relatives to have a better and a softer side.

(*Carry On, Jeeves*, 1956 repr., p. 93)

From an early age, Wodehouse took refuge in humorous fantasy. In later life, he supposed that he had spent his earliest years "just loafing" before he began to write—at age five. His earliest surviving story, written at the age of seven, already shows a sense of art as creating an enchanted world:

About five years ago in a wood there was a Thrush, who built her nest in a Poplar tree. and sang so beautifully that all the worms came up from their holes and the ants laid down their burdens. and the crickets stopped their mirth. and moths settled all in a row to hear her. she sang a song as if she were in heaven—going up higher and higher as she sang.
    at last the song was done and the bird came down panting.
    Thank you said all the creatures.
    Now my story is ended.

Pelham G. Wodehouse
(Donaldson, p. 46)

In this story, Wodehouse already displays a developed sense of prose rhythm, together with a clear image of himself as author, an emphasis on pleasing the audience, and an ironic awareness of the sheer labor involved in the process.

After ten years of frequent changes of locale, Wodehouse and his older brother Armine were sent to board at Dulwich, a school that was to have a decisive influence on him. There, his schoolmates became a new and better extended family. Though shy and uncomfortable in less stylized social settings, Wodehouse throve on the fellowship and rituals of school life. He excelled at cricket and other sports, succeeded his brother as editor of the school paper, and performed in amateur theatricals. The school, located on extensive grounds in a suburb of London, had been founded by Edward Alleyn, a famous seventeenth-century actor, and it continued to attract children of artistic as well as professional families.

Wodehouse was popular with his teachers as well as with his classmates; though never highly studious, he found that his innate love of language stood him in good stead in the classically oriented curriculum of the day. By the end of his time, his friends later recalled, he could compose Latin and Greek verse as swiftly as he could write English, and the beautifully modulated sentences of his later comic style owe as much to his reading of Virgil and Apuleius as to Charles Dickens and Oscar Wilde. "To me, the years between 1894 and 1900 were like heaven," he later remarked (Donaldson, p. 52).

The influence of Dulwich remained strong for Wodehouse in part because it unexpectedly proved to mark the end of his formal education. Wodehouse came from a prominent family, which traced its lineage back to Bertram of Wodehouse Tower in Yorkshire, who was said to have been an ally of William the Conqueror. A third cousin, the Earl of Kimberly, was William Gladstone's foreign minister during the early 1890s, and three other Wodehouses were Members of Parliament during Wodehouse's adolescence. On his mother's side, Wodehouse had a number of prominent ancestors, including his great-uncle, Cardinal Newman, famous both as a theologian and as one of the great masters of Victorian prose style. Yet Wodehouse's parents were younger children of younger children, and they had no inheritance to look forward to. Wodehouse's father had an adequate salary as a magistrate, and Wodehouse assumed that he would follow his brother Armine to Oxford upon graduation in 1900. His father's fortunes took a turn for the worse in the late 1890s, though, and for an appropriately Wodehousian reason. He made a bet that he could walk all the way around the island of Hong Kong in a single day; in the course of accomplishing this feat, he suffered severe sunstroke. He returned to England on medical leave, at the age of forty-five; unable to resume his duties, he took a disability pension in 1898, and remained on pension for the remaining forty years of his life.

Through connections of his father's, Wodehouse found work as a clerk for the Hong Kong and Shanghai Bank. After three years in the London office, he would be sent East. Wodehouse hated the work, shuddered at the thought of a career as a bank manager in Hong Kong, and set himself to become an established writer before he would be sent away from England. Writing at night and on the weekends, he began sending out a stream of stories to magazines that catered to the market for stories of schoolboy life. He also wrote humorous verse for *Punch* and the *Daily Express* newspaper, and began to contribute topical anecdotes to a humorous column at another paper, the *Globe*. In the fall of 1902 the editor of that column took a five-week vacation, and Wodehouse was offered the chance to write the column for those weeks. Forced to choose between the bank and this very temporary job, Wodehouse resigned from the bank on the spot and never looked back.

THE SCHOOL STORIES

BETWEEN 1900 and 1913, Wodehouse wrote a total of nine volumes' worth of school stories, mostly short stories or novels that were serialized in the *Public School Magazine* and *The Captain,* magazines read both by schoolboys and by Old Boys in later life. Journeyman work, these stories are interesting for the glimpses they give of the later concerns and techniques of the mature Wodehouse. His school stories are at once realistic and stylized, steeped in the conventions of the genre and yet mocking those conventions at the same time. In "Mike: A Public School Story" (1909), a new arrival is asked, "Are you the Bully, the Pride of the School, or the Boy who is Led Astray and takes to Drink in Chapter Sixteen?" (quoted in Usborne, p. 52). Elsewhere in the same book, Wodehouse brings on a lisping younger sister. Prattling children were staples of the genre, but in Wodehouse's story little Gladys Maud Evangeline gets only a single sentence of baby talk before her brother Bob growls, "Oh, put a green baize cloth over that kid, somebody!"

Wodehouse had an equally keen impatience with melodrama, the heart and soul of most school stories, and of much popular fiction in general. In 1901, at the age of twenty, he published an essay titled "School Stories" in the *Public School Magazine*, in which he remarked that "the worst of school life, from the point of view of a writer, is that nothing happens. A time may come when a writer shall arise bold enough and independent enough to retail the speech of school as it really is, but that time is not yet." He goes on to mock stories that feature thirteen-year-olds who develop philosophies of

life as they die of consumption, and adds: "No, the worst thing that ought to happen to your hero is the loss of the form-prize. . . . There should be a rule that no one under the age of twenty-one be permitted to die, unless he can get the whole thing finished in a space of time not exceeding two minutes" (quoted in Usborne, pp. 49–50).

In his school stories, Wodehouse set himself to capture the genuine speech of schoolboys and to show them engaged in plausible activities: winning at sports, dealing with friendship and rivalry, trying to outfox headmasters at exam time. The stories collected in 1903 as *Tales of St. Austin's,* for example, already show Wodehouse's sense of the ironic distance between the elevated diction of boys' adventure stories and the true speech of adolescents. Confronted with the announcement of a surprise examination, one boy "would have liked to have stalked up to Mr. Mellish's desk, fixed him with a blazing eye, and remarked, 'Sir, withdraw that remark. Cancel that statement instantly, or—!' or words to that effect. What he did say was: 'Oo, si-i-r!!'" (p. 9).

Wodehouse also distanced himself from the moralizing emphasis of many school stories; in "The Tom Brown Question," parodying theories of Homeric composition, the narrator discovers that the edifying second half of *Tom Brown's Schooldays* was actually written by a committee known as the S.S.F.P.W.L.W.T.R.O.E.B.A.S.T.H.G.I—"the Secret Society for Putting Wholesome Literature Within The Reach Of Every Boy, And Seeing That He Gets It" (p. 161).

Yet Wodehouse's school stories display certain values that remain strong in his later fiction. Loyalty to friends is all-important, and so are generosity and tolerance. A love of order coexists alongside a mockery of conventionality, of rules for their own sake. Work and self-discipline are valued, so long as they are freely chosen; work under compulsion, serving the arbitrary dictates of figures in authority, is to be avoided by any possible means. People who have ambition and who want to do things for themselves are likely to triumph over all obstacles; people who want to get other people to do things for them are highly suspect. In a sharply drawn story, "How Pillingshot Scored," the title character is manipulated by a big man on campus, Scott, who "could always get people to do things for him." Scott befriends Pillingshot and brings him to his room for tea, simply because his servant is out sick: "'Oh, by the way,' he said, with a coolness which to Pillingshot appeared simply brazen, 'I'm afraid my fag won't be here today . . . So would you mind just lighting that stove? . . . You'll find the toasting-fork on the wall somewhere. It's hanging up. Got it? Good man'" (pp. 13–14).

The St. Austin's stories feature the first in the long series of Wodehouse's amoralists, comic heroes or antiheroes who exist outside the normal conventions of society. Unlike the basely manipulative Scott, Frederick Wackerbath Bradshaw acts—or more often, avoids action—for pure pleasure, the sheer challenge of the game: "he had reduced cribbing to such an exact science that he loved it for its own sake, and would no sooner have come tamely into school with a prepared lesson than a sportsman would shoot a sitting bird" (p. 40). True, in later life, these sterling qualities will render him conspicuous in "the now celebrated affair of the European, African, and Asiatic Pork Pie and Ham Sandwich Supply Company frauds," but in school Bradshaw devotes himself to helping his friends evade the watchful eyes of their masters.

Like Rudyard Kipling, with whom he became friends, Wodehouse continued to see the world in terms of a great game (though not, in Wodehouse's case, the "Great Game" of British imperialism). In his view, at once ironic and deeply serious, adults are always adolescents at heart. The essence of Wodehouse's comedy is the construction of absurd scenarios in which the veneer of adulthood is stripped off and a person's essential immaturity is openly brought into play.

UKRIDGE AND PSMITH

THE immoralist germ of Bradshaw developed into Wodehouse's first two memorable characters, Ukridge and Psmith. Stanley Featherstonehaugh Ukridge was based in part on a schoolmaster Wodehouse knew of who tried to run a struggling chicken farm. Ukridge served as the chief comic character in Wodehouse's first adult novel, *Love Among the Chickens* (1906), though his role in the plot was subordinate to the love interest of a young couple. He later became the hero of a series of short stories. A rogue and a swindler, yet generous in spirit, good with dogs, and an opponent of all conventionality, Ukridge becomes, above all, a great talker, always hatching implausible schemes that will surely save him from the indignity of taking a steady job, always borrowing from his friends against the day when he will come into real cash.

Ukridge is at his best in small doses; Wodehouse went further with Psmith, initially a secondary character in the later school stories, then a hero in his own right once he went off to Cambridge. Psmith—who has added the silent "P" to his name to make it more interesting—is a natural aristocrat, a sublime talker, disinclined to work except on his friends' behalf; he floats through life with amused detachment, parodying every style he encounters and every author he reads, unflappable even when confronted by a gangster's gat. This occurs in *Psmith Journalist* (1915), the most memorable of the Psmith stories. In this book, Psmith visits New York, where he unexpectedly becomes involved in championing slum reform, combating both the gangsters and the politicians who prefer business as usual. In the process, Wodehouse gives a detailed picture of the mixed motives of the publishers of muckraking journalism—sincerely reformist, yet also sensationalistic, ever concerned with audience and the bottom line. The book is also a bravura exercise in style, counterpointing Psmith's Oxbridge English against Brooklynese and several other versions of "ordinary" English. Wodehouse never again wrote such a realistic work, and yet the more fantastical worlds of Blandings Castle and the Drones Club are similarly grounded through Wodehouse's sharp eye for psychologically revealing detail and his flawless ear for the nuances of many-leveled speech.

AMERICA AND MUSICAL COMEDY

WODEHOUSE was drawn to the American setting of *Psmith Journalist* because he was living in New York when he wrote it. He had been making extended visits since 1909 and was there when war broke out in 1914, making trans-Atlantic travel difficult. He stayed until 1919. American magazines were paying much better than British publications, and Wodehouse rapidly found a steady market for fanciful tales with aristocratic English settings. He had already begun to be active in British theater in the previous decade, and during his time in New York he quickly established himself in the world of musical theater. He became theater critic for *Vanity Fair* in 1915, and in December of that year he reviewed a musical composed by Jerome Kern, with book and lyrics by Guy Bolton. Within days, he had become friendly with Kern and Bolton, and they soon agreed to collaborate, with Bolton and Wodehouse creating stories and dialogue, and Wodehouse writing the lyrics.

The trio produced eight musicals in the next eight years, most of them enormous successes. Before then, musicals had generally been comic revues, with musical numbers loosely connected to a contrived farcical plot. Wodehouse, Bolton, and Kern worked to integrate story and music much more fully, and Wodehouse soon became famous as one of Broadway's premier librettists. He approached the writing of lyrics very differently from his contemporaries, for whom the usual method was to have the librettist write the song lyrics, to which the composer would then set a tune. Wodehouse felt that song lyrics should not be conceived independently of the music; instead, he preferred for Kern to give him a melody, to which he would set words. The result was more fluid and ear-catching, and Wodehouse soon found himself in great demand. Within two years, he became the most active writer on Broadway, with no fewer than five shows performing simultaneously in 1917; he later collaborated with George and Ira Gershwin, among others.

Wodehouse's attachment to America was strengthened by the fact that in New York he met his future wife, Ethel Newton Rowley, an English widow with a charming young daughter, Leonora. The courtship resembled the love-at-first-sight plots that are common in Wodehouse's stories: he met Ethel in August 1914, and they were married in September.

For the next twenty-five years, Wodehouse and his family commuted back and forth across the Atlantic, their movements closely related to the timing of theatrical productions in New York and London. By contemporary standards, Wodehouse's musicals and plays are highly contrived, and they are rarely performed today, but they had important effects on his fiction. His stories and novels took on a new scenic coherence; his complex plots flow unusually well because they are visually conceived and readily take shape in the mind's eye as one reads. Wodehouse applied many lessons from stagecraft to his fiction, as can

be seen in a comment from 1923 on the actions that are appropriate to major and minor characters respectively:

It is an error, I think, ever to have your villain manhandled by a minor character. Just imagine Moriarty socked by Doctor Watson. A villain ought to be a sort of scarcely human invulnerable figure. The reader ought to be in a constant state of panic, saying to himself: "How the devil *is* this superman to be foiled?" The only person capable of hurting him should be the hero.

(Edwards, pp. 96–97)

Wodehouse would complain hilariously about the unreasonableness of producers' demands, as in a depiction, in "The Agonies of Writing a Musical Comedy," of writing for a pair of ballroom dancers who wish to become musical comedy stars—"both artistes, though extremely gifted northward as far as the ankle-bone, go all to pieces above that level, with the result that by the time you reach the zone where the brains and voice are located, there is nothing stirring whatever" (in *The Uncollected Wodehouse*, 1977, pp. 30–31). But all his life, Wodehouse loved the craftsmanship of writing, and he was often stimulated to his best work by the requirements of editors and producers.

The interplay between Wodehouse's dramatic and fictional work is well illustrated by the story of *Spring Fever*, published as a novel in 1948. An actor and producer wished to put on the story as a play in New York, and Wodehouse rewrote the novel into a play, changing its locale from England to Hollywood in the process. The production fell through; never one to waste his work, Wodehouse rewrote the play as a new novel, differing from *Spring Fever* largely in its Hollywood setting and the names of the characters; this was published as *The Old Reliable* in 1951.

Above all, Wodehouse's theatrical work led him to make a decisive shift from realistically based comic romance to the more farcical, uniquely Wodehousian world of his mature style. Wodehouse once wrote that "I believe there are only two ways of writing a novel. One is mine, making the thing a sort of musical comedy without music, ignoring real life altogether; the other is going right down deep into life and not caring a damn" (Donaldson, p. 11). Like many of Wodehouse's remarks, this is an exaggerated and self-deprecating contrast, for the fascination of Wodehouse's work lies in his ability to present his farcical world with remarkable realism, even as his prose style provides all the music one could wish for; yet it remains true that from 1915 onward his books become something new in humorous writing, novels that can well be described as musical comedies in prose.

DURING 1914, as Wodehouse was writing of Psmith's slum-clearing adventures in New York, he was also beginning a novel set at the imaginary Blandings Castle, home of Clarence, Earl of Emsworth, and his ludicrous family. *Something New* (1915; published in England as *Something Fresh*) was Wodehouse's first best-seller, and it marked the decisive emergence of his own comic world. This world, however, is actually the site at which several very different spheres collide. The aristocratic leisure of the absent-minded Earl and his empty-headed son Freddie Threepwood is counterpointed against the energy of the go-getting American tycoon J. Preston Peters and his daughter Aline, to whom Freddie is engaged. Caught in the middle is a hero who looks remarkably like the young Wodehouse himself: Ashe Marson, struggling writer of dime novels, whom the Mammoth Publishing Company pays poorly for monthly installments of the implausible adventures of Gridley Quayle, Investigator. The author is caught in a sort of indentured servitude to his own character:

The unholy alliance had been in progress now for more than two years, and it seemed to Ashe that Gridley grew less human each month. He was so complacent and so maddeningly blind to the fact that only the most amazing luck enabled him to detect anything. To depend on Gridley Quayle for one's income was like being chained to some horrible monster.

(pp. 14–15)

Wodehouse, who himself had been anonymously turning out quick detective stories among his other ventures, pairs Ashe up with Joan Valentine, an anonymous writer for Mammoth's weekly paper "Home Gossip," which Joan describes as "a horrid little paper, all brown-paper patterns and advice to the lovelorn. I do a short story for it every week, under various names. A duke or an earl goes with each story. I loathe it intensely" (p. 17). These two young writers soon

find themselves involved in an absurd imbroglio involving theft and detection at the Earl of Emsworth's property, thereby bringing together the two genres in which they write. Lord Emsworth has wandered off with an ancient Egyptian scarab belonging to the tycoon Mr. Peters, believing it a gift, while Mr. Peters believes that Emsworth has stolen it from him. Joan and Ashe use their knowledge of the conventions of their own pulp fiction to sort out the tangled situation. In the process, they fall in love, and earn a reward that enables them to loosen the grip of their commercial writing.

Appropriately, this book that mocks the daily fare of the popular magazines sold for what was then an enormous sum, $3,500, to a leading popular magazine, the *Saturday Evening Post*, freeing Wodehouse himself to name his price and choose his audience for his work thereafter. So congenial did the world of Blandings prove that Wodehouse returned to it for a dozen later novels over the years; his last novel, uncompleted at his death at the age of ninety-three, was published posthumously under the title *Sunset at Blandings* (1977). Blandings mellowed somewhat over time, but for several decades there was a real edge to Wodehouse's depiction of this aristocratic world. When Ashe comes to Blandings on assignment from Mr. Peters to track down his missing scarab, his first view of the village of Market Blandings is none too encouraging:

The church is Norman, and the intelligence of the majority of the natives palaeozoic. To alight at Market Blandings Station in the dusk of a rather chilly Spring day, when the south-west wind has shifted to due east, and the thrifty inhabitants have not yet lit their windows, is to be smitten with the feeling that one is at the edge of the world with no friends near.

(p. 83)

The rolling acres of the Blandings estate are beautiful, but the host hides from his guests, who stroll listlessly around the grounds, having nothing in common and nothing to do but abuse their host. Both Ashe and Joan come to the estate in the guise of servants as they seek the scarab, and Wodehouse takes the opportunity to give a detailed picture of life in the servants' quarters. The servants are obsessed with hierarchy and status, snubbing or looking up to each other on the twin basis of their own duties and the social standing of their particular employer. Presiding over the servants' wing is the magisterial figure of Beach the butler, who "had that strained air of being on the very point of bursting which one sees in frogs and toy balloons" (p. 89). Butlers, Wodehouse continues, "seem to grow less and less like anything human in proportion to the magnificence of their surroundings. . . . Beach, accordingly, had acquired a dignified inertia which almost qualified him for inclusion in the vegetable kingdom." Beach's particular form of dignity is perfectly captured in his melancholy disquisitions on his health: "I Suffer Extremely From My Feet. Not only corns. I have but recently recovered from an Ingrowing Toe-Nail. . . . The Lining Of My Stomach is not what I could wish the Lining Of My Stomach to be" (pp. 90, 92–93).

Beach is a minor supporting character, a stock figure well known from the stage, but Wodehouse had found comrades among butlers and other servants during his childhood, when he was often sent off to play in the servants' hall while his aunts and uncles conversed in the drawing room; and he had observed his grown-up friends closely. Beach comes to life through brilliantly chosen descriptive touches: "Mr. Beach said grace somewhat patronizingly. The meal began" (p. 104); in *Pigs Have Wings* (1952), when someone ventures to address Beach as "Cocky," "ice formed on the butler's upper slopes" (p. 93).

Uneasily caught between the upper-class world where they are socially at home and the servants' world whose economic status is closer to their own, Ashe and Joan are fully alive to the incongruities of their situation. Hoping to garner the reward offered for the scarab's return, Joan proposes that her old school friend Aline, Mr. Peters' daughter, take her to Blandings in the guise of her maid. The wealthy Aline is unsure how she should treat Joan, so Joan instructs her to behave "kindly and yet distantly, as if I were a worm, but a worm for whom you felt a mild liking" (p. 65).

The master of Blandings is, nominally, the absent-minded Clarence; in actuality, the place is run by his strong-minded sister Constance, who treats Clarence in much the way an impatient aunt would treat a balky nephew. Inevitably, Emsworth heightens Constance's irritation by his very efforts to forestall it. Wodehouse developed a sly narrative voice, capable of underlining his characters' absurdity even as he seems to take their side. In the opening of *Pigs Have Wings*, Beach brings the mail in to Emsworth, who is ab-

sorbed in reading his favorite book, Whiffle's *On the Care of the Pig*. "Ah, the afternoon post?" Emsworth observes. "'The afternoon post, eh? Quite. Quite.' His sister, Lady Constance Keeble, might, and frequently did, complain of his vagueness—('Oh, for goodness' sake, Clarence, don't *gape* like that!')—but he could on occasion be as quick on the uptake as the next man. 'Yes, yes, to be sure, the afternoon post,' he said, fully abreast" (p. 1).

Constance is only one of three major irritants in Clarence's life, the others being his personal secretary and his younger son Freddie. His secretary, the Efficient Baxter, is always trying to get Emsworth to organize his affairs, and generally to do things, while Freddie would prefer to do nothing whatsoever, other than acquire gambling debts from which his father must bail him out. Kindly and lovable as he is, Emsworth has no visible affection for Freddie. In the British system of primogeniture, in which the eldest son inherits the title and the bulk of the estate, Freddie illustrates "the problem of What To Do With The Younger Sons. It is useless to try to gloss over the fact, the younger son is not required" (*Something New*, p. 23). When Freddie manages to get engaged to the wealthy Aline Peters, "such was the relief [Clarence] experienced that he found himself feeling almost affectionate towards Freddie" (p. 24).

Edenic Blandings may be, but not to Freddie, who chafes at captivity there, mooning about "with an air of crushed gloom which would have caused comment in Siberia" (p. 24). The innocence many readers have celebrated in the portrayal of Blandings is a selective sort of innocence. Lively young heroes and heroines remain pure before marriage and chaste thereafter; death is unknown; endings are always happy. And yet family relations are deeply strained, comically though those strains may be manifested; in *Blandings Castle* (1935), Emsworth still regards his son as "a worse menace to the happy life of rural England than botts, green-fly, or foot-and-mouth disease. The prospect of having him at Blandings indefinitely affected Lord Emsworth like a blow on the base of the skull" (p. 45).

Relations among the older generation are similarly uneasy. Clarence's own younger brother Galahad, a free-living character, is a thorn in the side of their sister Constance. In *Pigs Have Wings*, she recalls an occasion when he came close to drowning: "'just as he was sinking for the last time, one of the gardeners came along and pulled him out,' she added, speaking with a sort of wild regret" (pp. 155–156). Wodehouse underscores this regret, having Constance pause for a moment, "brooding on the thoughtless folly of the chuckle-headed gardener."

Blandings, then, is not simply seen through rose-colored glasses; it is, in fact, seen through monocles, pince-nez, and horn-rimmed glasses as well. At the time he was writing *Something New*, Wodehouse published "In Defense of Astigmatism," an essay on the modern novel, in which he used eyeglasses as his example of the real-life details his supposedly bold contemporaries were too timid to take up: "This is peculiarly an age where novelists pride themselves on the breadth of their outlook and the courage with which they refuse to ignore the realities of life. . . . why, you can hardly hear yourself think for the uproar of earnest young novelists proclaiming how free and unfettered they are. And yet, no writer has had the pluck to make his hero wear glasses" (in *The Uncollected Wodehouse*, pp. 19–20). Wodehouse goes on to imagine a scene involving a young lover named Clarence, who polishes his pince-nez tenderly as he woos his sweetheart. Next, Wodehouse gives a dramatic scenario ("Clarence adjusted his tortoise-shell-rimmed spectacles with a careless gesture, and faced his assassins without a tremor"), pointing out the wealth of new situations such an accoutrement can offer the novelist: "Have you ever considered the latent possibilities for dramatic situations in short sight? You know how your glasses cloud over when you come into a warm room out of the cold? Well, imagine your hero in such a position" (p. 21). He then sketches two hilarious scenes based on this problem.

At Blandings, Clarence does indeed wear pince-nez; the urbane Galahad sports a monocle whose mocking glitter alone can drive Constance up to her room to bathe her temples with eau de Cologne; the Efficient Baxter's suspicious eyes peer through rimless glasses. The world of Blandings, grounded in realistic detail and more socially and psychologically layered than it first appears to be, is a highly conventional world whose true heroes and heroines revel in the absurdity of all convention. This is why Galahad is so irritating to Constance, and why the narrator of *Pigs Have Wings* describes him as "the only genuinely distinguished member of the family" (p. 9). He is distinguished by a zest for eating

well, drinking abundantly, smoking profusely, and exerting himself endlessly on behalf of friends in need. "A pain in the neck to his sister Constance, his sister Julia, his sister Dora and all his other sisters, he was universally esteemed in less austere quarters, for his heart was of gold and his soul overflowing with the milk of human kindness" (p. 10).

Free of the class snobbery and money-consciousness of his sisters—perhaps just because, as a younger son, he has no secure social position and is always in need of cash—Gally befriends butlers, barmaids, and dukes alike. The plot of *Pigs Have Wings* turns on Lord Emsworth's anxiety that his scheming neighbor Sir Gregory Parsloe may steal his prize pig, the Empress of Blandings, so that his own pig can win first prize at an upcoming county fair. Gally rallies round to try to prevent this evil deed, moved both by pity for his brother and by his own financial interests, as he has wagered a hefty sum in Market Blandings that the Empress will carry the day. He is aided in his efforts by Beach the butler, who has evolved over the years into an almost friendly character, and who has also placed a substantial sum on the pig. Wodehouse portrays a sort of freemasonry of the enterprising, cash-starved soul; it is a mark of the sterling quality of the wealthy young heroine of this book, Penny Donaldson, that she too recognizes Beach as "a soulmate and a buddy" (p. 42).

The true coin of Wodehouse's realm is not cash at all but anecdotes; what his free spirits collect as they move through life is a fund of stories, and these tales bestow upon their owners both a wry detachment and also a toleration for the varieties of human conduct. Brought into contact with the earnest and humorless young Orlo Vosper, Gally Threepwood need not ignore him and go off in search of more congenial company, for to Gally all company is congenial: "Orlo Vosper belonged to the human race, and all members of the human race were to Gally a potential audience for his stories. It was possible, he felt, that the young man had not heard the one about the duke, the bottle of champagne and the female contortionist, so he welcomed him now with a cordial wave of his cigar" (p. 119).

Wodehouse had little patience for highbrow literature and satirized the exquisite aesthetes who were often producing it at the turn of the century; perhaps the early Marcel Proust stands behind the figure of Charleton (read: charlatan) Prout, author of *Grey Myrtles* and other Pastels in Prose (*Ukridge*, 1924, pp. 146–147). Yet the aristocratic world of Blandings had for Wodehouse something of the same attraction that the high society of the Guermantes had for Proust: an artificial world in which the social conventions are raised to a higher degree, susceptible of analysis and satire; freed of many of the constraints of ordinary life, the characters can pursue their desires, and vent their feelings, in an endless series of machinations and a constant stream of talk.

BERTIE AND JEEVES

THE snake-filled Eden of Blandings has an urban counterpart in the Drones Club, populated chiefly by the idle scions of aristocratic families and their sporadically active, impecunious younger brothers. The central figure in Wodehouse's Drones Club is Bertie Wooster, who first appeared in a short story in 1917; he soon became closely paired with his valet Jeeves in several stories (*My Man Jeeves*, 1919). Their relationship was fully developed in the stories collected in *Carry On, Jeeves* in 1925, and a full novel, *Thank You, Jeeves*, was devoted to their adventures in 1934. Thereafter Wodehouse returned regularly to them, up through his last completed novel, *Aunts Aren't Gentlemen* (1974; published in the United States as *The Cat Nappers*).

Closely similar in character to Freddie Threepwood, Bertie typically narrates his own adventures, giving Wodehouse the comic opportunity, and the challenge, of conveying complex events and the nuances of social interactions through the voice of an observer whose own devoted servant describes him as "mentally negligible." Bertie is often involved in helping his shiftless friends out of difficult situations, or in disentangling himself from problems, usually some social obligation foisted on him by an aunt, or an undesirable romantic involvement he has somehow backed into; over the years, Bertie is engaged at least nine times, never wisely.

Bertie and his friends are always bailed out by the brilliant counter-plotting of Jeeves, Bertie's valet or "gentleman's gentleman." Recounting his misadventures and Jeeves's miraculous solutions, Bertie plays Dr. Watson to Jeeves's Sherlock Holmes, a comparison often openly made in the stories themselves. Like Watson, Bertie is a kind of Everyman, through whose eyes the reader can indirectly appreciate the almost superhuman skills of the master detective; Bertie's own slowness on the uptake allows Wodehouse, like Conan Doyle, to have Watson/Bertie give the reader clues that he himself does not notice.

Unlike Watson, Bertie is wealthy, having been left a fortune by his deceased father—he never mentions his mother; yet Bertie's wealth earns him no respect. The censorious aunt of one of his friends views him as "a typical specimen of a useless and decaying aristocracy" ("The Aunt and the Sluggard," 1916, p. 110), while the celebrated loony-doctor Sir Roderick Glossop, no enemy to aristocrats in general, displays with Bertie "a knack of making a fellow feel like a waste-product" ("The Rummy Affair of Old Biffy," 1924, p. 133).[1] With the exception of his lively Aunt Dahlia, a sort of female Gally Threepwood, Bertie's own numerous aunts regard him with contempt. He lives in mortal fear of Aunt Agatha in particular, and will cross the Atlantic to avoid her.

Bertie himself is aware that he lacks a certain depth—"it was one of those jolly, peaceful mornings that make a chappie wish he'd got a soul or something" ("Jeeves and the Hard-Boiled Egg," p. 77)—and he becomes comically elated whenever he thinks that he has finally outflanked Jeeves. Though he is always wrong, he admits his failings with good grace, and he has many of the qualities that Wodehouse celebrates. He is intensely loyal to his friends and chivalrous to women—chivalrous to a fault, as he can never break even a dinner engagement, much less an engagement of marriage, however great a misunderstanding may be involved. He has no sense of snobbery and no love of money as such; he does love mystery novels, sunny weather, and the exquisite cooking of his Aunt Dahlia's French chef Anatole. Above all, he rebels instinctively against all sorts of pomposity, all adherence to conventionality for its own sake, all social duties that one is supposed to carry out simply because someone in authority says so.

Bertie's generosity and essential kindness do not prevent him from giving very pointed portraits of the less kindly souls he often encounters,

---

[1]Unless otherwise noted, page references to quoted passages from Wodehouse's short stories are from the 1956 reprint of *Carry On, Jeeves.*

and in Bertie's narratives Wodehouse carries to its highest level his ability to build comic scenes around a bumbling hero who can nonetheless give a very vivid account of his misadventures. By the 1920s, Wodehouse had succeeded in making far fuller use of farcical plots than the usual vaudeville pleasures that come from seeing stock figures stumbling through ridiculous situations. In Wodehouse's mature work, farcical plots work in parallel with the stylized aristocratic settings of Blandings and the Drones Club: absurd situations highlight the problems everyone finds in the stresses and strains of everyday life. When one story requires Bertie to stay at a country house in the guise of his friend Oliver Sipperley, Bertie comments, matter-of-factly, that "it is always a nervous job for a diffident and unassuming bloke to visit a strange house for the first time; and it doesn't make the thing any better when he goes there pretending to be another fellow. I was conscious of a rather pronounced sinking feeling, which the appearance of the Pringles did nothing to allay" ("Without the Option," 1925, p. 153).

Wodehouse's—and Bertie's—characterizations reinforce the effect of setting and plot. Bertie here finds himself in a house party from hell:

"No doubt you remember my mother?" said Professor Pringle mournfully, indicating Exhibit A.

"Oh—ah!" I said, achieving a bit of a beam.

"And my aunt," sighed the prof, as if things were getting worse and worse.

"Well, well, well!" I said, shooting another beam in the direction of Exhibit B.

"They were saying only this morning that they remembered you," groaned the prof, abandoning all hope.
(pp. 153–154)

These characters, moreover, express their inmost feelings with disorienting directness: "I remember Oliver," the mother says, believing Bertie to be Oliver; "she heaved a sigh. 'He was such a pretty child. What a pity!'" (p. 154). Her sister glares at Bertie, still burning with anger because the young Oliver had teased her cat many years before. Wodehouse works the cat theme into the fabric of the scene: a cat appears, and when Bertie stoops to tickle it under its ear, the eighty-six-year-old aunt rushes forward to save the cat, crying "Stop him! Stop him!" A page later, Bertie backs into the cat and steps on its foot, confirming the aunt's worst fears; her now-justified loathing in turn figures in the denouement of the plot.

During the decade before he wrote these stories, Wodehouse had already begun to play down the romantic plot around which comedies were traditionally constructed: the efforts of two young lovers to overcome all obstacles and marry. Wodehouse continued to use the romance plot, but he gave less and less attention to detailing the stages of young love or the emotions of the hero and heroine, concentrating instead on social interactions and on the play of languages and viewpoints. In the Bertie Wooster stories, Wodehouse went further, creating an *anti*-marriage plot that revolves around the need to extricate Bertie (or one of his friends) from an unsuitable marriage.

These marriages are never unsuitable for the social or financial reasons that concern conventionally minded characters like Lady Constance Keeble; they are unsuitable because they involve the wrong sort of person. Wodehouse employs three basic types of young women in his stories: his favored heroines, who always get their man, are energetic, fun-loving, resourceful young women, often self-supporting, a little androgynous in character and typically bearing masculine-sounding names like Bobbie and Corky; these women, however, are drawn to young men with some talent or energy that Bertie apparently doesn't possess. Bertie always becomes engaged to one of Wodehouse's two other types of young woman: gooey, sensitive souls, like Madeline Bassett, who thinks the stars are God's daisy chain, or domineering types who want to reform Bertie and generally buck him up.

When Jeeves first enters Bertie's service, as recounted in a story aptly titled "Jeeves Takes Charge" (1916), Bertie is engaged to Florence Craye, an athletic, philosophically inclined woman. She has set Bertie to reading *Types of Ethical Theory* and plans to send him on to Nietzsche thereafter. Jeeves prevents this marriage from taking place, both for Bertie's sake ("You would not enjoy Nietzsche, sir. He is fundamentally unsound," p. 30), and also out of self-interest, as he has observed that when a bride comes in the front door, the valet of the groom's bachelor days is asked to leave by the back door.

The archetypal threat to Bertie's peace of mind is Honoria Glossop, daughter of the loony-doctor Sir Roderick:

Honoria, you see, is one of those robust, dynamic girls with the muscles of a welterweight and a laugh like a squadron of cavalry charging over a tin bridge. A beastly thing to have to face over the breakfast table. Brainy, moreover. The sort of girl who reduces you to pulp with sixteen sets of tennis and a few rounds of golf and then comes down to dinner as fresh as a daisy, expecting you to take an intelligent interest in Freud.

("The Rummy Affair of Old Biffy," p. 125)

Many of Wodehouse's stories feature clever and athletic young women who deservedly win the hands of relatively passive young men; what distinguishes the Florences and Honorias are three faults: first, the sheer excess to which they take their abilities; second, the degree of mismatch with Bertie, who is not just relatively but absolutely passive; third, the insistence by the activist Florence, Honoria, or Heloise that Bertie must transform himself into their own image.

Wodehouse's passive young men typically have to do some kind of real work in order to overcome the obstacles to their marriage, obstacles often raised by an aunt or a parent who has been hoping for a better match, financially or socially. Even Emsworth's idle son Freddie Threepwood, after marrying Niagara Donaldson, becomes a successful partner in his father-in-law's business. Yet the good heroine always has complete faith in her man from the beginning, schemes to help him meet whatever challenge is posed, and does not herself take social censure seriously except as a practical problem. Florence Craye, by contrast, actually shares her aunts' values, and she is the one who enjoins upon Bertie a heroic act, in the reduced form of the requirement that he steal the manuscript of an uncle's memoirs. In classic conventionalist fashion, Florence is concerned for the social embarrassment that will spread among her parents' friends if Uncle Willoughby's salacious memoirs reach print; equally, she really lacks respect for Bertie as he is: "You may look on it as a test, Bertie. If you have the resource and courage to carry this thing through, I will take it as evidence that you are not the vapid and shiftless person most people think you. If you fail, I shall know that your Aunt Agatha was right when she called you a spineless invertebrate and advised me strongly not to marry you" ("Jeeves Takes Charge," p. 17).

While staying at the Pringle household in the guise of Oliver Sipperley, Bertie finds himself wooed by the formidable Heloise Pringle, who is, naturally, a cousin of Honoria Glossop's. Heloise

expresses her affection by suggesting that "Oliver" fire his valet Jeeves; then, in an eerie moment, she learns that "Oliver" is acquainted with Bertie Wooster, of whom she has heard so much from Honoria: "She gazed at me in a foul, motherly way. 'He can't be a good influence for you,' she said. 'I do wish you would drop him. Would you? . . . It only needs a little will-power'" (p. 161). Though she does not know it, Heloise's "foul, motherly" advice to Bertie is that he abandon himself, an all too accurate image of the effect she wishes to have on him. Her desire that he should exert a little "will-power" is, in reality, a demand that he surrender his will to hers.

When Jeeves intervenes to save Bertie or one of his friends from such a marriage, he displays many qualities in common with Sherlock Holmes: a vast knowledge of recondite information; a keen eye for clues and opportunities that others would miss; a focus on the psychology of the individual; an imperturbable calm even when things go awry. Yet he exercises his abilities very differently from Holmes: whereas Doyle's hero retraces and reveals a hidden plot, discovering what has happened to produce the crime or mystery, Jeeves acts above all to *keep* things from happening. Bertie's own love of inaction is considerable, and it can be carried even further among his friends, such as Rocky Todd in "The Aunt and the Sluggard." Rocky is a poet whose only wish is to stay at home and pen an occasional verse exhorting young people to live life to the fullest. Even Bertie's minimal occupations—dressing for dinner, going to nightclubs—strike Rocky as "a sort of St. Vitus's dance," since he prefers to stay in his pajamas until five in the afternoon, at which point he puts on an old sweater. ("I saw Jeeves wince, poor chap," Bertie comments; "this sort of revelation shocked his finest feelings," p. 98).

At times, characters rebel against the routines of life; at the extreme, they opt out of Wodehouse's world altogether, as in the notable instance of Florence Craye's father, Lord Worplesdon. First manifesting an impatient eccentricity by insisting on dressing for dinner in dress trousers, a flannel shirt, and a shooting coat, a few years later he "came down to breakfast one morning, lifted the first cover he saw, said 'Eggs! Eggs! Eggs! Damn all eggs!' in an overwrought sort of voice, and instantly legged it for France, never to return to the bosom of his family. This, mind you," Bertie adds, "being a bit of luck for the bosom of the family, for old Worplesdon had the worst temper in the county" ("Jeeves Takes Charge," p. 11).

Jeeves can always save the more temperate Bertie and his friends from the threat of change; typically, his method is psychological, grounded in analogy to someone else's response in a parallel situation. Jeeves's skills are less forensic than Holmes's and more narrative: he is a fund of stories of things that have happened to an aunt, a niece, a former employer, or a fellow valet's employer, and the resolutions to all these stories provide his chief resource in assessing unexpected situations. An aunt has been cured of a mania for driving about in hansom cabs; another relative has taken pride in having her stomach condition trumpeted in advertisements for a bromide; his uncle knew of a pair of cyclists named Nicholls and Jackson who were so badly mutilated by a truck that the coroners "collected as much as they could, and called it Nixon" (*Right Ho, Jeeves,* 1934, p. 232). All these anecdotes point the way at one or another difficult moment, and when stories fail, great literature can do the trick. Jeeves has read encyclopedically in Marcus Aurelius, the Bible, Shakespeare, and many more authors, and he always quotes from memory the passages Bertie can never quite dredge up from his school days.

Jeeves is variously compared to a father, mother, wife, and even a lover—Bertie pines for him when he is on vacation. Yet he is always also a servant, and he raises the servant's social invisibility to a semidivine level. In his preternatural skill at self-erasure he may even share traits with Wodehouse's older brother Armine, the one who went on to Oxford just before their father's fortunes faltered, and who became a theosophist and president of a theosophical college in India:

One of the rummy things about Jeeves is that, unless you watch like a hawk, you very seldom see him come into a room. He's like one of those weird birds in India who dissolve themselves into thin air and nip through space in a sort of disembodied way and assemble the parts again just where they want them. I've got a cousin who's what they call a Theosophist, and he says he's often nearly worked the thing himself, but couldn't quite bring it off, probably owing to having fed in his boyhood on the flesh of animals slain in anger, and pie.

("The Artistic Career of Corky," p. 37)

Jeeves is bound to his master by ties of affection and loyalty, by the frequent rewards paid him by Bertie and his grateful friends, and by the supreme malleability of his employer ("in an employer brains are not desirable," he tells us in "Bertie Changes His Mind," p. 230). Yet tensions occasionally arise between master and servant, for Jeeves is a stickler for propriety: not social or moral propriety as such, but the pure propriety of form, expressed above all in dress. He and Bertie recurrently disagree about some item of clothing that Bertie wishes to adopt; Jeeves's reward for solving the story's dilemma always includes—or even consists entirely of—Bertie's reluctant acquiescence to Jeeves's insistence that he give up the loud checked suit, or the soft collar, or even an unsightly moustache; "it seemed to me that it was getting a bit too thick if he was going to edit my face as well as my costume," Bertie complains ("Jeeves and the Hard-Boiled Egg," p. 73), but in the end he gives in.

Clothing displays the kind of order of which Wodehouse approves. The pleasures of dress, like those of the table at the hands of an inspired chef like Anatole, depend upon the creative modification of well-known recipes, the proper balance and harmonious concatenation of established ingredients. Like the detective fiction so many of Wodehouse's characters read and even write, clothes and meals provide pleasure for their own sake. The joy of clothing, like the joy of cooking, goes far beyond the simple provision of warmth or sustenance; in the hands of a Jeeves or an Anatole, it becomes a way of life. Sports work similarly. Wodehouse wrote many stories centered on golf, which becomes a virtual religion for its devotees, a religion with a self-sustaining code rather than divinely ordained commandments, a sublimely pointless and deeply gratifying pleasure.

Wrongly used—indeed, "used" for anything, even to promote good health—such pleasures become duties, ways to meet other people's expectations or else ostentatious signifiers of social status; rightly conceived, they cut across the divisions of society. In *Pigs Have Wings*, it is food that rekindles the love of the wealthy aristocrat Sir Gregory Parsloe for his long-lost sweetheart Maudie, a former barmaid who now heads a detective agency: "when I watched you wading into that Ambrosia Chiffon Pie, obviously enjoying it, I mean to say *understanding* it, not pecking at it the way most of these dashed women would have done but plainly getting its inner meaning and all that, I said to myself 'My mate!'" (p. 141). Food even crosses the boundaries separating species: Lord

Emsworth is never happier than when helping the Empress of Blandings to her daily 57,800 calories, and the rotund Sir Gregory must reject the dictates of an athletic aristocratic fiancée who has forced him onto a crash diet. As he bitterly reflects, "Why should there be one law for pigs and another for Baronets?" (p. 30).

WODEHOUSE AT WAR

IMMERSED in exploring the laws of his satirically skewed fictional world, Wodehouse took less and less interest in the outside world as such, apart from the hothouse worlds of the New York and London theater. In the spring of 1940, Wodehouse and his wife were living in a French village, in a beautiful half-timbered house conveniently located near a major casino; when the Germans occupied the area they were arrested, having resisted friends' appeals to come to safer territory in England, in part because of immunization problems involving their beloved Pekinese dogs. As an alien from a then-noncombatant nation, Wodehouse was interned by the Germans at a prisoner-of-war camp in Silesia for a little over a year; he was released just before his sixtieth birthday and allowed to stay in Berlin, joined by his wife and the dogs.

Wodehouse bore his internment with good humor, taking his share at peeling the few potatoes the prisoners were supplied and also writing away, not making any real concession to his uncomfortable environment. He wrote an entire novel, *Money in the Bank,* (1942), together with half of a second, *Full Moon* (1947); both are among his best books, showing no trace of the setting in which they were composed. Wodehouse seems actually to have enjoyed life in the camp. Refusing to dwell on the physical privation, the separation from his family, and worries about the future, Wodehouse enjoyed the camaraderie of the inmates and their covert resistance to their captors; the camp became for him a sort of adult boys' school.

His approach toward his situation made life there tolerable but caused enormous problems for him thereafter. While in the camp, he wrote a humorous sketch of camp life for an American magazine; getting wind of this, the German propaganda ministry inquired whether he might care to broadcast a few humorous talks to his American audi-

ence. Pleased at the chance to release some of his pent-up observations, Wodehouse never considered the fact that, as England by this time was locked in mortal combat with Germany, many of his countrymen would regard a humorous account of camp life as traitorous propaganda on behalf of the enemy, an implicit denial of the grim rumors that were beginning to circulate concerning the Nazi concentration camps.

Wodehouse made five radio broadcasts in the summer of 1941, which received little attention when broadcast to America but caused a storm of protest when they were rebroadcast to England. Wodehouse had no idea that people being nightly bombed by the Luftwaffe would take offense at an account of earnest, well-meaning German soldiers, described in a tone of ironic self-observation:

One's reactions on suddenly finding oneself surrounded by the armed strength of a hostile power are rather interesting. There is a sense of strain. The first time you see a German soldier over your garden fence, your impulse is to jump ten feet straight up into the air, and you do so. About a week later, you find that you are only jumping five feet. And then, after you have been living with him in a small village for two months, you inevitably begin to fraternize and to wish that you had learned German at school instead of Latin and Greek. All the German I know is *"Es ist schönes Wetter"* and this handicaps conversation with a Bavarian private who knows no English. After I had said *"Es ist schönes Wetter,"* I was a spent force and we used to take up the rest of the interview in beaming at one another.
(Donaldson, p. 224)

Unlike some of the British aristocracy who had been covertly or even overtly pro-fascist in the years before the war, Wodehouse was never a lover of authoritarianism in any form. In 1938 he had parodied the British fascist movement in his novel *The Code of the Woosters* (1938), in which Bertie sharply reproves Spode, a would-be dictator who has founded the Black Shorts party. Typically, Wodehouse focuses his satire on the fascists' clothing, which resembles the shorts worn by soccer players: "The trouble with you, Spode," Bertie remarks,

is that just because you have succeeded in inducing a handful of half-wits to disfigure the London scene by going about in black shorts, you think you're someone. You hear them shouting "Heil, Spode!" and you imagine it is the Voice of the People. That is where you make your bloomer. What the Voice of the People is saying is:

"Look at that frightful ass Spode swanking about in footer bags! Did you ever in your puff see such a perfect perisher?"

(p. 118)

Clear in his own mind about his scorn for Hitler and the whole Nazi ethos, Wodehouse saw nothing wrong with accounts of "beaming" at friendly young soldiers, to say nothing of the unfortunate choice of the term "fraternizing."

Bitter articles were written in England against his broadcasts; Sean O'Casey, for example, described the talks as "the pitiful antics of English Literature's performing flea." In a more measured vein, Malcolm Muggeridge, then a young intelligence officer, concluded that "it wasn't that he was other-worldly or un-worldly, as much as that he was a-worldly. Wodehouse's true offense was to have disinterested himself in the war" (Phelps, p. 223). The price of that disinterest was high. Questions were raised in Parliament, and for years thereafter, successive foreign ministers refused to rule out the possibility that Wodehouse might be tried for treason if he returned to England. He never did. He moved to New York in 1947; in 1955, he and his wife moved to a house on several wooded acres on Long Island, not far from the home of his close friend and theatrical collaborator Guy Bolton. Wodehouse lived there for the remaining twenty years of his life, rarely leaving home even for a night.

Wodehouse gradually came to understand the offense his broadcasts had caused, and he abandoned a book he had begun to write defending his talks, though he did continue to feel that the outcry had been excessive; he rejected out of hand the inflammatory accusations that had been made suggesting that he was a Nazi supporter. He even made an ironic point of pride of O'Casey's literary judgment of his work, and actually titled a 1953 volume of his theater correspondence *Performing Flea.*

Wodehouse's breach with England was symbolically healed in 1975, two months before his death, when he was made a Knight Commander of the British Empire.

THE LATER WODEHOUSE

WODEHOUSE wrote steadily to the end of his life, developing and refining his comic world, especially the worlds of Blandings and of Bertie Wooster and his circle of friends. Some of his best books appeared in his later years, such as *Ice in the Bedroom* (1961), *Galahad at Blandings* (1965; U.S. title *The Brinkmanship of Galahad Threepwood*), and *Much Obliged, Jeeves* (U.S. title *Jeeves and the Tie That Binds*), which he published in 1971 at the age of ninety. This remarkable late career—he published twenty-eight books after the age of seventy—involved mining familiar terrain rather than exploring new areas, but he could do so with considerable success, in part because he had always been inspired by the challenge of reworking established situations. In his early days, those situations were given to him by the conventions of existing popular fiction; from the late 1920s onward, the conventions were primarily those of his own creation or adaptation. As early as 1928, a critic accused him of virtual self-plagiarism, a charge that Wodehouse hilariously took up in the preface to his next novel, *Fish Preferred* (1929; published in London as *Summer Lightning*), a new Blandings story: "A certain critic—for such men, I regret to say, do exist—made a nasty remark about my last novel that it contained 'all the old Wodehouse characters under different names'. . . . With my superior intelligence I have outgeneralled the man this time by putting in all the old Wodehouse characters under the same names. Pretty silly it will make him feel, I rather fancy" (Phelps, p. 158).

In his later fiction, Wodehouse exploits to the full not only the charms of old acquaintance he can expect his characters to provide for his readers but also the surprises that can come when long-familiar characters appear in guises we never would have expected. Thus, in *How Right You Are, Jeeves* (1960), Sir Roderick Glossop surprises the reader no less than Bertie Wooster when he turns up at Aunt Dahlia's country house disguised as a butler named Swordfish. This apparition gives a severe jolt to the heroic sangfroid that Bertie believes himself to possess: "In the eyes of many people, I suppose, I seem one of those men of chilled steel you read about, and I'm not saying I'm not. But it is possible to find a chink in my armor, and this can be done by suddenly springing eminent loony-doctors on me in the guise of butlers" (p. 29). Bertie is somehow unprepared for this role change, even though in *Thank You, Jeeves* (1934), he and Sir Roderick had both donned blackface to disguise themselves as traveling minstrels. In *Uncle Fred in the Springtime* (1939), conversely, Frederick, fifth Earl of Ickenham and an inveterate impersonator, stays at Blandings Castle disguised as Sir Roderick himself.

In the late fiction, some of the emotional rough edges are smoothed; in *How Right You Are, Jeeves*, Bertie even discovers himself feeling fond of Sir Roderick a.k.a. Swordfish: "It seemed incredible that I could ever have looked on this admirable loony-doctor as the menace in the treatment" (p. 104). What has turned the tables for Bertie is a late-blooming sense of fellowship based on the fact that Sir Roderick's disguise, and the attendant plotting in which he becomes involved, restore the doctor to his youth, bringing back his school days, when he—like Bertie a generation later—would sneak into the headmaster's study late at night to steal some biscuits.

Even in this mellow late work, though, financial realities still assert themselves. The romantic lead in the story, "Kipper" Herring, hopes to marry Bobbie Wickham, one of Wodehouse's vivacious, mischief-making heroines, to whom Bertie once proposed but whom he came to see as "pure dynamite, and better kept at a distance by all those who aimed at leading the peaceful life" (p. 10). She and Kipper, however, are made for one another, but Kipper will be unable to marry if he loses his newspaper job. This will happen if his former headmaster sues the paper for libel on the basis of an article Kipper wrote concerning him. Kipper explains that if the suit should go forward, he would not only lose his job but be blacklisted among all the editors in London: "'Herring?' the latter [would] say when Kipper comes seeking employment. 'Isn't he the bimbo who took the bread out of the mouths of the *Thursday Review* people? Chuck the blighter out of the window and we want to see him bounce'" (p. 98). To the end, Wodehouse's artificial world was infused with a healthy dose of reality.

WODEHOUSE'S STYLE

THE paradox of Wodehouse's work is that his greatest gift, his magnificent style, came naturally and effortlessly to him. He labored at length over his plots, drafting and redrafting 30,000-word "treatments" of his novels; once the treatment was completed to his satisfaction, he wrote at great speed. As he remarked in a letter to a friend in 1944, "The actual writing of a story always gives me a guilty feeling, as if I were wasting my time. The only thing that matters is thinking the stuff out" (Donaldson, p. 30). Yet the result was anything but the forgettable, workmanlike prose that such methods would ordinarily produce; all his life, Wodehouse had an extraordinary stylistic gift, an ear for comical clashes of modes and manners of speech, a love of setting clichés and quotations askew, and the ability to convey action and character with great economy through long, hilarious sentences.

Like his plots and characterizations, Wodehouse's verbal play was grounded in close observation of reality. We may recall the early essay in which the twenty-year-old Wodehouse hoped for the day in which the real speech of schoolboys would be recorded in fiction; in his later work, his imaginary characters speak a highly realistic language in their unreal surroundings. Even their less articulate moments are rendered with precision: "Bicky laughed what I have sometimes seen described as a hollow, mocking laugh, a sort of bitter cackle from the back of the throat, rather like a gargle" (*Carry On, Jeeves*, p. 82). Later in the same book: "'On the liner going to New York I met a girl.' Biffy made a sort of curious gulping noise not unlike a bulldog trying to swallow half a cutlet in a hurry so as to be ready for the other half" (p. 121).

Wodehouse's own skill with metaphors is counterpointed against his characters' incompetence with them, and he specializes in circular conversations that occur when someone tries to use a comparison to clarify his meaning. In *Right Ho, Jeeves*, Bertie's shy friend Gussie Fink-Nottle wishes he were a male newt:

"Do you know how a male newt proposes, Bertie? He just stands in front of the female newt vibrating his tail and bending his body in a semicircle. I could do that on my head. No, you wouldn't find me grousing if I were a male newt."

"But if you were a male newt, Madeline Bassett wouldn't look at you. Not with the eye of love, I mean."

"She would, if she were a female newt."

"But she isn't a female newt."

"No, but suppose she was."

"Well, if she was, you wouldn't be in love with her."

"Yes I would, if I were a male newt."

A slight throbbing about the temples told me that this discussion had reached saturation point.

(p. 22)

P. G. WODEHOUSE

Wodehouse's omniscient narrative voice often displays a sort of manic precision, and even Bertie and Emsworth regularly drift into woolly moments of reflection on phrases or quotations they don't understand. Comparing his Aunt Dahlia at one point to Lot's wife, turned into a pillar of salt, Bertie adds, "though what was the thought behind this I've never been able to understand. Salt, I mean. Seems so bizarre somehow and not at all what you would expect" (*How Right You Are, Jeeves*, p. 99). At the start of *Pigs Have Wings*, Lord Emsworth is told that his nemesis Sir Gregory Parsloe is about to walk over to Blandings to see him. Emsworth is startled, but not from any concern about Sir Gregory's intentions:

> Lord Emsworth blinked.
> "Walk?"
> "So Sir Gregory gave me to understand, m'lord."
> "What does he want to walk for?"
> "I could not say, m'lord."
> "It's three miles each way, and about the hottest day we've had this summer. The man's an ass."
>
> (pp. 1–2)

Clarence's insistent focus on the trivial detail of Sir Gregory's mode of arrival would give Lady Constance a headache, but Clarence's surprise has a logic of its own. Sir Gregory, like Clarence himself, is a rotund, elderly man who would not normally engage in any activity more strenuous than ordering food for himself or his prize pig. Something unnatural has, in fact, intruded into Sir Gregory's life: the athletic fiancée who has put him on a crash diet and who is insisting that he get regular exercise to boot.

Having introduced the theme of walking, Wodehouse keeps it in Emsworth's mind; two pages later, when Constance asks him whether he has seen Galahad and another houseguest, Emsworth replies that "'I was looking out of the window and they came past. Going for a walk or something. They were walking,' explained Lord Emsworth, making it clear that his brother and the young visitor from America had not been mounted on pogosticks" (p. 5). This absurd alternative suddenly presents itself to the reader's eye, with a momentary plausibility to those who know Gally; and after all, in Wodehouse's fluid style, characters rarely do anything so simple as walking, even when they are simply walking. They are more likely to toddle, bound, leg it, nip, or charge, to

take just one sequence from a single paragraph in *Carry On, Jeeves*.

Wodehouse's verbal brilliance won him many admirers among his contemporary writers; in 1936 Hilaire Belloc called him "the best writer of English now alive. The head of my profession" (Phelps, p. 200). He was awarded an honorary Doctor of Letters from Oxford University in 1939—to the distress of some; in 1941 Sean O'Casey wrote that "the civilization that could let Joyce die in poverty and crown with an Litt.D. a thing like Wodehouse, deserves fire and brimstone from heaven: and is getting it" (Phelps, pp. 203–204). Yet Wodehouse and Joyce had more in common than either might have supposed: each had an abiding interest in concrete physical realities and the comedy they can provoke; each was a master of a many-leveled modern English prose style; each was steeped both in classics and in popular culture, though Joyce preferred to view that culture from a distance and transform it while Wodehouse remained immersed within it, playing with an ever-ramifying stock of images, quotations, characters, and events.

The ambiguous literary position of Wodehouse's work is perhaps best summed up by one of his own characters, Vladimir Brusiloff, a tragic Russian novelist and secret golf enthusiast who is giving a lecture tour in America in a story called "The Clicking of Cuthbert." Like any great novelist, at heart Brusiloff despises all of his contemporaries, most of all his eminent compatriots Nastikoff and Sovietski. Yet, though Brusiloff specializes in gray studies of hopeless misery, where nothing happens until a muzhik commits suicide on page 380, he does admit to a grudging admiration for one great predecessor and one contemporary writer: "No novelists anywhere any good except me. P. G. Wodehouse and Tolstoi not bad. Not good, but not bad. No novelists any good except me" (in *The Most of P. G. Wodehouse*, 1960, p. 394).

Among the most popular of popular writers, a lover of Shakespeare and of detective thrillers, trained equally on the Greek and Latin classics and on the works of W. S. Gilbert, Conan Doyle, and Kipling, all of whom he knew in his youth, Wodehouse moved all his life along the border between highbrow and lowbrow, just as he crossed and recrossed the Atlantic and turned novels into plays and back into novels again. A master of convention and a mocker of conventionality, he used the time-bound materials of his late-Victorian childhood to create a strangely timeless world: an artificial paradise shot through with reality.

SELECTED BIBLIOGRAPHY

I. NOVELS AND VOLUMES OF SHORT STORIES. When published under different titles in England and America, the later, alternate title follows in parentheses. Later reprints are listed when they have been cited in the text.

The Pothunters (London, 1902); *A Prefect's Uncle* (London, 1903); *Tales of St. Austin's* (London, 1903; repr. London, 1972); *The Gold Bat* (London, 1904); *William Tell Told Again* (London, 1904); *The Head of Kay's* (London, 1905); *Love Among the Chickens* (London, 1906; New York, 1909); *The White Feather* (London, 1907); *Not George Washington* (London, 1907); *The Swoop! or, How Clarence Saved England* (London, 1909); *Mike: A Public School Story* (London, 1909).

The Intrusion of Jimmy (New York, 1910; *A Gentleman of Leisure*, London, 1910); *Psmith in the City* (London, 1910); *The Prince and Betty* (London and New York, 1912); *The Little Nugget* (London, 1913; New York, 1914); *The Man Upstairs* (London, 1914); *Something New* (London, 1915; *Something Fresh*, New York, 1915; repr. as *Something New*, New York, 1943, 1972); *Psmith Journalist* (London, 1915); *Uneasy Money* (New York, 1916; London, 1918); *Piccadilly Jim* (New York, 1917; London, 1918); *The Man with Two Left Feet* (London, 1917; New York, 1933); *A Damsel in Distress* (London and New York, 1919); *My Man Jeeves* (London, 1919); *Their Mutual Child* (New York, 1919; *The Coming of Bill*, London, 1920).

The Little Warrior (New York, 1920; *Jill the Reckless*, London, 1921); *Indiscretions of Archie* (London and New York, 1921); *The Clicking of Cuthbert* (London, 1922; *Golf Without Tears*, New York, 1924); *Three Men and a Maid* (New York, 1922; *The Girl on the Boat*, London, 1922); *The Adventures of Sally* (London, 1923; *Mostly Sally*, New York, 1923); *The Inimitable Jeeves* (London, 1923; *Jeeves*, New York, 1923); *Leave It to Psmith* (London, 1923; New York, 1924); *Ukridge* (London, 1924; *He Rather Enjoyed It*, New York, 1925); *Bill, the Conqueror: His Invasion of England in the Springtime* (London and New York, 1924); *Carry On, Jeeves* (London, 1925; New York, 1927; repr. Harmondsworth, Eng., 1956, including "Jeeves Takes Charge," "The Artistic Career of Corky," "Jeeves and the Unbidden Guest," "Jeeves and the Hard-Boiled Egg," "The Aunt and the Sluggard," "The Rummy Affair of Old Biffy," "Without the Option," and "Bertie Changes His Mind"); *Sam the Sudden* (London, 1925; *Sam in the Suburbs*, New York, 1925); *The Heart of a Goof* (London, 1926; *Divots*, New York, 1927); *Meet Mr. Mulliner* (London, 1927; New York, 1928); *The Small Bachelor* (London and New York, 1927); *Money for Noth-*

ing (London and New York, 1928); *Mr. Mulliner Speaking* (London, 1929; New York, 1930); *Fish Preferred* (New York, 1929; *Summer Lightning*, London, 1929).

Very Good, Jeeves (London and New York, 1930); *Big Money* (London and New York, 1931); *If I Were You* (London and New York, 1931); *Doctor Sally* (London, 1932); *Hot Water* (London and New York, 1932); *Heavy Weather* (London and New York, 1933); *Mulliner Nights* (London and New York, 1933); *Thank You, Jeeves!* (London and New York, 1934); *Right Ho, Jeeves* (London, 1934; repr. Harmondsworth, Eng., 1972); *Brinkley Manor: A Novel About Jeeves* (Boston, 1934); *Blandings Castle* (London and New York, 1935); *The Luck of the Bodkins* (London, 1935; New York, 1936); *Young Men in Spats* (London and New York, 1936); *Laughing Gas* (London and New York, 1936); *Lord Emsworth and Others* (London, 1937; *The Crime Wave at Blandings*, New York, 1937); *Summer Moonshine* (New York, 1937; London, 1938); *The Code of the Woosters* (London and New York, 1938); *Uncle Fred in the Springtime* (London and New York, 1939).

Eggs, Beans and Crumpets (London and New York, 1940); *Quick Service* (London and New York, 1940); *Money in the Bank* (New York, 1942; London, 1946); *Joy in the Morning* (New York, 1946; London, 1947); *Full Moon* (London and New York, 1947), illus. by Paul Galdone; *Spring Fever* (London and New York, 1948), illus. by Paul Galdone; *Uncle Dynamite* (London and New York, 1948); *The Mating Season* (London and New York, 1949).

Nothing Serious (London, 1950; New York, 1951); *The Old Reliable* (London and New York, 1951); *Barmy in Wonderland* (London, 1952; *Angel Cake*, New York, 1952); *Pigs Have Wings* (London and New York, 1952; repr. New York, 1977); *Ring for Jeeves* (London, 1953; *The Return of Jeeves*, New York, 1954); *Jeeves and the Feudal Spirit* (London, 1954; *Bertie Wooster Sees It Through*, New York, 1955); *French Leave* (London, 1955; New York, 1959); *Something Fishy* (London, 1957; *The Butler Did It*, New York, 1957); *Cocktail Time* (London and New York, 1958); *A Few Quick Ones* (London and New York, 1959).

How Right You Are, Jeeves (New York, 1960; repr., New York, 1966; *Jeeves in the Offing*, London, 1960); *The Ice in the Bedroom* (New York, 1961; *Ice in the Bedroom*, London, 1961); *Service with a Smile* (New York, 1961; London, 1962); *Stiff Upper Lip, Jeeves* (London and New York, 1963); *Biffen's Millions* (New York, 1964; *Frozen Assets*, London, 1964); *The Brinkmanship of Galahad Threepwood* (New York, 1965; *Galahad at Blandings*, London, 1965); *The Purloined Paperweight* (New York, 1967; *Company for Henry*, London, 1967; reissued in 1986 by the Paperweight Press of Santa Cruz, Calif., with a preface stressing that "today, interest in paperweights is at an all-time high"); *Do Butlers Burgle Banks?* (London and New York, 1968); *A Pelican at Blandings* (London, 1969; *No Nudes Is Good Nudes*, New York, 1970).

The Girl in Blue (London, 1970; New York, 1971); *Much Obliged, Jeeves* (London, 1971; *Jeeves and the Tie that Binds*, New York, 1971); *Pearls, Girls, and Monty Bodkin* (London, 1972; *The Plot That Thickened*, New York, 1973); *Bachelors Anonymous* (London, 1973; New York, 1974); *Aunts Aren't Gentlemen* (London, 1974; *The Cat Nappers*, New York, 1975); *Sunset at Blandings* (London and New York, 1977).

II. SELECTED ANTHOLOGIES. *Jeeves Omnibus* (London, 1931); *Week-End Wodehouse* (London and New York, 1939); *Wodehouse on Golf* (New York, 1940); *The Best of Wodehouse* (New York, 1949), intro. by Scott Meredith; *Selected Stories by P. G. Wodehouse* (New York, 1958); intro. by John W. Albridge; *The Most of P. G. Wodehouse* (New York, 1960; including "The Clicking of Cuthbert"); *The World of Jeeves* (London, 1967); *Vintage Wodehouse* (London, 1977).

III. SELECTED PLAYS AND MUSICALS. Complete bibliographies for Wodehouse's theater work can be found in the biographies by Donaldson and Phelps listed below.

Sergeant Brue (London, 1904; book and one lyric); *A Gentleman of Leisure* (New York, 1911; book); *Miss Springtime* (New York, 1916; book by Guy Bolton, lyrics by Wodehouse, music by Emmerich Kalman and Jerome Kern); *Oh, Boy!* (New York, 1917; book by Guy Bolton and Wodehouse, lyrics by Wodehouse, music by Jerome Kern; 475 performances); *Oh, Kay!* (New York, 1926; book by Guy Bolton and Wodehouse; lyrics by Ira Gershwin, music by George Gershwin; 256 performances); *The Play's the Thing* (New York, 1926; repr. with three other plays in *Four Plays*, London, 1983); *Rosalie* (New York, 1928; lyrics by Ira Gershwin and Wodehouse; music by George Gershwin and Sigmund Romberg; 335 performances).

IV. ESSAYS AND LETTERS. *The Globe by the Way Book* (London, 1908); *Louder and Funnier* (London, 1932); *Bring On the Girls* (New York, 1953; London, 1954); *Performing Flea* (London, 1953; *Author! Author!*, New York, 1962); *America, I Like You* (New York, 1956; *Over Seventy*, London, 1957); *Plum Pie* (London, 1966; New York, 1967); *The Uncollected Wodehouse* (New York, 1976, including "In Defense of Astigmatism" and "The Agonies of Writing a Musical Comedy"); *Wodehouse on Wodehouse* (London, 1980); *Yours, Plum* (London, 1990).

V. BIOGRAPHICAL STUDIES. The two best biographies, giving very different views of Wodehouse, are Frances Donaldson, *P. G. Wodehouse: The Authorized Biography* (London, 1982), and Barry Phelps, *P. G. Wodehouse: Man and Myth* (London, 1992); both build on and quarrel with an earlier work, David A. Jasen, *P. G. Wodehouse: Portrait of a Master* (New York, 1974). Also of interest are Iain Sproat, *Wodehouse at War* (London, 1981), and N. T. P. Murphy, *In Search of Blandings* (London, repr. 1986).

VI. CRITICAL STUDIES. The best analytical books on Wodehouse are Owen Dudley Edwards, *P. G. Wodehouse: A Critical and Historical Essay* (London, 1977), and Richard Usborne, *Wodehouse at Work to the End* (London, 1977, rev. ed. of his *Wodehouse at Work*, 1961). A general overview is provided by Richard J. Voorhees, *P. G. Wodehouse* (New York, 1966). Other studies are George Orwell, "In Defense of P. G. Wodehouse," in *Dickens, Dali, and Others* (London, 1946); Geoffrey Jaggard, *Wooster's World* (London, 1967) and *Blandings the Blest* (London, 1968); Herbert Warren Wind, *The World of P. G. Wodehouse* (New York, 1972); Robert A. Hall, Jr., *The Comic Style of P. G. Wodehouse* (Hamden, Conn., 1974); J. H. C. Morris and A. D. Macintyre, *Thank You, Wodehouse* (London, 1981); Charles E. Gould, Jr., *The Toad at Harrow* (London, 1982).

VIRGINIA WOOLF

(1882-1941)

Bernard Blackstone

LIFE

VIRGINIA WOOLF's lifetime, a mere fifty-nine years, spans two world wars and the collapse of a civilization. Born on 25 January 1882, in the heyday of Victorian and imperial prosperity, she died by her own hand in 1941, as Hitler's bombs rained down on London. The fragility of intelligence and goodness, the frightening strength of evil and stupidity are the themes of her novels: she did not have to seek them anywhere outside the history of her own life and times.

Leslie Stephen, Virginia's father, the eminent Victorian literary critic and agnostic, had two daughters and two sons by his second wife, Julia Duckworth. Vanessa, his elder daughter, showed her talent for painting at an early age and became a leader of the English avant-garde. Virginia was equally committed, to literature. Without much formal education—she went neither to school nor to university—she had the run of her father's vast library and used it to full advantage. Her mother died in 1885 and her beloved half-sister, Stella Duckworth Hills, in 1897, blows from which Virginia never really recovered; after this her sister and various other maternal women figured in her life as substitutes, never with complete success, as is evidenced by the series of nervous breakdowns that pursued her from 1904, the year of her father's death, to her suicide by drowning.

Her childhood and young womanhood were passed in London, with summer holidays at St. Ives in Cornwall. As a novelist she is both a great Londoner, like Charles Dickens and William Makepeace Thackeray, and a great devotee of the sea and its coasts, like Joseph Conrad. After her father's death, she broke away from the respectable Victorian milieu of Kensington and migrated with her sister and two brothers, Thoby and Adrian, to Gordon Square, Bloomsbury. Bloomsbury at the turn of the century was felt to be shabby and disreputable, and the move earned the disapproval of Virginia's half-brothers by her mother's earlier marriage, George and Gerald Duckworth, and of most of their "society" friends. The offense was compounded when the Stephen sisters turned to a thoroughly bohemian way of life and chatted, unchaperoned, into the small hours with the young men their brother Thoby brought back with him from Cambridge. And so the celebrated or notorious Bloomsbury group came into existence.

Virginia Stephen married a member of the group, Leonard Woolf, in 1912. An ex-official of the Ceylon Civil Service and an old friend of Thoby Stephen's at Cambridge, Woolf was a stabilizing presence in her life. Together they founded the Hogarth Press (1917). The amateurish venture was a striking success. Profits, meager to begin with, expanded with the reputation of the press and provided funds for holidays on the Continent, which the Woolfs loved, and the purchase of a country cottage at Rodmell in Sussex—a refuge from the constant round of London parties to which Virginia was being invited, as the fame of her writing spread. Alternating solitude and society, she struggled hard to preserve a precarious equilibrium, frequently punctuated by the episodes of suicidal insanity that generally followed upon the completion of each of her novels.

The mounting pressure of horror from the outer as well as her own inner world assailed her—for she was hypersensitive to suffering—during the years of World War I, in which many of her Cambridge friends were killed or wounded. The period between the wars, in which her major creative and critical work was done, saw the rise of monstrous tyrannies on the Continent. With a Socialist and Jewish husband Virginia could not but be aware of the implications of these for her personal life as well as for European civilization. Could *notre vielle Europe aux anciens parapets* survive a second onslaught? The note of alarm sounds throughout *Jacob's Room* (1922), *Mrs. Dalloway* (1925), *To the Lighthouse* (1927), *The Waves* (1931), *The Years* (1937), and the posthumous *Between the Acts* (1941). She did not live to see the outcome. Walking into the river Ouse at Rodmell, her pockets filled with stones, she drowned on 28 March 1941, unable any longer to cope with her personal problems or "the monstrous agony of the world."

THE WRITER AND THE AGE

IN the maelstrom of "movements" that make up the literature of England in our time, we may distinguish two separate and contrary directions: the centrifugal and the centripetal. There is the literature of action—"in the destructive element immerse"; there is the literature of recollection—"be still and know." One current goes with the age; the other opposes it. Yet both are integral to our time: the maelstrom could not exist without them.

That double position accepted, there is no difficulty in pointing out the major figures. On the one hand, James Joyce, D. H. Lawrence, and the novel of violence; on the other, E. M. Forster, Virginia Woolf. In poetry, similar distinctions can be made. There are political overtones, more audible perhaps in the 1930's than today. Stretching a few points, we can sniff religious odors: here, incense and guttering candles; there, dusty hassocks and the cold stone of college chapels. One school, floating in a refined air of mystical agnosticism, looks askance on the sex-cum-blasphemy of the other.

If we ask ourselves in what consists the specific modernity of modern literature, of either the left or the right (as I shall call the two "currents," without political implication), we may find the answer far to seek. Is modern literature everything in "serious" prose and verse written after a particular date, say 1918? Hardly that; for it is notorious that a good deal of highly respected work done since that date might well have been written, as far as its concern with present-day living goes or as far as it shows an awareness of contemporary technique, at any point in the previous half-century. Moreover, a considerable amount of work that does display this awareness was written well before 1918—much of the verse of William Butler Yeats and Gerard Manley Hopkins, most of Forster's prose. We cannot leave

this out of account, or we may get a false perspective.

If modernity is not a matter of chronology, what is it? Well, of course chronology comes into the picture. The writer must deal with the events of his time; but if he is a good writer, in his hands they don't stay events—they become experiences. Such a writer is not a mere reporter; he is aware of the significance of what is happening in his age, able to encompass the broad pattern woven of separate events. The journalist cannot see the forest for the trees; the artist grasps the meaning behind phenomena. He is something of a philosopher, a seer, as well as a technician. But the technique comes in too. New wine won't go into old bottles. New ideas, new ways of experience, shatter the old forms. Inevitably, originality of thought and spontaneity of emotion create fresh designs, strange music, new rhythms. With some writers, like Joyce, they even create a new vocabulary. Indeed, if we find a poet using the old forms—the sonnet, the rondeau, blank verse, and so on—we may be suspicious of him—as suspicious as if we caught him aping the idiom of John Milton or Geoffrey Chaucer.

That is the first essential in the modern writer, I think: awareness of what is new and important, and adequate technical response to that awareness. Later we shall see that there is a second "note" of good writing, which I shall call *proportion*. But for the moment let us focus on this aspect, since it provides a useful introduction to our theme in this essay. Virginia Woolf is commonly held to be a difficult writer, which means that she did not use a conventional technique or seek to arouse stock responses in her readers. She was aiming at something new, and we may safely say that she achieved it. What was this something new?

To answer this question fully would entail a discussion of the position of the English novel when Virginia Woolf began to write—around 1915. But in an essay as brief as the present one there is no room for any but positive findings. I would like to make this not a conducted tour but a series of flashes focused now on one, now on another aspect of her art. What has she to offer the reader? What dimension of understanding? What particular insights? In discussing these questions we may find that we are also, in effect, probing into some of the general conditions of the modern novel, for it is futile to consider any writer other than in the context of his or her time. In the case of Virginia Woolf, we shall find especially profitable the distinction that I made first of all, between the two currents of the contemporary maelstrom.

The first characteristic that strikes me is her understanding of human insufficiency. There are affinities here, of course, with the left—with existentialism and the novel of violence; but where the existentialists give up in despair and the Lawrences and Graham Greenes seek their panacea in action—that is, in the movement away from the still center—Virginia Woolf works consistently inward, away from the world of events. Let us begin with an example from her last novel, *Between the Acts.* Here we have a positive statement, that is, a presentation of a moment of sufficiency; but we are shown how that moment can exist only under certain special conditions: in the mind of a child rather than an adult, in the absence of distraction, and exposed to the threat of instant destruction.

Amy was saying something about a feller when Mabel, with her hand on the pram, turned sharply, her sweet swallowed. "Leave off grubbing," she said sharply. "Come along, George."

The little boy had lagged and was grouting in the grass. Then the baby, Caro, thrust her fist over the coverlet and the furry bear was jerked overboard. Amy had to stoop. George grubbed. The flower blazed between the angles of the roots. Membrane after membrane was torn. It blazed a soft yellow, a lambent light under a film of velvet; it filled the caverns behind the eyes with light. All that inner darkness became a hall, leaf smelling, earth smelling, of yellow light. And the tree was beyond the flower; the grass, the flower and the tree were entire. Down on his knees grubbing he held the flower complete. Then there was a roar and a hot breath and a stream of coarse grey hair rushed between him and the flower. Up he leapt, toppling in his fright, and saw coming towards him a terrible peaked eyeless monster moving on legs, brandishing arms.

Little George's moment of sufficiency is flanked by two insufficiencies: the nursemaids with their talk of "fellers" and their sweets, the old man with his Afghan hound and the need to impose himself on his grandson. The vision, which consists in a perfect observation of and identification with that which *is* (in this case the flower, roots, and soil at the foot of a tree), is broken by the intrusion of an adult world. This is the final example in Woolf's work of a repeated pattern. Let us note in passing that there is no condemnation of the nursemaids for being stupid or of Bart for being tyrannical; things are what they

are, and we have moved out of the moral, discriminating world of Dickens and Thackeray. We might call this absence of judgment a note of modernity, indeed of maturity, for Virginia Woolf did not display it from the outset. Her early work, like Forster's, offers value-judgments, particularly in situations directed against organized religion and its ministers. There is, it is true, a survival of this trait in the clergyman of *Between the Acts,* but a balance is preserved with the sympathetic portrait of Lucy fingering her crucifix.

Yet Lucy, however sympathetically drawn, is plainly not a self-sufficient person. She fingers her crucifix; she relies on God. Let us, with George's experience in mind, watch her cutting a loaf of bread:

Why's stale bread, she mused, easier to cut than fresh? And so skipped, sidelong, from yeast to alcohol; so to fermentation; so to inebriation; so to Bacchus; and lay under purple lamps in a vineyard in Italy, as she had done, often.

We see what is happening: George perceives; Lucy muses. George experiences; Lucy reacts. The bread is there, but she does not *see* it. Her thoughts move in a chain; they are slung on the string of memory. Information, morality, nostalgia—all are there, all the debris that chokes the immediate and masks the strange. George's mind is a cavern filled with yellow light, smelling of earth, empty. He labels nothing, moves on to nothing. He experiences bliss. Lucy, in the same situation, would be naming everything she saw and relating it to past or future: "Ah, a worm, there goes a beetle, horrid thing, I must do something about these weeds, how stony this soil is." The screen of concepts would be set between her and reality.

And thus the uniqueness, the joy of the moment, escapes her—as, indeed, Virginia Woolf shows it escaping so many of her characters. Here is Mrs. Ramsay in *To the Lighthouse,* sensing much that is true and good; but she verbalizes it:

When life sank down for a moment, the range of experience seemed limitless. And to everybody there was always this sense of unlimited resources, she supposed; one after another, she, Lily, Augustus Carmichael, must feel, our apparitions, the things you know us by, are simply childish. Beneath it is all dark, it is all spreading, it is unfathomably deep; but now and again we rise to the surface and that is what you see us by.

(I.11)

Words fix her experience. Of course Virginia Woolf
knows the danger. Her art, in its development, aims
at finding a way out. The very stream-of-consciousness technique that we see at work in Lucy's interior
monologue, and that Virginia Woolf derived from
Laurence Sterne and Marcel Proust, is a means at
least of bringing the evil to the surface, of demonstrating how much we are bound in our mental processes by memories, reactions, obsessions. But need
the writer also be found in her art? That, for her, is
the question. And so we find her experimenting with
technique. Can words, phrases, the very structure of
the novel be stripped of their conventional trappings, made to evoke other than stock responses?
Can the reader be induced to expect something different or, if not to expect, at least to accept it? Is it
possible, above all, to emulate the technique of the
painter (we remember her interest in the postimpres-
sionists) and say, "There is what I saw—that is how
the thing you call a rose, a jam-jar, or a boat appeared to me, then, at the moment, under those conditions of light, inner and outer"? Can the novel present, as the pictures can, the thusness of each object
as it exists in relationship to blue sky, yellow sand, or
striped tablecloth?

Let us note how curiously the theme of insufficiency is again asserting itself—this time in the dubious
relationship of author and reader. It is the reader,
you or I, who now turns back from the immediate experience offered by the novelist. The writer comes
bearing gifts and is greeted by a "Timeo Danaos!" ("I
fear the Greeks, even though they bring gifts":
Vergil, *Aeneid* II. 49). I offer you, says the novelist, a
new slant on life, the fresh perception that I have
achieved; I doubt if you have been given anything
quite like it before. I don't want your new perception, replies the reader; I want Tarzan, or Forsyte, or
the mixture as before of Catholicism-and-violence.
Go away and leave me in peace. I don't want reality.
It bores me and frightens me. In any case, I don't
understand you. I can't follow what you are saying.

The reader cannot follow what the writer is saying
because she is trying to say it in a different way.
Virginia Woolf was, from first to last, intensely conscious of making a different thing out of the novel.
The genre had been developed and exploited by men;
but she was a woman, and she was sure that a
woman novelist had to create her own form. Jane
Austen had done it; but the Brontës and George Eliot
had stuck too close to the old masculine pattern. The
feminine mind, the feminine sensibility, cannot profitably imitate the masculine. A woman novelist has

something new to bring. And so Virginia Woolf experiments ceaselessly in new forms, fresh techniques,
always trying to get nearer to an integral expression of
life. For truth—her great devotion—is valid here as
well as in the realm of ideas, in how a thing is said as
well as in what is said. The form of the conventional,
commercial novel is not *true*; it is stereotyped, dealing only with certain detached aspects of living
(which it exaggerates and distorts) glued together by
the crude devices of set descriptions, coincidences,
catastrophes, transition passages of mere padding.
And all moves on the surface. How, thought Virginia Woolf, how could she find a form that would
convey the movement of things under the surface—
the free play of thought, emotion, insight?

She learned, of course, from others. Mostly from
her contemporaries, from Proust and Joyce and
Dorothy Richardson; but also from the older
masters in whose work she discerned the same experimental quality, the same focusing on an interior
world. There was Sterne, for instance, with his
technique of disintegration, his flouting of the time
sense and of the connecting link; there was Montaigne, with his delicately poised self-preservation,
his irony; there were also the great Russians.

In her first novels we feel rather strongly the influence of Forster. Indeed, these novels are not experimental in form; they are occupied more, after the
Forster pattern, in probing the niceties of human
relationships. She wants to find out what themes the
novel should deal with, what kinds of characters she
herself is best fitted to present. *The Voyage Out*
(1915) is a fairly straightforward narrative of a
young woman, Rachel Vinrace, who is thrust suddenly out of a backwater into the whirl of life, falls in
love, and dies. *Night and Day* (1919) is about
another young woman, Katharine Hilbery, more
self-possessed, more mature, who wonders whether
falling in love and marrying may not be a matter of
quitting life for a backwater. But in her next novel,
Jacob's Room (1922), and perhaps even more in the
little volume of short stories or sketches *Monday or
Tuesday*, which had appeared in the previous year,
we find her experimenting: experimenting with the
stream-of-consciousness technique, experimenting
above all with the disruption of time.

Time is a problem for most modern writers. They
feel bound, cramped, by the necessity of keeping to
the strict sequence of events: A followed by B, and C
following B; they envy the plastic artist his freedom
of movement in space, his power of presenting a
totality to the eye. Poetry, of course, is freer than

prose—poets have always enjoyed a certain license to jump about from present to past and from past to future, to organize their intuitions within a not strictly temporal pattern. But hitherto the novel had been bound. Restricted as it was to the sphere of action, to the telling of a story, it had to present the sequence of cause and effect. The reader wanted to know "what is going to happen now." In particular the Victorian convention (followed by Dickens, Thackeray, and Anthony Trollope) of serial publication prescribed a rigid scheme of "continued in our next" and made development and experiment impossible.

Perhaps the first note of revolt, in England at least, was sounded by Forster. Tentatively in his novels and more boldly in the course of lectures published as *Aspects of the Novel* in 1927, he criticized the time-obsession in fiction. Indeed, he assailed the story, the plot itself, as Virginia Woolf remarks in the review she wrote of his book:

Many are the judgements that we would willingly argue, many are the points over which we would willingly linger, as Mr. Forster passes lightly on his way. That Scott is a story-teller and nothing more; that a story is the lowest of literary organisms; that the novelist's unnatural preoccupation with love is largely a reflection of his own state of mind while he composes—every page has a hint or a suggestion which makes us stop to think or wish to contradict.
("The Art of Fiction")

As a reviewer, she had neither time nor space to debate these points; as a novelist, we find them influencing her increasingly. (The argument about Sir Walter Scott comes at a crucial point in *To the Lighthouse*.) She noted and she pondered. Even within the limits of her review she arrives at certain highly significant conclusions: "In England at any rate the novel is not a work of art. There are none to be stood beside *War and Peace*, *The Brothers Karamazov*, or *A la Recherche du Temps Perdu*." She calls upon the critic to be bolder:

He might cut adrift from the eternal tea-table and the plausible and preposterous formulas which are supposed to represent the whole of our human adventure. But then the story might wobble; the plot might crumble; ruin might seize upon the characters. The novel, in short, might become a work of art.

There can be no doubt that Virginia Woolf was stimulated and encouraged by *Aspects of the Novel*, with its first open statement of revolt; but she had already begun to put into practice most of Forster's

hints some six years earlier. *Monday or Tuesday*, however, was a mere collection of sketches. It was in 1925, with *Mrs. Dalloway*, that she first shattered the time-pattern within the space of a full-length novel. Here she made the bold experiment of restricting her scheme to the limits of a single day, a single district of London, a single character in the round (a return to the three unities already signaled in *Ulysses*), while employing the devices of memory and dramatic counterpoint (Septimus Warren Smith's day is linked harmonically with Clarissa Dalloway's, though the two characters never meet) to avoid thinness and monotony. Later, in *To the Lighthouse* (1927), we see her playing other tricks with time. In the first section the action is restricted to one evening, the hours between six o'clock and dinner, and in fact even these few hours are foreshortened to a single moment; for in obedience to Mrs. Ramsay's "Time stand still here!" there is a suspension similar to that imposed by Mr. Weston in T. F. Powys' novel *Mr. Weston's Good Wine* (1927) on the bewildered inhabitants of Folly Down. In the second section, "Time Passes," the human element is withdrawn; the house is left alone to decay. In the third section, memory comes into its own and the present is displaced by the past.

Why, we may ask, this preoccupation with time? Why this ceaseless experimenting with the devices of memory and foreshortening? It is probably not enough to reply that Virginia Woolf found the time sequence inadequate to her intuition of reality, though that is an important point for a writer who attempts, as she does, to give a this-worldly rendering of an other-worldly pattern or a series of patterns or glimpses of patterns. But there is another reason. I think she found the time sequence inadequate also to the simple rendering of character, to the display of her creatures' inner lives. This is most strikingly demonstrated in her next work, the fantasy *Orlando* (1928), in which the life of her heroine, which in *Mrs. Dalloway* and *To the Lighthouse* had been foreshortened to one day, is stretched out to the perspective of four centuries; in which, too, there is a change of sex from masculine to feminine. All this metamorphosis, this complication and explication, is necessary to elucidate that most mysterious entity, the human spirit. "One wanted fifty pairs of eyes to see with," Lily Briscoe had reflected in *To the Lighthouse*. "Fifty pairs of eyes were not enough to get round that one woman with, she thought." Very well, we can hear Virginia Woolf replying, let us see how many pairs of eyes, in four hundred years, are needed to pluck out the heart of Orlando's mystery. Let us show Orlando as first masculine, and then feminine; first in love, and then loved; first jilting, and then jilted; a man of action and a poet, a woman of fashion and a Victorian lady.

In *The Waves* (1931) the process is carried a step further; indeed, to what we can only imagine to be its conclusion, for further development can hardly be expected along a line that had led, as here, to the suppression of plot, dialogue, and exterior description. *The Waves* presents us with six characters who grow up from children to men and women, but who never, in the novel, address one another, never attain an effective relationship; they move in and out of a pattern as in the intricate steps of the ballet. Counterpointed against the changing emotions and sensations of six parallel lifetimes is the process of a solar day. We are presented with a tissue of infinite complexity in which each personality is mirrored in the minds of the other five; and that multiple image is again multiplied in the great glass of the novel, itself a fractional image reflected from the moving pageant of sea and earth and sky that forms the exordium to each of the nine sections of the book. "Mirror on mirror mirrored is all the scene." The undertaking is prodigious, and so, I think, is the effect; but many readers have found the effort of concentration they are called upon to make beyond their powers. More than any other of her books *The Waves* deserves to be labeled "difficult."

With her next novel, *The Years* (1937), she seems to be marking time. There is almost a regression to the early technique of *The Voyage Out* and *Night and Day*. The element of plot returns; there are hints of set descriptions. Time is disrupted, but in no very original manner. We are carried from 1880 to 1891, from 1907 to 1910, and so on, but the result is a series of fragmentary impressions rather than a bold and original perception. It is only with her final (indeed posthumous) novel, *Between the Acts*, that we get a hint of the new direction along which her art is going to develop—a direction that, with its suggestion of a marriage of poetic and prose technique, picks up a note sounded in *Monday or Tuesday* and a thread left hanging in her review of *Aspects of the Novel*:

The assumption that *fiction is more intimately and humbly attached to the service of human beings than the other arts* leads to a further position which Mr. Forster's book again illustrates. It is unnecessary to dwell upon her [fiction's] aesthetic functions because they are so feeble that they can safely be ignored. Thus, though it is impossible to imagine a book on painting in which not a word should be said about the medium in which a painter works, a wise and brilliant book, like Mr. Forster's, can be written about fiction without saying more than a sentence or two about the medium in which a novelist works. Almost nothing is said about words.

("The Art of Fiction")

THE LAW OF PROPORTIONS

I HAVE italicized a phrase in the last quotation because it serves to introduce the theme of the second part of this essay: What is the relation between fiction and the service of human beings? What is the *moral* task of the artist?

In the very rapid survey we have just made of Virginia Woolf's work there are clearly several gaps. It is hardly credible, for instance, that between 1931 (*The Waves*) and 1937 (*The Years*), or again between 1937 and 1941 (*Between the Acts*), she should have written and published nothing. In fact, these intervals in novel-writing (and there are others) were occupied in reviewing and essay-writing. Virginia Woolf's critical work, collected in the two series of *The Common Reader* (1925 and 1932) and a number of volumes published after her death, is delightful to read and adds a new dimension to our understanding of her. As a critic, she brought a spontaneous delight and a delicate humanism to the understanding of English literature; her taste was catholic, her discernment rapid and assured. Where she could praise, she did so, but not all she wrote was favorable. She disliked whatever was second-rate, middlebrow, and propagandist. She disliked the commercial novel; she disliked the political poetry of the 1930's; she had no patience with cant and pseudoscholarship. She was a highbrow.

Her occasional writing was not entirely taken up with literary criticism. Part of it was devoted to what we can only call invective. There was this side to Virginia Woolf; and indeed it is a corollary of the sensitiveness displayed in her creative work that she should be vulnerable to pity and indignation. She responded to the horrors of war in China, Spain, Abyssinia in a way we can hardly fathom. To her the remote was not tolerable because it was remote, nor the familiar acceptable by its familiarity. Hence *Three Guineas* (1938), hence *A Room of One's Own* (1929). I do not propose to discuss these books. They should, however, be read, and in reading them I recommend that the reader keep in mind two things: how Woolf died and this sentence of Schiller's, "Mit der Dummheit kampfen die Götter selbst vergebens" (With stupidity the gods themselves strive in vain).

It is to her credit as an artist that these sympathies did not blunt her perception, affect her detachment, or upset the balance of her work. They are there, but they are fully absorbed into the stuff of the novel. There are no bits and pieces left over. It is here that her writing differs so radically from that of the "left," the current of action. In speaking of Virginia Woolf's modernity, I suggested awareness of the contemporary situation and adequate expression of that awareness as essential notes; I also suggested a third essential: proportion. It is this note that we must now consider. There is a rightness of balance or perspective that enables a novelist to put first things first, to see in the turmoil of events the point of rest, the still center, that gives meaning and brings understanding. We know how poets mediate this understanding by symbol and allusion, by music and rhythm; but how is the novelist, weighed down by character and plot, to make it felt? This question links our consideration of the importance of technique and the importance of perspective.

The modern vogue of the novel stems undoubtedly from the perplexity of our time. The genre has quite lost its old tang of frivolity. For the Victorians, novels were a species of dissipation, classed with romps and visits to the zoo. Serenely conscious of the stability of their age, they devoted their reading hours to such works as William Paley's *Evidences of Christianity*, to books of travel, or to poetry. They needed no literary picture of their own time: they could see it (they thought) quite clearly for themselves. But for us the novel is a necessity, like modern hospitals or an efficient sanitation system. It performs for us, too, something of the function of a psychotherapist. We hardly feel that we exist unless we find ourselves within the covers of a book. The cinema, on a cruder plane, has the same raison d'être; and as our thoughts and feelings become cruder, other media will no doubt in time entirely replace the serious novel.

The first use of modern writing, I would suggest, is to hold a mirror up to the confusions of the age—or rather, perhaps, a number of mirrors. No single writer is equipped to deal with such chaos: "My soul, like to a ship in a black storm,/Is driven, I know not whither" (John Webster, *The White Devil*, V.vi.

248–249). On all sides the established things are cast down, on all sides a multitude of creeds call for acceptance. Incessantly, violently, we are buffeted by strange winds of doctrine. It is now, however, that the novelists come to our aid. In the camera obscura of the best writers, the raw material of life (so terrifying in its amorphous actuality) is reduced to manageable proportions. We are given a frame, a scale of reference. Certain aspects of chaos are detached and considered apart from the rest: they are thereby provided with a semblance of order. The writer need not distort, need not impose a false symmetry. The act of selection and separation is enough.

In reading the modern novel we pass from one viewpoint to another—from Lawrence to Forster, from Virginia Woolf to T. F. Powys, from Greene to William Golding—as though we walked past a series of windows. All look out upon the same turbulent scene, but each presents us, within the framework of art, with some new aspect of the whole. Lawrence stresses the physical and instinctive, Forster the civilized and the tolerant; Powys shows us the hidden horror of the village, Virginia Woolf the secret places of the heart; Greene presents the conflict of faith and passion, Golding the anatomy of strength in weakness. But through them all (if they do their job properly) there emerges, whatever their religious or political beliefs, a principle that is *the* principle of art and, in consequence, an important aid to satisfactory living: it is the rule of proportion.

The modern writer (let us say it again) is bound to deal with the events of his time. But in this very immediacy, this contemporaneity, lies a pressing danger—a danger to that rule of proportion which the good artist must observe. Approaching the raw material of his age too closely, the writer of talent rather than genius is sucked into the whirlpool and lost—lost, that is, as an artist. As a social writer, as a propagandist, he may continue richly to exist. It requires a powerful mind and an intense individuality—in short, genius—to dominate the dangerous stuff of life. Without genius the window (which I have pictured looking down on the foaming waters of the age) splinters as we press against it—and we fall headlong. The artist is submerged; the politician, the theorist, takes his place. "I am really sorry," said William Blake at the beginning of the last century, "to see my countrymen trouble themselves about politics. If they were wise, the most arbitrary Princes could not hurt them. If they are not wise, the freest government is compell'd to be a Tyranny. Princes appear to me to be fools. Houses of Commons and Houses of Lords appear to me to be fools; they seem to me to be something else beside Human Life."

"They seem to me to be something else beside Human Life"! Exact and pregnant phrase! And what would Blake say, if he were alive today, of the United Nations, of the World Court, of planning and nationalization? Precisely the same, I suspect. For these things *are* something other than human life. They are the frame, and only the frame, within which life may be lived. And, alas, they are too often the frame outside which life must be lived if it is to be *lived* at all. Yet it is with the frame that the men of talent are almost exclusively occupied. We remember H. G. Wells, who began his career with an agreeable flair for writing scientific romances and an observant eye for the oddities of lower-middle-class behavior, but who afterward, toppling into this slough of despond, set himself up as a purveyor of utopias to the world. We have the sad example of Aldous Huxley, whose genuine gifts as satirist and essayist were soon obscured under the mantle of a neo-Brahmin sage. With these, and with many more, the Moloch of abstraction has had its will. Overwhelmed, they either perish in the storm or are whirled away by it.

"In the destructive element immerse": Joseph Conrad's slogan is a true one, and essential to the writer. Yes, we must immerse, but we should not drown or dissolve. We may write about the eagles and the trumpets, about movements, about economic realities; but somewhere we must keep a place for the lovers in their trance of happiness, for the boy chasing a butterfly, for the old man asleep under the chestnut tree. We must observe the law of proportion. This is precisely what Virginia Woolf does. We feel, throughout her novels, the big abstract movements going on: the feminism of *The Years*, monarchy and the war in *Mrs. Dalloway*, the pressure of Europe's coming doom in *Between the Acts*; but these things don't submerge the delicate, exact understanding and handling of the human situation. Her people live; they are not Shavian puppets. The individual is at the center of the stage—and the subtle relations between individuals, what Mrs. Ramsay does *not* say to her husband, what a gesture conveys to Giles Oliver:

The wild child, afloat once more on the tide of the old man's benignity, looked over her coffee cup at Giles, with whom she felt in conspiracy. A thread united them—visible, invisible, like those threads, now seen, now not, that unite trembling grass blades in autumn before the sun rises. She had met him once only, at a cricket match. And then had been spun between them an early morning thread before the twigs and leaves of real friendship emerge. She looked before she drank. Looking was part of drinking. Why waste sensation, she seemed to ask, why waste a single drop that can be pressed out of this ripe, this melting, this adorable world? Then she drank. And the air round her became threaded with sensation. Bartholomew felt it; Giles felt it. Had he been a horse, the thin brown skin would have twitched, as if a fly had settled. Isabella twitched too. Jealousy, anger pierced her skin.

(*Between the Acts*)

It is in order to convey these moments of perception that writers like Proust and Virginia Woolf have forged a new technique of the novel. It is the task of the modern writer to catch these moments amid the increasing hubbub, the diminishing solitude, of modern life. Formerly it was the poets who did it. It was they who explored the secret springs of conduct, who made us see that under the flux of things the great passions still hold sway: love, friendship, hatred, along with birth and death, the rhythm of the seasons, the infinite pathos and splendor of man's destiny:

O what if gardens where the peacock strays
With delicate feet upon old terraces,
Or else all Juno from an urn displays
Before the indifferent garden deities;
O what if levelled lawns and gravelled ways
Where slippered Contemplation finds his ease
And Childhood a delight for every sense,
But take our greatness with our violence?

What if the glory of escutcheoned doors,
And buildings that a haughtier age designed,
The pacing to and fro on polished floors
Amid great chambers and long galleries, lined
With famous portraits of our ancestors;
What if those things the greatest of mankind
Consider most to magnify, or to bless,
But take our greatness with our bitterness?
(W. B. Yeats, *Meditations in Time of Civil War*)

And this is the use of literature in all ages: to show men and women amid the splendor of their environment—and yet, in a moment of passion, of betrayal, of reality, reduced to their essential humanity, to the greatness, the violence, and the bitterness of the lonely heart. In what else is Homer or Shakespeare or Dante great, if not in this? Consider some of the famous lines that color our waking hours and our dreams. The magnificence of Dante's Brunetto Latini, who, though in hell, ran like those who contend for the prize at Verona:

> e parve di costoro
> quegli che vince e non colui che perde.

And John Webster's Duchess, with all her bright world of love shattered about her: "I am Duchess of Malfi still." And, at the supreme height, Shakespeare's Cleopatra as she presses the asp to her breast:

> Dost thou not see my baby at my breast,
> That sucks the nurse asleep?
> (*Antony and Cleopatra*, V.ii)

It is the poets and the great novelists who reduce us to our pure humanity, to the "forked radish," the "unaccommodated man"; and, stripped of the trappings of grandeur and vanity, we see ourselves again as we are: solitary, vulnerable, and transient.

How tremendously helpful this is in a world that tries to persuade us that the important things are religious beliefs, social distinctions, political adherences. Let us listen again to the voice of Blake: "They seem to me to be something else beside Human Life." On all sides, by the radio, the cinema, the daily newspaper, the television we are bludgeoned into disproportion. From a billion loudspeakers, a million silver screens, the Antichrist bellows and gesticulates. It is salutary to be set naked beneath the stars. And it is salutary to see the others, the big imposing men who seek to dominate us, sub specie aeternitatis. Do not let us be worried by them, by their loud voices, their titles, their decorations. "Things are what they are," said Bishop Samuel Butler, "and the consequences of them will be what they will be: why therefore should we wish to be deceived?"

Virginia Woolf's standpoint is, above all, this standpoint of reality. It is for this that she praises the Greeks, that she loves Plato:

> For as the argument mounts from step to step, Protagoras yielding, Socrates pushing on, what matters is not so much the end we reach as our manner of reaching it. That all can feel—the indomitable honesty, the courage, the love of truth which draw Socrates and us in his wake to the summit where, if we too may stand for a moment, it is to enjoy the greatest felicity of which we are capable.

But for her there is not one kind of truth; there are two. There is the truth of the reason and the truth of the imagination. The truth of the reason is preeminently the masculine sphere, while the truth of the imagination is the feminine. Together, these make up what she calls reality. Some individuals combine the male and the female modes of perception more impartially than others; these are the artists, the poets and painters who mediate reality to us. They show us how neither the rational nor the intuitive can get on without the other. Mrs. Ramsay and Mr. Ramsay in *To the Lighthouse* need each other. Mrs. Dalloway, in the earlier novel, because she has married a politician, a sentimentalist, is unhappy: with all his kindness, with all the amenities of her life, she is out of touch with reality. Mr. Ramsay is a philosopher: intolerant, egotistical, eccentric; yet he is a better husband than the impeccable Richard Dalloway, who is a Member of Parliament. Virginia Woolf agrees with Blake: these things are not human life. The Houses of Parliament, the Law Courts, the Mansion House; she gives us her picture of them in *Three Guineas:*

> Your world, then, the world of professional, of public life, seen from this angle undoubtedly looks queer. At first sight it is enormously impressive. Within quite a small space are crowded together St. Paul's, the Bank of England, the Mansion House, the massive if funereal battlements of the Law Courts; and on the other side, Westminster Abbey and the Houses of Parliament. There, we [women] say to ourselves, pausing, in this moment of transition on the bridge, our fathers and brothers have spent their lives. All these hundreds of years they have been mounting those steps, passing in and out of those doors, ascending those pulpits, preaching, money-making, administering justice.
>
> (ch. 1)

And she goes on to show us how absurd it all is, how unreal. Against it she sets, in *A Room of One's Own*, this picture:

> What is meant by "reality"? It would seem to be something very erratic, very undependable—now to be found in a dusty road, now in a scrap of newspaper in the street, now in a daffodil in the sun. It lights up a group in a room and stamps some casual saying. It overwhelms one walking home beneath the stars and makes the silent world more real than the world of speech—and then there it is again in an omnibus in the uproar of Piccadilly.
>
> (ch. 6)

This is, let us note, no aesthetic attitude, no cult of beauty. Reality resides in the scrap of dirty paper as much as in the sunlit daffodil. The thing seen is not important in itself, or rather it is not important what our judgment is of the thing seen. Indeed, we must see it without judgment, without choice, with silent awareness; and then we know reality. This is the message of Virginia Woolf's novels, and it is a rather important message. No one was less of a teacher than she, no one less didactic, yet what she shows us here is of great importance for living. To be taught how to see—is not that a great thing? Because if we can learn to see in this way, there comes (she says it again and again) an extraordinary happiness.

This faculty of seeing directly can exist only in the mind that is concerned for what is, not for what ought to be or will be. That is why Virginia Woolf is antireligious. Belief of any kind blinds and binds. We cannot see what is when we have theories. It does not matter whether the beliefs are religious or political. In an essay called "The Leaning Tower" (originally a paper read to the Workers' Educational Association at Brighton in May 1940, and thus one of the last things she wrote), she discusses those modern writers who seemed to inhabit the leaning tower of Marxist class-consciousness:

If you read current literary journalism you will be able to rattle off a string of names—Day Lewis, Auden, Spender, Isherwood, Louis MacNeice and so on. . . . All those writers . . . are acutely tower conscious; conscious of their middle-class birth; of their expensive educations. Then when we come to the top of the tower how strange the view looks—not altogether upside down, but slanting, sidelong. That too is characteristic of the leaning-tower writers; they do not look any class straight in the face; they look either up, or down, or sidelong. There is no class so settled that they can explore it unconsciously. That perhaps is why they create no characters. Then what do we feel next, raised in imagination on top of the tower? First discomfort; next self-pity for that discomfort; which pity soon turns to anger—to anger against the builder, against society, for making us uncomfortable. Those too seem to be tendencies of the leaning-tower writers. Discomfort; pity for themselves; anger against society. And yet—here is another tendency—how can you altogether abuse a society that is giving you, after all, a very fine view and some sort of security? You cannot abuse that society wholeheartedly while you continue to profit by that society. And so very naturally you abuse society in the person of some retired admiral or spinster or armament manufacturer; and by abusing them hope to escape whipping yourself. The bleat of the scapegoat sounds loud in their work, and the whimper of the schoolboy crying "Please, Sir, it was the other fellow, not me."

We may regret that Virginia Woolf should devote her talents to castigating these writers of the 1930's, but we are concerned here with the implications rather than with the expediency of her remarks. Religion, political beliefs, moral codes: these things are among the blinders and binders. The writers she mentions were not, in her opinion, interested in what is, but only in their personal responses to what is: they never stood still to experience a situation, but reacted immediately with their stereotyped solutions. Thus the reality of the moment escaped them.

And in her novels it is the same. We can divide her characters, if we will, into those who are open to reality and those who are shut in—enclosed by various manias of faith, hatred, perversion, politics, morality. In the first division we have, to begin with, children. There is George in *Between the Acts.* There are Mrs. Ramsay's children in *To the Lighthouse:*

Then the door sprang open and in they came, fresh as roses, staring, wide awake, as if this coming into the dining-room after breakfast, which they did every day of their lives, was a positive event to them, and so on, with one thing after another, all day long, until she went up to say good-night to them, and found them nested in their cots like birds among cherries and raspberries, still making up stories about some little bit of rubbish—something they had heard, something they had picked up in the garden.

(I. 10)

The quality of eternal freshness, of wonder, surprise, the coming to each day as though it were the first and only day—this note of spontaneity exists in childhood, and is perceived and enjoyed by those who know. "One's children so often gave one's own perceptions a little push forward," thought Mrs. Ramsay. In *Mrs. Dalloway* too: the girl Elizabeth, dismissing the memory of the young men who are already comparing her to poplar trees and hyacinths (the personal, the sentimental, the desirous muddying the clear waters of perception), sees Wren's churches as "shapes of grey paper breasting the stream of the Strand." Jacob Flanders, in *Jacob's Room,* finds his direct vision blocked, like George's in the later novel, by the intruding adult element:

But there, on the very top, is a hollow full of water, with a sandy bottom; with a blob of jelly stuck to the side, and some mussels. A fish darts across. The fringe of yellow-brown seaweed flutters, and out pushes an opal-shelled crab. . . . Jacob was about to jump, holding his bucket in front of him, when he saw, stretched entirely rigid, side by side, their faces very red, an enormous man and woman.

(ch. 1)

And in *The Years* the pervert under the streetlamp wrecks little Rose Pargiter's fantasy.

But not all adults are closed to vision. There are the artists—the poets and painters who really have kept the innocent eye of childhood. These see reality whole from the beginning and express it in its untarnished brightness. Then there are the young men and women who are not artists but, because they are free from prejudice and interested in things as they are, succeed in battling their way toward reality. We have a whole gallery of these sympathetic figures— Jacob Flanders in *Jacob's Room*, Katherine Hilbery in *Night and Day*, Bernard in *The Waves*, and many others. All of them are steeped in the light of Cambridge, the good life that is devotion to truth and unremitting opposition to falsehood and cant, the life of scholarship and beauty. But that light in itself is not enough. It has to be surpassed. Behind truth there is reality; behind the constructs of the mind there lies the realm of pure being itself. It does not do to stay at Cambridge. "Is there not too much brick and mortar for a May night?" thinks Jacob, looking round him at the Great Court of Trinity.

In several of her novels Virginia Woolf gives us the portraits of people who have, in one way or another, "stayed at Cambridge": Ridley Ambrose and William Pepper in *The Voyage Out*, Mr. Ramsay and Charles Tansley in *To the Lighthouse*. And admirable people they are, superior, far superior, to the successful administrators, the Richard Dalloways and Colonel Pargiters, who direct the affairs of the great world from a blank center while the joy of living crumbles away from their wives' hearts little by little in attic rooms. But the "stayers" have become arrested at some point in their development. They have found truth, they are devoted to truth, but they have not pushed on to reality. They are stranded in the realm of the concept.

It is here that the third great class of the elect has its job to do. This is the class of women. The statement, thus flatly made, seems crass and stupid enough. Virginia Woolf is far from seeking to canonize her sex as a whole. What she does imply, throughout the course of her writing, is that the feminine personality is closer to earth, to the simplicity of things, to ob-

jects as objects and not as counters to be talked about; and by virtue of this concreteness women manage to achieve an adequacy of response to what is beyond the concrete. The woman's job, mainly, if she is not herself an artist of one sort or another, is to free the male intellect from its conceptual chains, to enrich and fertilize it.

Virginia Woolf has been called a feminist; and of course she was, in several of her writings, especially *A Room of One's Own* and *Three Guineas*. But more truly we might call her an androgynist: she puts the emphasis every time on what a man and a woman have to give to each other, on the mystery of completion, and not on the assertion of separate superiorities. If there is in woman a superiority, it is because *she* is the one to take the first step toward understanding, out of a compassion that is almost the Buddhist karma; more discerning than the male, she lays her light, healing touch on the source of conflict, the knot of refusal-to-be-what-one-is, and it loosens. The theme of Virginia Woolf's novels is often precisely this: the patient effort of the woman toward the reintegration of the man. His resistance is not always overcome. To show things thus would be to falsify; life, in fact, offers few happy endings.

We do not, then, find her placing the emphasis, in the man-woman relationship, on the sexual element; and in this respect she flows against the main current of modern writing. Just as she avoids the portrayal of violent action, so too she largely omits the passional. I don't think she could have given it to us successfully, but in any case it would not have fitted into the world where she is at home as an artist. For this is the world of *freedom*. Passion stultifies, distorts, and corrupts. The people she shows us as married, or thinking of marriage, all envisage the problem in terms of freedom. They are more than ordinarily intelligent persons. They enjoy a vigorous intellectual life of their own, and they want to preserve it inviolate. They don't appear to have very strong physical desires, but they are emotional. They have a lot of affection to give and to receive. They are fascinated and at the same time repelled by the idea of sharing. They see quite clearly the faults of those they love, but love deeply just the same. A movement of uncertainty, of discovery and relief, runs through the novels as a kind of inner action to make up for the lack of external events.

Virginia Woolf's work presents itself, then, as a study of the inner life of individuals as they exist, first of all, in solitude, and then in society; and as a counterpointing of these aspects. Solitude is a constant theme, the native air breathed by her characters when they are most themselves. In *A Room of One's Own* she records the importance of seeing "human beings not always in their relation to each other but in relation to reality; and the sky too, and the trees or whatever it may be in themselves." This is solitude. And since even solitude must have a locus, since one can't be alone without finding somewhere to be alone, her heroes and heroines enjoy their solitariness, as we should expect, among what William Wordsworth called the beautiful and permanent forms of nature. For the point of natural objects is their aloneness. Rocks, plants, rivers have achieved the secret of forming a society without impinging upon one another's privacy.

Virginia Woolf returns again and again to the proud aloofness of natural things. She pictures the tree standing alone in the field through the long summer nights. She sees, in *Orlando*, "those hyacinths—free from taint, dependence, soilure of humanity or care for one's kind." Yet though aloof, they are not inimical to the man or woman who approaches them without arrogance or prejudice. "Hills and trees accept one; human beings reject one," a character in *The Years* muses.

For a novelist, this taste for solitude plainly presents something of a problem. To be effective within the framework of a story, human beings must care for something more than hyacinths and hills: they must care for each other. How does Virginia Woolf solve this problem? In *Three Guineas* she writes: "Inevitably we ask ourselves, is there not something in the conglomeration of people into societies that releases what is most selfish and violent, least rational and humane in the individuals themselves?" These words were written under the (to her) almost unbearable horror of the Spanish Civil War and the growing shadow of Fascism. They represent a real attitude of hers, but not a final or complete one. They do suggest (what cannot be denied) that her scope is limited, that there are aspects of human life she will not touch and situations from which she shrinks back. Her world is a small one, a world of intellectuals and sensitive individuals, of artists and scholars. But it is what she does with that limited world that is important. Can she expand it to contain the great paradoxes of life: love and hate, solitude and society, and the freedom that springs from loving bondage?

And here, I think, she does succeed. By reducing the commitments of her characters to the simplest components—none of Arnold Bennett's bustle or Lawrence's complications for her—she shows us the pattern of lives that, even while harmonizing, preserve their individual melodies. A solitude is kept in the midst of society, sometimes by a deliberate act of withdrawal. Virginia Woolf's view is not far removed from the Blakean doctrine of salvation through art or the Taoist technique of *wei wu wei*. "If one wishes to better the world one must, paradoxically enough, withdraw and spend more and more time fashioning one's sentences to perfection in solitude." These words from the second *Common Reader* refer specifically to the writer, but they apply to every walk of life. Thus Mrs. Ramsay, in *To the Lighthouse*, finds her arduous duties as wife and mother and hostess bearable only if she can, from time to time, sink down to be "a wedge of darkness." "The supreme difficulty of being oneself," as Virginia Woolf calls it elsewhere, becomes insuperable if the world is too much with us. The subtler art of preserving solitude is not by withdrawal, but by fusion. And this, for Virginia Woolf, is the meaning of love. Human beings need one another—not for consolation, for protection, to form a closed circle—but for the joy of sharing. The moment of perception is heightened if it can be held in common:

Some spray in a hedge, or a sunset over a flat winter field, or again the way some old woman sits, arms akimbo, in an omnibus with a basket—these we point at for the other to look at. It is so vast an alleviation to be able to point for another to look at. And then not to talk.

But alas, with how few companions can such detached sharing, such shared detachment, be achieved.

There is always the question of whether it can be achieved at all. And that is why so many of her novels ponder the theme of compatibility or incompatibility. Can one really live with other people, and still be oneself, free to live, free to develop? The question haunts Mrs. Dalloway and Mrs. Ramsay; Katherine Hilbery and Jacob Flanders; Bernard in *The Waves* and Sara in *The Years*. The answer is given in terms of courage and common sense. What has been achieved can be achieved. The problem, we note, is radically a woman's problem. It would hardly occur to a man, unless he possessed a large measure of feminine sensibility. And it implies, radically, that absence of passion which we have already noticed in Virginia Woolf's work. We are here in a very cool, still, twilight region. (Many of her most effective scenes take place at evening.) The air of detachment, of aloneness, takes on an aspect of poignancy in her more elderly characters. I am thinking particularly of Mrs. Dalloway and Mrs. Ramsay. In the case of Mrs. Dalloway the poignancy is stressed: the note of regret, of nostalgia for opportunities that are past, the something lost that time in its swift course will not bring back again. Clarissa Dalloway, indeed, has missed her moment, has made the wrong choice in life's intelligence test, has opted for the successful Richard and not for the scapegrace Peter. But even with Mrs. Ramsay, who has achieved so much, whose life is so rich, there is the note of almost unbearable nostalgia—for what?

For what? That is the question. What is missing from Virginia Woolf's picture? For this note of melancholy tells us that something is missing; it is not a healthy sign. The greatest literature is not sad, though it may be tragic. Behind the brilliant, sensitive world she gives us there is an emptiness. And of course we know at once, in part, why this should be. The sensitivity entails the emptiness. Living in the world between two wars and in the world of war itself, she was unremittingly conscious of the fragility of the civilization that is Western Europe, of the transience of the values that her books so shiningly illustrate. But there is more than this. The lack is not only in her world: it is in herself. It is the lack of what we can only call faith; not the faith that is based on submission to authority or on wishful thinking—she could never have known that—but faith in the reality of her own intuitions, the faith that is really knowledge in its purest form, for there is nothing more certain or immediate to us than our own "feel" of reality. This contact she had, intermittently; the mystic (a word she disliked and for which I would prefer to substitute *poetic*) was strong in her. A dozen passages could be culled from her writing that would worthily stand by the side of Lao Tze's sayings or the gnomic aphorisms of Blake. But her upbringing was against her. Childhood years in an agnostic household, the company of intellectuals as an adult, had not taken the fine point off her spiritual perceptions, but they had effectively blocked the way to a synthesis.

But if the sadness is felt, it is, like the indignation and the pity, absorbed into the stuff of the novels; and the movement inward continues even if it is to a center of which Woolf could not say assuredly, "It is

there." The great artist—and she was a great artist—is used for purposes she may ignore or deny. No one can come away from a reading of these novels without feeling that his experience has been enriched, that he has been taught to see more clearly. There is sensationalism in her novels, the sensationalism of the painter entranced with color and form, of the poet drunk with scents and tastes; but she rises above or rather through sensation to a higher understanding. She is no Walter Pater. Her delight in the moment, the vivid crystal of the here and now, is always escaping into meaning. Just as often, distrustful of metaphysics, she hauls it back. The reality is always more than the sensation, but only in the sensation can reality be known. The ripple of the wave conceals beneath it the world of waters where swim strange, unthinkable shapes of fish and plant. And—if I may stretch my sea metaphor a little further—in the sensationalism of Virginia Woolf there is something one might call "salt," a tincture lacking in Pater and his like. The aesthetes cultivated sensation; she accepts it. The faint smell of decay is absent. They distrusted the intellect; she worships it—in its own place. They withdrew to the ivory tower; she writes *Three Guineas*, preaches feminism. Salt—the tincture of humor, responsibility, reverence for qualities not her own—keeps her writing sweet. Though her world is a limited one, vast perspectives are thrown open. And how wise she was to limit her scope to those intimate relationships that she knew so well.

It is because of this self-limitation, itself stemming from a shrewd assessment of her own resources, that her position in English fiction is, it seems to me, assured. She did supremely well what no one else has attempted to do. She mapped the world of the mind—especially the feminine mind—under certain precise conditions of character and environment. Her work forms a unity, the unity of great poems like T. S. Eliot's *The Waste Land* and *Four Quartets*. Within it we revolve, with Sir Thomas Browne alone in his study, the globe of ourselves:

I could never content my contemplation with those general pieces of wonder, the Flux and Reflux of the Sea, the increase of *Nile*, the conversion of the Needle to the North; and have studied to match and parallel those in the more obvious and neglected pieces of Nature, which without further trouble I can do in the Cosmography of my self; we carry with us the wonders we seek without us: There is all *Africa* and her prodigies in us; we are that bold and adventurous piece of nature, which he that studies wisely learns in a *compendium* what others labour at in a divided piece and endless volume.

(Religio Medici, pt. I, sec. 15)

Virginia Woolf's sphere is neither so bold nor so adventurous, perhaps; but it has its own unity. There, at the mouth of a river in South America, is the little town of Santa Marina. The climate is tropical, but the society might be that of the Cambridge of *Jacob's Room*. A flick of the hand sends the globe spinning to discover a large ramshackle house in the Hebrides—sea, mountains, barren shore are clearly visible, but as we eavesdrop on Charles Tansley and Mr. Bankes in *To the Lighthouse*, we fancy ourselves back again with Katherine Hilbery in Cheyne Walk, in *Night and Day*. It is good conversation: there is no room for stupidity or violence. The women are wise, witty, maternal; the men, whether old or young, wear rather shabby flannels and tweeds and stump up and down the terrace declaiming Tennyson, debating the nature of things. On the outskirts, it is true, certain sinister figures hover: clergymen, "irrelevant forked stakes in the flow and majesty of the summer silent world"; power-lovers and soul-destroyers, the Sir William Bradshawes and the Colonel Pargiters, the Miss Kilmans and the Minnie Marshes.

And beyond these figures of darkness there is the circumambient darkness itself, always felt, always pressing in upon the sphere and threatening to destroy it. There is the darkness deep in the nature of things, the tragedy and waste when Rachel Vinrace dies, her promise unfulfilled (death comes as the end); or when Sally Pargiter is dropped as a baby (death comes as the beginning). These are acts of God. But there are also the acts of men: the clang of war echoes through the early novels, the darkening horror of Fascism dominates the later ones. The colored and fragrant sphere vibrates in the chaos. There it hangs, fragile and iridescent. We tremble for its permanence. But there is no need to fear: this bubble is endowed with a surprising toughness. It will stand wind and weather; it will outlive the eagles and the trumpets. And, watching it, we may find that it focuses, within its little round, essences of human thought and action that escape the net of the blueprint and the interim report. The movement streams inward, toward the still center. But there is a plane of understanding on which the inward is also the outward, and the particular the most valid

representation of the universal. Virginia Woolf's world will survive as the crystal survives under the crushing rock masses. The juggernaut that destroyed its creator has no power over this globe of hers and its inhabitants:

> Forms more real than living man,
> Nurslings of immortality.

ACHIEVEMENT AND INFLUENCE

Since World War II many changes have come over the literary scene. We have seen the rise of the "angry young men" in Britain, of the beatniks in the United States, of the *chosistes* in France, to name only the most prominent among the "new bearings." The "novel of violence" has won hands down over the "be still and know" tradition. Virginia Woolf has had no successor. That fact in itself does not constitute an indictment; there are some writers so great (the greatest, indeed, need not be named) that there is no room in their circle for others. Jonathan Swift was an isolated phenomenon; Sterne had to wait two hundred years for his influence to be felt, and its possibilities are still unexhausted. We are just beginning to wake up to Blake. Byron is due for reassessment.

It must be admitted that Virginia Woolf's stock fell in the postwar years. Simultaneous revolutions may clash, as the Renaissance did with the Reformation, to produce the oddest results in the work of Edmund Spenser or Milton. Virginia Woolf was committed enough, as *Three Guineas* and *A Room of One's Own* show, but her true current, as we have seen, was interior, toward the still center. World War II, with its aftermath, deflected this current and the interest in subtleties of technique that went with it. We have seen its reemergence, perhaps, in a new and fascinating guise, in the interest in Zen. The technical revolution represented so brilliantly by Virginia Woolf has been short-circuited by insistent political and "existential" pressures: angry young men and beatniks write in a strangely outmoded idiom. The voice is Jacob's voice.

This is not to say that Virginia Woolf has been without influence. But her infiltration is pervasive, subtle, and unacknowledged. We can see it most clearly in Alain Robbe-Grillet and his school. Her intelligence was always more French than English in its

VIRGINIA WOOLF

lucidity, its poise, its irony. And just as we gave John Locke to France and got him back again via Jean-Jacques Rousseau and the *encyclopédistes*, so Virginia Woolf is returning to us quite quietly by way of the *chosistes*. Their admirable insistence on the thing seen, on the object *there* in space uncontaminated by impertinent comment, has long been anticipated in a score of passages in her novels, some of which are quoted in preceding pages, and most clearly, perhaps, in the short story "Solid Objects":

The only thing that moved upon the vast semicircle of the beach was one small black spot. As it came nearer to the ribs and spine of the stranded pilchard boat, it became apparent from a certain tenuity in its blackness that this spot possessed four legs; and moment by moment it became more unmistakable that it was composed of the persons of two young men. Even thus in outline against the sand there was an unmistakable vitality in them; an indescribable vigour in the approach and withdrawal of the bodies, slight though it was, which proclaimed some violent argument issuing from the tiny mouths of the little round heads. This was corroborated on closer view by the repeated lunging of a walking-stick on the right-hand side. "You meant to tell me . . . You actually believe . . ." thus the walking-stick on the right-hand side next the waves seemed to be asserting as it cut long straight stripes upon the sand.

This is the opening paragraph of a story in which the obsession of an adult mind with solid objects is as convincingly shown as that "inner darkness" of a child's mind which "became a hall, leaf smelling, earth smelling, of yellow light" in the first passage quoted in the present essay.

To go a little further afield: to Patrick White, the Australian novelist who seems to me by far the greatest talent to arise since the death of Virginia Woolf. *Voss* (1957) opens with a domestic interior that brings *Night and Day* directly to mind; there is no imitation, the settings are quite different; as far apart indeed as Cheyne Walk and Sydney, New South Wales, but the accents chime, the technique whereby place becomes an interpreter of grace (or its opposite); and might not this be an aside on Katherine Hilbery?

Already as a little girl she had been softly sceptical, perhaps out of boredom; she was suffocated by the fuzz of faith. She did believe, however, most palpably, in wood, with the reflections in it, and in clear daylight, and in water. She would work fanatically at some mathematical problem, even now, just for the excitement of it, to solve

and know. She had read a great deal out of such books as had come her way in that remote colony, until her mind seemed to be complete.

The self-existent life of buildings—particularly of houses—that bulks so large in Woolf, and their reactions to intruding human presences, also crystallizes out:

Not even the presence of the shabby stranger, with his noticeable cheekbones and over-large finger-joints, could destroy the impression of tranquillity, though of course, the young woman realised, it is always like this in houses on Sunday mornings while others are at church. It is therefore but a transitory comfort. Voices, if only in whispers, must break in. Already she herself was threatening to disintegrate into the voices of the past.

And here, finally, is the return to the assurance of the life of things, with a last twist in the paragraph that brings us back to the most characteristic of Virginia Woolf's novels, *The Voyage Out* and *To the Lighthouse*:

All this time Voss was standing his ground. He was, indeed, swaying a little, but the frayed ends of his trouser legs were momentarily lost in the carpet. How much less destructive of the personality are thirst, fever, physical exhaustion, he thought, much less than people. He remembered how, in a mountain gorge, a sandstone boulder had crashed aiming at him, grazing his hand, then bounding away, to the mutilation of trees and death of a young wallaby. Deadly rocks through some perversity inspired him with fresh life. He went on with the breath of life in his lungs. But words, even of benevolence and patronage, even when they fell wide, would leave him half dead.

We may summarize with a new note: on the possibility of a fusion of excellences between the novel of reflection and the novel of action, of the feminine fertilized by the masculine, of a new Conrad arising on a new continent, "nurslings of immortality" made flesh and bone in a new, all-inclusive vision. The ironic yet compassionate expression of the features that animates Virginia Woolf's portrait remains for me, at any rate, "the marble index" of a kind of greatness which, as Nicholas Ferrar remarked of the synthesis he established three centuries ago at Little Gidding, "might prove a pattern in an age that needs patterns."

THE UNCOMMON READER

SET side by side with the novels, Virginia Woolf's literary criticism must always be seen as marginal—an appendix, but one of astonishing resilience and strength, firmly rooted in her personal life, and casting no little light upon her aims and achievements as a novelist. She began her writing career with reviewing, contributing hasty appraisals of third- and fourth-rate books to the *Guardian*, a London weekly newspaper that aimed at readers among the clergy. From this she graduated to the *Times Literary Supplement*, John Middleton Murry's *Athenaeum*, Desmond MacCarthy's *New Statesman*, and even so mundane a periodical as *Vogue*. Most of the *Common Reader* essays took their first flight in these reviews. This was hack work—it brought in the bread and butter, paid for a WC to replace the outdoor privy at Monk's House, bought a second-hand car.

Virginia Woolf went on reviewing books for most of her life. When she achieved fame as a novelist she was free to pick and choose, and refused to write about books that didn't interest her. It was not all grind. Reviewing afforded a measure of relief from the tensions, the "screw," as she called it, of her creative work—the often agonizing intellectual and emotional complexities of *Mrs. Dalloway* or *The Waves*. Then back again she would spin from the "carpentry" of her critical essays with fresh vigor to the anguish, the color, and the flow of her novels. "What a fling I shall have into fiction and freedom when this [the second *Common Reader*] is off!" she writes in her diary on 8 July 1932. But—"at once, an American comes to ask me to consider writing articles for some huge figure."

These are dilemmas that face many artists. Virginia Woolf herself drew a firm line between criticism and reviewing: "Reviews seem to me more and more frivolous. Criticism on the other hand absorbs me more and more," she notes on 18 February 1922. In a letter to Madge Vaughan of December 1904, at the very outset of her career, she admits the tendency of reviewing to corrupt and to stifle: "My real delight in reviewing is to say nasty things; and hitherto I have had to [be] respectful." As late as 31 January 1920, when she had made her mark with *The Voyage Out* and *Night and Day*, she writes in her diary: ". . . I am equally able to write for [J. C.] Squire, Murry or Desmond MacCarthy—a proof of catholicity or immorality, according to your taste."

Friendly voices warned her of the threat to her integrity. And she came to be annoyed by editorial restraints. As early as December 1905 she had complained in a letter to Violet Dickinson that Dame Edith Lyttleton, who ran the Women's Supplement of the *Guardian*, "sticks her broad thumb into the middle of my delicate sentences and improves the moral tone." Bruce Richmond, editor of the *Times Literary Supplement*, coerced her into substituting "obscene" for "lewd" in a review of Henry James's ghost stories. Finally putting her foot down, she declares in September 1920: "I've taken the plunge of refusing my books from the Times, and dictated conditions for the future." She would now review the occasional volume, but only if she thought it worth reviewing; she would write the occasional essay, but only on subjects that interested her.

And what subjects did interest her? She was a catholic critic in the sense that she enjoyed all manner of books and wrote about them with enthusiasm and understanding. Her letters and diaries are full of the sheer delight of reading. After the stress of society, after the exertions of travel, after the clashes of personal relationships, back she slid into the healing world of books, some read for the first time, some for the fifty-first—like a sea creature returning to its element. There she too, like Blake "a mental prince," moved among her peers, and among those who were so devastatingly more than her peers that she was abashed in their presence. "[T]he power to make images . . . ," she notes in her 31 July 1926 diary: "Shakespeare must have had this to an extent which makes my normal state the state of a person blind, deaf, dumb, stone-stockish and fish-blooded. And I have it compared with poor Mrs. Bartholomew [her cook] almost to the extent that she has it compared with me."

Together with her many arrogances Virginia Woolf had her humilities too. Her awe in the presence of Shakespeare comes out most clearly—and to my mind most touchingly—in a diary entry of 9 May 1934 following a visit to Stratford:

I cannot without more labour than my roadrunning mind can compass describe the queer impression of sunny impersonality. Yes, everything seemed to say, this was Shakespeare's, here he sat and walked; but you wont find me not exactly in the flesh. He is serenely absent-present; both at once; radiating round one; yes; in the flowers, in the old hall, in the garden; but never to be pinned down. And we went to the Church, and there was the florid foolish bust, but what I had not reckoned for was the worn simple slab, turned the wrong way, Kind Friend for Jesus' sake forbear—again he seemed to be all air and sun smiling serenely; and yet down there one foot from me lay the little bones that had spread over the world this vast illumination. Yes, and then we walked round the church, and all is simple and a little worn; the river slipping past the stone wall, with a red breadth in it from some flowering tree, and the edge of the turf unspoilt, soft and green and muddy, and two casual nonchalant swans. The church and the school and the house are all roomy spacious places, resonant, sunny today, and in and out [illegible]—yes, an impressive place; still living, and then the little bones lying there, which have created: to think of writing The Tempest looking out on that garden; what a rage and storm of thought to have come over my mind.

"[W]hat a rage and storm of thought." From her own dementia, less controlled than Shakespeare's though infinitely less intense, she grasps for this moment at any rate the terror of creating the *Tempest, Lear,* and *Hamlet.* But even more instructive for us as students of Virginia Woolf is the marvelous phrase "one foot from me lay the little bones that had spread over the world this vast illumination." For in this phrase we find the essence of her critical method. First "the little bones": her concern for the immediate, the concrete, the perishable individual; here Shakespeare, elsewhere in her writing the Brontë sisters, Jane Austen, Sir Walter Scott, Daniel Defoe. She makes us aware of many things: of mortality, of "mighty poets in their misery dead," of the incommensurability of the work and its author; of the eternity of the work, of its resonance *in saecula saeculorum,* into the ages of ages, when everything else that remains of an era has vanished. At this point we can say, "She has understood." And if she is big enough to understand Shakespeare, then we shall follow her with confidence in what she has to say about Spenser, Thomas Hardy, Feodor Dostoyevsky.

For writers as diverse as these occupy the pages of the two *Common Reader* volumes and the selections of her critical work published after her death. I have just called her a catholic critic, and so she is in the "categorical" range of her interests. She hops from the Middle Ages to her own time and takes in poets, novelists, and biographers. Writing as a reviewer forced this diversity upon her, but I think a taste for it was part of her equipment. It was part of that concept of freedom for which the Bloomsbury group (which we shall look at) stood. But her freedom had serious limitations, as had the group's. It couldn't take in writers like Rudyard Kipling, the greatest short-story writer of his time (though Forster, on the fringe of the group, admired him). It couldn't take in genuine religious experience such as T. S. Eliot's, George Herbert's, and Hopkins'. It couldn't take in Lawrence and Joyce, advocates of "normal" sex; and there was little it had to say in favor of the younger demagogues, Stephen Spender, W. H. Auden, and Louis MacNeice.

This critical blindspot operates most unfortunately in the religious field. Oddly enough she can stomach Dante—her diary shows her returning to him again and again for sustenance—but she veers away from George Herbert, Sir Thomas Browne, and the devotional element in John Donne. Here she is firmly Leslie Stephen's daughter. She does not go as far as he does in speaking, grotesquely, of Herbert "skulking behind the Prayer Book"; she feels Herbert's charm and authenticity and regrets she cannot respond to it. She loves the baroque intricacies of Browne's prose, but his piety stumps her. Donne as lover, Renaissance man of all seasons, searcher of human motivations fascinates her, but his activities as dean of St. Paul's, master preacher of his age, God-intoxicated-man leave her cold. This lacuna is a major flaw in her critical equipment.

But what is of supreme interest in the letters and diaries, and in the collection of autobiographical fragments published after her death with the title *Moments of Being* (1978), is the light they throw on her aims as a writer, on the technical problems she came up against in the practice of her art and the strategies she devised to overcome them. "Suppose one thing should open out of another . . . doesn't that give the looseness and lightness I want: doesn't that get closer and yet keep form and speed, and enclose everything, everything?" she writes on 26 January 1920. But, "my doubt is how far it will [include] enclose the human heart." Her doubt and perhaps our doubt. With all the brilliant achievement of the novels, is there not something missing that engages us in Sterne, Fielding, Trollope, Hardy? Has anyone ever loved one of Virginia Woolf's characters? Where is her parallel to Uncle Toby, Mr. Harding, Tess, or Squire Western? Our demand may be, and very probably is, illegitimate. Virginia Woolf was not writing that kind of novel. And yet—the little doubt creeps in.

I have been distracted from the consideration of technique to an aside on emotional values, but with Virginia Woolf, can we draw a line between the two?

Her monologue continues: "My doubt is how far it will enclose the human heart—Am I sufficiently mistress of my dialogue to net it there?" We see how she relates heart to dialogue, emotion to technique. Of course there are other ways: plot, characterization, comment. She will have none of them. This limits her, but also it gives her an immense concentration.

The diaries open up further possibilities. What *shape* is the novel to take? There must be form without formality, freedom that escapes license. "The art must be respected. . . . At the same time the irregular fire must be there," she writes on 18 November 1924. The irregular fire burns up the excrescences: one is left with something like the glowing skeleton of a Victorian house in the blitz.

Constantly pondering form, she thinks also of texture. An early diary entry gives us a glimpse of a discussion on art with Clive Bell and Roger Fry: "Roger asked me if I founded my writing upon texture or upon structure; I connected structure with plot, and therefore said 'texture.' Then we discussed the meaning of structure and texture in painting and in writing" (22 November 1917). The painting side and the writing side of Bloomsbury cross-pollinate; when Virginia Woolf thinks of completing a friend's novel for her, she thinks in pictorial terms: "My brain at once spins to clothe her story for her,—how happiness is to be represented by a green here; a yellow there and so on" (14 January 1920).

"WHO'S AFRAID OF VIRGINIA WOOLF?"

QUITE a lot of people *were*, to judge from the evidence of the diaries and letters and of a wide range of contemporary comment. We have already noted her confession that as a reviewer she delights in saying nasty things about writers mainly unknown to her; now, in the mass of autobiography that has poured from the presses since her death, we see her talent for satire exercised upon her closest friends and acquaintances. This is a Virginia Woolf we should hardly guess at from a reading of the novels and critical essays.

Once again she admits her guilt. "I am alarmed by my own cruelty with my friends," she writes in her diary on 28 March 1929. The cruelty surfaces in the extraordinarily vivid portraits that the diaries and letters give us of the members of that elusive and notorious entity the Bloomsbury group. We may find both instruction and amusement in following what she herself has to say in the letters and diaries about the group's fluctuating fortunes.

The Bloomsbury group, or just "Bloomsbury," was in short the inner circle of friends, relatives, and fellow workers in the arts who gathered around Virginia and Leonard Woolf at Hogarth House, Richmond, where the famous Hogarth Press was established. The genesis of the group was actually much anterior to this period in the Woolfs' careers—may indeed be traced back to the Cambridge Apostles (a prestigious debating society); and the name of course became current only after the Woolfs had moved in 1924 from Richmond to 52 Tavistock Square in the Bloomsbury section of London, close to her sister, Vanessa, and Clive Bell, Vanessa's husband. The nucleus was familial: Virginia and Leonard, Clive and Vanessa and Vanessa's lover, Duncan Grant. Around this nucleus revolved the writers Lytton Strachey and Edward Morgan Forster, the painter and art critic Roger Fry, the economist and Cambridge don John Maynard Keynes. Vanessa, Clive Bell, and Duncan Grant were themselves avant-garde painters and decorators. On the fringe of the group hovered the portentous figure of Thomas Stearns Eliot—portentous but by that very token slightly ridiculous to the ironic Virginia, with his Americanisms, his Anglo-Catholicism, his pedantry—an intimate friend of the Woolfs but decidedly not a habitué of the group.

Bloomsbury was atheistic, cosmopolitan, sexually deviant. This combination aroused a good deal of opposition among the upholders of the status quo; perhaps even more was provoked by the group's exclusiveness and its ascetic ideals of intellectual and artistic integrity. "Lax in morals, priggish in taste" is not a good formula for winning friends. Almost the first reference to Bloomsbury in the diaries is to this intellectual snobbism—as it appeared to the non-elect: "Barbara . . . seems to be ashamed of the unintellectuality of Nick. She wont take him to see her Bloomsbury friends. Bloomsbury, I think, will have one more corpse to its credit; for poor B.'s attainments aren't such as to give her a very secure footing there" (January 1918). Complacent, mildly sadistic. In a conversation with Clive Bell noted in the entry of 14 January 1918, Virginia Woolf discusses "the hypnotism exerted by Bloomsbury over the younger generation": already the group is felt to be a force for good or evil. "In fact the dominion that

'Bloomsbury' exercises over the sane and the insane alike seems to be sufficient to turn the brains of the most robust." Strong words: perhaps not to be taken too seriously.

Virginia has "an amusing talk" with Lytton Strachey on 8 September 1920: "How far has our set justified its promise? Lytton maintains that in ourselves we are as remarkable as the [Samuel] Johnson set, though our works may perish—still we're still at the beginning of our works." Complacency modulating into arrogance. Johnson, Boswell, Garrick, Gibbon, Burke, Reynolds, Goldsmith—can one really dare to compare? But it is interesting evidence that the "Bloomsberries" already saw themselves as a *cenacle*. And "H[arcourt] Brace's catalogue talking of us all by name as the most brilliant group in Gordon Square!" (7 November 1922).

Many detested Bloomsbury. In the eyes of Hubert Henderson, editor of the *Nation and Athenaeum*, the group was a "pest"; Rupert Brooke thought it "corrupt"; Wyndham Lewis lampooned it ferociously in *The Apes of God* (1930). On 13 December 1924, Virginia Woolf records, Edward Sackville-West implored his cousin Vita "to resist the contamination of Bloomsbury, personified in the serpent destroyer, VW." She didn't, and the outcome was *Orlando*. Virginia's affair with Vita and her flirtation with Clive Bell are clear examples of that "ethical code" which "allows poaching" in the preserves of love and friendship (12 March 1922) and gave rise to cries of corruption and contamination. Even Forster, usually counted a member of the group, expresses some dismay: "I don't think these people are little," he confided to his diary, "but they belittle all who come into their power."

Bloomsbury, an early version of the permissive society, was never more permissive than in its penchant for indecency and scatology in the spoken and written word. The indecencies of Virginia Woolf's letters are more sporadic, but they could hardly be nastier. Most of the smut comes in letters to her sister, Vanessa, and one suspects that Virginia Woolf may be keeping her end up, as it were, in the running contest of "I am more liberated than you!" that went on between them.

The diaries are more free than the letters from these blemishes. (I call them blemishes because indecency is tolerable only when it is witty, as in Restoration drama, or contributes an essential part to a larger whole, as in *Ulysses*. Writing about in-

decency in the first *Common Reader*, Virginia Woolf herself makes a distinction between "the little clod of mud which sticks to the crocus of necessity, and that which is plastered to it out of bravado.") In the diaries she is not called upon to impress or shock; she can simply be herself and develop her own line of thought. The diaries are a gymnasium, a laboratory, a workshop. A gymnasium: Virginia Woolf herself thinks of the diary entries as muscle-flexing in readiness for the novels—practice in form, style, character, atmosphere. They affect the literary essays too: compare, for instance, "On Not Knowing Greek" (in the first *Common Reader*) and the diary entry of 19 August 1918. A laboratory, or, if you like, an analyst's consulting room—where Virginia Woolf herself is both doctor and patient. A workshop: perfecting the diary itself, for she refers to it as "this book," a work of art existing in its own right, to be brought to some sort of perfection. It is a masterpiece, as Quentin Bell rightly claims in the introduction to his biography of Virginia Woolf, and not inferior to *The Waves* or *To the Lighthouse*—though quite different from these: more free, more relaxed, less anguished in the making. Turning to her diary she has no reviewers to fear when the year's stint is done, nor even the dubious approval of her friends to contend with.

The letters and diaries are remarkable for their brilliant gallery of portraits of celebrities and noncelebrities. Many of these, as I have already emphasized, are painted with malice, but by no means all. She can be deeply respectful, even reverential, as in her account of a visit to Hardy at Max Gate on 25 July 1926; she can appreciate the greatness of Eliot while laughing at his mannerisms and remaining puzzled by his piety. Her accounts fascinate by the new light they throw on these great men and by the record of conversations with them on all manner of subjects. We overhear their talk on religion, politics, philosophy, art, and literature.

It is easy to see how some of the published essays in the *Common Reader* and elsewhere grew out of these meetings of minds. And this is another field in which the diaries help us to understand the novelist and the critic. They show conclusively that the "devices" of *Mrs. Dalloway* and the *Common Reader*—Virginia Woolf's use of aspects of the natural world to interweave with and enrich human happenings, her personal commitment to the author she is dealing with and his or her world—are in no sense contrived; they are quite simply the way her sensibility works. Of course in her published work she is more deliberate than she is in her diary entries, but the spontaneity is still there.

Brilliant glimpses of human character and natural phenomena vie for preeminence in her pages. "Human beings have figured less" in her 1919 diary, she notes rather guiltily at the start of the new year, "than the red berries, the suns and the moons risings" (7 January 1920). Is this true, perhaps, of her novels too? One of her discoveries in technique, in "texture," is expressed as a theory of "strata" (1 November 1934): the interweaving of the inner and the outer, the human and the nonhuman worlds, the life of the mind and the life of the senses. Virginia Woolf uses this sort of counterpoint supremely well. But, we may ask, is the stratum of suns and moons and berries and rivers and seas somewhat predominant over the stratum of Eleanor Pargiter and Kitty Malone, of Mr. and Mrs. Ramsay even? This first pair of characters is from *The Years*, where she tries to exploit her technique rather too systematically; the second is from *To the Lighthouse*, where the central section, "Time Passes," isolates the stratum of things-without-man and is considered by some to be her finest achievement.

Yet having said that, it is only fair to add that my observation applies much more to the novels than to the letters and diaries, which is rather odd: one might expect Virginia Woolf's delight in the natural scene to push the human element into the background more decisively here than in the fiction. But no. Side by side with marvels of natural observation like "the churchyard grass running over the old tombstones like green water" in the diary entry of 10 April 1920 and "up in the air across the meadows one sees the handful of grain flung in a semicircle—what birds they are I never know," we may set Mrs. J. C. Squire,

settled into a kind of whitish sediment; a sort of indecency to me in her passive gloating contentment in the arm chair opposite; like some natural function, performing automatically—a jelly fish—without volition, yet with terrifying potentiality. She breaks off into young (reproduces like a vegetable) on the least provocation.

(31 January 1920)

This last vision passes directly into *The Years*: "The men shot [birds], and the women—he looked at his aunt as if she might be breaking into young even there, on that chair—the women broke off into innumerable babies." (The problem of her own child-

lessness racked Virginia throughout her married life.) What a hatred of "the fury and the mire of human veins" is expressed here! Yet for tough, lonely old women, flower sellers or charwomen, she has a lasting admiration.

A bright night; with a fresh breeze. An old beggar woman, blind, sat against a stone wall in Kingsway holding a brown mongrel in her arms and sang aloud. There was a recklessness about her; much in the spirit of London. Defiant—almost gay, clasping her dog as if for warmth. How many Junes has she sat there, in the heart of London? How she came to be there, what scenes she can go through, I can't imagine. O damn it all, I say, why cant I know all that too? Perhaps it was the song at night that seemed strange; she was singing shrilly, but for her own amusement, not begging. Then the fire engines came by—shrill too; with their helmets pale yellow in the moonlight. . . . It was gay, and yet terrible and fearfully vivid.

(8 June 1920)

These human portraits in the letters and the diaries range from old beggar women to flamboyant duchesses and take in the bourgeoisie and the world of business and politics on their way. Virginia Woolf's own servants at Tavistock Square and Monk's House played an important role—often exasperating, always comic—in her life. They too were infected by the libertarian ethos of Bloomsbury and called themselves "the Bloomsbury clique" (12 November 1930): "And today, for the 165th time, Nelly has given notice—won't be dictated to: must do as other girls do. This is the fruit of Bloomsbury" (6 January 1925). Virginia Woolf analyzes their characters and motivations with considerable skill—as indeed she does those of the hundreds of figures, casual callers or intimate friends, who flit through these "fearfully vivid" pages.

The human "insufficiencies" I mentioned earlier most often come under scrutiny, and so do the masks, carapaces, and facades people adopt to conceal them. Of Ka Cox, for instance, she writes: "She has some worm gnawing at her, some passionate desire to impress us" (3 November 1923). Or again:

We have also seen [Richard] Aldington, who calls like a tradesman for orders; a bluff, powerful, rather greasy eyed, nice downright man, who will make his way in the world, which I dont much like people to do. All young men do it. No young women; or in women it is trounced; in men forgiven. It's these reflections I want to enmesh, in writing; or these are among them.

(21 December 1924)

We have already seen her "enmeshing" Mrs. Squire in *The Years.* With such powerful analytical equipment her aims in the novel—to be a social psychologist, or a psychologist of individuals in their gestalts, their circles—are attainable.

Virginia Woolf's character analyses are curiously interwoven with strictures on the London boroughs in which her subjects are resident. She has a feeling for London as a symbolic entity that often reminds us of Blake. Each district possesses its peculiar spiritual character—in every case inferior to that of Bloomsbury! Individuals are assessed in relation to their involvement with their particular gestalt. Can any good thing come out of Hampstead? No: for there the archvillain John Middleton Murry, king of "the Underworld," as she unkindly designates the higher journalism, holds his court. What of South Kensington, her own home of childhood and youth? Rose Macaulay, the poet and novelist, "has lived with the riff raff of South Kensington culture for 15 years, and is rather jealous, spiteful, and uneasy about Bloomsbury" (25 May 1928). Virginia Woolf meets Iolo Williams of the *London Mercury:* "Let me see, there's some failure of sympathy between Chiswick and Bloomsbury, I think, [Williams] said. So we defined Bloomsbury" (24 February 1926). Chelsea fares little better. On a tour of Ireland in 1934 the Woolfs encountered Cyril Connolly and his wife: "They brought the reek of Chelsea with them" (4 May 1934).

Mayfair is suspect for other reasons. It is the home of the aristocracy, and for the aristocracy Virginia Woolf has very mixed feelings. She admires the genuine grande dame or grand seigneur for the same qualities she finds in the old shepherd at Rodmell or the old blind woman in Kingsway: authenticity, spontaneity, indifference to comment, eccentricity, toughness, freedom from cant. The lower-middle and upper-middle classes lack these attributes: they are dull, conformist, timorous, respectable. But there is a false nobility also, a society of arrogant parasites and mindless nincompoops: "The fifth transmitter of a foolish face." So "if I'm Bloomsbury, you're Mayfair" is a defensive riposte to Philip Morrell at Garsington (3 July 1919) after a visit to a pigsty during which Fry and Forster were discussed "most carefully" (23 June 1919). That the pigsty should have been chosen as the venue for a serious literary and aristocratic discussion strikes Virginia Woolf as a lovable aristocratic oddity that should have been unthinkable for the Murrys and the Frank Swinner-

tons and the Squires. But Morrell's use of "Bloomsbury" as a term of abuse has to be countered.

Virginia Woolf can feel a certain admiration for aristocrats such as Morrell. But on 13 January 1915 she draws a devastating picture of the "aged Countesses and pert young millionairesses" who bully the assistants in Day's lending library:

Days at 4 in the afternoon is the haunt of fashionable ladies, who want to be told what to read. A more despicable set of creatures I never saw. They come in furred like seals and scented like civets, condescend to pull a few novels about on the counter, and then demand languidly whether there is *anything* amusing? . . . The West End of London fills me with aversion; I look into motor cars & see the fat grandees inside, like portly jewels in satin cases.

Conspicuous waste! The glance at *Lear* (fur and civets) opens up a new vein of social satire that we find difficult to associate with Virginia Woolf, despite all her husband's Socialist indoctrination; and indeed she does not pursue it in the novels. But that it is genuinely there and that it caused Virginia some heart-searching is clear from her comments on Knole, the Sackvilles' great Elizabethan house that is the background for *Orlando.* As an example of conspicuous waste Knole would be hard to beat. Virginia is torn between her love as a novelist for the magnificent and the historic and her conscience as a witness of the plight of the London poor. After a seigneurial luncheon alone with his lordship she is led into this moral reflection: "There is Knole, capable of housing all the desperate poor of Judd Street, and with only that one solitary earl in the kernel." Thinking the matter over a little later she comments, as an exercise in self-analysis: "Obviously I did not keep my human values and my aesthetic values distinct." Nor was it ever possible for her to do so.

SELECTED BIBLIOGRAPHY

I. BIBLIOGRAPHY. B. J. Kirkpatrick, *A Bibliography of Virginia Woolf* (London, 1957); R. Majumdar, ed., *Virginia Woolf: An Annotated Bibliography of Criticism* (New York, 1977).

II. COLLECTED WORKS. *Uniform Edition of the Works of Virginia Woolf,* 14 vols. (London, 1929–1952); L. Woolf, ed., *Virginia Woolf: Collected Essays,* 4 vols. (London, 1966–1967).

III. SEPARATE WORKS. *The Voyage Out* (London, 1915),

novel; *The Mark on the Wall* (Richmond, Surrey, 1919), short story; *Kew Gardens* (Richmond, Surrey, 1919), short story; *Night and Day* (London, 1919), novel.

Monday or Tuesday (Richmond, Surrey, 1921), short stories; *Jacob's Room* (London, 1922), novel; *Mr. Bennett and Mrs. Brown* (Richmond, Surrey, 1924), criticism; *The Common Reader* (London, 1925), criticism; *Mrs. Dalloway* (London, 1925), novel; *To the Lighthouse* (London, 1927), novel; *Orlando* (London, 1928), novel; *A Room of One's Own* (London, 1929), essay.

On Being Ill (London, 1930), essay; *Beau Brummell* (New York, 1930), essay; *The Waves* (London, 1931), novel; *A Letter to a Young Poet* (London, 1932), criticism; *The Common Reader: Second Series* (London, 1932), criticism; *Flush: A Biography* (London, 1932), fictionalized biography of Elizabeth Barrett Browning; *Walter Sickert: A Conversation* (London, 1934), essay; *The Years* (London, 1937), novel fragment; *Three Guineas* (London, 1938), essay; *Reviewing* (London, 1939), criticism.

Roger Fry (London, 1940), biography; *Between the Acts* (London, 1941), novel, published posthumously; *The Death of the Moth* (London, 1942), essays, with intro. by L. Woolf; *A Haunted House* (London, 1943), short stories, with preface by L. Woolf; *The Moment and Other Essays* (London, 1947), essays, with preface by L. Woolf.

The Captain's Death-Bed (London, 1950), criticism, with preface by L. Woolf; *Granite and Rainbow* (London, 1958), essays; J. Guiguet, ed., *Contemporary Writers* (London, 1965), contains articles and reviews by Virginia Woolf published from 1905 to 1921; *The London Scene* (London, 1975), essays; L. Ruotolo, ed., *Freshwater. A Comedy* (London, 1976); *Books and Portraits* (London, 1977), further selections from the literary and biographical writings; J. Schulkind, ed., *Moments of Being* (London, 1978), previously unpublished writings; M. Leaska, ed., *The Pargiters* (London, 1978), uncompleted novel-essay portion of *The Years.*

IV. LETTERS AND DIARIES. *A Writer's Diary* (London, 1953); L. Woolf and J. Strachey, eds., *Letters of Virginia Woolf and Lytton Strachey* (London, 1956).

The Letters of Virginia Woolf, vol. I: N. Nicolson and J. Trautmann, eds., *The Flight of the Mind (1888–1912)* (London, 1975); vol. II: N. Nicolson, ed., *The Question of Things Happening (1912–1922)* (1976); vol. III: N. Nicolson and J. Trautmann, eds., *A Change of Perspective (1923–1928)* (1977): vol. IV: N. Nicholson and J. Trautmann, eds., *A Reflection of the Other Person (1929–1931)* (1978); vol. V: N. Nicolson and J. Trautmann, eds., *The Sickle Side of the Moon (1932–1935)* (1979); vol. VI: N. Nicolson and J. Trautmann, eds., *Leave the Letters Till We're Dead (1936–1941)* (1980).

A. O. Bell, ed., *The Diaries of Virginia Woolf,* vol. I: *1915–1919* (London, 1977); vol. II: *1920–1924* (1978); vol. III: *1925–1930* (1980); vol. IV: *1931–1935* (1982).

V. TRANSLATIONS AND INTRODUCTIONS. F. M. Dostoyev-sky, *Stavrogin's Confession* (London, 1922), trans., with S. S. Koteliansky; *Talks with Tolstoy* (London, 1923), trans., with S. S. Koteliansky; *Tolstoy's Love Letters* (London, 1923), trans., with S. S. Koteliansky; intro. to J. M. Cameron, *Victorian Photographs* (London, 1926); intro. to L. Sterne, *A Sentimental Journey* (London, 1928); intro. to *Selections from the Works of George Gissing* (London, 1929); intro. to *Recent Paintings by Vanessa Bell* (London, 1930); intro. to M. L. Davies, ed., *Life as We Have Known It, by Co-operative Working Women* (London, 1931; repr. New York, 1975); intro to G. Gissing, *By the Ionian Sea* (London, 1933).

VI. BIOGRAPHICAL AND CRITICAL STUDIES. W. Holtby, *Virginia Woolf* (London, 1932); F. Delattre, *Le Roman psychologique de Virginia Woolf* (Paris, 1932); R. Gruber, *Virginia Woolf* (Leipzig, 1935); L. E. Rillo, *Katherine Mansfield and Virginia Woolf* (Buenos Aires, 1941); D. Daiches, *Virginia Woolf* (London, 1942); E. M. Forster, *Virginia Woolf* (Cambridge, 1942), the Rede Lecture; C. Segura, *The Transcendental and the Transitory in Virginia Woolf's Novels* (Buenos Aires, 1943); J. Bennett, *Virginia Woolf: Her Art as a Novelist* (London, 1945; pprbk. ed., 1975); R. L. Chambers, *The Novels of Virginia Woolf* (London, 1947); B. Blackstone, *Virginia Woolf: A Commentary* (London, 1949).

R. Brower, *The Fields of Light* (New York, 1951; repr. 1962); J. Lehmann, *The Open Night* (London, 1952), contains an appreciation; J. K. Johnstone, *The Bloomsbury Group* (London, 1954); J. Hafley, *The Glass Roof* (New York, 1954); A. Pippett, *The Moth and the Star: A Biography of Virginia Woolf* (Boston, 1955); J. Guiguet, *Virginia Woolf et son oeuvre* (Paris, 1962); D. Brewster, *Virginia Woolf* (London, 1963); R. Freedman, *The Lyrical Novel* (London, 1963); L. Woolf, *An Autobiography of the Years,* vol. III: *Beginning Again, 1911–1918* (London, 1964); vol. IV: *Downhill All the Way, 1919–1939* (1967); vol. V: *The Journey, Not the Arrival, Matters, 1939–1969* (1969); C. Woodring, *Virginia Woolf* (New York, 1966); M. Holroyd, *Lytton Strachey: A Critical Biography,* 2 vols. (London, 1967–1968).

Q. Bell, *Virginia Woolf: A Biography* (New York, 1972); A. V. B. Kelley, *The Novels of Virginia Woolf: Fact and Vision* (Chicago, 1973); A. McLaurin, *Virginia Woolf* (London, 1973); J. Naresmore, *"World Without a Self": Virginia Woolf and the Novel* (London, 1973); J. Lehmann, *Virginia Woolf and Her World* (London, 1975); R. Majumdar and A. McLaurin, eds., *Virginia Woolf: The Critical Heritage* (London, 1975); A. Fleishman, *Virginia Woolf: A Critical Reading* (Baltimore, 1977); H. Marder, *Feminism and Art: The Novels of Virginia Woolf* (London, 1977); I. M. Parsons and G. Spater, *"Marriage of True Minds": An Intimate Portrait of Leonard and Virginia Woolf* (London, 1977); J. Lehmann, *Thrown to the Woolfs* (London, 1978); J. O. Love, *Virginia Woolf: Sources of Madness and Art* (Los Angeles, 1978); R. Poole, *The Unknown Virginia*

Woolf (London, 1978); P. Rose, *Woman of Letters: The Life of Virginia Woolf* (London, 1978); L. Edel, *Bloomsbury: A House of Lions* (London, 1979); M. A. Leaska, *The Novels of Virginia Woolf* (London, 1979); M. Rosenthal, *Virginia Woolf* (London, 1979); B. A. Schlack, *"Continuing Presences": Virginia Woolf's Use of Literary Allusion* (University Park, Pa., 1979).

M. DiBattista, *Virginia Woolf's Major Novels: The Fables of Anon* (New Haven, 1980); R. Freedman, ed., *Virginia Woolf: Revaluation and Continuity* (Los Angeles, 1980); J. Hawthorn, *Virginia Woolf's "Mrs. Dalloway": A Study in Alienation* (Philadelphia, 1980); P. Meiser, *"Absent Father": Virginia Woolf and Walter Pater* (New Haven, 1980); L. A. de Salvo, *Virginia Woolf's First Voyage: A Novel in the Making* (London, 1980); F. Spalding, *Vanessa Bell* (New York, 1983).

WILLIAM WORDSWORTH

(1770-1850)

J. R. Watson

LIFE

IN his great autobiographical poem, *The Prelude*, Wordsworth tells the story of his early years; but it is important to remember that the truth was more complex than the poem suggests. *The Prelude*, like all poems, selects its own imaginative material from the experience on which it is based; and many of Wordsworth's poems are founded on his own life and his interpretation of it. To understand his poetry fully, we need to know something of Wordsworth's life, in more detail than we do with other poets whose imaginations are not so intricately connected to their own experience.

William Wordsworth was born at Cockermouth, Cumberland, on 7 April 1770, the second child of John and Ann Wordsworth. John Wordsworth was an attorney, the "agent" of Sir James Lowther, for whom he acted in legal and political matters. The Wordsworth children were born in a substantial house in Cockermouth, where the family lived until 1778; but in March of that year Ann Wordsworth died, and the family was split up. William's beloved sister Dorothy (born 25 December 1771) was sent to live at Halifax with her mother's cousin, and the boys were sent to school at Hawkshead. Fortunately they were well educated there and well cared for: they lived in a cottage with an old lady named Ann Tyson, who took in school boarders and who seems to have given them the right amount of affection and freedom. The impression conveyed by *The Prelude* is one of extraordinary energy and activity, but also of normality; he played games, both indoor and outdoor, with a natural exuberance and enthusiasm.

On 30 December 1783, when William was thirteen, his father died; years later he remembered the boyish anticipation of going home for the Christmas holidays and the sadness that followed. The house at Cockermouth had to be given up, and from then on the boys spent their holidays either with their uncle at Whitehaven or, more frequently, at Penrith with their maternal grandparents, the Cooksons, and their uncle, Christopher Crackanthorpe Cookson. There the boys were patronized and made to feel dependent, and William was rebellious: it is clear that his childhood was by no means as uniformly happy as *The Prelude* suggests, and it is of Hawkshead and not Penrith that the poet writes when he looks back to the happiness of the early years.

In October 1787, the young Wordsworth left the Lake District for the first time, to become an undergraduate at St. John's College, Cambridge. Although there were other boys from Hawkshead there, and he was in many ways contented, he was also uneasy in his mind and restless; just how restless may be seen from the marvelous fourth book of *The Prelude*, when he describes the joy of returning to Hawkshead for his first summer vacation. The most spectacular evidence of his unease came two years later, in the long vacation of 1790, when he and his friend Robert Jones undertook a strenuous walking tour through France and Switzerland. By then he had given up any intention of getting an honors degree, and his leaving Cambridge at a time when he might have been preparing for examinations was a snub to the academic life. The tour itself, which gave rise to *Descriptive Sketches* and later to the sixth book of *The Prelude*, was one of the great imaginative experiences of Wordsworth's life.

It was followed by an unsettled period: after graduating from Cambridge without honors in January 1791, he lived in London for some months before spending the summer in Wales, revisiting Cambridge, and then leaving for France in November.

His motive for visiting France was probably to learn the language: the results were very different. First, in a country that was experiencing a revolution he received his early political education, partly from his own observation and partly from his friendship with Michel de Beaupuy. Beaupuy was an unusual man, an army officer who was isolated from his fellow officers as a consequence of his revolutionary sympathies. Beaupuy's politics were simple and humane: he was against corruption and poverty, and looked forward to a time when men would live in liberty and brotherhood and the world would be a better place. Second, Wordsworth met Annette Vallon, the daughter of a deceased surgeon of Blois; they became lovers, and she became pregnant.

Thus, in a little over a year, Wordsworth had experienced a remarkable political and sexual awakening. Moreover, it was a time of great events: during his time in France the attack on the Tuileries, the September massacres, the abolition of the monarchy, and the split between the moderate Girondins (some of whom Wordsworth knew) and the Jacobins heralded the trial and execution of the king (21 January 1793) and the Terror. By late December 1792, however, Wordsworth had returned to England; his child, Anne-Caroline, was born and baptized on 15 December.

The following year, 1793, was of considerable importance to Wordsworth in several ways. In the first place, it saw the first publication of any of Wordsworth's poems: *An Evening Walk* and *Descriptive Sketches* appeared on 29 January. Three days later, France declared war on England, and England responded by declaring war on France on 11 February. Wordsworth's response, as he tells us in *The Prelude*, was painfully confused: his natural patriotism conflicted with his hope for the Revolution, and he must also have been disturbed by the separation from Annette and the child. Some of his anger is found in the "Letter to the Bishop of Llandaff," an unpublished reply to a sermon on *The Wisdom and Goodness of God in Having Made Both Rich and Poor*: the bishop's appendix to the sermon criticized the French and complacently preferred the British constitution and British justice. Wordsworth's reply demonstrates his impatience with what he called "the baleful influence of aristocracy and nobility upon human happiness and virtue" (p. 46) and his use of a classic argument for the revolutionary use of force:

> . . . a time of revolution is not the season of true Liberty. Alas! the obstinacy & perversion of men is such that she is too often obliged to borrow the very arms of despotism to overthrow him, and in order to reign in peace must establish herself by violence.[1]
>
> (I.33)

[1]All prose quotations are from W. J. B. Owen and J. W. Smyser, eds., *The Prose Works of William Wordsworth*, 3 vols. (Oxford, 1974). References are to volume and page numbers.

The "Letter" shows clearly Wordsworth's hatred of inherited rank and wealth, of rich clergy, and of the British system of justice (from which he and his brothers and sisters had suffered: after the death of their father, Lowther, now Lord Lonsdale, refused to pay for the work that he had done, and a long and inconclusive lawsuit followed).

It was at this moment that a friend, William Calvert, proposed a tour of the west of England, traveling in a small cart called a "whiskey": they began on the Isle of Wight, where Wordsworth's anger was probably further inflamed by the sight of the English fleet preparing for war. From there they set out across Salisbury Plain: an accident occurred to the whiskey, and Calvert took the horse, leaving Wordsworth to walk. Salisbury Plain was a desolate part of the country, and his solitude must have seemed to the young poet to be emblematic of his isolation and lonely frustration: he walked northward, past Stonehenge, having frightening visions (*The Prelude*, book XII, 1805 text) of ancient Britons engaged in savage war and human sacrifice. From there he traveled northwest, to Tintern Abbey and up the Wye valley to his friend Robert Jones in north Wales. The journey was remembered by him with a peculiar vividness: fifty years later he told Isabella Fenwick that it "left on my mind imaginative impressions the force of which I have felt to this day" (*Poetical Works*, I.330).[2] From it came experiences that represent two seminal themes of Wordsworth's poetry: his King Lear-like awareness of the houseless poverty of the outcasts of society, and his vivid appreciation of the beauty of a scene like that a few miles above Tintern Abbey. Meanwhile we may gain some insight into the kind of young man he appeared to be, if we realize that a tinker (who later became Peter Bell in the poem of that name) thought he might be a murderer. He had no doubt been sleeping rough and probably looked unkempt and farouche.

To the following months and years belong a variety of experiences, but none so significant as this remarkable journey on foot. Later in 1793, Wordsworth probably revisited France in secret, supposedly fleeing from Paris when his life was in danger; in 1794 he spent a happy few weeks with his sister Dorothy at Keswick; later in the year he stayed with a friend, Raisley Calvert (brother of William), being his companion during a terminal illness. Calvert died

[2]*The Poetical Works of William Wordsworth*, revised edition by E. de Selincourt and H. Darbishire, 5 vols. (Oxford, 1952–1959).

in January 1795, leaving Wordsworth a legacy that enabled him to live independently though simply. He returned to London, where he furthered his acquaintance with the radical political philosopher William Godwin, and in September he accepted the offer of a house in Dorset called Racedown (between Crewkerne and Lyme Regis) from some Bristol friends. There he and Dorothy settled down, and he began to recover from the upheavals of the previous years. He wrote much of the second version of a poem on the Salisbury Plain experience and a verse drama, *The Borderers*; though the main benefit of these years was a steady growth in the belief in his own powers. This was given a powerful boost by the developing acquaintance with Samuel Taylor Coleridge, whom Wordsworth had first met in 1794 and subsequently corresponded with. Coleridge visited Racedown in June 1797, leaping over a gate and bounding across a field in his eagerness to arrive. They read their poems to each other, with mutual delight; by mid-July, after Coleridge had brought William and Dorothy back with him to Nether Stowey (in North Somerset), they had moved into Alfoxden House nearby. There followed a year of buoyant spirits and happy activity, walking, writing, and preparing the *Lyrical Ballads* (1798). The final poem, "Lines Composed a Few Miles Above Tintern Abbey," was added in July after a short walking tour with Dorothy, in which they revisited the landscape that Wordsworth had seen in 1793; its confident tone of sustained and assured thankfulness indicates Wordsworth's joy at finding his imagination working at full stretch after the troublesome years that followed his return from France.

Throughout these years, it is difficult to overemphasize the importance of Dorothy Wordsworth's love and care: she continued to have faith in her brother and his poetry, and her vivid appreciation of nature (recorded in her journals) was an inspiration to both Wordsworth and Coleridge. The three left for Germany in September 1798, in the same month that saw the appearance of *Lyrical Ballads*. The plan was to settle near a university town, learn German, and attend lectures. They split up, to avoid speaking English all the time, and the Wordsworths settled in Goslar, during an unusually severe winter: deprived of books and company, William began to write again, composing some of the "Lucy" poems and the first parts of what was later to be book I of *The Prelude*. They left Goslar in February 1799, and after a short walking tour in Germany returned to England in the spring. In December 1799, they finally came to rest in the Lake District, in the cottage at Grasmere that is now called Dove Cottage. Except for occasional short periods or visits, Wordsworth lived in the Lake District for the rest of his life, at first at Grasmere and (after 1813) at Rydal, the next village.

The first years at Grasmere were years of great happiness, for Wordsworth seems to have felt a very deep sense of homecoming (which is expressed in "Home at Grasmere," a poem that remained unpublished at his death). In October 1802 he married Mary Hutchinson, after a brief visit to France to see Annette and the nine-year-old Anne-Caroline; he had known Mary Hutchinson and her family since childhood and stayed with them at their farm at Sockburn-on-Tees after returning from Germany. Meanwhile, Coleridge had settled at Keswick, thirteen miles away, though he was unhappy with his wife and often in poor spirits. He left Keswick for Malta in January 1804, and although the friends met again, there was never the same creative interchange and intimacy that had taken place in 1797–1798. Before leaving, however, Coleridge had introduced Wordsworth to Sir George Beaumont, a wealthy patron and connoisseur, who became a benefactor and friend until his death in 1827: it was to Beaumont that Wordsworth turned for support during the greatest crisis of his adult life, the death of his brother John at sea in February 1805.

The death of John Wordsworth, followed by the growth of the friendship with Sir George and Lady Beaumont, herald the later years of Wordsworth's life. They were, perhaps inevitably, less exciting than before: in 1813 he became distributor of stamps for Westmorland, a post that carried with it a commission on the sale of stamps, which amounted to some £400 a year, although clerks and other officials had to be paid out of this. Nevertheless, the post marked a significant change in Wordsworth's status and way of life; similarly, the friendship with Beaumont was with a man who was, unlike Coleridge, conventional and conservative in every way. We can only speculate on the reasons why Wordsworth wrote so little good poetry after 1807; but his increasingly respectable life, and the loss of Coleridge's stimulus, may have been partly responsible.

Apart from some Scottish and Continental tours, Wordsworth remained at Rydal Mount from 1813 to his death on 23 April 1850. In his later years, he was revered and honored: the University of Durham gave him an honorary degree in 1838, and Oxford followed in 1839; in 1843, on the death of Southey, he became poet laureate. His later years were clouded by the protracted illness of his sister, Dorothy, and by the death of his beloved daughter Dora in 1847; but he had the satisfaction of seeing his poems grow in popularity, and his fame spread through the English-speaking world. His faith that his poetry "must sooner or later work its way into the hearts and minds of the people"[3] had been fully justified.

EARLY POEMS

IN 1843, Wordsworth said that "no change has taken place in my manner for the last forty-five years." This dates Wordsworth's mature style at 1798, with the publication of *Lyrical Ballads*, and suggests that in the earlier poems he had failed to find his own individual voice. At first sight this seems to be the case: *An Evening Walk* and *Descriptive Sketches* (1793) are written in heroic couplets and contain many borrowings and influences from eighteenth-century poets; while another major poem of these years, the Salisbury Plain poem (in two versions), is written in Spenserian stanzas, another popular eighteenth-century form. In other respects, too, they seem conventional, with titles, diction, and description following the eighteenth-century patterns. They were later revised extensively by Wordsworth, and they are best read in the 1793 text, which is printed in many editions. There the reader can see the dominance of the contemporary style:

> —Then Quiet led me up the huddling rill,
> Bright'ning with water-breaks the sombrous gill;
> To where, while thick above the branches close,
> In dark-brown bason its wild waves repose,
> Inverted shrubs, and moss of darkest green,
> Cling from the rocks, with pale wood-weeds between;
> Save that, atop, the subtle sunbeams shine,
> On wither'd briars that o'er the craggs recline;
> Sole light admitted here, a small cascade,
> Illumes with sparkling foam the twilight shade.
> Beyond, along the visto of the brook,
> Where antique roots its bustling path o'erlook,
> The eye reposes on a secret bridge
> Half grey, half shagg'd with ivy to its ridge.
> (*An Evening Walk*, 71–84)

Here the reader notices immediately the personification of "Quiet," the use of words like "sombrous," "illumes," and "visto," the use of inversion, with a latinate postponement of the main verb, and the use of a Latin participial construction, "Sole light admitted here," to make an adjectival phrase. All these disappear in later versions, which suggests that Wordsworth himself came to regard them as blemishes on the poem. Yet the early poetry is not so unoriginal as it looks. It was *Descriptive Sketches* that first drew Coleridge's attention to Wordsworth, as he tells us in *Biographia Literaria*:

In the form, style, and manner of the whole poem, and in the structure of the particular lines and periods, there is an harshness and acerbity connected and combined with words and images all a-glow, which might recall those products of the vegetable world, where gorgeous blossoms rise out of the hard and thorny rind and shell, within which the rich fruit was elaborating. The language was not only peculiar and strong, but at times knotty and contorted, as by its own impatient strength; while the novelty and struggling crowd of images, acting in conjunction with the difficulties of the style, demanded always a greater closeness of attention, than poetry, (at all events, than descriptive poetry) has a right to claim.[4]

(I.56)

What Coleridge is describing here is a kind of individual voice, powerful and original, which he had detected: and it is true that the verse is full of energy, bursting out of the heroic couplets as a child outgrows its clothes. The subject matter, too, seems too big for the form of these poems: *An Evening Walk*, for instance, is principally about a landscape seen during the course of an afternoon, but it also contains a section in the middle that describes a destitute mother and her starving children. Similarly, *Descriptive Sketches*, which is about Wordsworth's tour of the Alps in 1790, contains a great diversity of material including descriptions of the mountain scenery, reflections on the lot of the Swiss and of mankind in general, and a prophecy of liberty. Both poems look two ways, in fact, to nature and to man, and in this we can see the beginnings of Wordsworth's continuous later concern with the interaction of the two. In these early poems they exist side by side, uncomfortably juxtaposed; in the later

---

[3]Mary Moorman, *William Wordsworth: A Biography*, vol. II: *The Later Years 1803–1850* (Oxford, 1965), p. 544.

[4]All references to *Biographia Literaria* are to the J. Shawcross edition (Oxford, 1907).

poetry there is a creative interaction, so that Wordsworth can portray himself.

> On Man, on Nature, and on Human Life,
> Musing in solitude. . . .
> (preface to *The Excursion*, 1–2)

The introduction of man and human life here is
not just a tautology: Wordsworth surveys man, and
nature, but also the larger significance that arises
from the interaction between the two, between man
and the world around him; he is to investigate the
nature and purpose of human life, its good and evil,
its joy and sorrow. These things are latent in *An
Evening Walk* and *Descriptive Sketches:* both are
filled with images of the beauty and sublimity of
nature, but they are also conscious that mankind,
besides having such enjoyments, often has to suffer
hardship and misery.

Descriptive Sketches, which was written during
Wordsworth's residence in France in 1792, contains a
good deal of explicit political suggestion. The
"Salisbury Plain" poems carry this further. They are
different versions of the same poem, which ends up
in the *Poetical Works*, somewhat toned down, as
"Guilt and Sorrow," though part of it was published
in the *Lyrical Ballads* under the title of "The Female
Vagrant." The first Salisbury Plain poem draws its
inspiration from Wordsworth's solitary wanderings
in 1793 and his angry state of mind at the time: the
first version ends with an impassioned plea for
revolution and a new order:

> Heroes of Truth pursue your march, uptear
> Th'Oppressor's dungeon from its deepest base;
> High o'er the towers of Pride undaunted rear
> Resistless in your might the herculean mace
> Of Reason; let foul Error's monster race
> Dragged from their dens start at the light with pain
> And die; pursue your toils, till not a trace
> Be left on earth of Superstition's reign,
> Save that eternal pile which frowns on Sarum's plain.
> (541–549)

The story of the poem concerns a good-hearted
sailor (the first stanzas of the second version show
him helping an aged soldier) who has been forced into the navy by a press-gang and dismissed without
reward. In his anger he robs and kills a traveler, and
now wanders homeless across the plain. In a ruined
building he meets a woman, the female vagrant, who
relates her story: her father was forced to leave his

home by a rapacious landowner, and her husband
joined the army to provide for the family; they
followed the army to America, where the husband
and children all died; and the woman was then
shipped back to England. On the following morning
the sailor and the vagrant continue their journey,
pacifying an angry father who is beating his child,
until they meet a dying woman, who turns out to be
the sailor's wife; her death affects the sailor so deeply
that he gives himself up to justice and is hanged.

In the later published version, entitled "Guilt and
Sorrow," the sailor is deemed to have suffered
enough; in the earlier (second) version, Wordsworth
drives home the message of the poem with a remorseless and fixed anger. The female vagrant is one victim of a society that allows the rich to deprive the
poor of their livelihood, and in which there is no
alternative to poverty but enlistment in the army.
The poor and helpless, however benevolent and well
disposed, are cast out to fend for themselves, while
old soldiers and sailors are thrown on the scrap heap.
The sailor is an example of a man who is driven to
desperation by the treatment he has received; even
more bitter, perhaps, is the way in which at the end,
he is surrounded by complacent people who bring
him to justice; like the judge in Camus's *L'Etranger*,
they make no attempt to understand him. After his
death, as he swings in chains on a gibbet, a fair is set
up beneath, in a final macabre touch. Meanwhile,
the housewife who cares for the dying woman in her
last hours stands out as a type of the Good Samar-
itan, and we are also allowed to see the deep humanity of the sailor and the female vagrant. The sustained
anger of the poem is matched only by the poet's admiration for those who can preserve their natural benevolence and kindness in the face of such adversity.

In the years following 1793 this relationship between individual behavior and the creation of the
good society was clearly much in Wordsworth's
mind, particularly in view of the later course of the
French Revolution. The motives of the Revolution
had been so good, and its outcome so disastrous
(especially, Wordsworth thought, under Robespierre), that some explanation was desirable. This
Wordsworth attempted to supply in *The Borderers*,
the other major work of these years. The complicated plot of this tragedy in verse is conducted to a point
at which a good man, Marmaduke, is persuaded to
leave an old blind man to die in a bleak wasteland;
Marmaduke has been deceived by Oswald, who had
committed a similar crime many years before, after

being manipulated by others. Marmaduke's motives are correct; he is a benevolent man who ends the play in remorse and penitence. Oswald, on the other hand, is driven by his crime to renounce remorse, to see in himself a terrible freedom from normal principles of benevolence and restraint. This is the freedom that he urges upon Marmaduke, and it was such a freedom that Wordsworth saw a man like Robespierre exercising. "Let us suppose," says Wordsworth, describing Oswald in the preface of *The Borderers*, "a young man of great intellectual powers, yet without any solid principles of genuine benevolence" (*Prose Works*, I.76). His action shows "the dangerous use which may be made of reason when a man has committed a great crime" (*ibid.*, p. 79). The note to *The Borderers* connects this clearly with the experience in France, for Wordsworth writes that "sin and crime are apt to start from their very opposite qualities," and that he had seen this "while the revolution was rapidly advancing to its extreme of wickedness" (*Poetical Works*, I.342).

When Coleridge heard Wordsworth read *The Borderers* he described it as "absolutely wonderful" (*Poetical Works*, I.344); he praised the work for its "*profound* touches of the human heart," seeing in it what later critics have come to recognize as a primary interest of Wordsworth's, the concern with the human heart, traditionally the seat of the affections and the organ of shared feeling between man and man. The concern for the human heart, and for what Wordsworth describes in the preface as "the primary laws of our nature," is brilliantly expressed in *Lyrical Ballads*. In *The Borderers* it is tangled up with a complicated plot and an undramatic scenario; in *Lyrical Ballads* it is produced in a marvelous series of spare, taut narrative poems, interwoven with concrete expressions of Wordsworth's own belief and ending with the triumphant "Tintern Abbey."

LYRICAL BALLADS

COLERIDGE described Wordsworth's part in *Lyrical Ballads* in his *Biographia Literaria*. While his own energies were to be directed toward the supernatural, Wordsworth

was to propose to himself as his object, to give the charm of novelty to things of every day, and to excite a feeling analogous to the supernatural, by awakening the mind's at-

tention from the lethargy of custom, and directing it to the loveliness and the wonders of the world before us; an inexhaustible treasure, but for which, in consequence of the film of familiarity and selfish solicitude we have eyes, yet see not, ears that hear not, and hearts that neither feel nor understand.

(II.6)

It will be seen that Wordsworth's role was to present the ordinary so that the reader would see it with new eyes; as he said himself about "The Thorn": "Cannot I by some invention do as much to make this Thorn permanently an impressive object as the storm has made it to my eyes at this moment?" (*Poetical Works*, II.511). The result is that *Lyrical Ballads* contains many poems that are concerned with simple people in ordinary surroundings, who have problems that are common, sometimes universal: old age, poverty, pregnancy and betrayal, cold, bereavement. Their stories are narrated in a style that is simple and direct, influenced by the street ballads in its dramatic abruptness. This style has sometimes been seen as unsuccessful, as Wordsworth's theory running away with his practice, yet its awkward simplicity is often peculiarly effective. Wordsworth writes a poetry the texture of which allows no escape, which is perhaps why it has been disliked: the lines shock the reader into a recognition of the suffering and the happiness of his fellow human beings, and there is no delicate transfusion of life into art, but, rather, a direct rendering of life into something more tactless and immediate than art. In its spirit it resembles Marianne Moore's poem "Poetry":

I, too, dislike it: there are things that are important
beyond all this fiddle.

And yet, paradoxically, Wordsworth's is a highly functioning poetic art, in the sense described by Marianne Moore in her last verse:

. . . if you demand on the one hand,
the raw material of poetry in
all its rawness and
that which is on the other hand
genuine, then you are interested in poetry.

Wordsworth certainly presents the raw material in all its rawness, in a way that, for many, commands respect; if he leaves himself open to the jeers of the cynic or the skeptic, this is a price he is willing to pay, for the greatest poets have always been vulnerable in this way. So we have Simon Lee's thick ankles, and the little pond in "The Thorn," which is three feet long and two feet wide, and poor Betty in "The Idiot Boy," "in a sad distemper." Not only is there a distinct rawness in these lines, but there is also "that which is on the other hand/genuine," the respect for the figures who appear in the poems, a respect that comes from love. Wordsworth is well aware of the danger of becoming a voyeur of human suffering: in "The Thorn," for instance, he introduces just such a figure, a retired sea captain who has too little to occupy his time, so that he becomes endlessly curious about his neighbors, and especially about the plight of one of them. We are presented, therefore, with a poem that is at once a narrative and a dramatic monologue; other examples of the sophistication of Wordsworth's art are found in "The Idiot Boy," where the diction creates its own rhetorical and rhythmical patterns, and "Simon Lee," where the colloquial simplicities of the earlier verses give way to a final quotation that requires the reader to think, sharply and suddenly, to penetrate beneath the conventional complaint of man's ingratitude to something more profound and more pathetic.

It is this respect for his fellow creatures, and this craft, that are the distinguishing marks of *Lyrical Ballads*: they are poems that challenge our very ideas about the nature of poetry and that also confound our expectations in other ways. If we accommodate ourselves to the rhetoric of "The Idiot Boy," we are surprised by the ritual game of "Expostulation and Reply" and "The Tables Turned," in which Matthew and William play out a game of statement and counterstatement. If we become accustomed to the simplicity of the ballad style, both in narrative poems and in reflective ones, we are surprised by the majestic reflections of "Lines Composed a Few Miles Above Tintern Abbey." This final poem, the last in the 1798 collection, is written in the eighteenth-century meditative blank-verse style, but with such individuality, originality, and organization as to make it a fitting conclusion to the volume; it should be seen not as the one success in a curious collection but as the open statement of what is explicit or implicit in so many of the other poems, a wonderful openness to feeling and experience. In the preface to *Lyrical Ballads*, published in the second edition (1800), Wordsworth writes of the poet that he is

a man speaking to men: a man, it is true, endowed with more lively sensibility, more enthusiasm and tenderness, who has a greater knowledge of human nature, and a more comprehensive soul, than are supposed to be common among mankind; a man pleased with his own passions and volitions, and who rejoices more than other men in the spirit of life that is in him; delighting to contemplate similar volitions and passions as manifested in the goings-on of the Universe, and habitually impelled to create them where he does not find them.

(*Poetical Works*, II.393)

The importance of this definition is not only in its splendid statement of a shared humanity between the poet and others; it is also concerned with the character of the poet as enthusiast, who is able to express his joy at being alive and finding himself in a world that is full of the same kind of passion and life. To be thus aware of the joy of the world is to be aware also of its variety and complexity, its pain as well as its joy; and Wordsworth is a great tragic poet as well as one who celebrates the happiness of man. He sees the pain of old age, the miseries of poverty, the tragicomedy of idiocy. The extraordinary feature of *Lyrical Ballads* is that they carry everywhere the evidence of the poet's love for life, for his fellow human beings, for those who are oppressed by society, for his sister, for the natural world around him. This energetic love of life is, in Wordsworth's eyes, evidence of a full humanity; in the preface he describes a poet as "singing a song in which all human beings join with him" (*Poetical Works*, II.396).

The fundamental conception of the poet as human being, sharing in the joys and sorrows of all mankind with a more than common enthusiasm, has tended to become obscured in the preface by Wordsworth's statements about poetic language. The principal object of *Lyrical Ballads* was, he said,

to choose incidents and situations from common life, and to relate or describe them, throughout, as far as was possible in a selection of language really used by men, and, at the same time, to throw over them a certain colouring of imagination, whereby ordinary things should be presented to the mind in an unusual aspect. . . .

(*ibid.*, II.386)

The phrase "a selection of language really used by men," and a similar one from the first paragraph, "a selection of the real language of men in a state of vivid sensation," have caused many problems to critics of Wordsworth, from Coleridge onward, who have wanted to know what is meant by "a selection" or by "real" language; other difficulties have been posed by those who have solemnly taken Wordsworth to task for what follows:

> Humble and rustic life was generally chosen, because, in that condition, the essential passions of the heart find a better soil in which they can attain their maturity, are less under restraint, and speak a plainer and more emphatic language; because in that condition of life our elementary feelings co-exist in a state of greater simplicity, and consequently, may be more accurately contemplated, and more forcibly communicated; because the manners of rural life germinate from those elementary feelings, and, from the necessary character of rural occupations, are more easily comprehended, and are more durable; and, lastly, because in that condition the passions of men are incorporated with the beautiful and permanent forms of nature.
>
> (*ibid.*, II.386–387)

We may disagree with Wordsworth about the need to choose humble and rustic life (although there are clear sociological indications that he may have been right), but his motives are clear and creditable: they are concerned with "the essential patterns of the heart," "elementary feelings," and "the passions of men" which are "incorporated with the beautiful and permanent forms of nature." His theory of language (partly set out in the appendix to the preface) is that primitive poets, although using a language of extraordinary occasions, spoke a language "which, though unusual, was still the language of men." In the course of time, the unusual became mistaken for the reality, so that diction became "daily more and more corrupt, thrusting out of sight the plain humanities of nature by a motley masquerade of tricks, quaintnesses, hieroglyphics, and enigmas" (*Poetical Works*, II.406). It is clear that Wordsworth was attempting to return to what he saw as a correct simplicity and directness, and that the choice of humble and rustic life, together with a predilection for ordinary language, is connected with this. The poetic results show how unprejudiced Wordsworth was about the matter, and how the actual language of his poetry varied according to the needs of the poem in question: the language of "Simon Lee" is very different from that of "We Are Seven," and the impassioned blank verse of "Tintern Abbey" is very different from the austere simplicities of "Michael." In every case the aim is to provide "little falsehood of description" and ideas "expressed in language fitted to their respective importance." So we have the hymnlike utterances of "To My Sister":

> And from the blessed power that rolls
> About, below, above,
> We'll frame the measure of our souls:
> They shall be tuned to love.
>
> (33–36)

or the nursery rhyme cadences of "We Are Seven":

> I met a little cottage Girl,
> She was eight years old, she said;
> Her hair was thick with many a curl
> That clustered round her head.
>
> (5–8)

The deliberate simplicity of this latter verse is characteristic of some of the shorter poems in *Lyrical Ballads*: critics have often found them naive and oversimple, but Wordsworth was not stupid and clearly had a specific effect in mind, an effect that may not seem as mature or complex as "Tintern Abbey" but that has an equal importance for an understanding of Wordsworth. He is a poet who is capable of writing with an amazing directness and hard sense, yet he is also capable of writing a poetry that has deeper and more elusive meanings.

As an example of the first kind, we may take "Simon Lee." It is a poem that underwent a number of changes after its first publication in 1798, but for convenience I shall take the version that appears in the Oxford Standard Authors edition, by Hutchinson. There the poem begins with a description of Simon Lee as a young man:

> In the sweet shire of Cardigan,
> Not far from pleasant Ivor-hall
> An old Man dwells, a little man, —
> 'Tis said he once was tall.
> Full five-and-thirty years he lived
> A running huntsman merry;
> And still the centre of his cheek
> Is red as a ripe cherry.
>
> (1–8)

Here the jingle of the rhythm, and the feminine rhyme at the end, encourage a curious jauntiness, an attention such as one gives to a straightforward, cheerful, and undemanding narrative: such a register is even clearer in the 1798 version of the second four lines:

> Of years he has upon his back
> No doubt, a burthen weighty;
> He says he is three score and ten,
> But others say he's eighty.

where the random guessing about Simon's age suggests the trivial and simple. In the reworked version of the poem, the first three verses, describing Simon in the past, continue this mood. They describe him as a huntsman in his prime, running, hallooing, and pushing himself to the limit of his endurance. Then comes the change, heralded by a phrase borrowed from Wordsworth's favorite, John Milton:

> But, oh the heavy change!—bereft
> Of health, strength, friends, and kindred, see!
>> (25-26)

The same deliberate simplicity is carried on in the following stanzas, which describe the aged and feeble man: it is as though a primitive painter had produced a diptych entitled "Youth" and "Age." Now the reader is given the facts with a hard matter-of-factness:

> And he is lean and he is sick;
> His body, dwindled and awry,
> Rests upon ankles swoln and thick;
> His legs are thin and dry.
>> (33-36)

After this, however, comes a surprise, as the poet himself enters the poem, with a direct address to the reader:

> My gentle Reader, I perceive
> How patiently you've waited,
> And now I fear that you expect
> Some tale will be related.
>
> O Reader! had you in your mind
> Such stores as silent thought can bring,
> O gentle Reader! you would find
> A tale in every thing.
> What more I have to say is short,
> And you must kindly take it:
> It is no tale; but, should you think,
> Perhaps a tale you'll make it.
>> (61-72)

Here the style seems to be the same, with the same insistent meter and feminine rhyme; the idea behind these lines, too, seems to be of the same order of simplicity as the earlier descriptive passages, and the continual addressing of the reader has a jocular effect. But beneath the simple words, especially "tale" and "think," there lie considerable reverberations. The point of these verses, which contain the central

analysis of how to consider Simon Lee and others like him, is that they emphasize the fact that Simon Lee *is*: he is a sad spectacle, an old man past his prime, living on in poverty and unable to perform the simplest task. There is ample matter for the feeling heart to consider here, and there will be no tale, for there should be none: we are contemplating old age, and there will be no escape into a story to take our minds off it. There is, as the poem's subtitle tells us, "an incident," but that is all: however, if we *think*, we can make much of that incident, that is, if we have hearts that feel, eyes that perceive, and minds that understand; if, in other words, we *think* about the plight of the elderly, we shall find a deep significance in the trivial incident that follows. It is a significance that is simple because it is universal, containing within itself the awareness of human life as brief, transitory, and often painful. So although it is no story, it contains a deep and inescapable truth:

> It is no tale; but, should you think,
> Perhaps a tale you'll make it.

The poem is given a final twist, as the traditional complaint against ingratitude is exploited to make something even more pathetic:

> —I've heard of hearts unkind, kind deeds
> With coldness still returning;
> Alas! the gratitude of men
> Hath oftener left me mourning.
>> (93-96)

There are times, it appears, when gratitude is actually worse than ingratitude: from the simplicity of the earlier verses the reader is now faced with a paradox, for the poet grieves more for the pathetic condition of Simon Lee (which makes him weep for the simplest kind of help) than for the usual ingratitude.

If "Simon Lee" moves from simplicity to a sudden complexity, surprising the reader by its final turn, the movement of "Tintern Abbey" is much more deliberate, and the poem modulates with consummate skill between different registers of simplicity and complexity. It is a poem that moves between the outer world of nature and the inner world of the mind in a way that beautifully suggests the interaction between the two. There is not space enough here to provide a full examination of the poem, but the way in which its reflective moments alternate with descriptions of the actual landscape is a feature that stands out, although it is most subtly and sensitively accomplished. The poem begins with the river Wye, bounded by its steep and lofty banks, with the pastoral farms and hedgerows, and the quiet sky; at the end the poem comes to rest in the same landscape, with a sense of having gone out and returned that is artistically very satisfying. Between the beginning and end, intertwining with the descriptions of landscape, is the exploration of the poet's mind and heart, and his expressions of confidence and love for his sister and the influence of nature upon her. The poem witnesses to his own experience and his trust that the same blessing will be hers.

The poem is dated "July 13 1798," and records a visit to the Wye some five years after the memorable walk of 1793. It records the effect of the landscape on the poet's mind as he remembered it, an effect that is both moral and mystical. The movement of the verse here is characteristic of a certain kind of Wordsworthian blank verse, which begins with a fairly straightforward idea, which it then expands; this leads to a further idea, or a further development, as one moment, or one insight, gives rise to another. The paragraph rises and falls, only to rise higher; the first statements of an idea are taken up and expanded a few lines later ("that blessed mood, . . . that serene and blessed mood"); moments of insight that the reader thinks have been described are suddenly taken up again:

> . . . These beauteous forms,
> Through a long absence, have not been to me
> As is a landscape to a blind man's eye:
> But oft, in lonely rooms, and 'mid the din
> Of towns and cities, I have owed to them,
> In hours of weariness, sensations sweet,
> Felt in the blood, and felt along the heart;
> And passing even into my purer mind,
> With tranquil restoration:—feelings too
> Of unremembered pleasure: such, perhaps,
> As have no slight or trivial influence
> On that best portion of a good man's life,
> His little, nameless, unremembered acts
> Of kindness and of love. Nor less, I trust,
> To them I may have owed another gift,
> Of aspect more sublime; that blessed mood,
> In which the burthen of the mystery,
> In which the heavy and the weary weight
> Of all this unintelligible world,
> Is lightened:—that serene and blessed mood,
> In which the affections gently lead us on,—
> Until, the breath of this corporeal frame
> And even the motion of our human blood

> Almost suspended, we are laid asleep
> In body, and become a living soul:
> While with an eye made quiet by the power
> Of harmony, and the deep power of joy,
> We see into the life of things.
>
> (22–49)

The same process is found in the great central passage describing the loss and gain of Wordsworth's imaginative development: if he has lost the dizzy rapture of his first coming to the Wye valley, he has gained a maturity that allows him both to learn and to feel. In this passage the second verb echoes the first, heralding a stronger and more assured statement of an inspiration ("For I have learned. . . . And I have felt"). The central section is in three parts, rising, declaiming, and descending, with the middle part ("a sense sublime . . .") containing a great enveloping conception of the whole of nature as interfused with spirit and movement, with a life that is found in the mind of man and in the external world:

> . . . For I have learned
> To look on nature, not as in the hour
> Of thoughtless youth; but hearing often-times
> The still, sad music of humanity,
> Nor harsh nor grating, though of ample power
> To chasten and subdue. And I have felt
> A presence that disturbs me with the joy
> Of elevated thoughts; a sense sublime
> Of something far more deeply interfused,
> Whose dwelling is the light of setting suns,
> And the round ocean and the living air,
> And the blue sky, and in the mind of man:
> A motion and a spirit, that impels
> All thinking things, all objects of all thought,
> And rolls through all things. . . .
>
> (88–102)

It is tempting to see the impassioned blank verse of "Tintern Abbey" as the true voice of Wordsworth, regarding "Simon Lee" or "We Are Seven" as unfortunate applications of a theory of simple language. This is the theory of Wordsworth as the poet of "two voices," which takes its name from J. K. Stephen's parody of Wordsworth's own sonnet:

> Two voices are there: one is of the deep;
> It learns the storm-cloud's thunderous melody,
> Now roars, now murmurs with the changing sea,
> Now bird-like pipes, now closes soft in sleep:
> And one is of an old half-witted sheep
> Which bleats articulate monotony,

And indicates that two and one are three,
That grass is green, lakes damp, and mountains steep:
And, Wordsworth, both are thine. . . .

This is a sensible and witty view to take, but it ignores so much of the idiosyncrasy that makes Wordsworth himself and no other: it neglects to observe the way in which Wordsworth clung tenaciously to the very lines that seem most ludicrous to modern readers. When his friend Henry Crabb Robinson told Wordsworth that he did not dare to read these lines aloud, the poet replied, "They ought to be liked." For us to write them off is to make Wordsworth into our own poet, the poet of "Tintern Abbey" and the other meditative or narrative blank verse poems. We would be truer to the spirit of the poet himself if we took *Lyrical Ballads* as a whole and observed it with the spirit that Wordsworth himself had in a letter he wrote in 1802. A young correspondent, John Wilson, had written to him, praising *Lyrical Ballads* but querying the suitability of "The Idiot Boy," which he thought not so likely to please. Wordsworth's reply (7 June 1802) was "please whom? or what?"

I answer, human nature, as it has been and ever will be. But where are we to find the best measure of this? I answer, from within; by stripping our own hearts naked, and by looking out of ourselves towards men who lead the simplest lives most according to nature men who have never known false refinements, wayward and artificial desires, false criticisms, effeminate habits of thinking and feeling, or who, having known these things, have outgrown them.[5]

And if this is the ideal, the poet is to point to it by leading men toward the good, rather than by reflecting the wishes and feelings of the majority of men:

You have given me praise for having reflected faithfully in my poems the feelings of human nature. I would fain hope that I have done so. But a great Poet ought to do more than this he ought to a certain degree to rectify men's feelings, to give them new compositions of feeling, to render their feelings more sane pure and permanent. In short, more consonant to nature, that is, to eternal nature, and the great moving spirit of things. He ought to travel before men occasionally as well as at their sides.

(*ibid.*)

[5]From E. de Selincourt, ed., *Letters of William and Dorothy Wordsworth, The Early Years, 1787–1805*, revised by C. L. Shaver (London, 1967), p. 355.

THE PRELUDE

THE first attempts at *The Prelude* are found in a small notebook, known as MS.JJ, which Wordsworth used in Germany during the autumn of 1798. By 1799 a two-part *Prelude* of nearly 1,000 lines was complete; this became an almost completed five-book poem, taking the account through the Cambridge years and into the dedication to poetry that is now in book IV. In 1804 and 1805 Wordsworth added the later books on London, the French Revolution, his despair at its outcome and at the war, and his developing confidence in himself as a poet through the help of Dorothy and Coleridge. The result is the 1805 text, which is the complete poem in thirteen books; this was revised and altered later, with the tenth book divided into two, so that the first publication of the poem in 1850 contained fourteen books. The 1850 text is in some ways more polished, and it contains some fine observations; but the 1805 text (which will be used here) is usually preferred for its freshness and its revelation of Wordsworth's mind at this time.

The Prelude is an extraordinary poem, both in conception and execution, principally because it is epic, history, and autobiography. It is a poem about a single person, a child growing up in the Lake District in the 1770's and 1780's and a young man experiencing the university and the French Revolution; yet it is also much more than this. It contains wonderfully vivid descriptions of the experiences of childhood, but they are contained and given significance by the structure and form of the poem. Basically the poem's experience is one of loss and gain: the loss of the intense childhood experiences and a corresponding gain in maturity and insight. But that experience of loss and gain is set in an epic pattern. In *Paradise Lost*, Milton had written a new kind of epic, as the opening to his book IX shows; Wordsworth, too, is writing a new kind of epic, challenging the traditional concepts of what heroic action consists of. In book III he claims that childhood itself is heroic:

> . . . Of genius, power
> Creation and divinity itself
> I have been speaking, for my theme has been
> What passed within me. Not of outward things
> Done visibly for other minds, words, signs,
> Symbols or actions, but of my own heart
> Have I been speaking, and my youthful mind.
> O Heavens! how awful is the might of souls,
> And what they do within themselves while yet

The yoke of earth is new to them, the world
Nothing but a wild field where they were sown.
This is, in truth, heroic argument,
And genuine prowess, which I wished to touch
With hand however weak, but in the main
It lies far hidden from the reach of words.

(III.171–185)

The suggestion that the poem's subject is "Not of outward things" recalls Milton's determination not to write about wars and battles,

> . . . the better fortitude
> Of Patience and Heroic Martyrdom
> Unsung. . . .
>
> (*Paradise Lost*, IX.31–33)

Wordsworth carries Milton's innovation a stage further, with an epic treatment of material that is traditionally not associated with the epic; in so doing he claims an epic significance for the growth of a mind, and particularly (as in this case) the growth of a poet's mind. That he had *Paradise Lost* in mind is suggested by an echo at the very beginning of *The Prelude*, where Wordsworth writes

> The earth is all before me—with a heart
> Joyous, nor scared at its own liberty,
> I look about, and should the guide I chuse
> Be nothing better than a wandering cloud,
> I cannot miss my way. . . .
>
> (I.15–19)

This takes up the final image of *Paradise Lost*, when Adam and Eve leave Paradise:

> The World was all before them, where to choose
> Thir place of rest, and Providence thir guide
>
> (XII.646–647)

Where *Paradise Lost* ends, *The Prelude* begins: Milton shows us Adam and Eve at the beginning of human history, faced with the choice of free will and guided by the providence of God; Wordsworth shows us a man in time, able to choose and confident of his ability to use his freedom. In *The Prelude* liberty has replaced the theologians' conception of free will, and the wandering cloud has replaced the workings of Divine Providence: Wordsworth is writing his epic on his own terms of natural goodness and human freedom. What the child does with that freedom is the subject of the early books of *The Prelude*;

how the young man survives the pressure of events and retains his imaginative power is the continuation. The whole conception is daring: it is, said Wordsworth, "a thing unprecedented in literary history that a man should talk so much about himself" (letter to Sir George Beaumont, 1 May 1805). He is, in effect, writing an individual *Paradise Lost*, a poem that sees the life of an obscure country boy in the northwest of England as its own kind of significant progress, its own kind of movement from innocence to experience, from paradise to the world outside. Wordsworth makes the reference to *Paradise Lost* clear in a passage of Miltonic pastiche in *The Prelude* (VIII.119–143), a long paragraph of exotic vocabulary and latinate syntax including a description of Gehol's gardens "for delight/of the Tartarian Dynasty composed" and the Great Wall of China, "that mighty Wall, not fabulous, /(China's stupendous mound!)."

Immediately afterward, Wordsworth swings into his own comparison:

> But lovelier far than this the paradise
> Where I was reared, in Nature's primitive gifts
> Favored no less, and more to every sense
> Delicious, seeing that the sun and sky,
> The elements, and seasons in their change,
> Do find their dearest fellow-labourer there
> The heart of man—a district on all sides
> The fragrance breathing of humanity,
> Man free, man working for himself, with choice
> Of time, and place, and object; by his wants,
> His comforts, native occupations, cares,
> Conducted on to individual ends
> Or social, and still followed by a train,
> Unwooed, unthought-of even: simplicity,
> And beauty, and inevitable grace.
>
> (VIII.144–158)

The curious sliding movement of the syntax here is not very common in Wordsworth; but although the elements occur in apposition, they allow a characteristic accumulation of different effects, so that paradise appeals to the senses and to the heart of man, and is a place that encourages the best side of man: man free to work as he wishes and to live in harmony with himself and his fellow men. The sense of living as a member of a community is very important in *The Prelude*: it underlies the happiness of the early years and the early enthusiasms of the French Revolution, while the lack of an organic community was one of the features of London. It is described by

Wordsworth at the beginning of book VII in one of those homely observations that he does so well:

> . . . Above all, one thought
> Baffled my understanding, how men lived
> Even next-door neighbours, as we say, yet still
> Strangers, and knowing not each other's names.
>
> (VII.117–120)

The Prelude describes this vital sense of a community in a number of ways. The child himself is part of it and knows his school friends, the villagers, and the landscape with a delighted familiarity. There are many instances of this, but perhaps the most vivid is the opening of book IV, where Wordsworth describes the feelings of a university student coming home for the long vacation. He bounds down the hill, shouting for the old ferryman, who greets him; he walks on a few miles to Hawkshead, where he sees the familiar church; he is welcomed, with tears of joy, by Ann Tyson and walks around the village with her, greeting everybody. He sees the old rooms, the old garden, the boxed-in stream; he takes his place at the well-loved table and sleeps in his accustomed bed. The whole first section of book IV is a most beautiful re-creation of the emotions of coming home to a well-known landscape and a well-loved community; it looks back, of course, to the scenes of books I and II, especially to the passages that describe the children playing together, skating, or playing cards with the battered and dirty pack (the cards themselves cherished like old soldiers), or rowing or riding. It looks forward, too, to the hopes for the French Revolution as the beginning of the new Jerusalem:

> For, born in a poor district, and which yet
> Retaineth more of ancient homeliness,
> Manners erect, and frank simplicity,
> Than any other nook of English land,
> It was my fortune scarcely to have seen
> Through the whole tenor of my schoolday time
> The face of one, who, whether boy or man,
> Was vested with attention or respect
> Through claims of wealth or blood; . . .
>
> . . .
>
> . . . It could not be
> But that one tutored thus, who had been formed
> To thought and moral feeling in the way
> This story hath described, should look with awe
> Upon the faculties of man, receive
> Gladly the highest promises, and hail

> As best the government of equal rights
> And individual worth. . . .
>
> (IX.217–226; 242–249)

The Prelude, then, is an epic that deals with the loss of paradise; it is Wordsworth's childhood seen as myth, in that he has constructed around his own experience a reading of events that corresponds to the paradise myth. We know that he was not happy at Penrith, and we can only guess at the effect of his mother's death when he was eight and his father's when he was thirteen. Both of these are referred to in *The Prelude*, but not until books V and XI respectively, and there is nothing in the early books to suggest unhappiness and bereavement. There is fear, but that is accepted—indeed, welcomed—as part of the educative ministry of nature:

> Fair seed-time had my soul, and I grew up
> Fostered alike by beauty and by fear
>
> (I.305–306)

But the individual development through beauty and fear is supported by the sense that the individual is part of the community. He can be himself, but he can also be one of a number, as the skating episode shows. The pronouns shift from singular to plural in a way that conveys the mixture of individual impression and communal feeling:

> . . . All shod with steel
> We hissed along the polished ice in games
> Confederate, imitative of the chace
> And woodland pleasures, the resounding horn,
> The pack loud bellowing, and the hunted hare.
> So through the darkness and the cold we flew,
> And not a voice was idle. With the din,
> Meanwhile, the precipices rang aloud;
> The leafless trees and every icy crag
> Tinkled like iron; while the distant hills
> Into the tumult sent an alien sound
> Of melancholy, not unnoticed; while the stars,
> Eastward, were sparkling clear, and in the west
> The orange sky of evening died away.
>
> Not seldom from the uproar I retired
> Into a silent bay, or sportively
> Glanced sideway, leaving the tumultuous throng,
> To cut across the image of a star
> That gleamed upon the ice. And oftentimes
> When we had given our bodies to the wind,
> And all the shadowy banks on either side
> Came sweeping through the darkness, spinning still
> The rapid line of motion, then at once

Have I, reclining back upon my heels,
Stopped short—yet still the solitary cliffs
Wheeled by me, even as if the earth had rolled
With visible motion her diurnal round.
Behind me did they stretch in solemn train,
Feebler and feebler, and I stood and watched
Till all was tranquil as a dreamless sleep.
                                        (I.460–489)

In this brilliant passage, with its wonderful re-creation of the movement and sound of skating, and of a Lake District winter twilight, the child is sharing in the experience and in the delight of the game with the others. Yet he is also able to retire "into a silent bay," and to perceive the way the earth seems to move, at a sudden stop. Like the poet of the preface to *Lyrical Ballads*, he is a child speaking to (or for) children, yet also a child endowed with more lively sensibility, rejoicing more than others in the spirit of life that is in him. The joyful energy of this passage is one of its most obvious characteristics, tempered as it is with a solemn awareness of the beauty and majesty of the earth. *The Prelude* as a whole is a striking combination of these qualities of individual energy and delight, with an equally important sense that the mind of the poet is, in many ways, a representative mind. It is aware, as we have seen, of the importance of the community; and the poem is also concerned with a major historical event, the French Revolution, an event of which the hopes and disappointments dominated the romantic movement. In the books on France, Wordsworth is recording the fact that he was present at the Revolution's various stages: when he first landed in France, on 13 July 1790, he and Robert Jones saw "benevolence and blessedness / Spread like a fragrance everywhere, like Spring" (VI.368–369). He had the enthusiasm and optimism of youth:

Bliss was it in that dawn to be alive,
But to be young was very heaven! . . .
                                        (X.692–693)

and this optimism was based upon observations, upon conversations with Beaupuy, upon a direct experience of a nation struggling to find its new liberty. In book X, Wordsworth relates, with a painful authenticity, how he was torn in sympathy when prayers for an English victory were offered in church, and how his attitudes to the Revolution changed as the French became "oppressors in their

turn" (X.791). He describes how he studied the problem relentlessly,

. . . endlessly perplexed
With impulse, motive, right and wrong, the ground
Of moral obligation—what the rule,
And what the sanction—till, demanding proof,
And seeking it in every thing, I lost
All feeling of conviction, and, in fine,
Sick, wearied out with contrarieties,
Yielded up moral questions in despair. . . .
                                        (X.893–900)

Book X of *The Prelude* is a most impressive record of a sensitive mind in confrontation with the great political events of the day: not only the French Revolution and the war, but the campaign for the abolition of the slave trade (X.202–226). He saw revolution become madness, and the rise and fall of Robespierre, with all the intense involvement of a contemporary; he remembered exactly where he was when he heard of the death of Robespierre, crossing Ulverston sands after visiting the grave of his beloved schoolmaster, William Taylor, at Cartmel. The scene (X.466–566), with the smooth sands of the Leven estuary in the foreground and the Lake District mountains in the background, is one of the most vividly pictorialized in *The Prelude*; the moment when the passing traveler told him that Robespierre was dead is sharpened by the poet's awareness of his surroundings and his feelings. It is no accident, of course, that the death of Robespierre is told to Wordsworth just after he had been thinking of the death of Taylor: the one famous and tyrannical, the other obscure and benevolent. In ways such as this, *The Prelude* is a record of what it was like to live through those years, to be a child at Hawkshead, a young man at Cambridge, a spectator in London, and an enthusiast in France.

Above all, however, these roles or stages were seen by Wordsworth in *The Prelude* as part of the growth of a poet's mind (the poem's alternative title). And if the poem is about the paradise myth, with the child growing up in the good community, and about history, with the child and young man responding to historical and social conditions around him, it is also about the development of a very special and very gifted man. Once again, it is possible to see Wordsworth referring back to Milton, who saw the role of the poet as a prophet or inspired teacher. In *Il Penseroso* the poet longs for the learning and wisdom of old age:

Till old experience do attain
To something like Prophetic strain.
                    (173–174)

and in *Paradise Lost* he remembers other figures who
have suffered the same fate as himself, the loss of
sight —

    So were I equal'd with them in renown,
    Blind *Thamyris* and blind *Maeonides*,
    And *Tiresias* and *Phineus* Prophets old.
                    (III.34–36)

Wordsworth, too, uses the word "Prophet"; and
in some ways the whole of *The Prelude* can be seen as
moving toward the final paragraph, in which he sees
himself and Coleridge as engaged in the teaching of
mankind:

    Prophets of Nature, we to them will speak
    A lasting inspiration, sanctified
    By reason and by truth; what we have loved
    Others will love, and we may teach them how:
    Instruct them how the mind of man becomes
    A thousand times more beautiful than the earth
    On which he dwells, above this frame of things
    (Which, 'mid all revolutions in the hopes
    And fears of men, doth still remain unchanged)
    In beauty exalted, as it is itself
    Of substance and of fabric more divine.
                    (XIII.442–452)

It is toward this end, with the poet as a responsible
member of society and an inspired teacher, that so
much of *The Prelude* has been moving. The range of
experience that contributes to this is considerable,
including the childhood episodes, education, books,
and the sublime experiences that remain in the
memory long after they have passed. Wordsworth
calls them "spots of time" in a crucial passage:

    There are in our existence spots of time,
    Which with distinct preeminence retain
    A renovating virtue, whence, depressed
    By false opinion and contentious thought,
    Or aught of heavier or more deadly weight
    In trivial occupations and the round
    Of ordinary intercourse, our minds
    Are nourished and invisibly repaired —
    A virtue, by which pleasure is enhanced,
    That penetrates, enables us to mount
    When high, more high, and lifts us up when fallen.
                    (XI.257–267)

Such moments, he goes on to say, are "scattered
everywhere" (XI.274), though they may be most
conspicuous in childhood; he gives an example of
two episodes that are vividly remembered, being lost
and finding himself beneath a murderer's gibbet, and
waiting for the horses to take him home just before
his father's death. In both cases there is a mysterious
intensity about the episode, a moment of perception
that remains with extraordinary sharpness. In the
first, the child, regaining the path, sees

    A naked pool that lay beneath the hills,
    The beacon on the summit, and more near,
    A girl who bore a pitcher on her head
    And seemed with difficult steps to force her way
    Against the blowing wind. . . .
                    (XI.303–307)

The poet recalls how he later revisited the spot and
remembered the earlier occasion:

    . . . So feeling comes in aid
    Of feeling, and diversity of strength
    Attends us, if but once we have been strong.
                    (XI.325–327)

We recognize this as one of Wordsworth's complex
states, in which "feeling comes in aid / Of feeling."
He is not clear exactly why the force of the episode is
so great, but he knows that it is: the greatness of man
is mysterious and deep, and it is by the exploration of
such episodes that we come to understand and acknowledge it. As a child, the poet was lost; as an
adult, looking back, he now says:

    I am lost, but see
    In simple childhood something of the base
    On which thy greatness stands—but this I feel,
    That from thyself it is that thou must give,
    Else never canst receive. . . .
                    (XI.329–333)

The sentiment is reminiscent of Coleridge's "we
receive but what we give" (from the "Letter to Sara
Hutchinson"), and it indicates something of the in-
teracting relationship between the mind and the external world that was so important to both poets. In
their most confident moments, both poets felt a great
union between man and nature, a profound interaction, or what Wordsworth describes as a "consummation" between the human mind and the natural
world. Sometimes this comes at unexpected mo-

ments, as it does in the second "spot of time" in book XI. This describes the poet and his brothers waiting for the horses to take them home at Christmastime: through the misty day he waited beside a stone wall, with a single sheep and a hawthorn tree for company (it is remarkable how often single trees or lonely people and animals occur in Wordsworth). He had been so impatient to get home, the poet records, and then ten days later his father died; he saw himself tritely as punished for his impatience, though clearly this is not the point of the passage. The long wait in the mist and rain, the strange company of sheep and tree (in his impatience he had left his brothers further down the pass), these constituents of the moment remained with him as a testimony to his imaginative grasp of a situation:

> And afterwards the wind and sleety rain,
> And all the business of the elements,
> The single sheep, and the one blasted tree,
> And the bleak music of that old stone wall,
> The noise of wood and water, and the mist
> Which on the line of each of those two roads
> Advanced in such indisputable shapes—
> All these were spectacles and sounds to which
> I often would repair, and thence would drink
> As at a fountain. . . .
> (XI.375–384)

In this description we notice not only the emphasis on the particular objects (the wind, the rain, the single sheep, the blasted tree) but an emphasis on what Wordsworth elsewhere calls the "goings-on" of the physical world. He animates the dreariness with unobtrusive life: "all the business of the elements," "the bleak music of that old stone wall," "The noise of wood and water," the mist that "Advanced in such indisputable shapes," all these suggest a mind that goes out to the universe and responds to what it is doing—a mind that apprehends the "business," hears the "music," and sees the shapes of the mist. Wordsworth is here celebrating not the power of nature, but the power of the imagination and the memory.

The same can be said of two other great passages in *The Prelude* that are concerned with the growth of the inspired prophet-poet. The first is the crossing of the Alps section in book VI (494 and following). Once again, as in the "spots of time" moments of book XI, there is a loss of direction, a momentary sense of failure, an unfulfilled expectation; as in those "spots of time," the failure and loss, the

mistaken hope, are suddenly transformed into an awareness of the power of the imagination. In book VI, it is addressed directly, in a startling apostrophe that erupts into the verse:

> Imagination!—lifting up itself
> Before the eye and progress of my song
> Like an unfathered vapour, here that power,
> In all the might of its endowments, came
> Athwart me. I was lost as in a cloud,
> Halted without a struggle to break through,
> And now, recovering, to my soul I say
> 'I recognize thy glory'. In such strength
> Of usurpation, in such visitings
> Of awful promise, when the light of sense
> Goes out in flashes that have shewn to us
> The invisible world, doth greatness make abode,
> There harbours whether we be young or old.
> Our destiny, our nature, and our home,
> Is with infinitude—and only there;
> With hope it is, hope that can never die,
> Effort, and expectation, and desire,
> And something evermore about to be.
> (VI.525–542)

Here the imagination itself is like a vapor or mist; the poet seems overcome by it, lost in it as he was on the Alpine path. But he suddenly sees the power of the imagination, not in the fact but in the promise, not in the material world but in the glimpse of something higher and beyond. As he sees this he becomes aware of the sheer power of an imagination that can so transcend its material circumstances as to become conscious of its activity. Similarly, in the "climbing of Snowdon" passage from the final book of *The Prelude*, the poet describes a night climb from Bethgelert through the mist, until suddenly he and his companions came out of the mist into the moonlight. They found themselves surrounded by a sea of mist, out of which the Welsh hills lifted their peaks and over which the moon looked down "in single glory." So strong is the impression of the mist as a sea that Wordsworth has to describe it as moving eventually

> Into the sea, the real sea. . . .
> (XIII.49)

The fact that Wordsworth has to describe it as "the real sea" is a testimony of how powerful his imagination has become. Before, the real world existed, and the imagination erupted from it; now the imagination seems to be supreme, and the real world has to be admitted. Between the mountain and the shore is a chasm, a fracture in the mist:

> A deep and gloomy breathing-place through which
> Mounted the roar of waters, torrents, streams
> Innumerable, roaring with one voice.
>
> (XIII.57–59)

The stupendous natural vision is one that Wordsworth sees as an emblem of the power of the mind; only with such a powerful landscape can he begin to say what the mind is capable of doing:

> . . . it appeared to me
> The perfect image of a mighty mind,
> Of one that feeds upon infinity,
> That is exalted by an under-presence,
> The sense of God, or whatsoe'er is dim
> Or vast in its own being—above all,
> One function of such mind had Nature there
> Exhibited by putting forth, and that
> With circumstance most awful and sublime:
> That domination which she oftentimes
> Exerts upon the outward face of things,
> So moulds them, and endues, abstracts, combines,
> Or by abrupt and unhabitual influence
> Doth make one object so impress itself
> Upon all others, and pervades them so,
> That even the grossest minds must see and hear,
> And cannot chuse but feel. . . .
>
> (XIII.68–84)

The imaginative minds are ever on the watch, building up greatness from the least suggestion, or from failure, or from ordinary expectations that have come to grief. This, the poet concludes, "this alone is genuine liberty" (XIII.122); the ability of the mind to transcend its surroundings, to become aware, even when it is least expected, of the strength of the imagination. For often it surprises, and surprise is a favorite idea of Wordsworth's. Moments come upon the imagination with strange suddenness: as the child rows a stolen boat out from the shore at Patterdale, he is astonished and terrified to see the mountain coming after him; as the child who is hooting to the owls (V.389 and following) fails to get a response, he is suddenly aware of something else:

> Then sometimes in that silence, while he hung
> Listening, a gentle shock of mild surprize
> Has carried far into his heart the voice

> Of mountain torrents; or the visible scene
> Would enter unawares into his mind
> With all its solemn imagery, its rocks,
> Its woods, and that uncertain heaven, received
> Into the bosom of the steady lake.
>
> (V.406–413)

Here the mind receives, but it receives because it is a mind that can give. The boy of Winander hooting to the owls is contrasted throughout book V with the fact-getting, well-behaved, unnatural child; the boy, who died young, was one of those with whom Wordsworth played:

> A race of real children, not too wise,
> Too learned, or too good, but wanton, fresh,
> And bandied up and down by love and hate;
> Fierce, moody, patient, venturous, modest, shy,
> Mad at their sports like withered leaves in winds;
> Though doing wrong and suffering, and full oft
> Bending beneath our life's mysterious weight
> Of pain and fear, yet still in happiness
> Not yielding to the happiest upon earth.
>
> (V.436–444)

And so, as so often with Wordsworth, the greatest sublimity is linked with the celebration of the ordinary; and to pursue the development of the prophet-poet, and the great creative imagination, is to be reminded that they are rooted in an ordinary childhood. It is all wonderfully simple, yet wonderfully mysterious and profound:

> Oh mystery of man, from what a depth
> Proceed thy honours! I am lost, but see
> In simple childhood something of the base
> On which thy greatness stands—. . .
>
> (XI.328–331)

and the greatness of *The Prelude* is that it does succeed in testifying to the power of the imagination while being firmly rooted in human experience.

SHORTER POEMS AFTER 1798

THE sheer ordinariness that is an essential part of Wordsworth is continued in the poems written after *Lyrical Ballads*; yet it is an ordinariness transformed, as in *The Prelude*, by an imaginative balance that seems to achieve just the right adjustment between the subject matter and its transformation.

In the "Lucy" poems, for instance, most of which were written in Germany during the winter of 1798–1799, Wordsworth writes of the death of a young girl who is an embodiment of all the natural forces of simplicity and grace. In one poem she is a "flower" and "sportive as the fawn"; she lives in the poet's memory as an ideal figure who has died while she is still in a fresh and youthful state of communion with nature. In the greatest of these poems, "A Slumber Did My Spirit Seal," she is first an ideal, almost spiritual creature and then a dead girl; yet even then she is reunited with nature in a way that seems appropriate and that turns her death into a fitting reunion with the world of which she was a part. She is both girl and nature form, shaped and molded by a force outside her; the poet sees her for a time, and loves her, only to lose her. Thus the "Lucy" poems are both elegies for a loved one and something more, a perception of an ideal and an indication of the transience of natural innocence. In his description of *Lyrical Ballads* in *Biographia Literaria*, Coleridge wrote of "the two cardinal points of poetry":

. . . the power of exciting the sympathy of the reader by a faithful adherence to the truth of nature, and the power of giving the interest of novelty by the modifying colors of imagination.

(II.5)

This is a remarkable insight into the working of Wordsworth's shorter poems: they are true to nature, that is, to a visible and recognizable external world, and yet that world is given a significance that it normally lacks. The significance is given to it by the perceiving mind, which allows the thing or person to be seen more vividly and yet as something more than its material self. So the sheepfold in "Michael" remains a sheepfold but becomes a symbol of all the unfulfilled hopes of the shepherd's life, and of more than that: it is a symbol and not an allegorical representation of something. So it has a life of its own: it exists in the eye of the passerby as he walks up the path beside Green-head Ghyll, and it has a history that sums up the whole life and fate of Michael and his family. They are simple, frugal people, who prefer to remain on the land rather than sell it to pay off the indemnity; Michael's work is with the elements, among the fields and hills, and he is summoned to work by the winds. His feelings, too, are elementary passions of the kind that Wordsworth saw as existing among rustic folk: his tenderness for his son and his love of the land on which he

has worked all his life. The laying of the cornerstone of the sheepfold, done by Luke at his request, is an act of faith and hope: the sheepfold becomes a covenant between the father and the son but also, in its way, an act of defiance against the destructiveness of the monetary and city world. Michael and Luke are forced to separate, and Luke comes to grief: Michael continues to go to the sheepfold, but he is unable to finish it, although he continues to work at it. The celebrated line

And never lifted up a single stone

(466)

has tended to make the reader forget that in fact Michael did continue to work at the sheepfold for seven years after Luke's downfall. Michael is a man of determination and perseverance; his life has been one of industrious labor, and the downfall of Luke does not alter this. But he has no heart to continue at times when the grief is too great; the sheepfold is an emblem of his purpose in life, the construction of something that will survive for Luke, as he hoped that the patrimonial fields would pass to him. Instead, in the city, Luke

. . . gave himself
To evil courses: ignominy and shame
Fell on him, so that he was driven at last
To seek a hiding-place beyond the seas.

(444–447)

In this poem, the sheepfold and the cottage are the foreground, and the city is far away; Luke's downfall is portrayed with a brisk absence of detail, whereas Michael's speeches are recorded verbatim. It is a masterly use of perspective to emphasize the quality of life and the destruction that comes into it from outside; as we know from *The Prelude*, Wordsworth had a particular admiration for shepherds, and "Michael" is a narrative poem that records the way in which the shepherd and his wife seem hardly to understand other ways. They are touchingly naive about Luke's departure, and presumably about life and conditions in the city; yet their naiveté is associated throughout with love. Michael loves the land and has an abiding love for Luke. He promises the boy that

". . . whatever fate
Befall thee, I shall love thee to the last,
And bear thy memory with me to the grave."

(415–417)

So too, after the brief account of Luke's fall, comes the resounding line

> There is a comfort in the strength of love;
> (448)

which indicates the contrary movements of love and despair that exist within Michael: he is a man who has experienced a lifetime of love, in his work and its surroundings, in the domestic happiness of his frugal home, in his land, and in the tenderness of his relationship with his son. When the last of these is broken the others remain; as so often in Wordsworth, the figures who are bereft of human relationships retain a strange and lonely dignity that comes from an affinity with nature. Michael is deeply moving because he represents every aging father with an only child in whom his hopes are centered; he is also awesome in his ability to go on loving. He is a man for whom the reader feels not tragic pity and fear but a mixture of pity and admiration.

The same is true of other solitaries in Wordsworth, most notably the leech-gatherer in "Resolution and Independence." If "Michael" is written in an austere and stately blank verse (for although the meter is the same, the language is quite different from the impassioned diction of "Tintern Abbey"), "Resolution and Independence" is written in stanza form, with a peculiar and very effective diction. It is metrically very formal, with an alexandrine at the end of each stanza, and the diction is often archaic, with a biblical cadence and rhythm:

> Motionless as a cloud the old Man stood,
> That heareth not the loud winds when they call;
> And moveth all together, if it move at all.
> (75–77)

The use of subjunctives ("if it move") and the older forms of the verb (heareth, moveth) are linked with rhythms that echo biblical ones ("consider the lilies of the field, how they grow": "That heareth not the loud winds when they call"). The result is a poem that describes an encounter with a poor old man in formal and stately terms, so that the old man himself is given dignity. In Dorothy Wordsworth's journal, he appears as "an old man almost double":

He had on a coat, thrown over his shoulders, above his waistcoat and coat. Under this he carried a bundle, and had an apron on and a night-cap. . . . His trade was to gather leeches, but now leeches are scarce, and he had not strength for it. He lived by begging. . . .

(3 October 1800)

When Wordsworth wrote "Resolution and Independence" some eighteen months later (in the productive spring of 1802), any of these details that might make the old man seem ludicrous were carefully removed. He enters the poem now at a moment when the poet is gloomily contemplating his own future: it is a brilliant fresh morning after rain, yet the poet feels uncertain about the fate of fellow poets and his own failure to provide; like the grasshopper in the fable, his whole life has been lived "in pleasant thought, / As if life's business were a summer mood" (36–37). Instead of being made to regret this by the hardworking ant, however, he meets the leech-gatherer, whose appearance is preceded by words such as "grace":

> Now, whether it were by peculiar grace,
> A leading from above, a something given,
> Yet it befell that, in this lonely place,
> When I with these untoward thoughts had striven,
> Beside a pool bare to the eye of heaven
> I saw a Man before me unawares:
> The oldest man he seemed that ever wore grey hairs.
> (50–56)

The great simplicities of Wordsworth's poetry appear to wonderful effect in a line like "I saw a Man . . . ," especially as Wordsworth goes on to qualify this:

> As a huge stone is sometimes seen to lie
> Couched on the bald top of an eminence;
> Wonder to all who do the same espy,
> By what means it could thither come, and whence;
> So that it seems a thing endued with sense:
> Like a sea-beast crawled forth, that on a shelf
> Of rock or sand reposeth, there to sun itself. . . .
> (57–63)

Here the old man is likened to a stone and to a strange sea beast; or, to complicate the process, he could be said to be likened to a stone that itself is like a sea beast. Either way, here is a strange combination of inanimate and animate, as though the old man is half immobile and insensate, and half strangely alive. It is interesting, too, to see how the rhythm of the line unobtrusively emphasizes the strangeness of the old man. He is like a stone "Couched on the bald

1437

top of an eminence," where the words "bald top" give two strong syllables in the middle of the line. Without the word "bald," the line would be regularly dactylic, with three feet:

/ x x / x x / x x
Couched on the top of an eminence

With "bald," it becomes strangely out of joint, especially when followed by the trochaic "Wonder" in the following line. But Wordsworth unerringly brings the reader back to the reality in the following line:

Such seemed this Man, . . .

which echoes "I saw a Man" and allows all the strangeness of the earlier verse to be clamped between the two occurrences of "Man." The man's humanity is asserted, even, it might be said, his basic humanity: he is Man, old and unaccommodated, and the poet's meeting with him has something of the meeting of the sophisticated with the elementary or primitive. The old man's physical condition is miserable: he is bent double with age, and like the stone *cum* sea beast, he seems "not all alive nor dead." Yet he returns a courteous answer to the poet's greeting, and replies to his inquiry "what are you doing?" The poet describes him thus:

Ere he replied, a flash of mild surprise
Broke from the sable orbs of his yet-vivid eyes.

His words came feebly, from a feeble chest,
But each in solemn order followed each,
With something of a lofty utterance drest—
(90–94)

The understated skill of Wordsworth's verse is brilliantly demonstrated here, in the contrast between the rhetorical and poetic language of the first two and the last two lines here, and the strong simplicity of the middle line. In the first two lines the diction ("sable orbs," "yet-vivid eyes") might have come from Milton; so might the image of words following each other dressed in their lofty utterance. In the center is the line full of effort, with the repetition of "feebly, . . . feeble," the alliteration of which suggests a difficulty in breathing or speaking freely. The contrast embodies the whole sense of strangeness that is found within the poem, the coexistence of an internal state that does not match the external conditions. The poet is miserable on a beautiful morning;

the decrepit man is firm in his courage and his optimism. As he describes his condition to the poet (and it is noticeable that in this version he is no longer begging) the poet becomes curiously abstracted; it is as though the individual situation becomes lost in its wider implications.

The old Man still stood talking by my side;
But now his voice to me was like a stream
Scarce heard; nor word from word could I divide;
And the whole body of the Man did seem
Like one whom I had met with in a dream;
Or like a man from some far region sent,
To give me human strength, by apt admonishment.
(106–112)

The idea of the old man as having been sent "from some far region" links up with the earlier description of him as "a something given"; he seems to be both natural and in some way supernatural. He comes to bring the poet human strength, yet in the last verse the poet turns to God:

"God," said I, "be my help and stay secure;
I'll think of the Leech-gatherer on the lonely moor!"
(139–140)

The leech-gatherer seems to stand for something, or rather to be something, above and beyond the customary experience and certainly above the worldly cares of the poet. It would be a great mistake to see him as an allegory of some kind of religious presence, but he is clearly an indication of something outside the poet, a strength and a resolution that contrasts forcibly with the poet's own failure to keep a serene mind. The leech-gatherer, in fact, embodies qualities that Wordsworth signally admired: an independence and a serenity that freed him from financial and other worldly responsibilities; this liberty is, for Wordsworth, a true freedom from anxiety, and it is connected with other freedoms that he celebrates in his poetry.

Politically, a love of freedom made him a supporter of the French Revolution, and later a fervent patriot; in social terms he admired societies like the one he had known in his youth, where men seemed to be independent and not bound together in a master-slave relationship; and in personal terms, he sought a freedom from anxiety, a freedom that does not seek to avoid misfortune but that comes from having the resources to bear it. Meanwhile, the relationship between this ideal freedom and the actual world of man continues to exercise Wordsworth; the ideal world is found in many forms, especially associated with nature and childhood, and the poet's delight in it is found in many of the poems written in these years, especially in the spring of 1802. Many of these poems, "The Tinker," "To a Butterfly," "Among All Lovely Things My Love Had Been," "To the Small Celandine," celebrate happiness and freedom, while others are aware of the forces that destroy these things. "The Sailor's Mother" is one, and the "Ode. Intimations of Immortality from Recollections of Early Childhood" is another. The great Ode, as it is sometimes called, balances a marvelous recapturing of the child's innocence and closeness to nature with an awareness of the later perception of an adult; the poet laments the inevitable process of growing into adulthood, embraced so enthusiastically by the child who acts grown-up parts, and yet the Ode is informed by a mature and responsible understanding that this process is necessary. A Neoplatonic sense of a reality elsewhere is joined to the memory of the child's experience, and through it our life on earth is seen to be an absence from a home in God. Yet the life on earth has its own precious moments, and not only in childhood:

> The thought of our past years in me doth breed
> Perpetual benediction. . . .
>
> (137–138)

The benediction comes not just from the memory of delight and liberty, but from something more elusive and profound:

> . . . those obstinate questionings
> Of sense and outward things,
> Fallings from us, vanishings;
> Blank misgivings of a Creature
> Moving about in worlds not realised,
> High instincts before which our mortal Nature
> Did tremble like a guilty Thing surprised. . . .
>
> (145–151)

With this praise for the mysterious and marvelous, there is another source of comfort, in the strength that the adult gains through contemplating life in all its confusion and limitations:

> In the primal sympathy
> Which having been must ever be;
> In the soothing thoughts that spring

> Out of human suffering;
> In the faith that looks through death,
> In years that bring the philosophic mind.
>
> (185–190)

The great Ode is a key poem in the understanding of the complexity of Wordsworth's beliefs. It contains, without fracturing into different pieces, the joy in childhood and liberty, the unity of this with the rejoicing natural world, and the sense, too, of the mature understanding of the role of man in the created world. The child is a prophet; the man can only remember, and understand, but his view of life involves an accommodation with things as they are that is a gain to compensate for the loss of the childhood vision.

Wordsworth's belief in the faith that looks through death was tested to the uttermost in February 1805, when his favorite brother, John, was drowned at sea. In his grief the poet turned to a favorite subject, the daisy, the "unassuming Common-place / Of Nature," which he saw as sleeping and waking upon the sailor's grave; even here there is a comfort from the simple things of nature. But in a greater poem, "Elegiac Stanzas, Suggested by a Picture of Peele Castle, in a Storm, Painted by Sir George Beaumont," Wordsworth chronicled a change. He had stayed near Peele Castle in fine weather, in 1794; now he saw Beaumont's picture, which showed it in a very different condition: a ruined tower beaten by the waves (the painting also contained a ship going down offshore, which would have reminded Wordsworth of his brother's death). The stormy sea he now sees as the true reflector of the condition of life, and the idea of a world governed by fine weather has disappeared:

> A power is gone, which nothing can restore;
> A deep distress hath humanised my Soul.
>
> (35–36)

As so often with Wordsworth, loss is turned into gain, and he sees himself as becoming more human and less likely to idealize in his bereavement. Certainly his poetry, from this time on, becomes less elusive and imaginative: even "Peele Castle" has an allegorical construction that is uncomfortably schematic—fine weather contrasted with bad weather, the castle standing against the storms of life, the sense of a "before" and "after" scene. It is saved by its austere diction and its stern sense of mourning tempered by hope:

Farewell, farewell the heart that lives alone,
Housed in a dream, at distance from the Kind!
Such happiness, wherever it be known,
Is to be pitied; for 'tis surely blind.

But welcome fortitude, and patient cheer,
And frequent sights of what is to be borne!
Such sights, or worse, as are before me here. —
Not without hope we suffer and we mourn.

(53–60)

SONNETS, THE EXCURSION, AND LATER POEMS

THE "Elegiac Stanzas," "Resolution and Independence," the "Immortality Ode," and many of Wordsworth's best-known shorter poems (such as "The Solitary Reaper" and "I Wandered Lonely as a Cloud") were published in *Poems, in Two Volumes* in 1807. This volume also contains some of Wordsworth's finest sonnets, a form in which he delighted. Once again his great master was Milton, and both poets use the same Italianate form, reveling in its compression and the artistic demands of its rhyme scheme. "Nuns fret not at their convent's narrow room," wrote Wordsworth, and he seems to have relished the discipline required to produce a good sonnet. Among the sonnets are some of the best patriotic poetry ever written, which links a love of England with qualities of spiritual nobility, as in "Milton! thou shouldst be living at this hour." The arresting first line is a feature of Wordsworth's sonnets: "Earth has not anything to show more fair" is perhaps the best-known example, but there are others, such as "Once did She hold the gorgeous east in fee" (another sonnet on a political subject, the extinction of the Venetian republic by Napoleon) and "It is a beauteous evening, calm and free." In this last example, the sonnet continues with a literally breathtaking image

The holy time is quiet as a Nun
Breathless with adoration; . . .
(2–3)

and then, as so often, Wordsworth anchors the image in straightforward natural description—

. . . the broad sun
Is sinking down in its tranquillity;
(3–4)

—only to invite the imagination to work again by the use of figurative language:

The gentleness of heaven broods o'er the Sea:
Listen! the mighty Being is awake,
And doth with his eternal motion make
A sound like thunder—everlastingly.
(5–8)

It is not clear to whom the word "Listen!" is addressed. Its introduction here gives it a general sense, as though anyone on a calm evening might, by listening, hear the workings of a mighty Being. But it then acquires a particular meaning, as Wordsworth turns to address his French daughter:

Dear Child! dear Girl! that walkest with me here,
If thou appear untouched by solemn thought,
Thy nature is not therefore less divine:
Thou liest in Abraham's bosom all the year;
And worshipp'st at the Temple's inner shrine,
God being with thee when we know it not.
(9–14)

There is a very delicate change of mood here, from the impersonal to the personal, with an equalizing movement from the ordinary to the sacred. A further balancing is found between the tender and the reflective as the poet notes the distance between the child's unconscious communion with heaven and her conscious ordinariness. The difference between the child's apparent state, walking on the sands with a mind "untouched by solemn thought," and her actual state is underlined by the biblical formality of the last lines, which apply to the child in a mysterious and remote, yet authoritative way. Yet throughout the grand reflections is the memory of "Dear Child! dear Girl!," the outburst of genuine feeling that is so much a part of Wordsworth's poetry.

Not all the sonnets are successful: some are plainly tedious, and others are mistakenly pretentious. The long series of *Ecclesiastical Sonnets*, written at the suggestion of Sir George Beaumont, has the air of a dull exercise. At their best, however, the sonnets have the same kind of forceful austerity that Wordsworth admired in Milton, and the characteristic blend of homely tenderness and lofty sentiment.

In the later sonnets something of the magic goes out of Wordsworth's poetry. It is difficult to say what it is, but the ideas that seemed so powerful now become commonplace. The same can be said of *The Excursion* (1814), with the exception of book I, and that is better read in its earlier version as "The Ruined Cottage" (written 1797–1798). There it is a moving story of the decline of a family and the ruin of their lives and hopes by sickness and economic recession (in some respects a return to the preoccupations of the Salisbury Plain poems). In *The Excursion* it is still very fine, though to some tastes the Christian conclusion is false and trite. The central figure of Margaret, the last human tenant of the ruined cottage (last human tenant as opposed to the natural creatures who later take up their abode there), is drawn with a sustained economy and gravity: she is

> . . . a Woman of a steady mind
> Tender and deep in her excess of love;
> (I.513–514)

while her husband is "Frugal, affectionate, sober, and withal / keenly industrious." A succession of calamities (bad harvests, war, and illness), however, causes him to lose his work and sense of purpose, and he finally leaves to join the army. Margaret has to part with her elder child to a kind farmer; the younger child dies; and she is left alone, waiting for the return that never comes. Her love and loyalty prevent her from leaving the cottage, and from having any other hope in life; her continued disappointment leads to her sickness and death.

Her story is told by a central figure in *The Excursion*, the Wanderer (in the earliest version, the Pedlar), who is one of those ideal Wordsworth characters who has given up a regular and settled employment for something that is freer and more haphazard. He has no interest in what Wordsworth called "getting and spending"; he is a traveling and solitary man, who possesses a tranquil and steady mind. The result is that his energies are not directed to his own problems:

> . . . and, by nature tuned
> And constant disposition of his thoughts
> To sympathy with man, he was alive
> To all that was enjoyed where'er he went,
> And all that was endured; for, in himself
> Happy, and quiet in his cheerfulness,
> He had no painful pressure from without
> That made him turn aside from wretchedness
> With coward fears. He could *afford* to suffer
> With those whom he saw suffer. . . .
> (I.362–371)

The Wanderer is an ideal figure, who is contrasted in the poem with the Solitary, a man who has ex-perienced the hopes and miseries of the French Revolution, and whose personal sufferings have made him misanthropic. A third character, the Pastor, is perhaps the most important of all: he dominates the latter part of the poem with his practical Christian wisdom, and the final book ends with a delightful scene of the Pastor and his family. This forms an obvious contrast to the first book of the poem: from the ruined family to the happy and prosperous one is a journey that involves a full acceptance and understanding of human misery, together with an ability to remain optimistic and benevolent. Both the Wanderer, in his solitude and peripatetic life, and the Pastor, who stands for the settled family life, are able to bring comfort to others and remain at peace with themselves.

The Excursion is thus an extended illustration of different ways of approaching the central problems of human life—the failure of hopes, the loss of loved ones, the doubtful consolations of religion. In its counseling of orthodox Christian belief, *The Excursion* looks toward the work of the later Wordsworth, and indeed the poet's orthodoxy may be one reason why his later poetry is not informed by the same intense conviction as the earlier poetry that expresses his sense of natural power. It is this awareness of the power of natural life and its relation to the mind of man that Wordsworth conveys so well: it is a power beside which the preoccupation of man with material things seems idle, and it is a power whose essential optimism is a counterbalance to the very real suffering and misery of men. If men were to behave with this power as their guide, there would be less misery, for human unhappiness often comes from a failure of society to provide properly for its members. Instead, there would be

> . . . a better time,
> More wise desires, and simpler manners. . . .
> (103–104)

These lines come from the preface to *The Excursion*, originally part of a longer poem entitled "Home at Grasmere." In it we see a summary of many of Wordsworth's most deeply held beliefs. As so often, Milton is in the background as Wordsworth thinks of the earthly paradise. He knows that he (like Milton visiting Hell) will have to travel

> . . . near the tribes
> And fellowships of men, and see ill sights

Of madding passions mutually inflamed;
Must hear Humanity in fields and groves
Pipe solitary anguish; or must hang
Brooding above the fierce confederate storm
Of sorrow, barricadoed evermore
Within the walls of cities—...

(73–80)

But he also intends to celebrate the beauties of paradise, not just as a concept or an idea, but as an actual possibility:

... Paradise, and groves
Elysian, Fortunate Fields—like those of old
Sought in the Atlantic Main—why should they be
A history only of departed things,
Or a mere fiction of what never was?
For the discerning intellect of Man,
When wedded to this goodly universe
In love and holy passion, shall find these
A simple produce of the common day.

(47–55)

The last beautiful line, with its utter simplicity (and the language really used by men), emphasizes the way in which Wordsworth regarded the universe that he found all around him. It was a world that contained its full share of human misery, but that had the power of being transformed by the human mind. In that process, the poet had his full part to play, and that is why Wordsworth always thought of himself as a teacher. The poet as he described him in the preface to *Lyrical Ballads* is many things, but above all

He is the rock of defence for human nature; an upholder and preserver, carrying everywhere with him relationship and love.

(*Poetical Works*, II.396)

SELECTED BIBLIOGRAPHY

I. BIBLIOGRAPHY. L. Cooper, *A Condordance to the Poems of William Wordsworth* (London, 1911); T. J. Wise, *A Bibliography of the Writings in Prose and Verse of William Wordsworth* (London, 1916); T. J. Wise, *Two Lake Poets: A Catalogue of Printed Books, Manuscripts etc., by Wordsworth and Coleridge* (London, 1927); J. V. Logan, *Wordsworthian Criticism: A Guide and Bibliography* (Columbus, Ohio, 1947); *Catalogue of the Library at Dove Cottage* (London, 1948); G. H. Henley, comp., *The Cornell Wordsworth Collection* (London, 1957); E. F. Henley and D. H. Stam, *Wordsworthian Criticism 1945-1964: An Annotated Bibliography* (New York, 1965); D. H. Stam, *Wordsworthian Criticism 1964-1973: An Annotated Bibliography, Including Additions to Wordsworthian Criticism 1945-1964* (New York, 1974).

II. COLLECTED WORKS. *Poems, Including Lyrical Ballads*, 2 vols. (London, 1915), the first collected ed.; *Miscellaneous Poems*, 4 vols. (London, 1820-1827), 5 vols. (London, 1832), 6 vols. (London, 1836-1846), 7 vols. (London, 1849-1850); *The Poems* (London, 1845); *The Poetical Works*, 6 vols. (London, 1857), with I. Fenwick's notes; T. Hutchinson, ed., *The Poetical Works* (London, 1895), rev. by E. de Selincourt (London, 1950), the Oxford Standard Authors series, also in Oxford Paperback (London, 1969); E. de Selincourt and H. Darbishire, eds., *The Poetical Works*, 5 vols. (Oxford, 1940-1949; rev. ed., 1952-1959); W. J. B. Owen and J. W. Smyser, eds., *The Prose Works of William Wordsworth*, 3 vols. (Oxford, 1974); J. O. Hayden, ed., *William Wordsworth: The Poems*, 2 vols. (Harmondsworth, 1977), does not include *The Prelude*; S. Parrish, ed., *The Cornell Wordsworth* (Ithaca, N.Y.-Hassocks, Sussex, 1975-): S. Gill, ed., *The Salisbury Plain Poems* (1975); S. Parrish, ed., *The Prelude, 1798-99* (1977); B. Darlington, ed., *Home at Grasmere* (1977); J. Butler, ed., *The Ruined Cottage and The Pedlar* (1979).

III. SELECTED WORKS. M. Arnold, ed., *Poems of Wordsworth* (London, 1879); T. Hutchinson, ed., *Poems in Two Volumes* (London, 1897), from the original ed. of 1807, edited by H. Darbishire (London, 1914), and rev. ed. (London, 1952); J. Butt, ed., *Wordsworth. Selected Poetry and Prose* (London, 1964); G. H. Hartman, ed., *William Wordsworth: Selected Poetry and Prose* (New York, 1969); R. S. Thomas, ed., *A Choice of Wordsworth's Verse* (London, 1971); W. J. B. Owen, ed., *Wordsworth's Literary Criticism* (London, 1974); W. Davies, ed., *William Wordsworth: Selected Poems* (London, 1975).

IV. SEPARATE WORKS. *An Evening Walk* (London, 1793), verse; *Descriptive Sketches* (London, 1793), verse; *Lyrical Ballads, with a Few Other Poems* (Bristol, 1798), also in R. L. Brett and A. R. Jones, eds. (London, 1965), W. J. B. Owen, ed. (London, 1967), and Scolar Press facs. ed. (London, 1971); *Lyrical Ballads, with Other Poems*, 2 vols. (London, 1800), also in D. Roper, ed., *Lyrical Ballads, 1805* (London, 1968); *Poems, in Two Volumes* (London, 1807), also in H. Darbishire, ed. (London, 1914); *Concerning the Relations of Great Britain, Spain, and Portugal to Each Other, and to the Common Enemy at This Crisis, and Specifically as Affected by the Convention of Cintra* (London, 1809), prose; *The Excursion, Being a Portion of "The Recluse"* (London, 1814), verse; *The White Doe of Rylstone* (London, 1815), verse, also in Scolar Press facs. ed. (London, 1971); *Thanksgiving Ode, 18 January 1816* (London, 1816); *Peter Bell, a Tale in Verse* (London, 1819); *The Waggoner* (London, 1819), verse; *The River Duddon, a Series of Sonnets* (London, 1820); *Memorials of* a Tour on the Continent (London, 1822), verse; Ecclesiastical Sketches (London, 1822), verse; A Description of the Scenery of the Lakes in the North of England; Originally Published with Select Views in Cumberland, Westmorland, etc., by the Rev. J. Wilkinson (London, 1822), prose; Yarrow Revisited, and Other Poems (London, 1835); A Guide Through the District of the Lakes in the North of England (London, 1835), prose, also in E. de Selincourt, ed. (London, 1906); The Sonnets of William Wordsworth (London, 1838); Poems Chiefly of Early and Late Years; Including the Borderers a Tragedy (London, 1842); Ode on the Installation of His Royal Highness Prince Albert as Chancellor of the University of Cambridge (London, 1847); The Prelude or Growth of a Poet's Mind; An Autobiographical Poem (London, 1850)—the standard ed. is that of E. de Selincourt, edited from the MSS with intro. and notes (London, 1926), rev. by H. Darbishire, Oxford English Texts (London, 1959); 1805 text, E. de Selincourt, ed., rev. by S. Gill (London, 1970); 1805 and 1850 texts, J. C. Maxwell, ed. (Harmondsworth, 1971); 1799, 1805, and 1850 texts, J. Wordsworth, M. H. Abrams, and S. Gill, eds. (New York, 1979); E. de Selincourt, ed., Journals of Dorothy Wordsworth, 2 vols. (London, 1941), also M. Moorman, ed. (London, 1971).

V. LETTERS. W. Knight, ed. Letters of the Wordsworth Family, 3 vols. (London, 1907); L. N. Broughton, ed., Wordsworth and Reed: The Poet's Correspondence with His American Editor: 1836-50 (London, 1933); E. de Selincourt, ed., Letters of William and Dorothy Wordsworth, 6 vols. (Oxford, 1935-1939), rev. ed. in progress: The Early Years, 1787-1805, rev. by C. L. Shaver (London, 1967), The Middle Years, Part 1, 1806-1811, rev. by M. Moorman (London, 1969), The Middle Years, Part 2, 1812-1820, rev. by M. Moorman and A. G. Hill (London, 1970), The Later Years, Part 1, 1821-1828, A. G. Hill, ed. (London, 1978); L. N. Broughton, ed., Some Letters of the Wordsworth Family (Ithaca, N. Y., 1942); P. Wayne, ed., Letters of William Wordsworth (London, 1954), in the World's Classics ed.; M. E. Burton, ed., The Letters of Mary Wordsworth, 1800-1855 (Oxford, 1958); C. H. Ketcham, ed., The Letters of John Wordsworth (Ithaca, N. Y., 1969).

VI. BIOGRAPHICAL AND CRITICAL STUDIES. S. T. Coleridge, Biographia Literaria (London, 1817)—there is a valuable modern ed., J. Shawcross, ed. (Oxford, 1907), also G. Watson, ed. (London, 1971); W. Hazlitt, Lectures on the English Poets (London, 1818); W. S. Landor, Imaginary Conversations of Literary Men and Statesmen, vol. I (London, 1824); W. Hazlitt, The Spirit of the Age (London, 1825); T. De Quincey, "Literary and Lake Reminiscences," in Tait's magazine (1834, 1839)—see also D. Masson, ed., Collected Writings of De Quincey (London, 1889-1890); J. Cottle, Early Recollections (London, 1837); J. Ruskin, Modern Painters (London, 1840-1860); C. Wordsworth, Memoirs of William Wordsworth, 2 vols. (London, 1851); J. Wilson, Recreations of Christopher North, vol. II (London, 1854); W. Knight, ed., Transactions of the Words-

worth Society (1882-1887); M. Arnold, Essays in Criticism, 2nd ser. (London, 1888); H. D. Rawnsley, Literary Associations of the Lakes (London, 1894); E. Legouis, La jeunesse de William Wordsworth (Paris, 1896), trans. by J. W. Matthews as The Early Life of William Wordsworth (London, 1897); W. Pater, Appreciations (London, 1899).

W. Raleigh, Wordsworth (London, 1903); A. C. Bradley, English Poetry and German Philosophy in the Age of Wordsworth (London, 1909); A. C. Bradley, Oxford Lectures on Poetry (London, 1909); E. J. Morley, ed., Blake, Coleridge, Wordsworth, etc.: Selections from the Remains of Henry Crabb Robinson (London, 1922); E. Legouis, William Wordsworth and Annette Vallon (London, 1922); H. W. Garrod, Wordsworth: Lectures and Essays (London, 1923); H. Read, Wordsworth (London, 1930; rev. ed., 1948); E. de Selincourt, Dorothy Wordsworth: A Biography (London, 1933); P. Burra, Wordsworth (London, 1936); E. L. Griggs, ed., Wordsworth and Coleridge: Studies in Honour of George McLean Harper (Princeton, N. J., 1939); J. D. Wilson, Leslie Stephen and Matthew Arnold as Critics of Wordsworth (London, 1939); G. W. Meyer, Wordsworth's Formative Years (Ann Arbor, Mich., 1943); J. C. Smith, A Study of Wordsworth (London, 1944); N. P. Stallknecht, Strange Seas of Thought: Studies in Wordsworth's Philosophy of Man and Nature (Durham, N. C., 1945); E. de Selincourt, Wordsworthian and Other Studies (London, 1947); N. Nicholson, Wordsworth: An Introduction and a Selection (London, 1949).

H. Darbishire, The Poet Wordsworth (London, 1950)—Clark Lectures (1949), Oxford Paperback (1966); Wordsworth at Cambridge: A Record of the Commemoration Held at St. John's College, Cambridge (London, 1950)—contains a detailed survey of Wordsworth portraits; G. T. Dunklin, ed., Wordsworth: Centenary Studies (Princeton, N. J., 1950); L. Abercrombie, The Art of Wordsworth (London, 1952); H. M. Margoliouth, Wordsworth and Coleridge (London, 1953); J. Jones, The Egotistical Sublime: A History of Wordsworth's Imagination (London, 1954); F. W. Bateson, Wordsworth: A Re-Interpretation (London, 1954; rev. ed., 1956); M. Moorman, William Wordsworth: A Biography, 2 vols. (Oxford, 1957-1965), reprinted in Oxford Paperback (London, 1968); B. R. Schneider, Wordsworth's Cambridge Education (London, 1957); K. Coburn, ed., The Notebooks of Samuel Taylor Coleridge, 2 vols. (London, 1957); F. M. Todd, Politics and the Poet: A Study of Wordsworth (London, 1957); Z. S. Fink, ed., The Early Wordsworthian Milieu (London, 1958)—a notebook of Christopher Wordsworth, with a few entries by William Wordsworth; D. Ferry, The Limits of Mortality: An Essay on Wordsworth's Major Poems (Middletown, Conn., 1959); F. Blanshard, Portraits of Wordsworth (London, 1959).

J. F. Danby, The Simple Wordsworth: Studies in the Poems, 1797-1807 (London, 1960); C. C. Clarke, Romantic Paradox: An Essay on the Poetry of Wordsworth (London, 1963); H. Lindenberger, *On Wordsworth's Prelude* (London, 1963); J. F. Danby, *William Wordsworth: The Prelude and Other Poems* (London, 1963); D. Perkins, *Wordsworth and the Poetry of Sincerity* (Cambridge, Mass., 1964); G. H. Hartman, *Wordsworth's Poetry, 1787–1814* (New Haven, Conn., 1964), contains a good critical bibliography; A. King, *Wordsworth and the Artist's Vision* (London, 1966); C. Salvesen, *The Landscape of Memory* (London, 1966); G. B. Groom, *The Unity of Wordsworth's Poetry* (London, 1966); M. L. Reed, *Wordsworth: The Chronology of the Early Years 1770–1779* (London–Cambridge, Mass., 1967); M. Rader, *Wordsworth. A Philosophical Approach* (Oxford, 1967); F. E. Halliday, *Wordsworth and His World* (London, 1969), with 140 illustrations; G. Durrant, *William Wordsworth* (London, 1969), Cambridge British Authors paperback; C. Woodring, *Wordsworth* (Cambridge, Mass., 1968); J. Wordsworth, *The Music of Humanity: A Critical Study of Wordsworth's "Ruined Cottage" Incorporating Texts from a Manuscript of 1799–1800* (London, 1969); J. A. W. Heffernan, *Wordsworth's Theory of Poetry: The Transforming Imagination* (Ithaca, N. Y., 1969); J. Wordsworth, *William Wordsworth: 1770–1969* (London, 1969), British Academy Chatterton Lecture.

D. Wesling, *Wordsworth and the Adequacy of Landscape* (London, 1970); G. Durrant, *Wordsworth and the Great System* (London, 1970); J. R. Watson, *Picturesque Landscape and English Romantic Poetry* (London, 1970); A. S. Byatt, *Wordsworth and Coleridge in Their Time* (London, 1970); W. Heath, *Wordsworth and Coleridge* (Oxford, 1970); S. Prickett, *Coleridge and Wordsworth: The Poetry of Growth* (Cambridge, 1970); J. Wordsworth, ed., *Bicentenary Wordsworth Studies in Memory of John Alban Finch* (Ithaca, N. Y., 1971); F. Garber, *Wordsworth and the Poetry of Encounter* (Urbana, Ill., 1971); G. K. Thomas, *Wordsworth's Dirge and Promise* (Lincoln, Nebr., 1971); J. R. Curtis, *Wordsworth's Experiments with Tradition* (Ithaca, N. Y., 1971); R. Noyes, *William Wordsworth* (New York, 1971); R. J. Onorato, *The Character of the Poet* (Princeton, N. J., 1971); G. McMaster, ed., *William Wordsworth* (Harmondsworth, 1972), Penguin Critical Anthology; A. R. Jones and W. Tydeman, eds., *Wordsworth, Lyrical Ballads* (London, 1972), a casebook; W. J. Harvey and R. Gravil, eds., *Wordsworth, The Prelude* (London, 1972), a casebook; R. Sharrock, *The Figure in a Landscape: Wordsworth's Early Poetry* (London, 1972), British Academy Warton Lecture; S. M. Parrish, *The Art of the Lyrical Ballads* (Cambridge, Mass., 1973); P. D. Sheats, *The Making of Wordsworth's Poetry* (Cambridge, Mass., 1973); A. Grob, *The Philosophic Mind* (Columbus, Ohio, 1973); A. O. Wlecke, *Wordsworth and the Sublime* (Berkeley, 1973); M. H. Abrams, ed., *Wordsworth, a Collection of Critical Essays* (Englewood Cliffs, N. J., 1973); L. M. Johnson, *Wordsworth and the Sonnet* (Copenhagen, 1973); F. D. McConnell, *The Confessional Imagination* (Baltimore, 1974); M. L. Reed, *Wordsworth: The Chronology of the Middle Years, 1800–1815* (Cambridge, Mass., 1975); R. E. Brantley, *Wordsworth's "Natural Methodism"* (New Haven, Conn., 1975); E. L. Stelzig, *All Shades of Consciousness: Wordsworth's Poetry and the Self in Time* (The Hague, 1975); S. Prickett, *Wordsworth and Coleridge: The Lyrical Ballads* (London, 1975); M. Jacobus, *Tradition and Experiment in Wordsworth's Lyrical Ballads (1798)* (Oxford, 1976); J. E. Jordan, *Why the Lyrical Ballads?* (Berkeley, 1976); F. Ferguson, *Wordsworth: Language as Counter-Spirit* (New Haven, Conn., 1977); J. Beer, *Wordsworth and the Human Heart* (London, 1977).

POETS OF WORLD WAR I

John Press

INTRODUCTION

WHEN Europe went to war in August 1914 it had not witnessed a major conflict since the defeat of Napoleon at Waterloo in 1815, although the war for the liberation of Italy and Bismarck's wars against Denmark, Austria, and France had reminded politicians that violence might be an effective instrument of policy. Britain's only adventure on the continent, the Crimean War, had revealed the criminal incompetence of the army command, the scandalous state of the hospital services as exposed by Florence Nightingale, and the blundering stupidity of military tactics, seen at its most notorious in the charge of the Light Brigade. But all that was over fifty years before. A study of the American Civil War might have prepared the men of 1914 for what lay before them: the employment of artillery on a very large scale; the devastation of the countryside; the destruction of towns and the wandering of refugees from homes they had been forced to abandon. Yet nobody would have believed that the particular kind of savagery endured in the United States in the 1860's would have marked a conflict between the chivalrous professional armies of Europe fifty years later.

Leonard Woolf describes how he walked over the Sussex Downs in the summer of 1914 and how they looked almost as if unchanged since Domesday. World War I was to transform far more than the landscape of Sussex and of the other English counties. The face of the world was changed and, together with the millions who perished on the battlefields or in the influenza epidemic after the war, the civilization of Europe died. The pages that follow record how some English poets fought in the trenches and wrote poems by which they are remembered.

SOME ESTABLISHED POETS

MANY of the older poets, who were well over military age, felt the impulse to write patriotic verse about the war. It is better not to quote Sir William Watson's lines about Germany or his address to the Kaiser, but to remark only that he sank to depths of vulgarity and hysteria unplumbed by any other poet in both world wars. Thomas Hardy's "Men Who March Away" is on a different level of achievement, but it moves with an uncharacteristic jaunty religious fervor that has not worn well. Charles Sorley, a great admirer of Hardy, believed that one line of the poem, "Victory crowns the just," was the worst Hardy had ever written.

Rudyard Kipling (1865–1936) summoned his fellow countrymen to brace themselves for the coming struggle and to gird themselves for sacrifice. "For All We Have and Are" is an accomplished call to arms, an attempt to stiffen the sinews and to strengthen the will. Kipling warns all patriots that "The Hun is at the gate," adroitly seizing on the Kaiser's admonition to his troops at the time of the Boxer rebellion that they should behave like the ancient Huns. Kipling's poems on the war are varied in mood and theme; some are diatribes against politicians who hid the truth before the war and sent men ill-equipped into battle after war had come. He also wrote some memorable epigrams, including one on a soldier executed for cowardice, toward whom he shows an unexpected compassion. Under most of his wartime poems one can detect anger and grief at the death in action of his beloved son.

Unlike Kipling, who was well attuned to the mood of the public, A. E. Housman (1859–1936) caused some offense by his tribute to the regular army, which fought with such courage in the early days of the war and saved the Allies from defeat. People objected to the title of his poem "Epitaph on an Army of Mercenaries," on the grounds that it was an insult to a heroic body of men, even though the word "mercenaries" was an accurate description of their calling. Nor did the pious relish the poem's last two lines:

What God abandoned, these defended,
And saved the sum of things for pay.

Today one admires the laconic precision of the phrasing, the lapidary force of the encomium bestowed by Housman on men who practiced two of the virtues he most cherished: stoical courage and devotion to duty.

One should pay a brief tribute to Ford Madox Ford (1873–1939), who insisted on joining the army and who fought in the trenches, even though overage. It is true that he was probably more of a menace to his military superiors than to the Germans, and that he had enlisted partly to get away from his mistress, Violet Hunt, who was proving even more tiresome than his wife. Nevertheless, it was a gallant gesture, and although Ford was not a very good poet, his "Antwerp" is an interesting example of an attempt to adapt and to enlarge imagistic technique for the purpose of describing war without emotion. The Belgian, with a smoking gun, is an uncomely man in an ugly tunic, and when he is killed he "lies, an unsightly lump on the sodden grass." As late as November 1917, T. S. Eliot described "Antwerp" as "the only good poem I have met with on the subject of the war," which makes one wonder what poems about the war Eliot had read.

"For the Fallen" by Laurence Binyon (1869–1943) is probably familiar to more people than any other poem of World War I. It is so widely known because it is frequently declaimed at memorial services, including services in memory of those who died in the Falkland Islands in 1982. The poem has a solemn, liturgical quality that commends it to those mourning their dead, and since it is free of any tincture of Christian devotion, it appeals to those who want religious dignity without Christian dogma:

They shall grow not old, as we that are left grow old:
Age shall not weary them, nor the years condemn.
At the going down of the sun and in the morning
We will remember them.

(st. 4)

Although there is no warrant in the text, congregations habitually supplement the words of the officiating clergyman by intoning a repetition of the last line: "We will remember them." The poem of an individual poet is transformed into a communal liturgical rite. None of Binyon's subsequent poems attained anything like the popularity of "For the Fallen." Halfway through World War II Binyon wrote a poem called "The Burning of the Leaves," which is concerned with the necessity of laying aside all that is ended and done. It may not be fanciful to suppose that he was looking back to the previous war and drawing courage from the experience of 1914–1918 when he achieved the mingled doubt and affirmation of the poem's final line: "Nothing is certain, only the certain spring."

Most of the younger poets who had begun to make a reputation by 1914 were associated, at least in the minds of poetry readers, with the Georgians or the imagists, although these were rough and often misleading classifications. D. H. Lawrence, for example, wandered cheerfully between the two camps, glad to win whatever sustenance he could from either group.

There were obvious links between the Georgians and the war poets, mainly because Edward Marsh printed their work in the anthologies with which he followed up his initial *Georgian Poetry 1911–1912*. His editorial labors did much to spread the fame of Rupert Brooke and to make more widely known the work of Siegfried Sassoon and of the largely forgotten but by no means untalented W. W. Gibson. Edmund Blunden and Ivor Gurney had strong affinities with Georgianism; and even Wilfred Owen was proud to be held peer by the Georgians, greatly though he surpassed them in technical mastery and imaginative force.

Imagism, on the other hand, had little influence on the war poetry written between 1914 and 1918. The younger imagist poets who served in the trenches included Richard Aldington (later famous as a novelist of the war), Herbert Read, and T. E. Hulme, who was killed in 1915, leaving no war poems. Long after the war Herbert Read sought to explain in *The Contrary Experience* (1963) why the aesthetic theories of imagism were inadequate to explain the "terrorful and inhuman events" of the conflict. Certainly Aldington's war poems, though well constructed, are too decorative and remote to move us greatly. Perhaps his best war poem is "Sunsets," the first stanza of which can be read simply as an impressionistic evocation of the sky at evening:

The white body of evening
Is torn into scarlet
Slashed and gouged and seared
Into crimson,
And hung ironically
With garlands of mist.

(1–6)

It is only after reading the second stanza that one understands the sinister import of the first, in which the bloody violence of war is mirrored upon the canvas of the natural world:

> And the wind
> Blowing over London from Flanders
> Has a bitter taste.
>
> (7–9)

Ezra Pound alone among the imagists found adequate expression for the inner meaning of the war, in *Hugh Selwyn Mauberley*; but that poem lies outside the scope of this essay, since it was written by a man who, though living in England, was a civilian and an American.

Just as the avant-garde poetry of the immediate prewar years exerted only a marginal influence on the war poets, so the poetry of 1914–1918 barely affected the modernist movement of the 1920's. Eliot, Pound, and William Butler Yeats seem to have learned nothing even from Owen and Isaac Rosenberg; and although W. H. Auden and the poets of the 1930's professed a deep reverence for Owen, they assimilated little of his achievement except a few technical devices and a tendency to invoke pity as an emotional gesture. It was left to the poets of World War II to discover that certain poems written between 1914 and 1918 gave imaginative shape to unchanging truths about the nature of war and of human life.

MORNING HEROES

WHATEVER might be said against the landed aristocracy and other members of the British ruling classes in 1914, nobody could gainsay their physical courage. The main fear of the young men among them was that the war might be over by Christmas, thus preventing them from killing Germans. Almost all of them had been educated at public schools, where they had absorbed the codes of honor and duty that governed all who grew up there. The poems of Henry Newbolt (1862–1938), though written mainly during the 1880's and 1890's, still expressed the ethics of the public schools. Indeed, Newbolt in 1914 had not felt it necessary to write any new poems: he merely published a collection of his earlier work, of which 70,000 copies were sold.

Poems such as "Vitai Lampada" may nowadays seem ludicrous, but young officers in 1914 accepted the injunction, "Play up! play up! and play the game!" Many of these young officers, most of whom were in no sense professional poets, wrote poems that recorded their experience of combat during the period of the war that ran from August 1914 to the end of June 1916, the eve of the Battle of the Somme. After that the world became darker: the experiences, terrifying but sometimes joyful, of Julian Grenfell and Charles Sorley were replaced by the purgatorial twilight in which Sassoon, Owen, and Rosenberg found themselves.

Raymond Asquith (1878–1916), eldest son of the prime minister, practiced at the bar after a career of exceptional brilliance at Oxford. He left no war poems and indeed was not a poet, although he wrote extremely skillful parodies and pastiches. He deserves to be remembered for his parody of Kipling's jingoistic "Soldiers of the Queen," which begins:

> The sun like a Bishop's bottom
> Rosy and round and hot. . . .

He was typical of his class and his generation in that he volunteered for military service when there was no pressure on him to do so; rejected a safe job as a staff officer for the danger and discomfort of the trenches; and died with courage and composure on the Somme in September 1916, during what the divisional commander called "the greatest of all the war achievements of the Brigade of Guards."

Herbert Asquith (1881–1947), Raymond's younger brother, managed to go through the war from beginning to end unscathed. He is remembered chiefly for a competent though old-fashioned and conventional sonnet, "The Volunteer," about a city clerk who is afraid that he will never break a lance in life's tournament. He volunteers, is killed, and lies content. This poem, with its imagery drawn from medieval knight errantry, is typical in its loftiness and total divorce from reality, the mood in which many young men went to war in 1914. This is not invalidated by the fact that Herbert Asquith wrote "The Volunteer" in 1912.

One of the closest friends of the Asquiths was Julian Grenfell (1888–1915). His father, William Grenfell, a remarkable athlete, was created Lord Desborough in 1905; his mother, "Etty," was probably the most celebrated hostess of her day. Before he was two he had displayed his vigorous enjoyment of killing: "Determined to kill a mouse. Hammer it with a hammer" (Mosley, *Julian Grenfell*, p. 13). He was a man of considerable intelligence, educated at Eton and Balliol, who in 1909 collected but did not publish a book of essays on social and political themes that his strong-minded mother and her friends heartily disliked. He received a commission in the Royal Dragoons in 1910, having passed first among all university graduate entrants to the army. After service in India and then in South Africa, Grenfell planned to give up his army career so that he might devote himself to painting. Etty, with whom his relations were always complex, mocked him and incited her circle of friends to join in the mockery. He capitulated.

On October 1914 Grenfell sailed for France. Although he had never enjoyed the mass slaughter that had characterized Edwardian and Georgian shooting parties, Grenfell had always loved solitary killing, because it represented a link with the earth and furthered his pursuit of primitive things. He perfected a technique that enabled him to stalk Germans after dark, to creep close to them and then shoot them. In mid-November he shot a German on each of two successive evenings, for which he was awarded the Distinguished Service Order. When he went home on leave he made an entry in his game book to the effect that on 16 and 17 November 1914 he had bagged a Pomeranian.

Grenfell's attitude to the war was unambiguous: it is to his credit that he did not drape his naked ferocity in sanctimonious moralizing. He was a killer from the egg, describing war as all the most wonderful *fun*. More sinister is his verdict on the life that he was leading:

I have never, never felt so well, or so happy, or enjoyed anything so much. It just suits my stolid health, and stolid nerves, and barbaric disposition. The fighting—excitement vitalises everything, every sight and word and action. One loves one's fellow-man so much more when one is bent on killing him.

(*Julian Grenfell*, p. 241)

Yet he was not devoid of human feelings. After a passage in a letter from Flanders written in October 1914: "I *adore* war. It is like a big picnic without the objectlessness of a picnic" (p. 239)—Grenfell goes on to express his sense of pity at the wretchedness of the inhabitants who had been forced to leave their homes.

At the end of January 1915 Grenfell returned to France, taking with him three greyhounds—he had always loved the breed and before the war had written a poem entitled "To a Black Greyhound." On 29 April he wrote "Into Battle," the poem that is his surest title to immortality. At 4:00 A.M. on 13 May he was grievously wounded, and although his friends believed that his toughness would pull him through, his wounds proved fatal. On his deathbed, presided over by the indomitable Etty, he quoted Phaedra's song from the *Hippolytus* of Euripides, a play that he had admired since his boyhood. When on 25 May a shaft of sunlight fell across his feet, Grenfell said, "Phoebus Apollo," and did not speak again except once to say his father's name. He died on 26 May with a radiant smile on his face.

"Into Battle" is one of those poems by gifted amateurs that have taken their place in the corpus of English poetry. It brings together many of the strands woven into Grenfell's nature: his love of killing that brought him closer to the earth; the sheer exhilaration of battle; a strain of mysticism. (At the age of thirteen, during a thunderstorm, he suddenly seemed to realize God, and he became devoted to Saint Thomas à Kempis.)

The poem opens with a celebration of the spring, which will enrich the fighting man. Then follows a section in which Grenfell affirms the kinship between the fighting man and the forces of the universe: "the bright company of Heaven"; the woodland trees; the kestrel and the little owls:

> The blackbird sings to him, "Brother, brother,
>   If this be the last song you shall sing,
> Sing well, for you may not sing another;
>   Brother sing."
>
> (st. 6)

Grenfell ends by envisaging the joy of battle, expressing his trust in the Destined Will, and committing himself to the powers of Day and Night.

Another intimate of the Asquith circle was Patrick Shaw-Stewart (1888–1917), whose career at Oxford was only slightly less brilliant than Raymond Asquith's. After leaving Oxford, he joined Baring's Bank, where he rapidly attained a senior position. Soon after the outbreak of war he became a lieutenant-commander in the Royal Naval Division and fought at Gallipoli. He was killed in action in France late in 1917, having refused to quit the field after his ear had been torn off by shrapnel. An untitled poem was found in Shaw-Stewart's copy of Housman's *A*

Shropshire Lad, a book whose influence on him it is difficult to overemphasize. The poem begins:

> I saw a man this morning
> Who did not wish to die.

It then considers the fighting in the Dardanelles, reflecting for a moment on Helen of Troy and incorporating into the poem a pun on her name that derives from Euripides. Shaw-Stewart's attainments as a classical scholar rivaled those of Raymond Asquith, and, like Julian Grenfell, he turned quite naturally in moments of crisis and fear to the world of classical Greece. He communes with Achilles, asking him if it was very hard to die, and the poem concludes on a note of affirmation, in which the figure of Achilles is invoked:

> I will go back this morning
> From Imbros over the sea;
> Stand in the trench, Achilles,
> Flame-capped, and shout for me.
>
> (25–26)

Robert Nichols (1893–1944), although now largely forgotten, was once a name to conjure with, cherished by the reading public as all that a young heroic poet should be, and admired by Edward Marsh as one of his favorite Georgian poets. Marsh was an influential figure, a cultivated member of the English upper classes, private secretary to Winston Churchill, a patron of the arts and editor of the widely read anthology *Georgian Poetry 1911–1912*, the first of five such collections. Although Nichols' army career was in no way discreditable, he was invalided home suffering from shell shock and after five months' treatment in military hospitals received his discharge. Robert Graves, who did not like Nichols, thought him almost a phony, perhaps because after leaving the army he scored a great success with his lectures in the United States on the war, in spite of having experienced active service only for what Graves would have regarded as a ridiculously brief period.

Nichols' wartime poetry, with its mixture of homosexual eroticism and religiosity, has not worn well. Even among his contemporaries there were those who found his work distasteful. Douglas Goldring savagely but justly called "The Assault" "a masterpiece of drivel"; and Wilfred Owen regarded him as "self-concerned and *vaniteux* in his verse" (*Wilfred Owen: Collected Letters*, p. 511). Yet some-

thing survives of the romantic vitality and élan that awoke a response in Nichols' first readers. His description of "Dawn on the Somme" was written during the Battle of the Somme while he was being treated for neurasthenia in a hospital:

> Oh, is it mist, or are these companies
> Of morning heroes who arise, arise
> With thrusting arms, with limbs and hair aglow,
> Towards the risen gold, upon whose brow
> Burns the gold laurel of all victories,
> Hero and heroes' gold, th'invincible Sun?
>
> (7–12)

After the war his reputation faded, although a selection of his poems, *Such Was My Singing*, appeared in 1942, and he edited *An Anthology of War Poetry* in 1943. Some of his lyrical pieces deserve to be remembered, while "The Sprig of Lime," a poem of about ninety lines, surpasses in gravity and tenderness everything else that Nichols wrote. It remains one of the neglected masterpieces of our time.

A far more formidable figure than Nichols was Rupert Brooke (1887–1915), for whom Edward Marsh felt a deeper affection than for any other Georgian poet. His legendary fame persists to the present day for a variety of reasons. He had many friends of widely different callings, ranging from Virginia Woolf to Geoffrey Keynes, the distinguished surgeon and literary scholar, and Hugh Dalton, chancellor of the exchequer in the Labour government of 1945. In conversations, diaries, memoirs, and letters they united to celebrate Brooke's physical splendor, intellectual power, and literary gifts. The cult of Rupert Brooke still flourishes, given fresh impetus by the revelation that he and Virginia Woolf once bathed naked; and it is possible even now to wax sentimental over the Old Vicarage, at Grantchester, and to get honey for tea in a tea shop in the village.

The building of Rupert Brooke into a legend began almost as soon as he was dead, and it is clear that, in part at least, those who fabricated the edifice did so in order to encourage young men to volunteer for the armed forces. Winston Churchill eulogized him as joyous, fearless, and ruled by high, undoubting purpose. Brooke confessed soon after the outbreak of war that the perils of the time and the darkness of the world made him uneasy and vaguely frightened. Nor was he joyous: he was deeply neurotic, especially in his dealings with women. In a letter of August 1912 to Ka Cox, with whom he had a long affair, Brooke confessed his fear that he was incapable of any fruitful sexual relationship, and testified to his self-disgust. He probably never recovered from the nervous breakdown that ended the affair. After he left Tahiti, where he had found brief happiness with a girl called Taatamata, Brooke received a letter from her full of misspellings in French and English, and he "gulped a good deal."

Brooke had achieved a reputation as a poet before 1914. He was one of the six people who met for luncheon in Edward Marsh's rooms on 20 September 1912 and planned the genesis of *Georgian Poetry*. He was probably the most valued contributor to the first anthology, *Georgian Poetry 1911–1912*, which appeared before the end of 1912.

Brooke's response to the war, a group of war sonnets, appeared in *New Numbers*, December 1914, without attracting much attention. In September, Brooke had received a commission in the Royal Naval Division, which early in 1915 sailed for the Dardanelles in the hope of striking a decisive blow against the Turks. Before he was able to accomplish anything of note, Brooke contracted blood poisoning caused by a bite from a mosquito or a scorpion. He died in a French military hospital on the Greek island of Scyros on Saint George's Day, 23 April. The firing party at his grave on the island, traditionally associated with Achilles, was commanded by Patrick Shaw-Stewart.

Even before Rupert Brooke's death one of his five war sonnets had begun to reach a wide audience. On 5 April 1915, Easter Day, the dean of Saint Paul's, W. R. Inge, had taken as the text for his sermon Isaiah 26:19—"The dead shall live, my dead bodies shall arise. Awake and sing, ye that dwell in the dust." Inge went on to quote one of Brooke's sonnets, "The Soldier," remarking that "the enthusiasm of a pure and elevated patriotism had never found a nobler expression." Three days after Brooke's death Winston Churchill praised the war sonnets in the *Times*. On 16 June 1915 the sonnets were gathered into *1914 and Other Poems*, edited by Edward Marsh. A few months later they were given a separate edition under the title *1914. Five Sonnets*.

Brooke had a gift for the striking phrase and the rhetorical assertion, as the opening lines of three of his sonnets demonstrate:

> If I should die, think only this of me:
> > That there's some corner of a foreign field
> That is for ever England.
> > > ("The Soldier")

> Blow out, you bugles, over the rich Dead!
> > There's none of these so lonely and poor of old,
> But, dying, has made us rarer gifts than gold.
> > > ("The Dead")

> Now, God be thanked who has matched us with His hour,
> > And caught our youth, and wakened us from sleeping,
> With hand made sure, clear eye, and sharpened power,
> > To turn, as swimmers into cleanness leaping,
> Glad from a world grown old and cold and weary,
> > Leave the sick hearts that honour could not move,
> And half-men, and their dirty songs and dreary,
> > And all the little emptiness of love!
> > > ("Peace")

Yet the sonnets are inadequate, poetically and morally. Even Julian Grenfell had been content to proclaim his love of killing without prating about the cleansing power of war. Nobody since the emotionally disturbed hero of Tennyson's *Maud* (1855), who resolved to plunge into the slaughter of the Crimea, had supposed that war was likely to offer a regenerative experience. Read in the light of what we know about Brooke's psychological difficulties, these sonnets represent the struggle of a highly strung, desperate man to escape from the emotional problems in which he lay trapped. There was a conscious drive toward simplification and self-sacrifice, a barely conscious drifting toward death.

It is significant that three of his contemporaries, all poets who died in battle, were unimpressed by Brooke's sonnets. In a letter to his mother dated 28 November 1914, Charles Sorley remarks that Brooke "is far too obsessed with his own sacrifice, regarding the going to war of himself (and others) as a highly intense, remarkable and sacrificial exploit. . . . He has clothed his attitude in fine words; but he has taken the sentimental attitude" (*Letters*, p. 263). Isaac Rosenberg, who was admittedly jealous of Edward Marsh's devotion to Brooke and to his memory, refers in a letter to Mrs. Cohen, probably written at midsummer 1915, to the commonplace phrases in Brooke's "begloried sonnets" (*Collected Works*, p. 237). Rosenberg thought that his "Clouds" was a magnificent poem, and, in a letter to Sydney Schiff dating from about August 1916, he singles out for praise Brooke's "Town and Country," but remarks of his other poems that "they remind me too much of flag days" (*Isaac Rosenberg 1890–1918: Catalogue with Letters*, p. 16). Edward Thomas, in a letter to Robert Frost of 19 October 1916, while acknowledging that Brooke had "succeeded in being youthful and yet intelligible and interesting (not only pathologically) more than most poets since Shelley," passes a severe judgment on him: "He was a rhetorician, dressing things up better than needed. And I suspect he knew only too well both what he was after and what he achieved" (*Rupert Brooke: A Biography*, p. 502).

It would be ungenerous to conclude on a sour note. When Brooke encountered the reality of war in the retreat from Antwerp in late 1914 he was moved to pity by the spectacle of refugees. In the "Fragment" written on his troopship in April 1915 he describes how, after dark, he remains on deck, watching his friends, unobserved by them. The poem is infused with a profound sadness, an awareness of human fragility. It is worlds away from the mood of the sonnets. Brooke's reaction to Dean Inge's sermon evinces something of his old irony and good sense. When he lay dying, his friend Denis Browne came to his cabin to talk about the dean's sermon, of which Brooke already knew, having received a newspaper clipping from Marsh. The clipping contained Inge's reservation about "The Soldier": "And yet it fell somewhat short of Isaiah's vision and still more of the Christian hope." Brooke murmured his regret that the dean didn't think him quite so good as Isaiah. They were his last coherent words.

Charles Hamilton Sorley (1895–1915) had an intense passion for truth:

The voice of our poets and men of letters is finely trained and sweet to hear; it teems with sharp saws and rich sentiments: it is a marvel of delicate technique: it pleases, it flatters, it charms, it soothes: it is a living lie.

(*The Letters with a Chapter of Biography*, pp. 37–38)

This passage has sometimes been quoted as Sorley's response to the jingoistic poetry of 1914: in fact, it comes from a paper on John Masefield read to the Literary Society of Marlborough College on 3 November 1912.

Sorley, who went to school at Marlborough, was planning to enter Oxford in September 1914, but, after leaving school at the end of 1913, he went to live in Germany in January 1914. He loved Germany, despite his loathing for such evil manifestations as the student corps, with their drunkenness, aggressiveness, and hatred of Jews. Nor did he care for Germany's bigotry and conviction of spiritual superiority. When war broke out he was on a walking tour; he was briefly imprisoned, released, and expelled. As soon as he reached England he applied for a commission.

Sorley was unique among English poets who fought in the war in having an intimate knowledge of Germany. He was in a very small minority of people who detested the tawdry elements in official propaganda, the nauseating humbug preached by journalists and churchmen, whom he stigmatized collectively as Annas and Caiaphas. Even his beloved Hardy's "Men Who March Away" incurred his displeasure. It is, he says, in a letter of 30 November 1914, "the most arid poem in *Satires of Circumstance*, besides being untrue of the sentiments of the ranksman going to war: 'Victory crowns the just' is the worst line he ever wrote—filched from a leading article in *The Morning Post*" (*Letters*, p. 246).

As early as August 1914 Sorley had grasped the truth that Britain and Germany were engaged in a fratricidal conflict. His sonnet "To Germany" opens:

> You are blind like us. Your hurt no man designed,
> And no man claimed the conquest of your land.

The theme of mutual blindness sounds at the end of the octet:

> And in each other's dearest ways we stand,
> And hiss and hate. And the blind fight the blind.

None of Sorley's poems compares in quality with the finest poetry written during the war: his command of poetic technique was inadequate to bear the charge of his imaginative vision. It is in his superb *Letters*, still available in the original edition of 1919, that one finds the best evidence of his intellectual keenness and searing honesty. Nowhere are these qualities more vigorously exhibited than in Sorley's letter to Arthur Watts of August 1915, describing the excitement of the encounter with the enemy:

. . . the wail of the exploded bomb and the animal cries of the wounded men. Then death and the horrible thankfulness when one sees that the next man is dead: "We won't have to *carry* him in under fire, thank God; dragging will do": hauling in of the great resistless body in the dark, the smashed head rattling: the relief, the relief that the thing has ceased to groan: that the bullet or bomb that made the man an animal has now made the animal a corpse. One is hardened by now: purged of all false pity: perhaps more selfish than before. The spiritual and the animal get so much more sharply divided in hours of encounter, taking possession of the body by swift turns.

(pp. 305–306)

One of Sorley's best poems is the untitled "All the hills and vales along," which owes something in mood to Housman. Written before Sorley had seen active service, it ironically celebrates the fact that the marching men are going to their death, urges them to be joyful, and reminds them that Nature will rejoice at their death as it rejoiced at the death of Socrates and of Christ:

> Earth that never doubts nor fears
> Earth that knows of death, not tears,
> Earth that bore with joyful ease
> Hemlock for Socrates,
> Earth that blossomed and was glad
> 'Neath the cross that Christ had,
> Shall rejoice and blossom too
> When the bullet reaches you.
>
> (st. 3)

Sorley's awareness of mortality and his sense of communion with the dead, which go back to his school days, find expression in two sonnets on death dated 12 June 1915 and in the sonnet "When you see millions of the mouthless dead," found among his possessions after his death in action on 13 October 1915. In that final sonnet, as in the June sonnets, one can detect an attempt to resolve a deep ambiguity in his attitude to death. Perhaps it would be truer to say that there coexisted in Sorley a devout belief in the Christian doctrine of the resurrection and a deep subconscious acceptance of the knowledge that death is final.

The final sonnet prefigures in certain ways Owen's apprehension of war as a tragedy in which numberless men meet their deaths:

> When you see millions of the mouthless dead
> Across your dreams in pale battalions go. . . .
>
> (1–2)

The sonnet emphasizes the deadness of the dead, the futility of praise or tears, the remoteness of the dead from the living. It might almost be a rejoinder to Rupert Brooke, whose war sonnets had not commended themselves to Sorley. The final line of the sonnet is difficult to read as other than a denial of immortality: "Great death has made all his for evermore."

During the last five months of his life Sorley wrote one or two poems that are no better than the average run of verse in a hymnal or the memorial tributes in a public school magazine. It is not easy to account for this descent into banality of thought and diction; but despite his rebellion against certain aspects of the ethos inculcated at Marlborough, Sorley remained deeply attached to the school and to the downs nearby, where he loved to take his long solitary runs. Perhaps, in the physical and emotional turmoil of the trenches, he at times found solace in reverting to the idiom and the values of his adolescence.

Sorley died so young that his potential as a poet had scarcely begun to develop. He had probably the keenest intelligence and the most admirable nature of all the poets of World War I. The visitor who wishes to enter the chapel at Marlborough, a splendid example of Victorian Gothic, must first pass through the antechapel. He will see, affixed to the walls, a number of memorial tablets that honor distinguished sons of the school. Most of them commemorate Victorian admirals, generals, and governors of remote colonies. One is in memory of Charles Hamilton Sorley: it is fitting that it should be there.

Sorley's view of the war was shared by few of those fighting in the trenches. When Siegfried Sassoon and Vivian de Sola Pinto, his platoon commander, first read Sorley's poems in 1916 they could scarcely believe that anybody who had died in action in October 1915 could have taken such an attitude to the war. Young poets continued to write under the influence of Rupert Brooke as late as mid-1916. One such was W. N. Hodgson (1893–1916), an athlete and an exhibitioner[1] of Christ Church, Oxford, who enlisted at the outbreak of the war and won the Military Cross in 1915. His poems, couched as they are in the deplorable idiom of late-nineteenth-century romanticism, display barely a vestige of talent. However, one poem, "Before Action," can still move the reader with its poignant intensity, partly because one knows that it was written by a brave man on 29 June 1916, two days before he died on the first day of the Battle of the Somme. The poet moves from a Ruskinian adoration of natural beauty in the opening stanza to a recognition that he has watched

> . . . with uncomprehending eyes
> A hundred of Thy sunsets spill
> Their fresh and sanguine sacrifice.
>
> (18–20)

Finally the poet faces the knowledge that he

> Ere the sun swings his noonday sword
> Must say goodbye to all of this;—
> By all delights that I shall miss,
> Help me to die, O Lord.
>
> (21–24)

[1] A student who attends school by benefit of a scholarship.

The Battle of the Somme ushered in a new and even darker phase of the war. Hitherto it had been just possible to keep up the pretense that there were elements of chivalry in the conflict. At Christmas 1914 in certain parts of the line British and German troops had fraternized, exchanging gifts, singing carols, playing football. The authorities had sternly forbidden the repetition of such gestures and court-martialed Sir Iain Colquhoun and another captain of the Scots Guards for permitting their men to fraternize with the Germans on Christmas Day 1915. A new era of mass slaughter was about to begin. Before the attack on 1 July 1916, Field Marshal Douglas Haig had bombarded the German trenches for a week. Unfortunately, the German dugouts were so deep and well constructed that their machine gunners were able to scramble into position unharmed and mow down the British soldiers as they mounted their assault. The British army lost 60,000 killed and wounded on 1 July, the heaviest casualties it had ever sustained on any one day in its annals. The pattern established on the Somme repeated itself from then on: artillery bombardment, waves of infantrymen assaulting positions defended by heavy concentrations of machine guns, and an advance of a few hundred yards. At Passschendaele the following summer, a new element of horror pervaded the fighting: the sea of mud where rain fell on ground churned up by the British artillery. Not until March 1918 was the stalemate broken, when a German offensive appeared to have won the war. Yet the impetus petered out; on 8 August an Allied counteroffensive broke through the German positions and on 11 November the war was over.

One needs to bear this background in mind when considering the work of Sassoon, Owen, and Rosenberg, all of whose best poems were written after the summer of 1916. The public at home still preferred the romantic falsities of Robert Nichols to the savage truths of Siegfried Sassoon. Nichols' *Ardours and Endurances*, published in May 1917, sold more copies than Sassoon's *The Old Huntsman*, which appeared at the same time. But no serious poet could write about the war with the devotional highmindedness that one finds in W. N. Hodgson. He was the last of the morning heroes.

Even before the Somme one or two poets were beginning to make some adequate response to the ghastly realities of the war. Sassoon was writing the first of his trench poems that aimed at presenting an objective picture of life at the front. There was also Arthur Graeme West (1891–1917), who suffered a total revulsion from the war in August 1916, returned to France, and was killed by a bullet in April 1917. His *Diary of a Dead Officer* (1919) records his growing disillusionment. It is mainly prose, with a few poems added, of which the finest is "Night Patrol," dated March 1916. West anticipates Sassoon in his determination to record the true visage of war:

>   . . . and everywhere the dead.
> Only the dead were always present—present
> As a vile sickly smell of rottenness.
> The rustling stubble and the early grass,
> The slimy pools—the dead men stank through all,
> Pungent and sharp. . . .
>   (19–24)

His polemic in "God! How I Hate You, You Young Cheerful Men," against those who wrote lyrical poetry in the manner of Rupert Brooke, forms part of his desire to clarify in his own mind the nature of the struggle in which he was enmeshed. In that same poem he makes a more subdued but perhaps more heartfelt protest against the popular concept of God, foreshadowing Wilfred Owen in his speculations about the love of God and the suffering on the battlefield:

>   Ah how good God is
> To suffer us be born just now, when youth
> That else would rust, can slake his blade in gore
> Where very God Himself does seem to walk
> The bloody fields of Flanders He so loves.
>   (34–38)

Even from these brief quotations one observes how far West had traveled from the landscape of the mind portrayed by Grenfell, Brooke, and Shaw-Stewart; how near he was to the no-man's land delineated by Sassoon, Owen, and Rosenberg. Before considering that somber region, one must turn to the achievement of three men who, belonging to no school, made highly distinctive contributions to the poetry of war.

EDWARD THOMAS, IVOR GURNEY, EDMUND BLUNDEN

In one sense Edward Thomas (1878–1917) can scarcely be called a war poet: he wrote no poems about fighting or about life in the trenches; almost all his poems that refer to the war do so glancingly; and he probably wrote no poems after he had landed in France. Yet in one way Thomas was essentially a war poet: he owed his existence as a poet to the war. He had married very young, and his struggle to support his wife and three children condemned him to a round of ceaseless publishing on a wide variety of subjects—the countryside, queens of England, English men of letters. Although some of his literary criticism, notably *Algernon Charles Swinburne* (1912) and *Walter Pater* (1913), contains perceptive insights and there are passages worth reading in most of his books, this merely proves his extraordinary stamina and his determination to do honest work for his meager pay. Being commissioned in the army meant that the worst of his financial worries were over and that he was free of the literary treadmill. Between 3 December 1914 and 24 December 1916, Edward Thomas wrote the body of verse by which he is primarily remembered.

It is not necessary to consider in any detail the debt owed by Thomas to Robert Frost. The strong-minded widows of the two poets turned into a matter of dispute something that Frost and Thomas would have discussed amicably. Frost certainly told Edward Thomas that he should write certain paragraphs of his prose in verse form and keep exactly the same cadence. This may account for the fact that although Thomas' poems are unmistakably poetry they never, even at their most formal, lose touch with the movement of prose.

Thomas' most overt declaration about the war occurs in "This Is No Case of Petty Right or Wrong," in which he disclaims all conventional patriotism. When Eleanor Farjeon asked him if he knew what he was fighting for, he picked up a pinch of the earth and said, "Literally, for this." So, in the poem, Thomas affirms his irrational love for his country:

> I am one in crying, God save England, lest
> We lose what never slaves and cattle blessed.
> The ages made her that made us from dust.
>
> (21–23)

A subtler, finer poem, "Tears," explores Thomas' feeling for his country and tells us even more about his own nature. Although not directly relevant to the war, it gives us more than a hint about his attitude toward the soldiers in the trenches and toward his native land. One April morning he stepped out of "the double-shadowed Tower" into a courtyard:

> They were changing guard,
> Soldiers in line, young English countrymen,
> Fair-haired and ruddy, in white tunics. Drums
> And fifes were playing "The British Grenadiers."
> The men, the music piercing that solitude
> And silence, told me truths I had not dreamed,
> And have forgotten since their beauty passed.
>
> (12–18)

There are poems by Thomas that seem to have no connection with the war until a phrase arrests one's attention, compelling one to read the poem in a new light. In "Rain," one of his most characteristic poems, one encounters a reference to those whose sympathy cannot relieve human suffering, but who lie awake,

> Helpless among the living and the dead,
> Like a cold water among the broken reeds,
> Myriads of broken reeds all still and stiff.
>
> (12–14)

The image of the last line is almost certainly suggested by the victims of slaughter on the battlefields of France and of Flanders.

The war is present even more explicitly in "The Owl." As in so many of his poems, Thomas writes here in the first person, describing how hungry, cold, and tired he was, until he had satisfied his needs at an inn. An owl's "most melancholy cry" leads him away from a preoccupation with his solitary pains into an imaginative sympathy with others:

> And salted was my food, and my repose,
> Salted and sobered, too, by the bird's voice
> Speaking for all who lay under the stars,
> Soldiers and poor, unable to rejoice.
>
> (st. 4)

The conjunction of soldiers and poor recalls Isaac Rosenberg's observation that privates in the army are akin to slaves. For Thomas, soldiers are not heroes or our gallant boys in the trenches, but rather men low on the social scale, on a level with the poor. They suffer passively, unable to rejoice.

The four-line poem "In Memoriam (Easter, 1915)" is both a beautiful elegy and a powerful comment on the war:

> The flowers left thick at nightfall in the wood
> This Eastertide call into mind the men,
> Now far from home, who, with their sweethearts, should
> Have gathered them and will do never again.

The emphasis falling on "should" makes us aware that it may be read in two ways: the simple observation that the soldiers would have gathered the flowers had they been home; and the implication that the war, by destroying the dead men, has broken the ritual of courtship, the gathering of flowers that the dead men ought to have performed. Once again Thomas is showing how a tiny incident in a peaceful countryside may help us to grasp the significance of war.

One observes the same kind of strategy in "As the Team's Head-Brass." A soldier who has not yet been out to the war is watching a man plowing a field. Lovers disappear into the wood, and the plowman stops from time to time to have a word with the soldier. Their conversation veers toward the war: the fallen elm on which the soldier is seated won't be taken away until the war is over; the soldier could spare an arm but would be reluctant to lose a leg; one of the plowman's mates died on his second day in France. The talk is inconsequential and casual, yet the poem gradually pieces together a picture of the way in which the war demands and deprives. The poem ends with what is almost certainly something more than a straightforward description of the landscape:

> The lovers came out of the wood again:
> The horses started and for the last time
> I watched the clods crumble and topple over
> After the ploughshare and the stumbling team.
> (34–37)

The menace hidden in the phrase "for the last time" may remind the reader that the soldier, like the men who will never again gather the flowers, will perhaps, as he fears, lose not just an arm or a leg in battle, but his head as well. There is even a hint that the lovers and the age-old relationship between man and the soil are under threat from the destructiveness of war.

Edward Thomas is the quietest, most introspective of all the war poets, but the keenness of his observation and the probing quality of his imagination enable him to penetrate beyond the outer semblance of things into the heart of sadness.

Ivor Gurney (1890–1937) was that rare creature, a poet who was also a composer, equally gifted in the two arts. The son of a Gloucester tailor, he grew up and was educated in the cathedral city that he never ceased to love. His intelligence and his musical gifts

augured well for his future, and nobody found it ominous that his fellow schoolboys gave him the nickname of "Batty Gurney."

In the autumn of 1911 Gurney won a scholarship to the Royal College of Music, where he showed his precocious skill in 1912 by his setting of five Elizabethan lyrics, a composition that he called "The Elizas." In 1912–1913 he began to write poetry, an activity that was not only of value in itself, but also an influence on his music; for Gurney was to set poems by most English poets of merit who flourished during the first two decades of the twentieth century. His joining the army did not put an end to his composition of music or of poetry: in 1916–1917 he achieved what may well be the unique feat of writing five songs while undergoing a spell of duty in the trenches. He sent home to a friend the poems that he had been writing, and in 1917 they appeared under the title *Severn and Somme,* names of the river that he had loved in childhood and the river associated with the terrible fighting that Gurney had known, and in which on 7 April 1917 he was wounded. In September 1917 he was gassed and sent home, then transferred to a mental hospital at Warrington and later to a similar hospital at St. Albans. His military career was over, formally terminating with his discharge in October 1918. There seems to be something mysterious about Gurney's last thirteen months in the army, since little is known about the circumstances of his gassing or of his confinement to the two mental hospitals. By 1919 he had apparently recovered.

From 1919 to 1921 he cut something of a figure at the Royal College of Music and in the literary world of London, a second book of poems, *War's Embers,* having appeared in 1919. Even so, he depended for his survival on a weekly allowance from a fund raised by his teacher Vaughan Williams and by friends. Back in Gloucester, he talked brilliantly and tumultuously, received financial help from Edward Marsh, and grew ever wilder. He was incarcerated in September 1922 at Barnwood House, Gloucester, and in December at the City of London Mental Hospital, Dartford, Kent. There he remained until his death on 26 December 1937, St. Stephen's Day, at a time of year that meant much to him.

Although Gurney's friends never deserted him, the story of his life at Dartford is heartrending. Apart from his bitter resentment at what he believed to be his betrayal by his country, Gurney was tormented by delusions that he was suffering from tortures inflicted from a distance by electricity. He claimed to have composed the works of Shakespeare, Beethoven, and Haydn. It is likely that he enjoyed (if that be the word) periods of lucidity. When in 1937 a friend told him that Oxford University Press was about to publish a collection of his songs, he merely said, "It is too late."

The poems written before he finally went mad are mostly acceptable exercises in the pastoral mode and reflections on various aspects of beauty. Two war poems stand out from the rest of those early poems. "To His Love," written when Gurney received a false report that his friend F. W. Harvey had died in battle, deploys in the first three stanzas the conventional properties of pastoral elegy—grazing sheep, the small boat on the Severn, the violets from the riverside. The final stanza opens decorously, but suddenly administers a shock:

> Cover him, cover him soon!
> And with thick-set
> Masses of memorial flowers
> Hide that red wet
> Thing I must somehow forget.
>
> (st. 4)

Calling a dead man a "red wet / Thing" strikes one with a raw violence, and it is almost as brutal to suggest that one should cover the corpse with masses of flowers partly in tribute and partly to blot it from sight.

Even finer is Gurney's "Ballad of the Three Spectres," a poem that somehow captures the spirit of the Border Ballads without lapsing into archaism or pastiche. The first two stanzas may yield some idea of the poem's merit:

> As I went up by Ovillers
> In mud and water cold to the knee,
> There went three jeering, fleering spectres,
> That walked abreast and talked of me.
>
> The first said, "Here's a right brave soldier
> That walks the dark unfearingly;
> Soon he'll come back on a fine stretcher,
> And laughing for a nice Blighty.

The curt off-rhymes in both stanzas enhance the atmosphere of menace and strangeness, just as it is sinister that one of the apparitions should speak the slang of the trenches, prophesying that the soldier will get a "nice Blighty"—a wound bad enough to ensure his return to England.

Yet the best of the poems that he wrote during his madness surpass even the most accomplished examples of his early work. One has to face the question of his insanity before turning to consider the poems composed in the asylums, and the evidence is probably inadequate for anybody to reach a verdict. The latest opinion is that he, like his mother, suffered from paranoid schizophrenia. Should this be so, one cannot lay the blame on the war for driving him mad, though the war almost certainly intensified his madness and determined the pattern that it took. Although the power to compose music left him after 1926, he was able to produce a mass of poetry throughout his confinement at Barnwood and at Dartford from 1922 to 1937.

Some of his poems are painful to read. Two long letters in verse to the metropolitan police ramble on about his war service and the pain that he is wrongfully enduring. All the sentences taken separately are logical, but something has gone wrong with the links between them, and gradually one realizes that the writer has lost his reason. A poem written at Barnwood House in December 1922 is far more controlled, despite the anguish that racks the poet as he draws up his indictment. The opening lines of "To God" are both tragic and comic in a pathetic way. Gurney's first example of God's cruelty toward him is that there are prayers with meals:

> Why have You made life so intolerable
> And set me between four walls, where I am able
> Not to escape meals without prayer, for that is possible
> Only by annoying an attendant.

What is so unnerving in the poem is the mixture of factual observation about forced meals, mere delusion about torture by electricity, and the prayer for death:

> Forced meals there have been and electricity
> And weakening of sanity by influence
> That's dreadful to endure. And there are others
> And I am praying for death, death, death.
>
> (9–12)

Gurney's bitter sense of having been betrayed by his country is certainly linked with his insanity, although nobody has explained precisely how. He seems to have felt outraged in that his sufferings during the war had not brought him merited fame. He may also have experienced anger and pity at the recollection of the suffering endured by others who fought. The prime emotion of "There Is Nothing" is certainly pain at his own betrayal. The poem, dated February 1925, bears the note "in torture":

Soldier's praise I had earned having suffered soldier's pain,
And the great honour of song in the battle's first gray show—
Honour was bound to me save—mine most dreadfully slain.

(12–14)

During the years at Dartford, Gurney continually reverts to his memories of the war. Some of the poems he wrote on that theme are so lucid that it is hard to believe he was other than sane when he was composing them. They display an unwavering control of mood and of tone as he remembers the killing of comrades or calls to mind with stoical irony those who for a while, until death took them, contrived to beat the system. These poems have no parallel in the work of any other war poet: the voice is Gurney's alone, speaking clearly and with authority from the depths of a mental hospital.

Two poems in particular yield a taste of Gurney's quality. "The Silent One" begins curtly in the middle of the story:

Who died on the wires, and hung there, one of two—
Who for his hours of life had chattered through
Infinite lovely chatter of Bucks accent:
Yet faced unbroken wires; stepped over, and went
A noble fool, faithful to his stripes—and ended.

It is all there in five lines: the tale of an honest countryman, a loyal NCO, obedient to his orders, who ended up hanging on the barbed wire. Then an officer, with "a finicking accent," unlike the Bucks accent of the dead man, politely asks the narrator of the poem if he'd mind crawling through a hole in the wire. The courteous exchange between the officer and the narrator derives its savor from the fact that it is taking place in the middle of the battlefield, where one might expect orders to be rapped out. There is a measure of anger smoldering away in the poem, whose irony points at the upper-class voice of the officer, at God, and at the narrator himself. The apparent casualness hides a cool artistry. The narrator lay down under unbroken wires,

Till the politest voice—a finicking accent, said:
"Do you think you might crawl through there:
      there's a hole"
Darkness, shot at: I smiled, as politely replied—
"I'm afraid not, Sir." There was no hole no way to
      be seen,
Nothing but chance of death, after tearing of
      clothes

Kept flat, and watched the darkness, hearing bullets
      whizzing—
And thought of music—and swore deep heart's
      deep oaths
(Polite to God). . . .

(9–16)

Equally fine is "The Bohemians," a portrait of Gurney and his friends, who found army regulations irksome, who wanted to be left alone:

Certain people would not clean their buttons,
Nor polish buckles after latest fashions,
Preferred their hair long, puttees comfortable.

(1–3)

He describes how they never adapted themselves to military ways,

Surprised as ever to find the army capable
Of sounding "Lights Out" to break a game of Bridge,
As to fear candles would set a barn alight.

(14–16)

Only in the last line of the poem does Gurney move almost imperceptibly from gentle irony into the starkness of an epitaph:

In Artois or Picardy they lie—free of useless fashions.

It is impossible to say just how good a poet Gurney was, because most of his work remains unpublished. Michael Hurd, who has labored so long and so effectively on the texts of Gurney's poems, reckons that 600 out of his 900 poems have not been published. About 300 are viable, many of them of the highest quality. It is sad to think that such richness lies neglected in the Gurney archive of the Gloucester public library. The cruel mischance that confined him to mental hospitals for the last fifteen years of his life still has the power to obscure his fame.

Edmund Blunden (1896–1974) remains an undervalued poet, partly because even his war poems are often held to be academic and pastoral, especially by those who have not read them. Joining the army early in 1915, he had already published two small collections and was to bring out a third in 1916, *Pastorals*, which was, like the two earlier volumes, devoted to the countryside in time of peace. Yet he was rapidly changing, as he tells us in *War Poets: 1914–1918*:

In May and June 1916, in my notebooks, the grimness of war began to compete as a subject with the pastorals of

peace. By the end of the year, when madness seemed totally to rule the hour, I was almost a poet of the shell-holes, of
ruin and of mortification.

(p. 24)

Blunden was awarded the Military Cross and saw
as much hard fighting as any other war poet. In Raymond Asquith's letters home, printed in John
Jolliffe's *Raymond Asquith: Life and Letters*, one
learns that, despite the killing, the pain, the fear, the
acute discomfort, and the boredom, there were
moments of exaltation and pleasure during the war:
the singing of nightingales or the enjoyment of splendid food and drink. Such moments seldom find their
way into the poems of the most powerful war poets,
such as Sassoon, Owen, or Rosenberg. It is a mark of
Blunden's rare honesty and range of sympathies that
he can reveal the less dark sides of war:

> O how comely it was and how reviving,
> When with clay and with death no longer striving
>> Down firm roads we came to houses
>> With women chattering and green grass thriving.
>>> . . .
>> Gazed on the mill-sails, heard the church-bell,
>> Found an honest glass all manner of riches.
>>> ("At Senlis Once," 1–4; 11–12)

It is typical of Blunden that the first, Miltonic line
should lead us not into deep metaphysical speculation but into a remembrance of lesser mercies.

Blunden knows that, in war, innocent relaxation
may for an hour or so charm away the ferocity of
killing. Both are aspects of war. In "Concert Party:
Busseboom," the audience, delighted by the entertainment, reluctantly leaves the world of illusion:

> We heard another matinée,
>> We heard the maniac blast
>
> Of barrage south by Saint Eloi,
>> And the red lights flaming there
> Called madness: Come, my bonny boy,
>> And dance to the latest air.
>
> To this new concert, white we stood;
>> Cold certainty held our breath;
> While men in the tunnels below Larch Wood
>> Were kicking men to death.
>>> (15–24)

Blunden grew up in a Kent village where, as in
Leonard Woolf's Sussex, life still went on much as in
the days of the Domesday Book. Even at school he

was a scholar and a poet, deeply versed in the
pastoral tradition of English poetry. But his own
poetry is pastoral not only because of his literary
learning but because he was genuinely a countryman. The weakness of his verse over the years is that
he tends to retreat into archaism and whimsy, but his
love for the fields and woods that he discovered in
France lends an element of strength and perceptive-
ness to his war poetry. He loathes the war because it
violates the pieties of nature no less than the sanctity
of man. As early as May 1916 he linked the two in
"Festubert: The Old German Line":

> Sparse mists of moonlight hurt our eyes
> With gouged and scourged uncertainties
> Of soul and soil in agonies.
>> (1–3)

One of his most moving poems, "Report on Experience," published in the collection *Near and Far*
(1929), takes up the earlier theme. The good man and
the enchanting Seraphina, "like one from Eden," are
victims of the war, which has also devastated a landscape:

> I have seen a green country, useful to the race,
> Knocked silly with guns and mines, its villages vanished,
> Even the last rat and the last kestrel banished—
>> God bless us all, this was peculiar grace.
>>> (st. 2)

The poem ends with an affirmation, not of faith as a
Christian would understand it, but of a belief that we
live in an ambiguous universe presided over by a distant God:

> Say what you will, our God sees how they run.
> These disillusions are His curious proving
> That He loves humanity and will go on loving;
>> Over there are faith, life, virtue in the sun.
>>> (st. 4)

The war continued to haunt Blunden's imagination. He collected many of his best war poems as a
supplement to the prose narrative of *Undertones of
War* (1928). One of the finest is a singularly beautiful
elegy, "Their Very Memory," that reveals Blunden
as a master of rhythmical subtlety. The imagery of
the poem evokes running water, green valleys, a
spring, a fountain, a greenwood, music. Although
Blunden's memory of his comrades is fading, it has
not wholly vanished:

1458

When they smiled,
Earth's inferno changed and melted
Greenwood mild;
Every village where they halted
Shone with them through square and alley.

(st. 3)

Even when Blunden is not ostensibly writing about the war, it presides over his meditations. His justly admired poem "The Midnight Skaters," from *English Poems* (1925), evokes death at watch within the pond's black bed:

What wants he but to catch
Earth's heedless sons and daughters?
With but a crystal parapet
Between, he has his engines set.

(9–12)

The word "parapet" intrudes into a tranquil, Wordsworthian scene like an icy wind blowing from no-man's-land.

Even after World War II, the memory of World War I steals into poems far distant in time and place. When Blunden was working in Hong Kong, the Communists allowed him to visit the Great Wall of China, because he was a poet and because they rightly believed that he would make no political use of his visit. His sonnet "At the Great Wall of China" is, sadly, one of the few poems of his later years fit to rank with the best of his work. The parapet reappears in the sonnet's octet, more appropriately perhaps than in "The Midnight Skaters." We look from a tower and imagine

Where these few miles to thousands grow, and yet
Ever the one command and genius haunt
Each stairway, sally-port, loop, parapet,
In mute last answer to the invader's vaunt.

(5–8)

It is in the sextet that the memories of Blunden's war loom unmistakably clear:

But I half know at this bleak turret here,
In snow-dimmed moonlight where sure answers quail,
This new-set sentry of a long dead year.

(9–11)

For there are two ghosts at the bleak turret: that of a young Chinese soldier and that of a British sentry on the Ancre or the Somme. They merge insensibly in the mind of an English poet.

Blunden's war poetry is tougher than commonly supposed. Even though he wrote pastoral verse and, at the end of *Undertones of War* (p. 314), called himself "a harmless young shepherd in a soldier's coat," he was adopting a strategy that enabled him to confront the war and record what he observed. In old age he went to live in Suffolk at the village of Long Melford with his wife and daughters, wrote a guide to the magnificent church, and composed an obituary for his old friend Siegfried Sassoon, who was, like Blunden, a survivor of the trenches, a holder of the Military Cross, and an honored poet.

It is time now to consider the work of two men whose view of the war is darker and more tragic than that of the poets so far discussed. (There will not be an account of Wilfred Owen, since he is the subject of a separate essay in this volume.)

SIEGFRIED SASSOON

SIEGFRIED SASSOON (1886–1967), who was born into a rich Jewish family, left Cambridge without taking a degree and in the years before 1914 devoted himself to hunting, cricket, golf, ballet, opera, and evenings at his London club. He also began to develop a taste for literature, bringing out his privately printed collection *Poems* in 1906 and *The Daffodil Murderer* in 1913. This poem, which appeared under the pseudonym Saul Kain, was a parody of John Masefield but also a serious attempt to portray the feelings of the poor and the degraded.

Sassoon, who had joined the army on the first day of the war, rapidly acquired a reputation for courage that bordered on the insane. He stood several inches over six feet, and was lean, athletic, and reckless: it is not surprising that this formidable killer acquired the nickname "Mad Jack." His poem "The Kiss," whatever he may have thought of it later, is written in praise of "Brother Lead and Sister Steel." In the Somme offensive of July 1916 he fought with such gallantry that he was awarded the Military Cross. But his attitude toward the war had already begun to change.

It is not easy to chart the logical progress of that change, if only because Sassoon lived by generous passion rather than by calm reason. He may have reacted strongly against lectures on "the spirit of the bayonet," given at the Fourth Army School at Flixé-court in the spring of 1916, lectures that aroused the disgust of poets as various as Edmund Blunden, Robert Graves, and David Jones.[2] He had begun writing early in 1916 what he himself called genuine trench poems that were the first things of their kind. Further stages in his pilgrimage include meetings at Garsington Manor, Oxfordshire, the home of Philip Morrell, MP, and Lady Ottoline Morrell, with a number of prominent pacifists, including Bertrand Russell; and a spell in a hospital after being invalided home with a bullet wound in his lung, sustained at the battle of Arras in April 1917, the engagement in which Edward Thomas was killed.

By February 1917 Sassoon was already losing his belief in the war, and in July he made a protest against its needless prolongation. This "act of wilful defiance of military authority," as Sassoon described it, rendered him liable to court-martial and imprisonment. Thanks largely to the intervention of Robert Graves, an alternative procedure was followed, and Sassoon, who had meanwhile thrown his Military Cross into the Mersey, agreed to appear before a medical board. Graves testified that Sassoon suffered from hallucinations typical of shell shock, and himself burst into tears three times while making his statement. The board dispatched Sassoon to Craiglockhart War Hospital, appointing as his escort Robert Graves, who missed the train that was carrying Sassoon to his destination.

At Craiglockhart the doctors cured Sassoon of whatever illness had prompted him to issue his act of defiance, and he asked for a posting abroad. He arrived in Egypt at the end of February 1918, then moved to France in May. His fighting days came to an end on 13 July 1918, when, on a daylight patrol, he was accidentally shot through the head by a British sentry and sent home to pass the rest of the war in a hospital.

Two volumes of poetry, *The Old Huntsman* (1917) and *Counter-Attack* (1918), contain almost all the enduring poems that Sassoon wrote about the war. The judgment that he is primarily a satirist is questionable, but his satirical poems retain to this day their incisiveness and power. In "They," Sassoon launches an attack not only on a complacent, stupid bishop but on the apparent subservience of the Anglican church to the state, and on the windy rhetoric that was one of the main civilian contributions to the war:

---

[2]Robert Graves is the subject of a separate essay in this series. Therefore, there is no discussion of his poetry here. His war poems form only a minor part of his work.

The Bishop tells us: "When the boys come back
They will not be the same; for they'll have fought
In a just cause; they lead the last attack
On Anti-Christ."

(st. 1)

The next stanza contrasts the stale abstractions by which the bishop lives with the raw truths that are the products of war:

"We're none of us the same!" the boys reply.
"For George lost both his legs; and Bill's stone blind;
"Poor Jim's shot through the lungs and like to die;
"And Bert's gone syphilitic; you'll not find
"A chap who's served that hasn't found *some* change."
And the Bishop said: "The ways of God are strange."

(st. 2)

In view of his official and social position, Edward Marsh showed courage when he published the poem: the mention of syphilis was an offense against decorum and an affront to patriotic feeling.

There are moments when Sassoon's rage may seem to be in excess of its object. In January 1917, just before returning to France, Sassoon went to a revue at the Hippodrome in Liverpool and wrote a poem designed to be his farewell to England:

. . . prancing ranks
Of harlots shrill the chorus, drunk with din;
"We're sure the Kaiser loves our dear old Tanks!"

I'd like to see a Tank come down the stalls,
Lurching to rag-time tunes, or "Home, sweet Home."
And there'd be no more jokes in Music-halls
To mock the riddled corpses round Bapaume.

("Blighters," 2–8)

It is a little hard on the inoffensive chorus girls to stigmatize them as harlots, and the audience hardly deserves to be massacred. But Sassoon believed that the ignorance of civilians about what was happening on the battlefield was criminal. Songs in music halls about tanks were blasphemous insults to the troops and to their dead comrades. Viewed in this light, "Blighters" is a valid testament of justified indignation. Its final line, particularly when spoken aloud, delivers a searing curse on those who thoughtlessly mock the agony of their fellow men.

Some of Sassoon's other satirical poems have become anthology pieces, such as "Base Details," "Glory of Women," "Does It Matter?" "The General," and "Fight to a Finish," a savage attack on civilians, especially journalists and members of Parliament.

Most of his poems have scarcely any satirical element, but take as their theme trench warfare, presented with an almost brutal realism, although the underlying tenderness aroused by the spectacle of the wounded and the dead redeems what would otherwise be almost intolerable. In "Attack," Sassoon, while playing down the worst of the horror, describes what it was like to go over the top:

> Lines of grey, muttering faces, masked with fear,
> They leave their trenches, going over the top,
> While time ticks blank and busy on their wrists,
> And hope, with furtive eyes and grappling fists,
> Flounders in mud. O Jesus, make it stop!
>
> (9–13)

Some reviewers of *Counter-Attack* condemned Sassoon for his insistence on the ugly aspects of war. In the title poem he portrays as faithfully as a Dutch seventeenth-century painter the contents of a captured trench:

> The place was rotten with dead; green clumsy legs
> High-booted, sprawled and grovelled along the saps
> And trunks, face downward, in the sucking mud,
> Wallowed like trodden sandbags, loosely filled;
> And naked sodden buttocks, mats of hair,
> Bulged, clotted heads slept in the plastering slime.
> And then the rain began,—the jolly old rain.
>
> (st. 1)

This is no mere catalog of horrifying items: the dense particularity of the description achieves a sensuous richness. The green legs are ghastly because the adjective suggests both the fertility of spring and the gangrenous texture of the rotting corpses. In a similar way the word "slept" has associations of repose that are mocked by the way in which the clotted heads sink into the slime. The stanza's last line, with its casual irony, provides a moment's relief from one's scrutiny of the dismembered bodies.

Although Sassoon wrote nothing else so richly complex as "Counter-Attack," he produced a number of memorable poems about various aspects of trench warfare. One of the most effective is "The Rear-Guard," set in a tunnel under the Hindenburg Line in April 1917 and based on an experience of his own. The narrator, who has not slept for days, is furious when a sleeping figure over whom he stumbles fails to wake up and answer his questions:

> Savage, he kicked a soft, unanswering heap,
> And flashed his beam across the livid face
> Terribly glaring up, whose eyes yet wore

> Agony dying hard ten days before;
> And fists of fingers clutched a blackening wound.
>
> (st. 3)

Two of Sassoon's poems are unusual in that they are explicitly elegiac. "To Any Dead Officer" mingles anger, mockery, and compassion, passing from a lament for one particular officer to a fine passage in which Sassoon mourns all who were reported "wounded and missing":

> Next week the bloody Roll of Honour said
>   "Wounded and missing"—(That's the thing to do
> When lads are left in shell-holes dying slow,
>   With nothing but blank sky and wounds that ache,
> Moaning for water till they know
>   It's night, and then it's not worth while to wake!)
>
> (st. 4)

"To One Who Was with Me in the War," written in 1926, is not so much a formal elegy as a "game of ghosts," in which the poet imagines going back with a fellow officer after the war to "some redoubt of Time," where they may relive their experience of the trenches. It is a less urgent, mellower poem than those Sassoon wrote during the war, yet it conveys something of his complex emotions toward that war:

>   Round the next bay you'll meet
> A drenched platoon-commander; chilled, he drums
>   his feet
> On squelching duck-boards; winds his wrist-watch;
>   turns his head,
> And shows you how you looked,—your ten-years-
>   vanished face,
> Hoping the War will end next week . . .
>   What's that you said?
>
> (32–37)

After the war was over Sassoon returned to his old life, combining his sporting interests with literary activity. He became widely known for a series of prose autobiographies that cover his life from the closing years of the nineteenth century to the end of the war. He continued to write poetry during the rest of a long life, happy to employ the diction and the meters of his youth, unswayed by the innovatory techniques of Pound, Eliot, and the imagists. His poems include gentle satires on, for example, the first performance of Stravinsky's *Rite of Spring* and the destruction of Devonshire House; reminiscences of the war; and explorations of religious and mystical themes. But it is by virtue of thirty or forty poems that delineate the agony of the fighting in the trenches that he holds an honored place among English poets.

ISAAC ROSENBERG

ISAAC ROSENBERG (1890–1918) is one of the few Englishmen to have achieved distinction as a poet and a painter. He was born in the East End of London and was the son of Lithuanian Jews who had emigrated to Britain in the 1880's. After leaving school in 1904 he was apprenticed to a firm of art publishers, but chafed at the narrowness of his life. Thanks to the generosity of some Jewish ladies, he was able in October 1911 to enroll at the Slade School, where he met gifted fellow students such as David Bomberg, Mark Gertler, Dora Carrington, Edward Wadsworth, Paul Nash, and Stanley Spencer. He published at his own expense in 1912 a booklet of poems, *Night and Day*, in which he was already expressing his perplexities about the significance of suffering and the nature of God.

On 10 November 1913 Gertler introduced Rosenberg to Edward Marsh at the Café Royal. For the rest of Rosenberg's life Marsh gave him all manner of help, buying his paintings, paying for the publication of his second book of poems, *Youth* (1915), and doing what he could to relieve Rosenberg's difficulties after he had joined the army.

The relationship between a man and his patron is always subject to strains of various kinds, and it must be admitted that Rosenberg and Marsh were seldom in perfect accord. Marsh was a cultivated member of the English upper classes, private secretary to Winston Churchill, a man of conservative tastes, editor of the Georgian anthologies, a passionate admirer of Rupert Brooke. It is easy to draw up an indictment of Marsh, pointing at his failure to recognize the genius of Rosenberg; at his exclusion of him from his anthologies, except for a speech from *Moses*; at his inability to admire "Dead Man's Dump." It is even held against Marsh that, years after the end of the war, he could still talk of "poor little Rosenberg."

Yet Marsh proved a true friend to Rosenberg. It was Marsh who ensured that Rosenberg's mother received from the army the allowance due her, just as it was Marsh who did all in his power to have Rosenberg moved to safer and less exacting military duties. Despite his failure to respond to "Dead Man's Dump," he took the trouble, before returning the manuscript to Rosenberg, to copy out the poem for fear that it might be lost. Nor did Marsh call him "poor little Rosenberg" in a spirit of upper-class condescension. Mark Gertler, a poor, working-class, East End, Jewish painter, described Rosenberg affec-

tionately as a "funny little man." It is possible to be a poet of the first order and also a poor, funny little man.

In June 1914 Rosenberg visited Cape Town, where he stayed with his married sister, Minnie. He wrote there "On Receiving News of the War," a poem that anticipates the end of the old order, a poem of foreboding deeper than any experienced by his compatriots at home. For over a year before the outbreak of war he had been concerned with the need to reject the orthodox male God, and at about the same time he was working on a poem on the outbreak of the war, he was composing a strange poem entitled "The Female God," an exploration of the sexual and the sacred.

Rosenberg went back to England in February 1915, although he could have stayed on in Cape Town indefinitely, especially as he was much in demand as a portrait painter. Apparently he felt that he had reached an emotional and spiritual dead end. But in London things were little better, and in the autumn of 1915 he enlisted in the army, partly to obtain an allowance for his mother and partly, it has been surmised, to fulfill a long-suppressed death wish. He wrote to Marsh that he had not joined the army for patriotic reasons.

Rosenberg's life in the army was unutterably wretched. He wrote to Lascelles Abercrombie on 11 March 1916: "the army is the most detestable invention on this earth and nobody but a private in the army knows what it is to be a slave" (*Collected Works*, p. 230). On 26 January 1918, in a passage canceled by the censor, he wrote to Edward Marsh: "what is happening to me now is more tragic than the 'passion play.' Christ never endured what I endure. It is breaking me completely."[3] Everything conspired to make Rosenberg's army life a long nightmare. He detested the coarseness of his fellow soldiers' behavior and the crudity of their minds. His lot was worsened by the anti-Jewish prejudice that he encountered among officers and private soldiers alike. Because the boots issued by the army did not fit him, he suffered the agony of sore heels, not nearly as trivial a matter as civilians at home might reckon. His awkwardness, stubbornness, and forgetfulness must have made matters worse: he was punished for leaving behind his gas helmet, and the injustice of army discipline rankled with him. The continual labor that was his lot imposed severe strains on his

---

[3]From an unpublished letter quoted in J. Cohen, *Journey to the Trenches* (London, 1975), p. 3.

physique. Dragging heavy coils of barbed wire into no-man's-land and setting them up, or digging latrines in the hard earth or in the excremental mud, weighed upon his body and his spirit. He refers several times to the difficulty of writing and of perfecting his poems in such conditions. The lives of officers were at least as dangerous as those of their men, but they enjoyed some compensations. They had the services of a batman, who would keep their uniform clean; their food and sleeping quarters were better; they were exempt from physical labor and from punishments such as pack drill for trivial breaches of discipline; they could afford to relax in decent hotels and restaurants on short leaves instead of in the bistros where private soldiers congregated; they might even make the acquaintance of cultivated Belgian or French civilians; and with luck they would find one or two congenial fellow officers in their regiment or company.

It is probably true that Rosenberg never met in the army a single person who cared for any of the arts or with whom he could have the kind of talk that meant so much to him. One of his officers, Frank Waley, asked Rosenberg for copies of some of his poems. Rosenberg was always short of paper, being obliged to write some poems on the backs of envelopes; nevertheless he gave Waley a few poems that baffled him so completely that he chucked them away. The only one Waley could remember was "Break of Day in the Trenches," and since he didn't think it was poetry he threw it out with the rest.

In 1916, at his own expense, Rosenberg published in a volume entitled *Roses* an unfinished play of that name, together with some shorter poems. It is convenient to group it with another play, *The Unicorn*, a work of only a few pages, completed in the summer of 1917, although in March 1918 he was planning to write a fuller treatment of the play, which he had always regarded as a sketch for a larger version.

Although only 470 lines long, *Moses* is an extremely complex work about whose significance there is still no general agreement. Rosenberg wrote to the poet R. C. Trevelyan in a letter postmarked 15 June 1916: "Moses symbolizes the fierce desire for virility, and original action in contrast to slavery of the most abject kind" (*Collected Works*, p. 235). Knowing Rosenberg's views about the slavery of private soldiers, one is entitled to say that *Moses* presents Rosenberg's situation in 1915–1916. It also marks the culminating stage in his rejection of the divinity whom he had scrutinized in a number of poems and stigmatized in "God" as "this miasma of a

rotting God." ("This miasma of a rotting god" also occurs as line 144 of *Moses*.) One may also read the play as Rosenberg's attempt to define the historical destiny of the Jews and of the proletariat. It expresses his preoccupation with violence as a force that may possibly regenerate a crumbling, sick society, a notion that he had played with even before the outbreak of war. The only overt act of violence occurs at the end of the play, when Moses strangles the brutal Egyptian overseer, Abinoah, father of his mistress, Koelue. She may also stand for the incarnate sexuality of the earth goddess whom Rosenberg had long envisaged as the supplanter of the orthodox male God.

The Unicorn is even shorter and stranger than *Moses*. It is about a decaying race who have never seen a woman, and whose chief, named Tel, is mounted on a unicorn. The two other main characters, Saul and his wife, Lilith, belong to another tribe, as does Enoch, the only other character. The climax of the play is best described in the final stage direction:

Through the casement they see riding under the rainbow a black naked host on various animals, the Unicorn leading. A woman is clasped on every one, some are frantic, others white or unconscious, some nestle laughing. ENOCH with madness in his eyes leaps through the casement and disappears with a splash in the well. SAUL leaps after him shouting "The Unicorn." TEL places the unconscious LILITH on the Unicorn and they all ride away.

(*Collected Works*, p. 173)

In a letter to Winifreda Seaton dated 8 March 1918 Rosenberg wrote of his ambitions for an expanded version of *The Unicorn*: "I mean to put all my innermost experiences into the 'Unicorn.' I want it to symbolize the war and all the devastating forces, let loose by an ambitious and unscrupulous will" (*Collected Works*, p. 270).

Some of the themes of *Moses* reappear in *The Unicorn*, notably those of sexuality and violence as the instruments of liberation and change. Before starting work on the fragments that became *The Unicorn* Rosenberg had contemplated writing a play about Judas Maccabeus, who reconquered Jerusalem from the Romans in 165 B.C. He may also have had in mind a quotation from the Book of Numbers: "God brought them out of Egypt; he hath as it were the strength of a unicorn."

It is the richness and complexity of the themes and the way in which they mirror Rosenberg's psychological turmoil that constitute the fascination of these plays, whether one ranks them among his greatest achievements or regards them as only partially successful despite their imaginative force and the magnificent passages of verse found in them.

Although Rosenberg was a mature artist by the outbreak of war and had written some hauntingly original poems by the spring of 1916, it is on a handful of poems written between midsummer 1916 and his death on 1 April 1918 that his reputation securely rests. He wrote to Edward Marsh on 4 August 1916, enclosing "A Worm Fed on the Heart of Corinth" and "Break of Day in the Trenches." The former prophesies, in ten astonishing lines, the destruction of England by a creature akin to the invisible worm of William Blake's "The Sick Rose." With this poem Rosenberg takes his place among the Hebrew prophets and the English poets. "Break of Day in the Trenches," actually written in the trenches, is a flawless, ironical meditation, that opens with an ominous strangeness:

> The darkness crumbles away.
> It is the same old druid Time as ever.

In his letter to Marsh, Rosenberg observes: "I am enclosing a poem I wrote in the trenches, which is surely as simple as ordinary talk. You might object to the second line as vague, but that was the best way I could express the sense of dawn" (*Collected Works*, p. 239). The sight of a rat that leaps over the poet's hand as he plucks a poppy to stick behind his ear moves him to meditate sardonically on the rat's cosmopolitan sympathies, which lead him to touch first an English, next a German, hand. He then imagines the rat's grin as he watches men in all their bodily pride reduced to short-lived creatures with terror in their eyes. At the very end of the poem the image of the poppy returns.

The poppy held great emotional potency for the soldiers in France and Flanders: indeed Englishmen still wear paper poppies in their buttonholes on Armistice Day. John McCrae, a Canadian, wrote the most popular poem of the war, "In Flanders Fields," which begins:

> In Flanders fields the poppies blow
> Between the crosses, row on row.

The first half of McRae's poem is reasonably competent versifying, although the second half represents a sad decline. But Rosenberg has made the symbol of the plucked poppy ironically resonant with our sense of life's brevity and of the mortality that is the lot of rat and poppy and men:

> Poppies whose roots are in man's veins
> Drop, and are ever dropping;
> But mine in my ear is safe—
> Just a little white with the dust.
> ("Break of Day in the
> Trenches," 23–26)

In May 1917, Rosenberg sent Marsh a seventy-nine-line poem, "Dead Man's Dump," based on his own experience of carrying wire up to the line on limbers and running over dead bodies. It contains Rosenberg's only realistic descriptions of the battlefield, yet his main concern is still his search for the meaning of human existence, his desire to discover the metaphysical significance of war. He is capable of writing lines that convey with horrifying exactness the sensation of driving a cart over dead bodies:

> The wheels lurched over sprawled dead
> But pained them not, though their bones crunched.
> (7–8)

The poem ends in a similar vein, but at the middle of it the sight of the dead moves Rosenberg to compose a passage unrivaled in any other poem of war except in Wilfred Owen's finest work:

> None saw their spirits' shadow shake the grass,
> Or stood aside for the half used life to pass
> Out of those doomed nostrils and the doomed mouth,
> When the swift iron burning bee
> Drained the wild honey of their youth.
> (27–31)

The imagery here of honey and iron occurs also in "August 1914," a beautiful short lyric written in the summer of 1916.

Two further poems of 1917 show Rosenberg's imagination at its strangest and most potent. "Daughters of War" evokes mysterious Amazons whose lovers are soldiers killed in battle and washed clean of mortal dust. He believed it to be his best poem, and during the year that he spent on it he had "striven to get that sense of inexorableness the human (or inhuman) side of this war has" (*Collected Works*, p. 260).

Again, in "Returning, We Hear the Larks," Rosenberg explores in this brief lyric themes to which he continually recurs: war, beauty, sexuality, the menacing power of women. The lark song that at first brings only joy carries a somber reminder:

> Death could drop from the dark
> As easily as song—
> But song only dropped,
> Like a blind man's dreams on the sand
> By dangerous tides,
> Like a girl's dark hair for she dreams no ruins lie there,
> Or her kisses where a serpent hides.
>
> (10–16)

Rosenberg continued to write poems of high quality until a few days before his death. In a letter to Marsh dated 28 March 1918 he enclosed his last poem, "Through These Pale Cold Days," the third of three meditations on Jewish history and Jewish destiny. On 30 and 31 March Rosenberg's regiment suffered heavy casualties while resisting the German advance, and in the early hours of the morning on 1 April his company was making its way back in order to gain a brief respite from the fighting. Rosenberg volunteered to return to the battle and within an hour was killed in close combat near the French village of Fampoux.

WHAT THE SOLDIERS SANG

THE British army sang on the march, in trenches, in billets, in bistros, and in concert halls. The songs that gave strength and comfort to the troops are often ignored by literary critics, who have failed to recognize in them the most considerable body of poetry in English composed and sung by the common man.

Not all the songs were anonymous products of the trenches. "Tipperary," arguably the most famous of marching songs, although the troops came to loathe it, was written in 1912 by a professional composer. "Keep the Home Fires Burning," which belongs to 1915–1916 and the march to the Somme, brought fame and money to the youthful Ivor Novello, who after 1918 wrote, acted in, and directed a long series of spectacular musical comedies at Drury Lane.

Yet the overwhelming majority of trench songs were by anonymous soldiers. Some of them may have been written by one man for performance at a concert, before being adopted, embroidered, or parodied by troops in different parts of the line. Others may have been the work of soldiers, put together during a rest period and then transmitted by word of mouth to men of other regiments. A few songs, some of which went back to the eighteenth and nineteenth centuries, were inherited from the pre-1914 regular army.

The words sung with such gusto were often parodies of well-known hymns, ballads, and musical comedy and music-hall songs: they were usually fitted to existing tunes, sacred and profane. The authors of these songs, whoever they may have been, portrayed themselves as cowardly, lecherous, skeptical of victory, disrespectful toward their military superiors, unappreciative of the charms or the morals of French women such as "Mademoiselle from Armenteers," longing only to get back to England. "I Don't Want to Die" begins:

> I want to go home,
> I want to go home,
> I don't want to go to the trenches no more,
> Where whizz-bangs and shrapnel they whistle and roar.

That inglorious declaration finds a parallel in "I Don't Want to Be a Soldier," a parody of "On Sunday I Walk Out with a Soldier," a song of the kind loathed by Sassoon, which was sung in a revue, *The Passing Show of 1914*, produced at the London Hippodrome:

> I don't want to be a soldier,
> I don't want to go to war.
> I'd rather stay at home,
> Around the streets to roam,
> And live on the earnings of a well-paid whore.

Not all the songs referred to the war. "Wash Me in the Water," widely sung throughout the war, seems to bear no relevance to the fighting, probably because it is said to have been sung by the regular army before 1914. It was set to a Salvation Army hymn tune:

> Wash me in the water
> That you washed your dirty daughter,
> And I shall be whiter
> Than the whitewash on the wall.

When no officers were present, "your dirty daughter" might become "the colonel's daughter."

But almost all the finest songs have deep roots in the daily lives of those who composed and sang them. "The Old Barbed Wire" provides a superb example of the way in which contemptuous humor, apparent callousness, and deadly accuracy combine to make an unforgettable song:

If you want to find the sergeant,
I know where he is, I know where he is.
If you want to find the sergeant,
I know where he is,
He's lying on the canteen floor.

The quarter-bloke (the quartermaster sergeant) is miles behind the line; the sergeant-major is boozing up with the private's rum; the CO is down in the deep dugouts. Then comes the final dramatic twist:

If you want to find the old battalion,
I know where they are, I know where they are.
If you want to find the old battalion,
I know where they are,
They're hanging on the old barbed wire.

In 1963 Joan Littlewood's musical extravaganza *Oh What a Lovely War* made brilliant use of these songs; yet it would be wrong to think of them merely as part of a theatrical entertainment. They commemorate, more fittingly than the headstones of the Imperial War Graves Commission, the lives and deaths of those gallant though unheroic common soldiers who, when the noise of the guns had died down, were found lying in the mud or hanging on the old barbed wire.

THE AFTERMATH:
HERBERT READ AND DAVID JONES

In the early 1920's and during the rest of the decade, English novelists tried to give order and coherence to their experience and memories of the war by writing prose fiction. No poet of any merit essayed this task by means of his art until the next decade. There then appeared two poems of some length, *The End of a War* (1933) by Herbert Read and *In Parenthesis* (1937) by David Jones. Neither can be described as a novel in verse or even as an orthodox narrative poem, yet both attempt to assimilate certain qualities of modern prose fiction and to build something less impressionistic and lyrical than the war poems that we have considered in this essay.

Herbert Read (1893–1968) fought with distinction in the war, earning the Distinguished Service Order and the Military Cross. His book of poems *Songs of Chaos* (1915) was followed by a second, *Naked Warriors* (1919). Although Read was to enjoy a long career as a literary critic and aesthetician, he had not in 1919 seen any of those works by Antonio Pollaiuolo or other Florentine painters conjured up by the book's title, whose progenitor is almost certainly Wordsworth's "Character of a Happy Warrior," a poem that is a happy source book of high-minded schoolmasters and of politicians eager to sanctify their wartime speeches with an edifying quotation from a great poet:

Who is the happy Warrior? Who is he
That every man in arms should wish to be?

Read gives his answer to Wordsworth's query of 1805:

Bloody saliva
Dribbles down his shapeless jacket.

I saw him stab
And stab again
A well-killed Boche.

This is the happy warrior,
This is he. . . .

(6–12)

"The Execution of Cornelius Vane" anatomizes the life and death of a soldier who shoots away his right index finger and works thereafter in a cookhouse. Required to fight in an emergency, he points to his mutilated hand that cannot fire a rifle, only to be told by a sergeant, "But you can stab." Vane deserts, is tried by court-martial, and is sentenced to death. His executioners, men of his own regiment looking very sad, blindfold him, and just before he is shot he says to the assembly:

"What wrong have I done that I should leave these:
The bright sun rising
And the birds that sing?"

(130–132)

"Kneeshaw Goes to War" analyzes a soldier whose passivity and failure to respond to the world of experience are perhaps more ignoble than Vane's cowardice. He loses a leg in battle and, after returning to England, accepts after long meditation the need to live by the truth and to discipline oneself. The poem anticipates, in its probing of a man's inner life, the intricate analysis of character found in Read's *The End of a War*.

Read's poetry is almost invariably marked by cool

intelligence and firm restraint. Very occasionally he permits his emotion to speak nakedly and movingly; such a moment occurs in "My Company":

> But, God! I know that I'll stand
> Someday in the loneliest wilderness,
>
> . . .
>
> I know that I'll wander with a cry:
> "O beautiful men, O men I loved,
> O whither are you gone, my company?"
> (26–27; 32–34)

It is this kind of passion, this kind of rhythmical vitality, that one finds wanting in Read's most ambitious poem, *The End of a War*.

The poem comprises three interwoven monologues: "Meditation of the Dying German Officer," "Dialogue Between Body and Soul," and "Meditation of the Waking English Officer." The prose Argument summarizes the main incident of the poem (it can hardly be called the main action, for it is an almost wholly static poem). Briefly, on 10 November 1918 a wounded German officer tells a British officer that a village nearby is undefended. German machine-gunners hidden in the church tower fire on the British battalion resting in the village square, killing or wounding a hundred men. The survivors bayonet the hidden machine-gunners and a corporal dispatches the German officer, who dies impassively. Later, the British find the dismembered body of a French girl who had been raped and tortured by the Germans. The English officer falls asleep, exhausted and nauseated. When he wakes in the morning the church bells are ringing in the armistice.

Despite the grandeur of his theme, Read fails to give his poem life, and the characters are only mouthpieces through whom the poet utters his leaden, monochrome soliloquies. The language remains so inert that even the armistice bells cannot stir it into activity. Extensive quotation would not substantiate that judgment, because the reader might suspect that the hostile critic had picked out the worst passages to prove his case. Here is a short extract, which shows Read in a comparatively sprightly mood, taken from the English officer's meditation:

> . . . First there are the dead to bury
> O God, the dead. How can God's bell
> ring out from that unholy ambush?
> That tower of death! In excess of horror
> war died.
> (26–30)

The reader must discover for himself whether that extract is representative of Read's poem.

The End of a War is a praiseworthy attempt to confront some philosophical questions that have preoccupied thoughtful men and women for centuries: the existence of God, the significance of war and violence in society, the limits of political obligation. Yet although the poem has won critical acclaim during the past half-century, it can rank only as an honorable failure. One suspects that *The End of a War* has been more often referred to than read, and more frequently read than enjoyed.

David Jones (1895–1974) was, like Isaac Rosenberg, both poet and painter. He was educated at Camberwell Art School from 1909 to 1914 and enlisted in the Royal Welsh Fusiliers, serving at the front as a private soldier from December 1915 to March 1918. He became a convert to Roman Catholicism in 1921 and lived by his painting until the mid-1930's, thereafter dividing his time between his work as painter, engraver, and typographer, and his work as a writer.

In Parenthesis, begun in 1928 and published in 1937, could be described as an epic in verse about World War I, although it is unlike traditional epic, contains long passages of prose, and celebrates wars much older than the conflict of 1914–1918. It is an extremely difficult, highly allusive poem, although Jones provides thirty-five pages of notes designed, unlike those of *The Waste Land*, to elucidate rather than to tantalize. Yet even the notes offer a formidable array of theological speculation, assorted myth, army jargon, and references to historical events.

Jones sets his poem between early December 1915 and early July 1916, telling us in the preface that after the Somme battle everything became more impersonal, mechanical, and relentless. He could not have written *In Parenthesis* about the mass slaughter that characterized the war after the midsummer of 1916.

The story concerns a battalion in an infantry camp in England preparing to embark for France. It lands in France and makes its way by stages to the trenches, these preliminary movements being completed on Christmas Day 1915. The opening three sections of the poem are followed by three sections that describe a typical day in the trenches and the southward marches toward the Somme. The final section concentrates on the part played in the disastrous Somme offensive in July 1916 by number 7 platoon, under the command of Lieutenant Jenkins. We follow in particular one of its members, Private Ball, who is indeed the sole survivor of the attack. The poem ends, after the nightmare of battle, with the garlanding of the dead by a figure from Jones's private mythology, the Queen of the Woods, who is in part the goddess Diana and in part the dryad of folklore.

The poem is difficult for a variety of reasons: Jones has at his fingertips and within his imagination a wealth of allusions drawn from heterogeneous and complex sources, of which the principal are Roman history, the Gospels, the so-called Matter of Britain (the Arthurian legends), the whole Romano-Celtic tradition, early English and medieval literature, and the rites of the Roman Catholic Church, especially the Mass. Jones attempts to fuse the raw material of the epic with the technique employed in a modernist poem such as *The Waste Land*, wherein the impressionistic use of imagery and evocative incantation of rhythm largely supersede the formal logic of argument and the orderly unfolding of narrative.

Yet behind these highly elaborate literary devices one senses the presence of the private soldiers with their routine blasphemies, their cockney speech, and their daily suffering. Nor must one forget Jones's constant sardonic humour. Even Private John Ball, hero of the epic tale (insofar as there is one), is so called not only because his namesake was the priest who led the Peasants' Revolt in 1381. As Jon Stallworthy observes in his *Survivors' Songs in Welsh Poetry* (1982), Ball's name has a further significance: coming after that of Private Leg in the sergeant's roster, and following the last two digits, 01, in his army number, it is both ballistic and anatomical.

When Private Ball lies wounded he finally abandons his rifle, even though he remembers the admonitions of the instructors in musketry:

> Marry it man! Marry it!
> Cherish her, she's your very own.
> Coax it man coax it—it's delicately and
>   ingeniously made
> —it's an instrument of precision—it costs us tax-payers
> money—I want you men to remember that.
>
>   (pp. 183–184)

That might well come from a work of naturalistic fiction, yet it coexists with the boast of Dai-Great-Coat, uttered after the men of number 1 section have shared a meager benefit of bread and rum. In his lengthy boast Dai, a character in Thomas Malory's *Morte Darthur*, who stands here for the private soldier throughout the ages, claims to have participated in all kinds of historical and mythical events involving the use of hand weapons from the war in Heaven onward:

>   I served Longinus that Dux bat-blind and bent;
> the dandy Xth are my regiment;
> who diced
> Crown and Mud-hook
> under the Tree, . . .
>
>   (p. 83)

This is a fairly simple example of Jones's elaborate allusiveness. The Xth Fretensis is reputed to have furnished the escort party at Jesus' crucifixion, and the dicing under the Cross is equated with the gambling game Crown and Mud-hook, or Crown and Anchor, that was popular among the troops in World War I. Jones's repeated collocation of exalted moments from the past with the brutal or trivial events of the war is not designed to glorify the war or, indeed, to diminish the splendor of history and legend. He wants us to apprehend the timelessness of human action. In a later poem, "The Fatigue," he imagines that the execution of Christ is carried out not by the Xth Fretensis but by a party of British soldiers of World War I.

The prose of *In Parenthesis* ranges from the demotic to the hieratic, the brutally simple to the densely allusive. The verse covers an equally wide gamut of form and of emotional resonance. The closing pages of the poem attain a climax of rare poetic intensity, when the Queen of the Woods comes to deck with garlands all who have died in the battle, officers and other ranks, the loved and the detested, German and British alike. Nothing in the poetry of the war excels this luminous requiem:

> For Balder she reaches high to fetch his.
> Ulrich smiles for his myrtle wand.
> That swine Lillywhite has daisies to his chain—you'd
> hardly credit it.
> She plaits torques of equal splendour for Mr. Jenkins and
> Billy Crower.
> Hansel with Gronwy share dog-violets for a palm, where
> they lie in serious embrace beneath the twisted tripod.
>
>   (p. 185)

Jones ends *In Parenthesis* with René Hague's translation of lines from the *Chanson de Roland*:

> The geste says this and the man who was on the field . . .
> and who wrote the book . . . the man who does not know
> this has not understood anything.
>
>   (p. 187)

Those words may serve as an epitaph for the poets of 1914–1918, whether they appear in the pages of this essay or not, and as a commemoration of all who suffered and bore witness on the battlefields of World War I.

SELECTED BIBLIOGRAPHY

LAWRENCE BINYON

I. COLLECTED WORKS. *The Four Years: War Poems* (London, 1919); *Collected Poems*, 2 vols. (London, 1931).

II. SEPARATE WORKS. *The Anvil* (London, 1916); *The Cause: Poems of the War* (Boston, 1917); *For the Fallen* (London, 1917).

EDMUND BLUNDEN

I. BIBLIOGRAPHY. B. J. Kirkpatrick, *A Bibliography of Edmund Blunden* (Oxford, 1979).

II. COLLECTED WORKS. K. Hopkins, ed., *Edmund Blunden: A Selection of Poetry and Prose* (London, 1950; New York, 1961); *Poems of Many Years* (London, 1957); R. Marsack, ed., *Selected Poems* (Manchester, 1982).

III. SEPARATE WORKS. *Undertones of War* (London, 1928), verse and prose, with new preface by author (New York, 1956); *War Poets 1914–1918* (London, 1958), criticism.

IV. CRITICAL STUDIES. A. M. Hardie, *Edmund Blunden* (London, 1958; rev. ed., 1971); M. Thorpe, *The Poetry of Edmund Blunden* (Wateringbury, 1971).

RUPERT BROOKE

I. BIBLIOGRAPHY. G. Keynes, *A Bibliography* (London, 1954; 2nd ed., rev., 1959).

II. COLLECTED WORKS. *Collected Poems: With a Memoir by E[dward]. M[arsh].* (London, 1918); G. Keynes, ed., *The Poetical Works* (London, 1947), paperback ed. (London, 1960); C. Hassall, *The Prose* (London, 1956); G. Keynes, ed., *Letters* (London, 1968).

III. SEPARATE WORKS. *Poems* (London, 1911); *1914 and Other Poems* (London, 1915); *John Webster and the Elizabethan Drama* (London, 1916); *Letters from America* (London, 1916), preface by Henry James.

IV. CRITICAL STUDIES. W. de la Mare, *Rupert Brooke and the Intellectual Imagination* (London, 1919); M. Browne, *Recollections of Rupert Brooke* (London, 1927); A. J. A. Stringer, *Red Wine of Youth: A Life of R. Brooke* (Indianapolis, 1948); C. Hassall, *Rupert Brooke: A Biography* (New York, 1964); M. Hastings, *The Handsomest Young Man in England: Rupert Brooke* (London, 1967), lavishly illus.; G. Keynes, *Rupert Brooke: Drafts and Fair Copies in the Author's Hand* (London, 1974).

FORD MADOX FORD

I. COLLECTED WORKS. *Collected Poems* (New York, 1936), intro. by W. R. Benét.

JULIAN GRENFELL

I. SEPARATE WORKS. *Battle: Flanders* (London, 1915).

II. CRITICAL STUDIES. V. Meynell, *Julian Grenfell* (London, 1917), memoir with poems; M. Mosley, *Julian Grenfell* (London, 1976), based on Grenfell family papers.

IVOR GURNEY

I. COLLECTED WORKS. *Poems by Ivor Gurney* (London, 1954), with memoir by E. Blunden; *Poems of Ivor Gurney, 1890–1937* (London, 1973), intro. by E. Blunden and bibliographical note by L. Clark; P. J. Kavanagh, ed., *Collected Poems of Ivor Gurney* (London, 1982), first major collection of Gurney's work, includes over 300 poems, 100 not previously collected; R. K. R. Thornton, ed., *War Letters of Ivor Gurney* (Manchester, 1983).

II. SEPARATE WORKS. *Severn and Somme* (London, 1917); *War's Embers, and Other Verses* (London, 1919).

III. CRITICAL STUDIES. M. Hurd, *The Ordeal of Ivor Gurney* (London, 1978).

W. N. HODGSON

I. COLLECTED WORKS. *Verse and Prose in Peace and War* (London, 1916; 2nd ed., 1917).

A. E. HOUSMAN

I. COLLECTED WORKS. *Collected Poems* (London, 1939; New York, 1940; 1959).

DAVID JONES

I. COLLECTED WORKS. H. Grisewood, ed., *Epoch and Artist: Selected Writings* (London, 1959), prose; R. Pryor, ed., *David Jones: Letters to Vernon Watkins* (Cardiff, 1976), foreword by G. Watkins, notes by ed.; R. Hague, ed., *Dai Greatcoat: A Self-Portrait of David Jones in His Letters* (Boston, 1980); J. Matthias, ed., *Introducing David Jones: A Selection of His Writings* (Boston, 1980).

II. SEPARATE WORKS. *In Parenthesis* (London, 1937), verse and prose; *The Anathemata: Fragments of an Attempted Writing* (London, 1952; 2nd ed., 1955), verse and prose; *The Sleeping Lord and Other Fragments* (London, 1974), verse and prose; although these later writings do not have World War I as their theme, they all throw light on *In Parenthesis*.

III. CRITICAL STUDIES. D. Blamires, *David Jones: Artist and Writer* (Manchester, 1971; Toronto, 1972); R. Hague, *David Jones* (Cardiff, 1975); J. Hooker, *David Jones: An Exploratory Study of the Writings* (London, 1975); R.

Mathias, ed., *David Jones: Eight Essays on His Work as Writer and Artist* (Llandysul, 1976); S. Rees, *David Jones* (New York, 1977), includes bibliography; W. Blissett, *The Long Conversation: A Memoir of David Jones* (London, 1981).

ROBERT NICHOLS

I. COLLECTED WORKS. *Such Was My Singing: A Selection from Poems 1915–1940* (London, 1942).

II. SEPARATE WORKS. *Invocation: War Poems and Others* (London, 1915); *Ardours and Endurances* (London, 1917).

HERBERT READ

I. COLLECTED WORKS. *Collected Poems* (London, 1966).

II. SEPARATE WORKS. *Songs of Chaos* (London, 1915), verse; *Naked Warriors* (London, 1919), verse; *In Retreat* (London, 1925), prose narrative; *Ambush* (London, 1930), prose narrative; *The End of a War* (London, 1933), verse.

III. CRITICAL STUDIES. F. Berry, *Herbert Read* (London, 1961).

ISAAC ROSENBERG

I. COLLECTED WORKS. G. Bottomley, ed., *Poems* (London, 1922), with memoir by L. Binyon; G. Bottomley and D. Harding, eds., *Collected Poems* (London–New York, 1949); I. Parsons, ed., *Collected Works* (London, 1979), rev. and enl. from 1937 ed., intro. by ed., foreword by S. Sassoon.

II. SEPARATE WORKS. *Night and Day* (London, 1912); *Youth* (London, 1915), poems; *Moses* (London, 1916), drama.

III. CRITICAL STUDIES. J. Cohen, *Journey to the Trenches: The Life of Isaac Rosenberg, 1890–1918* (London, 1975); J. Liddiard, *Isaac Rosenberg: The Half-Used Life* (London, 1975); J. M. Wilson, *Isaac Rosenberg, Poet and Painter* (London, 1975). Note: Catalogs of two exhibitions contain valuable material on Rosenberg: *Isaac Rosenberg 1890–1917: Catalogue with Letters*, ed. by M. de Sausmarez and J. Silkin, Leeds University Exhibition Catalog (Leeds, 1959), and the National Book League Exhibition Catalogue, ed. by J. Liddiard and C. Simmons (London, 1975).

SIEGFRIED SASSOON

I. BIBLIOGRAPHY. G. Keynes, *A Bibliography* (London, 1962).

II. COLLECTED WORKS. *The War Poems* (London, 1919); *The Complete Memoirs of George Sherston* (London, 1937), prose; *Collected Poems* (London, 1947); *Collected Poems 1908–1956* (London, 1961); *Selected Poems* (London, 1968), paperback ed.

III. SEPARATE WORKS. *The Old Huntsman and Other Poems* (London, 1917); *Counter-Attack and Other Poems* (London, 1918), intro. by R. Nichols; *Picture Show* (Cambridge, 1919), verse; *Satirical Poems* (London, 1926; enl. ed., 1933); *The Heart's Journey* (London, 1927), verse; *Memoirs of a Fox-Hunting Man* (London, 1928), memoirs; *Memoirs of an Infantry Officer* (New York–London, 1930), memoirs; *Sherston's Progress* (London, 1936), memoirs; *The Old Century and Seven More Years* (London, 1938), memoirs, paperback ed. with intro. by M. Thorpe (London, 1968); *The Weald of Youth* (London, 1942), memoirs; *Siegfried's Journey, 1916–1920* (London, 1945), memoirs; D. R. Hart, ed., *Diaries 1920–1922* (London, 1982), intro. by ed.

IV. CRITICAL STUDIES. M. Thorpe, *Siegfried Sassoon: A Critical Study* (London, 1966).

CHARLES HAMILTON SORLEY

I. COLLECTED WORKS. *Marlborough, and Other Poems* (London, 1916; 5th ed., rev. and enl., 1922); *Letters from Germany* (Cambridge, 1916); *The Letters with a Chapter of Biography* (Cambridge, 1919).

II. CRITICAL STUDIES. T. B. Swann, *The Ungirt Runner: Charles Hamilton Sorley, Poet of World War I* (Hamden, Conn., 1965).

EDWARD THOMAS

I. COLLECTED WORKS. *Collected Poems* (London, 1920), foreword by W. de la Mare; R. G. Thomas, ed., *Letters from Edward Thomas to Gordon Bottomley* (London, 1958); R. G. Thomas, ed., *Collected Poems* (New York–Oxford, 1978).

II. CRITICAL STUDIES. J. Moore, *The Life and Letters of Edward Thomas* (London–Toronto, 1939); H. Coombes, *Edward Thomas* (London, 1956); E. Farjeon, *Edward Thomas: The Last Four Years* (London, 1958); V. Scannell, *Edward Thomas* (London, 1965); W. Cooke, *Edward Thomas: A Critical Biography 1878–1917* (London, 1970); H. Thomas, *Edward Thomas* (Edinburgh, 1974), contains *As It Was* (New York–London, 1927) and *World Without End* (London, 1931), his widow's 2-vol. account of her life with him; A. Motion, *Edward Thomas* (London, 1980).

ARTHUR GRAEME WEST

I. SEPARATE WORKS. *Diary of a Dead Officer* (London, 1919).

ANTHOLOGIES

E. H. Marsh, ed., *Georgian Poetry* (London, 1914; 1916; 1918; 1919; 1922), eds. for 1911–1912, 1913–1915, 1916–1917, 1918–1919, 1920–1922; E. H. Marsh, ed., *1914 and Other Poems* (London, 1915); F. Brereton [Frederick T. Smith], ed., *Anthology of War Poems* (London, 1930), intro. by E. Blunden; R. M. B. Nichols, ed., *An Anthology of War Poetry* (London, 1943), with long intro. in form of dialogue between Nichols and J. Tennyson; J. Brophy and E. Partridge, eds., *The Long Trail: What the British Soldier Sang and Said in the Great War of 1914–1918* (London, 1965), rev. ed. of *Songs and Slang of the British Soldier 1914–1918* (London, 1938); B. Gardner, ed., *Up the Line to Death: The War Poets 1914–1918* (London, 1965), intro. by E. Blunden; I. M. Parsons, ed., *Men Who March Away: Poems of the First World War* (New York–London, 1965); M. Hussey, ed., *Poetry of the First World War* (London, 1967).

GENERAL CRITICISM

J. M. Johnston, *English Poetry of the First World War* (London, 1964), detailed study of the leading poets of the war; B. Bergonzi, *Heroes' Twilight: A Study of the Literature of the Great War* (London, 1965); J. Silkin, *Out of Battle: The Poetry of the Great War* (London, 1972); J. Stallworthy, *Poets of the First World War* (London, 1974); P. Fussell, *The Great War and Modern Memory* (New York, 1975).

WILLIAM BUTLER YEATS

(1865-1939)

G. S. Fraser

I

For just over ten years before he died in a hotel in the south of France, at the beginning of 1939, William Butler Yeats had been universally recognized by his peers as the greatest poet of this century writing in the English language. The recognition dated from the publication in 1928 of his finest volume, *The Tower*. In June of 1939 he would have been seventy-four. He had been writing verses since his teens and had been a poet of some reputation since his twenties. Since the turn of the century, he would probably have been mentioned by any critic in a list of the four or five most distinguished English poets, and in any consideration of Irish poetry he would have headed the list. He had won the Nobel Prize for literature in 1923, he had done more than any other man to bring about the birth of the Irish theater, and he had sat in the senate of the Irish Free State. Yet every critic knows that these public honors are never the full measure of a poet's reputation. At regular intervals during his long life, shrewd critics had been convinced that Yeats was finished. To George Moore, in the Edwardian decade, it seemed that all Yeats's best poems had been inspired by his hopeless love for Maud Gonne; this love was never to find physical fulfillment, and Moore thought that Yeats's lyrical gift would wither, like cut flowers in a glass. To the young T. S. Eliot, in the early Georgian era, Yeats seemed not much more than an interesting survival from the 1890's. The young Ezra Pound, sending some of Yeats's poems to an American magazine, took it upon himself to polish and improve them. The young John Middleton Murry, one of the best poetry critics of his period, dismissed *The Wild Swans at Coole*, which came out in 1917, as the work of a used-up aesthete. The interesting generation of writers who came to Oxford after World War I thought little of Yeats. "Surely," wrote T. E. Lawrence to Pound, "Yeats is no good?" Robert Graves, in the *Pamphlet Against Anthologies*, which

he wrote with Laura Riding, made jovial hay of "The Lake Isle of Innisfree." Thus, though Yeats had never been neglected, the full recognition of his greatness, like its full flowering, came very tardily.

To many critics it seemed that Yeats, wonderful as his gifts were, did not live wholly in the real world. Thus I. A. Richards, in *Science and Poetry* (1925), commenting on Yeats's interest in magic, wrote:

Now he turns to a world of symbolic phantasmagoria about which he is desperately uncertain. He is uncertain because he has adopted as a technique of inspiration the use of trance, of dissociated phases of consciousness, and the revelations given in these dissociated states are unsufficiently connected with normal experience.

Quoting this comment, T. S. Eliot, in *After Strange Gods*, had even more severe things to say as late as 1934:

Mr. Yeats's "supernatural world" was the wrong supernatural world. It was not a world of spiritual significance, not a world of real Good and Evil, of holiness and sin, but a highly sophisticated lower mythology summoned, like a physician, to supply the fading pulse of poetry with some transient stimulant so that the dying patient may utter his last words.

The centrally important critical problem about Yeats becomes clear if we contrast these passages with the noble tribute that Eliot paid to Yeats on his death:

There are some poets whose poems can be considered more or less in isolation, for experience and delight. There are others whose poetry, though giving equally experience and delight, has a larger historical importance. Yeats was one of the latter. He was one of the few whose history was the history of our own time, who are part of the consciousness of our age, which cannot be understood without them.[1]

[1]See Eliot's "The Poetry of W. B. Yeats" in *Purpose*, XII (1940), reprinted in *On Poetry and Poets* (London, 1957).

How are these pertinent strictures to be reconciled with this deserved praise? In what sense was the mental history of Yeats, which from a superficial point of view was so odd and eccentric, more profoundly "the history of our own time"? Was Eliot, feeling that every truly great poet must in some sense be representative of his time, and feeling intuitively sure of Yeats's major qualities, merely making a formal claim that Yeats *must* be representative? Or can Yeats's representative quality be illustrated in detail?

Since the first edition of this essay was published, a great deal of scholarly work has been done, by critics such as Frank Kermode, on Yeats's sources in the 1890's and what might be called the English symbolist tradition, one deriving from William Blake and the Pre-Raphaelites rather than from Stéphane Mallarmé. F. A. C. Wilson has also written interestingly on Yeats's debts to neo-Platonic and oriental mystical ideas, and Giorgio Melchiori on his use of themes suggested by Renaissance painting. The tendency of all this criticism has been to stress the fact that, in an informal way, Yeats was an extremely learned man and to stress also his lifelong interest in the supernatural. His correspondence with Sturge Moore reveals him as an amateur metaphysician of considerable ingenuity and eloquence. But though the above writers have very much deepened my own understanding in detail of Yeats, I remain convinced that his greatness as a poet lies in his realism, in his humanity, in his power to use fantasy and abstruse speculation as metaphors for, or means of exploring, the human situation; it lies at the pole of what Yeats himself called "self" or "heart," at the pole of the "mire and blood" of human veins, rather than at the pole of what he called "soul," or dreams of an abstract eternity. He had enough earthy strength and sap to be able to digest into true poetry a great deal of what Lord Castlereagh called "sublime mysticism and nonsense." What the poems record is the continuous conflict between the claims of a prophetic wisdom, a sense of insulation against the terrors of history, and, on the other hand, the claims, rewards, and pains of the moment.

II

When I. A. Richards, in *Science and Poetry*, suggested that a poet like Yeats, who took ghosts and fairies seriously, could hardly have anything quite centrally significant to say to the modern mind, he was making a crude but sensible point. The main debate of that mind, in England, since the 1880's, has been between an orthodox religious and an orthodox scientific attitude. Yeats was neither orthodoxly religious nor orthodoxly scientific; he had his own science, which was an occult one, and his own religion, or "sophisticated lower mythology," and in prose he sometimes reconciles them at the level of magic. In his better poetry, on the other hand, he often quietly jettisons both of them. The scientific attitude leads, in practice, to a kind of democratic humanitarianism. Yeats believed in aristocracy and, though his humane and fastidious temperament made him recoil from violence, he often allowed himself to romanticize violence when it was safely set in a mythological past. The modern Christian attitude tends to lead to a preoccupation with sin. From this, Yeats was quite free. In the last ten years of Yeats's life, these two contrasting attitudes were well represented in England by the work of W. H. Auden and Eliot. Auden, in the 1930's, was a kind of liberal semi-Marxist, profoundly but not always obviously affected by a Christian upbringing; Eliot was a Christian conservative, profoundly but not always obviously affected, particularly in his concern with social questions, by a liberal upbringing. These two poets, in fact, had much more in common with each other than either had with Yeats. Yet Auden, like Eliot, nobly saluted Yeats's passing:

> Earth, receive an honoured guest:
> William Yeats is laid to rest.
> Let the Irish vessel lie
> Emptied of its poetry. . . .
> ("In Memory of W. B. Yeats,")[2]

In saluting Yeats, neither Auden nor Eliot can have been merely saluting a great artist in verse. Given the deep seriousness of their critical attitudes, both must have found in Yeats's work a kind of wisdom, even though that expressed itself through ideas and gestures of which they disapproved. Yeats was as firmly set against Auden's attitude of the 1930's, which he symbolically described as "Moscow," as against Eliot's, which he symbolically described as "Rome." Just as he was never a political democrat, never at all sympathetic with the

> levelling, rancorous, rational sort of mind
> That never looked out of the eye of a saint
> Or out of a drunkard's eye,

[2]In *Collected Shorter Poems, 1930-1944* (London, 1950).

so he was very much farther, also, from any traditional Christian attitudes than many scientifically minded agnostics are. What may be called his morality was neither that of a diluted and imperfect Christianity nor that of a progressive humanitarianism. It could be better described as a morality of "style." It very much resembled (given that Yeats had a more genial and generous temperament) the morality of Nietzsche. Yeats's instinctive sympathies were with the strong and proud, not with the weak and humble; with the brilliant rather than the stupid, with the exceptional rather than the average. They were not, however, like those of Nietzsche, with the oppressor rather than the oppressed. Yet, as an Irish nationalist, Yeats identified himself with the liberal wing of the Protestant Ascendancy, with those like Jonathan Swift and Henry Grattan, "who gave though free to refuse," rather than with the masses of the Irish people. Yeats's frank admiration for such qualities as strength, beauty, recklessness, a dominating spirit, a "proper pride" set him against the obvious superficial currents of our age. If he does indeed have the central representativeness that Eliot claims for him, one reason may be that this aristocratic or "natural" morality—which is the morality of schoolboys, of film fans, of soldiers, a morality based on the instinctive admiration we feel for those who excel us—is more firmly rooted in us than we think, and that when we find it nobly expressed we instinctively respond to it. More broadly, for all our preoccupation today with "security," we still have hankerings after the heroic.

III

THE case for Yeats's representativeness, however, has never been properly argued. The mere exposition of the meaning of many of Yeats's poems, as related to his personal history, to his social background, and to his philosophical opinions, is in itself such a complicated task that very little that can properly be called "criticism" of his poems—criticism in the sense of concrete evaluation, of distancing and placing—has been written. Maud Gonne and Mme. Blavatsky and the Abbey Theatre and Irish politics and the esoteric symbolism of *A Vision* tend to bulk so large in accounts of Yeats that they crowd out any consideration of his diction, his rhythms, his way of constructing a poem, the coherence and sensitivity of his responses. What John Wain wittily calls "the

Gypsy Petulengro approach"—the painstaking exposition, with diagrams, of what Yeats meant by gyres and cones and "phases of the moon"—becomes so absorbing in itself that mere literary criticism no doubt seems dull by comparison. This sketch is not primarily concerned with Yeats as a magician or a mystic. Margaret Rudd may be perfectly right when, in her book about Yeats, she says that he is a rather inferior mystic if we compare him with Blake. What is also true is that the Blake of the prophetic books is a rather inferior artist if we compare him with Yeats—these have to be approached, as even Yeats's book of occult philosophy, *A Vision*, need not be, with a primarily extraliterary interest. And Yeats's prose poem *Per Amica Silentia Lunae*, a preliminary account of some parts of *A Vision*, needs no apology; it is an accomplished, even a moving, artifact in its own right. But we should remember a wise remark by his wife, George: "Willie," she is reported to have said, "you are a great poet, but you are no saint." The great poet is our subject. He was, of course, no saint; but we may make out a case in passing that he had many of the virtues of Aristotle's "magnanimous man" or of the *honnête homme* of the French seventeenth century. His representativeness for our own age does, as I have suggested, largely depend on the fact that he both possessed and praised what we think of as archaic virtues. He was the last quite wholehearted spokesman of the aristocratic idea.

IV

YEATS came from the outer fringe of the Irish Protestant Ascendancy, from a rather better family than George Bernard Shaw's, and perhaps from not quite such a good family as Oscar Wilde's. He spent his childhood between London and Ireland, and though in Ireland his family counted as minor gentry, in London, insofar as London bothers about such things, they probably counted as shabby-genteel bohemians. Yeats's father, J. B. Yeats, was a talented but unsuccessful painter who wrote brilliant letters and had a genius for friendship. As a painter he was influenced by the Pre-Raphaelites, and he handed down to his son the idea of a "religion of beauty" and a romantic taste in art and literature that even in Yeats's youth was a slightly old-fashioned one. There are certain great writers of the type of Henrik Ibsen whom the young Yeats could never absorb; to the

1475

end of his days his attitude toward the French painters Edgar Degas and Claude Monet was rather like that of Sir Alfred Munnings toward Pablo Picasso.[3] J. B. Yeats was also influenced in his ideas by the agnostic rationalism of Thomas Huxley and John Tyndall, and this in turn effected a change in his art to a naturalist impressionist portraiture. Against such beliefs and aesthetic practices the young Yeats violently reacted.

As a boy, Yeats was dreamy and backward, fond of long solitary walks. To his dying day, he never learned to spell properly, and diffidence about his scholarship prevented him from going to Trinity College, Dublin. This lack of a formal education is important in Yeats's development. He read very widely but never systematically. He was bad at languages; insofar as the French symbolist movement influenced him at all, it was through translations made by his friend Arthur Symons, and when in later life he said that he had "almost forgotten his Hebrew," he meant that at one period, for some occult purpose, he had memorized a few words of that language. Even for himself, the map of what he knew and did not know can never have had very firm outlines. Like many poets, he probably learned much from conversations with others, and, indeed, all his life he subjected himself to mentors, sometimes younger men than himself, who supplied the deficiencies in his stock of philosophy, connoisseurship, stagecraft, or mystical experience: Lionel Johnson, Charles Ricketts, John Synge, Gordon Craig, T. Sturge Moore.

The young Yeats began writing verses very early. This early work shows much vividness of imagery, but it was some time before Yeats learned to write in regular stanzas or even to make all his lines scan. The first drafts of his poems, to the end, often show a surprising technical hesitancy—a trite choice of words, a flat shaping of the line; the poems were perfected by a habit, early acquired, of endlessly patient revision. The young Yeats was lucky in that his father encouraged him to go on with his poetry and even actively discouraged him from tying himself down to the drudgery of regular newspaper work. Yeats, however, soon became a fluent freelance journalist, chiefly on topics of Irish folklore. By his early twenties, he had begun to make a reputation. In London, he became one of a group of minor poets, among them Symons, Johnson, and Ernest Dowson, whom today we tend to dismiss as "decadents."

This label has been attached to them partly because of their sense of the incurable materialism and philistinism of their own age, and of their self-created myth of themselves as doomed artists, and partly because of their almost exclusive devotion to their art. All of them—Lionel Johnson, Ernest Dowson, John Davidson, Arthur Symons, Aubrey Beardsley—had unhappy lives; most died young. A number were converts to Catholicism, and for them the possibility, ever present in their minds, of being damned gave not a relish but a momentousness to sin. Yeats's early poems are full of melancholy and falling rhythms, but have little to say about sin. The young Irishman was not haunted by the fear of damnation. He was chaste and temperate—the greatest love of his life, for Maud Gonne, was probably a chaste one, and his failure to win her did not drive him to prostitutes or to drink. In the middle 1890's he met a beautiful and talented woman, an unhappily married cousin of Lionel Johnson's, Olivia Shakespear, and for a short period they found happiness in their love affair. But before long, Maud Gonne appeared in London, asking for his help, and Olivia, sensing a divided loyalty, brought her affair with Yeats to an end. This renewed misery might well have brought him to the same end as the poets of "the tragic generation," had he not been rescued by the maternal kindness of Lady Gregory at the end of the decade. Shy and dreamy though Yeats was, he also was fundamentally a masterful man. Maud Gonne, dragging him at her heels on nationalist agitations, soon found that he was a natural orator and could easily dominate committees. His religion, far more than that of his companions, was genuinely a religion of poetry. Reacting against agnostic rationalism, he had not reacted in the direction of orthodoxy:

I was unlike others of my generation in one thing only. I am very religious, and deprived by Huxley and Tyndall of the simple-minded religion of my childhood, I had made a new religion, almost an infallible church of poetic tradition, of a fardel of stories, and of personages and of emotions, inseparable from their first expression, passed on from generation to generation by poets and painters with some help from philosophers and theologians.

(*The Trembling of the Veil,* 1926 ed., pp. 142–143)

How far, one wonders, was he right about himself? Was he really "very religious"? We wonder both about the word "fardel" with its dandified air and

---

[3]Munnings was a member of the Royal Academy and a painter of horses in the naturalist manner. He was intensely conservative and unsympathetic to the avant-garde work by Picasso.

about the word "stories," which shrugs off the question of whether the stories are true. The attitude is aesthetic rather than ethical or religious; in a sophisticated way the young Yeats is playing a child's game of Let's Pretend. There are late poems of his, such as "Among School Children," that do express an authentically religious attitude, one of mystical acceptance of a world experienced as contradictory; but the genuinely religious attitude that is often to be found in Yeats's poetry has little to do with—even tugs against—the pseudoreligious notions. It is not a playing with fantasies but a response to the whole. The very fact that the young man could so easily concoct a "new religion" for himself—out of Irish folklore and Blake and Mme. Blavatsky and anything that came handy—is evidence of a rather unreligious nature; evidence of a blithe and irresponsible temperament, that of a young man sure of his genius, and unconvicted of sin. The note of the 1890's, the genuinely religious note that is not to be found in Yeats's early poems, is that of Lionel Johnson's "The Dark Angel":

> Dark Angel, with thine aching lust!
> Of two defeats, of two despairs:
> Less dread, a change to drifting dust,
> Than thine eternity of cares.

Yeats's early religion, if it was properly a religion at all, was one without anguish or dread.

The charm of much of Yeats's early poetry is thus slightly equivocal—dreamy and melancholy, passive and self-indulgent, as indeed from this account of his poetical religion we might expect it to be. Robert Graves's attack on "The Lake Isle of Innisfree" is, in fact, an attack on a poet for not being properly awake. In the poem "A Faery Song" from Yeats's volume of 1892, *The Countess Cathleen and Various Legends and Lyrics,* a modern reader is embarrassed by the monotonous doleful music, by the yearning that seems neither to have nor to seek for an object:

> We who are old, old and gay,
> O so old!
> Thousands of years, thousands of years
> If all were told:
>
> Give to these children, new from the world,
> Silence and love;
> And the long dew-dropping hours of the night,
> And the stars above....
>   (1–8)

Even throughout the 1890's, however, there was a constant, slow, hidden growth in another direction. In *The Wind Among the Reeds,* the volume of 1899, the diction does indeed seem on the surface as formal and faded, the cadences as mechanically "beautiful," as ever; and the symbolism also, increasingly intricate but not increasingly vivid,

> a coat
> Covered with embroideries,

hangs now like a rich, worn tapestry between the poet and the hard stone walls of the world. But the yearning had now an object, Maud Gonne. The individual words clutch more at particular objects. There is a movement toward active feeling, positive grasp:

> I became a man, a hater of the wind,
> Knowing one, out of all things, alone, that his head
> May not lie on the breast or his lips on the hair
> Of the woman that he loves, until he dies;
> Although the rushes and the fowl of the air
> Cry of his love with their pitiful cries.
> ("He Thinks of His Past Greatness When a Part of
>   the Constellations of Heaven")

Yeats, at some time after 1909, changed the "dreamy Celtic" dying fall of the last two lines to an arrogant rhetorical question:

> O beast of the wilderness, bird of the air,
> Must I endure your amorous cries?

The poem had enough latent strength to stand the change.

We should look, in the early poems, for that latent strength. Their weary, withdrawn note is a kind of protective coloring that Yeats had taken from his friends of the 1890's. (He was often, throughout his life, ready to imitate admiringly his minor, but never his major, contemporaries. A natural leader, he liked to disguise himself as a follower, even of small men.) There is, of course, a paradox here. Yeats made himself a major poet, starting with the equipment and apparently the tastes of a good minor one —with a chaste but excessively "poetic" diction, with exquisite but trite cadences, with a tendency to use symbols in a way that was decorative and even fussy rather than deeply exploratory, with a narrow and rather willfully sad range of moods, always just on the verge of the literary pose or the stock response. He started, also, without much grasp of the outer world; his early poems rarely make us see

1477

anything; we can weave our own daydreams round them, which is another matter. And though he acquired unique rank among his contemporaries as a visionary poet, it is probable that the merely *visible* world left him, to the last, rather cold. Usually he evokes it for us by a kind of trick, not describing the thing but reminding us of our feelings about it:

> A sycamore and lime-tree lost in night
> Although that western cloud is luminous
>   . . .
> Back turned upon the brightness of the sun
> And all the sensuality of the shade. . . .
>   ("Coole Park," 3–4; 30–31)

We remember our feelings about staring toward a fading distance at sunset, about sharp contrasts in a garden of light and shade. We ourselves, most of the time, *make* Yeats's physical world for him. We believe in it, because we believe in Yeats, rather as we believe in a painted Elsinore when Hamlet is talking. We can, in fact, think perhaps most fruitfully of Yeats's poems as speeches made by him at crucial moments in a long noble drama. No poet lends himself so little to the cold-blooded examination of his poems as isolated objects; no poet gains more from being read as a whole, with a full knowledge of his life. Yeats, as he grows older, acts out, with growing assurance and spontaneity, the difficult part of himself. The acting in the end, having gone through the stages of lyrical mime and heroic and satirical tirade, becomes almost naturalistic.

V

THE Edwardian decade saw the masterful side of Yeats's nature coming to the surface. By 1908, when the first collected edition of his works came out, he had made a reputation not only as a poet and a dramatist, but as the man who had put the Abbey Theatre on its feet, who kept it going, and who had bravely defended Synge against local prejudice. Through Lady Gregory, who had become his patron, Yeats was now accepted by that "big house" society of which, in his childhood, he had only touched the fringes. He was becoming self-conscious about his ancestry. Some of the younger men in Dublin, and some older contemporaries like George Moore, thought him conceited and arrogant; but nobody any longer thought him a mere shy, ineffec-

tual dreamer. He had resigned himself to unfulfilled love and found public activity a distraction. Maud Gonne had made an unfortunate marriage, and though she was separated from her husband she had become a Roman Catholic, so there was no prospect of her divorcing her husband and marrying Yeats. He and she, in any case, were becoming estranged in a deeper sense. She felt that the Abbey Theatre had tempted Yeats away from the national cause. She would have liked cheaper seats and plays that were straight nationalistic propaganda. Maude Gonne remained the central figure in his poetry, a muse figure; but her presence in so many of his first lyrics should not deflect us from stressing that women played an important role as friends, even as muse figures: his wife, the young dancer Margaret Ruddock, Dorothy Wellesley (the duchess of Wellington), Lady Gregory, and, perhaps supremely, Olivia Shakespear. Their closeness survived the unhappiness of their affair in the 1890's and continued to the end of her life, a year before his own death; and it was to her that he wrote his warmest and most eloquent letters. She is also the subject of one of his most beautiful poems, "After Long Silence." Both Olivia and Lady Gregory are more sympathetic and more intelligent figures than Maude Gonne, and it is one of the achievements of later criticism that their roles in his life and art have emerged more clearly.

World War I, apart from the deaths of friends like Major Robert Gregory, hardly touched Yeats emotionally. But the Easter Rebellion of 1916, which took him by surprise (he was not in the confidence of any of the more extreme nationalists), made him regret his growing aloofness from the Irish cause. He remained a very moderate nationalist—he felt that England might still "keep faith"—and indeed the troubles of 1916 and after gave him a vivid sense of how violence can in a short time destroy values that it had taken the law centuries to build up:

> We had fed the heart on fantasies,
> The heart's grown brutal from the fare;
> More substance in our enmities
> Than in our love; O honey-bees
> Come build in the empty house of the stare.
>   ("The Stare's Nest by My Window," st. 4)

Yet he felt himself more profoundly identified with the Irish people than he had been for many years.

Yeats's long romance with Maud Gonne had meanwhile ended in a kind of comic fantasy. Her husband, one of the rebels of 1916, had been shot.

Yeats felt he ought to ask her to marry him again but was probably relieved when she refused. At the same time, he fell in love with her beautiful adopted daughter, who, as a young girl, had been half in love with him. The adopted daughter could not make up her mind. Yeats gave her a date by which to do so, and when her final decision was against marrying him, he suddenly married another young lady, George Hyde-Lees. Not unnaturally, after such a complication of emotions, he was in a state of depression and anxiety after his marriage—even if there had not been the business of Maud Gonne and her daughter, he was a man in his fifties, weighed down by anxiety for his country and married, after an unusually chaste bachelor existence, to somebody much younger than himself. It was partly to distract him that Mrs. Yeats started the experiments in automatic writing that ultimately gave him the material for *A Vision*. In judging Yeats's occult philosophy, we should always ask ourselves how far, at a fundamental level, he himself took it seriously; and how far it was a necessary plaything for a powerful and distressed creative mind.

VI

MANY critics agree that it is on the volumes published in the last twenty years of his life, from *The Wild Swans at Coole* of 1917 to the posthumous *Last Poems and Two Plays* of 1939, that Yeats's future fame will mainly rest. The sharpening and hardening of his attitudes, the development of the tough, complex, and ironical later style can in fact be traced farther back, to the significantly named *Responsibilities* of 1914. There is even a hint of the new style in "Adam's Curse," from a volume of 1903, *In the Seven Woods*:

> I said, "It's certain there is no fine thing
> Since Adam's fall but needs much labouring.
> There have been lovers who thought love should be
> So much compounded of high courtesy
> That they would sigh and quote with learned looks
> Precedents out of beautiful old books;
> Yet now it seems an idle trade enough."

It can, however, be agreed that there is a remarkable new maturity, a new "realism," in the work of Yeats's last twenty years; and this can be traced to several sources.

Yeats was now writing as a married man, a man with a house and children of his own, more rooted in everyday life than he had previously been. He was writing also as a man who had seen the dream of his youth, Irish independence, come true; and who was becoming aware of certain ironies, for him tragic ironies, involved in its coming true. His own personal dream had been of a free Ireland that would be a kind of replica, without the tensions or troubles, without the injustice to the majority, of the Ireland of Grattan's Parliament.[4] He wanted to go back to the eighteenth century rather than on into the twentieth. He hoped that the "big houses" would survive, that the Protestant Ascendancy would still, because of their wealth, their wit, and their manners, constitute a dominant group. He thought of the local grandees patronizing poets and the peasants touching their hats. He was romantically innocent about politics. He found, of course, that what had come into existence was not a Protestant-dominated aristocratic republic but a Roman Catholic farmers' democracy; and the farmers did not want to touch their hats to anybody. Some of the "big houses" were burned in the troubles, others were deserted because they cost too much to keep up and because they, like even the nationalistic aristocracy, had outlived their social function. Yeats had hoped that Dublin, as the capital of a free Ireland, would become a great cultural center; he saw the "blind, bitter town" becoming more rather than less provincial. The Dublin city fathers gave the freedom of the city to a retired Tam-

---

[4]Until 1780, the Irish Parliament could reject or accept, but not amend, laws relating to Irish matters passed by the British Parliament. Irish patriots like Henry Flood and Henry Grattan took advantage of the American Revolutionary War (which involved war with France) to claim and secure legislative independence for the Irish Parliament. The Volunteer Movement, a kind of unofficial defense militia ostensibly raised to resist invasion, was in fact used to put moral pressure on the viceregal government. The viceroy and his staff, however, retained practical control of Irish affairs by offering honors and sinecures to the progovernment parliamentary majority. The new Parliament did not represent the Roman Catholic masses of the people, or even their wealthier elements. Thus the short period of Irish parliamentary independence—or really, of independence for the Protestant Ascendancy—ended in the bloody troubles of 1798 and a little later in the union, secured partly by lavish bribery, of the Irish with the imperial Parliament. Nevertheless, the short period of Grattan's Parliament was marked both by splendid oratory and by a gay and brilliant social life in Dublin, and was thus often remembered nostalgically in the nineteenth century by Irishmen who saw Dublin, both socially and culturally, becoming more and more of a provincial city.

many boss, a Mr. Croker, but rejected the suggestion of Oliver St. John Gogarty that they should also give it to Yeats. Sean O'Casey's tragic masterpiece, *The Plough and the Stars*, aroused as passionate an opposition from the Abbey Theatre audience as Synge's *Playboy of the Western World* had done. Yeats's growing bitterness comes out as early as *The Wild Swans at Coole* in one of his most powerfully sustained shorter poems, "The Fisherman":

> All day I'd looked in the face
> What I had hoped 'twould be
> To write for my own race
> And the reality;
> The living men that I hate,
> The dead man that I loved,
> The craven man in his seat,
> The insolent unreproved,
> And no knave brought to book
> Who has won a drunken cheer,
> The witty man and his joke
> Aimed at the commonest ear,
> The clever man who cries
> The catch-cries of the clown,
> The beating down of the wise
> And great Art beaten down.
>
> (9–24)

Yeats, in this new Ireland, was not, in spite of the prestige that the Nobel Prize brought him, a centrally representative figure. He became a senator, but found himself allied in the senate, a little unromantically, with rich bankers and brewers; a speech that he made protesting, on behalf of the religious minority, against a proposal to make divorce illegal made him unpopular. The esoteric philosophy of *A Vision* is partly to be understood, as we have suggested already, in terms of Yeats's need for distraction. We should not take that book more seriously than Yeats did. He had a long philosophical correspondence with Sturge Moore about hallucinatory cats and other visions of that sort. Are they real beings to which we have access only at privileged moments? Yeats would have liked to think so. Or are they, on the other hand, hallucinations? It is interesting that in this correspondence he never refers to either the "facts" or the "arguments" of *A Vision* as having any relevant authority. He explicitly states elsewhere that it is not very profitable to discuss the theories of *A Vision* in terms of "belief." Many of the ideas in the book, like that of eternal recurrence, are not new; they can be found in the Italian philosopher Giovan-

ni Vico, and in Nietzsche. Yeats, after he had written the first draft of *A Vision*, also found them in Oswald Spengler. Their truth or otherwise cannot be discussed here. They provided props for Yeats's attitude to life, which was becoming a kind of tragic stoicism. He saw life as tragic and felt that it could be acted out with the style of a tragedy. We can embrace our destiny joyfully: "Hamlet and Lear are gay."

It should be particularly noticed, however, that Yeats's attitude toward the supernatural was a profoundly ambiguous one. He wanted, from a world beyond ours, in contrasting moods, two apparently quite contradictory kinds of assurance: one, that we are in fact bound, as the Buddhists tell us we are, to the "great wheel of existence" and shall reappear upon this stage in various roles again and again; the other that, as the Buddhists also tell us, we can escape ultimately from the "great wheel"—not to nonbeing, a concept that never attracted Yeats, but to some kind of timeless perfection. He was not sure (as perhaps no Western man who studies Eastern thought ever is) that he really wanted to escape from the wheel. Thus, in the face of his "symbolic phantasmagoria," he retains the freedom of inconsistency. His images of a Byzantine heaven in which he would be transformed into a golden bird (the artist becoming an eternal work of art) symbolize his desire to escape from the disorder, the irony, the failure of life; but so also other symbols—as when he says he would like to live again, even in a "foul ditch," as a "blind man battering blind men"—stand for a craving for life at any level, the "lust and rage" of which he speaks in his *Last Poems*, that grew stronger in him as he grew older. Often he hated life for not being perfection. Sometimes, also, he feared perfection for not being life.

VII

YEATS's early love poems are dreamily erotic, but those addressed to Olivia Shakespear, particularly through the use of hair imagery, possess a shadowy sexuality. Some of his later poems are so harshly sexual that they cease, in effect, to be erotic:

> From pleasure of the bed,
> Dull as a worm,
> His rod and its butting head
> Limp as a worm,

His spirit that has fled
Blind as a worm.
("The Chambermaid's
Second Song")

A glandular operation that Yeats underwent in his last years no doubt accentuated this tendency, but it was already there. It is best considered, however, as part of a more general tendency in his later poems toward self-questioning, self-stripping:

These masterful images because complete
Grew in pure mind, but out of what began?
A mound of refuse or the sweepings of a street,
Old kettles, old bottles, and a broken can,
Old iron, old bones, old rags, that raving slut
Who keeps the till. Now that my ladder's gone
I must lie down where all the ladders start
In the foul rag-and-bone shop of the heart.
("The Circus Animals' Desertion," st. 5)

The man who wrote that stanza also wrote:

We were the last romantics—chose for theme
Traditional sanctity and loveliness. . . .
("Coole Park and Ballylee," st. 6)

Anybody who wants to get the full range of Yeats must be able to respond to both kinds of statement—must be able to accept the tautness of a great poet's terrible sincerity. In that stanza from "The Circus Animals' Desertion," Yeats has become aware that the symbols of his poetry have a Freudian meaning of which for most of his life he has been unconscious. But we should notice also that this stanza, which bids farewell to the symbolist method, is a triumphant example of it; for we know what the poet is saying here, but we cannot say it in our own words. A merely clinical interpretation will not work. Is, for instance, "that raving slut/Who keeps the till" the Freudian censor—is the money she will give us in return for old rubbish a release of libido? Are the "old iron, old bones, old rags" and the "mound of refuse" symbols for the Freudian anal-erotic hoarding instinct? Is the "foul rag-and-bone shop of the heart" merely the sexual imagination, with its accumulated scraps of lustful memory? Quite obviously not, and quite obviously what Yeats is saying here is something more general and profound. There is something basically blind, grasping, insensate in all of us; something that hoards rubbish, that shuts doors, that hides away from the light. We climb up, but we never wholly get away. All is still

under our feet, in the cellarage. And the "heart" is what grasps and is insensate but also what loves and suffers, and the "ladders"—the ways upward and outward to the free air and the life of the spirit—do start there. And when we have said all this, of course, the stanza still retains, as all great symbolist poetry does, its eternal residue of mysterious suggestiveness.

The bare honesty of such poems, even more than the rich, dark mysteriousness of "Byzantium" or "The Statues," may partly account for Yeats's hold on the young. In his last volume he asks himself more frankly than most poets have done whether he may not have done as much harm as good:

Did that play of mine send out
Certain men the English shot?

Yet he can still strike a last attitude:

Cast a cold eye
On life, on death.
Horseman, pass by!
("Under Ben
Bulben")

He would not, like Rainer Maria Rilke (these lines were written out of irritation with Rilke), accept death as a final dark consummation. He would not accept life itself uncritically. And in the last thing he was working on, *The Death of Cuchulain*, the harlot (an eternal harlot, who has slept with "Conall, Cuchulain, Usna's boys") speaks of polarities and antinomies, of disgust and delight in physical love, of dread and delight in battle; speaks also of the Irish patriots of 1916, who were always in Yeats's heart, delighting in what they dreaded; speaks of gods and heroes whom we seem to embody, or who seem to stand behind us, in the crucial moments of our lives:

That there are still some living
That do my limbs unclothe,
But that the flesh my flesh has gripped
I both adore and loathe.
(*Pipe and drum music*)
Are those things that men adore and loathe
Their sole reality?
What stood in the Post Office
With Pearse and Connolly?
What comes out of the mountain
When men first shed their blood?
Who thought Cuchulain till it seemed
He stood where they had stood?

VIII

YEATS felt that there was a tension between his life and his poetry. He thought sometimes of the poem as a kind of antipersonality that the poet builds up to compensate for or conceal personal weakness, of the poem as a "mask." This idea has something in common with Ezra Pound's idea of the poem as a persona. Pound is a poet who, according to one of his most appreciative but also harshest critics, Percy Wyndham Lewis, has no "personality" of his own worth speaking of; he can function only by pretending to be somebody else, a Provencal troubadour or a Chinese sage. Yeats's masks in poetry are not of this sort; even in his earliest work his own personality—or at least an important aspect of it, the "poetic" aspect—seems to me to come over. Similarly, no doubt, at meetings of the Rhymers' Club in the 1890's, Yeats, fundamentally a very shy and diffident young man, put on a suitable "literary dandy" or perhaps sometimes a "dreamy Celt" personality. As Yeats's poetry matures, one of the things that happens is not so much that it becomes more personal, less of a mask, as that he gets more of his personality into it. He gets in things like irony, humor, arrogant irascibility, the coaxing manners of the professional Irish conversationalist, which in the 1890's he would probably have considered "antipoetic"; he gets in more of the prosaic detail of life, transformed by a poetic apprehension of it.

We might compare the generalized evocation of Maud Gonne, from "Fallen Majesty" in *Responsibilities*,

. . . A crowd
Will gather, and not know it walks the very street
Whereon a thing once walked that seemed a burning cloud,
(6–8)

with the prose bareness of a line and a half from "Beautiful Lofty Things," in *Last Poems:*

. . . Maud Gonne at Howth Station waiting a train,
Pallas Athene in that straight back and arrogant head. . . .
(10–11)

That line and a half evokes Maud Gonne, her setting, her bearing, her character (Pallas Athene, the goddess of wisdom, was severe and virginal). The more conventionally poetic phrase about "a burning cloud" tells us much about Yeats's feeling but does not evoke any image of a woman at all.

Often the force of the later poetry comes largely from this directness, like that of speech:

Before a woman's portrait suddenly I stand,
Beautiful and gentle in her Venetian way,
I met her all but fifty years ago
For twenty minutes in some studio.

. . .

And here's John Synge himself, that rooted man,
"Forgetting human words," a grave deep face. . . .
("The Municipal Gallery Revisited," st. 4 and 7)

Does the imagination dwell the most
Upon a woman won or woman lost?
If on the lost, admit you turned aside
From a great labyrinth out of pride,
Cowardice, some silly over-subtle thought
Or anything called conscience once;
And that if memory recur, the sun's
Under eclipse and the moon blotted out.
(The Tower)

There is no rhetoric in these passages; only in the latter of them any figures of speech, and these so commonplace (a human relationship as a labyrinth, the sense of loss seeming to blot out the sun and moon) that they could occur unaffectedly in ordinary conversation. Common turns of speech are also sometimes exploited for irony. In *The Tower* we are told the story of Mrs. French (it is in Sir Jonah Barrington's *Memoirs* of 1833) and how a footman at dinner one day clipped off the ears of a farmer who was behaving boorishly and brought them to her in a little covered dish. It is with a delighted shock that we meet the lady again, in a summary of the characters in the poems, as

Mrs. French,
Gifted with so fine an ear. . . .

Critics who have discussed to the verge of tedium Yeats's more obscure occult fancies might have discussed with more advantage this strong simplicity of his later style. Behind the strength is honesty of statement. The lines quoted above,

Does the imagination dwell the most . . .

express a complex of feelings that most of us have experienced but that few of us have the courage to put on record: a complex of feelings that might be called remorse or compunction. Yeats speaks for what he calls, in a poem addressed to Friedrich von Hügel, the "unchristened heart"; but with a dignity and passion that make it very unlikely that his words should ever cause scandal to Christians.

Yet if there were only pride and pagan courage and high art, only contempt for "this filthy modern tide," only the obstinate "lust and rage" of a "wild, wicked old man" in Yeats, should we turn to him as we do, not only for distraction, not only for stimulus, but for wisdom and consolation? We look in poetry for love. All great poets are more profoundly capable of love than common men, and they may be terrifyingly more capable of hate too. Yeats's capacity for hate distressed even close friends of his, like the duchess of Wellington. It was there to the last, as in the poem "A Bronze Head":

> Or else I thought her supernatural;
> As though a sterner eye looked through her eye
> On this foul world in its decline and fall;
> On gangling stocks grown great, great stocks run dry,
> Ancestral pearls all pitched into a sty,
> Heroic reverie mocked by clown and knave,
> And wondered what was left for massacre to save.
>
> (st. 4)

But he could hate like that *because* he could love. And the touchstones that I would choose from his poetry, to persuade an unsympathetic reader to reconsider it, all speak of love. I would choose these stanzas from "A Prayer for My Daughter":

> An intellectual hatred is the worst,
> So let her think opinions are accursed.
> Have I not seen the loveliest woman born
> Out of the mouth of Plenty's horn,
> Because of her opinionated mind
> Barter that horn and every good
> By quiet natures understood
> For an old bellows full of angry wind?
>
> Considering that, all hatred driven hence,
> The soul recovers radical innocence
> And learns that it is self-delighting,
> Self-appeasing, self-affrighting,
> And that its own sweet will is Heaven's will;
> She can, though every face should scowl
> And every windy quarter howl
> Or every bellows burst, be happy still.
>
> (st. 8–9)

I would choose a line or two from the gentle minor elegy "In Memory of Eva Gore-Booth and Con Markiewicz":

> Dear shadows, now you know it all,
> All the folly of a fight
> With a common wrong or right.
> The innocent and the beautiful
> Have no enemy but time. . . .
>
> (21–25)

I would choose the magnificent two last stanzas of "Among School Children":

> Both nuns and mothers worship images,
> But those the candles light are not as those
> That animate a mother's reveries,
> But keep a marble or a bronze repose.
> And yet they too break hearts—O Presences
> That passion, piety or affection knows,
> And that all heavenly glory symbolise—
> O self-mockery of man's enterprise;
>
> Labour is blossoming or dancing where
> The body is not bruised to pleasure soul,
> Nor beauty born out of its own despair,
> Nor blear-eyed wisdom out of midnight oil.
> O chestnut-tree, great-rooted blossomer,
> Are you the leaf, the blossom, or the bole?
> O body swayed to music, O brightening glance,
> How can we know the dancer from the dance?

And (though Yeats is not on the whole a poet of striking single lines, of lines that impress us out of their setting) I might choose a line and a half from "Nineteen Hundred and Nineteen":

> Man is in love and loves what vanishes,
> What more is there to say? . . .
>
> (st. 6)

Throughout his career, Yeats was a continuous reviser of his earlier work; and the student, when he quotes the work, needs to be careful that he is not basing his arguments on a text of 1908 or of the 1920's. This process is one of "making himself new." Essentially Yeats's poems are dramatic lyrics, and each of his volumes after *Responsibilities* (1914) consists of poems placed very carefully not in order of composition but in a cogent dramatic order, an unfolding, one poem commenting on its predecessor or its successor, amplifying or deflating. Each volume in turn leads on to its successor. So, for example, the last poem in *The Wild Swans at Coole*, "The Double Vision of Michael Robartes," with its figure of the dancer, is caught up in the little poem of the ensuing volume, *Michael Robartes and the Dancer* (1920).

I believe Yeats's poetry to be the centrally important part of his work. His work as a playwright is more difficult to assess.

IX

YEATS's approach is distinct from that of his contemporaries in the Irish dramatic revival. Theirs was to develop, first in the work of Synge and later in that of O'Casey, toward a drama of regional naturalism. Yeats on the other hand remained throughout his life the visionary of the movement, the one who aimed at a marriage of poetry and drama to be achieved by quite different methods. From the very beginning he took a vigorous and practical part in the artistic and technical development of the Irish theater, as well as in the day-to-day problems of administration, production, and experiment. He was by no means a Tennyson patronized by an Irving, but rather a combination of poet and man of the theater who created an integral dramatic form that was entirely new to his age. What distinguishes him from his dramatic contemporaries is his rejection of representation, a dramatic convention that had come to be accepted without question, because in Britain, at least, playwriting had for so long been overshadowed and dominated by the art of fiction. Yeats turned away not only from the large theater, with its sophisticated apparatus of illusion, and from the realistic conventions of performance, gesture, and details of staging and spectacle, but also from other conventions concerning dramatic composition:

One dogma of the printed criticism is that if a play does not contain definite character, its constitution is not strong enough for the stage, and that the dramatic moment is always the contest of character with character. . . . when we go back a few centuries and enter the great periods of drama, character grows less and sometimes disappears.
("The Tragic Theatre," in the
Mask [Florence], October 1910)

He sought, as he wrote elsewhere, "a deeper reality than any that can be reached by observation, for it is the reality of the imagination and comes from the withdrawal of the poet's mind into itself, not from the effort to see and record." His conception of the drama aimed at uncovering "not character, but those deeper forms of which character is merely a lineament."

Within these chosen limits, Yeats was to experiment for over thirty years to express his vision in dramatic form, first with the Irish Literary Theatre, then later with the Abbey; and his plays reveal a skill in the handling of his medium that increased slowly but unmistakably. In his early verse plays, such as *The Shadowy Waters* (1900), his aim is the realization of a vision of the transcendental. Next, in *Cathleen ni Houlihan* (1902)—the most popular of all his pieces—and *The Pot of Broth,* both written in collaboration with Lady Gregory, he begins to develop fluency in colloquial prose dialogue, coming down, as he put it, from the high window of dramatic verse. He returns to blank verse in a number of plays pitched in a more heroic key, notably *On Baile's Strand* (1903), centered on the episode of King Cuchulain's unwitting killing of his son, and *Deirdre* (1907), the tragic legend that was also dramatized by Synge. It is characteristic of Yeats's *Deirdre* that he contracts the action within a far smaller radius than that of Synge. Preparation is minimal and the attention of the audience is focused as soon as possible on the climax of love and death, the final tableau of queen, lover, and aged king, which constitutes the moment of insight of the play.

Yeats takes an even more radical step away from conventional dramaturgy in his *Four Plays for Dancers* (1921), which were shaped by the traditions of the Japanese *Noh* theater. "I wanted to create for myself an unpopular theatre," he wrote, and in these short pieces he strives to pare away still more rigorously what he regards as inessentials.

All imaginative art remains at a distance, and this distance must be firmly held against a pushing world. . . . Our unimaginative arts are content to set a piece of the world as we know it in a place by itself, to put their photographs, as it were, in a plush or plain frame, but the arts which interest me, while seeming to separate from the world and us a group of figures, images, symbols, enable us to pass for a few moments into a deep of the mind that had hitherto been too subtle for our habitation. . . .
(introduction to *Certain Noble Plays of Japan,* 1916)

The action in each of the four plays is framed by the presence throughout of masked musicians, who serve as prologue, chorus, and orchestra, and the plays mark a further stage in Yeats's perennial dramatic aim, to isolate particular moments of insight with the maximum of intensity.

The toughening and hardening of attitudes in Yeats's later years referred to in section VI of this essay—the replacing of music by fire, as B. Rajan has aptly put it—and its effect upon Yeats's poetic composition is paralleled by the continual effort to refine and purify his dramatic writing. Toward the end of his life his mastery of dramatic verse and dramatic prose became completely integrated, and his two finest pieces for the stage, albeit minor in scale, offer us an example of each: *Purgatory* (1939), a study of the imprisonment of people in themselves and in their heredity, is in verse; *The Words upon the Window Pane* (1934) is a histrionic tour de force in which the last days of Swift are described through the mouth of a spiritualistic medium in a state of trance.

X

YEATS wrote very delightful prose, and his reminiscences of the 1890's, in particular, are a primary document for a fascinating period. He was an erratic literary critic. His introduction to *The Oxford Book of Modern Verse, 1892–1935*, like his selection of poems in that book, is strikingly odd and eccentric; but it has the wit and charm of everything he wrote, and here and there, among statements that seem quite absurd, it has extremely penetrating paragraphs—particularly, perhaps, about his friend Ezra Pound, whose qualities and weaknesses no subsequent critic has estimated so justly. But it was into his poetry that he put himself most completely. The poetry, however, is better poetry because he gave himself to so many other things. His patriotism, his public spirit, his capacity for staunch friendship and passionate love all enrich it. The sense, which grew so strong in him in later life, that every victory he had worked for implied a defeat of something he perhaps cared about more, lends almost all his later work a pose of complex irony. The characteristics that some of his contemporaries disliked, such as his arrogance or "proper pride," are in his poems, too. Yet all true poets are fundamentally humble. Yeats was humble before the mystery of life. He never took either himself or his systems quite so seriously as some of his disciples have done. He was the last great poet in the English romantic tradition; and the only poet in that tradition, except Byron, with a genuine sense of humor and gift of wit. The true man, with the modesty and the generosity that underlay all his poses, comes out in the letters to Sturge Moore. Yeats writes about the Nobel Prize:

Yes, it will be a great help to me in several ways. Here especially it will help. I will find it easier to get the Government to listen to me on artistic things. I look upon it as a recognition of the Free State, and of Irish literature, and it is a very great help. People here are grateful because I have won them this recognition, and that is the distinction I want. If I thought it a tribute to my own capacity alone, I, being a very social man, would be far less pleased.

(23 November 1923)

All great poets tend to overawe us. They speak with "something above a mortal mouth." And they need their solitude to withdraw into. But it is as a lover, as a friend, and as a patriot, as "a very social man," that Yeats would like us to remember him. It is his broad and deep humanity that provides the substance of his art.

XI

THE first edition of this essay was published in 1954 and revised in Yeats's centenary year, 1965. How does Yeats's reputation now stand, and what light have scholarship and criticism thrown on his work since it was first printed? Only one critic, Professor Yvor Winters, has made a full-scale attack on Yeats's reputation (there has also been a skirmishing raid by Robert Graves). Professor Winters' case is that Yeats more or less invented his "romantic Ireland," that his philosophy is private and incoherent, that his images, however vivid, correspond to no clear structure of thought, that he overdramatizes and appeals to those in search of "easy emotions," and that he does not really write "pure poetry" in the tradition of the French symbolists. Professor Winters' attack is beautifully written and argued, but the brief answer is that he is wrong about Ireland—"Easter 1916" is one of the most "realistic" political poems in our language, and Yeats had a very thorough and complete understanding of Irish character and history—and that the rest of his attack is doctrinaire, an attack on Yeats for not being a kind of poet he did not set out to be.

Nevertheless, Professor Winters has put his finger on something, for it is a certain theatrical quality in Yeats, a certain occasional overeasy dramatization of certain stock attitudes, that has worried recent critics. Most contemporary critics would admit, for instance, that "Under Ben Bulben," however gallant as a deathbed gesture, is a little too stagy to be wholly satisfactory as a poem. In a lecture at Sligo in the 1960's, Professor Donald Davie suggested that the peak of Yeats's achievement lay in several late midperiod poems, like "A Prayer for My Daughter," which have a certain classical poise and balance that represent the survival in Yeats's milieu and temperament of Irish eighteenth-century decorum. The most interesting recent criticism, like that of T. Parkinson and J. Stallworthy, has made use of the variorum edition and the manuscript drafts to re-create for us Yeats's agonizingly slow, almost Flaubertian methods of composition. Yeats's first drafts, sometimes in prose, are always clear as outline sketches but remarkably hesitant and sometimes clumsy in rhythm and diction; the "grand style" was forged not easily or naturally, but with blood, sweat, and tears.

The labor that lay behind Yeats's style is perhaps one reason why, like another great, laborious poet, Milton, he has been a dangerous influence on subsequent poets. Direct imitation of him reads always like parody or pastiche; Irish poetry went through a dull period after his death and, in the work of Thomas Kinsella, Richard Murphy, and John Montague, has recently achieved a new liveliness largely by dint of resisting the temptation to overdramatize in a Yeatsian fasion. On the other hand, both Yeats's critical writings and his plays now seem much more important to his admirers than they did when I wrote the first version of this essay. We are perhaps moving away from an age of practical criticism to one of critical theorizing, and there are those who claim that as an aesthetic or philosophical critic Yeats is as important as T. S. Eliot is in the opposite field of direct scrutiny of texts. Yeats's plays have still, at least for Englishmen and Americans, to be practically tested on the stage; but Professor Peter Ure has made very high claims for Yeats's skill and readiness to experiment as a practicing playwright, and F. A. C. Wilson has emphasized the importance of the plays for the study of Yeats's "philosophy."

More recent criticism has also tended to suggest that while Yeats renewed his energies continuously throughout his career as poet, the commonly accepted notion that he somehow became a different, a finer, poet after 1908 has been overstressed. The earlier poems, particularly *The Wanderings of Oisin*, have attracted more admiration, and a number of the poems of the middle period appear to suffer from a certain dryness; the note is forced. *The Tower* now appears as the summit of the poet's achievement, although he continued to write master-

ly works. More attention has been directed to the prose works, and not simply as commentary on the poems. Argument continues as to the precise nature of Yeats's commitment to Irish politics, though we are perhaps less censorious about his alignment with bankers in the senate and his brief involvement with the Fascist General O'Duffy's Blueshirts in the 1930's.

It might be thought that the general currents of creative literature in the last ten years—the vogue of Brecht and Beckett in drama, for instance, and the vogue in poetry for low-toned or deliberately informal verse like that of Philip Larkin or Robert Lowell—as well as the tendency in all the arts toward a suspicion of the "high style" and toward the undermining of traditional standards of dignity and decorum, would have told against Yeats. I have heard T. R. Henn claim that modern undergraduates, democratic, humanitarian, anti-aristocratic, scientifically minded, practical, down-to-earth, peace-loving, are bound sooner or later to react violently against Yeats; but as a teacher of poetry to the young I have not yet come up against this hostility to Yeats. I think also that Henn perhaps underestimates the degree to which Yeats was himself, in some broad sense, a liberal; hating the violence and barbarism of the Irish troubles, stating in "Easter 1916" that "England may keep faith," and taking a firm stand in the Irish senate against the censorship and divorce laws. I find more sanity and realism about political and social affairs in Yeats than most critics have found; I think his reaction against images of violence more important than his dallying with them.

He was a poet who in his own way made as rich a use of "the tradition" as Pound or Eliot did in their ways; he could use both Donne and Spenser; there are elements in his poetry of broadsheet ballad style, Augustan formality, the self-exploration of the great romantics, Walter Pater's aestheticism and the world-weariness of the 1890's, French Symbolist mystification (as well as Blake's naked sense of symbolic mystery). He could think poetically in both emblems and abstractions. He incorporates the tradition in a new and personal way, as all great poets do. The antithetical movement of his mind, on the other hand, with its perpetual clashes against itself and its occasional precarious resolutions, is specifically modern. He combines in a strange way the virtues of two great, utterly opposite writers whom he admired: Landor's proud care for "perfection of the work"; Balzac's bursting unpredictableness (the *Autobiographies* are a great Balzacian novel). His whole oeuvre is a world, a world with elements in it of jumble, failure, pose, provinciality, but "changed, changed utterly" by his art, till "a terrible beauty is born."

SELECTED BIBLIOGRAPHY

Titles marked with an asterisk are those of books originally printed and published in limited editions by the Dun Emer (later the Cuala) Press, Dublin, founded by the poet's sisters. Yeats's texts were all republished in later editions and collections.

I. BIBLIOGRAPHY. W. M. Roth, *A Catalogue of English and American First Editions of W. B. Yeats* (New Haven, Conn., 1939); A. Wade, *A Bibliography of the Writing of W. B. Yeats* (London, 1951; rev. ed. with index, 1958), the definitive bibliography, incorporates valuable material contributed by P. S. O'Hegarty to the *Dublin* magazine (1939–1940) and includes full particulars of Yeats's contributions to books and periodicals, and a complete catalog of Cuala Press publications. Most of Yeats's poems were originally published in periodicals.

II. COLLECTED WORKS. *Collected Works in Verse and Prose*, 8 vols. (Stratford-on-Avon, 1908); *Plays for an Irish Theatre* (London, 1913), contains *Deirdre, The Green Helmet, On Baile's Strand, The King's Threshold, The Shadowy Waters, The Hour-Glass,* and *Cathleen ni Houlihan; Later Poems* (London, 1922), vol. I of the new *Collected Edition of the Works; Plays in Prose and Verse* (London, 1922), vol. II of the new *Collected Edition of the Works,* contains *Cathleen ni Houlihan, The Pot of Broth, The Hour-Glass, The King's Threshold, On Baile's Strand, The Shadowy Waters, The Unicorn from the Stars* (in collaboration with Lady Gregory), *The Green Helmet, The Player Queen, Notes and Music; Plays and Controversies* (London, 1923), vol. III of the new *Collected Edition of the Works,* contains "The Irish Dramatic Movement" and the following plays: *The Countess Cathleen, The Land of Heart's Desire, At the Hawk's Well, The Only Jealousy of Emer, The Dreaming of the Bones,* and *Calvary; Essays* (London, 1924), vol. IV of the new *Collected Edition of the Works; Early Poems and Stories* (London, 1925), vol. V of the new *Collected Edition of the Works; Autobiographies* (London, 1926), vol. VI of the new *Collected Edition of the Works,* contains *Reveries over Childhood and Youth* and *The Trembling of the Veil,* new ed. (1955), see below; *Poems* (London, 1927), the preface states that this ed. "contains what is, I hope, the final text of the poems of my youth."

The Collected Poems of W. B. Yeats (London, 1933; rev. and enl. ed., 1950); *The Collected Plays of W. B. Yeats* (London, 1934; 2nd ed., 1952); *Nine One Act Plays* (Lon-

don, 1937), contains *The Land of Heart's Desire, Cathleen ni Houlihan, The Hour-Glass, The Pot of Broth, On Baile's Strand, Deirdre, The Green Helmet, The Shadowy Waters, The Words upon the Window Pane; Poems,* 2 vols. (London, 1949), described as "the definitive edition" and lim. to 375 signed copies; *Autobiographies* (London, 1955), a new and enl. ed., the first of four vols. of Yeats's collected prose works, the others being *Mythologies, Essays and Introductions,* and *Explorations,* see below; P. Allt and R. K. Alspach, eds., *The Variorum Edition of the Poems* (New York, 1957); *Mythologies* (London, 1959); R. Pearce, ed., *The Senate Speeches of W. B. Yeats* (London, 1960); *Essays and Introductions* (London, 1961); *Explorations* (London, 1961); R. K. Alspach, ed., *The Variorum Edition of the Plays* (London, 1966).

III. SELECTED WORKS. A. N. Jeffares, ed., *Selected Poetry* (London, 1962); A. N. Jeffares, ed., *Selected Prose* (London, 1964); A. N. Jeffares, ed., *Selected Criticism* (London, 1964); A. N. Jeffares, ed., *Selected Plays* (London, 1964); J. P. Frayne, ed., *Uncollected Prose by W. B. Yeats: First Reviews and Articles, 1886–1896* (London, 1970); J. P. Frayne and C. Johnson, eds., *Uncollected Prose by W. B. Yeats: Reviews, Articles and Other Miscellaneous Prose, 1897–1939* (New York, 1976).

IV. LETTERS. H. Reynolds, ed., *Letters to the New Island* (Cambridge, Mass., 1934), letters; D. Wellesley, ed., *Letters on Poetry to Dorothy Wellesley* (London, 1940), K. Raine, ed., paperback ed. (London, 1964); C. Bax, ed., *Florence Farr, Bernard Shaw and Yeats: Letters* (Dublin, 1941); R. McHugh, ed., *Letters to Katherine Tynan* (Dublin, 1953); U. Bridge, ed., *Yeats and T. Sturge Moore: Their Correspondence 1901–1937;* A. Wade, ed., *Some Letters from W. B. Yeats to John O'Leary and His Sister from Originals in the Berg Collection* (New York, 1953), a lim. ed. published by the New York Public Library; A. Wade, ed., *Letters* (London, 1954), the fullest collection of Yeats's letters likely to be published, ed. with scholarly care by his bibliographer; R. McHugh, ed., *Ah, Sweet Dancer: W. B. Yeats and Margaret Ruddock. A Correspondence* (London–Basingstoke, 1970).

V. SEPARATE WORKS. American issues or eds., published more or less concurrently with the English, and successive reprs. of combinations of separate works are not as a general rule included in this section. *Mosada, a Dramatic Poem* (Dublin, 1886), first printed in *Dublin University Review* (June 1886), 100 copies of this pamphlet ed. printed; *The Wanderings of Oisin* (London, 1889), verse; *John Sherman and Dhoya* (London, 1891), stories, under the pseudonym of Ganconagh, no. 10 of the Pseudonym Library; *The Countess Cathleen and Various Legends and Lyrics* (London, 1892), verse, the verse drama *The Countess Cathleen* later rev. and published separately (1912); *The Celtic Twilight, Men and Women, Dhouls and Faeries* (London, 1893; rev. ed., 1903), verse, essays, stories; *The Land of Heart's Desire* (London, 1894), drama; *Poems* (London, 1895; rev. eds., 1899, 1901), verse; *The*

Secret Rose (London, 1897), stories; The Wind Among the Reeds (London, 1899), verse.

The Shadowy Waters (London, 1900), verse; Cathleen ni Houlihan (London, 1902), drama; Ideas of Good and Evil (London, 1903), essays; *In the Seven Woods (London, 1903), verse, includes the verse play On Baile's Strand; The Hour-Glass: A Morality (New York, 1904), drama, first published in the North American Review (September 1903), 12 offprints made for copyright purposes by Heinemann Ltd., London; The King's Threshold (New York, 1904), drama, 100 copies only, printed for private circulation, repr. in vol. V of Abbey Theatre series (Dublin, 1905); *Stories of Red Hanrahan (Dublin, 1904), stories; Poems, 1899–1905 (London, 1906); Deirdre (London, 1907), drama; *Discoveries (Dublin, 1907), essays; *The Green Helmet and Other Poems (Dublin, 1910), The Green Helmet, a "heroic farce," separately printed at the Shakespeare Head Press (London, 1911); *Synge and the Ireland of His Time (Dublin, 1911), with a note concerning a walk through Connemara with Yeats by J. B. Yeats; The Cutting of an Agate (New York, 1912; London, 1919), essays; Stories of Red Hanrahan: The Secret Rose: Rosa Alchemica (London–Stratford-on-Avon, 1913; New York, 1914), stories; *Responsibilities (Dublin, 1914; London, 1916), verse and a play; *Reveries over Childhood and Youth (Dublin, 1915; London, 1916), autobiography; *The Wild Swans at Coole (Dublin, 1917; London, 1919), verse and a play; Per Amica Silentia Lunae (London, 1918), essays; *Two Plays for Dancing (Dublin, 1919), contains The Dreaming of the Bones and The Only Jealousy of Emer.

*Michael Robartes and the Dancer (Dublin, 1920), verse; Four Plays for Dancers (London, 1921), contains At the Hawk's Well, The Only Jealousy of Emer, The Dreaming of the Bones, and Calvary; *Four Years: Reminiscences, 1887–1891 (Dublin, 1921), autobiography; *Seven Poems and a Fragment (Dublin, 1922); The Trembling of the Veil (London, 1922), autobiography, subscribers' ed. of 1,000 copies; "Speeches," in Parliamentary Debates Official Report, vols. I–X (Dublin, 1923); *The Cat and the Moon and Certain Poems (Dublin, 1924), drama and verse; A Vision (London, 1925), subscribers' ed. of 600 copies, rev. with additions (London, 1937), reiss. with corrections (London, 1962); Autobiographies (London, 1926) *Estrangement: Being Some Fifty Thoughts from a Diary Kept in the Year 1909 (Dublin, 1926), autobiography; *October Blast (Dublin, 1927), verse; The Tower (London, 1928), verse; Sophocles' "King Oedipus": A Version for the Modern Stage (London, 1928); *The Death of Synge and Other Passages from an Old Diary (Dublin, 1928), diary; *A Packet for Ezra Pound (Dublin, 1929), verse, an ed. of only 660 signed copies for sale; The Land of Heart's Desire [and] The Countess Cathleen (London, 1929), drama.

Stories of Michael Robartes and His Friends (Dublin, 1931), stories and a play, includes the play The Resurrec-

tion; *Words for Music Perhaps, and Other Poems (Dublin, 1932), incorporated in The Winding Stair and Other Poems (London, 1933); The Winding Stair and Other Poems (London, 1933), much enl. ed. of The Winding Stair (London, 1929) and incorporating the contents of Words for Music Perhaps . . . ; The Words upon the Window Pane (London, 1934), drama; Wheels and Butterflies (London, 1934), contains The Words upon the Window Pane, Fighting the Waves, The Resurrection, and The Cat and the Moon; The King of the Great Clock Tower: Commentaries and Poems (London, 1934), verse; A Full Moon in March (London, 1935), drama and verse, contains A Full Moon in March and The King of the Great Clock Tower; *Dramatis Personae (Dublin, 1935; London, 1936), autobiography; Modern Poetry (London, 1936), lecture, Broadcast National Lectures, no. 18; *Essays 1931–1936 (Dublin, 1937); The Herne's Egg (London, 1938), drama, published in America as The Herne's Egg and Other Plays (New York, 1938); *New Poems (Dublin, 1938); The Autobiography of William Butler Yeats (New York, 1938), autobiography, contains Reveries over Childhood and Youth, The Trembling of the Veil, and Dramatis Personae; *Last Poems and Two Plays (Dublin, 1939; London, 1940), contains The Death of Cuchulain and Purgatory; *On the Boiler (Dublin, 1939), essays and verse; *If I Were Four and Twenty: Swedenborg, Mediums and the Desolate Places (Dublin, 1940), essays; *Pages from a Diary Written in Nineteen Hundred and Thirty (Dublin, 1944), diary; D. R. Clark and G. Mayhew, eds., A Tower of Polished Black Stones: Early Versions of the Shadowy Waters (Dublin, 1971); W. H. O'Donnell, ed., The Speckled Bird (New York, 1976); G. M. Harper and W. K. Hood, eds., A Critical Edition of Yeats's "A Vision" (London–Basingstoke, 1978); P. Marcus, W. Gould, and M. J. Sidnell, eds., The Secret Rose: Stories by W. B. Yeats. A Variorum Edition (Ithaca, N. Y.–London, 1981).

VI. EDITED WORKS AND INTRODUCTIONS. W. B. Yeats, ed., Fairy and Folk Tales of the Irish Peasantry (London, 1888); W. Carleton, Stories from Carleton (London, 1889), intro. by Yeats; W. B. Yeats, comp., Representative Irish Names, 2 vols. (London, 1890), intro. and notes by Yeats; W. B. Yeats, ed., Irish Fairy Tales (London, 1892), intro. by Yeats; W. B. Yeats, ed., The Works of William Blake, 3 vols. (London, 1893), lim. ed. of 500 copies; W. B. Yeats, ed., The Poems of William Blake (London–New York, 1893; 1905), in Muses' Library series; A Book of Irish Verse (London, 1895; rev. ed., 1900), selected from modern writers with intro. and notes by Yeats; W. T. Horton, A Book of Images (London, 1898), intro. by Yeats; W. B. Yeats, ed., Beltaine. The Organ of the Irish Literary Theatre (Dublin, 1899–1900), 3 issues; W. B. Yeats, ed., Samhain (Dublin, 1901–1908), ed. for the Irish Literary Theatre from 1901 to 1908; Lady Gregory, ed., Cuchulain of Muirthemme (London, 1902), preface by Yeats; *L. Johnson, Twenty-one Poems (Dublin, 1904), selected by

Yeats; D. Hyde, trans., *The Love Songs of Connacht* (Dublin, 1904), preface by Yeats; Lady Gregory, ed., *Gods and Fighting Men* (London, 1904), preface by Yeats; *William Allingham, *Sixteen Poems* (Dublin, 1905), selected by Yeats; J. M. Synge, *The Well of the Saints* (London, 1905), intro. by Yeats; *Poems of Spenser* (Edinburgh, 1906), selected and with intro. by Yeats, in Golden Poets series; *J. Eglinton, *Some Essays and Passages* (Dublin, 1905), selected by Yeats; W. B. Yeats, ed., *The Arrow* (London, 1906–1907), 3 issues. *K. Tynan, *Twenty-one Poems* (Dublin, 1907), selected by Yeats; *W. B. Yeats and L. Johnson, eds., *Poetry and Ireland* (Dublin, 1908), essays; *W. B. Yeats, ed., *A Broadside* (Dublin, 1908); *J. M. Synge, *Poems and Translations* (Dublin, 1909), intro. by Yeats.

*J. M. Synge, *Deirdre of the Sorrows* (Dublin, 1910), intro. by Yeats; *Selections from the Writings of Lord Dunsany* (Dublin, 1912), intro. by Yeats; *R. Tagore, *The Post Office* (Dublin, 1914), a play with intro. by Yeats; *E. F. Fenellosa, *Certain Noble Plays of Japan* (Dublin, 1916), intro. by Yeats; R. Tagore, *Gitanjali* (London, 1919), intro. by Yeats; *The Complete Works of Oscar Wilde* (New York, 1923), vol. III intro. by Yeats; *J. B. Yeats, *Early Memories* (Dublin, 1923), preface by Yeats; *O. Gogarty, *An Offering of Swans* (Dublin, 1923), preface by Yeats; V. de Lisle Adam, *Axel*, H. P. R. Finberg, trans. (London, 1925), preface by Yeats; A. Ussher, trans., *The Midnight Court and the Adventures of a Luckless Fellow* (London, 1926), intro. by Yeats; *O. Gogarty, *Wild Apples* (Dublin, 1929), preface by Yeats; J. M. Hone, *Bishop Berkeley* (London, 1931), intro. by Yeats; Shri Purohit Swami, *An Indian Monk* (London, 1932), intro. by Yeats; Bhagwan Shri Hamsa, *The Holy Mountain*, Shri Purohit Swami, trans. (London, 1934), intro. by Yeats; D. Wellesley, *Selected Poems of Dorothy Wellesley* (London, 1936), intro. by Yeats; *The Oxford Book of Modern Verse, 1892–1935* (London, 1936), chosen and with intro. by Yeats; M. Ruddock, *The Lemon Tree* (London, 1937), intro. by Yeats; *The Ten Principal Upanishads* (London, 1937), put into English by Shri Purohit Swami and Yeats; O. Gogarty, *Others to Adorn* (London, 1938), preface by Yeats; Shri Purohit Swami, trans., *Aphorisms of Yoga* (London, 1938), with intro. by Yeats.

VII. BIOGRAPHICAL AND CRITICAL STUDIES. H. S. Krans, *William Butler Yeats and the Irish Literary Revival* (London, 1904), Contemporary Men of Letters series; F. Reid, *W. B. Yeats: A Critical Study* (London, 1915); P. Gurd, *The Early Poetry of William Butler Yeats* (Lancaster, Pa., 1916); J. M. Hone, *William Butler Yeats: The Poet in Contemporary Ireland* (London, 1916).

J. H. Pollock, *William Butler Yeats* (London, 1935); J. P. O'Donnell, *Sailing to Byzantium: A Study in the Development of the Later Style and Symbolism in the Poetry of William Butler Yeats* (Cambridge, Mass., 1939); *The Arrow*, W. B. Yeats Commemoration Number (Summer 1939); T. S. Eliot, "The Poetry of W. B. Yeats," in *Purpose*, III–IV, XII (London, 1940), the first Annual Yeats Lecture delivered in the Abbey Theatre, Dublin (30 June 1940), repr. in *On Poetry and Poets* (London, 1957).

L. S. Gwynn, ed., *Scattering Branches: Tributes to the Memory of W. B. Yeats* (Dublin, 1940); *J. Masefield, *Some Memories of W. B. Yeats* (Dublin, 1940); L. MacNeice, *The Poetry of W. B. Yeats* (London, 1941); J. M. Hone, *W. B. Yeats 1865–1939* (London, 1942; rev. ed., 1965), the standard biography; V. K. N. Menon, *The Development of William Butler Yeats* (London, 1942); P. Ure, *Towards a Mythology: Studies in the Poetry of W. B. Yeats* (Liverpool, 1946); D. A. Stauffer, *The Golden Nightingale: Essays on Some Principles of Poetry in the Lyrics of W. B. Yeats* (New York, 1949); R. Ellmann, *Yeats: The Man and the Masks* (London, 1949; paperback ed., 1961); A. N. Jeffares, *W. B. Yeats, Man and Poet* (London, 1949; rev. ed. and paperback ed., 1962).

J. Hall and M. Steinmann, eds., *The Permanence of Yeats: Selected Criticism* (New York, 1950); T. R. Henn, *The Lonely Tower: Studies in the Poetry of W. B. Yeats* (London, 1950; rev. ed., 1965); T. Parkinson, *W. B. Yeats, Self-Critic: A Study of His Early Verse* (Berkeley–Los Angeles, 1951); V. Koch, *W. B. Yeats: The Tragic Phase. A Study of the Last Poems* (London, 1951); A. Ussher, *Three Great Irishmen: Shaw, Yeats, Joyce* (London, 1952); M. E. Rudd, *Divided Image: A Study of William Blake and W. B. Yeats* (London, 1953); R. Ellmann, *The Identity of Yeats* (London, 1954; paperback ed., 1964); V. Moore, *The Unicorn: W. B. Yeats's Search for Reality* (New York, 1954); G. B. Saul, *Prolegomena to the Study of Yeats's Poems* (Philadelphia, 1957); F. Kermode, *Romantic Image* (London, 1957; paperback ed., 1961); F. A. C. Wilson, *W. B. Yeats and Tradition* (London, 1958); D. Donoghue, *The Third Voice: Modern British and American Verse Drama* (London, 1959).

Y. Winters, *The Poetry of W. B. Yeats* (Denver, Colo., 1960); G. Melchiori, *The Whole Mystery of Art: Pattern into Poetry in the Work of W. B. Yeats* (New York–London, 1960); A. C. Stock, *W. B. Yeats: His Poetry and Thought* (London, 1961; paperback ed., 1964); D. J. Gordon, *W. B. Yeats: Images of a Poet. Catalogue of the Yeats Exhibition at Whitworth Art Gallery, University of Manchester* (Manchester, 1961), with contributions from I. Fletcher, F. Kermode, and R. Skelton; D. J. Gordon, *W. B. Yeats: Images of a Poet* (Manchester, 1961); R. M. Kain, *Dublin in the Age of W. B. Yeats and James Joyce* (London, 1962); J. Stallworthy, *Between the Lines: Yeats's Poetry in the Making* (Oxford, 1963); P. Ure, *Yeats* (Edinburgh, 1963); P. Ure, *Yeats the Playwright: A Commentary on Character and Design in the Major Plays* (London, 1963), J. Unterecker, ed., *Yeats: A Collection of Critical Essays* (New York–London, 1963); H. Vendler, *Yeats's "Vision" and the Later Plays* (Cambridge, Mass.–London, 1963); S. M. Parrish, *A Concordance to the Plays* (Ithaca, N.Y.,

1963); E. Engelberg, *The Vast Design: Patterns in W. B. Yeats's Aesthetic* (Toronto, 1964); T. Parkinson, *W. B. Yeats: The Later Poetry* (Berkeley–Los Angeles, 1964); A. N. Jeffares and K. G. W. Cross, eds., *In Excited Reverie. A Centenary Tribute to William Butler Yeats, 1865–1939* (London, 1965); R. Skelton and A. Saddlerneyer, *The World of W. B. Yeats. Essays in Perspective. A Symposium and Catalogue* (London, 1965); E. Malins, ed., *The Dolmen Press Yeats Centenary Papers* (Dublin, 1965–   ); L. Miller, ed., *Yeats Centenary Papers* (London, 1965–   ); C. Bradford, *Yeats at Work* (Carbondale–Edwardsville, Ill., 1965); D. R. Clark, *Yeats and the Theatre of Desolate Anarchy* (Dublin, 1965); L. E. Nathan, *The Tragic Drama of W. B. Yeats* (London, 1965); B. Rajan, *W. B. Yeats: A Critical Introduction* (New York–London, 1965); C. Salvadori, *Yeats and Castiglione: Poet and Courtier* (Dublin, 1965); D. Donoghue and J. R. Mulryne, eds., *An Honoured Guest. New Essays on W. B. Yeats* (London, 1966); D. E. S. Maxwell and S. B. Bushrui, eds., *W. B. Yeats, 1865–1965. Centenary Essays on the Art of W. B. Yeats* (Ibadan, 1966); S. B. Bushrui, *Yeats's Verse Plays: The Revisions 1900–1910* (London, 1966); T. R. Whitaker, *Yeats's Dialogue with History: "Swan and Shadow"* (Chapel Hill, N. C., 1965); D. Hoffman, *Barbarous Knowledge: Myth in the Poetry of Yeats, Graves and Muir* (London, 1967); J. Stallworthy, ed., *Yeats's Last Poems: A Casebook* (New York–Oxford, 1968); R. Ellmann, *Eminent Domain: Yeats Among Wilde, Joyce, Pound, Eliot and Auden* (New York–London, 1967); J. Ronsley, *Yeats's Autobiography: Life as a Symbolic Pattern* (Cambridge, Mass.–London, 1968); A. N. Jeffares, *A Commentary on the Collected Poems of W. B. Yeats* (London, 1968; Stanford, 1969); R. Beum, *The Poetic Art of W. B. Yeats* (New York, 1969); A. R. Grossmann, *Poetic Knowledge in the Early Years* (Charlottesville, Va., 1969); J. Stallworthy, *Vision and Revision in Yeats's Last Poems* (London, 1969).

H. Bloom, *Yeats* (New York–London, 1970); P. L. Marcus, *Yeats and the Beginning of the Irish Renaissance* (Ithaca, N.Y.–London, 1970); J. R. Moore, *Masks of Love and Death: Yeats as Dramatist* (London, 1971); D. R. Albright, *The Myth Against Myth* (London, 1972); E. Domville, ed., *A Concordance to the Plays of W. B. Yeats* (Ithaca, N. Y., 1972); M. Brown, *The Politics of Irish Literature from Thomas Davis to W. B. Yeats* (London, 1973); G. Harper, *Yeats's Golden Dawn* (London, 1974); D. A. Harris, *Yeats: Coole Park and Ballylee* (Baltimore–London, 1974); R. Skene, *The Cuchulain Plays of W. B. Yeats* (London, 1974); P. Ure, *Yeats and Anglo-Irish Literature*, C. J. Rawson, ed. (Liverpool, 1974); G. Harper, ed., *Yeats and the Occult* (London, 1975); A. N. Jeffares and A. S. Knowland, *A Commentary on the Collected Plays of W. B. Yeats* (London, 1975); J. Johnson, *Florence Farr: Bernard Shaw's "New Woman"* (Gerrards Cross, 1975); W. M. Murphy, *Yeats's Early Poetry: The Quest for Reconciliation* (London, 1975); R. O'Driscoll and L. Reynolds, *Yeats and the Theatre* (Niagara Falls, N. Y., 1975); D. Young and C. Hulme, *Out of Ireland: A Reading of Yeats's Poetry* (London, 1975); D. Eddins, *Yeats: The Nineteenth Century Matrix* (University, Ala., 1976); J. W. Flannery, *W. B. Yeats and the Idea of a Theatre: The Early Abbey Theatre in Theory* (London, 1976); R. Taylor, *The Drama of W. B. Yeats: Irish Myth and the Japanese Nōh* (New Haven, Conn.–London, 1976); F. Tuohy, *Yeats* (London, 1976); A. N. Jeffares, *W. B. Yeats: The Critical Heritage* (London, 1977); L. Miller, *The Noble Drama of W. B. Yeats* (London, 1977); J. W. Flannery, *Yeats and Magic: The Earlier Works* (London, 1978); W. M. Murphy, *The Life of J. B. Yeats: Prodigal Father* (Ithaca, N.Y., 1978); A. Parkin, *The Dramatic Imagination of W. B. Yeats* (London, 1978); M. L. Rosenthal, *Yeats, Pound and Eliot: Sailing into the Unknown* (London, 1978); B. L. Reid, *W. B. Yeats: The Lyric of Tragedy* (London, 1978); A. Lynch, *Yeats: The Poetics of the Self* (Chicago, 1978).

M. H. Thuente, *Yeats and Irish Folklore* (Iowa City, 1980); E. Cullingford, *Yeats, Ireland and Fascism* (London, 1981); W. H. Pritchard, ed., *W. B. Yeats: A Critical Anthology* (Harmondsworth, 1982).

CHRONOLOGICAL LIST OF SUBJECTS

LIST OF CONTRIBUTORS

COMPLETE LISTING OF SUBJECTS
IN THE PARENT SET

Chronological List of Subjects

CHRONOLOGICAL LIST OF SUBJECTS

Contributors

Miriam Allott
John Keats

Nina Auerbach
Daphne du Maurier

John Bernard Bamborough
Ben Jonson

John Beer
William Blake

Bernard Benstock
Arthur Conan Doyle

Bernard Bergonzi
Graham Greene

Christopher Bigsby
Tom Stoppard

Bernard Blackstone
Virginia Woolf

Muriel Clara Bradbrook
T. S. Eliot
Sir Thomas Malory

Raymond Laurence Brett
Samuel Taylor Coleridge

Jocelyn Brooke
Aldous Huxley

John Butt
Henry Fielding

Ian Campbell
Thomas Carlyle

John Carey
William Makepeace Thackeray

Frederick Donald Coggan
The English Bible

Nevill Henry Kendal Aylmer Coghill
Geoffrey Chaucer

Philip Arthur Collins
James Boswell

Lettice Ulpha Cooper
George Eliot

Charles Brian Cox
Joseph Conrad

Anthony Curtis
W. Somerset Maugham

David Daiches
Robert Burns

David Damrosch
P. G. Wodehouse

Hugh Sykes Davies
Anthony Trollope

Philip Drew
Robert Browning

CONTRIBUTORS

Alastair David Shaw Fowler
Edmund Spenser

George Sutherland Fraser
William Butler Yeats

Philip Gardner
E. M. Forster

Ian Alstair Gordon
Katherine Mansfield

Barbara Hardy
Charles Dickens

Alethea Hayter
Elizabeth Barrett Browning

Richard Hoggart
W. H. Auden

Sir Tom Hopkinson
George Orwell

Arthur Raleigh Humphreys
Sir Richard Steele

Ian Robert James Jack
Alexander Pope

Alexander Norman Jeffares
Jonathan Swift

Malcolm Miles Kelsall
George Gordon, Lord Byron

John Frank Kermode
John Donne

Karl Kroeber
J. R. R. Tolkien

George J. Leonard
John le Carré

Randy Malamud
Alan Paton

Geoffrey Maurice Matthews
Percy Bysshe Shelley

Jean–Jacques Mayoux
Samuel Beckett

Stephen Medcalf
William Golding

Anne K. Mellor
Mary Shelley

Margery M. Morgan
George Bernard Shaw

William Francis Myers
Evelyn Waugh

Alastair Neil Robertson Niven
D. H. Lawrence

Leslie Norris
Dylan Thomas,

Sir Sydney Castle Roberts
Samuel Johnson

Alan G. Sandison
Rudyard Kipling

Sanford Schwartz
C. S. Lewis

Rolfe Arnold Scott-James
and Cecil Day Lewis
Thomas Hardy

Ian Stanley Scott-Kilvert
A. E. Housman

CONTRIBUTORS

Brian Charles Southam
Jane Austen
Alfred, Lord Tennyson

Gladys Bronwen Stern
Robert Louis Stevenson

John Innes Mackintosh Stewart
James Joyce

John Stokes
Oscar Wilde

Graham Storey
Gerard Manley Hopkins

James Sutherland
Daniel Defoe

Henri A. Talon
John Bunyan

John Russell Taylor
Harold Pinter

Michael Thorpe
Doris Lessing

E. M. W. Tillyard
John Milton

John Richard Watson
William Wordsworth

Stanley Wells
William Shakespeare

Kenneth Young
H. G. Wells

List of Subjects in the Parent Set

Joseph Addison
Eric Ambler
Kingsley Amis
Martin Amis
John Arden
Matthew Arnold
W. H. Auden
Jane Austen
Francis Bacon
Pat Barker
Julian Barnes
James M. Barrie
Francis Beaumont
Samuel Beckett
William Beckford
Max Beerbohm
Brendan Behan
Aphra Behn
Arnold Bennett
John Berger
John Betjeman
The English Bible
William Blake
Edward Bond
James Boswell
Elizabeth Bowen
Robert Bridges
The Brontës
Rupert Brooke
Christine Brooke-Rose
Anita Brookner
Sir Thomas Browne
Elizabeth Barrett Browning
Robert Browning
John Bunyan
Anthony Burgess

Edmund Burke
Frances Burney
Robert Burns
Samuel Butler
A. S. Byatt
Lord Byron
Thomas Carew
Thomas Carlyle
Lewis Carroll
Angela Carter
Joyce Cary
The Cavalier Poets
George Chapman
Bruce Chatwin
Geoffrey Chaucer
G. K. Chesterton
Agatha Christie
Caryl Churchill
Winston Churchill
Arthur Hugh Clough
Samuel Taylor Coleridge
William Collins
Ivy Compton-Burnett
William Congreve
Cyril Connolly
Joseph Conrad
Noel Coward
Abraham Cowley
William Cowper
George Crabbe
Richard Crashaw
Roald Dahl
Cecil Day Lewis
Thomas De Quincey
Daniel Defoe
Charles Dickens

Benjamin Disraeli

John Donne

Norman Douglas

Arthur Conan Doyle

Margaret Drabble

John Dryden

Daphne du Maurier

Lawrence Durrell

Maria Edgeworth

George Eliot

T. S. Eliot

William Empson

Sir George Etherege

John Evelyn

George Farquhar

Henry Fielding

Ronald Firbank

Edward FitzGerald

John Fletcher

John Ford

Madox Ford

E. M. Forster

John Fowles

James George Frazer

Christopher Fry

John Galsworthy

Elizabeth Gaskell

John Gay

Edward Gibbon

George Gissing

William Golding

Oliver Goldsmith

Nadine Gordimer

The Gothic Novel

John Gower

Robert Graves

Thomas Gray

Henry Green

Graham Greene

Lady Augusta Gregory

Thom Gunn

H. Rider Haggard

Thomas Hardy

David Hare

William Hazlitt

Seamus Heaney

George Herbert

Robert Herrick

Thomas Hood

Richard Hooker

Gerard Manley Hopkins

A. E. Housman

Henry Howard, Earl of Surrey

Ted Hughes

David Hume

Aldous Huxley

Christopher Isherwood

Kazuo Ishiguro

Henry James

P. D. James

Samuel Johnson

David Jones

Ben Jonson

James Joyce

John Keats

Rudyard Kipling

Arthur Koestler

Thomas Kyd and Early
    Elizabethan Tragedy

Charles Lamb

Walter Savage Landor

William Langland

Phillip Larkin

D. H. Lawrence

T. E. Lawrence

Edward Lear

F. R. Leavis

John le Carré

Doris Lessing

C. S. Lewis

Wyndham Lewis

David Lodge

Richard Lovelace

Malcolm Lowry

John Lydgate

John Lyly

Thomas Babington Macaulay

Louis MacNeice

Sir Thomas Malory

Katherine Mansfield

Christopher Marlowe

John Marston

Andrew Marvell

W. Somerset Maugham

Ian McEwan

George Meredith

Four Metaphysical Poets

Thomas Middleton

John Milton

George Moore

William Morris

Paul Muldoon

Iris Murdoch

V. S. Naipaul

Flann O'Brien

Sean O'Casey

George Orwell

John Osborne

Wilfred Owen

Walter Horatio Pater

Alan Paton

Thomas Love Peacock

George Peele

Samuel Pepys

Harold Pinter

Poets of World War I (British)

Poets of World War II (British)

Alexander Pope

Beatrix Potter

Anthony Powell

J. B. Priestley

V. S. Pritchett

Barbara Pym

Sir Walter Ralegh (Raleigh)

Herbert Read

The Restoration Court Poets

Jean Rhys

I. A. Richards

Samuel Richardson

Christina Rossetti

Dante Gabriel Rossetti

Salman Rushdie

John Ruskin

Charles Sackville, Earl of Dorset

Siegfried Sassoon

Dorothy L. Sayers

Olive Schreiner

Paul Scott

Sir Walter Scott

Sir Charles Sedley

Peter Shaffer

William Shakespeare

George Bernard Shaw

Mary Shelley

Percy Bysshe Shelley

Richard Brinsley Sheridan

Sir Phillip Sidney

Edith Sitwell

John Skelton

Stevie Smith

Tobias Smollett

C. P. Snow

Robert Southey

Muriel Spark

Steven Spender

Edmund Spenser

Christina Stead

Sir Richard Steele

Leslie Stephen

Laurence Sterne

Robert Louis Stevenson

Bram Stoker

Tom Stoppard

David Storey

Lytton Strachey

Sir John Suckling

Graham Swift

Algernon Charles Swinburne

J. M. Synge

Alfred Lord Tennyson

William Makepeace Thackeray

D. M. Thomas

Dylan Thomas

Edward Thomas

Francis Thompson

James Thomson

J. R. R. Tolkien

Cyril Tourneur

Thomas Traherne

G. M. Trevelyan

William Trevor

Anthony Trollope

William Tyndale

Sir John Vanbrugh

Henry Vaughan

Edmund Waller

Horace Walpole

Izaak Walton

Evelyn Waugh

John Webster

Fay Weldon

H. G. Wells

Rebecca West

Patrick White

Oscar Wilde

John Wilmot, Earl of Rochester

Angus Wilson

Jeanette Winterson

P. G. Wodehouse

Mary Wollstonecraft

Virginia Woolf

William Wordsworth

Sir Thomas Wyatt

William Wycherley

William Butler Yeats

INDEX

Index

Note: Page numbers in **boldface** indicate a major discussion.

Apuleius, 870

"Arabella" (Thackeray), 1244

Arabian Nights, The, 133, 135, 706

Arbuthnot, John, 1199, 1214

"Arcades" (Milton), 926

Arcadia (Sidney), 498, 1035

Archer, William, 1055, 1056, 1057

"Arctic Summer" (Forster), 520

Ardours and Endurances (Nichols), 1427

Areopagitica (Milton), 930, 931, 936, 941

Aretina (Mackenzie), 498

Argument . . . that the Abolishing of Christianity . . . May . . . Be Attended with some Inconveniences, An (Swift), 1206

Ariel Poems (Eliot), 478

Aristophanes' Apology (Browning), 197, 206, 209

Arms and the Man (Shaw), 1056, 1061, 1062, 1064, 1065, 1072

Arnold, Matthew, 210, 306-307, 489, 533, 599, 632, 633, 710, 721, 724, 1001, 1115, 1203, 1219, 1228

Arouet, François-Marie. *See* Voltaire

Arrow of Gold, The (Conrad), 332, 342, 345

"Arthur Snatchfold" (Forster), 525

"Artistic Career of Corky, The" (Wodehouse), 1388

"Artistic Temperament of Stephen Carey, The" (Maugham), 915

"Artists, The" (Thackeray), 1242

Art of D. H. Lawrence, The (Sagar), 807

"Art of Fiction, The" (Woolf), 1399, 1400

Art of Sinking in Poetry, The (Pope), 261

Arts and Crafts Movement, The (Naylor), 732

Ascent of F6, The (Auden and Isherwood), 2, 5, 7

Ash-Wednesday (Eliot), 470, 476, 477-478, 479, 480, 482

"As kingfishers catch fire" (Hopkins), 609

Asolando: Fancies and Facts (Browning), 198

Aspects of the Novel (Forster), 511, 525, 526, 1399, 1400

Asquith, Herbert, 1421

Asquith, Raymond, 1421, 1432

"Assault, The" (Nichols), 1423

"As the Team's Head-Brass" (Thomas), 1429

"Astronomy" (Housman), 631

Astrophel. A Pastoral Elegy (Spenser), 1115, 1127

As You Like It (Shakespeare), 657, 1030

Atalanta in Calydon (Swinburne), 766

"At Castle Boterel" (Hardy), 594

Athenaeum (periodical), 179, 894, 1340, 1410

Athenian Mercury (newspaper), 1148

Atkins, Robert, 804, 1046

"At last the secret is out" (Auden), 8

"At Lehmann's" (Mansfield), 892, 893

"At Senlis Once" (Blunden), 1432

"Attack" (Sassoon), 1435

Attempt to Describe Hafod, An (Cumberland), 319

"At the Bay" (Mansfield), 895, 897, 898, 899, 900

"At the End of the Passage" (Kipling), 737-739, 747, 748, 757

"At the Grave of Henry James" (Auden), 2

"At the Great Wall of China" (Blunden), 1433

"At the Mermaid" (Browning), 198

Auden, W. H., **1-21**, 28, 1116; on Eliot, 474; and Greene, 560; and Housman, 630; and Kipling, 740; and Waugh, 1319; on Yeats, 1474-1475

"Auguries of Innocence" (Blake), 101

"August 1914" (Rosenberg), 1438

Augustine, Saint, 84, 857

Augustus Does His Bit (Shaw), 1072

"Auld Lang Syne" (Burns), 236, 242

"Aunt and the Sluggard, The" (Wodehouse), 1377-1378, 1385

Aunts Aren't Gentlemen (Wodehouse; American title, *The Cat Nappers*), 1385

Aurora Leigh (Browning), 180, 181, 183-184, 185-186, 187

Austen, Jane, **23-46**, 515, 1057, 1058, 1089

Authorized Version. *See* King James Version of the Bible

"Author's Prologue" (Thomas), 1271, 1276

"Author upon Himself, The" (Swift), 1199, 1212

Autobiographies (Yeats), 1358, 1487

Autobiography (Russell), 774

Autobiography, An (Trollope), 1295, 1296-1299, 1302

"Autumn" (Pope), 1002

"Ave Imperatrix" (Kipling), 765

Aventures de Télémaque, Les (Fénelon), 498, 502

Awakened Conscience, The (Dixon Hunt), 731

Awakening Conscience, The (Holman Hunt), 367, 373

Ayala's Angel (Trollope), 1306

"Baa, Baa Black Sheep" (Kipling), 730

Babbitt (Lewis), 1287

Babees Book, The (Early English Poems and Treatises on Manners and Meals in Olden Time) (ed. Furnival), 286, 290

Babes in the Darkling Wood (Wells), 1334

Bacchae, The (Murray), 1070

Back to Methuselah (Shaw), 1073-1075, 1076, 1077

Bacon, Francis, 65, 1091, 1114, 1146

"Bad Idea, A" (Mansfield), 895

Bailey, Benjamin, 720, 722, 723

Baillet, Adrien, 47

Baillie, Alexander, 610, 612, 613, 617

Baines, Jocelyn, 331-332

"Baite, The" (Donne), 1223

Baker, Ida, 892, 894, 895, 896, 897

Balaustion's Adventure (Browning), 197

Bald, R. C., 397

Balfour, Arthur, 1332

Balfour, Graham, 1171

Balin or the Knight with Two Swords (Malory), 889

"Ballad of Bouillabaisse" (Thackeray), 1239

Ballad of Reading Gaol, The (Wilde), 1371-1372

"Ballad of the Long-legged Bait" (Thomas), 1269

"Ballad of the Three Spectres" (Gurney), 1430

Ballantyne, Robert Michael, 531, 532

Balzac, Honoré de, 906, 1237, 1487

Barber, Francis, 660